UNDERSTANDING REMEDIES

Second Edition

JAMES M. FISCHER

Professor of Law
Southwestern University School of Law

 LexisNexis

ISBN: 978-1-4224-8053-3

Library of Congress Cataloging-in-Publication Data

Fischer, James M.
    Understanding remedies / James M. Fischer. --2nd ed.
      p. cm.
    ISBN 0-8205-6343-9 (softbound)
  1. Remedies (Law)--United States. 2. Damages--United States. I. Title.
KF9010.F57 2006
347.73'77--dc22   2006012707

ISBN#: 0820563439

Editorial Offices
744 Broad Street, Newark, NJ 07102 (973) 820-2000
201 Mission St., San Francisco, CA 94105-1831 (415) 908-3200
701 East Water Street, Charlottesville, VA 22902-7587 (434) 972-7600
www.lexis.com

(Pub.00586)

DEDICATION

To Sue, Adam, Evan, Allison and Zachary with Love, Gratitude, and Affection; without Blame or Responsibility for errors and omissions.

PREFACE TO SECOND EDITION

The goal of this book is modest—a descriptive account of the law of remedies. Much modern scholarship is more ambitious seeking a normative account of the law of remedies, i.e., how much redress *should* the law allow to vindicate legal wrongs and restore individuals harmed by those wrongs to their rightful position.

Yet, to state that a work is descriptive is not to suggest that it is not difficult or complex. A descriptive account can illustrate the chance element of law; the fact that "law" is often either uncertain or unresolved. This open-endedness is particularly common with remedies. Much of the "law" here is stated in capacious language leaving much to individual interpretation. Remedies law tends to be situation sensitive; here, the usual feature is that the facts of the case control the result more than the remedies rule.

All this creates a large amount of uncertainty as to how remedies issues will be resolved. Law students (and lawyers) need to be comfortable with uncertainty. It is ever-present in the law, but "uncertainty" does not undermine the case for knowing the "law," such as it is. Chance, after all, does favor the prepared mind. *

This book states the "law," but also gives examples that illustrate that the "law" often bends, is bent, and courts often disagree as to how the issue before the court should be resolved. In other words, what is the law? This view of the "law" reflects, no doubt, the authors own biases. All authors simplify by collecting materials and omitting data based on their own view of what the end produte should resemble. I have tried to be attentive to that bias. How successful I have been is, ultimately, for the reader to judge.

An early Rolling Stone's song provides a compass that helps in learning, and ultimately understanding, the law of remedies:

> You can't always get what you want
>
> You can't always get what you want
>
> And if you try sometime you find
>
> You get what you need. **

Sometimes the law of remedies provides full redress, and perhaps even then some for harm sustained. Most often, however, other values conflict with

---

* Attributed to Louis Pasteur.
** Rolling Stones "You Can't Always Get What You Want," Let It Bleed Album (1969).

a full recovery (or restoration). Even here, however, the law does not leave the plaintiff unprotected. The law of remedies is a search (and a determination) as to what the law permits as rectification and reparation when legal wrongs have been committed.

Although this text is marketed primarily to law students, I have chosen to add extensive footnote references to authorities that support the propositions asserted, as well as references to other work that develop the materials further than can be accomplished in a single volume text that aspires to some degree of comprehensiveness. Any tour through the legal landscape is a sail through waters infested with legal icebergs. This book discusses the tips of those icebergs. As every sailor of the law, whether lawyer or judge, knows, much more lies beneath.

James M. Fischer
Professor of Law
Southwestern University School of Law
Los Angeles, California

CONVENTIONS USED IN THIS BOOK

Footnotes are consecutively numbered within each whole section. For example, all footnotes within Section 13 are consecutively numbered through that Section's subsections e.g., 13.1, 13.2, etc. Footnotes for each whole section begin with the number one.

The first time an authority is cited in a section, it is set forth in full; thereafter, *within that same whole section*, the authority is abbreviated, with only the page cite given. For example, a decision will be cited in full the first time it appears in Section 13, but only an abbreviated citation if the authority again is referenced in Section 13.1 or 13.2, etc. If that same authority is also cited in Section 14, it would again be fully set forth and abbreviated citations used for further references within Section 14's subsections.

Unless otherwise noted, all cross references are within the same whole section only. Thus, a reference in a footnote in Section 13, including subsections, to footnote 15 is to footnote 15 in Section 13, including subsections. A reference in a footnote in Section 21 including subsections, to text and notes 5–7 is to text and notes 5–7 in Section 21, including subsections, only.

PREFACE TO FIRST EDITION

Remedies are fundamental; yet, remedies are frequently overlooked. We often discuss remedies without realizing that it is a remedy about which we are talking. Consider, for example, the exclusionary rule, which is a staple of constitutional criminal procedure jurisprudence. The exclusionary rule is, at root, a remedy designed to vindicate the values courts have identified in the text of constitutional provisions. It rectifies the harm inflicted by excluding evidence acquired by the state in violation of constitutional and statutory guarantees. It is remedial in its field of operation as much as an injunction or damages award in the cases in which they apply.

Should it make a difference whether a legal issue is classified and analyzed as a remedy or as a substantive right or procedural device? There is the argument that the difference is simply one of category classification, no different from tort versus contract, substance versus procedure, or civil versus criminal. Yet, the very persistence of these category classifications tells us that there is more going on here than mere categorization or arrangement. Separate identification of a legal issue in the remedies category helps us focus on the essential nature of that legal issue and its role in the larger legal framework. By looking at an "issue" as a "remedies issue" we gain a better understanding of the capabilities of remedies, as well as their limits.

The approach taken in these materials is neither doctrinal nor theoretical; rather, the focus is educative. The objective is to identify the basic legal principles, rules, and standards that constitute the law of remedies as applied by courts in the United States. Of necessity, the focus is on general principles and general rules of application. This approach permits readers to begin the analysis of a problem by deciding which facts are relevant. General principles and general rules also enable the reader to discover the more precise rules that determine the particular case. Most importantly, however, general principles and general rules enable the reader to both gain a sense of the ambit of remedies and establish a base from which the relationship between the general and the particular may be investigated to determine whether the specific application of a remedial principle or rule is consistent and coherent with the larger body of substantive and remedies law.

Stating rules and principles is easy; it is their application that is difficult. Neither the most complex nor the most basic "How to" book can avoid that gap between knowledge and application. Yet, if knowledge of rules and principles is not a sufficient condition to the proper application of law, it is necessary condition. Even the most gifted athlete will be frustrated if his performance is crippled because he violates the rules of the game. The knowledge of law, particularly its component rules, principles, guidelines, and standards enables the good lawyer to practice her profession with skill and confidence. Knowing what a client's remedies are has an obvious connection to the work litigation lawyers do, but remedies are not solely the concern of trial lawyers. Transaction lawyers must know what consequences are likely to result if the transaction fails, or the deal the transaction spawns, is breached. Remedies are not the sum of a lawyer's work, but they are an important constituent part of what good lawyers do and think about when representing their clients.

I have attempted to provide in these materials a comprehensive, and I hope, readable overview of the law of remedies. I have selected those rules and principles that I believe are of general application, noting whenever possible significant splits and disagreements regarding the accepted canons of law. In this regard Newton's law works here as elsewhere: for every stated principle of law, there is an equal, and opposite, statement of the principle elsewhere. I have tried to bring many of these disagreements to the surface by presenting the views evenly. When I believe that a particular view is wrong, I have not, however, hesitated to say so, but always as my opinion, not disguised as a restatement of the law. I cite all, in my opinion, useful sources, oblivious (actually indifferent) to the critique that some sources are beneath academic usage.[*]

If courts use it, this text cites it.

I hope readers will find the work useful and interesting. I certainly encourage readers of this work to contact me at Southwestern University School of Law if they have comments or observations regarding the book.

James M. Fischer
Professor of Law

---

[*] See Patrick McFadden, *Fundamental Principles of American Law*, 85 Cal. L. Rev. 1749, 1750 n.9 (1997) (observing, I hope tongue in cheek: "Woe to the scholar who cites American Jurisprudence . . . ."

TABLE OF CONTENTS

Chapter 8 REMEDIES FOR BODILY INJURIES

Page

Chapter 1

UNDERSTANDING REMEDIES

§ 1 BASIC REMEDIAL GOALS

It is frequently stated that for every wrong there is a remedy.[1] The concept is at the very core of American constitutional government.[2] The concept was recognized by Blackstone, who noted in his commentaries: "It is a general and indisputable rule, that where there is a legal right, there is also a legal remedy by suit or action at law whenever that right is invaded."[3]

---

[1] Faria v. San Jacinto Unified Sch. Dist., 59 Cal. Rptr. 2d 72, 77 (Cal. App. 1996); Sanzone v. Board of Police Comm'rs, 592 A.2d 912, 921 (Conn. 1991); Burns v. Burns, 518 So. 2d 1205, 1208 (Miss. 1988).

[2] Marbury v. Madison, 5 U.S. 137, 163 (1803) ("The government of the United States has been emphatically termed a government of laws, and not of men. It will certainly cease to deserve this high appellation, if the laws furnish no remedy for the violation of a vested legal right").

[3] 1 WILLIAM BLACKSTONE, COMMENTARIES ON THE LAWS OF ENGLAND *23.

The linking of a remedy for the invasion of rights brings forth several important legal consequences. First, we should note the emotive value of the statement. A wrong will be rectified in fact, not just in principle. Yet, what does it mean to say that a wrong will be rectified? The essential elements of rectification are to undo the injurious effects of the wrong. It must be kept in mind, however, that it is not the injury that gives rise to the remedy, but the legal wrong.[4] An injury accomplished without the infliction of a legal wrong does not give rise to a legal right to remediation. Some injuries are tolerated, such as the harm a lawyer may inflict on a non-client when the lawyer is acting within the adversarial system.[5] Other harms are encouraged and promoted, such as the economic harm to some that is the inevitable consequence of competition that benefits the many.[6] Some harms are seen as beyond the ability of courts to redress, usually for reasons of deference and discretion.[7]

The coupling of the concepts of wrong and remedy helps demonstrate the essential purpose of remedies, which is to redress the wrong by creating the situation that would have existed had the wrong not occurred. This is often referred to as returning or restoring the plaintiff to the rightful position *i.e.*, the position plaintiff would have occupied had the wrong not occurred.[8] This, however, must be understood to be a process of creation.

---

[4] Lowery v. Mountain Top Indoor Flea Mkt., Inc., 699 So. 2d 158, 161 (Ala. 1997) (noting that "the law doesn't say for every injury there is a remedy. It says for every wrong there is a remedy") (citation omitted).

[5] Levin, Middlebrook, et al. v. United States Fire Ins. Co., 639 So. 2d 606, 608 (Fla. 1994) (stating that attorney's immunity for defamation in connection with litigation represents necessary accommodation to needs of adversary system); Stern v. Thompson & Coates Ltd., 517 N.W.2d 658, 666 (Wis. 1994) (noting attorney's qualified immunity from suits by non-clients for professional advice given client even though advice results in harm to non-clients).

[6] Brunswick Corp. v. Pueblo Bowl-O-Mat, 429 U.S. 477, 488 (1977) (holding that federal antitrust policies are not advanced by providing compensation for losses due to increased competition).

[7] San Francisco v. United Ass'n of Journeymen and Apprentices, of the Plumbing and Pipefitting Indus. of U.S. and Canada, Local 38, 726 P.2d 538, 541 (Cal. 1986) (holding that absent legislative authorization, the maintenance of an illegal strike by public employees was not redressable in damages by private employers injured by strike); Anderson v. St. Francis-St. George Hosp., Inc., 671 N.E.2d 225, 228–29 (Ohio 1996) (holding that no cause of action existed for wrongfully prolonging the life of a patient in disregard of prior instructions). The court noted: "There are some mistakes, indeed even breaches of duty or technical assaults, that people make in this life that affect the lives of others for which there simply should be no monetary compensation." *Id.* at 228 (citation omitted).

[8] Milliken v. Bradley, 433 U.S. 267, 280 (1977) (desegregation decree must be designed to restore victims to position they would have occupied in the absence of wrongful conduct); Albermarle Paper Co. v. Moody, 422 U.S. 405, 413–25 (1975) (stating that the purpose of Title VII remedies for unlawful discrimination is to make plaintiff whole and restore him to the position he would have occupied had the wrong not occurred); *cf.* Castillo-Perez v. I.N.S., 212 F.3d 518, 528 (9th Cir. 2000) (holding that the appropriate remedy to redress a lawyer's ineffective assistance to an alien subject to deportation was to remand the matter to the Board of Immigration Appeals with instructions to consider the matter based on the law as it existed at the time of the alien's hearing before the Administrative Law Judge rather than under current law, which had been changed by a statute subsequent to the hearing).

Unlike the traveler in the familiar Robert Frost poem who could save the road not taken "for another day,"[9] a party must demonstrate to the satisfaction of the court where that unbeaten path led and that but for the wrong he would have taken it.[10]

Placement of the plaintiff in the position he would have occupied but for the wrong is, by necessity, an inexact science given the vagaries of proof, the imprecision of forecasting, and the need to develop and rely on counterfactuals. Any construction of plaintiff's rightful position is also compromised by competing interests, values, and policies that claim a place at the decisionmaking table. These interests, values, and policies influence the extent to which the legal system may return or restore the plaintiff to the position he would have occupied but for the wrong.[11] It is these competing interests, values, and policies that ultimately dictate the rules, principles, and standards that constitute the law of remedies.

§ 2 TYPES OF REMEDIES

Remedies are flexible. They have been developed both to complement substantive law and to meet the needs of litigants. Because the scope of substantive law is broad and the needs of litigants are diverse, remedies law provides a broad and diverse array of approaches that may be used for the particular situation. Terminology in this area has a rich, historical tradition. In some cases, that tradition has continuing vitality. In other contexts, the tradition does not have the same claim for continued allegiance. The distinctions suggested by the terminology may no longer be valid or the distinction may be artificial, thus creating confusion. These conflicts should be kept in mind when reading the remedial classifications discussed in this section.

---

[9] Robert Frost, "The Road Not Taken" in COMPLETE POEMS OF ROBERT FROST 131 (1964).

[10] Ward v. Papa's Pizza To Go, Inc., 907 F. Supp. 1535, 1544 (S.D. Ga. 1995) ("Plaintiff's 'rightful place' appears to be roughly the position she now holds and the wage she now earns . . . [i]f it is not, no one can safely formulate the appropriate alternative"); *cf.* Munn v. Algee, 924 F.2d 568, 575 (5th Cir.) (refusing to compensate plaintiff for the "hypothetical" injuries she would have sustained had she acted properly to mitigate damages when, on the facts, she failed to mitigate damages), *cert. denied*, 502 U.S. 900 (1991); Meletio Sea Food Co. v. Gordons Transps., 191 S.W.2d 983, 985 (Mo. App. 1946) (stating that "basic principles of law of damages . . . contemplates that the remedy provided in a given case shall only afford compensation for whatever injury is actually sustained) (citations omitted).

[11] Kraemer v. Franklyn & Marshall College, 941 F. Supp. 479, 483 (E.D. Pa. 1996) ("[re]instatement [to one's former position with an employer] is not an appropriate remedy if it requires bumping or displacing an innocent employee in favor of the plaintiff who would have held the [position but for the wrong]") (citation omitted; brackets added). *But see* Lander v. Lujan, 888 F.2d 153, 156 (D.C. Cir. 1989) (adopting "bumping theory" when necessary to place plaintiff in rightful position by reinstatement to former job); Section 152 (Employee Reinstatement to Position).

[2.1] Legal vs. Equitable Remedy

The distinction between legal and equitable remedy is basic to the law of remedies, even as its importance is diminishing due to the merger of the two systems in most jurisdictions.

The distinction between law and equity serves as the beginning for the distinction between legal and equitable remedies. Put simply, legal remedies are those available in the law courts and equitable remedies are those available in equity courts. As will be abundantly clear throughout this book, nothing could be so easy, and easy it is not. For in fact remedies at law were often available in equity, under the equity clean-up rule, and many equity principles were adopted by the law courts. The reasons for this migration of rules and doctrine between supposedly independent law systems is addressed elsewhere.[1] The point here is that the current legal system reflects a hodgepodge of rules that both imitate past practice and reflect differences with the past.

The importance of the law-equity distinction today lies in the fact that some remedies are only available on one side of the distinction but not the other, *i.e.*, at law but not in equity or the opposite, in equity but not at law. The merger of law and equity notwithstanding, accessing legal rather than equitable remedies can generate procedural differences, primarily with regard to jury trial. Accessing equitable remedies may also require the satisfaction of different proofs and burdens of persuasion than would be imposed if only remedies at law are sought. The distinction between legal and equitable remedies remains important notwithstanding the formal merger of the two systems.

[2.2] Specific vs. Substitutional Remedies

A specific remedy is one that gives the plaintiff exactly what she would have had, or would have obtained, if the legal wrong had not been committed. An example of this is specific performance. The remedy gives the plaintiff exactly what she bargained for and is legally entitled to receive, defendant's performance under the contract. A substitutional remedy is something other than a specific remedy. Returning to the contract example, a substitutional remedy for breach would give the plaintiff the dollar value to plaintiff of defendant's performance, as opposed to the actual performance itself.

There is a tendency to attribute specific remedies to equity and substitutional remedies to law. As with any generalization there is a basis for the attribution, but it is entirely descriptive, not normative. Specific remedies claims appear to dominate in equity because, as a practical matter, a frequent invocation of equity is for injunctive relief. In fact, substitutional remedies are frequently sought in equity, as for example, relief for breach of fiduciary duty.

---

[1] Section 20 (The Historical Relationship Between Law and Equity).

The flip side of the issue is that while substitutional remedies appear to dominate at law, specific remedies are also available. For example, the common law legal remedies of ejectment and replevin were specific remedies for the recovery of real and personal property, respectively. Modernly, both remedies are available, sometimes under different names.

The distinction between specific and substitutional remedies is helpful in the sense that it focuses awareness on exactly what one is seeking, but aside from the context of prioritizing remedies,[2] the distinction has little importance. Moreover, money is often sought as a specific remedy, for example, as reimbursement under principles of indemnity for discharging another's obligation. Characterization of the remedy in this case as specific or substitutional does little more than encourage confusion by suggesting that the distinction is meaningful; in fact, it is simply a label.

[2.3] Damages

Damages is a term used today to identify the recovery of monetary compensation for loss caused by the legal wrong of another. For example, we commonly speak of breach of contract damages or personal injury damages. In both of these situations, the idea of damages refers to the losses caused by the defendant's breach of the contract or the defendant's breach of duty. The common practice is to award a sum of money to compensate the plaintiff for the "damages" sustained. This requires that the "damages" themselves be determined in the form of a monetary loss to the plaintiff. In other words, the loss due to a defendant's non-performance of a contractual obligation must be determined as a monetary loss, *i.e.*, what was defendant's performance worth to plaintiff and what was lost by non-performance.

Damages may be compensatory or punitive, general or special, or economic or non-economic. The common denominator for each form of damages is, however, that the award be in money for the loss or detriment caused by the defendant.[3] The idea is to place the plaintiff in the position she would have occupied but for the legal wrong by using money to ameliorate the consequences of that legal wrong to the plaintiff.

[2.4] Injunctions

Injunctions are a form of equitable relief by which a defendant is ordered to do something (mandatory injunction) or refrain from doing something (prohibitory or negative injunction). The purpose of an injunction is to induce compliance through the coercion of legal sanction for non-compliance. The injunction may prevent a plaintiff's legitimate legal position from being altered by a defendant. Alternatively, the injunction may restore or return

---

[2] Section 21 (Adequacy of the Remedy at Law/Irreparable Injury).

[3] BLACK'S LAW DICTIONARY 393 (Bryan A. Garner, ed. 1999) ("Damages": "Money claimed by, or ordered to be paid to, a person as compensation for loss or injury").

the plaintiff to the position he would have occupied but for defendant's wrongful conduct by undoing the continuing effects of that wrongful conduct. A defendant who violates the terms of an injunction may be sanctioned by the additional remedy of contempt.

[2.5] Restitution

Restitutionary remedies are designed to force the defendant to give up ("disgorge") a benefit when retention of that benefit would constitute unjust enrichment. The basic concern here is that the defendant is holding something that in fairness and justice should be held instead by the plaintiff. The plaintiff's claim may be inferior to that of a third party, but it is always superior to that of the defendant. While restitutionary remedies are guided by equitable principles of fairness and justice, the remedies themselves may be available in law (*e.g.*, quasi contract) or in equity (*e.g.*, subrogation). The location of the restitutionary remedy in law or equity is important when procedural issues are raised, as for example, the right to a jury trial in an action for rescission, or when additional equitable remedies, such as a constructive trust or equitable lien, are sought.

[2.6] Declaratory Relief

Declaratory relief provides a judicial statement of the parties' rightful legal position with respect to a particular matter. The most common example of this remedy is the declaratory judgment, but other remedies fall within this category, such as an action to quiet title.

The essential feature of declaratory relief is that it does not compel an immediate, specific obligation to do something. Such judgments lack an "operative command." A money judgment must be paid, although the enforcement of that obligation may prove difficult for the plaintiff (judgment creditor)—again another example of a remedy (damages) needing another remedy (levy or execution) to be effective.[4] An injunction must be obeyed under penalty of contempt. Declaratory relief does not, however, require or demand that the parties do anything. The full effect of the remedy lies in its educative value and the further remedy of a follow up action to enforce the rights, duties, and obligations recognized by the court in the declaratory action.[5] In some contexts, however, the line between a declaratory

---

[4] Levy or Execution refers to remedies available to a judgment creditor to obtain satisfaction of a judgment that remains unpaid. These remedies, including levy, execution, attachment, garnishment, examination, etc., were developed by the common law to secure payment, but have been largely codified today. *See* Dennis J. Drebsky & Lynn M. Barry, *Enforcing Money Judgments*, 686 PLI/Comm 27 (1994).

[5] Montana v. United States, 440 U.S. 147, 157–58 (1979) (declaratory judgment has precedential and collateral estoppel effect).

judgment and an action granting affirmative relief, such as damages, may be minimal.[6]

[2.7] Punitive Damages

Punitive damages are designed to punish a defendant for committing a legal wrong. A punitive remedy may be essentially freestanding, such as a punitive damages award,[7] or it may be interwoven into the fabric of the remedy itself, as in the case of contempt, which distinguishes between criminal and civil contempt.[8]

Because punitive damages are designed to punish, there is no need to assess whether they will restore or return the plaintiff to the position he would have occupied but for the defendant's wrongful conduct. On the other hand, a compensatory damages award may have a punitive component.[9] The restoration or return of the plaintiff to the position he would have occupied but for defendant's wrongful conduct is combined with the desire to punish the defendant. Alternatively, the purpose of the award may be seen as generously defining the position the plaintiff would have occupied but for defendant's wrongdoing. This latter view retains the compensatory focus of the award.

The line separating punitive from compensatory damages is further blurred by the existence of certain limitations on punitive awards that require courts to examine the nature of the award to ensure that the limitation is not evaded by artful labeling. For example, in *United States v. Halper*[10] the Court held that the imposition of civil, money penalties may in certain circumstances violate the Double Jeopardy Clause.[11] Similarly, in *Johnson v. Securities Exchange Commission*[12] the court held that a non-monetary sanction in the form of a suspension was punitive in nature.[13]

---

[6] Green v. Mansour, 474 U.S. 64, 67 (1985) (stating that a declaratory judgment against a state may be equivalent to a money judgment barred by the Eleventh Amendment because of the doctrine of res judicata and the absence of a continuing violation would give the declaration only retroactive application). *But cf.* Steffel v. Thompson, 415 U.S. 452, 480 (1974) (Rhenquist, J., concurring) (stating that issuance of injunction against state court prosecution should not occur as a matter of course after declaratory judgment that statute under which plaintiff would be prosecuted by state officials was unconstitutional).

[7] Chapter 23 (Punitive Damages).

[8] Chapter 22 (Contempt).

[9] Section 8.7 (Harsh or Mild Measures).

[10] 490 U.S. 435 (1989).

[11] *Id.* at 447–48. The ruling was later modified in *Hudson v. United States*, 522 U.S. 93 (1997) (holding that the Double Jeopardy Clause only prohibits multiple criminal punishments for the same offense and then only when multiple punishment occurs in successive proceedings). The Court in *Hudson* held that whether a penalty is civil or criminal is primarily a legislative function and "only the clearest proof will suffice to override legislative intent and transform what has been denominated a civil remedy into a criminal penalty." *Id.* at 100 (citations omitted).

[12] 87 F.3d 484 (D.C. Cir. 1996).

[13] *Id.* at 488–89. *But see* United States v. Merriam, 108 F.3d 1162, 1164 (9th Cir. 1997) (statutory bar against acting as broker-dealer imposed as a result of settlement was not punitive for purposes of the Double Jeopardy Clause), *cert. denied*, 522 U.S. 818 (1997).

A punitive remedy need not be labeled as such. Treble damage remedies are usually characterized as punitive in part.[14] Similarly, civil forfeiture remedies may be seen as punitive in character.[15]

[2.8] Nominal Damages

Nominal damages are designed to remedy violations of legal rights that cause no measurable actual loss or substantial injury. They are awarded in recognition that the plaintiff has sustained a legal wrong. Allowing a plaintiff to claim nominal damages permits the plaintiff to secure a public vindication of her legal claim.[16]

Although nominal damages are usually seen as a single concept, nominal damages actually consist of a mixture of different concepts that affect how the law treats nominal damages. First, a plaintiff may have been the victim of both legal and illegal conduct, but the plaintiff's injuries are only traceable to the legal conduct; alternatively, the defendant's illegal conduct may have produced no actual injury. Here, nominal damages reflects the law's disapproval of the illegal conduct. Second, the plaintiff's damages proof may have failed because plaintiff lacked credibility, when credibility is critical—as for example with claims for distress damages. Alternatively, the plaintiff's damages proof may fail because plaintiff's evidence is inadequate to satisfy the burden of proof. Here, the trier-of-fact may perceive that the plaintiff suffered actual injury, but be unable to award a specific sum as compensation.[17]

Nominal damages are available in a wide variety of actions, including breach of contract,[18] negligence,[19] constitutional[20] and business[21] torts.

---

[14] Section 207.2 (Augmented Damages and Punitive Damages).

[15] *Compare* Austin v. United States, 509 U.S. 602, 619 (1993) (treating in rem civil forfeiture as punishment for purposes of 8th Amendment excessive fines clause), *with* United States v. Ursery, 518 U.S. 267, 286–87 (1996) (treating in rem civil forfeiture as not being punishment for purposes of double jeopardy). The Court noted, however, that in some cases a civil penalty could be so punitive either in purpose or effect as to constitute criminal punishment for double jeopardy purposes. *Id.* at 289 n.3.

[16] Farrar v. Hobby, 506 U.S. 103, 121 (1992) (O'Connor, J., concurring) (noting "[n]ominal relief does not necessarily a nominal victory make," . . . "an award of nominal damages can represent a victory in the sense of vindicating rights even though no actual damages are proved"); Utah Animal Rights Coalition v. Salt Lake City Corp., 371 F.3d 1248, 1257 (10th Cir. 2004) (stating that nominal damages claim, unlike claim for declarative relief, is not rendered moot by cessation of challenged activity).

[17] Briggs v. Marshall, 93 F.3d 355, 360 (7th Cir. 1996) (discussing the concepts in the context of a police brutality claim).

[18] Scobell, Inc. v. Schade, 688 A.2d 715, 719 (Pa. Super. Ct. 1997); Magu Realty Co. v. Spartan Concrete Corp., 658 N.Y.S.2d 45, 45 (App. Dept. 1997).

[19] Nick v. Baker, 481 S.E.2d 412, 414 (N.C. App. 1997). *Contra* Bird v. Rozier, 948 P.2d 888, 892 (Wyo. 1997) (holding that "[n]ominal damages, to vindicate a technical right, cannot be recovered in a negligence action, where no actual loss has occurred").

[20] Carey v. Piphus, 435 U.S. 247, 266–67 (1978); Muhammad v. Lockhart, 104 F.3d 1069, 1070 (8th Cir. 1997).

[21] United States Football League v. National Football League, 842 F.2d 1335, 1377 (2d Cir. 1988) (antitrust action); Lodise v. Lodise, 9 F.3d 108 (6th Cir. 1993) (credit report improperly obtained but not used for improper purpose) (unpublished disposition).

Because an award of nominal damages will support an award of attorneys fees and costs in civil rights litigation, some attention has been devoted to the propriety of a plaintiff requesting only an award of nominal damages.[22]

Nominal damages must be requested; they are not awarded as a matter of right, although the Supreme Court has held that they are mandatory when plaintiff's constitutional rights have been violated, but he cannot prove actual injury.[23]

[2.9] Presumed Damages

Presumed damages originated in defamation actions. Words that were libelous were reasonably expected to cause harm by their use; thus, they were deemed actionable *per se*.[24] The cause of action did not require the plaintiff to prove that the publication of the libel caused any harm to reputation or injury to the plaintiff.[25]

Although the presumed damages rule was pegged to a causal relationship between act and harm, it is also clear that the rule was rooted in a realization that actual damage, while likely, would be a difficult proof. It is the combination of the causal element and the difficulty of proof that informs modern courts as to when presumed damages may be awarded.[26]

The doctrine of presumed damages in the common law of defamation *per se* has been referred to as "an oddity of tort law, for it allows recovery of purportedly compensatory damages without evidence of actual loss."[27] Notwithstanding the backhanded compliment, the doctrine of presumed damages has been recognized in other contexts, such as trespass[28] and certain forms of invasion of privacy.[29]

---

[22] *Farrar, supra*, 506 U.S. at 115 (plaintiffs who recovered only nominal damages on claim for $17 million in damages were not entitled to attorneys fee award under civil rights statute); Section 212 (Prevailing Party).

[23] *Farrar, supra*, 506 U.S. at 112.

[24] There is some disagreement whether "presumed damages" applied to all libel actions or only libel *per se*. Lawrence Eldredge, *The Spurious Rule of Libel Per Quod*, 79 Harv. L. Rev. 733 (1966); William Prosser, *Libel Per Quod*, 46 Va. L. Rev. 839 (1960). *See* Biondi v. Nassimos, 692 A.2d 103, 106 (N.J. Super. App. Dept. 1997) (applying principle to slander *per se*); Chapter 12 (Remedies For Defamation).

[25] Sisler v. Gannett Co., Inc., 516 A.2d 1083, 1096 (N.J. 1986).

[26] Memphis Community Sch. Dist. v. Stachura, 477 U.S. 299, 310–11(1986) (presumed damages may be appropriate when injury is likely but difficult to prove).

[27] Gertz v. Robert Welch, Inc., 418 U.S. 323, 349 (1974). The availability of "presumed damages" in defamation cases has been restricted due to First Amendment concerns. *Id.* at 349–50; Section 105 (Presumed Damages).

[28] Gross v. Capital Elec. Line Builders, Inc., 861 P.2d 1326, 1329 (Kan. 1993) (rule of presumed damages recognized when trespass constitutes tangible invasion, but not recognized when invasion is intangible, *e.g.*, airborne pollution); Bradley v. American Smelting & Refining Co., 709 P.2d 782, 790 (Wash. 1985) (same).

[29] Nolley v. County of Erie, 802 F. Supp. 898, 903 (W.D.N.Y. 1992) ("presumed damages are appropriate in a cause of action founded on the unwarranted disclosure of a person's HIV status").

The doctrine has received a mixed reception in the context of constitutional torts. The Supreme Court stated in *Carey v. Piphus*[30] that whether a constitutional tort would support an award of presumed damages depended on the nature of the constitutional right at issue.[31]

In *Carey* the Court rejected a claim of presumed damages when only procedural due process claims were involved. In *Memphis Community School District v. Stachura*,[32] the Court extended this proscription to First Amendment claims.[33] Lower courts have, however, evidenced a general willingness to apply the presumed damages rule to cases not expressly foreclosed by Supreme Court holdings. To this practice the Court itself has been somewhat ambivalent.[34]

§ 3 RIGHTS AND REMEDIES

[3.1] Relationship Between Rights and Remedies

Remedies do not exist in isolation, but are bound up with rights: the nature of the relationship is, however, subject to intense, critical debate. Should rights be seen as more important than remedies, or vice-versa?[1]

Is the rights-remedies issue simply a variation of the "chicken-egg" dilemma? Do rights necessarily precede remedies as a matter of form and practice and thereby claim a preference by priority? The questions are not

---

[30] 435 U.S. 247 (1978).

[31] *Id.* at 262–63.

[32] 477 U.S. 299 (1986).

[33] *Id.* at 312–13.

[34] *Id.* at 310–11:

> Presumed damages are a substitute for ordinary compensatory damage, not a supplement for an award that fully compensates the alleged injury. When a plaintiff seeks compensation for an injury that is likely to have occurred but difficult to establish, some form of presumed damages may possibly be appropriate. In those circumstances, presumed damages may roughly approximate the harm that the plaintiff suffered and thereby compensate for harms that may be impossible to measure. As we earlier explained, the instructions at issue in this case did not serve this purpose, but instead called on the jury to measure damages based on a subjective evaluation of the importance of particular constitutional values. Since such damages are wholly divorced from any compensatory purpose, they cannot be justified as presumed damages.

(citations omitted); Section 111 (Civil Rights/Constitutional Torts).

[1] Daryl J. Levinson, *Rights Esssentialism and Remedial Equilibration*, 99 Colum. L. Rev. 857 (1999) (discussing competing viewpoints as to whether constitutional rights are corrupted by the practical need to be expressed in a remedial format or whether constitutional rights and their corresponding remedial expression are complimentary and co equal); John C. Jeffries, Jr., *The Right-Remedy Gap in Constitutional Law*, 109 Yale L.J. 87 (1999) (arguing that limiting damages to cases involving both constitutional violations and fault, but allowing injunctive relief for constitutional violations regardless of fault, encourages a broad development of constitutional rights; limiting remedies encourages innovation in the field of constitutional rights by reducing the costs of the law's development).

simply rhetorical. Classification of remedies as "equal to" or "second order to" rights can have significant legal consequences.

Remedies are frequently characterized as procedural for a variety of purposes, such as choice of law[2] and retroactive application,[3] but how far should the distinction be taken? The nature of an available remedy is clearly tied to the substantive right at issue. Although the remedy may generically be labeled as damages, or injunctive, or restitutionary, the content of the remedy will be strongly influenced by the nature of the interests that comprise the right.[4] Property rights, for example, usually will not support emotional distress claims because such claims are not usually seen as part of the bundle of interests that comprise the right. That approach may seem counterintuitive to a layperson who is told that the defendant, who caused the loss of "Fido," the beloved household pet, need not respond to the emotional distress the loss has caused.[5] But unless the substantive bundle of interests is defined to include the owner's emotional attachment to property, the remedy will follow the law.

While remedies will follow the law, the law will provide appropriate remedies to protect the right. If an injunction is needed to protect a contract right, the remedy of an injunction is available in the form of specific performance. Likewise if an injunction is needed to prevent a trespass or a nuisance, it will be provided. If an injunction is not needed, but damages to redress the violation of a right are, the law will provide such a remedy. The law of remedies is essentially a study of the rules and principles that

---

[2] This was an area where the decisional law was in substantial flux over the proper characterization of remedies for choice of law purposes. *See* ROBERT LEFLAR, LUTHER MCDOUGAL & ROBERT FELIX, AMERICAN CONFLICTS LAW § 126 (4th ed. 1986). The modern trend has been to reject the substance-procedure distinction in this area due to inconsistency in the characterization of the issue and the perception that the distinction is unworkable. *See* WILLIAM RICHMAN & WILLIAM REYNOLDS, UNDERSTANDING CONFLICT OF LAWS § 59, at 166–67 (3d ed. 2002). *See generally* 16 Am. Jur. 2d *Conflict of Laws* § 137 (1979).

[3] The traditional rule is that legislation should be construed as operating prospectively absent express language to the contrary, but this rule does not apply to statutory remedies. First of Am. Trust Co. v. Armstead, 664 N.E.2d 36, 39 (Ill. 1996) (criticizing traditional approach); *see In re* Estate of DeWitt, 54 P.3d 849, 854 (Colo. 2002) (stating that retroactive application of a statute is permitted when the effected change is remedial). A common gloss on this rule is that retroactive application may not alter "vested rights." *Id.* (finding that a statute impermissibly has a retroactive application if "it operates on transactions that have already occurred or on rights and obligations that existed before its effective date"); Neiman v. American Nat. Property & Cas. Co., 613 N.W.2d 160 (Wis. 2000) (holding that statute that increased damages available for loss of society and companionship could not be retroactively applied to insurer that had contractually agreed to provide coverage for such losses before the statute's effective date).

[4] Ford v. Trendwest Resorts, Inc., 43 P.3d 1223 (Wash. 2002) (holding that plaintiff who established breach of an at-will employment contract could only recover nominal damages; lost earnings were not recoverable because such a recovery was incompatible with the right (at-will employment) possessed by the plaintiff).

[5] Section 82 (Pets).

have been developed to determine how much redress a person is entitled to once a right has been violated.[6]

The importance of the right will influence the court's desire to find a remedy. Not surprisingly it has been noted that "courts will be alert to adjust their remedies so as to grant the necessary relief" for the safeguarding of protected rights.[7] By the same token, judicial reluctance to recognize or protect a "right" may be demonstrated by a court's refusal to provide a remedy for the breach of a "right." For example, in *Anderson v. St. Francis-St. George Hospital, Inc.*[8] the court refused to recognize a distinct action for "wrongful prolongation of life." The court recognized the validity of a patient's right to refuse and anticipatorily reject life-saving treatment. It also found that the defendant had violated a patient's instructions to that effect. Nonetheless, the court refused to permit a suit for damages arising out of the patient's later suffering of a stroke. According to the court, it was necessary to show that the unauthorized treatment caused or contributed to the stroke. It was not sufficient to base the claim on the mere breach of instruction given by the patient. Nor was it sufficient merely to demonstrate that a stroke was reasonably foreseeable after the patient had been resuscitated in violation of his instructions.[9]

"Wrongful life" claims have proven to be particularly difficult and troubling for courts. While jurisdictions have recognized a person's right to decide whether to be administered life-saving treatment, as *Anderson* illustrates, courts have been reluctant to back up the right with an enforceable damages remedy. On the other hand, injunctive relief compelling compliance with the instructions has been recognized.[10] Here we see the rough balancing of interests that can be accommodated through the judicious blending of rights and remedies.[11]

---

[6] United States v. Sanchez, 917 F. Supp. 29, 34 (D.D.C. 1996) (noting that while "courts must ensure that for every right there is a remedy . . . courts 'need not provide for every right the same remedy' ") (citations omitted).

[7] Bivens v. Six Unknown Named Agents of Fed. Bureau of Narcotics, 403 U.S. 388, 392 (1971).

[8] 671 N.E.2d 225 (Ohio 1996).

[9] *Id.* at 229:

   We also observe that unwanted life-saving treatment does not go undeterred. Where a patient clearly delimits the medical measures he or she is willing to undergo, and a health care provider disregards such instructions, the consequences for that breach would include the damages arising from any battery inflicted on the patient, as well as appropriate licensing sanctions against the medical professionals.

[10] *In re* Fiori, 652 A.2d 1350 (Pa. 1995); Care and Protection of Beth, 587 N.E.2d 1377 (Mass. 1992).

[11] Chenault v. Huie, 989 S.W.2d 474 (Tex. Civ. App. 1999) (holding that child could not recover damages from mother due to mother's decision, whether negligent or grossly negligent under the circumstances, to use illegal drugs during pregnancy); *In re* Baby Boy Doe, 632 N.E.2d 326 (Ill. App. 1994) (holding that mother's decision to refuse delivery of child by cesarian section must be upheld even though harm to child is likely); Section 76.1 (Wrongful Birth/Wrongful Life).

[3.2] Common Law Remedies

The term "common law remedies" is often used, but rarely defined. The general understanding is that the phrase refers to remedies developed through judicial decision making as opposed to legislative or administrative action. The distinction is, however, not crisp; rather, the definition encompasses an evolving standard. As legislation and administrative action is incorporated into judicial decision making, it becomes part of the common law; thus, the term is dynamic, not static; Darwinian, not Newtonian. Nonetheless, at any particular point in time, the distinction between common law remedies, on the one hand, and statutory, administrative, or private (*i.e.*, arbitral) remedies on the other hand, helps identify respective areas of authority and responsibility, even if the exact meaning of the term "common law remedies" is somewhat opaque.[12]

[3.3] Statutory Remedies

We live in an "age of statutes."[13] This is not said to diminish the common law. Far from it. Nonetheless, as a source of law, the common law is often replaced or significantly augmented by statutes. The common law process is still dominant: it is judges who still declare what the law is. The source of that declared law is, however, no longer largely confined to prior decisions by courts; rather, the sources of law have been rapidly expanded to include legislative declarations.

[3.3.1] Express Remedies

A statute may expressly provide a remedy; thus, a statute may state that violations can be punished by damages, injunction, or restitutionary relief. When an express remedy is provided, the usual rule is that it will be applied to situations encompassed by the statute. Such applications are not surprising. The more difficult question is whether the express remedy is exclusive or supplementary to otherwise available common law remedies.

One approach to this question is to ascertain the intent of the legislature. This is the dominant approach and the approach used by federal courts assessing federal statutes.[14]

---

[12] C.J. Hendry Co. v. Moore, 318 U.S. 133, 148–49 (1943) (stating that: "Examination of the history of the Judiciary Act of 1789 does not disclose precisely what its framers had in mind when in § 9 [the former "Saving to Suitors" provision of federal Admiralty Law] they used the term "common law remedies") (brackets added). Similar uncertainty surrounds the 7th Amendment's preservation of the right to jury trial "[i]n Suits at common law." Section 20.2 (Right of Jury Trial).

[13] ANTONIN SCALIA, A MATTER OF INTERPRETATION: FEDERAL COURTS AND THE LAW (1997) (describing the modern era as the "age of statutes"); GUIDO CALABRESI, A COMMON LAW FOR THE AGE OF STATUTES (1982) (describing statutes as the primary source of law in modern America).

[14] Merrill Lynch, Pierce, Fenner & Smith, Inc. v. Curran, 456 U.S. 353, 378 (1982) (stating that "[w]hen Congress enacts new legislation, the question is whether Congress intended to create a private remedy as a supplement to the express enforcement provisions of the statute."). How that "intent" should be discerned (*e.g.*, statute's plain meaning or legislative history) is beyond the scope of these materials.

Another approach, or perhaps merely a variation of the first approach, is to determine whether the statute in question created a new right, *i.e.*, a right not previously recognized by the law of the jurisdiction, or merely enhanced an existing right. Under this approach, if the statute created a new right, the coupled statutory remedy is the exclusive remedy for violations of the statutorily created right. The theory behind this approach was the now largely discarded doctrine that statutes in derogation of the common law were to be strictly construed. A statute that created rights unknown at common law should, under this approach, be confined to the remedies the legislature saw fit to affix to the new right.[15] Many courts *today* use a different approach and examine the issue of exclusivity by asking whether the statutory remedy is adequate.[16]

A related issue is how courts should respond to positive statutory statements or declarations that the statutorily prescribed remedy is exclusive and controlling. The most common manifestation of the issue are "damages caps." Courts generally follow statutory mandates in this area unless the mandate itself is unconstitutional.[17]

[3.3.2] Implied Remedies

Whether courts should imply a remedy to a statutory scheme is one of the more contested issues of our times. There is an overlap here with the exclusivity issue addressed in section 3.3.1, but the question of implied remedies is usually treated as being analytically distinct. The distinction is often hard to maintain; however, implied remedy analysis is the usual approach taken when a party asks the court to redress a statutory violation by way of a remedy not expressly provided for in the statute. This approach dominants in cases addressing federal legislation because federal courts, unlike state courts, are courts of limited jurisdiction and are, thus, unable (or unwilling) to use common law as a substantive source of law; federal common law has largely developed as a gloss on statutory and constitutional law.[18]

Remedial statutes come in two types and are subject to independent yet overlapping concerns. Does the statute recognize an express remedy for the right(s) the statute creates? We often use the shorthand reference here of a statutory cause of action. Note, however, that *before* we get to that point,

---

[15] Fletcher v. Coney Island, Inc., 134 N.E.2d 371, 375 (Ohio 1956) (holding that civil rights statute prohibiting racial discrimination at places of public accommodation and providing criminal penalties and statutory damages could not be enforced by injunctive relief).

[16] Orloff v. Los Angeles Turf Club, 180 P.2d 321 (Cal. 1947) (holding that statutory remedy of damages was not exclusive remedy and that court could issue injunction to interdict violations of the statute barring discrimination at places of public accommodation); *see* Kulch v. Structural Fibers, Inc., 677 N.E.2d 308 (Ohio 1997) (distinguishing *Fletcher, supra*, and adopting the "adequacy" approach regarding the exclusivity of statutory remedies).

[17] *See* Mathew W. Light, Student Note, *Who's the Boss?: Statutory Damage Caps, Courts and State Constitutional Law*, 58 Wash. & Lee L. Rev. 315 (2001).

[18] Erwin Chemerinsky, Federal Jurisdiction §§ 6.1–6.3 (1989) (discussing the limits and breadth of "federal common law").

we have to identify the "right" (and the scope of that right) that the statute creates. Under modern jurisprudence, a distinction is made between "rights," "rights of action," and "remedies." A "right" imposes a duty upon another to act (or refrain from acting) for the benefit of the rightholder. A "right of action" is the mechanism by which a rightholder obtains judicial relief caused by a violation of that "right." A "remedy" is the form of redress a court provides through a "right of action."[19]

Recognizing that a statute creates an express right of action is, thus, only the beginning of the injury. It still must be determined: (1) what "rights" does the statute protect through the express "right of action"; (2) what "remedies" does the statute expressly provide for violations of statutory "rights"; and (3) to what extent, if at all, may the express "remedies" for the express "right of action" be "augmented" by the court?[20]

Federal law in this area has developed along two paths. One pathway is defined by cases that directly address the question whether a remedy should be implied for violations of the Constitution or Statute. The constitutional cases derive from *Bivens v. Six Unknown Named Agents of the Federal Bureau of Narcotics*.[21] *Bivens* adopted a liberal approach. The Court noted the presumption that damages are available for invasions of personal liberty and the absence of any exceptional circumstances counselling hesitation in implying a damages remedy when federal agents violate constitutional guarantees.[22] *Bivens* enjoyed, however, only a brief growth spurt; in its more recent decisions the Court has emphasized factors that counsel hesitation rather than expansion of *Bivens*. In *Schweiker v. Chilicky*[23] the Court refused to imply a remedy for alleged constitutional violations by federal officials "[w]hen the design of a Government program suggests that Congress has provided what it considers adequate remedial mechanisms for constitutional violations . . . ."[24] The congressional program need not be, (and invariably is not), as comprehensive or complete as the implied remedy a court would create.[25]

---

[19] Donald H. Zeigler, *Rights, Rights of Action, and Remedies: An Integrated Approach*, 76 Wash. L. Rev. 67, 68 n.3 (2001). Professor Zeigler criticizes this development in the body of his article, but he acknowledges its general acceptance. *Id.* at 69 n.6.

[20] Historically, federal courts took a rather broad view of their ability to expand on express statutory remedies. That approach has been challenged by the Court's decision in *Grupo Mexicano de Desarrollo, S.A. v. Alliance Bond Fund, Inc.*, 527 U.S. 308 (1999) (holding that federal courts lack equitable power to issue preliminary injunction ("freeze order") to preserve defendant's assets *pendente lite* when only legal remedies are sought). Judith Resnik, *Constricting Remedies: The Rehnquist Judiciary, Congress, and Federal Power*, 78 Ind. L.J. 223, 253–54 (2003) ("[E]ven when express congressional authority has been provided, courts have read *Grupo Mexicano* as 'counsel[ing] caution in' expansive reading of such statutory provisions") (citation omitted).

[21] 403 U.S. 388 (1971).

[22] *Id.* at 396–97.

[23] 487 U.S. 412 (1988).

[24] *Id.* at 423.

[25] Berry v. Hollander, 925 F.2d 311, 313 (9th Cir. 1991) (stating that *Bivens* claim may be precluded when Congress has created some mechanisms for relief even though the statutory remedial scheme is incomplete).

The Court has also found that *Bivens* remedies are inappropriate when the very threat of such remedies may undermine the attainment of other goals and purposes Congress is entitled to prefer. For example, in *Chappell v. Wallace*[26] the Court refused to recognize a *Bivens* claim brought by enlisted members of the United States armed forces who claimed racial discrimination by their military superiors. The Court stated that recognition of a *Bivens* action would impermissibly compromise the "unique disciplinary structure" of the military.[27]

Separate from the *Bivens* line of decisions is the question whether a remedy should be implied from a federal statute. Initially, the Court liberally implied remedies in this context.[28] In effect, under this approach, courts were authorized to imply a remedy when they thought that doing so would advance the congressional goals and purposes behind the statute. This liberal approach was, however, constrained in *Cort v. Ash*[29] and abandoned in *Touche Ross & Co. v. Redington*.[30] In *Cort v. Ash* the Court adopted a four factor test to determine whether a remedy should be implied. These factors were (1) legislative intent, (2) the consistency of the remedy with the underlying purposes of the legislative scheme, (3) whether the plaintiff was a member of the class for whose benefit the statute was enacted, and (4) whether the cause of action is one traditionally relegated to state law.[31] In *Touche Ross & Co. v. Redington* the Court completed the abandonment of *J.I. Case Co. and* raised the stakes by focusing the analysis on the question of legislative intent; the remaining *Cort* factors are now used to discern the relevant legislative intent.[32] In this area, the Court has not exhibited any willingness to read congressional acts liberally; quite the contrary in fact.[33]

The second pathway in which federal remedies may be judicially developed arises in the context of determining whether the statute or constitutional provision creates "specific, individual, enforceable rights." Law, whether of constitutional or statutory status, may create duties or liabilities but no enforceable rights or rights with limited remedies. Whether a federal statute creates a "right" (as opposed to a "right of action") was addressed in *Blessing v. Freestone*.[34] The distinction is critical in connection with

---

[26] 462 U.S. 296 (1983).

[27] *Id.* at 304–05; *cf.* Adams v. Johnson, 355 F.3d 1179, 1185 (9th Cir. 2004) (agreeing with decisions from the First, Fifth, and Seventh Circuits that recognition of a *Bivens* damages remedy in the field of tax collection by the Internal Revenue Service would "wreck (sic) havoc with the federal tax system").

[28] J.I. Case Co. v. Borak, 377 U.S. 426, 433 (1964) (holding that the broad remedial purpose behind section 14(a) of the Securities Exchange Act of 1934, 15 U.S.C.A. § 78n(a), warranted implying a damages remedy).

[29] 422 U.S. 66 (1975).

[30] 442 U.S. 560 (1979).

[31] 422 U.S. at 78.

[32] Love v. Delta Air Lines, 310 F.3d 1347, 1352 (11th Cir. 2002).

[33] Alexander v. Sandoval, 532 U.S. 275 (2001) (refusing to read longstanding agency interpretation as reasonable construction of statute).

[34] 520 U.S. 329 (1997).

Section 1983 actions[35] because that provision creates a cause of action for the violation of federal rights not just federal statutes. A federal right is an individual entitlement. A federal statute may create a right, but it need not; for example, the statute may create "a yardstick . . . to measure the system-wide performance of a State's" administration of a federal program.[36] In this case, the federal government can enforce the State's duties under the program, but a private individual, even one aggrieved by a violation of program obligations by the State, may not because a "yardstick" is not a "right."[37] The fact that there is no remedy for a statutory violation does not mean the plaintiff is completely without recourse to the courts. The defendant's conduct may violate common law duties that are independently available against the defendant. Of course, the common law remedies may have requirements not present in the statutory scheme. For example, the statutory action may not require the plaintiff to show "actual injury," but such a requirement may exist under the common law remedy.

Under *Blessing* a statute creates an *individual* right if: (1) Congress intended the provision to benefit the plaintiff; (2) the "right" is capable of judicial enforcement; and, (3) the statute unambiguously imposes a binding obligation on the defendant.[38] The factors are somewhat capacious and open to divergent application; however, as was the case with the decisional law applying the four factor test of *Cort v. Ash* to determine if a statutory remedy would be implied,[39] the *Blessing* factors may be in the similar process of coalescing around the first factor of congressional intent. An example of this may be found in *South Camden Citizens in Action v. New Jersey Dept. of Environmental Protection*,[40] which involved a challenge, by private parties brought under Section 1983, that the decision to site a "slag processing facility" in a low income, minority neighborhood violated disparate impact regulations promulgated by the EPA pursuant to Title VI of the Civil Rights Act of 1964.

The majority opinion in *South Camden* held that the disparate impact regulations could not be enforced in a private action. The majority held that the failure of Congress to provide expressly in the statute that "disparate impact" violated the law precluded private enforcement of that theory. The

---

[35] 42 U.S.C. § 1983.

[36] *Blessing, supra*, 520 U.S. at 343.

[37] Gonzaga University v. Doe, 536 U.S. 273 (2002) (holding that a student could not enforce federal education privacy laws through a Section 1983 action). In *Doe* the student claimed that the university had released personal information about the student to an unauthorized person in violation of the Federal Educational Rights and Privacy Act of 1974, 20 U.S.C. § 1232g. The Act prohibits schools from releasing information contained in school records without the consent of the student, or the student's parents if the student is a minor, or pursuant to a statutory exception. The Act denies federal funding to schools that have a "policy or practice" of releasing information in violation of the Act. The Court held the Act created no specific, individual, enforceable rights.

[38] *Blessing, supra*, 520 U.S. at 340–41.

[39] *See* text and notes 28–33, *supra*.

[40] 274 F.3d 771 (3d Cir. 2001), *cert. denied*, 536 U.S. 939 (2002).

fact that the EPA had adopted regulations prohibiting "disparate impact" was not helpful. A regulation cannot create an enforceable right because *Alexander v. Sandoval*[41] foreclosed that approach:

> [L]anguage in a regulation may invoke a private right of action that Congress through statutory text created, but it may not create a right that Congress has not.[42]

The current state of the law in this area is, thus, somewhat uncertain. A private plaintiff may secure judicial enforcement, and appropriate remediation, through Section 1983 of violations of federal rights even if the statute in which the right is contained does not contain an express or implied remedy. Whether that statute provides a federal right enforceable through Section 1983 is, however, the more difficult issue. *Blessing* points the way, but the law here appears to be more in the nature of a work in progress than a settled rule or even settled process.

Finally, it should be noted that implying a remedy is analytically different from construing an existing remedy, although the distinction may not always be honored. For example, in *Griggs v. Duke Power Co.*[43] the Court held that disparate impact claims could be directly asserted under Title VII of the Civil Rights Act of 1964. This approach avoids the need to imply a remedy; however, how far this approach may be taken is unclear.[44]

§ 4 PUBLIC POLICY

Lord Justice Burrough, when asked to invalidate a contract on public policy grounds, stated that public policy "is a very unruly horse, and once you get astride it you never know where it will carry you."[1] Other judges have expressed a more accepting role for public policy,[2] noting that it is

---

[41] 532 U.S. 275 (2000). *Sandoval* involved a direct action to enforce disparate impact regulations promulgated pursuant to Title VI by the Department of Justice. Justice Stevens suggested in dissent that Section 1983 could be used. *Id.* at 294. That approach appears, however, to be foreclosed by *Gonzaga University*, *supra*.

[42] *South Camden*, *supra*, 274 F.3d at 788, *quoting and citing Sandoval*, 532 U.S. at 291. The dissent is *South Camden* argued that *Sandoval* did not purport to address the issue of enforcement of disparate impact regulations through Section 1983, the point made by Justice Stevens in his *Sandoval* dissent. 523 U.S. at 299–300. *Gonzaga University*, *supra*, was not cited.

[43] 401 U.S. 424 (1971).

[44] Smith v. City of Jackson, Miss., 544 U.S. 228, 125 S. Ct. 1536, 1545–46 (2005) (holding that ADEA permits disparate impact claims, but to assert such claims a plaintiff must identify specific employment practices that caused the observed statistical disparities).

[1] Richardson v. Mellish, 2 Bing. 229, 130 Eng. Rep. 294, 303 (Comm. Pleas 1824); *see* Norwest v. Presbyterian Intercommunity Hosp., 652 P.2d 318, 323–24 (Or. 1982) (noting court's inherent limitations in gauging and weighing competing social interests presented as policy considerations).

[2] Pittsburg C, C & St. L.R. Co. v. Kinney, 115 N.E. 505, 507 (Ohio 1916):

> Public policy is the cornerstone — the foundation — of all constitutions, statutes, and judicial decisions, and its latitude and longitude, its height and its depth, greater than any or all of them. If this be not true, whence came the first judicial decision on matter of public policy? There was no precedent for it, else it would not have been the first.

impossible to divorce public policy considerations from the judicial decision making process.[3]

Public policy considerations are usually derived from constitutions and statutes.[4] While statutory text is usually determinative of public policy, statutory text is not a shackle. Courts possess inherent power as a coordinate branch of government to identify and declare public policy;[5] nonetheless, this power is gingerly exercised for the most part because courts also recognize that the term "public policy" is subjective and imprecise and more the product in a democratic society of group struggle than logic.

The conflicting judicial attitudes toward the role "public policy" in decision making tends towards three considerations. First, expressions of public policy are usually made as broad generalizations. Thus, it is frequently said that a person should not be permitted to profit from his own wrongdoing,[6] or that whether a contract violates public policy turns on whether the contract as made has a "tendency to evil, to be against the public good, or be injurious to the public."[7]

The second consideration flows from the first: Broad generalizations prove exceptionally difficult to apply with regularity and consistency in practice. The matter is often further complicated by the question whether "public policy" should be decided by the court or committed to the jury.[8]

Lastly, public policy issues are rarely unidirectional; rather, they tend to raise competing considerations. For example, the public policy in compensating individuals for another's tortious infliction of emotional distress may

---

[3] *See* Walter V. Schaefer, *Precedent and Policy*, 34 U. Chi. L. Rev. 3 (1966).

[4] Green v. Ralee Engineering Co., 960 P.2d 1046, 1048 (Cal. 1998) (stating that public policy is "tethered to fundamental policies that are delineated in constitutional or statutory provisions). The court went on to state: "[A]side from constitutional policy, the legislature, and not the courts, is vested with the responsibility to declare the public policy of the state." *Id.* at 1049 (citations omitted); *cf.* Dickerson v. United States, 530 U.S. 428 (2000) (holding that prophylactic remedy devised by the Court (*Miranda* Rule) could not be overruled by Congress because remedy was of constitutional dimension). The *Green* court recognized that in some cases statutory policy may be defined by administrative regulations. 960 P.2d at 1054.

[5] *Pittsburg C, C & St. L.R. Co., supra,* 115 N.E. at 507 ("Sometimes such public policy is declared by Constitution; sometimes by statute; sometimes by judicial decision. More often, however, it abides only in the customs and conventions of the people—in their clear consciousness and conviction of what is naturally and inherently just and right between man and man").

[6] Barker v. Kallash, 468 N.E.2d 39, 41 (N.Y. 1984) (voluntary participation in an illegal act).

[7] Marshall v. Higginson, 813 P.2d 1275, 1278 (Wash. App. 1991); *see* Petrillo v. Syntex Labs., Inc., 499 N.E.2d 952, 956 (Ill. App. 1986), *cert. denied, sub nom.* Tobin v. Petrillo, 483 U.S. 1007 (1987).

[8] Bovard v. American Horse Enters., Inc., 247 Cal. Rptr. 340, 343 (Cal. App. 1988) (stating that the illegality of contract is a question of law determined by the judge) (citation omitted); Vogel v. Liberty Mut. Ins. Co., 571 N.W.2d 704, 706 (Wis. App. 1997) (stating that application of public policy factors to determine existence of liability in tort is a function of the court); *cf.* 17A Am. Jur. 2d *Contracts* § 335, p.340 (1991) (stating that illegality of contract is question of fact for jury when determination whether contract violates public policy depends on circumstances or parties' intent).

conflict with the public policy that the intimacies of family life should be preserved against routine litigation when the parties are husband and wife.[9] The intersect of these considerations tends to turn many invocations of public policy into a surrogate for a balancing or cost/benefit oriented analysis.[10]

Public policy claims are best established when tied to a statute from which a legislative policy can be discerned. In these contexts, courts will apply the inferred public policy standards to the case before them.[11] The results of this process can, on occasion, be quite startling. For example, in *Hydrotech Systems Ltd. v. Oasis Waterpark*[12] the court refused to allow an unlicensed contractor to recover any remedies for work performed for which a license was required. Refusing an unlicensed party a recovery on the contract price was seen as consistent with the statutory scheme creating the license requirement in the first place. The court went on to hold, however, that the public policy behind the licensure requirement not only foreclosed a quantum meruit recovery for the value of any benefit realized by the party who hired the unlicensed contractor, but that public policy also foreclosed a promissory fraud claim that the hiring party retained the unlicensed contractor specifically because he knew the contractor was unlicensed and had no intention of paying for the services.[13] Not all jurisdiction would apply the policy as strictly.[14]

Public policy concerns are often tied to concrete issues that can give public policy considerations a conservative rather than progressive tone. For example, the absence of acceptable and easily applicable standards or the fear of opening a floodgate of litigation have been asserted as public policy reasons for not providing a remedy.[15] On other occasions the court may simply treat the wrong as de minimis:

> There are many wrongs which in themselves are flagrant. For instance, such wrongs as betrayal, brutal words, and heartless disregard of the feelings of others are beyond any effective legal remedy and any practical administration of law . . . . To attempt

---

[9] Hakkila v. Hakkila, 812 P.2d 1320, 1323–24, 1326 (N. Mex. App. 1991).

[10] Koestler v. Pollard, 471 N.W.2d 7, 12 (Wis. 1991) ("Public policy bars Koestler's claim because more harm than good will result if Koestler is allowed to pursue this action"); Rossman v. 740 River Drive, 241 N.W.2d 91, 93 (Minn. 1976).

[11] Weicker v. Weicker, 237 N.E.2d 876, 876–77 (N.Y. 1968).

[12] 803 P.2d 370 (Cal. 1991).

[13] *Id.* at 376:

Regardless of the equities, section 7031 bars all actions, however they are characterized, which effectively seek "compensation" for illegal unlicensed contract work. Thus, an unlicensed contractor cannot recover either for the agreed contract price or for the reasonable value of labor and materials. The statutory prohibition operates even where the person for whom the work was performed knew the contractor was unlicensed.

(citations omitted).

[14] Section 65.2 (Illegality).

[15] Ross v. Creighton Univ., 957 F.2d 410, 414 (7th Cir. 1992) (educational malpractice).

to correct such wrongs or give relief from their effects "may do more social damage than if the law leaves them alone."[16]

---

[16] Richard P. v. Superior Court, 249 Cal. Rptr. 246, 249 (Cal. App. 1988) (citations omitted) (rejecting tort claims by husband against another man for fathering two children with plaintiff's wife during plaintiff and his wife's marriage); Section 125 (Personal Relationships).

Chapter 2

GENERAL PRINCIPLES CONCERNING COMPENSATORY DAMAGES

SYNOPSIS

23

§ 6 THE PURPOSE OF COMPENSATORY DAMAGES

Damages are compensation in money for loss or detriment caused by the wrongful act of another. The act may be wrongful because it violates a prior promise (breach of contract) or because it violates public policy (tort). In theory, the amount of money awarded as compensation for the loss or detriment should equalize the loss or detriment so that it would be as if the loss or detriment never occurred; thus, the basic rule of damages is to place the plaintiff in the position she would have occupied had the wrong not occurred. This is often referred to as plaintiff's "rightful" position. In theory, compensation damages neither improves nor subtracts from the position the plaintiff would have found herself had the wrong not occurred.[1]

The very notion of compensation is to make even or be measurably the equivalent. For example, in *Harris v. Peters*[2] plaintiff leased an automobile that was subsequently declared a total loss after a collision with defendant's vehicle. Defendant paid plaintiff the fair market value of the car, which plaintiff turned over to his lessor. Plaintiff still owed money on the lease,

---

[1] Mountain View Coach Lines, Inc. v. Hartnett, 415 N.Y.S.2d 918, 918 (Sup. Ct. 1978) (stating that "[d]amages are to restore injured parties not to reward them").

[2] 653 N.E.2d 1274 (Ill. App. 1995).

however, because the total lease amount was greater than the fair market value of the leased vehicle. Plaintiff sued for the difference, but the court rejected the claim. The court held that plaintiff was made whole when he received the fair market value for the vehicle. Plaintiff's disadvantageous lease was a detriment he brought to the collision and was independent of the collision. If plaintiff could transfer the disadvantageous lease obligations to defendant, plaintiff would be better off than if the collision had not occurred.[3]

To state that the purpose of compensatory damages is to place the plaintiff in the position she would have occupied but for defendant's commission of a legal wrong is to state both a simple and a complex idea. There is intuitive appeal to the notion that the plaintiff should not bear a loss imposed on her by another in violation of plaintiff's legal right or the other's legal duty. Yet, the resolution of the issue is maddeningly difficult. Identification and measurement of the plaintiff's loss often requires construction of a counterfactual, *i.e.*, what would have happened to plaintiff had the legal wrong not occurred? Construction of that counterfactual world, a world that never existed but which we imagine to exist, can prove daunting.[4]

In assessing a plaintiff's loss in the counterfactual world should we consider events after the date of injury to calculate plaintiff's loss or should we fix the loss as of the date of injury? If the plaintiff's business is destroyed, is the proper measure of that loss the value of that business as of the destruction date without regard to events that occurred after that date or is the proper measure of that loss the earnings or profits the business would have made with those other events considered? For example, assume plaintiff had a contract to provide janitorial services to the World Trade Towers, but on September 1, 2000 that contract was wrongfully interfered with by defendant and plaintiff lost his business. In calculating damages should the subsequent destruction of the Towers by terrorists on September 11, 2001 be considered?[5] Should the result be different if instead of a business loss a plaintiff is injured in an automobile accident on September 10, 2001 and unable to work at her place of employment on the 85th Floor of the World Trade Towers North Tower. Is the subsequent destruction of that Tower the next day by terrorists relevant to the damages claim? Placing the

---

[3] *Id.* at 1276 (stating that "if [defendant] is forced to pay off [plaintiff's] lease, [plaintiff] will be enriched to the extent that he has rid himself of the negative net—the obligation to pay . . . which he had before the accident") (brackets added).

[4] *See generally* Symposium, *Baselines and Counterfactuals in the Theory of Compensatory Damages: What Do Compensatory Damages Compensate?*, 40 San Diego L. Rev. 1091 (2003).

[5] *See* George P. Roach, *Correcting Uncertain Prophecies: An Analysis of Business Consequential Damages*, 22 Rev. Litig. 1 (2003) (noting that in the context of business losses significant differences may arise if courts measure loss based on date of injury (general damages measure) or date of trial (special or consequential damages measure); Konrad Bonsack, *Damages Assessment, Janis Joplin's Yearbook, and the Pie-Powder Court*, 13 Geo. Mason U. L. Rev. 1 (1990) (discussing economic models that support both date of loss and *ex post* measuring and concluding that *ex post* approach is superior). Both articles cite decisions applying the date of loss or the *ex post* approaches).

plaintiff in the position she would have occupied had the legal wrong not occurred is, at root, a question of significant policy and philosophical importance and disagreement.[6]

Determining the proper measure of compensation also implicates a social policy calculus. Should compensation strive to exactly measure the plaintiff's loss; should it undercompensate to encourage conduct engaged in by the defendant; or, should it overcompensate because of underdetection of wrongdoing.[7] Should compensation be set, in situations when insurance is available, at the amount a rational person would deem prudent to insure against the loss or should compensation be based on the defendant's moral duty to make the person, whom the defendant has harmed, whole?[8] Should compensation restore the plaintiff to her pre-injury position or should the plaintiff be rehabilitated in light of changes to the plaintiff caused or resulting from the legal wrong?[9] When considering the doctrinal rules, principles, standards, guidelines, and approaches discussed in this chapter on compensation, readers should not lose sight of the underlying values and concerns that influence and determine the content of the law in this field.

(Expectation Damages) =Fulfilling an expected gain.

[6.1] Expectancy Interest

The expectancy interest refers to the fulfillment of an aggrieved party's expectancy of gain if the bargain to which he was a party had been carried out and performed. As suggested by the definition, the expectancy interest is generally confronted in the context of disrupted bargains. The most common reason for a disrupted bargain is breach of contract, but the basis for the disruption may sound in tort. In the latter case, courts may interpose a higher proof requirement to establish the authenticity of the expectancy.[10]

---

[6] *See* note 4, *supra* (particularly Michael Moore, *For What Must We Pay? Causation and Counterfactual Baselines*, 40 San Diego L. Rev. 1181 (2003), and Leo Katz, *What To Compensate? Some Surprisingly Unappreciated Reasons Why the Problems is so Hard*, 40 San Diego L. Rev. 1345 (2003)).

[7] Richard Crasswell, *Instrumental Theories of Compensation: A Survey*, 40 San Diego L. Rev. 1135 (2003).

[8] Ellen Smith Pryor, *The Tort Law Debate, Efficiency and the Kingdom of the Ill: A Critique of the Insurance Theory of Compensation*, 79 Va. L. Rev. 91 (1993); Margaret Jane Radin, *Compensation and Commensurability*, 43 Duke L. J. 56 (1993). Both papers discuss market and corrective justice approaches to compensation.

[9] Ellen S. Pryor, *Rehabilitating Tort Compensation*, 91 Geo. L.J. 659, 663–64 (2003):

In the realms of tort theory and tort practice, compensation is predominantly interpreted as making the victim whole by returning her to the status quo ante, to the extent possible, through cash payment. Rehabilitation, by contrast, focuses on the distance between the injured plaintiff and the plaintiff as restored to the maximum functioning possible. Specifically, one definition of rehabilitation is the process of helping the person achieve the fullest psychological, social, vocational, life activity (such as hobbies), and educational potential that is consistent with his or her disability and life plans.

(footnote omitted).

[10] Roboserve v. Kato Kagaku Co., Ltd., 78 F.3d 266, 274 (7th Cir. 1996) (applying higher standard when seeking expectancy under fraud theory of recovery); Section 122 (Damages).

The expectancy interest is frequently referred to as the "benefit of the bargain." The term "benefit of the bargain" may, however, have legal significance in its own right as a measure of fraud damages.[11] The linkage between the "expectancy" interest and the "benefit of the bargain" should be seen as illustrative rather than synonymous.

The compensatory aspect of the expectancy interest lies primarily in its functionality. A compensatory award equals what the plaintiff would have received had the bargain not been disrupted. The award and the loss being equal, the plaintiff is placed in the position she would have been had the bargain been performed.

A number of commentators have criticized the awarding of this expectancy interest on the ground that there is no actual loss against which the award is balanced. An expectancy is for these commentators just that, something too ephemeral and lightweight to warrant legal protection.[12] The main thrust of this argument has been rejected by other commentators and by the courts.[13]

The recognition and award of compensatory damages based on the loss of the bargained-for expectancy has been deemed fundamental; nonetheless, concern regarding the award of expectancy damages has not been abandoned by courts. The approach has been to burden the award for loss of expectancies with legal restrictions that address concerns over the speculative nature of the interest.[14] In some instances a court may determine that expectancy damages are an inappropriate recovery for reasons of public policy.[15]

---

[11] Section 122.1 ("Out-of-Pocket" or "Benefit-of-the-Bargain" Measure).

[12] PATRICK S. ATIYAH, THE RISE AND FALL OF FREEDOM OF CONTRACT 759 (1979); Louis E. Wolcher, *The Accommodation of Regret in Contract Remedies*, 73 Iowa L. Rev. 797, 876 (1988). Professor Crasswell has mounted a broader challenge to the expectancy interest. Richard Crasswell, *Against Fuller and Perdue*, 67 U. Chi. L. Rev. 99 (2000). Professor Crasswell argues that Fuller and Perdue's categorical approach to damages, which subdivides losses into expectancy, reliance, and restitutionary interests, is too imprecise and confused. The Fuller and Perdue taxonomy fails to contain relevant considerations that identify the proper measure of damages and ignores differences between types of damages that are consigned to one interest or the other. More fundamentally, Professor Crasswell challenges the concept of damages as redressive; rather the proper approach is instrumental—what behavior do we want remedies to encourage or deter.

[13] Caisse Nationale De Credit Agricole v. CBI Indus., Inc., 90 F.3d 1264, 1275 (7th Cir. 1996) (applying New York law). *See* Lon L. Fuller & William R. Perdue, Jr., *The Reliance Interest in Contract Damages*, 46 Yale L.J. 52, 57–63 (1936); DOUGLAS LAYCOCK, MODERN AMERICAN REMEDIES 44–48 (2d ed. 1995) (collecting authorities approving and disapproving of awarding expectancy interest as compensatory damages).

[14] Sections 8.1 (Certainty); 8.3 (Lost Profits); 8.4 (The New Business Rule).

[15] *E.g.*, Wilson v. Los Angeles County Metropolitan Transit Authority, 1 P.3d 63 (Cal. 2000) (refusing to allow a wrongfully denied bidder on a public contract the recovery of lost profits; rather, the bidder was limited to its bid preparation costs). The court relied on several factors. First, the right sounded in promissory estoppel, which permitted limitations as "justice may require." *Id.* at 69. Second, because the bidder did not know that its bid would be accepted or rejected, the public agency's actions necessarily had a limited impact on the bidder's decision to bid on other projects, yet it was the "loss" of the other projects that constituted the lost

[6.2]   Reliance Interest

The reliance interest refers to the loss or detriment caused by the legal wrong of another. This interest seeks to undo the loss or detriment by giving the plaintiff a sum of money equal to the loss or detriment sustained, thus "netting out" the loss with an equal gain, as represented by the award. Reliance as a remedial interest should be distinguished from reliance as a substantive law requirement for fraud or promissory estoppel.[16]

The reliance interest finds application in both contract, tort, and occasionally in unjust enrichment.[17] The reliance interest can be compared with the tort concept of "out-of-pocket losses." In fraud cases, for example, the "out-of-pocket" measure of recovery includes the loss or detriment caused to the plaintiff as a result of her reliance on the defendant's misrepresentation. Out-of-pocket losses can include losses for which there was no reliance, but which were caused by the defendant's legal wrong or breach of duty. We could classify these losses as reliance-related by saying that plaintiff "relied" on defendant not to commit a legal wrong or breach a duty. That approach runs the risk of confusing "reliance" with "causation"; nonetheless, it is an approach at times adopted by courts.

The reliance interest may be recovered in its own right or as an alternative to an expectancy or restitutionary recovery. For example, in *Glendale Federal Bank v. United States*,[18] Glendale Federal Bank (Glendale) sought damages for Congress's change of rules concerning capital requirements for federally insured savings and loans. The change aversely affected Glendale because it had agreed to acquire insolvent banking entities after the federal government promised that Glendale could include "supervisory goodwill" in the capital requirement and amortize the goodwill. This encouraged Glendale to acquire the insolvent banking entities and helped the federal government extricate itself from the Savings & Loan Crisis of the 1980s. When Congress enacted the 1989 Financial Institutions Reform, Recovery and Enforcement Act, it greatly restricted the use of goodwill in the capital account, thus breaching the agreement by which Glendale (and others) had

---

profits claim. *Id.* Third, the lowest bid may be an unprofitable one; hence, its rejection, even if wrongful, saved the bidder money which ought to be offset against any lost profits, yet, this "unprofitability is necessarily speculative and indeterminate. *Id.* at 70. Lastly, the court concluded that it would be against public policy to saddle taxpayers with lost profits awards. *Id.* at 72.

[16] Merex A.G. v. Fairchild Weston Sys., Inc., 29 F.3d 821, 825 (2d Cir. 1994), *cert. denied*, 513 U.S. 1084 (1995) (distinguishing between equitable estoppel and promissory estoppel for purposes of applying concept of reliance).

[17] Farash v. Sykes Datatronics, Inc., 452 N.E.2d 1245, 1246–47 (N.Y. 1983) (holding that plaintiff may recover in unjust enrichment even though defendant did not benefit from plaintiff's efforts; plaintiff may recover for those efforts that were to his detriment and that thereby placed him in a worse position). *Farash* involved a claim by a landlord against a prospective tenant for whom the landlord had made substantial leasehold improvements but who neither signed the lease nor occupied the building. The lease was unenforceable due to the statute of frauds and the leasehold improvements were apparently of no value to another tenant.

[18] 239 F.3d 1374 (Fed. Cir. 2001).

been induced to acquire insolvent banking entities. The Supreme Court held in *United States v. Winstar Corp.* that affected parties could assert breach of contract claims against the United States.[19]

Glendale asserted a *Winstar* claim, seeking expectancy, reliance, and restitutionary recoveries. The trial court awarded nearly $1 billion in restitution and non-overlapping reliance damages—the restitution award representing the benefit realized by the United States (expenses/costs avoided) by having Glendale acquire the insolvent banking entity. This was calculated by the trial court by taking the value of the insolvent banking entity's obligations (debts) and deducting the entity's assets. The resulting negative amount was deemed to be the amount the United States had benefitted from the transaction Congress subsequently repudiated. The appellate court, however, held that the benefit was speculative and indeterminate because it required an assessment of what might have occurred. The problem was, according to the court, whether the United States would have been required to expend money to bail out the entity and this determination was dependent on the direction interest rates took. At the time of the transaction with Glendale, future interest rate direction was an unknown and the United States received a benefit when the risk was assumed by Glendale. Interest rates subsequently trended downward, however, so neither Glendale (nor the United States) actually realized a loss on the transaction.[20]

Measuring the benefit was difficult and the court found that under the circumstances a restitution award would be improper:

> This case, then, presents an illustration of the problem in granting restitution based on an assumption that the non-breaching party is entitled to the supposed gains received by the breaching party, when those gains are both speculative and indeterminate. We do not see how the restitution award granted by the trial court, measured in terms of a liability that never came to pass, and based on a speculative assessment of what might have been, can be upheld; accordingly we vacate the trial court's damage award on this theory.[21]

On the other hand, the court found that reliance damages were appropriate and did not raise the problems of speculation and indeterminancy that the court associated with a restitution award:

---

[19] 518 U.S. 839 (1996). The Court did not address the remedy for this breach.

[20] 239 F.3d at 1382.

[21] *Id.* The "risk" had value in that some figure represented what the United States would have paid for someone to assume the risk. The problem was that no figure was contemporaneously determined when the bargain was struck and the court was unwilling to construct a surrogate figure—a number which the court believed reasonably approximated the value of the risk transferred from the United States to Glendale. We will see occasions when courts have been more liberal in allowing restitutionary recoveries notwithstanding difficulties in measuring the value of the benefit conferred. Section 45 (Valuation of the Benefit).

In a case like the one before us, for all the reasons we have explained, we conclude that, for purposes of measuring the losses sustained by Glendale as a result of the Government's breach, reliance damages provide a firmer and more rational basis than the alternative theories argued by the parties. We recognize the appeal in the restitution approach, but we find that keying an award to a liability that was at most a paper calculation, and which ignores the reality of subsequent events as they impacted on the parties, and particularly the plaintiff, is not justifiable. Reliance damages will permit a more finely tuned calculation of the actual losses sustained by plaintiff as a result of the Government's breach.[22]

Unlike expectancy damages, which derive from the defendant's failure to perform, reliance damages flow from the plaintiff's entry into the bargain itself.[23] Where expectancy damages seek to put the plaintiff in the position he would have been had the promised performance been rendered, reliance damages seek to place the plaintiff in the position he would have occupied had the contract itself not been entered into by the parties.[24]

Expectancy and reliance interests often are defined more by perspective than inherent distinctiveness. Wordsmanship can easily transform a benefit expected into something lost. The ability to state an interest in different ways by the creative use of language gives rise to opportunity and confusion. Confusion arises when the chameleon-like character of categories is not recognized and accepted; opportunity arises when the strategic use of categories is recognized and exploited. A good example of the latter is *Runyan v. Pacific Air Industries, Inc.*,[25] when plaintiff-franchisee sought compensatory damages for breach of contract by the defendant-franchisor. The court held that plaintiff's claim for loss of expectancy (anticipated future profits) failed due to insufficiency of proof. The court, however, awarded reliance damages calculated as salary foregone by plaintiff based on what he would have earned at another job had he not devoted his efforts to the franchise.[26]

In the disrupted bargain context, the reliance interest is occasionally subdivided into the categories of essential reliance and incidental reliance. Essential reliance refers to the expenses that are necessary, incidental

[22] *Id.* at 1383. Restitution has been allowed in *Winstar* claims, but under circumstances when it serves as a substitute for a reliance recovery. Landmark Land Co., Inc. v. F.D.I.C., 256 F.3d 1365 (Fed. Cir. 2001) (permitting restitution of acquiring S&L's contribution to insolvent S&L pursuant to agreement with the United States to takeover the insolvent S&L). Expectancy recoveries have generally failed for failure of proof. *Glendale Federal Bank, supra*, 239 F.3d at 1380; California Federal Bank v. United States, 54 Fed. Cl. 704, 712–13 (Fed. Cl. 2002).

[23] *In re* Yeager Co., 227 F. Supp. 92, 96–97 (N.D. Ohio 1963); Restatement (First) of Contracts § 333 (1932); 5 CORBIN ON CONTRACTS § 1031 (1964).

[24] Designer Direct, Inc. v. DeForest Redevelopment Authority, 313 F.3d 1036, 1049 (7th Cir. 2002).

[25] 466 P.2d 682 (Cal. 1970).

[26] 466 P.2d at 693.

reliance refers to expenses that are collateral.[27] The nomenclature has generated more acceptance from academics than judges. The underlying concept has been accepted, however, by courts under the formulation of expenses incurred in performing or preparing to perform the contract[28] which may be substituted for the essential reliance category.

[6.3] Restitutionary Interest

The restitutionary interest refers to the restoration, return, or transfer to the plaintiff of benefits received by the defendant due to or arising from the plaintiff's performance or efforts.[29] This interest is not "compensatory" in the sense used with regard to the expectancy and reliance interests, both of which seek compensation for something lost. The restitutionary interest seeks recovery of a benefit unjustly held by another. Nevertheless, the concept of restitution is frequently treated as a form of compensatory damages; the problem likely arising because in both instances the award is monetary. This interplay of dissimilar concepts can cause confusion. For example, in *Lempa v. Finkel*[30] a lease had been rescinded and the issue was the recoverability by the tenants of relocation and remodeling expenses incurred when the tenants moved to new premises. The issue was presented and considered by the court as one of "restitution damages." The court denied recovery on the ground that there had been no benefit realized by the landlord,[31] a theory consistent with "restitution" but not with "damages." The court was trapped in the oxymoron of "restitution damages":

> Upon closer inspection, it becomes apparent that, at a minimum, the "restitution damages" awarded the Finkels are not restitutionary. When the building lease was rescinded, the parties were required to return to each other the value of the benefits received under the rescinded contract. Although the relocation and remodeling expenses conferred a benefit on the Finkels, they did not confer a benefit on the Lempas. In other words, the Lempas did not receive any benefit from the expenses the Finkels incurred when they relocated to and remodeled their new location. As such, these expenses are not restitutionary.[32]

---

[27] Lon L. Fuller & William R. Perdue, *The Reliance Interest in Contract Damages*, 46 Yale L.J. 52, 78 (1936); Robert Hudec, *Restating the "Reliance Interest,"* 67 Cornell L. Rev. 704, 723 (1982) (noting the Restatement position that "reliance that is not essential is incidental").

[28] Baush & Lomb, Inc. v. Bressler, 977 F.2d 720, 729 (2d Cir. 1992); Hidalgo Properties, Inc. v. Wachovia Mortgage Co., 617 F.2d 196, 198 (10th Cir. 1980).

[29] Restatement (Second) of Contracts § 344 (1981) (remedies for breach of contract include expectation, reliance or restitution damages).

[30] 663 N.E.2d 158 (Ill. App. 1996).

[31] 663 N.E.2d at 165.

[32] *Id.*; Matter of Mediators, 190 B.R. 515, 530 (S.D.N.Y. 1995) (evidencing judicial tendency to conflate money awards with damages). Rescission damages have, however, been recognized in many jurisdictions. Section 135.1 (Rescission Damages). Some courts will award detriment-based compensation under an unjust enrichment theory. Farash v. Sykes Datatronics, Inc., 452 N.E.2d 1245, 1246 (N.Y. 1983).

The tendency to treat monetary awards as "damages" is probably too ingrained to be changed at this time. It is important nonetheless to distinguish damages recoveries from benefit disgorgement because damages doctrine pulls down a different menu of rules and principles than does restitution theory. The distinction is, however, not ironclad and in some cases the distinction is effectively ignored.[33] The relationship between damages and restitution is discussed in Section 47 (Restitution Damages).

[6.4] General Damages vs. Special or Consequential Damages

General or direct damages are those damages that flow necessarily and inherently from the wrong. Special or consequential (the terms are interchangeable) damages are all other damages that are caused by the wrong.[34] The distinction between general and special damages is well established but can be tricky. Each cause of action carries a basic measure of relief, although not necessarily a complete measure of relief. The basic measure is a part of the cause of action and is usually available as a matter of course on showing the defendant's breach or delict. In other words, general damages follow inevitably from the wrong; only their amount need be calculated. Special damages are not presumed to follow from the wrong; rather, the causal relationship between the loss and the wrong must be demonstrated by the plaintiff.[35]

Examples of the distinction between general and special damages can be seen in cases of landlord breach of a lease for which general damages would include the difference between the contract rent and the fair rental value of the leased property and special damages would be other expenses the tenant incurred because of the breach.[36] In a personal injury case involving

---

[33] Section 45 (Valuation of the Benefit) (discussing extent to which plaintiff's expenses may be used as a measure of the benefit unjustly held by the defendant); cf. Coleman Eng'g Co. v. North Am. Aviation, Inc., 420 P.2d 713, 728 (Cal. 1966) (Traynor, J., dissenting) (rejecting requirement of benefit to defendant when plaintiff performs at the request of the defendant).

[34] R.K. Chevolet, Inc. v. Hayden, 480 S.E.2d 477, 481 (Va. 1997). The court noted that classification of damages as general or direct on the one hand, or as special or consequential on the other hand was committed to the court. Id.

[35] The distinction is sometimes framed in terms of direct or indirect causation. Long v. Abbruzzetti, 487 S.E.2d 217, 219–20 (Va. 1997) (holding that attorneys fees incurred in specific performance action following breach of oral agreement to act as escrow were not direct damages caused by breach, but indirect (consequential) damages resulting from the seller's decision to eject the plaintiff-buyer from the premises subject to the contract). The seller refused to perform after the buyer allegedly failed to assume several notes on the property. The buyer was willing and had performed, but due to neglect the escrow relied on the seller's false representation that the buyer had not and cancelled the escrow. The seller assumed control of the property and was able to rebut the buyer's effort to reacquire possession by showing the escrow's cancellation letter to law enforcement personnel. It required legal action for the buyer to acquire control of the property. Id. at 218.

[36] Buck v. Morrow, 21 S.W. 398 (Tex. Civ. App. 1893) (special damages included extra help tenant was required to hire and personal property (cattle) lost when the cattle were moved from fenced, leased pasturage to the open range).

bodily injury, general damages usually include loss of earning capacity and pain and suffering; special damages may include medical expense and lost earnings.[37] Care must, however, be taken because the classification can differ from jurisdiction to jurisdiction. In a defamation action the general damages usually include the injury to the plaintiff's reputation caused by the publication while the special damages would include any loss of income or earnings resulting from the publication.[38]

In most cases the importance of the distinction between general and special damages lies in the fact that it demarks a rule of pleading.[39] In a number of cases, however, the distinction between general or special damages has significant remedial consequences.

First, the causation proof requirement for special damages imposes distinct requirements in the context of compensatory damages.[40] Special damages are also subject to mitigation requirements, an obligation not usually imposed on the recovery of general damages.[41]

Second, in some contexts, the substantive rule has developed that recoveries are limited to general damages only. This was traditionally the rule applied to actions for breach of a promise to pay money.[42] The reason for the rule appears to be the fungibility of money and the idea that the creditor could mitigate by borrowing an equivalent sum of money elsewhere to prevent losses that would be caused by the debtor's failure to repay in a timely manner. The rule is not applied when payment is owed to a third party or when the breach involves a promise to lend money.[43] The

---

[37] Handelman v. Victor Equip. Co., 99 Cal. Rptr. 90, 92 (Cal. App. 1971) (loss of earning capacity is general damages; loss of earnings is special damages).

[38] Sommer v. Gabor, 48 Cal. Rptr. 2d 235, 245 (Cal. App. 1995) (general damages include injury to reputation); McCune v. Neitzel, 457 N.W.2d 803, 811 (Neb. 1990); Ryan v. Herald Ass'n Inc., 566 A.2d 1316, 1320 (Vt. 1989).

[39] Special damages often must be specifically pleaded or else they are waived. Fed. R. Civ. P. 9(g). ("[W]hen items of special damages are claimed, they shall be specifically stated"). In some cases, this pleading requirement is even further particularized. Hogan v. Wal-Mart Stores, Inc., 167 F.3d 781, 783 (2d Cir. 1999) (stating that under New York law "aggravation of a pre-existing condition is an element of special damages which must be specially pleaded and proven before recovery therefor can be allowed") (quotations in original) (citations omitted); Harris Trust and Sav. Bank v. Phillips, 506 N.E.2d 1370, 1377 (Ill. App. 1987) (special damages must be pleaded to make out claim of libel *per quod*).

[40] Section 10 (Loss Causation). *But cf.* Restatement (Second) of Contracts § 351, cmt. b (1981):

> The damages recoverable for loss that results other than in the ordinary course of events are sometimes called "special" or "consequential" damages. These terms are often misleading, however, and it is not necessary to distinguish between "general" and "special" or "consequential" damages for the purpose of the rule stated in this Section.

The rule referred to is *Hadley v. Baxendale*, 9 Ex. 341, 156 Eng. Rep. 145 (1854), discussed at Section 10.2.2 ([Loss Causation] Policy Considerations).

[41] Section 13 (Duty to Mitigate Damages).

[42] Loudon v. Taxing Dist., 104 U.S. 771, 774 (1881) (limiting non-breaching party's recovery to sum "owed but not paid" plus "delay damages" in the form of prejudgment interest).

[43] John D. Calamari & Joseph M. Perillo, Contracts § 14–25, at 557 n.34 (2d ed. 1977); 5 Corbin on Contracts § 1078, at 447 (1964).

distinctions indicate the precarious vitality of the rule. It is increasingly being ignored in the one category of cases where its application would be most significant—insurer failure to pay the indemnity obligation. [44]

The limitation of recovery to general damages is sometimes sought to be justified on public policy grounds, although here it is difficult to determine if the limitation is really one of remedy or one of substantive liability. For example, in *Mutual Fire Ins. Co. v. Richardson* [45] the court observed that when an insured breached the insurance contract by making a fraudulent claim against the insurer, the insurer could *not* recover as consequential damages its attorney's fees and investigation costs incurred as a result of the insured's wrongdoing. It is difficult to identify what the insurer's general damages are in such a case and the practical consequences of a decision such as *Mutual Fire* is to insulate the insured's conduct from civil redress.

Third, the failure of the trier of fact to resolve general and special damage awards consistently with each other or with the underlying wrong may create verdict inconsistencies that warrant a new trial. For example, courts have split as to whether an award solely of special damages represents an irreconcilably inconsistent verdict. [46] The modern trend does appear, however, to reject the claim of irreconcilable inconsistency, [47] with some courts going to substantial lengths to reconcile seemingly conflicting verdicts. [48] Many of the inconsistent verdict awards involve the award of medical

---

[44] Marquis v. Farm Family Mut. Ins. Co., 628 A.2d 644, 650–52 (Me. 1993); *see* Olson v. Rugloski, 277 N.W.2d 385, 387–88 (Minn. 1979) (permitting the recovery of consequential economic damages when the insurer breached the insurance contract by unreasonably delaying payment, but requiring proof that the insurer committed an independent tort before permitting an award of punitive damages); Lawton v. Great Southwest Fire Ins. Co., 392 A.2d 576, 579–81 (N.H. 1978) (rejecting a bad faith action in tort for first-party claims because the insurer does not control the insured's fate as it does in third-party cases, but allowing recovery for consequential economic damages).

[45] 640 A.2d 205 (Me. 1994).

[46] *Compare* Bowers v. Sprouse, 492 S.E.2d 637, 639 (Va. 1997) (holding that a verdict which compensates plaintiff only to the extent of the exact amount of the claimed medical expenses is inadequate per se regardless of whether damages were controverted), *with* Wright v. Long, 954 S.W.2d 470, 472–74 (Mo. App. 1997) (holding that verdict awarding only the amount of medical expenses claimed was not inconsistent; the verdict may have resulted from juror compromise or juror belief that pain and suffering damages were minimal). *See generally* Todd R. Smyth, Annot., *Validity of Verdict Awarding Medical Expenses to Personal Injury Plaintiff, But Failing to Award Damages For Pain and Suffering*, 55 A.L.R. 4th 186 (1987).

[47] Snover v. McGraw, 667 N.E.2d 1310 (Ill. 1996); Peterson v. Reyna, 908 S.W.2d 472 (Tex. Civ. App. 1995); Childs v. Bainer, 663 A.2d 398 (Conn. 1995); Section 6.5 (Economic vs. Non-Economic Damages).

[48] Mary M. v. North Lawrence Community Sch. Corp., 951 F. Supp. 820, 826 (S.D. Ind. 1997):

> The language of this instruction allows a jury both to find liability and to award zero damages if, for instance, it finds that there was insufficient evidence of damages, or that plaintiff did not personally suffer or experience the damages proved, or that any damages proved were not proximately caused by the defendant's wrongful conduct.

rev'd on other grounds, 131 F.3d 1220 (7th Cir. 1998) (improper jury instruction).

expenses, but no award for pain and suffering. A frequent rejoinder to a claim of inconsistency is to note that the plaintiff was entitled to obtain medical treatment to determine if he was injured and to gauge the severity of the injury even if it turned out that he sustained no actual injury.[49] Courts have been largely unsympathetic to the claim that compromise verdicts may reflect juror dissatisfaction with the "all or nothing" approach of the law.[50]

General damages are usually measured by the value of the claim as of the date of injury; special damages by their nature flow from the injury and therefore must be assessed "ex post." The problem is that some claims may be easily cast as sounding in general or special damages. For example, assume a contract to build a structure is breached. Is the resulting loss to the contractor general damages because the benefit was in the contract itself and, therefore, lost at the point of breach or, on the other hand, is it special damages because the contractor lost profits that he would have realized on the contract?[51] Characterization of the loss as special damages subjects the recovery to more stringent proof requirements than are usually applied to general damages.[52] Treatment of the loss as general damages or special damages can also determine whether events subsequent to the loss will be considered in determining the amount of the loss.[53] Finally, the distinction between general damages and special damages is relevant to the construction and legality of contract provisions that purport to limit remedies for breach.[54]

[6.5] Economic vs. Non-Economic Damages

Economic damages generally are objectively verifiable monetary losses, such as medical expenses, lost earnings or profits, cost of repair, diminution in value, etc. Non-economic damages generally are subjective and non-verifiable losses, such as pain and suffering, emotional distress, injury to

---

[49] Waltrip v. Bilbon Corp., 38 S.W.3d 873, 880 (Tex. Cir. App. 2001); Wainwright v. Fontenot, 774 So.2d 70, 77–78 (La. 2000).

[50] *See* Michael Abramowicz, *A Compromise Approach to Compromise Verdicts*, 89 Cal. L. Rev. 231 (2001).

[51] Med Plus Properties v. Colcock Construction Group, Inc., 628 So.2d 370 (Ala. 1993) (concluding that such losses as described are part of the bargain and recoverable as general damages); *cf.* Century 21 Real Estate v. Meraj Intern. Inv. Corp., 315 F.3d 1271, 1282–83 (10th Cir. 2003) (questioning sufficiency of damages proof presented by the plaintiff, but affirming the verdict nonetheless because "Century 21 did almost nothing to undermine the assumptions on which [plaintiff] based his projections. It called no experts of its own. The cross-examination . . . on the matter was limited to having [plaintiff] repeat his assumptions and to asking him why he would let a business of such value go down the drain over a $14,000 dispute . . ."). The verdict was for $700,000! This represented the "value" of the plaintiff's business, according to the jury.

[52] 628 So. 2d at 376–77 (noting that special damages must be proven by "reasonable certainty" and must be the direct consequence of the breach). *See* Sections 9 (Future Losses), 10 (Loss Causation).

[53] Sections 6 (The Purpose of Compensatory Damages), 8.6 (Real or Hypothetical Losses).

[54] Section 186 (Negating Remedies by Contract).

reputation, loss of consortium, etc. Non-economic losses are increasingly being restricted or subjected to enhanced proof requirements due to concern that awards of non-economic damages have become a burden to the civil justice system. This is reflected in the rise of allocation requirements that substitute proportionate fault for joint and several liability for non-economic but not economic losses,[55] and damages caps that apply to non-economic but not economic losses.[56] In both situations characterization of a damages item may be critical to recovery because one or more of the defendants is insolvent, thus raising in importance joint and several liability, or because non-economic damages have already reached their cap.[57]

Proper identification of damages as economic or non-economic is also important for other reasons. Identification is necessary in cases where there has been a settlement with one or more but not all defendants and the court must determine the proper set off of the settlement against any award against the remaining defendants.[58] Identification is also necessary for evidentiary issues. For example, in *Shirley v. Smith*[59] the issue was whether a plaintiff's required self-catheterization constituted economic loss (loss of time) or non-economic loss (quality of life). The issue arose because some jurisdictions bar a witness from offering testimony as to the monetary value of non-economic damages.[60] The court held that the admission of the testimony regarding the monetary value of the time lost performing the self-catheterization was proper because it related to economic damages.[61]

Economic and non-economic awards also can raise consistency problems like those encountered with general and special damages.[62] For example, in *Lee v. Huntsville Livestock Services, Inc.*,[63] the court found a verdict which awarded economic damages ($30,000 for lost future earnings and $6,630 for future medical expenses) but no non-economic damages for future pain and suffering to be fatally inconsistent.[64] The jury did award damages

---

[55] Richards v. Owens-Illinois, Inc., 928 P.2d 1181 (Cal. 1997) (statutory immunity from liability precluded assignment of comparative fault for non-economic damages in suit in which the statutorily immune parties are not defendants).

[56] Bankert by Bankert v. United States, 937 F. Supp. 1169, 1184 (D. Md. 1996) (applying Maryland law) ($350,000 non-economic damages cap). Many jurisdictions have held, however, that damages caps violate state constitutional provisions.

[57] Wolfgang v. Mid Am. Motorsports, Inc., 111 F.3d 1515, 1529 (10th Cir. 1997) (stating that husband's inability to assist in household work characterized as economic loss and thus not subject to cap on non-economic damages).

[58] Wells v. Tallahassee Mem'l Reg'l Med. Ctr., Inc., 659 So. 2d 249, 253 (Fla. 1995); Greathouse v. Amcord, Inc., 41 Cal. Rptr. 2d 561, 566 (Cal. App. 1995).

[59] 933 P.2d 651 (Kan. 1997).

[60] Section 12.2 (Measuring Non-Economic Loss). *See generally* James O. Pearson, Annot., *Per Diem or Similar Mathematical Basis For Fixing Damages for Pain and Suffering*, 3 A.L.R. 4th 940 (1981).

[61] *Shirley, supra*, 933 P.2d at 655.

[62] Section 6.4 (General Damages vs. Special or Consequential Damages).

[63] 934 S.W.2d 158 (Tex. Civ. App. 1996).

[64] *Id.* at 160. Ironically, it was the plaintiff who was trying to save her verdict. Her argument that the zero dollar award for future suffering could be explained by the subjective nature of the damages item was rejected because the sole evidence supporting the future economic damages was plaintiff's claim of future suffering due to defendant's negligence).

for past economic and non-economic losses. These awards were not questioned. There are contrary decisions.[65] Many of the decisions are reconciled by identifying as an explanation for the alleged fatal inconsistency the speculative nature of future injury and treating the "inconsistency" as arising from the plaintiff's failure of proof.[66]

§ 7   VALUE

In order to compensate someone for the loss or injury to something we must be able to monetize what that something is that we are compensating. We use the concept of "value" to identify, for measurement purposes, the "worth" of the property or right that has been lost or damaged. This concept of value is not self-evident. Property and rights do not have inherent, preordained value for purposes of legal compensation. For damages purposes, value is constructed through the operation of rules and principles that seek to approximate what a neutral would identify as the economic worth of what was lost or damaged and express that worth in monetary terms.

The basic test is that the plaintiff is entitled to recover as compensatory damages the difference between value before loss or damage and value after loss or damage. A plaintiff whose property was damaged due to defendant's negligence would recover the difference between the pre-injury "value" of the property (say $10,000) and the post-injury "value" of the property (say $8,000), or $2,000. Plaintiff is restored to her rightful position because she now has cash ($2,000) and property ($8,000) that together equals her pre-injury position (property with a value of $10,000).[1] This test is easy to apply if we simply stipulate numbers, but how do we come up with these numbers? We need to know how the law calculates (1) pre-injury value and (2) post-injury value.

The calculation of value essentially reduces the inquiry into one over economic value. All interests can be valued as economic units, but that is not to say that, as a society, we always desire that losses be measured by their economic consequences only.[2] Economic value determinations are basic to many remedies calculations, but not all. Care must be taken when the determination of economic value is seen as properly part of damages

---

[65] Kinsella v. Berley Realty Corp., 657 N.Y.S.2d 771, 772 (App. Dept. 1997) (verdict of $0 for future pain and suffering and $202,176 for future lost earnings was not inconsistent; "jury obviously found that the injured plaintiff could no longer perform the strenuous work of an apprentice carpenter"); Staehler v. Beuthin, 557 N.W.2d 487, 491 (Wis. App. 1996).

[66] Allstate Ins. Co. v. Manasse, 681 So. 2d 779, 784 (Fla. App. 1996) (Klein, J. dissenting) (noting that inconsistencies involving awards of "future" damages can be explained by the "somewhat speculative nature of the injury"; past economic damages are based on a record of what happened and thus permit greater judicial scrutiny).

[1] The rightful position ignores transaction costs in transforming property to money, such as agent fees and costs, as well as litigation costs. Section 210 (Attorney's Fees—The "American Rule"). These omissions illustrate that the "rightful" position is a legal construct that approximates, but does not necessarily duplicate, the real world.

[2] Section 81 (Value to Owner).

calculations. Because the use of economic value is itself a judgment about the inherent quality and the worth of the matter before the court,[3] differences can be expected in the decisions as to whether economic value should be used in particular contexts. For purposes of Section 7.0, and its subsections, the assumption is that an economic measure of value is proper. The question then becomes how is economic value measured and determined?

[7.1] Determining Economic Value

There are numerous ways to calculate economic value, many of which are specific to certain types of property.[4] The three common measures of economic value are: (1) market (involving comparison of sales of like property); (2) replacement cost less depreciation (involving the cost of physically replacing that which was damaged); and (3) income or capitalization of earnings (involving the calculation of the income the property would have generated). The easiest way to see how these measures operate is to apply them to a common problem. Assume defendant negligently causes the complete loss of plaintiff's property. What has plaintiff lost?

If we use a market to measure economic value, we would ask what would a willing buyer have paid a willing seller for the property in the condition the property was prior to the loss? Depending on the thickness of the market, this may be an easy or difficult question to answer. If the property destroyed was a 3 year old, widely sold automobile, the used car market may be examined to determine what willing buyers and sellers are paying for a vehicle like the one plaintiff lost through defendant's negligence. The task may be more difficult if the market is thin, for example, the property lost is rare or the market is soft and not many sales of comparable properties can be identified. The more robust the market, the more confident we may be that the price for comparable properties accurately reflects the economic value of what plaintiff lost. That said, it must be recognized that economic value determined by comparable sales remains a hypothetical, counterfactual determination:

> The value of property springs from subjective needs and attitudes. As fixed by the market, value is no more than a summary expression of forecasts that the needs and attitudes which make up a demand in the past will have a counterpart in the future.[5]

---

[3] *See* Margaret Jane Radin, *Compensation and Commensurability*, 43 Duke L.J. 56, 56 (1993):

> I will suggest that our legal practice reflects in how compensation for personal injury is understood—that compensation is a contested concept. A commodified conception of compensation, in which harm to persons can be equated with a dollar value, coexists with a noncommodified conception, in which harm cannot be equated with dollars. In the commodified conception, harm and dollars are commensurable, and in the noncommodified conception, they are incommensurable

[4] American Institute of Certified Public Accountants Small Business Consulting Practice Aid No. 8, *Valuation of Closely Held Business* 10 (1987) (identifying seven approaches to valuing closely held corporations).

[5] Kimball Laundry Co. v. United States, 338 U.S. 1, 10 (1949).

A market measure of value that uses comparable sales should be distinguished from the term "fair market value" (FMV). FMV and value are interchangeable terms. FMV may be determined by the market measure, but FMV may also be determined through the use of approaches that do not emphasize comparable sales to determine economic value.

The replacement cost less depreciation measure uses purchase or reconstruction cost as the measure of value. The problem here, however, is that purchase or reconstruction gives us a new property, whereas what was lost is most often used property; therefore, the cost of purchase or construction must be reduced to reflect any betterment reflected by the substitution of new property for old. For example, returning to our earlier hypothetical involving the 3 year old motor vehicle. If we calculated the loss by the cost of a new vehicle to replace the destroyed vehicle, the plaintiff would now be in a better position than before the loss. Prior to the loss, plaintiff had a three year old vehicle; after the loss, plaintiff has a new vehicle. To adjust for this betterment of new for old we depreciate the new property to reflect the usage of the destroyed property. This concept is discussed in Section 7.5 (Betterment). The important point here is to recognize that valuing property by its replacement cost less depreciation focuses on the cost of acquiring a new replacement and then adjusting that economic cost to reflect the fact that the damaged property was "used."

The "capitalization of earnings" measure provides a valuation based on the earnings potential of the property damaged or destroyed. The measure may be based on current earnings using a capitalization factor[6] or it may be based on the capitalization of earnings from past[7] or future years.[8] The underlying premise of this measure is that property is worth what it earns, has earned, or is capable of earning. The capitalization of earnings measure essentially identifies, without explicit reference to other sales, what a buyer would pay and a seller would accept for each dollar of earnings.[9]

---

[6] Robert E. Hall & Victoria A. Lazear, *Reference Guide on Estimation of Economic Losses in Damages Awards*, in REFERENCE MANUAL ON SCIENTIFIC EVIDENCE 471, 498 (Fed. Jud. Center 1994) (the "capitalization factor is the ratio of the value of a stream of continuing income to the current amount of the stream; for example, if a firm is worth $1 million and its current earnings are $100,000, its capitalization factor is 10").

[7] Robert B. Labe, *Business Succession Planning*, 75 Mich. B.J. 940 (1996):

> The primary focus of the earnings based approach is on the capitalization of earnings when valuing a closely held business. This is done by taking the earnings data of the company over a period of years, and making certain adjustments, eliminating nonrecurrent or unusual items in the earnings, and then multiplying the result by a factor.

Id. at 946 (footnote omitted).

[8] Valuations based on projected future earnings should be discounted to present value. Section 9.3 (Discounting to Present Value).

[9] In practice the capitalization of earnings test is often leavened with subjective adjustments that are reflected in the capitalization factor. Allen S. Joslyn, *Measures of Damages for the Destruction of a Business*, 48 Brooklyn L. Rev. 431, 457 (1982) (adjustment by such factors as "the general economic outlook, the outlook for the specific industry, the past history of the business in general, and the prospect the business will continue").

In many cases all three measures are used to determine value. This is known as the "broad evidence" approach.[10] For example, there may be a good market for apartment complexes, the cost of construction (replacement value) is easily identified, and the earnings flow (capitalization of earnings) is ascertainable. Indeed, one formula or measure, such as capitalization of earnings, may influence the other, such as market. In other cases, one of the measures may be particularly well suited while others are not. For example, market is generally identified as a good measure for personal vehicles because the market for these "used" properties is usually thick and robust with many comparable sales, which facilitates the ascribing of value to the destroyed or damaged property. On the other hand, the capitalization of earnings test is rarely well suited to such properties because they are not used for income-producing purposes and, even if they are, the availability of substitutes makes it easy to replace the damaged property through the market.

When more than one measure is available, it is generally assumed that application of each measure will produce the same or nearly same result; thus, use of one method over another will not, in theory, lead to different results. However, the measures themselves are influenced by subjective judgments, such as what constitutes a "comparable" property for the market measure or how "net" earnings are calculated for the capitalization of earnings test.[11] This subjectivity can lead to significantly different results depending on which measure of value is used.

When valuation measures are used in special contexts, they can have meanings that are different from those given them in the general remedies context.[12]

In some cases, property may have value under one measure that is substantially different from another measure. This is usually due to market distortions or unique circumstances. For example, in *United States v. Crown Equipment Corporation*[13] a fire resulted in the loss of 11 million pounds of government surplus butter. The destroyed butter had been purchased as part of the government's price support program for $1.01/lb. The butter was used for a variety of programs that, in theory, did not compete with

---

[10] The "broad evidence" rule gives substantial latitude to the trier-of-fact to consider all relevant facts in determining the "value" of property. *See* Hills Bros. Coffee, Inc. v. Dairyland Transport, Inc., 460 N.W.2d 433, 435 (Wis. 1990). The rule finds primary application in insurance coverage cases involving the measure of loss when insured property is damaged or destroyed. Zochert v. National Farmers Union Property & Casualty Co., 576 N.W.2d 531, 533 (S.D. 1998) (identifying "broad evidence" rule as the "most widely accepted" test in insurance coverage context).

[11] Labe, *Business Succession Planning, supra,* 75 Mich. B.J. at 946 (noting that "valuation is a highly subjective process").

[12] General Cas. Co. v. Tracer Indus., Inc., 674 N.E.2d 473, 475–76 (Ill. App. 1996) (noting differences when replacement less depreciation measure is used in insurance context rather than remedies context); *see* United States v. 99.66 Acres of Land, 970 F.2d 651 (9th Cir. 1992) (condemnation—use of "lot method" or "developer's residual approach"); Mart v. Severson, 115 Cal. Rptr.2d 717 (Cal. App. 2002) (corporate dissolution—hypothetical sale model).

[13] 86 F.3d 700 (7th Cir. 1996).

the commercial market. Use of a market measure would be problematic because the nature of the destroyed product (surplus) would require the government to bid in the very market it was supporting. The defendant argued, unsuccessfully, that the government should be limited to its out-of-pocket expenses incurred in converting surplus milk to butter to replenish its destroyed inventory.

The court stated that the government's actual damages resulting from the loss of the butter were significant:

> When the fire . . . deprived the United States of 11 million pounds of surplus butter, it also deprived the government of an asset whose mere existence provided the national government with policy options and bargaining power it would not have had otherwise. The maintenance of these policy options is an integral part of the statutory scheme establishing the support program. As the text of the governing statute quite amply demonstrates, the government has many discretionary options for surplus commodities that do not affect the domestic butter market, including distributions to developing nations, the armed services, schools and prisons. These distributions facilitate the implementation of national policies. Surplus commodity also are bartered for critical materials produced abroad and for materials produced by other government agencies. Because many of these distributions cannot be anticipated by the government and vary with the tide of world events, the availability of stocks of surplus commodities gives the United States certain policy options—and bargaining power with other nations—that it would not otherwise have. Certain value accrues to the government, moreover, as a result of donating commodities for foreign and domestic aid.[14]

The court believed that the government's "losses" could be best measured by the cost of replacing the butter by purchase in the market.

[7.2] Diminution in Value

The difference in economic value pre-injury versus post-injury determines the amount of compensation the law allows for the damage. This is referred to as the "diminution in value" test.

One way to determine the "loss" is to calculate the pre-injury and post-injury values using one of the measures of value discussed in Section 7.1. The implicit assumption is that the same measure will be used for both calculations. The difference between the two calculations yields the monetary value of the loss.

Calculating before and after values for property damaged by another can be an expensive endeavor. To calculate a market value, an appraiser may be necessary; to calculate replacement cost, a contractor; to calculate

---

[14] *Id.* at 709 (citation and footnote omitted).

capitalization of earnings, an accountant. Frequently, a substitute test is used—cost of repair.

The underlying premise here is that the cost of repair is usually equal to diminution in value. The assumption is that the repaired property's value will equal its pre-injury value. Because this is not always the case, the presumption is rebuttable. For example, a Ming Vase that has been damaged by defendant's neglect may be repaired, perhaps restored is a better term. The restoration may be quite precise and undetectable except by a close inspection. Nevertheless, while the vase is now functional, it remains a "damaged" Ming Vase and this fact will be reflected in its value. It will not command the same price as a never damaged Ming Vase, all other things being equal.[15]

[7.3] Cost of Repair vs. Diminution in Value

Cost of repair is not itself damage or injury; rather, it is a means of measuring the loss, here diminution in value caused by the legal wrong inflicted on the plaintiff. Cost of repair is simply the expense necessary to restore damaged property to its pre-damaged condition. In making repairs, the plaintiff simply substitutes the cost of the repairs for another measure of loss—diminution in value.

Using cost of repair as a surrogate for diminution in value is efficient but raises problems of distortion, a problem commonplace with substitutes. For example, the case of *Hewlett v. Barge Bertie*[16] involved the issue of compensation for damage to a barge resulting from a collision. The barge had been declared a total loss before she was refloated and repaired by her current owner. The barge was used solely for carrying weather-proof cargo, such as pilings or logs. In the collision for which damages were sought it was noted by the court:

> Admittedly, the barge had no market value as an instrument of navigation and could be sold only for scrap. The skin of the barge was not pierced in the collision, and the only mark of impact was a dent in her starboard side. It produced no harmful effect upon the barge's seaworthiness or carrying capacity.[17]

The cost of repairing the "dent" was approximately $3,000; the diminution in value of the barge was $0, the barge had the same economic value

---

[15] Brennen v. Aston, 84 P.3d 99, 102 (Okla. 2003) (holding that when post-injury repairs fail to restore the property to its pre-injury condition, the plaintiff made recovery both cost of repair *and* the difference between pre-injury value and post-repair value); Papenheim v. Lovell, 530 N.W.2d 668, 672 (Iowa 1995); Byrne v. Western Pipe & Steel Co., 253 P. 776, 777 (Cal. App. 1927); *cf.* Gary v. Allstate Ins. Co., 250 So. 2d 168, 170 (La. App. 1971) (allowing cost of repairs plus remaining diminution in value because of stigma of structural damage to resale of vehicle). This concept of post-repair "stigma" has been applied in other contexts. Section 91.2 (Stigma Damages).

[16] 418 F.2d 654 (4th Cir. 1969), *cert. denied sub nom.* C.G. Willis, Inc. v. Hewlett, 397 U.S. 1021 (1970).

[17] *Id.* at 656.

pre-collision (no dent) as post-collision (dent).[18] The issue presented was whether the owner should recover the cost of repairing a dent that did not affect the economic value or functionality of the barge.

It is often stated that a plaintiff is limited to the lesser of the cost of repair or diminution in value.[19] Using this test, the owner would recover only nominal damages because diminution in value was $0. The majority in *Hewlett v. Barge Bertie* applied a different test. It permitted recovery of cost of repair as long as it did not exceed the pre-collision value of the property. In that case it did not, so the owner recovered as damages the cost of repair.

Decisions such as *Hewlett v. Barge Bertie* raise difficult policy decisions that permeate the law of remedies. The conflict is between awarding a plaintiff only his actual economic loss or, on the other hand, permitting the plaintiff to have his property restored to its pre-injury condition and thus reflect its value to the owner. The conflict between the two approaches is heightened by the fact that the plaintiff need not actually repair the property to recover under a cost of repair measure. The plaintiff may elect to keep the money and live with the dent. This raises the fear that rather than providing compensation, the award provides a windfall. As noted by the dissenting judge in *Hewlett v. Barge Bertie*:

> If my brothers are right, the libelant is unduly enriched. He must hope greatly that another errant navigator will hit his battered barge again, and still another yet again, so that each time he may happily pocket the estimated cost of theoretical repairs which neither he nor anyone else will ever dream of undertaking while retaining all along a barge as seaworthy and useful to him and of undiminished worth if he chooses to sell it.[20]

[7.4] Burden of Proof

It is the plaintiff's responsibility to establish her loss and the amount of compensation necessary to return her to her rightful position. Plaintiff's proof obligations are, however, aided by the presumption that cost of repair is equal to diminution in value; thus, plaintiff may satisfy her proof obligations by competent evidence establishing either diminution in value or cost of repair as the measure of the loss. The burden then shifts to defendant to rebut the presumption and demonstrate that plaintiff chose the "greater of" cost of repair or diminution in value rather than the "lesser

---

[18] *Id.* at 656, 659 (dissenting opinion) (noting that barge's market value remained at approximately $5,600 pre-and post-collision).

[19] Safeco Ins. Co. v. J & D Painting, 21 Cal. Rptr. 2d 903, 905 (Cal. App. 1993); Laska v. Steinpreis, 231 N.W.2d 196, 200 (Wis. 1975). In cases involving damage to real property, particularly residences, there is a growing tendency to allow cost of repair even if it exceeds diminution in value as long as repair will not constitute economic waste. *See generally* 13 Am. Jur. 2d *Building & Construction Contracts* § 79 (1964); Section 81 (Value to Owner).

[20] 418 F.2d at 661.

of."[21] Upon submission of the conflicting proofs, the issue will be resolved by the trier of fact.

The above rule applies specifically to tort claims. When the loss is remediable through a breach of contract action, the courts are more inclined to allow the plaintiff her cost of repair even if it exceeds diminution in value unless repair would constitute economic waste.[22] The reasoning here is that in contract the plaintiff is entitled to her expectancy; in tort the concern is out-of-pocket loss.

[7.5] Betterment

When damaged property is repaired or replaced, a problem of allocation may arise. Compensation is predicated on the basic notion of equivalency—"apples for apples" and "oranges for oranges." If the repairs transform the proverbial "sow's ear" into a "silk purse" or if the plaintiff purchases a "silk purse" to replace a damaged or destroyed "sow's ear" the plaintiff has not replicated the position he would have been in but for the wrong. The plaintiff has improved his position.

At one level the solution is easy. The law will not permit compensation recoveries that result in windfalls. If the damages proof consists solely of the value of "silk purses" when what the plaintiff lost was a "sow's ear," then the plaintiff has a failure of proof. At another level, however, the problem is more difficult, for often the plaintiff is not able to replicate through repair or purchase exactly what was lost or damaged. For example, if a pier or bridge is destroyed, the plaintiff cannot rebuild a "used" pier or bridge; the plaintiff must replace the pier or bridge with a new or newer structure. Similarly, if a used automobile is damaged, it is not always possible to repair it with like "aged" parts; oftentimes, the replacement parts are new.[23] This raises the question whether in calculating compensatory damages based on the cost of new parts and materials the plaintiff is being bettered at defendant's expense? One caveat should be noted. The betterment rule appears to be limited to tortious injury when the focus is on compensating the plaintiff for the harm inflicted. The betterment rule may not be applied in cases where the plaintiff's expectancy interest is being vindicated, as, for example, in a breach of contract case.[24]

---

[21] Green v. Bearden Enters., Inc., 598 S.W.2d 649, 652–53 (Tex. Civ. App. 1980); A.I.D. Ins. Servs. v. Riley, 541 P.2d 595, 599 (Ariz. App. 1975).

[22] Jacob v. West Bend Mut. Ins. Co., 553 N.W.2d 800, 807 (Wis. 1996); Redbud Coop. Corp. v. Clayton, 700 S.W.2d 551, 561 (Tenn. App. 1985). *But cf.* Hensic v. Afshari Enters., Inc., 599 S.W.2d 522, 525 (Mo. App. 1980) (noting conflicting Missouri authorities whether "lesser of" rule applied to breach of contract actions). *See generally* John P. Ludington, Annot., *Modern Status of Rule as to Whether Cost of Correction or Difference in Value of Structures is Proper Measure of Damages For Breach of Construction Contract*, 41 A.L.R.4th 131 (1986).

[23] Phillips Petroleum Co. v. Stokes Oil Co., Inc., 863 F.2d 1250, 1257–58 (6th Cir. 1988) (noting that "usually repairs are made with new materials").

[24] Shaw v. Bridges-Gallagher, Inc., 528 N.E.2d 1349, 1353 (Ill. App. 1988) (refusing to apply depreciation offset in breach of construction contract context to reflect enhanced value plaintiff received when his defective roof was replaced with a new roof with a longer expected useful life; the defendant was liable for the entire cost of the new roof).

[7.5.1] Determining Betterment

The first issue is one of definition. Apples and oranges are relatively easy, but determining whether something has been improved is a more difficult task. When the law speaks of betterment, it does so in an economic sense, not an aesthetic sense. When a used automobile has been repaired using new parts rather than used parts, the owner may feel subjectively better about the vehicle; however, if the economic value of the vehicle after the repairs is essentially the same as it was before the injury, then the owner has not received any betterment for which he need account. Betterment as "economic value" is reflected in a higher price because the repairs made the property more desirable than it was in its pre-injury state or the repairs extended the useful life of the property beyond that which it would have enjoyed in its pre-injury state. The basic issue is whether the repairs or replacement in fact added economic value to the pre-injury value.

[7.5.2] Allocating Betterment

If, as a result of replacement or repair, value is added, the defendant is entitled to a credit against the cost of repair or replacement for the added value or betterment. The repair or replacement costs are not always broken down in a way that facilitates this allocation; consequently, the process by which this is done can be, at its best, rough, and, at its worst, arbitrary.

When the betterment is immediately reflected in the market value of the property, the added value can be easily captured by the difference in value test. Oftentimes, however, the market is too thin to support such an approach; consequently, repair or replacement cost is normally used as the measure of loss. The added value is in turn calculated by depreciating the cost of repair or replacement to reflect the age of the repaired or replaced property. An example may help. Assume a furnace was 5 years old when it was damaged in 2000 due to defendant's negligence. When installed in 1995, the furnace had a useful life of 10 years; thus, at the time of damage, 5 years of the useful life had been used, 5 years remained. The repaired furnace has a useful life of 10 years from the date of repair in 2000. We may represent the example as follows:

$\longrightarrow$

1995 (Furnace Purchased and Installed)	2000 (Furnace Damaged and Repaired)	2005 (Original Useful Life Expended)	2010 (As Repaired, Useful Life Expended)

Figure 1

The term "useful life" does not mean the furnace's actual, productive lifespan. The original furnace may have operated quite satisfactorily past the year 2005. The repaired furnace may operate quite satisfactorily past the year 2010. The "useful life" reference is to depreciation schedules by which courts determine the amount of economic life a property has used. Functioning property may have zero useful life because the property is fully depreciated in an accounting sense. The concepts of "useful life" and "depreciation" are artificial. Moreover, they have been constructed more for taxation and accounting purposes than for remedies purposes; hence, their application to the calculation of compensatory damages and betterment is somewhat strained. A better measure waits, however, to be devised. Courts use what's available to accommodate the needs of the situation. As has been suggested, "necessity is the mother of law."[25]

Returning to the furnace example, we may solve the problem by applying an appropriate depreciation schedule, straight line or progressive. Straight line depreciation is used when the useful life of the repaired property equals the original useful life of the repaired property. Under the facts of the hypothetical, that is the case here. Both the original furnace and the repaired furnace have useful lives of 10 years. We assume that each year 10% of the value of the property has been expended. At the time the furnace is damaged, plaintiff had 50% of the useful life remaining; now, post repair, plaintiff has 100%. The court would allocate 50% of the cost of repair to defendant because that is what plaintiff lost. The remaining 50% would be borne by plaintiff. If cost of repairs was determined by the court to be $10,000, defendant would pay $5,000 (50% of $10,000) as compensatory damages. If the reader looks at the preceding graph (Figure 1), he or she will see that this conforms to the reality constructed by the useful life concept. But for the injury, plaintiff's furnace would have had economic value until the year 2005; due to the repairs, the furnace will have economic value until the year 2010. The additional 5 years are a betterment, and that portion of the new useful life, 50% (5/10), will be borne by the plaintiff as an offset against the total cost of repair.

This approach does not work, however, when the repairs give the property a useful life different from the property's original useful life.[26] For example, assume that due to new technology, the repairs give the furnace a new useful life of 15 years. We may represent the new facts as follows:

[25] *Cf.* City of El Paso v. Simmons, 379 U.S. 497, 534–35 (1965) (Black, J. dissenting) (stating that "Texas" necessity as seen by this Court is the mother of a regrettable judicial invention which I think has no place in constitutional law") (footnote omitted).

[26] If after repairs the remaining useful life is less that the repaired property's remaining useful life pre-injury, we have a situation when the cost of repair is not fully compensatory. Assume repairs can only give the property a new useful life of 4 years. In this situation, all economic value will be expanded in 2004, one year short of the original economic life span of the property. In this case there is no betterment and cost of repair is not fully compensatory. Section 7.2 (Diminution in Value).

→

1995	2000	2005	2015
(Furnace Purchased and Installed)	(Furnace Damaged and Repaired)	(Original Useful Life Expended)	(New Useful Life Expended)

Figure 2

If we allocated on the same basis as above using straight line depreciation, defendant would pay for 50% of the repairs even though the repaired furnace's new useful life had been greatly extended. Courts have found such a result to be a windfall for the plaintiff and unfair to the defendant.[27]

The solution courts have devised is to compare the pre-injury remaining useful life to the added useful life provided by the repairs.[28] Returning to the above hypothetical: as of the date of injury, the furnace had 5 years of useful life remaining (2000–2005). The repairs added 10 years (2005–2015). Of the 15 years of now existing useful life (2000–2015) 5 belonged to plaintiff, 10 to defendant. Thus, plaintiff should receive compensation for his loss (5/15). Alternatively, defendant should receive a credit for his contribution (10/15). Again assuming $10,000 to effect the repairs, plaintiff would receive an award of $3,333 (5/15 × $10,000). In other words, defendant would end up paying $3,333 for the repairs, plaintiff would have to pay the balance or $6,667. It must be remembered that the $6,667 reflects the extended useful life, after the year 2005 (when the furnace's original useful life would have expired) that has been added by the $10,000 in repairs.

It may be observed that the approach requires a plaintiff to expend a sum of money ($6,667) for repair or replacement prior to the time plaintiff would have expended the money (year 2005) but for the injury. Courts have, however, been unwilling to treat this advanced expenditure as a form of compensable injury.[29]

[7.6] Value as a Function of Time

When we value can often be as significant as how we value. What is valuable today may be worthless tomorrow, and vice versa. This point is particularly true with respect to items that fluctuate in value, but the point also holds true with other items when the passage of time may influence a thing's value. For example, should we value crops based on their value at the time of harvest or at some other time, such as the time of planting?

---

[27] E.I. DuPont de Nemours v. Robin Hood Shifting, 899 F.2d 377, 381–82 (5th Cir. 1990) (stating that only in rare cases will court use progressive as opposed to straight line depreciation; one such case is where useful life of property is extended).

[28] Freeport Sulphur Co. v. The S/S Hermosa, 526 F.2d 300, 306 (5th Cir. 1976) (holding that "the proper ratio is that which the useful life extension bears to the remaining useful life of the property after repairs").

[29] Id. at 307.

Should we value damaged property at the time the damage occurs, at the time damage is discovered, at the time of trial, or at the time the damaged property is repaired or replaced?

[7.6.1] General Rule

For breach of contract actions the general rule is that market fluctuations after the contract is breached are not relevant in measuring contract general damages, which are measured at the time of the breach.[30] This rule does not limit a plaintiff's right to recover consequential damages such as lost profits or reliance damages incurred prior to the breach. On the other hand, when breach denies or deprives the plaintiff of the very thing he was promised, value of that thing is determined based on the date performance was due,[31] not some earlier or later date unless the contract states otherwise.

The appropriate valuation date for tort actions is usually said to be the date of injury.[32] Tort actions are more likely, than contract actions, to raise the fluctuating value exception.[33] The reason is that the consensual nature of contract actions and the obligation to cover often limit the non-breaching party's ability to use a valuation date different from the date of breach. Tort's public policy foundation provides greater flexibility and a greater willingness to use a valuation date other than the date of misconduct. The linguistic connection between injury and loss in tort cases also facilitates this practice. When courts refer to date of loss, unlike date of breach, the term loss is sufficiently open-ended to accommodate a variety of different valuation dates. The loss occurs when the court identifies it as having

---

[30] Prospero Assoc. v. Redactron Corp., 682 P.2d 1193, 1198 (Colo. App. 1983); United Virginia Bank v. Dick Herriman Ford, Inc., 210 S.E.2d 158, 161 (Va. 1974); Crowe v. Estate of Harkins, 416 S.W.2d 770, 773 (Tenn. 1967) (holding that the measure of damages for plaintiffs when they sold the stock three and one-half years after date of purchase, when defendant had promised to buy back stock after two years, was difference between value of stock and purchase price at expiration of two years from date of purchase when breach occurred). *See generally* 22 Am. Jur. 2d *Damages* § 78. The problem of anticipatory breach may raise special issues. Section 166 (Buyer's Remedies), text and notes 10-13.

[31] Caisse Nationale De Credit Agricole v. CBI Indus., Inc., 90 F.3d 1264, 1276 (7th Cir. 1996):

> Therefore, the district court erred in calculating damages as a February 7, 1994, the date Credit filed suit. The proper date is January 19, 1994, the date Chameleon/ CBI gave unequivocal written notice disclaiming any obligation under the option or swap agreement. We therefore remand to the district court for a redetermination of damages using January 19, 1994 as the date of default. In so doing we note that under New York law Credit is entitled to "expectation damages," which means Credit should be placed "in the same economic position it would have been in had both parties fully performed."

[32] Browning v. Corbett, 940 S.W.2d 914, 925 (Mo. App. 1997) (conversion); Management Computer Servs., Inc. v. Hawkins, Ash, Baptie & Co., 557 N.W.2d 67, 79 (Wis. 1996) (conversion); Ryals v. Hunter, 638 So. 2d 2 (Ala. App. 1994) (trespass); Porras v. Craig, 675 S.W.2d 503, 504 (Tex. 1984) (trespass); Johnson v. Naugle, 557 N.E.2d 1339, 1343 (Ind. App. 1990) (fraud); Molnar v. Beriswell, 171 N.E. 593, 594 (Ohio 1930).

[33] Section 7.6.2 (Fluctuating Value).

occurred.[34] This date may be temporally distant from the date the defendant engaged in the loss-producing act. For example, if defendant causes a virus to lay dormant in plaintiff's computer until activated by a prearranged signal, the time span between act and injury may be short or long. Moreover, the resulting loss may not necessarily occur when the virus is activated. On the other hand, injury (and loss) may predate activation of the virus if plaintiff learns about it and seeks to vaccinate its computers before the virus strikes. For these reasons, valuation timing is usually less rigid in tort than in contract.

[7.6.2] Fluctuating Value

Some properties, particularly securities, may fluctuate in value due to the vicissitudes of the markets in which they are traded. When these properties are the subject of a legal claim, the selection of the valuation date can have significant consequences because the property's value may have moved dramatically over the relevant period of time.[35]

A number of approaches have been developed to deal with the situation.[36] As a general rule the more egregious the defendant's misconduct, the more leeway the court will allow plaintiff in selecting a valuation date that will maximize the recovery.[37] It should be borne in mind, however, that the fluctuating value rule is premised on the fact that the type and nature of property involved is subject to fluctuation. The mere fact that a property's value has changed does not mean that the rule should be applied.[38] Fluctuation suggests an "up and down" movement, not unidirectional movement.[39] In situations where property values are usually stable or

---

[34] United States v. Marshall, 338 F.3d 990, 993–94 (9th Cir. 2003) (holding that when the government wrongfully failed to give notice of forfeiture proceeding and was unable to return the specific property taken, the proper valuation date for a substitutional award of damages was the date the property was sold pursuant to the forfeiture proceedings; the court rejected contentions that the proper valuation date was the date of seizure or the date of forfeiture). In *Marshall*, the property had declined appreciably in value since the date of seizure and the government had discharged liens encumbering the property prior to sale. The court noted that the government's action had, in fact, benefitted Marshall. *Id.* at 993.

[35] Although the fluctuating value rule is most often applied in cases where property is converted or obtained by misrepresentation, it is not limited to such substantive claims. Mercantile Holdings, Inc. v. Keeshin, 633 N.E.2d 805, 806 (Ill. App. 1993) (applying fluctuating value rule to collateral lost through breach of contract).

[36] *See generally* C.B. Higgins, Annot., *Comment Note—Measure of Damages For Conversion of Corporate Stock or Certificate*, 31 A.L.R. 3d 1286, § 5 (1971).

[37] Patterson v. Wizowaty, 505 S.W.2d 425, 427 (Tex. Civ. App. 1974) (stating that "[t]he measure of damage in a stock conversion suit is the market value of the stock at the time of the conversion. If the conversion of the stock is attended by fraud, wilful wrong, or gross negligence, then the measure of damages is the highest market value between the date of the conversion and the filing of suit.") (citation omitted).

[38] Sullivan v. City of Philadelphia, 460 A.2d 1191, 1194 (Pa. Super. Ct. 1983) (noting that mere fact that property had appreciated in value after the date of loss did not mean that it was property that fluctuated in value).

[39] *Id.*

unidirectional, the traditional date of loss or breach rule is applied, notwithstanding the occasional case of value change after that date.

The dominant theme operating here is to restore to the plaintiff the range of elective action that defendant's wrongdoing deprived plaintiff from enjoying.[40] For example, if plaintiff was deprived of his property by defendant's fraud, act of conversion, or breach of contract, plaintiff has been deprived of the ability to own the property or to sell it. Because we have lost the opportunity to determine what plaintiff would have done with the property in the absence of defendant's wrong, we must create a counterfactual past, *i.e.,* a past that never was. Moreover, because the world moved on notwithstanding defendant's misconduct, we must align our counterfactual past with the world as it actually unfolded. For example, assume plaintiff's interest in 1000 shares in Widget, Inc., a company that trades on the New York Stock Exchange, is misappropriated. Assume further that the trading range of Widget over the relevant period is as follows:

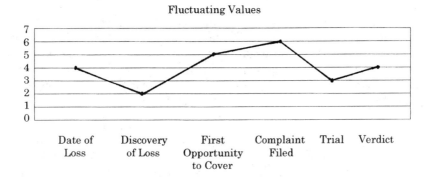

Figure 3

As noted earlier, the general rule is to use the date of misappropriation as the valuation date, which here would give each share a value of $4. When value is stable over time, the passage of time does not meaningfully affect, for remedies purposes, the plaintiff's range of elective action. Whatever plaintiff does or would have done is done against a constant—the value of $4/share. A claim by plaintiff that but for defendant's misconduct he would have sold the stock sometime after the date of misappropriation has no affect on damages, aside from prejudgment interest,[41] because the per share value never changed. When, however, values fluctuate, creation of an alternate past, (*i.e.,* the past we believe, or allow ourselves to believe, the plaintiff would have taken but for defendant's misconduct), has a significant impact. It does make a difference whether we select date of discovery ($2),

---

[40] *Cf.* Galigher v. Jones, 129 U.S. 193, 200 (1889) (noting that injury to rightful owner includes not only the loss of control, but the forced "sale of it at an unfavorable time, and for an unfavorable price").

[41] Section 16.3 (Accrual Date).

date of opportunity to cover ($5) date complaint was filed ($6), etc., as the appropriate valuation date. We could, of course, ignore this complication and continue to use the date of misappropriation ($4) as the valuation date, but this would require that we ignore completely the deprivation of plaintiff's right of elective action. Most jurisdictions refuse to do so because such an approach would be inconsistent with the basic compensatory goal of placing the plaintiff in the position he would have been in but for defendant's legal wrong.

Of course, creating an alternate past is not trouble free. What plaintiff will not believe that she would have sold at $6 rather than $2? There is always the risk that freeing the plaintiff from the date of misappropriation as the valuation date may lead to windfall recoveries as plaintiffs visualize a past through rose-colored glasses.[42] Some courts assume that plaintiff would have sold what was lost on the date the property reached its highest value between the date of loss and the date of trial,[43] or filing of suit.[44] It is customary to limit this approach to situations when the defendant's conduct manifested itself as fraud, willful wrong, or gross negligence.

Even with the wrongful conduct qualification, the above approach allows the plaintiff to shift all the speculative risk to the defendant and absolve herself of any obligation to mitigate damages. Indeed, it is illogical, under a compensation theory, to allow a plaintiff any recovery for value fluctuation of converted property before the plaintiff learns of the conversion. As noted by Judge Learned Hand in *Marcus v. Otis*:

> If a customer, who does not know that the broker has converted his shares, but supposes that he retains the power of selling them, does not order a sale throughout a given period, it is conclusive evidence that he did not wish to sell at any intermediate price; and he ought not to be allowed to charge the broker on the assumption that he might have . . . .[45]

A number of jurisdictions have adopted what has become known as the "New York Rule." The measure of damages is calculated based on the highest value of the property between the date of loss and a reasonable period of time after the plaintiff learns of the loss.[46] This approach precludes saddling the plaintiff with a potentially unfavorable sale, as may be the case if date of misappropriation is used, preserves the plaintiff's elective options, but subjects those options to a duty to mitigate within a reasonable period of time.[47] What constitutes a "reasonable period of time" will depend

---

[42] One response to this problem has been to require the plaintiff to prosecute the conversion claim with reasonable diligence. Friedman v. Renz, 87 P.2d 386, 387 (Cal. App. 1939).

[43] This is the common law rule for properly having a fluctuating value and is often referred to as the "English Rule." *Galigher, supra*, 129 U.S. at 200–01 (collecting decisions).

[44] Brougham v. Swarva, 661 P.2d 138, 144 (Wash. App. 1983).

[45] 168 F.2d 649, 657 (2d Cir. 1948) (footnote omitted).

[46] *Galigher, supra*, 129 U.S. at 200; Hoffman v. Dorner, 447 N.Y.S.2d 20, 22 (App. Dept. 1982).

[47] Broadwater v. Old Republic Sur., 854 P.2d 527, 531 (Utah 1993) (noting that New York

on the facts of the case.[48] At least for securities, the time periods tend to be rather short,[49] although periods of up to 60 days have been recognized.[50]

[7.6.3]   Foreign Currency Obligations

The problem arises when after having identified the appropriate valuation date for the cause of action itself, the court must make the further determination as to what exchange rate should be applied to convert the claim or judgment into United States dollars.[51]

Currency exchange rates are not always stable. Consider a relationship between American and Japanese companies during which time all obligations are to be paid in Japanese yen and during which time the dollar-yen exchange rate fluctuates form 1:120 to 1:80 to 1:100. As the dollar-yen rate deteriorates relative to the dollar, it costs the American company more dollars to acquire the necessary amount of yen to pay its contractual obligations. Initially, each dollar purchases 120 yen; later, each dollar purchases only 80 yen. Put another way, if the monetary obligation is 120 million yen, initially it costs the American company $1 million to comply (120,000,000 / 120); later, it costs the company $1.5 million (120,000,000 / 80). The situation is the converse for the Japanese company. When the dollar later improves relative to the yen (1:100), the cost to the American company is reduced to $1.2 million (120,000,000 / 100). If the contract is payable in dollars, the situation improves for the Japanese company as the dollar depreciates against the yen, *i.e.*, it takes fewer yen to purchase each dollar, and worsens as the dollar appreciates against the yen, *i.e.*, it takes more yen to purchase each dollar.

Rule "affords the owner of the stock a reasonable opportunity to consult counsel, employ other brokers, watch the market to determine when it would be advisable to purchase replacement stock, and raise funds should the owner decide to repurchase") (citations omitted). The plaintiff is entitled to the value of what was lost regardless of whether he reinvests. Letson v. Dean Witter Reynolds, Inc., 532 F. Supp. 500, 503 (N.D. Cal. 1982), *aff'd without opinion sub nom.* Shearson Loeb Rhoades, Inc. v. Bryant, 730 F.2d 769 (9th Cir. 1984).

[48] Schultz v. Commodity Futures Trading Comm'n, 716 F.2d 136, 140 (2d Cir. 1983) ("what constitutes a reasonable period between the act complained of and the time when reentry into the market would be both warranted and possible will vary from case to case . . ."); Caballero v. Anselmo, 759 F. Supp. 144, 149 (S.D.N.Y. 1991) ("no fixed period is prescribed . . . nor is there any rule of thumb") (citations omitted).

[49] Herman v. T&S Commodities, Inc., 592 F. Supp. 1406, 1421 (S.D.N.Y. 1984) (one day after unlawful reversal of short position); Cauble v. Mabon Nugent & Co., 594 F. Supp. 985, 996 (S.D.N.Y. 1984) (considering plaintiff's experience and capabilities as a trader and his immense wealth, two trading days was a reasonable period for determining damages); Mitchell v. Texas Gulf Sulphur Co., 446 F.2d 90, 105 (10th Cir.) (nine trading days after investors became informed of accurate information concerning status of corporation), *cert. denied,* 404 U.S. 1064 (1971); Flickinger v. Harold C. Brown & Co., 789 F. Supp. 616, 620 (W.D.N.Y. 1992) (because security was publicly traded, short period of time, no more than 10 days, would be reasonable).

[50] In the Matter of Sterling Navigation Co., Ltd., 6 B.R. 616, 617 (S.D.N.Y. 1980) (stating that "a reasonable time has been interpreted by some New York courts to be between 7 days and 60 days") (citation omitted).

[51] Aker Verdal A/S v. Neil F. Lampson, Inc., 828 P.2d 610, 613 (Wash. App. 1992).

Let us assume that a contract is breached when the dollar-yen exchange rate is 1:80 and a judgment is rendered in a Japanese court for the Japanese company in yen on the date the exchange rate is 1:100. When the judgment is sought to be enforced in the United States against the American company, the yen has depreciated so that the exchange rate is 1:120. The American court will enter a domestic judgment in dollars based on the foreign judgment, which is expressed in yen. What exchange rate should be used to convert the Japanese judgment into a domestic, dollar-valued judgment?

A number of approaches have arisen to address this issue. Much of the difficulty arises from a pair of United States Supreme Court decisions that are somewhat inconsistent. The two decisions are *Hicks v. Guinness*[52] and *Deutsche Bank v. Humphrey*,[53] both of which involved claims seeking to recover funds confiscated by the Germans during World War I. Substantial inflation of the German economy in the early 1920s and the resulting destruction of the integrity of the mark, the German unit of currency, figured prominently in both decisions. In *Hicks* the Court held that when the underlying debt is payable in the United States in a currency of a foreign country, the "breach date" rule should apply, *i.e.*, the currency exchange rate as of the date of breach. In *Deutsche Bank* the Court held that when a debt is payable in a foreign country in foreign currency, the "judgment day" rule should apply, *i.e.*, the currency conversion rate as of the date of judgment. The problem was that the decisions assumed a certain localization of decision making under the then dominant rule of *Pennoyer v. Neff*.[54] These cases could be brought either in the United States or a foreign court, but not both. Furthermore, the decisions were based on federal law and were not binding on the states.

One approach is to use the "breach date" as the determinative date for all currency conversion cases.[55] Another approach is to use the judgment date.[56] Several courts have attempted to reconcile *Hicks* and *Deutsche Bank* by adopting a blended rule:

> Under the first approach, the judgment day rule applies when the contract is payable in a foreign country in that country's currency; the breach day rule applies when the payment is to be made in the United States. Under the second approach, the judgment day rule applies if the obligation arises entirely under foreign law; the breach

---

[52] 269 U.S. 71 (1925).

[53] 272 U.S. 517 (1926).

[54] 95 U.S. 714 (1877).

[55] Vishipco Line v. Chase Manhattan Bank, N.A., 660 F.2d 854, 866–67 (2d Cir. 1981) (applying New York breach-date rule), *cert. denied*, 459 U.S. 976 (1982); *In re* Good Hope Chem. Corp., 747 F.2d 806, 811 (1st Cir. 1984), *cert. denied*, 471 U.S. 1102 (1985) (applying breach date rule).

[56] Competex S.A. v. Labow, 783 F.2d 333, 338 (2d Cir. 1986) (discussing approach).

day rule applies if the plaintiff could recover under United States law at the time of the breach.[57]

Several courts have adopted an approach that focuses on whether exchange rates have improved or worsened.[58] The rationale for this approach is described by the drafters of the Restatement:

> While the preference of the judgment creditor is to be taken into account, the decision is to be made by the court, which should assure that neither party receives a windfall or is penalized as a result of currency conversion. If the court gives judgment in United States dollars, as is the general practice, the date used for conversion should depend on whether the currency of obligation has appreciated or depreciated relative to the dollar. In general, if the foreign currency has depreciated since the injury or breach, judgment should be given at the rate of exchange applicable on the date of injury or breach; if the foreign currency has appreciated since the injury or breach, judgment should be given at the rate of exchange applicable on the date of judgment or the date of payment.[59]

The Uniform Foreign-Money Claims Act sets forth a third approach, the payment day rule. Under this approach, the court will award an amount the plaintiff would have collected had the plaintiff been able to recover on its claim or judgment in the foreign country. The exchange rate will be the rate in effect on the payment date. In *Manches & Co. v. Gilbey*[60] the court held that by using this date the appropriate award would reflect what the plaintiff (Manches & Co.) would have recovered had it been able to collect on its judgment in Great Britain.[61]

The issue can also be approached from a choice of law perspective to determine whether the foreign court would issue an award in U.S. dollars and, if that is the case, simply mimic what the foreign court would have done if the action had been brought there rather than in the United States.[62]

---

[57] El Universal, Compania Periodistica Nacional, S.A. v. Phoenician Imports, Inc., 802 S.W.2d 799, 802 (Tex. Civ. App. 1991), *citing In re* Good Hope Chem. Corp., 747 F.2d 806, 811 (1984), *cert. denied*, 471 U.S. 1102 (1985).

[58] Aker Verdal A/S, 828 P.2d at 613–14 (collecting decisions).

[59] Restatement (Third) of Foreign Relations Law of the United States § 823, cmt. c (1987). *But see* Competex S.A. v. Labow, 783 F.2d 333, 336 (2d Cir. 1986) (criticizing Restatement position as extreme creditor preference rule). The debtor can eliminate the preference, if any, by paying the debt. Nikimiha Secs. Ltd. v. The Trend Group Ltd., 646 F. Supp. 1211, 1227 (E.D. Pa. 1986) ("[The Restatement] rule prevents fluctuating exchange rates from causing the injured or non-breaching party to bear the loss. Here, defendants have resisted paying a debt owed for more than two years so that they should bear the risk of a fluctuating exchange rate.") (brackets added).

[60] 646 N.E.2d 86 (Mass. 1995).

[61] 646 N.E.2d at 88, *citing* Uniform Foreign-Money Claims Act § 1(3), 13 U.L.A. 42, 44 (Supp. 1994). According to the court 18 jurisdictions have adopted the Act. *Id.* at 88 n.6.

[62] Rose Hall, Ltd. v. Chase Manhattan Overseas Banking Corp., 566 F. Supp. 1558, 1570–72 (D. Del. 1983).

If the judgment was rendered in a foreign country, and enforcement of that judgment is sought in the United States, there is a greater tendency to use the judgment day rule.[63] This has been accomplished in breach-date jurisdictions by treating the failure to pay the judgment as the obligation being sued upon, thus conflating the breach date and judgment day approaches.[64] There is also authority for using the date the foreign judgment is merged into a judgment of the forum as the valuation date.[65]

[7.7]   Value as a Function of Place

[7.7.1]   Place in Chain of Distribution

Place like time can influence valuation. What is worth $X in one place, may be worth less or more in another. Perhaps, the most common example of this is the difference between manufacturing cost, wholesale cost, and retail cost. The value attributed to property will vary depending on its location in the chain of distribution when the valuation is made and the replacement market the plaintiff would enter to replace what was lost to mitigate or fix its losses.[66] If the plaintiff had sold the property, the market in which the property was sold would be the relevant market for loss of sale damages.[67] If the plaintiff is a manufacturer, courts split on whether to use manufacturing cost or invoice (selling) price.[68]

For example, assume plaintiff contracts with defendant in the wholesale market for goods for resale at plaintiff's retail outlet.[69] The property is destroyed while in transit. If the property was simply stock in trade, the relevant market is the market in which plaintiff purchased the property.[70] "[W]hen stock in trade is destroyed, retail value is an inappropriate measure of fair market value because the retail sales price includes a mark-up for overhead and profit. In lieu of evidence of retail price . . . only evidence as to the replacement value or wholesale value is admissible to prove

---

[63] Restatement (Third) of Foreign Relations Law, *supra*, § 823; *see* Pecaflor Constr., Inc., v. Landes, 243 Cal. Rptr. 605, 607 (Cal. App. 1988) (recognizing satisfaction of Canadian judgment made with devalued Canadian dollars); Teca-Print A.G. v. Amacoil Mach., Inc., 525 N.Y.S.2d 535, 540 (N.Y. Sup. Ct. 1988) (applying judgment date rather than breach date currency conversion rate to Swiss judgment sought to be enforced in the United States). *But see Manches & Co.*, *supra*, 646 N.E.2d at 88 (applying payment date rule to foreign judgment).

[64] *Competex S.A.*, *supra*, 783 F.2d at 334 (applying New York law).

[65] *In re* National Paper & Type Co. of Puerto Rico, 77 B.R. 355, 357–58 (Tex. Civ. App. 1987).

[66] United Truck Rental Equip. Leasing, Inc. v. Kleenco Corp., 929 P.2d 99, 107 (Haw. 1996).

[67] Chevron Chem. Co. v. Streett Indus., Inc., 534 F. Supp. 801, 803 (E.D. Mo. 1982).

[68] Acme Delivery Serv., Inc. v. Samsonite Corp., 663 P.2d 621, 625 (Colo. 1983) (using cost to manufacturer unless plaintiff can show actual lost sales). *But cf.* Tozzi v. Testa, 423 N.E.2d 948 (Ill. App. 1981) (adopting the invoice rule).

[69] The hypothetical is based on Stark Bros. Nurseries & Orchards Co. v. Wayne Daniel Truck, Inc., 718 S.W.2d 204 (Mo. App. 1986).

[70] J & H Auto Trim Co., Inc. v. Bellefonte Ins. Co., 677 F.2d 1365, 1369 (11th Cir. 1982) (collecting decisions).

market value."[71] As noted in *Ocean Electric Co. v. Hughes Laboratories, Inc.*:

> The appropriate economic market to be used in approximating reasonable market value is the usual market where the property or goods had been purchased. The usual market for the owner of goods held for subsequent resale, is the wholesale selling market, because a retailer will replace destroyed or damaged goods at the wholesale price, and thus be restored to the prior financial position.[72]

If, on the other hand, the destroyed property had been sold, the relevant market would be that in which the replacement sale would be made, the retail market.[73] Only in this market could plaintiff recover what he actually lost, the sale.

The concept of relevant market can have many unique applications. For example, in *Associates Commercial Corporation v. Rash*[74] a Chapter 13 debtor in bankruptcy opted to keep his automobile in what is euphemistically referred to as a "cramdown."[75] A "cramdown" permits the debtor to keep property of the bankruptcy estate over a creditor's objections as long as the debtor agrees to pay the creditor the "value" of the property. Usually, the payment schedule is over time and on terms more favorable to the debtor than the prior debt arrangement. The problem is: "what is value?" In *Rash* the debtor argued that the relevant market was the "foreclosure sale" market, which will typically generate a distress price. The creditor argued for a going concern value, which while not a retail market, envisioned a sale that was not forced or coerced. In *Rash* the difference between the two markets was $9,125. The Court sided with the creditor finding that the proper market was the replacement market in which a willing buyer in the debtor's trade, business, or situation would pay a willing seller to obtain property of like age and condition.

[7.7.2] Place in Terms of Physical Location

Valuation according to place can also raise questions of geography. Should the award include the cost of transportation to the place of loss? The problem arises when there is no market at the place of loss. The general rule is to include the cost of transportation if the plaintiff will use the property at the place of loss, but to subtract the cost of transportation if

---

[71] *Id.*; *Chevron Chem. Co.*, *supra*, 534 F. Supp. at 803; *United Truck Rental Equip. Leasing, Inc.*, *supra*, 929 P.2d at 107.

[72] 636 So. 2d 112, 114 (Fla. App. 1994) (citation omitted).

[73] *Stark Bros. Nurseries & Orchards Co.*, *supra*, 718 S.W.2d at 206 (noting that retail price was appropriate measure when "the testimony support[ed] a finding that the destroyed [property] had already been sold and that refunds and pro rata delivery to customers who had ordered [the destroyed property] was necessary") (brackets added).

[74] 520 U.S. 953 (1997).

[75] *Id.* (discussing 11 U.S.C. § 1325).

plaintiff would sell the property at a place other than the place of loss.[76] In some areas, the specialty of practice may have generated a specific rule. For example, in admiralty cases, the usual measure for damaged or lost cargo is the fair market value at its destination and at the time the cargo should have arrived.[77] This can lead to some interesting characterization issues. In *Roco Carriers, Ltd. v. M/V Nurnberg Express*[78] goods ("Zippo" cigarette lighters) were to be shipped from New York to Germany. The goods were lost. The court noted that under admiralty law the value at the place of destination (Germany) would control.[79] The law of the case, however, was that admiralty law did not attach on the facts; hence, the remedy lay in conversion. Defendant argued for the normal conversion rule of value at time and place of conversion,[80] in this case, New York. This was apparently less than the value of the goods in Germany, even adding shipping expenses. The court found that New York law was sufficiently flexible to permit invoice price, which was the price at destination (Germany).[81]

§ 8   MEASURING COMPENSATORY DAMAGES

Determining the proper measure of compensation to place the plaintiff in the position she would have occupied but for defendant's wrong raises a number of related issues. Although there is a general consensus at the core regarding the proper measure of compensatory damages, the myriad ways in which compensatory damages claims may arise, coupled with the subjectivity associated with essential aspects of compensatory damages calculations, ensures that there will be substantial disagreements and diversity of authorities regarding the measure of compensation.

[8.1]   Certainty

A requirement that damages be proven to a requisite degree of certainty involves two distinct inquiries. First is the element of causality or loss causation: did the defendant's misconduct result in or cause the plaintiff's damages. Because general damages are presumed to flow from the defendant's misconduct,[1] this element applies to special or consequential damages for most purposes. The primary exceptions are when the existence of

---

[76] Newbury Alaska Inc. v. Alaska Constructors, Inc., 644 P.2d 224, 226 (Alaska 1982), *quoting* DAN DOBBS, HANDBOOK ON THE LAW OF REMEDIES 375 (1973).

[77] Kanematsu-Gosho, Ltd. v. M/T Messiniaki Aigli, 814 F.2d 115, 118 (2d Cir. 1987).

[78] 1990 U.S. App. LEXIS 4542 (S.D.N.Y.).

[79] *Id.* at *2. Alternatively, the court noted that invoice price may be used if market value is not established.

[80] *Id.*; Section 83.1 (Conversion).

[81] The invoice price was apparently the value of the property in Germany. 1990 W.L. 270422, at *1. The court did not state whether invoice price should be offset by the saved transportation costs.

[1] Section 6.4 (General Damages vs. Special or Consequential Damages).

actual damages is intertied with and a part of the substantive claim, for example libel per quod,[2] or the issue is whether the type of injury claimed is the type of injury the legal system should redress,[3] or the cause of action itself requires a showing of actual injury.[4]

The second inquiry focuses on calculation: what quantum and quality of evidence is necessary and sufficient to establish the amount of damages. This inquiry is a part of both general and special damages awards.

Certainty is the antidote to speculation, which the law frowns upon.[5] The requirement that special damages be proven to have occurred and that all damages be proven as to their extent allays concerns that the damages award compensates hypothetical rather than actual injury or loss.[6] On the other hand, certainty requirements, particularly with respect to the quantum of injury or loss, will be relaxed when the court perceives that the accurate measure of damages has been made difficult by the defendant's misconduct.[7] In cases when the difficulties of proof are caused or attributed

[2] Battista v. United Illuminating Co., 523 A.2d 1356, 1360 (Conn. App. 1987); Barry College v. Hull, 353 So. 2d 575, 578 (Fla. App. 1977).

[3] Conduct which promotes competition as opposed to restraining competition, even if its injures competitors, would fall into this category. A plaintiff would have to show "unfair" competition. Thus, a violation of law that encouraged competition, and did not constitute unfair competition, would not be actionable. Brunswick Corp. v. Pueblo Bowl-O-Mat, 429 U.S. 477, 489 (1977) (stating that antitrust policies are not served by compensating for losses due merely to increased competition).

[4] Doe v. Chao, 540 U.S. 614 (2004) (holding that under Privacy Act of 1974, 5 U.S.C. § 552a, a plaintiff must show that the violation resulted in "some actual damages" in order to qualify for the minimum statutory award); Moseley v. V. Secret Catalogue Inc., 537 U.S. 418 (2003) (holding that to establish a violation of the Federal Trademark Dilution Act, 15 U.S.C. § 1125, the plaintiff must demonstrate actual economic harm resulting from dilution of the mark).

[5] Lexington 360 Assocs. v. First Union Nat'l Bank of N.C., 651 N.Y.S.2d 490, 492 (App. Dept. 1996) (stating that "where a party has failed to come forward with evidence sufficient to demonstrate damages flowing from the breach alleged and relies, instead, on wholly speculative theories of damages, dismissal . . . is in order"); Simmons H/W v. Pacor, Inc., 674 A.2d 232, 238 (Pa. 1996) (refusing to award damages for fear of contracting cancer because fear is speculative and awarding damages for speculative fear would lead to inequitable results). When, however, speculative fears have actual economic consequences, such as the depression of market prices, the court's treatment may be more lenient. Section 91.2 (Stigma Damages).

[6] Section 8.6 (Real or Hypothetical Losses).

[7] National Merchandising Corp. v. Leyden, 348 N.E.2d 771, 774 (Mass. 1976); see Bigelow v. RKO Radio Pictures, 327 U.S. 251, 265 (1946):

> The most elementary conception of justice and public policy require that the wrongdoer shall bear the risk of the uncertainty which his own wrong has created. That principle is an ancient one, and is not restricted to proof of damage in antitrust suits, although their character is such as frequently to call for its application. In cases of collision where the offending vessel has violated regulations prescribed by statute, and in cases of confusion of goods, the wrongdoer may not object to the plaintiff's reasonable estimate of the cause of injury and of its amount, supported by the evidence, because not based on more accurate data which the wrongdoer's misconduct had rendered unavailable. And in cases where a wrongdoer has incorporated the subject of a plaintiff's patent or trade-mark in a single product to which the defendant has contributed other elements of value or utility, and has

to the defendant, courts have permitted some latitude in quantifying damages.[8] One approach borrows from the standard used to grant remittitur for excessive awards:

> When damages are at some unascertainable amount below an upper limit and when the uncertainty arises from the defendant's wrong, the upper limit will be taken as the proper amount.[9]

The relationship between certainty requirements and compensatory damages awards is heavily influenced by public policy considerations and the realistic availability of satisfactory proofs. Thus, courts tend to be lenient when considering personal injury awards:

> Because the measure of damages in a personal injury case is not subject to precise mathematical calculation, each case must be measured by its own facts, and considerable latitude and discretion are vested in the jury. Therefore, the question of damages, if not excessive, is properly left for the jury to determine.[10]

On the other hand, courts have generally required greater certainty when the injury consists of a claim of lost profits. Evidence of lost profits must not be speculative. To recover "lost profits" the evidence must affirmatively show "with reasonable certainty both their occurrence and the extent thereof."[11] Notwithstanding the above, courts tend to be more lenient as to the fixing of the amount of lost profits once plaintiff has demonstrated with sufficient certainty that defendant's misconduct has actually interfered with a plaintiff's ability to calculate lost profits.[12] Courts may shift

---

derived profits from the sale of the product, this Court has sustained recovery of the full amount of defendant's profits where his own wrongful action has made it impossible for the plaintiff to show in what proportions he and the defendant have contributed to the profits.

[8] *Bigelow, supra*, 327 U.S. at 264.

[9] Raishevich v. Foster, 247 F.3d 337, 343 (2d Cir. 2001) (internal quotation marks and citation deleted).

[10] Owens-Corning Fiberglass Corp. v. Martin, 942 S.W.2d 712, 719 (Tex. Civ. App. 1997) (citations omitted).

[11] Sanchez-Corea v. Bank of Am., 701 P.2d 826, 836 (Cal. 1985) (citation omitted); *see* Wooton v. Viking Distrib. Co., Inc., 899 P.2d 1219, 1226 (Or. App. 1995) (stating that the evidence must show both existence and the amount of the loss); Kenford Co., Inc. v. County of Erie, 493 N.E.2d 234 (N.Y. 1986):

> Loss of future profits as damages for breach of contract have been permitted in New York under long-established and precise rules of law. First, it must be demonstrated with certainty that such damages have been caused by the breach and, second, the alleged loss must be capable of proof with reasonable certainty. In other words, the damages may not be merely speculative, possible or imaginary, but must be reasonably certain and directly traceable to the breach, not remote or the result of other intervening causes.

493 N.E.2d at 235 (citation omitted).

[12] Miami Int'l Realty Co. v. Paynter, 841 F.2d 348, 350 (10th Cir. 1988) (applying Colorado law) ("Once the *fact* of damages is proved by a preponderance of the evidence, 'uncertainty as to the *amount* of damages will not bar recovery'") (emphasis in original; citations omitted).

the burden of calculation of lost profits to the defendant when the difficulty is attributable to the defendant.[13] There is a general tendency to apply a more lenient standard of proof when the plaintiff's loss is due to defendant's tortious misconduct rather than defendant's breach of contract.[14]

While courts have required that damages proofs be individualized,[15] many courts have allowed the quantum of damages to be assessed indirectly, even though this may be seen as undermining the individualization requirement. For example, in *Avery v. State Farm Mutual Automobile Ins. Co.*[16] the court approved, in a class action context, the use of sampling to determine aggregate damages of the class.[17] The use of customer surveys to prove lost sales is common.[18] Perhaps it is more accurate to state that damages must be individualized to the extent it is reasonable to do so, but mathematical precision is not required: reasonably certain is certain enough. An example of this is *Tours Costa Rica v. Country Walkers, Inc.*[19] Defendant contracted with plaintiff to conduct a series of tours, but breached the contract after two of the tours were conducted. The court rejected defendant's contention that plaintiff was required to use costs and expenses incurred in preparing for the cancelled trips.[20] The court held that plaintiff could extrapolate from the conducted trips to calculate what it would have earned on the cancelled trips but for defendant's breach.[21]

---

[13] *Bigelow, supra*, 327 at 265 (stating that the "wrongdoer shall bear the risk of the uncertainty which his own wrong has created"); Eden United, Inc. v. Short, 653 N.E.2d 126, 131 (Ind. App. 1995) (same).

[14] Clipper Affiliates v. Checovich, 638 A.2d 791, 793 (N.H. 1994).

[15] United States v. Hatahley, 257 F.2d 920, 924–925 (10th Cir. 1958) (holding that (1) the trial court erred in applying the same formula to value animals lost due to defendant's wrongdoing without considering factors unique to each of the animals, such as condition, age, or sex; and (2) the court erred in awarding the same amount of distress damages to each plaintiff), *cert. denied*, Hatahley v. United States, 358 U.S. 899 (1958).

[16] 746 N.E.2d 1242 (Ill. App. 2001), *rev'd on other grounds*, 835 N.E.2d 801 (Ill. 2005), *cert. denied*, 126 S.Ct. 1470 (2006).

[17] *Id.* at 1260:

> In appropriate circumstances, it is considered feasible and reasonable to prove aggregate monetary relief for the class based upon (1) an examination of defendant's records, (2) the use of a common formula or measure of damages multiplied by the number of transactions, units, or class members involved, or (3) a reasonable approximation with proper adherence to recognized evidentiary standards. When determining which method to use, courts must be careful to balance the opposing interests of the parties, and a defendant must be given fair opportunity to contest the validity of individual claims.

(citations omitted).

[18] Schutt Mfg. Co. v. Riddell, Inc., 673 F.2d 202, 206–07 (7th Cir. 1982); U-Haul Int'l, Inc. v. Jartran, Inc., 601 F. Supp. 1140, 1149 (D. Ariz. 1984); *aff'd in part, modified in part, reversed in part on other grounds*, 793 F.2d 1034 (9th Cir. 1986). *See generally* M.C. Dransfield, Annot. *Admissibility and Weight of Surveys or Polls of Public or Consumers' Opinion, Recognition, Preference, or the Like*, 76 A.L.R.2d 619 (1958).

[19] 758 A.2d 795 (Vt. 2000).

[20] *Id.* at 804 ("Defendant has not cited, and we cannot find, any case that supports its contention that plaintiff was required to produce precise evidence of the expenses it would have incurred had the twelve tours gone forward").

[21] *Id.*

[8.2] Excessiveness

Excessiveness suggests an award that is overly compensatory to a fault. Courts routinely condemn excessive awards,[22] but like so much of the law, courts find it difficult to define, much less agree on, what constitutes excessiveness.

Excessiveness is easier to define when it involves economic damages rather than non-economic damages because the objective nature of the former usually provides a mean or baseline against which a court may measure the award. Disagreements concerning whether an award of economic damages was excessive are likely to be based on different views as to what was lost, rather than the value of what was lost. For example, in *Chatlos Systems v. National Cash Register*[23] the district court awarded $201,826.50 in expectancy damages for breach of warranty regarding a contract for the sale of a computer. The basis of the claim was that the computer system did not perform as it was represented that it would. The contract price was $46,020. An expectancy that was 5 times the contract price may seem a bit excessive. The majority held the district court's finding that the value of a computer that would do what defendant represented its computer would do was not clearly erroneous. The dissenting judge disagreed, concluding that the majority was comparing apples to oranges. The "hypothetical system" that would perform the functions represented by defendant as within the capabilities of its computer was, according to the dissent, entirely speculative.[24] The essential difference between the two positions is definitional. If a compact family sedan is represented to have the capabilities of a performance road car, and it fails to perform as warranted, is the car valued as a compact family sedan or as a performance road car? The answer is not self evident, for as *Chatlos* demonstrates, reasonable arguments can be made for either side of the proposition. The answer given does, however, significantly influence whether the award is ultimately seen as excessive.

The fact that the award is large or reflects a significant difference between the purchase or contract price and the item's fair market value does not necessarily mean the award is excessive. The critical issue is whether there is a plausibly reasonable explanation for the award. If a

---

[22] Some jurisdictions have statutory proscriptions on the award of over-compensatory damages. Cal. Civ. Code § 3359 ("Damages must, in all cases, be reasonable, and where an obligation of any kind appears to create a right to unconscionable and oppressive damages, contrary to substantial justice, no more than reasonable damages can be recovered"). In *Postal Instant Press, Inc. v. Sealy*, 51 Cal. Rptr. 2d 365, 372 (Cal. App. 1996), the court applied this principle to disallow an award to a franchisor of future royalties that the franchisee was obligated to pay under the franchise agreement. The franchisee breached the agreement and deprived the franchisor of its expectancy of future royalties; nonetheless, the court held that the expectancy was excessive and, thus, non-recoverable. *Cf.* Restatement (Second) Contracts § 351(3) (1979) (stating that "in the circumstances justice so requires in order to avoid disproportionate compensation" the court may exclude recovery of lost profits).

[23] 670 F.2d 1304 (3d Cir. 1982).

[24] *Id.* at 1307 (majority), 1309, 1311 (dissent).

plausibly reasonable explanation exists, the odds are good that the award will withstand judicial scrutiny.[25] If a statutory remedy sets forth a damages range, an award within the range will be respected.[26]

The analysis is fundamentally different when it comes to non-economic damages. The inherent subjectivity of this category of damages[27] makes it much more difficult to create a mean or baseline against which deviation may be measured. The subjectivity of the decision making process tends to result in affording substantial discretion to the decision maker, although discretion is not unlimited.[28]

One approach to this problem simply relies on the intuition of the judges to identify excessive awards.[29] While a judge's intuition may be no better than the jury's intuition on this matter, courts have, nonetheless, felt compelled by their responsibilities as judges to control awards.[30] It is not uncommon that this intuitive approach is leavened with the admonition that the damages award should be respected unless it "shocks the conscience" or evidences a "miscarriage of justice."[31] The maxims simply restate the idea that deference to the fact finder should be given; they do not control or inform decision making on review for the standards are too abstract to allow for meaningfully consistent application. Moreover, this is,

---

[25] American Nat'l Bank & Trust Co. of Chicago v. Regional Transp. Auth., 125 F.3d 420, 439 (7th Cir. 1997) (finding that differences in expert's assumptions explained large discrepancy between property's purchase price and its fair market value within a short period of time).

[26] Columbia Pictures TV v. Kyrpton Broadcasting 259 F.3d 1186, 1194–95 (9th Cir. 2001) (affirming compensatory damages award for copyright infringement of $31.68 million for 440 infringements ($72,000 per work infringed); the statute permits an award of statutory damages of up to $100,000 per infringement for willful infringement and the award was within the range), *cert. denied*, Feltner v. Columbia Pictures Television, Inc., 534 U.S. 1127 (2002). Ironically, the defendant had successfully appealed an earlier bench award of $8.8 million in statutory damages on the ground that a right to jury trial attached to the statutory damages determination. Feltner v. Columbia Pictures Television, Inc., 523 U.S. 340 (1998) (*discussed* at Section 20.2 (Right of Jury Trial)). This is perhaps a modern record for legal Pyrrhic victories.

[27] Gibbs v. United States, 599 F.2d 36, 39 (2d Cir. 1979) (stating that "measuring pain and suffering in dollars is inescapably subjective").

[28] Scala v. Moore McCormack Lines, Inc., 985 F.2d 680, 684 (2d Cir. 1993) (stating that "[w]hile a jury has broad discretion in measuring damages, it may not abandon analysis for sympathy for a suffering plaintiff and treat the injury as though it were a winning lottery ticket.") (citation omitted).

[29] David Baldus, John C. MacQueen & George Woodworth, *Improving Judicial Oversight of Jury Damages Assessments: A Proposal For the Comparative Additur/Remittitur Review of Awards For Nonpecuniary Harms and Punitive Damages*, 80 Iowa L. Rev. 1109, 1132–35 (1995).

[30] Consorti v. Armstrong World Indus., Inc., 72 F.3d 1003, 1012 (2d Cir. 1995), *vacated on other grounds*, 518 U.S. 1031 (1996), *on remand*, 103 F.3d 2 (2d Cir. 1996).

[31] *American Nat'l Bank, supra*, 125 F.3d at 439 (using in an economic damages case a "rationally related," "not monstrously excessive," nor "born of passion or prejudice" standard); Richardson v. Chapman, 676 N.E.2d 621, 628 (Ill. 1997) (using a "shocks the judicial conscience" standard).

at root, an evolving standard. What shocks one generation may not shock the next.[32]

One method sometimes used to establish a mean or baseline for determining whether awards, particularly these involving non-economic losses,[33] of damages are excessive is to compare the award with other awards.[34] When this approach is adopted, the critical issue is how much weight should be given to the comparable awards. One approach treats comparable awards as not binding but instructive.[35] A variant of this approach states that damages awards are not excessive if there is at least one other award in the same range.[36] Another approach is to determine whether the decision maker abused its discretion without direct reference to the other awards, but if an abuse of discretion is found, to use the comparable awards for guidance in fixing the appropriate award.[37] Some jurisdictions do not allow a "comparability" analysis on the ground that to do so would violate the parties' right to trial by jury.[38]

Review of damages awards for excessiveness can also be complicated by jurisdictional issues. For example, is federal judicial review of federal jury damages awards governed by federal or state law?[39] One court said both.

---

[32] Margaret Fisk, *Hard to Shock*, National Law Journal, September 3–10, 2001, at col. 4 (reporting that a National Law Journal survey of state and federal judges evidences a greater acceptance of large awards than in the past); Section 73.1.3 (Excessiveness).

[33] Section 12 (Non-Economic Damages).

[34] Baldus, et al., *Improving Judicial Oversight, supra*, 80 Iowa L. Rev. at 1134–40.

[35] Senko v. Fonda, 384 N.Y. S.2d 849, 851 (App. Dept. 1976).

[36] Lebron v. United States, 279 F.3d 321, 325–26 (5th Cir. 2002) (holding that deference to jury decision making requires that remittitur for excessiveness be limited to reducing award to the maximum recovery the jury could have awarded *and* that "maximum recovery" includes a multiplier or percentage enhancement to prior awards); Thomas v. Texas Dept. Criminal Justice, 297 F.3d 361, 369 (5th Cir. 2002) (stating that enhancements have ranged from 33 1/3—50% of the prior awards and adopting 50% enhancement as cap).

[37] Juge v. Judson, 650 So. 2d 312, 314 (La. App. 1995).

[38] Ritter v. Stanton, 745 N.E.2d 828, 845–46 (Ind. App. 2001) (refusing to apply comparative analysis to award of $55 million in compensatory damages to plaintiff who sustained massive injuries from vehicle collision). *But cf.* Paul DeCamp, *Beyond State Farm: Due Process Constraints on Non-Economic Compensatory Damages*, 27 Harv. J. Law & Pub. Pol'y 231 (2003) (arguing that unbridled discretion violates due process).

[39] *Cf.* Gasperini v. Center For Humanities, Inc., 518 U.S. 415 (1996) (holding that in diversity cases the 7th Amendment does not bar appellate review of excessiveness or inadequacy of damages verdict based on governing state law). The Court also held that under the *Erie* Doctrine, Erie R.R. Co. v. Tomkins, 304 U.S. 64 (1938), were a federal court not to follow state standards for reviewing damages awards, different results could result simply due to forum selection:

> It thus appears that if federal courts ignore the change in the New York standard and persist in applying the "shock the conscience" test to damage awards on claims governed by New York law, "substantial variations between state and federal (money judgments)" may be expected. We therefore agree with the Second Circuit that New York's check on excessive damages implicates what we have called *Erie's* "twin aims." Just as the *Erie* principle precludes a federal court from giving a state-created claim "longer life . . . than [the claim] would have had in the state courts" so *Erie* precludes

The trial court (District Court) checks the jury's verdict against the relevant state precedents. The appellate court (Circuit Court of Appeals) then reviews the trial court's decision under a federal abuse of discretion standard.[40]

[8.3] Lost Profits

Lost profits are by nature uncertain.[41] Lost profits are, however, recoverable when they are made legally certain by proof based on actual facts, using present data, and allowing for a reasonable, rationale estimate of their amount. An award cannot be based on pure, pie-in-the-sky speculation.[42] An accepted way to present lost profits claims is through expert witness testimony. The expert's opinion regarding lost profits will ordinarily be based on representative financial records of the plaintiff. The expert will then project from this financial data what the plaintiff's profits would have been had defendant's conduct not prevented their realization.[43] The expert's study cannot rest on unsupportable assumption or ignore distinctions crucial to arriving at a valid conclusion.[44] On the other hand, exact calculation is not required. The requirement that proof of damages be based on more than speculation "is intended to be flexible enough to accommodate the myriad circumstances in which claims for lost profits arise."[45] "[I]t will be enough if the evidence show[s] the extent of damages as a matter of just and reasonable inference, although the result be only approximate."[46] In

---

a recovery in federal court significantly larger than the recovery that would have been tolerated in state court.

Id. at 430 (citations omitted).

[40] Consorti v. Armstrong World Indus., Inc., 103 F.3d 2, 5 (2d Cir. 1996).

[41] Section 8.1 (Certainty).

[42] Schiller & Schmidt, Inc. v. Nordisco Corp., 969 F.2d 410 (7th Cir. 1992):

[P]eople who want damages have to prove them, using methodologies that need not be intellectually sophisticated but must not insult the intelligence. *Post hoc ergo propter hoc* will not do; nor the enduring of simplistic extrapolation and childish arithmetic with the appearance of authority by hiring a professor to mouth damages theories that make a joke of the concept of expert knowledge.

Id. at 415 (citations omitted; brackets added; emphasis in original); Wujcik v. Yorktowne Dental Assocs., Inc., 701 A.2d 581, 584 (Pa. Super. Ct. 1997) (holding that proof of industry-wide average for collection of accounts receivables failed to satisfy reasonable certainty standard in dentist's claim against employer for unpaid wages—the wages being based on a percentage of fees actually collected); Atlantic Mut. Ins. Co. v. Noble Van & Storage Co., 537 N.Y.S.2d 213, 214 (App. Dept. 1989) (rejecting as unreliable the use of an averaged value of costs to manufacture the destroyed property—hard and soft cover books, when damage was to particular books); Section 8.1 (Certainty) (noting use of sampling as permissible basis for calculating economic losses).

[43] *In re* Knickerbocker, 827 F.2d 281, 289 (8th Cir. 1987).

[44] McGlinchy v. Shell Chem. Co., 845 F.2d 802, 807 (9th Cir. 1988). The same expert was treated more kindly in *In re* James E. O'Connell, Co., Inc., 799 F.2d 1258, 1261–62 (9th Cir. 1986).

[45] Texas Instruments, Inc. v. Teletron Energy Mgmt., Inc., 877 S.W.2d 276, 279 (Tex. 1994).

[46] Story Parchment Co. v. Paterson Parchment Paper Co., 282 U.S. 555, 563 (1931).

some cases, courts have permitted plaintiff's loss of profits to be measured by defendant's actual profits,[47] or from similarly related businesses.[48]

The lost profit award is a "net" profit award,[49] although in the appropriate case "gross" profits may equal "net" profits.[50] The basic point is that the lost profits award should reflect the actual profits the plaintiff would have earned from the sales the plaintiff would have made had the defendant not interfered.[51]

In order to establish a lost profits claim, a plaintiff should give consideration to the following factors.

The period of damages. For how long a period of time is the plaintiff entitled to claim that defendant's misconduct has caused him a loss, here "lost profits"? Is it the life of the contract? Does it extend beyond the life of the contract? Is it less than the life of the contract?[52]

Lost revenues. How much in net sales was lost? "But for" the legal misconduct of defendant how much would the plaintiff have sold (X units), at what price ($Y per unit) and how much would have been returned (Z units). Net sales thus equals X minus Z times Y. This is why it is difficult for new companies to establish "lost profits" claims. Since they have no track record of profitability, it is difficult for them to establish lost revenues.[53]

---

[47] Ramona Manor Convalescent Hosp. v. Care Enters., 225 Cal. Rptr. 120, 129–30 (Cal. App. 1986) (involving a claim where the defendant (holdover tenant) prevented the plaintiff from occupying the premises and interfered with the plaintiff's contractual relationship with the landlord). This measure is used when defendant's profits tend to define plaintiff's loss. United States Naval Inst. v. Charter Communications, Inc., 936 F.2d 692, 696 (2d Cir. 1991).

[48] Lakota Girl Scout Council, Inc. v. Havey Fund Raising Mgmt., Inc., 519 F.2d 634, 641–43 (8th Cir. 1975); Pena v. Ludwig, 766 S.W.2d 298, 304 (Tex. Civ. App. 1989).

[49] Lipscher v. LRP Publications, Inc., 266 F.3d 1305, 1317 (11th Cir. 2001); Stern v. Satra Corp., 539 F.2d 1305, 1311–12 (2d Cir. 1976); Tom Sawyer Motor Inns, Inc. v. Chemung County Sewer Dist. No. 1, 305 N.Y.S.2d 408, 412 (App. Dept. 1969) (holding that a retrial of damages was necessary when it was unclear whether the opinion of the expert was based on a gross or net profit calculation).

[50] Cambridge Plating Co., Inc. v. NAPCO, Inc., 876 F. Supp. 326, 343 (D. Mass. 1995) (stating that the expert "equated lost gross profits with lost net profits by finding that [plaintiff's] expenses remained virtually constant in periods of increasing sales. In his words, lost gross profit, 'fell to the bottom line' as lost net profits") (footnotes omitted; brackets added), *aff'd on this point, vacated and remanded on other grounds*, 85 F.3d 752, 773 (1st Cir. 1996); F.L. Walz, Inc. v. Hobart Corp., 586 N.E.2d 1314, 1319 (Ill. App. 1992) (stating that the expert explained "that gross profits equalled net profits because the overhead expenses were already incurred . . . and would not have increased if the sale of parts and service would have been as projected rather than actual . . . [t]herefore, it was unnecessary to further reduce the gross profit by an actual overhead factor to determine net profit"); *cf.* Alaska Tae Woong Venture, Inc. v. Westward Seafoods, 963 P.2d 1055 (Alaska 1998) (holding that plaintiff should have recovered lost "revenue" caused by breach of contract because at that point it had already incurred all of its expenses).

[51] Central Sec. & Alarm Co., Inc. v. Mehler, 918 P.2d 1340, 1347 (N. Mex. App. 1996).

[52] Kirkland & Co. v. A & M Food Serv., 579 So. 2d 1278, 1287 (Ala. 1991) (14 years of lost profits awarded).

[53] Section 8.4 (The New Business Rule).

Determining costs. What costs would have been sustained in generating the revenues calculated above? The cost components are direct costs (those that vary proportionately with the amount of units produced, such as labor and materials), indirect costs (costs that must be paid regardless of the amount of units produced), and other costs (warranty, bad debt, depreciation, interest expense).[54]

Present value. All awards of future losses, which means those losses that are deemed to occur after the date of trial, must be calculated in terms of present value. All this means is that the present award, if invested, would generate the same stream of dollars as the future losses which plaintiff incurred because of defendant's legal misconduct.[55]

[8.4]   The New Business Rule

At common law, a business that lacked a baseline or record of profitability could not sue for lost profits either in contract or tort.[56] Some jurisdictions still apply the "New Business Rule" to prevent completely the recovery of lost profits.[57] In these jurisdictions "[i]n order to recover lost profits, a business must have been established and in operation for a definite period of time and calculations based on other similar businesses are too speculative and will not satisfy the [requirement that a] reasonable means of calculating [the amount be provided]."[58]

Many jurisdictions have, however, abandoned the "New Business Rule" as a per se rule. These jurisdictions permit the plaintiff to demonstrate that the "start-up" venture or business would have been profitable but for the defendant's wrongdoing.[59] New businesses, nonetheless, often have a difficult time demonstrating that "never was," "would have been."[60] In

---

[54] L&L Furniture v. Boise Water Co., 813 P.2d 918, 921–22 (Idaho App. 1991) (stating that the proper measure is "net profits lost"); *cf.* Foust v. Estate of Walters, 21 S.W.3d 495, 505–06 (Tex. Civ. App. 2000) (stating that "[t]he measure of damages for lost crops is their market value less all expenses of cultivating and bringing the crops to market"; claim fails if plaintiff does not introduce costs so as to enable trier-of-fact to calculate damages).

[55] Section 9.3 (Discounting to Present Value).

[56] Roger I. Abrams, Donald Welsch & Bruce Jonas, *Stillborn Enterprises: Calculating Expectation Damages Using Forensic Economics*, 57 Ohio State L.J. 809, 811 (1996).

[57] Western Pub. Co., Inc. v. Mindgames, Inc., 944 F. Supp. 754, 759 (E.D. Wis. 1996) (collecting decisions).

[58] H&P Research, Inc. v. Liza Realty Corp., 943 F. Supp. 328, 331 (S.D.N.Y. 1996) (citations omitted).

[59] Energy Capital Corp. v. United States, 302 F.3d 1314, 1325–26 (Fed. Cir. 2002); *In re Merrit Logan, Inc.*, 901 F.2d 349, 357 (3d Cir. 1990); Western Publ'g Co., Inc., 944 F. Supp. at 756 (collecting decisions). *See generally* Todd R. Smyth, *Recovery of Anticipated Lost Profits of New Businesses: Post-1965 Cases*, 55 A.L.R. 4th 507 (1987).

[60] Schonfeld v. Hillard, 218 F.3d 164, 172 (2d Cir. 2000) (applying New York law) (stating that "evidence of lost profits from a new business venture receives greater scrutiny because there is no track record upon which to base an estimate") (citation omitted); Maggio, Inc. v. United Farm Workers of Am., 278 Cal. Rptr. 250, 263 (Cal. App.) *cert. denied*, 502 U.S. 863 (1991).

general, a new business recovers "lost profits," if at all, by showing (1) the profits of another person who operated the business plaintiff would have but for the defendant's wrongdoing,[61] (2) by expert economic analysis,[62] or (3) by the profits defendant realizes as a result of its harming or destroying plaintiff's business or obtaining the benefits the plaintiff would have received but for defendant's legal wrong.[63]

The above factors are not litmus tests; a new business may recover its lost profits if it can persuade the court that its damages were caused by defendant's wrongdoing, were foreseeable, and have been established with reasonable certainty.[64]

Courts are likely to be influenced by the general level of success of new businesses in particular industries. For example, courts have noted the difficulties confronting new entertainment ventures as warranting caution and circumspection before lost profits are awarded.[65]

[8.5] Lost Volume Sellers

Damages rules have historically been transaction specific. If the buyer breached the seller was allowed to recover the lost benefit of the bargain; however, if the seller resold the subject matter of the transaction to a third party, the buyer was entitled to a credit of the proceeds against the seller's damages claim. This has come to be known today as "cover" and it operates both as a means by which the seller can fix his damages[66] and as an obligation on the seller to act reasonably to mitigate his damages after buyer's breach.[67]

One of the great debates in the law today is whether an exception to this traditional approach should be recognized when the seller claims that but for the buyer's breach he (seller) could have made two sales instead of just one sale. Requiring seller to credit buyer with the proceeds of sale #2 by treating it as a cover sale for buyer's benefit deprives seller of a profit he would have earned had buyer not breached. In this situation seller will

[61] SK Hand Tool Corp. v. Dresser Indus., 672 N.E.2d 341, 348–49 (Ill. App. 1996).

[62] Id.; Fera v. Village Plaza, Inc., 242 N.W.2d 372, 376 (Mich. 1976).

[63] Super Valu Stores, Inc. v. Peterson, 506 So. 2d 317, 330 (Ala. 1987).

[64] Energy Capital Corp., supra, 302 F.3d at 1326–28. But cf. Kids' Universe v. In2 Labs, 116 Cal. Rptr. 2d 158, 171–72 (Cal. App. 2002) (holding that plaintiff failed to produce sufficient evidence to sustain lost profits claim for new internet venture: (1) their prior experience as retailer did not involve e-business; (2) their prior experience with a web-site was unprofitable; (3) the new venture was in an unestablished market; (4) the venture was "rife with speculation"; (5) plaintiffs "presented no specific economic or financial data, market survey, or analysis based on business records or operating histories of similar enterprises; and (6) their expert relied on news articles not actual data in presenting his expert opinion that plaintiffs' venture would have successfully completed with eToys).

[65] Schonfeld, supra, 218 F.3d at 174–75.

[66] Seller will recover the difference, if any, between the cover (resale) price and the contract price as general damages, plus special and other damages as appropriate. U.C.C. § 2-706.

[67] Section 13 (Duty to Mitigate Damages).

argue that crediting buyer with the proceeds of sale #2 violates a fundamental rule of remedies—restoring the non-breaching party (seller) to the position he would have occupied had the breach not occurred.[68]

Although academic views on the subject are mixed,[69] the general approach of courts has been to recognize the loss volume seller exception. Within the courts the debate has been over the appropriate situations in which the exception may be recognized.

In general, for a party to qualify as a "lost volume seller," courts have required that the party demonstrate that it had the ability to supply both contracts *and* that it probably would have made the second sale.[70] Some courts require that the seller demonstrate that sale #2 would have been profitable; it is not simply assumed that the seller would have made sale #2 because the seller may have already been operating at maximum efficient levels of operation.[71]

Professor Harris, a proponent of the lost volume seller exception, argued that a causal relationship must exist between the breach and sale #2. Under this view the seller must demonstrate that the buyer in sale #2 would have been solicited by the seller had there been no breach and the solicitation would have been successful.[72] This approach is consistent with the two sale theory that underlies the exception. Courts, however, have generally opted for abstract tests that establish the seller's economic incentives to make two sales rather than Professor Harris' approach that asked whether the two sales would in fact have been made.

The lost volume seller exception was developed and is applied most frequently in the context of sales of goods; nonetheless, it has been extended to other areas, most particularly the sale of services.[73]

---

[68] Section 6 (The Purpose of Compensatory Damages).

[69] Much of the debate turns on the proper construction of the Uniform Commercial Code Section 2-708, which can be read and construed as both allowing and barring the "lost volume seller" exception. John Breen, *The Lost Volume Seller and Lost Profits Under U.C.C. § 2-708: A Conceptual and Linguistic Critique*, 50 U. Miami L. Rev. 779, 786–89 (1996) (arguing that the "due credit" language of U.C.C. § 2-708(2) is inconsistent with the "lost volume seller" exception). The doctrinal debate has largely turned on whether the seller's expectancy is fixed by the specific transaction in question or whether seller has a protectible interest in subsequent transactions. Breen, *id.* at 824–30; Daniel W. Mathers, *Should the Doctrine of Lost Volume Seller Be Retained? A Response to Professor Breen*, 51 U. Miami L. Rev. 1195, 1216 (1997).

[70] Islamic Republic of Iran v. Boeing Co., 771 F.2d 1279, 1290 (9th Cir. 1985), *cert. dismissed*, 479 U.S. 957 (1986).

[71] C.I.C. Corp. v. Ragtime, Inc., 726 A.2d 316 (N.J. Super. App. Div. 1999); R.E. Davis Chemical Corp. v. Diasonics, Inc., 826 F.2d 678 (7th Cir. 1987).

[72] Robert J. Harris, *A Radical Restatement of the Law of Seller's Damages: Sales Act and Commercial Code Results Compared*, 18 Stan. L. Rev. 66, 82 (1964).

[73] Gianetti v. Norwalk Hospital, 833 A.2d 891, 897 (Conn. 2003) (permitting surgeon to invoke exception as a defense to failure to mitigate damages).

[8.6] Real or Hypothetical Losses

Whether a plaintiff has sustained a loss is usually treated as basically a question of fact; occasionally, however, the issue is one of values—how does one look at the facts. In *United States v. Crown Equipment Corp.*[74] the defendant's negligence caused the government to lose a substantial quantity of surplus butter the government was withholding from the market pursuant to its agricultural product price support program. The government sued for the value of the lost butter,[75] but did the government really suffer a loss? Similarly, assume property has been condemned and the condemning authority intends to raze the existing structures on the property as part of a larger redevelopment project. If the structure is negligently destroyed before it is razed, has there been a loss?[76]

The question of the actuality of loss can also be time point sensitive. If the defendant negligently mars a baseball card with the picture of a young Hank Aaron,[77] should the loss be valued as of the date the card was marred or should the loss be valued as of the date of trial? Legal rules may provide litigants with the option to choose different valuation dates,[78] but the mere availability of legal rules should not cause us to ignore the underlying value judgments that are made when a litigant can freely elect differing valuation dates or when that choice is constrained. Free election places tremendous discretion in the hands of the plaintiff. If the market for baseball cards goes up, select the trial date; if the market goes down, select the date the card was actually marred. A constrained choice means that the decision is made by a public decision maker (court) rather than a private decision maker (litigant).

The actuality of loss can also be means directed or ends related. Assume a defendant promises to provide 300 private security police for a function, but only provides 200; nonetheless, the event is peaceful and the objective of having security achieved. Has the failure to perform completely resulted in a loss?[79]

One last example. Assume employer gives employee a $500 check to purchase coins for business use. At the bank, employee, a numismatist by a vocation, notices that one of the coins, a quarter, is very rare and worth

---

[74] 86 F.3d 700 (7th Cir. 1996).

[75] Section 7.2 (Diminution in Value) (discussing the valuation issue).

[76] The problem arises with some frequency in the insurance context when the structure that is to be demolished is insured and destroyed or damaged before demolition takes place or is completed. *See* ROBERT H. JERRY III, UNDERSTANDING INSURANCE LAW § 46[b] (3d ed. 2001) (collecting decisions).

[77] For those unfamiliar with the game of baseball, Hank Aaron was one of the premier players of the modern era. He is currently the record holder for most career home runs. There is a significant market for baseball cards and premium prices are paid for cards bearing the likeness of star players, particularly those that appeared before the player achieved stardom.

[78] Section 7.6.1 (Value as a Function of Time).

[79] This issue of so called "skimped performance" is addressed at Section 41.2 ([Restitution for Wrongdoing] Breach of Contract).

$10,000. Employee takes a quarter out of his pocket and exchanges it with the rare coin. Has employer suffered a loss?[80]

Real losses are presumed to warrant remediation through compensation; views to the contrary are rarely raised.[81] Yet, the line between real and hypothetical losses is not always clear and bright. Classification of the loss as real or hypothetical will, in these cases, represent a values judgment.[82]

[8.7] Harsh and Mild Measures

The amount of compensatory damages available to replace what was loss is not a fixed point. Compensatory damages often occupy a range and any point along that range may, based on the facts and circumstances of a case as they are presented and understood by the decision maker, serve as a proper place to fix the amount of compensatory damages available. Consider, for example, a defendant who infringes the plaintiff's patent. One measure of what is lost is the royalty the plaintiff would have received if the defendant had obtained a license to use the patent. An alternative measure is an award of the profits the plaintiff would have realized had the infringement not occurred. The usual assumption is that a lost profits award is more compensatory than a royalty award.[83]

We may identify these different measures of compensatory damages as "harsh" and "mild" measures. What influences a court to adopt a "harsh" measure rather than a "mild" measure usually turns on the nature or the degree of the defendant's culpability. The more the defendant's misconduct tends toward intentional, willful or wanton misconduct, the more inclined the court is to permit compensation by the harsh measure:

> The mild rule is applied where the wrong was innocently done, by mistake or inadvertence; the harsh, where the facts show the trespass to have been malicious, or with full knowledge of the title of the injured party, and in willful disregard of his rights. The former rule charges the defendant with the value of the coal, ore, or rock mined, in situ—usually measured by the royalty charged in the particular locality. The latter charges him with the value of

---

[80] Sections 41.1 ([Restitution for Wrongdoing] Tortious Conduct), 155 (Employer's Remedies for Employee's Breach of Duty).

[81] The law and economy school will, however, focus on the efficient allocation of losses. Efficiency concerns may dictate that some actual losses go uncompensated or only be partially compensated.

[82] *See* Jay M. Feinman, *The Jurisprudence of Classification*, 41 Stan. L. Rev. 661, 667 (1989) ("There are three possible methods of categorization: classification by tradition, classification by facts, and classification by principles. In practice, a classification system is likely to merge elements of all three").

[83] Hughes Tool Co. v. Dresser Indus., 816 F.2d 1549, 1558 (Fed. Cir. 1987) (reasonable royalty award should be structured to permit defendant to recover profit from infringing activities); Rite-Hite Corp. v. Kelley Co., 774 F. Supp. 1514, 1540 n.22 (E.D. Wis. 1991), *modified*, 56 F.3d 1538 (Fed. Cir.), *cert denied*, 516 U.S. 867 (1995) (stating that court has discretion in appropriate case to raise the royalty to preclude a defendant from realizing a profit from infringing activities).

the same after severance, without compensation for mining and preparing for market.[84]

Somewhat related to this distinction is the argument that harsh remedies should be reserved for unprincipled and inexcusable conduct, whereas mild remedies should be applied when the wrongdoing was compelled by exigent circumstances.[85]

Although the type of misconduct that supports the use of a harsh measure of compensatory damages bears similarities to the basic requirements for punitive damages,[86] the damages award is treated as compensatory. A punitive ("harsh") measure of damages is deemed distinct from punitive damages.[87] We should not ignore, however, the latent punitive element in the background for it will inform when the harsh measure will most often be invoked.[88]

The use of harsh and mild measures of compensatory damages is usually found in situations when liability is theoretically strict, but the defendant's level of misconduct may range from innocent mistake to deliberate wrong. Using harsh and mild measures of compensatory damages enables courts to match the remedy more closely to the actual nature of defendant's misconduct. Deliberate wrongdoing may be "punished" more severely than innocent wrongdoing. Even though both are actionable, the law's interest in deterring deliberate wrongdoing is likely greater than its interest in deterring innocent misconduct. Using a harsh measure permits this correlation of remedy and wrong at a level below that necessary for punitive

---

[84] Potter v. Tucker, 688 S.W.2d 833, 836 (Tenn. App. 1985) (citation omitted). Young v. Ethyl Corp., 444 F. Supp. 207, 211 (W.D. Ark. 1977); United States v. Marin Rock & Asphalt Co., 296 F. Supp. 1213, 1219 (C.D. Cal. 1969); Alaska Placer Co. v. Lee, 553 P.2d 54, 57–58 (Alaska 1976); Whittaker v. Otto, 56 Cal. Rptr. 836, 842–43 (Cal. App. 1967) (collecting decisions).

[85] *Cf.* Vincent v. Lake Erie Transp. Co., 124 N.W. 221 (Minn. 1910) (limiting plaintiff's recovery to actual damage to a dock when defendant's ship remained tied to dock during storm knowing that doing so would inflict damage to the dock; remaining tied to dock prevented risk of loss of the ship or damage to other property due to the storm). Professor Cohen has argued that in breach of contract actions expectation damages, which he treats as the harsh remedy, should be limited to opportunistic breaches; for non-opportunistic breaches the preferred remedy should be reliance damages (mild measure). George M. Cohen, *Finding Fault With Wonnell's Two Contractual Wrongs*, 38 San Diego L. Rev. 137, 138–39 (2001).

[86] Section 201 (Reason and Purpose For Punitive Damages); George M. Cohen, *The Fault Lines in Contract Damages*, 80 Va. L. Rev. 1225, 1226–27 (1994) (arguing that while contract liability is based on principles of "no fault," damages calculations for breach are influenced by the degree and scope of the breaching parties fault). An example of this approach was the traditional rule in cases of breach of a contract to sell land that the buyer was limited to reliance damages and could not recover his expectancy unless the buyer could show the seller breached in bad faith. Large v. Gregory, 417 N.E.2d 1160, 1163–64 (Ind. App. 1981) (discussing "English Rule"); Section 166.1 ([Buyer's Remedies] Damages).

[87] Glendale Federal Bank FSB v. United States, 239 F.3d 1374, 1330 (Fed. Cir. 2001) (stating that the purpose of compensatory damages is to make the plaintiff whole, not punish or deter).

[88] Alyeska Pipeline Serv. Co. v. Anderson, 629 P.2d 512, 530–31 (Alaska 1981), *cert. denied*, 454 U.S. 1099 (1982) (agreeing with trial court's decision not to award both punitive damages and harsh damages for trespass and conversion of timber).

damages. Conversion[89] and trespass[90] actions frequently present situations where a choice between a harsh and mild measure of compensatory damages must be made. In some cases, the choice may be between a contract-based recovery or a tort-based recovery. For example, in *Scully v. US WATS, Inc.*[91] the defendant failed to honor an obligation regarding plaintiff's stock options. What is the value of unexercised options that are not publicly traded? The court noted two approaches: (1) a contract model that measured damages based on the value of the security on the breach date; and (2) a tort (conversion) model. The court noted that the tort model was potentially more generous:

> The conversion theory extends the cover date to a "reasonable time" into the future, and therefore allows a plaintiff to recover from the defendant some prospective profit that may have accrued after the wrongful act. In contrast, the contract theory, as most strictly employed in the stock context, puts the onus on a plaintiff to cover immediately upon the breach because damages are fixed as of the breach date. Therefore, in the stock context, the contract theory does not allow a plaintiff to recover any prospective profit from the defendant.[92]

A statutory scheme may provide additional damages that are similar to the harsh measure. For example, under the Fair Labor Standards Act an employee who has not been paid for overtime work may recover unpaid overtime compensation and an equal amount as liquidated damages, in effect double damages. Should the employee also recover punitive damages? The answer appears to be "No,"[93] but the decisions are not consistent.[94] Similarly, copyright infringement may subject defendants to cumulative liability for both the plaintiff's lost profits and the defendant's earned profits from the infringement where the latter do not constitute part of the former.[95] Such a situation exists for example when the infringer makes sales the copyright owner could not have made.[96]

---

[89] National Lead Co. v. Magnet Cove Barium Corp., 231 F. Supp. 208, 217 (W.D. Ark. 1964); *Alyeska Pipeline, supra*, 629 P.2d at 526–27; Glaspey v. Prelusky, 219 P.2d 585, 587 (Wash. 1950).

[90] *See* notes 86, 88, *supra*; Section 7.6 (Value as a Function of Time).

[91] 238 F.3d 497 (3d Cir. 2001).

[92] *Id.* at 510.

[93] Skrove v. Heiraas, 303 N.W.2d 526, 532 n.4 (N.D. 1981); *cf.* Bhaya v. Westinghouse Elec. Corp., 624 F. Supp. 921, 923–24 (E.D. Pa. 1985) (stating that liquidated damages provision are punitive in nature), *vacated on other grounds*, 832 F.2d 258 (3d Cir. 1987), *cert. denied*, 488 U.S. 1004 (1989).

[94] Section 207.2 (Augmented Damages and Punitive Damages).

[95] Abeshouse v. Ultragraphics, Inc., 754 F.2d 467, 470 (2d Cir. 1985) (cumulative recovery allowed when plaintiff's lost profits are not reflected in defendant's actual profits from infringement); Deltak, Inc. v. Advanced Sys., Inc., 767 F.2d 357, 363 (7th Cir. 1985).

[96] *Abeshouse, supra*, 754 F.2d at 471 (applying the 1976 Copyright Act).

[8.8] Jury Discretion and Judicial Review

As noted earlier in the discussion of excessive awards,[97] juries are given substantial discretion to determine the proper amount of compensatory damages warranted in the particular case: "translating legal damage into money damages is a matter particularly within a jury's ken. . . ."[98] The more nebulous the interest, the more discretion is conferred on the jury:

> Damage resulting from loss of earning capacity is the loss of the ability to earn in the future. The impairment of the capacity to earn is the gravamen of the element. Proof of this element does not, however, require the same specificity or detail as does proof of loss of future wages. The reason is that the jury can observe the appearance of the plaintiff, his age, and the nature of the injuries that will impair his capacity to earn. A serious or permanent injury may sustain the submission of the issue of loss of earning capacity to the jury . . . . Thus, the relevant inquiry is whether there was some evidence of (the plaintiff's) loss of earning capacity.[99]

The general rule is to exercise deferential review when damages calculations are made by the jury.[100] This reflects the factual basis of the award and respect for the jury's role as the finder of fact. Deference is heightened when the trial judge has denied a motion for remittitur or new trial as to damages; thus, demonstrating the trial judge's implicit approval of the award.[101] In addition to the above process, the appellate court presumes the verdict is correct and the appellant faces a rigorous task in persuading the appellate court otherwise.[102] These principles are particularly strong because they are bound up in the constitutional guarantee of the right to trial by jury. That right would be of markedly less value if jury decision making was subject to rigorous scrutiny.[103]

Both too much and too little may be made of the discretion given to juries and the deference given their verdicts. Although the anecdotal view is that judge-jury disagreement is significant,[104] the empirical data tends to downplay the scope and extent of judge-jury disagreement.[105]

---

[97] Section 8.2 (Excessiveness).

[98] Trull v. Volkswagen of America, Inc., 320 F.3d 1, 9 (1st Cir. 2002) (citations omitted).

[99] Edwards v. Stills, 984 S.W.2d 366, 385 (Ark. 1998) (citations omitted); *Trull, supra,* 320 F.3d at 9 (noting that jurors are particularly well suited at calculating money damages "in cases involving intangible, non-economic losses").

[100] American Nat'l Bank & Trust Co. of Chicago v. Regional Transp. Authority, 125 F.3d 420, 437 (7th Cir. 1997).

[101] *Id.;* Lopez v. Price, 145 A.2d 127, 130 (Conn. 1958).

[102] Gaudio v. Griffin Health Services Corp., 733 A.2d 197, 205 (Conn. 1999); Westphal v. Wal-Mart Stores, Inc., 81 Cal. Rptr. 2d 46, 50 (Cal. App. 1998).

[103] *Gaudio, supra,* 733 A.2d at 214–15.

[104] Harvey Berkman, *Want Big Bucks? Try With Jury,* Nat'l L. J. (September 27, 1999) (stating that while judge's are more plaintiff-prone, juries are more generous).

[105] Kevin M. Clermont & Theodore Eisenberg, *Litigation Realities,* 88 Corn. L. Rev. 119, 144 (2002) (noting the high agreement rate between judges and juries). Ironically, in cases

Jurors are inexperienced participants in the legal process and this may tend to exaggerate cognitive biases that influence decision making, such as framing and hindsight bias. Courts have interposed some controls on naked appeals to juror self interest,[106] but arguments that seek to invoke cognitive biases, such as *per diem* guidelines and counsel's opinion as to an appropriate award receive mixed reviews.[107] In the consideration of damages by juries, it has been consistently noted that jury instructions are simply unhelpful.[108] Whether, in light of the above, this is desired or unintended cannot be said.

§ 9 FUTURE LOSSES

American jurisdictions historically have not recognized installment or conditional awards,[1] unless the rule is changed by statute or party agreement.[2] A plaintiff will receive a single, lump sum award for her injuries. That award represents compensation for all losses the plaintiff has sustained or will sustain as a result of her injuries that are the subject of the litigation. In determining the lump sum award it is common to distinguish past losses, such as past lost earnings or past lost profits, from future losses, such as future medical expenses or future pain and suffering. The point that separates the "past" from the "future" is not the date of wrongdoing but the date of trial. The pre-trial, realized losses are "past" damages; the unrealized losses, as of the date of trial, are future damages. "Past" damages may also be referred to as "present" damages in the sense that they have been realized as of the date of trial.

The award of future damages is based on a prediction as to how events will unfurl after the date of trial. The further into the future one goes, the more uncertainty, and risk of error, one encounters.[3] Some awards of future damages will over or under compensate the plaintiff because the future is

---

when disagreement was detected, the result was contrarian. *Id.* at 146 (noting that plaintiffs did better before judges than juries in product liability and medical malpractice cases in terms of win rates).

[106] For example, most jurisidications condemn the use of the so-called "Golden Rule" argument that asks the jury to award an amount of damages they would wish to receive if they had sustained the same injuries as the plaintiff. Lovett *ex rel.* Lovett v. Union Pacific R. Co., 201 F.3d 1074, 1083 (8th Cir. 2000).

[107] Section 12.2 (Measuring Non-Economic Loss) (discussing *per diem* guidelines and other devices used to structure jury discretion in awarding damages).

[108] *See* Edith Greene & Brian Bornstein, *Precious Little Guidance: Jury Instruction on Damages Awards*, 6 Psych., Pub. Pol'y & Law 743 (2000).

[1] Slater v. Mexican Nat'l R.R. Co., 194 U.S. 120, 128 (1904) (refusing to recognize foreign law that would permit an award in the form of periodic payments). This is also known as the "single recovery rule."

[2] Reilly v. United States, 863 F.2d 149, 170 (1st Cir. 1988) (noting that "[w]hen a tortfeasor loses at trial, then—absent a statute or the parties' contrary agreement—it must pay the judgment in one fell swoop") (footnote omitted).

[3] A risk of error attaches to any effort at predicting the future. JOHN MONAHAN & LAURENS WALKER, SOCIAL SCIENCE IN LAW: CASES AND MATERIALS 279–320 (2d ed. 1990).

predicted inaccurately. For example, the plaintiff may die prematurely or live exceptionally long; therefore, an award of future medical expenses may dramatically be wide of the mark.[4] To counter this vicissitude of life, there is an increasing turn to the use of periodic payments in lieu of lump sum judgments; todate, however, the use of periodic payments has been largely confined to hot button socio-legal issues, such as medical malpractice or municipal liability,[5] or consensually arrived at through settlement.

It would, of course, be possible to treat all losses as "future" if we used date of wrongdoing as the reference point. We generally do not do so. Courts distinguish losses temporally based on the world as it is when the decision regarding damages is made, *i.e.*, at the time of trial.[6] For example, assume losses extend over a ten-year period:

A = Date of Wrongdoing
B = Date Action Commenced
C = Date of Trial
D = End of 10-year period

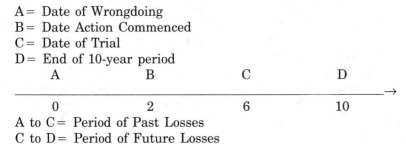

A to C = Period of Past Losses
C to D = Period of Future Losses

Figure 4

Looking backwards from the date of trial ("C"), we characterize those losses as "past"; looking forward, we characterize those losses as future. The distinction has several significant consequences. First, "past" losses have occurred, future losses are, by definition, less certain. It is the difference between the proverbial "bird in the hand" versus "the two birds in the bush." We have knowledge, or at least are "better informed," regarding losses that have incurred because the losses have happened. On the other hand, the future is always, to some decree, speculative; therefore, our confidence that future losses will actually be incurred is always necessarily less than our confidence in the actuality of past losses. That is not to say that the perception is entirely, or always, accurate. The past is only slightly more certain than the future and only because history is as much constructed

---

4 An example of this is *Frankel v. United States*, 321 F. Supp. 1331 (E.D. Pa. 1970), *aff'd sub nom.* Frankel v. Heym, 466 F.2d 1226 (3d Cir. 1972), in which the District Judge noted that while the 1960s had represented a period of unusually high inflation, federal efforts at the time of trial were likely to ameliorate the problem. Based on this insight the court refused to adjust upward future medical costs for a severely and permanently injured plaintiff. *Id.* at 1346. The fact was that inflation did not abate but increased throughout the 1970s.

5 *See* Ellen S. Pryor, *Rehabilitating Tort Compensation*, 91 Geo. L. J. 659, 673 n.55 (2003) (discussing modern movement to periodic payment judgment statutes).

6 Restatement (Second) of Torts § 924 cmt. d (1977) ("The extent of future harm to the earning capacity of the injured person is measured by the difference, viewed as of the time of trial, between the value of the plaintiff's services as they will be in view of the harm and as they would have been had there been no harm.").

as having happened.[7] Nonetheless, we feel more comfortable making decisions based on events that have occurred than events yet to come, even if only intuitively. Second, because future losses have not been realized but are compensated for in current dollars, the future damages must be reduced to present value when awarded as a lump sum.[8]

[9.1] Future Damage

It is important to distinguish the legal concept of damage or injury from the legal concept of damages, which is compensation for the damage or injury suffered. A person may be injured, as, for example, by exposure to toxic substances. As a consequence of that exposure, the person may become totally and permanently disabled. That disability is present injury. The damages awarded for that injury (damage) may consist of losses already incurred, such as past medical expenses or losses that will occur later, such as future pain and suffering resulting from the permanency of the injury. The viewpoint is the date of trial: losses incurred prior to trial are past losses; losses that will occur after trial are future losses.

In some cases the plaintiff may have been exposed to injury, but not yet have sustained injury, for example, exposure to a toxic substance may only increase the chance that the plaintiff will be injured in the future, *e.g.*, will contract cancer. The traditional and dominant rule is that the plaintiff may recover if she can show by a preponderance of the evidence, which is to say more likely than not, that the exposure will lead to cancer.[9] In this situation, the plaintiff is allowed to recover as if she presently has cancer due to the exposure. There is no discount reflecting the statistical chance that she will not contract cancer. If plaintiff cannot meet the minimal "more likely than not" threshhold, she must wait until she actually sustains the injury, in other words, she actually contracts cancer.[10] At that time, assuming her claim is not barred by the applicable statute of limitation or preclusion doctrine, such as res judicata, the plaintiff may now attempt to establish the causal link between the exposure and her injury. There is, however, an emerging rule, confined so far it appears to medical malpractice claims, that permits the plaintiff to recover when the risk of future injury is of a certain type, (reduction in length of life), but that injury is less than reasonably certain. The couplet to this extension is that the plaintiff's recovery is limited to reflect the probability of occurrence of the future

---

[7] EDWARD HALLETT CARR, WHAT IS HISTORY? (1961).

[8] Restatement (Second) of Torts § 913 cmt. a (1977) ("If damages are awarded for losses that will be incurred in the future, it would be over-compensation to give at the present time in cash their full amount. They should be reduced to their present worth, since they are being paid in advance."). *See* RICHARD A. POSNER, ECONOMIC ANALYSIS OF LAW § 6.11, at 177 (3d ed. 1986); Section 9.3 (Discounting the Present Value).

[9] Restatement (Second) of Torts § 328A (1965).

[10] This principle is modified in some cases by the "lost chance" doctrine, Section 10.5 (Lost Chance), and in toxic tort cases, Sections 10.4 (Future Losses), 72.4 (Medical Monitoring).

harm.[11] In this posture, the emerging rule parallels the lost chance doctrine, which is also confined to medical malpractice claims.[12]

The distinction between damage and damages is not always acknowledged or respected by the courts. In some contexts, respecting the distinction may raise difficult policy issues. For example, in the toxic exposure context, the plaintiff who is at risk of contracting cancer presents a case involving future damage. On the other hand, the "fear" the plaintiff has that she may contract cancer is a present injury. The same analysis holds with respect to the plaintiff whose skin is pricked by a hypodermic needle and who now fears contracting the HIV virus. The plaintiff's risk of contracting the disease is a future injury; her fear of contracting the disease is a present injury.

The analysis may be extended to property damage cases. For example, a building may have been constructed with asbestos-containing materials (ACMs). Removing the ACMs will be a costly and lengthy process. The incorporation of ACM may or may not be injury or damage.[13] What it will cost to remove the ACMs is damages.[14]

[9.2] Future Damages

The general requirement is that the likelihood of occurrence of future damages must, at the time of trial, be reasonably certain to follow, or probable, or reasonably probable.[15] The decision maker may not award damages for possible or conjectural losses.[16] The line separating reasonably certain from speculative is not cast in concrete. It is heavily influenced by the decision maker's value system. It is also significantly influenced by the real availability of proof. Bodily injury claims by individuals who have not achieved their likely career goals and who because of their injury have been deprived of the chance to achieve those career goals are often reviewed sensitively insofar as the plaintiff's claim for lost future earnings is concerned.[17] Less sensitivity tends to be exhibited in breach of contract

---

[11] Dillon v. Evanston Hosp., 771 N.E.2d 357, 370 (Ill. 2002).

[12] Sections 10.5 (Lost Chance), 73.4 (Hedonic Damages).

[13] Whether the incorporation of ACM into another product causes actual injury at the time of incorporation or at some other time, *e.g.*, when there is an actual release into the environment of asbestos, is a question of fact as to which there is some debate. *See* Richard C. Ausness, *Tort Liability For Asbestos Removal Costs*, 73 Or. L. Rev. 505 (1994) (arguing that incorporation equals injury in fact).

[14] In *Trinity Church v. John Hancock Life Ins. Co.*, 502 N.E.2d 532 (Mass. 1987), the court held that the fact that repair would be done in the future did not transform the damages into future damages that must be discounted to present value. Section 9.3 (Discounting to Present Value). Under this approach, repair or remediation costs should be based on current costs not future costs.

[15] Naughton v. Bankier, 691 A.2d 712, 720 (Md. App. 1997) (personal injury); S.C. Anderson, Inc. v. Bank of Am., 30 Cal. Rptr. 2d 286, 289–90 (Cal. App. 1994) (lost profits).

[16] *Naughton, supra*, 691 A.2d at 720.

[17] Maddox v. American Airlines, Inc., 298 F.3d 694 (8th Cir. 2002), *cert. denied*, 537 U.S.

cases when, in theory at least, the parties can bargain for damages *ex ante* should one of the parties breach.

[9.3] Discounting to Present Value

An award for future damages is thought to possess the potential for overcompensating the plaintiff. The plaintiff could take the money that he has not really "earned" because the future event has not yet occurred, invest it, and receive interest on the award in the interim.[18] The plaintiff would earn actual interest on a sum of money he would not have received at this time had the wrong not occurred. Plaintiff's receipt of interest on the accelerated payment of future compensation is seen as a betterment. All jurisdictions have responded to this "problem" by discounting all or some aspects of the award for future injuries to present value. "Present value" refers to the amount of money that if invested today would produce the future stream of payments the plaintiff would have received and in the manner he would have received them had he not sustained the legal wrong that is the subject of the claim.[19] For example, assume Paul, but for Dave's negligence, would have earned $100 a year for 5 years, beginning now. His total loss is $500 spread out annually over the 5-year period.[20] If Paul is awarded $500 now, Paul could invest that money. The accumulation of interest, when added to the principal sum of $500 would result in Paul actually receiving more than $500 over the 5-year period. Present value calculations are designed to avoid this situation. The present value of the $500 stream of earnings ($100/yr. for 5 years) is a sum, which if invested today would pay out, through principal and earned interest, $100 a year for 5 years before exhausting itself.

The calculation of the present value of future losses requires that we first ascertain the amount of future losses and then discount that amount by

---

1192 (2003) (noting that plaintiff, a college music major, was awarded $11 million as damages; plaintiff contended that the fire that accompanied the crash of the plane on which she was a passenger damaged her vocal chords and precluded a professional singing career). The opinion addressed issues other than damages calculation, but a newspaper account of the case indicated that the bulk of the award was for lost future earnings. Margaret Cronin Fisk, *$11 million for Silenced Opera Singer*, Nat'l L.J. (September 11, 2000). Defendant did not appeal the amount of the jury award. Sections 71.1 (Loss of Earnings), 71.2 (Loss of Earnings Capacity).

[18] Jones & Laughlin Steel Corp. v. Pfeifer, 462 U.S. 523, 536–37 (1983) ("It has been settled since . . . 1916, that in all cases where it is reasonable to suppose that interest may safely be earned upon the amount that is awarded, the ascertained future benefits ought to be discounted in the making up of the award") (citations, parantheses, and quotation marks omitted).

[19] PAUL A. SAMUELSON & WILLIAM D. NORDHAUS, ECONOMICS 273 (14th ed. 1992) (present value determination "is made by asking what quantity of dollars today would be just sufficient to generate the asset's stream of income at going market interest rates").

[20] Annualizing mistakes income to some extent because income is usually paid more frequently than once a year, but it is a simpler process than replicating exactly the future stream of income. William F. Landsea & David L. Roberts, *Inflation and the Present Value of Future Economic Damage*, 37 U. Miami L. Rev. 93, 101–02 (1982).

the appropriate discount rate. Let's return to our hypothetical involving Paul. Initially, we stipulated that Paul earned $100 per year and the relevant period was 5 years. In the real world, these figures are established by appropriate proofs. For example, we know what Paul was earning, assuming he was employed at the time of the injury, but how do we know what he will earn (or "would have earned") in the future? Expert testimony will normally be obtained whereby Paul's expected earnings will be projected for the relevant period, which is the period the injury will affect Paul's ability to earn.[21] This calculation may include wage and promotions increases Paul would have received, cost of living increases, productivity gains, etc.[22] The reader need simply reflect on his or her own life experiences and calculate how earnings have changed, or are hoped will change if the reader is a law student, over one's lifetime to date. As a person passes through life stages from law clerk, to associate, to junior partner, to senior partner, one's earnings increase as one becomes more experienced, more senior, more productive, and so on. Of course, there is the chance that the spiral may turn downward. It is important to keep in mind that the future is a forecast. One may expect that a plaintiff will have a somewhat different expectation of what the future will bring from that of the defendant.

Once the amount of future earnings (or future profits or future medical expenses) is calculated, it is necessary to select an appropriate discount rate. The discount rate is the interest rate that when applied to a sum yet to be determined will generate the future earnings we have just calculated. In effect we are working backwards. Once we have the appropriate discount rate and we know the amount of money we need to generate over the relevant time frame, we can calculate the principal sum that when invested at the discount rate will generate the stream of earnings.[23] That principal sum is the award or judgment the defendant pays as "damages."

---

[21] For example, if Paul were totally disabled and unable to work at his prior job, the relevant period would be Paul's remaining "work life." Even this figure may require some assumptions, however. Will Paul work to 62, 65, or 70? Will he take early retirement? Will he suffer periods of unemployment due to downsizing of the work force, etc. The expert will seek to support her testimony by reference to appropriate studies, particularly those from the U.S. Dep't of Labor, that permit her to offer an opinion as to the probable earnings Paul would have enjoyed but for the injury. Data on life expectancy is maintained and published by the United States Department of Health & Human Services, National Office of Vital Statistics.

[22] Fringe benefits may or may not be included. *Compare Jones & Laughlin Steel Corp.*, *supra*, 462 U.S. at 534 (noting that fringe benefits are usually excluded to simplify the calculation of the future earnings award), *with* Alaska Airlines, Inc. v. Sweat, 568 P.2d 916, 935 (Alaska 1977) (including fringe benefits, but at employer's cost to provide, to avoid subjectivity if "benefit to employee" standard were used).

[23] The issue here is more commonly encountered in Lottery payouts: (1) cash value; or (2) annual payments. Cash value is analogous to "lump sum" awards; annual payments to the projected stream of earnings. The cash value payout is less than the aggregate total of annual payments because money now is more valuable than money later. For example, if the Lottery advertises a $7 million prize, the aggregate of annual payments will total $7 million. The annual payments may be even or uneven, but in the end if you add the individual payments, the sum will be $7 million. Cash value, however, represents a sum of money that if invested today would duplicate the annual payments through the use of the principal (cash value) and the interest earned on the principal. Observe that if you take the annual payments, you will

What is the discount rate? It is composed of three elements: (1) the real interest rate, (2) the predicted inflation rate, and (3) the risk factor. The real interest rate is the actual value of the deferred enjoyment of money, without regard to inflation or risk of non-payment of the money loaned. The real interest rate reflects the time value of money. It has been judicially accepted that the annualized real interest rate is between 1% and 3%,[24] with 2% as the default figure.[25] In other words, a person would expect that she would receive between 1% and 3% annual interest if she loaned money to another and this interest would reflect only her inability to use that money for the period the money was loaned. The inflation rate refers to loss of the purchasing power of the money loaned.[26] If $1 will buy X quantity of goods today but it will take $1.02 to buy those same goods one year from today, then inflation has reduced the purchasing power of the dollar by 2%. If a person loaned money today, she would want an interest rate that would protect her from this loss. The risk factor refers to the likelihood of repayment of the money loaned. There is always a chance of default, but in some cases the chance is so remote as to be inconsequential. In other cases, the risk is high. United States government securities are considered risk free, whereas corporate securities are not. Depending on the debtor's solvency, the likelihood of repayment will be rated high, low, or somewhere in-between.

Given the above, why do some United States obligations have a lower interest rate than others? It should be observed that the components that make up an interest rate are to a large extent based on forecasts and assumptions. The real interest rates fluctuates because people disagree over the value of immediate access to money. Inflation forecasts may be accurate or wide of the mark. Similarly, what appears to be secure today, may be at risk tomorrow, particularly when the time horizon is short or mediate, *e.g.*, 10–25 years, rather than long, *e.g.*, 25–50 years. Finally, risk preferences vary. Some individuals are risk takers, others are risk adverse. Many factors may influence a person's identification of an appropriate interest rate necessary to generate the stream of dollars that was earlier defined as what the plaintiff would have received but for defendant's wrong. In effect, we have a process that is highly subjective at almost all stages of the inquiry. For this reason, many jurisdictions have adopted a broad evidence approach: they simply commit decision making in this area to the trier of fact to award damages from estimates based on sound and substantial economic evidence.[27] In some cases, the amount of deference accorded

---

receive in total $7 million. If, however, you take the cash value, all you are guaranteed is the cash value. Whether the cash value actual earns enough through investment to duplicate the annual payments income stream depends on the accuracy of the assumptions made to calculate the discount rate.

[24] *Jones & Laughlin Steel, supra*, 462 U.S. at 549.

[25] Ramirez v. New York City Off-Track Betting Corp., 112 F.3d 38, 41–42 (2d Cir. 1997).

[26] SAMUELSON & NORDHAUS, ECONOMICS, *supra* at 587.

[27] Rodriguez v. McDonnell Douglas Corp., 151 Cal. Rptr. 399, 419 (Cal. App. 1978).

to this process can be quite substantial,[28] but in other cases the process is reviewed quite rigorously.[29]

In order to reduce the amount of speculation that is inherent in the calculation of a future damages award, a number of alternative methods to this broad evidence test have developed. The common theme here is to eliminate one or more of the factors used to calculate the award under the assumption that simplification increases certainty.

One early approach was to not adjust the plaintiff's earnings for future developments. This approach, in effect, assumed that plaintiff's current earnings level would be static rather than dynamic. These earnings are then annualized, i.e., multiplied by the period of time defendant's wrong affects plaintiff's ability to obtain his current earnings, and then discounted to present value by an appropriate market interest rate.[30] The difficulties with this approach are several. First, it can only work when plaintiff is working, at the time of the injury, at his probable lifetime employment and mature earnings capacity. If the plaintiff is young or unemployed, or underemployed, using this approach will seriously misrepresent the economic effect of the injury on the plaintiff.[31] Second, using a market interest rate, which includes an inflation forecast, means that under the approach the plaintiff's earnings are not adjusted for inflation, but the discount rate, which reduces the aggregate amount plaintiff will receive, is adjusted upwards to reflect inflation.[32] The larger the discount rate, the less principal needed to generate the projected stream of earnings. For example, at an 8% compounded interest rate, principal doubles every 9 years; at a 6% interest rate, principal doubles every 12 years.[33] (The relationship is

---

[28] Reed v. Wimmer, 465 S.E.2d 199, 209 (W. Va. 1995).

[29] Myrlak v. Port Authority, 694 A.2d 575, 581–82 (N.J. Super. 1997); Novak v. Gramm, 469 F.2d 430, 432–33 (8th Cir. 1972).

[30] Day v. National U.S. Radiator Corp., 117 So. 2d 104, 127 (La. App. 1960); Wentz v. Connolly, 273 P.2d 485, 491 (Wash. 1954). The modern trend is to reject this approach. Kaczkowski v. Bolubasz, 421 A.2d 1027, 1031–32 (Pa. 1980) (rejecting prior decision in which the appellate court had affirmed the refusal to accept evidence of productivity gains in calculating projected lost earnings, but had discounted earnings at the market interest rate (6%) established by Pennsylvania precedents). See generally Michael Rosenhouse, Annot., Effect of Anticipated Inflation on Damages For Future Losses—Modern Cases, 21 A.L.R.4th 21 (1981).

[31] Jordan v. Bero, 210 S.E.2d 618, 636–37 (W. Va. 1974) (using impairment of earning capacity test rather than lost earnings because plaintiff was a minor); Florida Greyhound Lines v. Jones, 60 So. 2d 396, 397–98 (Fla. 1952) (homemaker); Section 71 (Lost Income).

[32] O'Shea v. Riverway Towing Co., 677 F.2d 1194, 1200 (7th 1982):

> [I]t is illogical and indefensible to build inflation into the discount rate yet ignore it in calculating the lost future wages that are to be discounted. That results in systematic under compensation, just as building inflation into the estimate of future lost earning and then discounting using the real rate of interest would systematically overcompensate.

[33] This is known as the Rule of 72. To approximate the amount of time it will take a principal sum to double using a compounded interest rate, divide 72 by the interest rate. The result is the number of years it will take for the principal to double.

similar but less dramatic for simple interest rates.)[34] Consequently, if the 8% discount rate is used, rather than the 6%, the defendant can put less money in and still generate, insofar as the legal system is concerned, the expected stream of earnings. In this regard, it helps to see the verdict or award as the amount of money the trier of fact considers necessary to generate the needed stream of earnings, given a discount rate. Because the trier-of-fact simply predicts the future, the actual future the plaintiff experiences may diverge from the prediction. That risk is borne by the parties.[35]

Other alternatives to the broad evidence approach are the "below market discount rate method" and the "offset" methodologies. Using the "below market" formula, the trier-of-fact calculates the future stream of earnings by estimating the earnings increases the plaintiff would have received each year because of all factors other than inflation.[36] The resulting earnings are then discounted by the real interest rate.[37] In some jurisdictions there is an further adjustment for the effects of any income tax.[38] The basic focus of this approach is to eliminate consideration of inflation from the calculation.[39]

The "offset" approaches are of two types: (1) total offset and (2) partial or qualified offset. Under the total offset method, it is assumed that all wage increases (expressed as a % of current earnings) will equal all interest earned on the award.[40] In other words, all upwards adjustments to the earnings stream are deemed, as a matter of law, to equal, and thus offset, all downward adjustments accomplished by discounting to present value. The award is then calculated by multiplying current annual earnings by the period the plaintiff will be unable to realize those earnings, e.g., 5 years or 10 years, etc.

---

[34] Jurisdictions are split whether the discount rate should be based on compound or simple interest calculations. In *Kirchgessner v. United States*, 958 F.2d 158, 162–63 (6th Cir. 1992), the court predicted that Michigan would adopt the compound measure because use of simple interest would undermine the statutory rate:

> The statute calls for the future damages to be reduced for each year, using the five percent rate. Were we to adopt a simple interest rate methodology, the later years would be discounted to present cash value at substantially less than five percent. We see no basis for utilizing a simple interest rate in determining "gross present cash value," and find no error in the compound method.

When the issue was later presented to the Michigan Supreme Court, it disagreed, holding that simple interest should be used because the common law favored that approach and it is easier and more convenient for jurors to apply. Nation v. W.D.E. Elec. Co., 563 N.W.2d 233, 235, 237–38 (Mich. 1997) (expressly rejecting *Kirchgessner*).

[35] Section 9 (Future Losses), *supra* at n.4 (discussing the erroneous prediction of inflation made by the district court in *Frankel v. United States*).

[36] Culver v. Slater Boat Co., 722 F.2d 114, 118 (5th Cir. 1983), *cert. denied sub nom.*, St. Paul Fire & Marine Ins. Co. v. Culver, 469 U.S. 819 (1984).

[37] *See* Ammar v. United States, 342 F.3d 133, 147–49 (2d Cir. 2003).

[38] *Culver, supra*, 722 F.2d at 118; Section 17.4 (Consideration of Taxability of Damages).

[39] *Culver, supra*, 722 F.2d at 121.

[40] Beaulieu v. Elliott, 434 P.2d 665, 671 (Alaska 1967).

The partial or qualified offset methodologies permit some limited upward adjustments to the stream of earnings, such as automatic wage increases[41] or productivity gains.[42] All other adjustments are deemed equal and offsetting to the discount rate.

The "below-market" approach has enjoyed substantial success. It received the Supreme Court's approval in *Jones & Laughlin Steel v. Pfeifer*.[43] The Court was, however, careful not to mandate use of the "below-market" approach,[44] a point it subsequently reiterated,[45] but apparently to little avail for it has been widely adopted by federal courts,[46] notwithstanding academic criticism of the methodology.[47]

Discounting future damages awards is generally limited to awards of economic damages.[48] There is limited contrary authority in the Second Circuit as to future pain and suffering awards.[49] There is also a conflict whether future loss of society and loss of consortium awards should be reduced to present cash value.[50] The split is the consequence of many courts characterizing loss of society awards as pecuniary in order to qualify the award under the jurisdiction's wrongful death statute.[51] Having characterized the loss of society award as economic for one purpose, some courts find it difficult to view the matter differently when the issue of discounting the award to present cash value is raised.

An interesting twist to computing "present value" was provided in *Energy Capital Corp. v. United States*.[52] The case involved future lost profits. The plaintiff claimed that the government had breached a contract that would have allowed plaintiff to make profitable loans. As damages, plaintiff sought the profits it would have earned on those loans. The government successfully argued that in discounting future lost profits to present value the court

---

[41] Alaska v. Guinn, 555 P.2d 530, 546 (Alaska 1976).

[42] *Kaczkowski, supra*, 421 A.2d at 1039.

[43] 462 U.S. 523, 545 (1983).

[44] *Id.* at 552–53 (stating that "[w]hatever the rate the District Court may choose to discount the estimated stream of future earnings, it must make a deliberate choice, rather than assuming that it is bound by the rule of state law").

[45] St. Louis Southwestern Ry. Co. v. Dickerson, 470 U.S. 409, 412 (1985) (stating that "no single method for determining present value is mandated by federal law").

[46] Hull by Hull v. United States, 971 F.2d 1499, 1511–12 (10th Cir. 1992); Scott v. United States, 884 F.2d 1280, 1286–87 (9th Cir. 1989).

[47] Rolando F. Pelaez, *Higgledy-Piggledy Awards for Lost Earnings*, 36 Jurimetrics 325 (1996) (arguing for the adoption of the "total offset" approach over the "below-market discount rate" approach and characterizing the latter as "an exquisite illusion").

[48] Brant v. Bockholt, 532 N.W.2d 801, 803–04 (Iowa 1995) (collecting decisions holding that non-economic damages, such as pain and suffering and emotional distress, should not be reduced to present cash value).

[49] Oliveri v. Delta Steamship Lines, Inc., 849 F.2d 742, 751 (2d Cir. 1988).

[50] Drews v. Gobel Freight Lines, Inc., 578 N.E.2d 970, 975–76 (Ill. 1991) (noting split in cases but identifying as majority rule the refusal to discount future loss of society awards); Section 74 (Loss of Consortium).

[51] Section 75.2 (Wrongful Death Actions).

[52] 302 F.3d 1314 (Fed. Cir. 2002).

should factor into the discount rate the riskiness of the venture plaintiff proposed to undertake pursuant to its contract with the government:

> [Plaintiff] argues that once the Court of Federal Claims determined that its profits were reasonably certain, no further consideration of risk was appropriate, because risk already had been considered in determining whether there would have been profits. We disagree. A venture that is anticipated to produce $1 million in profits and that has a 95% chance of success is obviously more valuable than a venture that is anticipated to produce $1 million in profits with only a 90% chance of success—and yet, both ventures would most likely be determined to have a reasonable certainty of producing profits. Therefore, the fact that the trial court has determined that the profits were reasonably certain does not mean that risk should play no role in valuing the stream of anticipated profits. In other words, by finding that [plaintiff's] lost profits were reasonably certain, the trial court determined that the probability that the AHELP venture wold be successful was high enough that a determination of profits would not be unduly speculative. The determination of the amount of those profits, however, could still be affected by the level of riskiness inherent in the venture.[53]

Whether court's willingness to subject a damages calculation to a riskiness discount will find favor with other courts remains to be seen.[54]

§ 10　LOSS CAUSATION

[10.1]　General Principles

One of the fundamental doctrinal distinctions between tort and contract is over the limits of responsibility for resulting damages. This is usually discussed in terms of causation and foreseeability. In the remedies context "causation" is often addressed as "certainty" that the loss was caused by or resulted from the injury. For example, are plaintiff's claimed lost profits properly attributed to defendant's breach of contract or tortious interference, or would the plaintiff not have realized any profits regardless of defendant's conduct? Should the answer turn on whether the claim sounds in tort (tortious interference) or contract (breach)? Should the scope of defendant's liability turn on that same question?

The concept of "foreseeability," and its related terminology, remoteness, directness, etc., that are used to define the limits of causation in this area of the law has no intrinsic, independent meaning. An event is not "foreseeable" simply because one classifies the dispute as arising in tort rather than

---

[53] *Id.* at 1333 (brackets added).

[54] Section 9.1 (Noting general rule that once plaintiff establishes likelihood of future damage by preponderance of evidence, no further diminution is made due to chance that future injury may not occur).

contract. Foreseeability is an artificial construct that reflects the context and purposes for which it is invoked. "Foreseeability" means different things in contract as opposed to tort because courts say it does and because courts want the concept to have a different meaning in the different contexts of tort and contract. In other words, events are not inherently or intrinsically foreseeability; events are deemed foreseeable or not because such a finding leads to legal results that are deemed to be socially, morally, and politically acceptable.

The contract approach is to assess "foreseeability" on the basis of the breaching party's knowledge at the time of contract formation rather than at the time of breach. Tort "foreseeability," on the other hand, is assessed at the time the breach of duty occurs rather than the time the duty attaches. Tort foreseeability is further based not on the defendant's actual knowledge of the foreseeable consequence of the breach, but on all detriment proximately caused thereby, whether it was or should have been anticipated or not, subject to a judicial doctrine of remoteness. The rationale for the distinction between contract and tort foreseeability is that contracts are voluntary transactions and the parties to the contract can, by contract provision, guard against any anticipated peril; consequently, each assumes the risk of certain losses that may be caused by the other's breach. Tort duties, in general, arise out of public obligations rather than consensual relationships and are designed to protect the body politic. Tort duties obligate the defendant to account for the ill he has caused, not just the ill he foresaw or should have foreseen.[1]

[10.2]   Contracts

[10.2.1]   Cause-in-Fact

The requirement that the contract losses be caused by the breach is usually captured by the certainty requirement. Damages must be sufficiently certain to avoid claims that they are speculative, *i.e.*, the plaintiff, non-breaching party must establish by competent evidence both the occurrence and extent of the claimed damages resulting from the breach.[2] This cause-in-fact requirement can have interesting repercussions for the non-breaching party. For example, in *Postal Instant Press, Inc. v. Sealy*,[3]

---

[1] Town of Alma v. Azco Constr., Inc., 10 P.3d 1256, 1262 (Colo. 2000) (holding that "[t]he essential difference between a tort obligation and a contract obligation is the source of the duties of the parties"). The court stated that because tort law is designed to protect all citizens from the risk of harm to their person or their property, tort duties are imposed by law "without regard to any agreement or contract." Contract obligations, in contrast, arise from promises between the parties; therefore, contract law is designed to allow rational actors to allocate risk and liability amongst themselves by consensual agreement. *Id.*; A.W. Byrom, *Do Damages Depend on the Same Principles Throughout the Law of Tort and Contract?*, 6 U. Queensland L.J. 118, 120–22 (1968), *reprinted* in DOUG RENDLEMAN, REMEDIES: CASES AND MATERIALS 65–68 (6th ed. 1999).

[2] Sanchez-Corea v. Bank of Am., 701 P.2d 826, 836 (Cal. 1985).

[3] 51 Cal. Rptr. 2d 365 (Cal. App. 1996).

plaintiff-franchisor terminated the defendant's franchise for late payment of royalties. The franchisor then sought to recover future lost royalty payments. The court rejected the claim, holding that the "loss" was caused by the franchisor's decision to terminate the franchise, not the franchisee's late payments. The court distinguished cases involving a total failure to perform from the mere failure to pay monies owed.[4]

The cause-in-fact issue is perhaps most significant in special or consequential damages cases, for here there is a concern that defendant's losses may exceed the parties' reasonable expectations. There can be a shading of cause-in-fact and proximate cause concerns.[5] Nonetheless, on a proper evidentiary showing courts frequently permit recovery of special damages caused by a defendant's breach.[6]

As in tort matters, in contract cases there may be many "causes" of the loss. The traditional contract test is that of "efficient" or "primary" cause rather than the tort "but-for" measure,[7] but the difference may involve only terminology, not substance.[8] In any event, the role of "cause in fact" is rarely addressed in contract damages cases.[9] The "efficient cause" test is subject to modification by contracts,[10] at least outside the insurance contract area.[11] Whether there can be more than one "efficient" cause

---

[4] *Id.* at 370.

[5] Olson v. Parchen, 816 P.2d 423, 427 (Mont. 1991) (stating that the prohibition against the awarding of speculative lost profits "does not necessarily apply to uncertainty about the amount of such profits, but applies to uncertainty about 'whether the loss of profits is the result of the wrong and whether such profit would have been derived at all").

[6] Hornwood v. Smith's Food King No. 1, 772 P.2d 1284 (Nev. 1989) (finding that special damages in the form of diminished property value could be awarded when anchor tenant breached lease by ceasing to operate store as a going concern drawing patrons to the mall).

[7] Vanguard Telecomm., Inc. v. Sou. New England Tel. Co., 900 F.2d 645, 651–52 (3d Cir. 1990) (brokerage contract); Graham v. Public Employees Mut. Ins. Co., 656 P.2d 1077, 1081–82 (Wash. 1983) (insurance contract).

[8] Garvey v. State Farm Fire & Cas. Co., 770 P.2d 704, 707–08 (Cal. 1989) (rejecting "but for" causation test in concurrent causation context in favor of "efficient" causation test and defining the latter as the "predominating cause of the loss").

[9] E. ALLAN FARNSWORTH, CONTRACTS § 12.1, at 757–58 (3d ed. 1999) (noting that cause-in-fact issues are less significant in contract than in tort because of the requirement that "the loss be foreseeable and proved with reasonable certainty"). *But see* Nielsen v. Farrington, 273 Cal. Rptr. 312, 316 (Cal. App. 1990) (holding that disappointed seller of real estate could not recover from nonperforming buyer the additional tax liability the seller incurred when he resold the property after the breach). The tax liability was due to an intervening change in law. The court held that the "cause" of the adverse tax consequences was not the buyer's breach but the seller's failure to resell the property before the change in the law! *Id.*

[10] *Vanguard Telecomm., supra*, 900 F.2d at 651.

[11] Most jurisdictions have concluded that insurers may contract around the efficient cause requirement. TNT Speed & Sport Ctr., Inc. v. American States Ins. Co., 114 F.3d 731, 733 (8th Cir. 1997) (collecting cases). *But see* Safeco Ins. Co. of Am. v. Hirschmann, 773 P.2d 413, 416 (Wash. 1989) (holding that parties to an insurance contract may not contract around the efficient cause standard).

remains unclear in the caselaw. The issue arises most frequently with insurance contracts,[12] which may present special circumstances.[13]

[10.2.2]   Policy Considerations

The time-honored general rule for recovery of breach of contract damages is found in *Hadley v. Baxendale*.[14] As modernly restated, the *Hadley* rule requires:

> 1) where no special circumstances distinguish the contract involved from the great mass of contracts of the same kind, the damages recoverable are those as would naturally and generally result from the breach according to the usual course of things, and 2) where there are special circumstances in the contract, damages which result in consequence of the special circumstances are recoverable, if, and only if, the special circumstances were communicated to or known by both parties to the contract at the time they entered the contract.[15]

The *Hadley* rule can have a significant, constricting effect on the award of breach of contract damages. The Hadley rule applies not just to the scope,[16] but to the extent of damages.[17] The *Hadley* rule may be triggered even if the breaching party reasonably contemplated the type of loss the non-breaching party would sustain, but did not appreciate the extent of the losses breach would entail. A defendant may expect the ordinary consequences of his breach, but is not responsible for extraordinary

---

[12] *Compare* Fidelity & Cas. Co. of New York v. A.H. Underwood, 791 S.W.2d 635, 646 (Tex. Civ. App. 1990) (noting that the "term producing cause" [means] an efficient, exciting or contributing cause, which in material sequence produces the injury or damages . . . . There can be more than one producing cause"), *with Garvey, supra*, 770 P.2d at 707 (efficient cause of loss is either covered or excluded).

[13] James M. Fischer, *Why Are Insurance Contracts Subject to Special Rules of Interpretation?: Text v. Context*, 24 Ariz. St. L. J. 995 (1992). *But cf.* Peter Nash Swisher, *Judicial Interpretations of Insurance Contract Disputes: Toward a Realistic Middle Ground Approach*, 57 Ohio St. L. J. 543 (1996) (disagreeing with Fischer).

[14] 156 Eng. Rep. 145, 151 (Ex. 1854).

[15] Florafax Int'l, Inc. v. GTE Market Resources, Inc., 933 P.2d 282, 292 (Okla. 1997).

[16] International Totalizing Sys., Inc. v. Pepsico, Inc., 560 N.E.2d 749, 753 (Mass. App. 1990) (finding that loss of lucrative acquisition was too remote to have been within reasonable contemplation of parties at time of contract to manufacture vending machine). Plaintiff's theory in this case was that it relied on anticipated profits from the contract when it rejected a third party's offer to acquire plaintiff.

[17] Macal v. Stinson, 468 N.W.2d 34, 36 (Iowa 1991) (holding that plaintiffs could not recover as damages higher interest rates they were required to pay on a loan they had to take out as a result of the breach because "drastic drop in [property] values which precipitated [defendants'] breach, [and] its consequences" were too remote to qualify as arising naturally from the breach. Nor was it foreseeable that plaintiffs would be required "to borrow money at a higher rate if [defendants] breached the contract") (brackets added); Automatic Poultry Feeder Co. v. Wedel, 28 Cal. Rptr. 795, 798 (Cal. App. 1963) (finding that plaintiff could not recover bonus he lost due to defendant's breach; while defendant was aware of plaintiff's contract with the third party, defendant was not aware of the bonus provision in the third party contract).

consequences,[18] unless those extraordinary consequences are brought home to the breaching party as required by the second part of *Hadley*.

The line dividing ordinary from extraordinary may be difficult to predict. For example, in *Redgrave v. Boston Symphony Orchestra, Inc.*,[19] plaintiff brought suit for damages after defendant cancelled plaintiff's contracted-for performance because of pressure from third persons upset with plaintiff's political views. Plaintiff sought damages for losses sustained as a result of the cancellation. The court noted the general rule that injury to reputation, professional or otherwise, is normally not compensable in a breach of contract action due to lack of foreseeability.[20] The court held, however, that if a plaintiff could allege specific refusal to hire, rather than mere damage to her general reputation as a professional, the concern over foreseeability would fade away. From this perspective, the damages claim would be treated as having naturally flowed from the breach and reasonably contemplated by the parties.[21]

One gloss on the *Hadley* rule is the "tacit agreement" test. This test applies when a defendant has been made aware, at the time of contract formation, that plaintiff will sustain extraordinary loss if the contract is breached. Such knowledge usually satisfies *Hadley's* second rule and subjects the defendant to the added liability. The tacit agreement test posits that the defendant must agree or acquiesce to being held liable for the greater exposure. Awareness alone is not enough; rather, there must be

---

[18] Starmakers Pub. Corp. v. Acme Fast Freight, Inc., 646 F. Supp. 780, 782 (S.D.N.Y. 1986) (denying recovery when plaintiff failed to show that defendant was made aware at the time of contract formation of the time-sensitive value of the material shipped and the likelihood of a "catastrophic loss in value if [the material was] not delivered in time") (brackets added); *see* Larry T. Garvin, *Disproportionality and the Law of Consequential Damages: Default Theory and Cognitive Reality*, 59 Ohio St. L. J. 339 (1998) (noting that traditional judicial reluctance to award consequential damages that are disproportionate to the contract price is inconsistent with standard economic analysis, but consistent with a behavioralist approach to human decision making and rationality).

[19] 855 F.2d 888 (1st Cir. 1988), *cert. denied*, 488 U.S. 1043 (1989).

[20] *Id.* at 892–93 (finding that reputation losses were deemed either non-foreseeable or speculative). There is a suggestion in *Ericson v. Playgirl, Inc.*, 140 Cal. Rptr. 921 (Cal. App. 1977), that a loss of professional publicity may be compensable in a breach of contract action. *Id.* at 926 (noting English decisions permitting such a recovery, but finding that plaintiff established only a "loss of mere general publicity that bears no relation to the practice of his art"). *See generally* Joel Smith, Annot., *Recovery by Writer, Artist, or Entertainer for Loss of Publicity or Reputation Resulting From Breach of Contract*, 96 A.L.R.3d 437 (1980).

[21] *Redgrave, supra*, 855 F.2d at 893:

> [I]f plaintiffs proved other employers refused to hire Redgrave after termination of the BSO contract because of that termination (that loss of the other employment "followed as a natural consequence" from the termination of the contract), that this loss of other employment would reasonably have been foreseen by the parties at the time of contracting and at the time of termination, and that damages are rationally calculable, then plaintiffs may be entitled to damages that include monies for loss of the other employment. Although plaintiffs have a heavy burden to carry here, it cannot be said with certainty at this time that they will not be able to meet this burden.

(citation omitted). Why the court added "time of termination" is unclear.

awareness plus some manifestation of assent on the part of the defendant at the time of contract formation to be responsible for the added exposure.[22]

The "tacit agreement" gloss on the *Hadley* rule is simply one of several ways courts address and control the perceived problem of excessive expectations, particularly when the expectancies are collateral to the bargain. Thus, the plaintiff who contracts with the defendant to purchase goods at price X and who expects to resell the goods at the much higher price Y may have an excessive expectancy. One way to ensure that the defendant is not faced with liability that is unreasonably difficult for him to bear is to insist that he be aware of it (*Hadley* rule) or in some way agree to bear it ("tacit agreement"). Another way to address the concern is to directly bar any recovery of excessive or disproportionate liabilities. There is, of course, some looseness in any approach that accepts open-ended terms such as disproportionality and excessiveness; yet, the validity of this approach has been recognized by both courts[23] and commentators[24] as consistent with the demands of fairness and justice.

Occasionally, courts frame the time when the breaching party must reasonably contemplate the breach-related damages to some point after contract formation. This occurs when the scope of the breaching party's obligation remains somewhat open until a point in time after contract formation. For example, in *Spang Industries, Inc. v. Aetna Casualty and Surety Company*[25] the parties entered into a contract whereby defendant's predecessor in interest was to supply structural steel at the job site as designated by plaintiff. The exact time and amount of material was not known at the time of contract formation; nevertheless, the court permitted a suit for breach of contract damages on defendant's breach:

> [W]hen the parties entered into a contract which, by its terms, provides that the time of performance is to be fixed at a later date,

[22] Globe Ref. Co. v. Landa Cotton Oil Co., 190 U.S. 540, 545 (1903) (holding that "mere fact of knowledge cannot increase the liability. The knowledge must be brought home to the party sought to be charged, under such circumstances that he must know that the person he contracts with reasonably believes that he accepts the contract with the special condition attached to it"). This decision was made during the now discredited reign of *Swift v. Tyson*, 41 U.S. 1 (1842), and has been rejected by modern federal courts. Krauss v. Greenbarg, 137 F.2d 569, 571 (3d Cir.), *cert. denied*, 320 U.S. 791 (1943). It is followed in some states, Camino Real Mobile Home Park Partnership v. Wolfe, 891 P.2d 1190, 1200 (N.Mex. 1995), but rejected by most. Twin City Fire Ins. Co. v. Philadelphia Life Ins. Co., 795 F.2d 1417, 1426 (9th Cir. 1986) (collecting authorities). Some jurists still look back longingly at the doctrine. Rexnord Corp. v. DeWolff Boberg & Assocs., Inc., 286 F.3d 1001, 1004 (7th Cir. 2002) (Posner, J.).

[23] Thurner Heat Treating Co. v. Memco, Inc., 30 N.W.2d 228, 233 (Wis. 1947) (noting that discrepancy between plaintiff's claimed lost profit ($2,337) on a job for which defendant earned $149.50 was "some evidence that the respondents would not have agreed to do the work if such damages were contemplated"); Sullivan v. O'Connor, 296 N.E.2d 183, 187–88 (Mass. 1973) (noting that damages that were "harsh and excessive" would not be awarded).

[24] Lon L. Fuller & William R. Perdue, *The Reliance Interest in Contract Damages*, 46 Yale L.J. 52, 88 n.58 (1936) (noting that disparity between benefits received versus liability imposed is a basis for denying relief); *see* Garvin, *Disproportionality*, *supra*, 59 Ohio St. L.J. 339; Restatement (Second) of Contracts § 351[3] (1979); Section 8.2 (Excessiveness).

[25] 512 F.2d 365 (2d Cir. 1975).

the knowledge of the consequences of a failure to perform is to be imputed to the defaulting party as of the time the parties agreed upon the date of performance. This comports, in our view, with both the logic and the spirit of Hadley v. Baxendale.[26]

[10.3] Tort Causation

Every cause produces more than one effect and every effect is the product of more than one cause. This reality, and the effort to deal with that reality in the law, has resulted in tort causation being seen as one of the most complex and complicated areas of the law. Here we address just a small subset of the field of problems in examining the relationship between causation and loss.

The relationship between causation and liability is not the same as the relationship between causation and loss,[27] although it may be contended that in some cases the distinction ignores or downplays the role of foreseeability and the notion that the defendant takes the plaintiff as she finds him. For example, a defendant's failure to provide a safe environment may breach a duty of care owed to another and be seen as a causal link in the injury (*e.g.*, assault and battery or slip and fall) inflicted on another. Whether, however, all the claimed injuries can be attributed to the defendant's wrong is another matter. If the plaintiff suffers a heart attack after a slip and fall caused by defendant's breach of duty, is there a causal link between the specific injury and defendant's act?[28]

A critical issue in establishing causation with respect to damages is the quantum and quality of proof required. This is a dangerous area in which to generalize: in some cases courts will require expert testimony on causation; in other cases lay testimony will be sufficient. A factor usually relied on by courts to police this divide is general experience and common

---

[26] *Id.* at 369. The items of damages awarded were the extra overtime expense incurred when the concrete had to be poured at an expedited rate due to defendant's breach in delivering the contracted-for steel.

[27] LHLC Corp v. Cluett, Peabody & Co., Inc., 842 F.2d 928, 931 (7th Cir.), *cert. denied*, 488 U.S. 926 (1988) (noting distinction in securities fraud context between acts that affect an investment decision and the separate inquiry whether the acts caused a loss, *i.e.*, would the investment consequences have been the same if the acts were not wrongful). In *McGonigle v. Combs*, 968 F.2d 810, 820–21 (9th Cir.), *cert. dismissed*, 506 U.S. 948 (1992), the court rejected the contention that loss causation is satisfied in securities fraud case by a showing that but for the misrepresentations plaintiff would not have acquired the devalued securities. The court held "that the plaintiffs were required to show that the alleged omissions adversely affected the objective value of their investment . . . causing the loss for which they seek to recover." *Id.* at 821 (footnote omitted); Bastian v. Petren Resources Corp., 681 F. Supp. 530, 533–535 (N.D. Ill. 1988) (collecting decisions); Sections 10.6 (Occurrence Causation vs. Loss Causation), 121.2 ([Fraud] Loss Causaton).

[28] *Cf.* Crinkley v. Holiday Inns, Inc., 844 F.2d 156, 163–165 (4th Cir. 1988) (noting that "[t]he doctrine of proximate cause which determines the existence of liability for negligence is equally applicable to liability for particular items of damage"). The majority found for the plaintiff based on medical testimony that assault-related stress triggered the heart attack for which plaintiff sought recovery.

sense. The more likely it is that the plaintiff's injuries are naturally understood to flow from the type of misconduct the defendant committed, the
more willing courts seem to be to permit before and after inferences to
satisfy the causation requirement.[29] On the other hand, when the factual
proof is beyond the ken of the average person, expert testimony will be
necessary to satisfy the causation requirement.[30] In *Tormenia v. First
Investors Realty Co., Inc.*[31] the court held that lay testimony is sufficient
if the claimed disability is the natural result of the alleged injury; expert
testimony is required only when "lay jurors confront causation issues that
are too complex to be understood without the assistance of specialized expert testimony." The *Tormenia* court cited *Kelly v. Borwegen*,[32] which held
that expert testimony was required to explain how an automobile accident
could cause plaintiff's alleged difficulty in sleeping because such pain and
suffering were "subjective" and were "not obviously related to an identifiable injury." The *Tormenia* court found that the plaintiff's injuries did not

---

[29] Morgan v. Campugraphic Corp., 675 S.W.2d 729 (Tex. 1984):

> Lay testimony is adequate to prove causation in those cases in which general
> experience and common sense will enable a layman to determine, with reasonable
> probability, the casual relationship between the event and the condition. Generally,
> lay testimony establishing a sequence of events which provides a strong, logically
> traceable connection between the event and the condition is sufficient proof of
> causation.

> In the instant case, the evidence shows that Morgan had always been in good health
> prior to returning to work from her vacation. Upon returning to her job, she worked
> with her face two inches from a typesetting machine which, it is admitted by default,
> was leaking chemical fumes. Soon after resuming her employment, that is, soon after
> being exposed to the fumes emanating from the typesetting machine, Morgan
> experienced problems with "breathing and swelling and the like." After four or five
> days of being constantly exposed to these fumes during her working hours, Morgan
> developed symptoms such as watering of the eyes, blurred vision, headaches and
> swelling of the breathing passages. We believe this evidence establishes a sequence
> of events from which the trier of fact may properly infer, without the aid of expert
> medical testimony, that the release of chemical fumes from the typesetting machine
> caused Morgan to suffer injury. We thus conclude that there is some evidence in
> the record to support the trial court's award of damages.

Id. at 733 (citations omitted).

[30] Baltimore v. B.F. Goodrich Co., 545 A.2d 1228 (D.C. 1988):

> To prevent the jury from engaging in speculation, we have held that in the absence
> of expert testimony, a jury may not consider the causal connection between a
> defendant's negligence and a plaintiff's claimed disability unless: (1) the disability
> first emerged coincidentally with or very soon after the negligent act, or (2) the
> disability was of a type which by its very nature reflected its cause, or (3) the cause
> of the injury related to matters of common experience, knowledge, or observation
> of laymen. Thus, in cases presenting medically complicated questions due to multiple
> and/or preexisting cases, or questions as to the permanence of an injury, we have
> held that expert testimony is required on the issue of causation.

Id. at 1231 (citations omitted); *see* Heinrich v. Sweet, 308 F.3d 48, 61 (1st Cir. 2002) (stating
that "[w]hether [a medical] treatment ultimately hastened a patient's death is not a topic of
common experience; it requires expert testimony") (brackets added; footnote omitted), *cert.
denied*, 539 U.S. 914 (2003).

[31] 251 F.3d 128 (3d Cir. 2000).

[32] 230 A.2d 532, 534 (N.J. Super. Ct. A.D. 1967).

meet the *Kelly* threshold when the record evidence as to how her injury occurred did not present a complex scenario regarding the injuries Tormenia claimed.[33] The fact that Tormenia had omitted mention of prior injuries and failed to seek prompt medical attention for her main medical problem went to credibility, not burden of proof.[34]

The dividing line between the simple and the complex causation situations is not always clean and precise. For example, Missouri has developed the "sudden onset" doctrine, which permits the plaintiff to dispense with direct proof of causation because causation is inferred. The sudden onset rule applies when the physical disability develops immediately after a negligent act and the injury is the type normally sustained by such negligence and is not the product of a preexisting condition.[35] Whether the injury falls within this paradigm is not, however, self-evident.[36] Sometimes courts use the term "before and after" to capture the intuitive linkage suggested by Missouri's "sudden onset" rule.[37] Both the "sudden onset" and "before and after" approaches are glosses on the general test as to when causation may be satisfied by lay testimony rather than expert opinion.[38]

As noted above the general standard for loss causation is substantial certainty; proof of a mere possibility is insufficient.[39]

---

[33] 251 F.3d at 132–33.

[34] *Id.* at 133; Williams v. Patterson, 681 A.2d 1147, 1150 (D.C. 1996) (holding that lay testimony as to injury causation is sufficient if no "complicated medical question" arises).

[35] Tucker v. Wibbenmeyer, 901 S.W.2d 350, 351 (Mo. App. 1995); Rech v. AAA Plumbing, 798 S.W.2d 194, 195–96 (Mo. App. 1990).

[36] Pihsiou Hsu v. Mound Yellow Cab Co., 624 S.W.2d 61, 63 (Mo. App. 1981) (holding that medical expert evidence was necessary to establish causal link between motor vehicle accident and plaintiff's claimed injuries of vertigo and pain; claims were too indefinite for the jury to resolve without medical evidence); Williams v. Jacobs, 972 S.W.2d 334, 341 (Mo. App. 1998) (same).

[37] Konieczka v. Mt. Clemens Metal Prods. Co., 104 N.W.2d 202, 204 (Mich. 1960); *cf.* Grant v. Sec'y Health & Human Resources, 956 F.2d 1144, 1148 (Fed. Cir. 1992) (noting that when inoculation results in injury within 10 days, child may recover under statutory tables created by Vaccine Act, 42 U.S.C. § 300aa-1 *et seq.*; but if child wants non-table measure of recovery or injury did not follow within 10 days of inoculation, child must prove cause in fact).

[38] Meyers v. Wal-Mart Stores, East, Inc., 257 F.3d 625, 630–31 (6th Cir. 2001) (applying Michigan law) (distinguishing claim that accident caused particular injury (rheumatoid arthritis), in which case medical evidence was required, from claim that accident exacerbated preexisting condition (rheumatoid arthritis), in which case the before and after test was sufficient). *But cf. Baltimore, supra,* 545 A.2d at 1231 (requiring expert testimony when plaintiff seeks recovery for aggration of preexisting condition).

[39] Sanderson v. I.F.F, 950 F. Supp. 981, 984 (C.D. Cal. 1996); Sebena v. AAA, 930 P.2d 51, 53 (Mont. 1996) (stating that "[d]amages must be proven by substantial evidence which is not the product of mere guess or speculation"); Hutcherson v. City of Phoenix, 933 P.2d 1251, 1258 (Ariz. App. 1996) (holding that defendant's act need not have been "large" or "abundant" cause of final result, as there is liability if result would not have occurred but for defendant's conduct, even if that conduct contributed "only a little" to plaintiff's injuries), *rev'd on other grounds,* 961 P.2d 449 (Ariz. 1998).

[10.4] Future Losses

Future losses are losses that accrue after the date of trial.[40] Under the American rule, a plaintiff must bring all her claims for losses attributable to a single event and obtain a single recovery. The plaintiff may not split or bifurcate her claims; hence, the judgment will resolve not only her past and present losses from her injuries, but also future losses attributable to her present injuries.

In the United States, the dominant rule is that damages for the future consequences of a present injury are limited to those that are reasonably certain to occur.[41] To meet this standard a plaintiff must show that it is more likely than not (greater than a 50% chance) that the future consequences will occur. If plaintiff prevails on her proof, the legal effect is to treat the future consequences as if they happened; in other words, the plaintiff receives full compensation for those future consequences.[42] If, on the other hand, plaintiff's proof fails to sustain the requisite certainty, her claim for future consequences fails and she is limited to her damages up to the date of trial.[43] This burden of proof applies to all claims of future losses.[44]

Recovery of future losses presupposes that the plaintiff has suffered, or is likely to suffer, injury.[45] This requirement has, however, been softened in the toxic tort field where the latency factor, as well as the background incidence of diseases allegedly "caused" by exposure to toxic materials, has engendered substantial indeterminacy that hampers the ability to determine cause-effect relationships.[46] The response of many courts has been to relax the standard for determining medical causation in toxic-tort litigation:

> In the toxic-tort context, "proof that a defendant's conduct caused decedent's injuries is more subtle and sophisticated than proof in cases concerned with more traditional torts." A less traditional

---

[40] Section 9.2 (Future Damages)

[41] Olmstead v. Miller, 383 N.W.2d 817, 822 (N.D. 1986); Jordan v. Bero, 210 S.E.2d 618, 629 (W. Va. 1974).

[42] *But see Energy Capital Corp.*, *supra*, 302 F.3D 1314 (adopting proportional test based on likelihood that future lost profits would have been realized) (discussed at Section 9.3 (Discounting to Present Value), text and notes 52–53, *supra*).

[43] Wilson v. Johns-Manville Sales Corp., 684 F.2d 111, 119 (D.C. Cir. 1982) (statute of limitations).

[44] Lone Cedar Ranches, Inc. v. D.B. Jandebeur, 523 N.W.2d 364, 370 (Neb. 1994) (loss of future profits).

[45] Potter v. Firestone Tire & Rubber Co., 863 P.2d 795, 815–16 (Cal. 1993) (involving negligent infliction of emotional distress due to fear of contracting cancer from wrongful exposure to toxic substances).

[46] Rubanick v. Witco Chem. Corp., 125 N.J. 421, 593 A.2d 733, 739–40 (1991) (noting difficulties in establishing causal relationships in toxic tort litigation); *see* Mark S. Ellinger, *DNA Diagnostic Technology: Probing the Problem of Causation in Toxic Torts*, 3 Harv. J.L. & Tech. 31 (1990); Charles Nesson, *Agent Orange Meets the Blue Bus: Factfinding at the Frontier of Knowledge*, 66 B.U. L. Rev. 521 (1986); Section 9.2 (Future Damages).

standard is essential because, unlike the typical personal injury action (where the connection between the conduct of the defendant and injury to the plaintiff is readily deducible) the toxic-tort case often involves, as here: (1) distribution of the offending substance by several manufacturers; (2) exposure of long duration, chronic and repeated; and (3) harm normally resulting from genetic or biochemical disruption rather than trauma or acute toxic response.[47]

This relaxed approach to causation has influenced the recognition of new remedial approaches in this area, for example, by allowing plaintiff to recover for their fear of contracting a disease even if they are presently asymptomatic.[48] Other jurisdictions have, however, expressed concern that, because this recovery is highly subjective and its genuineness is, therefore, difficult to determine, constraints on the recovery should be imposed. Some jurisdictions limit the recovery to cases when plaintiff presents objective symptomatology evidence of a disease in order to receive a "fear of" contracting a disease award.[49]

Toxic exposure claims have also given rise to the recognition of medical monitoring costs as an acceptable compensable recovery. Medical monitoring provides redress to a plaintiff who has not yet suffered a cognizable injury, but who is able to demonstrate that he faces an increased risk of injury due to the wrongful exposure.[50]

[10.5] Lost Chance

The traditional preponderance of the evidence or "but for" test may constrain a plaintiff's recovery that is predicated on an increase in risk, or alternatively a decrease in expectancy. For example, the plaintiff may claim that as a result of defendant's tortious wrong, plaintiff's chance of successful recovery from cancer through treatment and therapy has been reduced from 60% pre-tort to 45% post-tort. Alternatively, the doctrine may

---

[47] James v. Chevron U.S.A., Inc., 694 A.2d 270, 279 (N.J. Super. A. D.), aff'd, 714 A.2d 898 (N.J. 1997) (citations omitted).

[48] Carter v. Temple-Inland Forest Prods. Corp., 943 S.W.2d 221 (Tex. Civ. App. 1997) (holding that the plaintiff could recover emotional distress damages based on the fear of contracting cancer from exposure to asbestos even though plaintiff was presently asymptomatic and the reasonable medical probability was that he would not contract cancer; the critical issue was that plaintiff's fear was reasonable and he had been actually exposed to disease-causing agents). The "fear of" cases should be resolved by identifying the injury as present rather than future. Section 9.1 (Future Damage).

[49] Anderson v. Grace, 628 F. Supp. 1219, 1226–27 (D. Mass. 1986); Section 12.3 (Infliction of Emotional Distress).

[50] Buckley v. Metro-North Commuter R.R., 79 F.3d 1337, 1346–47 (2d Cir. 1996) (holding that plaintiff could recover medical monitoring costs necessary "in order to diagnose properly the warning signs of disease," but only for monitoring "which is necessary because of his exposure to asbestos," not to his smoking) (citations omitted), rev'd on other grounds, 521 U.S. 424 (1997). But cf. Ball v. Joy Techs., Inc., 958 F.2d 36, 39 (4th Cir.) (applying West Virginia law) (refusing to recognize claim for medical monitoring costs for plaintiffs who failed to show "present physical injury" resulting from exposure), cert. denied, 502 U.S. 1033 (1992); Section 72.4 (Medical Monitoring).

be invoked whenever it appears that the plaintiff's direct proof of cause in fact would be speculative.[51]

About one-half of Americans jurisdictions have adopted some variant of the lost chance doctrine for medical malpractice claims.[52] The extension of the doctrine into other areas has been slight.[53] The reasons for this were articulated in *Hardy v. Southwestern Bell Telephone Company*:

> The public policy considerations which are reflected in the judicial decisions creating this remarkable exception to the traditional rule of the standard of proof of causation focus on the special relationship of the physician and patient and the expression of apprehension that failure to adopt the loss of chance doctrine in medical malprac-tice suits would place patients with pre-existing conditions in peril.[54]

A number of courts have adopted a view expressed by Professor King[55] that the measure of the lost chance recovery is the value of the chance rather than the injury itself.[56] This is known as the percentage probability rule. Under this approach, the value of the lost chance is set, largely for expediency reasons and lack of a market, as the percentage reduction in "chance of survival" times the value of the claim itself if it could be proved conventionally. For example, assume a person had a 40% chance of survival if competently treated, but defendant's malpractice reduced that chance to 20%. The person dies.[57] Under the jurisdiction's wrongful death statute let

---

[51] Hardy v. Southwestern Bell Tel. Co., 910 P.2d 1024 (Okla. 1996) (plaintiff invoked doctrine because his emergency 911 call was delayed and his decedent died before help arrived). The court refused to extend the "lost chance" rule into ordinary negligence actions. *Id.* at 1026–27 (limiting doctrine to medical malpractice); Section 73.4 (Hedonic Damages).

[52] *See generally* John Hodson, Annot., *Medical Malpractice "Loss of Chance" Causality*, 54 A.L.R.4th 10 (1987) (collecting decisions). *But see* Smith v. Parott, 833 A.2d 843 (Vt. 2003) (rejecting doctrine).

[53] *Gardner v. National Bulk Carriers, Inc.*, 310 F.2d 284, 288 (4th Cir. 1962), *cert. denied*, 372 U.S. 913, (1963), is one of the few non-medical malpractice applications of the doctrine. In *Gardner* a ship's captain failed to attempt the rescue of a seaman, presumably "fallen overboard." There was no proof that the rescue would have been successful if attempted; only proof of the reasonable possibility of rescue.

[54] 910 P.2d 1024, 1028 (Okla. 1996). *Compare* John C. P. Goldberg, *What Clients Are Owed: Cautionary Observations on Lawyers and Loss of a Chance*, 52 Emory L. J. 1201 (2003) (arguing that application of "loss of chance" doctrine to legal malpractice claims would be unwise because liability should be limited to "realized injuries," not the "risk of injury"), *with* David A. Fischer, *Tort Recovery For Loss of A Chance*, 36 Wake Forest L. Rev. 605 (2001) (arguing for a limited expansion of the loss of chance doctrine beyond medical malpractice based on case-by-case application of several principles developed in the paper).

[55] Joseph King, Jr., *Causation, Valuation, and Chance in Personal Injury Torts Involving Pre-Existing Conditions and Future Consequences*, 90 Yale L. J. 1353 (1981).

[56] Fennell v. Southern Maryland Hosp., 580 A.2d 206, 212–13 (Md. 1990).

[57] Most cases invoking the "lost chance" doctrine involve death, but the doctrine has been applied to personal injury claims not involving death. Smith v. Washington, 734 N.E.2d 548, 550–51 (Ind. 2000) (applying "percentage probability rule" to claim involving loss of sight in eye).

us assume the value of the claim (*i.e.*, the loss caused by decedent's death) was $1 million. Under this version of the lost chance test, plaintiff would recover $200,000.[58] Alternatively, some courts attempt to measure the "lost chance" itself under a broad evidence standard.[59] Some cases suggest recovery of the entire $1 million if defendant's malpractice worked a substantial reduction in the decedent's chance of survival, but the suggestion has not been accepted.[60]

Perhaps the most difficult issue raised, besides that relating to acceptance of the "lost chance" doctrine itself, is determining what constitutes a substantial reduction in the chance of survival.[61] The issue is influenced by whether a court permits the recovery of all damages if defendant's malpractice resulted in "loss of chance" or whether a court permits only a pro rata recovery. In the former context the tendency is to require that the reduction be substantial, that there is a floor below which a plaintiff may not go, but to reject a mathematical approach. Courts that adopt a pure, pro rata approach are more likely to resist imposing any limit because a limit is theoretically inconsistent with the approach. A defendant who causes a 2% loss of chance is just as responsible for that lost 2% as a defendant who causes a 20% loss or a 50% loss.

An alternative to "loss of chance" is concurrent causation. Under this approach a plaintiff would argue that the negligent act and preexisting condition are concurrent causes and that she may prevail *if* the negligent act was a substantial factor in her ultimate injurious condition.[62] Under this approach, the defendant would likely be liable for the entire loss.

In cases when the claim is that the defendant's negligence hastened or accelerated the plaintiff's death, the accepted view appears to be that the defendant is responsible for the reduction only.[63] The hastening death cases are structurally identical in most respects to loss of chance cases and

---

[58] Twenty percent (40% − 20%) of $1 million equals $200,000. *See generally* Martin McMahon, *Medical Malpractice: Measure and Elements of Damages in Actions Based on Loss of Chance,* 81 A.L.R.4th 485, § 3 (1991).

[59] *See* Bointy-Tsotigh v. United States, 953 F. Supp. 358, 362 (W.D. Okla. 1996); Borgren v. United States, 723 F. Supp. 581, 582–83 (D. Kan. 1989); James v. United States, 483 F. Supp. 581, 587 (N.D. Cal. 1980).

[60] *See* Mays v. United States, 608 F. Supp. 1476, 1481 (D. Colo. 1985), *rev'd on other grounds,* 806 F.2d 976 (10th Cir. 1986), *cert. denied,* 482 U.S. 913 (1987). This decision can be read as allowing recovery of all damages relating to a loss chance of survivability that was less than 5%; however, on the facts the lost chance was a 35% reduction. The opinion is not entirely clear whether the award was the net loss attributable to the 35% reduction or the gross amount of the plaintiff's injuries. The consistent interpretation of *Mays,* however, is to read it as a pro rata, net loss decision. Scafidi v. Seiler, 574 A.2d 398, 404 (N.J. 1990).

[61] *Compare* James v. United States, 483 F. Supp. 581, 587 (N.D. Cal. 1980) (permitting recovery no matter how small the chance as long as some chance is shown); Pipe v. Hamilton, 56 P.3d 823 (Kan. 2002) (permitting loss of chance recovery when negligence of defendant reduced chance of survival by 5–10%), *with* McKellips v. Saint Francis Hosp., Inc., 741 P.2d 467, 474–75 (Okla. 1987) (requiring that loss be at least a better than even chance).

[62] Logacz v. Limansky, 84 Cal. Rptr.2d 257 (Cal. App. 1999).

[63] Alexander v. Scheid, 726 N.E.2d 272, 282–83 (Ind. 2000).

damages should be determined the same way in each case if a recovery is allowed.[64]

[10.6] Occurrence Causation vs. Loss Causation

A cause and effect relationship between the occurrence and the defendant's legal wrong may not be sufficient to impose liability for all succeeding losses. For example, assume that due to defendant's negligence plaintiff slips and falls sustaining some injury. Shortly thereafter, plaintiff goes into cardiac arrest and dies. Defendant's negligence (legal wrong) caused the fall (the occurrence). Is defendant also responsible for the injuries and death of the plaintiff (the loss)?

In most cases, a separate inquiry into loss causation is not required because the linkage between the occurrence and the loss is obvious. In other cases, the inquiry is aided by special rules, such as the fragile plaintiff doctrine.[65] In some cases, however, the wrong that induced the occurrence or event, *e.g.*, purchase, may not clearly have induced the loss, *e.g.*, a subsequent decline in the value of the item purchased. For example, a misrepresentation may induce the plaintiff to purchase a security; thereafter, a general market decline may cause the security to lose value independent of the misrepresentation. While the misrepresentation caused the bargain in the sense that "but for" the misrepresentation the plaintiff would not have purchased the security, the misrepresentation did not cause the loss; rather, the loss was the result of the general market decline. This idea is captured in the phrase "loss causation."

The concept of loss causation has been consistently applied to fraud claims,[66] but it has received inconsistent application elsewhere. In *Movitz v. First National Bank of Chicago*,[67] Judge Posner argued for a broader application of the loss causation principle. *Movitz* involved the negligent failure of a bank to evaluate an investment. The negligence induced the investment, which was the purchase of an office building in Houston, Texas, but the loss (decline in value) was the result of the Texas recession in the early 1980s, not the negligence.

Judge Posner relied on arguments of function and duty. He noted that there was little difference between the negligence and fraud theories insofar as the loss in *Movitz* was concerned. In Judge Posner's view, the legal wrong was disassociated from the events that caused the loss. Judge Posner also noted that the bank had not assumed a duty to protect the plaintiff from

---

[64] The general rule is to permit recovery of economic losses when plaintiff's work life expectancy is reduced by defendant's wrongdoing, Sections 71.1 (Loss of Earnings), 71.2 (Loss of Earnings Capacity), but not allow recovery of noneconomic losses. Section 73.4 (Hedonic Damages).

[65] Section 13.2.3 (The "Fragile" Plaintiff). The doctrine is also discussed in Section 10.7 (Apportionment of Damages), text and notes 78–80, *infra*.

[66] When a misrepresentation induces a bargain but not a loss, the plaintiff may be limited to rescission remedies. Sections 130 (Nature of Rescission), 134 (Restoration of Status Quo).

[67] 148 F.3d 760 (7th Cir. 1998), *cert. denied*, 525 U.S. 1094 (1999).

a recession-driven devaluation of the commercial real estate market in Houston.[68] The court refused to allow liability to proceed on the "for want of a nail a kingdom was lost" theory.[69] Whether Judge Posner's decision in *Movitz* will lead to an extended application of loss causation principles outside the context of fraud remains to be seen."[70]

The issue of loss causation has also arisen in contexts when the plaintiff claims that the defendant's negligence (1) exposed the plaintiff to a punitive damages award, *e.g.*, but for defendant's negligence the award would not have been entered against the plaintiff or (2) caused the plaintiff to lose a punitive damages award she would have received from a defendant. This complaint has arisen in legal malpractice[71] and insurance bad faith actions.[72] In both contexts, the decisions are split as to whether the lost punitive damages should be treated as recoverable under principles of loss causation[73] or should be evaluated in light of their purpose, which is to punish or deter,[74] and only awarded when the defendant's underlying conduct independently satisfies the criteria for awarding punitive damages.[75]

[10.7] Apportionment of Damages

As a general rule, the defendant is liable only for the injuries she causes. When the loss operates on a preexisting condition, this rule extends to injury that consists of aggravation or acceleration of the injury.[76] This raises two fundamental questions. First, how should the award be allocated between the plaintiff's current injuries and the plaintiff's former condition? Second, how does this rule differ from the "fragile" plaintiff doctrine?

With regard to apportionment, the defendant is responsible for that part of the plaintiff's aggregate injury that was caused by defendant's misconduct. The general approach distinguishes between divisible and indivisible injuries. When injuries are divisible, defendant is liable only for those injuries attributable to defendant's misconduct. When the injuries are indivisible, defendant's liability for the total injury turns on causation.[77] If

---

[68] *Id.* at 763–64.

[69] *Id.* at 764.

[70] *See* W. PAGE KEETON, PROSSER & KEETON ON TORTS § 43, 280–84 (5th ed. 1984) (criticizing loss causation as simply a variant of the "same hazard" principle and other limitations on tort liability that have been rejected).

[71] *See* Charles Marshall Thatcher, *Recovery of "Lost Punitive Damages" As "Compensatory Damages" in Legal Malpractice Actions: Transference of Liability or Transference of Character*, 49 S.D. L. Rev. 1 (2003).

[72] *Id.* at 30.

[73] Elliot v. Videan, 791 P.2d 639, 645–46 (Ariz. App. 1990) (holding that value of claim lost due to attorney's negligence included lost punitive damages claim).

[74] Section 201 (Purpose for Punitive Damages).

[75] Ferguson v. Lieff, Cabraser, Heimann & Bernstein, 69 P.3d 965, 974 (Cal. 2003) (rejecting inclusion of "lost punitive damages" in valuing claim lost by attorney's negligence).

[76] Reising v. United States, 60 F.3d 1241, 1244 (7th Cir. 1995).

[77] Lovely v. Allstate Ins. Co., 658 A.2d 1091, 1092 (Me. 1995) (adopting rule applied when

defendant's misconduct was a substantial factor in plaintiff's aggregate injury, defendant is liable for the whole. The distinction between preexisting injury and aggravation or acceleration of injury may be factually difficult and often is resolvable only on a case by case basis.

The "fragile" plaintiff doctrine is related to but distinct from the apportionment issue. The "fragile" plaintiff doctrine holds that a plaintiff's unusual sensitivity to injury is not a defense to defendant's responsibility for the complete, aggregate injuries sustained.[78] For example, if plaintiff is a hemophiliac and bleeds to death as a result of a touching that would cause only nominal discomfort to another person, the plaintiff's unusual, and more severe reaction, does not make the loss unforeseeable.[79] On the other hand, if plaintiff has a preexisting injury when defendant's misconduct inflicts additional harm, the defendant is only liable for that additional harm over the baseline established by the preexisting condition. The issue is whether the "fragile" plaintiff was already fractured at the time defendant acted or whether defendant's misconduct caused the "fragile" plaintiff to fracture.[80]

Allocation issues can become significant in jurisdictions that have capped certain types of recoveries, such as non-economic losses. In this context, the plaintiff will attempt to shift as much of the damages as possible into non-capped categories. For example, in *Gagliardo v. Connaught Laboratories, Inc.*,[81] the plaintiff was awarded $2.5 million for disability discrimination by her employer, of which $2 million was for compensatory damages and $0.5 million for punitive damages. The Americans with Disabilities Act caps damages at $300,000.[82] The district court permitted plaintiff to

---

two tortfeasors combine to cause aggregate injury and applying rule to case involving single actor aggravating preexisting injury); *cf.* Gross v. Lyons, 763 So.2d 276, 278 (Fla. 2000) (holding that if jury cannot apportion liability between successive tortfeasors, first tortfeasor is liable for the entire loss).

[78] Jordan v. Atchison, T & S Fe Ry., 934 F.2d 225, 228–29 (9th Cir. 1991); Stoleson v. United States, 708 F.2d 1217, 1220–21 (7th Cir. 1983) (discussing eggshell or thin headed plaintiff, which are alternative euphemisms for the "fragile" plaintiff concept); Maurer v. United States, 668 F.2d 98 (2d Cir. 1981):

> It is a settled principle of tort law that when a defendant's wrongful act causes injury, he is fully liable for the resulting damage even though the injured plaintiff had a preexisting condition that made the consequences of the wrongful act more severe than they would have been for a normal victim. The defendant takes the plaintiff as he finds him.

Id. at 99–100.

[79] Primm v. U.S. Fid. & Guar. Ins. Corp., 922 S.W.2d 319, 322 (Ark. 1996) (involving bone condition that rendered human bone unusually brittle and susceptible to breaking). The seminal case is *Vosburg v. Putney*, 50 N.W. 403 (Wis. 1891), in which a school boy kicked another boy in the shin; the other boy had an infection in his tibia and the kick caused his leg to break; the kick would not have seriously injured a normal, healthy person.

[80] *Reising, supra*, 60 F.3d at 1244 (noting that the judge did not abuse his discretion in allocating damages between the defendant's misconduct and plaintiff's degenerating back "which would have eventually caused him pain and limitations of mobility even without the accident"); Section 13.2.3 (The "Fragile" Plaintiff).

[81] 311 F.3d 565 (3d Cir. 2002).

[82] 42 U.S.C. § 1981a(b)(3)(D).

allocate all of her compensatory damages to a companion state law claim and apply the statutory cap only to the punitive damages claim. As a result plaintiff recovered $2.2 million rather than $0.3 million. The Third Circuit affirmed finding that the allocation was not prohibited by federal law.[83]

Allocation issues also arise in the context of contribution and indemnity among tortfeasors, good faith settlements, and comparative fault. These topics are, however, outside the scope of these materials.

§ 11   ECONOMIC LOSS RULE

[11.1]   Purpose and Scope of Rule

A significant tort-contract distinction is the general unwillingness of courts to compensate for negligent, tortious conduct that causes only economic loss.[1] Before the main principle is discussed, it should be noted that there are several glosses that limit the main principle. A party may recover its economic losses[2] caused by the defendant's negligence[3] when the loss is adjunct or derivative to injury to person (e.g., lost wages or medical expense incurred) or property (e.g., loss of value or use) and in which the plaintiff has an interest direct or related (e.g., the injured person is the plaintiff's spouse or with respect to damaged property the plaintiff has a legally recognized interest, such as lease, bailment, consignment, etc.). Economic losses are also recoverable when the negligent misconduct also constitutes a breach of contract or the tortious misconduct is intentional, e.g., inducing breach of contract.

This "no recovery for pure economic loss in negligence" rule (economic loss rule) is not a causation doctrine as the term is generally used and understood. In cases when the economic loss rule is applied, the defendant

---

[83] 311 F.3d at 570–71. *But cf.* Hoffman-La Roche, Inc. v. Zeltwanger, 144 S.W.3d 438 (Tex. 2004) (rejecting plaintiff's claim for common law intentional infliction of emotional distress that was brought to circumvent statutory cap on non-economic loss resulting from workplace sexual harrassment).

[1] Robins Dry Dock & Repair Co. v. Flint, 275 U.S. 303, 309 (1927); Nebraska Innkeepers, Inc., v. Pittsburgh-Des Moines Corp., 345 N.W.2d 124, 126 (Iowa 1984) (noting that "[t]he well-established general rule is that a plaintiff who has suffered only economic loss due to another's negligence has not been injured in a manner that is legally cognizable or compensable").

[2] Economic loss is harm to one's financial interests. It may include lost profits, diminution in value, consequential damages, etc. It does not include, as used here, the financial harm that is derivative of bodily injury or property damage, such as lost earnings, medical expense, or cost of repair. It is, therefore, not the nature of the expense but the origin of the expense that is critical.

[3] Leadfree Enters., Inc. v. United States Steel Corp., 711 F.2d 805, 808 (7th Cir. 1983) (finding no recovery for loss of business patronage and employment due to negligence of defendant resulting in closing of a public bridge that disrupted plaintiff's business); 532 Madison Avenue Gourmet Foods, Inc. v. Finlandia Center, Inc., 750 N.E.2d 1097 (N.Y. 2001) (rejecting economic loss claims brought by neighbors of defendant; neighbors' businesses suffered loss of patronage due to street closures caused by construction accident on defendant's property).

has caused actual economic loss to the plaintiff; the law, however, provides, in most cases, no remedy for that loss, absent conduct on the defendant's part resulting in or causing bodily injury or property damage to the plaintiff. The economic loss rule is bottomed on the view there is no independent duty or obligation flowing from general public policy that would warrant tort-based remedies being applied to remedy only economic loss caused by or resulting from defendant's negligence.[4] The economic loss rule is sometimes discussed in terms of lack of causation or remote cause, but the end result is the same—no recovery. The reasons for treating a cause as remote and the reasons for not recognizing a duty are increasingly seen as resting on the same ground of public policy.[5]

The origins of the economic loss rule are somewhat mysterious. The rule finds expression in both English[6] and American[7] precedents. The justification for the no recovery result varied, however, between no duty, no causation, etc. It is only recently that the concerns have been consolidated under the rubric "economic loss rule." As so consolidated, however, the full scope of the rule remains unclear. The rule remain a work in progress.

The modern origins of the economic loss rule likely derive from the expansion of tort liability in the mid part of the 20th Century. Tort liability, particularly product defect liability, grew exponentially during this period; yet, unlimited liability was never an option: tort liability was not intended to completely preempt bargain liability.[8] The economic loss rule was adopted to police this divide. As is the case with many legal doctrines, the economic loss rule escaped its initial area of application and entered virgin territories. In addition, the economic loss rule is neither uncritically nor

---

[4] AFM Corp. v. Southern Bell Tel. & Tel., 515 So. 2d 180, 181–82 (Fla. 1987); *see* Robert L. Rabin, *Tort Recovery for Negligently Inflicted Economic Loss: A Reappraisal*, 37 Stan. L. Rev. 1513 (1985).

[5] Patrick J. Kelley, *Proximate Cause in Negligence Law: History, Theory, and Present Darkness*, 69 Wash. U. L. Q. 49, 53 (1991) (arguing that this approach makes clear that the decision is based on policy, not science); David A. Fischer, *Products Liability—Proximate Cause, Intervening Cause, and Duty*, 52 Mo. L. Rev. 547, 549 (1987) (noting overlap between proximate cause and duty analysis).

[6] Cattle v. Stockton Waterworks Co., 10 LR-Q.B. 453, 457–58 (1875) (rejecting claim for increased cost of performing contract caused by defendant's negligence when defendant was not a party to the contract).

[7] *Robins Dry Dock & Repair Co.*, *supra*, 275 U.S. at 304–05 (rejecting claim for lost of use profits due to defendant's negligence in repairing property when no privity of contract existed between plaintiff and defendant); Connecticut Mut. Life Ins. Co. v. New York & New Haven R.R. Co., 25 Conn. 265 (1856) (rejecting claim by life insurance company seeking to recoup losses caused when defendant's negligence resulted in death of policyholder).

[8] The leading decision here is *Seely v. White Motor Co.*, 403 P.2d 145 (Cal. 1965) (Traynor, J.), which held that a plaintiff product owner could not recover in tort product liability for economic losses not associated with bodily injury or injury to other property; losses associated with the product itself must be asserted through bargain remedies, *e.g.*, damages for breach of warranty. Some courts see the economic loss rule as unique to product defeat claims, but that is incorrect. The application of the economic loss rule to product defeat claims is an adaption of the earlier ban on using negligence to evade contract doctrine.

unanimously accepted within its initial area of development or the areas it has invaded.[9]

The rationales for the economic loss rule vary depending on whether the claim for pure economic loss arises between (1) parties who are not in privity of contract with one another and (2) those who are. In the first context (absence of privity) justifications for the application of the economic loss rule have varied,[10] but the dominant fear has been that of open-ended liability:

> Courts which have addressed this issue have repeatedly expressed concern that a contrary rule would open the door to virtually limitless suits, often of a highly speculative and remote nature. Such suits would expose the negligent defendant to a severe penalty, and would produce serious problems in litigation, particularly in the areas of proof and apportionment of damages.[11]

It should not be surprising, however, that such a broad rule of no compensation would have its critics,[12] and more importantly, its exceptions:

> The tort process, like the law itself, is a human institution designed to accomplish certain social objectives. One objective is to ensure that innocent victims have avenues of legal redress, absent a contrary, overriding public policy . . . . This reflects the overreaching purpose of tort law: that wronged persons should be compensated for their injuries and that those responsible for the wrong should bear the cost of their tortious conduct.[13]

In cases when the parties are in privity the justification for the economic loss rule is different. Here the concern is not open-ended liability; indeed, the privity element limits the number of possible plaintiffs. Rather, the

---

[9] *See* Rabin, *Tort Recovery for Economic Loss, supra,* 37 Stan. L. Rev. at 1513–15 (noting that the economic loss rule must be understood within the larger context of the proper function of tort liability not as a separate, self-contained doctrine).

[10] *In re* Marine Navigation Sulphur Carriers, Inc., 507 F. Supp. 205 (E.D. Va. 1980), *aff'd,* 638 F.2d 700, 702 (4th Cir. 1981) (noting that "[t]he economic, non-physical losses as alleged were too remote to be legally compensable").

[11] General Foods Corp. v. United States, 448 F. Supp. 111, 113 (D. Md. 1978).

[12] John Minor Wisdom, *Admiralty Jurisdiction and Products Liability: Economic Loss,* 62 Tul. L. Rev. 325, 336 (1988) (criticizing "bright-line rule that there is no liability for purely economic loss" as representing "the dying hand of the past attempting and failing to grasp the realities of the present"); Rabin, *Tort Recovery for Economic Loss, supra,* 37 Stan. L. Rev. at 1514–15 ("[A]n identifiable type of economic loss case raises the specter of widespread tort liability—a characteristic which in itself has never been uniquely confined to economic loss situations—and . . . economic loss cases lacking this feature do not receive distinctive treatment") (citation omitted; bracket added).

[13] People Express Airlines Inc. v. Consolidated Rail Corp., 495 A.2d 107, 111 (N.J. 1985) (permitting recovery when commercial airline was forced to evacuate its premises and sustained economic loss due to business interruption as a result of defendant's negligent acts in allowing a dangerous chemical to escape from a nearby railing car). The court held that recovery would be permitted when the "plaintiff or plaintiffs [comprise] an identifiable class with respect to whom defendant knows or has reason to know are likely to suffer [economic loss] damages from its conduct." *Id.* at 116 (brackets added).

rationale for the rule in this context is that it prevents contracting parties from circumventing their bargained-for contract remedies by recovering purely pecuniary losses in tort.[14] Here also, however, the rule is not absolute but is sprinkled with exceptions.[15]

[11.2] Property Damage

It is well recognized that economic loss that is derivative of physical damage to property, such as loss of use damages, is recoverable. The more difficult issue is whether economic losses are recoverable when the property damaged is the subject of the privity relationship between the parties. Closely related to this is the definition of the "property" for purposes of applying the rule.

The majority rule in the United States is that producers are liable in tort (strict liability or negligence) to users of products for bodily injury or harm to other property caused by a defective product; however; tort liability does not extend to pure economic loss unrelated or unconnected to bodily injury or harm to other property.[16] In other words, when the defective product causes only economic loss, the plaintiff must look to contract, not tort, remedies for recovery. If contract remedies are limited or non-existent, plaintiff cannot enhance the bargain by suing in tort.[17]

---

[14] Town of Alma v. Azco Constr., Inc., 10 P.3d 1256 (Colo. 2000); Section 11.2 (Loss Resulting From Property Damage).

[15] Commercial Union Ins. Co. v. Roxborough Village Joint Venture, 911 F. Supp. 827, 831 (D. Colo. 1996) (noting exceptions for intentional misconduct and negligent misrepresentation).

[16] East River Steamship Corp. v. Transamerica Delaval Inc., 476 U.S. 858 (1986). *East River* involved a products liability claim brought under Admiralty jurisdiction. The decision collects and analyzes many of the leading decisions on this topic. The Court in *East River* reasoned that the no recovery position best advanced the interests of both the parties and the public:

> Damage to a product itself is most naturally understood as a warranty claim. Such damage means simply that the product has not met the customer's expectations, or, in other words, that the customer has received "insufficient product value." The maintenance of product value and quality is precisely the purpose of express and implied warranties.

Id. at 872 (footnotes and citations omitted). In *Florida Power & Light Co. v. Westinghouse Elec. Corp.*, 510 So. 2d 899 (Fla. 1987), this approach was adopted on the following grounds:

> The policy adopted by the majority of courts encourages parties to negotiate economic risk through warranty provisions and price. On the other hand, the minority view exposes a manufacturer to liability for negligence based on economic loss alone, replacing the freedom of bargaining and negotiation with a duty of care. A duty of care, as emphasized in *East River*, is particularly unsuited to the vagaries of individual purchasers' product expectations . . . . [U]nder the minority view, a manufacturer faced with this kind of liability exposure must raise prices on every contract to cover the enhanced risk. Clearly, product value and quality is covered by express and implied warranties, and warranty law should control a claim for purely economic losses.

Id. at 901.

[17] Bay Breeze Condominium Ass'n, Inc. v. Norco Windows, Inc., 651 N.W.2d 738, 742 (Wis. App. 2002) (stating that "when commercial parties have allocated their respective risks through contract, the economic loss doctrine instructs that it is more appropriate to enforce that bargain than to allow an 'end run' around that bargain through tort law") (citations omitted); *see* Rardin v. T&D Mach. Handling, Inc., 890 F.2d 24 (7th Cir. 1989).

When the dispute is between a buyer and seller of goods, the injury consists of damage to the goods themselves, and the measure of the injury is the cost of repair or lost profit that the transaction was expected to yield, the majority view holds the disappointed buyer to his contractual remedies.[18] There is a minority view that permits pure economic loss recoveries for defective products.[19] These distinctions are sometimes further broken down into subdistinctions between consumer transactions and commercial transactions.[20]

The problem in many product cases is that the defective product is not a stand alone product, but one that is incorporated into another product, or the defective product works with another product as part of a system. When the defective product malfunctions, its consequences may be said to have been visited on connected property. The dividing line between economic loss resulting from the defective product and damage to other property may be difficult to discern in these situations.

One distinction that has found some usage in the caselaw is the "external affects" test:

> When the defect causes an accident' involving some violence or collision with external objects,' the resulting loss is treated as property damage. On the other hand, when the damage to the product results from deterioration, internal breakage, or other non-accidental causes, it is treated as economic loss.[21]

The "external affects" test is designed to identify whether there is a single product or property ("property" that is subject to deterioration or internal breakage) or more than one property (a defective product or property that acts externally on other property). The concept is that a single property does not act externally on itself. The concept is intuitively sound, but it is questionable whether it is workable in fact. For example, assume the problem is a defective piston installed in an automobile engine. The engine seizes and the resulting violent vibrations result in the destruction of the engine and transmission. Does the "external affects" test guide us to an accurate assessment of whether the loss should be characterized as external property damage or mere economic loss? The distinction is elusive.

---

[18] Neibarger v. Universal Coop., Inc., 486 N.W.2d 612, 617 (Mich. 1992).

[19] Santor v. A&M Karagheusian, Inc., 207 A.2d 305, 312 (N.J. 1965) (finding that permitting economic loss recoveries furthers risk shifting and deterrence values by forcing parties who cause harm to internalize those costs rather than foisting them on innocent parties).

[20] Mt. Lebanon Personal Care Home, Inc. v. Hoover Universal, Inc., 276 F.3d 845 (6th 2002) (applying Kentucky law; noting state decisions declining to apply economic loss rule to consumer transactions, but concluding that rule would be applied to commercial transactions); cf. Quest Diagnostics, Inc. v. MCI Worldcom, Inc., 656 N.W.2d 858 (Mich. App. 2002) (limiting application of economic loss rule to cases when the parties had the opportunity to bargain over loss allocations).

[21] Moorman Mfg. Co. v. National Tank Co., 435 N.E.2d 443, 449 (Ill. 1982) (citation omitted); cf. Continental Ins. v. Page Eng'g Co., 783 P.2d 641, 668 n.14 (Wyo. 1989) (Urbigkit, J., dissenting) (noting different formulations of test).

Another approach (the "integrated product" rule) focuses on whether the product parts are seen as integrated or separate. Under this approach, when various components of a product are provided by the same supplier as part of a complete and integrated package, even if a defect in one component damages another component, there is no damage to other property of the plaintiff.[22] The rationale of the approach is that all but the simplest products are an assemblage of components and to divide an integrated product into its component parts to allow a finding that "other property" was damaged would eliminate the distinction between contract and tort.[23] As with any approach, however, the issue is not so much in its formulation, for the approach is plausibly sound, but in its application. For example, does the "integrated product" approach apply to replacement parts that are purchased separately and after the original purchase of the product? This was the issue in *Sea-Land Service Inc. v. General Electric Corp.*[24] The loss was caused by a defective replacement "connecting rod" that caused damage to the diesel engine in which it had been placed. Was the "product" the original diesel engine or the replacement rod? The plaintiff contended that timing was everything; therefore, its purchase of the replacement connecting rod after its purchase of the diesel engine resulted in damage to "other property." The court was not convinced. Using an "object of the bargain"[25] lens to examine the parties' reasonable expectations, the court concluded that it would be unreasonable to treat the replacement part as altering the parties' legal relationship as established by the initial purchase:

> It is a common commercial practice for the parties to a transaction to contemplate the integration of replacement parts subsequent to a purchase. In the instant case, it was expected that all the replacement parts would eventually have to be integrated into the engine. The GE connecting rod was purchased to be installed and to become integrated with the GE engine. It is a component of that engine; it has no use to Sea-Land otherwise. Moreover, in purchasing and installing replacement parts, the parties can, as with the

---

[22] New York State Elec. & Gas Corp. v. Westinghouse Elec. Corp., 564 A.2d 919, 925 (Pa. Super. Ct. 1989).

[23] *East River Steamship Corp.*, *supra*, 476 U.S. at 867–68. The fact that the "product" may be used in conjunction with other products does not mean that the entirety is a single product. *See* 2-J Corp. v. Tice, 126 F.3d 539, 544 (3d Cir. 1997) (holding that property stored within a prefabricated warehouse and damaged when the warehouse collapsed was not part of the warehouse (product) even though it was highly foreseeable that property would be stored in the warehouse).

[24] 134 F.3d 149 (3d Cir. 1998).

[25] *Id.* at 153 (citations omitted):

> One looks to the "object of the bargain"—the object purchased or bargained for by the plaintiff, in determining whether additions constitute "other property." We conclude then that every component that was the benefit of the bargain should be integrated into the product; consequently, there is no "other property." However, we distinguish from the product additional parts that are not encompassed in the original bargain but are subsequently acquired. These should not be integrated.

original purchase, negotiate the terms of the sale and of any warranties.[26]

Under the court's approach, it is unclear whether the fact that the replacement part came from the same supplier as the original part or a different supplier is material. Unless the source is critical, *i.e.*, quality control, it would seem that the subject matter of the transaction, a functioning diesel engine, is more significant than the identity, and sameness, of the contracting parties.[27]

Notwithstanding the apparent objectivity of the "integrated product"/ "bargained for" test, the actual process is more akin to context-based characterization. The decisions are in disarray.[28] Perhaps the point was put best in *Mainline Tractor & Equip. Co. v. Nutrite Corp.*, which involved damages claims arising out of reduced crop yield losses resulting from the failure of a herbicide to control crabgrass. The court noted:

> The line between property damage and economic loss can often be obscure, and this case is no exception. In the traditional property damage cases, the defective product damages other property. On the other hand, in an economic loss case, the product injures only itself and damages are sought for inadequate product value and consequent loss of profits.

> The case at bar is somewhat of a hybrid. Admittedly, the silage corn, property other than the defective product, was damaged. Nonetheless, the gravamen of Plaintiff's complaint is that the Micro-Tech proved inadequate for its purpose, causing plaintiffs to have a less successful yield and thereby to lose profits. Accordingly, this Court finds that Plaintiffs' harm is better characterized as economic loss than property damage.[29]

Some courts have added a gloss to the "integrated product" test that the component should be considered a separate product unless it has lost is distinct identity.[30]

---

[26] *Id.* at 154.

[27] *Cf.* Trans States Airlines v. Pratt & Whitney Canada, Inc., 682 N.E.2d 45, 55–59 (Ill. 1997) (adopting "product bargained for" test and stating that whether product and its components may constitute one or more "products" is determined by whether the parties bargained separately for individual components). The court concluded that the plaintiff had not separately bargained for an airplane's frame separate from its engines and held the airplane constituted a single product.

[28] For example, under the "integrated products" approach courts have held that windows installed in condominium units were part of an integrated system, *Bay Breeze Condominium Assn, Inc., supra*, 651 N.W.2d at 740 (holding that damage caused to portions of condominium units adjoining the defective windows was not damage to "other property"), and courts have held that they are not. Jimenez v. Superior Court, 58 P.3d 450 (Cal. 2002) (holding that whether a component product causes "other property" damage is to be resolved on a case-by-case basis by the trier-of-fact and declining to adopt a specific test).

[29] 937 F. Supp. 1095, 1101–02 (D. Vt. 1996) (citations omitted).

[30] *Jimenez, supra*, 58 P.3d at 458–59.

Other approaches in this area include differentiating between (1) disappointment (economic loss rule applied) and disaster or calamity (economic loss rule not applied) or (2) distinguishing between consumer (economic loss rule not applied) and commercial transactions (economic loss rule applied). These cases attempt to differentiate between "the disappointed users . . . and the endangered ones"[31] and permit only the latter to sue in tort. The recovery sought in these cases is usually the cost of remedying the defect before a loss to person or property occurs. Whether such recoveries should be permitted has been said to turn on the nature of the product defect, the type of risk, and the manner in which the injury arose.[32] The Alaska Supreme Court allows a tort action if the defective product creates a situation potentially dangerous to persons or other property, and loss is a proximate risk of that danger.[33] These approaches are simply variations of the main theme of assessing the parties' contemplated objectives in light of the goals and policies of tort and contract law.[34]

[11.3] Pollution-Caused Economic Losses

Pollution claims present a unique difficulty because the main impact of the harm often affects public lands. In *Union Oil Co. v. Oppen*[35] vast quantities of raw crude oil were released when the defendant oil company negligently caused an oil spill. The oil was carried by wind, wave, and tidal currents over large stretches of the California coast disrupting, among other things, plaintiffs' commercial fishing operations. While conceding that ordinarily there is no recovery for economic losses unaccompanied by physical damage, for which the plaintiffs suffered none because they did not own or possess the public lands harmed by the spill, the court concluded that commercial fisherman were foreseeable plaintiffs whose interest the oil company had a duty to protect when conducting drilling operations.[36] Similarly, in *Pruitt v. Allied Chemical Corp.*[37] the court allowed a limited recovery for pure economic losses caused by the discharge of a toxic chemical (Kepone) into the James River, which in turn empties into Chesapeake Bay. The introduction of Kepone damaged the marine life in the Bay and imposed substantial economic hardship on those who derived their livelihood from the bay. The court permitted certain categories of claimants to recover their

---

[31] Russell v. Ford Motor Co., 575 P.2d 1383, 1387 (Or. 1978).

[32] Pennsylvania Glass Sand Corp. v. Caterpillar Tractor Co., 652 F.2d 1165, 1173 (3d Cir. 1981).

[33] Northern Power & Eng'g Co. v. Caterpillar Tractor Co., 623 P.2d 324, 329 (Alaska 1981); *contra* Aas v. Superior Court, 12 P.3d 1125, 1140 (Cal. 2000) (stating that "whether the economic loss rule applies depends on whether property damage has occurred rather than on the possible gravity of damages that have not yet occurred").

[34] Citizens Ins. Co. of Am. v. Proctor & Schwartz, Inc., 802 F. Supp. 133, 140 (W.D. Mich. 1992), *aff'd on other grounds*, 15 F.3d 558 (6th Cir. 1994) (per curiam).

[35] 501 F.2d 558 (9th Cir. 1974).

[36] *Id.* at 570.

[37] 523 F. Supp. 975 (E.D. Va. 1981).

economic losses, under negligence and nuisance theories, but denied relief to others.[38]

Pruitt focused on the foreseeability of loss to potentially injured parties, but some courts have given *Pruitt* a narrower construction, holding that recovery will be allowed when a plaintiff's business is based on the exercise of a public right.[39] Thus, when a plaintiff did not have the recognized, lawful right to use public land, recovery of economic loss will be denied.[40] Courts have exhibited a general wariness in extending the pollution caused loss cases outside their relatively narrow banks.[41]

[11.4] Modern Applications

The general rule precluding recovery of pure economic loss for negligence may not be applied in the area of professional malpractice,[42] or breach of fiduciary duty,[43] at least when the professional's work product is not tangible.[44]

---

[38] *Id.* at 980 (permitting recovery for commercial fisherman, owners of boat, tackle, and bait shops, and marinas notwithstanding lack of physical injury or privity with defendant, but denying recovery for those who only benefited indirectly from activities on the water, *e.g.*, seafood restaurants).

[39] Adams v. Star Enters., 51 F.3d 417, 424–25 (4th Cir. 1995) (rejecting claims of landowners for economic loss relating to the proximity of oil spill to their property); Santa Fe Partnership v. Arco Products Co., 54 Cal. Rptr. 2d 214, 224 (Cal. App. 1996) (collecting decisions discussing recovery of "stigma" damages); Section 91 (Natural Resource Damage).

[40] Golnoy Barge Co. V. M/T Shinoussa, 841 F. Supp. 783, 785 (S.D. Tex. 1993) (rejecting claims of non-licensed commercial fisherman).

[41] Channel Star Excursions, Inc. v. Sou. Pac. Trans. Co., 77 F.3d 1135, 1138 (9th Cir. 1996) (limiting *Union Oil Co. v. Oppen* to its facts and refusing to extend rationale of decision to maritime tort). In *East River S.S. Corp. v. Transamerica Delaval, Inc.*, 476 U.S. 858 (1986), the Court reaffirmed *Robins Dry Dock & Repair Co. v. Flint*, 275 U.S. 303 (1927), and applied the economic loss rule to cases in Admiralty notwithstanding the erosion of the rule through exceptions over the prior twenty years.

[42] CHARLES WOLFRAM, MODERN LEGAL ETHICS § 5.6.3, at 222 (1986) (recognizing recovery of economic loss caused by lawyer's malpractice). A few jurisdictions have reserved judgment on the issue. Danforth v. Acorn Structures, Inc., 608 A.2d 1194, 1201 n.5 (Del. 1992). The primary effect of this application is on claims by persons not in privity with the professional. If privity exists, the action may sound in contract and contractual limitations on liability and recovery are frequently prohibited by professional standards. ABA Model R. Prof. Conduct 1.8(h) (prohibiting lawyer from prospectively limiting the lawyer's liability to the client for malpractice unless permitted by law).

[43] JAY FEINMAN, ECONOMIC NEGLIGENCE: LIABILITY OF PROFESSIONALS AND BUSINESSES TO THIRD PARTIES FOR ECONOMIC LOSS 63 (1995).

[44] Fireman's Fund Ins. Co. v. SEC Donohue, Inc., 679 N.E.2d 1197, 1201 (Ill. 1997). Illinois treats legal malpractice as an exception to its general rule that there can be no recovery for pure economic loss in negligence. Collins v. Reynard, 607 N.E.2d 1185, 1186 (Ill. 1992) (treating legal malpractice as limited, special exception to *Moorman* [Moorman Mfg. Co. v. National Tank Co., 435 N.E.2d 443 (Ill. 1982)] doctrine that bars a plaintiff from recovering pure economic loss under theories of strict liability, negligence, and innocent misrepresentation). By the same token, not all jurisdictions limit the economic loss exception for professional malpractice to case when no tangible product is produced. Southland Constr., Inc. v. The Richeson Corp., 642 So. 2d 5, 8–9 (Fla. App. 1994) (permitting general contractor to sue

The economic loss rule has been applied in a number of cases outside the traditional area of simple negligence. In a number of jurisdictions, the doctrine has been applied to a broad array of tort-based claims[45] as a means of preserving the tort-contract distinction.[46]

The economic loss rule is usually not applied when the cause of the loss is deliberate and intentional rather than negligent misconduct.[47] The concept commonly invoked in these situations is the "independent tort" doctrine: a tort recovery will be permitted if the defendant's misconduct constitutes an independent tort even if it is committed in a bargain-related transaction.[48] There has been an effort to create an exception to the economic loss rule when the parties are in a "special relationship." There is some support for this exception,[49] but the courts have not been generous in recognizing this exception in the absence of a professional relationship (e.g., lawyer-client) or traditional fiduciary relationship.[50] When the remedy is provided by statute rather than by the common law, the plaintiff may recover his statutory remedies even though they would be considered "economic loss;" however, the economic loss rule may apply to damages not directly encompassed by the statute.[51]

---

professional engineering service corporation for economic losses caused by the latter's malpractice even though no privity of contract existed between parties). This is an area that is highly nuanced. See Amanda Esquibel, The Economic Loss Rule and Fiduciary Duty Claims: Nothing Stricter Than the Morals of the Marketplace, 42 Vill. L. Rev. 789, 802–834 (1997) (discussing Florida and Illinois decisions addressing the tort liability of holders of fiduciary duties for pure economic loss caused by their breach of duty).

[45] Compare NBD Bank v. Krueger Ringier, Inc., 686 N.E.2d 704 (Ill. App. 1997) (applying the economic loss doctrine to a buyer's action against a seller for sale of property contaminated by a leaking underground storage tank, which exposed the buyer to costs of remediation), with Laidlaw Waste Sys., Inc. v. Mallinckrodt, Inc., 925 F. Supp. 624, 635 (E.D. Mo. 1996) (rejecting the application of the economic loss doctrine in the context of hazardous waste contamination clean-up claims); Section 11.3 (Loss Resulting From Pollution).

[46] Daanen & Janssen, Inc. v. Cedarapids, Inc., 573 N.W.2d 842, 846 & 14 (Wis. 1998); Section 11.1 (Economic Loss Rule] Purpose and Scope of Rule).

[47] Nautilus Marine, Inc. v. Niemela, 989 F. Supp. 1229, 1232–33 (D. Alaska 1996) (collecting decisions and refusing to extend exception to all intentional torts without requiring defendant's awareness that his actions were wrongful on the ground that knowledge was essential to avoiding open-ended tort liability for failed bargains); Aikens v. Baltimore & Ohio R.R., Co., 501 A.2d 277, 279 (Pa. Super. Ct. 1985).

[48] The point is developed in Section 121.3 ([Fraud] Economic Loss Rule).

[49] See text and notes 42–44, supra.

[50] Taunus Corp. v. City of New York, 279 F. Supp.2d 305 (S.D.N.Y. 2003) (rejecting contention that "special relationship" existed between city and property owners near World Trade Towers destroyed by terrorist attack on September 11, 2001; therefore, owners could not recover for economic losses caused by city control of "frozen zone" around Trade Towers even if city acted negligently).

[51] McKay v. State, 10 Cal. Rptr. 2d 771 (Cal. App. 1992) (permitting recovery of lost profits caused by negligently set fire, even though fire did not damage property, because of Cal. Health & Safety Code § 13007 (1984). This, of course, assumes a private right of action to recover statutory remedies. Stallings v. Kennedy Elec. Inc., 710 So. 2d 195, 196 (Fla. App. 1998) (stating that the economic loss rule may not be used to abrogate statutory remedies); cf. Standard Fish Co., Ltd. v. 7337 Douglas Enters., Inc., 673 So. 2d 503, 504–05 (Fla. App. 1996) (applying economic loss rule to common law tort remedies and noting that the plaintiff had adequate contractual and statutory remedies).

§ 12   NON-ECONOMIC DAMAGES

[12.1]   General Principles

Non-economic damages include such items as pain and suffering, emotional distress, fear of injury, humiliation, inconvenience, loss of bodily members or functions, disfigurement, loss of consortium, loss of companionship, loss of freedom, loss of enjoyment of life, and hedonic damages for loss of the pleasures of life. Non-economic damages have a unique position in American law. They are recognized as a legitimate item of recovery in many cases; yet, the difficulty in establishing boundaries for non-economic damages has caused courts to treat such awards warily and, in some cases, to reject recovery of non-economic damages altogether due to measurement and confirmation concerns. As recently noted by one court: "[a]n emotional distress claim is necessarily amorphous, in both its origins and its effects."[1] While it would be incorrect to state that non-economic damages are disfavored, it is probably accurate to state that they are often viewed and treated with care by courts, primarily due to concerns over genuineness, reliability, and the specter of unlimited liability for trivial losses.[2] As noted in *Kuehn v. Children's Hosp., Los Angeles*:

> The problem, which delayed the recognition of the tort and has circumscribed its scope, is the lack of a logical stopping point. Tens of millions of Americans were shocked by the assassination of President Kennedy; should they have been allowed to join in a class action against the FBI, the CIA, and the Secret Service for negligence in failing to anticipate and neutralize the threat that Lee Harvey Oswald posed the President? Should every case of wrongful death give rise to a claim by the victim's immediate relatives? It is difficult to believe that the expense of determining damages in such cases and of screening out the inevitable phony cases would be justified by the incremental contribution to the deterrence of wrongful conduct; and these hypothetical cases that we have put are not ones in which an award of damages is necessary to restore the plaintiff to the standard of living he enjoyed before the tort.[3]

---

[1] Karen L. v. State Dep't Of Health & Social Serv., Div. of Family and Youth Serv., 953 P.2d 871, 876 (Alaska 1998).

[2] Restatement (Second) of Torts § 436A cmt. b (1965) (noting concerns that claims for emotional distress can be easily falsified); *see* Hernandez v. McDonald's Corp., 975 F. Supp. 1418, 1428 (D. Kan. 1997) (stating that purpose behind limitation on emotional distress claims is to guard against fraud and exaggeration); Payton v. Abbott Labs, 437 N.E.2d 171, 179 (Mass. 1982):

> Courts have been troubled for many years by the problem of how to deal with claims for damages for emotional distress. They have recognized that emotional distress can be both real and serious in some situations, while trivial, evanescent, feigned, or imagined in others. The various methods of treating such claims . . . have been attempts by the judicial system to formulate a means of separating the former from the latter.

[3] 119 F.3d 1296, 1298–99 (7th Cir. 1997).

The most significant limitation on non-economic damages was the traditional reluctance to award these damages, except for a limited category of torts when emotional distress was either (1) the direct and necessary consequence of the injury, such as pain and suffering resulting from bodily injury, or (2) when emotional distress was seen as closely aligned with the underlying tort, for example, assault.

While this traditional reluctance has abated, it has not disappeared. Courts have defined the task as that of identifying meritorious claims for recovery of non-economic damages, particularly emotional distress, in a cost effective manner. When emotional distress is ancillary or connected to economic damage, the objectiveness of the economic damages claim often assuages concerns over the potential for abuse presented by the non-economic damages claim. Nevertheless, this still leaves a large body of pure emotional distress claims, where the only claim of injury is emotional distress.

Reliability concerns have been seen by courts as being of lesser magnitude when the distress damages follow naturally and directly from certain types of wrongful conduct captured by the concept of the so-called dignity torts, such as libel, invasion of privacy, and intentional infliction of emotional distress.[4]

Reliability concerns have also been relaxed when the plaintiff is within a zone of danger created by the defendant's negligence and suffers only emotional distress as a result of the experience. For example, a plaintiff may be in a crosswalk with others when a negligently driven vehicle strikes another pedestrian but misses the plaintiff. Under these facts, a plaintiff may recover.[5] The "zone of danger" test was itself a qualification of the "physical impact" rule that demanded that the plaintiff suffer an impact or touching as a result of defendant's negligence as a condition to recovery of emotional distress damages.[6] The genesis of the physical impact rule was a desire for some guarantee of the genuineness of the claim, coupled with concern over unlimited, unbounded liability. Requiring a physical impact served as an independent corroboration of the actuality of injury, leaving only measurement concerns. As courts became both more confident of their ability to discern genuine claims independent of physical impact and more concerned about the arbitrariness to which the physical impact rule had descended,[7] courts reevaluated their willingness to adhere to the rule,[8]

---

[4] Hubbard v. United Press Int'l, 330 N.W.2d 428, 438 (Minn. 1983).

[5] Dillon v. Legg, 441 P.2d 912, 915 (Cal. 1968) (discussing development of "zone of danger" test). The court ultimately rejected the "zone of danger" exception to the physical impact rule in favor of abolishing the physical impact rule altogether and adopting a test based on foreseeability. See text and notes 13–20, infra.

[6] Mitchell v. Rochester Ry., 45 N.E. 354, 355 (N.Y. 1896). The impact need only be slight, but it had to be meaningful. Gregorio v. Zeluck, 678 A.2d 810 (Pa. Super. 1996) (holding that distress caused by unpleasant body odor did not satisfy impact requirement); cf. Oliver v. Keller, 289 F.3d 623 (9th Cir. 2002) (stating that to satisfy "physical injury" requirement of Prison Litigation Reform Act plaintiff prisoner need not show that the injury was significant but it must be more than de minmis).

[7] Porter v. Delaware, L&W R.R., 63 A 860 (N.J. 1906) (dust in the eye); Morton v. Stack, 170 N.E. 869 (Ohio 1930) (smoke inhalation).

particularly when some other objective indicator of the genuineness of injury existed. The "zone of danger" test fit this requirement because the plaintiff's proximity to the negligent events served as an independent means of gauging the "reasonableness" of plaintiff's response.[9]

A critical limitation in some jurisdictions on the zone of danger test is that the plaintiff recovers for his distress arising out of fear for his own safety, not for his distress for his fear for the safety of others. For example, in *Williams v. Baker*,[10] a mother brought her child to a hospital emergency room for treatment. The child was diagnosed as having a minor ailment and discharged. Later that evening, at home, the child lapsed into unconsciousness. The child was diagnosed as having a much more serious ailment than previously and incorrectly identified. The mother sued for her distress caused by her witnessing her child's suffering. The court denied her claim because while her suffering was real, she did not reasonably fear for her own safety as a result of the defendant's negligence; her distress was over her child's safety.[11] Some jurisdictions have permitted a plaintiff within the "zone of danger" to recover for the distress suffered when "others" are endangered, but these jurisdictions have usually limited the exception to immediate members of the family.[12]

A number of courts have found even the relative freedom from the physical impact role provided by the zone of danger test to be unduly constricting. The leading decision is *Dillon v. Legg*,[13] in which a child pedestrian was killed by a negligently driven vehicle. The child's mother and sister observed the accident. The mother was not in the zone of danger. The court held that to allow or deny recovery simply because of the fortuity that the plaintiff was geographically close or distant to the accident created arbitrary distinctions between plaintiffs who could recover and those who

---

[8] Battalla v. State, 176 N.E.2d 729, 730 (N.Y. 1961), *overruling Mitchell, supra*; Schultz v. Barberton Glass Co., 447 N.E.2d 109, 110 (Ohio 1983), *overruling Morton, supra*. The physical impact test is today followed in only a small minority of states. Eastern Airlines, Inc. v. King, 557 So. 2d 574, 576 (Fla. 1990); M.B.M. Co. v. Counce, 596 S.W.2d 681, 684, 686–87 (Ark. 1980). These jurisdictions appear to only apply the impact test when the action sounds solely in negligence. Williams v. Baker, 572 A.2d 1062, 1065 & n.1 (D.C. 1990).

[9] Bovsun v. Sanperi, 461 N.E.2d 843, 848 (N.Y. 1984); Stadler v. Cross, 295 N.W.2d 552, 554 (Minn. 1980).

[10] 572 A.2d 1062 (D.C. 1990).

[11] *Id.* at 1063, 1073.

[12] Hamilton v. Nestor, 659 N.W.2d 321, 329 (Neb. 2003) (recognizing claim for emotional distress damages by one in the zone of danger who perceived death of another even though no intimate or family relationship existed between the plaintiff and the decedent); *but cf.* Trombetta v. Conkling, 626 N.E.2d 653, 653–54 (N.Y. 1993) (court held that a niece who was in the zone of danger could not recover distress damages arising out of her witnessing her aunt's death). *See generally* Dale Joseph Gilsinger, Annot., *Recovery Under State Law for Negligent Infliction of Emotional Distress Due to Witnessing Injury to Another Where Bystander Plaintiff Must Suffer Physical Impact or be in Zone of Danger*, 89 A.L.R. 5th 255 (2001).

[13] 441 P.2d 912 (Cal. 1968). *See generally* Dale Joseph Gilsinger, Annot., *Recovery Under State Law for Negligent Infliction of Emotional Distress Under Rule of* Dillon v. Legg *or Refinements Thereof*, 96 A.L.R. 5th 107 (2002) (citations omitted).

could not.[14] Of course, the distinction was arbitrary only if the underlying premise (that the zone of danger test provided courts with confidence as to the reliability and genuineness of the emotional distress claim) was erroneous or underinclusive. The court bypassed that approach and allowed emotional distress claims arising out of negligent conduct whenever a person could reasonably foresee that emotional distress would be a probable consequence of negligent conduct. While the court suggested some constraints on an overly-expansive application of the test,[15] the *Dillon* test did not address the core concern of reliability. Rather, it acknowledges that any effort permitting recovery for negligent infliction of emotional distress would result necessarily in some arbitrariness, a failing that contributed to the test's retrenchment.[16]

A number of jurisdictions have followed *Dillon v. Legg* in adopting a reasonable foreseeability test for negligent infliction of emotional distress claims. Some jurisdictions have adopted the constrained form of the test articulated in *Thing v. La Chusa*, which limits the scope of the defendant's duty to others not to negligently inflict emotional distress.[17] Other jurisdictions have rejected all or some of the constraints adopted in *Thing v. La Chusa* in favor of a purer rule.[18] Most importantly, however, rejection of the physical impact or zone of danger tests changes the orientation of the distress claim. Under the reasonable foreseeability test, it is proper to award damages based on the plaintiff's distress arising out of danger to another,[19]

---

[14] 441 P.2d at 915; *see* Clohessy v. Bachelor, 675 A.2d 852 (Conn. 1996).

[15] The *Dillon* court suggested that whether emotional distress was reasonably foreseeable would often turn whether: (1) the plaintiff was near the scene of the injury; (2) the plaintiff actually observed the injury; and (3) the plaintiff and the victim were closely related. 441 P.2d at 920. The history of *Dillon* in California has been the efforts of successive courts to elevate and refine one or more of these "suggestions" into rules. *See* Thing v. La Chusa, 771 P.2d 814, 829–30 (Cal. 1989).

[16] *Thing, supra*, 771 P.2d at 828 (stating that "drawing arbitrary lines is unavoidable if we are to limit liability and establish meaningful rules for application by litigants and lower courts"); *see* Migliori v. Airborne Freight Corp., 690 N.E.2d 413, 416 (Mass. 1998) (noting that limits on the recovery of emotional distress in the bystander context "are based more on the pragmatic need to limit the scope of potential liability, than on grounds of fairness or other imperatives of corrective justice"). The court went on to hold that a rescuer could not recover distress damages even though his presence was foreseeable since "foreseeability is not the real issue." *Id.* at 418.

[17] 771 P.2d 814 (Cal. 1989); *see* Cameron v. Pepin, 610 A.2d 279, 284 (Me. 1992) (holding that a "defendant's duty should be limited to the emotional vulnerability that arises in parents upon actually witnessing their child receiving an injury"); Heldreth v. Marrs, 425 S.E.2d 157, 164, 169 (W. Va.1992) (following the approach of *Thing*).

[18] Beck v. Dep't Of Transp. & Pub. Facilities, 837 P.2d 105, 110 (Alaska 1992) (stating that court would use *Dillon* guidelines rather than *Thing* rules). *See generally* Annot., *Recovery Under Rule of* Dillon v. Legg, *supra*, 96 A.L.R. 5th 107.

[19] *Clohessy, supra*, 675 A.2d at 860–62 (stating that "the emotional harm following the perception of the death or serious injury to a loved one is just as foreseeable as the injury itself"; that "the interest in emotional stability . . . is sufficiently important to warrant this protection"; and that "the sight of a loved one being injured can result in an emotional injury that is no less foreseeable than that experienced as the fear of injury to oneself"). The court held that a plaintiff should be allowed to recover, within certain limitations, for emotional distress as a result of harm done to third party.

as opposed to the physical impact and zone of danger tests, which focus on the plaintiff's fear for his own safety.[20]

There are, thus, four general approaches developed in the current case law addressing the issue of non-economic damages in the form of negligently inflicted emotional distress. Approximately 5 or 6 jurisdictions follow the physical impact rule, limiting recoveries to cases where the distress is tied to a physical impact on the plaintiff.[21] Approximately 13 or 14 jurisdictions have adopted and retain the zone of danger test, which permits emotional distress recoveries without physical impact when a plaintiff, in the zone of danger, reasonably fears for her own safety.[22] The remaining jurisdictions have adopted some variation of the reasonable foreseeability test, which permits a plaintiff to recover for her emotional distress caused by injury to herself or to another.[23] The classification of jurisdictions by approach is complicated, however, by the fact that for certain types of matters, such as exposure to toxic substances, the jurisdiction may adopt an approach different from that otherwise used for the generic negligent infliction case, such as observing the death or serious injury of a loved one.

Separate from the above approaches is the physical harm or manifestation requirement.[24] This requires a showing of physical injury related to the emotional distress. The physical injury need not be bodily injury; rather, it must reflect some objectively ascertainable discomfort that evidences the genuineness of the claim.[25] In order to recover for negligently inflicted emotional distress, the distress must be "serious and verifiable."[26] The

---

[20] See text and notes 10–11, *supra* (discussing *Williams v. Baker*, 572 A.2d 1062 (D.C. 1990)).

[21] *Payton, supra*, 437 N.E.2d at 176 n.6 (listing 5 states adhering to physical impact rule); *Williams, supra*, 572 A.2d at 1066 n.11 (listing 6 jurisdictions following impact rule).

[22] Consolidated Rail Corp. v. Gottshall, 512 U.S. 532, 548 n.9 (1994) (listing 14 jurisdictions following the "zone of danger" test); *Clohessy, supra*, 675 A.2d at 858 n.9 (listing 13 jurisdictions adopting the "zone of danger" test).

[23] *Consolidated Rail Corp., supra*, 512 U.S. at 548, n.10 (noting that "[t]he courts of nearly half the states now allow bystanders outside the zone of danger to obtain recovery in certain circumstances for emotional distress brought on by witnessing the death or injury of [another]"; and listing jurisdictions adopting "reasonable foreseeability" test); *Clohessy, supra*, 675 A.2d at 862 n.11 (same).

[24] Boyles v. Kerr, 855 S.W.2d 593, 599 n.2 (Tex. 1993) (collecting decisions); *Payton, supra*, 437 N.E.2d at 174 (same).

[25] Meracle v. Children's Serv. Soc'y of Wis., 437 N.W.2d 532, 535 (Wis. 1989) (noting that "hysteria" satisfied requirement); *Payton, supra*, 437 N.E.2d at 181 (holding that "a plaintiff's physical harm must either cause or be caused by the emotional distress alleged, and . . . the physical harm must be manifested by objective symptomology and substantiated by expert medical testimony"); Vance v. Vance, 408 A.2d 728, 733 (Md. 1979) (holding that "a plaintiff can sustain an action for damages for nervous shock or injury caused without physical impact, by fright arising directly from defendant's negligent act or omission and resulting in some clearly apparent and substantial physical injury as manifested by an external condition or by symptoms clearly indicative of a resultant pathological, physiological, or mental state"), *quoting* Bowman v. Williams, 165 A. 182, 184 (Md. 1933).

[26] Jones v. Howard Univ., Inc., 589 A.2d 419, 424 (D.C. App. 1991); *see* Restatement (Second) of Torts § 436 A, cmt. c (1965):

physical harm requirement was of limited significance when the traditional physical impact rule was applied because the impact supplied the genuineness and reliability desired by courts. As the impact rule eroded, more courts have emphasized the physical harm requirement as an independent guarantor of the genuineness of the emotional distress claim.

Not all jurisdictions impose a physical harm requirement.[27] Occasionally, the facts surrounding the events leading to the emotional distress claim may appear to the court to demonstrate patently the genuineness of the claim. For example, in *La Fleur v. Mosher*[28] the court found that the negligent, unjustified incarceration of a 14 year old girl in a jail cell for 13 hours warranted an emotional distress recovery, even absent physical injury. The court found the nature of the plaintiff's confinement, coupled with the obvious deprivation of liberty, demonstrated the genuineness of the claim.[29]

In some cases, the physical harm requirement has been read so broadly as to effectively negate the requirement.[30] The physical harm requirement seeks an objective verification of the genuineness of the emotional distress claim. The requirement seeks to distinguish trivial from meaningful claims. In this regard, the presence of subcellular injury is not a manifestation or verification of emotional distress. If the subcellular argument is used, it reflects the intent to claim emotional distress damages as ancillary to bodily injury.[31]

There is an ongoing dispute in the law today over recovery of distress damages based on the "fear" that the plaintiff will sustain injury or aggravation of existing injury in the future. The claim ("fear of") should be distinguished from the feared event (the future occurrence of injury or aggravation of injury). The "fear of" claim is a present claim[32] for which

---

> The fact that [the different forms of emotional disturbance] are accompanied by transitory, non-recurring physical phenomena, harmless in themselves, such as dizziness, vomiting, and the like, does not make the actor liable where such phenomena are in themselves inconsequential and do not amount to any substantial bodily harm. On the other hand, long continued nausea or headaches may amount to physical illness, which is bodily harm; and even long continued mental disturbance, as for example in the case of repeated hysterical attacks, or mental aberration, may be classified by the courts as illness, notwithstanding their mental character. This becomes a medical or psychiatric problem, rather than one of law.

[27] Bass v. Nooney Co., 646 S.W.2d 765, 772 (Mo. 1983); Molien v. Kaiser Found. Hosps., 616 P.2d 813, 820 (Cal. 1980); Leong v. Takasaki, 520 P.2d 758, 762 (Haw. 1974).

[28] 325 N.W.2d 314 (Wis. 1982).

[29] *Id.* at 317–18; *cf.* Rowell v. Holt, 850 So. 2d 474 (Fla. 2003) (rejecting "impact rule" in case when defendant's legal malpractice resulted in unwarranted incarceration of client for over 10 days).

[30] Anderson v. W.R. Grace & Co., 628 F. Supp. 1219, 1226–27 (D. Mass. 1986) (treating subcellular, chromosomal harm as satisfying the physical harm requirement for recovering negligently inflicted emotional distress damages).

[31] Potter v. Firestone Tire & Rubber Co., 863 P.2d 795, 806–07 (Cal. 1993) (treating emotional distress claim resulting from exposure to toxic materials as a claim of loss ancillary or parasitic to the bodily injury caused by the exposure rather than a "fear of" case).

[32] Sections 9 (Future Losses), 10.4 ([Loss Causation] Future Losses).

the remedy is damages to compensate for that fear.[33] The fear may continue into the future, but it remains a present injury.[34]

In deciding "fear of" cases, courts have adopted a number of approaches. Most courts categorically distinguish between persons who are presently injured (and the feared event is derivative of that injury, *e.g.*, the person has an asbestos related ailment and fears contracting cancer in the future) (hybrid "fear of" cases) and persons who are presently injury free but have been exposed to an injurious agent (pure "fear of" cases).[35] A minority of courts permit pure "fear of" cases. These courts do not require that the "fear of" claim be connected with another present injury.[36] This issue is further confused by the tendency to construe gently the majority requirement of physical manifestation of injury.[37] The "fear of" cases have centered around toxic, AIDS, asbestos, radiation, etc., exposures. The fear of insidious, latent disease in these contexts may or may not be well founded; they are, however, everpresent. Courts have struggled to define an appropriate balance in this area.[38]

[12.2] Measuring Non-Economic Loss

The very nature of non-economic loss, particularly emotional distress and its variant pain and suffering, preclude the preferred common law approach of objective measure. Distress and pain are inherently subjective. "Those who do not feel pain seldom think that it is felt; people in distress never think you feel enough."[39] As noted in *McDougald v. Garber*:

> An economic loss can be compensated in kind by an economic gain,
> but recovery for non-economic losses such as pain and suffering and

---

[33] Section 72.4 (Medical Monitoring).

[34] *See* Section 9.2 (Future Damages).

[35] Norfolk & Western Ry. Co. v. Ayers, 538 U.S. 135 (2003) (construing Federal Employers Liability Act (FELA) and holding in a 5-4 decision that plaintiffs who had developed an asbestos-related disease (asbestosis) could maintain a "fear of developing cancer" claim; persons who had been exposed to asbestos, but were at present disease free, could not).

[36] Madrid v. Lincoln County Medical Center, 923 P.2d 1154 (N.M. 1996) (permitting "fear of" claim to proceed when plaintiff had possibly been exposed to HIV virus, but had not, as yet, sustained AIDS-related injury).

[37] Mauro v. Owens-Corning Fiberglass Corp., 561 A.2d 257 (N.J. 1989) (permitting "fear of" claim when plaintiff had been exposed to asbestos and equating exposure with physical manifestation of injury). *Id.* at 259 (finding injury based on "pleural" asbestosis, which is thickening of tissue caused by exposure to foreign substance). Tissue thickening is, however, a normal, natural response when the human body encounters a foreign substance.

[38] *See* Andrew R. Klein, *Fear of Disease and The Puzzle of Futures Cases in Tort*, 35 U.C.D. L. Rev. 965 (2002); Thomas A. Delaney, *Actual Exposure or Reasonableness? What Policy Issues Drive the Ongoing Debate Over What Standards Should Govern The Recovery of Emotional Distress Damages for Fear of Contracting Infectious Diseases*, 5 Hth. Law. 11 (August 2001); Kenneth W. Miller, *Toxic Torts and Emotional Distress: The Case For an Independent Cause of Action For Fear of Future Harm*, 40 Ariz. L. Rev. 681 (1998).

[39] Samuel Johnson (quoted in part in United States v. Pastor, 557 F.2d 930, 942 (2d Cir. 1977) (Van Graafeiland, Jr., concurring and dissenting)).

loss of enjoyment of life rests on the legal fiction that money damages can compensate for a victim's injury . . . . We accept this fiction, knowing that although money will neither ease the pain nor restore the victim's abilities, this device is as close as the law can come in its effort to right the wrong. We have no hope of evaluating what has been lost, but a monetary award may provide a measure of solace for the condition created . . . .[40]

Non-economic loss introduces competing forces into the damages calculation, which courts have difficulty constraining or reconciling. On the one hand, the subjective nature of the loss suggests that the decision maker should have wide discretion to fashion an award that accurately compensates. On the other hand, confirming unbridled discretion, particularly in an area where objectives measures are lacking, commits courts to a process that portends both uncertainty and unlimited liability. Balancing these concerns has not proven to be easy. For example, in the context of property whose objective economic value does not equate with their cultural worth, such as heirlooms, cherished mementos, and the like, courts have struggled to come up with a formula that reflects both concerns. The result has been to permit recovery based on "value to the owner" but to require exclusion of "sentimental value,"[41] without acknowledging that sentimental value is what gives the property special value to the owner.

Concerns over the genuineness of distress claims, particularly when unaccompanied by bodily injury, have encouraged courts to impose several requirements that condition recovery. First, is the general rejection of negligent infliction of distress as an independent tort. The distress claim must flow from a separate, independent cause of action.[42] Second, and more significant is the threshold requirement that the distress must be severe in the sense of substantial or enduring as opposed to trivial or transitory; thus, distress that consists of anxiety, worry, anger, etc. will ordinarily not be of a level sufficient to justify an award of damages.[43] Some courts require that the distress be "medically diagnosable" before an award of damages

---

[40] 536 N.E.2d 372, 374–75 (N.Y. 1989); Section 73 (Pain and Suffering).

[41] *See generally* Annot., *Valuation of Wearing Apparel or Household Goods Kept by Owner For Personal Use, in Action For Loss or Conversion of, or Injury to, Such Property*, 34 A.L.R. 3d 816, § 3 (1971) (collecting cases permitting owner to recover actual economic value of goods to owner with no allowance for sentimental value); Section 81 (Value to Owner).

[42] *See* Gilchrist v. Jim Slemons Imports, Inc., 803 F.2d 1488, 1499 (9th Cir. 1986), *citing* Molien v. Kaiser Found. Hosp., 616 P.2d 813, 819 (Cal. 1980); Section 12.3 (Infliction of Emotional Distress).

[43] *Gilchrist, supra*; Parkway Co. v. Woodruff, 901 S.W.2d 434, 444–45 (Tex. 1995); Twaite v. Allstate Ins. Co., 264 Cal. Rptr. 598, 608–09 (Cal. App. 1989). This is not to say that the standard will be consistently applied or scrupulously honored. *See* Burlington Coat Factory Warehouse of El Paso, Inc. v. Flores, 951 S.W.2d 542, 548 (Tex. Civ. App. 1997) (*citing Parkway Co., supra*, and holding that a $10,000 mental anguish award arising out of a wrongful discharge claim would be sustained based on the plaintiff's testimony that his wrongful discharge from employment caused him "despair" and led to the brief "split-up" of his marriage for a short period of time).

may be entertained.[44] This concern parallels and overlaps the "physical manifestation" requirement discussed in Section 12.1 (General Principles).

The desire is to compensate individuals who suffer "severe" emotional distress without opening courts to any and all individuals who feel they have been slighted, denigrated, or otherwise made to suffer distress at the hands of another. Some inconvenience and annoyance is deemed the inescapable and the uncompensable price one pays for living in modern society. The law provides redress only when distress rises to a level beyond that which a reasonable person should endure.[45] Supplementing general allegations of distress with supporting incidents, such as crying or fainting, has also been held to be insufficient.[46] Some courts have applied the trivial-severe distinction, without expressly tying it to the absence of physical manifestation of injury. It is, however, unclear in this context whether the courts are applying the distinction as a general constraint or simply as a comment on the nature of the particular claim.[47]

---

[44] Hamilton v. Nestor, 659 N.W.2d 321, 329 (Neb. 2003) ("[E]motional distress must have been so severe that no reasonable person could have been expected to endure it and . . . the emotional [distress] must be medically diagnosable and must be of sufficient severity that it is medically significant") (citations deleted; brackets added).

[45] In this context, the test is similar to that applied as a threshold in intentional infliction cases, Howell v. New York Post Co., 612 N.E.2d 699, 702 (N.Y. 1993); Restatement (Second) of Torts § 46 (1977), but it is not as rigorously enforced.

[46] Matczak v. Frankford Candy & Chocolate Co., 136 F.3d 933, 940 (3d Cir. 1997) (holding that while crying may manifest distress, it does not rise to the level of bodily harm required to support an emotional distress recovery); Roark v. Kidder, Peabody & Co., Inc., 959 F. Supp. 379, 388 (N.D. Tex. 1997) (crying alone is not a sufficient response; fact that plaintiff also fainted is also insufficient given plaintiff's history of fainting). *But cf.* Avitia v. Metropolitan Club of Chicago, Inc., 49 F.3d 1219, 1229 (7th Cir. 1995) (reducing $21,000 damage to $10,500 because award is too much for the momentary "pang of distress at being fired, even distress enough to make a grown man cry . . .").

[47] Tabieros v. Clark Equip. Co., 944 P.2d 1279, 1305–06 (Haw. 1997) (holding that bystander girlfriend of injured victim could not state claim for negligent infliction of emotional distress because she did not show she sustained "serious emotional distress"). The court stated:

> In the case before us, just as the circuit court was not free to speculate regarding whether Wilson actually experienced pleasant relief that her companion had not died in the industrial accident, neither was it licensed to guess that Wilson had suffered serious and disabling mental anguish by virtue of her intimate companion's tragic injury. Reviewing the evidence produced at trial regarding the degree of Wilson's actual emotional distress, we agree with the circuit court that the plaintiffs failed to furnish any evidence of greater mental stress than transient "concern," "worry," and "upset." We therefore hold that no reasonable jury, considering this evidence, could have found that Wilson suffered "serious emotional distress," as that term has been construed in our case law.

Id. at 1306; Lawson v. Salt Lake Trappers, Inc., 901 P.2d 1013, 1016 (Utah 1995) (plaintiff must experience severe and not trivial distress); Boyles v. Kerr, 855 S.W.2d 593, 595 (Tex. 1993) (noting uncertainty whether negligent infliction of distress recovery was preconditioned on minimum threshold of distress and suggesting preferred approach was to commit the issue to the jury).

Although the decisions are split, many courts permit the plaintiff to establish the emotional distress claim by his own testimony.[48] The absence of corroboration feeds, however, judicial distrust of non-economic claims and, on occasion, the deficiency will prove dispositive and lead to the rejection of the emotional distress claim.[49] To the contrary, a few courts have suggested, or held, that any emotional distress is recoverable.[50] In each of these latter cases, however, there has been independent grounds to establish the genuineness of the distress claim; namely, substantial economic damages, which tended to validate the claim.[51]

Even if distress is severe and substantial, public policy considerations may preclude an award. For example, most courts have rejected, on public policy grounds, recovery of damages based on the distress of being sued,[52] unless the plaintiff is a victim of malicious prosecution.[53]

[12.2.1]   Excessiveness

Although the subjectiveness of non-economic losses presents the potential of both inadequate and excessive awards, the concern has been over the latter. The fear is that sympathy for the victim is more likely to exist and

---

[48] Alston v. King, 231 F.3d 383, 388–89 (7th Cir. 2000) (stating that "[w]hen the injured party provides the only evidence of emotional distress, he must reasonably and sufficiently explain the circumstances of the injury rather than relying on mere conclusory statements").

[49] Hitt v. Connell, 301 F.3d 240, 251 (5th Cir. 2002) (holding that plaintiff's uncorroborated testimony regarding his distress over his retaliatory dismissal from employment was insufficient to permit any award of distress damages); Section 12.2.3 (Quality of the Evidence).

[50] Gruenberg v. Aetna Ins. Co., 510 P.2d 1032, 1041–42 (Cal. 1973) (rejecting contention that distress must be limited to cases of outrageous conduct or that distress must be severe or of long duration; those requirements were applicable to intentional infliction claims). *Compare* Hetzel v. County of Prince William, 89 F.3d 169, 171 (4th Cir.), *cert. denied*, 519 U.S. 1029 (1996) (noting that plaintiff's general allegations of distress, lack of corroboration, and no observable injuries or ailments required rejection of his emotional distress claims), *with* Allabashi v. Lincoln Nat'l Sales Corp. of Colorado-Wyoming, 824 P.2d 1, 4 (Colo. App. 1991) (finding that emotional distress award was supported by evidence that plaintiff's behavior changed and that plaintiff "cried often, suffered sleeplessness, and experienced a loss of self-esteem").

[51] Clayton v. United Services Automobile Assn., 63 Cal. Rptr. 2d 419, 420–21 (Cal. App. 1997) (holding that once the plaintiff in an insurance bad faith case proves "some economic loss as a means of validating the seriousness of his or her emotional distress," the plaintiff is entitled to recover for all emotional distress proximately caused). The court rejected a requirement that the distress directly flow from the failure to pay the insurance proceeds or that distress be "severe, substantial, or enduring" before it is compensable. *Id.* at 421; *see* Leslie Benton Sandor & Carol Berry, *Recovery For Negligent Infliction of Emotional Distress Attendant to Economic Loss: A Reassessment*, 37 Ariz. L. Rev. 1247 (1995).

[52] Knussman v. Maryland, 272 F.3d 625, 642 (4th Cir. 2001) ("Generally speaking, litigation induced stress is never a compensable element of damages"); Picogna v. Board of Educ. of Township of Cherry Hill, 143 N.J. 391, 671 A.2d 1035, 1037–38 (N.J. Super. Ct. 1996) (holding that "litigation-induced stress" is not recoverable when defendant's conduct forced plaintiff to invoke court's assistance to vindicate legal rights).

[53] Section 112 (Litigation Torts).

thereby inflate awards than sympathy for the defendant will deflate awards.[54]

There is no bright line of demarcation that separates a reasonable award from an excessive award. The amount of the award is no doubt significant, but it forms no express component of the standard used to evaluate awards for excessiveness.[55] The general standard is that an award is not excessive "if it is within reasonable limits and there is any evidence in the record to sustain it."[56] This test is often stated as a "shocks the court's conscience" test.[57]

What shocks one court's conscience will not necessarily shock another. Excessiveness is inherently a subjective determination, containing a large degree of arbitrariness.[58] The most common way to attempt to smooth the differences subjectivity engenders is to compare awards entered in similar

---

[54] Occasionally, courts find that non-economic damages are inadequate but the finding is usually coupled to a finding that related economic damages are inadequate. *E.g.*, Doughty v. Ins. Co. of N. Am., 701 So. 2d 1225, 1228 (Fla. App. 1997) (holding that award of $8,000 for future medical expenses and for future pain and suffering to 9 year old who suffered permanent damage to her knee was inadequate). In some cases the court finds the verdict to be simply wrong. Foster v. Pyner, 545 N.W.2d 584, 587 (Iowa App. 1996) (holding that failure to award future pain and suffering damages to child permanently and conspicuously scarred was reversible error). *But see* Doe v. United States, 976 F.2d 1071, 1085–87 (7th Cir. 1992), *cert. denied*, 510 U.S. 812 (1993) (finding no reversible error in trial court's refusal to award future distress damages to 3 year old sexual abuse victim who suffered "night terrors" and obsessive conduct after the attacks. The court found that plaintiff had failed to establish a sufficient causal relationship between the abuse and the subsequently manifested distress).

[55] Generous awards have been upheld. Havinga v. Crowley Towing & Transp., 24 F.3d 1480, 1486–88 (1st Cir. 1994) (affirming $1.4 million award of non-economic damages to 5 crewmen who faced near-death experience, but survived); Molaison v. Denny's Inc., 592 So. 2d 916, 920 (La. App. 1991) (affirming award of $50,000 in distress damages to plaintiff who ate one or more worms in a salad); Young v. Bank of America, 190 Cal. Rptr. 122, 127 (Cal. App. 1983) (affirming $50,000 distress damages award to plaintiff who was humiliated and became afraid to shop after defendant negligently informed store that her credit was bad).

[56] Gerth v. American Star Ins. Co., 480 N.W.2d 836, 840–41 (Wis. App. 1992) (affirming award of $300,000 to severe burn patient who lived for 12 days with his injuries before he died).

[57] Moore v. Freeman, 355 F.3d 558, 564 (6th Cir. 2004); *Havinga, supra*, 24 F.3d at 1487; Knight v. Long Island College Hosp., 482 N.Y.S.2d 503 (App. Dept. 1984).

[58] Matthews v. Turner, 566 So. 2d 133, 135 (La. 1990) (considering distress claim from time of misdiagnosis of appendicitis until approximately 48 hours later when patient died). The court stated:

> We are mindful that this reduction is to a degree arbitrary; however, we find $50,000.00 to be the most that could have been awarded for the type of pain and suffering endured by Sabrina for nearly 48 hours. While we are not totally convinced that the reduced amount is appropriate, we are firmly of the opinion that the $200,000.00 awarded for Sabrina's pain and suffering was excessive and should be lowered.

See Kogan v. Dreifuss, 571 N.Y.S.2d 314, 316 (App. Dept. 1991) (finding that award of $1.05 million for distress between time of parent's call to pediatrician reporting child's worsening condition and time 50 hours later when child lapsed into coma was excessive and would be reduced to $350,000).

cases.[59] This, however, is a test for the court of review not the trier of fact.[60] The selected "comparable" cases may be an unsystematic and biased sample of relevant materials.[61] In *Geressy*[62] the court, nevertheless, suggested that if "comparable" awards could be collected, they should be subjected to statistical analysis to determine a range of reasonable verdicts.[63] The court went on to suggest that "[u]sing two standard deviations to define the group of values that constitute reasonable compensation supports the judiciary's efforts to sustain jury verdicts whenever reasonably possible."[64]

While the approach is attractive in its intimations of concreteness and objectivity, care must be exercised before it is adopted for its limitations are manifest.[65] Use of standard deviation simply informs us of the likelihood that a particular event falls within a certain range; it is not by itself evidence of the reasonableness of the event itself. It is no more appropriate to declare awards outside two standard deviations as unreasonable than it would be to say that grades of A or F are unreasonable or that too many As and Fs were awarded. Based on calculation of deviation, we may question whether a particular result was consistent or inconsistent with chance, but we cannot use statistics to prove the underlying fact, *i.e.*, the verdict or the grade's reasonableness. A verdict that lies outside two or three standard deviations may excite our attention simply because it is extreme insofar as the other comparable verdicts are concerned. That verdict remains, however, within the universe of possible, expected verdicts

---

[59] *Matthews, supra*, 566 So. 2d at 135 (comparing award with other awards to determine reasonable range but also noting that "[c]ourts cannot . . . mechanically adhere to prior quantum verdicts"); Gutierrez-Rodriquez v. Cartagena, 882 F.2d 553, 579–80) (1st Cir. 1989) (fact that award is "somewhat out of line with other cases of a similar nature" will not warrant overturning the verdict).

[60] Precopio v. City of Detroit, Dep't of Transp., 330 N.W.2d 802, 809 (Mich. 1982) (holding that comparison should be made at post-trial or appellate stage; fact finder should determine each case on its own merits). *See generally* D.C. Barrett, Annot., *Propriety and Prejudicial Effect of Reference By Counsel in Civil Case to Amount of Verdict in Similar Cases*, 15 A.L.R.3d 1144 (1968). The English rule is different with, apparently, no ill affects. Charles D. Cole, Jr., *Charging the Jury on Damages in Personal Injury Cases: How New York Can Benefit From English Practice*, 31 Syracuse J. Int'l L. & Comm. 1 (2004) (discussing English practice of informing juries of comparable awards to guide discretion in awarding damages).

[61] Geressy v. Digital Equip. Corp., 980 F. Supp. 640 (E.D.N.Y. 1997):

> In determining whether an award is reasonable, it is almost impossible to find cases for comparison where all relevant factors are identical to those in the case under consideration. Rather, the court must review the totality of the circumstances of the proffered sample cases to ascertain whether they can provide a basis for comparison. There are almost no "all fours" cases. As Appendix A indicates the decisions on comparability are somewhat arbitrary. The court's evaluation may be supplemented by expert testimony of practitioners and others familiar with state tort cases.

Id. at 657.

[62] *Supra*, 980 F. Supp. 640.

[63] *Id.* at 657–58.

[64] *Id.* at 658.

[65] *Id.* at 660 (noting that "[s]tatistical analysis alone can never be controlling. The court must always exercise independent discretion in its review of statistics").

and its reasonableness is a product of itself, not its likelihood of occurrence, which is all standard deviation measures. In other words, if a verdict is three standard deviations, all that means is that there is a 1% chance of that verdict being rendered. Chance in this sense is no indication of reasonableness. Statistical analysis tells us that we would expect in the normal course of events—a verdict of this size, 1% of the time.

As award for distress damages may be evaluated for excessiveness by comparing it with other components of the total award of damages to the plaintiff. For example, jurisdictions have divided on the issue whether a distress damages claim and a punitive damages claim are duplicative.[66] In a jurisdiction that treated the awards as duplicative, the issue of excessiveness should be addressed by aggregating the two awards.

[12.2.2] Discretion of the Decision Maker

Because the quantification of non-economic damages is a subjective decision, courts generally afford substantial discretion to the decision maker's evaluation of the evidence. Courts have, however, policed the process by which decision makers, particularly jurors, are encouraged by counsel to construe the evidence favorably toward counsel's client.

One method is the so-called "Golden Rule" argument. This approach asks the jurors to put themselves in the plaintiff's shoes or position and award a sum for non-economic damages they, the jurors, would like to receive if their injuries were the same as the plaintiff's injuries. Courts have uniformly concluded that such an argument is improper because it encourages jurors to decide cases based on bias, sympathy, and personal interest rather than on the evidence.[67] While the Golden Rule argument is normally made by the plaintiff, it is inappropriate for the defendant to raise the same argument to limit damages.[68]

Another form of argument used to influence jury calculation of the plaintiff's non-economic losses is the "per diem" argument. This tactic has received mixed reviews from the courts.[69] The essence of the per diem

---

[66] Tudor v. Charleston Area Medical Center, 506 S.E.2d 554, 572–76 (W. Va. 1997) (discussing issue and collecting decisions).

[67] Goutis v. Express Transp., Inc., Div. of F.V. Miranda, Inc., 699 So. 2d 757, 760 (Fla. App. 1997); Rodriguez v. Slattery, 194 N.W.2d 817, 819 (Wis. 1972) (holding that it was improper for counsel to ask jurors to consider "[I]f it was your seven-year old" in assessing damages); see Rojas v. Richardson, 703 F.2d 186, 191 (5th Cir. 1983); Waite v. Neal, 918 F. Supp. 133, 134 (E.D. Pa. 1996); Yerrick v. East Ohio Gas Co., 198 N.E.2d 472, 475 (Ohio App. 1964); Edward McCaffery, *Framing the Jury: Cognitive Perspectives on Pain and Suffering Awards*, 81 Va. L. Rev. 1341, 1384–85 (1995) (collecting arguments raised against the use of the Golden Rule argument); cf. Neal Feigenson, *Sympathy and Legal Judgment: A Psychological Analysis*, 65 Tenn. L. Rev. 1, 4-23 (1997) (discussing law's disapproval of decision making based on sympathy for the litigant). See generally Kevin Brown, Annot., *Propriety and Prejudicial Effect of Attorney's "Golden Rule" Argument to Jury in Federal Civil Cases*, 68 A.L.R. Fed. 333 (1984).

[68] Begley v. Kohl & Madden Printing Ink Co., 254 A.2d 907, 911 (Conn. 1969); see Adkins v. Aluminum Co. of Am., 750 P.2d 1257, 1265, *as clarified*, 756 P.2d 142 (Wash. 1988) (holding that it is improper for defendant to invoke the Golden Rule argument).

[69] Waldron v. Hardwick, 406 F.2d 86, 89 (7th Cir. 1969) (noting sharp split in authorities

argument is the attempt to quantify in everyday terms a quantum of non-economic loss: how much is the suffering for an hour or a day worth? Per diem arguments ask the jury to quantify non economic losses by affixing an amount of damages to the unit of time selected, *e.g.*, day or hour, and then multiply that amount by the number of units that the plaintiff will experience or has experienced, *e.g.*, days or hours of distress or pain. Thus, one minute of distress, measured as worth $1, becomes $60/hr., $1440/da.; $43,200/mo.; and $518,400/yr.

The position against permitting per diem argument rests on several arguments. First, there is no evidentiary basis in the record to support the transformation of non-economic losses into the unit of time allocation. Second, the per diem argument misdirects the jury into rendering excessive awards because it fails to consider the multiplier effect of the formula. Third, the per diem argument is simply a variant of the also forbidden attorney suggestion of the total amount of non-economic damages the jury should award, the "lump sum" argument.[70]

The justifications offered in favor of per diem arguments are essentially the converse of the opposition arguments. First, the jury should be given some reasonable and practical guidelines by which non-economic damages may be calculated. The decision should not be made in the abstract or by blind guess. Second, the contention that the per diem argument is not based on record evidence ignores the fact that the jury may ultimately make a calculation based on the same process counsel is barred from suggesting. Per diem arguments do no more than suggest an approach, which the jury may accept, reject, or apply with modifications, as an aid to making a reasonable estimate of an imprecise loss. Third, the dangers of per diem arguments are exaggerated because they are subject to rebuttal by opposing counsel and oversight by the trial judge.[71] It appears that a majority of the courts have accepted these reasons and permit per diem arguments, albeit with varying degrees of judicial control, such as cautionary instructions.[72] The use of per diem arguments may lead to some unintended consequences.[73]

---

regarding propriety of argument); Botta v. Brunner, 138 A.2d 713, 723–24 (N.J. 1958) (disapproving use of "per diem" arguments). *See generally* James Pearson, Jr., *Per Diem or Similar Mathematical Basis for Fixing Damages For Pain and Suffering*, 3 A.L.R. 4th 940 (1981).

[70] Debus v. Grand Union Stores of Vt., 621 A.2d 1288, 1291 (Vt. 1993); Affett v. Milwaukee & Suburban Transp. Corp., 106 N.W.2d 274, 278 (Wis. 1960), Ratner v. Arrington, 111 So. 2d 82, 88 (Fla. App. 1959).

[71] *Id.*

[72] *Compare Debus, supra*, 621 A.2d at 1290 (rejecting mandatory cautionary instruction in favor of case by case approach), *with* Weeks v. Holsclaw, 295 S.E.2d 596, 600 (N.C. 1982) (cautionary instruction is mandatory whenever per diem argument is presented to the jury) and Eastern Shore P.S.C. v. Corbett, 177 A.2d 701, 711 (Md. 1962) (suggesting that cautionary instruction should be given when requested by counsel).

[73] Future non-economic damages, such as pain and suffering are usually not discounted to present value owing to the inherent subjectivity of the calculation. In *Abernathy v. Superior Hardwoods, Inc.*, 704 F.2d 963 (7th Cir. 1983), the award of future pain and suffering damages

A third method is restricting the use of so-called "lump sum" arguments by which counsel suggests to the jury an amount counsel contends would appropriately compensate the plaintiff for her non-economic losses. The arguments in favor and against this approach largely parallel those made in connection with per diem arguments, although this has not prevented courts from taking inconsistent positions on the two approaches.[74]

Jurors may have no real appreciation as to the valuation of non-economic losses, and no objective measure for their calculation. In this context, jurors may be particularly susceptible to having their estimates influenced by counsel's lump sum requests. Cognitive psychologists refer to this as anchoring. Individuals make estimates by starting at an initial anchor position, which they adjust marginally to reach a final position. To the extent counsel can influence the initial anchor position, counsel can significantly influence the final position reached.[75] One study involving real estate brokers showed that their estimate of the properties appraised value was significantly influenced by the hypothetical listing price of the property.[76] A similar phenomena is observed in negotiation when extreme positions tend to produce on average better results than moderate positions.[77]

Because both sides have the ability to suggest an "anchor position" if the "lump sum" argument is allowed, the danger that jurors would be unfairly influenced by a unilateral argument is largely dissipated. Most jurisdictions appear to permit "lump sum" arguments.[78]

---

was discounted to present value. The court emphasized plaintiff counsel's use of the per diem argument and its apparent impact on the jury award. Having used an objective measure of the subjective, counsel was saddled by the court with the consequences of that approach, *i.e.*, if counsel wants the jury to award plaintiff $15 for an hour's suffering 40 years from the date of trial, the jury should award the present discounted value of that amount ($6.79, using a 2% discount interest rate). The court made the calculation and issued a remittitur.

[74] *Weeks, supra*, 295 S.E.2d at 600 (collecting decisions); *cf.* Bleau v. Ward, 603 A.2d 1147, 1150–51 (Conn. 1992) (rejecting contention that allowance of lump sum argument unfairly prejudices defense because it forces defendant to offer an opinion on damages while defendant is contesting liability).

[75] Amos Tversky & Daniel Kahneman, *Judgment Under Uncertainty: Heuristics and Biases*, 185 Science 1124, 1128–30 (1974).

[76] Max Bazerman & Margaret Neale, Negotiating Rationally 26–28 (1992) (noting that "[t]he listing price had a major impact on their valuation process; they were more likely to have high estimates on all four prices when the listing price was high than when it was low") (*discussed in* Russell Korobkin & Chris Guthrie, *Psychological Barriers to Litigation Settlement: An Experimental Approach*, 93 Mich. L. Rev. 107, 139 (1994)).

[77] Russell Korobkin & Chris Guthrie, *Opening Offers and Out of Court Settlement: A Little Moderation May Not Go a Long Way*, 10 Ohio St. J. Disp. Resol. 1, 4 (1994) (noting that "[b]oth empirical and experimental studies . . . have concluded that a litigant is likely to achieve a more advantageous settlement if he opens negotiations with an extreme, rather than a moderate, settlement offer") (footnotes omitted).

[78] *See generally* L.S. Groff, Annot., *Propriety and Prejudicial Effect of Reference by Plaintiff's Counsel, in Jury Trial of Personal Injuries or Death Action, to Amount of Damages Claimed or Expected by His Client*, 14 A.L.R.3d 541, § 2[a] (1968).

The role of rationality in decision making is under sustained study. Many, but not all, scholars have criticized assumptions that humans are inherently rational; rather, the emerging view appears to be that human decision making is frequently subject to erroneous assumptions that lead to inaccurate conclusions. As this subject is more fully explored in the literature[79] one expects that lawyers will seek to exploit, on their client's behalf, any cognitive biases individual or group decision makers possess.

[12.2.3] Quality of Evidence

Distress damages, particularly when bodily injury is absent, are often seen as (1) susceptible to fictitious and trivial claims; and (2) a legal intrusion into matters more the concern of social etiquette than legal redress.[80] For these reasons, and to abate these concerns, the quality of proof is often a significant factor. There is, however, no consensus as to when a non-economic damages claim is trivial as opposed to substantial; therefore, the approaches to the problem tend to be somewhat idiosynchratic.

A number of courts have suggested that a plaintiff's failure to document and treat for distress damages suggests that they are unsubstantial.[81] On the other hand, documentation may be evidence of falsification under the theory that the average person would not think to document his distress for use at trial.

Some courts have expressed the view that caution should be exercised when the distress claim is based solely on the plaintiff's testimony.[82] Other courts have held that the plaintiff's testimony is sufficient,[83] although the most common statement is to require corroboration[84] or require that the plaintiff's testimony be reasonable and sufficient.[85]

---

[79] Two recent papers that provide an overview of the scholarship in the field include: Russell B. Korobkin & Thomas S. Ulen, *Law and Behavioral Science: Removing the Rationality Assumption From Law & Economics*, 88 Cal. L. Rev. 1051 (2000), and Daniel Kahneman, *Maps of Bounded Rationality: Psychology for Behavior Economics*, 93 Am. Econ. Rev. 1449 (2003).

[80] Price v. City of Charlotte, N.C., 93 F.3d 1241, 1250–51 (4th Cir. 1996), *cert. denied*, 520 U.S. 1116 (1997).

[81] Dunn v. Medina Gen. Hosp., 917 F. Supp. 1185, 1194 (N.D. Ohio 1996) (intentional infliction of distress case); *see Price, supra*, 93 F.3d at 1254 (noting decisions treating, as a factor, the failure of the plaintiff to seek or obtain medical treatment as undermining the distress damages claim); Smith v. Hoyer, 697 P.2d 761, 764 (Colo. App. 1984) (stating that the plaintiff's failure to consult a physician or other professional does not preclude an award of damages).

[82] *Price, supra*, 93 F.3d at 1250.

[83] Gant v. Dumas Glass & Mirror, Inc., 935 S.W.2d 202, 209 (Tex. Civ. App. 1996) (stating that plaintiff's distress damages testimony "if not refuted, cannot be disregarded").

[84] Smith v. Norwest Financial Acceptance, Inc., 129 F.3d 1408, 1416–17 (10th Cir. 1997) (specifically noting presence of corroboration as reasons for not following decisions in which non-economic damages awards had been reduced); Page v. Columbia National Resources, Inc., 480 S.E.2d 817, 835 (W. Va. 1996) (holding that plaintiff's testimony, along with supporting testimony of plaintiff's husband and several others, was sufficient to support award of non-economic damages).

[85] Alston v. King, 231 F.3d 383, 388–89 (7th Cir. 2000) (*discussed* in Section 12.2 (Measuring Non-Economic Loss), text and notes 48–49 *supra*); Section 10.3 ([Loss Causation] Torts), text and notes 29–34, *supra* (discussing sufficiency of lay testimony to establish injury causation).

Most courts have not required that the plaintiff's non-economic damages be supported by expert testimony.[86] Occasionally a decision is rendered that suggests such a requirement,[87] but such decisions reflect the inadequacy of the plaintiff's testimony or the absence of corroboration, or both, more than the imposition of a mandatory requirement. On the other hand, the use of expert testimony is common in presenting the non-economics damages case to the trier-of-fact.[88] Although each case must be decided on its own merits, in general qualified experts may testify as to plaintiff's emotional distress, particularly when the expert has treated the plaintiff, so long as the testimony is necessary to assist the trier-of-fact in understanding matters not within their common knowledge or experience.

[12.2.4] Pre-Impact Fear of Death

Pre-impact distress claims are of relatively recent vintage. They involve cases where the victim is placed in a situation of imminent peril. The distinction is between pre-impact fear and post-impact pain and suffering or death. Courts have split whether they should distinguish between pre-impact and post-impact injury. The distinction was identified in *Montgomery Cablevision Limited Partnership v. Beynon*[89] as follows:

> [P]re-impact fright, mental distress caused by expectation or anticipation of impending doom, is an entirely different phenomenon from post-impact mental suffering or emotional distress. The latter results from and exacerbates bodily injuries sustained upon impact, *e.g.*, concern about the extent of recovery and the length of the recovery period; worry over the effect of the injuries and the duration of the recovery period on the victim's finances; and, if there is not a complete recovery, the loss of happiness or enjoyment of life suffered by one who has been rendered unable to do at all or do with the same degree of facility those things that formerly produced pleasure. All of those forms of mental distress are as much the natural, proximate, and foreseeable result of tortious conduct as bodily injury and physical pain. Pre-impact fright engendered by recognition of danger, however, does not result from bodily injuries and is compensable only to the extent that it causes or results in demonstrable or objectively determinable injury.[90]

---

[86] *See* Bolden v. Southeastern Penn. Transp. Authority, 21 F.3d 29, 34 n.3 (3d Cir. 1994) (collecting decisions).

[87] Patterson v. P.H.P. Healthcare Corp., 90 F.3d 927, 940 (5th Cir. 1996).

[88] Hurley v. Atlanta City Police Dept., 174 F.3d 95, 112–13 (3d Cir. 1999), *cert. denied*, 528 U.S. 1074 (2000).

[89] 696 A.2d 491 (Md. Ct. Sp. App. 1997), *rev'd*, 718 A.2d 1161 (Md. 1998). The Court of Special Appeals rejected the claim for pre-impact distress damages, but the Court of Appeals reversed and held that they may be awarded.

[90] 696 A.2d at 503. *But see* Haley v. Pan American World Airways, 746 F.2d 311, 314–15 (5th Cir. 1984) (rejecting distinction). *See* Brereton v. United States, 973 F. Supp. 752, 757 (E.D.Mich. 1997); Section 75.1 (Survival Actions).

While the decisional law is not uniform, many courts have permitted the award of pre-impact fear of death distress damages without requiring prior physical injury.[91] The more difficult issue in these cases is demonstrating that, in fact, the victim suffered pre-impact distress before his death. Courts have occasionally imposed significant proof hurdles before recovery. For example, in *Shatkin v. McDonnell Douglas Corp.*[92] the airplane lost an engine on the left side during takeoff. The plane rolled to its left and crashed nose-first into the ground. The entire event lasted approximately 30 seconds from the loss of the engine until impact. There were no survivors. The court rejected pre-impact distress claims because the court believed the evidence was insufficient to demonstrate an awareness on the part of the plaintiff of his imminent death or injury.[93] Courts have, however, permitted, as sufficient proof of awareness of imminent death or injury, evidence of skid marks before a fatal collision with another vehicle.[94]

When pre-impact claims are recognized, the awards have been quite substantial. For example, in one case the jury awarded $15,000 for 4–6 seconds of pre-impact distress.[95]

Courts do not appear to require death as a condition to recovering fear of impending death damages.[96] That said, there are few reported decisions valuing such claims.[97] The difficult issue raised here is whether and how

---

[91] Shu-Tao Lin v. McDonnell Douglas Corp., 742 F.2d 45, 53 (2d Cir. 1984) (recovery for aircrash decedent's pre-impact fear); Chapple v. Gangar, 851 F. Supp. 1481, 1487 (E.D. Wash. 1994) (awarding pre-impact mental distress damages in auto accident case); Livingston v. United States, 817 F. Supp. 601, 605 (E.D.N.C. 1993) (holding that victim who more likely than not "knew that he was faced with imminent bodily injury before impact" could recover pre-impact fear damages); Larsen v. Delta Air Lines, Inc., 692 F. Supp. 714, 721 (S.D. Tex. 1988) (stating that damages for decedent's pre-impact fear are recoverable).

[92] 727 F.2d 202 (2d Cir. 1984)

[93] *Id.* at 206–07 (noting that as far as the record was concerned "Shatkin could have dozed off in his seat" during the entire event). A number of cases have involved international flights governed by the Warsaw Convention. *See* Jack v. Trans World Airlines, Inc., 854 F. Supp. 654, 665 (N.D. Cal. 1994) (discussing various approaches to recovery of fear of death distress damages).

[94] Montgomery Cablevision Ltd. Partnership, *supra*, 718 A.2d at 1184–85 (holding that distress damages for pre-impact fright were recoverable in collision with tractor-trailer; existence of skid marks may permit inference that decedent experienced distress prior to impact); Smallwood v. Bradford, 720 A.2d 586, 591–92 (Md. 1998) (holding that evidence that decedent engaged in defensive maneuvering to avoid fatal automobile accident permitted recovery of pre-impact fear of death damages); Nelson v. Dolan, 434 N.W.2d 25 (Neb. 1989) (permitting trier-of-fact to award pre-impact fear of death damages when decedent feared death for 5 seconds while his motorcycle locked with automobile and traveled 268 feet before he was crushed to death). *But see* St. Clair v. Denny, 781 P.2d 1043, 1049 (Kan. 1989) (finding that evidence of 60' of skid marks before impact was insufficient to evidence pre-impact fear or fright).

[95] Haley v. Pan American World Airways, Inc., 746 F.2d 311, 317 (5th Cir. 1984); Section 75.1 (Survival Actions) (collecting additional decisions).

[96] Shu-Tao Lin v. McDonnell Douglas Corp., 574 F. Supp. 1407, 1417 (S.D.N.Y. 1983), *rev'd as to availability of damages*, 742 F.2d 45 (2d Cir. 1984); *cf. Havinga, supra*, 24 F.3d at 1486–88 (affirming award of distress damages to survivors of non-death experience).

[97] Gilbert v. Pan Am. World Airlines, Inc., 1989 U.S. Dist. LEXIS 6118 (June 2, 1989).

courts should value great distress of relatively short duration followed by the inevitable exhilaration of relief and elation when the danger has passed and the victim escapes unscathed except for the apprehension of a near-death experience. Is the relief of survival an offsetting benefit that balances out the prior fear and fright? Obviously, in individual cases, plaintiffs may contend that they have been traumatized by the experience, but courts may be expected to express some reluctance to open up this issue to tort liability.[98] Fear of claim proliferation may act to discourage courts from recognizing a right of recovery even if the technical requirements are met.[99]

Perhaps pushing the boundaries to the furthest limit is the question whether fear of death is required. In *Wooden v. Raveling*[100] the court held that a plaintiff could recover for emotional distress when the defendant negligently caused his vehicle to trespass onto plaintiff's property but missed the plaintiff, although plaintiff feared she might be killed or severely injured. How "near" the "near miss" was is not disclosed in the opinion.

[12.3] Infliction of Emotional Distress

Most jurisdictions do not treat negligent infliction of emotional distress as an independent tort.[101] The issue can be confused in jurisdictions that have adopted the "reasonable foreseeability" approach because that test often imports concepts of "duty" into the analysis.[102] A "duty" analysis suggests that an independent tort exists, but the suggestion is usually resisted.[103]

Because the emotional distress claim is simply a component of the loss, characterization of the claim is often critical. Emotional distress may not be recoverable under one theory of relief to which the facts are susceptible, but it may be available under another theory. For example, the general rule is that emotional distress damages are not recoverable when they arise out of negligent destruction of or damage to property.[104] If, however, the claim

---

[98] *Cf.* Jones v. United States, 698 F. Supp. 826, 835 (D. Haw. 1988) (stating that recovery for fear of future injury is dependent on existence of present injury).

[99] *Cf.* Kerins v. Hartley, 33 Cal. Rptr. 2d 172, 178–79 (Cal. App. 1994) (expressing need for caution in recognizing negligent infliction distress recovery with respect to exposure to HIV or AIDS due to widespread fear, absence of meaningful restrictions on scope and extent of claims, and the potential of crushing liability).

[100] 71 Cal. Rptr. 2d 891 (Cal. App. 1998).

[101] Boyles v. Kerr, 855 S.W.2d 593, 598–99 (Tex. 1993) (collecting both majority and minority decisions). *But see* State v. Hill, 963 P.2d 480, 485 (Nev. 1998) (holding that personal injury and negligent infliction of emotional distress were separate causes of action for purposes of municipal tort liability statute that had cause of action damages caps).

[102] Macy's Cal., Inc. v. Superior Court, 48 Cal. Rptr. 2d 496, 499 (Cal. App. 1995).

[103] *Id.* at 498 n.2

[104] Blagrove v. J.B. Mechanical, Inc., 934 P.2d 1273, 1276 (Wyo. 1997) (stating that emotional distress is not usually recoverable as element of property damage unless improper motive is involved); Cooper v. Superior Court, 200 Cal. Rptr. 746, 748 (Cal. App. 1984). *But cf.* Parkway Co. v. Woodruff, 910 S.W.2d 434, 444–45 (Tex. 1995) (stating that uniform test for recovery of distress damages is whether the plaintiff has introduced direct evidence of the

is capable of being asserted under theories of trespass or conversion, recovery of distress damages is possible.[105]

Emotional distress damages are generally not available for breach of contract.[106] A few cases have, however, recognized an exception when the subject matter of the contract is unique. For example, in *Windeler v. Scheers Jewelers*[107] the court permitted recovery of emotional distress damages when defendant, who had contracted to clean and repair personal property belonging to the plaintiff, failed to return the property. Because the property was "cherished mementos," the court held that recovery of distress damages was proper.[108]

A few courts have awarded emotional distress damages, arising out of the fear of being injured, under product liability theory. In *Walters v. Mintec/Int'l*,[109] the plaintiff escaped bodily injury when a crane collapsed but sought recovery for distress damages resulting from his near-injury experience. The court held that distress damages could be awarded under Restatement Section 402A.[110]

The presence of a fiduciary or quasi-fiduciary relationship may support an emotional distress award arising out of a breach even though the relationship itself is founded on contract. An example of this is the false positive case. A person seeks an HIV test from a licensed professional and the test comes back with the erroneous report that the test-taker is HIV positive. In *Chizmar v. Mackie*[111] the court held that the plaintiff test-taker

---

nature, duration, and severity of their mental anguish, thus establishing a substantial disruption in the plaintiff's daily routine; but holding that plaintiff's mere claims of anger, embarrassment, anxiety, and worry over the flooding of their land did not meet the required threshold); Sections 81 (Value to Owner), 82 (Pets).

[105] Gonzales v. Personal Storage, Inc., 65 Cal. Rptr. 2d 473, 479 (Cal. App. 1997). Section 83 (Damages For Loss or Interference With Possession).

[106] Valentine v. General Am. Credit, Inc., 362 N.W.2d 628, 629–30 (Mich. 1985) (holding that while emotional distress damages are foreseeable within rule of *Hadley v. Baxendale*, the general rule is to deny recovery); Meech v. Hillhaven West, Inc., 776 P.2d 488, 505 (Mont. 1989) (holding that distress damages are too remote to be recoverable in most breach of contract actions); Section 142 (Distress Damages).

[107] 88 Cal. Rptr. 39 (Cal. App. 1970).

[108] *Id.* at 44; *see* Maere v. Churchill, 452 N.E.2d 694, 697 (Ill. App. 1983) (noting exception when defendant had reason to know at time of contract formation that breach would cause mental distress for reasons other than mere pecuniary loss). *But see* Erlich v. Menezes, 981 P.2d 978 (Cal. 1999) (rejecting recovery of emotional distress in breach of construction contract matter; defendant had agreed to build plaintiffs' "dream house" but allegedly constructed a nightmare instead). The court found that the foreseeability of damage was not sufficient to permit an award of emotional distress damages when the defendant breached the contract but the breach caused no physical injury.

[109] 758 F.2d 73 (3d Cir. 1985).

[110] *Id.* at 79, *citing* Restatement (Second) of Torts § 402A, n.4 (1965) (collecting decisions permitting recovery "for physical harm resulting from emotional disturbance in strict liability cases"). *But cf.* Pasquale v. Speed Prods. Eng'g, 654 N.E.2d 1365, 1373 (Ill. 1995) (noting limitations on use of products liability theory in this context).

[111] 896 P.2d 196 (Alaska 1995).

could state a claim when the defendant stands in a contract or fiduciary relationship with the plaintiff and the nature of the relationship imposes on the defendant a duty to refrain from conduct that would foreseeably result in emotional distress to the plaintiff. In such cases, a plaintiff need not prove physical injury in order to recover emotional distress damages. The court held that the standard was met when the defendant-physician erroneously told his patient that she was HIV positive.[112] The court, however, refused to allow the plaintiff to recover her economic losses resulting from her subsequent divorce because of the false report.[113]

§ 13 DUTY TO MITIGATE DAMAGES

[13.1] General Principles

A plaintiff's recovery may be reduced if he fails to make reasonable efforts, post injury, to lessen damages. These efforts may be positive in the sense that the plaintiff must take affirmative, proactive steps to ameliorate the scope or severity of the loss, for example, submitting to reasonable medical procedures to reduce the injury or hasten the healing process. Alternatively, the obligation may be negative, in the sense that the plaintiff may be required to cease and desist from incurring further loss, as for example continuing as a contractor to expend labor and materials after the owner has breached the construction contract.[1]

The concepts of mitigation and avoidable consequences are frequently confused in this context. The "classical" distinction between "mitigation" or "reparation" (what defendant may do to avoid or lessen the plaintiff's damages) and "avoidable consequences" (what plaintiff must do to avoid or reduce his damages) reflects a definitional literalness that is rarely adopted by courts today.[2] The near universal tendency appears to be to use the term "mitigation" to describe the defendant's opportunity and the plaintiff's obligation to lessen damages. The plaintiff's "obligation" should not be understood as arising to the level of a legal duty, such as would create affirmative rights exercisable by the defendant. Rather, a plaintiff's failure to mitigate, when mitigation is reasonable and would operate to reduce the plaintiff's loss, will result in a dollar for dollar reduction in the recovery by the amount not mitigated.[3] For example, when a tort victim suffers

---

[112] *Id.* at 205; *see* Corgan v. Muehling, 574 N.E.2d 602, 607 (Ill. 1991) (permitting plaintiff to assert claim of emotional distress arising out of sexual relationship with her treating psychotherapist); Section 103.1 (Personal Tort Committed By Fiduciary).

[113] 896 P.2d at 211–12.

[1] Restatement (Second) Contracts § 350, cmts. a–b (1981).

[2] Courts have also used the terminology to distinguish between mitigation of contract damages and the avoidance of further damage from the actions of a tortfeasor. Olson v. Prosoco, Inc., 522 N.W.2d 284, 291 (Iowa 1994).

[3] Huffman v. Ace Elec. Co., Inc., 883 F. Supp. 1469, 1477 (D. Kan. 1995):

When a party fails to make reasonable efforts, which result in harm greater than

bodily injury but unreasonably fails to seek treatment for those injuries, the plaintiff may not recover for the aggravation of his initial injuries caused by the failure to seek medical aid.

Mitigation also resembles several liability doctrines, such as contributory negligence and comparative fault, in that the doctrines share a concern for causal responsibility for the loss. The technical line that separates mitigation from contributory negligence and comparative fault is the time of the wrong and resulting injury. Plaintiff's pre-accident activities that contribute to the loss are addressed through liability-based doctrines, such as negligence and comparative fault. Plaintiff's post-accident activities that contribute to the extent or magnitude of the loss are addressed through remedial-based doctrines, such as mitigation. The distinction can be significant since mitigation raises pure loss sharing issues, while contributory negligence does not and comparative fault may not. For example, in *Del Tufo v. Township of Old Bridge*[4] an arrestee died from a cocaine overdose while in police custody. His estate brought a wrongful death action alleging that the police had negligently delayed securing proper medical care for the decedent. Under New Jersey's comparative fault statute the plaintiff had to show that defendant was more than 50% responsible for the decedent's injuries. The court held that on these facts the trial court should have instructed the jury on comparative fault and the failure to do so constituted prejudicial error since the decedent's voluntary ingestion of cocaine was a substantial contributing factor to his death. Because New Jersey's comparative fault statute would bar recovery if the trier of fact found that the decedent was more responsible than defendant for his death from a cocaine overdose, the estate argued that on remand it could receive a mitigation instruction, which would allow for some recovery based on principles of pure fault. Thus, if decedent were found to be 80% responsible for his death, the estate could still recover 20% of its damages, which reflected defendant's share of responsibility. The court noted that while mitigation approaches had been allowed in medical malpractice cases, it would not extend the exception beyond that field. Since decedent's conduct contributing to the loss occurred prior to the accident, here decedent's arrest, the decedent's conduct must be evaluated against liability rules rather than remedial rules.[5] Similar problems have arisen when the claim involves the use of protective equipment, *e.g.*, safety googles,[6] helmets,[7]

---

would have otherwise occurred, the party may not recover damages for any amount which was avoidable. While the law does not penalize a party's inaction, it merely does nothing to compensate the party for the harm that a reasonable person would have avoided.

[4] 685 A.2d 1267 (N.J. 1996).

[5] *Id.* at 1282.

[6] Olson v. Prosoco, Inc., 522 N.W.2d 284, 291–92 (Iowa 1994) (holding that jury instructions on mitigation of damages were not warranted when plaintiff failure to wear safety goggles contributed to his injuries resulting from a lid exploding from a drum; wearing the goggles occurred before plaintiff's injury and thus before defendant committed a legal wrong; hence, no evidence demonstrated plaintiff could mitigate his damages); *cf.* Giannetti v. Darling Deleware Carting Co., 666 N.Y.S.2d 372, 374–75 (Sup. Ct. 1997) (applying mitigation principles

or seat belts.[8]

In some contexts the concept of mitigation may be folded into the substantive theory of liability to such an extent that separation is largely arbitrary. For example, a safe harbor exists that permits the employer to escape derivative liability for employee sexual harassment when the employer provides reasonable mechanisms in the workplace to prevent sexual harassment. Courts have recognized this defense under both substantive and remedial doctrine.[9]

[13.2] Reasonable Efforts

A person injured by the wrongful act of another, including breaches of contract, is required to exercise reasonable care and diligence to avoid further loss or minimize the resulting damage.[10] In other words, a plaintiff cannot recover losses that would have been avoided by reasonable expenditure or effort. Mitigation principles presuppose that damage will occur after the tort or breach of contract, which the plaintiff may ameliorate by reasonable efforts. Damages that are fixed as of the moment of the commission of the tort or breach of contract are not subject to mitigation requirements. For example, if buyer contracts with seller to purchase Blackacre for $90,000 and the fair market value of Blackacre is $100,000, buyer is entitled to his profit of $10,000 if seller breaches and buyer is not required to mitigate this loss.[11] This principle should not, however, be generalized into a rule that requires mitigation for consequential or special damages but not for general damages. Mitigation requirements are applied to general

to employee whose injuries were aggravated by his failure to wear safety glasses; the court analogized the situation to "seat belt" and failure to wear helmet cases where mitigation rules have been applied).

[7] Stehlik v. Rhoads, 645 N.W.2d 889 (Wis. 2002) (revising prior rule so that now failure to wear safety helmet, which leads to enhanced injuries, is treated as liability allocation issue rather than loss allocation issue). *See generally* Michael J. Weber, Annot., *Motorcyclist's Failure to Wear Helmet or Other Protective Equipment as Affecting Recovery For Personal Injury or Death*, 85 A.L.R. 4th 365 (1991).

[8] See the dueling annotations on this point: Christopher Hall, Annot., *Nonuse of Seat Belts as Reducing Amount of Damages Recoverable*, 62 A.L.R. 5th 537 (1998), and Thomas R. Trenker, Annot., *Automobile Occupants Failure to Use Seat Belts as Contributory Negligence*, 92 A.L.R. 3d 9 (1979).

[9] *Compare* Kolstad v. American Dental Ass'n, 527 U.S. 526 (1999) (holding that good faith efforts to comply with anti-discrimination laws provide defense to punitive damages claim for sex discrimination), *with* State Dept. Health Services v. Superior Court, 79 P.3d 556 (Cal. 2003) (holding that employer's reasonable efforts to prevent workplace sexual harassment may serve as mitigation defense).

[10] Valencia v. Shell Oil Co., 147 P.2d 558, 560 (Cal. 1944).

[11] Hickey v. Griggs, 738 P.2d 899, 902 (N. Mex. 1987); *see* Heller v. The Equitable Life Assurance Soc'y of the U.S., 833 F.2d 1253, 1256–57, 1258 n.10 (7th Cir. 1987) (refusing to impose mitigation obligation on disability insurance policyholder to submit to surgical procedure absent express contractual obligation to mitigate). *But cf.* Real Asset Mgmt., Inc. v. Lloyds of London, 61 F.3d 1223, 1229 (5th Cir. 1995) (finding that policyholder had duty to mitigate damages after insurance carrier breached liability insurance contract by refusing to settle the claim).

damages recoveries when those damages are experienced over time and could be reduced by reasonable effort in the interval between the commission of the tort or breach and the time the loss is sustained or the benefit would have been realized but for the legal wrong.[12]

A plaintiff need only expend reasonable efforts to mitigate damages; the plaintiff need not do what is unreasonable or impractical.[13] A plaintiff, who is financially unable to mitigate, need not do what he cannot do. The fact that mitigation efforts were unsuccessful does not mean that those efforts were unreasonable. Reasonableness is determined by the facts as they were at the time mitigation efforts were undertaken, not on the basis of 20/20 hindsight. If the choice was reasonable when made, it does not become unreasonable because it was unsuccessful. Moreover, if more than one reasonable choice for mitigation efforts presents itself, the person whose wrong forced the choice cannot complain that the unsuccessful choice was selected.[14] On the other hand, if a plaintiff's initial selection of a reasonable choice becomes, over time, unreasonable, the plaintiff cannot persist in pursuing a failed policy. The defendant's burden is, however, on this point, quite substantial.[15]

Whether a plaintiff has unreasonably failed to mitigate damages is a question of fact.[16] The burden of proof on the issue of mitigation lies with the defendant.[17] Moreover, it is not sufficient for defendant to show that plaintiff could have mitigated; rather, defendant must demonstrate by a preponderance of the evidence that mitigation efforts would have in fact reduced the scope or severity of plaintiff's losses.[18] To meet this standard, the defendant must demonstrate the reasonableness and effectiveness of the path not taken; the defense cannot rely on surmise or speculation.[19]

---

[12] Ford Motor Co. v. E.E.O.C., 458 U.S. 219, 231–32 (1982) (holding that a plaintiff in an employment discrimination action has a duty to mitigate his general damages by exercising reasonable diligence in seeking substitute employment that is substantially similar to his former employment or risk having the amount of any damages awarded reduced by the amount that could have been earned); Sections 13.2.2 (Employment Claims), 151 (Employee's Damages Against Employer).

[13] *Valencia, supra*, 147 P.2d at 561.

[14] Ellerman Lines, Ltd. v. The President Harding, 288 F.2d 288, 290 (2d Cir. 1961); Green v. Smith, 67 Cal. Rptr. 796, 800 (Cal. App. 1968).

[15] *Ellerman Lines, Ltd., supra*, 288 F.2d at 291 ("[I]n order to prove that a plaintiff's adherence to an initially proper decision as to how to mitigate damages has become unreasonable, the defendant must show that such adherence had become not merely erroneous but palpably so . . . .".

[16] Higgins v. Lawrence, 309 N.W.2d 194, 196 (Mich. App. 1981); Sackett v. Spindler, 56 Cal. Rptr. 435, 447 (Cal. App. 1967).

[17] Jackson v. Shell Oil Co., 702 F.2d 197, 202 (9th Cir. 1983); Sommer v. Kridel, 378 A.2d 767, 773 (N.J. 1977).

[18] Whitehouse v. Lange, 910 P.2d 801, 808 (Idaho App. 1996).

[19] Lewis v. Alfa Laval Separation, Inc., 714 N.E.2d 426, 430 (Ohio App. 1998) (holding that trial court properly rejected mitigation defense of failure to wear safety equipment when expert witness provided only equivocal testimony as to the effectiveness of the equipment in preventing injury).

[13.2.1] Bodily Injury Claims

The general rule is that the plaintiff in a personal injury action must make reasonable efforts to mitigate or ameliorate the extent or severity of her injuries.[20] What is reasonable will vary with the circumstances of the case and the character of the plaintiff.[21] The question arises frequently with respect to medical treatment to correct or repair injury caused by the defendant. The failure to seek medical treatment is frequently seen as failing to mitigate when such treatment would have effected a cure or minimized damages.[22] The more difficult issue involves surgery recommended by a treating physician to reduce the injury caused by the defendant. Here courts tend to distinguish between minor and major surgery:

> [A] person injured by another's wrong is obliged to exercise ordinary care to seek medical or surgical treatment so as to effect a cure and minimize damages. Failure or refusal to do so bars recovery for consequences which could have been averted by the exercise of such care. However, in this state the injured person is regarded as having the right to avoid if he chooses, peril to life, however slight, and undue risks to health, and anguish that goes beyond the bounds of reason. And a refusal to accept an operation is not unreasonable and therefore unjustifiable in the legal sense, unless it is free from danger to life and health and extraordinary suffering, and, according to the best medical or surgical opinion, offers a reasonable prospect of restoration or relief from the disability.[23]

Another difficult issue is the overweight plaintiff who is advised by his treating physician to lose weight to facilitate healing or recovery from harm inflicted by the defendant. The "failure to lose weight" approach has met with some success.[24] Whether this defense becomes widespread will likely turn on jury receptiveness to so-called "life style defenses" and the willingness of treating and testifying physicians to attribute plaintiff's lingering injuries to plaintiff's obesity rather than defendant's misconduct. The treatment of obesity as a handicap under the Americans With Disabilities Act may forestall this approach, but at present the issue whether obesity is a disability or perceived as such is unresolved.[25]

---

[20] Restatement (Second) of Torts § 918 (1979)

[21] Section 13.2.3 (The "Fragile" Plaintiff).

[22] Albert v. Monarch Federal Savings & Loan Assn., 743 A.2d 890, 892 (N.J. Super. App. Dept. 2000).

[23] *Id.* (citations and quotation marks omitted); Stein on Personal Injury Damages Treatise § 18.9 (Necessity of Surgery) (2003) (collecting decisions).

[24] Tamberg v. Ackerman Inv. Co., 473 N.W.2d 193, 196 (Iowa App. 1991), *overruled on other grounds* Greenwood v. Mitchell, 621 N.W.2d 200 (Iowa 2001). *See generally* Danny R. Veilleaux, Annot., *Failure To Lose Weight as a Basis For Reduction of Damages in Personal Injury Action*, 24 A.L.R.5th 174 (1994) (collecting decisions).

[25] *See* Christine L. Kuss, *Absolving a Deadly Sin: A Medical and Legal Argument For Obesity as a Disability Under the Americans With Disabilities Act*, 12 J. Contemp. Health L. & Pol'y 563 (1996).

There is a recent article noting the absence of decisions but suggesting that mitigation principles do not apply to non-economic damages. [26] The absence of decisions expressly addressing mitigation requirements is, however, not exceptional. The very method by which one would mitigate, *e.g.*, seek treatment for distress, is a medical expense the plaintiff would normally seek to recover. [27] Defendant could introduce evidence of failure to mitigate, but, as a trial tactic, it might be counterproductive as it would implicitly concede the validity and severity of plaintiff's claim of distress damage, *e.g.*, plaintiff should have treated, but didn't. When the issue has arisen, it has been in the context of the "fragile" plaintiff. [28]

[13.2.2] Employment Claims

A party harmed by an employment decision is required to mitigate damages. The obligation applies to both employees and employers; however, the much greater number of disputes brought by employees against employers in this area has generated a distinct body of mitigation law applicable to employee claims.

The rule is well established that a wrongfully discharged or terminated employee has a duty to mitigate. Wages or earnings the employee could have earned at a replacement job, but did not, will be offset against his recovery. [29] The reason for this rule is that (1) the plaintiff must act fairly toward the defendant notwithstanding the defendant's misconduct towards the plaintiff, (2) the plaintiff must act in a socially responsible manner, [30] and (3) the plaintiff should not be seen as the cause of his own losses. [31]

In order to establish that the employee-plaintiff failed to mitigate, the defendant must show that the damages could have been avoided. The defendant-employer must show that there were suitable employment opportunities available that plaintiff could have discovered and for which plaintiff was qualified and that plaintiff failed to act reasonably in searching out and finding those replacement employment opportunities. [32] It is

---

[26] *See* Eugene Kontorovich, Student Comment, *The Mitigation of Emotional Distress Damages*, 68 U. Chi. L. Rev. 491, 500–01 (2001) (noting absence of express rule but identifying implicit exception to general mitigation principle).

[27] Section 72 (Medical Expenses).

[28] Section 13.2.3 (The "Fragile" Plaintiff).

[29] *Ford Motor Co.*, *supra*, 458 U.S. at 231–32.

[30] California Sch. Employees Ass'n v. Personnel Comm'n, 106 Cal. Rptr. 283, 288 (Cal. App. 1973) (noting that "[r]ather than permitting the employee simply to remain idle during the balance of the contract period, the law requires him to make a reasonable effort to secure other employement").

[31] McClelland v. Climax Hosiery Mills, 169 N.E. 605, 609 (N.Y. 1930) (Cardozo, J. concurring):

> The servant is free to accept employment or reject it according to his uncensored pleasure. What is meant by the supposed duty is merely this, that if he unreasonably reject, he will not be heard to say that the loss of wages from then on shall be deemed the jural consequence of the earlier discharge. He has broken the chain of causation, and loss resulting to him thereafter is suffered through his own act.

[32] Aguinaga v. United Food and Commercial Workers Int'l Union, 993 F.2d 1463, 1474 (10th Cir. 1993), *cert. denied*, 510 U.S. 1072 (1994).

not enough that the employer show that the employee was lazy or idle in failing to secure alternative employment. The mitigation affirmative defense requires that the employer establish that had the employee acted reasonably to mitigate damages it is more likely than not that the employee would have been successful in finding suitable replacement work. The employer must establish that "like" or "comparable" positions were available and likely would have been offered to the employee had she sought alternative employment. Finally, the employer must present sufficient evidence to guide the trier-of-fact in determining those damages that are attributable to the employee's failure to mitigate.[33] On the other hand, it is not uncommon in this area to find judicial statements that suggest *strongly* that inadequate efforts by the plaintiff-employee may alone demonstrate the failure to mitigate.[34]

This latter view is not consistent with established law in this area. Whether it represents and evolutionary development of the common law's hostility towards idleness or *dicta* reflecting judicial exasperation at the plaintiff's lengthy absence from work is an open question.

What constitutes "suitable" alternative employment is sometimes difficult to determine. Although the employee need not go into another line of

---

[33] Ford v. GACS, Inc., 265 F.3d 670, 679 (8th Cir. 2001), *cert. denied*, 535 U.S. 954 (2002); Lamarca v. United States, 31 F. Supp. 2d 110, 131 (E.D.N.Y. 1998) (stating that the government failed to prove that plaintiff failed to mitigate by not applying for social security benefits: while the government established that plaintiff knowingly failed to apply, the government failed to show that had plaintiff applied, she would have received benefits).

[34] Mathieu v. Gopher News Co., 273 F.3d 769 (8th Cir. 2001):

> Of course, the burden to mitigate damages rests with the plaintiff, not the defendant. Even though Gopher News' proposed positions were not substantially equivalent, that fact does not relieve Mathieu of his burden to exercise reasonable diligence to find suitable employment with another employer. However, the evidence presented at trial tended to show that Mathieu applied with eight to ten employers during the first three months after he left Gopher News. For three months after that Mathieu devoted six to eight hours per week looking for work. Mathieu offered expert testimony that his job search was "very good." Certainly, a party in Mathieu's position might have exerted more effort looking for employment. We may have demanded more in the magistrate's position. However, on the evidence presented at trial we cannot say the magistrate committed a manifest abuse of discretion by finding that Mathieu made an honest effort and exercised reasonable diligence to mitigate his damages.

Id. at 784; *see also* Huffman v. Ace Elec. Co., Inc., 883 F. Supp. 1469, 1477 (D. Kan. 1995) (wrongful discharge claim):

> The court finds that plaintiff failed to use reasonable care and diligence in seeking employment and that most of her economic damages could possibly have been avoided had she attempted to look for work. Although defendant has not established that plaintiff would have been employed had she applied, defendant has established that positions were available for which plaintiff was qualified after January 9, 1993. Plaintiff may well have had some difficulty in obtaining employment due to her age, physical condition, and the circumstances of the termination of her employment had she made an effort to locate employment. However, her claim that she was embarrassed that she had been fired and consequently could not bring herself to admit such to prospective employers does not excuse her failure to attempt to mitigate her damages.

work, accept a demotion, or take a demeaning position,[35] the employee's claim of damages is diminished if he refuses a job substantially equivalent to the one he was contractually promised.[36] "Substantial equivalency" is a fluid term. In general, courts afford more leeway to individual, subjective wants when the employee's prospective work experience is influenced by the nature and type of the employee's prior employment. A plaintiff who reasonably believes that the replacement position would not be as career enhancing as the position she was wrongfully denied will be given more leeway in declining replacement employment than a plaintiff for whom a job is not career enhancing. For example, in *Parker v. Twentieth Century-Fox Film Corp.*[37] the court held that the lead in a western to be filmed in Australia was not equivalent to the lead in a musical to be filmed in Los Angeles, and affirmed a judgment for the full $750,000 fee promised actress Shirley MacLaine. Ms. MacLaine had contracted with Fox to play the female lead in the musical at a minimum compensation of $750,000. Before production started, Fox decided not to produce the picture and offered MacLaine the lead in a western for identical compensation. The western was to be filmed at the time scheduled for the musical. The musical contract gave MacLaine the power of director and screenplay approval, but the western contract provided only that the studio would consult with Mac-Laine on these issues. The studio argued that on these facts MacLaine had failed to mitigate damages. The court disagreed relying on the fact that (1) Ms. MacLaine would have less artistic control over the replacement film and (2) the differences between the two roles for an actress.

If the employee accepts a lower paying position and ceases looking for higher paying positions, does the employee forfeit her claim for damages post acceptance if the new position is unlike the previous position from which she was wrongfully terminated? In *Morris v. Clawson*[38] the Michigan Supreme Court said "No." The test was whether the plaintiff acted reasonably:

> We find no reason to require a plaintiff to search for "like employment," as defined by the Court of Appeals, in an effort to mitigate damages. The sole interest of the defendant, the courts, and the public, in the type of employment sought by the plaintiff in mitigation is the interest those parties have in avoiding unnecessary economic loss. "The principle of mitigation is a thread permeating the entire jurisprudence . . . it is part of the much broader principle of 'avoidable consequences.' " Thus, while a defendant may object to the "reasonableness" of the amount of compensation typical of

---

[35] *Ford Motor Co., supra,* 458 U.S. at 231–32.

[36] *Compare Mathieu, supra,* 273 F.3d at 783 (holding that plaintiff-employee's refusal to accept a lower paying position was effectively a demotion that plaintiff could reasonably reject), *with* Arkansas Oklahoma Gas Corp. v. Director, 94 S.W.3d 366 (Ark. App. 2002) (holding that loss of union protection and seniority did not provide good cause for unemployment compensation claimant turning down position and did not render offered employment unsuitable).

[37] 474 P.2d 689 (Cal. 1970).

[38] 587 N.W.2d 253 (Mich. 1998).

the jobs that the plaintiff seeks in mitigation, the "work conditions" and "type of work," are relevant only to the job seeker. Furthermore, there is no requirement that the plaintiff find employment with compensation equivalent to that of the job lost. "[T]he defendant must show that the course of conduct plaintiff actually followed was so deficient as to constitute an unreasonable failure to seek employment.[39]

On the other hand, in *Ford Motor Co. v. E.E.O.C.*[40] the Court refused relief to Ford employees who had been subjected to sex discrimination because the employees had refused Ford's offer of reparative promotion and taken alternative employment at General Motors.

Morris, more than *Ford Motor Co.*, recognizes that reasonableness is an illusive concept and that it is dangerous to indulge in criticism of prior mitigation decisions with the benefit (or critical smugness) of 20/20 hindsight. On the other hand, employment damages awards involve more than mitigation. The approach authorized by *Morris* may undermine other remedial goals, such as a preference for reinstatement over damages awards.[41] Remedy oriented decision making in this area should evidence a sensitivity and appreciation of these other concerns.

It is generally held that a plaintiff need not accept replacement employment that would compromise his claim against his former employer.[42] This approach is consistent with *Ford Motor Co.*'s holding that the plaintiff need not accept a position that constitutes a demotion or reduction in pay. When, however, the plaintiff does accept replacement employment, the trier of fact may consider the employee's failure to retain that replacement employment when determining whether plaintiff reasonably mitigated damages.[43]

---

[39] *Id.* at 258–59 (citations omitted); *cf.* Sellers v. Mineta, 358 F.3d 1058, 1066 (8th Cir. 2004) (holding that district court abused its discretion when it failed to reduce plaintiff's lost earnings award after plaintiff took post-termination alternative employment that was not comparable to her former employment with defendant).

[40] *Supra*, 458 U.S. 219.

[41] Section 152 (Employee Reinstatement to Position).

[42] Redman v. Dep't of Educ., 519 P.2d 760, 769–70 (Alaska 1974) (finding that an employee is not required to accept alternative employment that would compromise her claim to reinstatement); Billetter v. Posell, 211 P.2d 621, 623 (Cal. App. 1949) (stating that one employed for a definite period of time, at an agreed rate and wrongfully discharged before the expiration of his period of employment may refuse his employer's offer of reinstatement when the acceptance of such an offer would amount to a modification of the original contract or to a waiver of his rights to recover according to its terms).

[43] Stanchfield v. Hamer Toyota, Inc., 44 Cal. Rptr.2d 565, 568 (Cal. App. 1995) (noting absence of precedents on the point); *cf.* Boehm v. American Broadcasting Co., 929 F.2d 482, 488 (9th Cir. 1991) (noting that whether a plaintiff's move from his area of employment to Pebble Beach amounted to a voluntary leaving of the job market was a question of fact). *But cf.* Johnson v. Spencer Press of Maine, Inc., 364 F.3d 368, 381–82 (1st Cir. 2004) (stating in *dicta* that plaintiff's subsequent firing from replacement employment did not bar post-firing loss of earning damages in Title VII discrimination action; the court placed substantial weight on the plaintiff-employee's presumptive entitlement to back pay in Title VII actions).

[13.2.3] The "Fragile" Plaintiff

It is a basic tenet of tort law that the defendant takes the plaintiff as he finds him, including any preexisting conditions, vulnerability, or fragility the plaintiff presents.[44] The issue is occasionally presented whether in evaluating a plaintiff's decision making regarding mitigation, the same solicitude for a plaintiff's individuality should be rendered as under the fragile plaintiff rule. In general the reception has been mixed. For example, in *Williams v. Bright*,[45] the plaintiff, a Jehovah's Witness, refused medical treatment that defendant contended would have ameliorated her injuries. The majority rejected the notion that the plaintiff's religious values system formed a part of her pre-existing condition. Similarly, in *Munn v. Algee*,[46] the court refused to include within the "eggshell headed" doctrine's application situations where the plaintiff's pre-existing condition is "mental" rather than physical.[47]

Notwithstanding the statements in *Williams* and *Munn*, which are best understood as reflecting unease at incorporating religious issues and First Amendment complications into mitigation analysis, courts have provided some leeway so that the plaintiff's individual beliefs and risk aversion may be considered by the trier of fact when determining whether the plaintiff acted reasonably in responding to the fact of her loss or injury. For example, in *Small v. Combustion Engineering*,[48] the plaintiff refused low risk knee surgery that had a 92% chance of restoring his ability to walk. The court found the choice objectively unreasonable, but reasonable for plaintiff because he was manic-depressive and due to his mental disorder he considered only the risks and ignored the benefits.[49]

Because the plaintiff's duties are stated as being reasonable in nature and scope, there can be no hard and fast rule. Courts do permit the trier-of-fact to consider the "divergent personalities, beliefs, and fears" in gauging

---

[44] Colonial Inn Motor Lodge, Inc. v. Gay, 680 N.E.2d 407, 416 (Ill. App. 1997) (stating that "[a] negligence defendant must take the plaintiff as he finds him, even if the plaintiff's 'eggshell skull' results in his suffering an injury that ordinarily would not be reasonably foreseeable"); Avery v. Ward, 934 S.W.2d 516, 520 (Ark. 1996); Schafer v. Hoffman, 831 P.2d 897, 900 (Colo. 1992); McCall v. Weeks, 164 N.W.2d 206, 210 (Neb. 1969).

[45] 658 N.Y.S.2d 910, 913 (App. Dept. 1997).

[46] 924 F.2d 568 (5th Cir.), *cert. denied*, 502 U.S. 900 (1991).

[47] *Id.* at 576. *See generally* Gary Knapp, Annot., *Refusal of Medical Treatment on Religious Grounds As Affecting Right to Recover For Personal Injury or Death*, 3 A.L.R.5th 721 (1993).

[48] 681 P.2d 1081 (Mont. 1984).

[49] *Id.* at 1084–85; Tabieros v. Clark Equip. Co., 944 P.2d 1279, 1316 (Haw. 1997) (stating that "[t]he mere fact that the [treatment] might have been [efficacious] is not sufficient to hold that [the] plaintiff acted unreasonably in not resorting to such treatment. Other factors, such as the cost of the [treatment], the inconvenience resulting from it, and whether or not it had been recommended by a medical expert, [are] pertinent to the issue") (brackets in original; citation omitted); Jones v. Eppler, 266 P.2d 451, 455 (Okla. 1953) (holding that "as a matter of law, one who has been injured by the negligence of another is not bound to undergo a major surgical operation which would necessarily be attended with some risk of failure and of death, but such person must be permitted to exercise the liberty of choice in the matter . . . ."); Section 13.2.1 (Bodily Injury Claims).

the reasonableness of a plaintiff's refusal to mitigate damages in a particular fashion.[50] Many courts have held the defendant liable for the plaintiff's psychological injury even though the plaintiff's "personality structure" made the plaintiff more susceptible and vulnerable to psychological harm.[51] In this regard, a critical distinction must be made between application of the "fragile plaintiff" rule to lower the liability standard, (does the defendant owe a higher standard of care to the unusually sensitive plaintiff), or to tweak the damages standard, (does the plaintiff's greater sensitivity means greater damages when a defendant violates the basic liability standard).[52]

[13.3] Equal Opportunity to Avoid Losses Rule

It is consistently held that the plaintiff need not mitigate when the ability to lessen damages is equally available to both the plaintiff and the defendant.[53] This principle is, however, more limited than it facially appears. "Equal opportunity" means equal in fact not in theory. Thus, in *Toyota Industrial Trucks U.S.A., Inc. v. Citizens Nat'l Bank of Evans City*,[54] the court stated:

> Where both the plaintiff and the defendant have had equal opportunity to reduce the damages by the same act and it is equally reasonable to expect a defendant to minimize damages, the defendant is in no position to contend that the plaintiff failed to mitigate. Nor will the award be reduced on account of damages the defendant could have avoided as easily as the plaintiff. . . . The duty to mitigate damages is not applicable where a party whose duty it is primarily to perform the contract has equal opportunity for performance and equal knowledge of the consequences of the performance.[55]

---

[50] Allied Chem. Corp. v. Industrial Comm'n, 488 N.E.2d 603, 606 (Ill. App. 1986) (citation omitted); *cf.* Ortiz v. Bank of Am., 852 F.2d 383, 386–87 (9th Cir. 1988) (discharged employee's "mental condition" at time unconditional offer of reinstatement was made by employer constituted "special circumstances" and therefore whether employee failed to mitigate by accepting offer was for trier of fact to resolve).

[51] Jenson v. Eveleth Taconite Co., 130 F.3d 1287, 1294–95 (8th Cir. 1997) (collecting decisions applying fragile plaintiff rule in cases of emotional distress or psychological injury to plaintiffs who present special vulnerability to such injury).

[52] Poole v. Copland, Inc., 498 S.E.2d 602, 604–05 (N.C. 1998) (holding that the "fragile plaintiff" rule applied to sexual harassment claims, but rule applies to damages plaintiff sustains as a result of the harassment not to the defendant's standard of care, *i.e.*, the rule does not lower the standard as to the quantum or quality of conduct that constitutes a breach of duty rather it affects liability for the consequences of breach of duty).

[53] S.J. Groves & Sons, Co. v. Warner Co., 576 F.2d 524, 530 (3d Cir. 1978); Wartzman v. Hightower Prods., Ltd., 456 A.2d 82, 88 (Md. Ct. Sp. App. 1983).

[54] 611 F.2d 465 (3d Cir. 1979).

[55] *Id.* at 471; *see* Michael B. Kelly, *Defendant's Responsibility to Minimize Plaintiff's Loss: A Curious Exception to the Avoidable Consequences Doctrine*, 47 S.C. L. Rev. 391 (1996) (criticizing rule as unnecessary given that the plaintiff's basic obligation is to act reasonably under all the circumstances to mitigate losses).

[13.4] Disposal or Repair of Damaged Property

A plaintiff must make reasonable efforts to repair or recover property. For example, in *Stone Oil Distributor, Inc. v. M/V Miss Bern*[56] a vessel was seized pursuant to a maritime lien. The purchaser of the vessel sought damages from the seller. The court found, however, that the purchaser made no effort to mitigate any losses it suffered after the vessel was seized. The purchaser made no effort to post bond or any other security or to provide a letter of credit so that either seizure of the vessel could have been avoided or the vessel could have been released. There was no evidence that the purchaser attempted to negotiate to arrange for the vessel's release. The court found that the purchaser failed to exercise reasonable efforts to mitigate damages.

Another interesting case is *Sony Magnetic Products, Inc. v. Merivienti O/Y.*[57] The court found that Sony did not fail to mitigate damages by refusing to sell "damaged goods" to the account of the defendant. The court found that Sony had spent millions of dollars to establish a reputation for quality and the defendant did not show that Sony's fears the "unmarked" goods could be traced to it were unreasonable. Similarly, in *Urico v. Parnell Oil Co.*[58] the owner of a vehicle was permitted to recover loss of use damages beyond the normal repair period when defendant's delay in settling the dispute denied plaintiff the monies needed to pay for the repairs. This simply reemphasizes the core mitigation obligation to act reasonably and within one's capabilities.

[13.5] Continued Dealing with Defendant

Outside the employment cases, the mitigation rule does not require the non-breaching party to continue dealing with the breaching party in an effort to mitigate damages.[59] This reflects the homily, "fool me once, shame on you; fool me twice, shame on me." Employment cases tend to be different,[60] but many of these cases include claims by the plaintiff for reinstatement, so the plaintiff is hard pressed to complain that he cannot work successfully with the defendant. An offer of reinstatement may be

---

[56] 663 F. Supp. 773 (S.D. Ala. 1987).

[57] 668 F. Supp. 1505 (S.D. Ala. 1987), *aff'd*, 863 F.2d 1537, 1543 (11th Cir. 1989).

[58] 708 F.2d 852 (1st Cir. 1983).

[59] Zanker Dev. Co. v. Cogito Sys., Inc., 264 Cal. Rptr. 76, 79–80 (Cal. App. 1989) (holding that a landlord is not required to accept a breaching tenant's offer to re-rent); F & P Builders v. Lowe's of Texas, Inc., 786 S.W.2d 502, 503 (Tex. Civ. App. 1990) (holding that seller of goods on executed contract did not have to accept return of goods from breaching buyer).

[60] *Ford Motor Co.*, *supra*, 458 U.S. 219, 241 (holding that an employer charged with discrimination can toll the continuing accrual of damages by offering the claimant a job without conditions attached). This rule has been generally applied to employee discharge and termination cases. Martinell v. Montana Power Co., 886 P.2d 421, 440 (Mont. 1994) (noting that the purpose of the rule is to end discrimination and close cases more quickly); Section 13.2.2 (Employment Claims).

rejected when the plaintiff's experiences with the defendant would make it difficult for the plaintiff to return to that worksite.[61]

[13.6] Intentional Wrongs

The duty to mitigate is often excused or relaxed when the defendant engages in intentional misconduct, as, for example, when defendant intends to harm the plaintiff.[62] The reason for this approach is the concept that a party should not be required to surrender a right of substantial value in order to minimize a loss. It is understood that such a surrendering in the face of intentional misconduct is inconsistent with the concept of a right.[63] Even here, however, the plaintiff cannot intentionally or heedlessly fail to protect his interests.[64] In effect, a plaintiff's duty to act reasonably is influenced by the defendant's degree of culpability.

Casting the duty as one sounding in reasonableness ensures that jurisdictions will differ when they seek to elevate a fact-based inquiry to a legal rule. For example, courts have split on the question whether a plaintiff must submit to extortionistic demands in order to reduce his losses.[65] Complicating the issue is the view that a plaintiff's duty to mitigate does not require her to incur undue risk, burden, or humiliation.[66] While this principle applies directly to breach of contract claims, it suggests that a plaintiff's personal values should be included in the evaluation of the reasonableness of her resistance to extortionistic demands.[67]

[13.7] Compensation for Mitigation Efforts

Expenses incurred by the plaintiff in reasonably attempting to mitigate damages are recoverable even if the efforts are unsuccessful, provided the expenses do not exceed plaintiff's pre-mitigation damages.[68] An example of this principle is *Bendar v. Rosen*.[69] In *Bendar* the plaintiff was involved in an automobile accident. She had X-rays to determine the extent of her injuries. She did not know that she was pregnant at the time she was exposed to X-rays. Because of the exposure, she elected to have an abortion,

---

[61] Section 152 (Employee Reinstatement to Position).

[62] Restatement (Second) of Torts § 918(2) (1977).

[63] *Id.* at cmt. j.

[64] Flanagan v. Prudhomme, 644 A.2d 51, 61 (N.H. 1994).

[65] *Compare* Sinclair v. Fotomat, 189 Cal. Rptr. 393 (Cal. App. 1983), decertified per Cal. R. Court 976(c) (plaintiff was required to pay illegal charge of $1 to reacquire his property (film) in order to mitigate his damages), *with* O'Brien v. Isaacs, 116 N.W.2d 246 (Wis. 1962) (plaintiff not required to pay $1 illegal charge to retrieve his property (car)).

[66] Restatement (Second) of Contracts § 350(1) (1981).

[67] Compare the more rigorous approach taken in negligence cases when the plaintiff's religious beliefs and the duty to mitigate clash. Section 13.2.3 (The "Fragile" Plaintiff).

[68] Toledo Peoria and W. Ry. v. Metro Waste Sys., Inc., 59 F.3d 637, 640–41 (7th Cir. 1995); King World Prods. v. Financial News Network, 674 F. Supp. 438, 439 (S.D.N.Y. 1987); Hartong v. Partake, Inc., 72 Cal. Rptr. 722, 739 (Cal. App. 1968).

[69] 588 A.2d 1264 (N.J. 1991).

which resulted in complications. The court held that the driver was liable for the resulting injuries and abortion damages since submitting to the X-ray procedure was reasonable conduct by plaintiff to determine the nature of her injuries. An extension of this principle is *CUNA Mutual Life Ins. Co. v. Los Angeles County Metropolitan Transportation Authority.*[70] In *CUNA* the owner of an historic building sought to recover for the costs it had incurred *to protect* its building from damage during the construction of a portion of the Los Angeles subway system. No damages to its property was actually realized due to the mitigation work undertaken by the building owner. The court permitted a recovery based on mitigation principles. In effect, the owner recovered for reasonably avoiding anticipated injury.

[13.8]   Special Applications of the Mitigation Principle

In a number of cases the concept of mitigation must be addressed with an appreciation of other goals and objectives of the remedial system.[71] It is impossible to catalogue all of these applications; however, two occur with sufficient frequency to warrant discussion: (1) leases; and, (2) lost volume seller profits.

[13.8.1]   Leases

One recurring problem involves lessors who seek to sublet after a tenant breaches the lease. The traditional common law rule did not impose a duty to mitigate on the landlord. The primary reason for this rule was the characterization of the contract as involving property, a leasehold. As one court observed:

> [T]he ancient law of leaseholds was developed in the context of leases of agricultural land. Those leases generally ran from growing season to growing season. If a tenant vacated after planting time had passed, it was unrealistic to expect the landlord to find a new tenant interested in leasing land that was essentially useless . . . .[72]

The modern trend is to recognize the contractual nature of the landlord-tenant relationship and to impose a duty to mitigate, but there are many jurisdictions that retain the old rule.[73] These latter jurisdictions place greater reliance on the stability of precedent. As the New York Court of Appeals noted in a case involving commercial leases:

> In business transactions, particularly, the certainty of settled rules is often more important than whether the established rule is better than another or even whether it is the 'correct' rule . . . . This is

---

[70] 133 Cal. Rptr. 2d 470 (Cal. App. 2003).

[71] For example, the preference for employee reinstatement over damages was earlier noted as a gloss on the mitigation obligation. Section 13.2.2 (Employment Claims).

[72] Reid v. Mutual of Omaha Ins. Co., 776 P.2d 896, 905 (Utah 1989).

[73] *In re* Modern Textile, Inc., 900 F.2d 1184, 1189–90 (8th Cir. 1990) (collecting cases).

perhaps true in real property more than any other area of the law, where established precedents are not lightly to be set aside."[74]

This is a difficult area of the law because of the direct conflict between contract and property doctrine, the differences between consumer and commercial leases, the presence of statutes on this point in some jurisdictions, the nature of the tenant's breach, and the presence of contractual language regarding mitigation.[75]

[13.8.2]　Lost Volume Seller Profits

A lost volume seller is a seller who but for defendant buyer's breach would have made two sales and two profits rather than only one sale. When the buyer breaches, the question is whether the profits from the subsequent sale (sale #2) belong to the seller or are applied against the seller's damages claim arising out of the breached transaction (sale #1).[76] The general understanding is that, if the "lost volume seller" rule is applied and the seller is allowed to sue buyer for the lost profits of sale #1 without crediting the buyer for the profits of sale #2, there is no duty to mitigate on the part of the seller. The rationale is that the lost volume seller need not mitigate because mitigation is inconsistent with the seller's rightful position.[77] This exception to the mitigation requirement has also been applied to "services" contracts.[78]

§ 14　OFFSETTING BENEFITS

The usual assumption when a defendant inflicts a legal wrong on the plaintiff is that the plaintiff will suffer an actual, net loss. Every so often, however, this may not be the case. For example, plaintiff may sell property with a fair market value of $90 to defendant for $100. If defendant breaches and plaintiff is able to resell the property for $110, with additional costs of $5, plaintiff has not suffered any loss. If defendant had performed, plaintiff's expectancy was $10 ($100 − $90). As a result of defendant's

---

[74] Holy Properties, L.P., v. Kenneth Cole Prods., Inc., 661 N.E.2d 694, 696 (N.Y. 1995).

[75] Austin Hill Country Realty, Inc. v. Palisades Plaza, Inc., 948 S.W.2d 293 (Tex. 1997) (holding that landlord has duty to mitigate damages when tenant breaches commercial lease absent contrary contractual agreement); *see* Stephanie G. Flynn, *Duty to Mitigate Damages Upon a Tenant's Abandonment*, 34 Real Prop. Prob. & Tr. J. 721 (Winter 2000) (stating: "[T]he shift toward the view that a landlord should mitigate damages seems to have continued. Although courts often refer to the non-mitigation rule as the majority rule, twenty-eight states now impose an affirmative duty to mitigate on residential landlords"). *See generally* Christopher Vaeth, Annot., *Landlord's Duty, On Tenant's Failure to Occupy, or Abandonment of, Premises, to Mitigate Damages by Accepting or Procuring Another Tenant*, 75 A.L.R. 5th 1 (2000) (collecting decisions).

[76] Section 8.5 (Lost Volume Seller).

[77] C.I.C. Corp. v. Ragtime, Inc., 726 A.2d 316, 319–20 (N.J. Super. A.D. 1999).

[78] Gianetti v. Norwalk Hospital, 833 A.2d 891, 897 (Conn. 2003) ("Although the lost volume seller theory is commonly understood to apply to contracts involving the sale of goods, it applies with equal force to contracts involving the performance of personal service contracts") (footnote and citation omitted).

breach, plaintiff's expectancy increased to $15 ($110 − $90 − $5). Because of defendant's breach, plaintiff is in a better position than if defendant had performed. One may extrapolate this concept to other situations. Whether the result would be the same is, however, less clear. For example, a plaintiff may be the victim of governmental misconduct that causes her economic and emotional distress. Plaintiff becomes, however, a celebrity because of her plight and subsequently acquires substantial wealth by selling rights to her story to various media channels. Should plaintiff's new wealth be considered when measuring her damages caused by governmental misconduct?

Perhaps the most common example of the offsetting benefits rule is in employment disputes. If the discharged employee finds alternative work, salary received from that other work is credited against the damages award regardless of the mitigation rules discussed in Section 13.2.2. This offset applies whether the action for wrongful termination sounds in contract or tort.[1] The rule does not apply, however, if the plaintiff could have worked the alternative job had he not been wrongfully terminated.[2]

[14.1]   Special Benefits Rule in Tort

Most jurisdictions recognize what is commonly known as the "special benefits" rule for measuring tort damages. The rule essentially states that when a defendant's tortious conduct causes legal harm to the plaintiff or her property but in so doing also confers a special benefit to the interest that was harmed, the value of the benefit conferred is accounted for in mitigation of damages.[3] The rule reflects the basic compensatory orientation of tort damages. The rule restricts recovery to the net, actual harm incurred by the plaintiff.[4]

The critical feature of the "special benefit" rule is its focus on "interests." The benefit must relate to the same interest that was harmed; there is no offset if different interests are affected.[5] This can raise some interesting problems of classification. For example, in wrongful pregnancy cases[6] should the economic costs of raising the unplanned-for child be offset by the emotional benefit of having the child. Some courts bar the offset claim reasoning that the economic costs of raising a child are different from the non-economic benefits of having a child; moreover, the plaintiff should not

---

[1] Figueroa-Rodriguez v. Aquino, 863 F.2d 1037, 1046 (1st Cir. 1988) (federal civil rights action).

[2] Lily v. City of Beckley, 797 F.2d 191, 196 (4th Cir. 1986) (holding that if plaintiff could have worked both jobs—the one he lost and the replacement job— there is no offset).

[3] Turpin v. Sortini, 643 P.2d 954, 964 (Cal. 1982); Restatement (Second) os Torts § 920 (1977).

[4] Flowers v. District of Columbia, 478 A.2d 1073, 1080 (D.C. App. 1984) (Ferren, J., dissenting) (noting that "[the reason [behind the rule] is clear, if tautological: to the extent a plaintiff's interest benefits from negligence, [that interest] is not damaged") (brackets added).

[5] Restatement (Second) Torts § 920, illustrations 1–6 (1977).

[6] Section 76.2 (Wrongful Conception/Wrongful Pregnancy).

have to account for a benefit of uncertain value that was forced upon her by the defendant.[7] Other courts permit the offset reasoning that the interests are highly correlated and do not require speculation.[8]

This principle is similar to but different from concepts of betterment or unjust enrichment. The focus here is on the measure of the net injury to a particular interest of the plaintiff. The fact that defendant's misconduct may have conferred a benefit on the plaintiff does not necessarily invoke the "special benefit" rule. For example, in *Gits v. Norwest Bank Minneapolis*,[9] the bank converted bonds owned by Gits but also miscredited his account with funds, which Gits invested and on which he earned interest. The bank sought to offset its liability for conversion with the money Gits earned on the miscredited funds. The court refused to apply the "special benefits" rule on these facts since the benefit was not the result of the conversion but resulted from a related but independent act—the miscrediting of funds.[10] The bank should have sought recovery under a theory of unjust enrichment.[11] Similar results have been reached in cases where the plaintiff was induced either by fraud or misfeasance to sell an asset at a profit and invest the proceeds in a new asset, which thereafter depreciated in value. The courts have consistently refused to offset the plaintiff's damages claim from the second transaction with the profits from the first transaction.[12]

A plaintiff's benefits may be negative in the sense of expenses avoided because of defendant's misconduct that would have been incurred had defendant not engaged in the misconduct. Plaintiff's net, actual injury is the difference between where plaintiff is and where she would have been but for defendant's wrongful conduct. Unless plaintiff's damages award reflects those expenses avoided and saved, plaintiff will be better off as a result of defendant's wrongful conduct than she would have been had defendant acted legally. For example, in *Hanover Shoe, Inc. v. United Shoe Machinery Corp.*[13] defendant was found to be engaging in anticompetitive conduct when it refused to sell certain shoe manufacturing equipment and required persons, such as plaintiff, to lease the machinery instead. Because

---

[7] Lodato v. Kappy, 803 A.2d 160 (N.J. Super. Ct. A.D. 2002); Lovelace Med. Ctr. v. Mendez, 805 P.2d 603, 613–14 (N. Mex. 1991); Marciniak v. Lundborg, 450 N.W.2d 243, 249 (Wis. 1990).

[8] Burke v. Rivo, 551 N.E.2d 1, 5 (Mass. 1990) (permitting parents of unplanned for child to recover economic and non-economic damages as a result of child borne after negligent sterilization procedure, but permitting trier of fact to consider as offset benefit and joy plaintiff-parents realized from their child). The *Burke* court did not limit the offset to the non-economic portions of the award. Ochs v. Borrelli, 445 A.2d 883 (Conn. 1982).

[9] 390 N.W.2d 835 (Minn. App. 1986).

[10] *Id.* at 837–38.

[11] Chapter 5 (General Principles Governing Restitution).

[12] Kane v. Shearson Lehman Hutton, Inc., 916 F.2d 643, 646 (11th Cir. 1990) (rejecting "netting" theory); Nesbit v. McNeil, 896 F.2d 380, 385–86 (9th Cir. 1990) (rejecting argument that profits made from "churning" (excessive trading by broker) a securities account should be offset against the losses the customer incurred as a result of the practice).

[13] 392 U.S. 481 (1968).

persons, such as a plaintiff, would have purchased rather than leased the machinery if they had the opportunity to do so, the Court offset plaintiff's antitrust damages (gross rentals paid) against the amount plaintiff would have expended to purchase the machinery.[14]

The issue also arises in professional malpractice actions when the professional seeks to offset the plaintiff's damages award with the value or cost of services rendered. Courts have split as to whether such an offset is proper, although the focus tends to be on public policy rather than "special benefit."[15]

When a plaintiff benefitted from participating in the wrongful conduct she now seeks to assert as the basis for her damages claim, the plaintiff may have to account for the betterment as an offset against her damages. For example, in *Perma-Life Mufflers, Inc. v. International Parts Corp.*[16] the plaintiff participated in defendant's antitrust violations. While that participation did not bar the damages action under principles of "in pari delicto,"[17] the Court held that the benefits realized by the plaintiff should be deducted from plaintiff's gross antitrust damages to determine plaintiff's net, actual injury.[18]

[14.2] Special Benefits Rule in Contract

When a defendant's breach of contract has conferred a direct and immediate benefit on the plaintiff, the defendant is entitled to an offset against plaintiff's claimed damages.[19] The offset works more effectively in contract than in tort because the same economic interest is usually present for both the damages and benefit calculation. That said, the defendant must still quantify the benefit and the same rigor that attends the plaintiff's proof of his damages will accompany the defendant's proof of any offsetting benefit.[20]

---

[14] *Id.* at 487.

[15] Foster v. Duggin, 695 S.W.2d 526, 527 (Tenn. 1985) (holding that allowing deduction for attorney's fees plaintiff would have paid to the defendant would undercompensate the plaintiff since it would fail to reflect the additional attorney's fees plaintiff incurred in prosecuting the malpractice action); Restatement (Third) of Law Governing Lawyers. § 53 cmt. c (2000) (noting that denial of offset is appropriate sanction and prevents the defendant-lawyer from benefitting from a fee that she never earned). *See generally* John Theuman, Annot., *Measure and Elements of Damages Recoverable for Attorney's Negligence in Preparing or Conducting Litigation—Twentieth Century Cases*, 90 A.L.R. 4th 1033, § 14 (1992).

[16] 392 U.S. 134 (1968).

[17] Section 62.2 ("In Pari Delicto").

[18] 392 U.S. at 140.

[19] Macon-Bibb County Water & Sewerage Auth. v. Tuttle/White Constr., 530 F. Supp. 1048, 1055 (M.D. Ga. 1981); Louisiana Sulphur Carriers v. Gulf Resources & Chem. Corp., 53 F.R.D. 458, 461–62 (D. Del. 1971); *see* Restatement (Second) of Contracts § 347 cmts. c–e (1981).

[20] John Morrell & Co. v. Local Union 304A, 913 F.2d 544, 557 (8th Cir. 1990) (holding that defendant must prove the offset with "reasonable certainty" and finding defendant's proof deficient in that regard).

A plaintiff who is able to resell property or goods at a higher price due to defendant's breach of contract must credit the defendant with the net gain the breach permitted.[21] The situation may be different, however, when the plaintiff is a lost volume seller and, therefore, could have made two sales rather than one but for the defendant's breach.[22] In the lost volume seller context, giving the defendant a credit for the higher resale price could depreciate the two expectancies, which plaintiff would have realized but for defendant's breach, into one expectancy—the resale profit. Since giving the credit would not restore plaintiff to his rightful position, the argument may be made that an offset should not be given if the lost volume seller rule is applied.

[14.3] Taxes

The general rule is that a defendant may not capture, as an offset against a damages award, the tax benefits a plaintiff realized as a result of the defendant's misconduct.[23] This rule has been applied even when the primary motivation for the transaction is to secure a tax reduction.[24]

An example of the type of case that raises the tax benefit offset issue is *Cereal By Products Co. v. Hall*.[25] In that case the defendant-accountant was sued for negligence for failing to detect embezzlement by one of plaintiff's employees. Defendant sought, as a credit, the amount of tax benefits (federal tax refund) plaintiff received when it reported its theft losses as deductions to its gross taxable income. The court rejected the offset notwithstanding it was a fixed amount (the refund) on the ground that the issue of taxes was between the plaintiff and the government and did not concern the defendant.[26] The situation is seen as no different from that when the defendant destroys plaintiff's personal property, such as a valuable painting, and plaintiff is able to claim a casualty loss on his income tax return. It has not been successfully contended in such cases that plaintiff's tax benefit can be captured by defendant as an offset.[27]

---

[21] *Cf.* Heckert v. MacDonald, 256 Cal. Rptr. 369, 372 (Cal. App. 1989) (noting that while "appellants" suffered pecuniary damages by incurring attorney fees proximately caused by broker's tortious conduct, a preponderance of the evidence supported the conclusion that they also obtained a financial benefit in the form of an increased sale price as a result of that same conduct").

[22] Section 8.5 (Lost Volume Seller).

[23] Billings Clinic v. Peat Marwick, 797 P.2d 899, 912–13 (Mont. 1990); De Palma v. Westland Software House, 276 Cal. Rptr. 214, 217 (Cal. App. 1990).

[24] Randall v. Loftsgaarden, 478 U.S. 647 (1986) (holding that recovery should not be reduced by tax benefits received from a tax shelter investment that plaintiffs sought to rescind on the basis the shelter violated federal securities laws).

[25] 147 N.E.2d 383, (Ill. App.), *aff'd on other grounds*, 155 N.E.2d 14 (Ill. 1958).

[26] *Id.* at 384; *see* Fullmer v. Wohlfeiler & Beck, 905 F.2d 1394, 1402 (10th Cir. 1990); Coty v. Ramsey Assocs., Inc., 546 A.2d 196, 204 (Vt.), *cert. denied*, 487 U.S. 1236 (1988). Danzig v. Grynberg & Assocs., 208 Cal. Rptr. 336, 343 (Cal. App. 1984), *cert. denied*, 474 U.S. 819 (1985).

[27] Burdett v. Miller, 957 F.2d 1375, 1382–83 (7th Cir. 1992).

Other reasons given for not allowing tax benefits to be claimed by defendants as damages offsets include: (1) the "benefit" is illusory because the amount recovered for an item previously deducted must be reported as income in the year received;[28] and (2) tax benefits are usually too speculative to be considered.[29]

An interesting variation of this issue occurs in malpractice cases when the plaintiff claims that professional advice caused her to incur a tax liability with a deficiency assessment. The defendant will argue that if the plaintiff is entitled to recover the amount of the deficiency, or part thereof, as damages, the defendant should be allowed to claim, as an offsetting benefit, the use value of the money plaintiff did not pay in taxes until the tax assessment was paid. In *Ronson v. Talesnick*[30] the court permitted both the recovery of the interest paid as damages[31] and the claiming of an offset.[32]

§ 15 COLLATERAL SOURCE RULE

[15.1] Nature of the Rule

The Collateral Source Rule (CSR) holds that the plaintiff may recover damages that include amounts for which the plaintiff has already received compensation from sources independent of the defendant. The classic application permits the plaintiff in a tort action to recover, as damages, losses for which the plaintiff has received payment under an insurance policy maintained by her. For example, the plaintiff's medical expenses may be paid by her health care provider, but she may still claim medical expenses as damages. Similarly, the plaintiff's property insurer may compensate plaintiff for a property loss, but plaintiff may still claim repair costs or diminution in value losses as damages.

CSR may be seen as an exception to a pure compensation theory in several ways. First, to the extent a plaintiff has received payment, from someone other than the tortfeasor, for a loss, the plaintiff has been made whole and to the extent of the payment restored to the position plaintiff would have achieved but for the legal injury. Second, plaintiff's injuries have caused her to receive a benefit she would not have realized but for the legal injury; to the extent that benefit is not offset against plaintiff's losses, the plaintiff would recover duplicative damages. In effect, the plaintiff recovers twice: once from the collateral source and once from the tortfeasor.

---

[28] Randall v. Loftsgaarden, 478 U.S. 647, 660, 667 (1986); Burgess v. Premier Corp., 727 F.2d 826, 838 (9th Cir. 1984).

[29] *Randall, supra*, 478 U.S. at 664–65; *DePalma, supra*, 276 Cal. Rptr. at 220–21.

[30] 33 F. Supp. 2d 347 (D.N.J. 1999).

[31] *Id.* at 352–53 (noting split in jurisdictions as to recovery of interest paid to IRS as interest or penalty as damages).

[32] *Id.* at 355; *see* Caroline Rule, *What and When Can a Taxpayer Recover From a Negligent Tax Advisor?*, 92 J. Tax'n 176 (2000).

Several justifications for the exception to pure compensation accomplished by CSR have been offered. First, it is argued that there is no overcompensation of the plaintiff, or "double recovery" inconsistent with the ideal of compensatory damages, because the plaintiff is ordinarily under a legal or moral obligation to reimburse the benefit provider out of the proceeds received from the defendant. Second, the rule enhances deterrence by ensuring that defendants pay the fullest measure of damages for the legal injuries they inflict. It is thought that if defendants could capture the plaintiff's benefit, defendants would be less careful in avoiding wrongful conduct. Third, there is a quasi-moral belief that the wrongdoer ought not to obtain the benefit of the plaintiff's good judgment in obtaining, through a collateral source, insurance or the plaintiff's good fortune in having, for example, a compassionate employer who continues to pay the plaintiff's wages notwithstanding plaintiff's inability to work due to the injuries inflicted by the defendant.[1]

If CSR is applied, the provider of the benefit is usually subrogated to the interest of the person who received the benefit.[2] Subrogation may not be permitted for certain types of claims, such as personal injury because of concerns over trafficking in the claims.[3] Jurisdictions usually permit the benefit provider to assert liens securing a right to reimbursement from the proceeds realized from the litigation by judgment or settlement.[4] For example, assume X is injured due to the neglect of Y. Insurance company pays X's medical expenses in full. If X receives an award from Y that includes X's medical expenses, X must pay over that amount to Insurance Company. This can raise some difficult issues involving allocation. Assume X had $10,000 of medical expenses and $7,500 of lost earnings. X prays for $100,000 but settles for $35,000. Is Insurance Company entitled to full reimbursement? What if the parties (X and the defendant) specify that $25,000 of the settlement is for pain and suffering and $10,000 is for lost earning and, by implication, $0 for medical expenses?[5]

---

[1] Helfend v. California Rapid Trans. Dist., 465 P.2d 61, 69 (Cal. 1970) (stating that [t]he tortfeasor should not garner the benefits of his victim's providence"); Collins v. King, 545 N.W.2d 301, 312 (Iowa 1996) (stating that the plaintiff's duplicative recovery is preferable to the immunization of the tortfeasor for the full consequences of her wrongdoing).

[2] *Helfend, supra,* 465 P.2d at 69; Section 53 (Subrogation).

[3] *See generally* R.D. Hursh, *Assignability of Claims for Personal Injury or Death,* 40 A.L.R.2d 500 (1955 & Supp. 2000). The issue of the sale of personal injury claims has been the subject of recent scholarly activity, much of it critical of the common law prohibition. Michael Abramowicz, *On The Alienability of Legal Claims,* 114 Yale L.J. 697 (2005).

[4] *See* Erik V. Larson & Diana L. Panian, *Successfully Discharging Medical Liens in Personal Injury Cases,* 32 Cumb. L. Rev. 349 (2001–02). This has become a litigious area of the law with lienholders increasingly insistent and vigilant about protecting their right to reimbursement. *E.g.,* Kent M. Kostka, *Negotiating the Hospital Lien Minefield,* 68 Tex. B. J. 128 (2005); Roger J. Larue & Daniel Q. Posin, *Medicaid, ERISA and Other Medical Liens Against Personal Injury Recoveries,* 51 LA B.J. 334 (Feb./Mar. 2004); Section 72 (Medical Expenses).

[5] Ganley v. United States, 878 F.2d 1351, 1353 (11th Cir. 1989) (monies received by plaintiff from his benefits provider for past medical expenses could only be deducted from that portion of verdict representing same item of damages); *cf.* Jones v. Kramer, 838 A.2d 170, 178 (Conn. 2004) (construing Connecticut collateral source statute to require that a party seeking to reduce

[15.1.1]   Rule of Substance

CSR as a rule of substance is a rule of damages. CSR precludes reducing the damages award by the amount the plaintiff received from the collateral source. As a rule of substance, CSR applies to many forms of payments and benefits the plaintiff receives as a result of, or notwithstanding, his injuries, including: (1) wages;[6] (2) sick pay and vacation benefits;[7] (3) disability income insurance;[8] and (4) pensions.[9] For the most part, government benefits paid to the plaintiff as a result of personal injuries caused by the tortfeasor are subject to CSR.[10] This issue is addressed in more detail in Sections 15.3 (Gratuituous Benefits) and 15.4.1 (United States as Defendant).

[15.1.2]   Rule of Evidence

If CSR were only a rule of damages, a defendant might be able to present evidence of the collateral benefit at trial in the hope that it would influence the trier-of-fact. CSR also operates, however, as a rule of evidence. In this capacity CSR bars admission of evidence of the existence of the collateral source or the receipt of benefits. The concern here is that the trier of fact may use that evidence improperly to deny the plaintiff the full recovery to which he is entitled. CSR as a rule of evidence follows naturally from CSR as a rule of substance: evidence that cannot be used by the trier-of-fact to decrease the award is inadmissible. This has led to some disagreement whether it is proper to formulate CSR as a dual rule.[11] This dual formulation does, however, have several consequences. First, it tends to raise the

---

the amount of economic damages awarded . . . bears the burden of proving that the verdict includes items of damages for which the plaintiff has received a collateral source benefit"). On the priorities to proceeds as between plaintiff and the benefits provider, see *Rimes v. State Farm Mut. Ins. Co.*, 316 N.W.2d 348, 353–56 (Wis. 1982) (discussing various approaches); Section 53.3 (Subrogation Priorities).

[6] STEIN ON PERSONAL INJURY DAMAGES, *supra* at § 13.9 (collecting decisions); *see* Aaron v. Johnson, 794 S.W.2d 724, 727 (Mo. App. 1990) ("Continued payment of compensation by an employer to an employee during a time of the employee's disability may be gratuitous. If such continued pay is gratuitous, a third-person tortfeasor is not entitled to reduction of damages for the amount of such gratuity.").

[7] *Aaron*, *supra*, 794 S.W.2d at 727.

[8] Rotolo Chevrolet v. Superior Court, 129 Cal. Rptr. 2d 283, 286 (Cal. App. 2003) (stating that disability insurance payments could not be offset against lost earnings claim because of CSR).

[9] STEIN ON PERSONAL INJURY DAMAGES, *supra* at § 13.12 (collecting decisions). CSR bars the use of the pensions as an offset against the lost earnings claims. If, however, the plaintiff is claiming *pension-related* losses from his injuries, *e.g.*, his ability to earn a larger pension was harmed, CSR may not apply. *Rotolo*, *supra*, 129 Cal. Rptr. 2d at 286.

[10] STEIN ON PERSONAL INJURY DAMAGES, *supra* at § 13.6 (Federal Government Payments— Medicare, Medicaid, Social Security, etc.).

[11] Richard Maxwell, *The Collateral Source Rule in the American Law of Damages*, 46 Minn. L. Rev. 669 (1962). *But cf.* Joel Jacobsen, *The Collateral Source Rule and the Role of the Jury*, 70 Or. L. Rev. 523 (1991) (criticizing bifurcated view and contending that rule is solely one of damages and not evidence).

bar when the defendant seeks to introduce evidence of the collateral benefit for a purpose other than as an offset.[12] Second, it can raise some knotty issues when tort reform and CSR collide. For example, as part of an effort to "reform" medical malpractice and bring some relief to physicians faced with rising medical malpractice insurance premiums, the California Legislature enacted MICRA (Medical Injury Compensation Reform Act) in 1975. A part of that Act provides that a defendant in a medical malpractice case can introduce evidence at trial of all collateral source payments, and the plaintiff can introduce evidence of what he or she has contributed to get the benefit of these payments. The section is silent on the question of whether the jury can award the plaintiff medical damages that have been paid for by a collateral source.[13] In 1984 the California Supreme Court observed that the Legislature apparently assumed "that the trier of fact would take the plaintiff's receipt of such benefits into account by reducing damages."[14] Prior versions of the statute had required an offset, but the final version was silent.[15] The question thus arose whether the statute, as enacted, adopted CSR only as a rule of evidence or as both a rule of evidence and a rule of substance. In this case, the difference was material.[16]

CSR as a rule of evidence is also significant when the plaintiff seeks to recover medical expenses from the tortfeasor and the plaintiff's billings do not reflect the actual amount paid to the health care provider. This often occurs when the health care provider separately contracts with plaintiff's insurer and agrees to accept a set sum for the services.[17] In these cases the tortfeasor-defendant will seek to show that the payments are less than the billings. CSR, as a rule of evidence, may block this approach. For example, in *Rose v. Via Christi Health Systems, Inc.* the court barred a defendant hospital from limiting the plaintiff's medical expense damages claim to the amount actually paid for the plaintiff's treatment and services. The court found that permitting the defendant to introduce evidence of the amount paid would violate the collateral source rule.[18] This is a hotly contentious issue today and not all courts reach this result. Some courts limit the recovery to the amount paid;[19] other courts limit recovery to the reasonable value of medical services provided and allow both evidence of billing and payment to determine that issue.[20]

---

[12] Section 15.5 (Permissible Inquiries Into Collateral Sources).

[13] Cal. Civ. Code § 3333.1

[14] Barme v. Wood, 689 P.2d 446, 449 n.5 (Cal. 1984).

[15] *Id.*

[16] The court in *Barme, supra,* did not reach the issue. *See* Hernandez v. California Hospital Medical Center, 93 Cal. Rptr. 2d 97, 102 (Cal. App. 2000) (reversing trial court decision that had deducted collateral benefits and holding that issue was committed to jury's discretion under § 3333.1); Fein v. Permanente Medical Group, 695 P.2d 665, 685 (Cal. 1985) (noting that § 3333.1 does not require offset), *appeal dismissed,* 474 U.S. 892 (1985).

[17] Section 72.2 (Discounted Billing).

[18] 78 P.3d 798, 806 (Kan. 2003).

[19] Moorhead v. Crozer Chester Medical Center, 765 A.2d 786 (Pa. 2001).

[20] Haselden v. Davis, 579 S.E.2d 293 (S.C. 2003) (stating that evidence of actual payment should include a cautionary instruction to the jury that "such payments may not be used to limit recovery"). The issue is addressed in more detail in Section 72.2 (Discounted Billing).

Lastly, CSR as an evidentiary rule raises *Erie* Doctrine questions.[21] This issue arose in *Fitzgerald v. Expressway Sewerage Construction, Inc.*[22] when defendant sought to introduce evidence that the minor plaintiff's medical bills had been covered by insurance after the plaintiff's mother testified that the accident had imposed "quite a strain [on the family] both emotionally and financially."[23] Defendant argued that the mother's testimony created a false impression and that the evidence of the insurance benefits would put the mother's further testimony that the "medical bills were the source of financial strain" in proper perspective.[24] The district court allowed the evidence and the appellate court affirmed, finding that the lower court had not abused its discretion and that the admissibility of the evidence was governed by federal law.[25]

[15.1.3] Tort or Contract

CSR is usually limited to tort actions. Such a limitation is often assumed and occasionally explicitly stated.[26] The traditional common law rule is that CSR does not apply to contract actions.[27] The rationale for this approach is that in contract, unlike tort, the policy of deterrence is less significant and the policy against overcompensation is greater.[28] This approach can have some interesting applications. For example, in *Plut v. Fireman's Fund Ins. Co.*[29] plaintiffs sued their homeowner insurer for bad faith failure to pay insurance proceeds for property damage to their home. At the same time, plaintiffs sued and recovered a judgment against the tortfeasors responsible for the property damage. The question before the court was whether that award was a benefit subject to CSR.

Normally, an insurer, after paying the loss, is subrogated to the rights of its insured and may seek reimbursement of its payments from the

---

[21] Under *Erie R. Co. v. Tompkins*, 304 U.S. 64 (1938), and its progeny, in diversity cases damages issues are governed by state law, *in most cases*, while evidentiary issues are governed by federal law, *in most cases*.

[22] 177 F.3d 71 (1st Cir. 1999).

[23] *Id.* at 75 (brackets added).

[24] *Id.*; Section 15.5 (Permissible Inquiries Into Collateral Sources) (discussing exceptions to CSR).

[25] *Id.* at 74 ("To sum up, the Massachusetts collateral source rule must be given full credit in this case as a rule of damages. The evidentiary implications flowing from that rule, however, are governed by the Federal Rules of Evidence.").

[26] United States v. City of Twin Falls, 806 F.2d 862, 873 (9th Cir. 1986), *cert. denied*, 482 U.S. 914 (1987); Corl v. Huron Castings, Inc., 544 N.W.2d 278, 280–83 (Mich. 1996) (holding that CSR is concept of tort law and would not be extended to contract remedies; extension would conflict with compensatory goal of contract law); Amalgamated Transit Union Local 1324 v. Roberts, 434 S.E.2d 450, 452–53 (Ga. 1993) (same).

[27] Midland Mut. Life Ins. Company v. Mercy Clinics, Inc., 579 N.W.2d 823, 829–30 (Iowa 1998) (citing Restatement (Second) of Contracts § 347 cmt. e (1979) and collecting decisions that have refused to apply CSR in breach of contract actions).

[28] *Id.*

[29] 102 Cal. Rptr. 2d 36 (Cal. App. 2000).

tortfeasor.[30] In *Plut* the insurer had bypassed participation in the litigation with the tortfeasors and thus was barred from asserting its subrogation rights under California law until the insureds had recouped their entire loss from the tortfeasor, including litigation expenses.[31] In this posture, the insurer's ability to claim a portion of the award directly or by offset was subordinated to the insurer's interest in full recovery and was unlikely to have real economic value. On the other hand, because CSR did not apply to breach of contract actions, the insureds could not avoid an offset for the money they recovered from the tortfeasor legally responsible for the property damage for which they claimed coverage under their homeowner's policy.[32] The contract characterization of the bad faith action dominated the tort-based aspects of the claim.[33]

There are intimations in some cases that CSR applies to contract actions when the breach is willful and the action has tort-like elements of deceit or misrepresentation.[34] In some jurisdictions, the extension of CSR to contract actions has been explicit;[35] nonetheless, the decisions are probably limited to claims that can be asserted either as torts or breaches of contract. This issue has arisen with some frequency in wrongful discharge actions when the claim may be framed in some jurisdictions as sounding in tort or contract. In either context, the typical issue is whether the employee's lost earnings are subject to an offset for unemployment compensation received? The general response has been that an offset will be allowed, particularly if the action sounds in contract.[36]

Abrogation of the tort-contract distinction was championed by Professor John Fleming,[37] but the momentum has been toward restricting CSR's application in tort rather than extending it to contract.[38]

---

[30] Section 53 (Subrogation).

[31] 102 Cal. Rptr. 2d at 40–41.

[32] *Id.* at 42–44.

[33] Section 141 (Bad Faith Breach).

[34] City of Salinas v. Souza & McCue Constr. Co., 424 P.2d 921, 926 Cal. (1967) (holding that CSR was not applicable in breach of contract action possibly involving deceit because defendant was a governmental entity).

[35] Rutzen v. Monroe County Long Care Term Program, Inc., 429 N.Y.S.2d 863, 864 (Sup. Ct. 1980) (involving employment dispute, but court did not purport to limits holding to wrongful termination cases).

[36] *Corl, supra,* 544 N.W.2d at 285–86 (holding that the plaintiff employee's lost earnings claim must be reduced by unemployment compensation he received after his termination in breach of his contract). When the claim is characterized as other than a breach of contract, the result may differ. Craig v. Y&Y Snacks, 721 F.2d 77, 83 (3d Cir. 1983) (applying CSR in wrongful discharge case based on discriminatory termination in violation of Title VII); Hayes v. Trulock, 755 P.2d 830, 834–35 (Wash. App. 1988) (applying CSR in tort-based wrongful discharge case).

[37] John Fleming, *The Collateral Source Rule and Contract Damages,* 71 Cal. L. Rev. 56 (1983).

[38] Section 15.7 (Collateral Source Rule and Tort Reform).

[15.2] Collateral Source or No Damage

It can occasionally be difficult to determine whether a court will look at a third party payment and treat it as a collateral source or as an extinguishment or reduction of the loss. For example, in *Johnston v. Aiken Auto Parts* the plaintiff suffered personal injuries and property damage as a result of defendant's negligence. As part of his damages, plaintiff claimed the cost of a canceled vacation package he was unable to take because of his injuries. Defendant sought to introduce evidence that the cost of the vacation package had been refunded; thus, plaintiff had, in fact, suffered no economic detriment on this point. The court upheld rejection of defendant's evidence finding that the refund was a collateral source independent of the tortfeasor and, thus, within CSR[39]

On the other hand, in *Bates v. Hogg* the plaintiff was injured in an automobile accident. Plaintiff's medical treatment was paid by Medicaid, with the treatment provider accepting a discount from its customary charge in exchange for the Medicaid payment. Plaintiff wished to base her claim on the undiscounted amount, contending that the provider's willingness to accept the discount and the Medicaid payment as payment in full was in the nature of a benefit that was collateral to and independent of the defendant. The court rejected the argument, holding that CSR did not apply:

> Under the facts before us, we agree with a statement made by a federal court in North Carolina, which stated in a similar case: "It would be unconscionable to permit the taxpayers to bear the expense of providing free medical care to a person and then allow that person to recover damages for medical services from a tortfeasor and pocket the windfall."[40]

In *Shaefer v. American Family Mutual Insurance Company*[41] plaintiffs sought loss of inheritance damages resulting from the wrongful death of their parents. The plaintiffs had received the proceeds of a life insurance

---

[39] 428 S.E.2d 737, 739 (S.C. App. 1993) (noting that South Carolina "allows the plaintiff the benefit of both gratuitous benefits and nongratuitous benefits arising from employment, insurance or *other contractual agreements*") (citations omitted; emphasis in original); Section 72.2 (Discounted Billing).

[40] 921 P.2d 249, 253 (Kan. App. 1996), *citing* Gordon v. Forsyth County Hosp. Auth., Inc., 409 F. Supp. 708, 719 (M.D.N.C. 1976); *see* Amwest Sav. Ass'n v. Statewide Capital, Inc., 144 F.3d 885, 889–90 (5th Cir. 1998) (holding that agreement between Amwest and FSLIC (Federal Home Loan Bank Board), which guaranteed Amwest the "book value" of certain covered assets and obligated the FSLIC to pay the difference between the assets' sale price and its book value, if the sale price was less than book value, was not a collateral source), *cert. denied*, 525 U.S. 1105 (1999). Consequently, when Amwest sued certain individuals claiming that they had manipulated the bidding process so that certain assets sold below their market value, those individuals could claim that because of the Amwest-FSLIC agreement, Amwest suffered no actual injury to the extent the assets' "market value" did not exceed its "book value." In other words, any reduction in the price of the assets accomplished by the alleged manipulation of the bidding process by the individual was borne by the FSLIC, not Amwest.

[41] 514 N.W.2d 16 (Wis. App. 1994).

policy on their parent's lives. The court held that the plaintiffs' gain from the insurance proceeds could be offset against the loss of inheritance claim. The court noted that while CSR would bar consideration of the life insurance proceeds in the more typical "loss of support" context, CSR did not apply to a "loss of inheritance" claim. [42]

[15.3]   Gratuitous Benefits

The general rule is that the defendant is not permitted to introduce evidence that the benefit was provided gratuitously; rather, plaintiff can recover the reasonable value of the services actually provided. [43] The older rule was apparently to the contrary, [44] and some modern jurisdictions continue to reject application of CSR to gratuitously provided benefits or services. [45]

The relationship between CSR and gratuitous benefits can be complicated by the fact that other questions are often implicated in the analysis. For example, when benefits are gratuitously bestowed on the plaintiff, the issue might be framed as whether the plaintiff suffered any harm. [46] In other contexts, particularly when government benefits are involved, the issue may be framed in terms of the characterization of the benefit. [47] For example, many courts distinguish between federal medicare and medicaid benefits on the basis that medicare is funded, at least in part, by employee contributions; medicaid, on the other hand, is a benefits program funded directly by taxes. [48] Medicaid benefits, but not Medicare benefits, would be treated as gratuitous benefits based on the difference in source of funding. This does not mean that CSR will not apply, just that the effort may be more difficult. [49]

---

[42] *Id.* at 20 (noting that "life insurance proceeds are highly relevant to the primary issue . . . the difference between what the heirs would have inherited and what they *actually did* inherit") (emphasis in original).

[43] *See generally* J.A. Connelly, Annot., *Damages For Personal Injury or Death as Including Value of Care and Nursing Gratuitously Rendered*, 90 A.L.R.2d 1323 (1963).

[44] Gibney v. St. Louis Transit Co., 103 S.W. 43, 48 (Mo. 1907) (holding that injured mother could not recover as compensable damages value of nursing services gratuitously provided by daughter).

[45] Rutzen v. Monroe County Long Term Care Program, Inc., 429 N.Y.S.2d 863, 865 (Sup. Ct. 1980) (noting that "New York State has long belonged to a minority of jurisdictions which create an exception to the CSR for wholly gratuitous services and payments received by an injured plaintiff for which he gave no consideration and which he is not obligated to repay, absolutely or contingently")

[46] Section 15.2 (Collateral Source or No Damage); *see* Drinkwater v. Dinsmore, 80 N.Y. 390 (1880) (holding that when employer continued employee's wages after employee was injured by tortfeasor and unable to work, employee suffered no loss). *Drinkwater* is not the modern view. Section 15.1.1 (Rule of Substance).

[47] *See generally* Dag E. Ytreberg, Annot., *Collateral Source Rule: Receipt of Public Relief or Gratuity as Affecting Recovery in Personal Injury Action*, 77 A.L.R. 3d 366 (1977).

[48] Rose v. Via Christi Health System, Inc., 78 P.3d 798, 802–03 (Kan. 2003).

[49] Haselden v. Davis, 579 S.E.2d 293, 294 n.3 (S.C. 2003) (collecting decisions applying CSR to medicaid benefits); Section 15.4.1 (United States as Defendant).

[15.4] Independent Source

Application of CSR requires that the benefit be from a source independent from the defendant. When the plaintiff has arranged for the benefit and there is no relationship between the plaintiff and the defendant, the requirement is easily met. For example, if strangers meet and collide in an automobile accident, the benefits received from plaintiff's health care provider are not likely to be in any way connected with the defendant. As our world becomes smaller and more interconnected, however, complete independence is harder to achieve. Two recurring problem areas involve claims when the United States is a defendant and claims against employers.

[15.4.1] United States as Defendant

When the United States is sued, as for example under the Federal Tort Claims Act for the torts of its employees, the United States may claim that plaintiff's damages should be offset by benefits paid to the plaintiff as a result of the tortious conduct, such as medical treatment through Medicare, Medicaid, or Veterans benefits.

The general rule involving government benefits is to distinguish between payments made from special funds to which the plaintiff contributed as opposed to general funds made up of general tax revenues. Payments from special funds are generally deemed independent of the government.[50] Social Security and Medicare would generally be considered special funds even though the greater portion of the benefits payout, from an actuarial viewpoint, consists of a contribution from funds contributed by others.[51] On the other hand, benefits paid to veterans may be treated as from general funds.[52] This is not to diminish in any way the contributions of service veterans to the United States. It illustrates that the contribution must be

---

[50] Siverson v. United States, 710 F.2d 557, 560 (9th Cir. 1983).

[51] Manko v. United States, 830 F.2d 831, 836 (8th Cir. 1987) (federal medicare benefits are subject to CSR). Not all Social Security programs came from earmarked, special funds. For example, Supplemental Security Income (SSI) is a public welfare benefits program that provides financial assistance to those who qualify (e.g., developmentally disabled persons) and have not worked to qualify for social security benefits. 42 U.S.C. §§ 1381–1383f. If a developmentally disabled person works, she may qualify for SSDI (Social Security Disability Income), which is a special fund to which the employee contributes. 42 US.C. § 423(d)(1)(A). Whether SSI benefits would be subject to CSR appears to be an open question. But cf. Schroeder v. Triangulum Assoc., 789 A.2d 459, 470–71 (Conn. 2002) (holding that SSI benefits are not a collateral source as defined by the governing Connecticut statute, which controlled the classification; Connecticut law precludes giving CSR status to all social security benefits).

[52] Steckler v. United States, 549 F.2d 1372 (10th Cir. 1977); Feeley v. United States, 337 F.2d 924, 934 (3d Cir. 1964); United States v. Brooks, 176 F.2d 482, 484 (4th Cir. 1949); Green v. United States, 530 F. Supp. 633 (E.D. Wis. 1982), aff'd on other grounds, 709 F.2d 1158 (7th Cir. 1983); cf. Mays v. United States, 806 F.2d 976 (10th Cir. 1986) (Civilian Health and Medical Program of the Uniform Services (CHAMPUS) benefits for certain retired members of the armed services and their dependents), cert. denied, 482 U.S. 913 (1987). But cf. Brooks, 176 F.2d at 485 (excluding from offset government provided life insurance policy). See generally John Wagner, Annot., Application of Collateral Source Rule to Actions Under Federal Torts Claims Act (28 U.S.C.A. § 2674), 104 A.L.R. Fed. 492 (1991).

monetary for the subsequent benefit to be deemed as coming from a special fund.[53] It should be noted, however, that a plaintiff is not obligated to use a benefit that will evade treatment as a collateral source. A plaintiff may receive medical treatment with a private health care provider rather than at a Veterans Hospital and invoke CSR with respect to those private benefits.[54]

The emphasis on the source of the fund can be confusing. The critical issue is really the nature of the payment and the reason the payment is being made. CSR is not a single rule but an amalgamation of different policies.[55] It is the vindication of these policies that justifies the application of the Rule. In *Washington v. Barnes Hospital*[56] the court refused to apply CSR to exclude evidence of the availability of a free public special education when the plaintiff sought to recover the cost of private education necessitated by her disabilities.[57] The court reasoned that since plaintiff incurred no expense, obligation, or liability in connection with the benefit, CSR should not apply:

> Here, plaintiffs need not purchase the public school benefits, nor work for them as an employment benefit, nor contract for them. Hence, the "benefit of the bargain" rationale does not apply. Nor are these benefits provided as a gift by a friend or family member to assist plaintiffs specifically, such that it would be inequitable to transfer the value of the benefit from plaintiffs to defendants. Nor is this a benefit that is dependent upon plaintiff's indigence or other special status. Instead, public school programming is available to all by law. While to some extent public schools are funded by plaintiffs' tax dollars, they are also funded by defendants' tax dollars and no windfall results to either. We reject the concept that

---

[53] Overton v. United States, 619 F.2d 1299, 1307–08 (8th Cir. 1980) (rejecting application of CSR to benefits provided by government when plaintiff had not contributed directly to fund that provided benefits).

[54] Ulrich v. Veterans Admin. Hosp., 853 F.2d 1078, 1083–84 (2d Cir. 1988) (plaintiff should not have been denied future medical expenses award simply because he was eligible for free VA treatment); Molzof v. United States, 6 F.3d 461, 464 (7th Cir. 1993) (same).

[55] Washington v. Barnes Hosp., 897 S.W.2d 611, 619 (Mo. 1995):

> Numerous rationales have been used to justify the application of the CSR. Some courts state that plaintiffs who contract for insurance or other benefits with funds they could have used for other purposes are entitled to the benefit of their bargain. Some courts enforce the CSR to punish the tortfeasor. Other courts opine that, if one party will receive a windfall, it should be the plaintiff. Additional rationales supporting the CSR are: to protect plaintiffs against the inadequacy of public benefits or the uncertainty of their future availability, to recognize that the plaintiff, not the tortfeasor, was the intended beneficiary of gratuitous services, to compensate plaintiff for legal fees and expenses, and to avoid prejudices in the eyes of the jury because plaintiff was attempting to recover for an item for which he had not paid.

(citations omitted).

[56] 897 S.W.2d 611 (Mo. 1995).

[57] *Id.* at 619–20 (citing other jurisdictions refusing to apply CSR in the same situation).

[CSR] should be utilized solely to punish the defendant. Damages in our tort system are compensatory not punitive.[58]

CSR can raise some difficult questions that defy easy answers. The choice often is framed in either/or terms: either defendant pays and plaintiff receives a "windfall" or defendant receives a credit or offset against damages and to that extent receives a "windfall." In contrast to *Washington v. Barnes Hospital*, consider *Karsten v. Kaiser Foundation Health Plan, Inc.*,[59] in which plaintiff was injured by the same party that provided health insurance to the plaintiff. Should the plaintiff recover, as damages, medical expenses incurred, but paid by health insurance, or should defendant receive a credit or offset? The court held that CSR barred admission of evidence that defendant paid plaintiff's compensatory medical bills connected with plaintiff's medical malpractice claim against defendant and rejected defendant's contention that this amounted to double payment:

> Even though the same defendant is being asked to pay the same damages twice, it is patent that the nature of the two payments is different. The nature of the first is as a payment from defendant as insurer to the plaintiff insured. The nature of the second is as a payment from defendant as tortfeasor to the plaintiff as the party injured by the defendant's negligence. It is axiomatic that the plaintiff is entitled to receive the benefit of her bargain under the insurance contract, irrespective of the fact that the carrier servicing that contract may also be the tortfeasor . . . . To set off payments owed by the defendant as insurer against compensation owed by the defendant as tortfeasor allows the defendant to reap a windfall by allowing it to avoid its contractual obligations to the plaintiff.[60]

[15.4.2] Claims Against Employers

When an employee sues an employer for personal injuries, the employee may receive benefits from a fund to which the employer made payments, such as an Employer Sponsored Health & Welfare Plan. Do these benefits fall within CSR? Here there has been a greater willingness to reject the "source" rule. While a few courts have treated the fact of employee contribution as determinative of the benefits status under CSR,[61] the majority of courts appear to reject a *per se* rule. As noted in *Folkestad v. Burlington Northern, Inc.*:

---

[58] *Id.* at 621(brackets added).

[59] 808 F. Supp. 1253, 1256–57 (E.D. Va. 1992).

[60] *Id.* at 1257–58 (citations and footnotes omitted); *Molzof, supra,* 6 F.3d at 465–66 (permitting plaintiff, who treated and received free medical care at VA facility for injuries sustained while a patient at a VA facility, to recovery future medical expenses from the government; the court stated that while the government provided the free care to the plaintiff, it was not entitled to a credit because the source of the payment was different; the government provided free medical care because Molzof was a veteran, not because he was injured in a VA facility; the source of the benefit was independent of the wrongful conduct, therefore, CSR applied).

[61] Poole v. Baltimore & Ohio R.R., Co., 657 F. Supp. 1, 2 (D. Md. 1985).

The problem that has troubled the courts has been whether to treat the insurance as a fringe benefit in part compensation for the employee's work. If it is viewed as the product of the employee's labors, it is deemed to come from a source collateral to the employer/ tortfeasor rather than from the employer/tortfeasor itself. Setoff would permit avoidance of FELA liability, and such avoidance is prohibited by section 5. If, on the other hand, the insurance is viewed as a contribution by the employer intended to fulfill FELA obligations, it would appear to fall within the proviso, and setoff should be permitted.

In dealing with this issue both in the railroad and maritime cases, courts have been virtually unanimous in their refusal to make the source of the premiums the determinative factor in deciding whether the benefits should be regarded as emanating from the employer or from a "collateral source." Rather, courts have tried to look to "the purpose and nature of the fund and of the payments and not merely at their source."[62]

[15.5]   Permissible Inquiries into Collateral Sources

Even if the benefit qualifies as a collateral source, evidence that plaintiff is receiving the benefit may be admissible for reasons other than establishing plaintiff's actual loss. In *Evans v. Wilson*[63] the court recognized a broad range of situations when evidence of a benefit received by the plaintiff as a consequence of his injuries may be admissible notwithstanding CSR:

> There are unquestionably situations in which proof of a plaintiff's collateral income may be admissible for a particular purpose. We mention four such purposes: One, to rebut the plaintiff's testimony that he was compelled by financial necessity to return to work prematurely or to forego additional medical care. Two, to show that the plaintiff had attributed his condition to some other cause, such as sickness. Three, to impeach the plaintiff's testimony that he had paid his medical expenses himself. [F]our, to show that the plaintiff had actually continued to work instead of being out of work, as he claimed.[64]

The court's compilation was an amalgamation of exceptions recognized by diverse jurisdictions. That is probably still the case today; nonetheless, courts remain protective of CSR and exceptions are accepted with caution.[65]

---

[62] 813 F.2d 1377, 1381 (9th Cir. 1987); Perry v. Metro-North Commuter R.R., 716 F. Supp. 61, 62–63 (D. Conn. 1989) (employer not entitled to set off for medical expenses paid on employee's behalf absent specific provision in collective bargaining agreement to that effect).

[63] 650 S.W.2d 569, 570 (Ark. 1983).

[64] *Id.* at 570 (brackets added; citations deleted).

[65] Thornton v. Sanders, 756 So.2d 15, 19 (Miss. App. 1999) (citing *Evans, supra* (650 S.W.2d 569), but refusing to recognize exception to CSR without prior approval by Mississippi Supreme Court).

The plaintiff may open the door, by affirmatively stating he has not received the benefit or by raising an issue that evidence of the benefit would directly negate:

> It is familiar law that a plaintiff's collateral sources of compensation cannot be inquired into as part of a defendant's case, because of the danger that the jury may be inclined to find no liability, or to reduce a damage award, when it learns that plaintiff's loss is entirely or partially covered. We have held, however, for obvious reasons, that once a plaintiff asserts that he does not have coverage, then the defense may show that he does. We have also held that if a plaintiff is claiming emotional injury on account of financial stress following an accident, then defendant may inquire into collateral sources since these, if there are any, would tend to reduce the plaintiff's stress. In these limited kinds of situations, where plaintiff's case itself has made the existence of collateral sources of probative value, we have allowed proof of them.[66]

A number of jurisdictions have permitted inquiry into the plaintiff's receipt of benefits when offered to prove plaintiff is malingering[67] or that plaintiff was not injured as he claims. As noted in *Kish v. Board of Educ., City of New York*:

> The theory underlying the collateral source rule is simply that a negligent defendant should not, in fairness, be permitted to reduce its liability in damages by showing that the plaintiff is already entitled by contract or employment right to reimbursement for such items as medical expenses and lost wages. That rule is not necessarily violated where proof is offered showing that a plaintiff is not permanently disabled and has stopped working solely for a non-injury-related reason, such as voluntary retirement. While, to be sure, such evidence relates to the issue of damages, its purpose and effect may not at all be to offset specific amounts against the sum which a plaintiff might otherwise be awarded, but only to undermine the very basis for the claim—*i.e.*, that the plaintiff stopped working because of the effect of the injury.[68]

Some jurisdictions, however, refuse to recognize "malingering" as an exception to CSR. In some cases, the approach is categorical; the exception is simply deemed to be inconsistent with CSR.[69] In other cases, the issue is less clear because the courts point to the presence of other evidence of malingering.[70] This suggests the concern is more discretion-based than

---

[66] Moses v. Union Pac. R.R., 64 F.3d 413, 416 (8th Cir. 1995) (citations omitted).

[67] Gurliacci v. Mayer, 590 A.2d 914, 927–29 (Conn. 1991) (holding that issue is committed to trial judge's discretion).

[68] 558 N.E.2d 1159 1161 (N.Y. 1990) (footnote omitted).

[69] Proctor v. Castelletti, 911 P.2d 853, 854 (Nev. 1996) (*per curiam*) (holding that collateral source payments are inadmissible even if probative as to the issue of malingering).

[70] Lang v. Lake Shore Exhibits, Inc., 711 N.E.2d 1124, 1129 (Ill. App. 1999); Hrnjak v.

categorical: given the other evidence of malingering, the prejudicial effect of the evidence of collateral benefits in misleading the jury outweighed the evidence's probative value.

[15.6] Payments by Joint Tortfeasors

Payment from a joint tortfeasor does not qualify as a collateral source.[71] The payment must, however, be from a joint tortfeasor. In *In re W.B. Easton Construction Co., Inc.*[72] a bank brought a professional malpractice action against accountants who had prepared the borrower's financial statements. The court held that CSR barred consideration of any amount the bank recovered from guarantors of the borrower's obligation. The foresight of the bank in obtaining the guarantee was not capturable by the accountant-defendants. The guarantors' right of action in unjust enrichment against the bank supports the result since it negates concerns over double recovery by the bank. To the extent, if any, the bank's recovery against the accountant-defendants exceeds its losses on the loan to the borrowers, the bank is unjustly enriched and the guarantors can claim the excess.[73] Similarly, if the defendants harmed different interests of the plaintiff they may be co-defendants pursuant to liberal joinder rules, but that does not make them joint tortfeasors.[74]

A settlement with a defendant determined not to be a tortfeasor comes within CSR. In effect, the tortfeasor cannot capture the economic value a plaintiff acquires by suing the wrong person.[75] The admission of pretrial settlements into the record may also be restricted by concerns over jury prejudice; consequently, any offset that is allowed should be made by the judge after the jury has rendered its award.[76]

Graymar, Inc., 484 P.2d 599 (Cal. 1971) (limiting admission to cases where (1) defendant presents other evidence of malingering, (2) court gives cautionary instruction to jury, and (3) evidence sought to be admitted has substantial probative value).

[71] Porter v. Manes, 347 P.2d 210, 212 (Okla. 1959) (noting that CSR applies unless benefit is provided by tortfeasor or someone on the tortfeasor's behalf).

[72] 463 S.E.2d 317 (S.C. 1995).

[73] Gibson v. Harl, 857 S.W.2d 260, 268 (Mo. App. 1993); Northwest Otolaryngology Assocs. v. Mobilease, Inc., 786 S.W.2d 399, 402 (Tex. Civ. App. 1990); Pearlman v. Reliance Ins. Co., 371 U.S. 132, 136–37 (1962) (noting that "there are few doctrines better established than that a surety who pays the debt of another is entitled to all the rights of the person he paid to enforce his right to be reimbursed").

[74] Chisholm v. UHP Projects, Inc., 205 F.3d 731, 737 (4th Cir. 2000).

[75] Kiss v. Jacob, 650 A.2d 336 (N.J. 1994). Allocation rules applicable to settlements may change this if the jurisdiction permits a non-setting defendant to claim an offset based on the settlement without regard to the settling defendant's actual responsibility for the loss. New Jersey permits an allocation only to the settling defendant's actual fault. *Id.* at 339.

[76] *See* Johnson v. American Homestead Mortg. Corp., 703 A.2d 984, 988 (N.J. Super. Ct. App. Dept. 1997).

[15.7] Collateral Source Rule and Tort Reform Legislation

CSR has been a frequent target of tort reform advocates who believe the rule promotes overcompensation of plaintiff and hence encourages litigation.[77] This has proven to be particularly true in medical malpractice litigation. Modification of CSR has taken several forms. Some jurisdictions have restricted the rule to avoid double recovery.[78] Some jurisdictions have retained the substantive component of the rule (prohibiting deduction of benefits from collateral sources from plaintiff's damages), but they have abandoned the evidentiary component, which excludes evidence of collateral source benefits from the jury.[79] Another approach focuses on whether the plaintiff paid or gave something of value specifically as consideration for the collateral source benefit, for example, insurance premium payments.[80] In these contexts the statutes may allow the plaintiff to recoup the premiums she incurred for the benefits the defendant has now claimed to reduce the award.[81] The statute may provide for a recoupment period.[82] If it does not, there is little decisional law and it is conflicting, as one might expect.[83]

Courts have varied in their response to legislative modification of CSR. Some courts have embraced the statutes;[84] other courts have held that the

---

[77] *See* Deanna Goldsmith, *A Survey of the Collateral Source Rule: The Effects of Tort Reform and Impact on Multistate Litigation*, 53 J. Air L. & Com. 799 (1988).

[78] Fla. Stat. Ann. § 768.76 (limiting CSR to situations where right of subrogation or reimbursement exists).

[79] Ala. Code § 12-21-45 (permitting jury to consider collateral source benefits but not requiring reduction of award to account for collateral source benefits received); Cal. Civ. Code § 3333.1 (same).

[80] Colo. Rev. Stat. Ann. § 13-21 11.6 (limiting CSR to situations when benefits are received as a result of a contract); *cf.* Ind. Code § 34-4-36-1 (allowing admission into evidence of collateral source payments other than (1) life insurance or death benefits, (2) insurance benefits for which the plaintiff or his family paid for directly; and (3) certain governmental payments).

[81] Alvarado v. Black, 728 A.2d 500, 503 (Conn. 1999) (construing Conn. Gen. Stat. § 52-225a(c)).

[82] Minn. Stat. § 548.36, subd. 3(a) (permitting recovery of insurance premiums paid in the two years prior to the accrual of the cause of action).

[83] *Compare* Barme v. Wood, 689 P.2d 446 (Cal. 1984) (committing matter to the discretion of the trier-of-fact), *with* Woodger v. Christ Hospital, 834 A.2d 1047 (N.J. Super. Ct. App. Dept. 2003) (treating issue as involving statutory construction and equity and for the court). In *Woodger* the defendant was allowed to offset plaintiff's social security disability benefits against the future lost earnings award pursuant to New Jersey's CSR reform statute (N.J.S.A. 2A:15-97). Plaintiff sought as an offset her *lifetime* social security contributions. The court felt that was too much of a good thing and permitted an offset for the contributions made for the same number of years as the offset (5 years of benefits). *Id.* at 1052-53.

[84] Shirley v. Russell, 69 F.3d 839, 842 (7th Cir. 1995) (stating that Indiana statute (*see* note 80, *supra*) is "not an abrogation of the common law" but rather it "upholds the common law principle that a decision to protect oneself against certain risks cannot inure to the benefit of a tortfeasor . . .").

statutes must be narrowly construed.[85] In a number of cases, the "reform" of CSR has been declared violative of state constitutional guarantees.[86]

When a collateral source statute has been validly adopted, the critical issue is identifying those benefits that fall within the statute and those that do not. The statute and the common law rule do not generally overlap. A benefit may be included within the common law CSR but not within the collateral source statute.[87]

§ 16   PREJUDGMENT INTEREST

The award of interest is designed to compensate a plaintiff for delay in that party's actual receipt of money from the defendant. Prejudgment interest compensates a party for delay in the receipt of money prior to the date judgment is entered. Postjudgment interest compensates a party for delay in the satisfaction of a money judgment entered on behalf of that party against another.

Prejudgment interest has traditionally been governed by whether the action was brought in law or equity.[1] At common law, prejudgement interest was either available as a matter of right or it was not available at all.[2] In equity, recovery of prejudgment interest was committed in all cases to the discretion of the court.[3] In both cases, the rule has been substantially modified by statute or case law in most jurisdictions to provide that, within limits, prejudgment interest should be awarded as a matter of right or the presumption should be that prejudgment interest is available to prevailing

---

[85] *Compare* Oden v. Chemung County Indus. Dev. Agency, 661 N.E.2d 142, 144 (N.Y. 1995) (holding that legislation modifying CSR is "a statute enacted in derogation of the common law and, as such, is to be strictly construed"), *with* Parker v. Esposito, 677 A.2d 1159, 1162 (N.J. Super. Ct. A. D. 1996) (stating that in applying the collateral source statute a court should construe the provisions sensibly and "consonant to reason and good discretion") (citations omitted).

[86] O'Bryan v. Hedgespeth, 892 S.W.2d 571 (Ky. 1995); Denton v. Con-Way S. Express, Inc., 402 S.E.2d 269 (Ga. 1991).

[87] Kiss v. Jacob, 650 A.2d 336 (N.J. 1994) (involving settlement with defendant determined not to be a tortfeasor); *Oden, supra,* 661 N.E.2d at 143 (holding that under New York statute "the economic loss portion of the award should be reduced . . . only when the collateral source payment represents reimbursement for a particular category of loss that corresponds to a category of loss for which damages were awarded"). The court in *Oden* held that it would be proper to offset disability payments against the award of lost pension benefits because the disability payments were "in lieu of" that disability award. *Id.* at 146. On the hand, there would be no statutory offset for the lost earnings because while the disability payments were intended as a substitute for the plaintiff's lost earnings, the disability payments were contractually payable regardless of the plaintiff's future earnings; therefore, the payments did not replace the future earnings. *Id.* at 145–46.

[1] The history of the common law rule on prejudgment interest is traced in *General Motors Corp. v. Devex Corp.,* 461 U.S. 648, 651–52 & n.5 (1983).

[2] Dale Bland Trucking, Inc. v. Kiger, 598 N.E.2d 1103, 1106 (Ind. App. 1992).

[3] West Suburban Bank v. Lattemann, 674 N.E.2d 149 (Ill. App. 1996) (discussing equitable interest); Lightcap v. Mobil Oil Corp., 562 P.2d 1, 16 (Kan.), *cert. denied,* 434 U.S. 876 (1977) (same).

plaintiffs.[4] In a limited number of contexts, the common law recognized that for certain wrongs prejudgment interest was part of the general damages claim.[5] In other contexts, the court, applying the common law, simply noted that prejudgment interest was allowable, without specifying whether it was allowable as a matter of right or of discretion. As one court recently noted: "[w]e cannot deny that the issue of prejudgment interest has been a confusing area in our jurisprudence."[6]

The importance of prejudgment interest should not be minimized. To calculate the effect prejudgment interest on an award, one can apply the Rule of 72. Divide 72 by the prejudgment interest rate; the product is the number of years it takes a principal sum (the award) to double. Thus, at 6%, a principal sum will double in 12 years (72 ÷ 6). The calculation is based on compound interest rates, which are not available in all jurisdictions. At simple interest rates, the doubling effect is less dramatic but still significant. As a practical matter, litigation may be a lengthy process in many jurisdictions. Prejudgment interest cushions the cost of delay. In some cases, the interest award may exceed the compensatory damages award because of the passage of time.

Prejudgment interest, when awarded, is an element of complete compensation.[7] The award reflects the fundamental fact that money today is not a complete substitute for that same sum of money that should have been received in the past, but was not. Prejudgment interest is a means of redressing that deficit. It is designed to compensate the injured party, to make him whole by giving to him the accrual of wealth he would have obtained or produced had he received the money due him during the period of loss.[8] Awarding prejudgment interest has also been justified as ameliorating the

---

[4] United Phosphorus, Ltd. v. Midland Fumigant, Inc., 205 F.3d 1219, 1236–37 (10th Cir. 2000) (stating that "in the federal context, this court has adopted a preference, if not a presumption, for prejudgment interest") (citations omitted); Gorenstein Enters. Inc. v. Quality Care—USA, Inc., 874 F.2d 431, 435–36 (7th Cir. 1989) (same); cf. City of Milwaukee v. Cement Div. Nat'l Gypsum Co., 515 U.S. 189, 195 (1995) (noting that general rule is that prejudgment interest should be awarded in maritime collision cases, subject to limited exception for "peculiar" or "exceptional" circumstances).

[5] The two most important examples of this rule were (1) conversion damages, Universal CIT. Credit Corp. v. Stewart, 262 F.2d 745, 749 (5th Cir. 1959), and (2) damages for failure to pay money. Loudon v. Taxing District, 104 U.S. 771, 774 (1881).

[6] Woodline Motor Freight, Inc. v. Troutman Oil Co., Inc., 938 S.W.2d 565, 567 (Ark. 1997).

[7] West Virginia v. United States, 479 U.S. 305, 310 (1987); see Allison v. Bank One-Denver, 289 F.3d 1223, 1243 (10th Cir. 2002) (stating that an award of prejudgment interest is proper in ERISA cases to allow a ERISA beneficiary to "obtain appropriate equitable relief;" "[p]rejudgment interest is appropriate when its award serves to compensate the injured party and its award is otherwise equitable"); United States v. Seaboard Sur. Co., 817 F.2d 956, 966 (2d Cir.) (holding that pre-judgment interest could not accrue until the defendant wrongfully failed to reimburse the plaintiff; assessing interest prior to that date penalized the defendant rather than compensating the plaintiff), cert. denied, 484 U.S. 855 (1987).

[8] Cassinos v. Union Oil Co., 18 Cal. Rptr. 2d 574, 586 (Cal. App. 1993); Hanson v. Rothaus, 730 P.2d 662, 665 (Wash. 1986) (noting that prejudgment interest compensates the plaintiff for the loss of use of the principal sum awarded).

effect of inflation.[9] Viewed from another perspective, prejudgment interest awards have been justified as preventing the defendant's unjust enrichment through use of funds rightfully belonging to the plaintiff.[10]

The idea that prejudgment interest is compensatory is well intrenched in the law and may be used to challenge an award as improper or as an abuse of discretion. An excessive prejudgment interest rate may be deemed punitive rather than compensatory and vacated for that reason.[11]

In some instances the compensatory goal may be "enhanced" by a statutory rule that, as applied, provides an extracompensatory award. For example, in *Gussack Realty Co. v. Xerox Corp.*,[12] the court awarded prejudgment interest on a claim for clean-up costs at a contaminated waste site even though no money had actually yet been spent on the clean up. The court held that it was bound by the "affirmative mandate" contained in the governing state prejudgment interest statute.[13] In the absence of that "affirmative mandate," one suspects the court would have affirmed the district court's refusal to award prejudgment interest for money not spent by the plaintiff.[14] In another case, the court upheld an award of prejudgment interest on future (post judgment) losses, in effect awarding loss of use damages on money that had not yet been earned or expended. Again the result was deemed compelled by statute.[15]

---

[9] Ford v. Rigidply Rafters, Inc., 984 F. Supp. 386, 391 (D. Md. 1997) (noting that "[a]n award of interest ensures that inflation does not consume the value of [an] . . . award") (brackets added); In the Matter of Oil Spill By the Amoco Cadiz, 954 F.2d 1279, 1332 (7th Cir. 1992):

> Interest at what rate? Surely the market rate. That is what the victim must pay— either explicitly if it borrows money or implicitly if it finances things out of cash on hand—and the rate the wrongdoer has available to it. To return to the trust fund example, if the market rate were 12% it would be unthinkable to set a prejudgment rate of interest at 7.5%, order Amoco to turn over $154 million to the victims (the value of $60 million invested at 7.5% compound interest for 13 years), and authorize Amoco to retain the other $108 million. The victims would owe their creditors $108 million, and the tortfeasor would be the wealthier. Yet that would be the upshot of computing prejudgment interest at less than the market rate—an effect that does not depend on the existence of an express trust but is as powerful if the victims and the tortfeasor both use internal financing. All of this is just the flip side of discounting to present value in a tort case for future loss. As prepaid damages must be reduced at a market rate that takes account of inflation, so postpaid damages must be increased.

(citations omitted).

[10] Nedd v. United Mine Workers of Am., 488 F. Supp. 1208, 1220 (M.D. Pa. 1980), *aff'd sub nom.* Ambromovage v. United Mine Workers of Am., 726 F.2d 972 (3d Cir. 1984); *see Ford v. Rigidply, supra,* 984 F. Supp. at 391 (noting that an award of interest "ensures that a discriminating employer does not reap an unfair benefit from the inherent delays of litigation") (citation omitted).

[11] Ford v. Uniroyal Pension Plan, 154 F.3d 613, 618 (6th Cir. 1998).

[12] 224 F.3d 85 (2d Cir. 2000) (applying New York law).

[13] *Id.* at 93.

[14] *Seaboard Sur. Co., supra,* 817 F.2d 966.

[15] Reyes-Mata v. IBP, Inc. 299 F.3d 504, 507 (5th Cir. 2002) (applying Texas law). The court concluded that the statute had a rational basis and did not deny defendant due process of

In some contexts the award of prejudgment interest may have, by design, a non-compensatory purpose. For example, many states have "Offer of Judgment" provisions that encourage plaintiffs to offer compromises and provide that if the defendant rejects the compromise and plaintiff obtains a larger award at trial, the larger award shall include a mandatory heightened prejudgment interest rate.[16] These above-market, extracompensatory rates are upheld on the ground that they are designed to encourage settlement of disputes.[17]

[16.1] Ascertainability: Liquidated vs. Unliquidated Claims

Prejudgment interest is awarded as a matter of right to liquidated (ascertainable) claims. A claim is liquidated or ascertainable (the terms, as used here, are interchangeable) when the evidence furnishes data that makes it possible to compute the amount of damages with reasonable exactness, without reliance on opinion or discretion.[18] The fact that the claim is disputed does not render it unliquidated or change the nature of the claim.[19] The distinction to be made is between a dispute over the reasonableness of the award and a dispute over liability for the award. Only the former affects designation of the claim as liquidated.[20] The key fact is whether the amount of damages may be computed by reference to an objective source or formula, such as a property's fair market value. Whether the claim is liquidated or unliquidated is determined by the nature of the claim, not its legal classification as sounding in tort or contract.

Prejudgment interest is awarded as a matter of discretion when the claim is unliquidated; some jurisdictions, however, do not permit awards of prejudgment interest on unliquidated claims. A claim is unliquidated when the exact amount of the claim cannot be definitely fixed from the facts proved, but must, in the last analysis, depend on the opinion or discretion

---

law. *Id.* at 507–08; *see* Werremeyer v. K.C. Auto Salvage Co., Inc., 134 S.W.3d 633, 636 (Mo. 2004) (holding that statute compelled awarding of prejudgment interest on punitive damages award).

[16] Cal. Civ. Code § 3291 (fixing the rate at 10%; the default rate is a discretion-based 7%).

[17] Lakin v. Watkins Associated Industries, 863 P.2d 179, 191 (Cal. 1993).

[18] Agency of Natural Resources, State of Vermont v. Glens Falls Ins. Co., 736 A.2d 768, 774 (Vt. 1999); Fleming v. Pima County, 685 P.2d 1301, 1307–08 (Ariz. 1984); Prier v. Refrigeration Eng'g Co., 442 P.2d 621, 626–27 (Wash. 1968).

[19] City of Milwaukee v. Cement Division, National Gypsum Co., 515 U.S. 189, 198 (1995) (stating that in Admiralty cases the liquidated—unliquidated distinction should not be seen as talismanic because the existence of a legitimate difference of opinion on the liability issue is a characteristic of most ordinary litigation). The Court noted that the modern course is to award prejudgment interest as an element of just compensation and that this approach is not confined to Admiralty cases. *Id.* at 196–97.

[20] Miller v. Botwin, 899 P.2d 1004, 1013 (Kan. 1995) (stating that "[t]he fact that a good faith controversy exists as to whether the party is liable for the money does not preclude a grant of prejudgment interest") (citation omitted); Aker Verdal A/S v. Neil F. Lampson, Inc., 828 P.2d 610, 618 (Wash. App. 1992); *Fleming, supra,* 685 P.2d at 1307.

of the trier-of-fact.[21] In a case when damage to property could not be computed with reference to fair market value because the property was unique, the court held that the claim was unliquidated.[22] On the other hand, cost of repair has been recognized by some, but not all, courts as a suitably certain and definite measure to demonstrate that a claim is liquidated.[23] The unwillingness to use "cost of repair" in the context of "unique" property as liquidated appears to rest on the belief that repair cost is a surrogate measure of the usual measure of property damage (diminution in value);[24] therefore, the substitute (cost of repair) can rise no higher than what it replaces (diminution in value). The repair of "unique" property, without market value, may be seen as resting ultimately on opinion and discretion. There is no objective formula or test to apply to cap or limit the amount that may be spent to repair damaged "unique" property.

The existence of affirmative defenses, such as a duty to mitigate, does not affect the status of a claim as liquidated,[25] except in the most limited of circumstances.[26]

The "objective source or formula" test is not prescriptive. Stating the test and applying it consistently are two different matters. Indeed, it has been criticized as an unsound distinction and a number of courts have rejected its applicability as an absolute test.[27]

Fair market value may be seen as objective and a suitable formula for treating a claim as liquidated in one case, but not in another.[28] The court

---

[21] *Prier, supra*, 442 P.2d at 626.

[22] Maryhill Museum of Fine Arts v. Emil's Concrete Constr. Co., 751 P.2d 866, 869, 871 (Wash. App. 1988) (holding that claim by museum for water leakage damage was not liquidated because museum was unique property without readily ascertainable market value and measure of damages was committed to court's discretion); Marcotte Realty & Auction, Inc. v. Schumacher, 624 P.2d 420, 432 (Kan. 1981) (holding that a judgment based on quantum meruit is not liquidated until the determination of the amount of the claim at trial).

[23] *Aker Verdal, supra*, 828 P.2d at 617 (holding that property damage claim could be deemed liquidated when repair costs were determined by an outside source (third party adjustor)).

[24] Section 7.3 (Cost of Repair vs. Diminution in Value).

[25] *Fleming, supra*, 685 P.2d at 1308 n.5 (stating that "[i]t is neither good contract law nor equitable to allow the party responsible for the damage to claim that the damages are not 'liquidated' because the only difficulty in computation arises from . . . attempts to mitigate").

[26] Buckner, Inc. v. Berkey Irrigation Supply, 951 P.2d 338 (Wash. App. 1998). Buckner supplied products to Berkey, which Berkey resold. Some customers had claims that Buckner's products were defective. Berkey resolved these claims in some cases by payments to the claimants. Buckner eventually sued Berkey for nonpayment of amounts due on products sold to Berkey under the contract. Berkey counterclaimed for an offset for the costs it incurred in remedy the defects. The issue was whether prejudgment interest should run on Buckner's claim before or after the offset was applied. The court held that an after offset calculation is proper only when the offset "arises out of the same contract as the plaintiff's claim and is a result of defective workmanship or other defective performance by the plaintiff," which was the case here.

[27] *City of Milwaukee, supra*, 515 U.S. at 197 nn.9–10 (1995) (collecting decisions). *City of Milwaukee* was an Admiralty decision but that has not lessened its influence in non-Admiralty areas.

[28] St. Hilaire v. Food Servs. of Am., Inc., 917 P.2d 1114, 1119 (Wash. App. 1996) (rejecting use of "market value" formula as establishing that claim is liquidated and noting that "many variables can affect the assessment of market value").

may be impressed with the fact that the trier-of-fact split the difference between expert opinions as to market value offered by each side as evidencing that the award rested on jury opinion rather than objective formula. [29] The court may be influenced by a large discrepancy between the amount of damages demanded in the complaint and the size of the eventual award and conclude that the claim is unliquidated. Conversely, a match between the amount demanded and the amount awarded may support the contention the claim is liquidated. [30]

When the award of prejudgment interest is committed to the discretion of the trier-of-fact, a broad range of issues may be considered to determine if the award is appropriate. Discretion is guided by such factors as (1) the need to include prejudgment interest to compensate fully the plaintiff for his actual losses; and (2) the fairness and relative equities of the award. In one case, the court held that the award of prejudgment interest was proper in rescission notwithstanding that rescission is not effective until decreed by the court. The court noted that the defendant knowingly held onto plaintiff's purchase money after it was aware of the mistake that served to justify rescission of the transaction. The court found that the trial judge did not abuse his discretion in treating that fact as warranting the award of prejudgment interest on the monies withheld by the defendant from the date the existence of the mistake became known. [31] If statutory remedies are involved, the award of prejudgment interest is also keyed to the remedial purposes and goals of the statute. These factors include: (1) whether the legislative intent was to permit or preclude prejudgment interest; (2) whether the award of prejudgment interest would overcompensate the plaintiff; (3) the culpability of the defendant; and (4) whether the statute permitted punitive damages. [32]

When statutory remedies are sought, courts have usually interpreted statutory remedies liberally in favor of finding at least discretionary authority to award prejudgment interest. [33] The fact that the statute itself is silent on the issue of prejudgment interest is not controlling. [34]

The issue of delay is often critical to the award of prejudgment interest for both liquidated and unliquidated claims. When the plaintiff is solely responsible for delay in bringing the litigation to fruition, courts have

---

[29] Id.

[30] Cf. Wisper Corp. N.V. v. California Commerce Bank, 57 Cal. Rptr. 2d 141, 148–49 (Cal. App. 1996) (finding that significant disparity, due to finding that plaintiff was 75% at fault for loss, negated a conclusion that the claim was liquidated).

[31] Society Nat'l Bank v. Parsow Partnership, Ltd., 122 F.3d 574, 576–77 (8th Cir. 1997).

[32] Wickham Contracting Co. v. Local Union No. 3, Int'l Brotherhood of Elec. Workers, 955 F.2d 831, 834–35 (2d Cir.), cert. denied, 506 U.S. 946 (1992).

[33] Title VII Civil Rights Actions—Jones v. WMATA, 946 F. Supp. 1023, 1033 (D.D.C. 1996); Federal Securities Act and the Exchange Act—Blau v. Lehman, 368 U.S. 403, 414 (1962), and Chris-Craft Indus., Inc. v. Piper Aircraft Corp., 516 F.2d 172, 190 (2d Cir. 1975), rev'd on other grounds, 430 U.S. 1 (1977); Section 1983 Civil Right Actions—Golden State Transit Corp. v. City of Los Angeles, 773 F. Supp. 204, 220 (C.D. Cal. 1991).

[34] Rodgers v. United States, 332 U.S. 371, 373, (1947).

denied prejudgment interest.[35] The justification for this rule is that "[s]ubstantial, unexplained delay in filing suit . . . shifts the investment risk to the defendant, allowing the plaintiff to recover interest without bearing the corresponding risk."[36] Conversely, delay on the part of the defendant supports an award of interest.[37]

If a plaintiff fails to established that the claim is liquidated and that prejudgment interest is available as a matter of right, the plaintiff may still argue that prejudgment interest should be awarded as a matter of discretion on the unliquidated claim.[38]

[16.2] Interest Rate

[16.2.1] Determination of Rate

The generation of any consensus, at least in the absence of a specific statute,[39] as to the appropriate prejudgment interest rate has been impossible to achieve. The traditional approach has been to commit the matter to the discretion of the court.[40] In some jurisdictions, however, the presumption is that a particular rate or measure should be used and departures must be justified by the trial judge. Thus, in *Blanton v. Anzalone* the court noted: "We review the District Court's calculation of prejudgment interest for abuse of discretion. However, substantial evidence must support the district court's decision to depart from the treasury bill rate."[41]

The treasury bill rate has been accepted by other courts, albeit without the gloss that a departure requires substantial justification.[42] Other courts

[35] General Motors Corp. v. Devex Corp., 461 U.S. 648, 657 (1983) (patent infringement); *see* West Virginia v. United States, 479 U.S. 305, 311, (1987) (stating that laches could warrant a denial of interest); Section 61.1 (Laches).

[36] Williamson v. Handy Button Mach. Co., 817 F.2d 1290, 1298 (7th Cir. 1987). Perhaps a middle ground approach here would be to use an interest rate that reflects a "risk free" investment, *e.g.*, short term U.S. government notes.

[37] Matter of Milwaukee Cheese, 112 F.3d 845, 849 (7th Cir. 1997) (stating that "[d]elay is a reason to award interest, not to avoid interest; the longer the case lasts, the more of the stakes the defendant keeps even if it loses . . .").

[38] *Agency of Natural Resources, supra*, 736 A.2d at 774 (holding that trial court committed reversible error in failing to consider discretionary claim for prejudgment interest after determining that claim was not liquidated).

[39] Cal. Civ. Code § 3289 (providing that in contract actions the rate shall be as specified in the contact or, if no rate is specified, 10%); New York Civil Practice Law and Rules § 5004 (9% per year).

[40] Forman v. Korean Air Lines Co., Ltd., 84 F.3d 446, 450 (D.C. Cir.), *cert. denied*, 519 U.S. 1028 (1996).

[41] 813 F.2d 1574, 1576 (9th Cir. 1987) (defining "substantial justification" as "such relevant evidence as a reasonable mind might accept as adequate to support a conclusion") (citations omitted).

[42] N.Y. Marine & General Ins. Co. v. Tradeline (L.L.C.), 266 F.3d 112, 130–31 (2d Cir. 2001) (stating that while the rate of prejudgment interest is within the broad discretion of the court, interest generally "should be measured by interest on short-term, risk free obligations," "United States Treasury Bills") (citations omitted). Some federal courts have looked to state

have adopted the prime rate[43] and rejected the use of the treasury bill rate as undercompensatory[44] or some other alternative as overcompensatory.[45] The rationale for this approach is the treatment of the prevailing plaintiff as the involuntary creditor of the defendant; consequently, the appropriate prejudgment interest rate is that which the defendant would have had to pay to obtain the use of the funds that belong to the plaintiff.[46] The interest rate charged by the involuntary creditor (plaintiff) should reflect the market interest rate for borrowers.[47] None of these approaches preclude a court from engaging in more refined rate setting when necessary to provide fair compensation to a plaintiff,[48] although the decided preference is to use a · substitute, such as the treasury bill rate or the prime rate.[49] When there

---

law to determine the appropriate interest rate regardless of whether the claim arises under federal or state law. *See In re* Crazy Eddie Sec. Litig., 948 F. Supp. 1154, 1167 (E.D.N.Y. 1995). *But cf.* Turley v. New York City Police Dep't, 988 F. Supp. 675, 683 (S.D.N.Y. 1997) (rejecting use of state rate in favor of treasury bill rate in federal civil rights action brought under 42 U.S.C. § 1983 on the ground that the treasury bill rate is the "most commonly used basis for prejudgment interest in this Circuit").

[43] Alberti v. Klevenhagen, 896 F.2d 927, 938, *vacated in part*, 903 F.2d 352 (5th Cir. 1990) (instructing district court to use prime rate rather than municipal bond interest rate to calculate cost of delay in receiving payment). The "prime rate" is the rate banks charge for short-term unsecured loans to creditworthy customers.

[44] Matter of Oil Spill by Amoco Cadiz off Coast of France on March 16, 1978, 954 F.2d 1279, 1332 (7th Cir. 1992) (rejecting use of treasury bill rate in effect at time of judgment in favor of prime rate reflecting actual cost of borrowing money).

[45] Oldham v. Korean Air Lines Co., Ltd., 127 F.3d 43, 54 (D.C. 1997) (rejecting district court's use of Ibbotson index (stock market index that tracks rate of return on traded securities) rather than prime rate). The court stated:

> Although the court used the prime rate for all the other damage awards in these cases, it employed the Ibbotson Index in the case of the loss of inheritance award. The court reasoned that because that loss reflected what Mr. Kohn would have made as a stockbroker and what he had saved through stock market transactions, . . . the Ibbotson Index is the best tool for determining what interest the children could have made on the money if they had received it in 1983—when the accident occurred. We are not persuaded by this reasoning. What Mr. Kohn would have made and saved is irrelevant to the question of what constitutes appropriate compensation for a delay in a successful party's receipt of a cash payment. The time value of the money is the same whether paid in satisfaction of an award for a loss of inheritance or a loss of society.

Id. (citation omitted); *cf. Gamma-10 Plastics, Inc. v. American President Lines, Ltd.*, 839 F. Supp. 1359, 1362 (D. Minn. 1993) (discussed at text and notes 51–54, *infra*.

[46] Gorenstein Enterprises, Inc. v. Quality Care-USA, Inc., 874 F.2d 431, 436 (7th Cir. 1989). This approach is based on defendant's unjust enrichment (expense saved). *See* text and notes 51–54, *infra*.

[47] *Amoco Cadiz, supra*, 954 F.2d at 1332 (noting that "market interest rate reflects three things: the social return on investment (that is the amount necessary to bid money away from other productive uses), the expected change in the value of money during the term of the loan (*i.e.*, anticipated inflation), and the risk of non-payment").

[48] Refined rate setting is designed to determine what a party actually would have paid or received for the use of funds during the delay period. *Amoco Cadiz, supra*, 954 F.2d at 1332.

[49] *See* note 45, *supra*.

have been significant interest rate fluctuations during the period of the delay, an averaged rate may be applied.[50]

In some of the cases using the refined approach, the award of prejudgment interest may shift from a compensatory rationale to a preventing unjust enrichment rationale. Focusing on preventing defendant from gaining a windfall is different[51] from focusing on the plaintiff and asking whether the plaintiff could have made better use of the funds. As noted in *Gamma-10 Plastics, Inc. v. American President Lines, Ltd.*:

> The primary purpose of awarding prejudgment interest, however, is to fully compensate the injured party for the loss of use of money. If the injured party could have earned more with the money than the wrongdoer would have paid to borrow it, awarding interest at the wrongdoer's rate would undercompensate the injured party. Therefore, in determining the interest rate, the aim should be to award the greater of the cost of money to the wrongdoer or the return the injured party could have earned.[52]

The difficulty with this approach is more practical than doctrinal; few plaintiffs are able to demonstrate that they would have earned a better return as an investor than as an involuntary creditor of the defendant. For example, in *Gamma-10 Plastics* the plaintiff offered three theories: (1) return on reinvestment of the funds in the plaintiff's business; (2) the rate plaintiff would have had to pay to borrow the funds; and, (3) the return plaintiff could have achieved had it invested the funds in the market. The court found that each theory was speculative since plaintiff ceased operations, introduced no evidence that it could have borrowed the amount in question, and demonstrated no proclivities to invest in publicly traded securities.[53] Some courts appear to reject this approach altogether.[54]

Alternatively, some courts have used the rate charged by the Internal Revenue Service in cases involving underpayment of taxes, the rate applied to post-judgment interest, and the rate that reflects the average of inflation during the period prejudgment interest is to be awarded.[55]

---

[50] *Id.*; Cement Div. Nat'l Gypsum Co. v. City of Milwaukee, 31 F.3d 581, 587 (7th Cir. 1994), *aff'd*, 515 U.S. 189, (1995). *But cf.*, Webb v. GAF Corp., 949 F. Supp. 102, 108 (N.D.N.Y. 1996) (criticizing unexamined averaging and noting that while averaging may be appropriate over short periods of time when interests rates are stable, it may not be advisable in other contexts). The *Webb* decision contains a good discussion of competing interest calculation methodologies.

[51] *Amoco Cadiz, supra*, 954 F.2d at 1332.

[52] 839 F. Supp. 1359, 1362 (D. Minn. 1993), *aff'd in part, rev'd on other grounds*, 32 F.3d 1244 (8th Cir. 1994), *cert. denied*, 513 U.S. 1198 (1995).

[53] *Id.* at 1363.

[54] *See* note 45, *supra*.

[55] *Ford v. Rigidply, supra*, 984 F. Supp. at 391 (collecting cases and adopting average of inflation rate).

[16.2.2] Simple or Compound

The common law rule is to award simple interest.[56] "With simple interest, the interest is calculated each period on the original base amount."[57] The modern, but hardly universal, trend is to award compound interest.[58] "With compound interest, the interest is calculated each period by adding to the last period's ending base, the interest calculated over that period."[59] In effect, with simple interest, the interest rate works on a stable, static base—the principal sum; with compound interest, the interest rate works on an ever increasing base—the principal sum plus previously calculated interest.[60]

The rationale for using compound interest rates is said to be the same as the reason for awarding prejudgment interest in the first place—complete compensation.[61] When the interest rate is based on the deprivation of the plaintiff's use of the funds, compounding is thought to be reasonable because if the plaintiff had received the funds when due, she could have invested them and received the benefit of the investment. Since many money market investments are compounded, awarding compound interest replicates what was lost.[62] Compounding also allows the interest rate to reflect plaintiff's investment opportunities, not defendant's cost of borrowing. This suggests that if compounding is allowed, an investor rate of interest should be used (what would the investor earn as interest) rather than a debtor rate (what would a borrower pay), but the implication following from the use of compound interest rates have not been addressed by the courts.

When compound interest is awarded, the tendency is to do so on an annual basis. The possibility is left open, however, for daily or quarterly compounding on an appropriate showing.[63] Notwithstanding the central theme that prejudgment interest is designed to provide just compensation, compound interest awards are most common in contexts when a fiduciary has breached a duty of loyalty to the beneficiary.[64] In this context, the use

---

[56] Michael Knoll, *A Primer on Prejudgment Interest*, 75 Tex. L. Rev. 293, 306–07 nn.76–77 (1996); Sintra v. City of Seattle, 935 P.2d 555, 587 n.17 (Wash. 1997) (noting that "[c]ompound interest is never implied, and may be permitted only if there is express language in a statute or agreement providing for compound interest").

[57] Knoll, *A Primer on Prejudgment Interest, supra*, 75 Tex. L. Rev. at 306.

[58] *Id.* at 307 nn.77–80.

[59] *Id.* at 306.

[60] *Id.* (noting that at 10% simple interest, a principal sum of $1,000,000, earns $100,000 a year, each year; at 10% annualized compound interest, that same principal sum of $1,000,000 earns $100,000 the first year, $110,000 the second year (10% ($1,000,000 + $100,000)), $121,000 the third year (10% ($1,000,000 + $100,000, + $110,000)), etc.).

[61] American Tel. & Tel. Co. v. Jiffy Lube Int'l, Inc., 813 F. Supp. 1164, 1170 (D. Md. 1993).

[62] Cooper v. Paychex, Inc., 960 F. Supp. 966, 975 (E.D. Va. 1997); United States v. Mason Tenders Dist. Council of Greater N.Y., 909 F. Supp. 891, 895 (S.D.N.Y. 1995).

[63] Studiengesellschaft Kohle v. Dart Indus., Inc., 862 F.2d 1564, 1580 (Fed. Cir. 1988) (compounding quarterly); Trans-World Mfg. Corp. v. Al Nyman & Sons, Inc., 633 F. Supp. 1047, 1057 (D. Del. 1986) (compounding daily).

[64] Michelson v. Hamada, 36 Cal. Rptr. 2d 343, 353–54 (Cal. App. 1994).

of compound interest appears to be assessed more as a sanction for defecting agents than as compensation or injured plaintiffs.[65] It is sometimes stated that compound interest is allowed in equity,[66] but in most instances the cases involve breach of fiduciary duties, although there are occasional exceptions.[67]

[16.3] Accrual Date

The general rule is that prejudgment interest should be awarded from the earliest ascertainable date.[68] For liquidated claims, that date may be the date the claim accrues[69] or date of loss.[70]

In many cases involving liquidated claims, however, and in all cases when interest is a matter of discretion, computing the date from which interest begins is committed to the discretion of the court.[71] Courts exercise their discretion usually by selecting the date the obligation became ascertainable,[72] the date a demand was made on the obligation,[73] or the date suit was filed on the obligation.[74]

---

[65] *Cf.* Davis v. Davis, (1902) 2 Ch. 314 (stating English Rule that compound interest is allowed when fiduciary breached duty and commingled funds to fiduciary's profit).

[66] Ellis v. Sullivan, 134 N.E. 695, 697 (Mass. 1922).

[67] *Id.* (involving equity of redemption).

[68] NY Civ. Prac. L. & R. § 5001(b) (McKinney 1992 & 1995 Supp.).

[69] This is the common rule for breach of contract actions. Canady v. Crestar Mortgage Corp., 109 F.3d 969, 975 (4th Cir. 1997) (noting that under North Carolina law interest runs from date of breach not from date of plaintiff's demand).

[70] West Virginia v. United States, 479 U.S. 305, 311 (1987).

[71] United States v. Seaboard Sur. Co., 817 F.2d 956, 966 (2d Cir.); *cert. denied*, 484 U.S. 855 (1987); Gelfgren v. Republic Nat'l Life Ins. Co., 680 F.2d 79, 81 (9th Cir. 1982) (interpleader action involving assessment of interest against stakeholder); Van Hoove v. Mid-America Bldg. Maintenance Co., 841 F. Supp. 1523, 1536 (D. Kan. 1993) (COBRA violation involving terminated employees right to continuation insurance coverage); Huffman v. Hair Surgeon, Inc., 482 N.E.2d 1248, 1251 (Ohio 1985).

[72] Dallis v. Don Cunningham and Assocs., 11 F.3d 713, 718–19 (7th Cir.), *aff'd*, 273 U.S. 284 (1993) (finding that district court did not abuse his discretion in computing interest from date of stipulation of damages rather than date defendant received monies in dispute); Precision Automotive v. Northern Ins. Co., 61 Cal. Rptr. 200, 204 (Cal. App. 1967).

[73] McLemore v. Third Nat'l Bank in Nashville (*In re Montgomery*), 983 F.2d 1389, 1396 (6th Cir. 1993) (finding that court did not abuse its discretion in awarding interest from date of demand); Smith v. Mark Twain Nat'l Bank, 805 F.2d 278, 291 (8th Cir. 1986) (same); Isaac v. State Farm Mut. Auto. Ins. Co., 522 N.W.2d 752, 763–64 (S.D. 1994) (stating that demand for insurance policy benefits triggered accrual of interest).

[74] Conway v. Icahn & Co., 16 F.3d 504, 512 (2d Cir. 1994) (finding that the date the action was commenced was appropriate date for calculating interest); Cassinos v. Union Oil Co., 18 Cal. Rptr. 2d 574, 585–86 (Cal. App. 1993) (same). See *Lincoln Elec. Co. v. St. Paul Fire and Marine Ins. Co.*, 210 F.3d 672 (6th Cir. 2000) (applying Ohio Law), where the court stated:

> There are four points in time that courts could use to determine when prejudgment interest should begin to accrue against an insurer who wrongfully fails to defend on a claim against an insured: (1) the date when the insured submitted a claim to the insurer detailing funds expended in defense efforts; (2) the date when the insurer was made aware that the insured disagreed with the insurer's disposition of the

Prejudgment interest runs on accrued obligations. It should not be awarded as to future obligations, even when those future obligations are part of the award and have been discounted to present value.[75] This rule should not apply, however, when future damages are discounted back to the date of loss or injury:

> The cases cited by applicants, which state that prejudgment interest is not allowed on future lost wages, appear to involve (or contemplate) calculations in which future wages are discounted back to the date of trial, using the two-step method, rather than back to the date of loss, using the one-step method. The general proposition that prejudgment interest is not allowable on future losses, is inapplicable to the sum of the present value of future payments that have been discounted back to the date of loss.[76]

The two-step method envisions two damages calculations: first, a calculation of all damages from date of injury to date of trial; and second, a separate calculation for future losses after the date of trial. Only the future losses are discounted to present value; prejudgment interest may be awarded on the first calculation. In the "one-step method," all losses are calculated as of the date of injury and then that sum may be adjusted by an award of interest to reflect the period of delay from the date of injury to the date of trial. These calculations can become complex when settlements from joint tortfeasors are added to the mix as the plaintiff has the

---

defense-cost claim submitted to the insured; (3) the date when the insured filed a legal action against the insurer with a court or arbiter concerning legal costs; or (4) the date when (A) the insured has been incorrectly forced to expend or absorb defense costs, and (B) the insurer knew or should have known that it was not fulfilling its duty to defend.

In this case, the district court apparently adopted approach one, utilizing the "time between accrual of the claim and judgment." The court explicitly rejected approach two (St. Paul's argument), "that prejudgment interest should only run from February 1996—the point in time when Lincoln Electric first demanded a reallocation of defense and indemnity payments." The court adopted approach one even though "[d]efendants had no way of knowing of the claim," and there was a double-auditing procedure in place during the relevant time period to guard against mistakes and fraud. The court reasoned that "Lincoln Electric lost access and use of certain funds for the period through December 1997," and that the money would "fairly and reasonably compensate those losses flowing from St. Paul's breach."

Id. at 692. The court concluded that the district court erred in awarding interest prior to the date the defendant insurer was on notice that it was in violation of its contractual obligation to provide a defense. *Id.* at 694.

[75] Johnson v. Washington County, 506 N.W.2d 632, 640 (Minn. App. 1993) (remanding for recalculation of interest award when trial court initially awarded interest on entire award which consisted of past and future damages). *But see* C&H Nationwide, Inc. v. Thompson, 903 S.W.2d 315, 324 (Texas 1994) (construing state wrongful death statute as allowing prejudgment interest on future damages); Section 16 (Prejudgement Interest) (n.15).

[76] *In re* Complaint of Conn. Nat'l Bank, 928 F.2d 39, 44 n.5 (2d Cir. 1991) (citations omitted); *see* Blue Ribbon Beef Co., Inc. v. Napolitano, 696 A.2d 1225, 1230 (R.I. 1997) (finding no error in award of interest on total compensatory damages awarded even though trial court did not discriminate between past and future lost profits since trial court discounted all lost profits awarded to date of breach).

use of the settlement money and that fact should be factored into the award of interest.[77]

It is proper to award prejudgment interest to a damages award that superficially appears to consist of future damages but which actually consists of past losses. In *Commonwealth v. Johnson Insulation* the court upheld the award of interest on the entire amount of property damage caused by asbestos. Damages were measured by the cost of abatement through removal and mitigation efforts. Even though some of the abatement projects remained to be completed, the court held that the "damage" had already occurred and the costs of abatement were simply a measure of a past loss.[78] In some cases, the distinction between past and future losses can be strained. For example, in some jurisdictions prejudgment interest will not be awarded for future lost earnings, but will be awarded for impairment of earnings capacity, which is measured by future potential earnings.[79]

A defendant may stop the accrual of prejudgment interest by tendering the amount due. The offer must include the full amount the plaintiff is entitled to receive, including interest to the tender date,[80] and be unconditional.[81] The tender rules have both a statutory and common law basis.[82] Rule 68 of the Federal Rules of Civil Procedure does not penalize a plaintiff who rejects an offer of judgment and fails to do better at trial, by withholding or reducing the award of prejudgment interest,[83] but some state variations of Rule 68 do.[84]

§ 17   TAX CONSEQUENCES OF AWARDS AND SETTLEMENTS

An award of money represents income to the plaintiff; thus, the tax consequences should be considered to determine the net recovery the

---

[77] *In re* Joint Eastern District and Southern District Asbestos Litigation v. Keene Corp., 18 F.3d 126, 130–33 (2d Cir. 1994) (applying New York law).

[78] 682 N.E.2d 1323, 1333–34 (Mass. 1997) (stating that "[t]he Commonwealth's projected abatement costs are not "future damages," but are rather an estimation of damage that has already occurred, for which compensation is already due").

[79] Conway v. Electro Switch Corp., 523 N.E.2d 255, 258 (Mass. 1988); Karagiannis v. New York State Thruway Auth., 619 N.Y.S.2d 906, 907 (App. Dep't 1994) (treating plaintiff's personal injury claim as a "debt" and including within the "debt" plaintiff's future damages).

[80] Canady v. Crestar Mortgage Corp., 109 F.3d 969, 975 (4th Cir. 1997).

[81] Mercantile Bank of Sikeston v. Moore, 935 S.W.2d 762, 768–69 (Mo. App. 1996); Balder v. Haley, 441 N.W.2d 539, 542 (Minn. App. 1989); Lyons v. Ayala, 723 S.W.2d 254, 258 (Tex. Civ. App 1986) (stating that a conditional tender was insufficient to bar the continued accrual of interest even though the tender exceeded the ultimate jury award).

[82] Knab Bros., Inc. v. Town of Lewiston, 97 N.Y.S.2d 45, 46 (App. Dep't 1977) (discussing creditor's refusal to accept unconditional tender as raising an equitable estoppel against the creditors claim for post tender interest).

[83] Kehoe v. Keister, 727 F. Supp. 896, 899 (D.N.J. 1989) (noting Rule 68 does not bar plaintiff who fails to improve at trial from recovering interest up to the date of judgment).

[84] Mass. R. Civ. P. 68; Section 16 (Prejudgement Interest) (nn. 16–17).

plaintiff will receive.[1] The realization that the plaintiff may have to treat the entire award as taxable income may have significant consequences to the plaintiff who is required to use the award to pay litigation expenses, including attorney's fees. This problem is exacerbated when the plaintiff is unable to treat those expenses as a business deduction.[2]

The requirement that the plaintiff recognize the award as income is not avoided when attorney's fees are part of a fees award.[3] The decisional law in this field has generally treated fees awards as the property of the client, not the lawyer.[4] Does it make a difference if the attorney's fees a paid under a contingent fee arrangement? The argument is that the plaintiff does not receive the fees because the fees are the property of the attorney pursuant to the contingent fee agreement. The courts have split on this contention,[5] sometimes within a single circuit.[6] This issue proved to be most

---

[1] Section 61(a) of the Internal Revenue Code defines gross income subject to taxation as "all income from whatever source derived." Commissioner v. Glenshaw Glass Co., 348 U.S. 426, 431–32 (1955) (stating that gross income includes all "accessions to wealth" not excluded by statute). The early interpretation of the Income Tax Laws was that personal injury damages awards were includible in income. Frank Dotti, *Personal Injury Income Tax Exclusion: An Analysis and Update*, 75 Denv. U. L. Rev. 1, 65–67 (1997); Douglas Kahn, *Taxation of Damages After* Schleier—*Where Are We and Where Do We Go From Here?*, 15 Quinnipiac L. Rev. 305, 307 (1995).

[2] Alexander v. Internal Revenue Service, 72 F.3d 938, 944–45 (1st Cir. 1995) (requiring taxpayer to treat legal fees incurred in recovering monies due under employment contracts as "below the line" miscellaneous deductions rather than "above the line" trade or business expenses); *see* Biehl v. Commissioner of Internal Revenue, 351 F.3d 982, 985–86 (9th Cir. 2003) (holding that attorney's fees paid as part of settlement of wrongful termination action did not satisfy the business connection requirement of § 62(a)(2)(A) of the Tax Code, 26 U.S.C. § 62(a)(2)(A); therefore, the fees could only be deducted as miscellaneous deductions). The critical difference between "above the line" and "below the line" deductions is that the latter are subject to a 2% floor and are subject to reduction if the Alternative Minimum Tax provisions apply, which they almost surely will whenever the award is substantial.

[3] Chapter 24 (Attorney's Fees). There are tax horror stories that involve plaintiffs who end up owing more in taxes than they won by way of judgment or settlement. Marisa J. Mead, Student Notes and Comments, *Taxing the Victims: Compensatory Damage Awards and Attorney's Fees in Sexual Harassment Lawsuits*, 11 J. L. & Pol'y 801, 833 (2003) (describing situation of one litigant who won a modest award, on which taxes were paid, but who was subject to owing over $50,000 in taxes on the court awarded fees requested by the lawyer, fees on which the lawyer would also pay taxes).

[4] Section 214 (Standing to Collect Fees Award). There is a recent California Supreme Court decision that treated the attorneys fees awards as the property of the lawyer, not the client. Flannery v. Prentice, 28 P.3d 860 (Cal. 2001) (holding that an award of attorney's fees to the prevailing party under the Fair Employment & Housing Act, Cal. Gov. Code § 12900 *et seq.* belonged to the attorney(s) who earned the fee, not the prevailing party). By this holding, the court parted company with practically every other court that has considered the question of ownership of court awarded attorney's fees to prevailing parties. The *Flannery* court did not address the income recognition ramifications of its decision.

[5] Banks v. Commissioner of Internal Revenue, 345 F.3d 373 (6th Cir. 2003) (collecting decisions and noting that the Fifth, Sixth, and Eleventh Circuits have treated contingency fees as excludable from the client's income, while the Third, Fourth, Seventh, Ninth, Tenth, and Federal Circuits have disagreed), *rev'd*, 543 U.S. 426 (2005).

[6] *Compare* Sinyard v. Commissioner of Internal Revenue, 268 F.3d 756 (9th Cir. 2001) (not

contentious,[7] but the Supreme Court's resolved the issue in favor of the government holding that the entire award was the property of the plaintiff.[8] The "Civil Rights Tax Relief Act," which is part of the American Jobs Creation Act of 2004, will provide some relief to plaintiffs.[9] The Act provides that attorney's fees awarded in claims brought under certain federal and state anti-discrimination statutes need not be recognized as taxable income by the plaintiff, but only by the attorney who receives the fees award.

Most of the discussion in this area has involved Section 104(a)(2) of the Internal Revenue Code, which excludes personal injury awards from the calculation of gross income.[10] A related question is the extent to which the trier-of-fact should hear evidence on and receive instruction regarding the taxability of the award in making its damages calculation.[11]

[17.1] Personal Injury Awards

Section 104(a)(2) of the Internal Revenue Code excludes from gross income "the amount of damages received . . . on account of personal injury or sickness."[12] A number of justifications for the exclusion have been offered, perhaps the most favored are the arguments that (1) the plaintiff is simply being made whole, (2) the transaction that led to the damages award was involuntary, or (3) the damages award is equivalent to imputed income. Neither justification supports the full exclusion[13] and the best

---

excludable), *cert. denied sub nom.* Sinyard v. Rossotti, 536 U.S. 904 (2002), *with* Banatis v. Commissioner of Internal Revenue, 340 F.3d 1074 (9th Cir. 2003) (holding that attorney's fees paid pursuant to contingent fee arrangement were not includable in taxpayer's gross income; under Oregon law attorney had a vested property interest in the proceeds that could not be extinguished or discharged except by payment to the attorney), *rev'd*, 543 U.S. 426 (2005).

[7] *See* Gregg D. Polsky, *The Contingent Attorney's Fee Tax Trap: Ethical, Fiduciary Duty, and Malpractice Implications*, 23 Va. Tax Rev. 615 (2004).

[8] Commissioner v. Banks, 543 U.S. 426 (2005) (holding that litigant's recovery for tax recognition purposes includes portion of award encompassed by attorney's contingent fee).

[9] Pub. L. 108-357, 118 Stat. 1546, adding Section 62(a)(19) to the Internal Revenue Code, to be codified at 26 U.S.C. § 62(a)(19).

[10] Sections 17.1 (Personal Injury Awards), 17.2 (Non-Personal Injury Awards).

[11] Section 17.3 (Consideration of Taxability of Damages).

[12] The exclusion dates from 1918. Revenue Act of 1918, ch. 18, § 213(b)(6) (1919), codified as amended at 26 U.S.C. § 104(a)(2). The legislative history evidences that the exclusion was seen as a clarification rather than change in existing law (H.R. Rep. No. 767, 65th Cong., 2d Sess. 9–10 (1918)), but that position is inconsistent with the broad statement in Section 61(a) of the Code. Section 17 (Tax Consequences of Awards and Settlements) (note 1).

[13] Mark Cockran, *Should Personal Injury Damage Awards Be Taxed?*, 38 Case W. Res. L. Rev. 43, 45–49 (1987) (noting that (1) the "make whole" justification is inadequate to the extent it excludes from taxation all amounts recovered by the taxpayer in excess of basis; (2) the involuntary transaction justification substitutes the Code's legitimate rule of postponed recognition of gain in favor of complete non-recognition of gain; and, (3) the imputed income argument, which rejects including as income the benefits one derives from one's own efforts on one's own behalf, *e.g.*, fixing one's own car, is not sustainable once that benefit is reduced to an actual cash award); *see* Douglas Kahn, *Taxation of Damages After* Schieier, *supra*, 15 Quinnipiac L. Rev. at 309–18; *cf.* Frank Dotti, *Personal Injury Income Tax Exclusion: An Analysis and Update*, 75 Denv. U. L. Rev. 1, 63–64 (1997) (discussing "human capital" justification for exclusion, which is defined as "losses to a person's birthright—an uninjured body and mind").

rationale for the personal injury award exclusion remains that of humanitarianism.[14]

The critical issue has always been defining the scope of the personal injury/sickness exclusion. The simple, garden variety bodily injury claim does not pose a problem. Difficulties arise, however, because the exclusion is not framed in terms of bodily injury but personal injury and the term "personal injury" is not defined in the code. Traditional personal actions such as defamation and invasion of privacy usually do not present difficulties;[15] debate has arisen, however, with the expansion of statutory remedies, particularly in the area of employment rights. The key concern has been whether an award of lost earnings should be a non-taxable event when, had the wrong not occurred, the earnings would have been taxable as gross income. The problem has been confused by myriad lower court opinions and two somewhat inconsistent Supreme Court decisions.

In *United States v. Burke*,[16] the Court said the critical test for determining whether awards were excludible under Section 104 was to examine the underlying lawsuit and determine whether it "redresses a tort-like personal injury." *Burke* involved gender discrimination under Title VII, which, at the time, limited relief to back pay and equitable remedies.[17] The Court concluded that, because the Act did not provide for compensatory damages or provide traditional remedies, *e.g.*, pain and suffering, emotional distress, it did not redress a "tort-like personal injury" and thus was taxable.[18] In *Commissioner v. Schleier*,[19] an Age Discrimination in Employment Act case, the Court adopted a two part test for determining whether income is excludible under Section 104. First, the taxpayer must demonstrate that the underlying cause of action is based on tort or tort-type rights. Second, the taxpayer must show that the damages were received on account of personal injury or sickness.[20] This second prong extends *Burke* for it requires that the wrongful act cause personal injury. If the wrongful act only causes economic loss, the loss is not excludible.[21] It is only when the

---

[14] Bertram Harnett, *Torts and Taxes*, 27 N.Y.U. L. Rev. 614, 626–27 (1952).

[15] The IRS has taken the position that even in traditional tort cases a distinction should be drawn between excludible loss to personal reputation or privacy and non-excludible loss to business reputation and earning capacity. Rev. Rul. 85-143, 1985-2 C.B. 55. The Service's approach was rejected in the seminal lower court decision *Threlkeld v. Comm'r*, 87 T.C. 1294 (1986), *aff'd*, 848 F.2d 81 (6th Cir. 1988), which involved an award for damage to professional reputation caused by a malicious prosecution action. The tax court expansively defined personal injury by focusing attention on the nature of the claim (origin and character) rather than the consequences that resulted from the injury (loss of earnings).

[16] 504 U.S. 229 (1992).

[17] Title VII was modified in 1991 to permit limited awards of compensatory and punitive damages. Civil Rights Act of 1991, 42 U.S.C. § 1981(a) (discussed in *Kolstad v. American Dental Ass'n*, 527 U.S. 526 (1999)); Section 151 (Employee's Damages Against Employer).

[18] 504 U.S. at 241–42.

[19] 515 U.S. 323 (1995).

[20] *Id.* at 333–34.

[21] *Id.* (distinguishing between stigma injury resulting from being declared unfit to work (resulting from personal injury), in which case the measure of damages would be excludable under Section 104, and loss of income resulting from being denied the ability to work (economic not personal injury), in which case the damages would not be excludable).

economic loss results directly from the personal injury, that it will be excluded from income.[22] Notwithstanding the Court's pronouncements, the tests have proven to be difficult to apply and the distinctions are somewhat fine, if not evanescent.[23]

Recent amendments to Section 104(a)(2) have also scaled back the broad construction some courts were giving the provision. The Small Business Job Protection Act of 1996[24] contains provisions taxing both punitive and emotional distress damages if the emotional distress damages do not flow from a physical injury. The Act also provides that in certain cases emotional distress will not be considered a physical injury or sickness, except to the extent that the damages do not exceed the amount paid for medical care. Emotional distress damages recovered for non-physical personal injuries or sickness are taxable to the extent they exceed the costs of related medical care. On the other hand, damages (including emotional distress but excluding punitive damages) recovered for *physical* personal injury or sickness remain non-taxable. This includes any amount that compensates for lost wages on account of personal injury or sickness.

Unfortunately, the recent amendment to Section 104(a)(2) continues the past failure to define in the statute the term "personal injury or sickness." There are suggestions in the legislative history that Section 104(a)(2) should be limited to claims that involve "physical" injury or sickness.[25] If adopted, this could nullify excludability for many non-physical claims, such as loss of consortium, which have traditionally been treated as falling

---

[22] *Id.* (discussing surgeon who loses income as a result of severing his fingers, which prevents his continued employment as a surgeon).

[23] Fabry v. Commissioner, 223 F.3d 1261 (11th Cir. 2000) (holding that taxpayers who closed their business and concluded a settlement that included $500,000 for "damages to business reputation" did not have to recognize that money as taxable income under Section 104(a)(2)). The court held that the taxpayers were so closely connected to their business, that injury to the reputation of the business was, in effect, injury to the taxpayers individually. *Id.* at 1270. The court stated:

> The record indicates that both parties to the tort settlement undertook to evaluate the claims for damage to the business itself, then to evaluate the claims for damage done to the taxpayers as sole proprietors of the business. Here the tort directly disparaged the Fabrys in their business capacity, yet in this instance, the nursery business was the manifestation of the Fabrys, part and parcel of their persona. Their business reputation was their personal reputation.

Id. (citations omitted). The court further analogized the situation to that of a "reverse" piercing of the corporate veil. *Id.* at n. 28.

[24] Pub. L. No. 104-188, § 110 Stat. 1755.

[25] Small Business Job Protection Bill, House Conference Report No. 104-737, *reprinted in* 5 U.S. Code & Cong. News 1792–94 (1996) (discussing "emotional distress" exclusion from Section 104(a)(2)); Frank Dotti, *Personal Injury Income Tax Exclusion, supra,* 75 Denv. U. L. Rev. at 75 (noting the failure to define the terms "physical injury" or "physical sickness"). Dotti notes that while emotional distress damages are now generally includable as income, the Code is unclear whether severe distress resulting in significant physical injury, such as a heart attack or mental breakdown would be treated as includable emotional distress. *Id.*

within Section 104(a)(2). Some courts have limited the two-part *Schleier* test to the exact claim before the Court.[26]

Even if the claim is deemed to fall within Section 104(a)(2), not all components of the award may escape taxation. In *Rozpad v. Commissioner*, the court held that "prejudgment interest is not 'damages' received 'on account of' a personal injury, and is therefore taxable."[27] The court relied on the language of Section 104(a)(2), the characterization of prejudgment interest under state (Rhode Island) law, and, most importantly, on the fact that prejudgment interest is not awarded "on account of" injury but to compensate the plaintiff for delay in receiving the award.[28] Similarly, punitive damages awards are subject to taxation even when they are awarded for injuries that are otherwise within Section 104.[29]

The bottom line here that when possible the parties should contemplate the tax consequences of the award or settlement before-the-fact to avoid surprises after-the-fact.[30]

[17.2] Non-Personal Injury Awards

Non-personal injury awards, such as those arising out of breach of contract, have traditionally been understood as subject to taxation as gross

---

[26] Banks v. United States, 81 F.3d 874 (9th Cir. 1996) (taxpayer's settlement of claim against his Union for breach of duty of fair representation was of "tort-like" cause of action and thus excludible from income). The court stated:

> *Schleier*, however, was determined by the specific limitations of the ADEA and has no application here where neither punitive damages nor back wages were offered in the settlement. Unions do not pay wages to their members, and what the Union paid in settlement here to Banks did not constitute wages. It paid damages to compensate for its unfair and arbitrary treatment of Banks, conduct that the court had found to be in bad faith and in violation of the Union's duty to fairly represent Banks. We look to the nature of the injuries that were being compensated. Roemer v. Commissioner of Internal Revenue, 716 F.2d 693, 697 (9th Cir. 1983). Bank's injuries were, as the district court found, personal injuries. Consequently, the settlement was of a tort-like cause of action and the sum paid was on account of personal injuries and by statute excluded from gross income.

Id. at 876. Judge Rymer dissented on the ground the award was functionally the substitute for wages lost as a result of the Union's breach and function should control over form. *Id.* at 876–77.

[27] 154 F.3d 1 (1st Cir. 1998).

[28] *Id.* at 6; *see* Francisco v. United States, 267 F.3d 303, 313–14 (3d Cir. 2001); Aames v. Comm'r, 94 T.C. 189, 191 (1990) (holding that interest on damages awarded to taxpayer is taxable even though damages themselves are excludable under Section 104(a)(2)).

[29] Small Business Jobs Protection Act of 1996 § 1605, Pub. L. No. 104-188, § 110 Stat. 1755 (amending § 104(a)(2) (26 U.S.C. § 104(a)(2)). The Court reached the same conclusion for claims predating the 1996 statutory amendments. O'Gilvie v. United States, 519 U.S. 79 (1996).

[30] Crosby v. U.S. Postal Service, 243 F.3d 560 (Fed. Cir. 2000) (Table) (holding that language in settlement of employment dispute, which provided that employee would receive $400,000 and that employer would make "standard deductions," authorized employer to deduct income and social security taxes, reducing the actual payment to approximately $260,000. Query: if the employee was represented by a lawyer with a contingent fee arrangement, on which figure ($400,000 or $260,000) should the contingency percentage be calculated?

income;[31] however, it is perhaps more accurate to identify what the damages award is designed to replace. If damages, such as lost profits, are awarded in lieu of ordinary income, which is the typical case, the award is taxable. If, however, damages are awarded to replace a capital asset, *e.g.*, compensation for goodwill or for property damage, the award is not taxable.[32] The more difficult issue is whether the jury should hear evidence and receive instruction on the issue.

When taxes are a part of plaintiff's compensatory damages, evidence of taxes is evidence of plaintiff's loss and thus admissible. For example, if defendant contracts to pay plaintiff's taxes and breaches, plaintiff's damages are measured in part by what plaintiff lost—here the payment of taxes.[33]

A few cases gave extended this recovery to cases where tax benefits were lost directly as a result of breach. In *Walker v. Signal Companies*[34] the defendant's failure to perform timely a construction contract caused plaintiff to lose the benefit of a capital gains tax rate instead of the income tax rate. The differential, representing the tax consequences of the breach, were allowed as damages.[35] On the other hand, the mere accretion in wealth, and the resulting higher taxes, caused by the award is generally not seen as a compensable item of recovery.[36]

When calculating lost "net profit" recoveries the preferred figure is a "before tax" amount.[37] This approach is supported by two rationales. First, the issue of taxation is a collateral matter between the plaintiff and the government.[38] Second, since the plaintiff will have to pay taxes on the award, using an "after-tax" figure would result in the effective double taxation of this plaintiff, placing her in a worse position than she would have been had the legal wrong not been inflicted on her.[39]

When calculating punitive damages, the tax consequences to the plaintiff are disregarded.[40]

---

[31] Casas Office Mach., Inc. v. Mita Copystar Am., Inc., 961 F. Supp. 353, 359 (D.P.R. 1997); Alexander v. Comm'r, T.C. Memo 1995-51 (Tax Ct. 1995) (stating that "damages received for breach of an employment contract are in the nature of compensation and taxable as ordinary income to the recipient"), *aff'd*, 72 F.3d 938 (1st Cir. 1995).

[32] Raytheon Production Corp. v. Commissioner, 144 F.2d 110, 113 (1st Cir. 1944).

[33] Community Dev. Serv. Inc. v. Replacement Parts Mfg., Inc., 679 S.W.2d 721 (Tex. Civ. App. 1984); Forbes v. Wells Beach Casion, Inc., 409 A.2d 646 (Me. 1979).

[34] 149 Cal. Rptr. 119 (Cal. App. 1978).

[35] Ehly v. Cady, 687 P.2d 687 (Mont. 1984) (allowing plaintiff to recover the tax benefits he would have obtained from the use of tax credits if the contract had been performed).

[36] Paris v. Remington Rand, Inc., 101 F.2d 64, 68 (2d Cir. 1939) (holding that additional amount taxpayer had to pay because it recovered award in particular year was not an additional item of damages); *Ehly, supra*, 687 P.2d at 695 (same); Section 17.5 (Enhanced Taxation as Additional Damages).

[37] Eason v. Federal Broad. Co., 697 So. 2d 435, 438 (Miss. 1997).

[38] Section 17.2 (Non-Personal Injury Awards) (notes 31–32).

[39] *Supra* notes 1&2.

[40] Geressy v. Digital Equip. Corp., 950 F. Supp. 519, 523 (E.D.N.Y. 1997); Section 209 (Tort reform—punitive damages) (discussing share-with-state requirement).

[17.3] Effect of Settlement Allocation

Because a lawsuit may contain includible and excludible items for purposes of taxation, the parties may be able to maximize joint gains by structuring a settlement that emphasizes the excludible items. For example, a defendant has the incentive to shift settlement dollars away from punitive damages, which are uninsurable in many jurisdictions,[41] toward compensatory damages, which are insurable. The plaintiff has the incentive to shift settlement dollars away from punitive damages, which are taxable,[42] and toward those compensatory damages that are excludable. When there is coherence and alignment of interests in the direction the settlement is structured, settlement will be facilitated to the extent the parties' interests, as reflected in the settlement, will be respected by the IRS.

Both the courts and the IRS have taken a somewhat mixed approach toward settlement allocations. In general, the allocation will be accepted when the courts or the IRS are convinced that it is the product of an arms-length, adversarial process. For example, in *Delaney v. Commissioner of Internal Revenue*[43] the taxpayer had received a $287,000 judgment, which included $112,000 prejudgment interest that was taxable.[44] The parties then settled for $250,000 with a stipulation that no part of the settlement reflected an award of interest. The court held that on these facts the tax court was not bound by the stipulation.[45]

The Service has taken the position that written findings of a judge supervising a settlement of a lawsuit is a relevant but not conclusive factor that the Service uses in classifying the settlement amount for tax purposes.[46]

Whenever possible, allocation should be made in the settlement since the failure to do so may result in the entire settlement being including in

---

[41] *See generally* Michael Rosenhouse, Annot., *Liability Insurance Coverage as Extending to Liability For Punitive or Exemplary Damages*, 16 A.L.R.4th 11 (1982) (noting split in authorities but finding majority of courts bar insurability of punitive damages for one's own, personal misconduct).

[42] Section 17.1 (Personal Injury Awards) (note 29).

[43] 99 F.3d 20 (1st Cir. 1996).

[44] Section 17.1 (Personal Injury Awards) (notes 27–28).

[45] 99 F.3d at 24–25. In *Edward E. Robinson et ux v. Comm'r*, 102 T.C. 116 (1994), it was held that the Tax Court was not bound by an allocation agreed to between the parties and as entered in the final judgment by the state court; the allocation was not the product of *bona fide* adversarial negotiations, there was a lack of bargaining, and the state court had merely approved the settlement and had not made an independent review of the allocation. The Tax Court decision was affirmed on this part in *Robinson v. Comm'r*, 70 F.3d 34, 37–38 (5th Cir. 1995), *cert. denied*, 519 U.S. 824 (1996); *see* King-Knoll v. Commissioner, T.C. Memo 2003-277 (Tax Ct. 2003) (holding that settlement allocation of claimed distress damages was not bona fide when (1) same amount of damages had previously been claimed as economic losses that were subject to taxation; (2) distress damages claims were added to litigation after taxpayer learned of their excludability under Section 104; and (3) defendant was unaware of nature of taxpayers distress claims for which money was being paid).

[46] IRS Priv. Ltr. Rul. 84-37084 (June 13, 1984).

taxable income.[47] In cases when the settlement is silent the guiding allocation factor is the parties' intent, which is ascertained from all non-privileged materials relevant to the parties' dispute that resulted in the settlement. The Service may look at pleadings and discovery as well as settlement correspondence and negotiations. Moreover, because the tax-payer always has the burden of proof on the excludability of income from taxation, to persuade the Service or a court the taxpayer may be required to use privileged materials to carry its burden. Once privileged materials are used, all privileged materials will likely become accessible to the Service as the taxpayer will not be permitted to engage in selective disclosure.

[17.4] Consideration of Taxability of Damages in Arriving at Damages Awards

When the damages award is excludable from taxation under Section 104 of the Internal Revenue Code,[48] should this influence the award of damages by the trier-of-fact? The majority view appears to be that income tax consequences should not be taken into consideration in calculating damages for loss of earnings or for impairment of earning capacity, notwithstanding excludability under Section 104. The award of damages should be based upon a plaintiff's gross earnings that would have been realized but for the wrong. Courts have generally reasoned that the amount of taxes is too conjectural and would not only unduly complicate and confuse the damages issue but overshadow the basic issue of liability.[49] An alternative approach has been most consistently adopted by courts applying federal law. In *Norfolk & Western Ry. Co. v. Liepelt*[50] the Court held that it was error to exclude evidence offered to show the effect of income taxes on plaintiff's estimated future earnings in an FELA case. The Court stated: "It is his after-tax income, rather than his gross income before taxes, that provides the only realistic measure of his ability to support his family. It follows inexorably that the wage earner's income tax is a relevant factor in calculating the monetary loss . . . ."[51] The *Liepelt* rule has been applied outside the context of FELA (Federal Employers Liability Act) actions.[52]

---

[47] Taggi v. United States, 835 F. Supp. 744, 746 (S.D.N.Y. 1993), aff'd 35 F.3d 93 (2d Cir. 1994). But cf. Rozpad v. Commissioner, 154 F.3d 1, 3 (1st Cir. 1998) (stating that "[w]hen the interest component of a personal injury settlement is difficult to delineate, there is every reason for courts . . . to . . . treat the entirety as free from tax). The court noted that personal injury settlements result from a "multitude of factors" and "in the absence of an allocation" it is too speculative to isolate a portion of the settlement as representing taxable prejudgment interest. Id. On the facts, however, the settlement did allow for separate itemization and allocation and therefore that portion of the award representing interest was taxable. *Id.* at 4.

[48] Section 17.1 (Personal Injury Awards) (discussing general rule of exclusion from taxation).

[49] Exchange Nat'l Bank of Chicago v. Air Ill., Inc., 522 N.E.2d 146, 152 (Ill. App. 1988); Hoge v. Anderson, 200 Va. 364, 106 S.E.2d 121, 123 (1958). See generally John Theuman, Annot., *Propriety of Taking Income Tax Into Consideration in Fixing Damages in Personal Injury or Death Action*, 16 A.L.R. 4th 589 (1981).

[50] 444 U.S. 490 (1980).

[51] *Id.* at 493–94.

[52] Gulf Offshore Co. v. Mobil Oil Corp., 453 U.S. 473, 487 n.17 (1981) (noting that *Liepelt*

While there is some contrary authority,[53] the decided federal trend since *Liepelt* has been to use an after-tax figure.[54]

Because of the conflict between the majority (state) and alternative (federal) approaches to using before (gross) or after (net) tax dollars to compute damages awards, a question often arises when one jurisdiction provides the substantive rule but another jurisdiction the forum. For example, assume a FELA action is tried in state court. Must the state apply the federal *Liepelt* rule or may it apply its own majority rule? Conversely, if a federal court is exercising diversity jurisdiction, must it apply the state rule under *Erie*,[55] or may it apply the federal *Liepelt* rule? The better approach is to find that the issue is governed by the jurisdiction that provides the rule of decision rather than the forum.[56] There are, as might be expected, divergent views on this point,[57] but these appear to be a distinct minority view to proper treatment of the *Erie* issue. Some courts have skirted the issue by assuming that a state court would revise its position after *Liepelt*; hence, under this view a federal court should instruct the jury on the taxable status of the award absent a contrary, post-*Liepelt* state decision.[58]

---

stated a federal common law rule not necessarily limited to FELA actions); *cf.* Felder v. United States, 543 F.2d 657, 669–70 (9th Cir. 1976) (using net earnings rather than gross earnings to calculate economic losses in Federal Tort Claim Act (FTCA) matter; use of gross earnings would, according to the court, constitute a variant of punitive damages, which are prohibited under the FTCA). *See generally* Ethel Alston, Annot., *Propriety of Considering Future Income Taxes in Awarding Damages Under Federal Tort Claims Act*, 47 A.L.R. Fed. 735 (1980) (collecting decisions).

[53] Adams v. Fuqua Indus., 820 F.2d 271, 276 (8th Cir. 1987) (limiting *Liepelt* rule to FELA cases).

[54] *See* Randall G. Vaughn, *Tax Issues of Personal Injury and Wrongful Death Awards*, 19 Tulsa L. J. 702, 712 (1984).

[55] Erie R. Co. v. Tompkins, 304 U.S. 64 (1938) (requiring federal courts to apply state "rules of decision" when exercising diversity jurisdiction). This approach has proven to be quite challenging to apply with predictive accuracy.

[56] Childs v. United States, 923 F. Supp. 1570, 1583 (S.D. Ga. 1996) (applying Georgia law that lost earnings award not be reduced by anticipated federal and state income taxes that would have been paid had decedent actually earned the wages; the action was brought under the Federal Tort Claims Act, 26 U.S.C. § 2674, which makes the federal government responsible for the acts of its employees that constitute tortious conduct under the law of the state where the tortious act was performed); Van Holt v. Nat'l R.R. Passenger Corp., 669 N.E.2d 1288, 1297 (Ill. App. 1996), *cert. denied*, 520 U.S. 1211 (1997) (finding that when FELA claim is brought in state court, federal after-tax rather than state before tax rule applies); Fenasci v. Travelers Ins. Co., 642 F.2d 986, 989 (5th Cir.) (*per curiam*), *cert. denied*, 454 U.S. 1123 (1981) (holding that state "before tax" rule applied to diversity claim in federal court).

[57] *In re* Air Crash Disaster Near Chicago, Ill., 701 F.2d 1189, 1195 (7th Cir.), *cert. denied*, 464 U.S. 866 (1983) (holding that federal court sitting in diversity may view *Liepelt* as establishing a procedural rule on the admissibility of evidence, which may be applied notwithstanding contrary state law).

[58] Grant v. City of Duluth, 672 F.2d 677, 683 (8th Cir. 1982).

[17.5]   Enhanced Taxation as Additional Damages

Unless the tax code provides otherwise, awards and settlements are treated as income and subject to taxation.[59] Because tax rates are graduated, a plaintiff who receives a damages award that consists of multiple year losses, *e.g.*, lost earnings, might find that his effective tax rate is higher because his losses have been telescoped into a single tax year rather than being spread over a multi-year period.[60] For example, if the plaintiff would have been taxed at an effective rate of 10% had he not been injured, but he is taxed at an effective rate of 20% because his lost earnings for several years are awarded to him in one lump sum, has the plaintiff been made whole by the award?

The tradition rule in this area is that enhanced taxation due to the aggregation of income in a single tax period is not an item of compensable damages.[61] Several recent decisions have, however, challenged the traditional approach. In *Jordan v. CCH Inc.*,[62] the plaintiff secured a verdict of $350,000 in an age discrimination case. The verdict reflected lost wages that would have been received over several years, but were compressed into a single year. To redress the additional taxes plaintiff was required to pay due to the compression, the trial court awarded an additional $33,124 for "negative tax consequences." A similar result was reached in *Blaney v. International Association of Machinists etc.*[63] *Blaney* treated the enhancement as a form of equitable relief permitted by the "other appropriate relief" provision in state law addressing wrongful discrimination.[64] Not all courts have accepted this recent trend to permit additional damages due to the enhanced tax consequences of the award.[65]

The legal system has not yet developed a coherent, consistent approach towards the issue of taxes as damages. One view holds that there is no economic difference between money obtained and money saved or money not obtained and an expense incurred.[66] The other view holds that

---

[59] Sections 17.1 (Personal Injury Awards).

[60] United States v. Cleveland Indians Baseball Co., 532 U.S. 200, 209 (2001) (holding that back pay awards should be taxed based on rates in existence when back pay awards are made, not rates in existence when pay was earned and should have been paid).

[61] Paris v. Remington Rand, Inc., 101 F.2d 64 (2d Cir. 1939). *See generally* John H. Derrick, Annot., *Damages For Breach of Contract As Affected By Income Tax Considerations*, 50 A.L.R. 4th 452 § 3 (1986) (Income tax due on lump-sum damages awarded).

[62] 230 F. Supp. 2d 603 (E.D. Pa. 2002).

[63] 87 P.3d 757 (Wash. 2004); *cf.* Sears v. Atchison, Topeka & Santa Fe Ry. Co., 749 F.2d 1451, 1456 (10th Cir. 1984) (allowing "gross-up" to reflect increased taxation caused by protracted litigation).

[64] 87 P.3d at 762–63.

[65] Meacham v. Knolls Atomic Power Laboratory, 185 F. Supp. 2d 197, 238 (N.D.N.Y. 2002); Arneson v. Callahan, 128 F.3d 1243 (8th Cir. 1997); Dashnaw v. Pena, 12 F.3d 1112, 1116 (D.C. Cir. 1994) (rejecting claim that award should be "grossed-up" to reflect increased taxes plaintiff will have to pay on the award); *cf. Blaney, supra*, 87 P.3d at 764 (refusing to treat tax enhancement as "damages," but permitting recovery as "other appropriate relief").

[66] United Housing Foundation, Inc. v. Forman, 421 U.S. 837, 863–64 (1975) (Brennan, J., dissenting).

treatment of taxes as damages introduces speculative and collateral issues into the litigation.[67] The issue has begun to attract the attention of the academy[68] and one must expect much more to come on this point.

---

[67] De Palma v. Westland Software House, 276 Cal. Rptr. 214, 217 (Cal. App. 1990); *Blaney*, *supra* 87 P.3d at 764 (stating that enhanced taxation is caused by tax laws not defendant's wrongdoing).

[68] *See* Gregg D. Polsky & Stephen F. Befort, *Employment Discrimination Remedies and Tax Gross Ups*, 90 Iowa L. Rev. 67 (2004); Charlotte Crane, *Some Explicit Thinking About Implicit Taxes*, 52 S.M.U. L. Rev. 339, 367–71 (1999).

Chapter 3

GENERAL PRINCIPLES CONCERNING EQUITABLE REMEDIES

SYNOPSIS

§ 20   THE HISTORICAL RELATIONSHIP BETWEEN LAW AND EQUITY

Equity and law developed as independent legal systems with different forms of practice and methods of redress that reflected the institutional origins of each system. Law developed out of the methods for resolving disputes involving the writs (or orders) of early English Kings after the Norman conquest. The Normans conquest did not operate to erase existing legal institution in England; rather, the Norman established a supplementary system of courts emanating from the King's Council in the twelfth and thirteenth centuries. At this early stage, law and equity were intertwined.[1] By the thirteenth century, this process was organized around three courts, King's Bench, Common Pleas, and Exchequer, although we use the term "courts" loosely for they are not courts as we know them, but courts in the sense that they are ancestral to modern forms.[2] With organization comes bureaucratization and professionalism within both the Bench and Bar.[3] This process has a price. The forms of justice ossify and collect around established recognized procedures. The former ability of the "courts" to respond to new developments is lost.

While the "courts" are in stasis, the world outside the courts is dynamic. Life goes on, and if the established legal system will not respond, another pathway must be found. Legal systems must evolve or they will be bypassed. We see this today. In the mid-twentieth century, when some state courts proved unresponsive to appeals for justice and fair treatment by minorities, litigants moved across the street, across town, or across the state to the federal courthouse. Today, at the beginning of the century, we see increased use of so-called "alternative dispute resolutions" programs, fueled in large part by dissatisfaction over the quality and availability of "justice" in the traditional courts.

By the fifteenth century, the alternative dispute resolution system in England was chancery, which we now know as equity, headed by the Chancellor, a churchman.[4] Into this "court" came individuals seeking justice. We may reflect for a moment on the type of justice available in chancery as opposed to the law courts. The law courts had by this time developed the principle of "deciding like cases alike;" chancery, however, knew no such principle. In chancery, each case was distinct and precedent was not consciously used as a method of resolving disputes.[5] The reasons

---

[1] THEODORE PLUCKNETT, A CONCISE HISTORY OF THE COMMON LAW 681 (5th ed. 1956) (noting that "equity is inseparable from the duty of the king to do justice and his power to exercise discretion . . . this power is . . . as old as the conquest").

[2] F.W. MAITLAND, EQUITY AND THE FORMS OF ACTION 1–7 (1909).

[3] PLUCKNETT, A CONCISE HISTORY, *supra* at 80–81; MAITLAND, EQUITY, *supra* at 10–11.

[4] For a discussion of the English Court of Chanery during this period, see Timothy Haskett, *The Medieval English Court of Chanery*, 14 Law & Hist. Rev. 245 (1996). *But cf.* S.F.C. MILSOM HISTORICAL FOUNDATIONS OF THE COMMON LAW 74 (1969) (stating: "Nothing in the history of English institutions is so obscure as the rise of . . . chancery").

[5] Fry v. Porter, 86 Eng. Rep. 898, 902 (1670) (stating that "if there be equity in a case, that equity is a universal truth, and there can be no precedent in it"). This "tradition" was reported lost by the 1700s. PLUCKNETT, A CONCISE HISTORY, *supra*, at 692:

> It is in the period from Restoration in 1660 down to the beginning of the eighteenth century that equity finally achieves its new form of a consistent and definite body of rules, and the chancellors accept the conclusion that equity has no place for a vague

for this were twofold. First, the procedure was practical. The reason litigants chose chancery was because they fell outside the regime established by the "law courts." This was not a case of concurrent jurisdiction with litigants selecting the most favorable forum for tactical reasons;[6] litigants went to chancery because the "law courts" did not provide a remedy.

The second factor had to do with the person of the Chancellor. He was, until the sixteenth century, a churchman. While the law courts were applying a body of law largely built on the unenacted, non statutory law common to all Englishmen,[7] chancery was developing a body of law based on canon law, which, in turn borrowed heavily from Roman law.[8] Most importantly, the law courts focused on the claim, as encapsulated by the writ; chancery focused on the person of the defendant. If the hallmark of the law court was a judgment declaring legal rights and remedies, the hallmark of chancery was an order commanding the defendant to do, or refrain from doing, something.

Over time both legal systems moved toward the other. The law courts relaxed their rules and opened themselves up to entertaining new rights and remedies, while chancery began to formalize its practice. By the early 1600s, however, the two systems were in conflict, and the conflict was over more than legal process. The law courts were identified with Parliament; equity or chancery was identified with the king. In the early 1600s, before

---

and formless discretion; in short, equity is now, for practical purposes, a body of law which can only be defined as the law which was administered by the chancellors.

Blackstone noted in the mid century that precedent has established a firm hand on equity—a point Dickens would again emphasize a century later in BLEAK HOUSE (1853). 3 WILLIAM BLACKSTONE, COMMENTARIES ON THE LAWS OF ENGLAND *432; *see generally* Michael Lobban, *Preparing For Fusion: Reforming The Nineteenth-Century Court of Chancery Part I*, 22 Law & Hist. Rev. 389 (2004) (discussing the status and state of English equity practice in the 1800s).

[6] For example, in many instances both state and federal courts have concurrent jurisdiction over a matter. Litigants may seek to place the matter in the forum that they believe is most favorable to their position. Factors that will influence the placement decision include tactical benefits arising out of state court-federal court differences over: (1) scope of discovery; (2) venue transfer; (3) rules of evidence; (4) jury pool; and (5) judicial assignment.

[7] MAITLAND, EQUITY, *supra* at 2. This is not entirely correct; some of the common law of the period is based on Acts of Parliament and the local law of the manorial courts. Perhaps it is easier to see the common law as the law applied in the law courts as distinct from the law applied in the feudal or manorial courts, although the distinction is not crisp as there was substantial borrowing. There are again parallels to this in our country's history. The federal common law under Swift v. Tyson, 41 U.S. 1 (1842) was not wholly distinct from its state law counterparts; federal common law during this period was developed by a different authoritative voice using the same materials available to state courts. In the field of procedure, the results were even closer owing to the Conformity Act, Act of May 8, 1792, ch. 36, § 2, 1 Stat. 275, 276 (repealed 1872), which directed federal courts to use the "forms and modes of proceedings" used by the State in which the court was located.

[8] It is generally understood that notwithstanding the obscurity of the early history of equity, its roots lay in Roman law. HENRY MAINE, ANCIENT LAW: ITS CONNECTION WITH THE EARLY HISTORY OF SOCIETY AND ITS RELATION TO MODERN IDEAS 44-69 (Peter Smith ed. 1997) (reprint of 10th ed. of 1864). How deeply the roots were in Roman law is, however, a matter of dispute. Haskett, *The Medieval Court of Chancery, supra*, at 256–57.

the English Civil War, the king recognized the priority of equity; a law court must respect a chancery order enjoining a litigant from appearing before the law court and seeking redress.[9] Yet, the preference for equity was limited, and not for reasons relating to the civil war and its aftermath. Rather, it is recognized and accepted that law and equity had developed into complimentary systems, each of which filled gaps that one system alone would present. This recognition of the compatibility of law and equity preserved the two systems in England throughout the turbulence of "The Restoration" and the "Quiet Revolution" in the last half of the seventeenth century.

The compatibility of law and equity allowed both systems to survive in this country after the American Revolution, even though equity was identified with King George III. What accounts for equity's longevity, notwithstanding its association with two failed kings, Charles I (who lost his head to the victorious Cromwell) and George III (who lost his colonies to the victorious Washington)? The simple answer is the utility of alternative systems, each of which covers for shortfalls in the other. The closest analogy is to rules and standards. Which is preferable, decision making by rule or decision making by standards? Both sides have their defenders and their critics. The test of time is that we seem to prefer both, operating in some uneasy equilibrium. There are situations when decision making by rule seems superior to decision making by standard; in other situations, the opposite holds true. Such an approach lacks theoretical neatness, but decision making has always been a human enterprise with all the flaws (and benefits) that humans bring to any enterprise.

[20.1] Judicial Power

Equity derives from the ideal that a judgment should be based on the particulars of the person and the situation.[10] This is not to say that "justice" was found only in equity; rather, each legal system—law and equity—held (and perhaps to some extent today still "holds") a different view of justice. In equity, "justice" was seen as encompassing individualized decision making; in law "justice" was seen as generalized decision making by consistent application of rules.

As noted previously, the War of Independence did not act to abolish equity practice in the newly formed United States. The states continued to recognize equity and the Constitution expressly extends the judicial power "to all Cases, in law and equity, arising under this Constitution, the laws

---

[9] WILLIAM HOLDSWORTH, A HISTORY OF ENGLISH LAW 461–62 (7th ed. 1956) (discussing political and legal dispute between the common law courts and chancery that was resolved in favor of chancery by King James 1 in 1616). A more detailed recounting of these events can be found in David Raack, *A History of Injunctions in England Before 1700*, 61 Ind. L.J. 539, 573–583 (1986).

[10] Martha C. Nussbaum, *Equity and Mercy* in LITERATURE AND LEGAL PROBLEM SOLVING 15, 17–19 (Paul J. Heald, ed. 1998) (noting that equity permits, if it does not demand, that the qualities of mercy, leniency, and sympathy be applied to resolve the dispute fairly).

of the United States, and Treaties made. . . ."[11] This constitutional conferral does not, however, mean that federal judges, or their state court counterparts, have unfettered power to resolve a dispute under law or equity or both. This holds true notwithstanding the formal merger of the two legal systems.[12] The ability of a judge to decide a case at law or in equity is often a difficult question because the answer depends on distinctions that are dated and bear little relation to contemporary problems. The English legal historian Maitland once observed that the old forms of action are dead, but they still rule us from their graves.[13] The same can be said for the law-equity distinction notwithstanding the merger of the two systems.

Recently, the Supreme Court has reinvigorated the law-equity distinction and in so doing has limited the ability of federal courts to redress legal wrongs through remedies in equity. In *Grupo Mexicano de Desarollo S.A. v. Alliance Bond Fund* holders of unsecured notes issued by Grupo Mexicano de Desarollo, S.A. ("the company") brought an action against the company based on its failure to make scheduled payments on the notes. The holders sought a preliminary injunction restraining the company from transferring its assets pending resolution of their claims. The district court issued the requested preliminary injunction and the Court of Appeals affirmed. The Supreme Court, by a 5/4 division, reversed the lower courts' decision. The Court focused on the history of equitable relief and the nature of the relief requested. The Court noted that the equity power of federal courts was generally fixed at the time of the Judiciary Act of 1789. According to the Court, at that time, the "well-established general rule was that a judgment fixing the debt was necessary before a court in equity would interfere with the debtor's use of his property."[14] The Court concluded that in the absence of congressional modification of that rule, federal courts have no authority for granting the requested relief. The salient aspect of the case is, however, that the plaintiffs did not seek any final equitable relief that the preliminary injunction would preserve or protect. The requested "asset freeze" order was solely designed to protect a prospective money judgment. The case would be different if final injunctive relief was sought and the purpose of the interim relief was to protect the court's power to award meaningful, "equitable" relief. The reason for the distinction is that the

---

[11] U.S. Const. Art III, § 2. On the Supreme Court's approach to and understanding of the grant of equitable jurisdiction, see John R. Kroger, *Supreme Court Equity, 1789–1835, and the History of American Judging*, 34 Hous. L. Rev. 1425, 1440–71 (1998).

[12] Section 20.3 (Merger of Law & Equity).

[13] MAITLAND, EQUITY, *supra*, 1–2.

[14] 527 U.S. 308, 321 (1999); Section 31.5 (Freeze Orders). Prior to *Grupo Mexicano de Desarollo*, the lower federal courts had split on the issue. *Compare* Estate of Ferdinand Marcos, Human Rights Litig., 25 F.3d 1467, 1476–79 (9th Cir.), *cert. denied*, 513 U.S. 1126 (1994) (collecting decisions and affirming issuance of preliminary injunction (asset freeze order) when the only final relief sought was money damages), *with* Rosen v. Cascade Int'l Inc., 21 F.3d 1520, 1530 (11th Cir. 1994) (holding that preliminary injunctive relief (asset freeze order) was not appropriate when plaintiff sought only legal remedies); *and In re* Fredeman Litig., 843 F.2d 821, 826 (5th Cir. 1988) (same).

equity courts power to protect its own jurisdiction was well recognized by 1789.

A similarly grudging view of judicial power has been exhibited by the Court when construing federal statutes that authorize equitable remedies. In *Great-West Life & Annuity Co. v. Knudson*[15] the Court continued a practice begun a decade earlier in *Mertens v. Hewitt Associates*[16] of sharply limiting the authority of federal courts to read liberally a statutory grant of equitable relief. The Court, again in a series of narrow 5/4 rulings, has held that, unless Congress expressly indicates otherwise, statutory grants of equitable redress should be read against the historic division between law and equity, along with the fine distinctions that accompanied dual legal systems that were both separate yet interconnected.

Knudson involved a claim for reimbursement of money expended by the defendant for her medical care. Under the contracts between plaintiffs and defendant, and under the law in general, a health plan that pays for another's medical care is entitled to obtain reimbursement from the tortfeasor who caused the injuries.[17] If the victim sues the tortfeasor and recovers, the victim holds the money for the benefit of the health plan. That was the situation in *Knudson*, except that the victim (Knudson) did not pay any of the settlement proceeds of her action against the tortfeasor to the plaintiffs to reimburse them for expenses they had incurred in having her injuries treated. The plaintiffs sued Knudson for reimbursement. Because the relationship between the parties was governed by ERISA, plaintiffs' sole remedy lay in Section 502(a)(3) of the Act, which provides for injunctive relief and "other appropriate equitable relief."[18] All other remedies are preempted; thus, whether plaintiffs recovered turned on whether their claim for reimbursement could be characterized as "equitable relief."

The Court stated that "restitution in equity" was available when money or property belonging to the plaintiff could be traced to money or property now in the hands of the defendant; otherwise, "restitution at law" was the only available relief.[19] The inability of the plaintiffs to trace their money or property into the hands of the defendant meant they had no equitable remedies under the applicable statute and, in fact, no remedy at all because the statute preempted all state remedies and only provided equitable remedies.

This narrow view of judicial power (1) was vigorously contested by strong dissents in both *Mertens* and *Knudson*; (2) has been strongly criticized in

---

[15] 534 U.S. 204 (2002).

[16] 508 U.S. 248 (1993). In *Mertons* the Court held that the statutory conferral of authority to federal courts in ERISA allowing plan participants to secure "appropriate equitable relief" did not extend to damages claims against non-fiduciaries who colluded with plan fiduciaries to breach their fiduciary duties owed to the plan participants.

[17] Section 53 (Subrogation).

[18] Employee Retirement Income Security Act of 1974, 29 U.S.C. §§ 1001-1461 at § 1132(a)(3).

[19] 534 U.S. at 213; Section 59 (Tracing Principles for Constructive Trusts, Equitable Liens, and Equitable Accounting).

the academic literature;[20] and is neither binding on nor necessarily followed by state courts.[21]

How far the *Mertins-Knudson* approach will be taken is unclear. In *Parke v. First Reliance Standard Life Ins. Co.* the court refused to foreclose recovery of prejudgment interest on wrongfully delayed or suspended ERISA benefits and rejected arguments that the relief sought was not equitable. The court found that the recovery of prejudgment interest was sufficiently close to the traditional equitable remedy of an "accounting" as to survive *Knudson's* strict test. In effect, prejudgment interest was awarded to deprive defendant of the profits it earned by its wrongful conduct.[22]

This law-equity distinction can arise in many ways that may not be facially apparent. For example, in 1991 Congress amended Title VII to permit the award of compensatory and punitive damages;[23] however, these awards were capped at $300,000.[24] Prior to 1991 courts had been limited to providing equitable relief and this was construed to permit the awarding of lost earnings as "back pay" or "front pay" awards. "Back pay" refers to earnings lost prior to the date of trial; "front pay" is future lost earnings. The "back" and "front" pay awards were deemed equitable because they were awarded in lieu of reinstatement. The 1991 Amendment raised, however, a characterization problem: were future lost earnings awards subject to the statutory damages cap.[25] For ten years the issue was contested with the federal courts split on the issue in part along the lines as to whether the future lost earnings awards were seen as equitable in nature (and not subject to a *damages* cap) or legal in nature (and, thus, subject to the cap). Ultimately, the Court resolved the split although not on the basis of the law-equity distinction.[26]

[20.2]   Right of Jury Trial

One other area in which the law-equity distinction remains significant is in the context of the right to jury trial. This results from the constitutional

---

[20] John H. Langbein, *What ERISA Means by "Equitable": The Supreme Court Court's Trail of Error in Russell, Mertens, and Great West*, 103 Colum. L. Rev. 1317 (2003); Judith Resnik, *Constricting Remedies: The Rhenquist Judiciary, Congress, and Federal Power*, 78 Ind. L.J. 223 (2003). The Court's narrow approach also has its defenders. John Choon Yoo, *Who Measures the Chancellor's Foot? The Inherent Remedial Authority of Federal Courts*, 84 Cal. L. Rev. 1121 (1996).

[21] Section 23 (Equitable Discretion); Section 33.1 ([Permanent Injunctions] Scope of Relief).

[22] 368 F.3d 999, 1007–09 (8th Cir. 2004); Section 54 (Constructive Trust).

[23] Kolstad v. American Dental Ass'n., 527 U.S. 526, 533–34 (1999) (noting that such damages are only available in cases involving intentional, as opposed to disparate impact, discrimination); Section 151 (Employee's Damages Against Employer).

[24] 42 U.S.C. § 1981a(b)(3).

[25] "Back pay" is specially mentioned in Title VII, but "front pay" is not; nonetheless, the federal courts held that "front pay" could be awarded in lieu of reinstatement. Pollard v. E.I. du Pont de Nemours & Co., 532 U.S. 843, 850–51 (2001) (discussing trend to award "front pay").

[26] *Pollard, supra*, 532 U.S. at 853–54 (holding that "front pay" was merely an extension of "back pay" and that Congress exempted "back pay" from the statutory cap).

guarantee of the right to jury trial in the federal and state constitutions and the general tendency to frame the scope of the guarantee in terms of the right as it existed at some point in the past.[27] This approach raises several issues. First, it requires the classification of claims on the basic of historical fact rather than current usage.[28] Second, it requires that the defendant be suable at law as of the relevant reference date.[29] Since the formal merger of law and equity accomplished by the Rules Enabling Act in 1938, federal courts have tended to view the historical test contextually. For example, a matter triable in equity in 1791 because there was no legal remedy, but modernly triable at law may now give rise to a right to jury trial notwithstanding the historical pedigree that placed the matter in equity.[30] In state courts the approaches vary. While most courts retain the historical test, modern actions may create difficult problems of classification that have resulted in conflicts: Two examples of this are (1) promissory estoppel;[31] and (2) breach of fiduciary duty.[32]

The right to jury trial may also be provided by statute even if it is not guaranteed by the Constitution. This issue is essentially one of defining

---

[27] Ford v. Blue Cross & Blue Shield of Connecticut, 578 A.2d 1054, 1059 (Conn. 1990) (stating that the "test is whether the issue raised in the action is substantially of the same nature or is such an issue as prior to 1818 would have been triable to a jury"). For federal courts, the relevant date is 1791, when the Seventh Amendment guaranteeing the right to jury trial in civil actions was adopted. Pernell v. Southhall Realty, 416 U.S. 363, 373–74 (1974); Curtis v. Loether, 415 U.S. 189, 193 (1974). States vary in their reference date, but the usual reference is to the date the state constitution was adopted.

[28] *Ford, supra,* 578 A.2d 1054 (holding that right to jury trial attached to claim of wrongful termination of employee for seeking statutory worker's compensation benefits because the claim has its roots in the common law); American Universal Ins. Co. v. Pugh, 821 F.2d 1352, 1356 (9th Cir. 1987) (holding that claim for "money had and received" and imposition of constructive trust were not triable to a jury). The court reasoned that "the imposition of a constructive trust is purely an equitable remedy." *Id.* While the award of monetary relief is usually done at law, when the monetary award is integral to the equitable remedy the action remains one in equity. *Id.*

[29] Williams v. Shipping Corp. of India, 653 F.2d 875, 881–83 (4th Cir. 1981), *cert. denied,* 455 U.S. 982 (1982) (finding that non-jury provision of Foreign Sovereign Immunities Act did not violate Seventh Amendment because foreign sovereigns were not suable at common law in 1791).

[30] *See* CHARLES ALAN WRIGHT, LAW OF FEDERAL COURTS § 92, at 609–15 (4th ed. 1983).

[31] *Compare* C&K Engineering Contractors v. Amber Steel Co., 587 P.2d 1136, 1140 (Cal. 1998) (holding that promissory estoppel is an equitable action unknown at law before California Constitution was adopted in 1850), *with* ECCO Limited v. Balimay Manufacturing Co., 446 N.W.2d 546, 548 (Mich. App. 1989) (when damages rather than relief traditionally provided by equity, e.g., cancellation of document, is requested, right to jury trial attaches). The issue is extensively discussed in *Olson v. Synergistic Technologies Business Systems, Inc.,* 628 N.W.2d 142 (Minn. 2001), particularly in Justice Anderson's concurring opinion. *Id.* at 155.

[32] *Compare* Interactive Multi-Media Artists, Inc. v. Superior Court, 73 Cal. Rptr.2d 462, 468–69 (Cal. App. 1998) (holding that no right to jury trial existed in breach of fiduciary duties case when claim alleged breach of trust and the sole method assessing damages is by equitable principles), *with* Mortimer v. Loynes, 168 P.2d 481, 486 (Cal. App. 1946) (holding that right to jury trial attached to claim against association officer for secret profit).

legislative intent.[33] The approach taken in these cases is first determine whether a right to jury trial exists as a matter of statutory grant. Alternatively, the right to jury trial may be implied.[34] If the statute does not provide for a right to jury trial, the constitutional guarantee is examined using the approach discussed above.[35]

The right to a jury trial can be substantially affected by the equity clean-up doctrine. The doctrine holds that once equity jurisdiction attaches, the court possesses the power to resolve the entire controversy, including those legal claims triable to the jury,[36] even when the equitable claims have been dismissed and only legal claims remain before the court.[37] While the equity court can decline to consider the remaining legal claims, it is not obligated to surrender jurisdiction to a law court.[38] The power of an equity court to provide legal remedies under the "clean-up" doctrine is generally restricted to those cases when the plaintiff first establishes that a right to equitable relief existed at the time the action was commenced.[39]

In federal courts, the equity clean-up doctrine has been significantly limited by the Supreme Court. In *Beacon Theatres, Inc. v. Westover*[40] and *Dairy Queen, Inc. v. Wood*,[41] the Court held that when jury and non-jury issues are before a federal court in a single dispute, the jury issues must be tried first. The merger of law and equity, particularly as it facilitated claim joinder, strongly influenced this development.[42] Federal courts have

---

[33] Brown v. Sandimo Materials, 250 F.3d 120, 125 (2d Cir. 2001).

[34] Lorillard v. Pons, 434 U.S. 575, 580–81 (1978).

[35] Feltner v. Columbia Pictures Television, Inc., 523 U.S. 340, 352–54 (1998) (noting that the right to have a jury determine the amount of statutory damages for copyright infringement has long been recognized); *Id.* (noting the practice of trying copyright damages actions at law before juries before 1791). *Feltner* had an interesting denouement. The initial award by the court was for $8.8 million, based on $20,000 per statutory violation, of which there were 440. Feltner obtained a reversal of that award because it was by the court rather than a jury. On remand, a jury awarded $31.68 million, based on an award of $72,000 per violation. Feltner appealed, but this time unsuccessfully. 259 F.3d 1186 (9th Cir. 2001), *cert. denied*, 534 U.S. 1127 (2002). Feltner's victory cost him over $20 million!

[36] Camp v. Boyd, 229 U.S. 530 (1913); Priest v. Polk, 912 S.W.2d 902, 906 (Ark. 1995).

[37] New Castle Co. Vol. Fire A. v. Belvedere Vol. Fire Co., 202 A.2d 800, 802 (Del. Ch. 1964).

[38] Getty Refining & Marketing Co. v. Park Oil, Inc., 385 A.2d 147, 150 (Del. Ch. 1978).

[39] Ziebarth v. Kalenze, 238 N.W.2d 261, 266 (N.D. 1976) (noting contrary authorities but adopting approach permitting the award of legal relief even though equitable relief is ultimately denied). In *Ziebarth* the defendant rendered specific performance impossible by selling the contract goods to another. The plaintiff was, however, unaware of this development until after the action was commenced. The court held that when the plaintiff commenced the action for equitable relief in good faith, the loss of the equitable remedy did not bar the awarding of legal relief.

[40] 359 U.S. 500, 509 (1959).

[41] 369 U.S. 469 (1962).

[42] Ross v. Bernhard, 396 U.S. 531, 539 (1970). The merger is not complete. The right to jury trial requires the assertion of a claim; the pleading of a legal defense to an equitable claim does not give rise to a right to a jury. Medtronic, Inc. v. Benda, 689 F.2d 645, 661 (7th Cir. 1982); *cert. denied*, 459 U.S. 1204 (1983) (holding that defendant's pleading of legal defense of lack of consideration in action for specific performance did not convert the equitable action into an action at law); Burlington N. R.R. Co. v. Nebraska Pub. Power Dist. 931 F. Supp. 1470, 1481 (D. Neb. 1996) (same).

extended this principle to disputes raising legal claims through procedures that were equitable in origin, such as derivative actions.[43] The equitable clean-up doctrine has received greater application, notwithstanding the merger of law and equity, in state courts.[44]

[20.3] Merger of Law and Equity

Today, in the United States, law and equity have been formally merged in all but two states. The extent and consequences of this merger continue to draw the attention of academics and courts.[45] All would agree that merger has had a profound impact on the former separateness of law and equity and this impact has affected substantive legal doctrine in many ways. How far the merger will go remains a matter of debate.[46]

[20.3.1] Procedural or Substantive

The formal merger of law and equity should not be viewed as a singular act; rather, merger should be seen as an evolving process in which both law and equity have borrowed from each other while still retaining their individual nature. Merger of the two systems into a single system has blurred the distinctions somewhat, but not completely. Notwithstanding the formal merger, courts still recognize equity as a separate, freestanding body of law in many respects.[47]

[20.3.2] Remedial Defenses

The most immediate impact on Remedies of the merger of law and equity has been in the area of defenses, most particularly, the extension of equitable defenses, with their moralistic heritage, to actions at law. The movement has today been largely one-way; but this generally parallels an earlier movement in the seventeenth and eighteenth centuries of equitable rights and remedies over to the law side in the areas of fraud and quasi contract remedies. Chapter 7 will examine the more frequently encountered equitable defenses.

---

[43] *Ross, supra*, 396 U.S. at 539.

[44] Demoulas v. Demoulas Super Markets, Inc., 677 N.E.2d 159, 178 (Mass. 1997) (treating derivative action as unitary equity action and denying right to jury trial on law issues); Colclasure v. Kansas City Life Ins. Co., 720 S.W.2d 916, 917 (Ark. 1986) (noting that equity clean-up doctrine is compatible with state constitutional guarantee of a jury trial); Rankin v. Frebank Co., 121 Cal. Rptr. 348, 358 (Cal. App. 1975) (holding that no right to jury trial attached to shareholder derivative action). *But see* Higgins v. Barnes, 530 A.2d 724, 728 (Md. 1987) and Miller v. Carnation Co., 516 P.2d 661 (Colo. App. 1973) (following *Beacon Theatres*).

[45] Symposium, *Modern Equity*, 56 Law & Contemp. Prob. 1 (1993).

[46] Stephen N. Subrin, *How Equity Conquered the Common Law, The Federal Rules of Civil Procedure in Historical Perspective*, 135 U. Pa. L. Rev. 909 (1987); Douglas Laycock, *The Triumph of Equity*, 56 Law & Contemp. Prob. 53 (1993). *But see* Thomas D. Rowe, Jr., *No Final Victories: The Incompleteness of Equity's Triumph in Federal Public Law*, 56 Law & Contemp. Prob 105 (1993).

[47] Section 20.1 (Judicial Power).

Because law and equity developed as separate legal systems, each system came to recognize defenses that were applied only within that system. Remedial defenses tend to reflect the culture of each system. Legal defenses, such as "in pari delicto" or statutes of limitations, reflect the rule orientation of the common law courts. Equitable defenses, such as unclean hands or laches, reflect the flexible and discretion-based orientation of equity courts. Owing to equity's historical tie to ecclesiastic courts, the Chancellor was comfortable resolving disputes on the merits based on principles of fairness and justice; the situation was otherwise with the Royal Judges.[48]

Even before the modern efforts to merge law and equity, the distinctiveness that separated law from equity was blurring due to the tendency to select judges for law courts and equity courts from the same group of lawyers. By the time of the Glorious Revolution in 1688, equity had lost its ecclesiastical chancellors and its judges were entirely secular.[49] Of course, in the United States, the ecclesiastic lineage of equity was never more than a distant memory; American chancellors and judges have always been secular and, aside from the populism of Jacksonian Democracy, have always been lawyers.

The merger of law and equity, largely, but not completely, a twentieth century phenomenon, has tended to accelerate this change, but we should not overemphasize this event. Even before merger, many equitable rights and defenses began, and completed, their journey over to the law side and became part of the accepted jurisdiction of law courts. For reasons of history and inertia, however, the transfer of equitable defenses over to the law side, and vice versa, has not been complete. A number of courts have observed that the merger of law and equity suggests any formal separation is anachronistic.[50] Nevertheless, the law-equity distinction perseveres, albeit with ever decreasing force. The law-equity distinction seems to resemble a glacier that while formidable is ever retreating as the environment changes and warms.

[20.4]   Law and Equity

There is an old equitable maxim that "Equity follows the law" ("Equitas Sequitur Legem"). The concept is something reformatted as "A court in equity may not do that which the law forbids."[51] As with equitable maxims in general, care must be taken not to take the principle too literally or too far.[52] The maxim expresses the modern commitment to accommodate dual

---

[48] Maitland, Equity, *supra*, 2–11.

[49] *Id.*

[50] Byron v. Clay, 867 F.2d 1049, 1052 (7th Cir. 1989) (Posner, J.) (stating that "with the merger of law and equity, it is difficult to see why equitable defenses should be limited to equitable suits any more . . ."). The issue has also attracted the attention of legal scholars. Emily L. Sherwin, *Law & Equity in Contract Enforcement*, 50 Md. L. Rev. 253 (1991); Edward Yorio, *A Defense of Equitable Defenses*, 51 Ohio St. L. J. 1201 (1990).

[51] United States v. Coastal Ref. And Mktg., Inc. 911 F.2d 1036, 1043 (5th Cir. 1990).

[52] The origins of the maxims of equity are shrouded in history and lore. A good review of

legal systems. As a general rule, equity will not act "wherever the rights or the situation of the parties are clearly defined and established by law."[53] Of course, if the principle were applied literally, there would be little room for equity. The fact is that equity does step in when law provides a rule that clearly defines the rights and situation of the parties and, in so doing, equity provides a remedy or redress when law would not. For example, in *Navajo Academy v. Navajo United Methodist Mission School* the court held that the tenant had no legal right to hold over after the lease had been properly terminated, but permitted the tenant to remain on property for 3 additional years, rent free, due to the long standing relationship between the parties, the work done by the tenant in educating Native-American children, and the "equities" of the case.[54] Similarly, an equity court might deny equitable relief to protect a legal right that was clear and absolute. In *Brown v. Voss* the court refused an injunction to prevent the holders of a private easement from using the easement to access after-acquired property. The court held that the original estate and the after-acquired parcel could be legitimately combined and the use of the easement to access the after-acquired property resulted in no additional burden on the servient estate.[55] The owners of the subservient estate had been granted nominal damages reflecting the legal correctness of their position.[56]

The fact that equity steps in *occasionally* to reach a result inconsistent with the result prescribed at law should not be read as a mandate to do so or even a tendency to do so. The maxim "equity follows the law" expresses the general rule. A party who wishes the court to do otherwise must reckon that the odds the court will agree are long.

---

the maxims is Roger Young & Stephen Spitz, *SUEM—Spitz's Ultimate Equitable Maxim: In Equity Good Guys Should Win and Bad Guys Should Lose*, 55 S.C. L. Rev. 175 (2003). *See also* Howard Brill, *The Maxim's of Equity*, 1993 Ark. L. Notes 29:

> Unlike the maxims of Solomon, the maxims of equity do not span millenia, are not traceable to a single author or Author, and do not promise eternal rewards. Unlike statutes, they lack the precision and clarity necessary to resolve specific issues, do not specify any sanctions, and are not invalid for vagueness. Some maxims are merely pretext or justification for the decisions of chancery; some are inconsistent or contradictory; some are consumed by their exceptions. One treaties suggests their only role is to provide "some utility as memory aids." On the other hand, equally extreme is the statement that the maxims are "the fruitful germs" and the "judicial principles of morality which thus constitute the ultimate sources of equitable doctrines . . . ." If nothing else, the maxims, developed over the centuries, offer an insight into equitable discretion and provide the opportunity for creative lawyering.

Id. (footnotes omitted).

[53] Hedges v. Dixon County, 150 U.S. 182, 192 (1893). Often the concept is shortened to "Equity follows the law."

[54] 785 P.2d 235 (N. Mex. 1990).

[55] 715 P.2d 514, 517–18 (Wash. 1986).

[56] Section 2.8 (Nominal Damages).

In some instances courts are expressly authorized to change the legal result when certain equitable principles are found, e.g., undue hardship. As a general rule, these situations are both rare and limited.[57]

§ 21 ADEQUACY OF THE REMEDY AT LAW/ IRREPARABLE INJURY

[21.1] Justification for the Requirement

The traditional ticket to admission to equitable remedies was the requirement that the remedy at law be inadequate. This requirement originated at an early date to avoid conflicts between the Chancellor and the Royal Judges. As independent yet parallel systems of dispute resolution the two courts needed principles of coexistence that would govern their relationship.[1] The guiding principle that developed was that, for most cases, recourse to equity would demand a showing that the remedy at law was inadequate. Equity was to be, for the most part, a supplemental rather than alternative legal system.

Coexistence between equity and the common law courts led to equity's jurisdiction being a divided into two categories. In the first category were those matters that had historically and traditionally been heard in equity. These included matters involving fiduciaries, which arose out of equity's long-standing and recognized jurisdiction over "uses," fraud, mistake, and bankruptcy, to name but a few.[2] Here, equity's jurisdiction was primary and a party was not required to demonstrate that his remedy at law was inadequate. This primary jurisdiction is still recognized.[3]

The second category encompassed the inadequacy of the remedy at law concept and gave rise to the irreparable injury requirement—irreparable not in terms of severity but in terms of the injury's remediability at law. To say the remedy at law is inadequate (or perhaps more accurately

---

[57] *In re* Saxman, 325 F.3d 1168 (9th Cir. 2003) (discussing limited exception in bankruptcy to general rule barring discharge of student loan debt). The court held that the equitable power prescribed in the Bankruptcy Act regarding student loan debt could not expand or exceed the statutory criteria; otherwise equitable power would eviscerate statutory provisions. *Id.* at 1173–74 (rejecting contrary approach reached in *Tennessee Student Assistance Corp. v. Hornsby*, 144 F.3d 433 (6th Cir. 1998)).

[1] Competition between parallel dispute resolution systems is not confined to ancient legal systems. We see the problem albeit with substantial variance due to the different contexts, in the relationships between state and federal courts, judicial and administrative decision making, and judicial and private alternative dispute resolutions processes, such as arbitration and mediation. Section 20.3 (Merger of Law and Equity).

[2] PLUCKNETT, A CONCISE HISTORY, *supra*, 688–92.

[3] *In re* Evangelist, 760 F.2d 27, 29 (1st Cir. 1985) (noting that "[a]ctions for breach of fiduciary duty, historically speaking, are almost uniformly actions 'in equity' . . ."); Nayee v. Nayee, 705 So. 2d 961, 963 (Fla. App. 1998) (noting that proceedings involving trusts are generally within the exclusive jurisdiction of equity; therefore, court could hear matter involving accounting by fiduciary without need to show inadequacy of remedy at law, *e.g.*, that the accounts were too complicated for a jury); Section 55 (Equitable Accounting).

"insufficiently adequate") is to say that the injury is irreparable at law. A plaintiff had to show that the remedy at law was inadequate, in the sense described above, before she could access remedies in equity.[4]

How stringently the irreparable injury requirement is enforced today is a matter of debate. Professor Douglas Laycock has argued that the former stridency with which the irreparable injury requirement was enforced has largely abated.[5] Other commentators have expressed a less confident view of the demise of the irreparable injury requirement.[6]

While the irreparable injury requirement has been reduced in significance, it has not been abolished. That much is probably agreed to by the commentators. The merger of law and equity, accomplished in most American jurisdictions in the first half of the twentieth century, has undermined the traditional "dual jurisdictions" justifications for the irreparable injury requirement; nevertheless, the requirement remains in place.[7] To paraphrase Mark Twain, the reports of the death of the irreparable injury requirement appear to have been exaggerated; the debate is over the extent of the exaggeration. Several factors may account for this. First, while courts have abated the rule through application, they have not expressly negated the rule in doctrine. Any review of modern cases will evidence frequent invocations of the irreparable injury requirement.[8] A judge or advocate looking solely for a statement of law will find many expressions of the

---

[4] It is important to understand that the two categories are not clear and distinct. For example, certain equitable actions, such as subrogation, indemnity, and constructive trusts, are sometimes placed in the first category; other times, they are placed in the second category. The distinctions between the two categories, while useful, are not absolute. There is some confusion in the application of the distinctions when concrete problems arise.

[5] Douglas Laycock, *The Death of the Irreparable Injury Rule*, 103 Harv. L. Rev. 687 (1990).

[6] Doug Rendleman, *Irreparability Irreparably Damaged*, 90 Mich. L. Rev. 1642 (1992) (agreeing with Laycock's major theme but questioning Laycock's deemphasis of the power of equitable remedies (injunctions) vis a vis substitutional legal remedies); Gene Sheve, *The Premature Burial of the Irreparable Injury Rule*, 70 Tex. L. Rev. 1063 (1992) (questioning plausibility of the premise that the irreparable injury rule is dead).

[7] The issue of irreparable injury figured prominently in the case that decided the outcome of the 2000 Presidential election, *Bush v. Gore*, 531 U.S. 98 (2000) (holding that the Florida Supreme Court's recount order violated the 14th Amendment's Equal Protection Clause). Three days earlier, however, the Court had issued a stay of the Florida Supreme Court's order that stopped the recount process, which had already begun, in its tracks. Bush v. Gore, 531 U.S. 1046 (2000) (granting application for stay). Because of the entry of the stay, when the Court decided the case three days later George Bush was still leading Al Gore in the Florida popular vote. Would the decision have been the same if during that interval the ongoing vote count had reversed the positions? Laurens Walker, *The Stay Seen Around the World: The Order that Stopped the Vote Recounting in* Bush v. Gore, 18 J. L. & Pol. 823 (2002) (arguing the Supreme Court precedents warranted granting of the stay to preserve George Bush's "tactical advantage," the loss of which would amount to irreparable injury).

[8] Citibank, N.A. v. Citytrust, 756 F.2d 273 (2d Cir. 1985):

Perhaps the single most important prerequisite for the issuance of a preliminary injunction is a demonstration that if it is not granted the applicant is likely to suffer irreparable harm before a decision on the merits can be rendered.

Id. at 275 (citation omitted).

irreparable injury requirement and given the volume of decisions, not infrequent harsh applications of the irreparable injury requirement in a particular case. Whether this reflects the intended application of the rule, the unthinking application of the rule, or the devious application of the rule to avoid addressing other issues remains a matter of interpretation and debate. It is unclear whether we are to follow what commentators say or what courts do and this confusion extends to the courts themselves.

Second, the irreparable injury requirement may be seen as a mechanism for regulating access to a remedial system (equity) whose remedies and methods of decision making are seen as raising policy issues that warrant subordinating that system to the law-based remedial system. This distinction is not based on the form of relief for both equity and law provide in appropriate cases specific remedies, e.g., injunctions (equity) and replevin and ejectment (law) and substitutional remedies, e.g., monetary awards to replicate what was lost or damaged or taken away. Rather, the difference lies in the authority of the court to enforce its decisions and the methods by which its decisions are reached. In this regard, equity courts differ from law courts in several significant ways.[9] Equity decisions are by the court not by a jury; equity court decisions normally order and direct the defendant to engage in specific acts; and equity courts may enforce compliance with their orders through the remedy of contempt.[10]

Professor Douglas Laycock in his casebook and other writings examines and critiques four arguments that he identifies as underlying, in the post-merger era, the preference for monetary awards at law over specific remedies in equity. Should modern legal systems require a plaintiff to justify a preference for an equitable remedy (specific performance) over a remedy at law (damages) to redress the breach of any contract? Should remedy election be essentially the same as cause of action selection where litigants are generally given a free hand? Professor Laycock believes that the arguments he examines fail to support the preference and this suggests that use of the irreparable injury requirement as a gatekeeper to restrict access to equity is at worst unwarranted and at best overused.

The first consideration is the idea that injunctive relief imposes greater supervisory burdens on the court than a monetary award. Because an injunction acts on the person, requiring specific action by that person, the court's involvement in the defendant's post-order activities will likely be more detailed than when the court awards money and concludes the matter insofar as the court is concerned. The plaintiff-judgment creditor's ability to collect the money awarded is not of direct and immediate concern to the law court; defendant's compliance with the injunction is of direct and immediate concern to the equity court. A money judgment generally ends the law court's involvement in the dispute; post-judgment collection remedies normally raise only peripheral court involvement. An injunction, on

---

[9] These issues are discussed in greater depth by Rendleman, *Irreparability*, *supra*, 90 Mich. L. Rev. 1642 (1992).

[10] Chapter 22 (Contempt).

the other hand, is often but a mid-step in the equity court's involvement. As much effort as went into fashioning the injunction may now be expended in policing the injunction. This drain on scarce judicial resources is ameliorated by the irreparable injury requirement.[11]

Laycock does not completely disagree with the "burden on the court" argument as much as he rejects it as a general justification for the irreparable injury requirement. In cases when the "burden of supervision" is real, a reason exists for not permitting free access to equity. Such a burden should not, however, be presumed, which is the case when it is used as a general justification for the irreparable injury requirement.

"Burden of supervision" has long been a discretion-based factor a court could invoke to refuse to provide equitable remedies.[12] Laycock's argument that it should not be invoked as a general justification for the irreparable injury requirement avoids "double-counting" the "burden" factor. It also recognizes that the "burden" factor has been substantially relaxed not just in public law litigation but in private dispute litigation as well.

The second consideration is the concern that specific equitable relief constitutes a greater intrusion on the defendant's liberty than a monetary award. Equity orders require the defendant to do something. Even when the orders are framed in the negative, e.g., do not trespass onto plaintiff's land, they may require specific conduct, such as the removal of the encroaching structure that constitutes the trespass. A legal judgment, on the other hand, declares a state of legal relations, e.g., defendant owes plaintiff money, but does not specifically require that the defendant do anything, such as pay the judgment.

Laycock notes that any judicial decision in this context will have consequences to both parties. He criticizes a viewpoint that examines only the consequences to one party, the defendant. The effect of emphasizing the effect of the order on the defendant's liberty is that it ignores the effect of the defendant's conduct on the plaintiff. If both legal and equitable remedies were equally effective in remedying defendant's conduct, the concern over liberty might serve a role as a tie-breaker, ensuring that the plaintiff was fully remedied at the least cost possible. The determination that the remedies are equivalent is not, however, made; rather, the decision is avoided because of external concerns (liberty). As a consequence, defendant's liberty is preserved by relegating the plaintiff to a less desired, and possibly less effective, remedy.

---

[11] These concerns led Judge Tjoflat to propose an extremely restrictive test for issuing injunctive relief in *Chandler v. James*, 180 F.3d 1254, 1266 (11th Cir. 1999) (Tjoflat, J., concurring). Judge Tjoflat argued that only when violations of an injunction would be remedied by coercive civil contempt (Section 194) should the remedy at law be deemed inadequate. *Id.* at 1266–77. Judge Tjoflact's proposal, which would substantially (and wrongly) constrict federal equity is discussed and critiqued in Doug Rendleman, *Irreparability Resurrected?: Does a Recalibrated Irreparable Injury Rule Threaten the Warren Court's Establishment Clause Legacy*, 59 Wash. & Lee L. Rev. 1343, 1388 (2002).

[12] Section 24 (Burden on the Courts/Supervision).

The liberty interest cannot be viewed in isolation. Surely ordering the defendant not to cut plaintiff's timber is on a different order of magnitude than ordering a defendant not to speak or protest.[13] Any concern over intrusion on a defendant's liberty must be calibrated to reflect the value of the interest that the injunction is supposed to protect and affect. Expressing this concern through the irreparable injury requirement suffers from the "one size fits all" problem; the solution is both over and under-inclusive because the underlying concerns are too variegated. The defendant's liberty interest may on occasion warrant restricting a plaintiff to the substitutionary remedy of a monetary award. On other occasions, the plaintiff's interests may warrant significant intrusions on the defendant's liberty. If the analysis of the irreparable injury requirement is conducted in an informed manner, with an awareness of these concerns, no harm is done. Such an approach gives real meaning to the concept of irreparable injury. The danger, however, is that the requirement will be pulled off the shelf and applied because of the underlying generalization, which may or may not apply to the facts.

The third consideration is timing. Because an injunction operates to remedy future injury (whether from past or future acts),[14] an injunction requires the court to frame a remedy based to some extent on assumptions whether the acts will continue or the injury will happen. The defendant may cease or refrain from engaging in the conduct the remedy seeks to affect or the injury may abate without judicial intervention. Although legal remedies often raise issues regarding future effects (future lost profits, future injuries), these issues are deemed to be structurally different because they flow from a completed past act. Folding these concerns into the irreparable injury requirement avoids judicial decision making that, because it is based on speculation as to what the defendant may do, may be unnecessary or inaccurate or both.

Laycock notes that even if the concern is justified at least in some cases involving equitable remedies regarding future acts that cause harm to plaintiff, the response to that concern is over-inclusive. The irreparable injury rule does not differentiate an order to remediate a past act having future consequences from an order to remediate a future act having future consequences; yet the "past acts—future consequences" situation is functionally equivalent to the legal remedy for future consequences (future lost profits) of past acts. We may extend the criticism and ask whether "speculation" is structurally different when equitable relief is sought from when legal relief is sought. Is it different in kind to ask what a defendant will do in the future from what effect a defendant's past act will have in the future when calculating the plaintiff's future losses? Both inquiries involve a "probabilistic" determination regarding future conduct. In the case of

---

[13] Elrod v. Burns, 427 U.S. 347, 373 (1976) (plurality opinion) (stating that "[t]he loss of First Amendment freedoms, for even minimal periods of time, unquestionably constitutes irreparable injury"); Section 21.2.4 ([Irreparable Injury] Nature of the Injury).

[14] Section 30 (Ripeness, Mootness, and Standing).

injunctive relief, the focus is on what the defendant will do; in the case of damages, the focus is on what the plaintiff would have done had the legal wrong not occurred. On an intuitive basis, the call in the equity case appears to be the easier because fewer variables are involved. Equity only has to ask itself what the defendant will do, and this decision is largely shaped by ripeness and mootness concerns that if overcome can instill in the decision maker a high degree of confidence that the probabilistic call is correct. Legal remedies for future consequences are, on the other hand, subject to numerous variables and counterfactuals that make prediction difficult, a point effectively conceded by the law of damages, which allows relaxed proofs regarding the quantitive measurement of future loss.[15] Reliance on the timing issue is counterintuitive; rather than supporting the irreparable injury requirement, it undermines its use as a support for a policy that subordinates equitable remedies to those provided at law.

The last consideration is the preservation of the parties' right to jury trial in actions at law. A preference for adjudication in law courts rather than in equity, accomplished through invocation of the irreparable injury requirement, prevents diminishment through avoidance. The irreparable injury requirement is said to serve a legitimate gate-keeping role by restricting access to equity (non-jury trial) to only those matters for which the legal (right to jury trial) remedy is inadequate. Laycock observes that there is a noticeable irony in a forum selection rule that is based on the defendant's preference for a jury trial, but the constitutional guarantee was driven by that preference.[16] The popular literature suggests that juries tend to favor plaintiffs over defendants.[17] This bias, if it exists in fact, is, however, counter balanced by the numerous studies that evidence substantial judge-jury agreement.[18] It may be that defendants invoke the right to jury trial strategically to reduce the value to plaintiffs of the remedies potentially available, but that conduct is no different from the plaintiff's strategic conduct in selecting claims to pursue. It also may be that the preference for damages over injunctive relief reflects a preference that

---

[15] Section 8.1 (Certainty); Section 8.3 (Lost Profits).

[16] While this election may be remedy-driven, occasionally it appears to be decision-maker driven. The plaintiff may prefer a bench trial and wish to avoid a jury trial. This was a concern that drove the adoption of the Seventh Amendment—guaranteeing defendant-debtors a jury trial in collection claims by plaintiff-creditors. *See* Ann Woolhandler & Michael S. Collins, *The Article III Jury*, 87 Va. L. Rev. 587, 594–600 (2001); Mathew P. Harrington, *The Economic Origins of the Seventh Amendment*, 87 Iowa L. Rev. 145, 188–89 (2001).

[17] Actual verdicts may not tell the whole tale because of the bias affecting cases selected for trial. Only weak cases may go to trial; strong cases are settled. A high rate of defense verdicts may be skewed due to the fact that "tried" cases do not reflect the actual universe of disputes in that field. *See* Samuel R. Gross & Kent D. Syverud, *Don't Try: Civil Jury Verdicts in a System Geared to Settlement*, 44 UCLA L. Rev. 1 (1996).

[18] Valerie P. Hans & Stephanie Albertson, *Empirical Research and Civil Jury Reform*, 78 Notre Dame L. Rev. 1497, 1509–10 (2003) (collecting studies).

defendants be permitted, even encouraged, to breach and pay damages rather than perform, when it is in their economic interests to do so.[19]

Laycock correctly exposes the tactical considerations that underlie the defendant's decision to invoke the irreparable injury requirement to close off a plaintiff's access to equity, but many dearly held "rights" are protected by a litigant's tactical self-interests. It is, no doubt, a happy coincidence when ideals cohabitate with practice. The fact remains that the right to a jury trial continues to serve as a cornerstone of the civil justice system for all litigants. Perhaps the larger question is whether the "right" could be better preserved and protected by extending the right to jury trial to equity fact finding. This has largely occurred in the federal courts through the Supreme Court's Seventh Amendment jurisprudence, although the reach of those decisions has not been extended to, nor completely embraced by, the states.[20]

We are left with a series of compromised justifications for a requirement that expresses a preference for legal over equitable remedies in many cases. Well directed scholarly criticism of the irreparable injury requirement has succeeded in the softening of the irreparable injury requirement, but not its demise. Perhaps its survivability reflects its serviceability as a utilitarian doctrine that courts can invoke to avoid hard decisions or unpopular ones. It may reflect the failure of scholarly criticism to persuade. Courts may believe the rationales and not be persuaded that the criticisms are well taken. Whatever the case may be, the irreparable injury requirement exists and must be addressed even though it is encountered today in a weakened form than in the past.

[21.2] The Content of the Requirement

Articulations of the content of the "irreparable injury requirement" are often less than informative although they do provide minimal guidance. The modern formulations vary. One test is comparative: is the legal remedy as "complete, practical, efficient, etc." as the equitable remedy.[21] If the legal remedy is not as "complete, etc." as the equitable remedy, the plaintiff satisfies the irreparable injury requirement. While this formulation provides a focus, it uses terms that are general and vague. Does "practical" mean practical for the parties or practical for the court? How is "practicability" or "efficiency" defined? Other formulations focus more on the nature of the injury, defining irreparable injury as "substantial injury to a material

---

[19] *Compare* RICHARD POSNER, ECONOMIC ANALYSIS OF LAW 88–89 (2d ed. 1977) (contending that permitting specific performance to be granted routinely would impair economic efficiency), *with* Alan Schwartz, *The Case For Specific Performance*, 89 Yale L.J. 271 (1979) (contending that plaintiff's preference for specific performance over damages is itself evidence of the superior efficiency of the former).

[20] Section 20.2 (Right of Jury Trial).

[21] McArdle v. Rodriguez, 659 N.E.2d 1356, 1365 (Ill. App. 1995); IBM Corp. v. Comdisco, Inc., 602 A.2d 74, 78 (Del. Ch. 1991); Liza Danielle, Inc. v. Jamko, Inc., 408 So. 2d 735, 738 (Fla. App. 1982); Citizens Bldg., Inc. v. E.L. Azios, 590 S.W.2d 569, 574 (Tex. Civ. App. 1979).

degree.[22] or downplaying the severity or magnitude of the injury in favor of an analysis of the "quality" of the injury.[23] These approaches, however, confuse the severity of the injury with the need for equitable as opposed to relief at law. A money damages award can compensate for severe injuries as well as minor injuries, all other things being equal. Equitable relief is necessary in those cases when "all other things are not equal." Injury severity does not necessarily demonstrate that damages will be inadequate. Something more is needed, but that something more is not always required by courts; sometimes, severity of injury suffices.

[21.2.1] Frustration of Relief Sought

Irreparable injury has been found when delay in obtaining legal redress would effectively deprive the plaintiff of the beneficial use of the right he seeks to establish. For example, in *Muhammad Ali v. Division of State Athletic Comm'n Dep't of State of New York*[24] the court held that the suspension of the plaintiff's boxing license caused irreparable injury in view of the limited number of years remaining in which plaintiff would meet the physical standards for boxing. Similarly, in *Jensen v. IRS*[25] the court enjoined the defendant IRS from levying on the plaintiff's earning notwithstanding the general rule discussed in Section 21.2.2 that mere economic harm usually does not constitute irreparable injury. The court observed that were the plaintiff required to pay the tax through the levy he would lose the very administrative remedy he claimed he was illegally being deprived of because of the IRS's failure to give him proper notice of the claimed deficiency. The loss of the right to litigate the tax liability before paying the tax was itself, under the circumstances, a "substantial hardship."[26]

[21.2.2] Economic Harm

Mere "economic harm" is usually not sufficient to constitute irreparable injury.[27] For example, in *General Textile Printing & Processing Corp. v. Expromtorg, Int'l Corp.*[28] the court refused to enjoin the defendant from

---

[22] Tully v. Mott Supermarkets, Inc., 337 F. Supp. 834, 850 (D.N.J. 1972).

[23] Doe v. Bellin Mem'l Hosp., 479 F.2d 756, 759 (7th Cir. 1973) (noting that the threatened invasion of the constitutional and sensitive right to an abortion satisfied the irreparable injury requirement notwithstanding that other facilities besides the defendant's could perform the procedure).

[24] 316 F. Supp. 1246, 1252 (S.D.N.Y. 1970).

[25] 835 F.2d 196 (9th Cir. 1987).

[26] *Id.* at 199; Textile Unlimited, Inc. v. A. BMH Co., Inc., 240 F.3d 781, 786 (9th Cir. 2001) (stating that party would suffer irreparable injury if it were forced to contest the existence of an arbitration agreement in a venue dictated by the disputed arbitration agreement); *A.W. Chesterton Co., Inc.*, note 38, *infra*.

[27] Central Nebraska Broad. Co., Inc. v. Heartland Radio, Inc., 560 N.W.2d 770, 772–73 (Neb. 1997) (holding that possibility that competitor's installation of second antenna on radio tower that also supported plaintiff's antenna would cause the collapse of the tower and prevent plaintiff from earning advertising revenue from broadcasting was fully compensable by a damages award; hence, request for injunction to bar erection of tower would be denied).

[28] 862 F. Supp. 1070 (S.D.N.Y. 1994).

breaching his contract with the plaintiff and selling the contracted goods to another party at a higher price. The court noted that the plaintiff presented no evidence that it was unable to cover, that the defendant could not respond and satisfy a monetary award, or that plaintiff would suffer a loss of goodwill as a result of the breach. The court refused to find that the mere potential that defendant would be unable to satisfy a judgment evidenced irreparable injury.[29]

Irreparable injury has been found when the economic harm rises to the level of the potential destruction of the plaintiff's business.[30] Destruction of business means just that. It is insufficient proof of irreparable injury if all the plaintiff can show is decreased profitability.[31] Even substantial, potential loss may be insufficient if the court believes that the loss can be made good by a monetary award.[32] On the other hand, potential destruction has been found to constitute irreparable injury under both the "difficult to measure" test[33] and the "severity of injury" test.[34] The latter characterization may be questioned. Complete destruction or loss does not appear to differ, for measurement purposes, from partial destruction of a business, both of which are measured by loss of profits. Perhaps the persistence of the distinction in the cases reflects the impact of language—destruction is linked to irreparable, at least in terms of usage and meaning. Destruction of a business may also be perceived as creating more third party effects on employees, suppliers, etc., such that injunctive relief is deemed appropriate.

Mere loss of employment, even though it is accompanied by severe financial hardship, is usually rejected as a sufficient basis for finding irreparable injury.[35] These loss of employment cases, however, typically arise in the

---

[29] *Id.* at 1075; Section 21.2.6 (Insolvency).

[30] Travellers Int'l AG v. Trans World Airlines, Inc., 684 F. Supp. 1206, 1216 (S.D.N.Y. 1988) (holding that loss of customer that represented 95% of plaintiff's customer base constituted irreparable injury); see Doran v. Salem Inn, Inc., 422 U.S. 922, 932 (1975) (stating that a "substantial loss of business," coupled with the threat of bankruptcy, constitutes irreparable injury).

[31] Watkins, Inc. v. Lewis, 346 F.3d 841, 845–46 (8th Cir. 2003). In *Tri-Nel Mgt. v. Bd. of Health of Barnstable*, 741 N.E.2d 37 (Mass. 2001), the court rejected claims of irreparable injury based on the effect of a government-mandated smoking ban on restaurant revenues. The plaintiffs' proof (statistical studies) evidenced that the ban had little or no actual impact on restaurant profitability. *Id.* at 46.

[32] District of Columbia v. Group Ins. Admin., 633 A.2d 2, 23 (D.C. 1993) (holding that potential loss of 50% of revenue did not amount to irreparable injury).

[33] Semmes Motors Inc. v. Ford Motor Co., 429 F.2d 1197, 1205 (2d Cir. 1970) (holding that loss of dealership could not be measured monetarily); Section 21.2.3 (Problems in Measuring The Legal Remedy).

[34] *Semmes Motors Inc.*, *supra*, 429 F.2d at 1205 (holding that economic hardship that is so great as to threaten the plaintiff's ongoing business constitutes irreparable injury); Canterbury Career School, Inc. v. Riley, 833 F. Supp. 1097, 1105 (D.N.J. 1993) (holding that when denial of injunction would deprive school of funds (financial aid programs) necessary to continue its operations, irreparable injury was established).

[35] Remlinger v. State of Nevada, 896 F. Supp. 1012, 1015–16 (D. Nev. 1995) (holding that fact that plaintiff lives paycheck to paycheck is not sufficient to deem loss of employment as irreparable injury).

context of a request for temporary injunctive relief where the irreparable injury requirement is looked at somewhat differently.[36]

[21.2.3] Problems in Measuring the Legal Remedy

Irreparable injury has been found when the proof needed to establish the amount of legal damages would be difficult to establish, measure, or quantify. Reputational interests and business goodwill[37] frequently fall into this category. *A.W. Chesterton Co., Inc. v. Chesterton*[38] involved a minority shareholder who sought to transfer his shares, which if accomplished, would threaten the plaintiff corporation's S-corporation status. The court found the potential damages difficult to measure because measurement depended on the plaintiff's future income, which was uncertain. The court noted that loss of "tax-advantaged status" also constitutes irreparable injury.

In *Continental Airlines Inc. v. Intra Brokers, Inc.*[39] Continental had published coupons that provided for discounts on its fares. All the coupons contained restrictions stating they could not "be bartered, sold, or redeemed for cash." Intra acquired the coupons and sold them to travel agents for resale to the agent's customers. Continental sought to enjoin Intra's transfer of the coupons. Intra countered that Continental had an adequate remedy at law—damages for financial losses from passengers' use of the coupons Intra sold. The court noted: (1) that Continental did not demonstrate any financial harm; and, (2) that discount coupons would tend to increase Continental's volume, but decrease the average fare received. Continental's revenues could be higher, lower, or the same, depending on how much the brokering affected passenger volume and average price.[40] Given the variables, expert witness testimony might be conflicting, and the appropriate economic analysis would be "difficult and uncertain" and

---

[36] Section 31.2.2 ([Temporary Injunctive Relief] Irreparable Injury).

[37] Graham v. Mary Kay Inc., 25 S.W.3d 749, 753 (Tex. Civ. App. 2000) (stating that "[a] company's loss of goodwill, clientele, marketing techniques, office stability and the like are not easily assigned a dollar value but they qualify as "probable injury" [Irreparable injury] for purposes of injunctive relief") (citations omitted; brackets added); Robert W. Stark, Inc. v. New York Stock Exchange, 346 F. Supp. 217, 232 (S.D.N.Y.), *aff'd*, 466 F.2d 743 (2d Cir. 1972) (holding that expulsion of member of a securities exchange, which adversely affected the person's standing in the community, credit rating, and reputation, satisfied irreparable injury requirement); Cutler-Hammer, Inc. v. Universal Relay Corp., 285 F. Supp. 636, 639 (S.D.N.Y. 1968) (finding that injury to reputation and goodwill is not easily measurable in monetary terms and hence is viewed as irreparable injury). *But see* United Retail Inc. v. Main Street Mall Corp., 903 F. Supp. 12, 14 (S.D.N.Y. 1995) (finding the loss of goodwill from mall closing was insufficiently substantial when the mall was run down).

[38] 907 F. Supp. 19, 23–24 (D. Mass. 1995), *aff'd*, 128 F.3d 1, 8–9 (1st Cir. 1997). The defendant was using the threatened loss of S-corporation status to force the plaintiff to purchase his minority interest. The court held that the plaintiff did not have to acquiesce to the very conduct plaintiff claimed violated its rights. *Id.* at 24; *cf.* Section 13.6 ([Duty to Mitigate] Intentional Wrongs) (discussing whether a plaintiff must mitigate damages intentionally caused by the defendant).

[39] 24 F.3d 1099 (9th Cir. 1994).

[40] *Id.* at 1105.

"[e]xpensive accounting and economic analysis might be necessary."[41] The court concluded:

> Continental was entitled to control whether its coupons were transferred. The difficulty and probable expense of establishing the amount of economic harm supports the proposition that damages would be an inadequate remedy and so cuts in favor of equitable relief.[42]

It is not enough, however, to claim that damages are difficult to measure or determine. The claim must be credible and supported by the record. If the court believes that monetary damages can be reasonably calculated, it may find that no irreparable injury exists.[43]

[21.2.4] Nature of the Injury

Irreparable injury is presumed to exist in certain cases. When a defendant's conduct infringes or deprives one of a constitutional right or guarantee, courts often find that no further showing of irreparable injury is needed.[44] This is particularly true in the case of First Amendment guarantees.[45] When the sought to be enjoined conduct threatens the plaintiff's bodily safety, irreparable injury is usually found. Monetary awards are deemed a poor substitute for good health and well being.[46] When injunctive

---

[41] *Id.*

[42] *Id.* at 1105 (citations omitted); R.I. Turnpike & Bridge Auth. v. Cohen, 433 A.2d 179, 184 (R.I. 1981) (finding that plaintiff failed to establish that retailer's offer to provide meals in exchange for turnpike tokens and retailer's desire to use acquired tokens to increase business by providing the tokens to patrons caused plaintiff any injury; hence, plaintiff failed to show on the record any irreparable injury).

[43] General Textile Printing & Processing Corp v. Expromtorg, Int'l Corp., 862 F. Supp. 1070, 1076 (S.D.N.Y. 1994):

> Plaintiff also contends that the actual damages suffered will be difficult to calculate, and thus injunctive relief should be granted. This Court finds plaintiff's argument unpersuasive. [E]ven if the market for greige goods proves to be in such short supply that plaintiff cannot purchase cover, and thus cannot calculate cover damages, plaintiff may be entitled to lost profits. "Lost profits, though typically 'difficult to prove with exactitude' may be recovered 'to the extent that the evidence affords a sufficient basis for estimating their amount with reasonable certainty.' " Since plaintiff is a middleman, its lost profits could be calculated as the difference between the contract price, and the downstream market price, less expenses not incurred. Thus, so long as plaintiff can reasonably calculate the profits that were lost due to defendant's failure to honor the contract, money damages are still an adequate remedy.

Id. at 1076 (Citations omitted) "Greige" is a raw, textile fabric.

[44] Doe v. Bellin Mem'l Hosp., 479 F.2d 756, 759 (7th Cir. 1973) (right to an abortion); *see* 11A CHARLES WRIGHT, ARTHUR MILLER & MARY KANE, FEDERAL PRACTICE & PROCEDURE § 2948.1, at 161 (1973 & 1995 Supp.)

[45] Elrod v. Burns, 427 U.S. 347, 373 (1976) (stating that "loss of First Amendment freedoms, for even minimal periods of time, unquestionably constitutes irreparable injury") (citations omitted). Although this quote is taken from Justice Brennan's plurality opinion, it has been repeatedly cited and accepted as a general constitutional principle.

[46] Henderson v. Bodine Aluminum, Inc., 70 F.3d 958, 961 (8th Cir. 1995) (stating that "pre-

relief is expressly authorized for breach of statutory duty, irreparable injury is usually presumed to exist.[47]

The irreparable injury requirement often can be driven by a party's ability to command the characterization of the issue before the court. A good example of this is *Lee v. State of Oregon*,[48] which involved the constitutionality of Oregon's assisted suicide law.[49] The law permits a person with less than 6 months to live to request a lethal dose of drugs, which can be administered by a physician. The district court enjoined enforcement of the law finding that the possibility of death by assisted suicide constitutes irreparable injury. Of course, the issue could have been phrased as whether prolonging life and subjecting persons to suffering by denying them the ability to die constitutes irreparable injury.

[21.2.5] Loss of Chance or Advantage

In *McCardle v. Rodriquez* plaintiff sought a preliminary injunction requiring defendant to promote him to the position of lieutenant in the Chicago Police Department. The court found that the loss of experience and prestige the plaintiff would sustain as a result of defendant's improper promotions could not be compensated by a legal remedy. Further, the loss of actual time in the position to which plaintiff claimed he should have been promoted would affect his future promotability. Damages and credit for time that would have been served if the promotion had been properly granted could not duplicate actual time in the position. The court found that the irreparable injury requirement was satisfied by difficulties of proving monetary damages, coupled with the finding that money was not the equivalent of time on the job when that factor was critical to future promotions.[50] A similar approach can be seen in a case involving a non-custodial parent who was involved in a dispute with the custodial parent of their child whether the child would attend a particular private school. The non-custodial parent wanted an injunction requiring the custodial parent to enroll the child. The court found that the failure to enroll the child pending resolution of the issue between the parents would result in the loss of the child's place for several years and the likely loss of the opportunity

---

liminary injunctions become easier to obtain as the plaintiff faces progressively graver harm" . . . [i]t is hard to imagine a greater harm than losing a chance for potentially life-saving medical treatment) (citations omitted); Smith v. Western Elec. Co., 643 S.W.2d 10, 13 (Mo. App. 1982) (finding irreparable injury in plaintiff's workplace exposure to second-hand smoke).

[47] Section 26.1 (Statutes Expanding Equitable Remedies).

[48] 869 F. Supp. 1491, 1501 (D. Or. 1994), *rev'd on other grounds*, 107 F.3d 1382 (9th Cir.), *cert denied sub nom.* Lee v. Harcleroad, 522 U.S. 927 (1997).

[49] In *Washington v. Glucksberg*, 521 U.S. 702 (1997), the Court held that "assisted suicide" did not fall within the liberty interest protected by the 14th Amendment; consequently, a state could, but was not required to, preclude assisted suicide.

[50] 659 N.E.2d 1356, 1365 (Ill. App. 1995). *But see* Richenberg v. Perry, 73 F.3d 172, 173 (8th Cir. 1995) (finding that reinstatement and back pay award, if plaintiff, an Air Force Captain, prevailed on his claim that he had been improperly separated from the military under the "don't ask, don't tell" policy, precluded finding of irreparable injury).

to ever attend the school. This, according to the court, constituted irreparable injury.[51]

There are a number of cases that Professor Laycock has labelled "loss of legitimate tactical advantage."[52] The idea here is that a litigant is entitled to injunctive relief to protect the party's existing position.[53] Professor Walker argued that this concept justified the stay entered by the Court in *Bush v. Gore* that effectively enabled George Bush to claim the Presidency after the November, 2000 elections.[54]

The "loss of tactical advantage" concept is similar to the "frustration of relief" concept discussed is earlier.[55] The basic idea is that of entitlement and that the law should protect directly what one is legally entitled to have. There is also a sense of irreplaceability, that some positions cannot be fully replicated by legal relief. To require a party to surrender or cede that position to secure a judicial declaration that one was right along effectively defeats the very right the law is protecting.[56]

[21.2.6]   Insolvency

The inability of the defendant to respond to a monetary award is recognized as irreparable injury.[57] A legal remedy that exists only as an abstraction is not equal to an equitable remedy that will provide real redress. A remedy that is only illusory is not a remedy. On the other hand, the threat of insolvency must be real. The record must support the contention of defendant's insolvency.[58]

A frequently encountered issue today is whether the potential that the defendant will render himself judgment proof satisfies the irreparable injury requirement. Increasingly, plaintiffs are seeking "asset freeze" orders, which are designed to prevent a defendant from dissipating or transferring assets so as to prevent satisfaction of a judgment the plaintiff may obtain. This remedy is discussed in Section 31.5 (Freeze Orders).

---

[51] Foulke by Foulke v. Foulke, 896 F. Supp. 158, 160–61 (S.D.N.Y. 1995).

[52] Douglas Laycock, The Death of the Irreparable Injury Rule 81–82 (1991).

[53] Lucas v. Townsend, 486 U.S. 1301 (1988) (Kennedy, Circuit J.) (granting a stay to bar an election when conducting the election would deprive the moving parties of the benefit of the status quo granted by the governing statute).

[54] Walker, *The Stay Seen Around the World*, *supra*, Section 21.1 (Justification for the Requirement).

[55] Section 21.2.1 (Frustration of Relief Sought).

[56] In a different context, but illustrative of the point, in cases of privilege, courts permit appeals even though a party is disobeying an order to disclose (Section 198.2 (Exceptions to Collateral Bar Rule)), recognizing that requiring a party to comply (disclose), would defeat the purpose of an appeal. Appeal is, however, not from the order, but from the contempt citation. This raises the stakes because if the party guesses wrong not only will she have to disclose, but she may be punished for not disclosing.

[57] Roland Mach. Co. v. Dresser Indus., Inc., 749 F.2d 380, 386 (7th Cir. 1984) (stating that insolvency is a basis for finding irreparable injury).

[58] JSG Trading Corp. v. Tray-Wrap, Inc., 917 F.2d 75, 79 (2d Cir. 1990); Wurttembergische Fire Ins. Co. v. Pan Atlantic Underwriters, Ltd., 519 N.Y.S.2d 57, 58 (App. Dep't 1987).

[21.2.7] Multiple Lawsuits

The need to bring additional or multiple lawsuits to vindicate a legal right has often been seen as evidencing the inadequacy of the remedy at law.[59] The prospective burden, expense, and inconvenience of multiple lawsuits and involvement in multiple litigation is often seen as evidencing that the legal remedy is inadequate when compared to the equitable remedy that can provide complete relief within a single lawsuit. For example, an injunction barring the defendant from trespassing on plaintiff's property may be seen as superior to a legal remedy, which permits a damages recovery only for trespasses that have occurred prior to the date of trial. How many lawsuits constitute a multiplicity is difficult to state. The need to bring three actions at law when the same relief could be accomplished by one action in equity was held to demonstrate the inadequacy of the former;[60] usually, however, the courts simply refer to the prospect of multiple lawsuits.[61]

[21.2.8] Uniqueness

Equity jurisdiction was originally centered on protecting interests in real property. Today, that focus has ebbed, but equity jurisdiction is commonly asserted when the dispute involves real property under the fiction that each piece of real property is unique and therefore a substitutional remedy (monetary damages) will not adequately compensate the plaintiff for what has been lost.[62] The monetary award can purchase a different piece of property, but not the property at issue.

Notwithstanding this focus on real property, care must be taken not to read it too far. Many actions involving real property are properly brought at law, for example, ejectment.[63] The issue is not land per se, but the

---

[59] Garrett v. Bamford, 538 F.2d 63, 71 (3d Cir.), *cert. denied*, 429 U.S. 883 (stating that "[w]here legal remedies require multiple suits involving identical issues against the same defendant, federal equity practice has recognized the inadequacy of the legal remedy and has provided a forum") (citations omitted); Allstate Ins. Co. v. Hill, 128 S.E.2d 321, 324 (Ga. 1962) (holding that "[e]quity will assume jurisdiction for the purpose of preventing a multiplicity of suits, the general principle being that the necessity of multiple suits in itself constitutes the inadequacy of remedies at law which confers equitable jurisdiction"); 4 J. POMEROY, EQUITY JURISPRUDENCE § 1357, at 964–65 (5th ed. 1941) (stating that if repeated acts of wrong are done or threatened, although each of these acts, taken by itself, may not be destructive, and the legal remedy may therefore be adequate for each single act *if it stood alone,* then also the entire wrong will be prevented or stopped by injunction, on the ground of avoiding a repetition of similar actions) (emphasis in original).

[60] Homer Enters., Inc. v. Daake, 957 S.W.2d 353, 357 (Mo. App. 1997).

[61] Almond v. Capital Properties, Inc., 212 F.3d 20, 25 (1st Cir. 2000) (stating that "to recover these amounts in breach of contract suits would involve substantial and complicated litigation").

[62] New Life Community Church of God v. Adomatis, 672 N.E.2d 433, 438 (Ind. App. 1996) (noting that specific performance of contracts involving the purchase of real estate is a "matter of course" because "each piece of real estate is unique") (citation omitted); *cf.* Schumacher v. Ihrke, 469 N.W.2d 329, 335 (Minn. App. 1991) (noting that "[i]f real property is involved, specific performance is a proper remedy, even if the other remedies would be adequate").

[63] Sections 58 and 92 (Ejectment).

uniqueness of the subject matter as it affects the remedy sought. An action to specifically enforce a contract to purchase[64] or sell[65] real property is usually deemed to sound in equity because the issue is the acquisition or transfer of unique property, although there are occasional murmurs to the contrary.[66] The uniqueness argument can, moreover, be extrapolated to contracts in general, as for example, contracts for the sale of personal property that is unique[67] or contracts to provide services that are unique and, thus, not easily replaceable.[68] Uniqueness is, however, not self-defining or obvious. What makes a product or service unique depends on context. Some factors courts have considered in deciding this point include:

- ease of purchase of substitute or replacement.[69]

- inherent nature of the service or product, e.g., "artwork."[70]

---

[64] Okaw Drainage Dist. v. National Distillers & Chem. Corp., 882 F.2d 1241, 1248 (7th Cir. 1989); Anderson v. Onsager, 455 N.W.2d 885, 889 (Wis. 1990).

[65] Although the seller wanted money, which is hardly unique, equity thought it was irregular to permit one party but not the other party to the contract to secure specific performance. Section 167.2 ([Seller's Remedies] Specific Performance); Section 173 (Mutuality of Remedy).

[66] Centex Homes Corp. v. Boag, 320 A.2d 194, 198–99 (N.J. Super. Ct. A.D. 1974) (refusing seller remedy of specific performance against defaulting purchaser of condominium unit on ground that seller's damages were easily measurable and thus remedy at law was adequate); Section 170 ([Specific Performance] Introduction).

[67] U.C.C. § 2-716 (authorizing buyer's remedy of specific performance when contracted for goods are unique).

[68] Hopper, D.V.M. v. All Pet Animal Clinic, Inc., 861 P.2d 531, 546 (Wyo. 1993) (enforcing covenant not to compete by enjoining breach because ex-employee's exposure to employer's trade secrets, customer contacts, and special training makes the ex-employee a particularly, and uniquely, dangerous competitor); cf. Ormco Corp. v. Johns, 869 So. 2d 1109, 1115–16 (Ala. 2003) (holding that if employer demonstrated that it had valid, enforceable non-compete agreement, a rebuttable inference of irreparable injury arises if an employee violates the agreement). Section 154 (Employer's Injunction Against Employee).

[69] See Klein v. PepsiCo., Inc., 845 F.2d 75, 80 (4th Cir. 1988) (holding airplane not so unique as to merit specific performance when three roughly comparable airplanes existed on the market).

[70] Turnick, Inc. v. Kornfield, 838 F. Supp. 848 (S.D.N.Y. 1993):

> [P]rints, unlike petroleum or produce, are not purchased for strictly utilitarian reasons. A print is selected by a purchaser because the traits of that print please the purchaser's aesthetic sensibilities. Thus, whether prints in a series are largely similar or slightly different is of no critical importance. The real fact to be considered is that the purchaser chose a given print because he viewed it as uniquely beautiful, interesting, or well suited to his collection or gallery. Nothing else will satisfy that collector but that which he bought. For these reasons, prints are not interchangeable. Thus, each print is, by definition, unique. Hence, there can be no exact substitute for a given print purchased by a collector. In the case at bar, plaintiff did not enter into a contract to purchase a print of Le Minotauromachie signed by Picasso; rather, plaintiff bid for and purchased the specific print of Le Minotauromachie that Mr. Tunick viewed prior to the auction, which was signed by Picasso and in the condition Mr. Tunick observed at the time of purchase. In this context it would be fundamentally unfair, and unsound policy, to impose on plaintiff a duty to accept another—inherently different—print of Le Minotauromachie as a substitute for the one plaintiff actually viewed, bid for, and purchased.

- customized or modified product or service.[71]

§ 22   EQUITY ACTS IN PERSONAM

The phrase "equity acts in personam" traces at least as far back as Lord Ellesmere's decision in the Earl of Oxford case that equity may enjoin a litigant from enforcing a judgment obtained in a common law court "[not] for any error or defect in the judgment, but for the hard conscience of the party."[1] A modern statement of this principle can be found in *PMZ Oil Co. v. Lucroy*:

> Equity acts in personam, and in this instance equity has acted in personam. Where within the rules of law described above a court of equity determines that an estoppel should be enforced, it is entirely appropriate that the defendant should be personally directed to do that which is necessary to achieve compliance with the condition upon which the plaintiff has relied to his detriment.[2]

As a practical matter this means that equity can enforce its judgments through the contempt remedy over individual defendants.[3]

For this power to be meaningful and effective it was traditionally necessary that the equity court have jurisdiction over the person of the defendant. Well into the modern era an equity court would assert jurisdiction only when it could secure the personal appearance of the defendant before the court,[4] although the rule had exceptions and could be modified by statute.[5] Much of the jurisdictional limitations of the principle have been erased by the abolition of the power rationale of jurisdiction expressed by *Pennoyer v. Neff*.[6]

The idea that equity acted "in personam" had important consequences, particularly insofar as relations with the law courts were concerned. Because equity, as the expression of the Chancellor's conscience, could compel personal compliance, it could order a defendant to do something that was foreclosed by the law courts or not do something that was permitted by the law courts. As noted by one early commentator:

---

[71] *In re* Ballet Jet Charter, Inc., 177 B.R. 593, 599 (N.D. Ill. 1995) (customized long range aircraft); Kawa Leasing, Ltd. v. Yacht Sequoia, 544 F. Supp. 1050, 1069 (D. Md. 1982) (ordering specific performance because of ship's uniqueness, noting that "she is, after all, the only Presidential yacht this nation has ever had").

[1] 21 Eng. Rep. 484, 487 (1615).

[2] 449 So. 2d 201, 208 (Miss. 1984).

[3] Chapter 22 (Contempt).

[4] Indemnity Ins. Co. of N. Am. v. Smoot, 152 F.2d 667, 670 (D.C. Cir.), *cert. denied*, 328 U.S. 835 (1946) (noting that principle that equity acts in personam normally requires personal service on the defendant; service by publication is inadequate since it is normally reserved for actions in rem).

[5] Mendrochowicz v. Wolfe, 95 A.2d 260, 261 (Conn. 1953) (noting state statute permitting equity court to act in rem by passing title without having jurisdiction over the person of the defendant).

[6] 95 U.S. 714, 727 (1878), *overruled* in Shaffer v. Heitner, 433 U.S. 186 (1977).

[T]he fundamental difference between law and equity . . . [is] that the law acts in rem, while equity acts in personam. The difference between the judgment at law and the decree in equity goes to the root of the whole matter. The law regards chiefly the right of the plaintiff, and gives judgment that he recover the land, debt, or damages, because they are his. Equity lays the stress upon the defendant, and decrees that he do or refrain from doing a certain thing because he ought to act or forebear. It is because of this emphasis upon the defendant's duty that equity is so much more ethical than law.[7]

For example, if an action at law was time barred, but the plaintiff's delay was caused by the defendant's inequitable conduct, equity could enjoin the defendant from asserting the statute of limitations against the plaintiff's claim in the law court.[8] By acting on the person of the defendant, equity could influence the proceedings at law without being directly involved in the action at law.

While the Chancellor declaimed any right to adjudicate title to foreign situated real property, when the holder of title to that foreign real property was before the equity court, the Chancellor could remedy a breach of trust or contract or remedy fraud by ordering the holder of legal title to execute a conveyance.[9] Once having power over the person of the defendant, the Chancellor was not restricted by geographic boundaries, but could enforce any appropriate decree, not directly on the property outside the territorial jurisdiction of the court,[10] but indirectly by coercing the defendant to respect the decree.[11]

---

[7] James Ames, *Law and Morals*, 22 Harv. L. Rev. 97, 105–06 (1908).

[8] Sheer Bros. v. Marlboro, 383 A.2d 1225, 1227 (N.J. Sup. Ct. 1978). In the *Earl of Oxford's Case, supra,* the Chancellor enjoined enforcement of a judgment obtained in King's Bench on the grounds of unconscionability.

[9] Muller v. Dows, 94 U.S. 444, 449 (1877); Mills v. Mills, 305 P.2d 61, 67 (Cal. App. 1956) (noting that "[a]fter the court has obtained jurisdiction of the parties it may, by a decree operating in personam against them, control their actions with respect to property situated without its jurisdiction . . ."); Summers v. Martin, 295 P.2d 265 (Idaho 1956) (same); Kimbrough v. Hardison, 81 So. 2d 606 (Ala. 1955) (same).

[10] The long accepted rule in the United States is that Full Faith & Credit need not be given to foreign (in the sense of "out of state") decrees that affect title to land, such as a court ordered deed. Fall v. Eastin, 215 U.S. 1 (1909). A number of states now provide that they will give Full Faith & Credit to such decrees (Restatement (Second) of Conflict of Laws § 102, cmts(c)-(d) (1971); however, the Supreme Court has not modernly addressed the issue. Even if Full Faith & Credit is not required, many states will recognize foreign land decrees as a matter of courtesy ("comity"), but comity is discretionary. *See* David Currie, *Full Faith & Credit to Foreign Land Decrees,* 21 U. Chi. L. Rev. 620 (1954).

[11] Steele v. Bulova Watch Co., 344 U.S. 280, 285–86 (1952) (restraining extraterritorial acts by defendants); Leman v. Krentler-Arnold Hinge Last Co., 285 U.S. 448, 451 (1932) (stating that "[t]he decree . . . bound the respondent personally. It was a decree which operated continuously and perpetually upon the respondent in relation to the prohibited conduct. The decree was binding upon the respondent, not simply within the District of Massachusetts, but throughout the United States"); *see* Ernest J. Messner, *The Jurisdiction of a Court of Equity Over Persons to Compel the Doing of Acts Outside the Territorial Limits of the State,* 14 Minn. L. Rev. 494, 514–29 (1930) (collecting cases and authorities).

A variation of this theme was recognized when the plaintiff complained in equity that the defendant had instituted legal proceedings against him. While the Chancellor lacked the power to restrain proceedings in another court, he had the power to compel the defendant, over whom the Chancellor did have power, to refrain from prosecuting, or to initiate prosecution of, an action in another court.[12] Cross-injunctions, each enjoining the litigants from proceeding in the other jurisdiction, while rare are not unknown.[13] This power is cautiously exercised when the other court is in a foreign jurisdiction,[14] but it is occasionally exercised.[15]

The issue of enjoining litigants from commencing or participating in related proceeding is of critical importance when the laws of the competing jurisdictions differ. The Full Faith & Credit (FF&C) Clause obligates states to recognize and respect the judgments of sister states even if that judgment violates the receiving state's public policy.[16] The FF&C Clause does not prevent a state from refusing to apply a sister states laws on the ground that to do so would violate the forum state's public policy.[17] Vindication of the forum's public policy permits the forum to apply its own law; that course will, however, be foreclosed if another interested state has rendered a judgment applying its conflicting law to the dispute between the litigants. To protect its ability to apply its law to a dispute, a state may seek to prevent another state from rendering a decision (judgment) that would bar the forum state from deciding the dispute using the law of the forum. The forum state cannot enjoin the other state, but it may seek to control indirectly the other state's ability to affect the dispute by controlling the action of the disputing parties.[18]

The concept that equity acts in "personam" and not "in rem" should not be confused with the concepts of judgments or jurisdiction "in personam" and "in rem." The idea that equity acted "in personam" meant that equity

---

[12] Archibald v. Cinerama Hotels, 544 P.2d 947, 950 (Cal. 1976); see General Atomic Co. v. Felter, 434 U.S. 12, 19–21 (1977) (Rehnqist, J., dissenting).

[13] James v. Grand Trunk Western Railroad Co., 152 N.E.2d 858 (Ill. 1958), cert. denied, 358 U.S. 915 (1959) (involving Illinois decree prohibiting enforcement of Michigan decree enjoining the prosecution of the Illinois lawsuit).

[14] Bano v. Union Carbide Corp., 361 F.3d 696, 716 (2d Cir. 2004) (stating that the court may deny a request for an injunction that would primarily apply extraterritorially when the injunction would interfere with another nation's sovereignty).

[15] Laker Airways Ltd. v. Sabena, Belgian World Airlines, 731 F.2d 909, 930 (D.C. Cir. 1984) (enjoining defendants from participating in foreign judicial proceedings aimed at depriving American court of its jurisdiction); Seattle Totems Hockey Club, Inc. v. National Hockey League, 652 F.2d 852, 856 (9th Cir. 1981), cert. denied, 457 U.S. 1105 (1982) (enjoining defendant from engaging in parallel, vexatious litigation in Canada).

[16] Fauntleroy v. Lum, 210 U.S. 230 (1908).

[17] Alaska Packers Ass'n v. Indus. Acc. Comm'n, 294 U.S. 532 (1935).

[18] Having the power does not mean that the court will exercise the power. Advanced Bionics Corp. v. Medtronic, Inc., 59 P.3d 231 (Cal. 2002) (holding that California's policy of not enforcing post-employment noncompetition agreements did not overcome principle of comity (respect) that should be afforded other state's judicial system; consequently, injunction barring party from litigating claim before court of another state should not have been entered).

enforced its decrees on the person of the defendant through contempt or similar process.[19] Judgments of the law courts were enforceable through seizure and sale of the judgment debtor's property. A judgment that was enforceable through seizure of non-exempt property came to be known as a personal judgment, and resulted from the exercise of personal jurisdiction. A judgment enforceable only through the seizure and sale of certain specific property came to be known as an "in rem" judgment, and resulted oftentimes from the exercise of "in rem" jurisdiction. Moreover, even the concept of acting on the person of the defendant was not alien to common law courts. If a defendant attempted to hide his property from levy and execution by his judgment creditors, he could be fined or imprisoned in order to compel disclosure and disgorgement of the hidden property.[20]

The concept that equity acts "in personam" (upon the person), not "in rem" (upon the thing) can be overused. First, there are instances where equity enforced equitable rights by acting in rem.[21] Second, equity courts could appoint a surrogate for the defendant and have the surrogate act for the defendant. For example, in *Rowe v. Hayden* the court noted:

> We have no statute which provides for the transfer of title by the mere recording of a decree in equity ordering the transfer. However, if the whereabouts of Hayden are still unknown, or if known and he is personally without the jurisdiction of the court, the court below, upon application therefor, will in aid of the decree appoint a Master to make conveyance to the plaintiff of Hayden's title to the plaintiff's property.[22]

§ 23 EQUITABLE DISCRETION

It is commonplace when speaking about equity and equitable remedies to refer to "discretionary decision making." The concept derives from equity's canon law tradition and its non-reliance on precedent, at least in its early years.[1] Each case in equity was to be decided on its own merits and with the goal of achieving fairness and justice with reference to the facts of the particular case. The ideal that "like cases should be decided alike" was achieved only through happenstance, not as a goal of decision making. This individualistic, free wheeling approach led to the comment

---

[19] In fact the practice in equity was broader than the remedy of contempt. Equity compelled obedience to its process and decrees by restraint of a party through the stages of attachment, attachment with proclamations, commission of rebellion, warrant to sergeant at arms or sheriff to take into custody, and commission of sequestration. *In re* Portland Elec. Power Co., 97 F. Supp. 903, 911 (D. Ore. 1947), *quoting* 1 OWEN BARBOUR, TREATISE ON THE PRACTICE OF THE COURT OF CHANCERY Chapter II, § II, pp. 54–75 (2d ed. 1874).

[20] PLUCKNETT, A CONCISE HISTORY, *supra*, at 389–90.

[21] State v. Porter, 91 P. 1073, 1074 (Kan. 1907) (enjoining public nuisance); *Mendrochowicz, supra*, 95 A.2d at 262 (passing title when permitted by statute); *see* 1 JOHN POMEROY, A TREATISE ON EQUITY JURISPRUDENCE 134–35 (5th ed. 1941).

[22] 101 A.2d 190, 195 (Me. 1953); Phelps v. Kozakar, 194 Cal. Rptr. 872 (Cal. App. 1983).

[1] Section 20 (The Historical Relationship Between Law and Equity), n.5.

by detractors that the equity of a case depended upon the length of the Chancellor's foot, which suggests uncertainty, arbitrariness, and partiality:

> Equity is a rougish thing: For law we have a measure, know what to trust to; equity is according to the conscience of him that is Chancellor, and as that is larger or narrower, so is equity. 'Tis all one, as if they should make his foot standard for the measure we call a Chancellor's foot; what an uncertain measure would this be! One Chancellor has a long foot, another a short foot, a third an indifferent foot; tis the same thing in the Chancellor's conscience.[2]

Many modern legal scholars view "discretion" with distaste. It has been suggested that where law ends, discretion begins,[3] paraphrasing William Pitt's famous aphorism "where law ends, tyranny begins." The analogy is obvious. Judges, however, tend to be more accepting, recognizing that discretion is a necessary component of any functioning dispute resolution system,[4] and, at times, courts gush with praise over the ability of equity to provide individualized justice to the case at hand:

> The essence of equity jurisdiction has been the power of the Chancellor to do equity and to mold each decree to the necessities of the particular case. Flexibility rather that rigidity has distinguished it. The qualities of mercy and practicality have made equity the instrument for nice adjustment and reconciliation between the public interest and private needs as well as between competing private claims.[5]

The fundamental debate is over the concept of "justice." The idea that "like cases should be decided alike" is as basic to our jurisprudence as is the notion that "each case should be decided on its own merits." We are concerned that the evenhanded application of rules may perpetrate injustice in particular applications and we are also concerned that unbridled discretion may result in favoritism or capriciousness based on conflicts over what is "fair."[6] In the end we want both and the debate then turns to the

---

[2] Gee v. Pritchard, 36 Eng. Rep. 670, 679 (1818), *quoting* JOHN SELDEN, "Equity," TABLE-TALK (1689), reprinted in TABLE TALK OF JOHN SELDEN 43 (Frederick Pollock ed., 1927).

[3] KENNETH DAVIS, DISCRETIONARY JUSTICE: A PRELIMINARY INQUIRY 3 (1971); *cf.* Cass R. Sunstein, Daniel Kahneman & David Schkade, *Assessing Punitive Damages (With Notes on Cognition and Valuation in Law)*, 107 Yale L.J. 2071, 2077 (1998) ("If similarly situated people—plaintiffs and defendants alike—are not treated similarly, erractic awards are unfair").

[4] AHARON BARAK, JUDICIAL DISCRETION (1989) (discretion is inherent in any legal system and an asset to that system); Henry Friendly, *Indiscretion About Discretion*, 31 Emory L.J. 747 (1982) (discretion is a necessary part of a legal system but the exercise of discretion must be guided and controlled to prevent misuse).

[5] Hecht Co. v. Bowles, 321 U.S. 321, 329–30 (1944).

[6] How do you define "fair" to guide the court's discretion?:
- economic efficiency
- libertarianism
- utilitarianism
- egalitarianism

proper relationship that should exist between rule and discretion, a topic beyond the scope of this work, but a question, nonetheless, that underlies and underscores many legal decisions.

Discretion itself is an elusive concept, hard to define and harder to apply if one wants to make any claim of consistency. As a legal term, discretion acts like a chameleon, changing its content to suit the applicable legal background. In some contexts discretion is used as a synonym for choice. Here to state that a decision maker (e.g., trial judge) has discretion is to mean that his range of decision is unfettered, to varying degrees, by rules or standards that would limit the available options the judge can select. In other instances discretion means not choice but deference to choice. The decision maker's options are limited, but the decision maker's selection is reviewed only to determine whether the actual choice conformed to one of the available options. In practice it is often difficult to determine how the term discretion is being used. It does after all make a difference whether a decision maker is told she has unfettered choice or constrained choice. Similarly, it is significant whether choices actually made will be reviewed with scrutiny, with deference, or with diffidence. Unfortunately, the practice is often to treat the issue of discretion cursorily, leading to substantial uncertainty as to what it means when it is said that a decision maker has discretion.

This elusiveness can be seen in the standard formulation of the test used by appellate courts to review the decision by a trial court to grant or deny a request for injunctive relief:

> Although the grant of permanent injunctive relief is generally reviewed for an abuse of discretion, "if the trial court misapplies the law we will review and correct the error without deference to that court's determination. [I]f the court misapplied the law in making its decision [to grant the preliminary injunction] we do not defer to its legal analysis." We review questions of law de novo.[7]

This current formulation is different from the more traditional test that simply stated that the decision whether to grant or deny injunctive relief was within the "sound discretion of the trial court."[8] It should be observed that the modern formulation is overtly more restrictive of the trial court's "choice" than the traditional test. Indeed, some courts have stated that the rigor with which a discretion-based standard of review will be applied is related to the significance of the issue before the court. The more important the issue, the less likely the lower court's decision will be accepted with

----

- Rawlism social justice
- individual intuitivism

The above categories themselves have many different variations and schools.

[7] Hughey v. JMS Dev. Corp., 78 F.3d 1523 1528–29 (11th Cir.) (citations omitted), *cert. denied*, 519 U.S. 993 (1996). In some jurisdictions review in equity is said to be de novo in its entirety, *e.g.*, Neb. St. § 25-1925; Owen v. Owen, 579 P.2d 911, 913 (Utah 1978), but the practice is to exhibit deference to the trial court, nonetheless. *Owen.*

[8] Virginian R. Co. v. System Fed'n No. 40, 300 U.S. 515, 551 (1937).

deference. On the other hand, the less likely the appellate court can identify a right course of action from a group of reasonable alternatives, the more likely it is that deference will be exhibited to the lower court's decision.[9] The difficulty here, as elsewhere, is characterization of the issue to be reviewed as being important or unimportant and the confidence to identify a particular option as the most appropriate choice.

These concepts are illuminated when we examine cases involving equitable remedies when an appellate court has reviewed a trial court's decision. The articulated standard is "abuse of discretion." This term is significant for two reasons. First, as noted above, it frequently consists of more than pure discretionary review; concepts such as "clearly erroneous" and "de novo" are often also involved. Second, the use of the term "abuse" suggests a moralist judgment that is absent in most cases of appellate review.[10] A trial court may err, or the trial court may commit "clear error," but to suggest that the trial court has "abused" its discretion is to suggest conduct that is more than mistaken. An "abuse" of discretion standard suggests that the trial court will be reversed only when it is shown that the trial court's decision is tainted. For example, many courts equate "abuse of discretion" with a "miscarriage of justice."[11] Again, the language used creates an image that a high degree of inappropriate judicial conduct must exist before the trial judge's discretion-based decision will be set aside. We see that a rather simple test, "abuse of discretion," contains within itself divergent strands; some strands pointing to deference, other strands pointing toward scrutiny.

The decisions implicitly accept this "balancing" approach. For example, in *Schering Corp. v. Illinois Antibiotics Corp.* the court noted that "the term abuse of discretion covers a range of degrees of deference rather than denoting a point within that range . . . , and whether a particular case falls in the range depends on the precise character of the ruling being reviewed."[12]

Courts can find an "abuse of discretion" when there is no reasonable basis for the trial court's decision,[13] or when the trial court makes an error of law in determining that the plaintiff showed "a likelihood of success on the merits" sufficient to support granting a preliminary injunction.[14] While the

---

[9] Langton v. Johnston, 928 F.2d 1206, 1220 (1st Cir. 1991) (stating that trial court discretion-based decision making will be reviewed "flexibly, with due regard for the circumstances").

[10] Friendly, *Indiscretion, supra*, 31 Emory L. J. at 762 (suggesting that the term "abuse" should be replaced with the term "misuse").

[11] Baggett v. Gates, 649 P.2d 874 (Cal. 1982):

Where, as here, a trial court has discretionary power to decide an issue, its decision will be reversed if there has been a prejudicial abuse of discretion. "'To be entitled to relief on appeal . . . it must clearly appear that the injury resulting from such a wrong is sufficiently grave to amount to a manifest miscarriage of justice . . . .'"

Id. at 882 (citations omitted); Valente v. Secretary of Health and Human Servs., 733 F.2d 1037, 1041 (2d Cir. 1984).

[12] 62 F.3d 903, 908 (7th Cir. 1995) (citations omitted), *cert. denied*, 516 U.S. 1140 (1996).

[13] Tollis Inc. v. San Bernardino County, 827 F.2d 1329, 1331 (9th Cir. 1987).

[14] Genentech, Inc. v. Novo Nordisk, A/S, 108 F.3d 1361, 1362 (Fed. Cir. 1997).

trial court's decision how to weigh and balance the various factors that go into the determination whether to award injunctive relief will be reviewed deferentially under an "abuse of discretion" standard,[15] within that same standard lies the power to exercise more rigorous scrutiny of the trial court's determination of the particulars and components of the factors. Was the law correctly stated and applied (de novo) or were the facts correctly found (clearly erroneous)?[16] A court may use those sub-factors to undermine and sap the vitality out of the deferential abuse of discretion standard.[17]

The deference afforded trial court discretion-based decision making by reviewing courts may vary depending on the significance of the issue. A good example of this is *Project B.A.S.I.C. v. Kemp.*[18] The court stated that review of discretion-based decisions finding a person in civil contempt will be reviewed more rigorously than a discretion-based decision exonerating a person from a charge of contempt.[19] The difficulty with this approach is that the interest(s) considered can be unduly narrow. The charged contemnor's interest are certainly affected differently depending on whether she is convicted or exonerated, but the interest(s) of a person seeking performance by the contemnor are also in play. Focusing on one, to the exclusion of the other, skews the reviewing process. This is particularly true in cases of civil contempt since the primary force of the remedy is to vindicate the plaintiff's entitlement.[20]

Courts may have different opinions as to when discretion-based decision making should be rigorous or deferential even on the same issue. For example, First Circuit decisions suggest that "greater deference" is owed to the trial court in public law litigation than in purely private litigation.[21] Ninth Circuit decisions suggest the opposite approach.[22]

Equity's balancing of discretionary and rule-based decision making is difficult to cabin. On the one hand, courts frequently exalt equity's focus

---

[15] Roland Mach. Co. v. Dresser Indus., Inc., 749 F.2d 380, 390 (7th Cir. 1984).

[16] Northern Indiana Pub. Serv. Co. v. Dozier, 674 N.E.2d 977, 989 (Ind. App. 1996) (in determining whether the trial court abused its discretion "we determine whether the findings validly support the court's decision. The finding will not be set aside unless clearly erroneous").

[17] Section 32 (Appellate Review of Order Granting or Denying Temporary Injunctive Relief).

[18] 947 F.2d 11 (1st Cir. 1991).

[19] *Id.* at 16.

[20] Roe v. Operation Rescue, 919 F.2d 857, 868 (3d Cir. 1990) (noting that the "purpose of civil contempt is primarily remedial and is to benefit the complainant" and that even when sanctions coerce they do so to aid the complainant by ensuring that the order is complied with by the defendant); Chapter 22 (Contempt).

[21] Langton v. Johnson, 928 F.2d 1206 (1st Cir. 1991):

> [In public law litigation] the district court's construction of a consent decree should be accorded considerable deference, because broad leeway is often necessary to secure complicated, sometimes conflicting, policy objectives.

Id. at 1221 (brackets added).

[22] Toussaint v. McCarthy, 801 F.2d 1080, 1088–89 (9th Cir. 1986), *cert. denied*, 481 U.S. 1069 (1987) (noting factors that in context of "public law litigation" weigh in favor of deference, such as familiarity with the record, also weigh against deference; familiarity with the parties and issues may lead to "excessive involvement and a breakdown of institutional perspective").

on the pursuit of justice while at the same time noting equity's commitment to regularity.[23] Where the balance will be struck in the particular case will be hard to predict with confidence. Perhaps we should say that equity is a body of rules equitably applied.[24]

§ 24   BURDEN ON THE COURT/SUPERVISION

Equity acts in personam;[1] therefore, enforcement of equitable remedies may require a greater degree of judicial involvement in oversight and involvement than would be encountered after the rendition of a judgment at law. Because equity acts on the conscience of the defendant, equity must ensure that the defendant heeds equity's pronouncements. Successful avoidance or evasion of an equity court's demands would diminish the moral and legal standing of the court. This concern has been reflected in the reluctance of equity to involve itself in matters that would require substantial judicial efforts to ensure compliance.[2] Equitable relief has been refused when the required performance would be unreasonably difficult to enforce[3] or require lengthy judicial supervision,[4] the cost of which would be disproportionate to the net advantages gained from the injunction.[5]

Although the burden/supervision concept has a long history, the modern trend is to treat burden/supervision concerns not as complete defenses to

---

[23] *Compare* Yuba Consol. Gold Fields v. Kilkeary, 206 F.2d 884, 889 (9th Cir. 1953) (stating that "[e]quity jurisdiction being recognized, the question whether it will be exercised rests in the sound discretion of the chancellor. It must be a legal discretion based on principles of law and not on the arbitrary will of the chancellor"), *with* Youngs v. West, 27 N.W.2d 88, 91 (Mich. 1947):

> [T]he granting of equitable relief is ordinarily a matter of grace, and whether a court of equity will exercise its jurisdiction, and the propriety of affording equitable relief, rests in the sound discretion of the court, to be exercised according to the circumstances and exigencies of each particular case. Of course, this discretion is not an arbitrary one, but must be exercised in accordance with the fixed principles and precedents of equity jurisprudence, and in accordance with the evidence.

[24] *See* Lonchar v. Thomas, 517 U.S. 314, 323–24 (1996) (noting in connection with equitable remedy of habeas corpus that availability of the writ is a product of rules and precedents controlling equitable principles).

[1] Section 22 (Equity Acts in Personam).

[2] Besinger v. National Tea Co., 221 N.E.2d 156, 159 (Ill. App. 1966) (stating that the court would be hesitant to grant specific performance of a construction contract "for the decree would necessitate constant and prolonged judicial supervision of the construction operations") (citations omitted).

[3] Restatement of Contracts § 371 (1932) (stating traditional rule that equity will not order the performance of a contract when it would be unreasonably difficult to monitor compliance).

[4] The traditional rule has been that equity will not grant injunctive relief when enforcement requires supervision by the court over an extended period of time. Bach v. Friden Calculating Mach. Co., 155 F.2d 361, 366 (6th Cir. 1946); Canteen Corp. v. Republic of Texas Properties, Inc., 773 S.W.2d 398, 400 (Tex. Civ. App. 1989); Long Beach Drug Co. v. United Drug Co. 88 P.2d 698, 703–04 (Cal. 1939) (exclusive distribution or sales agency); Poultry Producers, etc. v. Barlow 208 P. 93, 97 (Cal. 1922) (output poultry sales contract); Pacific Etc. Ry. Co. v. Campbell-Johnston, 94 P. 623, 626–27 (Cal. 1908) (railroad construction or operation).

[5] Suchan v. Rutherford, 410 P.2d 434, 440 (Idaho 1966).

injunctive relief,[6] but as one of the factors that go into the assessment whether equitable injunctive relief should issue.[7] It is not burden or supervision per se that will warrant denial of equitable relief, but the degree and extent of judicial involvement the decree will require. The salient fact is that there is no hard and fast rule for determining whether an injunction should be denied because it will impose unreasonable burdens on the court in the form of supervision and oversight;[8] rather, the critical focus involves a "weighing of the need for ongoing[9] judicial supervision with the importance of enforcement to the plaintiff."[10] The scope and extent of judicial supervision is also a factor:

> [W]e view the critical inquiry in the instant case to be not simply whether FPI is seeking specific performance of a construction contract, but rather, whether if specific performance is granted, the court will be required to become involved in prolonged supervision of the building's construction if disputes arise. If the trial court will not be required to become embroiled in continuing disputes and decisions regarding the building's construction, specific performance may be an appropriate remedy.[11]

When the court believes that the nature of the parties' relationship will reduce or eliminate the need for constant judicial oversight, injunctive relief may be granted when in the absence of that belief it would not.[12] Similarly, the ability of the parties to draft specific language in a proposed order[13]

---

[6] Grayson-Robinson Stores, Inc. v. Iris Constr. Corp., 168 N.E.2d 377, 379 (N.Y. 1960) (arbitration award) (noting that "[m]odern writers think that the 'difficulty of enforcement [of specific performance of a construction contract] is exaggerated' and that the trend is towards specific performance") (citations omitted; brackets added). Because the case involved arbitration, some courts have construed the decision narrowly. Niagra Mohawk Power Corp. v. Graver Tank & Manf. Co., 470 F. Supp. 1308, 1326 (N.D.N.Y. 1979).

[7] The Original Great American Chocolate Chip Cookie Co., Inc. v. River Valley Cookie, Ltd., 970 F.2d 273, 277–78 (7th Cir. 1992) (noting that judicial difficulty in supervising injunction requiring parties to a franchise agreement to maintain a cooperative relationship favored the denial of equitable relief).

[8] Franklin Point, Inc. v. Harris Trust & Sav. Bank, 660 N.E.2d 204, 206 (Ill. App. 1995) (citing Grayson-Robinson Stores, supra, 168 N.E.2d at 378).

[9] The mere length of the time of performance is not critical. Portland Section of the Council of Jewish Women v. Sisters of Charity, 513 P.2d 1183, 1187 (Or. 1973) (holding that hospital must perform contract to maintain a charity bed in perpetuity).

[10] Franklin Point, Inc., supra, 660 N.E.2d at 206 (citing City Stores Co. v. Ammerman, 394 F.2d 950 (D.C. Cir. 1968).

[11] Franklin Point, Inc., supra, 660 N.E.2d at 206.

[12] Compare The Original Great Am. Chocolate Chip Cookie Co., Inc., supra, (expressing concern over parties' ability to maintain cooperative relationship if ordered to do so), with Travelers Int'l AG v. Trans World Airlines, Inc., 722 F. Supp. 1087, 1105 (S.D.N.Y. 1989) (rejecting argument that injunctive relief should be denied because compliance would require constant judicial monitoring of parties' ongoing business relationship and noting that while order will require parties to work together "the long history of these relationships indicates they can do just that without judicial intervention"). The court further noted at the operations level the relationship was less troubled than at the leadership positions. The court indicated that any "disputes" by the parties should be resolved based on established, past practice. Id.

[13] Section 34 (Specificity of Injunctive Relief).

may assuage a court that is concerned that the order will occasion significant judicial involvement and supervision.[14]

§ 25 NATURE OF RIGHTS PROTECTED

It is occasionally said that equity distinguishes between property rights, which it will protect if the remedy at law is inadequate, and "personal rights," which it will not protect even though the remedy at law is inadequate. The property/personal rights distinction is attributed to Lord Eldon's decision in *Gee v. Pritchard*, which involved the effort of the sender of a personal letter to enjoin its republication by the recipient.[1] In finding for the sender, Lord Eldon stated:

> I do not say that I am to interfere because the letters are written in confidence, or because the publication of them may wound the feelings of the plaintiff; but if mischievous effects of that kind can be apprehended in cases in which this court has been accustomed, on the ground of property, to forbid publication, it would not become me to abandon the jurisdiction which my predecessors have exercised, and refuse to forbid it.

As noted by one court, however, the distinction was "known chiefly by its breach rather than by its observance."[2] Indeed the same court referred to the doctrine as a "fiction" stating:

> [C]ourts with greatest uniformity have based their jurisdiction to protect purely personal rights nominally on an alleged property right, when, in fact, no property rights were invaded. This is . . . as it should be because the personal rights of citizens are infinitely more sacred and by every test are of more value than things that are measured by dollars and cents.[3]

It is doubtful, aside from an occasional spurious and chance decision, that the rule was ever other than that "equity will protect personal rights by injunction upon the same conditions upon which it will protect property rights by injunction."[4] The true rule here, if it can really be called a "rule,"

---

[14] *Franklin Point, Inc.*, *supra*; *cf.* Bituminous Coal Operators' Ass'n, Inc. v. Int'l Union U.A.W., 585 F.2d 586, 592 (3d Cir. 1978) (noting that difficulty in drafting appropriate relief may be grounds for denial of relief, but that decision should be deferred until the scope of the parties' obligations are a matter of record).

[1] 2 Swanst. 402, 36 Eng. Reprint 670 (Ch. 1818); *see* Chappell v. Stewart, 33 A. 542, 543 (Md. 1896) (refusing to enjoin actions that were annoying and inconvenient to plaintiff and raised suspicions about him because no property right was involved and stating that a "court of equity has no jurisdiction in matters merely criminal or merely immoral which do not affect any right to property"), *cert. dismissed*, 169 U.S. 733 (1898).

[2] Hawks v. Yancey, 265 S.W. 233, 237 (Tex. Civ. App. 1924).

[3] *Id.*

[4] Kenyon v. City of Chicopee, 70 N.E.2d 241, 244–45 (Mass. 1946); *see* Everett v. Harron, 110 A.2d 383, 387 (Pa. 1955). *See generally* Annot., *Jurisdiction of Equity to Protect Personal Rights, Modern View*, 175 A.L.R. 438 (1948).

is that the decision whether to protect the "right" turned not on its characterization as property or personal but on the substance of the right— was the interest such that it should be protected in equity. Cases evidencing a judicial disinclination to provide equitable relief can in turn be subdivided into several categories: (1) cases where the claimed "right" raises collateral issues that warrant non-intervention by an equity court; (2) cases where the claimed "right" is legally insignificant and not deserving of protection on the merits; and (3) cases that raise concerns over the propriety and advisability of judicial involvement.

Cases in the first category involve claims that would embroil courts in political disputes with coordinate branches of the government[5] or implicate courts in religious controversies. For example, in *Weiss v. Weiss*[6] the parties signed a pre-nuptial agreement in which the mother had agreed to raise any children of the marriage in a particular religious faith. After the divorce the ex-husband sought enforcement of the agreement in equity. The court refused on the ground that enforcement would entangle the court in religious issues in contravention to the Free Exercise and Establishment Clauses of the First Amendment.[7] Judicial involvements becomes more likely, however, if it becomes apparent that the parents religious practices are affecting the general welfare of the child.[8] Similarly, an equity court will resolve a property dispute between members of a church or religious organization when the dispute can be resolved under "neutral principles of property law" rather than religious dogma.[9] This principle is not limited to actions in equity but also extends to actions at law.[10]

The second category involves claims that have marginal legal merit based on current legal standards. This formulation accepts that a claim that was once deemed marginal may, through the evolution of contemporary legal standards, become a claim that is mainstream. Rights of association and membership in a private organization are examples of claims that have gone through this metamorphasis:

---

[5] Kavanagh v. Coash, 81 N.W.2d 349, 351 (Mich. 1957) (holding that court of equity may not properly enjoin an act that is political in nature and does not involve property, personal, or civil rights).

[6] 49 Cal. Rptr. 2d 339 (Cal. App. 1996).

[7] *Id.* at 346. This is an area where courts have differed. *See generally* Annot., *Religion As Factor in Child Custody and Visitation Cases*, 22 A.L.R. 4th 971 (1983) (collecting decisions).

[8] Burnham v. Burnham, 304 N.W.2d 58 (Neb. 1981) (reversing award of custody when evidence disclosed that custodial parent would elevate religious beliefs over welfare of child); *see also* Munoz v. Munoz, 489 P.2d 1133, 1135 (Wash. 1971) (requiring "clear and affirmative showing"); see Barbara Handschu & Mary Kay Kisthardt, *Religion as a Custody Issue*, Nat'l L. J., Feb. 1, 2000, at A17 (collecting decisions and noting that "harm to child" is key consideration).

[9] Presbyterian Church v. Mary Elizabeth Blue Hull Mem'l Presbyterian Church, 393 U.S. 440, 449 (1969).

[10] Natal v. Christian and Missionary Alliance, 878 F.2d 1575 (1st Cir. 1989) (rejecting clergyman's wrongful termination claim; the court refused to intrude into church rules, policies, or decisions).

When courts originally declined to scrutinize admission practices of membership associations they were dealing with social clubs, religious organizations and fraternal associations. Here the policies against judicial intervention were strong and there were no significant countervailing policies. When the courts were later called upon to deal with trade and professional associations exercising virtually monpolistic control, different factors were involved. The intimate personal relationships which pervaded the social, religious and fraternal organizations were hardly in evidence and the individual's opportunity of earning a livelihood and serving society in his chosen trade or profession appeared as the controlling policy consideration. Public policy strongly dictates that this power [of exclusion] should not be unbridled but should be viewed judicially as a fiduciary power to be exercised in reasonable and lawful manner for the advancement of the interests of the medical profession and the public generally.[11]

Recent decisions have substantially expanded the types of associations that are now subject to judicial supervision regarding their admission, discipline, and expulsion of members.[12]

Many cases is this category declining to provide a remedy may also be seen as effectively refusing to recognize a right.[13] In some instances courts have expressly treated the interest as too trivial to warrant protection through an equitable remedy.[14] Of course, what is trivial to one may be of fundamental importance to another, e.g., disputes over officiating at Little League games or high school athletic contests. Many courts continue to use the property-personal right dichotomy to resolve these disputes or

[11] Falcone v. Middlesex County Med. Soc'y, 170 A.2d 791, 799 (N.J. 1961) (citations omitted; brackets added). See Chapter 11 (Remedies for Injury to Relationships) (particularly Section 101 (Social and Professional Relationships).

[12] Cf. Brounstein v. American Cat Fanciers Assoc., 839 F. Supp. 1100, 1108, 1110 (D.N.J. 1993) (plaintiff "cat fancier" stated claim against defendant organization for revoking her license as "all breed" cat judge). The "organization" in this case was held to be subject to New Jersey's Law Against Discrimination. Plaintiff claimed her license was revoked because she was Jewish.

[13] Mathew Bender & Co. v. West Publishing Co., 158 F.3d 674, 681 n.4 (2d Cir. 1998) (stating that mere corrections to a text, such as providing or changing punctuation or spelling may be trivial and not amount to sufficient "creativity" to warrant copyright protection); cf. Hollister v. Tuttle, 210 F.3d 1033, 1035–36 (9th Cir. 2000) (holding that "[a] professor has no property right in the number of units assigned to his academic course; nor can a reduction in the number of units be generally treated as a kind of demotion") (same as to appointment to college committee). But cf. Associated Press, June 28, 2005 (reporting decision by University of Montana President to accept committee's decision that law school professor Rob Natelson was qualified to teach constitutional law class; earlier Natelson had filed, and prevailed, in a grievance that he was improperly denied teaching assignment of that course due to his conservative political views).

[14] Blatt v. University of Southern California, 85 Cal. Rptr. 601 (Cal. App. 1970) (involving admission to law school honor society).

to simply hold that the interest is too insignificant to warrant protection,[15] but there are exceptions.[16]

A third category raises issues of judicial management as a reason for non-intervention. In the area of academic performance, courts have generally rejected claims of negligent evaluation[17] or negligent instruction[18] on the ground that recognition of such claims is impractical and would involve the judiciary in matters better left to educational authorities. Courts have recognized the importance of education and the consequences of a poor education can hardly be denied.[19] Courts have also recognized that students may bring breach of contract claims[20] and collect damages, although the full scope of the remedy has not been addressed.[21] The basis for the reluctance to intervene is a combination of (1) a recognition of the volume of claims that would result from recognition of "educational malpractice" as a cause of action, and (2) the inherently subjective nature of the evaluation of academic performance.[22]

Another area where courts have expressed a reluctance to intervene are matters involving intimate personal decisions. For example, courts have refused to require a pregnant woman to have her baby by cesarean section even though medical evidence indicated that a natural childbirth would be

---

[15] Georgia High School Assn v. Waddell, 285 S.E.2d 7 (Ga. 1981) (holding that courts are without authority to review officiating decisions of football referees in high school sports); see Jeff Nemerofsky, What is a "Trifle" Anyway?, 37 Gonzaga L. Rev. 315 (2001/2002) (discussing legal system's treatment of "de minimis" harm).

[16] Cf. Hornstine v. Township of Moorestown, 263 F. Supp.2d 887 (D.N.J. 2003) (enjoining school district from having 3 valedictorians at high school commencement instead of 1— plaintiff). Plaintiff's claim was based in large part on the ground that the school district discriminated against her in violation of the Americans with Disabilities Act and the Rehabilitation Act.

[17] Hoffman v. Board of Educ. of City of N.Y., 400 N.E.2d 317, 319–20 (N.Y. 1979) (denying claim of student negligently classified as "retarded" and placed in special education program); see Tarka v. Cunningham, 917 F.2d 890 (5th Cir. 1990) (rejecting action to change grade on the ground that plaintiff failed to state claim). But cf. Sylvester v. Texas S. Univ., 957 F. Supp. 944 (S.D. Tex. 1997) (holding that student was entitled to equitable remedy requiring university law school to change student's course grade due to the university's failure to follow its own procedures regarding disputed grades).

[18] Ross v. Creighton Univ., 957 F.2d 410, 414 n.2 (7th Cir. 1992) (collecting decisions refusing to recognize claim of educational malpractice).

[19] Peter W. v. San Francisco Unified Sch. Dist., 131 Cal. Rptr. 854, 858 (Cal. App. 1976).

[20] Ross v. Creighton Univ., supra, 957 F.2d at 417 (collecting decisions recognizing breach of contract action). The breach of contract claim, however, cannot be a subterfuge to address the deficiencies of the academic services provided. Houston v. Mile High Adventist Academy, 872 F. Supp. 829, 836 (D. Colo. 1994); cf. Gupta v. New Britain Gen. Hosp., 687 A.2d 111, 118 (Conn. 1996) (holding that residency agreement between physician and hospital created educational rather than employment relationship).

[21] Zumbrun v. University of S. Cal., 101 Cal. Rptr. 499, 504 (Cal. App. 1972) (permitting partial refund of tuition as remedy for refusal of instructor to teach last month of class). A critical side issue is whether consequential damages are available to a student for breach of contract by an educational institution.

[22] Tarka v. Cunningham, supra, 917 F.2d at 891–92; Ross v. Creighton Univ., supra.

harmful to the fetus.[23] In *Curran v. Bosze* the court refused to order siblings to submit to bone marrow harvesting in order to donate bone marrow. The sibling's natural mother objected to the harvesting procedure.[24] Courts have rejected requests for organ donation from minors and incompetents even when all the interested parties agree to the procedure.[25] Contracts to sell bodily organs have been deemed unenforceable.[26]

§ 26 STATUTORY EQUITABLE REMEDIES

Judicial power must find its source in some enabling law or it must be deemed inherent. The question of the court's inherent equity power has proven to be somewhat controversial and intractable. At one end, some courts have taken a strong stance that "the power of a [court] to [provide equitable remedies] does not in the first instance depend on a statutory grant of power. Rather, the authority derives from the inherent power of a court of equity to fashion effective relief."[1] A somewhat less expansive view of inherent power was expressed in *Freeman v. Pitts* when the Court stated that "[t]he essence of a court's equity power lies in its inherent capacity to adjust remedies in a feasible and practical way to eliminate the conditions or redress the injuries caused by unlawful action."[2] How far these conceptions should be extended has provoked extensive discussions regarding the role of courts in American society.[3] That is, however, not a

---

[23] *In re* Baby Boy Doe v. Mother Doe, 632 N.E.2d 326 (Ill. App. 1994). *But cf.* Jefferson v. Griffin Spaulding County Hosp. Auth., 274 S.E.2d 457, 460 (Ga. 1981) (holding that mother in last week of pregnancy lacked the right to refuse medical treatment necessary for her unborn fetus).

[24] 566 N.E.2d 1319 (Ill. 1990).

[25] *See generally* Lisa Gregory, Annot., *Propriety of Surgically Invading Incompetent or Minor for Benefit of Third Party*, 4 A.L.R.5th 1000, 1008 (1992) (stating that basis of decision in this area is whether "from an objective point of view what course of action will confer [upon] the [person whose organs are to be harvested] the greatest net benefit") (brackets added).

[26] Wilson v. Adkins, 941 S.W.2d 440, 441–42 (Ark. App. 1997) (holding that agreement to sell bone marrow to another violated federal law prohibiting the transfer of human organs for valuable consideration (42 U.S.C. § 274(e)); Section 65.2 (Illegality).

[1] Securities & Exch. Comm'n v. Wencke, 622 F.2d 1363, 1369 (9th Cir. 1980) (receivership) (brackets added). A related, albeit distinct, concept is that courts have inherent power to grant equitable relief as necessary to protect the integrity of their judgments and proceedings. Chambers v. NASCO, Inc., 501 U.S. 32, 43–44 (1991); Winkler v. Eli Lilly & Co., 101 F.3d 1196, 1202–03 (7th Cir. 1996) (federal court has authority under All Writs Act (28 U.S.C. § 1651) to enjoin litigatant from engaging in forum shopping in derogation of the integrity of federal proceedings).

[2] 503 U.S. 467, 487 (1992); ABC Int'l Traders, Inc. v. Matsushita Elec. Corp. of Am., 931 P.2d 290, 303 (Cal. 1997) (stating that in absence of statutory restriction, court of equity retains "full range of its inherent powers in order to accomplish complete justice . . . ."); Armstrong Sch. Dist. v. Armstrong Educ. Ass'n, 595 A.2d 1139, 1143 (Pa. 1991) (stating that once equity jurisdiction attaches, court may provide complete relief). *But cf.* State v. Morales, 869 S.W.2d 941, 947 (Tex. 1994) (stating that there is no such legal concept as inherent power of a court; no court may exercise a power without a law authorizing it).

[3] Missouri v. Jenkins, 515 U.S. 70 (1995) (particularly the concurring opinion of Justice Thomas, *id.* at 126–130, discussing role of equity in England and America); *see* ERWIN

question we need to resolve here except to note that at least as to federal courts the claim is well established that they possess "all of the common law equity tools of a Chancery Court (subject, of course, to congressional limitation) to process litigation to a just and equitable conclusion."[4] The principle is also accepted in state courts as a general proposition of law.[5]

[26.1]   Statute Expanding Equitable Remedies

When a statute expressly authorizes equitable remedies, the most common consequence is a judicial finding that one or more of the requirements of the prima facie case for injunctive relief have been satisfied.[6] For example, when the legislature expressly provides for injunctive relief to remedy statutory violations, the irreparable injury requirement is usually satisfied by the fact of the violation.[7] The fact of violation will also usually satisfy the requirement of balancing of hardships.[8] In effect, the presence of an express equitable remedy for a violation of a statute means that the equitable remedy is available "as a matter of course" upon establishment of the statutory breach.[9] A good example of this principle is copyright infringement; courts have consistently noted that the rules for statutory injunctive relief for copyright infringement are different from the rules generally applied for injunctive relief. A plaintiff who makes out a prima facie case of statutory infringement is entitled to statutory injunctive relief as a matter of course.[10] In the usual case, the statutory violation creates a

---

CHEMERINSKY, FEDERAL JURISDICTION 147–180 (1989); LAWRENCE H. TRIBE, AMERICAN CONSTITUTIONAL LAW 42–61 (2d ed. 1988); Section 20.1 (Judicial Power) (discussing recent trend of the Supreme Court to read narrowly statutory provisions for equitable remedies).

[4] ITT Community Dev. Corp. v. Barton, 569 F.2d 1351, 1359 (5th Cir. 1978) (citation omitted); see In re Prevot, 59 F.3d 556, 565 (6th Cir. 1995) (listing "inherent" powers of equity court as contempt, sentences for abuse of judicial process, dismissal for failure to prosecute, disciplinary power over attorneys, and the power to dismiss an action for lack of jurisdiction). The above list is not exclusive.

[5] Sims v. Sims, 930 P.2d 153, 159 (N. Mex. 1996); Brenner v. Berkowitz, 634 A.2d 1019, 1031 (N.J. 1993); Trindle v. State, 602 A.2d 1232, 1234 (Md. 1992).

[6] Section 33.2 ([Permanent Injunctions] Entitlement to Relief). But cf. Bates v. Bates, 793 S.W.2d 788 (Ark. 1990) (holding that Domestic Abuse Act, which eased requirements for abused spouses to obtain equitable relief, violated separation of powers; legislature was without authority to give equity court any jurisdiction other than that which equity court could exercise at time state constitution was adopted).

[7] United States v. City and County of San Francisco, 310 U.S. 16, 31 (1940); Atchison, T. & S.F. Ry. v. Lennen, 640 F.2d 255, 259–60 (10th Cir. 1981) (collecting cases); Section 31.2 (Traditional Tests for Issuance of Temporary Injunctive Relief); Section 33.2 ([Permanent Injunctions] Entitlement to Relief).

[8] Burlington N. Ry. Co. v. Bair, 957 F.2d 599, 601–02 (8th Cir.), cert. denied, 506 U.S. 821 (1992).

[9] Burlington N. Ry. Co. v. Bair, supra, 957 F.2d at 602; United States v. Fang, 937 F. Supp. 1186, 1196 (D. Md. 1996).

[10] Johnson Controls, Inc. v. Phoenix Control Sys., Inc., 886 F.2d 1173, 1174 (9th Cir. 1989); Apple Computer, Inc. v. Franklin Computer Corp., 714 F.2d 1240, 1254 (3d Cir. 1983); cf. Maier Brewing Co. v. Fleischmann Distilling Corp., 390 F.2d 117, 120–21 (9th Cir. 1968) (allowing equitable remedy of "accounting of profits" as a matter of right upon establishment of Lanham Act (trademark) violation).

presumption that the prima facie case for statutory equitable remedies has been satisfied, but the presumption is rebuttable.[11]

A defendant may still be able to show, however, that, in the particular case, the court should exercise its discretion to refuse to award equitable relief. For example, a court may consider a plaintiff's delay in enforcing its statutory rights in determining whether the presumption of irreparable injury should be applied.[12] In *California Grocers Ass'n, Inc. v. Bank of America*[13] plaintiffs sought to enjoin aspects of defendant's policy regarding checks written against insufficient funds on the ground that defendant's policy was unconscionable. The court assumed that the objected to practices could come within California's Unfair Business Practices Act,[14] which does expressly provide for injunctive relief to remedy violations.[15] The court, nonetheless, reversed the trial court's grant of injunctive relief as an abuse of discretion finding that the case involved a matter of economic policy— whether service fees charged by banks are too high and should be regulated—that was better left to legislative rather than judicial oversight and control.[16]

If a statute expressly provides for temporary equitable relief, the matter is handled as described above.[17] The absence of express statutory authorization for temporary equitable remedies does not, however, defeat the court's power to award them. The general approach is to recognize that courts have inherent power to issue temporary equitable remedies ancillary to the court's authority to provide final equitable relief.[18] Several courts had permitted temporary equitable remedies to issue even if the plaintiff did not seek final injunctive relief, but this approach is likely foreclosed, at least in federal courts when applying federal law, under *Grupo Mexicano de Desarrollo S.A. v. Alliance Bond Fund*, in which Court held that federal courts do not have general equitable power to grant temporary equitable relief when no final equitable remedy is sought.[19] On the other hand, a federal statute may confer such authority.[20] *Grupo Mexicano* illustrates the

---

[11] Bourne Co. v. Tower Records, Inc., 976 F.2d 99, 101 (2d Cir. 1992) (noting that acquiescence in another's infringement rebuts the presumption of irreparable harm).

[12] Tom Doherty Assocs., Inc. v. Saban Entertainment, Inc., 60 F.3d 27, 39 (2d Cir. 1995).

[13] 27 Cal. Rptr. 2d 396 (Cal. App. 1994).

[14] California Business & Professions Code § 17200 *et seq.*

[15] 27 Cal. Rptr. 2d at 404, *citing* Cal. Bus. & Prof. Code § 17203.

[16] *Id.*; Jacobs v. Citibank N.A., 462 N.E.2d 1182, 1183 (N.Y. 1984).

[17] 17 U.S.C. § 502 (specifically authorizing courts to grant temporary injunctive relief to "prevent or restrain infringement of copyright"); Country Kids 'N City Slicks, Inc. v. Sheen, 77 F.3d 1280, 1288 (10th Cir. 1996) (holding, that plaintiff was entitled "to preliminary injunction enjoining copyright infringement upon showing of likelihood of success on the merits); *Apple Computer, Inc., supra,* 714 F.2d at 1254.

[18] Reebok Int'l. Ltd. v. Marnatech Enters., Inc., 970 F.2d 552, 559 (9th Cir. 1992); F.T.C. v. U.S. Oil & Gas Corp., 748 F.2d 1431, 1433–34 (11th Cir. 1984).

[19] 527 U.S. 308, 327 (1999). The decision is discussed in Section 20.1 (Judicial Power), at text and note 14.

[20] *In re* Dow Corning Corp., 280 F.3d 648, 657–58 (6th Cir.) (noting that Court in *Grupo*

desirability in federal court of tying the request for temporary injunctive relief whenever possible to an express statutory grant or to a request for final equitable relief. .

The fact that a statute makes a general reference to equitable remedies does not mean that a court will expansively construe the language.[21]

[26.2]　Statute Restricting Equitable Remedies

Statutes restricting a court's power to provide an equitable remedy, though otherwise appropriate, are viewed much more critically by courts than statutes that expand equitable remedies by relaxing elements of the remedies' prima facie case. The issue is fundamentally one of separation of powers. Some would not put the issue so forcefully.[22] This has been, however, the central focus of the Supreme Court in reviewing legislative efforts to restrict the power of federal courts to provide equitable remedies.[23] American constitutions usually confer the judicial power upon the courts. That conferral creates a delicate balance when measured against the legislature's acknowledged power over remedies. The first and primary rule here is strict construction against remedy restriction. In *Weinberger v. Romero-Barcelo* the Court stated:

> [E]quitable jurisdiction is not to be denied or limited in the absence of a clear and valid legislative command . . . . 'The great principles of equity, securing complete justice, should not be yielded to light inferences, or doubtful construction.'[24]

The rationale for this approach is that the courts assume that a jurisdictional grant is conferred with the understanding of the court's equitable

---

Mexicano distinguished a prior decision (United States v. First National City Bank, 379 U.S. 378 (1965)) on that basis (527 U.S. at 326)), *cert. denied sub nom.* Class Five Nevada Claimants v. Dow Corning Corp., 537 U.S. 816 (2002).

[21] Section 20.1 (Judicial Power), at text and notes 15–21 (discussing *Mertens* and *Knudson*, both of which gave a narrow construction to the phrase "other equitable remedies" used in ERISA (Federal Employee Retirement Income Security Act)).

[22] Zygmunt Plater, *Statutory Violations and Equitable Discretion*, 70 Cal. L. Rev. 524 (1982) (treating separation of powers as an influential factor).

[23] Miller v. French, 530 U.S. 327, 341–50 (2000) (addressing and discussing whether "automatic stay" provision of Prison Litigation Reform Act of 1995, which provides for a statutorily imposed "stay" of equitable relief ordered by a federal court, violates doctrine of separation of powers); *cf.* Weinberger v. Romero-Barcelo, 456 U.S. 305, 319 (1982) (stating that "the legislative history [of the Federal Water Pollution Control Act] does not suggest that Congress intended to deny courts their traditional equitable discretion"); Hecht Co. v. Bowles, 321 U.S. 321, 330 (1944) (stating that "if Congress desired to make such an abrupt departure from traditional equity practice . . . it would have made its desire plain")

[24] 456 U.S. 305, 313 (1982), *quoting* Brown v. Swann, 35 U.S. 497, 503 (1836); *In re* Reighard's Estate, 84 N.E.2d 345, 352 (Ill. 1949) (stating that "[w]here abrogation or abridgment of this jurisdiction of courts of equity is attempted by statute, such statutes are to be strictly construed").

power to provide complete relief.[25] If the legislature wishes to negate that assumption it must do so expressly, clearly, and comprehensively.[26]

The test is difficult and courts are often creative in finding that the Legislature did not really mean what it appeared to say. For example, in *Syring v. Tucker* a statute imposed restrictions on the use of HIV testing. Plaintiff sued defendant for assault and battery and sought an order compelling defendant to undergo HIV testing. The court held that the statute, which imposed restrictions on HIV testing, dealt with "informed consent" for testing and "disclosure" of test results;[27] it did not address the circumstances confronted by the case at hand and did not warrant reading the restrictions in the statute as limiting the court's authority to order defendant to submit to HIV testing.[28]

During the Vietnam War the federal courts held that students who had their draft deferment status changed, so that they could be inducted into the Armed Forces, in retaliation for the students' anti-war activities could obtain injunctive relief. Congress responded by enacting Section 10(b)(3) of the Selective Service Act of 1967:

> No judicial review shall be made of the classification or processing of any registrant by local boards, appeal boards, or the President, except as a defense to a criminal prosecution instituted under section 12 of this title, after the registrant has responded either affirmatively or negatively to an order to report for induction, or for civilian work in the case of a registrant determined to be opposed to participation in war in any form: Provided that such review shall go to the question of the jurisdiction herein reserved to local boards, appeal boards, and President only when there is no basis in fact for the classification assigned to such registrant.[29]

In *Oestereich v. Selective Service Sys. Local Board No. 11* the plaintiff had a student deferment. He turned in his draft card as an antiwar protest and was reclassified by his draft board. He sought equitable relief, which the Court held he could receive. In addressing the jurisdictional limitation imposed by Congress, the Court stated:

> No one, we believe, suggests that § 10(b)(3) can sustain a literal reading. For while it purports on its face to suspend the writ of habeas corpus as a vehicle for reviewing a criminal conviction under the Act, everyone agrees that such was not its intent. Examples are legion where literalness in statutory language is out of harmony

---

[25] Mitchell v. Robert De Mario Jewelry, Inc., 361 U.S. 288, 291–92 (1946).

[26] Porter v. Warren Holding Co., 328 U.S. 395, 398 (1946):

> Unless a statute in so many words, or by a necessary and inescapable inference, restricts the court's jurisdiction in equity, the full scope of that jurisdiction is to be recognized and applied.

[27] 498 N.W.2d 370, 376 (Wis. 1993).

[28] *Id.* at 374–75.

[29] Military Selective Service Act of 1967. 81 Stat. 104, 50 U.S.C.A. App. § 460(b)(3).

either with constitutional requirements, or with an Act taken as an organic whole.[30]

The fact that Oestereich sought injunctive relief against his induction and that the statute did not suspend the writ of habeas corpus was not controlling. The Court held, without expressly saying, that Congress's effort to restrict equitable relief in cases of clear wrongdoing would not be accepted, at least in the context of the times and the case.

This is not to suggest that the Court will always reject Congress's efforts to limit the authority of federal courts to provide equitable relief. In *Miller v. French* the Court found that Congress "intended to prohibit federal courts from exercising their equitable authority to suspend operation of the [statutory] automatic stay."[31] The Court held that a more limited construction that would preserve some modicum of judicial authority to suspend the automatic stay "would subvert the plain meaning of the statute."[32] The Court went on to hold that the limitation was not an unconstitutional violation of separation of powers.[33]

Statutory restrictions on the timing of equitable relief are more likely to be upheld over statutory preclusion of equitable remedies.[34] Similarly, it has been suggested that statutory restrictions are more likely to be upheld when they are part of a comprehensive enforcement scheme for addressing statutory violations.[35] That suggestion cannot, however, be taken too far. It was made in the context of a decision addressing whether a court should imply an equitable remedy into a comprehensive remedial scheme that was silent on the issue;[36] it did not address a restriction on

---

[30] 393 U.S. 233, 239 (1968).

[31] 530 U.S. 327, 341 (2000) (brackets added). The Court noted:

> [A]lthough we should not construe a statute to displace courts' traditional equitable authority absent the "clearest command," or an "inescapable inference" to the contrary, we are convinced that Congress' intent to remove such discretion is unmistakable. And while this construction raises constitution questions, the canon of constitutional doubt permits us to avoid such questions only where the saving construction is not "plainly contrary to the intent of Congress."

Id. (citation omitted; brackets added).

[32] *Id.* at 340.

[33] *Id.* at 342–50 (finding that the statutory limitation did not amount to an improper usurpation of judicial power).

[34] Beck v. Atlantic Richfield Co., 62 F.3d 1240 (9th Cir.) (*per curiam*):

> We conclude that the district court does not have jurisdiction over West Side's claim for injunctive relief because that claim constitutes a "challenge" to the CERCLA cleanup effort over which the district court would not have jurisdiction until the cleanup was completed.

Id. at 1242–43 (citations omitted), *cert. denied*, 517 U.S. 1167 (1995).

[35] Reebok Int'l, Ltd. v. Marnatech Enters., Inc., 970 F.2d 552, 561 (9th Cir. 1992).

[36] Religious Tech. Ctr. v. Wollersheim, 796 F.2d 1076, 1077–89 (9th Cir. 1986) (refusing to imply injunctive relief as part of civil remedies created for private right of action under Racketeer Influenced and Corrupt Organizations Act (RICO) based on review of RICO's legislative history and statutory language).

the equitable remedy, except by silence. Ironically, the same circuit later recognized the limitation directly in an unpublished decision.[37]

§ 27 INJUNCTION OF CRIMINAL ACTIVITY

Although enforcement of penal statutes through the English Court of Chancery was not unusual in the period after the Norman Conquest, this jurisdiction effectively abated by the fifteenth century.[1] A rule developed that equity courts would not interfere through the issuance of an injunction to prevent a breach of the penal code.[2] The idea that equity could enjoin certain types of criminal activity began to revive in the nineteenth century.[3] During the latter part of that century, equity's rediscovered its power to enjoin "public nuisances," used this rediscovery to enjoin labor unrest,[4] and, as such, found that its use of the injunctive power would again be called into question.[5]

Although the use of injunctions to prevent violations of the penal code has had an ebb and flow quality to it, the general contours of the modern approach are relatively well defined. The first principle is that equity possesses no criminal jurisdiction, but the mere fact that an act sought to be enjoined is punishable as a crime will not preclude equitable relief.[6]

The second principle is that equity will enjoin threatened criminal activity when the injunction is directed at activity that unreasonably interferes with the public health and safety and is defined as a public nuisance by the legislature.[7] In order to constitute a public nuisance:

> Conduct must be "injurious to health, . . . indecent or offensive to the senses, . . . an obstruction to the free use of property, so as to interfere with the comfortable enjoyment of life or property, or unlawfully obstruct[] free passage or use, in the customary manner,

---

[37] Securities Exchange Comm'n v. KS Resources, 110 F.3d 69 (9th Cir. 1997) (Table).

[1] The infamous "Star Chamber" operated in the 16th and 17th centuries until it was abolished in 1641 during the English revolution. Star Chamber is sometimes referred to as a court of "criminal equity."

[2] United States v. Fang, 937 F. Supp. 1186, 1193 (D. Md. 1996); People ex rel. Oakland County Prosecuting Attorney v. Kevorkian, 534 N.W.2d 172, 174 (Mich. App. 1995); cf. Bates v. Bates, 793 S.W.2d 788 (Ark. 1990) (refusing to issue injunction preventing spousal abuse on ground that remedy at law (criminal prosecution) was adequate).

[3] 2 STORY'S EQUITY JURISPRUDENCE § 1250 (14th ed. 1918) (noting use of injunction to abate "public nuisances").

[4] Edwin Mack, *The Revival of Criminal Equity*, 16 Harv. L. Rev. 389, 397 (1903).

[5] Penn. R.R. Co. v. Commonwealth, 7 A. 374 (Pa. 1886); L. & N. R. R. v. Commonwealth, 31 S.W. 476 (Ky.), *aff'd*, 161 U.S. 677 (1896).

[6] United States v. Santee Sioux Tribe of Neb., 135 F.3d 558, 565 (8th Cir.) (stating that, in general, equity will not enjoin the commission of a crime, but that the rule recognizes three exceptions: (1) cases of national emergency; (2) wide spread public nuisance; and (3) when a statute grants the court the power to enjoin a crime), *cert. denied*, 525 U.S. 813 (1998). *See generally* 42 Am. Jur. 2d, *Injunctions*, § 157 (1969).

[7] People v. Lim, 118 P.2d 472, 474 (Cal. 1941).

of any . . . public park, square, street or highway." In addition, the conduct must affect "an entire community or neighborhood, or any considerable number of persons."[8]

This authority "to declare a given act or condition a public nuisance rests with the legislature" and recognition of legislative preemption "serves as a brake on any tendency in the courts to enjoin conduct and punish it with the contempt power under a standardless notion of what constitutes a 'public nuisance.' "[9] It is generally not required that the act or conduct that constitutes the public nuisance also be proscribed as criminal.[10] Examples of acts or conduct that have been deemed public nuisances include: (1) gang activity,[11] (2) operating brothels,[12] (3) obscenity,[13] (4) gambling,[14] and (5) firearms.[15]

A third, and perhaps today the broadest principle, is the ability of a court to enjoin illegal or illicit activity by reason of statutory authorization.[16] This principle is frequently used by bar associations to enjoin the unauthorized practice of law by nonlawyers.

An injunction is binding on the parties until dissolved or modified. A party in violation of an injunction and cited for criminal contempt is often barred from challenging the validity of the injunction.[17] For this and other reasons, and because injunctions against criminal activity often implicate constitutionally guaranteed rights of association, expression, and speech,

---

[8] People ex rel. Gallo v. Acuna, 929 P.2d 596, 614–15 (Cal. 1997) (citations omitted).

[9] *Gallo, supra*, 929 P.2d at 606.

[10] *Id.* at 606; *see* Restatement (Second) of Torts, § 821(B), cmt. d (1979).

[11] *Gallo, supra*, 929 P.2d at 618; People v. Englebrecht, 106 Cal. Rptr.2d 738 (Cal. App. 2001) (rejecting contentions that injunction restricting gang members from throwing gang signs, wearing gang clothing, and congregating with other gang members in public, even gang members who are related by blood or marriage, violated gang members' right to jury trial or gang members' rights of association and speech).

[12] City of Minneapolis v. Fisher, 504 N.W.2d 520, 527 (Minn. App. 1993) (operation of sauna in connection with provision of "sexually oriented services" enjoined).

[13] People ex rel. Busch v. Projection Room Theater, 550 P.2d 600, 608 (Cal. 1976).

[14] *People v. Lim, supra*, 118 P.2d at 475.

[15] Cincinnati v. Beretta U.S. A. Corp., 768 N.E.2d 1136 (Ohio 2002) (rejecting contention that public nuisance doctrine cannot be extended to defectively manufactured and improperly marketed firearms). This issue has proven to be particularly contentious. *See* City of Gary ex rel. King v. Smith & Wesson Corp., 801 N.E.2d 1222, 1232 n.8 (Ind. 2003) (collecting decisions rejecting and accepting public nuisance theory as applied to firearms manufacturers). *Compare* Donald G. Gifford, *Public Nuisance As a Mass Products Liability Tort*, 71 U. Cinn. L. Rev. 741 (2003) (concluding that public nuisance theory provides a poor fit for mass tort litigation against the handgun industry), *with* Jean Macchiaroli Eggen & John C. Culhand, *Gun Torts: Defining A Cause of Action for Victims in Suits Against Gun Manufacturers*, 81 N.C. L. Rev. 115 (2002) (arguing for liability using product defect doctrine).

[16] People of the State of Cal. v. Steelcase, Inc., 792 F. Supp. 84, 85 (C.D. Cal. 1992) (action to enjoin unfair business practices; injunctive relief specifically authorized by statute); City of Minneapolis v. Fisher, 504 N.W.2d at 523–24 (injunction to abate public nuisance specifically authorized by statute).

[17] Section 198 (Collateral Bar Rule).

courts are frequently advised to exercise caution before issuing such injunctions.[18]

The counterpart to the injunction against criminal activity is the injunction against criminal prosecution. The tendency here is hesitancy. As the Supreme Court stated in *Younger v. Harris*:

> Courts of equity should not act, and particularly should not act to restrain a criminal prosecution, when the moving party has an adequate remedy at law and will not suffer irreparable injury if denied equitable relief. Certain types of injury, in particular, the cost, anxiety, and inconvenience of having to defend against a single criminal prosecution, could not, by themselves be considered 'irreparable' in the special legal sense of that term.[19]

The Court's decision in *Younger v. Harris* was in the special context of a federal court being asked to enjoin a threatened state court prosecution,[20] but the principles of that case have been generally applied to all cases seeking to enjoin a criminal prosecution.[21]

§ 28   INJUNCTIONS AND PRIOR RESTRAINTS

The traditional rule in equity was that equity would not enjoin a libel:

> [T]he maxim that equity will not enjoin a libel has enjoyed nearly two centuries of widespread acceptance at common law. The welter of academic and judicial criticism of the last seventy years has, in truth, done little more than chip away at its edges.[1]

---

[18] *People v. Lim, supra*, 118 P.2d at 476 (noting hesitancy of equity courts to grant injunctions against criminal activity because of collateral effects, such as deprivation of jury trial, burden of proof, and multiple punishment); *see* Kwang Hung Hu v. Morgan, 405 F. Supp. 547, 548 (E.D.N.C. 1975) (holding that criminal penalties were adequate sanction and use of injunction and contempt in lieu thereof would deny defendant's right to jury trial); *cf.* People ex rel. Lemon v. Elmore, 177 N.E. 14, 16 (N.Y. 1931) (statute, which authorized "penalty tax" in addition to injunction to close houses of prostitution as public nuisances, violated defendant's right to jury trial). *But cf. Englebrecht, supra*, 106 Cal. Rptr.2d at 743–49 (rejecting contention that "gang injunction" infringed on individual's right to jury trial or fair mode of decisionmaking).

[19] Younger v. Harris, 401 U.S. 37, 43–46 (1971) (noting that an injunction should not issue except in "very unusual circumstances" when an injunction is necessary to prevent "both great and immediate" irreparable injury); Metro Med. Supply, Inc. v. Shalala, 959 F. Supp. 799, 802 (M.D. Tenn. 1996). The *Younger v. Harris* exceptions include criminal prosecution (1) brought in "bad faith," (2) for purposes of "official harassment," or (3) based on statutes that are "patently and flagrantly unconstitutional." Kevorkian v. Thompson, 947 F. Supp. 1152, 1164 (E.D. Mich. 1997).

[20] 401 U.S. at 45 (noting that "the normal thing to do when federal courts are asked to enjoin pending proceedings in state courts is not to issue such injunctions"); Freedberg v. Dep't of Justice, 703 F. Supp. 107, 112 (D.D.C 1989) (finding that ongoing Grand Jury investigations of plaintiff did not establish that government prosecution had "begun" so as to prevent injunction against "threatened" prosecution).

[21] McCall v. Roman, 640 N.Y.S.2d 152 (App. Dep't 1996); Campbell v. Sundquist, 926 S.W.2d 250, 266 (Tenn. App. 1996); Billy Dot, Inc. v. Fields, 908 S.W.2d 335, 337 (Ark. 1995).

[1] Kramer v. Thompson, 947 F.2d 666, 677 (3d Cir. 1991), *cert. denied*, 504 U.S. 940 (1992).

This view while well entrenched is not unanimous.[2]

The traditional rule that equity would not enjoin a libel was the culmination of a number of sub-rules, such as the belief (1) that the remedy at law was adequate, (2) that libels involved personal rather than property rights; (3) that equity would not enjoin a crime; and (4) that an injunction was a form of prior restraint of speech that was legally disfavored. Many of these objections, save the last, have lost their status as a bulwark against the exercise of equitable relief.[3] The concept of "prior restraint" remains, however, as a significant restriction on the availability of injunctive relief against defamatory statements and other restrictions on speech.[4]

Current restrictions on the availability of injunctive relief against defamatory statements flow from the prior restraint doctrine, which was initially developed to limit the power of the executive to censor speech.[5] As is often the case when a newcomer is allowed to migrate from its native habitat to a new area, the effect of the newcomer on the new area cannot always be predicted. In many instances, the newcomer overwhelms the existing inhabitants. That has been the case with the "prior restraint" doctrine. It has been embraced by courts and elevated to the central altar of American jurisprudence. This is not, however, the place to examine critically the role of the "prior restraints" doctrine;[6] rather, the focus in these materials is more limited. How, as a remedial matter, has the "prior restraints" doctrine been applied modernly when a litigant seeks to enjoin speech? The emphasis here is on speech that is defamatory, but the analysis applies to other situations, such as speech that is offensive or invades privacy, as well.

---

[2] Roscoe Pound, *Equitable Relief Against Defamation and Injuries to Personality*, 29 Harv. L. Rev. 640 (1916) (passim) (stating that the decisions espousing the maxim that "equity will not enjoin a libel" blindly follow an old English decision that is no longer followed in England). The English decision is *Gee v. Pritchard*, 2 Swanst. 402, 36 Eng. Reprint 670 (Ch. 1818), discussed at Section 25 (Nature of Rights Protected), n.2.

[3] Section 21 (Adequacy of the Remedy at Law/Irreparable Injury); Section 25 (Nature of Rights Protected); Section 27 (Injunction of Criminal Activity).

[4] Our Lady of the Lake Regional Medical Center v. E.R., 879 So.2d 167 (La. App. 2004) (holding that Federal Patient Confidentiality Law does not justify a "prior restraint" that prevents a person from making public statements about his mistreatment at a substance abuse treatment facility); Brammer v. KB Home Lone Star L.P., 114 S.W.3d 101 (Tex. Civ. App. 2003) (holding that injunction barring statements by home buyer critical of home seller was unconstitutional "prior restraint"); *cf.* In re Marriage of Suggs, 93 P.3d 161, 165–66 (Wash. 2004) (holding that anti-harassment order that barred ex-spouse from making untruthful allegations about the other ex-spouse was overbroad and, therefore, invalid as a prior restraint). *See generally* Floyd Abrams, *Prior Restraints*, 811 PLI/Pat 275 (Nov. 2004) (comprehensive restatement of the law of prior restrain with extensive case compendium).

[5] LAWRENCE TRIBE, AMERICAN CONSTITUTIONAL LAW, §§ 12-34–12-39 (1988) (discussing development and modern application of "prior restraint" doctrine in the United States).

[6] For commentary critical of this development, see Martin H. Redish, *The Proper Role of the Prior Restraint Doctrine in First Amendment Theory*, 70 Va. L. Rev. 53 (1984); Marin Scordato, *Distinction Without a Difference: A Reappraisal of the Doctrine of Prior Restraint*, 68 N.C. L. Rev. 1 (1989).

It is helpful to begin by noting that not all speech is constitutionally protected. "Fighting words,"[7] "obscenity,"[8] and knowingly false defamatory statements[9] are not protected by the First Amendment. The general prohibition against "prior restraints" *by the judiciary* is primarily a restriction on *temporary* injunctive relief against the publication of defamatory statements. This results because the proceeding that leads to the issuance of temporary equitable relief lacks the protections, particularly discovery and the ability to present, examine and cross-examine witnesses, that are associated with plenary, or full, trial proceedings.[10]

The concern over "prior restraints" is reduced once it has been determined, after a plenary trial on the merits, that the statements are defamatory and, if the First Amendment is implicated, that the statements were published with the requisite actual malice.[11] Some courts have accepted this principle that the "prior restraints" doctrine should not be applied when the defamatory statements have been determined to be actionable after a plenary, adversarial trial on the merits. For example, in *O'Brien v. University Community Tenants Union* a landlord successfully sued a tenant's group for defamation. The Ohio Supreme Court held that issuance of an injunction barring the tenant group from further publishing the defamatory statements may be proper because the judicial determination that the statements were actionable and defamatory had been made prior to any restraint.[12]

There is, nonetheless, resistance to this approach. The concern here is that a post-trial injunction on speech may impermissibly chill otherwise lawful speech, to the detriment of First Amendment values.[13] How far courts will go before they will find that speech determined in plenary proceedings to be wrongful will, nonetheless, not support an injunction against reutterance is unclear. In *Aguilar v. Avis Rent A Car Systems, Inc.* a plurality of the California Supreme Court upheld an injunction prohibiting the use or utterance of racial epithets in a workplace setting:

> Defendants contend that, although it is proper to punish a defendant after the fact for a violation of the FEHA based upon spoken words, the trial court's injunction against the use of future epithets is an invalid prior restraint of speech. Under well-established law, however, the injunction at issue is not an invalid prior restraint,

---

[7] Chaplinsky v. New Hampshire, 315 U.S. 568, 572 (1942).

[8] Roth v. United States, 354 U.S. 476, 484–85 (1957).

[9] New York Times Co. v. Sullivan, 376 U.S. 254, 279–80 (1964) (holding that a civil prosecution of an action for libel by a public official against a media defendant was prohibited by the First Amendment "unless he proves that the statement was made with actual malice . . .").

[10] Sid Dillon Chevrolet v. Sullivan, 559 N.W.2d 740, 746–47 (Neb. 1997).

[11] TRIBE, AMERICAN CONSTITUTIONAL LAW, *supra*, at §§ 12–37, pp. 1054–55.

[12] 327 N.E.2d 753, 755 (Ohio 1975). Many courts had reached this position prior to the constitutionalization of the law of defamation. *See generally* W.E. Shipley, Annot., *Injunction As Remedy Against Defamation of Person*, 47 A.L.R.2d 715 (1956).

[13] *See* John Calvin Jeffries, Jr., *Rethinking Prior Restraint*, 92 Yale L.J. 409, 425–29 (1983).

because the order was issued only after the jury determined that defendants had engaged in employment discrimination, and the order simply precluded defendants from continuing their unlawful activity.[14]

The concurring Justice was unwilling to uphold the injunction against a prior restraint challenge merely because the speech had been previously determined in plenary proceedings to be unprotected. In addition to the adjudication that the specific speech was unprotected, the restraint had to be justified as a reasonable time, place, and manner restriction.[15]

In shaping an injunction to enjoin the publication of speech, courts will be particularly concerned that the injunction is not overbroad and does not intrude upon or chill protected speech.[16] A court will likely insist on a strong and compelling showing that the objectionable statements are part of continuing course of conduct designed to harm the plaintiff.[17] The injunction will also be limited to those statements found to be unprotected although this does not mean that an enjoined party can avoid the injunction by recourse to a Thesaurus.[18] On the other hand, framing the injunction in broad terms, such as barring the utterance of speech that is "fraudulent" or "defamatory" regarding the plaintiff, increases the likelihood that the court will see the order as a prior restraint.[19] When an injunction issues in an area of constitutionally protected activity, care must be taken that it not improperly intrude into and chill that activity. This issue has arisen with some frequency in the context of restricting public protests by injunctions.[20] The issue arose in connection with planned anti-war protests at the Democratic and Republican Presidential Nominating conventions in 2004. At both sites, judges upheld substantial restrictions on political demonstrations that effectively cordoned off the protests and marginalized their effectiveness.[21]

---

[14] 980 P.2d 846, 856–57 (Cal. 1999), *cert. denied*, 529 U.S. 1138 (2000). The California Supreme Court did note that it was not presented with the exact words that were uttered in the work place. *Id.* at 852.

[15] *Aguilar, supra*, 980 P.2d at 863 (Werdegar, J. concurring).

[16] Georgia Soc'y of Plastic Surgeons, Inc. v. Anderson, 363 S.E.2d 140, 144 (Ga. 1987).

[17] Lothschueltz v. Carpenter, 898 F.2d 1200, 1208–09 (6th Cir. 1990) (Wellford and Hull, Js., concurring) (involving the publication of defamatory material).

[18] Section 34 (Specificity of Injunctive Relief).

[19] *E.g.*, Metropolitan Opera Ass'n, Inc. v. Local 100, Hotel Employees and Restaurant Employees Int'l Union, 239 F.3d 172, 178 (2d Cir. 2001) (finding that order that enjoined statements regarding the plaintiff that were fraudulent or defamatory was unconstitutionally vague and amounted to a prior restraint).

[20] Section 33.1 ([Permanent Injunctions] Scope of Relief), n.10 (discussing limits on abortion protests).

[21] National Council of Arab Americans v. City of New York, 331 F. Supp.2d 258, 266–67 (S.D. N.Y. 2004) (upholding regulations prohibiting demonstrations in New York's Central Park in connection with Republican National Convention in New York City as reasonable time and place restriction); Coalition to Protest Democratic Nat'l Convention v. City of Boston, 327 F. Supp.2d 61, 71 (D. Mass. 2004) (upholding ban on demonstrations during the time the Democratic National Convention in Boston was open); *see* Bl(a)ck Tea Society v. City of Boston, 378 F.3d 8 (1st Cir. 2004) (upholding district courts limiting protesting surrounding Democratic National Convention in Boston).

An interesting example of this issue occurred in a decision involving a disaffected client of the lawyer Johnnie L. Cochran. The client and his wife picketed Cochran's Los Aneles law offices to demonstrate their complaint over the lawyer's handling a matter some years earlier. Cochran sued his former client claiming that the placards that were used in the picketing were defamatory. After plenary proceedings, the court agreed and issued a sweeping injunction that effectively precluded further picketing, *i.e.*, the client was barred from "[s]tanding, assembling or approaching within [300 yards] of (i) Cochran; or (ii) Cochran's place of business . . ." or "[i]n any public forum . . . (i) picketing Cochran [or] Cochran's law firm; (ii) "displaying signs, placards, or other written material or printed material about Cochran [or] Cochran's law firm; (iii) orally uttering statements about Cochran [or] Cochran's law firm."[22]

Prohibiting a person from being within 300 yards of another (3 football fields) seems excessive on its face,[23] as is an injunction that completely bars a person from speaking about another person! In the *Cochran* case, the death of Mr. Cochran pending the appeal complicated the issues, but the injunction also ran in favor of the Cochran Law Firm, which saved the case from mootness. The Court held that Mr. Cochran's death necessarily implicated the justification for the breadth of the injunction. Based on that point the Court reversed and vacated the injunction without reaching the underlying issue of the validity of the injunction as a prior restraint due to its terms, breadth, or length of application.

---

[22] Cochran v. Tory, 2003 Cal. App. Unpub. LEXIS 10227 (October 29, 2003) (unreported opinion), *vacated*, 125 S. Ct. 2108 (2005).

[23] *Cf.* Galella v. Onassis, 487 F.2d 986, 998 (2d Cir. 1973) (holding that injunction that barred photographer from approaching within 100 yards of Jacqueline Kennedy Onassis was overbroad and would be reduced to 25 feet); Section 33.1 (Scope of Injunctive Relief), n. 10 (collecting decisions).

Chapter 4

INJUNCTIONS

SYNOPSIS

36.4   **Effect of Appeal on Power of Trial Court to Supervise or Modify Injunction**

§§ 37—39 RESERVED

§ 30   RIPENESS, MOOTNESS, AND STANDING

Courts have been reluctant to provide certain equitable remedies, particularly injunctive relief, unless the relief is sought in the context of disputes that are proper and appropriate for judicial resolution. The terms "ripeness," "mootness," and standing have increasingly been used to describe this basic concern. The terms originated in a specific type of dispute involving judicial review of executive or agency action.[1] Today, the terms are used to describe subsets of the larger constitutional doctrine of justiciability.[2] Ripeness, mootness, and standing issues are grounded in both jurisdictional (justiciability) and equitable (prudential) concerns.[3] The basic focus for "ripeness" is an inquiry whether the threatened harm or wrong, which the injunction is designed to remedy, will occur. The basic focus for "mootness" is whether the threatened harm or injury, which the injunction is designated to remedy, will reoccur. Although the two concepts overlap, there is a distinction in that a moot case was once ripe; thus, mootness reflects the view that a claim has lost its ripeness and the question is whether it is sufficiently likely that the claim will rejuvenate later to warrant granting equitable relief now against that possible occurrence later. The core concern with "standing" is over injury-in-fact that can be redressed by court ordered injunctive relief. Standing also shares common concerns with ripeness and mootness over the appropriateness of judicial involvement in and resolution of the dispute. In many ways the distinctions between the doctrines are unauthentic; the concepts represent a single continuum rather than separate tests.[4]

---

[1] 4 KENNETH DAVIS, ADMINISTRATIVE LAW 369 (2d ed. 1983).

[2] *See* ERWIN CHEMERINSKY, FEDERAL JURISDICTION 35-145 (1989). Although in this form, the doctrines are most frequently discussed in connection with federal court decisions, the doctrines occasionally arise in the same context in state court proceedings. Pacific Legal Found. v. California Coastal Comm'n, 655 P.2d 306, 313–14 (Cal. 1982) (discussing issue of ripeness in context of review of state administrative proceeding); Alfred Eng'g, Inc. v. Illinois Fair Employment Practices Comm'n, 312 N.E.2d 61, 67 (Ill. App. 1974) (same).

[3] With respect to ripeness, see *Thomas v. Union Carbide Agric. Prods. Co.*, 473 U.S. 568, 579–82 (1985) (discussed as constitutional doctrine) and *Buckley v. Valeo*, 424 U.S. 1, 117–18 (1976) *(per curiam)* (discussed as prudential doctrine). With respect to mootness, see *United States v. W.T. Grant Co.*, 345 U.S. 629, 632 (1953) (noting that the doctrine has jurisdictional and prudential components). With respect to standing, see *Allen v. Wright*, 468 U.S. 737, 750–51 (1984) (identifying both constitution (jurisdictional) and equitable (prudential) components of the doctrine).

> All of the doctrines that cluster about Article III—not only standing but mootness, ripeness, political question, and the like—relate in part, and in different through overlapping ways, to an idea, which is more than an intuition but less than a rigorous and explicit theory, about the constitutional and prudential limits to the powers of an unelected, unrepresentative judiciary in our kind of government.

Vander Jagt v. O'Neill, 699 F.2d 1166, 1178–1179 (D.C. Cir. 1983) (Bork, J., concurring), *cited with approval in Allen v. Wright, supra*, 468 U.S. 737.

The use of ripeness, mootness, and standing in actions challenging the legality of federal, state, or local actions can be partially explained by the fact that such actions are typically brought in equity against the office holder or person charged with the responsibility to take (or not take) the challenged action. Actions are brought in this manner because the federal government and the States possess extensive sovereign immunity. That immunity, however, does not extend to the person who is acting in an allegedly illegal manner when the remedy sought is a directive or order that the person cease acting illegally or begin acting legally, or both.[5]

Ripeness, mootness, and standing concepts reflect a common concern that injunctive relief is appropriate and available to prevent future injury or harm. If the wrongful act is completed, there is little on which the injunction can act. A court will not issue an injunction to prevent the construction of a road that has been already built[6] or the demolition of a building that has already been wrecked[7] or continue a lease that has expired.[8] Injunctive relief operates prospectively and a plaintiff must show that there are future acts, or future consequences of completed acts,[9] that the requested relief will prevent or repair. The fact that the threatened act has occurred does not absolutely preclude injunctive relief, but the plaintiff's focus must move from the act to the consequences of the act. The plaintiff must show that the injunction will restore her to the position she was legally entitled to have, and would have had, but for the defendant's wrongdoing. If the completed act, e.g., construction of a road, is itself a continuing violation of the plaintiff's rightful position, she may seek injunctive relief to have the road removed or modified consistent with her legal entitlement.

[30.1]   Ripeness

It is well settled that equity will not interfere when the apprehended injury or harm is doubtful or speculative. Reasonable probability that the harm will occur is usually sufficient to negate the concern, but courts may insist on a higher standard, such as reasonable certainty of harm or a

---

[5] *Ex Parte* Young, 209 U.S. 123 (1908) (permitting federal suit for injunction against enforcement of state law by state official to proceed notwithstanding 11th Amendment limitation on suits against States in federal courts); *see* CHEMERINSKY, FEDERAL JURISDICTION, *supra*, at § 7.5.1 (Suits against state officers for injunctive relief), § 9.2.2 (Injunctive relief against the United States) (noting in both instances the use of injunctive relief directed at government officials as a time-honored means of avoiding the defense of sovereign immunity).

[6] Griffith v. Dept. Public Works, 345 P.2d 469 (Cal. 1959) (freeway).

[7] Flood v. Goldstein (E.L.) Co., 110 P. 916 (Cal. 1910).

[8] *Id.*; *see* Friends of the Earth, Inc. v. Bergland, 576 F.2d 1377, 1379 (9th Cir. 1978) (stating that "[w]here the activities sought to be enjoined have already occurred, and the appellate courts cannot undo what has already been done, the action is moot").

[9] Sahlobei v. Providence Healthcare, 5 Cal. Rptr. 3d 598 (Cal. App. 2003) (physician who was terminated sought injunction restoring his staff privileges pending the hearing he was wrongfully denied before he was terminated); Bell v. Southwell, 376 F.2d 659 (5th Cir. 1967) (candidate defeated in local election sought injunction requiring new election on ground prior election had been conducted in atmosphere of racial fear and intimidation); Section 30.2.3 (Continuing Effects).

showing that there will necessarily be a wrong.[10] Injunctive relief is granted to prevent threatened infractions of legally protected interests, not to allay mere fears that legal interests will be harmed.[11]

An injunction should not be granted under a "can't hurt" theory.[12] This rule derives from the general principle that every person is presumed to obey the law and, absent credible evidence to the contrary, a court should not use its equity powers, backed up by the sanction of contempt, to enjoin a person who has not demonstrated a desire, propensity, or intent to do wrong.[13] Decisions applying these principles, admittedly to not always consistent results, are legion. For example, in *Hudson v. School District of Kansas City*[14] plaintiff sought to enjoin the defendant school district from violating the state open meeting requirements (Sunshine Law). The court rejected the injunction noting:

> On the issue of a continuing injunction to restrain future violations of the Sunshine Law, there was no proof of any sort in the hearing before the trial court that the school board contemplated, planned, or even threatened to conduct any future meetings in a manner violative of the Sunshine Law. In fact, it is apparent from the record that the school district was attempting to comply with what its understanding was of the restrictions of Chapter 610 and, in the absence of authoritative judicial interpretation of the provisions of the statute, they failed to properly observe its mandate. In this respect, the instant case is very much like *St. Louis 221 Club*, in which there was a dispute between the parties with respect to the meaning of the lease contract, and the court held that a continuing injunction was not necessary since there was no reason to believe that once the contract issue had been settled, the defendants would not comply with its terms. Here, too, there is no evidence and

---

[10] Beck Dev. Co., Inc. v. S. Pac. Transp. Co., 52 Cal. Rptr. 2d 518, 540 (Cal. App. 1996) (enjoining a nuisance).

[11] Osborn v. Grant County, 896 P.2d 111, 113 (Wash. App. 1995); Manufacturers Hanover Trust Co. v. Kingston Investors Corp., 819 S.W.2d 607, 611 (Tex. Ct. App. 1991); *cf.* Chalk v. United States Dist. Court, Central Dist. Cal., 840 F.2d 701, 706–07 (9th Cir. 1988) (stating that possibility that AIDS infected teacher's return to classroom would produce fear and apprehension on part of students and parents did not warrant denial of injunctive relief when fear and apprehension were unfounded in fact).

[12] Humble Oil & Refining Co. v. Harang, 262 F. Supp. 39, 42 (E.D. La. 1966) (stating that "[t]he necessity for the injunction [to prevent destruction of documents] must be demonstrated clearly. Injunctions will not be issued merely to allay the fears and foreboding or to soothe the anxieties of the parties"); City & County of San Francisco v. Market Street Ry. Co., 213 P.2d 780, 785 (Cal. App. 1950) (stating that an "injunction is not a proper remedy to prevent a person from doing an act which he has never undertaken or threatened to undertake").

[13] East Bay Mun. Util. Dist. v. Department of Forestry & Fire Prot., 51 Cal. Rptr. 2d 299, 309 (Cal. App. 1996); *cf.* Paraco, Inc. v. Owens, 333 P.2d 360, 363 (Cal. App. 1959) (stating that in order to obtain injunctive relief to prevent a former employee from disclosing confidential information, the former employer must show an actual, real threat of disclosure).

[14] 578 S.W.2d 301 (Mo. App. 1979).

certainly no implication that the school board will not conduct future meetings in accordance with the statute as here construed.[15]

Similarly, in *Tubular Threading, Inc. v. Scandaliato*[16] the trial court enjoined the defendant, who had designed and built a "pipe handling system" for plaintiff, from using, selling, distributing, or otherwise disseminating any shop drawing or other document related to the system. The appellate court agreed that the system qualified as a trade secret, but reversed as to the issuance of the injunction reasoning:

> In the instant matter, the trial judge said that he was not convinced that Scandaliato had violated any ethical canons of the engineering profession, duplicated Tubular Threading's drawings or violated any trade secret law. The injunction was ". . . to forestall future problems." The trial judge's language indicates that his order was not necessitated by a clear and present need. The trial judge found no actual or threatened misappropriation of a trade secret . . . and the record does not show that there was either an actual or threatened misappropriation. Accordingly, the injunction was inappropriate, no matter how well-intentioned the trial judge was.[17]

On the other hand, it is not required that a defendant engage in conduct analogous to the law of criminal attempt before the case will be deemed ripe. The critical issue is the likelihood that the defendant will engage in conduct that will violate the plaintiff's legally protectible interests. As the Supreme Court noted in the context of justiciability ripeness: "[R]ipeness is peculiarly a question of timing."[18] "[I]ts basic rationale is to prevent the courts, through avoidance of premature adjudication, from entangling themselves in abstract disagreements."[19] The critical focus is future oriented and probablistic.[20]

In most instances, proof of a "reasonable likelihood" of future harm is all that is required to satisfy the equitable ripeness test. The more likely it is that the future violation or injury will occur, the more likely a court is to grant an injunction to prevent the violation or injury from happening. Evidence that the defendant is inclined or disposed to engage in future violations will tend to satisfy the likelihood standard,[21] particularly, if the

---

[15] *Id.* at 313 (citation omitted).

[16] 443 So. 2d 712 (La. App. 1983).

[17] *Id.* at 715 (citation omitted). *Compare* Air Prods. and Chems., Inc. v. Johnson, 442 A.2d 1114 (Pa. Super. Ct. 1982) (finding that protection of trade secrets may require prohibiting former employee from engaging in certain lines of work), *with* Lemmon v. Hendrickson, 559 N.W.2d 278 (Iowa 1997) (rejecting injunctive relief barring former employee from soliciting or servicing customers from an alleged misappropriated customer list because there was no evidence the former employee had appropriated list for his use or disclosed its contents to another). *See* Section 154 (Employer's Injunction Against Employee).

[18] Thomas v. Union Carbide Agric. Prods. Co., 473 U.S. 568, 580 (1985).

[19] Abbott Labs. v. Gardner, 387 U.S. 136, 148 (1967).

[20] *Cf.* Steffel v. Thompson, 415 U.S. 452, 460 (1974) (noting that likelihood of future injury must be "of sufficient immediacy and reality to warrant the issuance of declaratory judgment").

[21] *Id.* at 458 ("The prosecution of petitioner's handbilling companion is ample demonstration

court perceives that the defendant's past wrongdoing, even in another area, makes him particularly disposed to engage in conduct the injunction would prevent.[22]

The "reasonable likelihood" requirement serves several basic policies inherent in the ripeness doctrine. First, injunctive relief is necessarily future oriented:

> Equity acts in the present tense and not in the past tense. An injunction will not be granted where, at the time of the hearing, conditions have so changed that no unlawful act is threatened. The injunctive power is not wielded as a punishment for past acts. It will be ordered only when there is evidence the acts enjoined will probably recur.[23]

The "reasonable likelihood" requirement helps assure that the exercise of equity jurisdiction will not be an idle act. Unless courts have some reasoned basis for believing that the injury or harm will occur, courts have no basis for enjoining a defendant to prevent that injury or harm from occurring. In other words, courts need a basis for believing that the defendant will not obey the law.[24] The requirement may be relaxed for particular cases when public policy warrants.[25]

Second, the "reasonable likelihood" requirement helps ensure that the issues presented by the case are fit for judicial resolution at the time adjudication is sought.[26] By requiring that a certain probability threshold be met,

---

that petitioner's concern with arrest has not been 'chimerical,'" *quoting*, Poe v. Ullman, 367 U.S. 497, 508 (1961)). The petitioner in *Stefel* had been twice warned before to cease the handbilling activity and warned that if he disobeyed a warning to stop, he would be arrested.

[22] Dodge, Warren & Peters Insurance Services v. Riley, 130 Cal. Rptr. 2d 385 (Cal. App. 2003) (holding that the California Discovery Act did not constitute an adequate remedy at law so as to preclude an injunction barring the potential destruction of material subject to discovery). The court's opinion never really addressed the likelihood of destruction issue rather, it was apparently sufficient that defendant was a bad person who might engage in document destruction that would amount to irreparable injury. *Cf. Humble Oil & Refining Co.*, *supra*, 262 F. Supp. 39 (discussed at note 12, *supra*).

[23] Engle v. City of Oroville, 47 Cal. Rptr. 630, 632 (Cal. App. 1965) (citations omitted).

[24] Aulenback, Inc. v. Federal Highway Admin., 103 F.3d 156, 166 (D.C. Cir. 1997) (ripeness doctrine serves "to prevent courts, through avoidance of premature adjudication, from entangling themselves in abstract disagreements . . . to protect . . . agencies from judicial interference until an administrative decision has been formalized, and its effects felt in a concrete way . . .", *quoting*, Abbott Labs. v. Gardner, 387 U.S. 136, 148–49 (1967)).

[25] State ex rel Missouri Bd. For Architects, Prof'l Eng'rs and Land Surveyors v. Henigman, 937 S.W.2d 757, 759 (Mo. App. 1997) (holding that to obtain injunction against unauthorized practice without a license it is not necessary to show that the person might again engage in unauthorized conduct in the future).

[26] *Abbott Labs.*, *supra*, 387 U.S. at 149; Bauer v. Waste Mgmt. of Conn., Inc., 686 A.2d 481, 486 (Conn. 1996) (stating that "[w]hether a party is entitled to injunctive relief is determined by the situation that has developed at the time of trial, not by the situation that existed when the action was commenced") (citations omitted); Mallon v. City of Long Beach, 330 P.2d 423, 430 (Cal. App. 1958) (noting that the critical viewpoint is the condition existing at the time of the hearing, not the time the action accrues or is commenced).

the ability to frame the issues, present a defense, and draft a specific order, if warranted, is enhanced. The "reasonable likelihood" requirement helps to narrow the case, particularize it, and make it more focused by making it less abstract and general.[27]

Third, the "reasonable likelihood" requirement helps avoid any unnecessary hardship being visited on the plaintiff. A hardship may exist, for example, when a plaintiff is forced to choose between alternatives, each of which carries significant costs if the choice is wrong.[28] For this "hardship" argument to be meaningful, the risk must be real not speculative. The "reasonable likelihood" test helps insure that the risk is real, which is to say that the plaintiff will likely be required to make the choice and incur the costs the choice will entail even though the directive may be illegal and no choice should be required and no costs, associated with that choice, should be incurred.

[30.2] Mootness

If the central concern with ripeness is whether the claim of future harm is sufficiently alive to warrant application of equitable remedies, mootness addresses whether the claim is really dead. In this context there are two types of death. A claim that is truely dead, *i.e.* there is no realistic chance of revival, is jurisdictionally moot. In other words, there is no case or controversy.[29] A claim that has a possibility of revival, even one that is slim, permits the discretionary exercise of equity jurisdiction and the providing of equitable remedies to prevent the harm that revival of the wrongful practice would engender.[30] As is the case with ripeness, the concern here is over the likelihood that equitable relief is needed to address future injury.[31]

What distinguishes mootness from ripeness is the emphasis on the likelihood that the wrongful conduct will be revived, whereas with ripeness the concern was whether it would ever occur at all. "Injunctive power is

---

[27] Allstate Ins. Co. v. Wayne County, 760 F.2d 689, 696 (6th Cir. 1985).

[28] *Aulenback, Inc., supra*, 103 F.3d at 167–68 (stating that "hardship" is shown when plaintiff is forced to choose between serious sanctions for non-compliance or substantial costs of compliance with allegedly illegal directive).

[29] Commodity Futures Trading Comm'n v. Board of Trade of City of Chicago, 701 F.2d 653, 655 (7th Cir. 1983) (stating that "[a]lthough mootness is sometimes painted in black and white . . . it really should be painted in shades of gray, since few controversies are wholly beyond the power of changed circumstances to revive; but the probability of revival is too small in this case to allow a federal court to exercise jurisdiction") (citation omitted). This can be more than a metaphor. Bowman v. Corrections Corp. of America, 350 F.3d 537, 549–50 (6th Cir. 2003) (holding that death of claimant rendered moot claim for injunctive relief concerning prison medical policies that harmed claimant).

[30] United States v. W.T. Grant Co., 345 U.S. 629, 633 (1953) ("holding that [a]long with its power to hear the case, the court's power to grant injunctive relief survives discontinuance of the illegal conduct").

[31] Weiss v. Pederson, 933 P.2d 495, 499 (Wyo. 1997); Bouma v. Bynum Irrig. Dist., 364 P.2d 47, 49 (Mont. 1961).

not used as punishment for past acts and is ordered against [past acts] only if there is evidence they will probably recur. . . . A court of equity will not afford an injunction to prevent in the future that which in good faith has been discontinued, in the absence of any evidence that the acts are likely to be repeated in the future."[32] A case may become moot when the relevant law changes[33] or when the allegedly wrongful behavior has ceased and is not expected to reoccur.[34]

In one very meaningful sense ripeness and mootness are flipsides of the same coin. The same past acts that help establish that the threatened act will occur (ripeness) can be conceptualized as evidencing that established conduct will reoccur (mootness). What distinguishes the two doctrines is that a mootness inquiry is usually generated by the added fact that the defendant has acted in the interim in some manner that suggests that the past pattern of conduct has stopped or the plaintiff's circumstances have changed so that she is no longer affected by the conduct. The first situation is captured by the "voluntary cessation of activities" doctrine; the second situation by the "capable of repetition yet evading review" doctrine.

[30.2.1] Voluntary Cessation

The mere fact that a defendant has ceased the conduct that threatens future injury does not necessarily mean that a claim for injunctive relief is moot. Were the practice otherwise, a defendant could skillfully evade the imposition of injunctive relief by stopping and starting the wrongful conduct. Once the threat of judicial intervention passed, the defendant could revert to its old ways.[35] The voluntary cessation rule is based on practicalities. It recognizes that once past wrongdoing has been established, the "likelihood" of future repetition confers power and discretion on the court to provide injunctive relief. The critical inquiry in these matters is "how" likely must the prospect or threat of reoccurrence be before equitable relief is available. Unlike the ripeness cases, where a "reasonable likelihood" test appears to be the dominant approach, cases in this area tend to use a lesser probability threshold. The reason appears to be the presence of a baseline of wrongful activity, a fact not present in ripeness cases, when

---

[32] Dawson v. East Side Union High Sch. Dist., 34 Cal. Rptr. 2d 108, 130 (Cal. App. 1994) (citations omitted; brackets added); see Dufresne v. Veneman, 114 F.3d 952, 954–55 (9th Cir. 1997) (per curiam) (holding that action to enjoin airborne spraying of pesticide to eradicate Medfly was moot; state had no plans in foreseeable future to resume airborne application of pesticide; mere speculative fear that airborne application may be renewed is insufficient).

[33] United States v. Alaska S.S. Co., 253 U.S. 113, 115 (1920) (holding that change in law party was challenging rendered challenge moot).

[34] S.E.C. v. Medical Comm. For Human Rights, 404 U.S. 403, 405–06 (1972) (noting that subsequent acquiescence of company in placing proposal before shareholders, who rejected it by margin negating any further legal obligation to place similar proposal before shareholders, mooted challenge to earlier rejection by company of similar proposal).

[35] United States v. W.T. Grant Co., 345 U.S. 629, 635 (1953); Chaffin v. Kansas State Fair Bd., 348 F.3d 850 (10th Cir. 2003) (stating that defendant's dilatory and diffident efforts to bring itself in compliance with the Americans With Disabilities Act counselled against treating the case as moot notwithstanding the fact that defendant was currently in compliance).

the wrongful conduct is only threatened. This baseline provides a factual foundation demonstrating a defendant's proclivity for wrongful conduct. [36] Ripeness asks whether the defendant will "do it." In mootness cases the defendant "did do it," the only inquiry here is whether the defendant has really been cured of its proclivity or is he a recidivist who will do it again if given the chance. We see, therefore, much lower thresholds than "reasonable likelihood" in many of the decisions. Many courts articulate a "mere possibility" test. [37] In some cases this has been reduced, at least linguistically, even further to a "reasonable fear" test. [38] The cases reflect some uncertainty whether the mere presence of past violations, now ceased, will support injunctive relief. Some courts will draw an inference that violations will continue and use this inference to support the award of injunctive relief. [39] Other courts refuse to do so. [40] Perhaps the dominant and most sensible approach is one that emphasizes the facts of each case and the types of factors that support or diminish the likelihood of reoccurrence: A court should not issue an injunction unless there exists some cognizable danger of recurrent violation. The determination that such danger exists must "be based on appropriate findings supported by the record." The Court identified a number of factors in *United States v. W.T. Grant*:

- Bona fideness of the expressed intent to comply with the law (versus, I suppose, recalcitrance or intent to test or challenge the law).

- Effectiveness of the discontinuance of the activity.

- Character of past violations. [41]

---

[36] City of Los Angeles v. Lyons, 461 U.S. 95, 102 (1983) (stating that " '[p]ast wrongs' [are] evidence bearing on 'whether there is a real and immediate threat of repeated injury' ") (citations omitted).

[37] Atlantic Richfield Co. v. Oil, Chem. and Atomic Workers Int'l Union, AFL-CIO, 447 F.2d 945, 947 (7th Cir. 1971) (stating that "[i]f past wrongs have been proved, and the possibility of future misconduct survives, so does the court's power"); *cf. Engle, supra,* 47 Cal. Rptr. at 633 (holding that court abused its discretion in granting permanent injunction when conditions creating need for injunctive relief had abated and there was "no possibility" that conditions would reoccur).

[38] United States v. Massachusetts Maritime Academy, 762 F.2d 142, 157 (1st Cir. 1985) (enjoining sex discrimination).

[39] S.E.C. v. Washington County Util. Dist., 676 F.2d 218, 227 (6th Cir. 1982) (stating that evidence of past violations provide basis for inference that future violations may occur); United States v. Hopkins Dodge Sales, Inc., 661 F. Supp. 1155, 1158 (D. Minn. 1987) (same); *see* N.A.A.C.P. v. City of Evergreen, Ala., 693 F.2d 1367, 1370 (11th Cir. 1982) (stating that "in cases presenting abundant evidence of consistent past discrimination, injunctive relief is mandatory absent clear and convincing proof that there is no reasonable probability of further noncompliance with the law") (citation omitted).

[40] *Mallon, supra,* 330 P.2d at 431 (stating that injunction should not issue unless "reasonable probability that past acts complained of will recur"). *See also* Home Placement Serv., Inc. v. Providence Journal Co., 573 F. Supp. 1423, 1427 (D.R.I. 1983) (showing must consist of "some cognizable danger of recurrent violation, something more than the mere possibility which serves to keep the case alive").

[41] 345 U.S. at 633.

Additional factors that a court may consider in making this finding include the degree of scienter involved; the isolated or recurrent nature of the infraction; the defendant's recognition of the wrongful nature of his conduct; the extent to which the defendant's professional and personal characteristics might enable or tempt him to commit future violations; and the sincerity of any assurances against future violations.[42] Courts have also been more willing to find that the complained of activities will reoccur when they are embedded in a policy that is "deeply rooted and long standing."[43] In determining whether a defendant may resume the activity, a court may also consider the cost of resumption, the time it would take to resume the activity, and the visibility, *i.e.,* detectability, of resumption efforts. The more difficult it would be for the defendant to resume the wrongful activities, the more likely it is that cessation is permanent.

[30.2.2] Capable of Repetition

The "capable of repetition, yet avoiding review" doctrine applies to situations where: "(1) the challenged action was in its duration too short to be fully litigated prior to its cessation or expiration, and (2) there was a reasonable expectation that the same complaining party would be subjected to the same action again."[44] The focus of most decisions is on the second prong of the test, the "capable of repetition" issue; satisfaction of the durational element tends to be self evident. The critical issue is how likely must it be that the action will reoccur and affect the complaining party?[45] This resolution can be subtly influenced by the position of the court making the decision. Evasion of review is usual a greater concern when appellate review is concerned because of the time delay involved. For example, in *Super Tire Engineering Co. v. McCorkle* an employer sought declaratory relief that a state practice of paying striking employees unemployment compensation violated federal law. The strike settled, but the Court stated that the case was not moot because the employees could go on strike again.[46] If that event occurred, the employer could obtain relief at the trial level and perhaps even at the interim appellate level through expedited review. It was, however, unlikely, absent a lengthy, prolonged

---

[42] United States v. Laerdal Mfg. Co., 73 F.3d 852, 854–55 (9th Cir. 1995); S.E.C. v. National Student Mktg. Corp., 402 F. Supp. 641, 651 (D.D.C. 1975).

[43] Westbrook v. Teton County Sch. Dist. No. 1, 918 F. Supp. 1475, 1497 (D. Wyo. 1996).

[44] Spencer v. Kemna, 523 U.S. 1, 17 (1998); *see* General Land Office of State of Tex. v. Oxy U.S.A., Inc., 789 S.W.2d 569, 571 (Tex. 1990). *But cf.* Majors v. Abell, 317 F.3d 719, 723 (7th Cir. 2003) (noting disagreement as to consistent application of the "same complaining party" requirement); Van Vie v. Pataki, 267 F.3d 109, 114 (2d Cir. 2001) (same). *See* text and notes 52–53, *infra.*

[45] The rules differ slightly in class action contexts insofar as it concerns the requirement that the reoccurrence affect the same complainant. A jurisdiction that does not use "class action" procedures may adopt a modified "capable of repetition" exception. Mississippi High Sch. l Activities Ass'n, Inc. v. Coleman, 631 So. 2d 768, 773 (Miss. 1994) (applying exception when it is shown that (1) duration of challenged action is short, but (2) time required to complete an appeal is lengthy).

[46] 416 U.S. 115, 125 (1974).

strike that the employees would remain on strike for the duration of all appeals. Application of the mootness doctrine would frustrate a complete legal challenge to the state practice. [47] On the other hand, it was not shown that the practice could not have been challenged in another format, as, for example a suit for refund of increased taxes or charges due to the increase in the employer's unemployment compensation tax rate resulting from the increased number of claims. If such an alternative existed it would undermine a claim that the practice was "avoiding review." [48]

There must also be a realistic possibility of reoccurrence. A unique, isolated event is unlikely to generate reasonable claims of the possibility of "reoccurrence" after the event is completed. For example, in *Boston Herald, Inc. v. Superior Court Department of Trial Court* [49] plaintiff challenged a closed arraignment held at the intensive care unit of a hospital as a violation of the public's right of access to judicial proceedings. The court held the issue was moot since the arraignment had already been held. It rejected application of the "capable of repetition" exception on the ground that the likelihood of the event occurring again was highly speculative. [50] This is a consistent theme. Characterization of the likelihood of reoccurrence as a "theoretical possibility" means the court will find the claim moot. [51]

Some courts have expressly combined the "capable of repetition" exception with a public policy gloss. In *Loisel v. Rowe* the court added to the standard two part requirement of "short duration" and "reasonable likelihood" the additional requirement that the matter have a public, as opposed to merely personal, import. [52] The test is substantially similar to the

---

[47] The frustration of review can occur at lower levels. Time is the critical factor. It will most frequently frustrate appellate review, but may occasionally frustrate even lower level review. Mendonza v. Commonwealth, 673 N.E.2d 22, 27 (Mass. 1996) (involving a pretrial detention statute).

[48] Lawson v. City of Santa Barbara, 310 F.3d 1134, 1136–37 (9th Cir. 2002) (holding that state provision of expedited review of decisions denying parade permits undermined claim that time delays would frustrate the providing of judicial relief if the defendant were improperly denied a permit under its applicable local ordinance), *opinion withdrawn and memorandum disposition filed instead*, 314 F.3d 1070 (9th Cir. 2002) (granting plaintiffs leave to amend their complaint to allege that permit requirement would affect planned future parades). In *Lawson*, after the plaintiff brought a lawsuit challenging the permit requirement, the City dropped all of its conditions save one and the parade was held. Plaintiffs wished to continue the lawsuit challenging the permit requirement on First Amendment grounds. The City argued the case was moot because the parade had already taken place.

[49] 658 N.E.2d 152 (Mass. 1995).

[50] *Id.* at 154.

[51] Haley v. Pataki, 60 F.3d 137, 141 (2d Cir. 1995); *see* Trane Co. v. O'Connor Secs., 718 F.2d 26, 27 (2d Cir. 1983) (holding that the likelihood that defendant would again obtain 5% ownership interest in plaintiff so as to trigger requirements of Section 13D of the 34 Securities & Exchange Act was only "abstractly conceivable"; therefore, the contention was moot).

[52] 660 A.2d 323, 330 (Conn. 1995); *see* Bradway v. Cohen, 642 A.2d 615, 617 (Pa. Comm. Ct. 1994) (stating that the court may decide moot cases "where issue presented is of great public importance, involves exceptional circumstances, or is capable of repetition . . .").

traditional test except that it relaxes the requirement that the reoccurrence affect the complaining party. It is sufficient if it affects a similarly situated person for whom the complaining party serves as a surrogate or representative. The test effectively incorporates approaches the United States Supreme Court has developed to deal with mootness in class action contexts, when much of the focus is on the representatives's ability to present the claims of those not directly before the court,[53] to cases not using class action procedures.

An appeal of a preliminary injunction may be rendered moot when the action required by the injunction is completed and unlikely to reoccur. In *Harris v. Blue Cross/Blue Shield of Missouri*[54] the plaintiff obtained a preliminary injunction requiring the defendant to fund chemotherapy treatments. The treatments were provided. Defendant appealed from the decision granting temporary equitable relief. The court held that while irreparable injury surely existed at the time the injunction was granted, it does not exist now. Plaintiff had received the treatment and was not a candidate for repeat treatment. The issue was therefore limited to money damages and moot as to the claim that the district court abused its discretion in granting the preliminary injunction.[55] This mootness application only extends, however, to the decision to grant injunctive relief; it does not extend to any collateral issues that remain alive notwithstanding the inability to challenge directly the decision to grant the injunction. For example, if the preliminary injunction was bonded,[56] the matter remains alive and the propriety of the issuance of the injunction may be considered to determine if relief against the bond should be afforded.[57]

[30.2.3] Continuing Effects

The fact that the complained of activity has occurred or been completed does not necessarily mean that the case is moot. If the completed activity is still generating harmful effects, injunctive relief may be appropriate to remove the source of the continuing harm. A defendant that has ceased committing wrongful acts may still be required to prevent further and future harm flowing from those past acts.[58] On the other hand, if it is clear

---

[53] County of Riverside v. McLaughlin, 500 U.S. 44, 50–51 (1991).

[54] 995 F.2d 877 (8th Cir. 1993).

[55] *Id.* at 879; Honig v. Students of Cal. Sch. For the Blind, 471 U.S. 148, (1985) (per curiam) (holding that challenges to preliminary injunction ordering seismic safety testing was moot when tests had been completed and were not likely to be undertaken again).

[56] Section 31.7 (Bond Requirement).

[57] University of Texas v. Camenisch, 451 U.S. 390, 397 (1981).

[58] Legal Assistance for Vietnamese Asylum Seekers, et. al. v. Department of State, Bureau of Consular Affairs, 104 F.3d 1349, 1352 (D.C. Cir. 1997); Lampkin v. District of Columbia, 886 F. Supp. 56, 62 (D.D.C. 1995). These orders are common in environmental clean up disputes. E.g. Comprehensive Environmental Response, Compensation, and Liability Act of 1980 (alternatively known as CERCLA or Superfund Act), 42 U.S.C. § 9601 *et. seq.* and Resource Conservation & Recovery Act of 1976, 42 U.S.C. § 690 *et. seq.*, particularly § 6972. Note that in this context, injunctive relief may be more efficient than a damages award. A

that the completed acts have neither continuing effects nor the possibility of reoccurence, the case is moot.[59]

The question may arise whether the defendant may attempt to strategically preempt claims so as to moot the controversy. For example, may a defendant settle or concede liability by making a Rule 68 offer to named representatives of a class to prevent class certification? The few decisions that have considered the issue have held that the tactic may not be used purposively to defeat class certification.[60]

[30.3] Standing

The law in this area has been characterized both as "a morass that confuses more than it clarifies[61] and as "remarkably well settled."[62] Both views are correct. The law of standing has been consistently described by the Court as consisting of both a core constitutional component and a broader prudential penumbra. The constitutional core consists of a three part test that is designed to demonstrate that the legal dispute has the requisite "concrete adverseness" to satisfy the constitutional "case or controversy" requirement.[63] The core constitutional tests requires that the plaintiff demonstrate that:

---

damages award may miscalculate the actual remediation costs, but injunctive relief avoids this problem because there is no time lag between determining the cost of remediation and doing the remediation when an injunction is issued.

[59] Freedom from Religion Found., Inc. v. Romer, 921 P.2d 84, 88 (Colo. 1996) (stating that challenge to temporary closure of public park to facilitate visit of Pope was moot since return visit unlikely); cf. Fishbeck v. State of N.D., 115 F.3d 580 (8th Cir. 1997) (finding that mother of male circumcised child could not challenge, as underinclusive, state statute that criminalized female but not male circumcision; relief could not help already circumcised male and likelihood that woman would have another male child and be forced by father to circumcise child against her will was too speculative to confer standing on her to challenge statute as underinclusive).

[60] Weiss v. Regal Collections, 385 F.3d 337 (3d Cir. 2004) (noting conflict between Rules 23 and 68 of the Federal Rules of Civil Procedure as to whether an offer of judgment to named class representative prior to class certification moots claim). The court resolved the conflict by holding that in such cases the appropriate procedure is to relate class certification back to the date the class complaint was filed, which prevents the mooting of the claim by the offer of judgment to only the named class representative(s). Id. at 348; Nasca v. GC Services L.P., 2002 U.S. Dist. LEXIS 16992, 53 Fed. R. Serv. 3d 1089 (S.D.N.Y. 2002) (rejecting tactic as improper "pickoff" strategy that frustrates class action procedures prescribed by Fed. R. Civ. P. 23)

[61] Erwin Chemerinsky, A Unified Approach to Justiciability, 22 Conn. L. Rev. 677 (1990). Admittedly, Professor Chemerinsky was addressing the broader topic of justiciability rather than its subpart "standing", but the characterization fits the part as well as the whole. Professor Chemerinsky makes the same point in his discussion of "standing" in his treatise. CHEMERINSKY, FEDERAL JURISDICTION, supra at § 2.3, p. 48.

[62] Gene R. Nicol, Jr., Standing For Privilege: The Failure of Injury Analysis, 82 B. U. L. Rev. 301 (2002) (speaking "in the most superficial sense").

[63] Whether the constitution requires, or should require, "concrete adverseness" as that term is used by the Court is beyond the scope of this work. For commentary on the point, see David M. Driesen, Standing For Nothing: The Paradox of Demanding Concrete Context For Formalistic Adjudication, 89 Corn. L. Rev. 808 (2004) (criticizing reliance on "concrete adverseness" as meaningful device to identify appropriate instances for exercise of judicial

- the injury she has suffered is concrete, particularized, and actual or imminent ("injury in fact")

- the injury is fairly traceable to the conduct of the defendants ("cause in fact")

- the requested relief would likely redress the injury suffered ("redressibility in fact")[64]

There is also a prudential (discretionary) component to standing. The exact scope of this prudential doctrine is unclear. It is invoked most often in cases when the plaintiff is attempting to assert the rights of third parties, e.g., physicians asserting rights of patients or organizations asserting the rights of their members. The difficulty here is the myriad ways in which one party, e.g., the plaintiff, may have a relationship with another, e.g., the third party. A test formulated to deal with one relationship, e.g., organizations and their constituents[65] may be illsuited and provide a poor fit if it is extrapolated to other relations, e.g., physician-patient.

As with all contentious doctrines, the problem in comprehending standing lies not just in the blackletter law, but in the application. It is here that characterization of the doctrine as a "morass" is perhaps most accurate for it is difficult to identify a principled, consistent application of the doctrine in the cases. Much of the difficulty exists in the blurred lines that separate ripeness, mootness, and standing and the different results that can arise if a problem is characterized as falling under one doctrine rather than another. In *Steffel v. Thompson*[66] the plaintiff sought a declaratory judgment that he could distribute anti-war handbills at a shopping center. The Court held that the case was ripe because on prior occasions the police had responded to complaints by owners of the center and, on one occasion, plaintiff's companion had been arrested when he failed to leave the center.[67] On the other hand, in *Park v. Forest Service*[68] the plaintiff sought injunctive relief against the use of checkpoints that plaintiff claimed were targeted at her group. The court held that the past use of an unconstitutional checkpoint with respect to plaintiff's group was insufficient to establish standing.[69] The court also deemed irrelevant the fact that the

---

review); Ann Woolhander & Caleb Nelson, *Does History Defeat Standing Doctrine*, 102 Mich. L. Rev. 689 (2004) (responding to commentators who contend that the law of standing is a judicial makeweight).

[64] Friends of the Earth, Inc. v. Laidlaw Envtl. Servs., 528 U.S. 167, 180–81 (2000).

[65] Hunt v. Washington State Apple Advertising Comm'n, 432 U.S. 333, 343 (1977):

[A]n association has standing to bring suit on behalf of its members when: (a) its members would otherwise have standing to sue in their own right; (b) the interests it seeks to protect are germane to the organization's purpose; and (c) neither the claim asserted nor the relief requested requires participation of individual members in the lawsuit.

[66] 415 U.S. 452 (1974).

[67] *Id.* at 462.

[68] 205 F.3d 1034 (8th Cir. 2000).

[69] "Past exposure to illegal conduct does not in itself show a present case or controversy

defendant had continued to use the unconstitutional checkpoints in 1997, 1998, and 1999 because "these events occurred after Ms. Parks filed her original complaint.[70]

Cases in which plaintiffs seek injunctive relief to prevent a recurrence in the future of a course of conduct engaged in by the defendant in the past are sometimes treated under "ripeness" analysis and sometimes under "standing" analysis. In *Shotz v. Cates*[71] plaintiffs claimed that architectural barriers impeded their attendance at a public courthouse in violation of the Americans with Disabilities Act (ADA). The court held that the facility was in violation of the ADA, but injunctive relief would not be granted because plaintiffs' injuries were conjectural—they had not alleged an intent or attempt to revisit the courthouse since their earlier unsuccessful effort.[72] "Ripeness" analysis would ask how likely is it that were plaintiffs to revisit the facility they would meet the same obstacle that frustrated their earlier visit.[73] The plaintiffs past effort to access the courthouse, coupled with the court's concession that an ADA claim was stated, would have likely satisfied a "ripeness" inquiry because the issues in the dispute were "fit" for judicial decision.[74] When, on the other hand, the "possibility of future harm" is related to injury-in-fact, the courts undertake a standing analysis.[75] Unfortunately, we do not have a "meta-rule" that tells us when courts will adopt one approach over the other.

§ 31 TEMPORARY INJUNCTIVE RELIEF

[31.1] Forms of Relief

Temporary injunctive relief consists of two closely related remedies: the temporary restraining order (TRO) and the preliminary injunction. Both are designed to provide immediate but durationally limited injunctive relief.

---

regarding injunctive relief . . . if unaccompanied by continuing, present adverse effects." *Id.* at 1037, *citing and quoting* O'Shea v. Littleton, 414 U.S. 674 (1974), but ignoring that the key fact in *O'Shea* was that the personnel enforcing the allegedly unconstitutional policy changed after the complaint was filed and the complained of actions were not repeated by the new administration.

[70] *Id.*:

> We believe that it is Ms. Parks' burden to show that, at the time she filed her suit in 1996, there was a real and immediate threat that she would again be subjected by the Forest Service to an unconstitutional checkpoint. We do not think that she may use evidence of what happened after the commencement of the suit to make this showing.

[71] 256 F.3d 1077 (11th Cir. 2001).

[72] *Id.* at 1081–82.

[73] National Rifle Ass'n of America v. Magaw, 132 F.3d 272, 280, 284 (6th Cir. 1997) (stating that "ripeness" focuses on whether future events may or may not occur).

[74] Cleveland Branch, N.A.A.C.P. v. City of Parma, Ohio, 263 F.3d 513, 533–34 (6th Cir. 2001), *cert. denied*, 535 U.S. 971 (2002).

[75] *Park v. Forest Service, supra,* 205 F.3d 1034.

While permanent injunctive relief is obtained at the conclusion of a plenary trial on the merits as part of the final judgment, temporary injunctive relief is usually obtained in less complete proceedings.

The TRO is usually described as an extraordinary remedy reserved for emergency situations.[1] The procedures surrounding the obtaining of a TRO tend to be less formal given the time constraints that attend to true emergency situations and the need for immediate legal relief. TROs are normally of short duration, e.g., 10–20 days, and are usually designed to bridge the gap and maintain the status quo until the request for a preliminary injunction can be heard by the court.

The procedures surrounding the obtaining of a preliminary injunction tend to be more formal,[2] which reflects the usual longer duration of a preliminary injunction vis à vis a TRO. Nonetheless, "formality" is relative. As noted by the Court:

> The purpose of a preliminary injunction is merely to preserve the relative positions of the parties until a trial on the merits can be held. Given this limited purpose, and given the haste that is often necessary if those positions are to be preserved, a preliminary injunction is customarily granted on the basis of procedures that are less formal and evidence that is less complete than in a trial on the merits. A party thus is not required to prove his case in full at a preliminary-injunction hearing . . . .[3]

Preliminary injunctions are usually sought through noticed motions.[4] They are normally subject to the requirements that Findings of Fact and Conclusions of Law accompany their issuance;[5] however, the findings and conclusions "made by a court granting a preliminary injunction are not binding at the trial on the merits."[6]

The differences between TROs and preliminary injunctions should not, however, be overemphasized. Both require notice of the intent to seek relief; the exception for ex parte TROs without notice are rare.[7] Both TROs and

---

[1] Geiger v. Espy, 885 F. Supp. 231, 232 (D. Kan. 1995) (stating that "[a]s opposed to a preliminary injunction, a temporary restraining order ("TRO") is sought and heard on an emergency basis").

[2] Rosen v. Siegel, 106 F.3d 28, 31 (2d Cir. 1997) (noting that the "Federal Rules of Civil Procedure prescribe a stylized ritual for the entry of a preliminary injunction").

[3] Univ. of Texas v. Camenisch, 451 U.S. 390, 395 (1981) (citations omitted).

[4] *Rosen, supra,* 106 F.3d at 31–32; Parker v. Ryan, 960 F.2d 543, 544 (5th Cir. 1992).

[5] Fed. R. Civ. P. 52(a). When a jurisdiction imposes such a rule, it will be deemed mandatory. *Rosen, supra,* 106 F.3d at 32–33 (remanding for failure of district court to provide Findings of Fact and Conclusions of Law in support of preliminary injunction). *But see* F.T.C. v. H.N. Singer, Inc., 668 F.2d 1107, 1109 (9th Cir. 1982) (holding that failure of trial court to provide required findings and conclusions did not necessitate remand when record evidenced that trial court had considered all relevant materials and absence did not impinge meaningful appellate review).

[6] *Camenisch, supra,* 451 U.S. at 395.

[7] Section 31.6. (Notice and Hearing Requirement).

preliminary injunctions require that any temporary equitable relief provided be specific in terms and describe in reasonable detail the act(s) enjoined.[8] Both usually require a bond.[9]

A preliminary injunction can be sought as a complement to a TRO or independent of a TRO. Likewise, a request for a TRO is not dependent on a future request for a preliminary injunction. In the typical case, however, a TRO will be sought at the outset of the litigation and will be accompanied or followed by a request for a preliminary injunction. By these means a plaintiff can obtain temporary injunctive relief throughout the pretrial and trial phases of dispute resolution. The need for temporary injunctive relief may, however, arise at any time during the dispute resolution process. As the situation dictates, a party may seek appropriate, temporary injunctive relief through a TRO, a preliminary injunction, or a combination of the two.[10]

The Court has limited the ability of a plaintiff to obtain temporary injunctive relief ("Freeze Order") in the absence of a claim for permanent equitable relief.[11]

Although not an equitable remedy per se, stays are a form of extraordinary relief that are often discussed in terms that mirror the providing of temporary equitable relief. A stay is an order from a court to a lower court, administrative agency, or governmental authority. A stay is usually issued on less than a complete record and full hearing and is necessarily tentative and transient. The factors used to assess the propriety of issuing a stay (likelihood of success on the merits, irreparable injury, harm to others, and public policy)[12] are similar to those applied to deciding whether to provide temporary injunctive relief.[13]

---

[8] Section 34 (Specificity of Injunctive Relief).

[9] Section 31.7 (Bond Requirement).

[10] A related procedural remedy is the Order to Show Cause (OSC). The OSC directs a party to appear or respond before the court and state why certain requested relief or a threatened order should not be granted. No presumption that a party is entitled to relief is created by the OSC; it is simply a mechanism for bringing the matter before the court for further proceedings. Parties must closely check Local Rules of Court to determine the proper method for seeking temporary equitable relief. Paisa, Inc. v. N & G Auto, Inc., 928 F. Supp. 1004, 1007 n.2 (C.D. Cal. 1996) (noting that under District Court's local rule, filing of ex parte application for TRO and a separate motion for a preliminary injunction was improper. "When a TRO is sought, application for a preliminary injunction shall be made by order to show cause," *citing* Local Rule of Court, Rule 7.17).

[11] Section 20.1 (Judicial Power).

[12] *See* John Y. Gotanda, *The Emerging Standards For Issuing Appellate Stays*, 45 Baylor L. Rev. 809 (1993).

[13] Similar, but not the same. Wisconsin Right to Life, Inc. v. Federal Election Comm'n, 125 S. Ct. 2 (2004) (Rhenquist C.J., Circuit Justice) (stating that "an injunction pending appeal . . . would be an extraordinary remedy"). The Chief Justice went on to state that such relief "is only appropriately exercised where (1) 'necessary or appropriate in aid of [our] jurisdictio[n]' and (2) the legal rights at issue are 'indisputably clear.'" *Id.*; Section 31.2 (Traditional Tests For Issuance of Temporary Injunctive Relief).

It is not uncommon that a court, to avoid ruling on a request for a TRO, will inquire whether the defendant will "stipulate" to not engage in the conduct that would be subject to the TRO and thus preserve the status quo pending a hearing on the motion for a preliminary injunction. A stipulation is an agreement between the parties, not an order of the court. In deciding whether to enter into the stipulation a lawyer should insure that she has the authority to do so. In addition, the moving party should recognize that violation of a stipulation is not the same as a violation of a court order; therefore, the sanctions (and remedies) may not be as favorable. To preserve those remedies, the stipulation should be confirmed as a court order.[14]

[31.2] Traditional Tests for Issuance of Temporary Injunctive Relief

Courts have developed a basic formula for determining whether to order temporary injunctive relief. The specific articulations of that formula may vary somewhat. The basic formula may be articulated as a four-part test that requires the plaintiff to show that:

- there exists the likelihood of success on the merits;
- irreparable injury will result if temporary relief is not granted;
- the balance of hardships (or equities) lies with the plaintiff; and
- ordering temporary relief will serve the public interest.[15]

[31.2.1] Likelihood of Success on the Merits

The great deterrent to awarding temporary injunctive relief is the fear of error. Unlike a permanent injunction, which is issued at the conclusion of a plenary trial on the merits after the court has the opportunity to hear the evidence and have the evidence scrutinized under the adversary system, temporary injunctive relief is by motion or application, usually based largely on papers filed with the court, and resolved by proceedings less formal than a plenary trial on the merits. While the court has the power to hear testimony, the practice is to rule on the request based on declaration or affidavit evidence presented by the interested parties.[16] Because these materials are not tested through cross examination, coupled with the time constraints imposed on the parties and the court, the belief is that the risk of an erroneous decision is greater at the temporary injunction stage than at the permanent injunction stage. Set in this context, the "likelihood of

---

[14] Section 193 (Elements of Civil Contempt) (particularly Section 193.1 (Order)).

[15] Opticians Ass'n v. Independent Opticians, 920 F.2d 187, 191–92 (3d Cir. 1990); Cunningham v. Adams, 808 F.2d 815, 819 (11th Cir. 1987); Vision Center v. Opticks, Inc., 596 F.2d 111, 114 (5th Cir. 1979), *cert. denied*, 444 U.S. 1016 (1980); Lockheed Missile & Space Co. v. Hughes Aircraft Co., 887 F. Supp. 1320, 1322 (N.D. Cal. 1995) (noting that test is essentially the same for both TROs and preliminary injunctions).

[16] There are, of course, exceptions to this practice. Roland Machinery Co. v. Dresser Industries, Inc., 749 F.2d 380, 389 (7th Cir. 1984) (noting that "many preliminary injunction hearings take as long as the average federal trial, which lasts only three days").

success" element exists to reduce the chance of an erroneous result, or at least a result different from that which would be reached at the permanent injunction stage. The "likelihood of success" element imposes some consistency in approach by limiting temporary injunctive relief to those who are most likely to prevail on the merits at the conclusion of the trial.

"Likelihood of success" is not the same as "certainty of success."[17] Many articulations of this factor use a strong descriptive term, such as "strong" or "substantial probability" in place of "likelihood," as an indication of the required certainty or confidence in "success." On the other hand, under one or more of the variants of the traditional test for injunctive relief, "likelihood" may be reduced to "possibility."[18]

"Likelihood of success" means that the claim for temporary injunctive relief must be supported by appropriate legal authority. If a court temporarily enjoins a demonstration, an ordinance, a breach of contract, or a trespass, the applicable law must support the court's position. If the governing law does not, the court is usually deemed to have abused its discretion.[19]

The decision to order temporary injunctive relief must be accurately grounded in law. This introduces a subtle twist to the decision making process. While the decision to grant or deny temporary equitable relief is reviewed under an abuse of discretion standard, the law applied by the court is reviewed de novo.[20] Although the line is blurry at best, one way to understand the distinction is to think of the applicable law as the ground rules. These must be stated correctly by the trial court and whether they have been stated correctly is reviewed de novo by the appellate court. How the ground rules are factored into the decision to grant or deny equitable relief is committed to the court's discretion.[21] Although the process can be stated with relative precision, the playing out of the process is murky. The

---

[17] O'Connor v. Peru State College, 728 F.2d 1001, 1002 (8th Cir. 1984).

[18] Section 31.3 (Modern Variations of Traditional Test).

[19] NCAA v. Lasege, 53 S.W.3d 77 (Ky. 2001) (reversing trial court and vacating award of temporary injunctive relief that permitted collegiate basketball player to play on the University of Louisville basketball team notwithstanding that the player had previously signed a contract to play professional basketball; the court found that plaintiff's chances of success on the merits were "too remote" to warrant temporary injunctive relief); Philip Morris, Inc. v. Harshbarger, 159 F.3d 670 (1st Cir. 1998) (affirming granting of temporary injunctive relief against enforcement of state statute requiring manufacturers of tobacco products to disclose ingredients of products; the court found that plaintiffs were entitled to injunctive relief as they had made a strong showing that disclosure constituted an impermissible taking of proprietary information); cf. Philip Morris, Inc. v. Reilly, 312 F.3d 24 (1st Cir. 2002) (en banc) (finding that permanent injunctive relief was warranted under "regulatory taking" doctrine).

[20] Section 23 (Equitable Discretion); see Virginian Ry. Co. v. System Fed'n, 300 U.S. 515, 551 (1937) (granting or denying a preliminary injunction is within the sound discretion of the trial court).

[21] Sports Form, Inc. v. United Press International, 686 F.2d 750, 753–59 (9th Cir. 1982) (holding that the appellate court would review de novo whether the district court identified the correct legal standard, but would apply a deferential standard of review as to whether those standards were correctly applied).

line between "Rule" and "Application of Rule" can easily be ignored. Those who hope for precision in this area are likely to be disappointed.[22]

The "likelihood of success" factor is influenced by the substantive law of the subject matter area to which the temporary injunctive relief applies. For example, in *Mutual of Omaha v. Novak*,[23] a deceptive trade practices case brought under the Lanham Act, Mutual of Omaha had acquired trademark protection for several marks, e.g., "Wild Kingdom," "Mutual of Omaha" and an "Indian Head" logo. The defendant produced a design, which he placed on T-shirts that used the words "Mutant of Omaha," a side view of a feather-bonneted, emaciated human head, along with the words "Nuclear Holocaust Insurance." Mutual was not amused and sought to enjoin further sale of the T-shirts. Resolution of the dispute involved certain legal issues pertinent to trademark law, such as "likelihood of confusion," which in turn raises its own specific sub-issues, such as the strength of the mark, similarity between the mark and defendant's usage, competition, actual confusion, etc. A related issue was that of "parody," which raised First Amendment concerns and its own sub-set of legal issues related to commercial speech. The correct construction of these legal rules directly affected the determination of the plaintiff's "likelihood" of success.

[31.2.2] Irreparable Injury

The traditional articulation of the "irreparable injury" standard is that the plaintiff has no "adequate remedy at law."[24] It is important to recognize that irreparable injury must be examined in the context of the specific remedy requested—here, temporary injunctive relief.

Temporary injunctive relief controls the defendant's conduct until it expires by its terms or further injunctive relief is granted or denied. In this context, irreparable injury is not harm that the plaintiff would sustain if the permanent injunction is not granted, but harm that will be sustained if the preliminary injunction is not granted. The proper question to ask is whether, at the time a permanent injunction would be granted, the court would be able to award adequate legal remedies for any losses or injury suffered by the plaintiff during the period the preliminary injunction would have been effective had it been issued. For example, assume that a plaintiff complains of personal and property damage because of defendant's nuisance. Plaintiff wants temporary relief enjoining the nuisance pending trial. The critical perspective is what the parties and the court would know at the time the permanent injunction was sought, not what they know now. If plaintiff's losses up to the time of trial could be properly compensated at the time of trial by a monetary award, plaintiff will not sustain irreparable injury if the temporary injunction is not granted. In other words "[t]he

---

[22] James M. Fischer, *"Preliminarily" Enjoining Elections: A Tale of Two Ninth Circuit Panels*, 41 San Diego L. Rev. 1647 (2004) (discussing different approaches of two Ninth Circuit panels in reviewing district court's decision not to grant a preliminary injunction enjoining the holding of a recall election).

[23] 836 F.2d 397 (8th Cir. 1987), *cert. denied*, 488 U.S. 933 (1988).

[24] Section 21 (Adequacy of the Remedy at Law/Irreparable Injury).

possibility adequate compensatory or other corrective relief will be available at a later date, in the ordinary course of litigation, weighs heavily against a claim of irreparable harm."[25] The analysis is usually applied to requests for preliminary injunctions because of their potential length—the entire pretrial period. The analysis is usually not applied to TROs. Their short duration usually requires only application of traditional irreparable injury considerations, albeit within the context of "emergency" relief.

This particular showing of irreparable injury when a preliminary injunction is sought is dramatically illustrated in wrongful discharge cases. Here courts have refused reinstatement of terminated employees pursuant to temporary injunctive relief on the ground that the employee's damages (lost wages) can be satisfactorily calculated at the time of judgment.[26] Courts have noted that in "genuinely extraordinary circumstances" irreparable injury might be found warranting temporary equitable relief in the form of reinstatement;[27] however, courts have generally imposed a high threshold here. For example, courts have rejected claims that injury to reputation, increased work load if ultimately successful, or the possibility of replacement constitute irreparable injury.[28] On the other hand, courts have been willing to find the threshold has been met when the basis for the wrongful discharge would chill the assertion of constitutional and statutory rights by employees, as for example, in discrimination cases. Even here, however, courts require proof of a chilling effect; a mere allegation is insufficient. Some courts reject the "chilling effect" theory altogether.[29] A few courts have found irreparable injury sufficient to warrant temporary reinstatement when the loss of employment would render the plaintiff destitute: "[I]n essence the plaintiff must literally find herself being forced into the streets or facing the spectre of bankruptcy before a court can enter a finding of irreparable harm."[30]

A plaintiff's ability to obtain temporary injunctive relief is often difficult when the basis for the claim of irreparable injury is uncertainty of proof as to the amount of damages. The future is often uncertain, but the past is less so, at least, so it seems. If the appropriate decision date is a point in the future and the question is whether from that vantage point we can compensate the plaintiff for any actual losses sustained up to that point, we are going to have fewer findings of irreparable injury than if the decision

---

[25] United States v. Jefferson County, 720 F.2d 1511, 1520 (11th Cir. 1983).

[26] Sampson v. Murray, 415 U.S. 61, 90 (1974) (holding that "temporary" loss of income associated with termination from employment would not be deemed "irreparable").

[27] *Id.*

[28] Jayaraj v. Scappini, 66 F.3d 36, 39 (2d Cir. 1995).

[29] American Postal Workers Union v. United States Postal Serv., 766 F.2d 715, 722 (2d Cir. 1985) (rejecting "chilling of rights" theory as establishing irreparable injury).

[30] Adam-Mellang v. Apartment Search, Inc., 96 F.3d 297, 301 (8th Cir. 1996) (collecting cases) (noting that "chilling effect of unrestrained retaliation" satisfies irreparable injury requirement). Compare Porter v. Adams, 639 F.2d 273, 278 n.8 (5th Cir. 1981) (noting that after *Sampson* irreparable injury may not be presumed in discrimination, wrongful termination cases, but must be demonstrated in fact).

date is when injunctive relief is requested and the question is whether we can ascertain the amount of damages the plaintiff will sustain in the future. Hindsight is 20/20 because it is based upon an actual record rather than a forecast. When we decrease uncertainty connected with decision making, we reduce the need for temporary injunctive relief to avoid the costs uncertainty imposes. A plaintiff claiming wrongful discharge can usually obtain temporary injunctive relief (immediate reinstatement) only when he can show extreme hardship, a collateral consequence, such as "chilling effect," or, a statutory entitlement to immediate reinstatement.[31]

Claims involving certain types of harms may resist monetary compensation as a complete remedy. An injunction to prevent threatened bodily injury is an example of this category. While courts customarily award compensation for past bodily injury, it is consistently recognized to be inadequate compensation. Good health is not tradable for money.[32] Similarly, certain rights may be intrinsically valuable in themselves and resist accurate assessment for awarding compensation even when evaluated retrospectively. For example, in *Metropolitan Sports Facilities Comm'n v. Minnesota Twins Partnership*[33] the court upheld a temporary injunction requiring the Minnesota Twin, a major league professional baseball team, to play its home games at the plaintiff's public facility. The Twins had been widely rumored to be a candidate for elimination from professional baseball. The injunction forestalled this move. In finding the requisite "irreparable injury" to support temporary injunctive relief, the court noted that the benefits to the plaintiff of having the Twins play at its stadium were not just monetary, e.g., rent and concessions revenues, but "intangible benefits" not easily quantifiable.[34] In some cases, a statute may ease the plaintiff's burden of establishing "irreparable injury."[35]

[31.2.3] Balancing of Hardships or Equities

The irreparable injury requirement addresses the ability at the time of trial to compensate adequately for "harm" to the plaintiff if the request for temporary injunctive relief is not granted. The balancing of hardships or equities test weighs the harm to the defendant *if the injunction is granted*

---

[31] *Sampson v. Murray, supra*, 415 U.S. at 67.

[32] Section 21.2.4 (Nature of Injury) (discussing loss of good health as satisfying irreparable injury requirement).

[33] 638 N.W.2d 214 (Minn. App. 2002).

[34] *Id.* at 225; Glenwood Bridge, Inc. v. City of Minneapolis, 940 F.2d 367, 371–72 (8th Cir. 1991) (noting that intangible injuries, such as being allowed to bid on public contract without an illegal term, warranted finding of irreparable injury even though the disappointed bidder could receive "lost profits" as damages).

[35] For example, the Copyright Act specifically provides for temporary and permanent injunctive relief against infringers. 17 U.S.C. § 502(a). Under § 502(a) a "showing of a reasonable likelihood of success raises a presumption of irreparable harm." Johnson Controls v. Phoenix Control Systems, 886 F.2d 1173, 1174 (9th Cir. 1989); Section 26.1 (Statutes Expanding Equitable Remedies).

against the harm to the plaintiff *if the injunction is denied.* The interests of third parties may also be factored into the decision. [36]

In assessing the harm realized by the grant or denial of temporary injunctive relief, the focus must be on actual harm not speculative harm. [37] The record must reflect and support the claim of "harm." [38] Moreover, the court must evaluate the threatened harm based on the situation as its exists when the court is considering the request for injunctive relief, not as the situation existed in the past.

The "balancing of hardships or equities" test used here should be distinguished from the "balance of hardship" test that is applied to requests for permanent injunctive relief. [39] The "balance of hardship" test used for permanent injunctive relief weighs the benefit of the injunction to the plaintiff against the cost of the injunction to the defendant. The test is essentially a "cost-benefits" analysis. The "balancing of hardships or equities" test used for temporary equitable relief ultimately seeks to ascertain the cost of granting or denying relief to each. The comparison is between the cost to the plaintiff if the temporary injunction is denied and the cost to the defendant if the temporary injunction is granted. Unlike the "balance of hardship" test for permanent injunctive relief, where the costs to defendant of compliance must be disproportionate to the benefits realized by the plaintiff from compliance, no disproportionality test per se is used when determining the propriety of temporary injunctive relief. The test favors whichever party would suffer a greater loss.

In some formulations the balancing of hardships test is combined with the likelihood of success factor to create a test that awards or denies temporary injunctive relief based on the greater cost of an erroneous decision, determined at the time temporary injunctive relief is sought. This approach is discussed in Section 31.3 (Modern Variations of the Traditional Test).

[31.2.4] Public Policy or Public Interest

"Public policy" is often spoken of metaphorically as an "unruly horse" courts are cautioned to avoid saddling up. [40] The public policy concept is,

---

[36] *Glenwood Bridge, Inc., supra*, 940 F2d at 372 (noting affect of denial of injunctive relief on public interest); Holford USA Ltd., Inc. v. Cherokee, Inc., 864 F. Supp. 364, 371 (S.D.N.Y. 1994) (noting effect of granting injunctive relief on creditors of defendant). Alternatively, third party interests are considered under the public policy factor. Section 31.2.4 (Public Policy or Public Interest).

[37] Frank B. Hall & Co., Inc. v. Alexander & Alexander, Inc., 974 F.2d 1020, 1023 (8th Cir. 1992).

[38] Stuart Circle Parish v. Bd. of Zoning Appeals of City of Richmond, 946 F. Supp. 1225, 1236 (E.D. Va. 1996) (finding no significant harm to defendant if injunction issues when the record failed to show that generalized complaints that defendant relied on in restricting plaintiff's activities could be attributed to plaintiff).

[39] Section 33.2 ([Permanent Injunctions] Entitlement to Relief).

[40] Section 4 (Public Policy).

nonetheless, well ingrained in the traditional test. The "public interest" factor frequently invites courts to indulge in broad observations about conduct that is generally recognizable as costly or injurious upon third parties or the public in general."[41] Thus, courts have held that "the public interest is not served by a court's prohibition of advertising that is not false or misleading,"[42] or by allowing "consumer confusion,"[43] or breach of contract.[44] The "public interest" usually follows legislative enactments,[45] but it may have "homegrown" judicial origins.[46] The two terms, "public policy" and "public interest" are essentially synonymous and are interchangeable. On the other hand, when the public interest is identified as the *effect* of the injunction on third parties, the public interest factor has some concreteness so long as the third party affects are real, and immediate rather than abstract and general.

The public interest must be based on actualities not supposition. Moreover, the interest must be legitimate. An "irrational" community belief, however real to the community, may not override a party's right to equitable redress.[47] The fact that a party is a public agency does not create a presumption that its litigation position represents the public interest.[48] It is usually the case that both sides can state their positions as implicating the public interest.[49] Indeed, the ability to identify the public interest as

---

[41] Heather K. v. City of Mallard, 887 F. Supp. 1249, 1260 (N.D. Iowa 1995); Laura Stein, *The Court and the Community: Why Non-Party Interests Should Count in Preliminary Injunction Actions*, 16 Rev. Litig. 27, 29 (1997) ("Many courts interpret the public interest factor as a license to consider the impact that granting or denying injunctive relief will have on non-parties . . .") (footnotes omitted).

[42] J&M Turner, Inc. v. Applied Bolting Tech. Prods., Inc., 1997 U.S. Dist. LEXIS 1835 at *57–58 (E.D. Pa. Feb. 19, 1997).

[43] Gougeon Brothers, Inc. v. Hendricks, 708 F. Supp. 811, 817 (E.D. Mich. 1988) (finding that evidence of consumer confusion supports finding that public interest will be advanced by issuance of injunctive relief); Calamari Fisheries, Inc. v. Village Catch, Inc., 698 F. Supp. 994, 1015 (D. Mass. 1988) ("preventing consumer confusion is clearly in the public interest").

[44] The Score Board, Inc. v. Upper Deck Co., 959 F. Supp. 234, 240 (D.N.J. 1997) (preventing tortious interference with contract rights furthers public interest).

[45] Schulz v. United States Boxing Ass'n, 105 F.3d 127, 134 (3d Cir. 1997) (applying New Jersey law).

[46] Falcone v. Middlesex County Med. Soc'y, 170 A.2d 791, 795 (N.J. 1961) (noting that "while earlier day judges displayed hesitancy in its acknowledgment, modern day judges display no comparable hesitancy; in recent decisions our courts have repeatedly acknowledged that public policy is the dominant factor in the molding and remolding of common law principles to the high end that they may soundly serve the public welfare and the true interests of justice").

[47] Chalk v. United States Dist. Court, Cent. Dist. of Cal., 840 F.2d 701, 711 (9th Cir. 1988) (holding that community's "fear of AIDS" would not support denial of equitable relief to teacher reassigned from his employment because of his condition).

[48] Carey v. Klutznick, 637 F.2d 834, 839 (2d Cir. 1980).

[49] Tri-State Generation & Transmission Assoc., Inc. v. Shoshone River Power, Inc., 805 F.2d 351, 357 (10th Cir. 1986).

being served, or subverted by the injunction is so easy as to reduce often the requirement to a banality.[50]

[31.3] Modern Variations of the Traditional Test

Dissatisfaction with the traditional test lead a number of courts to reformulate their test for temporary injunctive relief. The basis or cause of the dissatisfaction was never expressly articulated, but the general theme of the new tests was to make it easier to obtain temporary injunctive relief.

The movement to new tests was also fueled by scholarly criticism of the functionality of the traditional tests. Professor Dobbs argued that the proper approach to analyzing a request for temporary injunctive relief was to strike an appropriate balance between the factors that were considered under the traditional test. The factors should guide decision making, but courts should reject a formulaic approach that allowed the factors to control or dictate results.[51]

Professor Leubsdorf argued that the decision to grant or deny temporary injunctive relief should focus on the risk of error. The decision whether to grant temporary injunctive relief should favor the party with the most to lose if the court decides the request incorrectly, *i.e.*, grants temporary injunctive relief when it should deny or denies when it should grant.[52]

The modern formulations come in a variety of packages and, in some instances, the differences between the formulations may be more verbal than real. One formulation treats the four factors of the traditional test as just that—factors—rather than as elements of a prima facie test, which is the traditional approach.[53] This variation does not treat each element as having separate and independent thresholds, the satisfaction of which is necessary to obtaining the remedy. Courts adopting this approach often note that the elements "do not establish a rigid and comprehensive test for determining the appropriateness of [temporary] injunctive relief."[54] Rather, the "factors" simply guide the discretion of the court and are to be balanced and weighed against one another to ensure a just result.[55] What this means

---

[50] *E.g.*, *Stuart Circle Parish, supra*, 946 F. Supp. at 1240 (finding that public interest is served because injunction "provides a federal forum for the vindication of federal rights"); C.P.M. v. D'ilio, 916 F. Supp. 415, 422 (D.N.J. 1996) (finding that injunction preventing parole authorities from notifying employer of employee's parole status served public interest of "rehabilitation and reassimilation of offenders into productive, employed, tax-paying citizens"); Canterbury Career Sch., Inc. v. Riley, 833 F. Supp. 1097, 1106 (D.N.J. 1993) (finding that operation of private school "benefits the public by providing quality education to persons who are below the poverty level prior to enrolling . . .").

[51] DAN DOBBS, LAW OF REMEDIES § 2.11(2) (1973).

[52] John Leubsdorf, *The Standard For Preliminary Injunctions*, 91 Harv. L. Rev. 525 (1978).

[53] Black Fire Fighters Ass'n v. City of Dallas, Tex., 905 F.2d 63, 65 (5th Cir. 1990) (*per curiam*) (on rehearing) (holding that denial of preliminary injunction was proper if the applicant fails to establish any one of the four factors).

[54] Friendship Materials, Inc. v. Michigan Brick, Inc., 679 F.2d 100, 102 (6th Cir. 1982) (brackets added).

[55] *In re* Eagle-Picher, Indus. Inc., 963 F.2d 855, 859 (6th Cir. 1992); Washington Metropoli-

is that a plaintiff does not have to reach a threshold with respect to each factor. A weakness of proof with respect to one factor may be offset by the strength of the proof of another factor. No single factor is itself dispositive; in each case, all the factors must be considered to determine whether, on balance, they weigh toward granting temporary injunctive relief.[56] This approach is also known as the "sliding scale" approach:

> Our analysis of the four factors governing these stays is necessarily case-specific. [T]he party seeking a preliminary injunction must first demonstrate "some" likelihood of succeeding on the merits, and that it has no adequate remedy at law and will suffer irreparable harm if the preliminary relief is denied. In deportation cases, . . . the lack of an adequate remedy at law is always present. No one suggests that the United States government could be required to pay money damages later on to a person whose asylum application was erroneously denied. As is the case in many areas of traditional equity jurisprudence, this is a situation where specific relief is the only possible solution. The other two factors, numbered 1 and 2 . . . , require more comment. [I]f the moving party cannot establish some likelihood of success and irreparable injury, the court's inquiry is at an end and the injunction must be denied. If the applicant meets those threshold requirements, the court will consider the balance of hardships to the moving and non-moving parties, from the denial or grant of injunctive relief respectively, and the public interest, which [we have] defined as "the consequences of granting or denying the injunction to non-parties."

> These factors do not have absolute weights. Instead, this court uses a sliding scale approach, under which "the more likely it is that plaintiff will succeed on the merits, the less the balance of irreparable harms need weigh towards its side; the less likely it is the plaintiff will succeed, the more the balance need weigh toward its side." Although there is thus a minimum threshold for likelihood of success, we held . . . that it is a low one: "[i]t is enough that the plaintiff's chances are better than negligible . . . ." That does not mean, of course, that applicants for interim injunctive relief with relatively weak cases will always obtain injunctions. The less compelling the case on the merits, the greater the showing of irreparable harm must be.[57]

---

tan Area Transit Comm'n v. Holiday Tours, Inc., 559 F.2d 841, 844 (D.C. Cir. 1977) (rejecting minimum 50% requirement for probability of success factor of four-factor test; "necessary showing on the merits is governed by the balance of equities as revealed through an examination of the other three factors").

[56] Baker Elec. Coop., Inc. v. Chaske, 28 F.3d 1466, 1472 (8th Cir. 1994); FMC Corp. v. United States, 3 F.3d 424, 427 (Fed. Cir. 1993); United States v. Alameda Gateway, Ltd., 953 F. Supp. 1106, 1109 (N.D. Cal. 1996) (noting that "[a]s the likelihood of irreparable harm increases, the required degree of probable success decreases") (citation omitted).

[57] Sofinet v. I.N.S., 188 F.3d 703, 707 (7th Cir. 1999) (citations omitted) (brackets added); cf. White v. Davis, 68 P.3d 74, 91 (Cal. 2003) (stating that grant of preliminary injunction

Another approach is to give preferential treatment to several of the factors. Usually this is accomplished by grouping several of the factors into subtests. For example, the Ninth Circuit has held that a party is entitled to temporary equitable relief if the party can establish either:

1)   a combination of probable success on the merits and the possibility of irreparable harm; or

2)   that serious questions are raised and the balance of equities tips sharply in the moving party's favor.[58]

The Second Circuit has adopted a different version of the alternative test. To obtain a preliminary injunction, the plaintiff must "demonstrate . . . (1) irreparable harm and (2) either (a) likelihood of success on the merits or (b) 'sufficiently serious questions' on the merits and a balance of hardships 'tipping decidedly' in the [plaintiff's] favor."[59] These "combination" or "hybrid" tests are usually identified as alternatives to the traditional test;[60] however, the general tendency is to discuss all of the traditional factors even when the "combination" or "hybrid" tests are used.[61]

Another factor driving the tendency to combine elements of the traditional test into "combination" tests is the recognition that although the elements are stated separately, there is in fact some overlap. A finding of irreparable injury is related to an evaluation whether, on balance, the hardship of avoiding that injury is greater than the hardship inflicted on the defendant by granting relief, particularly when defendant's hardship may be ameliorated by an injunction bond. Likewise, the plaintiff's likelihood of success is interwoven with the assessment of injury and hardship, for it is hardly an injury or a hardship, in any legally meaningful sense, if the harm is not caused by defendant's actionable misconduct. Occasionally, courts attempt to reduce these concepts to more precise formulas. Judge Posner expressed his approach as a mathematic formula he believed followed in the footsteps of Judge Learned Hand's famous formula for negligence:

> These mistakes can be compared, and the one likely to be less costly can be selected, with the help of a simple formula: grant the preliminary injunction if but only if [$P \times Hp > (1-P) \times Hd$ (where P is the probability of success, Hp is harm to the plaintiff, and Hd is harm to the defendant], or in words, only if the harm to the

"involves two interrelated factors: (1) the likelihood that the plaintiff will prevail on the merits, and (2) the relative balance of harms that is likely to result from the granting or denial of interim injunctive relief"). One pronounced consequence of this approach is to ease the obtaining of preliminary injunctive relief when constitutional violations are alleged; in such cases irreparable injury is often presumed. Section 21.2.4 (Nature of the Injury).

[58] Rodeo Collection, Ltd. v. West Seventh, 812 F.2d 1215, 1217 (9th Cir. 1987).

[59] Brooks v. Giuliani, 84 F.3d 1454, 1562 (2d Cir.), *cert. denied sub nom.* Brooks v. Pataki, 519 U.S. 992 (1996).

[60] Cassim v. Bowen, 824 F.2d 791, 795 (9th Cir. 1987).

[61] *See* Fischer, *Enjoining Elections, supra,* 41 San Diego L. Rev. at 1656–63, 1667–73 (discussing use of "hybrid" tests in connection with effort to enjoin holding of recall election).

plaintiff if the injunction is granted, multiplied by the probability that granting the injunction would be an error (that the plaintiff, in other words, will win at trial), exceeds the harm to the defendant if the injunction is granted, multiplied by the probability that granting the injunction would be an error. The probability is simply one minus the probability that the plaintiff will win at trial; for if the plaintiff has, say, a 40 percent chance of winning, the defendant must have a 60 percent chance of winning $(1.00 - .40 = .60)$. The left-hand side of the formula is simply the probability of an erroneous denial weighted by the cost of denial to the plaintiff, and the right-hand side simply the probability of an erroneous grant weighted by the cost of grant to the defendant.[62]

The formula requires the court to quantify the party's respective hardships resulting from an erroneous decision and then discount that hardship by the likelihood the party should not suffer the hardship. For example, if we could quantify plaintiff's hardship if the preliminary injunction is not granted as $1 million and defendant's hardship if the preliminary injunction is granted as $1 million, and the probability of success as 60%/40% respectively, the injunction should issue because:

$$60\% \text{ times } \$1 \text{ million} \quad > \quad 40\% \text{ times } \$1 \text{ million}$$
$$(\$600,000) \qquad\qquad (\$400,000)$$

Under this test even a small likelihood of success warrants temporary injunctive relief when the hardship resulting from an erroneous denial is manifestly greater than the hardship resulting from an erroneous grant.

The approach has generated strong criticism.[63] Nevertheless, the recognition of overlap may be inducing courts to compress the elements of the traditional test so as to avoid double counting and provide more streamlined tests to determine the appropriateness of temporary injunctive relief.

As is the case with many cost-benefit approaches, it is often easier to calculate costs with precision than benefits. This may induce a defendant's bias if the court requires objective verification, but a plaintiff's bias if the court is willing to value benefits subjectively.[64]

It remains unclear how significant the adoption of the "balancing" or "combination" tests have been in affecting results. Is the change largely symbolic because the same relief would invariably be given under the traditional test as under one of the modified versions? It is always difficult to determine what the view would be on the "path not taken." We should

---

[62] American Hospital Supply Corp. v. Hospital Products, Ltd., 780 F.2d 589, 593 (7th Cir. 1986) (brackets added); RICHARD A. POSNER, ECONOMIC ANALYSIS OF LAW 605–06 (5th ed. 1998).

[63] Schultz v. Frisby, 807 F.2d 1339, 1347 (7th Cir. 1986) (Swygert J.) (discounting formulaic approach), rev'd on other grounds, 487 U.S. 474 (1988); Linda S. Mullenix, Burying (With Kindness) The Felicific Calculus of Civil Procedure, 40 Vand. L. Rev. 541, 543 (1987) (contending that "Judge Posner's efforts to Benthamize civil procedure are an abomination in theory and practice").

[64] Section 91 (Natural Resource Damage).

not, however, overestimate the rigor of the traditional factors test, nor underestimate the rigor of the modified versions of the traditional test. Temporary injunctive relief remains an area committed to discretionary decision making insofar as evaluating "elements" are concerned. Whether the test involves two, three or four elements, reviewing courts often extend substantial deference to this aspect of the trial court's decision making, although, at times, the scope of review may be colored by the court's view of the better end result.

[31.4] Maintenance of the Status Quo

The idea that temporary injunctive relief should not give the plaintiff the ultimate relief requested is loosely captured by the often cited requirement that temporary injunctive relief should preserve the status quo.[65] As Judge Posner has, however, observed, that concept is both "inaccurate" and "empty."[66] In an appropriate case, the court may use temporary injunctive relief to alter the status quo and even if the status quo is maintained, there may be substantial disagreement as to the state of the status quo. Both points are developed in this section. Temporary injunctive relief is not a final determination of a matter, but the exercise of the trial court's discretion to maintain or alter the status quo between the litigants until a final judgment is rendered.[67]

The first issue is determining the status quo. Is the status quo defined by plaintiff's or defendant's claim of right? For example, if Able has been crossing Baker's land to reach a particularly desirable fishing pond, and Baker seeks to enjoin Able's continued crossing of the land, what is the status quo? Crossing or not crossing? If Baker employs a security guard who bars Able from crossing the land and Able seeks to enjoin Baker's acts barring Able's access to the pond, has the status quo changed?

Although some courts simply assume that the "status quo" is the state of affairs the temporary injunctive relief seeks to affect, the dominant, modern test is to focus on the "last, uncontested status preceding the commencement of the controversy."[68] Using this test, the unimpeded

---

[65] Granny Goose Foods, Inc. v. Brotherhood of Teamsters and Auto Truck Drivers Local No. 70, 415 U.S. 423, 439 (1974); MacIntyre v. Metropolitan Life Ins. Co. 634 N.Y.S.2d 180, 181 (App. Dept. 1995); *see* Phillip v. Fairfield Univ., 118 F.3d 131, 134 (2d Cir. 1997).

[66] Praefke Auto Electric & Battery Co., Inc. v. Tecumseh Products Company, Inc., 255 F.3d 460, 464 (7th Cir. 2001).

[67] Fernandex-Roque v. Smith, 671 F.2d 426, 429 (11th Cir. 1982); Blaylock v. Cheker Oil Co., 547 F.2d 962, 964 (6th Cir. 1976).

[68] O Centro Espirita Beneficente Uniao Do Vegetal v. Ashcroft, 342 F.3d 1170, 1177–78 (10th Cir. 2003) (rejecting government's contention that enforcement of Controlled Substances Act (CSA) was the status quo; rather, plaintiffs' use of "hoasca," which contained substances banned by the CSA, free from government interference was the status quo), *aff'd on other grounds*, 389 F.3d 973 (10th Cir. 2004) (*en banc*), *aff'd on other grounds sub nom.*, Gonzales v. O Centro Espirita Beneficiente Uniao Do Vegetal, 126 S.Ct. 1211 (2006); Washington Capitols Basketball Club, Inc. v. Barry, 419 F.2d 472, 476 (9th Cir. 1969).

crossing of Baker's land by Able would be the last peaceable or uncontested act and the maintenance of the status quo should reflect that fact. The argument is not, however, unassailable. For example, if we change the hypothetical and have Baker decide to employ a security guard without reference to Able's action, it becomes more difficult to select Able's prior conduct as the last peaceable or uncontested act. Why isn't Baker's conduct deemed peaceable or uncontested, particularly if it is done without the specific intent to frustrate Able's continuing access? The last peaceable or uncontested act test helps resolve some cases, but the test is insufficiently precise to resolve all the cases.[69]

Courts have cautioned against giving the status quo concept a wooden application.[70] Courts have repeatedly warned against using the status quo concept to lock a party into a situation that would result in his irreparable injury. "[T]he maintenance of the status quo is only one of the reasons for which a preliminary injunction may be granted. It may also be granted to prevent irreparable injury."[71] The desire to maintain the status quo should not be done at the cost of permitting the inflicting of irreparable injury on the party seeking temporary equitable relief. When issuance of a preliminary injunction is necessary to avoid irreparable injury, the fact that status quo will be altered is not controlling.[72]

Courts often draw distinctions between mandatory and prohibitory temporary injunctions. A mandatory temporary injunction alters rather than maintains the status quo.[73] When a plaintiff wishes to alter the status quo by a temporary injunction, the court will often insist on a greater showing of the likelihood of success than when a prohibitory injunction, (which maintains the status quo) is sought.[74] The form of the order is not controlling. As one commentator has noted, "The 'mandatory injunction' has

---

[69] *Praefke Auto Electric & Battery Co., Inc.*, *supra*, 255 F.3d at 464 (using as an example a hypothetical contract that gave one party the right to terminate on 30 days notice; notice is given; and, on the 29th day the noticed party seeks temporary injunctive relief to keep the contract in force past the 30 days). Judge Posner asked rhetorically:

> Would such an injunction "maintain the status quo" because an established dealership would continue, or change the status quo by suspending a term of the contract, making Praefke a dealer with at least temporary tenure rather than a dealer subject to termination at the will of his supplier?

Id.

[70] Nat'l Ass'n of Letter Carriers, AFL-CIO v. Sombrotto, 449 F.2d 915, 921 (2d Cir. 1971).

[71] Ross-Whitney Corp. v. Smith Kline & French Laboratories, 207 F.2d 190, 199 (9th Cir. 1953).

[72] United States v. Barrows, 404 F.2d 749, 752 (9th Cir. 1968), *cert. denied*, 394 U.S. 974 (1969).

[73] Tom Doherty Assocs., Inc. v. Saban Entertainment, Inc., 60 F.3d 27, 33 (2d Cir. 1995).

[74] *Id.* at 34 (noting that plaintiff must make "clear showing" of entitlement to relief); *see* SEG Sports Corp. v. State Athletic Comm'n, 952 F. Supp. 202, 204 (S.D.N.Y. 1997) (stating that "[w]hen injunctive relief is mandatory in the sense that it will alter, rather than maintain the status quo, a heightened standard is applied"); Sportsmen's Wildlife Def. Fund v. U.S. Dep't of Interior, 949 F. Supp. 1510, 1523 (D. Colo. 1996) (same).

not yet been devised that could not be stated in 'prohibitory terms.' "[75] If the order accomplishes significantly more than the maintenance of the status quo, it may be subject to heightened proof requirements, even though the order uses prohibitory language.[76]

[31.5] Freeze Orders

A form of temporary relief that is enjoying some popularity is the "asset freeze" order. The order prevents the defendant from using or removing her assets, except as permitted by the court. The purpose of the order is to preserve the defendant's ability to comply with any final orders or judgments of the court. "Asset freeze" orders are permitted under a number of federal statutes, such as RICO (Racketeering Influenced & Corrupt Organization Act).[77] Freeze orders are also permitted as a common law remedy. Courts have, however, disagreed whether a freeze order is more like a preliminary injunction or a writ of attachment.[78]

"Asset freeze" orders are commonly available in international disputes; in this setting they are known as "Mareva" injunctions. The Supreme Court, however, restricted the availability of common law "asset freeze" orders in the recent case of *Grupo Mexicano de Dessarrollo S.A. v. Alliance Bond Fund*,[79] to cases when the interim freeze order was connected to related final equitable relief[80] or interim relief was authorized by Congress.[81] If

---

[75] *Developments in the Law-Injunctions*, 78 Harv. L. Rev. 994, 1062 (1965).

[76] Securities and Exch. Comm'n v. Unifund SAL., 910 F.2d 1028, 1040 (2d Cir. 1990). *But cf.* Phillip v. Fairfield University, 118 F.3d 131, 133–34 (2d Cir. 1997) (finding that heightened standard of proof was not applicable to injunction preventing NCAA from barring plaintiff's participation in University's basketball program and denying him financial aid; by preventing NCAA interference injunction preserved relationship between student (plaintiff) and university).

[77] 18 U.S.C. §§ 1961–1968 (2000); *see* Teresa Bryan, et al., *Racketeer Influenced and Corrupt Organizations*, 40 Am. Crim. L. Rev. 987, 1022–25 (2003).

[78] Republic of the Philippines v. Marcos, 862 F.2d 1355, 1361 (9th Cir. 1988) (characterizing a freeze order as not a writ of attachment, and therefore subject to F.R.C. P. Rule 64, but rather an injunction subject to Rule 65); *SEC v. Unifund SAL*, *supra*, 910 F.2d at 1040–41 (stating that while the SEC had not made out a sufficient claim for a preliminary injunction, it was entitled to an asset freeze order).

[79] 527 U.S. 308 (1999) (*discussed* in Section 20.1 (Judicial Power)); David Capper, *The Need For Mareva Injunctions Reconsidered*, 73 Fordham L. Rev. 2161, 2166–67 (2005) (stating that on its facts *Grupo Mexicano* stated a weak case for a "Mareva" injunction).

[80] United States ex rel. Rahman v. Oncology Associates, P.C., 198 F.3d 489, 498 (4th Cir. 1999) (holding that court could grant interim freeze order when plaintiff sought constructive trust and equitable rescission (setting aside of fraudulent conveyance); *cf.* Dateline Exports, Inc. v. Basic Const., Inc., 306 F.3d 912, 914 (9th Cir. 2002) (*per curiam*) (suggesting that *Grupo Mexicano* decision is limited to pre-default claims by unsecured creditors).

[81] United States, v. DBB, Inc., 180 F.3d 1277, 1283–84 (11th Cir. 1999) (finding that Congress intended to permit interim assets freezes by preliminary injunction even though statute (False Claims Act) did not expressly authorize remedy); *cf.* S.E.C. v. Hickey, 322 F.3d 1123, 1128 (9th Cir. 2003) (holding that federal courts have inherent equity power to freeze non-party's assets in aid of S.E.C.'s enforcement action).

the federal courthouse is closed, however, a state court may provide the desired remedy.[82]

In general, the availability of an "asset freeze" order requires some "misconduct" on the defendant's part that exacerbates the risk of insolvency. Courts will usually condition an "asset freeze" order on a showing of fraud or mismanagement on the part of the defendant that makes it unlikely that defendant will be able to respond to the monetary award.[83] There is much in this area that borrows from the law of fraudulent conveyances.[84]

Courts frequently admonish that "asset freeze" orders are extraordinary remedies that are not to be used in run of the mill cases. The mere fact that the damages claim exceeds the defendant's net worth is not, standing alone, a sufficient showing of the need for a freeze order.[85] An "asset freeze" order will be easier to obtain when the order attaches to property a plaintiff seeks to have restored to him and as to which he was unlawfully deprived by the defendant, for example, property given to the plaintiff but misappropriated by the defendant.[86] Some courts limit "asset freeze" orders to misappropriation cases.[87]

[31.6] Notice and Hearing Requirement

The general preference is that temporary injunctive relief should not be granted unless notice is provided to the defendant of plaintiff's intent to seek such relief. This is done so that the defendant may have a "fair opportunity" to marshal evidence and arguments in opposition to the requested relief.[88] It is important, however, when applying the preference to distinguish between the forms of temporary injunctive relief.[89] For preliminary injunctions, the notice requirement is usually mandatory; for TROs, *in cases involving exigent circumstances*, the order may be sought ex parte and without notice.[90]

---

[82] All Season Excavating Co. v. Bluthardt, 593 N.E.2d 679 (Ill. App. 1992) (allowing "asset freeze" under state common law and equity jurisdiction of court).

[83] Elliott v. Kiesewetter, 98 F.3d 47, 58 (3d Cir. 1996); U.S. Dep't of Housing & Urban Dev. v. Cost Control Mktg. & Sales Mgmt. For Virginia, 64 F.3d 920, 927 (4th Cir. 1995), *cert denied*, 517 U.S. 1188 (1996).

[84] Pashaian v. Eccelston Properties, Ltd., 88 F.3d 77, 85 (2d Cir. 1996) (noting that transfers were made " 'without a fair consideration' at a time when [defendant] '[was] or [would] be thereby rendered insolvent in violation of Debtor and Creditor Law . . . .' ").

[85] *Elliott, supra*, 98 F.3d at 58 n.8.

[86] *Id.* at 58.

[87] Mitsubishi Int'l Corp. v. Cardinal Textile Sales, Inc., 14 F.3d 1507, 1521 (11th Cir. 1994), *cert. denied*, 513 U.S. 1146 (1995); *In re* Fredeman Litig., 843 F.2d 821, 824 (5th Cir. 1988).

[88] Weitzman v. Stein, 897 F.2d 653, 657 (2d Cir. 1990).

[89] Fed. R. Civ. P. 65(a) (1992)

[90] Fed. R. Civ. P. 65(b) (1992).

The notice requirement at its most fundamental level derives from constitutional due process concerns.[91] Those concerns have, however, been largely subsumed within express statutory requirements that specify when notice is required and when notice may be excused due to other concerns.

The form of notice required will usually differ depending on whether the plaintiff is seeking a TRO or preliminary injunction. Notice for a TRO may be informal, for example, a telephone call informing the defendant that the plaintiff intends to seek a TRO before Judge X at a particular time, date, and place.[92] Notice for a preliminary injunction tends to be more formal as the process is usually begun by motion. In either case, the procedure is often controlled by local rules of court, which should be consulted before initiating the request for temporary injunctive relief.

Because motions for preliminary injunctions are usually prescribed by rules of court, the amount of advance notice that the plaintiff must give the defendant of the intent to seek this form of injunctive relief is preset.[93] That is rarely the case with TROs; rather, the rules are often silent as to how much advance notice must be given. This silence in the rules creates an incentive for plaintiffs to delay till the last minute the giving of notice so that the defendant's preparation time before the hearing may be reduced. Such tactics must, however, be tempered by the realization that the trial judge may view dimly the plaintiff's "delayed-noticed" tactic and use that factor to continue the hearing to give the defendant more time to respond or deny the requested relief due to plaintiff's inequitable conduct. While no fixed time line can be adduced in the abstract, a reasonable approach would suggest that notice should be given to defendant of plaintiff's intent to seek the TRO around the point in time plaintiff commits to seek that remedy. If a time line is prescribed by the rules, the rule must be obeyed, at least absent good cause excusing strict compliance.[94]

---

[91] Fidelity Mortgage Investors v. Camelia Builders, Inc., 550 F.2d 47, 51 (2d Cir. 1976), *cert. denied*, 429 U.S. 1093 (1977) (stating that to be bound by an order party must have knowledge of the order); *cf.* Carroll v. President of Comm. of Princess Anne County, 393 U.S. 175, 181 (1968) (holding that First Amendment precluded court from issuing, without notice, ex parte TRO that prohibited participation in protest rallies); *In re* Snow, 201 B.R. 968, 976 (C.D. Cal. 1996) ("due process requires that a party in interest be given an opportunity to be heard after due notice before the party may be bound by a court order").

[92] G&J Parking Co. v. City of Chicago, 522 N.E.2d 774, 777–78 (Ill. App. 1988) (telephone call); *see Fidelity Mortgage Investors, supra*, 550 F.2d at 51; *In re* Rubin, 378 F.2d 104, 108 (3d Cir. 1967) (formal notice not required as long as party has actual notice).

[93] Courts have not, however, been receptive to claims that inadequate time was provided by the notice to prepare an adequate defense. Dominion Video Satellite, Inc. v. EchoStar Satellite Corp., 269 F.3d 1149, 1153–54 (10th Cir. 2001) (holding that one day notice of hearing on motion for preliminary injunction did not violate defendant's right of due process; defendant neither objected to nor requested more time to respond to the motion). *But see* Four Seasons Hotels and Resorts, B.V. v. Consorcio Bar, S.A., 320 F.3d 1205, 1212 (11th Cir. 2003) (holding that foreign defendant was provided with inadequate notice when only two days notice of the hearing was given).

[94] Cal. Rules of Court 379(b) (requiring 24 hours notice, "absent a showing of exceptional circumstances").

There are occasions when the plaintiff fears that if notice of the intent to seek a TRO is given, the defendant will use the opportunity to frustrate the realization of the benefits of obtaining a TRO. For example, the plaintiff may seek a TRO freezing defendant's assets, but fears that if defendant has advance notice of plaintiff's intentions, defendant will move or conceal his assets, making enforcement of the TRO difficult if not impossible.[95] Increasingly, legislation has been adopted that recognizes that in certain discrete areas, as diverse as counterfeit goods or stalking, the dangers associated with giving notice may outweigh the benefits.[96] It must, however, be recognized that in these cases the plaintiff must still make a factual proof, by declaration or otherwise, that a real, palpable danger exists that is associated with the giving of notice of the intent to seek a TRO.[97] Moreover, if a TRO without notice issues from the court, the defendant must be given the opportunity to appear promptly before the court to seek the dissolving or modification of the TRO.[98]

A lawyer appearing on behalf of the plaintiff seeking a TRO ex parte must recognize that her professional duties will be altered by her appearance ex parte. A lawyer in this setting must "inform the tribunal of all material facts known to the lawyer that will enable the tribunal to make an informed decision, whether or not the facts are adverse."[99] The reasons for this

---

[95] Vuitton et Fils, S.A. v. Crown Handbags, 606 F.2d 1, 2 (2d Cir. 1979) (per curiam) (reversing district court's denial of ex parte relief and noting that if alleged counterfeiter of plaintiff's recognized goods was allowed to evade TRO by being given notice "the community of counterfeiters will be permitted to continue to play its 'shell game' at great expense and damage to Vuitton"). The court continued: "[W]hen a proper showing is made . . . a plaintiff is entitled to have an ex parte temporary restraining order." Id. at 4.

[96] Fimab-Finanziria Maglificio Biellese Fratelli Fila Sip. A. v. Helio Import/Export, Inc., 601 F. Supp. 1, 2 (S.D. Fla. 1983) (counterfeit goods); Michigan Comp. Laws Annotated § 600.2950(a)(8) (permitting issuance of ex parte "personal protection orders" without written or oral notice to enjoined party); see Vuiton v. White, 945 F.2d 569, 575 (3d Cir. 1991) (addressing use of ex parte seizure orders in trademark infringement cases):

> In essence, both the Senate and House bills permitted issuance of an ex parte seizure order if the applicant could show that the defendant would not comply with a lesser court order, such as a temporary restraining order, and there was no means of protecting the court's authority other than to seize the property in question on an ex parte basis. The legislative history thus indicates that Congress considered "ex parte seizures . . . a necessary tool to thwart the bad faith efforts of fly by night defendants to evade the jurisdiction of the court," and intended seizure orders to be available whenever a temporary restraining order and the threat of contempt for a violation thereof are unlikely to result in preservation of the evidence and the removal of the counterfeit merchandise from commerce.

(citations omitted).

[97] G&J Parking Co., supra, 522 N.E.2d at 778; Lorillard Tobacco Co. v. Bisan Food Corp., 377 F.3d 313, 320 (3d Cir. 2004) (holding that plaintiff was not entitled to an ex parte seizure order absent proof that defendant had failed to appear in court when required or was likely to fail to appear); Vuitton et Fils, supra, 606 F.2d at 3.

[98] Fed. R. Civ. P. 65(b) (enjoined party must be given calendar preference by issuing court to move to dissolve or modify TRO).

[99] Rule 3.3(d), ABA Model Rules of Professional Conduct; In re Anonymous, 786 N.E.2d 1185 (Ind. App. 2003) (imposing discipline of private reprimand on lawyer who failed to disclose

heightened duty of disclosure lies in the deficiencies of ex parte proceedings in an adversarial system. The defendant's absence prevents the testing of proofs and the presentation of opposing arguments; consequently, plaintiff's attorney must fill the gap.

The ability, under limited circumstances, to dispense with the giving of notice of the intent to seek a TRO does not apply to the requirement that before a person is deemed bound by an order that person must have notice of the order.[100] There are no exceptions to this requirement; however, the means by which notice of the order is given may be quite loose and in some circumstances the person enjoined may be under what can only be described as "inquiry notice." For example, many state and federal courts have standing orders that govern conduct before the court. Knowledge of these orders is often presumed, although the better course is to inform the party of the existence of the order. Only if disobedience persists should a sanction be issued.

Notice of the issuance of an order is communicated to a client-party through its counsel. If counsel appears at the hearing, counsel's knowledge of the order is imputed to counsel's client(s) under the law of principal and agent.[101]

Notice of the order should be provided by personal service or other approved means.[102] In appropriate situations, notice may be relatively informal. For example, notice that a parade or protest is in violation of a court order may be given by bullhorn warning to the demonstrators.[103] The notice must, however, be by means that, under the circumstances, are reasonably calculated to inform the party of the substance of the order and the party's

---

to judge when seeking *ex parte* TRO why notice should not have been required); Goodsell v. Mississippi Bar, 667 So. 2d 7 (Miss. 1996) (finding that lawyer who failed to disclose that paper submitted to court was signed by lawyer rather than by client breached duty of candor); Jill Dennis, *The Model Rules and the Search For the Truth: The Origins and Applications of Model Rule 3.3(d)*, 8 Geo. J. Legal Ethics 157 (1994).

[100] Fed. R. Civ. P. 65(d) (providing that a TRO or preliminary injunction is binding only on those "who receive actual notice of the order by personal service or otherwise").

[101] Restatement (Second) of Agency §§ 9(3), 268, 283 (1957).

[102] I.A.M. Nat'l Pension Fund, Benefit Plan A v. Wakefield Indus., Inc., 699 F.2d 1254, 1259–60 (D.C. Cir. 1983) (holding that contempt proceeding against President of enjoined party must be predicated upon proper service upon President who was not named a defendant in the action in which the injunction was issued); PILF Investments, Inc. v. Arlitt, 940 S.W.2d 255, 260 (Tex. Civ. App. 1997) (holding that "notice on motion for injunctive relief is inadequate to the extent a non-movant party, who is ultimately enjoined, is not served with notice of the hearing").

[103] Allison v. City of Birmingham, 580 So. 2d 1377, 1379 (Ala. Crim. App. 1991) (holding that notice over bullhorn of revocation of consent to enter premises adequately informed persons on premises that their continued presence constituted a trespass); Roe v. Operation Rescue, 919 F.2d 857, 871–72 (3d Cir. 1990) (notice by bullhorn was sufficient to bind protester nonparty; formal service not required); United States v. Baker, 641 F.2d 1311, 1317 n.8 (9th Cir. 1981) (suggesting that in limited circumstances notice by publication in areas frequented by persons to be bound may suffice).

obligations under the order.[104] Notice, however, will be effective when the person to be bound engages in concerted effort to defeat notice.[105] The jurisdiction may require that notice of the issuance of the order be given by someone other than the party benefitted by the order.[106]

The general rule is that a party is entitled to an evidentiary hearing before the court enters or continues a preliminary injunction.[107] "Only when the facts are not in dispute, or when the adverse party has waived its right to a hearing, can that significant procedural step be eliminated."[108] Sometimes the phraseology changes so that the hearing is required only when the facts are in dispute,[109] but phraseology does not appear to affect the core entitlement to a hearing to contest disputed facts relevant to the issuance of preliminary injunctive relief. The fact that the defendant has submitted a written opposition does not conclusively evidence his acquiescence to the resolution of the claim for preliminary relief without a hearing.[110] It is also recognized that "a decision [to enter an order] may be based on affidavits and other documentary evidence if the facts are undisputed and the relevant factual issues are resolved."[111] Perhaps the point was put best in *Consolidated Gold Fields PLC v. Minorco, S.A.*:

> This Court has held that "[o]n a motion for a preliminary injunction, where 'essential facts are in dispute, there must be a hearing . . .

[104] Mullane v. Central Hanover Bank & Trust Co., 339 U.S. 306, 319 (1950) (holding that notice by publication of a claims bar date was insufficient because it was not reasonably calculated to inform known claimants of the existence of the bar date).

[105] Vermont Women's Health Ctr. v. Operation Rescue, 617 A.2d 411, 415 (Vt. 1992) (finding attempts to "drown out" reading of order ineffective); Neshaminy Water Resources Auth. v. Del-Aware Unlimited, Inc., 481 A.2d 879, 883–84 (Pa. Super. Ct. 1984) (singing in unison while terms of order were read did not defeat notice).

[106] Caldwell v. Coppola, 268 Cal. Rptr. 453, 456 (Cal. App. 1990) (holding that improper personal service by plaintiff on defendant renders any judgment or order arising from the proceeding void despite the defendant's actual notice).

[107] Williams v. McKeithen, 939 F.2d 1100, 1105 (5th Cir. 1991) (stating that notice requirement of Rule 65 "implies a hearing in which the defendant is given a fair opportunity to oppose the application and to prepare for such opposition"); Professional Plan Examiners of New Jersey, Inc. v. LeFante, 750 F.2d 282, 288 (3d Cir. 1984).

[108] *Professional Plan Examiners, supra,* 750 F.2d at 288 (citations omitted).

[109] Cumulus Media Inc. v. Clear Channel Communications, Inc., 304 F.3d 1167, 1178 (11th Cir. 2002).

[110] *Four Seasons Hotels and Resorts, B.V., supra,* 320 F.3d at 1209 n.2; Charlton v. Estate of Charlton, 841 F.2d 988, 989 (9th Cir. 1988); Fengler v. Numismatic Americana, Inc., 832 F.2d 745, 748 (2d Cir. 1987) (holding that "[a] party against whom an injunction is sought will be found to have waived his right to a hearing only where that party was demonstrably "content to rest on affidavits submitted to the court") (citations omitted).

[111] Elliott v. Kiesewetter, 98 F.3d 47, 53 (3d Cir. 1996); *see* Ty, Inc. v. GMA Accessories, Inc., 132 F.3d 1167, 1171 (7th Cir. 1997) (noting that while affidavits are ordinarily inadmissible at trial, they are "fully admissible in summary proceedings, including preliminary-injunction proceedings") (citations omitted); Schraer v. Berkeley Property Owners' Ass'n, 255 Cal. Rptr. 453, 460–61 (Cal. App. 1989) (holding that the trial judge committed an abuse of discretion by refusing to permit the introduction of oral testimony at hearing on request to enjoin alleged harasser).

and appropriate findings of fact must be made.' " However, [that authority] does not stand for the proposition that a hearing must be held in all preliminary injunction cases. As Judge Feinberg has noted, "[T]here is no hard and fast rule in this circuit that oral testimony must be taken on a motion for a preliminary injunction or that the court can in no circumstances dispose of the motion on the papers before it." While some factual disputes may require an evidentiary hearing, more global matters, such as determination of the relevant market, may be decided by a judge on the basis of the paper record.[112]

It is generally required that the factual showing in support of the request for temporary injunctive relief be under oath. The rationale for this requirement is that the issuance of an injunction is a delicate power, requiring great caution; doubtful cases should be resolved against issuance.[113] Requiring that the proofs be affirmed under oath provides additional security in the form of confidence that the temporary decision will likely be consistent with the final decision.

[31.7] Bond Requirement

A plaintiff awarded temporary injunctive relief is usually required to obtain a bond. This bond requirement serves two functions. First, it provides a secure source of funds from which a wrongfully enjoined defendant may collect damages. Second, in most jurisdictions it caps the amount of damages that can be collected from the plaintiff when the defendant is wrongfully enjoined.

Notwithstanding the apparent mandatory language of most bonding regulations, a split has developed. Some courts require a bond in all cases, absent a specific statutory exception.[114] Other courts, emphasizing the last phrase of Rule 65(c),[115] permit discretionary exceptions.[116] Examples of

---

[112] 871 F.2d 252, 256 (2d Cir.) (citations omitted; brackets added), *cert. dismissed*, 492 U.S. 939 (1989). In specific situations, a statute may require more process. Bravo v. Ismaj, 120 Cal. Rptr.2d 879, 889–90 (Cal. App. 2002) (stating that under Vexatious Litigant statute a person was entitled to a noticed motion and oral hearing before being declared a vexatious litigant whose access to court could thereafter be controlled).

[113] Ancora-Citronelle Corp. v. Green, 115 Cal. Rptr. 879, 880 (Cal. App. 1974).

[114] Hoechst Diafoil Co. v. Nan Ya Plastics Corp., 174 F.3d 411, 421 (4th Cir. 1999) (holding that "failure to require a bond upon issuing injunctive relief is reversible error"); Evar, Inc. v. Kurbitz, 468 P.2d 677, 678 (Wash. 1970) (holding that the failure to require bond rendered order invalid); Brunzell Constr. Co., Inc. v. Harrah's Club, 404 P.2d 902, 905 (Nev. 1965). A common exception is that no bond is required of a governmental entity. Cedar-Al Prods., Inc. v. Chamberlain, 748 P.2d 235, 236 (Wash. App. 1987) (noting exception from bonding requirement for governmental entities). The exemption may apply to private parties when a governmental party joins in the request for temporary injunctive relief. Dangberg Holdings v. Douglas Co., 978 P.2d 311, 320–21 (Nev. 1999).

[115] Fed. R. Civ. P. 65(c) provides: "No restraining order or preliminary injunction shall issue except upon the giving of security by the applicant, in such sum as the court deems proper . . . ."

[116] Connecticut General Life Ins. Co. v. New Images of Beverly Hills, 321 F.3d 878 (9th Cir. 2003):

discretionary exceptions include: (1) cases where the plaintiff would have difficulty posting the bond and the defendant faced a low burden of harm from its absence;[117] (2) cases where there was no proof that the defendant would be harmed by the issuance of the injunction;[118] (3) cases where the amount in dispute was deposited into court;[119] (4) cases where the plaintiff is indigent;[120] (5) cases where a bond requirement would deprive a group access to court to litigate an issue affecting the "public interest,"[121] and (6) cases where the injunction issued to aid in the preservation of the jurisdiction of the court, e.g., enjoining a defendant from removing property, (vesting the court with in rem jurisdiction), from the control of the court.[122]

Even if the bond is required, a court may have discretion to set the bond at a nominal amount.[123] This approach is more consistent with the

---

The district court is afforded wide discretion in setting the amount of the bond, and the bond amount may be zero if there is no evidence the party will suffer damages from the injunction. Because Haya failed to request a bond or submit any evidence regarding her likely damages, we will not entertain this argument for the first time on appeal

We recognize that some other circuits have held that a motion to set bond is not required to preserve the issue for appeal. We do not, however, believe that the language of Rule 65(c) absolves the party affected by the injunction from its obligation of presenting evidence that a bond is needed, so that the district court is afforded an opportunity to exercise its discretion in setting the amount of the bond. Without such evidence before it, the district court did not abuse its discretion by not reaching the bond issue.

Id. at 882 (citations omitted); Temple Univ. v. White, 941 F.2d 201, 219–20 (3d Cir. 1991), *cert. denied*, 502 U.S. 1032 (1992).

[117] Crowley v. Local No. 82, Furniture & Piano Moving, 679 F.2d 978, 999 (1st Cir. 1982), *rev'd on other grounds*, 467 U.S. 526 (1984).

[118] International Controls Corp. v. Vesco, 490 F.2d 1334, 1356 (2d Cir. 1974), *cert. denied*, 417 U.S. 932 (1974); Continental Oil v. Frontier Refinery, 338 F.2d 780, 782–83 (10th Cir. 1964).

[119] Corrigan Dispatch Co. v. Casa Guzman, S.A., 569 F.2d 300, 302 (5th Cir. 1978).

[120] Wayne Chem., Inc. v. Columbus Agency Serv. Corp., 567 F.2d 692, 701 (7th Cir. 1977).

[121] People of State of Cal. ex rel. Van De Kamp v. Tahoe Regional Planning Soc'y, 766 F.2d 1319, 1325 (9th Cir. 1985); City of Atlanta v. Metropolitan Atlanta Rapid Transit Dist., 636 F.2d 1084, 1094 (5th Cir. 1981):

[The] parties were seeking to protect citizens in the Atlanta area from perceived adverse economic and social consequences. In a real sense, therefore, plaintiffs were engaged in public interest litigation, an area in which the courts have recognized an exception to the Rule 65 security requirement.

The beneficiary of this discretionary act need not be a "public interest" organization. Zenith Radio Corp. v. United States, 518 F. Supp. 1347, 1350 (C.I.T. 1981) (dispensing with bond requirement in suit brought by private litigants (domestic manufacturer) to enforce anti-dumping laws and challenging settlement between United States and foreign manufacturer).

[122] Magidson v. Duggan, 180 F.2d 473, 479 (8th Cir.), *cert. denied*, 339 U.S. 965 (1950).

[123] *Id.*; State of Ala. ex rel. Baxley v. Corp of Eng'rs of U.S. Army, 411 F. Supp. 1261, 1276 (N.D. Ala. 1976):

This court is simply unwilling to close the courthouse door in public interest litigation by imposing a burdensome security requirement on plaintiffs who otherwise have standing to review (the challenged) governmental action . . . . Accordingly, the

language of bonding rules than the "no bond" approach, although in fact there is little that functionally distinguishes the two approaches. For the defendant who is subject to an erroneously issued injunction, recourse against a nominal bond is a Phyrric victory.

Distinct from the issue of the power of the court to dispense with the bond is the issue of the failure of the plaintiff to post a required bond. The failure to post a required bond may render the injunction void.[124] Some jurisdictions take a more generous approach treating the failure as a mere irregularity, which only makes the injunction voidable.[125] The difference is a voidable injunction must be obeyed until it is dissolved; a void injunction is a nullity. Failure to file the required bond makes dissolution of the injunction mandatory, although the plaintiff may cure the deficiency by posting a bond before the hearing date for the motion to dissolve.[126]

Injunction bond determinations may be affected by special legislation creating rights or duties different from those prescribed by a general rule, such as Rule 65(c). For example, in *International Association of Machinists & Aerospace Workers v. Eastern Airlines., Inc.* the court held that the damages provision of the Norris-LaGuardia Act[127] expanded upon the costs recoverable against an injunction bond issued pursuant to Rule 65(c).[128] Similarly, an order issued pursuant to the All Writs Act,[129] in aid of and in preservation of the federal court's jurisdiction, need not be bonded. Thus, an injunction without bond may issue to keep a case from becoming moot.[130]

The general rule is that the wrongfully enjoined defendant is limited to the bond for all damages caused by the injunction.[131] This is known as the

---

injunction to be issued will be conditioned upon the giving of security in the amount of one dollar.

Brown v. Artery Org., Inc., 691 F. Supp. 1459, 1462 (D.D.C. 1987) (finding that requiring poor plaintiffs to post a bond that would provide real security would stifle the purpose of the Fair Housing Act and preclude judicial review until after irreparable injury had been inflicted; accordingly, the court set bond at $500).

[124] Christo v. Tuscany Inc., 454 A.2d 1042, 1044 (Pa. Super. Ct. 1982). *But cf.* Kaiser v. Market Square Discount Liquors, 992 P.2d 636, 643 (Colo. App. 1999) (finding that failure to post *nominal* bond did not invalidate injunction; evidence showed that defendant was unlikely to suffer compensable injury if injunction issued).

[125] Guiliano v. Carlisle, 653 N.Y.S.2d 635, 637 (App. Dept. 1997); Vanguard Transp. Sys., Inc. v. Edwards Transfer & Storage Co., 673 N.E.2d 182, 186 (Ohio App. 1996).

[126] Abba Rubber Co. v. Seaquist, 286 Cal. Rptr. 518, 521 (Cal. App. 1991).

[127] 29 U.S.C. § 107 (1997).

[128] 925 F.2d 6, 9 (1st Cir. 1991) (noting that Rule 65(e) "states that the Rule does not modify any statute of the United States relating to . . . preliminary injunctions in actions affecting employer and employee . . . .")

[129] 28 U.S.C. § 1651.

[130] Zenith Radio Corp. v. United States, 518 F. Supp. 1347, 1348–49 (Ct. Int'l Trade 1981) (collecting cases).

[131] Coyne-Delany Co., Inc. v. Capital Dev. Bd. of State of Ill., 717 F.2d 385, 393 (7th Cir. 1983). *Contra* Nat'l Sanitary Supply Co. v. Wright, 644 N.E.2d 903, 905 (Ind. App. 1994) (stating that a "wrongfully enjoined defendant's recovery is not limited to the amount of security provided . . ."). *See generally* Jay M. Zitter, Annot., *Recovery of Damages Resulting From Wrongful Issuance of Injunction As Limited to Amount of Bond*, 30 A.L.R. 4th 273 (1984).

"injunction bond rule." The bond requirement may be likened to a contract in which the court and the plaintiff "agree" to the bond amount as the "price" of a wrongful injunction. Under this view, the defendant becomes the involuntary "beneficiary" of the agreement.[132] Absent a bond, the wrongfully enjoined defendant may have no remedy.[133] Under this view, a court should not excuse the bond requirement when the plaintiff is fiscally solvent[134] because the damages remedy may be illusory.[135] Similarly, the court should not condition relief from the bond requirement on the plaintiff agreeing to waive the protection of the injunction bond rule.[136] The parties may, however, stipulate or voluntarily provide that excusing the bond requirement waives the injunction bond rule. There are, however, few decisions addressing this tactic.[137]

It appears that the court may not retroactively increase the amount of the bond. The bond amount permits the injunction holder to know what its liability is if the injunction was wrongfully issued.[138] The caveat here is that this issue has arisen in the context of the dissolution of a preliminary injunction. If the injunction is dissolved, there is no purpose for a bond.[139] Prospective modification of bonds is permitted[140] and the court's power to continue the injunction may include the implied power to impose retroactive exposure on the injunction holder who, if it disagrees with the increase in exposure, can withdraw the request for further injunctive relief.

A defendant may appeal the bond amount and in some instances substantial relief has been granted.[141]

The calculation of damages arising from a wrongfully issued injunction is not constrained other than being limited in most jurisdictions to the amount of the bond. Within that constraint, the damages recoverable in an action on the bond include all damages sustained as a result of the

---

[132] Continuum Co., Inc. v. Incepts, Inc., 873 F.2d 801, 803 (5th Cir. 1989).

[133] W.R. Grace & Co. v. Local Union 759, Int'l Union of United Rubber, Cork, Linoleum & Plastic Workers, 461 U.S. 757, 770 n.14 (1983) (stating that "[a] party injured by the issuance of an injunction later determined to be erroneous has no action for damages in the absence of a bond") (citations omitted).

[134] *Continental, supra,* 338 F.2d at 782–83.

[135] *Continuum Co., Inc., supra,* 873 F.2d at 803.

[136] Pharmaceutical Soc'y of State of N.Y., Inc. v. New York State Dep't of Social Servs., 50 F.3d 1168, 1174 (2d Cir. 1995).

[137] Republic Inc. Co. v. Masters, Mates and Pilots Pension Plan, 843 F. Supp. 914, 920 (S.D.N.Y. 1994) (noting waiver exception), *rev'd on other grounds,* 77 F.3d 48 (2d Cir. 1996).

[138] Sprint Communications Co., L.P. v. Cat Communications Int'l, 335 F.3d 235, 241 (3d Cir. 2003).

[139] *Id.*; Mead Johnson & Co. v. Abbott Labs., 209 F.3d 1032, 1033–34 (7th Cir.) (*per curiam*), *cert. denied,* 531 U.S. 917 (2000).

[140] *Coyne-Delany, supra,* 717 F.2d at 394; Standard Forms Co. v. Nave, 442 F. Supp. 619 (E.D. Tenn. 1976).

[141] Northern States Power Co. v. Federal Transit Admin., 270 F.3d 586, 588 (8th Cir. 2001) (*per curiam*) (holding that district court abused its discretion in setting bond amount at $50,000; the appellate court raised the bond requirement to $8,000,000).

injunction's wrongful issuance. General rules governing the measure of damages apply.[142] Damages may include "lost profits" resulting from the wrongful enjoining of the defendant.[143]

Damages for wrongfully issued temporary injunctive relief must be attributable to the issuance of the injunction. In *Phoenix Aviation, Inc. v. MNK Enterprises. Inc.*[144] a creditor was temporarily enjoined from selling collateral when the debtor defaulted. After the injunction was dissolved, the creditor sought to recover prejudgment interest on the amount owed by the debtor and storage costs relating to the collateral against the injunction bond. The creditor could not show, however, that it would have been able to dispose of the collateral through a creditor's sale if the injunction had not issued. Absent proof of a lost sale, the creditor lost no interest on potential sale proceeds; rather, the lost interest represented the debtor's failure to pay the underlying debt, a fact distinct from the issuance of the injunction. Similarly, the creditor could not show that it could have disposed of the collateral and avoided additional storage charges had it been free of the injunction. No recovery of prejudgment interest or storage costs was permitted against the bond.

Some jurisdictions permit the prevailing party to recover attorney fees incurred in defending against a wrongfully issued injunction.[145] Recoverable attorney's fees must be separated from the fees incurred in defending against the claim itself,[146] although if the fees were incurred on a matter that benefits both aspects of the defense, recovery may be allowed.[147]

The connection between bond and damages is that ordinarily the bond amount or undertaking should be sufficient to compensate for the damages likely to be sustained by an erroneously enjoined defendant. The bond amount should be calculated based on the assumption the injunction will

---

[142] Global Contact Lens, Inc. v. Knight, 254 So. 2d 807, 808 (Fla. App. 1971); *Abba Rubber Co., supra*, 286 Cal. Rptr. at 523 (stating that "sole limit . . . is that harm must have been proximately caused by the wrongfully issued injunction").

[143] *Abba Rubber Co., supra*, 286 Cal. Rptr. at 523 ("When an injunction restrains the operation of a business, foreseeable damages include 'the profits' which [the operator] would have made had he not been prevented by the injunction from carrying out his business"); *see* Nintendo of Am. Inc. v. Lewis Galoob, Toys, Inc., 16 F.3d 1032, 1038–39 (9th Cir. 1994) (upholding award of lost profits due to lost sales caused by injunction).

[144] 919 P.2d 348 (Idaho App. 1996).

[145] NewMech Cos., Inc. v. Independent Sch. Dist., 558 N.W.2d 22, 24 (Minn. App. 1997); *Hampton, supra*, 654 N.E.2d at 10; *Abba Rubber Co., supra*, 286 Cal. Rptr. at 525; Collins & Hermann, Inc. v. St. Louis County, 684 S.W.2d 324, 326 (Mo. 1985). *Contra* Fireman's Fund, Ins. Co. v. S.E.K. Constr. Co., Inc., 436 F.2d 1345, 1351 (10th Cir. 1971) (applying Fed. R. Civ. P. 65(c) and holding that attorney's fees are not recoverable as damages in an action on injunction bond); *but cf.* Alton & Southern Ry. Co. v. Brotherhood of Maintenance of Way Employees, 899 F. Supp. 646, 650–51 (D.D.C. 1995) (permitting recovery of attorney fees against bond pursuant to § 7 of the Norris-LaGuardia Act).

[146] *NewMech Cos., Inc., supra*, 558 N.W.2d at 24. If the injunction dissolves by its own terms, no attorney's fees would be recoverable. Label Printers v. Pflug, 616 N.E.2d 706, 708 (Ill. App. 1993).

[147] *Phoenix Aviation, supra*, 919 P.2d at 354; Section 213.1 (Calculation of Fees Award).

be deemed to have been erroneously issued,[148] and should include all elements of damage the wrongfully enjoined defendant would be entitled to recover. Nevertheless, in practice, the amount of the undertaking is usually committed to the trial court's discretion.[149]

In order to recover damages against the bond, the defendant must demonstrate that he was wrongfully enjoined. This is determined by a final judgment or order that the plaintiff was not entitled to temporary injunctive relief.[150] The issue is whether the defendant actually had the right to do that which he was enjoined not to do.[151] The issue is not whether the trial court committed any irregularities when it issued the injunctive relief. Based on the record at the time the preliminary injunction was issued, the trial court may not have abused its discretion in issuing injunctive relief; however, on a fuller record after a trial on the merits, it may be determined that the defendant was wrongfully enjoined.[152]

A dissolution of the temporary injunction for reasons that do not go directly to the merits will preclude recovery against the bond. The dissolution of an injunction due to the failure to post the required bond may not constitute a determination that the injunction itself was wrongfully issued.[153] Reversal or dissolution due to the failure to render required findings of fact and conclusions of law may not permit recovery on the bond.[154] If the parties settle the dispute and the temporary injunction is dissolved, a recovery may not be made against the bond.[155] The result may be different, however, if the settlement occurs post-trial and does not affect the underlying final relief ordered by the trial court.[156]

---

[148] *Abba Rubber Co., supra,* 286 Cal. Rptr. at 524

[149] *Id.* at 523 (stating that the "estimation is an exercise of the trial court's sound discretion and will not be disturbed on appeal unless it clearly appears that the trial court abused its discretion by arriving at an estimate that is arbitrary or capricious, or is beyond the bounds of reason"); State of Ala. ex rel Siegelman v. EPA, 925 F.2d 385, 389 (11th Cir. 1991) (using "abuse of discretion" standard). *But cf.* Nintendo of Am., Inc., 16 F.3d at 103 (holding that the calculation of damages suffered by erroneously enjoined defendant is reviewed under the "clearly erroneous" standard). The court in *Siegelman, supra,* 925 F.2d at 388–89, also noted that some courts use either an "automatic damages" or a "malicious prosecution" standard for determining whether a recovery should be had against the injunction bond.

[150] Blumenthal v. Merrill Lynch, Pierce, Fenner & Smith, Inc., 910 F.2d 1049, 1054–55 (2d Cir. 1990).

[151] *Nintendo of Am., Inc., supra,* 16 F.3d at 1036.

[152] *Blumenthal, supra,* 910 F.2d at 1054–55.

[153] *Phoenix Aviation, Inc., supra,* 919 P.2d at 353 n.9 (noting but not deciding the issue).

[154] *National Sanitary Supply Co., supra,* 644 N.E.2d at 906.

[155] Aetna Cas. & Sur. Co. v. Bell, 603 P.2d 692, 694 (Nev. 1979).

[156] *Cf.* Siebel v. Mittlesteadt, 12 Cal. Rptr.3d 906, 914 (Cal. App. 2004) (holding that settlement did not deprive plaintiff his ability to show a "favorable termination" of the underlying claim necessary to support a malicious prosecution action; the "settlement" only provided for the abandonment of each party's appeals and did not alter or change the underlying judgment), *hearing granted sub nom.* Siebel v. Buell, 97 P.3d 72 (Cal. 2004). Under California law, the granting of a hearing by the California Supreme Court results in the depublication of the intermediate court of appeals decision. Cal. Rules of Court 976(d).

If the court determines the defendant was wrongfully enjoined, courts have suggested that the defendant is presumptively entitled to recover on the bond.[157] Such statements must be carefully received. The defendant must still prove his actual damages. Moreover, courts occasionally state that even a wrongfully enjoined defendant who proves actual damages may be denied a recovery against the bond if good cause otherwise exists.[158]

The injunction bond rule does not bar actions for malicious prosecution[159] or litigation sanctions[160] related to obtaining temporary injunctive relief. In *Microsoft Corporation v. A-Tech Corp.*,[161] this principle was extended to permit a wrongfully enjoined party to maintain an abuse of process claim against the plaintiff. Microsoft had sought and obtained a pretrial "asset freeze" order. Defendant contended that Microsoft had requested an order that froze assets "substantially in excess of the amount of damages which Microsoft could recover . . . ."[162] The court found that defendant stated a valid claim for abuse of process based on plaintiff's "alleged illegitimate use of the asset freeze process to tie up more assets than is reasonably necessary to secure [its] claims."[163]

It has been suggested that the injunction bond rule should not be applied to claims for restitution based on plaintiff's unjust enrichment resulting from the wrongful enjoining of defendant.[164] The suggestion is sound. The injunction bond rule is designed to provide certainty and security as to the potential "loss" the enjoined party may sustain as a result of good faith efforts to secure temporary injunctive relief. The injunction bond rule is not designed to confer a collateral benefit or windfall on the party who obtained injunctive relief by immunizing that party from any obligation to disgorge the benefit to another with a superior claim to the benefit. Whether on the facts a claim for restitution is made is, of course, different from the question whether the right to make the claim should be barred.[165]

---

[157] National Kidney Patients Ass'n v. Sullivan, 958 F.2d 1127, 1134 (D.C. Cir. 1992), *cert. denied*, 506 U.S. 1049 (1993).

[158] City & County of Denver v. Ameritrust Co., 832 P.2d 1054, 1057–58 (Colo. App. 1992) (holding that presumption was outweighed by fact that action was brought in the public interest).

[159] DeSantis v. Wackenhut Corp., 793 S.W.2d 670, 686 (Tex. 1990).

[160] Martinez v. Roscoe, 100 F.3d 121, 123 (10th Cir. 1996).

[161] 855 F. Supp. 308 (C.D. Cal. 1994).

[162] *Id.* at 311.

[163] *Id.* at 312.

[164] *Republic Ins. Co.*, *supra*, 843 F. Supp. at 920; State v. Zahourek, 935 P.2d 74, 77 (Colo. App. 1996); *aff'd on other grounds, sub nom.* Graham v. State, 956 P.2d 556 (Colo. 1998); Dan Dobbs, *Should Security be Required as a Pre-Condition to Provisional Injunctive Relief?*, 52 N.C. L. Rev. 1091, 1136 (1974); Note, *The Triggering of Liability on Injunction Bonds*, 52 N.C. L. Rev. 1252, 1255 & n.18 (1974).

[165] Chapter 5 (General Principles Governing Restitution); Chapter 6 (Restitutionary Actions).

§ 32 APPELLATE REVIEW OF ORDERS GRANTING OR DENYING TEMPORARY RELIEF

Many jurisdictions, including the federal system, permit an aggrieved party to appeal an order granting or denying a request for a preliminary injunction.[1] The granting or denying of a Temporary Restraining Order (TRO) is ordinarily not appealable.[2] While a TRO usually expires at the conclusion of a set period of time, the preliminary injunction remains in effect until dissolved or until the rendering of final judgment. Unfortunately, Rule 65 of the Federal Rules of Civil Procedure and its state counterparts do not define TROs and preliminary injunctions; thus, it is not always clear whether the entered "order" is a TRO or preliminary injunction. The task then is to distinguish preliminary injunctions from TROs—a task that is often difficult because the distinction can be illusive.[3]

Trial courts are not always careful to identify the form of relief that is being provided (or denied) and matching it with the correct procedures.[4] One factor used by courts is whether the order changed the status quo. If it did, the order will often be deemed a preliminary injunction, at least after the 10th day, for purposes of determining its appealability.[5] This approach is problematic because the assumption is that TROs only preserve the status quo. Preliminary injunctions, however, no more, and no more frequently, change the status quo than do TROs. On the other hand, neither the label affixed to the order nor its duration are controlling.[6] As one commentator has noted "[a]pplication of these tests is not easy to fathom."[7] Uncertainty over the nature of the order may affect a party's understanding of its obligation to comply with, and its ability to appeal, that order.

Rule 65 provides that a TRO issued *without notice* expires at the end of ten days, unless extended by order of court.[8] The difficulty is that Rule 65 is silent as to the term of a TRO issued with notice. Rule 65 is also silent as to the proper characterization of such an order for purposes of appealability. For example, assume plaintiff gives notice of her intent to seek a

---

[1] 28 U.S.C. § 1292(a)(1) (permitting appeals of orders granting or denying a preliminary injunction).

[2] First Eagle SoGen Funds, Inc. v. Bank of Int'l Settlements, 252 F.3d 604, 607 (2d Cir. 2001); Gon v. First State Ins. Co., 871 F.2d 863, 865 n.1 (9th Cir. 1989).

[3] *Gon, supra* (stating that "[a]n injunction may be defined as an order that is directed to a party, enforceable by contempt, and designed to accord or protect some or all of the substantive relief sought by a complaint *in more than temporary fashion*") (emphasis added; footnote omitted). Nicely tautological!

[4] Such as Findings of Fact and Conclusions of law when preliminary injunctions are *granted* (Fed. R. Civ. P. 52), or expiration dates for TROs, which are not always required, but are always helpful.

[5] Fernandez-Roque v. Smith, 671 F.2d 426, 429 (11th Cir. 1982).

[6] Sampson v. Murray, 415 U.S. 61, 86–87 (1974).

[7] CHARLES ALAN WRIGHT, LAW OF FEDERAL COURTS § 102, at 708 (4th ed. 1983).

[8] Fed. R. Civ. P. 65(b) (1992) states that such extensions of the TRO beyond the 10 day limit require the consent of the party to be bound unless a hearing is afforded. The form of hearing is not specified. *See also* Cal. Code of Civ. P. § 527 (West 1997) (permitting the ex parte TRO without notice to be valid for 15 days or 22 days if good cause is shown).

TRO, defendant appears and argues, the court grants the TRO and sets the hearing on the preliminary injunction for 15 days hence. The order is silent as to its termination date. On the 11th day, may defendant act free of the obligations of the TRO or is it implied that the term of the TRO extends through the 15th day? Did defendant's silence and failure to object constitute "consent" as contemplated by Rule 65(b)?[9] If the judge on his own (*sua sponte*) vacates the hearing date for the preliminary injunction and continues the order until a new hearing date is held 90 days hence, has the nature of the order changed? Is it now sufficiently akin to a preliminary injunction to be appealable? If defendant violates the order on the 81st day, is defendant subject to contempt or has the order expired?

The Supreme Court addressed this problem in two decisions. In *Sampson v. Murray* the trial court issued a TRO with notice that lasted more than 10 days.[10] The Court held "that a temporary restraining order continued beyond the time permissible under Rule 65 must be treated as a preliminary injunction, and must conform to the standards applicable to preliminary injunctions . . . ."[11] The Court ultimately reversed and remanded because in granting the equitable relief the district court had not prepared findings of fact and conclusions of law as required by Rule 52 of the Federal Rules of Civil Procedure.[12] The refusal to dissolve the TRO was deemed to be tantamount to a grant of a preliminary injunction, the words used by the district court were not controlling.[13] The effect of the *Sampson* ruling was to treat Rule 65(b) as if the 10-day rule applies to all TROs, even though a literal reading of Rule 65(b) indicates that the 10-day rule only applies to TROs issued without notice.[14] Courts have so applied *Sampson*,

---

[9] Fed. R. Civ. P. 65(b) provides in part:

> Every temporary restraining order granted without notice . . . shall expire by its terms within such time after entry, not to exceed 10 days, as the court fixes unless within the time so fixed . . . the party against whom the order is directed consents that it may be extended for a longer period. The reasons for the extension shall be entered of record.

[10] 415 U.S. 61 (1974) (a wrongful termination action). The trial court initially granted a TRO and extended it after a hearing until a witness could testify about the reasons for the plaintiff's dismissal from employment. 415 U.S. at 66–67.

[11] 415 U.S. at 86.

[12] This not uncommon. Hoechst Diafoil Co. v. Nan Ya Plastics Corp., 174 F.3d 411, 423 (4th Cir. 1999) (noting that the order specified no duration, but had been in effect for over 18 months; the district court had failed to provide Findings and Conclusions required for a preliminary injunction granted by the court; the failure to provide the required Findings and Conclusions rendered the order invalid).

[13] *Cf.* Professional Plan Examiners of New Jersey, Inc. v. Lafante, 750 F.2d 282, 287 (3d Cir. 1984) (noting that the absence of an identifiable date when the TRO became a preliminary injunction warranted a broader scope of appellate review than normally applied to the modification of an injunction).

[14] Many courts proceed under the erroneous assumption that the durational limits applies to all TROs, those "with" and those "without" notice. *Hoechst Diafoil Co.*, *supra*, 174 F.3d at 423 ("restraining orders may be issued only for a limited duration"). The order in *Hoechst* was apparently preceded by telephonic notice and both sides participated in the hearing. *Id.* at 415 ("During this hearing . . . in which Nan Ya's attorneys participated, Hoechst requested an injunction . . .").

notwithstanding the language in Rule 65(b).[15] *Sampson* and its progeny thus treat an injunctive order of indefinite duration as a preliminary injunction, at least after the 10th day, for purposes of determining the order's appealability.[16]

The judicial gloss placed on the 10-day rule is usually limited to the issue of appealability. When other issues are involved, a court may assess the order in a more limited manner. For example, in *Granny Goose Food, Inc. v. Brotherhood of Teamsters and Auto Truck Drivers*[17] the Court was again confronted with a TRO with notice that extended more than 10 days. Here, however, the issue was not appealability but contempt. Plaintiff filed a complaint in state court alleging a breach of the collective-bargaining agreement. Plaintiff also secured a TRO prohibiting certain activity. The opinion states that the TRO was issued ex parte and the defendant was served with the order. The defendant removed the matter and also sought simultaneously to dissolve the order. Lack of notice was not raised; rather, defendant raised a jurisdictional challenge. The specific issue before the Court in *Granny Goose* involved the effect of 28 U.S.C. § 1450, which provides that the removal of a case does not invalidate an injunction issued by the state court. The question before the court was the effect of that statute on a TRO issued by the state court, which had not been dissolved, and which was arguably violated by defendant over six months after its issuance. This raised an issue similar to *Sampson v. Murray* in that a TRO had been extended beyond duration provided for TROs without notice.[18] In *Granny Goose* the extension was the result of the removal action and defendant's unsuccessful effort in state court to dissolve the injunction.

In *Granny Goose*, unlike *Sampson v. Murray*, the Court had no difficulty finding that the order was a TRO that expired, as if it had been issued without notice, before the alleged violations of the order occurred. The Court noted the unique nature of the TRO remedy,[19] but provided little insight as to why the TRO was deemed to have expired given the events surrounding its issuance. *Sampson v. Murrary* was not cited. It appears that the *Granny Goose* Court saw the primary issue as the construction of 28 U.S.C. § 1450. In cases involving contempt sanctions a court may be likely to view an order of uncertain classification in its most restrictive category, akin to

---

[15] *Id.; see* Nutrasweet Co. v. Vit-Mar Enters., Inc., 112 F.3d 689, 693–94; (3d Cir. 1997); Manbourne, Inc. v. Conrad, 796 F.2d 884, 887 n.3 (7th Cir. 1986); Lewis v. S.S. Baune, 534 F.2d 1115, 1121 (5th Cir. 1976); National City Bank v. Battisti, 581 F.2d 565, 568 (6th Cir. 1977).

[16] Phillips v. Chas. Schreiner Bank, 894 F.2d 127, 131 n.5 (5th Cir. 1990).

[17] 415 U.S. 423 (1974).

[18] The state provision in effect at the time allowed a TRO *without notice* to be in effect for 20 days. No durational time was specified for TROs with notice. Cal. Code Civ. P. § 527(a) (1979).

[19] *Granny Goose, supra*, 415 U.S. at 439 (noting that "under federal law [TROs] should be restricted to serving their underlying purpose of preserving the status quo and preventing irreparable harm just so long as necessary to hold a hearing, and no longer") (brackets added; footnote omitted).

the Rule of Lenity.[20] Such an approach would reconcile *Sampson* and *Granny Goose*; however, not all courts follow a Rule of Lenity when considering whether a person may be cited for contempt for violating, after the 10th day, a TRO issued with notice.

In *Levine v. Comcoa, Ltd.*[21] an attorney's conduct in violating a district court's order not to transfer funds from his firm's client trust account to the firm's operating account resulted in a finding of contempt. The order arose out of an application for temporary equitable relief by the Enforcement Division of the Securities & Exchange Commission. The district court granted a TRO, freezing Comcoa's assets and appointing a Receiver on May 6, 1994. The court notified the parties of a hearing on May 16, 1994, to consider a preliminary injunction. On May 16–17, 1994, the court held a preliminary injunction hearing. No ruling was forthcoming, but the court did continue the May 6th order "until the court ruled on the substantive motions." On June 6, 1994, the attorney called the court to inquire whether the preliminary injunction had issued. On being told that it had not, the attorney transferred funds from Comcoa's client trust account to the firm's operating account. The court accepted for purposes of the appeal that the attorney did not consent to the extension of the May 6th order.

The court held that the attorney was properly cited for contempt. The court relied extensively upon *Sampson*'s language that a TRO continued beyond the time permissible for an *ex parte* TRO "without notice" (10 days) should be treated as a preliminary injunction. According to the court, the proper course of conduct for the attorney was to treat the "TRO as an erroneously granted preliminary injunction."[22] The court placed particular emphasis on the contemnor's status as an attorney and the need to maintain proper respect for court processes.[23] *Granny Goose* was relegated to a footnote and distinguished as a decision where the TRO had issued with "no notice to the parties and no hearing on the various factors involved in considering a preliminary hearing."[24]

The court's decision is troubling in several respects. The limitation of *Granny Goose*, a decision directly addressing the issue of contempt, in favor

---

[20] The Rule of Lenity provides that criminal statutes should be read narrowly when there is reasonable doubt as to the scope of the statute. Moskal v. United States, 498 U.S. 103, 108 (1990) (court should apply lenity when language, structure, legislative history, and motivating policies do not remove reasonable doubt as to the meaning and scope of statute); People ex rel. Lungren v. Superior Court, 926 P.2d 1042, 1053 (Cal. 1996) ("defendant entitled to the benefit of every reasonable doubt, whether it arises out of a question of fact, or as to the true interpretations of words or the construction of language used in a statute") (citation omitted). It is unclear whether plaintiff sought criminal or civil contempt remedies in *Granny Goose*.

The quasi-criminal nature of contempt has, however, been noted. Section 190 (Nature of Contempt). The use of a restrictive rule of construction given the uncertainty over the proper characterization of the order would seem appropriate.

[21] 70 F.3d 1191 (11th Cir. 1995).

[22] 70 F.3d at 1193.

[23] 70 F.3d at 1194 ("for [attorney] just to disregard the district court's clear order, based on his personal belief that it was invalid was not merely bold; it was bad").

[24] 70 F.3d at 1193 n.7.

of *Sampson*, a decision addressing appealability, is perplexing. The emphasis on the "hearing" rather than the issuance of an "order" from the hearing puts the proverbial cart before the horse. Whether or not there was a hearing was not a critical factor. Hearings are not appealed; orders granting or denying a preliminary injunction are. The court distinguished *Granny Goose* based on an irrelevant factor and ignored the striking similarities between the two cases.[25]

A few cases have suggested that, in limited circumstances, a TRO may be immediately reviewable when the TRO effectively grants full and complete relief.[26] The converse, however, tends not to be the case; the denial of a TRO is not deemed an appealable order.[27] Some formulation of the exception do not distinguish, at least literally, between the grant or denial of the TRO. For example, in *Carson v. American Brands, Inc.*[28] the Court recognized that an interlocutory (non-final) order could be immediately appealed when the "order effectively disposes of the litigation" and "might have a 'serious, perhaps irreparable consequence,' [that] . . . "can be effectively challenged' only by immediate appeal."[29] Situations that satisfy this test tend to be extraordinary.[30]

---

[25] 70 F.3d at 1194, 1197. Judge Hill concurring *dubitante* was troubled by the intersect between *Sampson* and *Granny Goose*. Section 199 (Attempted Contempt) (particularly Section 199.2 (Evasion of Anticipated Order)) (noting split in authorities whether a person can be held in contempt for violating an order that has not *yet* been entered).

[26] Romer v. Green Point Savings Bank, 27 F.3d 12 (2d Cir 1994):

> As a preliminary matter we note that the district court's order, although in the form of a TRO, had the effect of a final permanent injunction. By restraining all activity on the conversion until at least February 3, 1994, making it impossible for Green Point to meet the 45-day sale-date, the district court's order would have prevented Green Point's conversion plan from taking effect within the time allowed by law. After the January 29 sale-date, depositors who had subscribed to buy shares in the conversion would be released from their commitments, and any conversion would need to begin with a resolicitation. Thus the district court's order had a far more drastic effect than is normal for a TRO. It effectively granted the Plaintiffs final victory. "[W]hen a grant or denial of a TRO "might have a serious, perhaps irreparable, consequence" and . . . can be 'effectively challenged' only by immediate appeal," we may exercise appellate jurisdiction. Because the district court's order met this standard, this court had jurisdiction to entertain Green Point's appeal, as well as the motion for a stay that accompanied it.

Id. at 15 (citations omitted); Adams v. Vance, 570 F.2d 950, 953 (D.C. Cir. 1978); *see* WRIGHT, FEDERAL COURTS, *supra* at § 102, p. 709 n.15 (collecting cases and commentary suggesting "that [when] the effect of the ruling on the [TRO] is sufficiently grave to make it, in effect, the grant or denial of a preliminary injunction, [it is] appealable under . . . § 1292(a)(2)") (brackets added). *See generally* K.H. Larsen, Annot. *Appeability of Order Granting, Extending or Refusing to Dissolve Temporary Restraining Order*, 19 A.L.R. 3d 403 (1968).

[27] Office of Personnel Mgmt. v. American Fed'n of Gov't Employees, AFL-CIO, 473 U.S. 1301, 1304–05 (1985) (Burger, C.J., Circuit Judge) (distinguishing *Adams v. Vance*, *supra*, when request for TRO is denied). *See generally* K.H. Larsen, Annot., *Appealability of Order Refusing to Grant or Dissolving Temporary Restraining Order*, 19 A.L.R. 3d 459 (1968).

[28] 450 U.S. 79 (1981).

[29] *Id.* at 84, *quoting* Baltimore Contractors, Inc. v. Bodinger, 348 U.S. 176, 181 (1955).

[30] Woratzeck v. Arizona Bd. of Executive Clemency, 117 F.3d 400 (9th Cir. 1997) (*per curiam*):

An order that has the "practical effect" of denying preliminary injunctive relief is appealable to the same extent as the denying of a preliminary injunction if the denial is causing the aggrieved party irreparable injury.[31] This gloss on the rule of appealability is primarily applied when the court denies a request for an order and contained in the order is a request for injunctive relief, for example, as in *Carson* declining to enter a proposed consent decree that contained injunctive relief. Similarly, the granting of summary judgment or summary adjudication may be immediately appealable when the effect of the order is to deny a request for injunctive relief.[32] On the other hand, the requirement of "irreparable harm" should not be minimized.[33]

If an appellate court remands a case awarding equitable relief to the district court due to procedural irregularity, such as for failing to provide findings of facts and conclusions of law in connection with the issuance of a preliminary injunction, the appellate court may, in its discretion, continue the injunction pending further consideration of the matter by the district court on remand.[34]

The modification or denial of modification of a preliminary injunction is immediately appealable when the judicial act has injunctive effect, as for example by requiring the defendant to do something new and now, such as immediately paying another party's attorney's fees and expenses.[35] This raises the related issue of the type of orders that have injunctive effect so as to be immediately appealable. The fact that specific relief is granted is

---

Woratzeck, an Arizona state prisoner sentenced to death tomorrow morning at 12:05 a.m., appeals from the district court's denial of his motion for a temporary restraining order (TRO) and stay of his execution. Denial of a TRO is normally not a final appealable order. However, since Woratzeck faces imminent execution, "the court will not require (Woratzeck) to go through the futile act of reapplying for permanent relief and the denial of a TRO may be treated as a de facto denial of a permanent injunction.

Id. at 401 (citation omitted).

[31] Carson v. American Brands, Inc., 450 U.S. 79, 84 (1981) (involving interlocutory order refusing to enter "consent decree").

[32] Transworld Airlines v. American Coupon Exch., 913 F.2d 676, 680 (9th Cir. 1990).

[33] Simon Property Group, L.P. v. MySimon, Inc. 282 F.3d 986, 990 (7th Cir. 2002) (holding that appellant did not show that delay of final injunctive relief caused irreparable injury; hence, order was not appealable). The court paid particular emphasis to the fact that appellant abandoned its request for a preliminary injunction relief after the district court denied the application for a TRO. *Id.* at 990–91.

[34] *Hoechst Diafoil Co.*, *supra*, 174 F.3d at 424; Inverness Corp. v. Whitehall Labs., 819 F.2d 48, 51 (2d Cir. 1987); *see* TEC Eng'g Corp. v. Budget Molders Supply, Inc., 82 F.3d 542, 546 (1st Cir. 1996) (continuing injunction after remand but modifying so that it will expire two months from issuance of court's mandate); Allied Mktg. Group, Inc. v. CDL Mktg., Inc., 878 F.2d 806, 814 (5th Cir. 1989) (continuing injunction after remand absent substantive, reversible error).

[35] Hook v. Arizona Dep't of Corrections, 107 F.3d 1397, 1401 (9th Cir. 1997). *See generally* Robert Morse, Annot., *When Does Interlocutory Order of Federal District Court, Concerning Previously Issued Injunction, Modify or Continue Such Injunction so as to be Appealable Under 28 U.S.C. § 1292(A)(1)?*, 106 A.L.R. Fed. 500 (1992).

not controlling. For example, an order granting a provisional remedy may not be deemed injunctive in nature.[36] The tests tend to be somewhat conclusory and circular, but the focus is often on whether the order seeks to avoid irreparable injury, direct a party to do or not do something, and, is enforceable by contempt.[37] The fact that a request for judicial action is brought in the form of injunctive relief does not necessarily mean that orders arising from the proceedings will be treated as an injunction.[38]

§ 33 PERMANENT INJUNCTIONS

A permanent injunction is one that is issued after a plenary trial on the merits. It is designed to provide final and complete relief and is thus distinguishable from temporary injunctive relief, which is primarily designed to maintain the status quo until the plaintiff's right to a permanent injunction can be determined.

[33.1] Scope of Injunctive Relief

It is often said that the basic principle applicable to injunctions is that relief "should be narrowly tailored to fit specific legal violations."[1] Injunctive relief should be only as burdensome as necessary to restore plaintiff to her rightful position, which is the position she would have occupied but for defendant's misconduct.[2] That principle is, however, easier to articulate than to apply, for it is also recognized that the injunction should provide complete relief and limiting the remedy or providing only a limited remedy may not accomplish that goal.

---

[36] *In re* Lorillard Tobacco Co., 370 F.3d 982 (9th Cir. 2004) (holding that a "seizure order" authorized by federal trademark law was not an injunction; therefore, the district court's decision was not immediately appealable under 28 U.S.C. § 1292(a)(1) as an order granting or denying injunctive relief). The court stated that an injunction must have three elements: (1) directed to a party; (2) enforceable by contempt; and (3) designed to accord or protect some or all of the substantive relief sought. *Id.* The court found the "seizure order" deficient on all three grounds:

> The ex parte seizure order misses the mark on all three criteria of an injunction. It is not "directed to a party." Instead, the order commands action from a federal or local law enforcement officer. It is not enforceable by contempt. And finally, it does not protect "the substantive relief sought by [the plaintiff] in more than [temporary] fashion."

Id. at 986 (citations and footnote omitted). *Contra* Lorillard Tobacco Co. v. Bisan Food Co., 377 F.3d 313, 318 (3d Cir. 2004).

[37] HBE Leasing Corp. v. Frank, 48 F.3d 623, 632 (2d Cir. 1995); 16 Charles A. Wright et al, Federal practice and procedure § 3922 (1977).

[38] DHR International, Inc. v. Winston & Strawn, 807 N.E.2d 1094 (Ill. App. 2004) (holding that denial of plaintiff's motion for a preliminary injunction enjoining defendant law firm from representing another party in an arbitration adverse to plaintiff was *not* the denial of injunctive relief; rather, the order was more in the nature of a motion to disqualify, which is not appealable under state law).

[1] Waldman Publ'g Corp. v. Landoll, Inc., 43 F.3d 775, 785 (2d Cir. 1994); Haynes v. North State Law Enforcement Officers Ass'n, 10 F.3d 207, 217 (4th Cir. 1993).

[2] Califano v. Yamasaki, 442 U.S. 682, 702 (1979).

Should the injunction operate only to protect the plaintiff[3] or should it also protect those similarly situated?[4] The answer to this question lies perhaps more in the nature of the claim(s) actually litigated and the court's belief as to whether extending relief beyond the plaintiff would be fair under the circumstances. For example, in *Jones v. WMATA*[5] the plaintiff brought sex and age discrimination claims against the defendant. Plaintiff sought a broadly-worded injunction that would protect her and other similarly situated employees of defendant from retaliation for engaging in protected job related activities. The court recognized that in an appropriate case such relief would be proper even if class action status was not sought or obtained.[6] Under the facts, however, the court deemed narrow relief more appropriate. The critical facts were that "[i]n this instance, the jury was not asked to find retaliation against other employees; nor was [plaintiff's] case built upon statistical evidence of disparate impact."[7] Since plaintiff had not attempted to prove a broad case, she was not entitled to a broad remedy.

Perhaps a workable approach to the problem can be found in *Armstrong v. Davis*, when the court observed:

> System-wide relief is required if the injury is the result of violations of a statute or the constitution that are attributable to policies or practices pervading the whole system (even though injuring a relatively small number of plaintiffs), or if the unlawful policies or practices affect such a broad range of plaintiffs that an overhaul of the system is the only feasible manner in which to address the class' injury. However, if injunctive relief is premised upon only a few isolated violations affecting a narrow range of plaintiffs, its scope must be limited accordingly.[8]

---

[3] Brown v. Trustees of Boston, Univ., 891 F.2d 337, 361 (1st Cir. 1989) (limiting injunctive relief in sex discrimination case to named plaintiff).

[4] Bailey v. Patterson, 323 F.2d 201, 205–06 (5th Cir. 1963) (enjoining discriminatory policy of common carrier and requiring that all passengers be treated equally).

[5] 946 F. Supp. 1023 (D.D.C. 1996), *vacated in part and aff'd in part on other grounds*, 205 F.3d 428 (D.C. Cir. 2000).

[6] *Id.* at 1033. Courts may enjoin the enforcement of unconstitutional or illegal statutes without narrowing the injunction to benefit only those before the court. *E.g.*, Larkin v. State of Michigan Dept. of Social Services, 89 F.3d 285 (6th Cir. 1996) (upholding injunction enjoining state from enforcing statute restricting location of adult foster care homes and requiring neighbor notification, without limiting the injunction benefitted to the named parties); *cf.* Doe 1-13 ex rel. Doe Sr. 1-13 v. Bush, 261 F.3d 1037 (11th Cir. 2001) (affirming contempt citation based on failure of defendants to provide relief to non-parties consistent with relief court ordered to be provided to parties; order was intended to provide "system-wide" remedy even though claim was not certified as class action), *cert. denied sub nom.* Kennedy v. Does 1-13, 534 U.S. 1104 (2002).

[7] 946 F. Supp. at 1033.

[8] 275 F.3d 849, 870 (9th Cir. 2001) (footnote omitted), *cert. denied*, 537 U.S. 812 (2002); *cf.* Virginia Society for Human Life, Inc. v. Federal Election Comm'n, 263 F.3d 379, 393–94 (4th Cir. 2001) (citing, as reason for not issuing a nationwide injunction against enforcement of FEC regulation found to unconstitutionally restrict free speech, that such an injunction would prevent other circuits from addressing the issue).

The tension between use of a remedy to provide class-wide relief without the providing of class certification has been commented on by several courts.[9]

Another area evidencing the intersect between the scope of injunctive relief and the specific legal violation is abortion protests. Courts have tried to walk the fine line between respecting the rights of protesters and those who are the objects of or subject to the protests. Courts have scrutinized the extent to which protesters can be enjoined from (1) approaching facilities where abortions are performed, (2) approaching women entering those facilities for abortions, and (3) approaching physicians who provide services at the facilities.[10] The concept applied here is usually captured by the phrase that the equitable remedial power of courts is not unlimited,[11] but is to be exercised in a manner not disruptive of constitutional or statutorily protected rights.[12]

Injunctive relief may not be relied on to create rights not recognized at law.[13] For example, in *California Grocers Ass'n Inc. v. Bank of America*[14] plaintiff sought an injunction requiring defendant to reduce the charge it imposed on member grocers for "deposited items returned" because of non-sufficient funds by the item payor on the ground that the charge was

---

[9] Sharpe v. Cureton, 319 F.3d 259, 273 (6th Cir. 2003), *cert. denied*, 540 U.S. 876 (2003); *Armstrong v. Davis, supra*, 275 F.3d at 870–72; *cf.* Kraus v. Trinity Management Services, Inc., 999 P.2d 718 (Cal. 2000) (holding that the court could not order defendant to provide restitution to non-parties who were harmed by same unfair business practice that harmed the named parties, and for which court properly ordered restitution, unless restitution claims were brought as class action).

[10] Planned Parenthood Ass'n of San Mateo County v. Operation Rescue California, 57 Cal. Rptr. 2d 736 (Cal App. 1996) (providing 15' space between protestors and facility but rejecting 250' space between protestors and residence of physician(s) who provided services at facility), *cert. denied sub nom.* Cochran v. Planned Parenthood Ass'n of San Mateo County, 522 U.S. 811 (1997); Murray v. Lawson, 649 A.2d 1253, 1268 (N.J. 1994) (limiting antiabortion protesters to area 100' from physicians residence and limiting number of protesters and duration of protests), *cert. denied*, 515 U.S. 1110 (1995). *Compare* Madsen v. Women's Health Center, Inc., 512 U.S. 753 (1994) (upholding injunction, against First Amendment challenge, which restricted protestors from coming within 36' of abortion facility), *with* Schenck v. Pro-Choice Network, 519 U.S. 357 (1997) (rejecting "bubble" or floating concept which requires protestor to withdraw to a defined distance away from the person when that person is entering or leaving the facility).

[11] Sixty-Seventh Minn. Senate v. Beens, 406 U.S. 187, 199 (1972) (*per curiam*).

[12] *Madsen, supra*, 512 U.S. at 765:

> Our close attention to the fit between the objectives of an injunction and the restrictions it imposes on speech is consistent with the general rule, quite apart from First Amendment considerations, "that injunctive relief should be no more burdensome to the defendant than necessary to provide complete relief to the plaintiffs."

See Carter v. Gallagher, 452 F.2d 315, 324 (8th Cir. 1971), *cert. denied*, 406 U.S. 950 (1972); Rice v. Garrison, 898 P.2d 631, 637–38 (Kan. 1995).

[13] Rees v. City of Watertown, 86 U.S. 107, 121–22, 22 (1873); Valenzuela v. Aquino, 853 S.W.2d 512, 513 (Tex. 1993) (holding that because state did not recognize a claim for negligent infliction of emotional distress, trial court improperly enjoined, on that ground, picketing of plaintiff's residence).

[14] 27 Cal. Rptr. 2d 396 (Cal. App. 1994).

unconscionable. The court refused the injunction, reasoning that uncons-cionability was traditionally only a defense to contract enforcement; there-fore, it normally cannot be used offensively to support a claim for injunctive relief.[15] The court distinguished situations in which a statute provides an affirmative cause of action for unconscionability, but found that no such statute applied to the plaintiff's claim.[16]

Perhaps a more accurate way to state the scope of injunctive relief is to recognize that equity courts will fashion injunctive relief as necessary to meet the needs of the case.[17] Of course, the "needs of the case" is an imprecise standard, and this simply reflects the futility of a search for an all-encompassing rule in this area. Rather, the emphasis should be placed on the nature of the defendant's conduct, e.g., is it isolated or part of an institutionalized policy, practice, or pattern.[18]

Just as the measure of damages is often calibrated to reflect factors that are not strictly compensatory,[19] injunctive relief often reflects similar influences. The natural flexibility of equitable remedies to fit the needs of the particular case was noted by the Supreme Court in *Hecht Co. v. Bowles*:

> The essence of equity jurisdiction has been the power of the Chan-cellor to do equity and to mold each decree to the necessities of the particular case. Flexibility rather than rigidity has distinguished it. The qualities of mercy and practicality have made equity the instrument for nice adjustment and reconciliation between the public interest and private needs as well as between competing private claims.[20]

While injunctive relief, like damages, seeks to place the plaintiff in the position in which he would have been absent defendant's wrongful conduct, that position is not preordained; rather, it is created by the evidence and found to be true by the decision maker.[21] At times, reasonable minds may

---

[15] 27 Cal. Rptr. 2d at 403.

[16] *Id.* at 404; Section 26.1 (Statutes Expanding Equitable Remedies).

[17] Syring v. Tucker, 498 N.W.2d 370, 374 (Wis. 1993); *see* Lemon v. Kurtzman, 411 U.S. 192, 200–01 (1973) (stating that "equitable remedies are a special blend of what is necessary, what is fair, and what is workable . . . . [I]n equity, as nowhere else, courts eschew rigid absolutes and look to the practical realities and necessities inescapably involved in reconciling competing interests"); Rosario-Torres v. Hernandez-Colon, 889 F.2d 314, 321 (1st Cir. 1989) (*en banc*) (noting that a central feature of equity was "the ability to assess all relevant facts and circumstances and tailor appropriate relief on a case by case basis").

[18] Next Level Communications LP v. DSC Communications Corporation, 179 F.3d 244, 247 (5th Cir. 1999) (holding that when the plaintiff had received full monetary compensation for trade secret misappropriation, it would amount to an impermissible double recovery to also award the plaintiff an injunction barring defendant from using the trade secret); *cf.* Spencer v. General Elec. Co., 894 F.2d 651, 660 (4th Cir. 1990) (affirming lower court's denial of injunction in sexual harassment case when the employer had fully remedied the problem by terminating the offending employee and instituted company-wide anti-sexual harassment pol-icy).

[19] Section 8.7 (Harsh or Mild Measures).

[20] 321 U.S. 321, (1944); *see* note 17, *supra*.

[21] David S. Schoenbrod, *The Measure of an Injunction: A Principle to Replace Balancing*

disagree whether the plaintiff's equitable remedy simply makes him whole or confers a windfall on him. *Bailey v. Proctor* illustrates this point.[22] In *Bailey* the investment policy of an investment trust was changed from a concentration in public utilities to a concentration in investments in the horse racing industry for the principal purpose of allowing an individual who controlled the trust to control the racetrack. The trust was subsequently placed in receivership; however, the racetrack investment proved profitable and new management wished to terminate the receivership. New management's motivation was the fact that (1) this type of trust could be used for highly leveraged investments that would be disproportionately profitable to the owners of the trust, (2) changes in federal law barred these types of investment vehicles, but (3) this particular trust survived under "grandfather" provisions in federal law. The effort to terminate the receivership, and restore control to the new management, was opposed by bondholders, whose monies had been used to engage in the highly leveraged activities. The bondholders received interest on their investment, but did not participate, as the owners did, in capital appreciation. Realizing the risk/reward calculus was not in their favor, the bondholders sought to liquidate the trust. The court agreed with the bondholders.

It may be observed that the bondholders received a remedy that was better than available at law. Because there was no fraud in the inducement, the bondholders could not escape the bargain they had struck. Once equity acquired jurisdiction, however, the bondholders could invoke the court's power to liquidate the trust—a power well established.[23] Yet, the availability of a power is not a command that it be exercised.[24] The exercise of the power to liquidate the trust is independent of the power to appoint the receiver for the trust. The key is whether liquidation was appropriate. The court in *Bailey* found it was, given the legislation disapproving the future use of such investment vehicles. Perhaps it was too strong an exercise of equity power for the court to cause the owners to lose the advantage they had bargained for (highly leveraged investment vehicle) because of the intervening acts, which necessitated the receivership, but whose ill effects had been cured and were no longer harming the bondholders. On the other hand, given the precarious legal status of the investment trust, perhaps it was also permissible to require that the trust be operated at all times properly, if the grandfathered status was to be retained. It was not, and the court found greater equity in relieving the bondholders of a bargain

---

the Equities and Tailoring the Remedy, 72 Minn. L. Rev. 627, 678 (1988) (noting that "[t]he injunction's aim must be the plaintiff's rightful position, but to achieve that aim, its terms may impose conditions on the defendant that require actions going beyond the plaintiff's rightful position").

[22] 160 F.2d 78 (1st Cir.), *cert. denied*, 331 U.S. 834 (1947).

[23] Riehle v. Margolies, 279 U.S. 218, 223 (1929) (holding that appointment of receiver permitted consideration of all questions incident to the preservation, collection, and distribution of the assets of the receivership).

[24] Los Angeles Trust Deed & Mortgage Exch. v. Securities and Exch. Comm'n, 285 F.2d 162, 182 (9th Cir. 1960) (upholding part of district court's order conserving assets but rejecting further direction to liquidate).

than in permitting the continued use of an investment vehicle deemed by Congress to be violative of public policy.

Occasionally courts may provide more injunctive relief than is necessary to ensure that the plaintiff will receive the amount of injunctive relief to which he is entitled.[25] These forms of injunctive relief have come to be known as "prophylactic" injunctions.[26] The primary reason for providing additional (or "prophylactic") relief is ensuring compliance: In fashioning injunctive relief a court must have authority "to address each element contributing to the violation" and may issue an injunction broad enough to avoid "the risk of inadequate compliance."[27] For example, an employee, having confidential information, may wish to work for a competitor. An order limited to barring disclosure of the confidential information may be difficult to enforce because detecting violations may be difficult. Barring the employee from working for the competitor makes compliance easier to assess. Relief of this type is commonly used to police lawyer-client conflicts. The concern is that the lawyer's loyalty to her current client may cause her to breach the duty to maintain the confidences of a former client. The usual remedy is to require disqualification;[28] more limited remedies, such as screening, are generally rejected as ineffective and difficult to police.[29]

A prophylactic injunction may also be justified under the precautionary principle. The problem is similar to the "ensuring compliance" justification, although here the concern is not so much detection but the negation of opportunity to engage in the prohibited conduct. The injunction is broadly phrased to make violation more difficult. For example, an abusive ex-husband may be barred from living in the same neighborhood as his ex-wife

---

[25] People Who Care v. Rockford Bd. of Educ., 111 F.3d 528 (7th Cir. 1997):

> The discretionary power of a district court to formulate an equitable remedy for an adjudicated violation of law is broad. Where necessary for the elimination of the violation, the decree can properly fence the defendant in by forbidding conduct not unlawful in itself.

Id. at 533 (citations omitted); Schoenbrod, *The Measure of An Injunction*, *supra*, 72 Minn. L. Rev. at 671 (noting that "a property tailored injunction may sometimes contain terms that go beyond the plaintiff's rightful position to avoid falling short of it").

[26] The concept of "prophylactic" relief is also found in the area of constitutional remedies. Here the question has arisen in several contexts. For example, are constitutional-based remedies, such as the exclusionary rule or the *Miranda* warning, core constitutional rights, incidental rights, or something else? *See generally* Michell N. Berman, *Constitutional Decision Rules*, 90 Va. L. Rev. 1 (2004). The issue as also arisen regarding Congress' powers under Section 5 of the 14th Amendment, particularly in the context of the Voting Rights Act. *See* Tracy A. Thomas, *Congress' Section 5 Power and Remedial Rights*, 34 U.C. Davis L. Rev. 673 (2001).

[27] Hutto v. Finney, 437 U.S. 678 (1978) (noting failure of defendants to comply with prior orders).

[28] In some cases by an independent action in equity. Maritrans GP Inc. v. Pepper, Hamilton & Scheetz, 602 A.2d 1277, 1284 (Pa. 1992). *But see* DHR Int'l, Inc., *supra* (treating preliminary injunction to remove attorney from case as non-appealable motion to disqualify).

[29] CHARLES WOLFRAM, MODERN LEGAL ETHICS § 7.6.4 (1986) (noting limited use of screening mechanism outside context of government lawyers reentering private practice).

to prevent opportunities for confrontation.[30] A proven infringer may be required to keep a greater distance away from the plaintiff's protected activity than would a non-infringer because the proven infringer's past actions have demonstrated a weakness to temptation.[31] Prophylactic remedies have been criticized as illegitimate and improper extensions of judicial power,[32] but courts have not agreed with the critics; rather, the courts have acknowledged a "necessary and proper" approach to the issue that, in effect, justifies what "needs" to be done to provide effective relief.[33]

Broad injunctive relief may be made necessary due to the nature of the enjoined party's wrongful acts. For example, in *Dr. Seuss Enterprises L.P. v. Penguin Books, U.S.A., Inc.*[34] plaintiff sought to enjoin further publication of defendant's book. The book (Dr. Juice) was a spoof of the O.J. Simpson criminal trial patterned after plaintiff's "The Cat in the Hat." Unfortunately, the court found the fit a little too close and therefore violative of plaintiff's copyright. The problem for defendant was that between the time the district court denied the request for a TRO and the time it granted a preliminary injunction, defendant had gone forward with its production schedule. Complying with the injunction would require defendant to refrain from selling or distributing its book even though only a portion of the book was found to infringe on plaintiff's copyright. The court's response was that the difficulty was of defendant's own making:

> Because only the back cover illustration and the Cat's stovepipe hat were deemed infringing by the district court, Penguin and Dove argue that the court should not have enjoined the entire book. However, they created the all-or-nothing predicament in which they currently find themselves. Even though the book had not yet been bound when Seuss initiated this action, Penguin and Dove still went forward with their production schedule and completed the stitching and binding. As a result, the publisher can no longer alter the final product to eliminate the infringing elements. Penguin and Dove's decision left the court no choice but to enjoin the entire book.[35]

---

[30] Zappaunbulso v. Zappaunbulso, 842 A.2d 300 (N.J. Super. App. Div. 2004).

[31] Oral-B Laboratories, Inc. v. Ni-Lor Corp., 810 F.2d 20 (2d Cir. 1987):

> [A] party who has once infringed a trademark may be required to suffer a position less advantageous than that of an innocent party.

Id. at 24; 5 J.T. McCarthy, McCarthy on Trademarks and Unfair Competition § 30:4, at 30–12 (4th ed. 2002).

> [A]n infringer, once caught, must expect some fencing in . . . . [A] court can frame an injunction which will keep a proven infringer safely away from the perimeter of future infringement.

[32] Tracy Thomas, *Understanding Prophylactic Remedies Through the Looking Glass of* Bush v. Gore, 11 Will. & Mary B.R.J. 343, 363–370 (2002) (discussing competing views).

[33] United States v. Holtzman, 762 F.2d 720, 724 (9th Cir. 1985):

> A federal court's equity jurisdiction affords it the power to enjoin otherwise lawful activity when necessary and appropriate in the public interest to correct or dissipate the evil effects of past unlawful conduct.

[34] 109 F.3d 1394 (9th Cir.), *cert. dismissed*, 521 U.S. 1146 (1997).

[35] *Id.* at 1406.

[33.2] Entitlement to Permanent Injunctive Relief

The requirements for permanent injunctive relief resemble, but are not the same as, those for temporary injunctive relief. It is important to keep each remedy separate and not confuse the tests. Not infrequently, courts use language loosely, suggesting that the tests are interchangeable.[36] They are not; the differences through small are meaningful. Most importantly, the availability of permanent injunctive relief is frequently affected by statutory language liberalizing the requirements for granting relief.[37]

To be entitled to permanent injunctive relief a plaintiff must establish (1) that she has a valid claim against the defendant,[38] (2) that future harm is imminent and irreparable,[39] and (3) that the hardship to defendant of compliance is not disproportionate to the benefit to plaintiff of compliance.[40] Many formulations include the express requirement that issuance of the injunction be in the public interest,[41] but this element is always implied.

It may be helpful to contrast the requirements here with those identified earlier in conjunction with temporary injunctive relief.[42] The permanent injunction will issue, if at all, only after a plenary trial on the merits. The risk of an erroneous interim decision, which pervasively influences temporary injunctive relief jurisprudence, does not apply here. The risk of an erroneous decision to grant an injunction after a plenary trial is no greater, and no less, than inherent in any decision after a trial on the merits. Plaintiff either proves her claim or she does not; the "probability of success"

---

[36] Amoco Prod. Co. v. Village of Gambell, 480 U.S. 531, 546 n.12 (1987); Bank One, Utah v. Guttau, 190 F.3d 844, 847 (8th Cir. 1999), *cert. denied sub nom.* Foster v. Bank One, Utah, 529 U.S. 1087 (2000).

[37] *Bank One, Utah, supra,* 190 F.3d at 847–48 (holding that once plaintiff established actual injury from statutory violation, plaintiff was entitled to injunctive relief and did not have to address balance-of-harm or public policy factors for obtaining injunctive relief; 3 NIMMER ON COPYRIGHT § 14.06[B] at 14–101 (1996) (noting that as a general rule, "a copyright plaintiff is entitled to a permanent injunction when liability has been established and there is a threat of continuing violations"); Section 26.1 (Statutes Expanding Equitable Remedies).

[38] Avery Dennison Corp. v. Sumpton, 189 F.3d 868, 881 (9th Cir. 1999).

[39] A. W. Chesterton Co., Inc. v. Chesterton, 128 F.3d 1, 8–9 (1st Cir. 1997); Green v. Unauthorized Practice of Law Comm., 883 S.W.2d 293, 296 (Tex. Civ. App. 1994); American Nat'l Bank & Trust Co. v. Carroll, 462 N.E.2d 586, 595 (Ill. App. 1984); Willing v. Mazzocone, 393 A.2d 1155, 1158 (Pa. 1978).

[40] Harrisonville v. W.S. Dickey Clay, Mfg., 289 U.S. 334, 338 (1933) (involving claim of nuisance and denying equitable relief when injunction would cause grossly disproportionate hardship and payment of money would provide substantial redress); Kratze v. Independent Order of Oddfellows, Garden City Lodge #11, 500 N.W.2d 115, 120 (Mich. 1993) (noting that "unless the burden to the defendant of removing the encroachment is disproportionate to the hardship to the plaintiff in allowing the encroachment to remain, the injunction will issue"). This hardship factor is, for reasons noted later in this section, often more an affirmative defense than an element of plaintiff's prima facie case.

[41] Harlem Wizzards Entertainment Basketball, Inc. v. NBA Properties, Inc., 952 F. Supp. 1084, 1091 (D.N.J. 1997); Restatement (Second) of Torts § 951, cmt. a (1979) (noting that countervailing public interest may support denial of otherwise proper award of injunctive relief); Section 4 (Public Policy).

[42] Section 31.2 (Traditional Test For Issuance of Temporary Injunctive Relief).

calculus, which is so influential at the temporary injunctive relief stage, is inapplicable here. This also illustrates another distinction between temporary and permanent injunctive relief; the granting of the former does not establish any entitlement to the latter. The decision whether to grant a temporary injunction is only a prediction by the court as to the ultimate resolution of the issue. Regardless of the disposition of the request for temporary injunctive relief, a court is free to consider the claim according to the evidence adduced at the trial on the merits.[43]

The requirement that harm be imminent is simply another way of saying that the claim be ripe and not moot. Injunctive relief operates to prevent future harm. The threat of future harm must be real and not remote. These concepts are captured by the "imminency" requirement.

The requirement that harm be irreparable is functionally different for permanent injunctions from that used for preliminary injunctive relief. For preliminary injunctive relief the trial judge must ask whether she will be able to remediate, by a monetary award, harm realized by the plaintiff during the period prior to trial.[44] In contrast, irreparable injury for purposes of a permanent injunction is prospective in orientation. The trial judge must ask whether she can quantify in money the harm plaintiff will sustain after the trial is concluded if an injunctive is not granted. Because the future is usually less certain than the past, at least the immediate past, irreparable injury tends to be less of a hurdle to an award of permanent injunctive relief than it is to temporary injunctive relief.[45] Moreover, many statutes provide that equitable relief should be available as a matter of course to the plaintiff who establishes a statutory violation by the defendant.[46]

The requirement that the hardship of compliance by defendant not be disproportionate to the benefit of compliance for plaintiff creates a modified cost/benefit calculus.[47] The underlying premise here is the avoidance of

---

[43] Univ. of Texas v. Carmenisch, 451 U.S. 390, 395 (1981). The decision to grant or deny temporary injunctive relief does not affect other pretrial issues. Morris ex rel. Estate of Morris v. Hoffa, 361 F.3d 177, 189 (3d Cir. 2004) (stating that decision to grant preliminary injunction for plaintiff does not preclude court from later granting summary judgment for defendant).

[44] Section 31.2.2 (Irreparable Injury).

[45] Irreparable injury is usually presumed when the plaintiff seeks to enjoin a constitutional violation. In some cases, a finding of actual breach of contract will be deemed to create an inference of irreparable injury. Overholt Crop Ins. Serv. Co. v. Travis, 941 F.2d 1361, 1371 (8th Cir. 1991) (breach of restrictive covenant); Ormco Corp. v. Johns, 869 So.2d 1109 (Ala. 2003) (breach of non-compete clause); Jim Rutherford Inv. v. Terramar Beach Com., 25 S.W.3d 845–849 (Tex. Civ. App. 2001) (breach of restrictive covenant); Cherne Indus. Inc. v. Grounds & Assocs., Inc., 278 N.W.2d 81, 92 (Minn. 1979) (breach of non compete clause).

[46] Max 100 L.C. v. Iowa Realty Co. Ltd., 621 N.W.2d 178, 181 (Iowa 2001); Section 26.1 (Statutes Expanding Equitable Remedies).

[47] In some situations the issue is so pervasive that it may be folded into the very fabric of the substantive law. For example, in nuisance cases, a cost/benefit analysis may be treated as part of the basic determination whether a nuisance exists or as part of the decision as to the type of remedy, damages or injunction, to provide. Section 94 (Nuisance).

economic waste. Should we require the defendant to spend $100 for compliance to generate $1 of benefit for plaintiff? A related concern is over settlement leverage. Will the victorious plaintiff, who earlier claimed that damages were not an adequate remedy, now be inclined to negotiate a cash settlement and will defendant now find that any settlement which costs less than $100 is preferable to compliance?[48]

An example of this concern is presented in encroachment cases. Assume Able builds a structure that encroaches onto Baker's property. Both Able and Baker own acre plots and Able's encroachment consumes 1% of Baker's land. The market value of each plot (without structures) is $100,000. The cost of removing the portion of Able's structure that encroaches on Baker's land is $20,000. If Baker is limited to damages, we may assume that his recovery would be limited to a sum around $1,000 (1% of $100,000).[49] We can see that complying with injunctive relief is much more costly for Able than damages because Able's liability, whether in law or equity, is solely expressed in dollars. For Able, the end result is an expenditure whether relief for Baker is at law or in equity: $1,000 to pay as damages for taking Baker's land or $20,000 to comply with the injunction to remove the encroachment.

The benefits of compliance for Baker are more difficult to measure. If we look at the problem strictly in monetary terms, we might agree on the $1,000 figure since that measures the economic value of the portion of Baker's land occupied by Able and which Able could continue to occupy if only damages at law were permitted. A strict economic view, however, marginalizes Baker's rights as an owner.[50] It also fails to reflect an emerging view that residential property, both real and personal, should be valued under the more liberal "value to owner" rule.[51] Finally, a purely

---

[48] Although the intuitive and rational belief is that a defendant would buy itself out of an expensive injunction, the few empirical studies find otherwise. Ward Farnsworth, *Do Parties to Nuisance Cases Bargain After Judgment? A Glimpse Inside the Cathedral*, 66 U. Chi. L. Rev. 373 (1999) (observing that most plaintiffs were unwilling to trade injunctions for dollars). The study data remains small and the nature of disputes studied may create distortions, but the studies do indicate that this is an area where generalizations are perilous. On the other hand, so-called "patent trolling," which is the acquisition of patents for the purpose of suing others for patent infringement, does suggest that injunction leverage is not a fanciful theme.

[49] The valuation should reflect what a willing seller (Baker) would demand and receive from a willing buyer (Able) in an arm length transaction. I assume the portion encroached upon has no unique features (e.g., roadside access) that would warrant a premium.

[50] Guido Calabresi & A. Douglas Melamed, *Property Rules, Liability Rules, and Inalienability: One View of the Cathedral*, 85 Harv. L. Rev. 1089 (1972).

[51] As to real property, see *Orndorff v. Christiana Community Builders*, 266 Cal. Rptr. 193, 196 (Cal. App. 1990) (permitting homeowners cost of repair recovery even though it exceeded diminution in value resulting from soil destabilization; the court emphasized the "personal use" by plaintiffs of the property as their residence). *Cf.* Housley v. City of Poway, 24 Cal. Rptr. 2d 554, 559 (Cal. App. 1993) (refusing to permit larger cost of repair over diminution in value when former was 3 1/2 times larger than the latter and thus bore no reasonable relationship to market value of property). As to personal property, see *Bond v. A.H. Belo Corp.*, 602 S.W.2d 105 (Tex. Civ. App. 1980) (awarding damages for loss of personal effects based on "special value" to the owner); Section 81 (Value to Owner).

economic approach gives to Able a power of private eminent domain, a power that is usually deemed to be solely governmental.[52] These factors may cause us to reassess upward the "benefits" side of the equation, thus reducing the "disproportionality" that was initially suggested.

After we have reached some accommodation with the numbers, we still have to address the way in which we will relate the numbers to the concept of "disproportionality." How much is too much? Is a 20-1 cost to benefit ratio disproportionate? Is a 5-1 ratio disproportionate? The answer is "it depends." "Disproportionality" has not been reduced to a rule or even a rule of thumb. Disproportionality is required, but whether a particular cost-benefit ratio is disproportionate is resolved on a case by case basis.

One rule that is often applied here is that a defendant can only argue that an injunction should not issue because of cost-benefit disproportionality when the defendant did not act inequitably in connection with the encroachment. There is much in this rule that borrows from parallel equitable defenses such as laches and unclean hands and in many instances it will be difficult to identify with precision how a court is approaching the problem. It is, however, generally recognized that a defendant who engages in deliberate misconduct, e.g., intentionally encroaches on another's land, will be barred from raising disproportionality as a reason for refusing equitable relief.[53] Similarly, certain types of violations may not be amenable to cost-benefit balancing.[54]

The last requirement is that the injunction be in the public interest. As noted elsewhere, this concept is so malleable that it is rarely dispositive in any particular case.[55] It may, however, require that the court proceed more cautiously because the injunction will operate in a way that could prove inimitable to established rights. On the other hand, the public interest may be served by an expansive view of the court's injunctive power when a statute so states or implies.

---

[52] Town of Vidalia v. Unopened Succession of Ruffin, 663 So. 2d 315, 318 (La. App. 1995) (noting that "[e]minent domain is the inherent right of the sovereign to acquire private property for public purposes without the consent of the owner, provided just compensation is paid"); Customer Co. v. City of Sacramento, 895 P.2d 900, 905 n.3 (Cal. 1995) (same); McCoy v. Peach, 251 S.E.2d 881, 884 (N.C. App. 1979) (noting that power of eminent domain is inherent right available only to federal government and states, and to those bodies to whom the states properly delegate the power).

[53] Hollis v. Garwall, Inc., 974 P.2d 836, 845 (Wash. 1999); *Kratze, supra*, 500 N.W.2d at 120–21.

[54] Atlantic Coast Demolition & Recycling Inc. v. Board of Chosen Freeholders of Atl. County, 112 F.3d 652, 669–72 (3d Cir.) (vacating two year stay of injunction against enforcement of waste control statutes, which trial court had determined to burden interstate commerce; financial cost of compliance is not a justification for withholding the remedy of injunctive relief for constitutional violations), *cert. denied*, 522 U.S. 966 (1997).

[55] Section 31.2.4 ([Temporary Injunctive Relief] Public Policy or Public Interest). The exception would be when third party interests are analyzed and assessed under this factor rather than the "balance-of-hardship" factor. *Id.*

[33.3] Length of Permanent Injunctive Relief

A permanent injunction need not be a perpetual injunction. Permanent refers to the injunctive relief that is provided after a plenary trial on the merits. It is permanent in the sense that it is final, but its duration is determined by the particular case. A plaintiff is entitled only to that amount of injunctive relief needed to restore her to her rightful position.[56]

A defendant who has entered into a valid non-competition clause that has a *three*-year duration should not be enjoined from competing with his former employer for *five* years, unless the additional time is needed to remediate consequential damages flowing from defendant's breach.[57] If the plaintiff is lawfully entitled to three-years of non-competition, that is all the injunctive relief she is entitled to receive. Similarly, if a plaintiff seeks equitable relief compelling his appointment to a position for a three-year term, as promised, the injunction should do just that, no more, no less.[58]

In some cases, the court must determine from the facts what would be an appropriate time period for the permanent injunction to run before it expires by its own terms.[59] For example, in *Lamb-Weston, Inc. v. McCain Foods, Ltd.*[60] the court found that defendant/competitor had wrongfully acquired and used trade secrets owned by plaintiff. The district court issued a permanent injunction barring defendant from producing, using or selling products derived from the misappropriated information for eight months.[61] The appellate court affirmed and stated the basic test as follows:

> [T]he appropriate duration for the injunction should be the period of time it would have taken [the defendant], either by reverse engineering or by independent development, to develop [the product] legitimately without use of [plaintiff's] trade secrets.[62]

The length of the injunction should be sufficient to deprive a defendant of any commercial advantage his illegal activity conferred upon him.[63]

---

[56] 3M v. Pribyl, 259 F.3d 587, 609 (7th Cir. 2001) (applying Wisconsin law).

[57] Presto-X -Company v. Ewing, 442 N.W.2d 85, 89–90 (Iowa 1989) (noting that extending non-competition injunction for additional year beyond contract term was necessary: (1) to discourage litigation delay by defendants; (2) to protect usefulness of restrictive covenants; and (3) to give the plaintiff adequate time to recover sales and customers lost through defendant's breach).

[58] Gleicher, Friberg & Assoc. v. University of Health Sciences, Chicago Med. Sch., 586 N.E.2d 418, 425 (Ill. App. 1991) (holding that the court properly granted plaintiff a permanent injunction requiring that he be appointed for a three-year term).

[59] A permanent injunction is always subject to modification on a showing of good cause. Section 36.2 ([Modification of Injunctions] Permanent Injunctions).

[60] 941 F.2d 970 (9th Cir. 1991).

[61] Injunctions for wrongful use of trade secrets or confidential information are often classified as "production" or "use" injunctions. A "production" injunction is usually deemed broader in scope than a "use" injunction because it prohibits the defendant from producing or selling any product that is connected with the misappropriated information. General Elec. Co. v. Sung, 843 F. Supp. 776, 779–80 (D. Mass. 1994) (collecting cases).

[62] *Lamb-Weston, supra,* 941 F.2d at 974 (citations omitted); *see* Eastern Marble Prods., Corp. v. Roman Marble, Inc., 364 N.E.2d 799, 804 (Mass. 1977).

[63] *Lamb-Weston, supra,* 941 F.2d at 975.

§ 34 SPECIFICITY OF INJUNCTIVE RELIEF

An injunction must be "specific and definite" if it is to be enforceable.[1] This requirement is codified in most jurisdictions.[2] A corollary principle is that injunctions should be construed narrowly in order to make sure that persons who are subject to them have clear notice as to what the injunction requires them to do or not do.[3] This principle is designed both to avoid confusion and uncertainty on the part of persons subject to the injunction and to provide guidance to an appellate court reviewing the injunction as to what the injunction purports to enjoin.[4]

Decisional law in this area reveals two somewhat divergent approaches to the issue of how specific and definite the injunction must be to be enforceable through contempt. The strict approach "cautions [courts] to read court decrees to mean rather precisely what they say."[5] The order must be "clear and unambiguous"[6] and "ambiguities must be resolved in favor of persons charged with [violating the order]."[7] Under this approach, for an order to be sufficiently specific and definite to be enforceable, the enjoined party " 'must be able to ascertain from the four corners of the order' what acts are required or forbidden."[8] A less strict approach is evidenced in *Schering Corporation v. Illinois Antibiotics Company* when the court held that an injunction barring defendant from sale of gentamicin sulfate *solution* was properly interpreted to include its *powdered* equivalent:

> [S]trict construction of injunctions should not be pressed to a dryly logical extreme. If narrow literalism is the rule of interpretation, injunctions will spring loopholes, and parties in whose favor injunctions run will be inundating courts with requests for modification in an effort to plug the loopholes. It is enough protection for

---

[1] N.L.R.B. v. Cincinnati Bronze, Inc., 829 F.2d 585, 590 (6th Cir. 1987); *In re* Rubin, 378 F.2d 104, 108 (3d Cir. 1967); *cf.* Hispanics United of Du Page County v. Village of Addison, 248 F.3d 617, 620–21 (7th Cir. 2001) (noting that district court's disposition was "Delphic" in that it was unclear whether the district judge had "meant to command something" or had simply given "the parties a piece of his mind").

[2] Fed. R. Civ. P. 65(d) (requiring that the injunction be "specific in terms" and "describe in reasonable detail . . . the act or acts sought to be restrained"); Tex. R. Civ. P. 683 (same).

[3] CPC International, Inc. v. Skippy, Inc., 214 F.3d 456, 459 (4th Cir. 2000); Schering Corp. v. Illinois Antibiotics Co., 62 F.3d 903, 906 (7th Cir. 1995).

[4] *CPC International, Inc., supra*; Calvin Klein Cosmetics Corp. v. Parfums de Coeur, Ltd., 824 F.2d 665, 669 (8th Cir. 1987).

[5] NBA Properties, Inc. v. Gold, 895 F.2d 30, 32 (1st Cir. 1990) (brackets added).

[6] Project B.A.S.I.C. v. Kemp, 947 F.2d 11, 16 (1st Cir. 1991) (collecting cases).

[7] Grace v. Center For Auto Safety, 72 F.3d 1236, 1241 (6th Cir. 1996) (holding that order limiting access to deposition to "parties and their attorneys and office staff" was not violated when deposition was shown to consultant retained by party); *NBA Properties, Inc., supra* (stating that ambiguities in an order must be read in the light most favorable to the person charged with contempt).

[8] Red Ball Interior Demolition Corp. v. Palmadessa, 947 F. Supp. 116, 121 (S.D.N.Y. 1996) (citations omitted); *see Project B.A.S.I.C., supra*, 947 F.2d at 17 (stating that "the contempt power ought not to be deployed against a backdrop of uncertainty").

defendants if close questions of interpretation are resolved in the defendant's favor in order to prevent unfair surprise . . . .[9]

In *United States v. Young* the court emphasized that whether an injunction is adequately specific is necessarily a case by case determination:

> In determining whether an order is sufficiently clear and specific to justify a contempt conviction, we apply an objective standard that takes into account both the language of the order and the objective circumstances surrounding the issuance of the order: " 'Whether an order is clear enough depends on the context in which it is issued and the audience to which it is addressed.' "[10]

Care must be exercised not to overemphasize differences between the two approaches.[11] They are approaches, not tests. More importantly, they are both "strict" approaches that neither tolerate nor encourage loose or sloppy draftsmanship. The decision to adopt one approach over the other will often reflect the court's intuitive sense of fairness given the purpose of the injunction and the motives of the person alleged to have violated the terms of the injunction. Parallel but somewhat inconsistent legal authority may permit flexibility, albeit at the cost of some certainty. For example, in *Grace v. Center For Auto Safety* the court looked pragmatically at the language of the order, which limited access to depositions to certain individuals, and the conduct of the defendant. The court noted:

> We do not mean to suggest, of course, that Mr. Ditlow was free to send the Timm deposition to any personal injury lawyer in the country as long as he took the precaution of asking the lawyer for some free legal advice. The Patel affidavit shows without dispute, however, that Mr. Butler's firm had been assisting in the defense of the Grace case for months before Mr. Timm was deposed. The firm was still doing so when it received the deposition transcript, and it continued to do so thereafter. The record contains no evidence whatever to suggest that Ms. Patel and Mr. Ditlow turned to Mr. Butler for legal counsel in Grace as a smokescreen to mask a conscious violation of the spirit, if not the letter, of the protective order.[12]

An injunction that simply instructs a person to "obey the law" or "follow or comply with an agreement" is usually held to be too broad and

---

[9] 62 F.3d 903, 906 (7th Cir. 1995) (citations omitted); Williams v. City of Dothan, Alabama, 818 F.2d 755, 761 (11th Cir. 1987) (stating that "Rule 65(d) should not be applied strictly; rather, the inquiry should be whether the parties subject to the injunctive order understood their obligations under the order").

[10] 107 F.3d 903, 907–08 (D.C. Cir. 1997) (citations omitted).

[11] *Schering Corp., supra*, 62 F.3d at 906 (noting that court had "no quarrel with the general rule that injunctions should be construed narrowly . . .").

[12] *Supra*, 72 F.3d at 1241; *see* Riccard v. Prudential Ins. Co., 307 F.3d 1277, 1296–97 (11th Cir. 2002) (holding that injunction that prohibited Riccard from filing action against Prudential "in state court, federal court, or any other forum" barred Riccard from filing claim before administrative agency, " 'any other forum' language has to refer to non-judicial fora, because all state and federal courts were already covered by the language which preceded that phrase").

non-specific to be enforceable.[13] An injunction must contain "an operative command capable of enforcement."[14] A few examples may help illustrate the point. In *Hughey v. JMS Development Corp.*[15] the defendant was ordered as follows:

> Defendant shall not discharge stormwater into the waters of the United States from its development property in Gwinnett County, Georgia, known as Rivercliff Place if such discharge would be in violation of the Clean Water Act.

The court held that the order was unenforceable as drafted:

> Not only was this an "obey the law" injunction, it was also incapable of enforcement as an operative command. The court's order merely required JMS to stop discharges, but failed to specify how JMS was to do so. Discharges, though not defined by the order, occurred only when it rained, and any discharge was a violation of the order. Rain water ran into the subdivision's government-approved streets and storm sewers; then into the small stream that started on the subdivision property; on into a tributary stream; and eventually into the Yellow River. Was JMS supposed to stop the rain from falling? Was JMS to build a retention pond to slow and control discharges? Should JMS have constructed a treatment plant to comply with the requirements of the CWA? The injunction's failure to specifically identify the acts that JMS was required to do or refrain from doing indicates that the district court-like the CWA, the EPA, Georgia EPD, and Mr. Hughey-was incapable of fashioning an operative command capable of enforcement. As such, we must vacate this "obey the law" injunction.[16]

In *Peregrine Myanmar Ltd. v. Segal*[17] the injunction barred defendant from:

> [T]rying to intimidate plaintiffs' officers, directors, employees and agents in the exercise of their duties with threats of spurious lawsuits, provided that nothing in this Final Judgment shall be

---

[13] Sterling Drug, Inc. v. Bayer AG, 14 F.3d 733, 748 (2d Cir. 1994); Epstein Family Partnership v. Kmart Corp., 13 F.3d 762, 771 (3d Cir. 1994). As noted in *NLRB v. Express Pub. Co.*, 312 U.S. 426 (1941):

> [T]he mere fact that a court has found that a defendant has committed an act in violation of a staute does not justify an injunction broadly to obey the statute and thus subject the defendant to contempt proceedings if he shall at any time in the future commit some new violation unlike and unrelated to that with which he was originally charged.

Id. at 435–36.

[14] International Longshoremen's Ass'n Local 1291 v. Philadelphia Marine Trade Ass'n, 389 U.S. 64, 73–74 (1967).

[15] 78 F.3d 1523 (11th Cir.), *cert. denied*, 519 U.S. 993 (1996).

[16] *Id.* at 1531–32 (footnote omitted).

[17] 89 F.3d 41 (2d Cir. 1996).

deemed to impinge upon or to impede Segal's right to interpose all legitimate counterclaims; . . . .

The court found the language to be imprecise, particularly since defendant, a non-lawyer, was unlikely to know in advance "which 'threatened' lawsuits are 'spurious' and which are not."[18] The court found that the plaintiff's ability to suggest "hypothetical" cases that would trigger the language was not curative of the drafting deficiency.[19] The court remanded, suggesting that the "plaintiffs may want to define more specifically the types of lawsuits that, based on the district court's legal conclusions, would be spurious."[20]

Orders that simply prohibit conduct in broad terms, such as "discrimination,"[21] "monopolization,"[22] or "slandering and disparaging"[23] are usually deemed too broad; consequently, they violate the command of Rule 65(d) that orders be specific in term and descriptive in reasonable detail. On the other hand, breadth of language will be allowed when more specific language is not feasible. For example, in *United States v. V-1 Oil Company* the court upheld, against a charge of lack of reasonable specificity, an injunction that required "V-1 to allow warrantless administrative searches for the purpose of enforcing the [Hazardous Materials Transportation Act] and its implementing regulations."[24] If the order had specifically identified and barred the past courses of conduct that defendant engaged in to frustrate the government's right of entry and search, defendant could simply devise new tactics because the range of alternatives is vast. To avoid encouraging a game of "cat and mouse," the court believed that some broadness in language was necessary and unavoidable.

Occasionally, language will be found in an opinion suggesting that a person is bound by an "obey the law" order. Closer inspection usually reveals that the suggestion is erroneous. For example, "obey the law" language may be found when the court is asked to "balance the hardships" in deciding whether to award injunctive relief. It is not a legal hardship to obey the law. Courts consistently find that a directive to "obey the law" in this context is not burdensome.[25]

---

[18] *Id.* at 51.

[19] *Id.*

[20] *Id.*

[21] Payne v. Travenol Labs., Inc., 565 F.2d 895, 898 (5th Cir. 1978).

[22] Schine Chain Theatres, Inc. v. United States, 334 U.S. 110, 125–26 (1948), *overruled on other grounds*, Cooperweld Corp. v. Independence Tube Corp., 467 U.S. 752, 765, 777 (1984).

[23] Wynn Oil Co. v. Purolator Chem. Corp., 536 F.2d 84, 85 (5th Cir. 1976); see Mazzacone v. Willing 369 A.2d 829, 834 (Pa. Super. Ct. 1977) (holding that in connection with injunction against defamation it is incorrect to order the defendant to go forth and defame no more; rather, the order must describe the statements the defendant is no longer permitted to utter), *rev'd on other grounds*, 393 A.2d 1155 (Pa. 1978).

[24] 63 F.3d 909, 913 (9th Cir. 1995).

[25] Scott on behalf of N.L.R.B. v. Pacific Custom Materials, Inc., 939 F. Supp. 1443, 1456 (N.D. Cal. 1996); TKR Cable Co. v. Cable City Corp. (D.N.J. 1996), 1996 U.S. Dist. LEXIS 11941, at *29 (noting that "[d]efendant will suffer no harm if any injunction is issued which

"Obey the law" language is permissible if it is tied to specific requirements. For example, in *Public Interest Research Group of New Jersey, Inc.
v. Powell Duffryn Terminals, Inc.* the court recognized that a broad "obey
the laws in the future" mandate would be unenforceable; however, an order
requiring the defendant to comply with a discharge permit was sufficiently
specific:

> We will strike that portion of the injunction which purports to en-
> join PDT from violating future permits. We do not find the portion
> of the injunction directing PDT not to discharge in violation of its
> current permit lacking in specificity. PDT's permit provides detailed
> and very specific limitations on PDT's discharge. Thus we will
> affirm the portion of the injunction prohibiting PDT from discharg-
> ing in violation of its permit.[26]

In *Meyer v. Brown & Root Construction Co.* the court held that an
injunction that enjoined the defendant from "engaging in the stated
unlawful employment practice" was not impermissibly vague or broad. The
judgment rendered in the case had specified that defendant "violated Title
VII by constructively discharging plaintiff when she was pregnant . . .
defendant failed to treat plaintiff in the same manner as other temporarily
disabled workers who were given the opportunity to perform light or limited
work during the period of disability."[27] The court held that the statement
in the judgment adequately informed defendant of the conduct prohibited
in the future.

The above two cases point out another aspect of "specificity"; the injunction must be a complete document; incorporation by reference is not
permitted.[28] This is often referred to as the "four corners rule."[29] The four
corners of the order itself must describe and set forth, in words of operative
command, the defendant's duties and obligations. Even if a defendant has
knowledge of the incorporated document, and its terms, the injunction may
still be defective.[30] As is the case, however, with the basic specificity

---

simply requires them to obey the law"), *quoting* Storer Communications v. Mogel, 625 F. Supp.
1194, 1203 (S.D. Fla. 1985), *vacated in part and aff'd in part on other grounds*, 267 F.3d 196
(3d Cir. 2001); *cf.* Nat'l Org. For Women, Inc. v. Scheidler, 267 F.3d 687 (7th Cir. 2001):

> Here, we do not disagree with the proposition that some language in this injunction,
> taken in the abstract, is rather general. But the key question is: Compared to what?
> Any effort to deal with a case of this complexity will inevitably involve some
> imprecision.

Id. at 706, *rev'd on other grounds*, 537 U.S. 393 (2003).

[26] 913 F.2d 64, 83 (3d Cir. 1990), *cert. denied*, 498 U.S. 1109 (1991).

[27] 661 F.2d 369, 373 (5th Cir. 1981).

[28] Fed. R. Civ. P. 65(d).

[29] Drywall Tapers, Local 1974 v. Local 530, 889 F.2d 389, 395 (2d Cir. 1989).

[30] Red Ball Interior Demolition Corp. v. Palmadessa, 947 F. Supp. 116, 121 (S.D.N.Y. 1996):

> Although this Court is of the opinion that the actions required by the June 25 Order
> should have been clear to the parties, the Order operates by reference to the motion
> papers, and does not expressly set forth its requirements within the four corners
> of the Order. Therefore, a contempt order is inappropriate at this time.

requirement, some courts distinguish between material and minor deviations from the requirement.[31] In *Combs v. Ryan's Coal Company, Inc.* the
district court's order referenced several other documents, the contents of
which were critical to giving the order its necessary specificity. Although
the order violated the no incorporation requirements of Rule 65(d), the court
held that the failing was immaterial and non-prejudicial when the enjoined
party "understood their obligation, for they complied with the decree for
almost three months."[32] The *Combs* court did not, however, indicate
whether defendants' obedience was knowing or fortuitous, a critical fact
given the court's approach to Rule 65(d) compliance. The court also suggested that the failure of an enjoined defendant to seek clarification of an
order defendant believes is vague or ambiguous may undermine the
contention that the order is vague or ambiguous. Similarly, in *Chathas v.
Local 134 IBEW* the court found that the issuance of a permanent injunction
that incorporated by reference the terms of the preliminary injunction was
not fatally defective:

> When the terms of an injunction, although not set forth in a
> separate document as the rule requires, can be inferred from the
> documentary record with sufficient clarity to enable a violation of
> those terms to be punished as a contempt, the injunction is enforce-
> able.[33]

Some courts have rejected a strict construction of the "no incorporation by
reference" rule in favor of an "actual notice" rule. This approach emphasizes
the purpose of the "four corners requirement" ("Notice") over strict, literal
compliance with Rule 65(d). As noted by one court:

> By incorporating the order into the injunction, the district court
> acted consistently with the rationale of Rule 65(d). The defendants
> were aware of the order because it was physically attached to the
> injunction itself. Thus, the defendants received adequate notice that

---

[31] Chathas v. Local 134 IBEW, 233 F.3d 508, 512–13 (7th Cir. 2000) (noting that violation
of the anti-incorporation rule may be "harmless error"), *cert. denied*, 533 U.S. 949 (2001).

[32] 785 F.2d 970, 979 (11th Cir. 1986).

[33] *Chathas, supra*, 233 F.3d at 513 (citations omitted) (finding that language in injunction
referring to "likelihood of success" on the merits rather than "actual success" as required for
permanent injunction was not material defect). Similarly in *Marseilles Hydro Power, LLC v.
Marseilles Land and Water Co.*, 299 F.3d 643 (7th Cir. 2002), the court noted:

> [Rule 65(d)] is not jurisdictional, however, and thus the repair plan incorporated by
> reference may be looked to for assistance in deciding whether the injunction is
> sufficiently definite to be enforceable by means of a contempt proceeding. That is
> an inquiry of jurisdictional significance because if the injunction is not at least that
> definite the canal company can disobey it with impunity and thus, not being hurt
> by it, would lack standing to challenge it, since an unenforceable order is no order
> at all. But the order in this case is that definite, at least. Although there are a number
> of open issues, there is a core of ascertainable duty imposed by the injunction. If
> the canal company flatly refused without excuse to allow the power company onto
> its property for the purpose of formulating a definite plan of repair, it would be
> punishable for contempt.

Id. at 646–47 (citations omitted; brackets added).

they could face contempt if they violated the order. Under these circumstances, the district court did not err by attaching the order to the injunction.[34]

Ultimately, the guiding principle here is that of reasonable specificity and detail. Injunctions must deal with myriad possibilities and the risk of artful evasion. What the Supreme Court once noted in the related context of statutes is true here:

> [F]ew words possess the precision of mathematical symbols. . . . [No] more than a reasonable degree of certainty can be demanded. Nor is it unfair to require that one who deliberately goes perilously close to an area of proscribed conduct shall take the risk that he may cross the line.[35]

Limited as we are to words, we can neither expect nor demand mathematical certainty from our language.[36]

§ 35 PERSONS BOUND BY INJUNCTIVE RELIEF

[35.1] In Active Concert or Participation With

Rule 65(d), Federal Rules of Civil Procedure provides that an order granting equitable relief "is binding only upon the parties to the action, their officers, agents, servants, employees, and attorneys, and upon those persons in active concert or participation with them. . . ."[1] This principle speaks to both temporary and permanent injunctive relief.

The effect of an injunction or order on one other than the enjoined party was set forth by Judge Learned Hand in *Alemite Manufacturing Corp. v. Staff*:

> "[A] person who knowingly assists a defendant in violating an injunction subjects himself to civil as well as criminal proceedings for contempt . . . . On the other hand no court can make a decree which will bind any one but a party; a court of equity is as much so limited as a court of law; it cannot lawfully enjoin the world at large . . . ."[2]

From this statement we may elicit several principles. First, a court of equity has no power to punish, through contempt, a non-party acting solely in pursuit of his own interests merely because that person has notice of

---

[34] State of California v. Campbell, 138 F.3d 772, 789 (9th Cir.), *cert. denied*, 525 U.S. 822 (1998).

[35] Boyce Motor Lines, Inc. v. United States, 342 U.S. 337, 340 (1952) (citation omitted).

[36] Grayned v. City of Rockford, 408 U.S. 104 110 (1972).

[1] State practice is generally the same. Ind. Trial R. 65(D); Tex. R. Civ. P. 683; Mo. Sup. Ct. R. 92.02(d). A jurisdiction may accomplish the same end through case law. Gallo v. Acuna, 929 P.2d 596, 617–18 (Cal. 1997), *cert. denied sub nom.* Gonzales v. Gallo, 521 U.S. 1121 (1997).

[2] 42 F.2d 832, 832 (2d Cir. 1930) (citations omitted).

the court's order.[3] Second, a nonparty may violate an order and be liable in his own right if he acts in concert or participation with persons who are bound by the order.[4] Third, the enjoined party may violate an order through the acts of a nonparty.[5]

The principles of *Alemite* derive from the common law doctrine that an injunction not only binds the parties, but also those identified with them (1) in interest, (2) in privity, (3) represented by them, or (4) subject to their control.[6] An injunction could easily be frustrated if a court could only enforce its orders against parties because parties could enlist the aid of nonparties to defeat the order.[7] While the court could still impose sanctions against the parties, this would require proof that the parties were acting through the nonparties. While such relief would not be ineffective, it is not as effective as relief that operates directly upon both the party *and* the person actually engaging in the acts that constitute a violation of the order.

The common law precedents, and their current statutory counterparts, require for the most part that the nonparty be acting with the party. The operative language here is "in concert or participation with."[8] This language distinguishes between a third person who acts independently from the party and for the third person's own account, on the one hand, and a third person who acts with, for, or on behalf of a party and for that party's account, on the other hand. The former is not bound by an injunction to which he is

---

[3] Chase Nat'l Bank v. City of Norwalk, Ohio, 291 U.S. 431, 436–37 (1934) (holding that injunction that sought to bind "all persons to whom notice of this order shall come" was invalid to the extent it sought to bind persons who merely had notice of the order); *cf.* Additive Controls & Measurement Systems, Inc. v. Flowdata, Inc., 96 F.3d 1390 (Fed. Cir. 1996):

> Having a relationship to an enjoined party of the sort set forth in Rule 65(d) exposes a non-party to contempt for assisting the party to violate the injunction, but does not justify granting injunctive relief against the non-party in its separate capacity.

Id. at 1395–96.

[4] People of State of N.Y. by Vacco v. Operation Rescue Nat'l, 80 F.3d 64, 70 (2d Cir.), *cert. denied sub nom.* Broderick v. United States, 519 U.S. 825 (1996); Stotler & Co. v. Able, 870 F.2d 1158, 1163 (7th Cir. 1989). *See generally* Ronald I. Mirvis, Annot., *Who, Under Rule 65(d) of Federal Rules of Civil Procedure, Are Persons "In Active Concert or Participation" With Parties to Action so as to be Bound by Order Granting Injunction?*, 61 A.L.R. Fed. 482 (1983); Annotation, *Violation of State Court Order by One Other Than Party as Contempt*, 7 A.L.R. 4th 893 (1981).

[5] Roe v. Operation Rescue, 919 F.2d 857, 871 (3d Cir. 1990) (holding that "[t]he law does not permit the instigator of contemptuous conduct to absolve himself of contempt liability by leaving the physical performance of the forbidden performance to others. As a result, those who have knowledge of a valid order and abet others in violating it are subject to the court's contempt powers") (citations omitted); People v. Conrad, 64 Cal. Rptr. 2d 248, 251 (Cal. App. 1997) (noting that "enjoined parties may not play jurisdictional 'shell games.' They may not nullify an injunctive decree by carrying out prohibited acts with or through non-parties to the original proceeding") (citations omitted).

[6] Regal Knitwear Co. v. N.L.R.B., 324 U.S. 9, 14 (1945).

[7] E.E.O.C. v. International Longshoremen's Ass'n, 541 F.2d 1062, 1063 (4th Cir. 1976).

[8] *Ex Parte* Lennon, 166 U.S. 548, 555 (1897); McGraw-Edison Co. v. Preformed Line Prod. Co., 362 F.2d 339, 344 (9th Cir. 1966); Bird v. Capital Site Mgmt. Co., 667 N.E.2d 826, 831 (Mass. 1996).

not a party; the latter is bound, even though he is not a party, and may be punished by contempt if his acts constitute a violation of the order.[9]

Nonparty liability for violating an order is conditioned on that nonparty's assistance being rendered to the party to violate the order. The relationship necessary to support a finding of "assistance" can be loose and informal. For example, in *Reliance Insurance Co. v. Mast Construction Company* the court rejected the district court's construction of "in concert with" language as limited to those situations when there is " 'a showing something akin to alter ego, collusion, or identity or interest' between a party and a nonparty." The court went on to hold that while the above would satisfy the "in concert with" language, the language in Rule 65(d) also encompasses situations when the nonparty "aids and abets" a violation of the order by the party.[10]

Whether a nonparty is acting for her own account, independent of the party, or to aid and abet a party's violation of an order is a question of fact.[11] That the non-party and the enjoined party have common agendas and goals is insufficient, standing alone, to support holding the non-party in contempt for aiding and abetting a violation of a court order.[12] That the nonparty has assisted the enjoined party in the past in the activities now subject to the injunction may not establish that the nonparty is currently in active concert with the enjoined party,[13] although it may be probative evidence of active concert.[14]

---

[9] Zenith Radio Corp. v. Hazeltine Research, Inc., 395 U.S. 100, 112 (1969) (stating that "a nonparty with notice cannot be held in contempt until shown to be in [active] concert or participation" with the enjoined party); O&L Assocs. v. Del Conte, 601 F. Supp. 1463, 1465 (S.D.N.Y. 1985) (finding that a nonparty was not in violation of order when it acquired trademark covered by order in arm's length transaction involving entities distinct from the parties to the order).

[10] 84 F.3d 372 (10th Cir. 1996). In general, "aiding and abetting" requires that the abettor knowingly and intentionally lends material assistance to further and facilitate the commission of the act that violates the legal rights of another. *See* Nye & Nissen v. United States, 336 U.S. 613, 619 (1949); Restatement of Torts § 876 (1939) (Persons Acting in Concert).

[11] Thompson v. Freeman, 648 F.2d 1144, 1147 (8th Cir. 1981) (requiring a factual examination of each case as it arises).

[12] *Id.* (holding that nonparty federal Department of Health & Human Services was not acting in concert with state enjoined party and therefore could not by mere notice be included within scope of injunction issued against state agency); State Univ. of N.Y. v. Denton, 316 N.Y.S.2d 297, 300 (App. Dept. 1970) (refusing to hold faculty members in contempt for aiding and abetting violations of order enjoining students from engaging in certain acts when faculty members independently performed those same acts). The court held:

> The mere fact that an actor may be sympathetic to the desires of one properly bound by an injunction, or that by his conduct the former accomplishes what the party enjoined wants accomplished, is not sufficient to establish beyond a reasonable doubt that the conduct was carried out in combination with or collusion with the named enjoinee.

316 N.Y.S.2d at 302. Faculty in concert with students? Perish the thought!

[13] Howlett v. Kentucky Bd. of Dentistry, 823 S.W.2d 461, 463 (Ky. App. 1991)

[14] Planned Parenthood Ass'n of San Mateo v. Operation Rescue of Cal., 57 Cal. Rptr. 2d 736, 745 (Cal. App. 1996) (holding that individual's prior association with enjoined defendant

One area that has created difficulties is that of "successors-in-interest." Such persons could be bound at common law;[15] they are not, however, specifically listed in Rule 65(d). The issue is whether a successor-in-interest can be bound in its own right or only when it aids and abets a violation by acting in concert or participating with an enjoined party. For example, a transfer of ownership to evade an order made by the party, and assisted by the nonparty, may be addressed by the "in concert with" language of Rule 65(d).[16] If, however, the nonparty acts solely for its own account, can it still bound *solely* as a successor-in-interest?

A line of decisions supports binding the successor when the successor acquires the assets and property of the enjoined party.[17] Under this approach, it is sometimes said that for the successor-in-interest rule to be applied, the successor must have received a transfer of assets from the enjoined party. "It is not enough to prove that the first entity went out of existence and that the second entity entered into the enjoined type of business activity, knowing about the injunction but without having acquired the business, or a relevant part of it, from the first entity."[18] Other courts take a more liberal approach.[19]

could "justify treating [the individual] as either a member of Operation Rescue, or as sufficiently associated with it that he is bound by the injunction against that entity"), *cert. denied sub nom.* Cochran v. Planned Parenthood Ass'n of San Mateo County, 522 U.S. 811 (1997); Horizon Health Center v. Felicissimo, 722 A.2d 611, 613 (N.J. Super. Ct. A.D. 1999) (same).

[15] Garden State Bottling Co., v. N.L.R.B., 414 U.S. 168, 179 (1973) (stating that "[p]ersons acquiring an interest in property that is subject to litigation are bound by . . . a subsequent judgment, despite lack of knowledge") (citations omitted).

[16] Regal Knitwear Co. v. N.L.R.B., 324 U.S. 9, 14 (1945) (noting that "successors" may be instrumentalities through which a defendant seeks to evade an order and thus successors may come within the description of persons "in active concert or participation with" in the violation of an injunction); *see* Rockwell Graphic Sys., Inc. v. DEV Indus., Inc., 91 F.3d 914, 919 (7th Cir. 1996) (collecting cases); G&C Merriam Co. v. Webster's Dictionary Company, Inc., 639 F.2d 29, 36 (1st Cir. 1980) (suggesting that "it may be doubted that a successor can be within the permissible scope of contempt proceedings absent a finding that the succession was an instrumentality through which the enjoined party, and not merely the successor, sought to evade the injunction"); *cf.* People ex rel. Gwinn v. Kothari, 100 Cal. Rptr.2d 29 (Cal. App. 2000) (holding that injunction enjoining operation of motel on grounds it was a public nuisance ("brothel") was not operative against successor-in-interest who was a BFP).

[17] Additive Controls & Measurement Sys., Inc. v. Flowdata, Inc., 154 F.3d 1345 (Fed. Cir. 1998):

> In a series of cases, the Supreme Court described successorship liability as turning on whether there is a "substantial continuity of identity" between the two organizations. Although the original formulation of the test arose in the labor relations context, the "substantial continuity of identity" test has been adopted as a general expression of the degree of closeness that Rule 65(d) requires for a non-party successor to be subject to the injunction.

Id. at 1355 (citations omitted).

[18] G&C Merriam Co., 639 F.2d at 36 (collecting decisions); *cf.* E&J Gallo Winery v. Gallo Cattle Co., 967 F.2d 1280, 1298 (9th Cir. 1992) (deleting language from injunction extending its reach to "descendants" of the enjoined defendant).

[19] *Additive Controls & Measurement Sys., Inc., supra*, 154 F.3d at 1355:

A somewhat different approach can be seen in some cases raising successor liability for consent decree violations involving work force discrimination. Here the considerations focus not so much on assistance given to the enjoined party but on "fairness" and "necessity." In *Bates v. Pacific Maritime Association* the court identified a three-part test for successor liability in the context of workforce discrimination orders: (1) continuity in operations and work force of the successor and predecessor employers; (2) notice to the successor employer of its predecessor's legal obligation; and (3) ability of the predecessor to provide adequate relief directly.[20] In commenting and approving this approach, the court in *Musikiwamba v. Essi, Inc.*, observed:

> [T]wo factors [notice and ability to provide relief] are critical to the imposition of successor liability. The successor doctrine is derived from equitable principles, and it would be grossly unfair, except in the most exceptional circumstances, to impose successor liability on an innocent purchaser when the predecessor is fully capable of providing relief or when the successor did not have the opportunity to protect itself.[21]

[35.2] Personal Jurisdiction Over Non Party

If a nonparty acts in concert with an enjoined party, the nonparty has been held subject to the jurisdiction of the court that issued the order even if the nonparty would otherwise not be subject to the jurisdiction of the court.[22] For this rule to apply, however, there must be a strong "identity of interests" between the enjoined defendant and the nonparty such as to evidence "a commonality of incentives and motivations" between the two.[23]

> In making its finding on that issue, the district court properly recognized that Cotton was the incorporator, president, and majority stockholder of both AdCon and Truflo, and that both entities shared phone lines and office space at his home. In our previous opinion, we noted that any entity "created in order to evade the original injunction" could be subject to contempt under Rule 65(d). The facts as found by the district court adequately support its conclusion that Truflo was such an entity formed to evade the injunction.

(citation omitted)

[20] 744 F.2d 705, 709–10 (9th Cir. 1984).

[21] 760 F.2d 740, 750 (7th Cir. 1985) (citation omitted; brackets added).

[22] Waffenschmidt v. Mackay, 763 F.2d 711, 718 (5th Cir. 1985), *cert. denied*, 474 U.S. 1056 (1986) (holding that "[b]y actively aiding and abetting [a party to the order], [the nonparties] placed themselves within the personal jurisdiction of the district court") (brackets added). According to the court, under traditional in personam jurisdiction rules the acts would not have constituted sufficient forum contacts. *Id.* at 714; Brooks v. United States, 119 F.2d 636, 644 (9th Cir. 1944) (holding that court had power to hold non-resident successors in contempt whether or not decree was deemed to be in rem or in personam); Teele Soap Mfg. Co. v. Pine Tree Prods. Co., Inc., 8 F. Supp. 546, 551 (D.N.H. 1934) (holding that court could adjudicate non-resident, who, outside of the state, aided and abetted enjoined part's violation of court order, in contempt).

[23] Lynch v. Rank, 639 F. Supp. 69, 72 (N.D. Cal. 1985).

The presence of divergent and conflicting interests and motivations will refute the exercise of jurisdiction over the nonparty under the "in concert with" rationale.[24] The fact that the nonparty is subject to conflicting obligations under the law of the nonparty's domicile cautions against finding the nonparty subject to the obligations imposed by the injunction or liable for aiding in its violation.[25]

Alternatively, a court may broadly define its "jurisdiction." For example, in *United States v. International Brotherhood of Teamsters et al.* the court held that its injunction extended to local affiliates of the enjoined defendant:

> Finally, appellants argue that the district court could not enjoin non-New York affiliates because it lacked personal jurisdiction over them. This argument is also without merit. Injunctions may be issued against non-parties under the All Writs Act. We believe that the All Writs Act requires no more than that the persons enjoined have the "minimum contacts" that are constitutionally required under due process. Appellants correctly note that the Act does not enlarge the jurisdiction of the federal courts. However, all we hold is that if jurisdiction over the subject matter of and the parties to litigation is properly acquired, the All Writs Act authorizes a federal court to protect that jurisdiction even though non-parties may be subject to the terms of the injunction.[26]

It is unclear whether the "minimum contacts" reference is to the United States or the state in which the district court is located.[27]

[35.3] Agents and Employees

A second category of nonparties who are bound by an injunction are those persons who are "legally identified" with the enjoined party. These persons are usually listed by category type and include the "officers, agents, servants, employees, and attorneys"[28] of the enjoined party. The principle at play here is that those who act as agents of the enjoined defendant, and, thus, are legally identified with the defendant within the scope of that agency relationship, are bound by the terms of the injunction that bind the principal (defendant).[29] The concept of "legally identified" normally means

---

[24] *Id.* (noting that enjoined party (Secretary of Health & Human Services) had a strong incentive in seeing that terms of order were carried out whereas nonparty (State Administrative Officer) had counter incentives due to costs associated with administering the type of program envisioned by the order).

[25] Reebok Intern. Ltd. v. McLaughlin, 49 F.3d 1387, 1392 (9th Cir. 1995).

[26] 907 F.2d 277, 281 (2d Cir. 1990) (citations omitted).

[27] Royal Ins. Co. v. Quinn-L Capital Corp., 759 F. Supp. 1216, 1228 (N.D. Tex. 1990) (finding nonparties to be bound by injunction issued pursuant to "All Writs Act," had "minimum contacts" with Texas), *rev'd in part on other grounds*, 960 F.2d 1286 (5th Cir. 1992), *cert. denied*, 511 U.S. 1032 (1994).

[28] Fed. R. Civ. P. 65(d).

[29] Pahlavi v. Laidlaw Holdings, Inc., 580 N.Y.S.2d 303, 305 (App. Dept. 1992) (attorney required to comply with TRO obtained against client precluding client from using funds which client used to pay attorney's retainer).

that an active, ongoing relationship is in place. A person who is no longer employed or associated with the party bound by the injunction is, himself, no longer bound unless the "in concert with" rule is satisfied. As noted in *Saga Intern., Inc. v. John D. Brush & Co:*

> Therefore, there is no merit to Brush's claim that because Stuhlbarg was an officer at the time of the settlement agreement, he is automatically bound by the injunction. An injunction is not like a tattoo. It does not permanently stick to every person employed by the party enjoined for the rest of his or her life, regardless of what course their lives might later take. Even if that is what Brush and Saga intended by the language in their stipulation, such a broad reading would be void under Rule 65(d). The reference in Rule 65(d) to "officers" means only current officers, and Stuhlbarg is no longer an officer of Saga. [30]

The doctrine of privity may, however, bind the ex-employee to the order as if he were a directly enjoined party. [31] Whether a nonparty is "legally identified" with a party subject to an injunction is not determined by labels, but by facts. As noted in *Metro-Goldwyn Mayer v. 007 Safety Products, Inc.*:

> The "legal identification" test focuses on whether Ronald Pasqualino's participation in Safety Products was sufficiently significant to make him a *de facto* participant in the Settlement Agreement. Safety Products acknowledges that the factual finding of "legal identification" may not be disturbed unless clearly erroneous. [32]

This category of persons "legally identified" with the enjoined party raises two questions. First, how far does the category reach. Courts have held that the category reached corporate officers "officially responsible for the conduct of [the enjoined corporation's] affairs" [33] and union officials. [34] These results

---

[30] 984 F. Supp. 1283, 1286 (C.D. Cal. 1987) (citation omitted).

[31] *Id.* at 1287, *citing* G&C Merriam Co., 639 F.2d at 37–38 (holding ex-officer bound by injunction because of his control over litigation that resulted in the injunction).

[32] 183 F.3d 10, 16 (1st Cir. 1999) (citation omitted). The court concluded that the facts supported the finding that the "legal identification" test was satisfied when the nonparty (Pasqualino) (1) co-founded defendant, (2) designed and applied for a trademark for the infringing product, (3) received substantial compensation for services performed for defendant, (4) consulted during settlement negotiations with the plaintiff, and (5) received copies of the final agreement that was the subject of the litigation. *Id.*

[33] Reich v. Sea Sprite Boat Co., Inc., 50 F.3d 413, 417 (7th Cir. 1995) ("A command to the corporation is in effect a command to those who are officially responsible for its affairs. If they, apprised of the writ directed to the corporation, prevent compliance or fail to take appropriate action within their power for the performance of the corporate duty, they, no less than the corporation itself, are guilty of disobedience and may be punished for contempt"), *quoting* Wilson v. United States, 221 U.S. 361, 376 (1911)); United States v. Hochschild, 977 F.2d 208, 211 (6th Cir. 1992) (collecting cases).

[34] National Labor Relations Bd. v. Sequoia Dist. Council of Carpenters, AFL-CIO, 568 F.2d 628, 633–34 (9th Cir. 1977).

are not surprising, but the "reach" has also extended to municipal workers employed by an enjoined city.[35]

The liability imposed on individuals who assist in non-compliance by the enjoined defendant does not require the presence of facts that would support the piercing of the corporate veil.[36] The liability of persons legally identified with the enjoined party is indirect; it is due to the aid they provide the enjoined party in violating the injunction. Liability does not affect them directly unless they are named in the order.[37] In one case liability, albeit not for contempt, was extended to a lawyer who "recklessly advised his client that an injunction (TRO) was not effective and thereby assisted in the violation of the injunction.[38]

The second issue is that of notice. Legal identification for purposes of Rule 65(d) is not the same as identicality. The fact that the enjoined party has received notice does not mean that the person legally identified with the enjoined party has received notice. Some courts have suggested that actual notice is not required to bind a nonparty legally identified with the enjoined party to the order.[39] The majority view is, however, to require actual notice.[40] It may be noted that the cases suggesting that actual notice may be dispensed with involved situations when the court found or suggested actual notice had been given;[41] hence, the statements were dicta.

Finally, a person, such as a corporate officer, who is responsible for a party's compliance with an order, cannot escape liability by "merely removing himself from the day-to-day operations of the corporation and washing his hands of responsibility."[42]

---

[35] Shakman v. Democratic Org. of Cook County, 533 F.2d 344, 351 (7th Cir. 1976), *cert. denied*, 429 U.S. 858 (1976) (holding that city employee could be held in contempt for violation of order enjoining city).

[36] Connolly v. J.T. Ventures, 851 F.2d 930, 935 (7th Cir. 1988).

[37] Spallone v. United States, 493 U.S. 265, 276 (1990); *Project B.A.S.I.C., supra*, 947 F.2d at 17–18.

[38] Pacific Harbor Capital, Inc. v. Carnival Air Lines, Inc., 210 F.3d 1112, 1118–19 (9th Cir. 2000) (affirming award of sanctions imposed pursuant to 28 U.S.C. § 1927). Sanctions awarded under § 1927 are different from sanctions imposed by contempt.

[39] *Pacific Harbor Capital, Inc., supra*, 210 F.3d 1112; Morales-Feliciano v. Hernandez-Colon, 704 F. Supp. 16, 19 (D.P.R. 1988). Both decisions note that while some notice is constitutionally required, the notice provided need not be actual notice.

[40] *In re* Slaiby, 73 B.R. 442, 444 (D.N.H. 1987); *cf. Hochschild, supra*, 977 F.2d at 212 (noting ample evidence of actual notice of order as supporting conviction for contempt).

[41] *Shakman, supra*, 533 F.2d at 351; Morales-Feliciano, *supra*, 704 F. Supp. at 19.

[42] United States v. Voss, 82 F.3d 1521, 1526 (10th Cir.), *cert. denied*, 519 U.S. 889 (1996), *quoting* Colonial Williamsburg Found. v. Kittinger Co., 792 F. Supp. 1397, 1406 (E.D. Va. 1992), *aff'd*, 38 F.3d 133 (4th Cir. 1994); *Reich, supra*, 50 F.3d 413 (7th Cir. 1995) (stating that officers cannot avoid liability by "fail[ing] to take appropriate action within their power. . . .").

[35.4] Duty to Participate

There is decisional law *suggesting* that a nonparty who deliberately bypasses an opportunity to intervene is bound by the adjudication.[43] That suggestion has been questioned, however,[44] and the *current* view appears to be that failure to intervene does not *per se* bind a nonparty to an adjudication.[45] The issue was tangentially addressed in *Microsystems Software, Inc. v. Scandinavia Online, AB*,[46] but the decision involved standing by a nonparty to appeal an injunction, not the direct issue of the liability of the nonparties to the injunction. The opinion noted that a litigant should not be able "to have its cake and eat it too," which suggests that the nonparty should be bound, although the court's language must be read against the backdrop that the nonparty did participate in the proceedings before the District Court, albeit not as a party of record.[47] On the other hand, the court noted that denying standing to appeal did not deprive the nonparty of due process of law because for the nonparty to be found guilty of violating the injunctive, the court would have to find "active concert with," which is the traditional test for nonparty liability.[48]

§ 36 MODIFICATION OF INJUNCTIONS

An injunction, unlike a damages award,[1] is subject to modification when it would no longer be fair or just to require continued obedience to the existing terms of the injunction. The damages award resolves the dispute between the parties. All the plaintiff's past and future losses associated with the claim will be represented in the award. "Res Judicata" will prevent subsequent relitigation over the dispute except for extreme circumstances, such as a judgment procured by extrinsic fraud. An injunction on the other hand has continuing benefit for the plaintiff and impact on the defendant after the injunction is entered—that is the injunction's *raison d'etre*. Those continuing effects are, moreover, backed up by the contempt power of the court; if the defendant violates the injunction, the plaintiff can seek sanctions through contempt proceedings. The court's power and duty of continuing oversight and supervision of the injunction provides the justification for post-judgment modification of the injunction.

In determining the circumstances under which an injunction will be modified, it is helpful to distinguish between preliminary injunctions,

---

[43] Provident Tradesmens Bank & Trust Co. v. Patterson, 390 U.S. 102, 114 (1968).

[44] Martin v. Wilks, 490 U.S. 755, 766–67 (1989).

[45] 18A WRIGHT, MILLER & COOPER, FEDERAL PRACTICE AND PROCEDURE: JURISDICTION 2D § 4452, at 390–420 (Duty to Participate) (extensively surveying the decisions and the literature on this point).

[46] 226 F.3d 35 (1st Cir. 2000).

[47] *Id.* at 41–42.

[48] *Id.* at 43.

[1] Lake Thunderbird Property Owners Ass'n, Inc. v. Lake Thunderbird, Inc., 680 S.W.2d 761, 763 (Mo. App. 1984) (when judgment fully disposes of matter leaving nothing further for court to do, court's power to control the judgment ceases).

permanent injunctions, and consent decrees. One should not, however, invest too much in these distinctions, as they are not rigid. All efforts to modify any type of injunction share many more similarities than dissimilarities. Temporary Restraining Orders are of such short duration that they are unlikely to raise modification issues. If they do, they should be handled as modification of preliminary injunctions would be handled.

[36.1] Preliminary Injunctions

Because preliminary injunctive relief is often obtained in truncated proceedings, it is not uncommon for such an injunction to be modified on appeal.[2] Modification to correct error is not the issue here; rather, the focus is on whether a change in circumstances warrants modification of the injunction to prevent unfairness. In this regard, care must be taken not to overemphasize the occasional statement that a trial court may vacate or modify a preliminary injunction as necessary or that trial courts have the same power to modify a preliminary injunction as they do to issue or deny such relief.[3] Such statements should not be construed as suggesting a liberal, relaxed judicial approach to modification of a preliminary injunction.

The general standard here, as with permanent injunctions, is that modification of a preliminary injunction is proper only when there has been a change in circumstances between the time the injunction was issued and the time modification is sought.[4] While modifications are usually made because of changes in fact or law occurring after the issuance of the injunction, they can also be made for "any good reason."[5] Courts will, however, police motions to modify preliminary injunctions to ensure that the motion is not used to evade formal requirements associated with the granting or denying of a request for a preliminary injunction. A request for modification of a preliminary injunction is usually independently appealable. A party that failed to appeal in a proper, timely fashion from the earlier granting of a preliminary injunction will not be permitted to simply repackage its arguments as a request for modification and thereby obtain

---

[2] Parkmed Co. v. Pro-Life Counselling, Inc., 457 N.Y.S.2d 27, 29 (App. Dept. 1982) (modifying overly broad preliminary injunction).

[3] Museum Boutique Intercontinental Ltd. v. Picasso, 880 F. Supp. 153, 161 (S.D.N.Y. 1995); Section 36.4 (Effect of Appeal on Power of Trial Court to Supervise or Modify Injunction).

[4] Canal Authority of Fla. v. Callaway, 489 F.2d 567, 578 (5th Cir. 1974); Hunter v. Dennies Contracting Co., Inc., 693 So. 2d 615, 616 (Fla. App. 1997) (holding that when enjoined party participated in hearing from which temporary injunction issued, to demonstrate abuse of discretion in declining to adjust injunction "it was incumbent [on enjoined party] to prove some change of circumstances that would have justified the dissolution or modification of the injunction") (citations omitted; brackets added).

[5] *Canal Authority, supra,* 489 F.2d 567; Gammon, Inc. v. Lemelson, 442 F. Supp. 211, 216 n.2 (D.N.J. 1977).

a second opportunity for appellate review. This evasion of time limits on appeal is not permitted.[6]

[36.2] Permanent Injunctions

Permanent injunctions are final judgments in that they conclude the matter before the court and leave no issue to be determined between the parties except compliance. A permanent injunction is issued primarily to prevent future harm and, unless otherwise specified in the order, is unlimited in respect to time.[7] A time-limited permanent injunction expires by its own terms[8] unless the injunction is modified to extend its time limit. As a practical matter, however, a permanent injunction is permanent so long as the conditions that produce the injunction remain in place.[9] After the conditions that create the need cease, the need for the injunction ceases. If the permanent injunction completely resolves the matter between the parties, modification would not be needed. When, however, the permanent injunction places a continuing burden of compliance on the defendant, it is consistently recognized that the defendant may seek to modify the injunction when changed circumstances render continued compliance with the terms of the original injunction inequitable.[10] The doctrine of "res judicata" does not bar a court from modifying a previously entered injunction.[11]

A plaintiff may seek modification of a permanent injunction even when doing so would materially add to the defendant's burden of compliance. In such cases, the focus is on whether modification is needed to achieve the injunction's original purpose.[12]

Whether a permanent injunction should be modified is based on equitable principles acting on the circumstances of the case.[13] A court may grant a

---

[6] Favia v. Indiana Univ. of Pa., 7 F.3d 332, 338 & n.8 (3d Cir. 1993) (noting that proper method to secure review of order granting a preliminary injunction is to seek reconsideration under Rule 59(e), F.R. Civ. Proc., or to seek appellate review under 28 U.S.C. § 1292(a)(1); to ensure compliance the motion to modify will be reviewed to see whether the motion alleges a change in circumstances or simply represents an untimely appeal).

[7] Bear v. Iowa Dist. Court for Tama County, 540 N.W.2d 439, 441 (Iowa 1995).

[8] Section 33.1 ([Permanent Injunctions] Scope of Relief).

[9] Condura Constr. Co. v. Milwaukee Bldg. & Constr. Trade Council AFL, 99 N.W.2d 751, 755 (Wis. 1959).

[10] Merrell-Nat'l Lab., Inc. v. Zenith Lab., Inc., 579 F.2d 786, 791 (3d Cir. 1978).

[11] Jefferson v. Big Horn County, 4 P.3d 26, 32 (Mont. 2000); see Fardig v. Fardig, 56 P.3d 9, 11–12 (Alaska 2003) (holding that principles of "res judicata" and collateral estoppel did not bar court from modifying custody order); Saenz v. Saenz, 602 So.2d 973, 974 (Fla. App. 1992) (holding that modification of temporary custody order does not require "change in circumstances" because temporary order is not "res judicata").

[12] United States v. United Shoe Mach. Corp., 391 U.S. 244, 248–49 (1968). This approach also applies to consent decrees. Building & Constr. Trades v. NLRB, 64 F.3d 880 (3d Cir. 1995) (stating that "[d]ifferent considerations apply when the party seeking to modify the consent decree wishes to strengthen its prohibition because the purpose for which the decree had been framed has not been fully achieved"); United States v. Western Elec. Co., 46 F.3d 1198, 1202 (D.C. Cir. 1995) (stating that "[a]t the request of the party who sought the equitable relief, a court may tighten the decree in order to accomplish its intended result").

[13] First Protestant Reformed Church v. DeWolf, 100 N.W.2d 254, 257 (Mich. 1960).

request to modify a permanent injunction when warranted by a change in circumstances. A change in circumstances consists of a change in facts relevant to the underlying injunction or a change in law (decisional or statutory) relevant to the underlying injunction.[14]

The reasons for permitting modification rest on the unique function of the injunction. Once an injunction is issued, its future effects cannot be ignored.[15] When an injunction has continuing legal effects on the parties, backed up by the formidable sanction of contempt for disobedience, the ability to modify ensures that the injunction does not impose obligations on the defendant, the performance of which are, because of changed circumstances, absurd, unwarranted, unnecessary, or unduly burdensome.[16]

The fact that circumstances have changed does not mean that a request to modify an injunction will be well received by the court. The change must be substantial and unexpected.[17] There is language in the decisional law that modification requires a showing of extraordinary circumstances[18] and should be approachable with caution.[19] These glosses all derive from *United States v. Swift & Co.*,[20] a decision addressing modification of a consent decree;[21] nevertheless, the language has been extended to injunctions that are the product of litigation rather than agreement.[22] One may distill from the above a three-part test for the modification of a permanent injunction: (1) a clear showing of substantial change in circumstances since the injunction was issued; (2) extreme and unexpected hardships in compliance with the injunctions existing terms; and (3) good reason why the court

---

[14] System Fed'n No. 91 v. Wright, 364 U.S. 642, 647 (1961) (stating that "the court cannot be required to disregard significant changes in law or facts if it is satisfied that what it has been doing has been turned through changing circumstances into an instrument of wrong"); Toussaint v. McCarthy, 801 F.2d 1080, 1090 (9th Cir. 1986), *cert. denied*, 481 U.S. 1069 (1987). *See generally* John F. Wagner, Annot., *Construction and Application of Rule 65(b)(5) of Federal Rules of Civil Procedure, Authorizing Relief From Final Judgment Where its Prospective Application is Inequitable*, 117 A.L.R. Fed. 419 (1994). Similar results are reached under state law. See Sontag Chain Stores Co. v. Superior Court, 113 P.2d 689, 690 (Cal. 1941) (holding that a court has inherent power to modify or dissolve an injunction based on "a change in the controlling facts upon which the injunction rested, or the law has been changed, modified, or extended, or where the ends of justice would be served by modification").

[15] *Toussaint, supra*, 801 F.2d at 1090 (stating that the court must be sensitive to the need for modification because permanent injunctive relief controls future conduct); C.L. Smith Indus. Co., Inc. v. Matecki, 914 S.W.2d 873, 877 (Mo. App. 1996) (stating that "a court has authority to modify a permanent injunction which is based on a condition subject to change").

[16] Edlis v. Miller, 51 S.E.2d 132, 139 (W. Va. 1948); *see* Timothy Jost, *From* Swift *to Stotts and Beyond: Modification of Injunctions in Federal Courts*, 64 Tex. L. Rev. 1101, 1116 (1986) (stating that the "courts have been willing, even absent change in the law, to modify or dissolve an injunction in the interest of fairness and efficiency").

[17] Transgo, Inc. v. Ajac Transmission Parts, Corp., 911 F.2d 363, 365 (9th Cir. 1990).

[18] *Id.*

[19] Humble Oil & Ref. Co. v. American Oil Co., 405 F.2d 803, 813 (8th Cir. 1969).

[20] 286 U.S. 106 (1932).

[21] Section 36.3 (Consent Decree and Structural Injunctions).

[22] Rufo v. Inmates of Suffolk County Jail, 502 U.S. 367, 378–80 (1992).

should modify the injunction.[23] In this regard, unexpected or unforeseen does not mean unforeseeable:

> Respondents urge that modification should be allowed only when a change in facts is both "unforeseen and unforeseeable." Such a standard would provide even less flexibility than the exacting *Swift* test; we decline to adopt it. Litigants are not required to anticipate every exigency that could conceivably arise during the life of a consent decree.[24]

As further noted by the Court (again, in the context of a consent decree):

> Ordinarily, however, modification should not be granted where a party relies upon events that actually were anticipated at the time it entered into a decree. If it is clear that a party anticipated changing conditions that would make performance of the decree more onerous but nevertheless agreed to the decree, that party would have to satisfy a heavy burden to convince a court that it agreed to the decree in good faith, made a reasonable effort to comply with the decree, and should be relieved of the undertaking under Rule 60(b).[25]

Factual change in circumstances is a fundamental condition in many cases for modification of an injunction. In order to satisfy that requirement, a party may show: (1) changed factual conditions make compliance "substantially more onerous";[26] (2) compliance with the injunction proves unworkable due to "unforeseen obstacles";[27] or (3) enforcement of the injunction in its present form would be "detrimental to the public interest."[28]

Change in law can represent a difficult political issue when the change is the result of statute rather than decision. Under standard separation of powers doctrine, the legislature does not have the power to nullify a judicial decision because a judicial decision would then lack an essential characteristic—finality.[29] When permanent injunctive relief is provided, that principle is not applied as to the prospective aspect of the order:

---

[23] Securities & Exch. Comm. v. Worthen, 98 F.3d 480, 482 (9th Cir. 1996).

[24] *Rufo, supra*, 502 U.S. at 385.

[25] *Id.* (citations omitted).

[26] *Id.* at 384 (finding that the unforeseen explosion of pretrial detainees makes it substantially more onerous to build a jail that houses all the detainees in single-cell occupancy as required by the injunction).

[27] *Id.*; New York State Ass'n For Retarded Children Inc. v. Carey, 706 F.2d 956, 965 (2d Cir. 1983) (involving inability to relocate mentally disabled to specifically designed community placements due to tight housing market).

[28] *Rufo, supra*, 502 U.S. at 384; Duran v. Elrod, 760 F.2d 756, 760 (7th Cir. 1985) (observing that compliance with injunction forbidding double bunking of inmates would result in the release of dangerous accused felons on their own recognizance).

[29] Plaut v. Spendthrift Farm Inc., 514 U.S. 211, 222 (1995) (stating that "[a] legislature without exceeding its province cannot reverse a determination once made, in a particular case; though it may prescribe a new rule for future cases").

[I]f the remedy in this case had been an action at law, and a judgment rendered in favor of the plaintiff for damages, the right to these would have passed beyond the reach of the power of congress. It would have depended, not upon the public right of the free navigation of the river, but upon the judgment of the court . . . . But that part of the decree, directing the abatement of the obstruction, is executory, a continuing decree . . . . [W]hether [the bridge] is a future existing or continuing obstruction depends upon the question of whether or not it interferes with the right of navigation. If . . . since the decree, this right has been modified by the competent authority, so that the bridge is no longer an unlawful obstruction, it is quite plain that the decree of the court cannot be enforced. [30]

A change in the relevant statutory law is a fully adequate basis on which an injunction may be modified. [31] Change in decisional law also supports modification of an injunction. [32] Unlike the situation involving a factual change, courts often state that a change in the law, which authorizes what was previously forbidden, requires modification. [33]

Neither compliance with the terms of a permanent injunction nor the mere passage of time warrants modification. [34] The burden is on the party seeking the modification to show the requisite "changed circumstances." [35]

An effort to modify an injunction calls into play different considerations from those that arise during direct appellate review of an order granting an injunction. Modification attacks settled expectations; direct review does not. When exercising direct appellate jurisdiction, the court sits as a court of correction; correspondingly, a party's expectation that injunctive relief will be provided does not merit legal protection until all appeals have been

---

[30] State of Penn. v. Wheeling & Belmont Bridge Co., 59 U.S. 421, 431 (1855); see Class v. Norton, 507 F.2d 1058, 1061 (2d Cir. 1974) (finding that *Wheeling & Belmont Bridge Co.* created a "doctrine of deference to legislative revision of a statute upon which a prospective court order is based").

[31] Wang v. Reno, 81 F.3d 808, 815 n.11 (9th Cir. 1996); Hodge v. Dep't of Housing & Urban Dev., 862 F.2d 859, 865 (11th Cir. 1989); Jacobson v. County of Goodhue, 539 N.W.2d 623, 625 n.3 (Minn. App. 1995).

[32] Nelson v. Collins, 659 F.2d 420, 424 (4th Cir. 1981); Coca-Cola Co. v. Standard Bottling Co., 138 F.2d 788, 790 (10th Cir. 1943). Change in constitutional interpretation may support modification of equitable decrees. Agostini v. Felton, 521 U.S. 203 (1997) (vacating an injunction against a state program offering educational services by public school teachers on parochial school campuses when the injunction was based on First Amendment Establishment Clause principles no longer followed).

[33] *Toussaint, supra,* 801 F.2d at 1090; American Horse Protection Ass'n, Inc. v. Watt, 694 F.2d 1310, 1316 (D.C. Cir. 1982).

[34] Securities & Exch. Comm'n v. Advance Growth Capital Corp., 539 F.2d 649, 652 (7th Cir. 1976).

[35] Latenser v. Intercessors of the Lamb, Inc., 553 N.W.2d 458, 462 (Neb. 1996).

concluded.[36] This but reemphasizes that a motion to modify an injunction is not a substitute for a timely appeal.[37]

Vagueness and ambiguity do not require modification of an injunction.[38] However, vagueness and ambiguity may be eliminated by motion so that the enjoined party's obligations are clarified. The motion is limited, however, by its purpose. A motion for clarification is not designed to change, expand, or reduce a party's obligations under an injunction.[39]

[36.3]   Consent Decrees and Structural Injunctions

Consent decrees like permanent injunctions seek to remedy a particular harm by ordering the enjoined party's future conduct. They differ from permanent injunctions only in that they are products of assent rather than adjudication,[40] but too much can be made even of that distinction. Consent decrees are not freely negotiated in arms length transactions between willing parties of equal bargaining strength. They are a product of compulsion—the threat of litigation and an adverse or unsatisfactory judgment. How much compulsion exists in any particular case will, of course, vary as the facts and circumstances vary. Consent decrees represent a unique mix of bargained for and compelled injunctive relief. As noted in *Local No. 93, Int'l Ass'n of Firefighters, AFL-CIO C.L.C. v. City of Cleveland*:

> [C]onsent decrees "have attributes both of contracts and of judicial decrees," a dual character that has resulted in different treatment for different purposes . . . . The question is not whether we can label a consent decree as a "contract" or a "judgment," for we can do both.[41]

One unique factor of consent decrees, however, is that "a defendant may agree, within limits, to do more than a judicially imposed injunction could have required."[42] This may also lead to creative uses of consent decrees

---

[36] *Toussaint, supra*, 801 F.2d at 1091 n.7.

[37] Railway Labor Executives Ass'n v. Metro-North Commuter R.R. Co., 759 F. Supp. 1019, 1021 (S.D.N.Y. 1990).

[38] Wyatt by and through Rawlins v. King, 803 F. Supp. 377, 390 (M.D. Ala. 1992).

[39] Walshon v. Walshon, 681 A.2d 376, 379 (Conn. App. 1996) (referred to as a "motion for articulation" under Connecticut law).

[40] United States v. Armour & Co., 402 U.S. 673, 681 (1971):

> [By entering into a consent decree the parties] waive their right to litigate the issues involved in the case and thus save themselves the time, expense, and inevitable risk of litigation. Naturally, the agreement reached normally embodies a compromise; in exchange for the saving of cost and elimination of risk, the parties each give up something they might have won had they proceeded with the litigation.

[41] 478 U.S. 501, 519 (1986) (citation omitted).

[42] Labor/Community Strategy Center v. Los Angeles County Metropolitan Transp. Autho., 263 F.3d 1041, 1050 (9th Cir. 2001) ("[S]everal courts have held that federalism concerns do not prevent a federal court from enforcing a consent decree to which state officials have consented. MTA's consent to this form of dispute resolution relieves many federalism concerns") (internal quotation marks and citations omitted), *cert. denied*, 535 U.S. 951 (2002); Alexander v. Britt, 89 F.3d 194, 200 (4th Cir. 1996).

to authorize unpopular actions thought to be socially desirable.[43] When a party has voluntarily assumed an extralegal obligation, a court may be more reluctant to relieve a party of the added obligations.[44]

Structural injunctions are a particularized form of permanent injunctive relief. Structural injunctions operate on the large scale rather than the traditional, bipolar private dispute between a plaintiff and a defendant. Structural injunctions have come to dominate institutional reform litigation that came of age in the latter half of the twentieth century in cases involving school desegregation, prison administration, and mental health facility reform.

Structural injunctions envision a fluid future in which the form of injunctive relief must reflect the changing contours of both the evolving facts and the often evolving law.[45] Much of the modern decisional law addressing modification of permanent injunctions have arisen in the context of structural injunctions. Many of these structural injunctions are in the form of consent decrees. A critical issue is whether modification rules should reflect, on the one hand, the changing contours and fluidity of the setting to which the injunction applies or should reflect, on the other hand, the bargain elements of the decree. The former suggests a liberal, relaxed approach to modification; the latter a tighter approach reflecting respect for the bargain struck by the parties.

Traditionally, courts have required a party seeking modification of a consent decree to demonstrate that continued obedience to the existing decree would result in "grievous wrong" on account of new and unforeseen conditions.[46] With the rise in institutional reform litigation, courts began to question whether such a rigorous approach was consistent with the objectives of institutional reform remedies.[47] In 1992, the Supreme Court agreed with these courts. In *Rufo v. Inmates of Suffolk County Jail*[48] the Court

---

[43] Cleveland County Ass'n for Government by the People v. Cleveland County Bd. of Commr's, 965 F. Supp. 72 (D.D.C. 1997) (rejecting challenge to consent decree settling Voting Rights Act case, which plaintiffs contended created minority preferences; court held that failure of defendant to admit or court to find violation of Voting Rights Act was not a prerequisite to awarding equitable relief to achieve the objectives of the Act); *cf.* Lawyer v. Department of Justice, 521 U.S. 567 (1997) (holding that district court was not required to determine liability before settlement could be reached by some of the parties regarding redistricting plan even though settlement frustrated judicial review of the reapportionment plan).

[44] *Alexander, supra,* 89 F.3d 194; *cf.* LaShawn A. v. Barry, 69 F.3d 556, 567 (D.C. Cir. 1995) (noting difference between approach that should be taken between enjoined party who consents to decree "only to the extent necessary to remedy legal violations" and an enjoined party who "accept[s] and continue[s] to embrace extra obligations") (brackets added), *vacated on other grounds,* 74 F.3d 303 (D.C. Cir. 1996), *cert. denied,* 520 U.S. 1264 (1997).

[45] Newman v. Graddick, 740 F.2d 1513, 1518 (11th Cir. 1984) (finding that a Supreme Court intervening decision along with changed factual circumstances warranted modification of structural injunction governing the Alabama prison system).

[46] United States v. Swift & Co., 286 U.S. 106, 119 (1932).

[47] *New York State Ass'n for Retarded Children, supra,* 706 F.2d at 969; Philadelphia Welfare Rights Org. v. Shapp, 602 F.2d 1114, 1120–21 (3d Cir. 1979).

[48] 502 U.S. 367 (1992).

adopted a two-pronged test for modification of structural injunctions. First, the party seeking modification must demonstrate that "a significant change in circumstances warrants revision of the decree."[49] Second, the proposed revision "must be suitably tailored to the changed circumstances,"[50] and responsive to the situation the changed circumstances present.[51] The modification should be consistent with the decree's purpose;[52] however, even a modification that frustrates the decree's purpose may be acceptable if changed circumstances so warrant, although a court should proceed with caution in this latter setting.[53]

The primary issue that lower courts have addressed, post *Rufo*, is the extent to which *Rufo* should be applied, if at all, outside the context of institutional reform litigation. The specific holding in *Rufo* was that "the *Swift* 'grievous wrong' standard does not apply to requests to modify consent decrees stemming from institutional reform litigation,"[54] although the Court did not expressly state that its holding could not be applied in other contexts. Because courts, like nature, abhor a vacuum, post-*Rufo* decisions have tended to expand the approach;[55] indeed, the Court in a pre-*Rufo* decision, suggested that the *Swift* strict test was inappropriate to apply to a litigated, school desegregation decree.[56] Even courts that have rejected a broad application of *Rufo* have suggested that the *Rufo* approach may be appropriate in non-institutional reform litigation when the public interest is implicated in the request for modification.[57]

Rufo is largely the culmination of a retreat the Court had been taking from *Swift* for many years.[58] In *United States v. United Shoe Machinery Corp.* the Court noted that the "grievous wrong" test was in large part the product of the unique facts of *Swift*—an enjoined party seeking to avoid a consent decree a short period of time after the decree's adoption and before the purposes of the decree had been achieved.[59] The state of the law in this area is, "at bottom, guided by equitable considerations."[60] Consistent

---

[49] *Id.* at 384.

[50] *Id.* at 383.

[51] *Id.* at 390–91.

[52] *Id.* at 381.

[53] *Id.* at 388.

[54] *Id.* at 393.

[55] Building & Contr. Trades Council of Philadelphia v. N.L.R.B., 64 F.3d 880, 886–87 (3d Cir. 1995) (collecting cases).

[56] Board of Educ. of Oklahoma City Public Sch. v. Dowell, 498 U.S. 237 (1991).

[57] Alexis Lichine & Cie v. Sarcha A. Lichine Estate Selections, Ltd., 45 F.3d 582, 586 n.2 (1st Cir. 1995).

[58] *New York State Ass'n For Retarded Children, supra*, 706 F.2d at 970 (noting that "[a]s experience with [structural injunction] litigation increases, a consensus is emerging among commentators in favor of modification with a freer hand") (brackets added).

[59] 391 U.S. 244, 248 (1968).

[60] United States v. Eastman Kodak, Co., 63 F.3d 95, 101 (2d Cir. 1995); *Building and Construction Trades Council, supra*, 64 F.3d at 888 (stating that "[a] court of equity cannot rely on a simple formula but must evaluate a number of potentially competing considerations to determine whether to modify or vacate an injunction entered by consent or otherwise").

with this approach is the realization that requests to modify a consent decree, which seek "to implement minor changes in extraneous details" of a consent decree, should be considered under a more relaxed standard of "reasonableness."[61]

A consent decree encompasses obligations the parties have agreed to assume without litigation; therefore, the parties should be afforded notice and an opportunity to be heard before their legal obligations and rights are changed by modifying the decree.[62] Even if notice and a hearing are provided, however, the power to modify a consent decree is not unlimited:

> Even given their distinctive character as agreements backed by the authority of the court, consent decrees are to be interpreted as contracts. The binding force of a consent decree comes from the agreement of the parties. A federal district court may not use its power of enforcing consent decrees to enlarge or diminish the duties on which the parties have agreed and which the court has approved.[63]

Parties who contract against a backdrop of uncertainty may be deemed to have assumed the risk that the future will unfold differently from what they envisioned.

[36.4]   Effect of Appeal on Power of Trial Court to Supervise or Modify Injunction

It is generally recognized that the appeal of the injunction does not divest the trial court of authority to supervise compliance with the injunction, including punishment by contempt for violations of the injunction.[64] A more difficult issue is the extent to which the trial court may modify the injunction after a party has appealed the order to a higher court. The issue is one of allocation of power and the concern that the trial court could effectively divest the appellate court of jurisdiction by changing the injunction and mooting the appeal.[65] Although the decisions can not be completely

---

[61] Police Ass'n of New Orleans v. City of New Orleans, 100 F.3d 1159, 1171 (5th Cir. 1996):

> The standard we set forth applies when a party seeks modification of a term of a consent decree that arguably relates to the vindication of a constitutional right. Such a showing is not necessary to implement minor changes in extraneous details that may have been included in a decree . . . but are unrelated to remedying the underlying constitutional violation. Ordinarily, the parties should consent to modifying a decree to allow such changes. If a party refuses to consent and the moving party has a reasonable basis for its request, the court should modify the decree.

quoting Rufo, supra, 502 U.S. at 383 n.7.

[62] United States v. Western Elec. Co., 894 F.2d 430, 434–35 (D.C. Cir. 1990) (distinguishing between interpretation and modification of a consent decree; the notice and hearing requirements apply to modification, not interpretation, of the consent decree).

[63] Johnson v. Robinson, 987 F.2d 1043, 1046 (4th Cir. 1993) (citations omitted).

[64] A&M Records, Inc. v. Napster, Inc., 284 F.3d 1091, 1099 (9th Cir. 2002).

[65] There is a separate and distinct issue whether an appeal automatically stays the injunction issued by the trial court or whether the appellant must seek affirmative relief, by way of a stay, from the appellate court.

reconciled, the general view is to recognize a limited power on the part of the trial court to modify the injunction, usually in response to a party's request for clarification.[66] Rule 62(c) recognizes a somewhat liberal gloss to this limited right:

> When an appeal is taken from an interlocutory or final judgment granting, dissolving, or denying an injunction, the court in its discretion may suspend, modify, restore, or grant an injunction during the pendency of the appeal upon such terms as to bond or otherwise as it considers proper for the security of the rights of the adverse party.[67]

Some courts, however, suggest a more limited power to modify pending appeal. The trial court may modify the injunction, but the modification must not meaningfully alter the status quo or change the core questions before the appellate court.[68]

---

[66] *A&M Records, Inc.*, *supra*.

[67] Fed. R. Civ. P. 62(c).

[68] Natural Resources Defense Counsel, Inc. v. Southwest Marine Incorporated, 242 F.3d 1163, 1166 (9th Cir. 2001).

Chapter 5

GENERAL PRINCIPLES GOVERNING RESTITUTION

§ 40   RESTITUTION

Restitution is said to be an often overlooked remedy.[1] If true, that is unfortunate for restitution provides an alternative approach to assessing

---

[1] Andrew Kull, *Rationalizing Restitution*, 83 Cal. L. Rev. 1191, 1191 (1995) (observing that "[s]ignificant uncertainty shrouds the modern law of restitution. Few American lawyers, judges, or law professors are familiar with even the standard propositions of the doctrine.");

and redressing civil liability. Restitutionary remedies may also provide redress that is otherwise unavailable under the law of damages. The essence of restitution is the recovery of the benefit realized by the defendant not compensation for the harm or injury sustained by the plaintiff.[2]

Restitution is based on the goal of avoiding unjust enrichment; unjust enrichment is, however, a concept of some indeterminancy. Unjust enrichment exists as a separate basis of civil liability, wholly independent of tort or contract. Examples of actions based on the idea of unjust enrichment, for which there is no direct tort or contract counterpart, include actions for indemnity, subrogation, quasi contract, and rescission. Unjust enrichment also exists within the traditional contract and tort framework. A breach of contract or breach of duty may give rise to restitution when, as a consequence of that breach, the defendant has been unjustly enriched. The distinction between unjust enrichment as a separate, independent action and as a derivative, dependent part of an action in tort or contract is important. The absence of a traditional damages remedy in tort or contract may not foreclose restitution based on a finding of unjust enrichment as a consequence of the breach. Assume, for example, that a landlord and tenant orally agree to a 5-year lease and pursuant to that "agreement" the tenant makes improvements to the leasehold. The parties are unable to memorialize their oral agreement and the landlord bars the tenant from the premises. Assume that the oral lease is unenforceable due to the statute of frauds. Assume further that the tenant's leasehold improvements were insufficient to avoid the statute of frauds defense under the part performance exception. This does not mean that the tenant is remediless against the landlord. The tenant may still obtain compensation for the "value" of the benefit the tenant conferred on the landlord by the tenant's part performance, even though the contract that induced the tenant's performance is unenforceable. On the other hand, assume the parties enter into an enforceable agreement, but the agreement is silent as to tenant improvements. Should the law of unjust enrichment now be invoked to allow the tenant to claim a benefit that the contract did not address? Should it matter that the default rule in the jurisdiction is that tenant improvements belong to the landlord unless the contract otherwise provides?[3]

The resolution of the proper role for restitution also extends to nomenclature. Should the right to recover a benefit held by another be called restitution or should restitution be designated the remedy and the right be called

---

Douglas Laycock, *The Scope and Significance of Restitution*, 67 Tex. L. Rev. 1277, 1277 (1989) (noting that "restitution is a relatively neglected and underdeveloped part of the law. In the mental map of most lawyers, restitution consists largely of blank spaces with undefined borders and only scattered patches of familiar ground").

[2] *Laycock, Restitution, supra*, 67 Tex. L. Rev. at 1282–83 (noting that restitution must be distinguished from compensation either by its focus on restoration of the loss in kind as a measure of recovery or by the focus on defendant's gain as a measure of recovery); Paschall's, Inc. v. Dozier, 407 S.W.2d 150, 155 (Tenn. 1966) (noting that "[t]he most significant requirement for a recovery on quasi contract is that the enrichment to the defendant be unjust").

[3] Section 41.2 ([Restitution for Wrongdoing] Breach of Contract).

"unjust enrichment."[4] The debate is fundamental because beneath the labels is an important debate over the extent to which, if at all, the private law formed by the parties (contract) or law based on general social policy (tort) should be displaced by a legal doctrine based on moral concepts of right and wrong, fairness and justness, with all the ambiguity and uncertainty that such terms import. For example, if the dispute would normally be treated as a breach of duty or contract, but the defendant has not inflicted any harm on the plaintiff, should the law leave the parties alone and provide plaintiff with no remedy or should the law, nonetheless, intervene and require disgorgement of any benefit(s) defendant obtained by his breach?[5]

The treatment of Restitution as a distinct body of substantive law is generally attributed to the First Restatement of Restitution. Professors Seavey and Scott, the Reporters for the First Restatement of Restitution, collected a disparate, but related, body of legal concepts and formulated them into a discrete category that has at times since been referred to as Restitution, Unjust Enrichment, or both. The problem is that unjust enrichment has always been, and remains, an area somewhat outside the accepted domains of tort and contract. As long as unjust enrichment was limited to areas largely outside the concern of tort and contract, such as mistaken payments, the presence of this alternative body of legal rights posed no significant problem. Modernly, however, the concept of unjust enrichment has been extended into areas that are also of interest to tort and contract. It is this potential conflict between competing views as to how "law" should respond to legal controversies that pushes the debate today.

Without in anyway minimizing the debate over taxonomy in this area, these materials will distinguish between restitution for wrongdoing,[6] restitution for breach of contract,[7] and restitution for unjust enrichment.[8] As noted above, the division and distinctions drawn are not uncontroversial,[9] but the approach will, it is hoped help clarify the law in this area

[4] Stephen A. Smith, *The Structure of Unjust Enrichment Law: Is Restitution a Right or a Remedy?*, 36 Loy. L.A. L. Rev. 1037 (2003); Coleen P. Murphy, *Misclassifying Monetary Restitution*, 55 SMU L. Rev. 1577,1578 (2002) ("Modern scholars have debated whether restutition should be defined solely as the law of unjust enrichment or whether it also includes 'restoration' remedies") (footnote omitted).

[5] *In re* New Motor Vehicles Canadian Export Antitrust Litigation, 350 F. Supp. 2d 160 (D. Me. 2004):

> In contemporary United States common law, restitution based upon unjust enrichment takes at least two forms. "It may arise from contracts, torts, or other predicate wrongs." Then it is sometimes called "parasitic." Alternatively, unjust enrichment alone "may also serve as independent grounds for restitution in the absence of mistake, wrongdoing, or breach of contract." Then restitution is sometimes called "autonomous" or "freestanding." Academic commentary debates the wisdom of this structure, but there is little debate that it exists.

Id. at 207–08 (citations and footnotes omitted).

[6] Section 41.1 ([Restitution for Wrongdoing] Tortious Conduct).

[7] Section 41.2 ([Restitution for Wrongdoing] Breach of Contract).

[8] Section 42 (Restitution for Unjust Enrichment).

[9] Symposium, *Restitution and Unjust Enrichment*, 79 Tex. L. Rev. 1763 (2001).

and the approaches courts usually adopt when confronted with problems of this ilk.

This overlap between restitution as a remedy for distinct, substantive claims of unjust enrichment, restitution as a remedy for breaches of contract or breaches of duty, and restitution as a substantive right has generated the inevitable confusion and imprecision in the case law. It is not always clear in which context the language of restitution is being used. This can lead to idiosyncratic applications and care must be taken when reading decisions not to read more into the decision than it will support. This is an area of the law where it is probably safest to read decisions cautiously, at least insofar as particular applications of general principles are concerned. The general principles retain broad acceptance; consensus dissipates in the individual applications. This is, of course, true throughout the law—the "devil is in the details" problem. It is simply particularly true here.

§ 41   RESTITUTION FOR WRONGDOING

There is a view that the law of restitution went out of fashion in the United States sometime in the 1950s and remained so until it was rediscovered in the 1980s.[1] This view, held and promoted largely by law professors, is overstated. It is, after all, not the case that before the 1950s mistaken payments were returned to their payors, as the law of restitution requires, but after 1950 they were retained by their payees because the law of restitution had become extinct. In fact, the period between the 1950s and 1980s saw a tremendous growth in the use of restitution, both as a substantive and as a remedial principle. What did happen is that law schools and academics lost interest in restitution as a separate, free standing, self-contained body of law that warranted its own law school courses(s) and law journal recognition.

Why restitution was ever lost, much less who lost it, is hard to say. Perhaps interest in the law of restitution waned as academic interest in "rights" based doctrines and "law and economics" increased. Restitution is often seen as guided by case-sensitive equitable concerns and restitution remedies may have seemed "inefficient." Restitution may have appeared to have lost the Darwinian battle to a "more evolved law." This new law was seen as more just because it was based on rules rather than discretion-based standards and guidelines and was perceived to be more scientific and precise because it was based on economic science rather than moral intuition.[2] Yet, the argument that restitution is inefficient has always been implied rather than proved. The idea that restitution is more ambiguous, and consequently less certain, than contract or tort, likely rests or restitution's association with the concept of unjust enrichment. Whether, as a body

---

[1] Section 40 (Nature of Restitution) at n.1.

[2] John H. Langbein, *The Later History of Restitution*, in RESTITUTION: PAST, PRESENT AND FUTURE 57, 61–62 (W.R. Cornish, et. al. eds. 1998); *see* Ernest J. Weinrib, Book Review, *Restoring Restitution*, 91 Va. L. Rev. 861, 862 (2005).

of law, unjust enrichment is more or less ambiguous, than contract or tort, is more a statement of perception than of fact. No means exist to make that determination; nor would the effort necessarily prove productive.

What would it prove about restitution, to say that it was more or less ambiguous than another body of law, such as tort or contract damages. Such an inquiry profoundly misperceives what is being studied and why. Restitution, as a part of private law, exists, as does all private law, for the purpose of facilitating human interaction by means and for ends that are deemed socially proper and advantageous. Whether restitution does well, or poorly, in this regard is surely a matter of legitimate inquiry, analysis, and criticism. Whether restitution's purpose is better achieved by rules, principles, standards, or guidelines is also a legitimate inquiry. Whether, however, restitution law is more or less ambiguous than some other body of law is irrelevant for it does not shed any light on whether restitution law is good or whether the "compared to" body of law is good. The inquiry, moreover, assumes that restitution law is ambiguous in some significant way that deviates from the situation found with other law that establishes a baseline norm of "certainty."

By the same token, restitution does not deserve a free pass. Restitution law must justify its seat at the table. Restitution must show that it is a useful component of private law. The breadth, depth, and scope of restitution law must be justified.

What role then does restitution play in private law? To answer this question we need to examine what restitution is. Much of the modern concern over restitution followed from the effort by the American Law Institute to systematize disparate legal doctrines, such as quasi contract, constructive trusts, indemnity, subrogation, etc., into a new body of law titled "Restitution."[3] That effort created a term "restitution" that had both a substantive and a remedial connotation. Restitution could refer to doctrine that would provide a right outside the traditional categories of contract and tort—and thus a right that both complemented and competed with tort and contract. In this form, restitution was distinct from contract and tort and restitution was largely saved for situations when neither contract nor tort provided relief but it was thought nonetheless that relief should be provided. This point is significant for it is not sufficient to value law by what it does and does not provide, we must also ask what does law refuse and resist providing. Not providing relief is not necessarily the same as refusing and resisting relief. Refusal reflects a value directly; not providing reflects that value indirectly. When law provides relief in restitution (unjust enrichment) while denying relief in contract or tort, that statement by the law has special significance as compared to when law permits relief both in restitution and in contract or tort.

Restitution can also refer to the nature of relief provided. In this form, restitution is seen as measuring relief by identifying the defendant's gain

---

[3] Restatement of Restitution (1937). The Reporters for the project were Professors Warren Seavey and Austin Scott.

rather than the plaintiff's loss. For example, if defendant fraudulently induces plaintiff to pay $10 for a widget that is worth $1, plaintiff has lost $9 and defendant has gained $9. As the example indicates, in many cases, restitution, as an additional remedy, is not needed because traditional tort or contract remedies fully redress plaintiff's loss. There are, however, situations when defendant's gain exceeds plaintiff's loss or plaintiff does not sustain a loss, but defendant realizes a gain. In these cases, the plaintiff will necessarily prefer the remedy of restitution (recovery of defendant's gain) over damages (recovery of plaintiff's loss).

Confusion may especially be encountered in cases when the defendant's wrongdoing not only inflicts harm on the plaintiff but produces gain for the defendant. Not all cases fit the scenario. A defendant who negligently runs a red light and collides with the plaintiff's car, damaging the car and injuring the plaintiff, sustains no gain in the usual sense. Even in cases of this ilk when some gain may be envisioned, as when the defendant manufactures and sells a defective product, saving as a gain the amount needed to expend to produce a non-defective product, the gain (per product) will usually fall far short of the loss sustained by the plaintiff (per accident).[4] There are, however, cases when wrongdoing does produce gains that exceed losses, for example, a defendant who wrongfully takes property from the plaintiff and improves the property or uses the property to generate additional gain. In the first situation (improvement of property wrongfully taken) the law traditionally recognized the right of the original owner to get his property back without compensating the wrongdoer for the improvements provided. This availability of a remedy of specific restitution, (return of the very thing taken), provides support for an alternative or substitute damages remedy that compensates the plaintiff for what he lost, measured not by what he originally lost but by what he was entitled to get back but did not get back either because the property was destroyed, would not be returned, could not be returned, or the plaintiff now preferred cash rather than the specific property.

A different case arises when defendant's gain cannot be reconciled with any property or loss sustained by the plaintiff. For example, A takes B's property, incorporates that property into A's own property and uses the admixture to reap profits that only the admixture could generate. Here, the gain cannot be seen as something B had and lost because it is not a gain B could acquire by the use of his property or his own efforts. Permitting B to acquire the entire gain or any portion that exceeds B's actual contribution must be justified by reasons that transcend giving B back what he lost for the simple reason that B is getting back more than he lost. Most importantly, if that broader relief is sought, the law must address whether it wishes to provide or resist providing that relief.

---

4 The result may be different if the plaintiff can claim the aggregate of defendant's savings across the product line. This usually requires a heightened showing of wrongdoing by the defendant. Section 41 (Restitution for Wrongdoing). Section 51 (Disgorgement Orders); Chapter 23 (Punitive Damages).

Permitting a plaintiff to acquire gains that transcend the plaintiff's loss is most commonly justified by tying the relief to the defendant's wrongdoing. Separating a wrongdoer from his ill gotten gains is a time honored legal tradition. Here the inquiry necessarily focuses on whether the defendant's wrongdoing warrants disgorgement of the gain that exceeds plaintiff's loss. When the plaintiff seeks damages for what was lost rather than return of the specific property, whether those damages are measured based on the property's value at the time it was lost or at the time it was not returned often turns on the wrongfulness of the means by which the defendant acquired the plaintiff's property or the wrongfulness of the defendant's refusal to return the property, thus forcing the plaintiff's recourse to damages.

In making this inquiry much weight is borne by the concept of "wrongfulness", which itself is a term of some ambiguity. For example, it is wrong to breach a contract, it is wrong to convert property, and it is wrong to acquire property by misrepresentation; yet, the law distinguishes between simple breaches and opportunistic breaches, between innocent converters and wrongful converters, and between non-intentional misrepresentations and intentional misrepresentations. We distinguish between legal wrong and moral wrong both within and outside the law. Of course, we do not always do this consistently or clearly and that is the root of the problem in this area.

[41.1] Tortious Conduct

Restitution of benefits and gains acquired by tortious wrongdoing has been long accepted in the law, but the acceptance has been guarded and the rationales for the acceptance have been controversial.

Restitution has most consistently been allowed in cases of fraud,[5] conversion,[6] and misappropriation.[7] Recently, a number of courts have permitted restitution in cases involving trespass, but the decisions are in conflict.[8] Courts have rejected efforts to bring restitution claims for defamation[9] and nuisance,[10] although large mass tort settlements have

---

[5] Heldenfels Bros. v. City of Corpus Christi, 832 S.W.2d 39, 41 (Tex. 1992) ("A party may recover under the unjust enrichment theory when one person has obtained a benefit by fraud, duress, or the taking of an undue advantage").

[6] Olwell v. Nye & Nissen Co., 173 P.2d 652 (Wash. 1946); Restatement of Restitution § 151 cmt. f (1937).

[7] *Compare* Edwards v. Lee's Adm'r, 96 S.W.2d 1028 (Ky. App. 1936) (permitting recovery of portion of defendant's profits gained by trespass), *with* R.O. Corp. v. John H. Bell Iron Mountain Ranch Co., 781 P.2d 910, 912–13 (Wyo. 1989) (rejecting recovery of defendant's profits gained by trespass).

[8] Infinity Products, Inc. v. Quandt, 810 N.E.2d 1028 (Ind. 2004); Jet Spray Cooler, Inc. v. Crampton, 385 N.E.2d 1349, 1356 (Mass. 1979).

[9] Hart v. E.P. Dutton & Co., 93 N.Y.S.2d 871 (N.Y. Sup. Ct. 1949), *aff'd* 98 N.Y.S.2d 773 (App. Dept. 1950).

[10] Doug Rendleman, *Common Law Restitution in the Mississippi Tobacco Settlement: Did the Smoke Get in Their Eyes?*, 33 Ga. L. Rev. 847, 904–05 (1999).

been concluded based on theories of public nuisance and unjust enrichment.[11]

Criticism over the use of restitution in cases involving tortious wrongdoing largely center on the appropriateness of benefits or gain disgorgement as a remedy for actions the law deems unacceptable due to the "harm" the actions cause relative to the benefits the actions engender. Traditionally, the methods by which restitution was obtained, e.g., quasi-contract, subrogation, indemnity, and constructive trust, operated in areas largely untouched by tort or contract and were based on principles for which the defendant's wrongdoing was only "incidental" to his enrichment.[12] Put another way, should the law provide a remedy if the defendant's "wrongful" conduct produced no harm to the plaintiff but generated a gain for the defendant?

Perhaps the best way to conceptualize and state the scholarly disagreement over the role of restitution in this area is to distinguish between "unjust" enrichment and "wrongful" enrichment.[13] One view holds that restitution for tortious wrongdoing falls into the "wrongful" enrichment category. Under this view, restitution would be available when the purpose of the tort is to prevent enrichment caused by conduct the tort proscribes or the remedy of restitution advances the goals of the tort.

A different view deemphasives the notion of wrongfulness insofar as the right of action is concerned; however, the nature of the wrongdoing may influence the measure of restitution. The recovery may be limited to the benefit the plaintiff would likely have obtained rather than the greater benefit or gains the defendant did in fact obtain.[14]

Notwithstanding scholarly disagreement over the use of restitution to redress tortious misconduct, the availability of benefit or gain disgorgement is fairly common. As suggested earlier, the remedy is usually limited to situations when the defendant has obtained something from the plaintiff from which it can be deduced that the gain or benefit directly derived;

---

[11] *Id.* (discussing settlement of tobacco litigation between states and major tobacco companies). *See* Hanoch Dagan & James J. White, *Governments, Citizens, and Injurious Injuries,* 75 N.Y.U. L. Rev. 354 (2000) (discussing the use of restitution-oriented remedies in mass-tort litigation).

[12] Restatement of Restitution Ch. 7 (Introductory Note) (1937); Christopher T. Wonnell, *Replacing the Unitary Principle of Unjust Enrichment,* 45 Emory L.J. 153, 153–54, 177–90 (1996); *see* Mark P. Gergen, *What Renders Enrichment Unjust?* 79 Tex. L. Rev. 1927, 1933–38 (2001) (arguing that restitution as a remedy for tortious wrongdoing satisfies both normative and utilitarian criteria).

[13] *Compare* Peter Birks, *Unjust Enrichment and Wrongful Enrichment,* 79 Tex. L. Rev. 1767, 1783 (2001) (arguing that "wrongfulness" rather than "unjustness" defines availability of restitution here), *with* Daniel Friedmann, *Restitution of Benefits Obtained Through the Appropriation of Property or the Commission of a Wrong,* 80 Colum. L. Rev. 504, 504 (1980) ("This Article argues that restitutionary claims should be recognized in a wide variety of cases in which one person's interests have been 'appropriated' by another, whether or not the appropriation was tortious").

[14] Daniel Friedmann, *Restitution for Wrongs: The Measure of Recovery,* 79 Tex. L. Rev. 1879 (2001).

consequently, restitution is most widely obtained when the misconduct involves conversion, misappropriation, or fraud.[15] When the claim may be seen as, at best, involving incidental benefit of an interest that the plaintiff wishes to protect, e.g., her reputation, the law resorts to the traditional remedy of compensatory damages.[16]

Some of the older decisions use the term "waive the tort," as the plaintiff could waive the tort (conversion) and sue for restitution.[17] The language is a holdover from the old practice of actions on the writ. The action for conversion was brought by the writ of trover; restitution was brought by the writ of assumpsit. At common law, a plaintiff could sue on one writ at a time; hence, when the plaintiff bypassed the traditional action (trover) the idea developed that he had "waived the tort." Although code pleading, developed in the 19th Century, abolished the forms of action, the codes still had strict joinder rules that often prohibited joinder of tort and contract actions.[18]

Today, with the relatively free joinder permitted in American practice, the idea that a plaintiff "waives the tort" is antiquated and wrong. A plaintiff can seek both tort damages and restitution of benefits or gains resulting from the defendant's misconduct. The general rule is that the plaintiff cannot recover both remedies.[19] At some point (usually post-verdict) plaintiff must elect the remedy on which he wished to have judgment entered,[20] but even here there are occasional relaxations of the rule.[21]

---

[15] Text and notes 5–8, *supra.*

[16] Text and note 9, *supra.*

[17] *Olwell, supra,* 173 P.2d at 653.

[18] Felder v. Reeth, 34 F.2d 744, 746 (9th Cir. 1929).

[19] Telex Corp. v. IBM, 510 F.2d 894, 930 (10th Cir.) (stating that "a plaintiff may recover either, but not both [unjust enrichment and lost profits damages], because to allow both would permit double recovery"), *cert dismissed,* 423 U.S. 802 (1975); Jet Spray Cooler, *supra,* 385 N.E.2d at 1356 (stating: "Of course, a plaintiff is not entitled to both the profits made by the defendant and his own lost profits.")

[20] Section 133 (Election of Remedies).

[21] Mackie v. Rieser, 296 F.3d 909, 914 (9th Cir. 2002) (noting that under Section 504(b) of the Copyright Act a plaintiff may recover "the actual damages suffered" and "any profits of the infringer that are attributable to the infringement and are not taken into account in computing the actual damages"), *cert. denied,* 537 U. S. 1189 (2003); see Michael Anthony Arciero, *Trademark, Infringement and Plaintiff's Damages: LANHAM ACT § 35(A),* 12 J. Contemp. Legal Issues 320 (2001):

> The grammar of Lanham Act § 35(a) appears to authorize an award of both the mark owner's damages and the infringer's profits, but the law is unsettled whether such an award may be granted. Some circuits have held that an award of both plaintiff's damages and defendant's profits amounts to impermissible double recovery. Other courts reject this inflexible approach and have crafted awards that compensate the plaintiff by whatever remedy fits the specifics of the case. A recent study of monetary awards under the Lanham Act found that the case law is equally split between awards based on plaintiff's damages and awards based on defendant's profits, thus indicating that courts mandate the election of one remedy or the other; but the study also determined that ten percent of the awards included both damages and profits.

Id. at 321–22 (footnote omitted).

[41.2] Breach of Contract

Whether restitution should be available for breach of contract has proven to be one of the most contentious issues today. Part of the difficulty arises from the fact that some contracts create relationships that have significant third party effects or create heightened duties of loyalty between the contracting parties, such that the relationship is ultimately more defined by the law of agency, or professional codes (e.g. lawyer-client), or fiduciaries, than the private law of contract. That situation is addressed in Section 41.3 (Other Examples of Restitution in Contractual Settings). In this section, the question addressed is restitution for breach of the simple commercial contract. When the owner breaches and throws the contractor off the job, should the contractor be limited to damages or should she be able to seek disgorgement of the benefits or gains realized by the owner from the contractor's performance under the contract? When the security company promises to provide 20 guards for an event but provides only 10, is the promissee limited to damages or should the promissee be allowed to recover the benefits and gains realized by the promissor from his breach?

The difficulty in this area is that courts and commentators may be inclined to see contract actions as varied. Thus, even while expressing a general disapproval of restitution as a contract remedy,[22] case exceptions may be recognized when other policies come into play, e.g., discouraging opportunistic breaches.[23] Some commentators have argued that restitution should be freely available in breach of contract actions.[24]

---

[22] Andrew Kull, *Restitution as a Remedy for Breach of Contract*, 67 S. Cal. L. Rev. 1465 (1994):

> The central proposition of restitution for breach, in standard American doctrine, is that every material breach of contract—more precisely, every breach of contract permitting the injured party to "terminate," thereby discharging his own remaining obligation of performance—affords the plaintiff this radical election between enforcement and avoidance: between a contractual and an extra-contractual recovery for benefits conferred. The argument of this Article is that such a rule, assessed from a variety of perspectives, is anomalous and wrong.
>
> Judged by principals of contract law, an unconstrained election between enforcement and avoidance as a remedy for material breach is inconsistent with our assumptions about the stability of the contractual exchange. It is indefensible as a "default rule," or as the product of "hypothetical consent," because such a remedial option is not one that contracting parties would agree to give the plaintiff in ex ante negotiation. Judged by principles of restitution, the remedy fails again. The standard account of restitution for breach relies heavily on the proposition that a quantum meruit recovery is justified by the need to prevent the unjust enrichment of the party in breach, but on closer examination it may be seen that a party who is liable in damages is not unjustly enriched by a breach of contract and indeed is not enriched at all. Judged finally in terms of remedial efficiency, restitution for breach fails a third time, notably because of its invitation to opportunism: in this context, a party's ability to readjust the terms of the exchange by exploiting the shortcomings of contract enforcement.

Id. at 1466–67.

[23] Andrew Kull, *Disgorgement for Breach, The "Restitution Interest," and the Restatement of Contracts*, 79 Tex. L. Rev. 2021, 2021 (2001).

[24] Stephen A. Smith, *Concurrent Liability in Contract and Unjust Enrichment: The Fundamental Breach Requirement*, 115 Law. Q. Rev. 245 (1999).

The focus on breach is critical. There is little disagreement with the principle that a party who has entered into a contract should not be able to claim benefits derived from the contract by the other party. This holds true whether the benefits are direct or indirect. Many judicial statements that a party may not avoid a valid contract by bringing a claim in unjust enrichment reflect the core fact that there was no breach and the allocation of benefits (and risks) was expressly agreed to by the parties to the contract.[25] Disagreement does, however, arise once the inquiry is expanded to include the issue of breach. Does (should?) breach entitle the benefit conferer to "waive the contract" and seek recovery of the benefit or gain under principles of unjust enrichment? Resolution of that question will often require the analysis of separate but related issues. First, do any benefits exist that absent breach would be subject to a claim of unjust enrichment? As suggested above these instances will be rare. Courts sometimes distinguish (implicitly) the case when the contract is unenforceable, but the plaintiff provided a benefit nonetheless. In most of these cases when a non-contractual recovery is allowed, the recovery is limited to the putative contract price. These cases do, however, constitute a "no breach" category. Second, what policies support a non-contractual recovery for a contractual breach? This may beg the question for a proponent of non-contractual recoveries may shift the burden of proof: what policies support limiting recoveries in cases of breach to traditional contract remedies? Third, are all breaches equal or are some breaches more deserving of non-contractual recoveries than other breaches?[26]

The above considerations evidence disagreement over the appropriate resolution of this issue that is reflected in the caselaw. On the whole, however, courts appear to be somewhat wary of non-contractual remedies for breach of contract. This is reflected in a number of statements that preclude restitution (other than return of consideration) for breach of contract.

First, the remedy of restitution will not be recognized when an enforceable binding, unrescinded agreement exists defining the rights of the parties.[27] This approach bars restitution to avoid unjust enrichment when the basis of the quasi contract claim parallels a party's contractual obligations.[28] In its most extreme form, the fact that the contract does not cover

---

[25] United States for the Use and Benefit of Walton Technology, Inc. v. Weststar Eng'g, Inc., 290 F.3d 1199, 1204 (9th Cir. 2002) (applying Washington law).

[26] Earthinfo, Inc. v. Hydrosphere Res. Consultants, Inc., 900 P.2d 113, 119 (Colo. 1995) (holding that while "mere breach" of contract would not permit restitution of gains obtained by breach; when "the defendant's wrongdoing is intentional or substantial, or there is no other means of measuring the wrongdoer's enrichment, recovery of profits is permitted").

[27] Paracor Finance v. General Elec. Capital Corp., 96 F.3d 1151, 1167 (9th Cir. 1996); cf. Cromeens, Holloman, Sibert, Inc. v. AB Volvo, 349 F.3d 376, 397 (7th Cir. 2003) ("Quasi contract is not a means for shifting a risk one has assumed under a contract") (citations omitted). Quasi contract is an action to prevent unjust enrichment. Section 44 (Quasi Contract and Unjust Enrichment).

[28] Id. (noting that the subject matter of the dispute was covered by several provisions of the contract); Robinson v. Durabilt Mfg. Co., 260 S.W.2d 174, 175 (Tenn. 1953).

the specific subject on which the unjust enrichment claim is based is not dispositive. It is enough that the "contract governs the relationship between the parties."[29] The approach is based on the view that the parties' consensual, voluntary arrangements should be preferred over court imposed obligations based on amorphous values, such as equity, fairness, and justice.

Second, a party who has fully performed his contractual obligations and is only owed the performance of payment by the other contracting party is denied the right to sue for restitution and is relegated to an action for the contract price.[30] The motivation for seeking recovery in restitution, usually quasi contract, is the belief that the reasonable value of the performance is greater than the agreed upon price. The plaintiff's preference illustrates the reason for the restriction. When the parties have expressly determined their expectancy interests if the contract is fully performed by the non-breaching party, courts should not reevaluate the parties determination.[31]

Third, contrary to the first approach is the view that the non-breaching party may elect to sue in either quasi contract or on the contract when the defendant is the breaching party *and* the breach occurs before the plaintiff has fully performed.[32] The most famous case in this area of the law is *Boomer v. Muir*. A contractor breached a contract with a subcontractor on a dam construction contract. The subcontractor would have lost a substantial sum of money had he been relegated to an action on the contract. The court permitted an action for unjust enrichment based on the value of the goods and services provided by the subcontractor. The resulting recovery significantly exceeded the contract price.[33] The underlying theory is that the defendant's substantial breach allows the plaintiff to treat the contract as rescinded and abandoned and recover the value of services provided rather than losses sustained.[34]

The "abandonment" language is rather critical here. Many of the *Boomer* type cases involve unprofitable contracts. If the contractor was required to sue on the contract, there would be no recovery; in some cases, the owner's

---

[29] Williams v. National Hous. Exch., Inc., 949 F. Supp. 650, 653 (N.D. Ill. 1996) (citations omitted); *cf.* Clark-Fitzpatrick, Inc. v. Long Island R.R. Co., 516 N.E.2d 190, 193 (N.Y. 1987) (stating that "[t]he existence of a valid and enforceable written contract governing a particular subject matter ordinarily precludes recovery in quasi contract for events arising out of the same subject matter") (citation omitted).

[30] Restatement (Second) of Contracts § 373(2), cmts. a, d (1979).

[31] 3 E.A. FARNSWORTH, CONTRACTS § 12.20, p. 311 (1990).

[32] Feng v. Dart Hill Realty, Inc., 601 A.2d 547, 548 (Conn. App. 1992); Lee v. Foote, 481 A.2d 484, 486 (D.C. App. 1984).

[33] 24 P.2d 570 (Cal. App. 1933). Ironically, *Boomer* is non-precedential authority. A hearing was granted by the California Supreme Court but the appeal was subsequently dismissed. *See* Lessing v. Gibbons, 6 Cal. App. 2d 598, 45 P.2d 258, 262 (1935) (discussing subsequent history of *Boomer v. Muir*). Under California law, the granting of a hearing by the California Supreme Court operates to nullify the precedential value of a Court of Appeal decision. Cal. R. Ct. 976[d].

[34] United States for Use of Wallace v. Flintco, Inc., 143 F.3d 955, 965 n.9 (5th Cir. 1998); Section 163 (Losing Contracts and Restitution).

breach actually benefitted the contractor in that contractor was excused from expending more resources on a losing contract. Many of these cases also involve "change orders"[35] and the question arises whether the resolution would be any different if the action was brought in contract, but the court would treat the original contract as abandoned in favor of the new contract formed by the change orders.[36] The restitutionary remedy is often fixed in these cases as the plaintiff's cost of providing the services (and materials) to the defendant. In effect, the restitutionary recovery and the breach of contract recovery on the new agreement are the same. This point has been made by a number of commentators.[37] The use of restitution may also be justified as a form of risk shifting. In this class of cases, it may be difficult to determine whether the contract was unprofitable for the contractor from the beginning or whether it became so due to the change orders. Restitution may be seen as a simpler (and fairer) method of addressing the issue as opposed to a lengthy examination of the consequences of the defendant's conduct leading to (or constituting) the breach.

Notwithstanding acceptance of the abandonment theory and the allowance of restitution, the amount of restitution is always an issue. In some cases, the recovery is limited to the contract price.[38] In other cases, the recovery may exceed the contract price.[39] This rule that contract price does not limit recovery has been applied to restitution claims in which the United States is a defendant;[40] however, that approach is questionable given the doctrine of sovereign immunity and the United State's limited waiver of that defense to contract claims.[41]

Restitution has also been sought in cases when the defendant breached, but the breach carried only the potential of harm, not its actuality. For example, a defendant may promise to provide protection against injury. Unless the promise is unqualified, (any harm equals a breach), it is difficult

---

[35] These are also referred to a "cardinal changes". *See* 1 BRUNER & O'CONNOR ON CONSTRUCTION LAW § 4.13.

[36] Section 162.3 ([Contractor's Remedies] Change Orders).

[37] Mark P. Gergen, *Restitution as a Bridge Over Troubled Contractual Waters*, 71 Fordham L. Rev. 709 (2002).

[38] Johnson v. Bovee, 574 P.2d 513, 514 (Colo. App. 1978) (holding that use of the "contract price as a ceiling on restitution is the better reasoned resolution . . . [since] had [plaintiff] fully performed, his recovery would be limited to the contract price . . . . It is illogical to allow him to recover the full cost of his services when, if he had completed the house, he would be limited to the contract price . . .") (citation omitted).

[39] Dravo Corp. v. L.W. Moses Co., 492 P.2d 1058, 1069 (Wash. App. 1971) (stating that the "balance of judicial opinion does not limit recovery under restitution to the contract price") (citation omitted); *see* United States v. The Western Cas. & Sur. Co., 498 F.2d 335, 338 (9th Cir. 1974) (stating that "[t]he contract price, while evidence of reasonable value, is neither the final determinant of the value of performance nor does it limit recovery").

[40] Acme Process Equip. Co. v. United States, 347 F.2d 509 (Ct. Cl. 1965), *rev'd on other grounds*, 385 U.S. 138 (1966).

[41] A good review of the problem and the precedents is Michael F. Noone Jr. & Urban A. Lester, *Defining Tucker Act Jurisdiction After* Bowden v. Massachusetts, 40 Cath. U. L. Rev. 571 (1991).

to specify what is being promised. The usual approach is to address the problem quantitatively, e.g., the defendant will provide 20 security guards or 12 manned fire trucks. Providing less than that number is clearly a breach, but if no harm actually results, the traditional rule would give the plaintiff only nominal damages. That limited remedy might encourage the defendant to accept the risk and deliberately breach by skimping the contracted—for performance. Although there are not a lot of decisions in this area, there is a tendency to permit restitution based recoveries that require the defendant to disgorge the gains derived from its breach, here the savings from under-performance of the contract.[42] These cases can also be treated as "opportunistic breaches."[43]

[41.3]   Other Examples of Restitution in Contractual Settings

A contractual relationship may serve as a springboard for non-contractual duties and obligations. In these contexts, the breach of a contract obligation may also constitute a breach of the non-contractual duty or obligation. In these cases, the remedy may follow from the non-contractual source. Benefit disgorgement is a common remedy for breach of trust even though the breach caused no actual injury to the party owed the duty. This principle is frequently applied to lawyers, who have a fiduciary relationship with their clients. Fees disgorgement may be ordered when the lawyer breaches her duty of loyalty, e.g., fails to address a conflict of interest, even though the breach causes no harm to the client.[44] Disgorgement is also a frequently sought remedy in cases when corporate insiders have wrongfully taken a corporate opportunity and earned consequential profits.[45] This principle has also been extended to employees who are deemed by the courts to have wrongfully exploited the employee-employer relationship. The signature case here is *Snepp v. United States*.[46] Snepp served two tours of duty in South Vietnam as a CIA employee. He became disillusioned with the Vietnam war and the actions of the United States Government and resigned from the CIA in 1976. During his tenure with the CIA, Snepp signed and was subject to a secrecy agreement that required him to maintain the

---

[42] City of New Orleans v. Firemen's Charitable Ass'n, 9 So. 486 (La. 1891).

[43] Kull, *Disgorgement For Breach*, *supra*, 79 Tex. L. Rev. at 2046–47. This principle has been further developed in the English cases. James Edelman, *Restitutionary Damages and Disgorgement Damages for Breach of Contract*, 8 Restitution L. Rev. 129 (2000).

[44] Burrow v. Arce, 997 S.W.2d 229, 232 (Tex. 1999) (recognizing that actual damages need not be proven for a client to be entitled to fee forfeiture as a remedy for an attorney's breach of fiduciary duty); *see* Restatement (Third) of the Law Governing Lawyers § 37 (2000) (noting that "[a] lawyer engaging in clear and serious violation of duty to a client may be required to forfeit some or all of the lawyer's compensation for the matter"). The Reporter's Notes include numerous examples of breaches justifying fee forfeiture. *Id.* at § 37, cmt. c.

[45] Section 51 (Disgorgement Orders).

[46] 44 U.S. 507 (1980). There is an English case that is strikingly parallel to *Snepp*. Attorney General v. Blake, [2000] 4 ALL E. R. 385 (H.L.) (Eng.). The House of Lords reached the same result as the Supreme Court, although by a different line of reasoning.

confidentiality of classified information he had access to as a CIA employee, including information regarding intelligence sources and methods. As part of that agreement, Snepp promised that he would provide the CIA with a pre-publication right to review his manuscripts that contain information gained by Snepp as a result of his CIA employment.

Snepp submitted to Random House for publication a non-fiction book entitled "Decent Interval," which was based, in large part, on information gain by Snepp in the course of his employment with the CIA. Snepp did not submit the manuscript for pre-publication review as he was required to do by his secrecy agreement with the CIA. Random House published that book. The U.S. sued Snepp for breach of contract and breach of fiduciary duty. The U.S. did not seek to enjoin publication of "Decent Interval." The U.S. did seek: (1) a declaratory judgment that Snepp had breached the secrecy agreement;[47] (2) an injunction requiring Snepp to submit future manuscripts to the CIA, and (3) a constructive trust over all profits Snepp would earn from the publication of "Decent Interval."

The Court upheld the constructive trust remedy.[48] Snepp's status with the CIA made him a trusted employee and created a confidential relationship between him and his employer. Constructive trusts are often invoked when a fiduciary (Snepp) breaches a duty owed to the beneficiary, here the United States. The use of a constructive trust in *Snepp* is debateable under American law, but the Court did not address the technical issues of the remedy. Constructive trusts usually require property of some kind that can be identified to the claimant. What "property" of the United States could be traced into the royalties Snepp received and the United States claimed?[49] In the English counterpart to *Snepp*, *Attorney General v. Blake*, *supra*, the House of Lords did not rely on constructive trust; it went directly with a disgorgement theory. This disgorgement approach may also be criticized because Snepp did not withhold or deprive the United States of royalties, he deprived the United States of its contractual right of review. There was no showing in *Snepp* that the breach (failure to provide pre-publication review) contributed to Snepp's royalties.

§ 42 RESTITUTION FOR UNJUST ENRICHMENT

Traditionally, the law of unjust enrichment was understood as limited to discrete legal relationships that fell outside the broader legal regimes of tort and contract. Perhaps the most prominent example of this category was mistake: should the law intervene when a party conferred, or cause to be conferred, a benefit on another party by mistake, such as an overpayment of rent or erroneous discharge of a debt. The issues tended to be

---

[47] Snepp claimed that the U.S. had breached the agreement and thus he was relieved of his duty of performance. Snepp's arguments are collected in the District Court's opinion. United States v. Snepp, 456 F. Supp. 176, 177–78 (D.D.C. 1978).

[48] Section 54 (Constructive Trust).

[49] Recall that the government disclaimed that Snepp's book contained any classified information over which the government could assert a proprietary interest.

unique; hence, the law in this area was more gap filling than coordinated. Nonetheless because the overreaching concern was the same—the avoidance of "unjust" enrichment—some common themes developed among the disparate legal entities that constituted the universe of unjust enrichment. Traditionally, the law of unjust enrichment consisted of specific actions, such as quasi-contract, indemnity, contribution, subrogation, constructive trust, etc., as well as the general action called either "unjust enrichment" or restitution. This verbal imprecision and overlap can generate confusion[1] but also opportunity.

The very nature (and language) of unjust enrichment suggests the utility of restitution as the remedy. The party who is "unjustly" enriched should cede so much of the enrichment so that the label "unjustly" no longer applies. This close connection between unjust enrichment and restitution can present some definitional difficulties. Courts may treat unjust enrichment as a separate, substantive cause of action, or as a concept applicable to other cases of action. Courts may treat restitution as a substantive right or as a remedy. Care must always be taken to determine how exactly the terms "unjust enrichment" and "restitution" are being used.[2]

§ 43 NATURE OF UNJUST ENRICHMENT

It is difficult to posit a bright line which separates unjust enrichment cases from simple enrichment cases. One finds a large degree of fact specificity influences decision making in this area. For example, in *United States v. Allstate Insurance Co.*[1] the United States was granted restitution against an insurer for the value of medical benefits provided to military personnel involved in automobile accidents. The insurer had agreed to provide personal injury protection (a form of medical insurance) to those personnel. The court held that if the United States was not granted restitution, the insurer would be granted a "windfall" since it would have collected premiums without having to pay claims. It was not demonstrated that the insurer consciously sought, at the time the contract was entered into, to obtain the advantage of providing an illusory benefit. It simply fortuitously (for the insurer) worked out that the insured sought and received the free treatment from the United States to which the insured was entitled. The court did not explain why the government should be able to shift the cost of its promise to its employees to a party—the insurer—with whom the government had no relationship.

In *United States v. House*[2] the United States sued the defendant-prisoner for the cost of an autopsy, funeral, and burial of the defendant's victim, who was a fellow prisoner and confined to a federal penitentiary at the time of his death. The court declined the defendant's invitation to offset the

---

[1] *See* Andrew Kull, *Rationalizing Restitution*, 83 Cal. L. Rev. 1191 (1995).

[2] Section 40 (Restitution) (discussing problem of nomenclature and terminology).

[1] 910 F.2d 1281 (5th Cir. 1990).

[2] 808 F.2d 508 (7th Cir. 1986).

amount the United States saved by no longer having to feed and house the prisoner-victim. There can be no question but that the defendant's conduct improved the United States' position from a strict balance sheet point of view. The costs of incarceration are great and those costs had been made to disappear by defendant's act of homicide. The court, nonetheless, and again without much discussion, rejected the claim for an offset. No doubt the court was troubled by the thought that the remedy could be construed as rewarding the wrongdoer. On the other hand, the government sought an economic recovery against a party who arguably had improved the government's economic position rather than harmed it. Yet, not only did the court not see enrichment, it saw a cause of action for redress against the party who had benefitted the government economically.

Unjust enrichment is an area of the law in which the individual facts of the case often dominate the broader legal pronouncements. Given the nature of the problem not much more can be expected. If a party mistakenly plows my field is my "windfall" meaningfully different from the hailstorm that ruins my neighbor's crop, but leaves mine unharmed? Why should the law intervene in one case, but not the other?[3] As noted in *Reisenfeld & Co. v. Network Group, Inc.*:

> Defining a given situation as either just or unjust is subjective and not necessarily open to a clear and decisive answer; as one court explained, "[t]he notion of what is or is not 'unjust' is an inherently malleable and unpredictable standard."[4]

The fact that the law of unjust enrichment is rich and varied in its approaches to the conferral and receipt of benefits and gains does not mean that it is formless. Some general principles have developed that courts consistently rely upon to shape and influence their decisions in this area.

[43.1] The Volunteer Principle

The terms volunteer or officious intermeddler are frequently applied as a justification for denying a claim for unjust enrichment.[5] The rule essentially provides that a person who, without request, at his own insistence, and without a valid reason confers a benefit upon another, is not entitled to restitution. This rule exists to protect persons who have unsolicited benefits thrust upon them.[6] The concepts of volunteer and officious intermeddler

---

[3] The issue has been provocatively discussed in the context of public goods in Eric Kades, *Windfalls*, 108 Yale L. J. 1489 (1999) (arguing that "public windfall" are different from "private windfalls" in that the former can be captured and redistributed through an equitable system of taxation).

[4] 277 F.3d 856, 860 (6th Cir. 2002), *quoting* DCB Constr. Co. v. Central City Dev. Co., 965 P.2d 115, 120 (Colo. 1998).

[5] Curtis v. Becker, 941 P.2d 350, 354 (Idaho. App. 1997) (stating that "[t]he principle of unjust enrichment . . . . is applicable only if the person conferring the benefit is not an "officious intermeddler"). An "officious intermeddler" is an turn defined as "a mere volunteer." *Id.* at 354.

[6] Chinchuretta v. Evergreen Mgmt., Inc., 790 P.2d 372, 374 (App. 1989); Siskron v. Temel-Peck Enters., Inc., 26 N.C. App. 387, 216 S.E.2d 441 (1975).

are not, however, self-defining in the sense that we intuitively know when and whether a plaintiff confers a benefit as a volunteer or with the expectation of payment or whether the plaintiff has officiously meddled, thrust herself upon, or unreasonably involved herself in the affairs of the defendant. Even the Restatement of Restitution could do little more, in attempting to state a guiding principle, than define the concept in terms of itself, noting that "[o]fficiousness means interference in the affairs of others not justified by the circumstances under which the interference takes place."[7]

Some general contours of the volunteer-officious intermeddler concept can, however, be discerned from the case law. First, a person who acts to protect his own legal interest, even though it is ultimately determined that he had no legal liability, is not a volunteer.[8] A defendant who settles a claim for the benefit of another may obtain restitution for the value of the benefits conferred on that other.[9] Restitution is, however, usually subject to a good faith requirement. A plaintiff who out of spite pays the debt of the defendant so that the defendant will be indebted to the plaintiff may find that his claim for restitution will be rejected even though he acted without the intent to confer a gift and with the expectation of repayment.[10]

A person who acts under a legal obligation is generally deemed not to be a volunteer. For example, in *Goldin v. Putnam Lovell, Inc. (In re Monarch Capital Corp.)* a business broker made a telephone call, after an involuntary petition for bankruptcy was filed against the debtor, to a prospective buyer of the debtor's subsidiary. The telephone call lead to the sale of the debtor's subsidiary to that buyer. The court held that the broker was entitled to

---

[7] Restatement of Restitution § 2 (1937).

[8] Perkins v. Worzala, 143 N.W.2d 516, 518 (Wis. 1966) (stating that because the insurer was potentially liable, the insurer's settlement payment was not voluntary even though the insurer had in fact no coverage obligations); Restatement of Restitution § 7(12) (1937) (stating that "[a] person who has paid the debt of another in response to the threat of civil proceedings by a third person, whether or not that third person is acting in good faith, is entitled to restitution from the other if the payor acted to avoid trouble and expense"); *but cf.* Gallagher, Magner & Solomento, Inc. v. Aetna Cas. & Sur. Co., 252 A.2d 206, 207 (Pa. Super. Ct. 1969) (holding that the plaintiff insurance brokerage firm acted as a volunteer when it paid the loss after the insurance company denied coverage; the plaintiff discharged no liability it owed, potentially or otherwise, to its client). The court noted, however, that plaintiff's argument that it acted to preserve its "business goodwill" was not before the court. *Id.* at 208.

[9] Rowley Plastering Co., Inc. v. Marvin Gardens Dev. Corp., 883 P.2d 449, 451 (Ariz. App. 1994) (finding that a non-negligent subcontractor was entitled to restitution from the negligent general contractor for a settlement of a worker's claim; the contract between the subcontractor and the general contractor required the subcontractor to indemnify the general contractor for any damage if the subcontractor were found to be partially at fault. The subcontractor was entitled to seek a liability release from the worker or the subcontractor would have remained exposed to a possible judgment by the worker against the general contractor in excess of the settlement amount).

[10] Norton v. Haggett, 85 A.2d 571, 573–74 (Vt. 1952) (refusing restitution to the plaintiff who had paid the defendant's mortgage apparently with the expectation that he could acquire the obligation and assume the role of creditor. It also appeared that the parties had a hostile relationship and that the plaintiff sought to acquire the obligation not for business reasons but for spite and malice toward the defendant).

restitution for post-petition services because the broker was in the unenviable position of being bound to its prepetition contract with the debtor and yet unable to obligate the bankruptcy estate under contract to do anything other than pay expenses incurred after entry of the order for relief.[11] This is an application of the earlier noted usage of unjust enrichment in contexts where the plaintiff confers a benefit on the defendant pursuant to a supposed contract.[12]

While it is often stated that one who receives a benefit may be under a moral obligation to return the benefit, in kind or in specie,[13] the converse is not true. When the person conferring the benefit does so only out of a moral duty, rather than a legal duty or a desire to protect her own interests, the conferrer of the benefit will be deemed a volunteer. Rescuers fall into this category. The consensus view is that while rescuers act out of the noblest of motives, they may not recover the value of the benefit conferred even though the law encourages rescues and recognizes the likelihood that rescues will be attempted.[14]

---

[11] 163 B.R. 899, 907 (D. Mass. 1994).

[12] *In re* Snowcrest Dev. Group, Inc., 200 B.R. 473, 480 (D. Mass. 1996) (noting that the presence of the executory contract in *Goldin, supra,* which placed the broker under an obligation to perform but gave the estate the freedom to refuse to pay under the contract for the benefit of the broker's "contracted for performance," was critical to the recognition of the remedy of restitution); *cf.* NLRB v. Bildisco & Bildisco, 465 U.S. 513, 531 (1984) (holding that if the debtor-in-possession elects to continue to receive benefits from the other party to an executory contract pending a decision to reject or assume the contract, the debtor-in-possession is obligated to pay for the reasonable value of those services, which, depending on the circumstances of a particular contract, may be what is specified in the contract).

[13] Rice v. Wheeling Dollar Savings & Trust, 99 N.E.2d 301, 305 (Ohio 1951) (stating that "the moral obligation to make restitution . . . rests upon a person who has received a benefit which if retained by him, would result in inequity and injustice").

[14] Ross Albert, *Restitutionary Recovery For Rescuers of Human Life,* 74 Cal. L. Rev. 85 (1986):

> Two interrelated mechanisms in the common law that operate to deny a rescuer a recovery are (1) a finding that the rescuer was an 'officious intermeddler' and (2) an irrebuttable presumption that an unofficious rescuer was a 'mere volunteer' who intended to make a gift of his services—in legal parlance, to 'act gratuitously.' The combined effect of these mechanisms, however, creates a 'no-win' situation for a plaintiff rescuer seeking restitution.

74 Cal. L. Rev. at 88 (footnotes omitted). Saul Levmore notes that the law's resistance to affording restitutionary recoveries is puzzling:

> The rescuer who seeks to recover expenses after risking life and property creates only a minor valuation problem, comes on the scene too late to interfere with any bargaining, presents no wealth-dependency problem inasmuch as rich and poor alike would normally choose to be rescued, and does not create a market-encouragement issue because the victim can hardly call in a more efficient rescuer.

Saul Levmore, *Explaining Restitution,* 71 Va. L. Rev. 65, 102 (1985). Levmore suggests that in the case of rescuers, the reluctance to award restitution may be justified by the benefits the rescuer receives from the rescue (public accolade), the perception that doing good is its own reward, that any incentives to rescue provided by awarding restitution are unnecessary, and, conversely, that providing restitution might encourage too many rescuers and the resulting confusion the incentives would create. *Id.* at 102–03.

A person may, however, recover in restitution when she mistakenly believes that she has a moral obligation to act and acts in conformity to her belief. In these circumstances, the law does not treat her as a volunteer, even though she acts altruistically, because of her mistake. As noted in *Deskovick v. Porzio*:

> We think the foregoing authorities would apply in favor of sons, who, during their father's mortal illness, believing him without means of meeting medical and hospital bills as a result of what he had previously told them, and wishing to spare him the discomfort of concern over such expenses at such a time, themselves assumed and paid the obligations. The leaving by the father of an estate far more than sufficient to have met the expenditures would, in such circumstances, and absent others affecting the basic equitable situation presented, properly invoke the concept of a quasi contractual obligation of reimbursement of the sons by the estate.[15]

Likewise the moral "obligation" of family members to care for one another has also been recognized as justifying restitution to avoid unjust enrichment.[16]

[43.2] Bypassing the Person Benefitted

The idea that restitution should be denied when the benefactor denied or frustrated the recipient's ability to reject the benefit was popularized by Professor Dobbs as the "choice" principle.[17] The ability to choose is, however, not absolute but a factor to be considered.[18] A defendant is not unjustly enriched when he retains a benefit that he is not able to reject easily or divest himself of without substantial cost.

---

[15] 187 A.2d 610, 613 (N.J. Super. Ct. A.D. 1963),

[16] Estate of Cleveland v. Gordon, 837 S.W.2d 68 71 (Tenn. App. 1992) (noting that a moral obligation to support a family member rebuts a claim that the benefits were provided officiously). The court further noted that while the usual presumption is that services provided other family members are given with donative intent, *i.e.*, as a gift, the presumption is rebuttable and was rebutted in the case before the court. *Id.* at 71–72 (noting evidence that benefits were provided after benefactor was told she would be reimbursed, expected to be reimbursed, and provided benefits beyond that which would have been expected of family members under the circumstances, given that the benefactor and the recipient of the benefits were not close relatives and had never lived together in a family relationship).

[17] McCoy v. Peach, 251 S.E.2d 881, 883 (1979), *citing*, DAN DOBBS, REMEDIES § 4.9 (1973).

[18] *McCoy, supra*, 251 S.E.2d at 883 (noting that the choice principle "does not apply with absolute rigidity but yields at times to special situations . . . which override a . . . right of free choice"); St. Paul Fire & Marine Ins. Co. v. Indemnity Ins. Co. of N.A., 158 A.2d 825, 827 (N.J. 1960) (suggesting that restitution may be imposed in the appropriate case "even against a clear expression of dissent") (citations omitted).

[43.3] Mistaken Payment

Mistake may be a basis for restitution, but not all mistakes give rise to restitution.[19] The fact that a payment is mistakenly made does not mean that there is unjust enrichment. For example, in *Lincoln National Life Ins. Co. v. Brown Schools, Inc.*[20] the insurer sought restitution for payments made to a hospital on behalf of the insured. The insurer claimed that its payments exceeded its contractual obligations. Generally, claims of mistaken performance that result in overpayment (e.g., computer error causes two checks instead of one to be sent) are well received by courts.[21] Here, however, the court felt there was no unjust enrichment because the hospital had rendered services to the insured without knowledge that the insurer claimed or would claim mistake as to the amount of the payment the hospital would receive.[22]

When a person receives a benefit with knowledge of the circumstances evidencing that the transfer is mistaken, that person may be held to have been unjustly enriched.[23] The fact that the person conferring the benefit acted negligently does not excuse the recipient's duty to make restitution.[24] On the other hand, when a party enters or concludes a bargain consciously aware that it is uncertain as to the true facts, that party may not seek restitution on the ground of mistake.[25] The lines separating "good faith"

---

[19] James J. White & Robert S. Summers, Uniform Commercial Code 618 (5th ed. 2000) ("If a bank is mistaken about its customer's creditworthiness, that is not a payment mistake, but a credit mistake and the bank has no right of restitution").

[20] 757 S.W.2d 411 (Tex. Civ. App. 1988).

[21] United States v. Fowler, 913 F.2d 1382 (9th Cir. 1990); County of Morris v. Fauver, 153 N.J. 80, 707 A.2d 958, 968 (N.J. 1998); Restatement (Third) of Restitution and Unjust Enrichment § 6 (Tentative Draft No. 1, 2001).

[22] *Lincoln Nat'l Life, supra,* 757 S.W.2d at 414; Federated Mut. Ins. Co. v. Good Samaritan Hosp., 214 N.W.2d 493, 495 (Neb. 1974) (holding that in cases of mistaken payments to hospitals there is no unjust enrichment of the hospital that is paid for services rendered; unjust enrichment lies with patient who received medical services for which plaintiff mistakenly paid); City of Hope Nat'l Med. Ctr. v. Superior Court, 10 Cal. Rptr.2d 465, 467 (Cal. 1992) (holding that restitution for mistaken payment will be denied when payment is made to bona fide creditor of third party, a creditor without fault who made no misrepresentations to the payor and who had no notice of the payor's mistake at the time the payment was made); Section 66 ([Remedy Defenses] Change in Position and Hardship).

[23] First Nationwide Savings v. Perry, 15 Cal. Rptr. 2d 173, 177 (Cal. App. 1992), *citing* Restatement of Restitution § 13 (1937).

[24] Naugle v. O'Connell, 833 F.2d 1391, 1398 (10th Cir. 1987).

[25] Bennett v. Shinoda Floral, Inc., 739 P.2d 648 (Wash. 1987):

> A contract is voidable on grounds of mutual mistake when both parties independently make a mistake at the time the contract is made as to a basic assumption of the contract, unless the party seeking avoidance bears the risk of the mistake. A party bears the risk of a mistake when "he is aware, at the time the contract is made, that he has only limited knowledge with respect to the facts to which the mistake relates but treats his limited knowledge as sufficient."

Id. at 653 (citations omitted); *cf.* Chris Albritton Constr. Co. v. Pitney Bowes, Inc., 304 F.3d 527 (5th Cir. 2002) (applying Mississippi law) (holding that lessee could not recover payments voluntarily made to lessor; lessee who with knowledge of the facts, actual or implied, responds to demand for payment cannot later seek reimbursement).

from "doubt" from "conscious awareness of uncertainty" are not well defined, but are determined on a case by case basis.

[43.4] Expectation of Payment or Compensation

It is frequently stated, in situations when goods or services have been provided, that the benefit must be conferred on the defendant under circumstances that raise an expectation, on the provider's part, of payment or compensation.[26] When goods or services are provided for that person's own benefit, e.g., to obtain a business advantage, no unjust enrichment exists. As noted in *Salamon v. Terra*:

> Compensation on a quasi contract theory is not mandated where the services were rendered simply to gain a business advantage or where the plaintiff did not contemplate a personal fee. "[C]hagrin, disappointment, vexation, or supposed ingratitude cannot be used as a subsequent basis for a claim of compensation where none was originally intended or expected."[27]

Some courts have limited the use of the "expectation of payment" concept to actions for quasi contract and have not applied the concept to actions for unjust enrichment.[28] This confuses the nature of the claim with nomenclature. An action for quasi contract is a part of the broader category of claims for unjust enrichment.[29] Unjust enrichment may include situations where a benefit was conferred under circumstances when it would make no sense to speak of an expectation of payment or compensation, for example, when property was given as a gift by mistake or a judgment was paid and then the judgment was later reversed on appeal. The fact, however, that in some cases restitution may be required without requiring that the conferrer of the benefit expected payment does not mean that the

---

[26] Heller v. Fortis Benefits Ins. Co., 142 F.3d 487, 495 (D.C. Cir. 1998), *cert. denied*, 525 U.S. 930 (1998); Thomas v. Kearney Little League Baseball Ass'n, 558 N.W.2d 842 (Neb. App. 1997) (holding that no unjust enrichment occurs when party provides benefits for charitable, religious, or humane motives, even if the services were requested; services provided by a Little League coach fell into this category).

[27] 477 N.E.2d 1029, 1033 (Mass. 1985); *see* Holmes v. Torguson, 41 F.3d 1251, 1256 (8th Cir. 1994) (finding no unjust enrichment when expenditures were made by the plaintiff for its own benefit even though defendant benefitted as well) (citations omitted); Allstate Ins. Co. v. Reeves, 440 So. 2d 1086, 1089 (Ala. App. 1983) (holding that automobile repairman, who repaired vehicle, which he then operated for his own use and enjoyment, could not recover in restitution against rightful owner; a contrary rule would "encourage others in such business to assume ownership and control the property of others without consent or duty . . . and recover the value of repairs if discovered").

[28] Yoh v. Daniel, 497 S.E.2d 392, 394 (Ga. App. 1998) (stating that "unlike quantum meruit, a claim for unjust enrichment does not require a showing of the anticipation of compensation); D.A. Collins Constr. Co., Inc. v. ICOS/NCCA, A Joint Venture, 1994 U.S. Dist. LEXIS 9001 at *27 n.17 (N.D.N.Y., June 28, 1994) (stating that "there is a difference between the elements of a quantum meruit claim and those of a claim for unjust enrichment" and noting that an expectation of payment was part of the former but not the later).

[29] Harmon v. Rogers, 510 A.2d 161, 164 (Vt. 1986); Section 44 (Quasi Contract and Unjust Enrichment).

presence (or absence) of an expectation of payment is limited to certain types of actions for restitution. The inquiry is always relevant when it sheds some light on whether the benefit was conferred under circumstances that demonstrate the defendant-recipient has been unjustly enriched. As noted in *Knott v. Pratt*:

> In the instant case, the trial court found that plaintiff's father received a benefit which he was aware of, due to his visits to the property, and which he accepted. The court concluded, however, that it would not be inequitable for her father, and the estate, to retain the benefit without compensating plaintiff. The evidence fully supports the court's conclusion. By her own admission, plaintiff cared for the property as a "labor of love" and as her own residence. She did the work for her own benefit with the expectation, which proved unfounded, that she would eventually own the property. See Restatement of Restitution § 57 (1937) (person who confers a benefit to another, without a manifest intent to claim compensation, is not entitled to restitution, "merely because his expectation that the other will make a gift to him . . . is not realized"); 2 G. Palmer, The Law of Restitution § 10.7(b), at 422 (1978) (restitution generally denied "where a person in pursuit of his own interests improves the land of another").[30]

If the motive behind the benefit was altruistic or donative, restitution may be inappropriate because, absent other factors, we would not say that the increase in the defendant's wealth (enrichment) was *unjust* enrichment.[31]

[43.5] Irreparable Injury

Confusion is sometimes encountered over the relationship between the action for unjust enrichment and the irreparable injury requirement because of the equitable nature of the unjust enrichment claim.[32] As a general rule, the irreparable injury requirement is not applied to unjust enrichment claims.[33] This is consistent with the fact that many forms of unjust enrichment, such as quasi contract, are maintainable at law.[34] Yet, the scope or availability of relief in unjust enrichment may be influenced by irreparable injury concerns. The form of unjust enrichment may be a

---

[30] 609 A.2d 232, 234 (Vt. 1992).

[31] Goldstick v. ICM Realty, 788 F.2d 456, 467 (7th Cir. 1986) (Posner, J.) (stating that "restitution does not make altruism a paying proposition").

[32] Moses v. Macfarlan, 2 Burr. 1005, 97 Eng. Rep. 676 (K.B. 1760) (describing the action for "money had and received" (an early form of an action for unjust enrichment recognized at law) as "This kind of equitable action"); *see* First Heights Bank, FSB v. Gutierrez, 852 S.W.2d 596, 605 (Tex. Civ. App. 1993) (noting that "[equity] seeks to prevent unjust enrichment") (footnote omitted); 1 GEORGE PALMER, THE LAW OF RESTITUTION § 1 (1978) (noting the connection between the development of remedies for unjust enrichment (restitution) at law and in equity).

[33] Mobil Oil Corp. v. Dade County Esoil Mgmt. Co., 982 F. Supp. 873, 880 (S.D. Fla. 1997).

[34] Section 44 (Quasi Contract and Unjust Enrichment).

constructive trust and this will often trigger the observation that the plaintiff must demonstrate that her remedy at law is inadequate.[35] This results not from the unjust enrichment claim, but from the equitable vehicle (constructive trust) through which the remedy is provided.[36]

Nonetheless, courts have, on occasion, used the historic connection of unjust enrichment and equity to impose a broad irreparable injury requirement. For example, in *McKesson HBOC, Inc. v. New York State Common Retirement Fund, Inc.*[37] the acquiring corporation brought an action for unjust enrichment against the shareholders of the acquired corporation alleged they have been overpaid for their stock and therefore unjustly enriched. The court noted the novelty of the claim and invoked the irreparable injury requirement holding that the plaintiff had adequate remedies against the third parties (corporate officers and directors, etc.) who were directly responsible for the alleged over-valuation of the acquired corporation.

[43.6] Plus-Minus Rule

Traditionally, restitution for unjust enrichment was limited by the concept that the defendant's benefit had to be related to the plaintiff's loss (the "plus-minus" rule).[38] This issue should not be confused with the basic requirement that the defendant's conduct, which underlies the claim of unjust enrichment, must relate to the benefit the defendant holds unjustly against the plaintiff. The plus-minus rule is often ignored today. The issue is simply whether the defendant has unjustly realized a benefit even if the plaintiff has not suffered an actual, or equal, loss.[39] If the plaintiff has sustained a loss, she may be permitted to claim the greater of either her loss or the defendant's gain.[40]

[43.7] Benefits vs. Harms

Unjust enrichment rests on the core premise that some benefits should be transferred; however, the doctrine rests on the implicit understanding that the requirement is exceptional. With respect to harms, however, the

---

[35] Section 54 (Constructive Trust).

[36] PALMER, RESTITUTION, *supra*, at § 1.6:

> The availability of restitution is not dependent upon inadequacy of the alternative remedy. This is a historic limitation on the assertion of equity jurisdiction which must be taken into account when restitution is sought in equity, but there is no independent principle that confines restitution to cases in which alternative remedies are inadequate.

[37] 339 F.3d 1087, 1093–94 (9th Cir. 2003) (applying Delaware law).

[38] PALMER, RESTITUTION, *supra* at § 2.6.

[39] PALMER, RESTITUTION, *supra*, at § 2.10, pp. 133–34; Restatement of Restitution § 150 (1937).

[40] Developers Three v. Nationwide Ins. Co., 582 N.E.2d 1130, 1133–34 (Ohio App. 1990) (collecting decisions permitting election although ultimately "reluctantly" concluding that court would not permit a plaintiff to assert a restitutionary remedy in tortious interference cases).

orientation of the law is just the opposite: most inflictions of harm require compensation.[41] This distinction was perceptively observed by Professor Gordon:

> If Harriet erects a reeking cattle feedlot next to Peter's residential neighborhood, for example, Peter will probably be able to obtain damages or an injunction against her, in nuisance. If, by contrast, Harriet builds a luxury resort hotel next to Peter's land, absent contract she will have no legal right to obtain monies from him, no matter how high his land values rise as a result of her development. For injuring her neighbor, Harriet must pay. But for benefitting him, she cannot use the law to demand compensation he has not agreed to pay. As Saul Levmore has observed, "The law appears ready to create missing bargains in tort where harms are concerned, but is reluctant to do so in restitution where benefits are at stake."[42]

This ambivalence, for lack of a better term, reflects some uncertainty as to how far law should go in redressing unconsented to gains.

§ 44 QUASI CONTRACT AND UNJUST ENRICHMENT

The relationship between quasi contract and unjust enrichment is both difficult and often confused. Quasi contract is a legal device for redressing particular types of unjust enrichment. The device has ancient roots in the action of assumpsit, but it also incorporates equitable principles of fairness and justice into its content. Its hybrid nature has caused it to wax and wan in popularity. With the merger of law and equity and the abolition of the forms of action and code pleading in most jurisdictions today, there is little call for insistence that the quasi contract format be used rather than the more general form of unjust enrichment. Nonetheless, the use of quasi contract remains commonplace, no doubt a vestige of judicial and lawyer familiarity with the device, coupled with the extremely liberal pleading rules that apply to quasi contract actions.[1] The device, like the human appendix, remains in place today even though it is no longer useful or needed and its presence occasionally results in mischief.

[44.1] Nature of Quasi Contract

An action in quasi contract (contract implied-by-law) is a means for avoiding unjust enrichment. The term "quasi contract" is also used to refer to implied-in-fact contracts. Implied-in-fact contracts are real contracts based on the conduct of the parties as manifesting bargaining intent. In the implied-by-law version of quasi contract, a fictional contract is presumed in order to use the contract form to redress the aspects of the

---

[41] "Most" in the sense of relative to cases when a benefit rather than a harm is inflicted.

[42] Wendy Gordon, *Of Harms and Benefits: Torts Restitution, and Intellectual Property,* 21 J. Legal Studies 449, 452 (1992).

[1] *See* Fed. R. Civ. P. Forms 5, 7 & 9.

relationship that constitutes unjust enrichment. As observed in *Kozlowski v. Kozlowski*:

> A quasi-contract is not a contract at all, but a legal concept rationalizing a sanction to prevent unjust enrichment based upon the equitable principle that whatsoever it is certain that a man ought to do, the law supposes him to have promised to do.[2]

Use of the term "quasi contract" in both contexts generates unnecessary confusion but is probably too ingrained to be excised.

Quasi contract derives from the common law action for assumpsit. Originally, a plaintiff was permitted to plead in a short, concise manner that the defendant had received a benefit that in fairness and justice belonged to the plaintiff. The format while concise was somewhat stylized and came to be known as common counts. They were arranged around generic reoccurring situations. *Quantum meruit* was for the reasonable value of services rendered on the theory that reasonable value measured the benefit a defendant received when the plaintiff performed work for which the defendant benefitted but did not pay. Similarly, if the defendant received goods and did not pay, the action sounded in *quantum valebat*. The same assumption about a "promise" to pay reasonable value for the goods also applied here. Perhaps the broadest common count was for "money had and received," which could be used in a wide variety of situations by implying a promise to pay even when such a promise was counter-intuitive, as for example, when a defendant procured a fraudulent judgment.[3] In this situation, the court would imply a promise to repay the plaintiff the sum owed, thus netting out the debt. Of course, the defendant intended no such promise; indeed, if anything, the intent was just to the contrary. The promise was simply a fiction to accommodate the form of the action (assumpsit); no real promise existed in fact.[4]

The action in quasi contract thus rested on a fictional promise that in turn supported a remedy (restitution or disgorgement of the benefit) in order to prevent unjust enrichment.[5] It is in this form that the action is recognized today.[6] Real contracts may be distinguished from quasi contracts by recognizing that, in cases of the former, the agreement defines the parties' duties, while in cases of the latter, the duties define the parties' "agreement." A quasi contract is based on duties imposed by law not by

---

[2] 395 A.2d 913, 918 (N.J. Super. Ch. 1978).

[3] Moses v. Macfarlan, 2 Burr. 1005, 97 Eng. Rep. 676 (K.B. 1760) (Lord Mansfield, J.).

[4] Perhaps all legal fictions are counterintuitive else the need for the fiction would not exist. *See* Lon Fuller, *Legal Fictions*, 25 U. Ill. L. Rev. 363, 513, 877 (1931).

[5] It must be reemphasized, for the point is often forgotten, that the quasi contract action we address here is the "implied-by-law" variety, not the "implied-in-fact" contract that is also known as a quasi contract. Implied-in-fact contracts arising out of the conduct of the parties are real contracts; implied-by-law contracts are not contracts at all, but simply legal constructs to prevent unjust enrichment.

[6] Biggerstaff v. Vanderburgh Humane Soc'y, Inc., 453 N.E.2d 363, 364 (Ind. App. 1983); Tipper v. Great Lakes Chem. Co., 281 So. 2d 10, 13 (Fla. 1973).

the parties.[7] The duties themselves are equitable in nature, resting on the moral obligation to do what is right[8] and prevent that which would be deemed inequitable or unjust.[9] It is another example of equitable consideration being adopted by law courts for infusion into the common law. Nonetheless, the quasi contract action remains one at law not in equity.[10]

A few cases have expanded the concept to include a fictional benefit. For example, in *Earhart v. William Low Co.*, the court ordered restitution when the plaintiff, at defendant's request but without an enforceable contract, improved property belonging to a third party. The court held that the defendant received a benefit on the "theory that performance at another's request may itself constitute a benefit."[11] The measure of that benefit was not the value to the defendant of the plaintiff's performance, but the reasonable cost of providing that performance. Decisions such as *Earhart* are more accurately characterized as cases of "unjust detriment" rather than unjust enrichment, but courts appear more comfortable extending artificially the concept of benefit to meet the situation.[12]

While the action for quasi contract is based on unjust enrichment, the "contract" usage may generate confusion. Occasionally, a court will speak in terms of "damages" or "restitution damages" in this area.[13] The usage usually accompanies the decision to allow recovery based on cost of providing rather than increase in value. While cost of providing can be used as a measure of "benefit,"[14] the closeness of the approach to a damages measure is obvious and sometimes the distinction is missed.

---

[7] Callano v. Oakwood Park Homes Corp., 219 A.2d 332, 334 (N.J. Super. Ct. A.D. 1966).

[8] *See Kozlowski, supra*, 395 A.2d 913.

[9] Hummel v. Hummel, 14 N.E.2d 923, 927 (Ohio 1938); *see* Western Nat'l Bank of Casper v. Harrison, 577 P.2d 635, 642 (Wyo. 1978) (noting that the touchstone of the rule that the plaintiff may recover a benefit derived from the wrongdoer is "the moral obligation arising out of the unjust enrichment to the tortfeasor").

[10] Parsa v. State of New York, 474 N.E.2d 235 (N.Y. 1984):

> The action [for restitution in quasi contract] depends upon equitable principles in the sense that broad considerations of right, justice and morality apply to it, but it has long been considered an action at law.

Id. at 237 (citations omitted; brackets added); *see* Colleen P. Murphy, *Misclassifying Monetary Restitution*, 55 S.M.U. L. Rev. 1577, 1598–1607 (2002) (discussing the development of quasi contract in the English common law courts and the similarity of the action to other remedies available in equity).

[11] 600 P.2d 1344, 1349 (Cal. 1979).

[12] *Cf.* Farash v. Sykes Datatronics, Inc., 452 N.E.2d 1245 (N.Y. 1983) (permitting owner to recover "build-out" expenses incurred to prepare premises for tenant who made oral commitment to lease). The tenant repudiated the commitment, which was unenforceable under the Statute of Frauds. Because the tenant never occupied the premises, the "build-out" could not be said to have benefitted the tenant. Nonetheless, the court permitted the owner to recover his "losses" under a theory of unjust enrichment.

[13] Paffhausen v. Balano, 708 A.2d 269, 271 (Me. 1998) (stating that "[d]amages in unjust enrichment are measured by the value of what was inequitably retained. In *quantum meruit*, by contrast, the damages are not measured by the benefit realized and retained by the defendant, but rather are based on the value of the services provided by the plaintiff") (citations omitted).

[14] Section 45 (Valuation of the Benefit); Section 47 (Restitution Damages).

[44.2]   Critical Elements of Quasi Contract

A number of factors have been developed by the courts to identify and channel the concept of unjust enrichment.[15] These factors are often reformulated as elements of quasi contractual relief:

- A benefit conferred upon the defendant by the plaintiff with the expectation of payment;

- Awareness, appreciation, or knowledge by the defendant of the benefit; and

- Acceptance or retention of the benefit by the defendant under such circumstances as to make it inequitable for the defendant to retain the benefit without payment to the plaintiff.[16]

Consider how these concepts were applied in *Bailey v. West*.[17] Defendant bought a horse named "Bascom's Folly." The horse was shipped to defendant-buyer, inspected, determined by the buyer to be lame, and returned to the seller. Seller refused to accept delivery of the horse. The delivery driver took the horse to plaintiff's farm where the horse remained (May 3, 1962) until it was sold to a third party on July 3, 1966, 4 years later. There was a conflict in the testimony whether the driver transporting the horse was instructed by defendant-buyer to take the horse to plaintiff's farm. Plaintiff billed defendant for the care of the horse, but defendant returned the bills to plaintiff with a notation that defendant did not own the horse and was not responsible for its board and care. In a related action, the court had found that defendant-buyer was liable to the seller on the contract to purchase the horse. Plaintiff sued defendant, seeking compensation for the 4 years he stabled the horse. The trial court held that an "implied-in-fact" contract existed between plaintiff and defendant to board the horse until plaintiff received notice to the contrary from defendant. It granted plaintiff limited relief. Both plaintiff and defendant appealed.

The Rhode Island Supreme Court first held that even if the conflict regarding the driver's instructions was resolved in the plaintiff's favor, no actual contract (implied-in-fact) was formed. Any inference of an actual bargain or bargaining intent was completely negated by plaintiff's conduct after taking delivery of the horse, in particular, his knowledge there was a dispute over ownership, his inquiries as to ownership, and his billing both buyer and seller.

The court then addressed whether plaintiff could recover under a theory of quasi contract. The court ultimately denied plaintiff a recovery by finding that plaintiff acted as a "volunteer" because of his knowledge that a dispute existed between the defendant-buyer and the seller. The court held that its resolution was consistent with the conferral, awareness, and acceptance

---

[15] Section 43.1 (The Volunteer Principle); Section 43.2 (Bypassing the Person Benefited); Section 43.4 (Expectation of Payment or Compensation).

[16] Martens v. Metzgar, 524 P.2d 666, 674 (Alaska 1974); Home Sav. Bank v. General Fin. Corp., 103 N.W.2d 117, 121 (Wis. 1960).

[17] 105 R.I. 61, 249 A.2d 414 (R.I. 1969).

test, but the contrary result can also be justified. For example, a benefit was conferred upon the defendant—a horse he owned was boarded and cared for by plaintiff. Second, defendant knew that plaintiff was boarding the horse and that plaintiff was in the horse-boarding business. Third, defendant accepted the benefit in that he did not cause the horse to be moved.

It might be argued that a distinction should be drawn between active and passive acceptance. If the defendant-buyer had claimed the horse from plaintiff, it is unlikely the court would have treated plaintiff as a volunteer. Affirmative conduct may be seen as a benchmark, or tolerable limitation, on an open-ended doctrine predicated on notions of equity and fairness. Yet, the line between passive and active acceptance of a benefit may be hard to sustain. On the one hand are cases where the defendant is unable to reject the benefit *ex post*, for example, when the plaintiff improves defendant's property by trimming defendant's trees or clearing the land of debris. On the other hand are cases where the plaintiff has the power to accept or reject but temporizes, which was the case in *Bailey v. West*. It is a stronger case for acceptance of the benefit, (the exercise of free choice), when the defendant can return or reject the benefit, but elects not to do so.[18]

A person cannot be unjustly enriched unless that person receives a "benefit."[19] For example, in *National City Bank, Norwalk v. Stang* the court denied restitution against an innocent husband for monies fraudulently obtained by his wife. The refusal was not based on the husband's non-involvement in the fraud. Even an innocent donee may be compelled to return that which he unjustly holds against another with a superior claim to the property or money. The court found, however, that since the wife had used the money she fraudulently obtained for her own purposes and to discharge debts for which her husband bore no responsibility or liability, the husband had not benefitted from the wrongful conduct. Therefore, there was no basis to claim that he had been unjustly enriched.[20] The benefit requirement has been criticized,[21] but rather than being rejected the general approach is to construe the requirement liberally.[22]

---

[18] Tom Growney Equip., Inc. v. Ansley, 888 P.2d 992, 994–95 (N. Mex. App. 1995) (noting the general rule that an owner who is neither aware of nor encourages the repair of his property is not unjustly enriched by repairs that improve, (increase the market value), of the property). The court further noted that the general rule is "founded upon the owner's fundamental right of free choice: the exclusive right to determine whether his property shall be repaired and, if so, by whom." *Id.*, *citing* DOBBS, REMEDIES, *supra*, § 4.9(2), (5) (2d ed. 1993).

[19] Restatement of Restitution § 1 (1937).

[20] 618 N.E.2d 241, 243 (Ohio App. 1992).

[21] John Dawson, *Restitution Without Enrichment*, 61 B.U. L. Rev. 563 (1981).

[22] Ogden Martin Sys., Inc. v. San Bernardino County, Cal., 932 F.2d 1284, 1287–88 (9th Cir. 1991) (holding that defendant benefitted from Environmental Impact Report (EIR) prepared for specific project that defendant decided not to build because of the project's negative environmental impact). The court noted that the defendant relied on the EIR in making its decision and that the defendant acknowledged that it could use the environmental, social, and other data compiled in the EIR in subsequent EIR's. *Id.*; Section 44.1 (Nature of Quasi Contract) (text and notes 10–11).

If goods are delivered, services are rendered, or money or property is transferred, a benefit can usually be found quite readily. Yet, some cases escape easy classification. Resolution of the issue may be one of public policy: is the underlying conduct one which the law wishes to discourage or encourage? Because the definition of "benefit" is here tied to public policy, the existence of a benefit may change as public policy changes. For example, during the "frontier" period of American history clearing land of vegetation was deemed a benefit; in the modern era clearing land of vegetation may be deemed environmentally hazardous.[23] If a person innocently and in good faith clears the land of another of natural vegetation, has he conferred a benefit or inflicted a harm?

Even when a specific benefit is conferred, analysis of the larger relationships and the burden restitution would impose may negate a finding of unjust enrichment. For example, the use of the doctrine of collateral estoppel by a third party represents the free expropriation of the efforts of others to establish the defendant's liability. Courts have not required that third parties invoking collateral estoppel provide compensation to the parties whose efforts and expense generated the benefit. Courts have treated the doctrine as a public good, analogous to the use of precedent.[24]

A party who in seeking to advance her own interest confers a benefit upon another is generally denied restitution of that benefit.[25] How far this principle will be taken is difficult to predict. One the one hand, the party's existing interest in engaging in the activities that generated the benefit would seem to serve as adequate incentive or reward. On the other hand, a third party has received a windfall. Given the competing considerations, divided authority is the usual result. For example, when a lawyer represents a client for a fee, but the representation results in the conferral of direct economic benefits to a non-client, should the lawyer be limited to the fee agreement with the client or should the lawyer be allowed to recover in quasi contract ("money had and received") against the non-client? The issue arises with some frequency and with disparate results.[26]

---

[23] John Sprankling, *The Antiwilderness Bias in American Property Law*, 63 Un. Chi. L. Rev. 519, 577 (1996) (criticizing the view that the destruction of wilderness constitutes "compensable improvement" and arguing that an "expanded good faith-improver doctrine rewards despoliation"); Section 86 (Good Faith Improvers of Personal Property); Section 96 (Good Faith Improvers of Real Property).

[24] *Cf. In re* Chicago Flood Litig., 682 N.E.2d 421, 427–28 (Ill. App. 1997) (finding that while opt-out class members had received some benefit from efforts of counsel for class, counsel could not recover under theory of *quantum meriut* for the reasonable value of the services rendered in creating the benefit; the opt-out class members simply exercised a legal right). The court also observed that the use of public documents, generated by class counsel through pretrial preparation, by the opt-out class members was unlikely to generate disincentives to the use of class actions and thus did not warrant a restitutionary recovery to prevent free riding. *Id.*

[25] Restatement of Restitution § 106 (1937).

[26] *Satisfaction of third party liens in personal injury litigation*: White v. St. Alphonsus Regional Medical Center, 31 P.3d 929, 932 (Idaho App. 2001) (collecting decisions permitting and rejecting recovery of fees against lien holders); *Prosecution of Wrongful Death Action*: Morris B. Chapman & Assoc. v. Kitzman, 739 N.E.2d 1263, 1271–72 (Ill. 2000) (discussing

[44.3] Connected Relationships

Oftentimes parties have connected relationships with other parties. For example, a tenant may contract with a contractor to repair a leasehold. This tenant-contractor relationship exists alongside the tenant-landlord relationship. If the contractor subsequently subcontracts all or a portion of the work, that relationship (contractor-subcontractor) now also coexists alongside the other relationships.

These multiple relationships have long perplexed our legal system, a system that largely developed along bipolar, rather than multilateral, lines. When damages are sought, the issue is usually framed in terms of duty: did the party not in privity of contract owe a duty. For example, assume A (Contractor) agrees to repave a parking lot owned by B (Landlord). A breaches and pays liquidated damages to B. A's breach also causes economic harm to C (Tenant) because construction delays impede access to C's business. Can C recover his economic losses from A? The "Economic Loss" rule generally prevents recoveries of economic loss when the cause of the loss is simple negligence and the loss was not the result of bodily injury or property damage.[27] Nonetheless, many courts recognize a right of action when the economic loss is highly foreseeable because of the interconnected network of relationships.[28]

The converse of the damages claim is when parties contract for a benefit to be realized by one of the contracting parties, but the benefit is realized by a third person. For example, assume A (Contractor) is hired by B (Tenant) to improve the leasehold. A does the work, but B fails to pay. Thereafter, C (Landlord) evicts B and occupies or relets the improved leasehold. Has C been unjustly enriched?

The traditional rule in the United States was that C was not unjustly enriched.[29] The more recent decisions have, however, not followed this rule slavishly. The easiest departures from the rule are when C engaged in misconduct that is seen by the court as contributing to the creation of the benefit.[30] The result may differ if the landlord authorized the work before

---

competing views whether lawyer hired by one client to prosecute wrongful death action should receive compensation from non-clients who shared wrongful death recovery as statutory wrongful death beneficiaries).

[27] Section 11 (Economic Loss Rule).

[28] See JAY M. FEINMAN, ECONOMIC NEGLIGENCE: LIABILITY OF PROFESSIONALS AND BUSINESS TO THIRD PARTIES FOR ECONOMIC LOSS (1995). The hypothetical is based on *J'Aire Corp. v. Gregory*, 598 P.2d 60 (Cal. 1979) (finding contractor owed duty to tenant).

[29] Kossian v. American Nat'l Inc. Co., 62 Cal. Rptr. 225, 226 (Cal. App. 1965) ("Had the circumstances been simply that defendant, by foreclosure, took the property improved by plaintiff's debris removal, there would be a benefit conferred upon defendant by plaintiff, but no unjust enrichment."); Restatement of Restitution § 110 (1937).

[30] DCB Constr. Co., Inc. v. Central City Develp. Co., 965 P.2d 115, 121–23 (Colo. 1998) (holding that for enrichment to be unjust in context of receipt of benefits not contracted for "requires some type of improper, deceitful, or misleading conduct by the landlord"); Associate Eng'g Co. v. Webbe, 795 S.W2d 606, 608–09 (Mo. App. 1990) (stating that work performed by a contractor for tenant did not unjustly enrich the landlord who reclaimed the property; the fact that the landlord knew of and acquiesced in the work did not make the landlord liable since the contractor looked to the tenant for payment).

it was done or ratified the work after it was done,[31] although how far courts will extend this point is unclear. Most leases require landlord consent for significant leasehold work and a broad interpretation of this exception could swallow the rule. If the improvements can be removed from the leasehold, the landlord's refusal to permit removal may be deemed acceptance of the benefit[32] or alternatively, conversion.[33]

If we vary the hypothetical slightly, however, we see a significant change in result even though the absence of privity is not cured. Assume A (Contractor) is hired by B (Tenant) to improve the leasehold. A contracts with S (subcontractor). S performs, but A fails to pay. May S look to B under principles of quasi contract for restitution of the gain B received. If B paid A, the general rule is that no recovery by S against B is allowed. This result is sensible because when B pays there is no enrichment in most cases. Should the result be different if B hasn't paid A? Some courts today say that it should. Even though S contracted with A and agreed, per the contract, to look to A for payment for services rendered and even though courts acknowledged a hesitancy "to impose obligations in the absence of a contract,"[34] here the equities are seen as weighing in favor of S rather than B.[35] The key factor in these cases is that B agreed to pay for the work; transferring B's obligation from A to S does not harm B and avoids S's impoverishment. In such cases, transfer is deemed fair, just, and equitable.[36] Not all courts follow this approach. Some jurisdictions refuse to allow S to escape the improvident bargain with A by seeking a quasi contractual recovery against B, absent exceptional circumstances.[37]

[44.4]   Recovery by Party in Breach of Contract

The traditional rule has been that a party in breach of contract may not sue in quasi contract for the net value of the benefits conferred on the non-breaching party—the difference between the value of goods or services

---

[31] *Associate Eng'g Co., Inc., supra*, 795 S.W.2d at 609.

[32] Section 44.2 (Elements of Quasi Contract) (text and note 15 (acceptance of benefit)).

[33] General Leasing Co. v. Manivest Corp., 667 P.2d 596, 598 (Utah 1983).

[34] *DCB Constr. Co., Inc., supra*, 965 P.2d at 121.

[35] Mid Coast Aviation, Inc. v. General Elec. Credit Corp., 907 F.2d 732 (7th Cir. 1990) (applying Illinois law). The court also noted that the failure to file mechanic's liens did not preclude a recovery in quasi contract. *Id.* at 740–41; *see* Doug Rendleman, *Quantum Meruit For The Subcontractor: Has Restitution Jumped Off Dawson's Dock?*, 79 Tex. L. Rev. 2055 (2001).

[36] Ontiveros Insulation Co., Inc. v. Sanchez, 3 P.3d 695, 700 (N. Mex. App. 2000) (finding that trial court's implied finding that owners had paid general contractor 52% on the underlying contract did not preclude a quasi contract action against the owners by the unpaid subcontractor); Zalenznik v. Gulf Coast Roofing Co., Inc., 576 So.2d 776, 778–79 (Fla. App. 1991).

[37] Haz-Mat Response, Inc. v. Certified Waste Services Ltd., 910 P.2d 839, 847 (Kan. 1996) (limiting quasi contract recovery to cases when subcontractor can show misconduct by owner that induced subcontractor to provide the benefit). *See generally* J.R. Kemper, Annot. *Building and Construction Contracts: Right of Subcontractor Who Has Dealt Only With Primary Contractor To Recover Against Property Owner in Quasi Contract*, 62 A.L.R.3d 288 (1975).

provided prior to breach less damages to the non-breaching party caused by the breach.[38] This rule has, however, been under sustained attack for its harshness and many jurisdictions have rejected it and permitted an action in quasi contract by the breaching party *when the breach is not willful or opportunistic.*[39] The traditional rule is usually not applied in the settings where it would inflict the most pain—construction contract disputes[40] and land contracts.[41]

§ 45   VALUATION OF THE BENEFIT

The purpose of restitution is taking away the "benefit" unjustly held by the defendant. When specific restitution is sought, valuation is usually not a problem as the benefit is the very "thing" that is to be turned over to the plaintiff.[1] For example, if the defendant unjustly holds a painting that belongs to the plaintiff, requiring the defendant to turn over the painting does not raise concerns over the value of the benefit. When, however, the benefit is less tangible, as, for example, when goods and services have been provided under circumstances that retention of those goods and services without payment would be unjust, the valuation of the "benefit" can prove both challenging and important. An good example of the difficulties in this area is *Campbell v. Tennessee Valley Authority.*[2]

Campbell, pursuant to a request by Earl Daniel, Director of the TVA Technical Library, reproduced 13 sets of technical trade journals on 16 mm film. The journals were then destroyed by Campbell pursuant to Daniel's instruction. It developed that Daniels did not have actual authority to commit the government to the contract with Campbell, the government refused to ratify Daniels' actions, and the government refused to pay Campbell the contract price of $30,240.00. Campbell sued the government and proceeded to trial on the theory of quasi contract (*quantum meruit*).[3]

---

[38] Collar City Partnership I v. Redemption Church of Christ of the Apostolic Faith, 651 N.Y.S.2d 729, 730 (App. Dept. 1997); J. CALAMARI & J. PERRILLO, CONTRACTS § 320, p. 492 (1970).

[39] Vines v. Orchard Hills, Inc., 435 A.2d 1022, 1026 (Conn. 1980) (collecting what court characterized as more recent decisions permitting quasi contractual recovery by breaching party). *See generally* James Pearson, Annot., *Modern Status of Defaulting Vendee's Right to Recover Contractual Payments Withheld by Vendor as Forfeited,* 4 A.L.R. 4th 993 (1981).

[40] Section 163 (Losing Contracts and Restitution).

[41] Section 168 (Installment Land Sale Contracts).

[1] A problem may arise if the property has greatly appreciated in value (Section 51 (Disgorgement Orders)), or the benefit is not entirely attributable to the defendant's illegal acts (Section 46 (Apportionment of Benefit), Section 59 (Tracing Principles for Constructive Trusts, Equitable Liens, and Equitable Accounting)).

[2] 421 F.2d 293 (5th Cir. 1969).

[3] Normally, the United States cannot be sued under a theory of unjust enrichment because it has not waived the defense of sovereign immunity as to that claim. New America Shipbuilders, Inc. v. United States, 871 F.2d 1077 (Fed. Cir. 1989) (holding that oral agreement entered into by SBA Regional Administrator was legally ineffective and that government could not be sued under alternative theories of quasi contract or estoppel when approval was outside

The court had little difficulty finding that the government had been unjustly enriched at Campbell's expense; the question was "how much." The government contended "not much." It argued that the materials had little intrinsic value, had been used only slightly, and, on Campbell's refusal to accept their return, the materials (microfiche) had been place in storage and were unavailable for usage by library patrons. The court rejected the government's position as to the ways of valuing the benefit. The court found that the government had obtained a benefit from Campbell, although it also recognized that the amount of benefit, being as it was intangible, was not easy to quantify. Under these circumstances the court allowed use of an alternative measure—the market value of the microfilm, which the court found to be equal to Campbell's cost of production ($30,240.00).

There are three general approaches to measuring a benefit: (1) cost of producing; (2) market value of the thing produced; and, (3) the value to the defendant of the thing produced. The first and third measures are subjective to the extent they reflect a party's personal taste and concerns. The plaintiff who expends resources to produce something to her standards or to contract specifications creates a thing (product or service) that reflects in significant part the value the individual parties place in the thing created. Market value is, however, objective in that it reflects what third parties would pay. While third parties may have individual tastes, just as the parties to the transaction have, the use of a market value smooths out individual preferences in favor of an average, which reflects a market clearing price.[4] None of this works in practice as cleanly as it does on paper; nonetheless, the perceived objectivity of market value causes it to be used as the preferred measure of benefit. This does not, of course, prevent a plaintiff from claiming, and as *Campbell* evidences a court from accepting, that her cost of production reflects the market price, but again it must be emphasized that the measure is "reasonable cost," not necessarily the amount actually expended.[5]

The market measure does not preclude the inclusion of profit in the calculation of reasonable value,[6] but the decisions are conflicting on this

---

administrator's actual authority). The *Campbell* court allow the action to go forward by the use of the term "quasi contract." The United States has waived sovereign immunity for implied-in-fact contracts. The *Campbell* court, without expressly discussing the point, used quasi contract in this sense for jurisdictional purposes, 421 F.2d at 296, but used the implied-by-law form of the action when addressing the substantive claim and remedy. *Id.* at 304 (Rives, J. dissenting).

[4] Asphalt Prods. Corp. v. All Star Ready Mix, Inc., 898 P.2d 699 (Nev. 1995) (finding that trial judge erred in relying on contract price to establish reasonable rental value of vehicle used by defendant. The contract price was based on an arrangement to purchase the vehicle; thus, it did not reflect the normal, customary charges that would be imposed for excessive use by the defendant).

[5] Chase Manhattan Bank, N.A. v. T&N plc, 905 F. Supp. 107, 122 (S.D.N.Y. 1995), *citing* Restatement of Restitution § 115 (1937).

[6] City of Portland v. Hoffman Constr. Co., 596 P.2d 1305, 1314 (Or. 1979); *see* United States v. Stringfellow, 414 F.2d 696 (5th Cir. 1969) (involving excavation work performed by a subcontractor):

point.[7] In some jurisdictions the issue of profit recovery is addressed indirectly. The test of "reasonable value" is "the amount it would have cost the defendant to obtain the services of another."[8] While the plaintiff does not capture his own profit (to do so he would need a contract), the plaintiff captures the average profit obtained by the market clearing price for the services provided by the plaintiff to the defendant.

In deciding which measure to use to value the benefit, the particular circumstances of the case control and the trial court is generally given substantial discretion.[9] There is a tendency in the cases to calibrate the harshness of the remedy with the seriousness of the culpability.[10] In *W.H. Woolley & Co. v. Bear Creek Manor* the court held that the trial court did not abuse its discretion in awarding restitution measured by the cost of providing or obtaining the benefit from others rather than the higher enhancement of the value of the property as a result of the benefits conferred because of the defendants' misconduct:

> Where, as here, the parties seeking restitution have themselves committed a material breach, uncertainties as to the amount of the benefit may properly be resolved against them.[11]

It is sometimes suggested that the proper measure of recovery in unjust enrichment cases is the greater of either enhancement of market value or cost of providing the benefit. The suggestion is, however, qualified in practice as exemplified by *Robertus v. Candee*:

> There may be cases where the enhancement to the defendant's property will be far less than the quantum meruit value of the

---

The value of West's [subcontractor] performance is to be determined "not by the extent to which (Stringfellow's) [contractor] total wealth has been increased thereby [benefit to defendant], but by the amount for which such services and materials as constituted the part performance could have been purchased from one in (West's) position at the time they were rendered.

Id. at 700 (parentheses in original) (citations omitted; brackets added).

[7] Price v. H.L. Coble Constr. Co., 317 F.2d 312, 317 (5th Cir. 1963) (noting that if a "contractor cannot include a profit, he would not be in business"). *Compare* Rowland v. Hudson County, 80 A.2d 433, 437 (N.J. 1951) (stating that when market value measure is used, the measure includes an allowance for profit), *with* Hudson City Contracting Co. v. Jersey City Incinerator Auth., 111 A.2d 385, 391 (N.J. 1955) (stating that quasi-contractual recovery against municipal corporation would be limited to expenses incurred without allowance for profit). The preferred approach appears to be to include an allowance for profit (market price), absent circumstances that call for its exclusion. V.C. Edwards Contracting Co., Inc. v. Port of Tacoma, 514 P.2d 1381, 1386 (Wash. 1973).

[8] Maglica v. Maglica, 78 Cal. Rptr. 2d 101 (Cal. App. 1998).

[9] Far West Federal Bank, S.B. v. Office of Thrift Supervision-Director, 119 F.3d 1358, 1367 (9th Cir. 1994), *citing*, Restatement (Second) of Contracts § 371 cmt. a (1981) (stating that "[t]o the extent that the benefit may reasonably be measured in different ways, the choice is within the discretion of the court").

[10] Murdock-Bryant Constr., Inc. v. Pearson, 703 P.2d 1197, 1204 (Ariz. 1985) (stating that "the amount of recovery should correspond to the reasons underlying that recovery"), *citing*, Dobbs, Remedies, *supra*, § 4.5, 261–62 (1973); Section 8.7 (Harsh or Mild Measures).

[11] 735 P.2d 910, 912 (Colo. App. 1986).

plaintiff's efforts. For example, where the improvement did not enhance the value of the property but did result in a pecuniary saving to the defendant, the enhancement measure would not reflect the unjust enrichment. Conversely, there may be cases where the value of the enhancement greatly exceeds the cost of the improvement, as in this case.

Thus, the rule has evolved that the proper measure of damages in unjust enrichment should be the greater of the two measures. We adopt this rule. But this rule must be tempered with the idea that it is only so much of the enrichment which is unjust that may be awarded the plaintiff. For example, the cost of surveying a tract of land into lots may be $5,000, while the total value of the subdivided lots may be $50,000 greater than the undivided tract. The landowner is justly entitled to the majority of the increase in value for his risk, idea, decision making and development activity. He is only unjustly enriched to the extent that the unpaid surveyor contributed to or caused the increase.[12]

When "benefit" is measured by "costs incurred" as a surrogate for market, the usual rule is to limit the recovery to incurred costs, not future expenses.[13]

An interesting example of the valuation issue is *Chodos v. West Publishing Co., Inc.*[14] in which the parties contracted to publish a legal text, but the defendant breached. The court held that the breach was sufficient to allow the plaintiff to treat the contract as rescinded and seek restitution under quasi contract,[15] the measure of which would be the reasonable value of the services provided.[16] The court in a subsequent opinion rejected the author's claim that the proper measure was the value to the author of his time as valued by what he could have earned had he not been writing the manuscript the defendant refused to publish.[17] Nonetheless, the court upheld a $300,000 *quantum meruit* recovery based on the market for the services the author did provide the defendant finding that:

> It was within the competence of the jury to determine the value of Chodos' services based on West's testimony on the hourly or per unit compensation that West would have offered to have the treatise written and Chodos's testimony on what a practicing attorney would have accepted to produce the treatise. The district court's "open market" jury instruction, which gave the jury discretion to do so, was not in error.[18]

---

[12] 670 P.2d at 540, 543 (Mont. 1983) (citations omitted); Section 46 (Apportionment of Benefit).

[13] Motor Ave. Co. v. Liberty Indus. Finishing Corp., 885 F. Supp. 410, 426 (E.D.N.Y. 1994).

[14] 292 F.3d 992 (9th Cir. 2002).

[15] *Id.* at 1001; Section 41.2 ([Restitution for Wrongdoing] Breach of Contract).

[16] Section 44 (Quasi Contract and Unjust Enrichment).

[17] 92 Fed. Appx. 471, 2004 U.S. App. LEXIS 4109 (9th Cir. 2004).

[18] *Id.*

§ 46   APPORTIONMENT OF BENEFIT

The defendant may receive a benefit, but the scope and extent of the benefit may be imprecise. For example, if a defendant misappropriates or wrongfully acquires the plaintiff's proprietary or confidential information and uses that information in his trade or business, to what extent has the defendant benefitted? Should the "benefit" be measured by the entirety of the profits realized or should an apportionment be attempted between the contributions made to the end product (benefit) by the wrongful conduct (use of misappropriated information) and the contributions made by the defendant's lawful conduct (use of untainted efforts to obtain the benefit)? It is rarely the case that the defendant's benefit was solely the product of its misconduct. The defendant will usually have invested capital and incurred expenses in producing the benefit that are not directly tied to the misconduct, for example, purchasing raw materials and incurring production and distribution costs. To what extent, if at all, should these connected but lawful activities be considered when determining the "benefit" that must be disgorged to the plaintiff?

The apportionment issue can arise in a number of different contexts, such as actions for rescission, trademark or copyright violations, or misappropriation. Particularly, in cases of statutory violations, such as trademark and copyright, the statutory remedial scheme may influence the calculation of the "benefit" in a manner that is not transferrable across cases. In this context, the individual features of the case and the cause of action may dominate the general principles discussed in these materials.[1]

A guiding general principle in this area was voiced in *Earthinfo, Inc. v. Hydrosphere Resource Consultants, Inc.*:

> No easy formulas exist for determining when restitution of profits realized by a party is permissible. Instead, the court must resort to general consideration of fairness, taking into account the nature of the defendant's wrong, the relative extent of his or her contribution, and the feasibility of separating this from the contribution traceable to the plaintiff's interest. Thus, the more culpable the defendant's behavior, and the more direct the connection between the profits and the wrongdoing, the more likely that the plaintiff can recover all defendant's profits. The trial court must ultimately decide whether the whole circumstances of a case point to the conclusion that the defendant's retention of any profit is unjust.[2]

Two factors or considerations predominate in the benefit allocation analysis: (1) the feasibility of the apportionment and (2) the culpability of the defendant.

---

[1] For a more specific discussion of these issues in the field of intellectual property, see Dane S. Ciolino, *Reconsidering Restitution in Copyright*, 48 Emory L.J. 1 (1999); 1a GILSON, TRADEMARK PROTECTION AND PRACTICES § 80.0 [1] (1990).

[2] 900 P.2d 113, 118 (Colo. 1995) (citations omitted).

[46.1]   Feasibility

An apportionment will not be made if the court treats the benefit as indivisible. For example, in *Belford Clark & Co. v. Scribner*[3] it was found that the defendant had incorporated many copyrighted recipes into a cookbook. The cookbook contained both recipes that were lawfully published by the defendant and those that were infringed. The court noted:

> The rule is well settled, that, although the entire copyrighted work be not copied in an infringement, but only portions thereof, if such portions are so intermingled with the rest of the piratical work that they cannot well be distinguished from it, the entire profits realized by the defendants will be given to the plaintiff.[4]

The reason for this approach was set forth in *Hamilton Brown Shoe Co. v. Wolf Brothers & Co.*; it is that the risk of over-remediation should be placed on the defendant who caused the confusion in the first place:

> No one will deny that on every principle of reason and justice the owner of the trademark is entitled to so much of the profit as resulted from the use of the trademark. The difficulty lies in ascertaining what proportion of the profit is due to the trademark, and what to the intrinsic value of the commodity; and as this cannot be ascertained with any reasonable certainty, it is more consonant with reason and justice that the owner of the trademark should have the whole profit than that he should be deprived of any part of it by the fraudulent act of the defendant. It is the same principle which is applicable to a confusion of goods. If one wrongfully mixes his own goods with those of another, so that they cannot be distinguished and separated, he shall lose the whole, for the reason that the fault is his; and it is but just that he should suffer the loss rather than an innocent party, who in no degree contributed to the wrong.[5]

---

[3] 144 U.S. 488 (1892).

[4] *Id.* at 508.

[5] 240 U.S. 251, 262 (1916); Business Trends Analysts, Inc. v. The Freedonia Group, Inc., 887 F.2d 399, 407 (2d Cir. 1989) (stating that when apportionment is rendered impossible by defendant's conduct, the entire profit should go to the plaintiff); *cf.* Securities Exch. Comm'n v. Hughes Capital Corp., 124 F.3d 449 (3d Cir. 1997):

> The burden is on the tortfeasor to establish that the liability is capable of apportionment, and the district court has broad discretion in subjecting the offending parties on a joint-and-several basis to the disgorgement order. Imposing the burden upon the defendant of proving the propriety of the apportionment of the disgorgement amount in securities cases is appropriate and reasonable. Although in some cases, a court may be able easily to identify the recipient of ill-gotten profits and apportionment is practical, that is not usually the case. Generally, apportionment is difficult or even practically impossible because defendants have engaged in complex and heavily disguised transactions. Very often defendants move funds through various accounts to avoid detection, use several nominees to hold securities or improperly deprived profits, or intentionally fail to keep accurate records and refuse to cooperate with investigators in identifying the illegal profits. Hence, "the risk of uncertainty should fall on the wrongdoer whose illegal conduct created that uncertainty."

Id. at 455 (citations omitted). A similar approach is found in the calculation of damages. Section 8.1 (Certainty).

Whether a benefit is indivisible and not subject to apportionment or divisible and subject to apportionment is resolved on a case-by-case basis. The defendant has the burden of proving what portion of the total benefit resulted from lawful activities, *i.e.*, activities that did not result in the defendant's unjust enrichment.[6] Many of the decisions in this area involve statutory remedies that award *as damages* the profits earned by the wrongdoer, e.g., copyright infringement profits. These statutory remedies may have statutory accounting provisions. For example, the Copyright Act provides that the copyright owner is entitled to recover "any profits of the infringer that are attributable to the infringement and are not taken into account in computing actual damages." Moreover, that section explicitly allocates the burden of proof as follows:

> In establishing the infringer's profits, the copyright owner is required to present proof only of the infringer's gross revenue, and the infringer is required to prove his or her deductible expenses and the elements of profit attributable to factors other than the copyright work.[7]

Any risk of uncertainty is borne by the wrongdoers who created the uncertainty, not the victim; however, the concept cannot be taken too far. Courts will reject extreme applications of this principle.[8]

When there exists a rational basis for apportioning the benefit, the court should divide the benefit between the plaintiff and the defendant in a manner that is fair and equitable. Precise mathematical certainty is not required.[9] As noted in *Cream Records, Inc. v. Jos. Schlitz Brewing Company*:

> [W]e are resolved to avoid the one certainly unjust course of giving the plaintiffs everything, because the defendants cannot with certainty compute their own share. In cases where plaintiffs fail to prove their damages exactly, we often make the best estimate we can, even though it is really no more than a guess and under the guise of resolving all doubts against the defendants we will not deny the one fact that stands undoubted. By claiming only 1.37% of

---

[6] Sheldon v. Metro-Goldwyn Pictures Corp., 309 U.S. 390, 402, 405–06 (1940) (stating that the defendant carries the burden of proof as to apportionment and that the evidence produced must be "sufficient to provide a fair basis of decision").

[7] 17 U.S.C. § 5-4(b).

[8] Bouchat v. Baltimore Ravens Football Club, Inc., 346 F.3d 514 (4th Cir. 2003) (rejecting claim that all of defendant's profits could be recovered based on copyright infringement involving team's logo; the statutory presumption does not extend to revenues that have no conceivable connection to the infringement), *cert. denied* 541 U.S. 1042 (2004); Mackie v. Rieser, 296 F.3d 909, 911 (9th Cir. 2002) (stating that to survive summary judgment a plaintiff seeking the recovery of "indirect profits" under the Copyright Act (17 U.S.C. § 504(b)) must show a causal relationship between the defendant's infringement and the indirect profits), *cert. denied*, 537 U.S. 1189 (2003).

[9] Sygma Photo News, Inc. v. High Soc'y Magazine, 778 F.2d 89, 93 (2d Cir. 1985) (noting that even though defendants failed to show "exact" amount of their expenses, they were entitled to a credit for the "minimum amount they in all likelihood spent").

Schlitz's malt liquor profits, Cream recognizes the impropriety of awarding Cream all of Schlitz's profits on a record that reflects beyond argument that most of these profits were attributable to elements other than the infringement. As to the amount of profits attributable to the infringing material, "what is required is . . . only a reasonable approximation," and Cream's calculation is in the end no less speculative than that of the court.[10]

In *Abkco Music, Inc. v. Harrison Songs Music, Ltd.* the court recognized that a defendant's infringement may contribute to the profits realized by non-infringing material. When that occurs a portion of the profit realized by the non-infringing material should be recovered.[11]

In apportioning the benefit between the plaintiff and the defendant, the court may look at the individual units or factors that, when combined, create the finished product from which the benefits or profits are derived. For example, in *Sheldon v. Metro-Goldwyn Pictures Corp.*[12] the Court addressed the apportionment of profit when the movie "Letty Lynton" infringed upon plaintiff's play, "Dishonored Lady." The Court found that in performing the apportionment it was proper to take into account the popularity and drawing power of the motion picture's stars. The Court also noted the dissimilarity between the name of the play and of the movie and that the picture had been licensed to its distributors in advance simply on the name of the film's star. Based on these facts, the Court found that it was proper to apportion the profits based on an approximation of the value of the contribution of the screenplay (which was infringing upon the plaintiff's copyrighted work) to the other factors of production.[13] In other

---

[10] 754 F.2d 826, 829, *quoting* Hand, L., J. (citations omitted).

[11] 508 F. Supp. 798 (S.D.N.Y. 1981):

Mechanical royalties attributable solely to "My Sweet Lord" total $260,103. Plaintiff contends that it is also entitled to some portion of the mechanical royalties Harrison received for the relatively unsuccessful songs on the same discs with "My Sweet Lord" which, it argues, whold not have been earned but for the unusual popularity of "My Sweet Lord." In assessing plaintiff's argument, two things must be kept in mind. First, on the single record, the song "My Sweet Lord", a hit, was teamed with "Isn't It A Pity," a non-hit; on the twelve-inch album, "All Things Must Pass," "My Sweet Lord" was one of twenty-two Harrison songs, only one other of which achieved even modest popularity. Second, exactly the same mechanical royalty is payable to Harrison for each of his songs on any given record, whether memorable or not. Common sense dictates that a hit song contributes more to the sale of a record than does a less popular song. In such circumstances, mechanical royalties paid to a composer for a less-than-memorable song on the record are, in fact, earned by the memorable song which has caused the public to purchase the record. While not susceptible to quite the precision one might prefer, a reasonable determination of the total earnings allocable to "My Sweet Lord" can be made here and is an appropriate item of damage for the court to award.

Id. at 800 (footnote and citations omitted), *modified on other grounds*, 722 F.2d 988 (2d Cir. 1983).

[12] 309 U.S. 390 (1940).

[13] 309 U.S. at 407.

words, only the contribution made by the infringing factor should be apportioned to the plaintiff. To the extent the benefit (profits) were attributable to factors other than the infringement, those profits were properly retained by the defendant.[14]

[46.2] Defendant's Culpability

The moral culpability of the defendant has been identified by commentators as a significant consideration in determining the extent of any apportionment of a benefit between the plaintiff and the defendant.[15] On the other hand, the Supreme Court has expressed reservation on this point:

> Petitioners stress the point that respondents have been found guilty of deliberate plagiarism, but we receive no ground for saying that in awarding profits to the copyright proprietor as a means of compensation, the court may make an award of profits which have been shown not to be due to the infringement. That would be not to do equity but to inflict an unauthorized penalty.[16]

Courts have been willing to allow the defendant's relative culpability to influence the type of remedy permitted, *e.g.*, injunction versus damages,[17] damages versus restitution,[18] or the selection of the measure of damages.[19]

---

[14] *E.g.*, Rogers v. Koons, 960 F.2d 301, 313 (2d Cir. 1992) (stating that an apportionment of profits was proper when the defendant improperly incorporated copyrighted work in a larger work). The court noted that the profits were attributable to factors other than the infringement, particularly the defendant's notoriety and ability to command high prices for his works. *Id.*; *Abkco Music, Inc., supra*, 508 F. Supp. 798:

> Next, I must determine the portion of the above income which should be attributed to factors, other than the plagiarized music, affecting public interest in the song "My Sweet Lord." Several matters must be considered. Harrison, an artist with an international "name," supplied his own text. How much of the income is attributable to the text, to the selling power of his name? Although this is not an area susceptible to precise measurement, I conclude that three-fourths of "My Sweet Lord's" success is due to plagiarized tune and one-fourth to other factors, such as the words and the popularity and stature of George Harrison in this particular field of music. I weigh the music heavily in this case because the music had already demonstrated its outstanding "catchiness" in 1963 when it carried the rather unexceptional, romantic text of "He's So Fine" to first place on the Billboard charts in the United States for five weeks.

Id. at 801–02 (footnotes omitted).

[15] Douglas Laycock, *The Scope and Significance of Restitution*, 67 Tex. L. Rev. 1277, 1289 (1989); Dale Oesterle, *Deficiencies of the Restitutionary Right to Trace Misappropriated Property in Equity and in U.C.C. § 9-306*, 68 Cornell L. Rev. 172, 200–202 (1983).

[16] *Sheldon, supra*, 309 U.S. at 405; *but see Earthinfo, Inc., supra*, 900 P.2d at 118 (noting defendant's culpability as a relevant factor in considering the issue of apportionment).

[17] Maier Brewing Co. v. Fleischmann Distilling Corp., 390 F.2d 117, 123 (9th Cir.), *cert denied*, 391 U.S. 966 (1968) (stating that in cases of deliberate trademark infringement a plaintiff should not be limited to injunctive relief but should be allowed to recoup diverted profits).

[18] Olwell v. Nye & Nissen Co., 172 P.2d 652, 653–54 (Wash. 1946).

[19] Section 8.7 (Harsh or Mild Measures).

Extensions of this principle expressly to the apportionment issue have been inconclusive. The decisional law is mixed. For example, *Truck Equip. Serv. Co. v. Fruehaf Corp.* supports using culpability to measure apportionment:

> [E]quity requires that Fruehauf relinquish all of its profits from the sales in the three states wherein TESCO has acquired protectable trademark rights. We proceed upon the theory that such relief is necessary as a deterrence to willful infringement.[20]

Yet, *Truck Equip. Serv.* relied upon *W.E. Bassett Co. v. Revlon, Inc.*, which is more accurately classified as a type of remedy case rather than a measure of apportionment case.[21] Thus, the court in *W.E. Bassett* stated:

> An accounting should be granted if the defendant is unjustly enriched, if the plaintiff sustained damages from the infringement, or if an accounting is necessary to deter a willful infringer from doing so again.[22]

Notwithstanding the disagreement in the decisions, using the defendant's culpability as a factor in determining the extent of any apportionment is certainly consistent with the general approach of courts when addressing remedies.[23]

The decisional law is clearer when the issue is the deductibility of income taxes paid by the defendant when determining the amount of profit subject to disgorgement. There is a willingness to permit the defendant to claim an offset for taxes paid, unless the defendant is guilty of "conscious wrongdoing."[24]

---

[20] 536 F.2d 1210, 1222 (8th Cir.), *cert. denied*, 429 U.S. 861 (1976).

[21] 435 F.2d 656 (2d Cir. 1970)

[22] *Id.* at 664. A strong statement of the utility of culpability in this context is found in Hill v Names & Addresses, Inc., 571 N.E.2d 1085, 1096 (Ill. App. 1991) (involving misappropriation of business expectancy by former employee in breach of duty of loyalty).

[23] *Abkco Music Co., supra*, 508 F. Supp. at 801 n.10 (stating that "[h]ad I found that Harrison deliberately plagiarized the music, I would award the entire earnings of "My Sweet Lord.") (citation omitted); *see* McCarthy on Trademark & Unfair Competition § 30.65 (4th ed. 1996).

[24] Julius Hyman & Co. v. Velsicol Corp., 233 P.2d 977, 1010 (Colo. 1951); *see* Weiss v. Weiss, 984 F. Supp. 675 (S.D.N.Y. 1997):

> There remains a question as to whether, in calculating defendant's "profits" from the breach of trust, he is entitled to a credit for any taxes that he may have paid on those profits. Not surprisingly, the parties have not cited, and we have not located, any controlling authority on this point. We may, however, analogize to the law regarding profit awards in other contexts and conclude that federal income taxes actually paid may be offset from profits in the absence of "conscious and deliberate wrongdoing."

Id. at 680 (citations and footnote omitted); *but cf.* USM Corp. v. Marson Fastener Corp., 467 N.E.2d 1271, 1280–81 (Mass. 1984) (allowing credit for taxes paid in case of deliberate misappropriation of confidential information).

[46.3] Extent of Apportionment

When the wrongdoer contributes his own time or money to create or enhance a benefit, the issue of apportionment of the value of the benefit or value of the property created or enhanced will often arise. The effort or expense must enhance or change that which was obtained by the defendant from the plaintiff.[25] The analysis is more case-by-case than by general rule.[26] Several approaches have been identified:

> Profit claims can be calculated first by identifying and deducting legitimate business expenses from gross income. The defendant usually has the best access to this information and may properly be required to prove such expenses. Second, gross income of the defendant is produced at least in part "by investment, enterprise, and management skill of the defendant," and the defendant should receive credit for its own efforts and investments. The court must determine which part of the profit results from the defendant's own independent efforts and which part results from the benefits provided by the plaintiff. The court must seek to determine a fair apportionment that will result in a reasonable approximation or informed estimate of the relative contributions of the two parties.[27]

The identification of legitimate expenses which may be credited against the benefit (profits) tends to be rigorous. For example, in *Hill v. Names & Addresses, Inc.* an employer sought an accounting based on a former employee's misappropriation and diversion of six customers. The court held that the former employee was liable for the profits the diverted customers generated. The former employee sought an offset for the expenses incurred. The court held that an offset would only be permitted from gross profits for "those expenses incurred for the purpose of servicing the six diverted customers."[28] This would permit the crediting to the defendant of direct but not fixed (e.g., general overhead) costs.

§ 47 RESTITUTIONARY DAMAGES

The term "restitution damages" will strike some as anathema, or, at best, an oxymoron. Restitution is benefit oriented, damages are harm oriented; where, when, and how do the parallel lines merge?

While the term "restitution damages" generates some academic hostility, it is generally well received by the courts, albeit with little analysis or

---

[25] Will of Rothko, 392 N.Y.S.2d 870, 874 (App. Dept. 1987):

> Increase in value by the labor of the wrongdoer without change in the character of the property improved inures to the benefit of the wronged party, and the wrongdoer is entitled to no credit thereof. (citations omitted).

[26] *Earthinfo, Inc., supra,* 900 P.2d at 120–21 (noting that "no single rule governing the burden of proving apportionment is adequate for all cases or all facets of a single case").

[27] *Id.* at 120–21 (citations omitted).

[28] 571 N.E.2d at 1084, 1097 (Ill. App. 1991).

discussion of the tension between the two terms. The idea of "restitution damages" is not new. Traditionally, the legal system recognized that a plaintiff could recover, as damages, the consideration paid when the defendant materially breached the contract. Alternatively, the plaintiff could seek recovery of the consideration through an action in unjust enrichment. As Fuller and Perdue famously noted, the recovery of consideration sounded both in damages (plaintiff had been harmed) and in unjust enrichment (defendant had benefitted).[1] The recovery of one's consideration thus looked and sounded like restitutionary damages. We could extrapolate this usage to any case when plaintiff's loss equaled and consisted of defendant's gain, e.g., the profits defendant earned are the same profits plaintiff would have realized but for defendant's wrongdoing.

While this use of the term "restitution damages" raises nomenclature issues, it probably doesn't trouble most commentators because the usage does not contribute to, or result in, a different result in unjust enrichment with restitution than would be found in contract or tort with damages. Concern arises, however, when use of the term "restitution damages" may confuse or cause courts to ignore long settled boundaries established in tort[2] or contract.[3]

Notwithstanding the early association of "restitution damages" with return of consideration, courts do not limit use of the term today to that situation, although how often this occurs is hard to say. The term "restitution damages" is broadly applied to situations when a defendant has acquired a benefit, usually "profits," as a result of misconduct that may or may not have harmed the plaintiff. Even if the plaintiff is harmed, the benefit may bear no relationship, at least quantitatively, to plaintiff's loss. In this context, it is helpful to understand how courts *might* be using the term "restitution damages." The monetizing of benefits may reflect the liberal use of the terms "damages" when in fact the court means "money."

Secondly, the term may reflect a "punitive" gloss on the availability of restitution. In many instances the scope of restitution is conditioned on a required finding of deliberate wrongdoing.[4]

Thirdly, the term may reflect the tendency to require a causal connection between the defendant's conduct and the resulting unjust enrichment.[5] Linking causation and profits may suggest a *damages* orientation that in turn is melded into the concept of restitution.

Lastly, perhaps the most likely explanation for the development of the term is the sense that awarding restitution of defendant's profits serves

---

[1] Lon L. Fuller & William R. Perdue, Jr., *The Reliance Interest in Contract Damages*, 46 Yale L. J. 52, 373 (1937).

[2] Section 41.1 ([Restitution for Wrongdoing] Tortious Conduct).

[3] Section 41.2 ([Restitution for Wrongdoing] Breach of Contract).

[4] Section 46.2 (Defendant's Culpability) (text and note 24).

[5] Taylor v. Meirick, 712 F.2d 1112, 1122 (7th Cir. 1983) ("If General Motors were to steal your copyright and put it in a sales brochure, you could not just put a copy of General Motor's corporate tax return in the record and rest your case for an award of infringer's profit.")

as a substitute for plaintiff's lost profits, which would clearly be damages.[6] This linkage between restitution of defendant's profits as the second best replacement for plaintiff's lost profits can be seen in the unfair competition cases.[7] Initially, the recovery of defendant's profits in lieu of plaintiff's lost profits was limited to cases when the party's were competitors and a "zero sum" assumption could be used, *i.e.,* defendant's gain came from plaintiff's share of a limited pie—the "pie" being aggregate available profits. Over time, many courts dropped the "direct competition" requirement,[8] but did not preclude recovery of defendant's profits! Now, however, the rationale for restitution was the defendant's deliberate wrongdoing, but the remedy remained even though it had been dislodged from its initial mooring.

These explanations are necessarily speculative because the courts have largely chosen to use the term "restitution damages" without defining it. The very impreciseness of the term allows it to be (mis) applied to a variety of situations. When the term is limited to its traditional area of "return of consideration," it does little damage. When, however, the term is extended aggressively to capture benefits held by the defendant that were never possessed, or capable or likely to be possessed, by the plaintiff, care must be taken that the imagery of the term "restitution damages" doe not blind us to what is occurring.

---

[6] Section 8.3 (Lost Profits).

[7] Restatement (Third) of Unfair Competition § 37 (1995).

[8] Maier Brewing Co. v. Fleischmaun Distilling Corp., 390 F.2d 117, 121–22 (9th Cir.), *cert. denied,* 391 U.S. 966 (1968).

Chapter 6

RESTITUTIONARY ACTIONS

§ 50 INTRODUCTION

The remedies described in this chapter share one common theme—they are designed to separate the defendant from property (real or personal, tangible or intangible) that the defendant holds, possesses or controls. The remedies discussed in this Chapter developed in both law and equity and today still retain attributes of their separate origins, e.g., irreparable injury requirement.[1] Although the remedies may be generally classified by their origin in law or equity, this does not mean that there is a high degree of homogenization within each category. The remedies were designed to address specific problems and those problems provide a more reliable insight into the remedy than the legal system of origin.

The remedies described in this chapter tend to be self contained and limited to precise problems. While the damages remedy attaches to a wide set of legal relationships defined by the Law of Contract or the Law of Torts, the remedies discussed here do not. For example, subrogation is not widely available; rather, the remedy exists to address problems that arise out of specific relationships. In many respects, the remedies discussed in this chapter may be best seen and understood as self-contained rights of action with their own specific remedy(ies).

§ 51 DISGORGEMENT ORDERS

The purpose of disgorgement is to deter violations of the law, particularly statutory law, by depriving wrongdoers of their ill gotten gains,[1] and thus make violations unprofitable. Disgorgement is an ancillary equitable remedy, which a court may exercise under its general equitable power to afford complete relief.[2]

Disgorgement is based on restitution. Sometimes the terms are used interchangeably, sometimes they are treated as distinct both in purpose and effect. A distinction between disgorgement and restitution was made by the court in *Securities and Exchange Commission v. Huffman*:

> Despite some casual references in our caselaw to the contrary, (describing disgorgement order in one isolated phrase as "this restitution"), disgorgement is not precisely restitution. Disgorgement wrests ill-gotten gains from the hands of a wrongdoer. It is an equitable remedy meant to prevent the wrongdoer from enriching himself by his wrongs. Disgorgement does not aim to compensate the victims of the wrongful acts, as restitution does. Thus, a

---

[1] Section 21 (Adequacy of the Remedy at Law/Irreparable Injury).

[1] Securities and Exch. Comm'n v. Fischbach Corp., 133 F.3d 170, 175 (2d Cir. 1997).

[2] Securities and Exch. Comm'n v. Randolph, 736 F.2d 525, 529 (9th Cir. 1984); State v. Southwest Mineral Energy, Inc., 617 P.2d 1334, 1337 (Okla. 1980).

disgorgement order might be for an amount more or less than that required to make the victims whole. It is not restitution.[3]

There is always some looseness of language in attempting to define terms. Restitution is a concept that focuses on avoiding unjust enrichment, although, as *Huffman* indicates, courts may conflate the term with damages. At times, disgorgement is treated as a specific remedy much like an injunction or quasi contract are remedies, and this is perhaps unfortunately loose if it generates confusion. More accurately, disgorgement is a form of restitution in equity, a vehicle by which unjust enrichment is avoided and redressed. Disgorgement restores the defendant to the status quo by stripping him of the gains he unjustly obtained by his misconduct. In this sense, disgorgement and restitution are the same for each seeks to take away from the defendant that which in equity and fairness the defendant should not retain.[4] Disgorgement may be most accurately seen as a stylized form of restitution, used in particular cases, such as securities fraud or insider trader, where the policy of completely stripping the wrongdoer of his profits is particularly strong.[5] Most disgorgement claims are brought by administrative agencies, e.g., the SEC,[6] but the power of the remedy attracts many civil litigants. When a defendant is required to restore to a plaintiff money or property wrongfully obtained from the plaintiff, courts have no difficulty seeing this as restitution. When, however, the plaintiff is a governmental agency and the restoration includes gains derived from property wrongfully acquired from a private party, many courts prefer to

---

[3] 996 F.2d 800, 802 (5th Cir. 1993) (citations omitted); *see* Kraus v. Trinity Management Services, Inc., 999 P.2d 718, 725 (Cal. 2000):

> An order that a defendant disgorge money obtained through an unfair business practice may include a restitutionary element, but is not so limited. As in this case, such orders may compel a defendant to surrender all money obtained through an unfair business practice even though not all is to be restored to the persons from whom it was obtained or those claiming under those person. It has also been used to refer to surrender of all profits earned as a result of an unfair business practice regardless of whether those profits represent money taken directly from persons who were victims of the unfair practice.

[4] Branch v. Mobil Oil Corp., 788 F. Supp. 539, 540 (W.D. Okla. 1992) (noting that "[d]isgorgement is a restitutionary remedy or remedy for restitution. The underlying basis for disgorgement and other restitutionary remedies or tools like quasi-contracts is the prevention of unjust enrichment") (citations and footnote omitted).

[5] *See* SEC v. Texas Gulf Sulphus, 446 F.2d 1301, 1307 (2d Cir.) (stating that "[t]here is little doubt that § 27 of the [1934] Act confers general equity power upon the district courts," and later, "we hold that SEC may seek other than injunctive relief in order to effectuate the purposes of the Act, so long as such relief is remedial relief and is not a penalty assessment"), *cert. denied*, 404 U.S. 1005 (1971); H.R. REP. NO. 335, 98th Cong., 2nd Sess. 7 (1984), *reprinted in* 1984 U.S.C. C.A.N. 2274, 2280 ("Once the equity jurisdiction of a court has been invoked on a showing of a securities violation, the court possesses the necessary power to fashion an appropriate remedy. Thus, the Commission may request that the court order certain equitable relief, such as the disgorgement (giving up) of illegal profits . . . .").

[6] SEC v. MacDonald, 699 F.2d 47 (1st Cir. 1983); SEC v. Blavin, 557 F. Supp. 1304, 1316 (E.D. Mich. 1983) ("The deterrent effect of the SEC enforcement action would be greatly undermined if . . . violators were not to disgorge illegal profits"), *aff'd*, 760 F.2d 706 (6th Cir. 1986).

deem the remedy disgorgement. The differences in terminology can also have instrumental consequences.[7]

Disgorgement diverts focus away from the "victim," and any sense of "compensating" the victim by transferring the benefit to her, and toward the sole goal of deterrence.[8] Disgorgement is usually effected through a disgorgement "order." A disgorgement order may be enforced as an injunction. As noted in *Huffman*:

> We have not traditionally understood a disgorgement obligation to be "a mere money judgment or debt" but rather more akin to "an injunction in the public interest . . .". Because disgorgement is more like a continuing injunction in the public interest than a debt, we held in *Pierce* that the disgorgement order could be enforced by contempt sanctions.[9]

Disgorgement orders emanating out of federal courts are particularly powerful. Such orders may transcend state laws on levy and execution of judgments[10] and state laws on vicarious liability.[11] Courts have entered disgorgement orders on nominal defendants over whom the court could not impose direct remedies.[12]

Once the disgorgement order is enforced, the funds collected should be distributed in an equitable manner. The usual practice is to return the funds disgorged to the victims of the wrongdoing; however, restoration is not required. When restoration is too costly, as, for example, when numerous victims have sustained relatively small or minor losses or when the

---

[7] *Compare* Texas Am. Oil Corp. v. United States Dept. of Energy, 44 F.3d 1557, 1569 (Fed. Cir. 1995) (treating concepts differently when doing so allowed court to change government's priority against creditors of bankrupt from class 7 to lower class 9), *with* People v. Martinson, 233 Cal. Rptr. 617, 621 (Cal. App. 1987) (treating the concepts the same when doing so allowed state to obtain disgorgement order even though statute referred only to "restitution or damages" as remedy).

[8] Securities and Exch. Comm'n v. Commonwealth Chem. Sec., Inc., 574 F.2d 90, 102 (2d Cir. 1978) (Friendly, J.) (stating that "the primary purpose of disgorgement is not to compensate investors. Unlike damages, it is a method of forcing a defendant to give up the amount by which he was unjustly enriched"). *But cf.* People v. Beaumont Inv. Ltd., 3 Cal. Rptr.3d 429, 455 (Cal. App. 2003) (stating that focus of statutory restitution order requiring defendant to give up profits gained through unfair business practices is not to restore defendant to status quo ante but to restore money to victim). The *Beaumont* court then, somewhat inconsistently, stated that "statutory restitution is not solely intended to benefit the [victims] by the return of money, but instead is designed to penalize a defendant for past unlawful conduct and thereby deter violations." *Id.*

[9] 996 F.2d at 802–03.

[10] Securities and Exch. Comm'n v. Hickey, 322 F.3d 1123, 1131 (9th Cir. 2003).

[11] Pension Benefit Guaranty Corp. v. Ouimet Corp., 711 F.2d 1085, 1093 (1st Cir.), *cert. denied*, 464 U.S. 961 (1983).

[12] Commodity Futures Trading Comm'n v. Kimberlynn Creek Ranch, Inc., 276 F.3d 187, 191–92 (4th Cir. 2002) (freezing assets in hands of innocent party who received assets from wrongdoer; assets were ill gotten gains of wrongdoer's activities; and, innocent party had no legitimate claim to assets).

victims cannot be identified, it is proper to remit the disgorged funds to the public treasury.[13]

Disgorgement has been limited to those profits that directly relate to the wrongdoing,[14] but, as noted previously, the dominant rule is to the contrary.

Disgorgement orders are usually only available to public enforcement agencies, rather than as a private remedy for civil litigants. The first reason is that a disgorgement order that strips the defendant of all gains risks subjecting the defendant to multiple punishment as he is still liable for the plaintiff's losses. The court may attempt to ameliorate this exposure by crediting disgorgement against damages, but there is no general rule requiring such as offset.[15]

Secondly, the strong use of disgorgement to capture gains that do not belong to the plaintiff(s) prosecuting the action bypasses the usual focus of American litigation on individualized justice and transforms the action into one seeking public redress. Such broad actions may be brought by private individuals, but usually only in the form of class actions, with the attendant protections for defendants and individuals not party to the action. Permitting private individuals to use disgorgement to evade class action requirements may be deemed unacceptable by courts.[16]

Disgorgement orders are generally limited to cases involving statutory violations and the statute permits or authorizes disgorgement as a remedy. The statute need not use the term "disgorgement", but the court must be satisfied that the remedy is consistent with the goals and purpose of the statute.[17] In some contexts, courts have suggested that disgorgement,

[13] Securities and Exch. Comm'n v. Lorin, 869 F. Supp. 1117, 1129 (S.D.N.Y. 1994), *aff'd.* 76 F.3d 458 (2d Cir. 1996).

[14] Commodity Futures Trading Comm'n v. Am. Metals Exch. Corp., 991 F.2d 71, 77–78 (3d Cir. 1993) (rejecting disgorgement of profits in excess of victim's losses as an improper penalty assessment when the district court failed to hold a hearing to determine the amount of defendant's actual gains). The court suggested that the harsher method might be appropriate if a defendant's misconduct made the calculation of "profits" impossible. *Id.* at 77; Securities and Exch. Comm'n v. First City Fin. Corp., 890 F.2d 1215, 1230 (D.C. Cir. 1989) (allowing disgorgement only of those profits directly related to wrongdoing in question—failure to file Schedule 13D).

[15] American Bar Association Section of Antitrust Law, Comment on Remedial Use of Disgorgement (2002), discussed and criticized in Robert Pitofsky, *Antitrust at the Turn of the Twenty-First Century: The Matter of Remedies,* 91 Geo. L. J. 169, 175–76 (2002).

[16] *Kraus, supra,* 999 P.2d at 128–29 (rejecting use of disgorgement ("fluid recovery remedy") absent compliance with class action requirements when action is brought by private, as opposed to public, plaintiffs).

[17] *In re* Multidistrict Vehicle Air Pollution, 538 F.2d 231, 233–34 (9th Cir. 1976) (rejecting claim of disgorgement of profits under the Clayton Act (15 U.S.C. § 26)); *cf.* F.T.C. v. Mylan Laboratories, Inc., 62 F. Supp.2d 25, 43 (D.D.C. 1999) (permitting disgorgement of profits under state statutes that permit, or have been construed to permit, the remedy). In both *Multidistrict* and *Mylan* the courts used the term "restitution" in the sense that "disgorgement" is used here, *i.e.*, as inclusive of gains derived from possession, use, or control of the wrongfully obtained property.

outside the federal securities litigation context, requires a prior relationship between the parties such that the benefit to the defendant is at the cost of the plaintiff.[18] The statement is probably an accurate descriptive statement of the law insofar as private litigants are concerned; however, if a relationship does exist between the parties, the plaintiff may be able to claim additional gains, which the defendant realized, as part of the restoration remedy.[19] The rationale for this approach was set forth in *Janigan v. Taylor*:

> [I]f the property is not bought from, but sold to the fraudulent party, future accretions not foreseeable at the time of the transfer even on the true facts, and hence speculative, are subject to another factor, viz., that they accrued to the fraudulent party. It may, as in the case at bar, be entirely speculative whether, had plaintiffs not sold, the series of fortunate occurrences would have happened in the same way, and to their same profit. However, there can be no speculation but that the defendant actually made the profit and, once it is found that he acquired the property by fraud, that the profit was the proximate consequence of the fraud, whether foreseeable or not. It is more appropriate to give the defrauded party the benefit even of windfalls than to let the fraudulent party keep them. We may accept defendant's position that there was no fiduciary relationship and that he was dealing at arm's length. Nonetheless, it is simple equity that a wrongdoer should disgorge his fraudulent enrichment.[20]

Janigan has been praised, criticized, limited, and followed. The remedy it provides is generally addressed today through the law of constructive trust,[21] or through statutory construction.[22]

---

[18] Smith v. Pacific Properties and Development Corp., 358 F.3d 1097, 1106 (9th Cir. Cir. 2004) (rejecting disgorgement in context of alleged profitable violations of Fair Housing Amendment Act), *cert. denied*, 125 S. Ct. 106 (2005). The plaintiffs sought to capture profits ("expenses saved") the defendant allegedly realized by constructing premises that discriminated against disabled individuals.

[19] Janigan v. Taylor, 344 F.2d 781 (1st Cir.) (permitting plaintiffs to capture appreciated value of stock that they had lost to defendant as a result of his fraud), *cert. denied*, 382 U.S. 879 (1965). The appreciation of the stock was largely due to defendant's post-fraud actions, but the gain was embedded in the value of the stocks, which were returned to plaintiffs when the transaction was rescinded. Section 134 ([Rescission] Restoration of Staus Quo).

[20] *Id.* at 786 (citations omitted).

[21] Lawton v. Nyman, 327 F.3d 30, 45–46 (1st Cir. 2003) (applying Rhode Island law); Section 54 (Constructive Trust).

[22] Danielle Conway-Jones, *Remedying Trademark Infringement: The Role of Bad Faith in Awarding An Accounting of Defendant's Profits*, 42 Santa Clara L. Rev. 863 (2002) (discussing split in the federal court as to whether disgorgement of profits for trademark infringement requires a showing of "bad faith" or only "willfulness"); *see Kraus, supra*, 999 P.2d at 128–29 (refusing to construe California Unfair Business Practices Act (Cal. Bus. & Prof. Code § 17200 *et seq.*) to permit disgorgement unless class certification is obtained or action is brought by public actor, e.g., State Attorney General).

The benefits of disgorgement may be muted by the decision to apportion the benefit between the defendant's lawful and wrongful conduct.[23]

§ 52 INDEMNITY

The remedy of indemnity provides for reimbursement when one person pays or discharges a debt or liability, which another person should have paid or discharged.[1] The essential element is that one party (indemnitee) has paid more than its fair share and another person (indemnitor) has been unjustly enriched to that extent. Indemnity is thus a form of restitution, an action developed in equity to prevent unjust enrichment.[2] There are occasional references to indemnity actions at law, but these references are marginal.[3]

Indemnity comes in two forms: (1) contractual and (2) equitable (remedial). Contractual indemnity is a consensual, risk sharing agreement between parties. The most common example of contractual indemnity is insurance. For a fee (premium) the insurer agrees to indemnify the insured for certain losses up to certain amounts. Equitable indemnity, on the other hand, arises by operation of law. Historically, equitable indemnity's most common application was in matters involving joint tortfeasors when one tortfeasor was passively liable and the other tortfeasor was actively liable. It was deemed unfair that a defendant whose culpability was less, relative to the other defendant, should bear the losses generated by the tortious misconduct of the active wrongdoer. This application of equitable indemnity was generally limited to cases where the person seeking indemnity (the "indemnitee") was only vicariously liable for the tort of the other (the "indemnitor"). For example, in *Manning v. Loidharmer* the court held that three elements are necessary to create a claim for equitable indemnity: "(1) a wrongful act or omission by A towards B; (2) such act or omission exposes or involves B in litigation with C, and (3) C was not connected with . . . the original wrongful act or omission of A towards B."[4] Thus, if A (agent) commits a tort on B (victim) and B successfully sues C (principal) under

---

[23] Section 46 (Apportionment of Benefit) (particularly Section 46.2 (Defendant's Culpability)).

[1] Central Wash. Refrigeration, Inc. v. Barbee, 946 P.2d 760, 762 (Wash. 1997); Restatement of Restitution § 76 (1937).

[2] City of Willmar v. Short-Elliott-Hendrickson, Inc., 512 N.W.2d 872, 874 (Minn. 1994); *cf.* Signal Cos. v. Harbor Ins. Co., 612 P.2d 889, 895 (Cal. 1980) (involving multiple insurers seeking allocation of losses incurred by their common insured):

> The reciprocal rights and duties of several insurers who have covered the same event do not arise out of contract, for their agreements are not with each other . . . . Their respective obligations flow from equitable principles designed to accomplish ultimate justice in the bearing of a specific burden.

[3] George Lee Flint, Jr. & Phillip W. Moore, Jr., *ERISA: A Co-Fiduciary Has no Right to Contribution and Indemnity*, 48 S.D. L. Rev. 7, 9–15 (2003) (discussing English and American roots of the remedy of indemnity).

[4] 538 P.2d 136, 138 (Wash. App. 1975).

the theory of respondeat superior (vicarious liability), C could recover his costs and expenses against A under the remedy of indemnity.

Indemnity was also recognized in contexts where the parties had a "relationship" but had failed to expressly address risk of loss issues within the relationship. As noted by one court:

> A suit for indemnity is often, though presumably not here, contractual. And often—and here—it is at least quasi-contractual in the following sense: the parties have a preexisting contractual relationship and the suit asks the court to find in effect that they would have provided expressly for indemnity had they foreseen the incident that has given rise to the indemnity claim. If, as the cross-claim alleges, the oil spill was due not to any fault on Amoco's part but to Astilleros' negligence in designing or constructing the ship, this implies that Astilleros could have avoided a disastrous accident, for which both parties may be liable, more easily than Amoco could have. Therefore, if the parties had foreseen the possibility of such a disaster, they would have agreed that Astilleros would bear the full cost, for this would have created the right incentives for avoiding the disaster at the lowest possible cost. They would in other words have inserted an explicit provision for Astilleros to indemnify Amoco in the event that disaster struck, Amoco was sued, and judgment was entered against it. This reasoning shows that Amoco's claim for indemnity, though not strictly contractual, has the form of a contractual argument—enough so that it can be said to "arise from" the negotiation and signing of the shipbuilding contract.[5]

This form of "implied" indemnity was not equitable per se as it was derived from the contract and based on the supposed intent of the contracting parties.[6] Nonetheless, the situations when courts will "imply" an obligation to indemnify often overlap with the equitable considerations[7] making it difficult to differentiate the two tests in practice.

Equitable (or implied contractual) indemnity will generally be applied, as the term suggests, in an equitable fashion:

> Although [a party's] rights arose out of a contractual agreement, the right of indemnity is essentially equitable in nature. "Indemnification is a flexible, equitable remedy designed to accomplish a fair allocation of loss among parties[.] . . .The right to indemnity stands upon the principle that everyone is responsible for the consequences

---

[5] *In re* Amoco Cadiz Oil Spill, 699 F.2d 909, 915 (7th Cir. 1983), *cert. denied*, 464 U.S. 864 (1984) (citations omitted).

[6] Haynes v. Kleinewefers and Lembo Corp., 921 F.2d 453, 456 (2d Cir. 1990) (applying New York law) ("Express language need not be used as long as the contract demonstrates an 'unmistakable intent' to indemnify") (citation omitted).

[7] Jinwoong, Inc. v. Jinwoong, Inc. 310 F.3d 962, 965 (7th Cir. 2002) (applying Illinois law) (requiring for implied contractual indemnity the same showing of indemnitor fault and indemnitee blamelessness as required in equity).

of his own acts[.]" Thus, an award of indemnity should follow traditional concepts of equity, and granting [a party] reimbursement for losses, expenses, or fees unnecessarily and unreasonably incurred would be error.[8]

Parties who have consensually agreed among themselves as to the desired allocation of prospective losses will usually find their agreement respected and enforced by the courts.[9]

The decision to separate express contractual indemnity from equitable or implied contractual indemnity reflects the legal system's general reluctance to allow restitutionary remedies to trump consensual bargains. When, however, the cause of the loss is a legal wrong independent of the contract, equitable indemnity, irrespective of the contractual allocation, may be applied.[10]

At common law, the rule was to reserve equitable indemnity to matters when the proposed indemnitee was relatively free from fault.[11] That rule has been substantially relaxed, largely in response to the development of comparative fault that, unlike contributory negligence regimes, expressly envisions proportionate responsibility. When a joint tortfeasor seeks to reallocate the loss among the other joint tortfeasors, many courts permit

[8] Carpenter-Vilquartz Redevelopment Corp. v. James H. Barickman Assocs., 886 S.W.2d 634, 638 (Mo. App. 1994) (citation omitted).

[9] E.L. White, Inc. v. City of Huntington Beach, 579 P.2d 505 (Cal. 1978):

> Express indemnity reflects its contractual nature, permitting great freedom of action to the parties in the establishment of the indemnity arrangements while at the same time subjecting the resulting contractual language to established rules of construction.

Id. at 510 (footnote ommited); cf. Gibbs-Alfano v. Burton, 281 F.3d 12 (2d Cir. 2002) (applying New York law):

> It is axiomatic that an indemnity contract is interpreted to effectuate the intention of the parties as expressed in the unequivocal language of the contract. Thus, "[w]hen a party is under no legal duty to indemnify, a contract assuming that obligation must be strictly construed to avoid reading into it a duty which the parties did not intend to be assumed." Nevertheless, "[a] contract of indemnity need not explicitly state an intent that the undertaking extend to the indemnitee's own negligent acts." Instead, where there is all-encompassing language in an indemnification agreement, the New York Court of Appeals has divined the "unmistakable intent of the parties" to indemnify against the indemnitee's negligent acts.

281 F.3d at 19 (citations omitted).

[10] Galt G/S v. JSS Scandinavia, 142 F.3d 1150, 1156 (9th Cir. 1998) (holding that the "vessel owner's breach of its duty to care for a cargo gives rise to liability in tort, irrespective of the contractual obligations of the parties"; consequently, "[t]he existence of a contract between Safeway and Galt does not preclude Hapag-Lloyd's equitable indemnity claim against Safeway") (citation omitted).

[11] Russell v. Community Hosp. Ass'n, 428 P.2d 783, 787 (Kan. 1967) (stating that traditionally equitable indemnity was not available unless the proposed indemnitee was "not in pari delicto" and his negligence was "substantially different, not merely in degree but in character" from that of the proposed indemnitor); see Trustees of Columbia Univ. v. Mitchell/Giurgola Assocs., 492 N.Y.S.2d 371, 374–75 (App. Dept. 1985).

reallocation under principles of equitable indemnity. In these cases, indemnity may be proportionate rather than all or nothing,[12] or equal, as the case with the remedy of contribution.

The remedy of indemnification is not available unless the indemnitor can be held directly liable to the person injured. For example, if A (victim) sues B (tortfeasor), B cannot claim equitable indemnity from C for the monies paid A to resolve the claim unless C would be liable to A. For example, under the Jones Act[13] an action for injuries resulting from the negligence of a seaman (employee) lies only against the master (employer).[14] If a person is injured by the negligence of a seaman and sues the master, the master has no equitable indemnity claim against the seaman. However, if the injuries were also caused by third party negligence or product defect, the master could claim equitable indemnity from that third party.[15] Similarly, the manufacturer of a defective product will be denied a remedy of equitable indemnification against a husband for the payment of the wife's loss of consortium claim notwithstanding the manufacturer's claim that the husband's negligence, as the driver of the defective motor vehicle, was greater than the manufacturer's liability for product defect. The denial rests not upon the differing degrees of culpability, an abstract exercise in its own right, but on the fact that the wife cannot sue the husband for loss of consortium, therefore, the proposed indemnitor (husband) has no liability to which a claim of equitable indemnity by the manufacturer against the husband can attach.[16]

As a general rule, a claim for equitable or implied contractual indemnification does not accrue until the person seeking indemnification has paid

---

[12] City of Huntington Beach v. City of Westminster, 66 Cal. Rptr. 2d 826 (Cal. App. 1997):

> Rather than recognizing different forms of equitable indemnity, California has but a single comparative indemnity doctrine "which permits partial indemnification on a comparative fault basis in appropriate cases." Comparative equitable indemnity includes the entire range of possible apportionments—from no indemnity to total indemnity. Rather than being different in kind from comparative indemnity, total equitable indemnity is merely a possible result at one end of the spectrum when one party bears 100 percent of the fault and another bears none. Even with a total shifting of loss, "the indemnitee's equitable indemnity claim does not differ in its fundamental nature from other comparative equitable indemnity claims."

Id. at 828 (citations omitted). *See generally* J.R. Kemper, Annot., *Comment Note—Contribution or Indemnity Between Joint Tortfeasors on Basis of Relative Fault*, 53 A.L.R.3d 184 (1974).

[13] 46 U.S.C.A. § 688 *et seq.*

[14] California Home Brands, Inc. v. Ferriera, 871 F.2d 830, 833 (9th Cir. 1989).

[15] Cooper Stevedor Co. v. Fritz Kopke, Inc., 417 U.S. 106, 112–14 (1974).

[16] General Motors Corp. v. Doupnik, 1 F.3d 862, 866 (9th Cir. 1993) (involving manufacturer, which was found to be 20% liable for catastrophic injuries rendering husband quadriplegic). The manufacturer paid the entire loss of consortium claim of the wife and then sought equitable indemnification from the husband based on the finding that the husband was 80% responsible for his injuries. The court denied the remedy. *Cf.* United Pac. Ins. Co. v. Hanover Ins. Co., 266 Cal. Rptr. 231, 237 (Cal. App. 1990) (holding that equitable reapportionment doctrines would not be applied to shift liability to a party that had no liability under the insurance contracts in question).

the debt or discharged the obligation that is more justly owed by another.[17] Some courts, however, recognize an "interest of justice" exception that permits assertion of the claim *before* it has legallly accrued.[18] Under this approach, a claim for equitable indemnity may be pleaded and proved prior to accrual, although enforcement of the judgment will be stayed until payment or discharge is made.[19]

Equitable indemnity among joint tortfeasors is a difficult, complex area of the law. The interests in providing finality through settlements may conflict with the interests in allocating responsibility through equitable indemnity.[20] For example, to encourage settlement the jurisdiction may permit a defendant who enters into a "good faith" settlement to avoid claims for common law or statutory contribution or indemnity. This topic is outside the scope of this book, but exclusion from these materials does not mean that it can be excluded from consideration in practice. As noted by one commentator:

> Courts have expressed divergent views regarding the relative merits of the various state rules governing the interrelated issues of contribution and settlement. The chief motivation in fashioning these rules has been a desire to increase the likelihood that a particular rule will encourage the settlement and early resolution of the action. Yet, no strong consensus exists regarding the best method for achieving this result. Indeed, as this Paper will show, no single "magic" rule will satisfy all participants—plaintiffs, defendants, their attorneys, and the judicial system—in all circumstances.[21]

The reference in the quoted materials to "contribution" should not mislead. At common law, contribution permitted a pro rata (equal) sharing of the loss; indemnity was all or nothing. Contribution was, however, severely limited in its availability. With the advent of comparative fault, many jurisdictions have effectively melded contribution and indemnity into "equitable contribution." Again, the approach here is varied and unsystematic. Each jurisdiction's approach must be plumbed and generalizations must be cautious.

---

[17] State v. Syracuse Rigging Co., Inc., 671 N.Y.S.2d 801, 802 (App. Dep't 1998); General Acc. Ins. Co. of Am. v. Schoendorf & Sorgi, 537 N.W.2d 33, 38 (Wis. App. 1995); Dawson Lumber Sales, Inc. v. Bonneville Inv., Inc., 794 P.2d 11, 19 (Utah 1990).

[18] Fonda v. Paulsen, 363 N.Y.S.2d 841, 846 n.4 (App. Dept. 1975) (stating that a defendant could be kept in a lawsuit for purposes of a third party action, even though the action for indemnity had not accrued, in the interest of justice and judicial economy).

[19] Walker Mfg. Co. v. Dickerson, Inc., 510 F. Supp. 329, 331–32 (W.D.N.C. 1980), *aff'd*, 660 F.2d 494 (4th Cir. 1981) (Table); Adams v. Lindsay, 354 N.Y.S.2d 356, 358 (Sup. Ct. 1974).

[20] Bay Dev. Ltd. v. Superior Court, 791 P.2d 290 (Cal. 1990) (holding that a "good faith" settlement will bar all claims for contribution and indemnity against the settling party, except those claims based on express contractual indemnity). *But see* Medallion Dev. Inc. v. Converse Consultants, 930 P.2d 115, 119–20 (Nev. 1997) (permitting parties to bring claim of equitable indemnity against one another notwithstanding good faith settlement).

[21] Jean Eggen, *Understanding State Contribution Rules and Their Effect on the Settlement of Mass Tort Actions*, 73 Tex. L. Rev. 1701, 1702 (1995) (footnotes omitted).

§ 53 SUBROGATION

Subrogation is based on the principle that when A has paid to C the obligation of B, who is primarily liable to C, it is fair and just that A receive reimbursement from B, otherwise B would be unjustly enriched by the payment of its obligation to C. In the language of subrogation, the person who pays the obligation (A) is referred to as the subrogee, the person whose obligation is paid (B) is referred to as the subrogor.

Subrogation may be judicially created (legal subrogation) or may result from contract (conventional subrogation), e.g., insurance policy or settlement agreement.[1] Legal subrogation has its origin in equity.[2] Legal subrogation arises by operation of law. Conventional subrogation is based on contract or agreement; consequently, the right to conventional subrogation is governed by the agreement and the body of law that has developed in this field.[3] The relationship between legal and conventional subrogation is difficult. In some cases the two forms are treated as substantially identical; in other cases the two forms are treated as distant, albeit related, cousins. One important difference between legal and conventional subrogation is the volunteer rule. Legal subrogation, as a form of restitution, requires a showing of unjust enrichment. If the person discharging the debt or obligation acts as a volunteer or intermeddler, there is no unjust enrichment.[4] On the other hand, in cases of conventional subrogation, the right of subrogation is granted by the contract or agreement and exists irrespective of whether the payer acted to protect his own interest.[5] To avoid the volunteer tag in this setting, a court may require that the

---

[1] There are two other forms of subrogation: statutory subrogation and subrogation by assignment. Subrogation by assignment occurs when a person is contractually obligated to assign a claim to another. This is really a form of conventional subrogation. *See* Security Ins. Co. of New Haven v. Mangan, 242 A.2d 482, 485 n.7 (Md. 1968). Statutory subrogation may or may not provide broader remedies than its common law counterpart. Davis v. Idaho Dep't of Health and Welfare, 943 P.2d 59, 61–62 (Idaho App. 1997) (stating that statute entitled subrogee to priority claim to proceeds of settlement over subrogor).

[2] 1 GEORGE E. PALMER, LAW OF RESTITUTION § 1.5(b), at 21–22 (1978).

[3] Dade County Sch. Bd. v. Radio Station WQBA, 731 So.2d 638, 647 (Fla. 1999) (stating that conventional subrogation "depends upon a lawful contract, and occurs when one having no interest in or relation to the matter pays the debt of another and by agreement is entitled to the securities and rights of the creditor so paid").

[4] Rock River Lumber Corp. v. Universal Mortgage Co., 262 N.W.2d 114, 116 (Wis. 1978); Smith v. Sprague, 222 N.W. 207, 208 (Mich. 1928); Section 43.1 (The Volunteer Principle).

[5] *Security Ins. Co. of New Haven, supra,* 242 A.2d at 485–86. The court also noted:

> A conventional subrogee may maintain an action for a pro tanto recovery, which a legal subrogee, who must pay in full in order to establish his rights, can never do. The conventional subrogee is not necessarily entitled to subrogation as a matter of legal right if there are intervening equities and his rights may be limited or denied him by the terms of his agreement, or extinguished by his creditors [sic] course of conduct.

Id. at 486.

contractual obligation to pay be meaningful. If it is not, a court may deny subrogation notwithstanding the contractual right.[6]

Before one may assert a claim in subrogation, one must have paid the primarily liable party's debt, obligation, or loss. As noted in *Reliance Ins. Co. v. United States Bank of Wash., N.A.*:

> As of the time the bank received the money, and as of the time the bank setoff the progress payment against its loan to the contractor, the surety had not yet paid any subcontractors. Subrogation would mean that, having paid them, the surety would step into their shoes and take over their rights to recover the money they had been entitled to. But because the surety had not yet paid them, the unpaid subcontractors still owned the rights to payment. At common law, a surety does not become subrogated to its principal's right to payment from a third party until the surety performs the principal's obligation.[7]

[53.1] Derivative Claim

Subrogation is in function a form of equitable assignment; consequently, the subrogee's (assignee's) rights can rise no higher, nor be any greater, than those of the subrogor (assignor). This is often euphemistically referred to as "stepping into the shoes of." The effect of this principle is that the subrogee can recover only if, and only to the extent that, the subrogor could recover on the same claim.[8] Defenses available against the subrogor are generally available against the subrogee.[9] The subrogee must walk the

---

[6] Gearing v. Check Brokerage Corp., 233 F.3d 469, 472 (7th Cir. 2000) (holding that party that purchased checks under full recourse provision, which allowed party to return checks within 60 days with full cancellation rights, could not sue payor of checks as subrogee of payee). As noted by the court:

> Although Check Brokerage purchased Gearing's bad checks from Ayerco, it was not required to eat the checks if its collection efforts were unsuccessful. Indeed, the recourse provision granted Check Brokerage the absolute right to cancel its purchase of the checks after 60 days. This escape hatch shows that Check Brokerage did not act under any sort of "compulsion." It was a mere volunteer, and its claims to the contrary are illusory.

Id. (footnote omitted) (noting that failure of Check Brokerage to exercise its recourse rights did not change the result).

[7] 143 F.3d 502, 504 (9th Cir.) (citations omitted), *cert. denied*, 525 U.S. 964 (1998); *In re Southwest Equip. Rental, Inc.*, 193 B.R. 276, 283–84 (E.D. Tenn. 1996) (noting that in cases of legal subrogation, the entire debt must be paid before the party may equitably assert the rights of another); Copeland Enters. Inc. v. Slidell Mem'l Hosp., 657 So. 2d 1292, 1296 (La. 1995); Cook v. Cook, 174 P.2d 434, 436 (Utah 1946). Total payment of the debt may not be required in cases of conventional subrogation as a condition precedent to asserting rights in subrogation. *See* note 5, *supra*.

[8] Dix Mut. Ins. Co. v. La Framboise, 597 N.E.2d 622, 624 (Ill. 1992) (noting that "[o]ne who asserts a right of subrogation must step into the shoes of, or be substituted for, the one whose claim or debt he has paid and can only enforce those rights which the latter could enforce"); Section 53.4 (Loss of Subrogation Rights).

[9] Grinnell Mut. Reinsurance Co. v. Recker, 561 N.W.2d 63, 70–71 (Iowa 1997) (noting that subrogors settlement with tortfeasors barred subrogation claim against those same tortfeasors); *cf.* Century 21 Prods., Inc. v. Glacier Sales, 918 P.2d 168 (Wash. 1996):

subrogor's walk in the subrogor's shoes, not a different pair. If that fit is uncomfortable, it is all that subrogation provides.

The subrogee can assert all of the subrogor's rights. If the subrogated claim involves a contract that contains an attorneys fees provision, the subrogee may avail itself of that provision.[10] Of course, the doctrine works both ways, if the subrogee litigates and loses, the attorneys fees provision may be asserted against it.[11]

Subrogation entails the assertion of another's right. If the "subrogee" acted to discharge her own obligation she may be denied the right to seek subrogation if the debt the "subrogee" discharges is separate and distinct from the debt owed by the "subrogor," even though the beneficiary of the payment is the same person.[12] This concept should not be misunderstood. The insurer who pays the insured's loss pays an obligation it owes under the insurance contract; yet, the insurer may seek reimbursement from the tortfeasor under principles of subrogation. This distinction is that the insurer does not have a separate, independent obligation. The insurer's obligation is secondary to that of the tortfeasor who is the wrongdoer and thus primarily responsible for the loss. The distinction is fine, but significant and is addressed in Section 53.2 ("Superior Equities" Principle).

[53.2] "Superior Equities" Principle

The ability to assert the claim of another through subrogation may be subordinated to the "superior equities" doctrine. This doctrine holds that the right of subrogation "may be invoked against a third party only if he

---

> In order to enforce a guarantor's obligation, a creditor generally must not impair the collateral. In other words, if collateral is provided, the creditor cannot diminish or sacrifice it and then demand that a guarantor meet its obligation to the creditor. The defense of impairment of collateral is based on equitable considerations and promotes a guarantor's right of subrogation: a guarantor has the right to step into the shoes of the creditor and sue the debtor for collateral securing the debt. If the creditor has impaired this collateral, then the guarantor is denied the right of subrogation. By impairing the collateral, a creditor prevents a guarantor from suing the debtor to recover the collateral.

Id. at 170 (citations omitted).

[10] Rushing v. Inten. Aviation Underwriters, 604 S.W.2d 239, 243–44 (Tex. Civ. App. 1980).

[11] Allstate Ins. Co. v. Loo, 54 Cal. Rptr. 2d 541, 544 (Cal. App. 1996).

[12] Nova Information Systems v. Greenwich Ins. Co., 365 F.3d 996, 1005–06 (11th Cir. 2004). The facts of the case are somewhat complex, but interesting. *Nova Information Systems* involved a bankrupt cruise line and passengers who wanted refunds for pre-paid cruises that never occurred. The passenger payments were made by credit card and the payments were guaranteed by the cruise line's insurer. The "subrogee" processed the credit card transactions for the cruise line's bank. When the bank reimbursed the passengers, the "subrogee" reimbursed the bank under the contract between the parties. The "subrogee" then sought reimbursement for itself and eyed the cruise line's insurer that had posted a bond for the cruise line. The court refused to permit subrogation against the insurer holding that the obligations were separate and distinct. The "subrogee" had discharged its own obligation to the bank pursuant to its contract and could not shift that obligation to the cruise line's insurer by invoking legal subrogation.

is guilty of some wrongful conduct which makes his equity inferior to that of the [subrogee]."[13] This rule applies when an insurer has paid its insured's losses and seeks recovery against a third party tortfeasor. For example, a tortfeasor causes property damage to the victim's motor vehicle. The victim receives $20,000 from his insurance company to cover the losses sustained as a result of the property damage. The insurance company is now subrogated to the claim of the victim and may obtain recovery of the $20,000 from the tortfeasor. Under this approach, the victim is made whole, the risk of loss and litigation is borne by the insurance company, and the tortfeasor avoids reaping a windfall from the victim's prudence in having obtained insurance. In this situation, it is more equitable that the loss (payment for damage to the motor vehicle) be borne by the tortfeasor rather than the insurance company; hence; the concept that the company has the better claim vis-a-vis the tortfeasor ("superior equities") to reimbursement.[14]

This concept of "superior equities" helps define when subrogation is warranted. A party that discharges or pays in full a debt of another *and* does so in order to protect its own legal rights, e.g., to fulfill a contractual obligation of indemnification it has with its payee or pursuant to the request of the original, primary debtor,[15] possesses a superior claim to reimbursement from the original, primary debtor than that debtor has in escaping responsibility for payment of the initial debt. If the original, primary debtor were not required to reimburse the payor, that debtor would be unjustly enriched. On the other hand, when the party seeking reimbursement is as responsible for the debt as the original debtor, the equities are in equipoise and denial of reimbursement is not seen as resulting in that debtor's unjust enrichment.[16]

[53.3] Priorities

The subrogee may be required, or desire, to stand aside and permit the subrogor to prosecute the claim. This may result (1) because of public policy restrictions on the assignment of claims,[17] (2) because the subrogee did not

---

[13] Golden Eagle Ins. Co. v. First Nationwide Fin. Corp., 31 Cal. Rptr. 2d 815, 822–23 (Cal. App. 1994) (brackets added). *But see* National Union Fire Ins. Co. of Pittsburgh, Pa v. Riggs Na'l Bank of Wash., D.C., 646 A.2d 966, 979 (D.C. App. 1994) (holding that doctrine of superior equities did not apply in conventional, as opposed to legal, subrogation cases). The *National Union* opinion collects decisions discussing the issue.

[14] The equities here are similar to those identified in connection with the application of the Collateral Source Rule. Section 15 (Collateral Source Rule). A mutual goal of the two doctrines is to assign the risk and responsibility for the loss to the most deserving party—the tortfeasor.

[15] St. Paul Fire & Marine Ins. Co. v. Murray Guard, Inc., 37 S.W.3d 180, 183 (Ark. 2001).

[16] Meridian Title Ins. Co. v. Lilly Homes, Inc., 735 F. Supp. 182, 186 (E.D. Va. 1990) (denying subrogation when subrogee was separately and independently responsible for the debt it paid), *aff'd*, 934 F.2d 319 (4th Cir. 1991) (Table).

[17] Block v. California Physicians' Service, 53 Cal. Rptr. 51, 53 (Cal. App. 1966) (noting that "it is the established rule in California that an assignment of a cause of action for personal injuries is void and that, in the absence of a statute, a cause of action for tortious injury to the person is not subject to subrogation") (citations omitted). *See generally* Andrea Nadel,

pay the loss in full,[18] or (3) because, for tactical reasons, the subrogee prefers that the claim be brought in the name of the subrogor.[19]

[53.3.1] Make Whole Requirement

When the subrogor has not been made whole, notwithstanding the payment by the subrogee, claims over priority may arise as to monies subsequently received from third persons. The subrogor (victim) wishes a preference to the monies to make itself whole; the subrogee wishes a preference to make itself whole. Who gets made whole first? There are several approaches to the problem.

One approach permits the subrogee to be made whole first. This approach usually relies on conventional rather than legal subrogation because the subrogee's preference is provided for by contract language.[20] A second approach requires the subrogor be made whole before the subrogee may claim any of the additional monies.[21] This second approach relies on the general rule that the right to subrogation does not exist until the underlying "debt" is fully discharged. It is usually identified as the dominant rule,[22] but the situations involving subrogation are so varied that generalizations on this point must be cautious. The jurisdictions are split as to whether the subrogee may specifically contract for a priority over the subrogor. Jurisdictions that permit the subrogee to claim a priority emphasize freedom of contract.[23] This approach is claimed to be more efficient than

---

Annot., *Assignability of Proceeds of Claim for Personal Injury or Death*, 33 A.L.R.4th 82 (1981), at § 2 (noting that general rule is to bar assignment of personal injury claims prior to judgment).

[18] Section 53.3.1 (Make Whole Requirement).

[19] June Entman, *More Reasons For Abolishing Federal Rule of Civil Procedure 17(a): The Problem of Proper Plaintiff and Insurance Subrogation*, 68 N.C. L. Rev. 893, 896 (1990) (noting the conventional wisdom that insurers prefer not to be identified as party plaintiffs because of jury prejudice against insurers). A number of devices are used to allow the insurer to litigate in the name of the insured. *Id.* at 925 (discussing use of "loan receipts").

[20] Peterson v. Ohio Farmers Ins. Co., 191 N.E.2d 157 (Ohio 1963):

> In summary then, we conclude that, where the policy subrogation provisions and the subrogation assignment to the insurer convey all right of recovery against any third-party wrongdoer to the extent of the payment by the insurer to the insured, the insurer, who has cooperated and assisted in proceedings against the wrongdoer, is entitled to be indemnified first out of the proceeds of any recovery against the wrongdoer.

Id. at 159–60.

[21] Sapiano v. Williamsburg Nat'l Ins. Co., 33 Cal. Rptr. 2d 659 (Cal. App. 1994) (holding that the insurer, which had paid policy limits for property damage to the plaintiff-insured's motor vehicle, must hold its subrogation claim against tortfeasor in abeyance until the plaintiff's property damage was fully remedied); *cf.* Wimberly v. American Cas. Co. of Reading, Penn. (CNA), 584 S.W.2d 200, 203 (Tenn. 1979) (holding that subrogor (insured) was entitled to be made whole, notwithstanding assignment through conventional subrogation of all of the subrogor's rights against the tortfeasor to the subrogee (insurer)).

[22] 16 COUCH ON INSURANCE § 223:134 (3d ed. 1997).

[23] *Sapiano, supra*, 33 Cal. Rptr. 2d at 661–62 (assuming that parties could explicitly provide

the subrogor preference approach.[24] The contrary approach, which denies subrogee preference, even in the context of a specific contract right to priority, emphasizes the equitable nature of the action:

> It is our conclusion that the equitable nature of subrogation requires that no distinction need be made between equitable and conventional rights of subrogation. An insured's right to subrogation takes precedent over that of an insurer, so the insured must be wholly compensated before an insurer's right to subrogation arises; therefore, the insurer's right to subrogation arises only in situations where the recovery by the insured exceeds his or her total amount of damages incurred.[25]

This approach has been extended by some courts to employee benefits.[26] A contractual provision for subrogee priority will usually encounter strict construction.[27]

[53.3.2] Settlement or Compromise

Priority issues are further complicated when the subrogor receives funds, in which the subrogee claims an interest, and the subrogor contends that the additional funds reflect a compromise; thus, even with the additional funds, the subrogor has not been made whole. This situation arose in *Associated Hospital Service of Philadelphia v. Pustilnik*.[28] Pustilnik was injured when he was struck by a subway car operated by SEPTA. He incurred medical treatment expenses as a result of his injuries of $30,200.87. His health insurer paid $18,960, pursuant to its contractual obligations to Pustilnik. Pustilnik sued SEPTA for his personal injuries. On the 5th day of trial, Pustilnik and SEPTA settled for $235,000. The insurer made a claim for reimbursement. Pustilnik contended that the settlement reflected

---

in their contract that the subrogee (insurer) would have a priority regardless whether the subrogor (insured) was first made whole); Samura v. Kaiser Foundation Health Plain, Inc., 22 Cal. Rptr. 2d 20 (Cal. App. 1993) (enforcing explicit contract language giving subrogee a priority over subrogor and rejecting challenge that priority constituted unfair business practice).

[24] Alan O. Sykes, *Subrogation and Insolvency*, 30 J. Legal Studies 383 (2001) (arguing that the subrogor "make whole" rule is inefficient in the context of a partially insolvent tortfeasor).

[25] Franklin v. Healthsource of Ark., 942 S.W.2d 837, 844 (Ark. 1997) (relying on fact that insurance contracts are "adhesion contracts" and that the insurer (subrogee) had been adequately protected against the risk of loss by the premium it received); *see* Hare v. State, 733 So.2d 277 (Miss. 1999) (same).

[26] Hiney Printing Co. v. Brantner, 243 F.3d 956 (6th Cir. 2001) (applying subrogor make whole rule to ERISA plan that contained express subrogee priority term).

[27] *Sapiano, supra*, 33 Cal. Rptr. 2d at 661 (stating that "[a]lthough insurers may place subrogation clauses in their policies, those provisions typically are general and add nothing to the rights of subrogation arising by law") (citations omitted); Medical Ctrs. Health Care v. Ochs, 854 F. Supp. 589, 592 (D. Minn. 1993) (stating that "Minnesota's full recovery rule requires that the subrogation clause must be explicit regarding priority of payments (and the plan's recovery regardless of full recovery) or the full recovery rule will bar subrogation"), *aff'd*, 26 F.3d 865 (8th Cir. 1994) (parentheses added); note 25, *supra*.

[28] 396 A.2d 1332 (Pa. Super. Ct. 1979), *vacated on other grounds*, 439 A.2d 1149 (Pa. 1981).

the discounted value of his claim; therefore, he had not been made whole and the claim for reimbursement was premature.[29]

A critical issue was whether Pustilnik was bound by his settlement as to the amount of his loss for "make whole" purposes. The court stated that he was:

> The trial court also erred in reducing Blue Cross' recovery by 50% on the grounds that Pustilnik had settled with SEPTA for less than the full value of his claim. In *Illinois Automobile Insurance Exchange v. Braun*, the [Pennsylvania] Supreme Court held that when a subrogor settles instead of pressing his suit against an alleged tortfeasor to verdict, he cannot defeat a subrogee's claim by asserting that his loss exceeded the settlement recovery. Sound policy requires this result. It is of course possible that in some cases a subrogor will be well advised to settle for substantially less than his claim because of the tenuous proof establishing the alleged tortfeasor's liability. This possibility, however, does not imply that the subrogor should be permitted to assert against the subrogee that after all, his claim against the tortfeasor really was worth more than he had settled for which is what the trial court permitted to happen here. Such a procedure would encourage unethical practice, if not perjured testimony: a representation in the court where the suit against the tortfeasor was tried that the case for liability was strong, to obtain a high settlement, followed by a representation in the court where the subrogation claim was tried that the case for liability was weak. Liability should be determined, whenever possible, in one proceeding. When a subrogor settles, he waives his right to a judicial determination of his losses, and conclusively establishes the settlement amount as full compensation for his damages.[30]

A contrary approach was advanced in *Rimes v. State Farm Mut. Auto. Ins. Co.*[31] In *Rimes* the plaintiff was injured in a multi-vehicle accident. Rimes ultimately settled his claims on the second day of trial. The settlement included a $50,000 policy limits payment from one defendant and a $75,000 payment, out of $300,000 policy limits, from the other defendant. The plaintiff and his subrogated insurer then agreed to a trial regarding the insurer's claim for reimbursement. The court held a trial and determined that the plaintiff's total damages exceeded $300,000. Because the settlement fell short of that amount, the trial court denied reimbursement.

On appeal, the Wisconsin Supreme Court affirmed the trial court's ruling. The court noted that the settlement did not state that the settlement had made the plaintiff whole and the evidence indicated that the plaintiff did not consider himself to have been made whole by the settlement. The court stated:

---

[29] *Id.* at 1334.

[30] 396 A.2d at 1337 (citation omitted; brackets added).

[31] 316 N.W.2d 348 (Wis. 1982).

Under Wisconsin law the test of wholeness depends upon whether the insured has been completely compensated for all the elements of damages, not merely those damages for which the insurer has indemnified the insured. Thus the mere fact that the settlement figure of $125,000 exceeded the insurer's claim for subrogation is immaterial. The injured or aggrieved party is not made whole unless all his damages arising out of a tort have been fully compensated.[32]

While some jurisdictions seemingly embrace the position that the settlement is not conclusive on the "make whole" issue,[33] many jurisdictions either disagree (as in *Pustilnik*) or adopt a qualified approach that may permit the subrogor some leeway to contend that he has not been made whole by the settlement.[34]

A related issue here is allocation. If the settlement is for a lump sum, it may require a hearing or mini-trial to determine what portion, if any, should be identified and credited to the subrogated claim. For example, if the subrogee is entitled to reimbursement of medical expenses, should reimbursement be made against the entire settlement or award, or only that portion that reflects compensation for medical expenses?[35]

[53.4]   Loss of Subrogation Rights

Subrogation rights are derivative; therefore, the subrogee may lose its claim because the subrogor has no claim. Perhaps the most common way in which this happens is when the subrogor enters into some form of pre-loss exculpatory or indemnity agreement with the tortfeasor. For example, a subcontractor may agree to hold the contractor harmless from the contractor's negligence. The contractor then negligently causes the subcontractor to incur a loss, which the subcontractor's insurer pays. If the insurer attempts to assert a claim in subrogation against the contractor, the claim will fail. The insurer's (subrogee's) claim is no stronger than the subcontractor's (subrogor's) claim and that claim is barred by the exculpatory agreement.

When a party has contractually agreed to subrogation, that party may commit a breach of contract if she causes the other party to the contract

---

[32] *Id.* at 355.

[33] *Rimes, supra*; Powell v. Blue Cross and Blue Shield of Ala., 581 So. 2d 772 (Ala. 1990).

[34] Esparza v. Scott and White Health Plan, 909 S.W.2d 548, 552–53 (Tex. Civ. App. 1995) (stating that contrary positions "underscore the conflict of interests in subrogation which cannot be resolved by a bright-line test that curtails a trial court's discretion to apply equity based on the facts of the case").

[35] Ludwig v. Farm Bureau Mut. Ins. Co., 393 N.W.2d 143 (Iowa 1986):

> Allocation of the separate amounts could be done in the settlement documents, as in this case. In the case of trial it could be done by special interrogatories, or by separate findings by the court in a non-jury case.

Id. at 146 (citations and footnote omitted). Section 17.3 ([Tax Consequences] Effect of Settlement Allocation).

to lose his subrogation rights.[36] There is, however, a strong presumption against a finding of breach.[37]

Priority issues also arise in commercial and consumer contexts. A junior creditor may discharge a senior lien to prevent the senior creditor from foreclosing and extinguishing the junior's interest. The junior is protecting its interest and would not be deemed a volunteer; nonetheless, the question arises as to the status of the junior's claim for reimbursement. Is it subject to a homestead exemption that does not apply to the senior debt but does apply to the junior debt? If the senior debt is collateralized, but the junior debt is not, is the reimbursement claim collateralized?

When a debt is discharged under circumstances that give rise to a right of subrogation, the general rule is to vest the subrogee with all the rights and privileges of the subrogor, at least to the amount of the payment for which reimbursement is sought.[38] In this context, subrogation may allow the subrogee to avoid homestead rights[39] or tax liens,[40] that would not attach to the senior creditor's rights.

[53.5] Duties to Fund Creators

When the subrogee claims an interest in a fund created by others, the subrogee may be required to pay the fund's creator the reasonable value of her services, else the subrogee would be unjustly enriched. The most common example of this is when the subrogee had furnished medical benefits to the subrogor. The subrogor then retained an attorney, and brought a personal injury action against the tortfeasor. When that claim is resolved, the subrogee may seek reimbursement against the fund

---

[36] Great Northern Oil Co. v. St. Paul Fire & Marine Ins. Co., 189 N.W.2d 404, 406–07 (Minn. 1971) (collecting decisions and discussing various approaches).

[37] Continental Cas. Co. v. Homontowski, 510 N.W.2d 743, 746 (Wis. App. 1993) (holding that contractual language that required insured to "secure [insurer's] rights and do nothing to impair those rights after a loss occurred" did not prohibit the insured from affecting those rights at anytime). The court stated that if the insurer wanted to bar pre-loss acts that caused the insurer to lose its subrogation rights, then the insurer must use explicit language. *See* Hendershot v. Charleston Nat'l Bank, 563 N.E.2d 546 (Ind. 1990) (holding that compromise between subrogor and third party did not defeat subrogee's subrogation rights against the third party notwithstanding that compromise provided that it constituted full settlement of claim). The court stated:

> We believe that focusing on words like "full satisfaction" and "final release" in an agreement between creditor and debtor wrongly ignores the reservation of rights against the surety. When the creditor clearly reserves his rights against the surety, the debtor is notified that the release is no more than a covenant not to sue. Consequently, the principal debt remains alive, the surety's rights to reimbursement and subrogation are unimpaired, and the surety is not discharged.

Id. at 549 (citations omitted).

[38] Newberry v. Scruggs, 986 S.W.2d 2d 853, 857 (Ark. 1999); East Boston Sav. Bank v. Ogan, 701 N.E.2d 331, 333–35 (Mass. 1998).

[39] Vogel v. Veneman, 276 F.3d 729, 735 (5th Cir. 2002).

[40] Han v. United States, 944 F.2d 526, 529–30 (9th Cir. 1991).

generated by the subrogor's personal injury action. To what extent, if at all, should the costs of the attorney's retention be borne by the subrogee?

Courts have split whether the subrogee should bear a portion of those costs in this setting. As noted in *Travelers Insurance Co. v. Williams*:

> There are, of course, many situations in which the work of an attorney proves useful to persons other than his own client. The normal rule in such cases is that he must look only to his client, with whom he has contracted, for his compensation, notwithstanding the acceptance of benefits by others. But, an exception to this rule is made whenever one person, having assumed the risks and expense of litigation, has succeeded in securing, augmenting, or preserving property or a fund of money in which other people are entitled to share in common. In that event, the expenses of the action are borne by each participant according to his interest. The fairest and most efficient means of distributing these costs is thought to be to make them a charge upon the fund itself. This device, known as the "fund doctrine," was invented by courts of equity to prevent passive beneficiaries of the fund from being unjustly enriched. It is, therefore, never applied against persons who have employed counsel on their own account to represent their interests. Thus, the right to employ counsel of one's own choosing is preserved.
>
> Varied fact situations are disclosed by the reported cases dealing with the problem. We doubt the advisability of attempting to devise a single "rule" to govern all such cases, whatever the facts might be. Instead, each case, with its peculiar facts must be decided by applying general, fundamental principles of contract law.
>
> It follows that whether or not an attorney is entitled to collect from the insurer a fee with respect to a subrogation claim depends upon whether an express or implied contract or a quasi contractual relation exits between them.[41]

The application of common fund doctrine to personal injury action is not recognized in all jurisdictions.[42]

The subrogor's right to reimbursement is dependent on the recognition of a benefit to the subrogee flowing from the subrogor's actions. Normally, this benefit will be expenses avoided, primarily attorneys fees. The subrogee may contend that the subrogor's litigation expenses were unnecessary or unreasonable.[43] Generally, these issues must be resolved on a case-by-case

---

[41] 541 S.W.2d 587, 589–90 (Tenn. 1976) (citations omitted).

[42] *See* Lovett v. Carrasco, 73 Cal. Rptr. 2d 496, 499–501 (Cal. App. 1998) (rejecting recovery of attorney's fees because retainer agreement with client fully compensated lawyer for services provided; therefore, third party was not unjustly enriched); White v. St. Alphonsus Reg. Med. Ct., 31 P.3d 926, 932 (Idaho App. 2001) (collecting decisions); ROBERT L. ROSSI, ATTORNEYS' FEES § 7:20 (Insurance Subrogation) (3d ed. 2003) (collecting decisions).

[43] Jennings v. Nationwide Ins. Co., 669 A.2d 534, 535–36 (R.I. 1996).

basis. In some cases, however, the court will excuse the subrogee from any duty to effect restitution to a litigation fund creator, as, for example, when inexpensive alternatives to litigation are available to the subrogee.[44]

§ 54 CONSTRUCTIVE TRUST

A constructive trust is an equitable remedy that provides for specific restitution, *i.e.*, return or restoration of property that has been wrongfully acquired by the defendant.[1] The defendant is said to hold the property involuntarily "as a trustee" for the benefit of the person with a superior equitable claim to the property. In the often repeated words of Justice Cardozo, the constructive trust was described as follows:

> A constructive trust is the formula through which the conscience of equity finds expression. When property has been acquired in such circumstances that the holder of legal title may not in good conscience retain the beneficial interest, equity converts him into a trustee.[2]

A constructive trust confers on the non-possessory but rightful owner of property an equitable interest superior to that of the non-owning, wrongful possessor of the property.[3] Unlike an express trust, a constructive trust does not arise because of an intent to create it. It is just to the contrary. A constructive trust is imposed by law to prevent the possessor's unjust enrichment that would result were the possessor allowed to retain title and possession.[4]

[54.1] Trust By Analogy or Metaphor

A constructive trust is a remedy, not a trust. The reference to "trust" is metaphorical:

---

[44] Cockman v. State Farm Auto. Ins. Co., 854 S.W.2d 343, 345 (Ark. 1993) (noting that inter-insurer agreement obligated insurers to arbitrate all claims involving physical damage to motor vehicles; hence, the insurer-subrogor's efforts to litigate property damage claims against the insured tortfeasor violated the arbitration agreement).

[1] Covert v. Nashville, C. & St. L. Ry., 208 S.W.2d 1008 (Tenn. 1948):

> [A constructive trust] arises contrary to the intention and in invitum, against one who, by fraud, actual or constructive, by duress or abuse of confidence, by commission of wrong, or by any form of unconscionable conduct, artifice, concealment, or questionable means, or who in any way against equity and in good conscience, either has obtained or holds the legal right to property which he ought not, in equity and good conscience, hold and enjoy.

Id. at 1012.

[2] Beatty v. Guggenheim Exploration Co., 122 N.E. 378, 380 (N.Y. 1919).

[3] *In re* N.S. Garrett & Sons, 772 F.2d 462, 467 (8th Cir. 1985).

[4] Omohundro v. Mathews, 341 S.W.2d 401, 405 (Tex. 1960).

> An express trust and a constructive trust are not divisions of the same fundamental concept. They are not species of the same genus.[5]

This American approach represents a change from the English rule.[6] A constructive trust is not a resulting trust. A resulting trust arises out of the "intent" of the parties.[7] Because a resulting trust arises by implication, rather than express agreement, the distinctions between resulting trust and a constructive trust may appear minor. Courts appear to confuse the matter by stating that resulting trusts arise by "operation of law."[8] The language must be understood in the context of the case. The law effectuates the parties' intent when it recognizes a resulting trust. A constructive trust does not arise out of the parties' intent; indeed the exact opposite is often the case: a constructive trust is used to remedy a party's attempt to defraud another.[9] Much like a quasi contract is a fictional contract, a constructive trust is a fictional trust.[10] The terminology is used to impress upon judges the realization that the defendant, who wrongfully acquires property, holds the property for another, much like a real trustee holds property for another—the beneficiary. And just as an equity court may require that the trustee transfer the trust corpus to the beneficiary, an equity court may

---

[5] Restatement of Restitution § 160 cmt. a (1937) (noting that "[t]he term 'constructive trust' is not altogether a felicitous one").

[6] H. Jefferson Powell, *"Cardozo's Foot": The Chancellor's Conscience and Constructive Trusts*, 56 Law & Contemp. Probs. 7 (1993):

> Although both U.S. and English lawyers are familiar with the term "constructive trust," as is so often the case similar language disguises substantive differences. English law has always thought of the constructive trust as an institution . . . as opposed to the American attitude that the constructive trust is purely a remedial device. The English constructive trust is a trust, or at least something very much like one; as understood in most U.S. courts, the constructive trust is a remedy, available whenever specific restitution in equity is appropriate on the facts. These divergent uses of the same term can be understood only in the light of the two societies' diverging legal histories.

Id. at 9 (quotation marks deleted).

[7] Scott v. Commissioner of Internal Revenue, 226 F.3d 871 (7th Cir. 2000) (applying Illinois law):

> [A] resulting trust is established when one person furnishes consideration for property and title is taken in the name of someone else with the intent that the person furnishing consideration retains beneficial ownership of the property. The pivotal question in determining whether a resulting trust has been created is "whether the nominal purchaser intended the actual payor to have an ownership interest in the good."

Id. at 874 (citations omitted).

[8] Wait v. Cornette, 612 N.W.2d 905, 911 (Neb. 2000).

[9] American Nat'l Bank & Trust Co. v. United States, 832 F.2d 1032, 1035 (7th Cir. 1987) ("A resulting trust, unlike a constructive trust, seeks to carry out a donative intention rather than thwart a wicked scheme"); Martin v. Kehl, 193 Cal. Rptr. 312, 317–18 (Cal. App. 1983).

[10] Shaffer v. Lambie, 667 N.E.2d 226, 229 (Ind. App. 1996) (stating that "[a] constructive trust is a fiction of equity, devised for the purpose of making equitable remedies available against one who through . . . wrongful means acquires property of another"); *see* BOGERT'S, THE LAW OF TRUSTS AND TRUSTEES § 471 (rev. 2d ed. 1992).

require that the defendant, who has wrongfully acquired property, transfer the property to the party with a superior equitable claim.

The inability (or refusal) to distinguish remedy from trust has led to substantial confusion and conflicting precedent. For example, early on many courts took the view that a constructive trust would not lie against a thief. The rationale was both legalistic and simplistic. A real trustee has title, a thief cannot have title; therefore, a thief cannot be a trustee, real or constructive.[11] Alternatively, some courts simply held that a constructive trust could only be imposed on a fiduciary.[12] The fault line in the process was the failure to realize that the purpose for referencing to trusts, trustees, and trust law in developing the constructive trust doctrine was not to create a new form of trust, but to recognize a remedy to avoid unjust enrichment. A person is unjustly enriched by thievery as by other forms of misconduct, such as fraud, which operate to confer at least a voidable title. Denying the plaintiff an equitable remedy simply because the defendant acquired a void rather than voidable title makes no sense, and the weight of modern authorities so hold.[13]

Recognizing that a constructive trust is a remedy not a real trust also affects the defendant's duties while he is in possession of property subject to the constructive trust. A trustee hold the trust corpus for the use and benefit of the trust beneficiaries. This fiduciary obligation imposes substantial duties of care and management on the trustee, the breach of which may result in substantial personal liability. A constructive trustee is not a real trustee but a fictional trustee; therefore, he is generally not held to owe anyone, in his capacity as a constructive trustee, fiduciary duties of care and management of property subject to a constructive trust.[14] Judge Hand, concurring in *Marcus v. Otis*, noted that a person might be both a real and a constructive trustee:

> We all agree that the defendants, as "constructive trustees," are not subject to the same measure of damages as though they had converted the shares; and my brothers hold that their liability does not go beyond the actual profits which they have made. They regard Automatics' right to follow the converted funds into the shares as a remedy for the conversion no different because the wrongdoers were also fiduciaries. They think that, although the victim may trace his money into any substitute into which the wrongdoer may have changed it, and reclaim it though it had remained in specie,

[11] *See generally* J.A. Bryant, Annot., *Imposition of Constructive Trust In Property Brought With Stolen or Embezzled Funds*, 38 A.L.R.3d 1354 § 4 (1972) (discussing early cases denying constructive trust when property acquired by theft.).

[12] Banton v. Hackney, 557 So. 2d 807, 820 (Ala. 1989) (noting early authorities limiting constructive trust to misappropriation by fiduciaries). *But see* Koffman v. Smith, 682 A.2d 1282, 1291 (Pa. Super. Ct. 1996) (collecting modern authorities imposing constructive trust notwithstanding absence of fiduciary relationship).

[13] Nannow Corp. v. Egger, 668 P.2d 265, 267 (Nev. 1983). *See generally* J.A. Bryant, Annot., *Imposition of Constructive Trust, supra*, 38 A.L.R. 3d 1354.

[14] Marcus v. Otis, 168 F.2d 649 (2d Cir. 1948).

the law does not in addition impose upon him, even though he be a fiduciary, any of those duties as to the substitute which he would have been under, had the substitute been part of the trust res. It follows that the liability of the defendants at bar must be limited to their actual profits; and, in the case of those who may not have sold the shares, to a return of these and any dividends received, upon payment of $1.20 a share.[15]

Judge Hand raised the above criticism because he believed that the defendant's status as corporate fiduciaries continued after they appropriated the corporate opportunity (stock) on which the lost profits claim was based. Judge Hand did not disagree with the majority's view that constructive trustees do not have a duty to care for or manage the property subject to a constructive trust; rather, he believed, on the facts, that the defendants' fiduciary duties continued to apply after the sale to them of the corporate opportunity property. The position taken in *Marcus v. Otis* was also taken by the Restatement.[16]

Occasionally, there is language in the decisional law suggesting that a constructive trustee has a fiduciary duty of care toward the property impressed with a constructive trust.[17] The language cannot be based on the idea that a constructive trustee has "fiduciary" duties, for those duties would require a real trust or a confidential relationship. In *Elliot* the facts were that the defendant deliberately acted to render worthless the plaintiff interest in property held by the defendant. The property was a note and a marital asset held by the ex-husband defendant, who refused to enforce the note until the debtor could invoke the statute of limitations as a bar.[18] In *David v. Russo* the constructive trustee's obligations were effectively the same as a command not to commit "waste."[19] In both cases, the reference to the constructive trustee's *duties* added little to the defendant's legal obligations that otherwise would have been imposed by other law.

[54.2] Elements of Constructive Trust

The imposition of a constructive trust requires: (1) a wrongful act; (2) specific property acquired by the wrongdoer that is traceable to the wrongful behavior; and (3) an equitable reason why the person now holding

---

[15] *Id.* at 657.

[16] Restatement of Restitution § 160 cmt. a (1937) (noting that a "constructive trust, unlike an express trust, is not a fiduciary relation. . . .").

[17] Elliott v. Elliott, 41 Cal. Rptr. 686, 688 (Cal. App. 1964) (stating that "[t]he constructive trust is a remedial device which would lose its efficacy if a trustee were permitted to defeat recovery by wrongfully permitting the res to become valueless . . ."); David v. Russo, 456 N.E.2d 342, 347–48 (Ill. App. 1983) (holding that a constructive trustee must act prudently in caring for and maintaining the property).

[18] 41 Cal. Rptr. at 688 (observing that defendant exercised exclusive control over the note and invoked a judicial stay to prevent the plaintiff from enforcing the note before the limitations period expired).

[19] 456 N.E.2d at 346.

the property should not be allowed to keep or retain possession of the property.[20]

The reference to "wrongful act" in the definition, while commonplace, can be misinterpreted. Some decisions appear to limit the remedy of constructive trust to egregious misbehavior, such as fraud,[21] or breach of a fiduciary or confidential relationship;[22] however, most jurisdictions construe "wrongful" liberally. A constructive trust may be imposed when, due to mistake or breach of contract, unjust enrichment has resulted.[23] A constructive trust has been imposed based on simple negligence.[24]

While some degree of wrongdoing is a necessary element of the remedy of constructive trust, it is not required that the wrongdoing be by the constructive trustee, *i.e.*, the person presently having possession of the property. As noted in *Simonds v. Simonds*:

> Unjust enrichment, however, does not require the performance of any wrongful act by the one enriched. Innocent parties may frequently be unjustly enriched. What is required generally is that the party hold property under such circumstances that in equity and good conscience he ought not to retain it.[25]

---

[20] *In re* Independent Clearing House Co., 41 B.R. 985, 1000 (D. Utah 1984).

[21] *In re* North Am. Coin & Currency, Ltd., 767 F.2d 1573, 1575 (9th Cir.), *as amended,* 774 F.2d 1390) (1985), *cert. denied,* 475 U.S. 1083 (1986) (stating that under Arizona law only active misconduct will support the imposition of a constructive trust); Greenly v. Greenly, 49 A.2d 126, 129 (Del. Ch. 1946) (stating that in order to impose a constructive trust "[s]ome fraudulent or unfair or unconscionable conduct is essential").

[22] Meadows v. Bierschwale, 516 S.W.2d 125, 128 (Tex. 1974).

[23] Berger v. Cas' Feed Store, Inc., 577 N.W.2d 631, 632 (Iowa 1998) (noting that a constructive trust may be based "on equitable principles other than fraud," which may include: "bad faith duress, coercion, undue influence, abuse of confidence, or any form of unconscionable conduct or questionable means by which one obtains the legal right to property which they should not in equity and good conscience hold"); Prince v. Bryant, 275 N.W.2d 676, 680 (Wis. 1979) (stating that "[e]ven if we were to assume that Prince's conduct was entirely innocent and the change in beneficiary was made in the honest mistaken belief that such an act was permissible, it would not necessarily follow that a constructive trust could not be imposed. Mistake may be sufficient to impose a constructive trust"); Rubenstein v. Mueller, 225 N.E.2d 540, 542–43 (N.Y. 1967), *remanded on other grounds* (imposing a constructive trust on property that passed under a second will that violated terms of an earlier will that had become irrevocable). *But cf.* In re Vappi & Co., Inc., 145 B.R. 719 (Bankr. D. Mass 1992):

> [T]he circumstances under which courts declare constructive trusts must involve fraud, mistake, duress, undue influence, breach of a fiduciary duty or prevention of unjust enrichment. Clearly, and the Court so holds, breach of contract alone does not justify the imposition of a constructive trust. Moreover, [the creditor] has failed to cite one case in which a court in the absence of a suretyship relationship or statutory authority has imposed a constructive trust in favor of a subcontractor on funds pertaining to the prime contract for breach of contract.

Id. at 725 (citations omitted); note 1, *supra.*

[24] *In re* Unicom Computer Corp., 13 F.3d 321, 325 (9th Cir. 1994) (applying California law).

[25] 380 N.E.2d 189, 194 (N.Y. 1978) (citations omitted); Boyd v. La Master, 927 F.2d 237, 239 (6th Cir. 1991) ("Illinois law does not require that there be wrongful conduct by the person in possession before a constructive trust can be declared").

In *Simonds* the court imposed a constructive trust on life insurance proceeds, payable to the insured's current wife, in favor of the insured's former wife. The insured had agreed, when he divorced his former wife, to maintain a life insurance policy for the benefit of his former wife. Notwithstanding that agreement, the insured allowed an existing policy, to which the divorce decree made reference, to lapse and the insured obtained a new life insurance policy in which he named his new wife and daughter as beneficiaries. The new beneficiaries did not participate in any wrongdoing and, it appears, were unaware of any "wrongdoing" by the insured toward his former wife. Nevertheless, the court imposed a constructive trust.[26]

[54.3] Application of Irreparable Injury Requirement

Because a constructive trust is an equitable remedy, the application of the irreparable injury requirement may arise. The decisional law on this topic is surprisingly diverse. In many decisions, the issue is simply not raised. It is always dangerous to read meaning into silence, but the omission of any mention of an irreparable injury requirement may reflect the lingering presence of the trust metaphor and equity's inherent jurisdiction over trusts.[27] In some decisions, the presence of a fiduciary obligation may substitute for the irreparable injury requirement.[28] In some cases, the irreparable injury requirement appears to have been abrogated.[29]

In other cases, however, courts have refused to impose a constructive trust citing the availability of an adequate remedy at law.[30] The issue is

---

[26] 380 N.E.2d at 194–95. While there are contrary cases, the view expressed in *Simonds* dominates the modern decisions. Norton v. City of Chicago, 690 N.E.2d 119 (Ill. App. 1997):

> Where a defendant has obtained money to which he is not entitled, under such circumstances that "in equity and good conscience he ought not retain it," the rightful owners of the money can claim it through a constructive trust to avoid unjust enrichment. That the person receiving the money acted in good faith does not prevent recovery of the sum paid.

Id. at 126 (citations omitted).

[27] Section 21.1 ([Adequacy of the Remedy at Law/Irreparable Injury] Justification for the Requirement).

[28] *Cf.* Security Nat'l Bank v. Educators Mut. Life Ins. Co., 143 S.E.2d 270, 276 (N.C. 1965) (holding that constructive trust will not be imposed when there is no fiduciary relationship or irreparable injury).

[29] Bregman, Berbert & Schwartz, L.L.C. v. United States, 145 F.3d 664, 669 (4th Cir. 1998) (stating that "[u]nder Maryland law, the equitable remedy of a constructive trust is applied by operation of law where property has been acquired by fraud, misrepresentation, or other improper methods. . . .") (internal quotations omitted); Heckman v. Ahmanson, 214 Cal. Rptr. 177, 187 (Cal. App. 1985) (stating that "[i]n California . . . . an action in equity to establish a constructive trust does not depend on the absence of an adequate legal remedy"). *But cf.* Wilkison v. Wiederkehr, 124 Cal. Rptr.2d 631, 639 (Cal. App. 2002) (rejecting action for specific performance of contract to make a will and imposition of constructive trust on property devised to estate beneficiary on the ground that adequate remedy at law existed—action for breach of contract against testator's estate).

[30] *In re* Broadview Lumber Co., Inc., 118 F.3d 1246, 1253 (8th Cir. 1997) (holding that bankruptcy court correctly declined to impose a constructive trust when the plaintiff had an adequate remedy at law); *cf.* United States v. Ribadeneira, 105 F.3d 833 (2d Cir. 1997):

difficult to resolve because many cases involve claims against fiduciaries or actions involving land for which equity jurisdiction is inherent without reference to the irreparable injury requirement. The precedent is equivocal whether a constructive trust may be obtained without regard to the adequacy of the remedy at law.

[54.4] Reasons for Seeking a Constructive Trust

The remedy of a constructive trust is not freely available for every legal wrong. While a constructive trust may be asserted over property, such as a fund or money, a constructive trust is generally not afforded simply because the defendant failed to pay a debt.[31] Even if a court does not treat "irreparable injury" as a formal requirement to obtaining a constructive trust, "irreparable injury" helps identify situations when a constructive trust is a needed remedy that should be afforded despite possible third party effects.

A party's invocation of a constructive trust should be animated by purpose and reason. For example, a person may desire specific restitution of property through a constructive trust because a money judgment would be largely uncollectible. In *Hicks v. Clayton* a lawyer defrauded his clients and obtained title to the client's residence. Because the lawyer was insolvent, a money judgment would be largely uncollectible. In these circumstances, a money judgment would not be as effective a remedy as the return of the residence to the plaintiffs-clients, which could be accomplished by deeming the lawyer a constructive trustee of the residence—the remedial trust res.[32]

The value of a money judgment may also be compromised by the claims of other creditors. In *Hicks v. Clayton* the lawyer's estate was beset by the claims of other creditors, including the Internal Revenue Service. If the plaintiffs' received a money judgment, the assets that could be seized to discharge that judgment debt were subject to competing and prior claims. The constructive trust remedy allows the plaintiffs to contend that the subject property was theirs and therefore not really subject to claims by the creditors of the lawyer-constructive trustee.[33] Again the analogy is to

---

In particular, we note that the district court correctly declined to establish a constructive trust on Appellants' behalf both because Appellants have not met the elements required by New York law for a constructive trust *and* because § 853(I) provides a legal remedy which obviates the need for application of an equitable remedy.

Id. at 836 n.5 (emphasis added). The use of the conjunctive "and" confuses the matter. It is unclear whether the court is providing cumulative or independent reasons.

[31] Bender v. Centrust Mortgage Corp., 51 F.3d 1027, 1030 (11th Cir. 1995).

[32] 136 Cal. Rptr. 512, 520–21 (Cal. App. 1977).

[33] Not surprisingly this has raised difficult problems in bankruptcy. Emily Sherwin, *Constructive Trusts in Bankruptcy*, 1989 Univ. Ill. L. Rev. 297. *See generally* Alan Skutt, Annot., *Power of Trustee In Bankruptcy to Defeat Rights of Beneficiaries of Constructive Trust Under § 544(a) of Bankruptcy Code (11 U.S.C.A. § 544(a))*, 96 A.L.R. Fed. 100 (1990); Section 54.6 (Priority); Section 59.3 (Limitations on Tracing).

the law of trusts. The trust corpus is not for the use or enjoyment of the trustee; the trustee holds legal title, but no beneficial interest. Trustees are barred from commingling their own and trust property in a common fund in order to preserve and identify the property (in which the trust beneficiaries have an interest) from non-trust property (in which the trustee has a beneficial interest). A constructive trust allows the plaintiff to obtain a preference against other creditors of the debtor-constructive trustee by claiming that the property, nominally in the name of the debtor, is really the plaintiff's property. Because the property truly belongs to the plaintiff, other creditors of the debtor should not be permitted to use the plaintiff's property to satisfy their claims against the debtor. Not surprisingly, the imposition of constructive trusts in this context is strictly controlled to prevent unfairness to those other creditors.[34]

A constructive trust is appropriate when the plaintiff must trace her property into new, evolved forms of property. While legal remedies, such as replevin, are often equivalent to a constructive trust, and therefore adequate,[35] when replevin is unavailable, a constructive trust may be appropriate. The most common example of this is when tracing is necessary to identify property belonging to the plaintiff. Tracing is inextricably tied to equitable remedies;[36] consequently, the need to trace warrants a finding that the remedy at law is inadequate and a constructive trust is necessary and proper.

[54.5] Scope of Constructive Trust

Because a constructive trust is a specific restitutionary remedy, the "beneficiary" recovers the property with any and all enhancements and improvements made to the property by the possessor. In this sense, a constructive trust is little different in function from replevin.[37] When, however, a constructive trust is sought over the profits derived from the investment of property impressed with a constructive trust, a question of allocation may arise. How much of the profits, if any, should be given to the beneficiary of the constructive trust?[38]

---

[34] Section 54.6 (Priority).

[35] Alger v. Davis, 76 N.W.2d 847, 851 (Mich. 1956) (refusing to impose a constructive trust over personal property when immediate possession could be obtained by a replevin action); Section 57.1 ([Replevin] Nature of the Action); Section 84.2 (Equitable Replevin).

[36] *In re* Advent Mgmt., 104 F.3d 293, 295 (9th Cir. 1995) (stating that the inability to trace and identify an interest in property held by another precludes imposition of a constructive trust on that property). Section 59 (Tracing Principles for Constructive Trusts, Equitable Liens, and Equitable Accounting).

[37] Section 84.1.1 (Superior Title or Equity in Another). It is possible that the constructive trustee could have an action to recover the value of the improvements. Section 86 (Good Faith Improvers of Personal Property); Section 96 (Good Faith Improvers of Real Property).

[38] Section 46 (Apportionment of Benefit); Section 51 (Disgorgement Orders); Section 59 (Tracing Principles for Constructive Trusts, Equitable Liens, and Equitable Accounting).

The constructive trustee may be required to account for actual profits,[39] but what constitutes actual profits? When specific property is simply held and sold for a price, the determination of "actual profit" may be easy to calculate as the difference between acquisition cost and sale price. When, however, the profit is a byproduct, in whole or in part, of the efforts of the constructive trustee, courts may hesitate awarding the entire profits to the beneficiary, as the apportionment and disgorgement cases indicate.[40]

[54.5.1] Purchase of Life Insurance

Cases when the constructive trustee has not contributed any "sweat equity" to the wrongfully acquired property may raise allocation concerns, as the life insurance cases illustrate. The typical fact pattern involves a person who uses funds impressed with a constructive trust to purchase life insurance. The person then dies and a dispute arises over entitlement to the life insurance proceeds, which are usually much larger than the invested premium(s). In this context, courts have been reluctant to award the entire proceeds of the life insurance to the beneficiary, even when the insurance was maintained solely by the use of funds impressed with the constructive trust.

One approach is to limit the beneficiary to a recovery of the premiums paid. In other words, the beneficiary is deprived of any profits from the investment. This result is sometimes justified by specific exemption statutes applicable to insurance,[41] sometimes by reference to the fact that the wrongful acts are merely alleged not established,[42] and sometimes out of concern that absent some higher equity, there is no reason to prefer the constructive trust beneficiary over the named beneficiaries of the insurance policy. As noted in *Succession of Onorato*:

> In our opinion, in this case the civil law doctrine should not be applied to the extent that the proceeds of exempt life insurance, when the premiums are paid or the insurance purchased with stolen funds, should be given to the owner of the property thus stolen, but he is entitled to recover the amount of the stolen funds which was used by the thief in payment of premiums or purchase of the insurance itself. By permitting this recovery, the fraud is made ineffective, equity and justice are served, and the public good and the policy of the statute creating the exemption are in no way

---

[39] *See* text and notes 14–19, *supra* (discussing general rule that constructive trustee is not responsible for losses resulting from the failure to prudently manage the property subject to a constructive trust).

[40] Section 46 (Apportionment of Benefit); Section 51 (Disgorgement Orders).

[41] Ahmad v. Gruntal & Co., Inc., 882 F. Supp. 391, 393 (D.N.J. 1995) (noting that under New Jersey law, creditors cannot assert legal or equitable claims against group life insurance policies; creditors' recoveries are limited to premiums paid from funds or monies wrongfully obtained).

[42] *Id.* at 393 (collecting decisions); Succession of Onorato, 51 So. 2d 804, 812 (La. 1951) (collecting decisions).

impaired since the family and loved ones of the insured are assured of the proceeds that the misappropriated money bought.[43]

Another approach permits the beneficiary of a constructive trust to a proportionate recovery of the life insurance proceeds. The recovery is based on the proportion of the total insurance as the amount of premiums that have been paid from money subject to a constructive trust bears to the total amount of premiums paid.[44] For example, if $1,000 worth of premiums have been paid to maintain a $100,000 life insurance policy and the beneficiary can establish that $100 of the premiums paid was subject to a constructive trust, the beneficiary could claim up to $10,000 (10% (*100/1000*) of $100,000).[45] One open question appears to be whether the constructive trust beneficiary can recover more than she lost. There is little decisional law directly on point.

In *McKissick v. McKissick*[46] a decedent failed to maintain life insurance in favor of his former wife (Barbara) as he had agreed to do in their property settlement agreement. The agreement specified that the decedent was to maintain $50,000 worth of life insurance with a specified company that was in fact non-existent. The decedent did at the time of his divorce have several policies with a total face value of $40,000. At the time of the decedent's death, those policies named his second wife (Dorothy) as the beneficiary. Because of an accidental death provision in the policies, the actual benefits paid on the decedent's death was $112,848.59. The trial court limited Barbara's recovery to the $50,000 specified in the agreement. The Nevada Supreme Court disagreed:

> The divorce decree obligated Howard to maintain insurance with Barbara as the irrevocable beneficiary. This constituted an equitable assignment for her benefit. He violated the agreement and decree when he designated his second wife, Dorothy, as the beneficiary of the insurance policies. In such circumstances it is permissible to conclude, as did the district court, that the second wife holds the insurance proceeds in a constructive trust for the first wife. The problem remains however, as to the extent of that trust. The district court limited the trust to $50,000 since that was the sum mentioned

---

[43] 51 So. 2d at 812. The civil law doctrine referenced in the quoted materials is the rule that a thief cannot obtain or convey title; hence title to the stolen property remains in the original owner. On this point the common law does not differ. Note, however, that the common law rule does not extend to negotiable instruments and money. Here the rule is that a thief can convey good title to a BFP, *i.e.*, a person who pays fair value and takes without notice of the superior claim to the instrument or money. *In re* Mushroom Transp. Co., 227 B.R. 244, 258 (Bankr. E.D. Pa. 1998); *In re* Whiteacre Sunbelt, Inc., 211 B.R. 411, 417 (Bankr. N.D. Ga. 1997); Hinkle v. Cornwell Quality Tool Co., 532 N.E.2d 772, 777 (Ohio App. 1987); Portland v. Berry, 739 P.2d 1041, (Or. App. 1987); *see* Andrew Kull, *Defenses to Restitution: The Bona Fide Creditor*, 81 B.U. L. Rev. 919, 936 (2001). *See generally* 53A Am. Jur. 2d *Money* § 23.

[44] *Succession of Onorato, supra*, 51 So. 2d at 812 (collecting decisions); Brodie v. Barnes, 132 P.2d 595, 599 (Cal. App. 1942) (collecting decisions).

[45] PALMER, LAW OF RESTITUTION, *supra* § 2.15(b), at 187–193 (collecting decisions).

[46] 560 P.2d 1366 (Nev. 1977).

in the property settlement agreement. We believe that the court erred in so limiting the trust. The figure of $50,000 in the insurance paragraph of the property settlement was a part of the misdescription of the life insurance 'presently insuring his life.' He did not have life insurance in that amount. Notwithstanding this mistake, it is clear that Howard intended to secure his obligation to provide for the support and education of his children in the event of his untimely death by means of the life insurance he had when the agreement was made. Consequently, Barbara and the children are entitled to the proceeds of that insurance including the increase in amount by reason of Howard's accidental death since such increase properly belongs to the person or persons for whose benefit the insurance was required to be carried. We, therefore, conclude that the life insurance proceeds received by Dorothy in the amount of $112,848.59 are held by her as constructive trustee for the benefit of Barbara and the children.[47]

Baxter House v. Rosen[48] is another decision that appears to fall into this category. In *Baxter House* creditors of an insolvent debtor were able to impress a constructive trust on insurance premium payments made by the debtor from monies the court held should have been preserved for the benefit of creditors due to the debtor's insolvency.[49] The amount of debt totaled $43,000. The amount collected by the named beneficiaries under the life insurance policies was $1,939,329.39. The total premium payments made by the debtor were $290,403.80. Under a pro rata approach, the creditors could claim approximately 14.9% of the paid insurance proceeds, or approximately $289,000. The court held that the creditors could claim a pro rata share.[50]

[54.5.2] Failure to Maintain Life Insurance

A constructive trust may be used when a person fails to comply with a promise (usually encompassed in a court order) to name the plaintiff as the beneficiary of a designated sum of insurance on the life of the promissor. The cases usually involve divorced parties who provided that one of the parties, e.g., the husband, would maintain insurance on his life for the benefit of his former wife or children or both. The husband then remarries and starts family #2, which becomes the focus of his attention to the detriment and exclusion of former family #1. The husband breaches his

---

[47] *Id.* at 1369 (citations and footnotes omitted).

[48] 278 N.Y.S.2d 442 (App. Dept. 1967).

[49] *Id.* at 445 (treating premium payments as fraudulent conveyances as to the creditors); *In re* Gurley, 222 B.R. 124, 134 (Bankr. W.D. Tenn. 1998) (stating that "the imposition of a constructive trust may be an appropriate remedy when transfers are made in fraud of third persons, such as creditors of the transferor. It is said that [w]here a person holding property transfers it to another in violation of his duty to a third person, the third person can reach the property in the hands of the transferee, unless the transferee is a bona fide purchaser") (citations omitted).

[50] 278 N.Y.S.2d at 447.

promise to designate his ex-wife or children of family #1 as life insurance beneficiaries; rather, he takes out a new life insurance policy in which he names his new wife or the children of family #2 as the life insurance beneficiaries. When husband dies, the question arises, who owns the insurance proceeds?[51]

Courts have responded in several ways to this problem. One line of decisions permits the former wife to assert a constructive trust over the insurance proceeds notwithstanding that the former wife cannot identify "property" that has been wrongfully acquired by the life insurance beneficiary.[52] In most of these cases, even if the husband had a life insurance policy in effect at the time of the divorce, that policy lapsed or expired and a different policy (the "after-acquired" policy) was purchased that named a different beneficiary than promised. One method courts use to bridge this gap is to treat the policy(ies) existing at the time of the divorce as "property" that has been maintained in the new policy. A fiction is employed that the husband intended that the new policy serve as a replacement of the old policy, as to the limits of the old policy.[53] In some cases, courts do not limit the recovery to the old policy limits.[54]

Other courts take a contrary approach, finding that a constructive trust should not be imposed in the setting described by the hypothetical. These courts emphasize the absence of a property interest that is *acquired* by the life insurance beneficiary.[55] This is particularly effective when the plaintiff is unable to establish the existence of an insurance policy *at the time of the divorce*,[56] a not uncommon fact given the passage of time that often occurs in these cases.[57]

---

[51] Most jurisdictions permit the insurer to pay the named beneficiary(ies); however, if a competing claim is received by the insurer before payment is made, the insurer may (and probably will) elect to interplead the proceeds in court. In this setting, the competing claimants may litigate who is entitled to the proceeds. Alternatively, the promisee may bring an action against the promisor's estate for breach of promise. This may be unsatisfactory. The estate may be insolvent or the period within which to bring claims may have expired. The life insurance proceeds would not be part of the husband's probate estate unless he failed to designate a beneficiary or the designation failed as a matter of law.

[52] Simmond v. Simmond, 380 N.E.2d 189 (N.Y. 1978) (holding that first wife could assert constructive trust to claim portion of insurance proceeds received by second wife when husband common to both wives failed to maintain insurance for benefit of first wife as he promised in divorce decree).

[53] Rollins v. Metropolitan Life Ins. Co., 912 F.2d 911, 915–16 (7th Cir. 1990).

[54] McKissick v. McKissick, 560 P.2d 1366 (Nev. 1977) (discussed in Section 54.5.1.)

[55] Oregon Pacific State Ins. Co. v. Jackson, 986 P.2d 650 (Or. App. 1999) (refusing to recognize constructive trust when husband failed to name first wife as insurance beneficiary as required by dissolution agreement when insurance policy was not created to fund future obligation); Rindels v. Prudential Life Ins. Co., 489 P.2d 1179 (N. Mex. 1971); *see* Carpenter v. Carpenter, 722 P.2d 298 (Ariz. App. 1985) (collecting decisions on equitable interests in after-acquired insurance policies), *vacated in part on other grounds*, 722 P.2d 230 (Ariz. 1986).

[56] Parge v. Parge, 464 N.W.2d 217, 219 (Wis. App. 1990); *cf.* Burch & Cracchiolo P.A. v. Pugliani, 697 P.2d 674, 679 (Ariz. 1985) (stating that a general claim for money damages will not support a constructive trust; the plaintiff must identify specific property belonging to him held by the defendant).

[57] *Rollins, supra*, 912 F.2d at 915 (noting that divorce decree was ambiguous and sparse

[54.6] Priority

A constructive trust treats the plaintiff as the actual owner of the property impressed with the constructive trust. That property is, therefore, not subject to claims by creditors of the defendant-constructive trustee. The creditors cannot seek a recovery out of property that does not belong to their debtor. Thus, if a creditor can transform her claim from one of debt to restitution, as, for example, by claiming that the property held by the debtor was obtained by fraud, duress, or some other wrongful act permitting the imposition of a constructive trust, that creditor may obtain a preferential position as against the other creditors of the debtor. Not surprisingly, such claims are viewed cautiously by the courts. As noted in *In re Matter of United Imports, Inc.*:

> Although the Eighth Circuit apparently recognizes constructive trusts imposed in bankruptcy in sufficiently extreme circumstances, "[e]ven in courts where constructive trusts are recognized in bankruptcy, the remedy is rarely granted and only in the most egregious of circumstances, and usually where a trust is sought on property in which the party claims an ownership interest." The equities of bankruptcy are not the equities of the common law.[58]

Claims of priority as between the plaintiff-beneficiary of a constructive trust and others (creditors of the defendant-debtor/constructive trustee) tend to arise in two situations: (1) Insolvency (primarily bankruptcy) when the beneficiary seeks to claim a larger share of the debtor's estate than would be available to her as a general unsecured creditor;[59] and (2) Taxation when the beneficiary seeks to escape tax liens filed against property to which the constructive trustee has legal title.[60]

Priority conflicts can also arise between (1) beneficiaries of a constructive trust and bona fide purchasers (BFP) for value[61] and (2) beneficiaries of

---

as to details about the duty to maintain a policy and the records of the proceeding had been lost).

[58] 203 B.R. 162, 169–70 (Bankr. D. Neb. 1996) (citations omitted).

[59] First Federal of Mich. v. Barrow, 878 F.2d 912, 915 (6th Cir. 1989) (distinguishing between priority afforded beneficiary of constructive trust in bankruptcy context from that afforded general creditor); *cf. In re* Liquidation of Security Casualty Company, 537 N.E.2d 775 (Ill. 1989) (distinguishing between priority afforded lenders and investors (insureds) in failed insurer's insolvency proceedings).

[60] Blachy v. Butcher, 221 F.3d 896 (6th Cir. 2000) (holding that federal tax lien attached to property later determined to be impressed with a constructive trust), *cert. denied*, 532 U.S. 994 (2001); Securities & Exch. Comm'n v. Levine, 881 F.2d 1165, 1175 (2d Cir. 1989) (involving insider trading profits made by Levine that were subject to disgorgement order). The conflict in *Levine* was over the government's tax liens on the profits as against the defrauded investors ability to take the profits free of the liens.

[61] Hunnicutt Constr., Inc. v. Stewart Title & Trust of Tucson Trust No. 3496, 928 P.2d 725, 730 (Ariz. App. 1996) (denying general contractor, who held unrecorded judgment imposing constructive trust on property, priority against BFP). The court placed particular emphasis on the contractor's failure to record materialmen or mechanics liens that would have given notice of the claims to the BFP. *Id.*; Osin v. Johnson, 243 F.2d 653, 656 (D.C. Cir. 1957) (same).

constructive trusts and judgment creditors.[62]

The questions of priority tends to be issue specific; however, several generalization are possible. First, courts are sensitive to the fact that recognition of a constructive trust may operate to give a preference to one group of otherwise similarly situated creditors. When the general orientation of the law is to treat like groups alike, as is the case in bankruptcy proceedings, courts will scrutinize claims for constructive trust that seek to establish a preference or priority to limited assets.[63]

Second, courts will be sensitive to whether recognition of a constructive trust, and the priority it affords, will interfer with a legislative model of risk sharing, as, for example, statutorily prescribed classes of creditors for insolvency proceedings.[64] Third, courts appear to place some emphasis on the state of mind of the defrauded party insofar as recognizing a constructive trust that will afford that party a preference vis à vis other "similarly situated" parties, e.g., unsecured creditors of the debtor. A victim of fraud who voluntarily enters the bargain may be treated more harshly than an unknowing victim of fraud. In the first case, the court may perceive that the "victim" is in a "heads I win, tails you lose" position. Affirm the bargain if all goes well, disaffirm the bargain and seek a constructive trust if it does not. As noted by the Illinois Supreme Court in *In re Liquidation of Security Casualty Company*:

---

[62] Sherwin, *Constructive Trusts in Bankruptcy, supra*, 1989 Ill. L. Rev. at 324 (noting that "the prevailing rule of priority outside bankruptcy holds that a judgment lien is subject to a constructive trust or equitable lien on specific property").

[63] *In re* California Trade Technical Schools, Inc., 923 F.2d 641, 646–47 (9th Cir. 1991) (distinguishing between express trusts and constructive trusts insofar as property subject to either is deemed property of the bankruptcy estate); *In re* North American Coin & Currency, Ltd., 767 F.2d 1573, 1575 (9th Cir. 1985):

> While we agree that any constructive trust that is given effect must be a creature of [state] law, we cannot accept the proposition that the bankruptcy estate is automatically deprived of any funds that state law might find subject to a constructive trust. A constructive trust is not the same kind of interest in property as a joint tenancy or a remainder. It is a remedy, flexibly fashioned in equity to provide relief where a balancing of interest in the context of a particular case seems to call for it . . . . Moreover, in the case presented here it is an inchoate remedy; *we are not dealing with property that a state court decree has in the past placed under a constructive trust.* We necessarily act very cautiously in exercising such a relatively undefined equitable power in favor of one group of potential creditors at the expense of other creditors, for ratable distribution among all creditors is one of the strongest policies behind the bankruptcy laws.

(citations omitted; emphasis added), *cert. denied sub nom.* Torres v. Eastlick, 475 U.S. 1083 (1986). Note the express comment in the quote "suggesting that *only* a constructive trust declared *prior* to filing for bankruptcy will be respected by the bankruptcy court. *See* text and notes 77–80, *infra*.

[64] *In re Liquidation of Security Casualty Compay, supra*, 537 N.E.2d 775 (noting that recognition of constructive trust would be denied as it would contravene priorities established by statute for claims against insolvent insurer). In some cases this point is taken to the extreme. *In re* Omegas Group, Inc., 16 F.3d 1443, 1452 (6th Cir. 1994) (stating that "[c]onstructive trusts are anathema to the equities of bankruptcy . . ."); *see* Andrew Kull, *Rationalizing Restitution*, 83 Cal. L. Rev. 11191, 1217 (1995) (criticizing *Omegas Group* statement as "discount[ing] a century of judicial authority to the contrary") (brackets added).

Where the debtor corporation is insolvent and is about to undergo complete liquidation, the equities favor the conventional general creditors rather than the allegedly defrauded stockholders. In such circumstances, "[t]he real party against which [the stockholders] are seeking relief is the body of general creditors of their corporation. Whatever relief may be granted to them in this case will reduce the percentage which the general creditors will ultimately realize upon their claims." We will not allow stockholders whose claims are based solely on the alleged fraud that took place in the issuance of stock to deplete further the already meager pool of assets presently available to the general creditors. In so deciding, we heed the observation made many years ago by the Eighth Circuit: 'When a corporation becomes bankrupt, the temptation to lay aside the garb of a stockholder, on one pretense or another, and to assume the role of a creditor, is very strong, and all attempts of that kind should be viewed with suspicion."

Imposing a constructive trust in this case for the benefit of the defrauded shareholders advances their claims ahead of the claims of Security Casualty's policyholders and creditors. Such a recovery by the shareholders diminishes the pool of assets available for distribution to other claimants. In effect, it shifts the risk of illegally or fraudulently issued securities from the investors, where the risk properly lies, to other, equally innocent parties who chose not to expose themselves to the potential burdens and benefits of owning stock in the enterprise.[65]

On the other hand, a more generous approach may be discerned when the victim of the fraud is unaware of the wrongdoing, as in the case of embezzlement.[66]

[54.7] Time Interest Attaches

An equitable lien[67] or constructive trust gives the holder of the equitable claim a priority over other claimants to the property. Priority necessarily references a certain point in time before which both an equitable lien and a constructive trust may be cut off by the superior interests of third parties, such as a good faith purchaser for value (BFP) who takes the property without notice of the adverse interests and whose interest predates the priority date of the equitable remedies.[68]

One advantage of claiming an equitable lien or constructive trust is the ability to provide notice through a lis pendens to prospective purchasers

---

[65] 537 N.E.2d at 781 (citations omitted).

[66] *In re* NewPower, 233 F.3d 922, 931 (6th Cir. 2000) (holding that "embezzled" funds were not property of the bankruptcy estate and that property purchased with embezzled funds could be impressed with a constructive trust).

[67] Section 56 (Equitable Lien).

[68] Nachazel v. Mira Co., Mfg., 466 N.W.2d 248, 253 (Iowa 1991).

to cut off their claim of BFP,[69] although not all jurisdictions permit the use of a lis pendens in this context.[70] This is important since a BFP will not take subject to an unrecorded equitable interest of which there is no notice.[71] Care must be exercised, however. The equitable interest must involve the property on which the lis pendens is filed.[72] If the interest is unrelated, the holder has no right to file the lis pendens and doing so may constitute the tort of slander of title.[73]

The equitable interest will attach as against a third party from the time the third party has actual notice of the interest. Actions taken after that date by the third party are taken subject to the risk that the court will find that the interest is valid. If, for example, monies are paid inconsistent with the rights of the holder of the known equitable interest, the risk of loss falls on the third party who may find that he paid full value for property subject to the valid claims of another.[74]

---

[69] Fingerhut Corp. v. Suburban Nat'l Bank, 460 N.W.2d 63, 67 (Minn. App. 1990) (stating that a constructive trust establishes an equitable lien which brings the action within the lis pendens statute).

[70] Flores v. Haberman, 915 S.W.2d 477 (Tex. 1996) (*per curiam*) (holding that a constructive trust would not support a lis pendens when a party converted funds and used the money to acquire other assets, which plaintiff sought to impress with the lis pendens). The allowance of a lis pendens would prevent a person who became a creditor of the debtor after the lis pendens attached from claiming the status of a bona fide creditor who could assert a superior or equal equitable claim to the property.

[71] *Hunnicutt Constr. Co., supra*, 928 P.2d at 730. A lis pendens provides constructive notice; however, if the purchaser has actual notice of the equitable claim, he may take subject to it. Bishop Creek Lodge v. Scira, 54 Cal. Rptr. 2d 745, 753 (Cal. App. 1996).

[72] Suess v. Stapp, 407 F.2d 662, 665 (7th Cir. 1969).

[73] Busch v. Doyle, 141 B.R. 432, 436 (Bankr. D. Utah 1992) (holding that equitable interest claimed in action for breach of an oral employment contract was improper; cause of action did not affect title to the land on which the lis pendens was filed); Coventry Homes, Inc. v. Scottscom Partnership, 745 P.2d 962, 965 (Ariz. App. 1987) (holding that action for breach of personal services contract would not support lis pendens or equitable lien on defendant's property as security for the claim because the contract claim was unrelated to the property).

[74] Blue Fox, Inc. v. Small Business Admin., 121 F.3d 1357, 1362–63 (9th Cir. 1997) (holding that defendants could not claim credit for money paid to contractor in derogation of equitable interest of subcontractor of which defendant had notice). As noted by the court:

> Blue Fox gave notice to the Army on May 26, 1994 and June 15, 1994 that it had not been fully paid. The Army subsequently paid Verdan $86,132.33 before terminating the contract. Thus, at the time the Army received notice from Blue Fox, it retained funds to which the equitable lien attached. The fact that the Army has since paid out the monies to which the lien attached does not thwart Blue Fox's equitable lien claim. In the suretyship context, the Federal Claims Court has noted:
>
> > Where the government has on hand contract funds owing for work done and is alerted . . . to the possibility of unpaid materialmen's claims . . . it may not dispense those funds to the contractor—at least not without running the distinct risk of having to pay twice.
>
> The Army cannot escape Blue Fox's equitable lien by wrongly paying out funds to the prime contractor when it had notice of Blue Fox's unpaid claims.

Id. (citations omitted), *rev'd on other grounds sub nom.* Dept. Of the Army v. Blue Fox, Inc., 525 U.S. 255 (1999) (holding that the doctrine of sovereign immunity barred contractor from asserting lien against the United States).

A court will be more willing to allow the equitable interest to attach at an earlier date when the legitimate interests of third parties will not be frustrated. For example, in *In re Stoffregen*[75] the bankrupt (debtor) had received a 1/4 interest in property years earlier from his parents. When he became bankrupt, his creditors sought to apply the 1/4 interest to his debts. To avoid this scenario, the debtor reconveyed the interest to his mother. His creditors sought to set aside the conveyance as fraudulent; the. mother resisted claiming an equitable interest in her son's 1/4th interest as of the date of the initial transfer to her son. The court agreed. The court found that the initial transfer was done for estate planning purposes and the avoidance of probate.[76] The debtor-son received only the barest of legal title and not a beneficial interest that could be attached by creditors. No evidence was adduced that any creditor relied on the debtor's 1/4 interest in extending credit. Under the circumstances, the recognition of the mother's equitable lien as of the date of initial transfer was not seen as subtracting anything of the debtor's to which the creditors could legitimately claim.

The timing issue is of critical importance when litigating tax liens or bankruptcy preferences. A court is much more willing to recognize an equitable interest that predates the filing of the lien or the bankruptcy petition.[77] Some courts have expressed the position that an inchoate claim that property is subject to an equitable interest, such as a constructive trust, is ineffective; the equitable interest must be judicially declared *before* the other interest (federal tax lien, bankruptcy trustee's "strong arm" powers) attaches or is invoked.[78] This point has become highly contestable and produced a split within the federal courts. Some courts reject the approach that the equitable interest must be judicially declared before the tax lien attaches or "strong arm" power is exercised.[79] Even courts that adhere to the view that federal law trumps an inchoate state claim have not applied the rule consistently, but have created ad hoc exceptions.[80]

[54.8] Fraudulent Conveyance v. Constructive Trust

The law of fraudulent conveyance and the law of constructive trust share the similar goal of effecting the transfer of property from one less deserving

---

[75] 206 B.R. 939 (Bankr. E.D. Wis. 1997).

[76] *Id.* at 944.

[77] *Blachy, supra*, 221 F.3d at 904–05 (noting that constructive trust was declared ten years after tax lien attached to property).

[78] *In re Omegas Group, Inc.*, 16 F.3d 1443, 1449 (6th Cir. 1994) (refusing to subject property brought into the bankruptcy estate by the exercise of the trustee's "strong arm" power to an after-acquired declaration that the property was impressed with a constructive trust).

[79] *In re Paul J. Paradise & Associates, Inc.*, 249 B.R. 360, 370–71 (Bankr. D. Del. 2000) (stating that power of states to define "property" includes power to determine beneficial interests in property).

[80] *In re Morris*, 260 F.3d 654 (6th Cir. 2001); *see* Ashley S. Hohimer, Notes & Comments, *Constructive Trusts in Bankruptcy: Is An Equitable Interest in Property More Than Just a Claim?*, 19 Bankr. Dev. J. 499 (2003).

to retain it to one more deserving to have it. The way the two legal doctrines operate is, however, fundamentally different.

A constructive trust is based on principles of unjust enrichment. The holder of the property has acquired or retains the property in some way or by some means that render the acquisition and retention unjust.[81] A fraudulent conveyance on the other hand is a transaction designed to defeat the rights of a creditor who can claim an interest in the property transferred.[82] A constructive trust is an equitable interest subject to equitable limitations and defenses. Fraudulent conveyance law is based on statute in most jurisdictions, although the statutes have been augmented by judicial construction. Most importantly, as between the conveyancing parties, a fraudulent conveyance is generally immune from challenge. As noted in *Estates of Kalwitz*:

> Only a creditor may bring an action to set aside a fraudulent conveyance . . . . [A] conveyance of property in fraud of creditors is generally valid and binding as between a fraudulent grantor and grantee, their privies, heirs and devises, and persons claiming under them.[83]

In effect, constructive trust law focuses on the defendant's effort to enrich himself or others by acquiring, retaining, or transferring property that more rightfully belongs to the plaintiff. Fraudulent conveyance law, on the other hand, focuses on the defendant's efforts to defraud the plaintiff. Notwithstanding these distinctions, a creditor may assert a constructive trust over property conveyed by the debtor. This will be particularly useful in circumstances when the plaintiff-creditor is unable or fails to plead and prove fraud.[84] A conveyer, or one taking through him, may be able to challenge a fraudulent conveyance, even though the challenger is not a creditor of the conveyer, by obtaining a constructive trust over the conveyed property.[85]

In *Morganroth & Morganroth v. Norris, McLaughlin & Marcus, P.C.*[86] the Third Circuit held that lawyers acting for their client in opposing collection efforts by a client's judgment creditor, can themselves be held liable for fraud when "they actively, knowingly, and intentionally

---

[81] Melloh v. Gladis, 309 N.E.2d 433, 338–39 (Ind. 1974).

[82] Uniform Fraudulent Transfer Act § 3439.04(a), which provides:

> A transfer made or obligation incurred by a debtor is fraudulent as to a creditor, whether the creditor's claim arose before or after the transfer was made or the obligation was incurred, if the debtor made the transfer or incurred the obligation as follows: (a) With actual intent to hinder, delay, or defraud any creditor of the debtor.

[83] 717 N.E.2d 904, 910 (Ind. App. 1999).

[84] Goya Foods, Inc. v. Unanue, 233 F.3d 38, 45 (1st Cir. 2000), *cert. denied*, 532 U.S. 1022 (2001); In re McGavin, 189 F.3d 1215, 1218–19 (10th Cir. 1999).

[85] *Estates of Kalwitz, supra*, 717 N.E.2d at 913–14. *But see* Section 62.1 (Unclean Hands), notes 16–18.

[86] 331 F.3d 406 (3d Cir. 2003).

participated in their client's unlawful efforts to avoid execution on his property."[87] The case involved efforts by creditors (lawyers) of John DeLorean to collect on a $6.23 million judgment for legal fees. The court held that the allegations in the complaint stated a viable claim against the law firm that assisted DeLorean in avoiding (evading?) the payment of the judgment. Among other things, plaintiff alleged that the defendant firm prepared a sham lease and deed they knew to be false and knowingly made false representations to a county clerk so the sham lease could be recorded. In other words, the lawyers had "papered" the fraudulent transactions that DeLorean used to avoid his creditors. Of course, the plaintiff still must show, as opposed to allege, that the transfer was fraudulent as to creditors.

§ 55 EQUITABLE ACCOUNTING

An accounting is an equitable remedy that is closely associated with constructive trusts, so much so that it is often difficult to determine whether the accounting flows from the recognition of a constructive trust or vice versa.[1] The remedy is popularly known as an accounting of profits or an accounting for profits, the terms being interchangeable. Although the remedy is designed to prevent unjust enrichment, in some contexts, particularly trademark infringement, the recovery is often seen as a surrogate for the plaintiff's lost profits.[2] This does not, however, nullify the equitable nature of the remedy.[3] An equitable accounting should also be distinguished from the legal action for an Account Stated, a point of distinguishing complicated, however, by the various ways the remedy of an accounting is used today.

An equitable accounting historically, and modernly, was justified on two primary grounds. First, when a fiduciary duty existed between the parties, equity, as part of its traditional jurisdiction over fiduciaries, would require the wrongdoing fiduciary to account for his unjust enrichment and disgorge the benefit wrongly obtained to the plaintiff. Many jurisdictions purport to limit equitable accounting to claims arising out of breach of fiduciary

---

[87] *Id.* at 414; McElhanon v. Hind, 728 P.2d 273, 278 (Ariz. 1986) (noting lower court upholding of civil conspiracy award against debtor's lawyer, but not addressing merits); *see* Henry J. Lischer, *Professional Responsibility Issues Associated With Asset Protection Trusts*, 39 Real Prop. Prob. & Tr. J. 561 (2004); Craig H. Averch & Blake L. Berryman, *Attorney Liability For the Client's Fraudulent Transfer: Two Theories*, 7 J. Bankr. L & Prac. 495 (1998).

[1] Parke v. First Reliance Standard Life Ins. Co., 368 F.3d 999, 1008 (8th Cir. 2004); *see* Kevin C. Kennedy, *Equitable Remedies and Principled Discretion: The Michigan Experience*, 74 U. Det. Mercy L. Rev. 609, 653–54 (1997); DAN DOBBS, HANDBOOK OF THE LAW OF REMEDIES 253 (1973) ("The principle of tracing used in constructive trust cases is the same principle applied here, so that it is possible to think of the accounting for profits in [cases against nonfiduciaries] as simply a special form of constructive trust.").

[2] Danielle Conway-Jones, *Remedying Trademark Infringement: The Role of Bad Faith in Awarding An Accounting of Defendant's Profits*, 42 Santa Clara L. Rev. 863, 879–80 (2002).

[3] Mark A. Thurmon, *Ending the Seventh Amendment Confusion: A Critical Analysis of the Right to Jury Trial in Trademark Cases*, 11 Tex. Intell. Prop. L.J. 1, 98–99 (2002).

or quasi-fiduciary, (or confidential), relationships,[4] although this requirement can be liberally applied.[5]

Historically, an equitable accounting was also allowed when the accounts between the parties were confused, complicated, or, preferably both. Confusion and/or complexity distinguished these claims from the action at law for an Account Stated and justified resolution by an expert (chancellor or special master) in equity rather than lay decision makers (jury) at law.[6] The Supreme Court largely rejected this basis of equitable jurisdiction in *Dairy Queen, Inc. v. Wood*,[7] but that decision is not binding on the states, which may continue to use confusion and/or complexity as a basis for the equitable remedy of an accounting. Note, however, that when the basis for the remedy is confusion and/or complexity, the focus largely moves off of unjust enrichment. The equitable remedy, combined with discovery historically available in equity but not at law, facilitated determining what the defendant had gained, which usually was what the plaintiff had lost. Discovery is now freely available at law; thus, the main consequence of recognizing confusion and/or complexity as justifying an equitable accounting is to substitute the judge for the jury as the decision maker.

Characterization of the remedy of an accounting as legal or equitable is also important when a statute permits only one form of relief, e.g., equitable but not legal, as, for example, is the case with ERISA.[8]

The remedy of an accounting may be made available by statute, as, for example, under the Lanham Act for trademark violations. In such cases, the availability of the remedy will be largely governed by statutory, rather than common law concerns.[9] Similarly, because a statute may have a retributive or deterrent function, an accounting may be an appropriate remedy as part of a restitutionary disgorgement order.

---

[4] Rodgers v. Roulette Records, Inc., 677 F. Supp. 731, 738–39 (S.D.N.Y. 1988).

[5] *See generally* 1 Am. Jur. 2d *Accounts and Accounting* § 55.

[6] Joel Eichengrum, *Remedying the Remedy of Accounting*, 61 Ind. L.J. 463 (1985). *See generally* 1 Am. Jur. 2d *Accounts and Accounting* §§ 54, 57.

[7] 369 U.S. 469, 478 (1962) (holding that "complexity" did not permit decision to be made in equity rather than by jury; court could appoint master under Fed. R. Civ. P. 53(b) to assist the jury, if assistance was necessary; therefore, the remedy at law was not inadequate and the exercise of equitable jurisdiction on the ground of "complexity" was not warranted).

[8] *Parke, supra*, 368 F.3d at 1006 (permitting award of prejudgment interest on benefits wrongly withheld under theory that plaintiff's claim for an accounting was equitable for purposes of ERISA and prejudgment interest represented "profits" defendant realized by wrongful withholding of benefits); *cf.* Jones v. Dorsey, 91 P.3d 762, 764–65 (Or. App. 2004) (stating that while interest is usually not awarded in accounting between partners, equity court had discretion to award prejudgment interest).

[9] Danielle Conway-Jones, *Remedying Trademark Violations, supra*, 42 Santa Clara L. Rev. at 865 (noting that for trademark dilution, as opposed to infringement, claims "a mark owner must show a willful violation" to recover defendant's profits).

§ 56 EQUITABLE LIEN

The origins of the equitable lien are shrouded in murkiness.[1] The common law recognized a number of liens, as for example, the seller's possessory lien,[2] the attorney's retaining lien,[3] or the repairman's lien.[4]

An equitable lien is a judicially created remedy, based on principles of avoiding unjust enrichment and is awarded when general equitable considerations so warrant.[5] An equitable lien creates a security interest in property held by the defendant. In effect the property collateralizes the money judgment that the plaintiff-lienholder obtains against the defendant. As noted in *Watson v. Hobson*:

> An equitable lien is the right to have property subjected, in a court of equity, to the payment of a claim. It is neither a debt nor a right of property but a remedy for a debt. It is simply a right of a special nature over the property which constitutes a charge or encumbrance thereon, so that the very property itself may be proceeded against in an equitable action and either sold or sequestered under a judicial decree, and its proceeds in one case, or its rents and profits in the other, applied upon the demand of the creditor in whose favor the lien exists. Equity recognizes, in addition to the personal obligation, in some cases, a peculiar right over the thing concerning which a contract deals, which it calls a 'lien,' and which, though not property, is analogous to property, by means of which the plaintiff is enabled to follow the identical thing and to enforce the defendant's obligation by a remedy which operates directly upon that thing.[6]

The holder of an equitable lien can foreclose on the property to which the lien attaches to satisfy her judgment,[7] but the remedy does not allow for direct capture of the property.[8]

---

[1] *See* Fiona Burns, *The Equitable Lien Rediscovered: A Remedy For the 21st Century*, 25 U. New South Wales L.J. 1 (2002) (discussing use of equitable lien from Roman origins to modern English and commonwealth cases).

[2] *See* Donald L. Kreindler, *Priority Rights Between Seller in Possession and a Good Faith Third Party Purchaser*, 82 Comm. L. J. 86 (1977).

[3] Sinclair, Louis, Siegel, Heath, Nussbaum & Zavertnik, P.A. v. Baucom, 428 So. 2d 1383, 1384 (Fla. 1983).

[4] General Motors Acceptance Corp. v. Colwell Diesel Serv. & Garage, Inc., 302 A.2d 595 (Me. 1973).

[5] Nachazel v. Mira Co., Mfg., 466 N.W.2d 248, 253 (Iowa 1991).

[6] 81 N.E.2d 885, 898 (Ill. 1948) (citations omitted).

[7] What priority the lienholder will have to the funds received is a different matter. Small v. Beverly Bank, 936 F.2d 945, 948 (7th Cir. 1991) (stating that Bank's perfected security interest would likely trump plaintiff's claimed equitable lien); Section 54.6 (Priority); 54.7 (Time Interest Attaches).

[8] The lienholder could acquire the property at the foreclosure sale, but this would require that the lienholder outbid all other bidders. Moreover, because the process was by judicial foreclosure, the debtor would likely have a period of time to redeem the property after the sale; hence, the marketability of the title would be, at least temporarily, compromised.

An equitable lien thus differs from a constructive trust in that it provides security for the equitable debt whereas a constructive trust provides specific restitution of the property or the property's cash equivalent.[9] For example, assume a defendant embezzles $100,000 from the plaintiff and uses the money to purchase 1000 shares of X Corp at $100/share. The plaintiff may use a constructive trust to claim the shares.[10] In the alternative, the plaintiff may seek a judgment for the losses sustained ($100,000), secured by an equitable lien on the shares. The plaintiff can then foreclose on the lien and apply the proceeds of the foreclosure sale against the judgment debt.

These alternatives suggest that the plaintiff will prefer the remedy of a constructive trust when the shares have appreciated in value since a constructive trust allows for the capture of the appreciation inherent in the property. On the other hand, if the shares are now worth less than the monetary loss, as, for example, because of a general market decline, then the plaintiff will usually prefer an equitable lien. The constructive trust is a specific restitutionary remedy. The general rule is that the plaintiff can claim the property, but not damages resulting from the wrongdoing. However, since an equitable lien merely secures a debt, it can be used in conjunction with a damages award.

An equitable lien is superior to a judgment lien in that it provides a greater priority, just as a constructive trust does.[11] In fact, for all intents and purposes, an equitable lien is available under the same terms and circumstances as a constructive trust.[12] The converse is not, however, true. In some circumstances an equitable lien, but not a constructive trust, is available. As noted in *Frambach v. Dunihue* (involving a good faith improver of property owned by another):

> As a general rule, a court of equity may give restitution to a plaintiff and prevent the unjust enrichment of a defendant by imposing a constructive trust or by imposing an equitable lien upon the property in favor of the plaintiff. However, where the plaintiff makes improvements upon the land of another under circumstances which

---

Marshall E. Tracht, *Renegotiation and Secured Credit: Explaining the Equity of Redemption*, 52 Vand. L. Rev. 599, 605–13 (1999) (discussing "equity of redemption" as right of mortgagor to reacquire the foreclosed property by paying the debt within a specified period of time after the foreclosure sale).

[9] Dixon v. Smith, 695 N.E.2d 284, 291 (Ohio App. 1997) (stating that "[a] constructive trust is not a right to recover on a debt owing; it creates a right to recover property wrongfully held") (citation omitted).

[10] Section 54 (Constructive Trust).

[11] The priority may be limited. *In re* Commercial Inv., Ltd., 92 B.R. 488 (Bankr. D.N.Mex. 1988) (suggesting that while equitable lien to amount of "earnest money" (down payment) paid by plaintiff to secure repayment of the "debt" might lie, the lien would not be afforded a priority over existing encumbrancers of the property).

[12] Martian v. Martian, 399 N.W.2d 849 (N.D. 1987) (noting that "one form of equitable lien is equivalent to a constructive trust"), *citing* Restatement Restitution § 161 (1937) and 51 Am. Jur. 2d *Liens* § 24.

entitle him to restitution, he is entitled only to an equitable lien upon the land and he cannot charge the owner of the land as constructive trustee and compel the owner to transfer the land to him. Neither a constructive trust nor a resulting trust arises in favor of a person who pays no part of the purchase price even though he pays for improvements on the property. The person does not become, in whole or in part, a beneficial owner of the property although he may be entitled to reimbursement.[13]

The rule reflects the common law apprehension that the law should not provide a remedy that would improve an owner out of his property.[14]

Consistent with the theme of unjust enrichment, to assert an equitable lien the plaintiff must show enrichment. For example, if the plaintiff expended time, effort, or funds on property, but the property was not improved, an equitable lien will not lie because there is no benefit.[15]

§ 57   REPLEVIN

[57.1]   Nature of the Action

At common law several distinct remedies were recognized for the actual, physical recovery of personal property from another. Detinue (unlawful detention) was used when the defendant wrongfully refused to return property over which she had initially obtained lawful possession, as through a bailment or consignment. Replevin (unlawful taking) was used when the defendant wrongfully obtained possession of the property from the defendant, as through theft or conversion. As was the case with the correlative equitable restitutionary action, the legal restitutionary actions effectively collapsed the right/remedy distinction. The remedy of specific restitution was the right.

The focus of these common law personal property actions was possession not the determination of title.[1] In many modern jurisdictions, the personal

---

[13] 419 So. 2d 1115, 1117 (Fla. App. 1982) (citations omitted).

[14] Section 96 (Good Faith Improvers of Real Property); *cf.* Jacoby v. Jacoby, 100 P.3d 852, 855 (Wyo. 2004) (holding that there was no unjust enrichment when parents-in-law reclaimed residence daughter-in-law had helped construct while married to parents-in-law's son; services were not rendered to in-laws, and daughter-in-law provided services without expectation of payment; equitable lien denied).

[15] Price Dev. Co. v. Redevelopment Agency, 852 F.2d 1123, 1127 (9th Cir. 1988) (involving effort to obtain reimbursement of option deposit that plaintiff had paid for exclusive negotiating rights over a 41 acre parcel of land and remedy of equitable lien to secure reimbursement); *cf.* Seward v. Mentrup, 622 N.E.2d 756, 758 (Ohio 1993) (refusing to recognize action for unjust enrichment following termination of same-sex relationship during which plaintiff contributed to upkeep and maintenance of defendant's residence; the court held there was no unjust enrichment because plaintiff enjoyed the benefits of the improvements while living in the home); *see* Laura Weinrib, *Reconstructing Family: Constructive Trust at Relational Dissolution*, 37 Harv. Civ. Rts.-Civ. Lib. Rev. 207 (2002) (criticizing *Seward v. Mentrup* and discussing contrary authorities and theories of recovery).

[1] Wurdeman v. Miller, 633 F. Supp. 20, 22 (S.D.N.Y. 1986); *see* Ferrell Mobile Homes, Inc.

property possessory actions have been combined into one action commonly known as replevin.[2] This statutory replevin action should be distinguished from the common law replevin action, which was a summary, pre-judgment remedy.[3] The modern derivations of the old common law action can vary widely; hence, the best that can be accomplished here is to stay within rather large generalizations about the nature of replevin today.

In order to prevail in a replevin action, the plaintiff must show that she has an immediate and superior right to actual possession of the personal property at issue over that of the defendant.[4] And while the determination of title is not the focus of the action, the plaintiff may establish her right to possession by demonstrating her title and that the defendant holds the property in derogation of plaintiff's title that gives plaintiff the right of immediate possession.[5] One might have rights to property superior to everyone but the true owner. This is the situation with "treasure trove" and "mislaid property."[6] Thus, one in that situation should be able to replevin property from anyone other than the true owner.

At common law replevin could not be maintained against a defendant who no longer had possession of the personal property. The usual focal point was the time of commencement of the action, but occasionally the principle extended to the time of trial. Such a principle invited mischief because a defendant could defeat the action by divesting himself of possession. Modern joinder rules limit the effectiveness of this tactic and the transfer can be challenged as a fraudulent conveyance. If the court has assumed jurisdiction over the property by an attachment, the transfer can be challenged as an improper effort to divest the court of its lawful jurisdiction. Finally, in some jurisdictions the plaintiff may obtain replevin damages in lieu of specific relief; therefore, a defendant who divests himself of or destroys the personal property becomes subject to a judgment that

---

v. Holloway, 954 S.W.2d 712, 714 (Mo. App. 1997) (stating that "[r]eplevin is a possessory action to obtain from defendant property he possesses, . . . [and such action] relies upon a right to possession, not ownership") (citation omitted).

[2] In many jurisdictions the common law actions are controlled by statute. N.Y. Civ. Prac. L. & R., Art. 71; Cal. Civ. Proc. Code §§ 512.010 et seq. (Writ of Possession), 482.010 et seq. (Writ of Attachment) (prejudgment remedies).

[3] Section 84.1.3 (Pre-Trial or Judgment Remedy).

[4] Future Tech Int'l, Inc. v. Tae Il Media, Ltd., 944 F. Supp. 1538, 1549–51 (S.D. Fla. 1996) (noting that the seller may not replevin property from a defaulting buyer unless the default vests in the seller the right to immediate possession of the property); Dubied Mach. Co. v. Vermont Knitting Co., 739 F. Supp. 867, 872 (S.D.N.Y. 1990).

[5] United States v. Lindberg Corp., 882 F.2d 1158, 1160–61 (7th Cir. 1989) (holding that government title in personal property created pursuant to procurement contract entitled it to replevin property from subcontractor who had created property pursuant to agreement with contractor and was holding the property because of nonpayment). But cf. Valley Gypsum Co. v. Pennsylvania State Police, 581 A.2d 707, 710 (Pa. Commw. Ct. 1990) (involving an impounded vehicle and stating that "[r]eplevin is a possessory action in which the issues are plaintiff's title and right of possession").

[6] Ritz v. Selma United Methodist Church, 467 N.W.2d 266, 269 (Iowa 1991).

represents the value of the property as of the time of trial in addition to loss of use damages.[7]

[57.2] Identification of Property (Accession and Confusion)

A plaintiff may follow his property, as long and as far as necessary, in order to recover it through replevin.[8] An example of this was published in a Los Angeles newspaper in 1992:

> Harold Johnson of St. Louis admits he lost hope after someone stole his prized 1962 Corvette, but last week a sharp-eyed Missouri state cop got it back when he ran a computer check on a suspicious registration and discovered the vehicle belonged to Johnson. Sounds routine except the car was stolen in 1971 and had passed through several "owners." Johnson not only recovers a classic car but stands to turn a handsome profit; he paid $1,300 for the car in 1969 and today it is valued at $25,000.[9]

Perhaps more common, however, was the experience of the owner of another Corvette recounted in *Capitol Chevrolet Co. v. Earheart*.[10] In this case, a 1965 Corvette was stolen from Revis. Subsequently, the Corvette was stripped and the hull was bought by Pack from Howard's Used Cars. Pack sold the hull to Horn who in turn sold it to Sartin for $200. Sartin used the hull to build a functioning Corvette with his own labor and materials. Sartin then sold the Corvette to Bennett for $4,750. Bennett sold the car to Earheart for $4,775. Earheart then traded the Corvette to Capitol for a 1979 Corvette. Capitol allowed $6,052 on the trade-in. Capitol in turn sold the Corvette to Crass. The saga ends when the car was stolen from Crass, recovered by the Atlanta, Georgia Police and returned to Revis, the original owner. Crass refused to pay Capitol alleging Capitol had sold him a stolen car—a good defense if true.[11] Capitol sued Crass and Earheart,

---

[7] Section 83.2 (Replevin).

[8] Autocephalous Greek-Orthodox Church of Cyprus v. Goldberg & Feldman Fine Arts, Inc., 717 F. Supp. 1374 (S.D. Ind. 1989), aff'd, 917 F.2d 278 (7th Cir. 1990) (involving recovery of Mosaics taken during Turkish occupation of Cyprus in 1974); O'Keeffe v. Snyder, 416 A.2d 862, 867 (N.J. 1980) (involving painting lost in 1946 and found in 1976).

[9] L.A. Daily J., September 2, 1992, at B1. The vehicle had been stolen and the owner deprived of possession for approximately 21 years before it was returned.

[10] 627 S.W. 2d 369 (Tenn. App. 1981).

[11] A thief cannot, with limited exceptions convey good title. Suburban Motors, Inc. v. State Farm Mut. Auto Ins. Co., 268 Cal. Rptr. 16, 19 (Cal. App. 1990) (noting that a purchaser can only take those rights the seller possesses in the property; since a thief has neither title nor the power to convey title, even a BFP does not acquire title from a thief. Absent title there is a failure of consideration and the performing party may recover her consideration. Chapter 15 (Rescission (Disaffirmance) of Bargain). The primary exception involves negotiable instruments and money when possession is deemed to constitute title if a transfer to a BFP is involved. Section 54.5.1 [Constructive Trust] Purchase of Life Insurance (note 43) (collecting decisions).

and cross claims, counterclaims and third party claims spawned exponentially. The court ultimately held that when Sartin "rebuilt" the Corvette he acquired title to the Corvette by accession and thus could convey good title. Consequently, Capitol was granted judgment against Crass.[12]

This was a phyrric victory for Capitol Chevrolet. Recall that Earheart had sold the '65 Corvette to Capitol Chevrolet as a trade-in for a '79 Corvette. Earheart paid the balance in full. Capitol Chevrolet subsequently sold the '65 Corvette to Crass. If Capitol Chevrolet is determined to have title, it loses its claim against Earheart! This results because the essence of Capitol Chevrolet's argument is that no one other than Revis had good title; therefore, Earheart had not paid good consideration for the '79 Corvette and Capitol Chevrolet had a security interest (equitable lien) in the '79 Corvette equal to the trade-in value of the '65 Corvette. Capitol's dissatisfaction is increased if Crass is judgment proof. Moreover, since both Revis and the '65 Corvette were apparently not subject to the jurisdiction of the Tennessee courts, Capitol Chevrolet needed to come up with a theory of liability that gave it an effective remedy over those persons or things over which the court did have jurisdiction. Capitol Chevrolet's appeal suggests it did not see its victory as providing it with an effective remedy.

The doctrine applied in *Capitol Chevrolet* is that of Accession and Confusion. The doctrine derives from civil law by which the owner of property becomes entitled to all which the property produces, and to all that is either added or united to the property, either naturally or artificially by the labor or skill of another. The doctrine is applied even when the addition extends to a change of form or materials.

In its most common form accession occurs when a mortgagee or secured creditor forecloses on property that has been improved by the debtor and takes free of the debtor's or a third party's claim of reimbursement for improvements made. In its more controversial setting, accession permits the cutting off of the original owner's right of specific restitution, even when possession was lost due to theft! This was the situation in *Capitol Chevrolet*.

The doctrine itself is imprecise as to when the converter adds sufficient new material and workmanship to the converted property to cut off the original owner's title. The general understanding is that the doctrine is not available to willful converters,[13] but it is unclear how far the point can be

---

[12] How far can you take this? As long as you can identify your property, you can replevin the property. Historically, the law was very generous in its treatment of this issue, especially when the defendant was morally blameworthy. Union Naval Stores Co. v. United States, 240 U.S. 284, 290–91 (1916) (holding that trespassers who converted sap in government owned trees and transformed sap into turpentine could not avoid replevin by invoking doctrine of accession and confusion); Farm Bureau Mutual Auto Ins. Co. v. Moseley, 90 A.2d 485, 487–88 (Del. Sup. Ct. 1952) (holding that thief who installed motor in stolen car could not reclaim motor from rightful owner who reclaimed vehicle from thief). *But cf.* Wetherbee v. Green, 22 Mich. 311 (1871) (holding that plaintiff could not replevin barrel-hoops that had been manufactured from timber taken from plaintiff's land by defendant, who acted on good faith belief that he had right to harvest the timber). The "hoops" are the bands that surround the barrel and hold the barrel staves (the outside of the barrel) together.

[13] Restatement of Restitution § 158 cmt.

taken. For example, Professor Laycock hypothesizes a famous artist, Leonardo DaVinci, stealing paints, brushes, and canvas and painting the Mona Lisa.[14] Could the store from which the goods were taken replevin the painting from a bona fide purchaser or has the stolen property been so transmuted that it has ceased to exist in identifiable form?[15]

The doctrine of Accession and Confusion has two principle applications today. First, in the area of security interests in personal property, (collateral), improvements made or affixed to property become subject to the creditor who has a lien on the whole.[16] This application often turns on the ease with which the improvements may be separated from the property.[17] The second application is the one of interest here: application of the doctrine of accession and confusion is a means of acquiring title or an equitable interest in the improved property, which may give the improver enforceable rights against the true owner. As noted in *Bancorp Leasing and Fin. Corp.*:

> The common-law doctrine of accession was taken from Roman law by Bracton and was said by Blackstone to have been grounded on the right by occupancy. 2 Blackstone, Commentaries *404–05. Thus, the owner of a parchment acquired title to writings on the parchment, and the owner of a garment acquired title to embroidery on the garment. *See id.* at *404–07. The concept of title by occupancy precluded joint ownership of the combined substances, although in certain circumstances, for example, when a writer used the parchment of another by mistake, the person acquiring title to goods by accession would be required to compensate the former owner of the goods. *See* 2 Gaius, Institutes §§ 77-78; 2 Justinian, Institutes, title 1, §§ 26-34.[18]

---

[14] DOUGLAS LAYCOCK, MODERN AMERICAN REMEDIES 610 (3d. ed. 2002); note 15, *infra.*.

[15] Austrian Motors Ltd. v. Travelers Ins. Co., 275 S.E.2d 702, 705 (1980) (recognizing general rule that doctrine of accession is not available to the wrongdoer but only to an innocent party against the original owner); Burroughs v. Garrett, 352 P.2d 644, 648 (N. Mex. 1960) (same); Farm Bureau Mut. Auto. Ins. Co. v. Moseley, 90 A.2d 485, 487 (Del. Super. Ct. 1952) (same). *But cf.* Janigan v. Taylor, 344 F.2d 781, 787 (1st Cir.) (suggesting that restitution would not be allowed to capture the enormous profit created by the willful wrongdoer), *cert. denied,* 382 U.S. 879 (1965). The court noted: "If an artist acquired paints by fraud and used them in producing a valuable portrait, we would not suggest the defrauded party would be entitled to the portrait or to the proceeds of its sale." *Id.*

[16] *See generally* 1 Am. Jur. 2d *Accession and Confusion* § 4.

[17] Bucci v. IRS, 653 F. Supp. 479, 483 (D.R.I. 1987) (collecting decisions finding that creditor's liens did not attach to easily removable improvements to motor vehicle, such as mobile phone, new tires, radio, etc.); *In re* Lyford (General Motors Acceptance Corp.), 22 B.R. 222, 224–25 (D. Maine 1982) (finding that the creditor's lien attached to a factory-installed hydraulic boom and grapple attached to a truck chassis to pick up logs and load them onto truck). The fact that certain of the components were merely bolted, not welded to the chassis was not controlling given that separation would require two workers a full day or more to accomplish the task. Bancorp Leasing and Fin. Corp. v. Stadeli Pump & Constr., Inc., 739 P.2d 548, 553 (Or. 1987) (finding that the doctrine of accession did not apply to an engine placed in a vehicle; the court noted that while a vehicle without an engine was incomplete, the vehicle was capable of receiving a new engine with relative ease).

[18] 739 P.2d at 552 (citations in original).

Accession and confusion are distinct although, as here, they are often combined. Accession refers specifically to the enhancement of property by its improvement by one other than the true owner; confusion refers to the commingling of property so that it loses its separate identity. When combined, the term refers to improvements of such a nature as to raise questions as to the essential identity of the property: Is it still the property of the original owner or have the improvements created a new property, separate and distinct from the earlier version possessed by the original owner? One often cited decision here is *Wetherbee v. Green* in which the plaintiff sought to replevin timber wrongfully cut from his land. The defendant had, however, obtained possession of the timber in good faith and fashioned it into barrel-hoops. The court held that the plaintiff's rights in the property could be cut off by the doctrine and that replevin would not lie against the superior title of the improver who provided nearly all of the value represented by the property sought to be replevined. [19]

Courts have developed a number of approaches to determine if the doctrine attaches to improved property. Under the "physical identity" test, the court determines whether the physical identity of the property has so changed that it can no longer be considered the same property. [20] Consider, for example, timber cut from land, milled into lumber, and then used to manufacture a piano. We would probable concede that the timber retained its physical identity into the cut lumber, but lost its identity as timber once it was incorporated into the piano. A second test is the "relative value" test, which vests title in the party who produces the greatest contribution to the finished product. [21] This test is less intuitive than the "physical identity" test and more fact based. For example, using the earlier timber to lumber to piano hypothetical, it may be argued that the greatest contribution to the lumber is produced by the transportation, cutting, and milling rather than the raw product. If so, the miller may claim title by the doctrine and cut off replevin and conversion remedies asserted by the original owner. This was essentially the case in *Wetherbee v. Green* when the defendant mistakenly took timber worth $25 from plaintiff's land and manufactured barrel-hoops worth $700, a 2700% increase in value. The court held that the disparate values vested title in the defendant. [22]

California has adopted an interesting variation to the doctrine of accession and confusion that appears to codify the *Wetherbee* approach, but with

---

[19] 22 Mich. 311 (1871).

[20] Roy Hardiman, *Toward The Right of Commerciality: Recognizing Property Rights in the Commercial Value of Human Tissue*, 34 U.C.L.A. L. Rev. 207, 253 (1986).

[21] *Id.*; *Wetherbee, supra*, 22 Mich. at 319 (noting that even if the original owner could identify his wood in the piano or his wood in the beam of a house, it would be unreasonable to allow him to claim the whole or to demand destruction of the whole to claim his part); *see* Jay L. Koh, *From Hoops to Hard Drives: An Accession Law Approach to the Inevitable Misappropriation of Trade Secrets*, 48 Am. U. L. Rev. 271 (1998) (providing a comprehensive discussion of the doctrine of accession in a unique, modern context).

[22] Hardiman, *Property Rights in Human Tissue, supra*, 34 U.C.L.A. L. Rev. 207, *discussing Wetherbee, supra*, 22 Mich. 311.

a twist. The California Civil Code distinguishes between the principal part, defined as the more valuable part, and the other part, and whether the enhancement consists of goods or services. When the improver acts in good faith and enhances the property by adding materials, the whole belongs to the owner of the principal part.[23] When the improver enhances the property through her services, but the enhancement does not constitute the principle part, the owner must compensate the enhancer for the value of the services provided if the owner wishes to recover the improved property. Alternatively, if the enhancement constitutes the principal part, the improver may claim the property and pay the "owner" the fair market value of the property prior to enhancement. The Civil Code provisions do not bar an action for damages.[24]

§ 58 EJECTMENT

Ejectment is an action to recover immediate possession of real property. In this sense, it is a specific restitutionary remedy that seeks to give the plaintiff the very thing that was lost. The elements of ejectment were noted in *Soffer v. Beech*:[1]

> Ejectment originally rested on a claim of actual or constructive ouster of the plaintiff.
>
> The writ of ejectment, however, has changed dramatically in the centuries since its narrow origin. Today, the right to possession is the central element of the action—not the claim of ouster. The writ of ejectment has long been the general method for obtaining possession of real property. The writ has expanded from a tenant's remedy and has long since been available to fee claimants and all others who assert the right to possession of estates in real property.

Ejectment differs from trespass in that ejectment is used when the defendant is in possession of land and the plaintiff has superior title. When the element of defendant's holding onto the land under a claim of right is absent, the proper action is trespass.[2] Ejectment differs also from trespass in that ejectment gives the plaintiff the very thing he seeks (possession of real property), whereas trespass gives a remedy for the harm caused.[3] Similarly, ejectment is distinguishable from quiet title. Ejectment can be brought if the plaintiff has the right to immediate possession and the right to demand that the defendant vacate the property.[4] The plaintiff need not

---

[23] California Civil Code §§ 1025–1028; *see* International Atlas Servs., Inc. v. Twentieth Century Aircraft Co., 59 Cal. Rptr. 495, 497 (Cal. App. 1967) (applying Civil Code provisions to dispute between legal owner of component part and legal owner of principal property), *cert. denied*, 389 U.S. 1038 (1968).

[24] Cal. Civ. Code §§ 1032–1033.

[1] 409 A.2d 337, 340 (Pa. 1979) (citations omitted).

[2] *See generally* 25 Am. Jur. 2d *Ejectment* § 3.

[3] Sweat v. Atlantic Coast Line R. Co., 81 F.2d 492, 493 (5th Cir. 1936).

[4] Moore v. Duran, 687 A.2d 822, 827 (Pa. Super. Ct. 1996).

be in actual possession to maintain the action for ejectment, it is sufficient that plaintiff has the right to immediate possession.[5] Quiet title, on the other hand, traditionally required that the plaintiff be in actual possession of the property in controversy, although the concept of "possession" could be liberally construed. For example, in *Moore v. Duran* Duran used the land for pasturing cattle; Moore used the land for hunting. The court found that Duran's use, coupled with the presence of fences he repaired, could be sufficient to give him actual possession to maintain an action to quiet title by adverse possession. In reaching this result, the court observed:

> There is no precise definition of what constitutes possession of real property; the determination of possession is dependent upon the facts of each case, and to a large extent upon the character of the land in question. In general, however, actual possession of land means dominion over the property; it is not the equivalent of occupancy. Thus, the trial court must determine which party exercised dominion and control over the property before determining what is the proper form of action in such a case.[6]

Many jurisdictions have created statutory actions to obtain possession of real property, but these actions still contain common law antecedents that must be respected.[7] The creation of these statutory actions, coupled with the abolition of the old forms of action can lead to some interesting problems.[8]

In addition to specific relief—recovery of the real property, a party bringing an action for ejectment may recover loss of use damages—called "mesne profits."[9]

---

[5] The modern view is that a *lessee* who is denied possession, as, for example, because of a holdover tenant, may use ejectment to obtain possession of his estate. *Soffer, supra,* 409 A.2d at 342 (making remedy available to lessees before entry and collecting authorities supporting position). Many jurisdictions today have summary statutory remedies that the lessor may invoke against a lessee, but these statutory remedies may not be available to a person other than the lessor.

[6] 687 A.2d at 827 (citations omitted).

[7] Tobin v. Stevens, 251 Cal. Rptr. 587, 589 (Cal. App. 1988) (discussing California statutory provision requiring that party (or his ancestor, predecessor, or grantor) seeking to quiet title show that he "was seised or possessed" the property in question within five years before commencement of the action). The court construed the term "seised" as meaning that the plaintiff possessed legal title.

[8] J&M Land Co. v. First Union Nat'l Bank, 766 A.2d 1110 (N.J. 2001) (resolving conflict between time period of adverse possession and time period for bringing action for ejectment). Part of the problem in this case was that the ancient Writ of Right of Entry, for which there was no limitations period and which allowed for recovery of possession along with the action for ejectment, had been abolished, leading to a conflict between adverse possession rules and ejectment rules. *Id.* at 1115–17.

[9] Section 92 (Ejectment).

§ 59 TRACING PRINCIPLES FOR CONSTRUCTIVE TRUSTS, EQUITABLE LIENS, AND EQUITABLE ACCOUNTING

[59.1] Equitable Principles

Tracing developed in equity, but we must be careful that this statement does not suggest too much. What was unique about tracing in equity was the ability to follow specific property as it was bartered, sold, or exchanged for new property. At common law a party could follow property but he could not follow that property into new forms. For example, if defendant wrongfully acquired plaintiff's timber, plaintiff could follow that property even though it was improved and even though it was acquired by third parties until some higher equity or principle cut off that right, such as a BFP[1] or the doctrine of Accession and Confusion.[2]

Tracing, on the other hand, permitted the equity court to do what the common law court would not—follow the property into its new forms and attach an equitable interest in that new form; hence, the connection between tracing and the equitable remedies of constructive trust, equitable lien, and accounting. The defendant who exchanged plaintiff's timber for a horse could find that plaintiff now had an equitable interest in the horse because the plaintiff could trace from his property (timber) to the new property (horse) through the exchange. At common law, a plaintiff could replevin the timber from the new possessor, unless the possessor could claim a superior right or equity, but plaintiff could not claim the horse, which was never his to begin with in the eyes of the law. The only way the plaintiff could get the horse would be to obtain a money judgment against the defendant and then levy and execute against the horse. By then the defendant and the horse might be long gone or the horse might be exempt from levy and execution. In either case, the defendant had the horse—all the plaintiff had was his judgment.

Tracing developed along side equity's supervision over trustees. When a trustee violated his fiduciary duties and converted trust funds, equity followed those funds and required the trustee to account for his wrongdoing. The funds themselves, and the gains, profits, and new forms the funds took, were subject to an equitable interest that permitted recapture of the funds, and their progeny and substitutes, for the beneficiaries of the trust.[3] As equity expanded by broadly defining who was subject to fiduciary (and quasi-fiduciary) obligations, tracing became a common remedy in cases of fraud and misappropriation whenever the defendant occupied a position of trust or confidence with the plaintiff. As noted in *Hicks v. State*:

> It was formerly held that these rules came to an end the moment the means of ascertaining the identity of the trust property failed.

---

[1] Section 84.1.1 ([Replevin] Superior Title or Equity in Another).

[2] Section 57.2 ([Replevin] Identification of Property (Accession and Confusion)).

[3] Section 54.6 ([Constructive Trust] Priority).

In the case of trust moneys commingled by the trustee with his own moneys, it was held that money has no ear-marks, and when so commingled the whole became an indistinguishable mass and the means of ascertainment failed. But equity, adapting itself to the exigencies of such conditions, finally determined that the whole mass of money with which the trust funds were commingled should be treated as a trust. And if the trustee deposited the trust funds with his own funds in bank, and then drew upon the commingled funds, he was presumed to have drawn out his own funds first, and that the remaining funds belonged to the trust. It is not to be presumed that the trustee would commit a wrong and use the trust funds when he had moneys of his own idle in the bank. The above rules applied only to express trusts. But many cases arose in which it was impossible to trace the trust funds beyond the point of conversion. The means of ascertainment failed. And many cases arose which were not express but resultant or constructive trusts

. . . It was [thus] held that if money be received by a person in a fiduciary character, though not as a technical trustee, and he pays it into his own account in bank, the person for whom he received the money might follow it and have a charge on the balance in the bank as shown by the account.[4]

Today, notwithstanding the merger of law and equity, tracing remains firmly tied to the equitable remedies of constructive trust, equitable lien, and accounting. Tracing outside these remedies is usually accomplished by legislative edict, such as when a statutory remedy authorizes disgorgement,[5] an accounting for profits,[6] or creditor's remedy.[7]

[59.2] Nature of Tracing

The essential element of tracing is the idea that the rightful owner of "property" is entitled to follow what is his through subsequent transactions in which the "property" is sold, exchanged, or transferred. As long as the owner can identify his "property," he can trace it through an unlimited number of transactions.[8] This principle was well known at common law, which allowed the rightful owner to replevin his stolen property "no matter what changes and transmutations it may have undergone and however much it may be increased in value by the expenditure of labor upon it." The caveat was that at common law the "property" had to remain composed of its original materials. Once it was transformed into new or different property, the original owner lost the right to reclaim it against a bona fide

---

[4] 535 N.E.2d 1151, 1156 (Ind. App. 1994) (citations and quotation marks omitted).

[5] Section 51 (Disgorgement Orders).

[6] Section 55 (Equitable Accounting) (discussing trademark infringement v. trademark dilution).

[7] *E.g.*, U.C.C. § 9-306 (granting secured party right to trace proceeds of sale of property by debtor in which creditor had security interest).

[8] 1 George E. Palmer, The Law of Restitution § 2.14, at 178 (1978).

purchaser for value who took without notice of the wrongful deprivation. Moreover, the owner could only follow his property. He could not elect to take a substitute, such as the property the defendant received when the defendant sold, exchanged, or transferred the original owner's property. One limited exception was when the defendant sold the plaintiff's property or money. The plaintiff could invoke the common court of money had and received and treat the transaction as a fictional sale for the plaintiff's benefit. The remedy was, however, limited. It would not encompass property exchanges or subsequent transactions.

Equity, however, allowed the holder of an equitable interest in property to follow the "property" further that he could at law. In equity, property could be followed if it was co-mingled with the property of others.[9] Moreover, equity would allow the holder of the equitable interest to follow his property into new property:

> It is established beyond debate that no change of form can divest a trust fund of its trust character, and that the cestui [beneficiary] may follow and reclaim his funds so long as he is able to trace and identify them, not as his original dollars or necessarily as any dollars, but through and into any form into which his dollars may have been converted . . . . The underlying principle of this rule is that the cestui que trust [beneficiary of the trust] has been wrongfully deprived of that which belongs to him; that his right to his funds has not been lost or destroyed by the misappropriation; and that if, and to the extent, the cestui is able to follow and identify the amount of the misappropriation funds as having been used in the acquisition of other property he may recovery.[10]

For example, if the defendant stole a car, the rightful owner could replevin it at law.[11] If, however, the defendant exchanged the stolen car for a motorcycle, the owner could not replevin the motorcycle. However, when, as here, the owner could trace his property into the new and different property (the motorcycle), he could claim an equitable interest in that property. Tracing could be further extended as, for example, if the defendant sold the motorcycle for cash. To prevent the defendant's unjust enrichment and profiting from his own misconduct, equity characterized the defendant as an "involuntary trustee." In other words, the defendant held only bare legal title to the property in his possession. The remedy of a constructive trust would be imposed and the defendant-constructive trustee would be directed to return the property to the holder of the beneficial, equitable interest (the plaintiff). If the motorcycle was more valuable than the car, the plaintiff could seek specific restitution of the

---

[9] National Bank v. Insurance Co., 104 U.S. 54, 69 (1881) (stating that "equity will follow the money even if it is put into a bag or an undistinguishable mass, by taking out the same quantity").

[10] Republic Supply Co. of California v. Richfield Oil Co., 79 F.2d 375, 377 (9th Cir. 1935) (citations omitted) (brackets added).

[11] Section 57 (Replevin).

motorcycle through the remedy of a constructive trust. If the converse were true, the plaintiff could replevin the car.

Tracing in equity also allowed the plaintiff to follow property, usually money, into co-mingled funds. The problem here, however, was that once the plaintiff's property was co-mingled, it became "confused"[12] and lost its separate identification. How could the commingled fund, or transactions in or out of that fund be traced to determine what was the plaintiff's and what was not? To aid a victim in this situation, equity developed fictions to enable the victim to trace his property into and out of funds commingled with the victim's and the wrongdoer's property. As initially formulated, these fictions did not precisely distinguish between funds that consisted of commingled property of the victim and the wrongdoer and funds that consisted of commingled property of victims. In the first situation, the victim's focus is on identifying his property as against claims by a wrongdoer, although there may be an incidental effect on the claims of the other creditors of the wrongdoer; in the latter situation, the victim's claim for a constructive trust directly depreciates the value of other victims' property in the fund. Courts are generally unwilling to permit a constructive trust in this latter context. As a rule, the wrongdoer has filed for bankruptcy and recognizing a constructive trust would give certain victims greater recoveries than other similarly situated victims in derogation of Bankruptcy's prime directive of equal treatment among members of a creditor class.[13]

The tracing fictions that were developed mirrored approaches used by accountants and bookkeepers to manage inventories, which are constantly being depleted by sales to customers and enhanced by purchases from suppliers. Courts recognized the fiction of FIFO (first in, first out) and LIFO (last in, first out), and others, as means to create order out of the chaos and the complexity of the commingled fund. The formula was arbitrary. In fact, the first in (deposit) may not have been used in the first out (expenditure), but the nature of a commingled fund prevented an actual proof; hence, the resort to fictions.

[59.3] Limitations on Tracing

It is one thing to allow a person rather open-ended tracing as against a wrongdoer, it is another thing to apply the same principles when the consequence is to give the person a preference over non-wrongdoers, such as creditors or other victims of the wrongdoer. This is reflected in the insolvency and bankruptcy cases when recognition of a constructive trust or equitable lien would run counter to the dominant bankruptcy theme of equal treatment within classes of creditors of the bankrupt[14] and priority

---

[12] Section 57.2 (Identification of Property (Accession and Confusion)).

[13] Section 54.6 ([Constructive Trust] (Priority); Section 59.3 (Limitations on Tracing) (particularly 59.3.1 (Strict Rule in Bankruptcy)).

[14] Berger v. IRS, 496 U.S. 53, 58 (1990) (stating that equal distribution with creditor classes is fundamental goal of bankruptcy law); *cf.* Goldberg v. New Jersey Lawyers' Fund For Client Protection, 932 F.2d 273, 280 (3d Cir. 1991) ("In general, courts favor a pro rata distribution of funds when such funds are claimed by creditors of like status").

as between classes of creditors of the bankruptcy.[15] This conflict has been addressed in a number of ways.

[59.3.1] Strict Rule in Bankruptcy

The general approach of bankruptcy courts is to impose on the party seeking to trace property out of commingled funds "the burden of tracing the alleged trust property 'specifically and directly' back to the illegal transfers giving rise to the trust."[16] This requirement is further hardened by the presumption that transactions from commingled accounts under the control of the debtor, which can be used by the debtor, are presumptively property of the bankrupt-debtor's estate.[17] While this presumption is rebuttable, the courts tend to require specific and direct evidence that the debtor dealt with the plaintiff's property. This is consistent with the rule that "the degree of identification required in an action between the [beneficiary] and the trustee is far less than where the trustee is insolvent, and the rights of other creditors are involved."[18] In *Bullion Reserve of North America*[19] identification of the property to be impressed with a constructive trust was deemed insufficient when the investor could not show a direct linkage between the money he gave and the gold he received. The investor had purchased gold and had it stored at Bullion Reserve of North America [BRNA]. BRNA represented that the gold would be segregated for each investor. It was not. BRNA frequently had to purchase gold on the open market to meet delivery demands. In the particular case, the investor (Bozek) became an investor in December, 1981. Between 1981 and 1983 he made substantial purchases of gold, which he stored at BRNA. On August 22, 1983, forty-two days before BRNA filed for bankruptcy, Bozek liquidated his account and took possession of "his" gold. Unfortunately for Bozek, he was unable to show that his money had purchased the very gold now in his possession and he was forced to return the gold as a preferential transfer because the transfer was within 90 days of the bankruptcy filing. On these facts, Bozek was unable to meet the strict tracing requirement.

The decisions evidence how narrow the presumptions are when the effect of recognizing a constructive trust would be to grant the beneficiary a preference over other creditors of the bankruptcy estate.[20] When the recognition of a constructive trust would not harm other creditors, courts

---

[15] *See* 11 U.S.C.A. § 726 (distribution of property of bankruptcy estate).

[16] *In re* Advent Mgmt. Corp., 104 F.3d 293, 295 (9th Cir. 1997) (citations omitted).

[17] *In re* Bullion Reserve of N. Am., 836 F.2d 1214, 1217 (9th Cir.), *cert. denied*, 486 U.S. 1056 (1988).

[18] Kobida v. Hinkelman, 127 P.2d 657, 661 (Cal. App. 1942).

[19] 836 F.2d 1214 (9th Cir.), *cert. denied*, 486 U.S. 1056 (1988).

[20] *In re* Foster, 275 F.3d 924, 928 (10th Cir. 2001):

> A tracing fiction should not be employed to elevate Kinzler's claim over the claims of other creditors if those creditors are similarly situated. The court did not determine if the other creditors are similarly situated and thus erred in employing the tracing fiction.

may exhibit a more relaxed tracing requirement.[21] For example, when a debtor mistakenly receives a check that should have gone to a third party and deposits the funds in its account, a constructive trust as to those funds will be recognized in favor of the third party because a direct link can be shown between the funds and the wrongfully diverted check and it is unlikely that others would be prejudiced by the correction.[22]

Tracing rules may be relaxed when doing so would advance a victim-compensation function and not subtract from the rights of interested creditors. For example, in *United States v. Benitez*[23] the wrongdoer turned over the fruits of his criminal activity to the government and disclaimed any interest in the fund created. The court adopted a constructive trust in order to facilitate distribution of the fund to the victims and relaxed the tracing requirements that each claimant would normally be obligated to satisfy to identify a property interest in the fund.

[59.3.2] Lowest Intermediate Balance Rule

The Lowest Intermediate Balance Rule (LIB Rule) applies when a trustee, actual or constructive, commingles "trust" funds with other funds in a single account. The LIB Rule provides that once the single account is reduced, the amount expended is dissipated and cannot be deemed to reappear in subsequent deposits.[24] In other words "[o]nce traced proceeds are withdrawn . . . they are treated as lost, even though subsequent deposits are made into the account."[25]

When funds are commingled, it is very difficult to reconstruct with precision the movement of funds into and out of the account. When money is deposited into a bank account, the bank credits the account in an amount equal to the deposit. The opposite occurs when a withdrawal is made; the account is debited in an amount equal to the withdrawal. At any point in time, however, the account balance represents the cumulative and current result of all transactions affecting the account. Moreover, the account itself is not a physical thing but simply an electronic entry maintained by the account custodian.[26]

The order in which deposits and withdrawals are made can be influential if accounts are seen as physical things. For example, if the wrongdoer (WD)

---

[21] *In re* Goldberg, 168 B.R. 382, 385 (Bankr. 9th Cir. 1994) (stating that "it is not an abuse of discretion to allow liberal tracing when no creditors will be harmed").

[22] *In re* Unicom Computer Corp., 13 F.3d 321, 325 (9th Cir. 1994); *see* Crestar Bank v. Williams, 462 S.E.2d 333, 335 (Va. 1995) (stating that "a claimant's money must be 'distinctly traced' into the . . . fund, or other property which is to be made subject to the trust").

[23] 779 F.3d 135, 138–40 (2d Cir. 1985).

[24] Schuyler v. Littlefield, 232 U.S. 707, 710 (1914).

[25] *In re* Dameron, 155 F.3d 718, 724 '(4th Cir. 1998); Meyer v. Norwest Bank Iowa, Nat'l Ass'n, 112 F.3d 946, 948 (8th Cir. 1997).

[26] *Cf.* United States v. Banco Cafetero Panama, 797 F.2d 1154, 1158 (2d Cir. 1986) ("Banks are not bailees of their depositors' money, and a depositor may not replevy his money as a specific res or follow it into the hands of another bank customer . . .") (citations omitted).

takes $100 of the victim's (V) money and deposits it into an account and the next two transactions are $100 in then $100 out, we can conceive that V still has his $100 in the account since the last two transactions effectively net themselves out. But if we reverse the order, $100 out and $100 in, there is still $100 in the account but is it WD's or V's? Similarly, the concept of an account is abstract. Using the same hypothetical facts, assume the $100 taken from V is deposited in account A at Bank and that WD also has another account (account B) at the same bank. Should the transactions be aggregated or kept separate by account?[27] Should transactions be separated by banks or bank branches? There is tremendous fortuitousness and arbitrariness in the identification of a fund and the fixing of interests in the fund.[28]

Any effort to affix a priority to certain events will necessarily be arbitrary. Courts have, nonetheless, evidenced a willingness to adopt certain fictions to assist in the identification of an equitable interest, if any, in property held by another. Many of the cases initially adopted one or more fictions that borrow those used in accounting, such as LIFO (last in, first out) and FIFO (first in, first out).[29] LIFO allows the last depositor to take her funds out first, then the next to last depositor, and so on. FIFO simply reverses the order. The bulk of an inadequate fund will go to those assigned to the head of the line. This may affect which approach a court may adopt.[30]

The modern approach is to combine the LIB Rule with the fiction that the wrongdoer acts for the benefit of the victim. This is consistent with trust theory that the trustee acts for the benefit of the beneficiary, but clearly is a fiction when applied to a wrongdoer. This approach directs that the beneficiary's interests in a commingled account are "preserved to the greatest extent possible as the account is depleted."[31] Withdrawals are considered as having come first from the wrongdoer's interest in the fund when the withdrawal benefits the wrongdoer. In other words, the LIB Rule allows the beneficiaries to assume that their funds are withdrawn last from

---

[27] *In re* MJK Clearing, Inc., 371 F.3d 397, 402–03 (8th Cir. 2004) (holding that creditor could not use aggregate of accounts maintained by debtor against which to apply LIB Rule, but would be limited to specific account in which creditor's funds were deposited; because that specific account had been depleted, creditor could not claim an equitable interest in the other accounts of the debtor).

[28] United States v. Moore, 27 F.3d 969, 976 (4th Cir. 1994) (noting that distinguishing between interests in commingled fund "cannot be traced to any particular source, absent resort to accepted, but arbitrary accounting techniques") (citations omitted); Dale Oesterle, *Deficiencies of the Restitutionary Right to Trace Misappropriated Property in Equity and UCC § 9-306*, 68 Cornell L. Rev. 172 (1983).

[29] The Chase Manhattan Bank, N.A. v. Traditional Inv. Corp. (S.D.N.Y.), 1995 W.L. 72410 (applying LIFO).

[30] *Cf.* First Wisconsin Financial Corp. v. Yamaguchi, 812 F.2d 370 (7th Cir. 1987) (discussing whether LIFO or FIFO would be appropriate method of determining scope of guarantor's obligation on past debt in light of effect of the Rule on each approach).

[31] *In re Dameron, supra,* 155 F.3d at 724; C.O. Funk & Sons, Inc. v. Sullivan Equip., Inc., 431 N.E.2d 370, 372 (Ill. 1982).

a commingled account.[32] The beneficiary also has the option, however, of treating a withdrawal as involving "trust property" and tracing her interest from the commingled fund into the acquired property.[33] The beneficiary is allowed the liberality of characterizing transactions out of the commingled fund in whatever manner preserves the beneficiary's interest to the maximum extent possible, subject, however, to the rule that once "trust funds" are dissipated they are not replenished.[34]

It may help to visual the concept by working through a hypothetical. Assume that Stu stole $20,000 from Marc on May 2nd. The transactions with regard to Stu's account are as follows:

DATE		AMOUNT	BALANCE
May 1			$ 2,500
May 2	Deposit	$20,000	22,500
May 3	Check 215 (Rent)	2,500	20,000
May 4	Checks 216-18 (food and utility bills)	500	19,500
May 5	Check 219) (vacation in Las Vegas)	1,500	18,000
May 8	Deposit	10,000	28,000
May 9	Check 220 (Classic 1958 Mercedes Benz 190SL)	18,000	10,000
May 10	Check 221 (Lottery Tickets, none successful)	10,000	0
May 11	Deposit	25,000	25,000

(The May 2nd deposit consisted of the money stolen from Marc).

Because the account balance was $0 as of May 10, the LIB Rule denies Marc the ability to assert an equitable interest in the $25,000 balance as of May 11th. Marc may claim an interest in the account as a general creditor, but Marc's ability to claim all or a portion of the $25,000 balance will depend on whether Stu has other creditors and whether the $25,000

---

[32] *In re* Columbia Gas Sys., Inc., 997 F.3d 1039, 1063 (3d Cir. 1993), *cert. denied sub nom.* Official Comm. Of Unsecured Creditors of Columbia Gas Transp. Corp. v. Columbia Gas Trans. Corp., 510 U.S. 1110 (1994).

[33] Sony Corp. of Am. v. Bank One, West Virginia, Huntington N.A. 85 F.3d 131, 138–39 (4th Cir. 1996).

[34] *In re Dameron, supra,* 155 F.3d at 724; Chrysler Credit Corp. v. Superior Court, 22 Cal. Rptr. 2d 37, 44–45 (Cal. App. 1993).

is subject to levy and execution by a judgment creditor. The presumption applied to the modern version of the LIB Rule may, however, give Marc another option. After the May 2nd deposit of money stolen from Marc, Marc can claim an equitable interest in the account. As of May 2nd, Marc's claim was $20,000 of the total balance of $22,500. The withdrawals on May 3rd, 4th, and 5th were first credited against Stu's interest in the account (the difference between the total value of the account ($22,500) and Marc's interest ($20,000) which was $2,500. Stu's interest was, however, consumed by the May 3rd withdrawal; therefore, the May 4th and 5th withdrawals reduced Marc's interest in the account to $18,000 ($20,000 less $500 less $1500). The deposit on May 8th, while it increased the account, did not replenish the prior, partial dissipation of Marc's interest in the account. Notwithstanding the deposit, Marc's interest in the account remained fixed at $18,000. On May 9th Stu purchased a vehicle for $18,000, which equaled Marc's interest in the account. Marc may trace his interest in the account into the purchase of the vehicle and assert a constructive trust over it. Since the vehicle's purchase price equaled Marc's interest in the account, Marc may claim a 100% interest in the vehicle. If the vehicle cost more than $18,000 Marc would own a proportionate share of the vehicle as his $18,000 bore to the total purchase price. Thus, if the vehicle costs $24,000, Marc would own 3/4ths ($18,000/$24,000) and Stu would own 1/4th. Alternatively, Marc may sue Stu for damages and assert an equitable lien over the vehicle because he can trace his property ($20,000) to the vehicle.[35]

[59.3.3] Tracing and Equal Treatment

Tracing issues arise in a variety of contexts. In a divorce, a spouse may seek to trace whether marital funds were used to acquire property held in the name of only one spouse.[36] In a securitized transaction, one party may seek to trace proceeds to which it can claim a security interest superior to other creditors of the debtor.[37] In a forfeiture matter, the government may seek to trace illegally obtained monies into assets held by the defendant.[38] While there are substantial similarities and overlaps in the way tracing and its fictions are applied in the various contexts, there are also substantial divisions. For example, the use of accounting fictions to identify

---

[35] These and other fictions are discussed in PALMER, RESTITUTION, *supra* § 2.18, at 214–17; Restatement of Restitution §§ 202-215 (1937); and Section 59.3.3 (Tracing and Equal Treatment).

[36] Hart v. Hart, 497 S.E.2d 496, 505–06 (Va. App. 1998) (using formula characterized by the court as "hybrid tracing methodology").

[37] Security State Bank, Sheldon Iowa v. Firstar Bank Milwaukee, 965 F. Supp. 1237 (N.D. Iowa 1991) (involving proceeds from sale of collateral); *Chrysler Credit Corp., supra*, 22 Cal. Rptr. 2d at 45–46 (involving maintenance of cash collateral account).; *C.O. Funk & Sons, Inc., supra*, 431 N.E.2d at 370 (involving proceeds from sale of collateral).

[38] United States v. Banco Cafetero Panama, 797 F.2d 1154 (2d Cir. 1986) (involving civil forfeiture proceedings instituted by the United States to recover assets purchased with profits from trafficking in illegal drugs).

interests in commingled funds has been more readily accepted in forfeiture cases than in other cases.[39]

The ability to trace one's property and identify it in the hands of another does not guarantee that an equitable interest in the property will be recognized. Constructive trusts and equitable liens are remedies, not rights. Unlike an express trust in which the equitable interest truly belongs to the beneficiary, a remedial interest is bottomed on the desire to accomplish substantial justice. When recognition of a constructive trust would accomplish an injustice, such as by giving the plaintiff an unfair preference over similarly situated individuals, the remedy of a constructive trust may be denied.[40] The Supreme Court took note of this in the *Cunningham v. Brown* decision, involving efforts by some defrauded investors in the infamous "Ponzi scheme" to obtain a preferential position over other defrauded investors. The Court rejected efforts to use equitable remedies to create a preference among creditors observing that in some cases "equality is equity."[41] Charles Ponzi defrauded thousands of people by promising them $150 within 90 days for every $100 they lent him. Ponzi stated that he was able to avail himself of currency fluctuations in post-WWI Europe. He couldn't and didn't. In fact, Ponzi was using current investors to pay off earlier investors. Eventually the market of fools dried up and the scheme collapsed. Nevertheless, Ponzi became associated with all schemes of the same ilk; hence, "Ponzi Scheme." It is important to note, however, that not all creditors may be deemed "equal." For example, in *In re Teltronics*[42] the court permitted defrauded investors to claim a priority as against other unsecured general creditors of the bankrupt wrongdoer. The court noted that assets obtained by fraud are not deemed part of the bankrupt's estate[43]

[39] *Banco Cafetero Panama, supra,* 797 F.2d at 1158–59 (identifying three approaches that could be used when illegal and legitimate funds are commingled in a single account: LIFO; FIFO; and pro rata averaging). The court held that the government could use either LIFO or FIFO, but since the government had not requested pro rata averaging the court did not approve its use. Although the use of these accounting fictions has been questioned, they are generally applied in the forfeiture context. *See* United States v. BCCI Holdings (Luxembourg), S.A. 961 F. Supp. 287, 304 (D.D.C. 1997).

[40] United States v. Real Property Located at 13328 and 13324 State Highway 75 N., Blaine County, Idaho, 89 F.3d 551 (9th Cir. 1996):

> Wymer defrauded many innocent parties. The fund created to make these parties whole is insufficient to allow full restitution to all victims. Rather than participate in the SEC's plan to distribute this inadequate fund pro rata, the PDRA seeks to better its position by using tracing fictions to make a claim to all proceeds from the sale of the Idaho property. To allow PDRA to succeed with this claim would frustrate equity.

Id. at 553.

[41] 265 U.S. 1, 13 (1924); *Real Property Located at 13328 and 13324 State Highway 75 N., supra,* 89 F.3d at 553–54 (collecting decisions rejecting tracing fictions when their use would permit an inequitable distribution).

[42] 649 F.2d 1236 (7th Cir. 1981).

[43] *Id.* at 1239. The accuracy of this point in the broad sense articulated by the court may be questioned. *In re* Deephouse Equip. Co., Inc., 22 B.R. 255, 257 (Bankr. D. Conn. 1982).

and relaxed the usual strict tracing requirement in bankruptcy.[44] Abandoning the strict tracing requirement was not seen as violating the equal treatment principle since all "defrauded" victims would share pro rata in the "trust" property excluded from the bankruptcy estate. As noted by the *Teltronics* court:

> The present case also calls for an exception to the tracing requirement. The funds held by the state court receiver are those of the consumers. Fraud is established. Unlike the common law exception rejected in *Cunningham*, however, the Illinois Consumer Fraud Act provides a mechanism by which the consumers will share equally in the fund. The receivership is expressly designed to fairly distribute a fund among customers. Application of the Illinois Consumer Fraud Act thus realizes the equitable result sought by *Cunningham*. Where such a procedure is provided, an exception to the tracing requirement should be recognized. Otherwise, as noted in *Paragon Securities*, the creditors would obtain a windfall at the expense of the defrauded customers, who did not enter into their contracts with a creditor's acceptance of the risk of failure of the debtor.[45]

Tracing, however, was not expressly abandoned. The court stated that the defrauded investors could "roughly" identify which property was theirs.[46] Statements by courts that "tracing" is not required should be viewed cautiously. They invariably mask a policy based decision that aspecific creditor or class of creditors should be favored in the particular case.

---

[44] Section 59.3.1 ([Tracing Principles] Strict Rule in Bankruptcy).

[45] 649 F.2d at 1240–41.

[46] *Id.* at 1240; *cf.* People of the State of Ill., ex rel. Hartigan v. Peters, 871 F.2d 1336, 1345 (7th Cir. 1989) (rejecting claim of equitable interest when Attorney General could not trace illegally obtained monies into accounts).

Chapter 7

REMEDY DEFENSES

§ 60 COMPARED WITH LIABILITY DEFENSES

This chapter examines the more frequently encountered remedial defenses. In a number of sections equitable and legal defenses are paired, for example, laches (traditionally equitable) and statute of limitation (traditionally legal). A number of defenses that go to the merits of the claim are also included because of their widespread use, for example, waiver and estoppel. More specialized equitable defenses, such as "misuse,"[1] are omitted.

Although the focus here is on defenses to remedy claims, a defense may be asserted against a remedial defense.[2]

The basic issue addressed is the character of the remedy defense. As the term suggests, the defense is limited to the specific remedy. A liability defense, if successful, negates a party's right of action, for example truth as a defense to libel. If the statement is true, there is no cause of action for libel; however, there may be a cause of action for invasion of privacy for which truth is not a defense. A remedy defense operates on the remedy, not the underlying right. An equitable remedy defense, such as laches, precludes equitable remedies, such as an injunction, but does not, by its terms, preclude legal remedies, such as damages.[3]

The fact that the remedial defense goes to the remedy rather than the right gives legislatures and courts greater leeway to alter retroactively the content of remedial defenses.[4] Perhaps the most common modern example of this has been legislative alteration of statutes of limitation to permit time-barred actions to proceed under new, more generous limitation periods.[5] Although it is commonplace to speak of the action as being time barred, the limitation defense affects the remedy, not the right; this distinction is critical to allowing retroactive application of the statute altering or abridging the defense.[6] That said, the distinction between extending a limitation period as to an active, not time-barred, claim and

---

[1] Lasercomb Am., Inc. v. Reynolds, 911 F.2d 970 (4th Cir. 1990) (involving copyright infringement).

[2] E.T. Manufacturing Co., Inc. v. Xomed, Inc., 679 F. Supp. 1082, 1085–86 (M.D. Fla. 1987) (considering defense of unclean hands to defense of laches).

[3] Section 20.3.2 (Remedial Defenses).

[4] Section 3.1 (Relationship Between Rights and Remedies).

[5] Campanelli v. Allstate Life Ins. Co., 322 F.3d 1086 (9th Cir. 2003) (rejecting constitutional challenges to retroactive extension by California legislature of time period within which to bring claims against insurers arising out of the 1994 Northridge earthquake), *cert. denied sub nom.* Allstate Ins. Co. v. Noah, 124 S. Ct. 1038 (2004). The challenges were based on the impairment of contracts proscription in the United States (Art. 1, § 10, cl.1) and California (Art. 1, § 9) constitutions and the due process provisions of both constitutions. 322 F.3d at 1097–1101.

[6] This distinction is longstanding. Sturges v. Crowninshield, 17 U.S. 122, 200 (1819) ("The distinction between the obligation of a contract and a remedy given by the Legislature to enforce that obligation exists in the nature of things, and, without impairing the obligation of the contract, the remedy may be modified as the wisdom of the nation may direct").

reviving a time-barred claim by extending the limitation period is one that continues to trouble courts.[7]

Generalizations regarding retroactive application of new, longer statutes of limitation must be cautious because analysis tends to focus on statutory language and legislature intent. The analysis tends to be two pronged. First, did the legislature clearly intend to extend the limitation period. Second, did the legislature clearly intend to revive time-barred claims.[8]

A true statute of limitation affects only the right to enforce the remedy not the right itself. Occasionally, however, the limitation period is seen as part of the right itself, such that the passage of the limitation period operates to extinguish the right itself. These are referred to as Statutes of Repose and retroactive application of these statutes may be viewed differently and more restrictively.[9] Statutory rights of action often occupy this category:

> Statutes of limitation are to be distinguished from statutes which create a right of action not existing at common law and restrict the time within which action may be brought to enforce the right. Although the general rule is that a true statute of limitations extinguishes only the right to enforce the remedy and not the substantive right itself, the limitation of time for commencing an action under a statute creating a new right enters into and become part of the right of action itself and is a limitation not only of the remedy but of the right also; the right to recover depends upon the commencement of the action within the time limit set by the statute, and if that period of time is allowed to elapse without the institution of the action, the right of action is gone forever.[10]

The distinction between right and remedy can be particularly significant in conflict of laws contexts when the forum's own period of limitation may "revive" a cause of action barred in the jurisdiction that created the right of action.[11]

---

[7] Deutsch v. Turner Corp., 317 F.3d 1005, 1020 n.4 (9th Cir.) *amended and superseded on denial of reh'g en banc*, 324 F.3d 692 (9th Cir.) (stating that revival of time-barred claim with accompanying exposure to civil liability and "upsetting the repose of potential defendants . . . is troubling"); *cert. denied sub nom.* Tenney v. Mitsui & Co., Ltd., 540 U.S. 820 (2003). The court did not, however, address the due process claim.

[8] Kansas Pub. Employees Act. Sys. v. Reimer & Koger Associates, Inc., 61 F.3d 608, 615 (8th Cir. 1995); Chenault v. United States Postal Service, 37 F.3d 535, 539 (9th Cir. 1994); Hymowitz v. Eli Lilly & Co., 539 N.E.2d 1069, 1079 (N.Y. 1989).

[9] William Danzer Co. v. Gulf & Ship Island R.R. Co., 268 U.S. 633, 637 (1925).

[10] Jamerson v. Miles, 421 F. Supp. 107 811 (N.D. Tex. 1976); *see* J&M Land Co. v. First Union Nat'l Bank, 766 A.2d 1110, 1123 (N.J. 2001) (same).

[11] Bournias v. Atlantic Maritime Co., Ltd., 220 F.2d 152, 155 (2d Cir. 1955) (holding that expired limitation period of jurisdiction that created right of action (Panama) did not bar forum from enforcing right that was still alive under forum's limitation period).

§ 61 LACHES AND STATUTES OF LIMITATION

The general focus of both of these defenses is a concern over delay in bringing the action. The effect of the valid assertion of either the defense of laches or statute of limitation is to bar the remedy for the cause of action to which the defense applies.

[61.1] Laches

The defense of laches developed in equity at a time that system's remedies were not bound by statutes of limitation.[1] Laches was premised on the maxim that equity aids the vigilant not those who sleep on their rights.[2] However, laches cannot be used to force action on the plaintiff when the obligation to act lies with the defendant. For example, laches is not a defense to a claim of adverse possession; the obligation is on the owner of record to bring an action, after adverse possession commences, to clear title.[3]

Laches policy base is analogous to that which underlies statutes of limitation, the discouragement of stale demands:

> The doctrine of laches is based upon grounds of public policy, which requires for the peace of society the discouragement of stale demands; and where the difficulty of doing entire justice by reason of the death of the principal witness or witnesses, or from the original transactions having become obscured by time, is attributable to gross negligence or deliberate delay, a court of equity will not aid a party whose application is thus destitute of conscience, good faith and reasonable diligence.[4]

Rather than adopting a rule-based jurisprudence to deal with the issue of delay, equity courts continue in their policy of a case-by-case approach. Consequently, laches is not framed by clearly delineated time periods for bringing equitable claims; rather, equity determines whether in the particular case delay and its consequences warrant denial of equitable relief in the interests of justice and fairness.[5]

The essence of laches is unreasonable delay by the plaintiff causing material prejudice to the defendant. The precise verbal formulations of the laches defense vary slightly but all carry this core concept. For example, in *Lingenfelter v. Keystone Consolidated Industries, Inc.* the court spoke of

---

[1] 2 JOHN POMEROY, EQUITY JURISPRUDENCE §§ 418–19a (5th ed. 1941).

[2] Jarrow Formulas, Inc. v. Nutrition Now, Inc., 304 F.3d 829, 835 (9th Cir), *cert. denied*, 537 U.S. 1047 (2002); Richardson v. Richland County, 711 P.2d 777, 782 (Mont. 1985).

[3] Marriage v. Keener, 31 Cal. Rptr. 2d 511, 513–14 (Cal. App. 1994).

[4] Mackall v. Casilear, 137 U.S. 556, 566 (1890); Schroeder v. Schlueter, 407 N.E.2d 204, 207 (Ill. App. 1980).

[5] Cornetta v. United States, 851 F.2d 1372, 1379–80 (Fed. Cir. 1988); National Wildlife Fed'n v. Burford, 835 F.2d 305, 318 (D.C. Cir. 1987); *cf.* Holmberg v. Armbrecht, 327 U.S. 392, 396 (1946) (stating that "[e]quity eschews mechanical rules; it depends on flexibility").

a two-part test consisting of (1) lack of diligence by plaintiff in asserting the claim and (2) prejudice to the defendant.[6] In *Leinoff v. Louis Milona & Sons, Inc.* the court articulated the same test as a three-part formula: In order to assert the defense the defendant must demonstrate by a preponderance of the evidence (1) that plaintiff delayed bringing the action; (2) that plaintiff's delay was unreasonable and inexcusable; and (3) that defendant was materially prejudiced by the delay.[7] The distinction is insignificant because "lack of diligence" and "unreasonable and inexcusable delay" are legal equivalents.[8]

The first factor is delay. The mere passage of time does not constitute delay.[9] Delay occurs when a plaintiff, with actual or constructive knowledge of the facts that support the claim for relief in equity, fails to act to secure his legal rights.[10] There is only a fine, if imprecise, line between "delay" and "unreasonable delay." Indeed, when stated in the abstract, the test is somewhat circular: "An inexcusable or unreasonable delay may occur . . . by facts otherwise indicating a lack of vigilance."[11] The particular facts of the matter give meaning to whether there was delay and whether it was unreasonable.

The most accurate measure of reasonableness or unreasonableness is also the simplest. Delay becomes unreasonable when there is no good explanation for delay. For example, in *Marriage of Capetillo* the plaintiff delayed 10 years in seeking to recover unpaid child support from the defendant. The court held that 10 years delay was not necessarily unreasonable because there was evidence defendant abused the children, and this explained plaintiff's reluctance to move more aggressively to collect the unpaid support.[12] It is reasonable to delay to await a change in law that will allow the claim to go forward.[13] It is reasonable to delay until the plaintiff has a claim to bring. As noted in *What-a Burger of Virginia, Inc. v. Whataburger, Inc.* when the plaintiff was aware that a distant potential

---

[6] 691 F.2d 339, 340 (7th Cir. 1982); *see* Costello v. United States, 365 U.S. 265, 282 (1961).

[7] 726 F.2d 734, 741–42 (Fed. Cir. 1984); National Parks and Conservation Ass'n v. Hodel, 679 F. Supp. 49, 53 (D.D.C. 1987).

[8] White v. Daniel, 909 F.2d 99, 102 (4th Cir. 1990), *cert denied*, 501 U.S. 1260 (1991).

[9] Tray v. Whitney, 192 N.W.2d 628, 631 (Mich. App. 1971) (noting that "[i]t is well established that the doctrine of laches consists of more than the mere passage of time").

[10] Baker Mfg. Co. v. Whitewater Mfg. Co., 430 F.2d 1008, 1111 (7th Cir. 1970) (stating that the "doctrine of laches requires not only the passage of time but an acquiescence . . . acquiescence must be predicated on knowledge . . . either express or implied . . .") *cert. denied*, 401 U.S. 956 (1971); National Parks and Conservation Ass'n v. Hodel, 679 F. Supp. 49, 53 (D.D.C. 1987) (noting that record was "replete with evidence" that plaintiffs had knowledge of the facts underlying their claim approximately 3 1/2 years prior to commencement of action); North Bay Council, Inc. v. Grinnell, 461 A.2d 114, 116 (N.H. 1983) (holding that "laches, as a general rule, cannot be imputed to a party who is ignorant of the facts creating his right").

[11] *White v. Daniel, supra*, 909 F.2d at 102.

[12] 932 P.2d 691, 695 (Wash. App. 1997). The "fear" was that enforcing the child support obligations would encourage the defendant to insist on his visitation rights, which the plaintiff feared would lead to abuse of the children.

[13] *In re Beaty*, 306 F.3d 914, 927 (9th Cir. 2002).

competitor was using a similar name, but the defendant was not yet infringing on the plaintiff's mark:

> Logic dictates that "unreasonable delay" does not include any period of time before the owner is able to pursue a claim for infringement— otherwise, a trademark owner could be punished for not bringing a claim he had no right to bring. For this reasons, we have recognized that laches "assumes the existence of an infringement for an extended period prior to the commencement of litigation.[14]

On the other hand, the plaintiff cannot delay to make the case *factually* better. In *White v. Daniel* the court held that plaintiff's 17 year delay in challenging redistricting as violative of the Voting Rights Act was unreasonable. Plaintiffs' reason for delay, the need for more elections to substantiate their statistical evidence of racially polarized elections, was rejected by the court because plaintiffs' failed to demonstrate that earlier elections were not sufficient to support their claims.[15]

Courts should consider and weigh "any justification offered by the plaintiff for the delay."[16] Perhaps the most common justification is delay caused by time reasonably spent by a plaintiff seeking to negotiate a resolution of the dispute with the defendant. Time spent reasonably attempting to resolve a dispute is excluded from the determination whether the delay was "unreasonable."[17]

The rule is that laches follows the analogous statute of limitation, but not slavishly. An equitable claim filed within the period of time specified in the analogous statute of limitation is rebuttably presumed to have been brought without unreasonable delay.[18] The analogous statute of limitation

---

[14] 357 F.3d 441, 449 (4th Cir. 2004).

[15] 909 F.2d at 103.

[16] A.C. Aukerman Co. v. R.L. Chaides Constr. Co., 960 F.2d 1020, 1033 (Fed. Cir. 1992) (collecting cases noting that courts have considered justifications for delay such as other litigation, poverty, illness, and wartime conditions) (citations omitted). *But cf.* Vernon Fire Fighters Ass'n, Local 2312 v. City of Vernon, 223 Cal. Rptr. 871, 878 (Cal. App. 1986) (questioning whether a party may delay commencing litigation because of other litigation pending).

[17] Meyers v. Asics Corp., 974 F.2d 1304, 1307 (Fed. Cir. 1992) (negotiating with defendant and other persons for a license was reasonable and excused delay in commencing action); *In re* GVF Cannery, Inc., 188 B.R. 651, 669 (N.D. Cal. 1995) (same); *cf.* Bomba v. W.L. Belvidere, Inc., 579 F.2d 1067, 1071 (7th Cir. 1978) (stating that contrary to the rule for laches, settlement negotiation does not toll an applicable statute of limitation).

[18] This applies most strongly to statutory remedies. Lyons Partnership, L.P. v. Morris Costumes, Inc., 243 F.3d 789, 797–98 (4th Cir. 2001) (stating that judicially created doctrines (laches) should not be used to undermine legislatively crafted remedies):

> [T]his principle is equally relevant when Congress creates a cause of action for traditional equitable remedies, such as injunctions, and specifies a statute of limitations for that action. Thus, when Congress creates a cause of action and provides both legal and equitable remedies, its statute of limitations for that cause of action should govern, regardless of the remedy sought.

Id. at 798. This principle was, however, questioned in Teamsters & Employers Welfare Trust

provides guidance in determining the reasonableness of any delay, but it is not necessarily conclusive.[19] On the other hand, laches may in the appropriate case operate to bar equitable relief even though legal relief for the same violation would not be barred.[20]

A modified version of this approach is to use an analogous statute of limitation as a linchpin. When the equitable claim is filed within the analogous statute of limitation, the defendant has the burden of proof to show unreasonable delay. As to claims filed after the analogous statute has expired, the burden shifts and a presumption of laches is created.[21] The approach derives from early equity practices to apply the statute of limitation to an equitable claim when the reasons for repose were equally applicable and the equitable and legal remedies were equivalent. As noted in *Russell v. Todd*:

> In the application of the doctrine of laches [equity] recognized that prejudice may arise from delay alone, so prolonged that in the normal course of events evidence is lost or obscured, and the English Court of Chancery early adopted the rule, followed in the federal courts, that suits to assert equitable interests in real estate will, without more, be barred after the lapse of twenty years when ejectment or the right of entry for the assertion of a comparable legal interest in the land would be barred. And where resort was had to equity in aid of a legal right, equity, following the law, would refuse its aid if the legal right had been barred by the applicable statute of limitations.[22]

The principle has been extended to situations where legal and equitable claims are not the same but analogous.[23]

---

of Illinois v. Gorman Bros. Ready Mix, 283 F.3d 877, 881 (7th Cir. 2002) (arguing that courts do not reject the application of equitable principles to lengthen limitation periods and a double standard should not be applied). The "equitable principles" referred to by the court are discussed in Section 61.2.2 (Discovery of Injury or Harm).

[19] Goodman v. McDonnell Douglas Corp., 606 F.2d 800, 804–05 (8th Cir. 1979) (stating that the running of the analogous statute of limitation is merely one factor to be considered); Kay v. Kay, 334 A.2d 585, 587 (Pa. 1975).

[20] Holmberg v. Armbrecht, 327 U.S. 392, 396 (1946); Marriage of Plescia, 69 Cal. Rptr. 2d 120, 124–25 (Cal. App. 1997) (holding that notwithstanding legislature's abolition of statute of limitation and due diligence requirement for commencing action for accrued, unpaid spousal support, defense of laches was still available). The California legislature has limited *Plescia*. Cal. Fam. Code § 4502(c) (precluding laches unless claim is brought by governmental entity).

[21] Puerto Rican-Am. Ins. Co. v. Benjamin Shipping Co., Ltd., 829 F.2d 281, 283 (1st Cir. 1987); Dameron v. Sinai Hosp. of Baltimore, Inc., 595 F. Supp. 1404, 1416 (D. Md. 1984). *But cf.* Stevens v. TVA, 712 F.2d 1047, 1056 (6th Cir. 1983) (cautioning against a mechanical application of the approach).

[22] 309 U.S. at 287 (citations omitted; brackets added); United States v. Banks, 115 F.3d 916, 919 (11th Cir. 1997) (noting "concurrent remedy rule" under which "equity will withhold its relief . . . where the applicable statute of limitation would bar the concurrent legal remedy" (citation and footnote omitted), *cert. denied*, 522 U.S. 1075 (1998); Federal Election Comm'n. v. The Christian Coalition, 965 F. Supp. 66, 71 (D.D.C. 1997).

[23] A.C. Aukerman & Co. v. R.L. Chaides Constr. Co., 960 F.2d 1020, 1030, 1034 (Fed. Cir.

Even unreasonable delay is not sufficient to bar a plaintiff's equitable claim, the defendant must still show material prejudice resulting from the unreasonable delay.[24] Prejudice has been found in a variety of circumstances and may be organized around the following categories: (1) defense prejudice; (2) economic prejudice; or (3) unfair exposure to risk. Defense prejudice involves injury to the defendant's ability to defend against the claim. It includes "loss of records, destruction of evidence, fading memories, or unavailability of witnesses."[25] In support of its claim of defense prejudice the defendant cannot rely on mere conclusory assertions; rather, defendant must demonstrate both the existence of the event, such as "loss of records," and its impact upon defendant's ability to defend against the claim.[26] For example, in *E.E.O.C. v. CW Transport, Inc.* the court rejected the defendant's claim that it was materially prejudiced by the unavailability of witnesses due to plaintiff's unreasonable delay:

> In this case, the facts before the court are insufficient to establish that CWT is materially prejudiced by the unavailability of witnesses. The facts establish only that key CWT personnel-the manager in charge of the Chicago terminal and the vice president of personnel/corporate compliance officer-do not know where the majority of the supervisory ex-employees are located. These statements imply that those officers do know where some of the former employees are located. If the company knows the location of certain witnesses, then it does not "face the hardship of locating" those persons. Without more specific information as to which employees are unavailable in the sense that their locations are not known, I cannot determine when material prejudice resulting from the unavailability of witnesses attaches to CWT.[27]

A defendant who has an affirmative duty to keep and maintain records may be hard pressed to claim prejudice even if the period of delay is unreasonable as the duty to preserve is independent of the plaintiff's (in)action.[28]

The second type of prejudice is economic. When by reason of the unreasonable delay, a defendant's liability is enlarged, courts have found material prejudice.[29] Again, however, prejudice must be proved not presumed from

---

1992) (applying 6 year limitations period for damages action based on patent infringement (35 U.S.C.A. § 286) to a patent infringement action brought in equity, for which there is no statute of limitations).

[24] Lake Caryonah Improvement Ass'n v. Pulte Home Corp., 903 F.2d 505, 509–10 (7th Cir. 1990).

[25] Cornetta v. United States, 851 F.2d 1372, 1378 (Fed. Cir. 1988); E.E.O.C. v. Dresser Indus., Inc., 668 F.2d 1199, 1203 (11th Cir. 1982).

[26] United States v. Rodriguez Aguirre, 264 F.3d 1195, 1208–09 (10th Cir. 2001).

[27] 658 F. Supp. 1278, 1293 (W.D. Wis. 1987). *But cf.* Whitfield v. Anheuser-Busch, Inc., 820 F.2d 243, 245–46 (8th Cir. 1987) (finding prejudice when key employees responsible for terminating the plaintiff could no longer recall details of termination after 10 year delay).

[28] *Rodriguez Aguirre, supra,* 264 F.3d at 1208–09.

[29] E.E.O.C. v. Alioto Fish Co., Ltd., 623 F.2d 86, 89 (9th Cir. 1980).

conclusory allegations. For example, in *Cornetta v. United States* the plaintiff, a retired Marine Corp officer, sought back pay as part of his wrongful discharge claim against the government. The court rejected the government's claim of economic prejudice. The government argued that plaintiff's delay would force it to pay two salaries for one position if plaintiff was successful; one salary for plaintiff and one salary for the substitute the government employed during the period of delay. The court held that because the government used a "pool" of individuals who are assigned as needed, the government incurred no real additional costs resulting from the delay. The court found that the government failed to show that it must pay a second officer when it discharges the first officer, that it will be forced to recruit a replacement, or that any vacancy resulting from the discharge would be promptly filled.[30]

Economic prejudice can arise when the defendant makes expenditures based on the reasonable assumption that the status quo will continue. For example, in *Lake Caryonah Improvement Ass'n v. Pulte Home Corp.* plaintiff sought specific performance by defendant of a contract to convey realty that had been entered into by defendant's predecessor in interest. However, during the period of delay prior to commencement of the specific performance action against it, defendant had paid taxes, carried insurance, and maintained the property. Defendant had also spent time and expense in an effort to develop the property only to then be confronted with the specific performance claim. The court found that defendant suffered material prejudice from the delay and barred the equitable claim.[31]

The third form of material prejudice is unfair exposure to risk. This form is close to "economic prejudice" because the risk exposure is usually monetary. The difference is that where economic prejudice requires some actual monetary harm, exposure to risk simply requires exposure to a "risk" of monetary loss due to unreasonable delay. While the two concepts are occasionally folded into a single articulation of the rule,[32] the concept of "exposure to risk" as a form of material prejudice is well recognized:

> A person may not withhold his claim awaiting the outcome of a doubtful enterprise and, after the enterprise has resulted in financial success favorable to the claimant, assert his interest, especially where he has thus avoided the risks of the enterprise. The injustice of permitting one, holding the right to assert an interest in property of a speculative character, to voluntarily await the event and then decide, when the danger is over and the risk has been that of another, to come in and share the profit, is obvious.[33]

---

[30] 851 F.2d 1372, 1379 (Fed. Cir. 1988).

[31] 903 F.2d 505, 510 (7th Cir. 1990).

[32] Baylie v. Swift & Co., 670 N.E.2d 772, 779 (Ill. App. 1996) (stating that "[a] party is guilty of laches [when] he remains passive while an adverse claimant incurs risk, enters into obligations, or makes expenditures for improvements or taxes").

[33] Pfister v. Cow Gulch Oil Co., 189 F.2d 311, 315 (10th Cir.), *cert. denied*, 342 U.S. 887 (1951); *see* Martin v. Adams County Area Vocational Tech. Sch. Auth., 313 A.2d 785, 786–87 (Pa. Commw. Ct. 1973); Duncan v. Colorado Inv. & Realty Co., 178 P.2d 428, 430 (Colo. 1947).

On the other hand, a party that knowingly incurs expenses in the face of a possible claim for equitable relief cannot claim material prejudice. Costs voluntarily incurred in the face of a known risk of litigation cannot be later used to support a claim of material prejudice due to unreasonable delay. [34]

Some courts have held that the presence of unreasonable delay creates a presumption of prejudice. [35] Generally these cases require extreme unreasonable delay. [36] This rule has, moreover, been entirely limited to patent infringement litigation. Efforts to extend the principle to other equitable actions have been unsuccessful. [37] The reason for the rejection of a presumption is that it converts a dual prong test (unreasonable delay and material prejudice) into a single prong test (unreasonable delay). When the presumption is accepted, it is recognized that the presumption should not be applied when it is shown that the defendant engaged in "particularly egregious conduct which would change the equities significantly in plaintiff's favor." [38]

Conduct may fall short of amounting to laches, yet still influence judicial resolution of the case. This is particularly so when plaintiff's delay increases defendant's costs. For example, in *Headwaters, Inc. v. Bureau of Land Management, Medford District* the court observed that had plaintiff not delayed nearly 6 months before bringing suit, much of one of the defendant's economic costs in complying with the requested injunctive relief could have been avoided. While the court was unwilling to find that the delay was "unreasonable," it did conclude that delay influenced the balance of hardship and operated to deny plaintiff injunctive relief. [39] Similarly, delay may influence a court's finding whether plaintiff will sustain irreparable injury necessary for an award of injunctive relief. [40]

---

[34] Sandy City v. Salt Lake County, 827 P.2d 227, 230 (Utah 1992) (noting that defendant's claim that it incurred substantial costs as a result of plaintiff's delay in commencing suit was without merit; defendant "ran up these costs with full knowledge of [plaintiff's] position and of the risk that the project would later be found in violation of the . . . law . . . . [A]ny losses incurred by [defendant] were taken as the result of a calculated risk that [plaintiff] would not prevail . . .").

[35] E.E.O.C. v. Great Atl. & Pac. Tea Co., 735 F.2d 69, 80–81 (3d Cir.), *cert. denied*, 469 U.S. 925 (1984); *Baker Mfg. Co.*, *supra*, 430 F.2d at 1011–15.

[36] Hall v. Aqua Queen Mfg., Inc., 93 F.3d 1548, 1552–1553 (Fed. Cir. 1996) (involving delay of 6 or more years); Odetics, Inc. v. Storage Tech. Corp., 919 F. Supp. 911, 918 (E.D. Va. 1996), *vacated on other grounds*, 116 F.3d 1497 (Fed. Cir. 1997) (Table).

[37] *Cornetta*, *supra*, 51 F.2d at 1378–79 (involving wrongful discharge action against government by military personnel).

[38] TWM Mfg. Co, Inc. v. Dura Corp., 592 F.2d 346, 349 (6th Cir. 1979).

[39] 665 F. Supp. 873, 876 (D. Or. 1987).

[40] Costello v. McEnery, 767 F. Supp. 72, 78 (S.D.N.Y. 1991), *aff'd*, 948 F.2d 1278 (2d Cir. 1991) (table), *cert. denied*, 504 U.S. 980 (1992); Century Time Ltd. v. Interchron Ltd., 729 F. Supp. 366, 369 (S.D.N.Y. 1990) (noting that delay may preclude awarding temporary injunctive relief due to absence of irreparable injury, but when delay does not amount to laches it does not necessarily preclude award of permanent injunctive relief or even another request for preliminary injunction).

Before a plaintiff can be found guilty of laches, the plaintiff must be shown to have knowledge of the claim or action he delayed bringing;[41] although the knowledge may be constructive.[42]

The ability to assert the defense of laches may be restricted when the defendant engaged in willful misconduct.[43]

[61.2] Statutes of Limitation

In actions at law, a party will invariably be given a set, specific amount of time within which to commence the claim.[44] Failure to timely file results in barring the plaintiff from obtaining affirmative relief; hence, while we speak of these time bars (statutes of limitation) as barring the action, the correct legal principle is that they act on the remedy.[45]

Statutes of limitation are said to serve a number of purposes. The primary justifications are twofold: (1) to provide peace of mind so people may cleanse their books of potential liabilities that occurred before a certain date,[46] and (2) to prevent the perpetration of fraud by precluding the prosecution of stale claims because "evidence has been lost, memories have faded, and witnesses have disappeared."[47] Other less frequently offered considerations include: (3) enhancing commercial intercourse by freeing individuals from the distraction and disruption of litigation;[48] (4) testing whether claims are meritorious (the assumption is that meritorious claims will be diligently prosecuted); (5) controlling dockets; and (6) discouraging courts from reaching dubious, difficult to support decisions based on stale evidence.[49]

---

[41] Davis v. Coleman, 521 F.2d 661, 667 (9th Cir. 1975); see Frederick Road Ltd., Partnership v. Brown & Sturm, 756 A.2d 963, 985 (Md. 2000).

[42] Advanced Cardiovascular Sys., Inc. v. Sci Med Life Sys., Inc., 988 F.2d 1157, 1161 (Fed. Cir. 1993).

[43] Danjaq LLC v. Sony Corp., 263 F.3d 942, 957 (9th Cir. 2001) (willful infringement); Section 62.1 (Unclean Hands).

[44] At early common law actions were perpetual, and it was not until the Limitation Act of 1623 that periods of limitation were engrafted onto the forms of action. *Developments in the Law—Statutes of Limitations* 63 Harv. L. Rev. 1177, 1177–78 (1950). The perpetuity concept still exists in very limited form today. *See* Cal. Civ. P. Code § 348 (action to recover money or property deposited in a bank or savings and loan); Cal. Civ. Code § 3490 (public nuisance).

[45] Section 60 (Compared With Liability Defenses).

[46] United States v. Kubrick, 444 U.S. 111, 117 (1979) (stating that "'the right to be free of stale claims in time comes to prevail over the right to prosecute them'"), *quoting* Order of R.R. Tel. v. Railway Express Agency, 321 U.S. 342, 349 (1944); *Developments in the Law— Statutes of Limitations, supra*, 63 Harv. L. Rev. at 1185.

[47] American Pipe and Constr. Co. v. Utah, 414 U.S. 538, 554 (1974), *quoting* Order of R.R. Tel. v. Railway Express Agency, 321 U.S. 342, 349 (1944)); *see* Davies v. Krasna, 535 P.2d 1161, 1168 (Cal. 1975); *Developments in the Law—Statutes of Limitations, supra*, 63 Harv. L. Rev. at 1185–86.

[48] Wood v. Carpenter, 101 U.S. 135, 139 (1879) (discussing Indiana's six year statute of limitation for fraud); *Developments in the Law—Statutes of Limitations, supra*, 63 Harv. L. Rev. at 1185–86.

[49] James Martin, *Constitutional Limitations on Choice of Law*, 61 Cornell L. Rev. 185, 221–22 (1976).

The fundamental distinction between the defenses of statute of limitation and laches is that laches is applied based on an analysis of historical facts. For laches to apply the critical issue is was there was actual delay, was the delay actually unreasonable; was the defendant actually materially prejudiced?[50] Statutes of limitation are, however, based on policy fact, derived from the assumptions that underlie the factors justifying the defense. An action brought after the statutorily fixed period of limitation has expired is time barred even if the evidence is fresh, memories are acute, and witnesses are available. Statutes of limitation are based on the legislative policy determination that the public interest is better served by dismissal of the time-barred claim, whereas equity focuses on the individual interests of the parties as to whether a matter should be heard.[51]

Determining whether a claim has been timely filed requires a three-step analysis. First the claim must be correctly identified and matched with the appropriate statute of limitation. Usually this is a simple process, but no task escapes completely the web of legal complexity. Is an action seeking relief for breach of the implied covenant of good faith and fair dealing matched with the contract statute, the tort statute or with the usual catch-all, cleanup statute? Is a legal malpractice action matched with the contract statute (because of the retainer), a fiduciary statute (because of the lawyer's status and role), a negligence statute (because of the nature of the misconduct), or some other statute? If there is a specific legal malpractice statute of limitations, is it supplementary to other applicable statutes or preemptive? These questions while important to ask are much too jurisdictionally sensitive to be answered here. Nevertheless, one should pay particular care when dealing with claims that have multiple remedies to consider that each remedy may trigger a different (and longer or shorter) statute of limitation.

Steps two and three raise the issues of accrual and tolling, which are often either confused or erroneously conflated. Accrual identifies the point when an action can first be maintained. Tolling is the suspension of a limitation period applicable to an accrued claim.

[61.2.1] Accrual

When a "suit may be maintained" is an elusive concept. It can be the date of the defendant's wrongful act; the date the plaintiff is first injured, substantially injured, or last injured by the wrongful act; or some other date. The usual date of accrual of the claim for limitation purposes is the date the plaintiff sustains injury, but "injury" comes in many forms. For example, in a case involving wrongful discharge, accrual injury may occur when the employee is notified that she will be terminated,[52] leaves her employment,[53] or when the employee is prevented from resuming her

---

[50] Section 61.1 (Laches).

[51] S.V. v. R.V., 933 S.W.2d 1, 5 (Tex. 1996).

[52] Delaware State College v. Ricks, 449 U.S. 250, 259 (1980).

[53] Rubin v. O'Koren, 621 F.2d 114, 116 (5th Cir. 1980).

employment if she left reasonably expecting to return.[54] Moreover, injuries can vary. A plaintiff exposed to injurious substances, for example, may manifest different injuries at different times, such as asbestosis and cancer. Does the cause of action for cancer accrue when the cancer occurs, or earlier when asbestosis was diagnosed? Many, but not all jurisdictions recognize that a separate limitation period applies to the second injury when the second injury is distinct from the first injury.[55] Courts have been very liberal in determining critical dates for accrual of actions and have avoided a "mechanical analysis" of the issue,[56] although at the obvious cost of less certainty regarding the actual period within which a lawsuit must be commenced. Nevertheless, liberal application will not be extended to eviscerate the values that underlie statutes of limitation.[57] The general rule is that the plaintiff's ignorance that she has sustained injury does not postpone accrual.[58] Two major exceptions to this rule are the discovery doctrine and the continuing injury/continuing violation rule.

[61.2.2] Discovery of Injury or Harm

Initially, the law did not distinguish between a plaintiff who was "blamelessly ignorant" of his right of action and a plaintiff who "slept on his rights." To ameliorate what was perceived as a harsh result courts developed the discovery rule, which holds that a cause of action "accrues" when the plaintiff knows or should have known that actionable harm was committed.[59] For the discovery rule to apply, plaintiff's excusable ignorance must go to the fact of his injury, not the scope of his injury.[60]

---

[54] Kline v. North Tx. State Univ., 782 F.2d 1229, 1233 (5th Cir. 1986).

[55] Cigna Ins. Co. v. Oy Saunatec, Ltd., 241 F.3d 1, 9–10 (1st Cir. 2001) (holding that two fires 9 years apart at the same location caused by the same defective product constituted two causes of action and the limitation period for each commenced with the date of each separate fire); Fearson v. Johns-Manville Sales Corp., 525 F. Supp. 671, 673–74 (D.D.C. 1981); Martinez-Ferrer v. Richardson-Merrill, Inc., 164 Cal. Rptr. 591, 596 (Cal. App. 1980).

[56] See Associated Indem. Corp. v. State Indus. Accident Comm'n, 12 P.2d 1075, 1076 (Cal. App. 1932) (adopting manifestation of injury test for accrual because of long latency nature of injury).

[57] Hecht v. Resolution Trust Corp., 635 A.2d 394, 401 (Md. 1994); see Piper v. IBM, 639 N.Y.S.2d 623, 626–27 (App. Dept. 1996) ("delaying accrual until last use of product or actual awareness of the nature of the injury, [would give the plaintiff] the power to put off the running of the Statute of Limitations indefinitely") (brackets added); Miller v. Lakeside Village Condo. Ass'n, 2 Cal. Rptr. 2d 796, 804 (Cal. App. 1991) (holding that plaintiff's cause of action accrued when she suffered actual and appreciable harm in form of extreme allergic reaction and severe asthma, and not later when her medical condition was diagnosed as immune dysregulation; fact that plaintiff's condition was not diagnosed correctly does not delay the running of the statute of limitation).

[58] Fairfax Sav., F.S.B. v. Weinberg & Green, 685 A.2d 1189, 1201 (Md. Ct. Sp. App. 1996); Pederson v. American Lutheran Church, 404 N.W.2d 887, 889 (Minn. App. 1987); Curran v. Time Ins. Co., 644 F. Supp. 967, 972 (D. Del. 1986) (applying Delaware law).

[59] Doe v. Maskell, 679 A.2d 1087, 1089–90 (Md. 1996), cert. denied, 519 U.S. 1093 (1997).

[60] Albertson v. T.J. Stevenson & Co., Inc., 749 F.2d 223, 228–29 (5th Cir. 1984) (stating that "[i]f some injury is discernible when the tortious act occurs, the time of event rule respecting statutes of limitations applies, and the plaintiff's cause of action is deemed to have

The discovery doctrine does not have the same broad application as the accrual concept. A court will apply the discovery doctrine: (1) when a statute so provides; or (2) when it is equitable to do so. In this latter context, courts have been most prone to apply the discovery doctrine to postpone accrual when the injury was latent, insidious, or concealed.[61]

If a court applies the discovery doctrine to postpone accrual, it must decide the relevant discovery date. This can be the date the plaintiff: (1) discovers any manifestation of the injury (whether physical or psychological); (2) discovers that she has been substantially harmed; (3) discovers that she has been harmed as a result of a specific defendant's conduct; or (4) discovers that her injuries are permanent. Remember, these tests are applied when the injury is latent, insidious, or concealed. The tests are not applied when the injury is obvious or commonplace; then the general accrual rule is applied.

Standard one reflects the traditional test. This standard is most consistent with the basic accrual rule because the existence of actual injury (which completes the prima facie case) and the awareness of that injury generally will coincide.[62]

Standard two allows the plaintiff more time to confirm that she has sustained an injury and to identify the cause of that injury. Many courts apply this standard.[63]

Standard three allows postponement of accrual until the plaintiff knows she has a cause of action she probably can successfully assert against a defendant.[64]

---

accrued. If the plaintiff later discovers that his injuries are more serious than originally thought, his cause of action nevertheless accrues on the earlier date, the date he realized that he had sustained harm from the tortious act"); *cf.* Beauchamp v. Amedio, 751 A.2d 1047 (N.J. 2000) (stating that plaintiff's claim accrued on date she was injured, not on date she learned that her injuries were permanent).

[61] Matter of New York County DES Litig., 678 N.E.2d 474, 478, (N.Y. 1997) (stating that purpose of statutory enactment of "discovery of injury" rule in toxic tort cases was to overrule judicial precedents adopting exposure or impact tests that were thought to be overly harsh given latency and non-manifestation of injuries for lengthy period of time); *In re* Estates of Hibbard, 826 P.2d 690 (Wash. 1992):

> Application of the rule is limited to claims in which the plaintiffs could not have immediately known of their injuries due to professional malpractice, occupational diseases, self-reporting or concealment of information by the defendant. Application of the rule is extended to claims in which plaintiffs could not immediately know of the cause of their injuries.

Id. at 696.

[62] Section 61.2.1 (Accrual).

[63] Brown v. Bleiberg, 651 P.2d 815, 818 (Cal. 1982).

[64] Hughes v. United States, 263 F.3d 272, 276 (3d Cir. 2001) (holding that medical malpractice action based on physicians failure to treat and monitor plaintiff's reaction to medication he was administering did not accrue until plaintiff learned of physician's error). As noted by the court:

> When a physician's failure to diagnose, treat, or warn a patient results in the

The fourth standard—the action accrues on the date plaintiff discovers his injuries are permanent—has generally been rejected by courts as inherently inconsistent with the statute of limitation doctrine.[65]

Closely related to the above is the question of "how certain" or knowledgeable the plaintiff must be that she has sustained harm as a result of "wrongdoing." The general approach here is to use a layperson's sense of wrongdoing, not a lawyer's sense.[66] When a plaintiff becomes aware of an injury and its possible cause, she must act or run the risk that her cause of action will be lost due to delay. The penultimate questions are often "what should the plaintiff have known," and "when should the plaintiff have known it?" A plaintiff is required to exercise good judgment notwithstanding her condition. Courts may expect plaintiffs to be aware of "alerting events," as for example, media stories about the plaintiff's condition.[67] General media attention has also been deemed sufficient, even absent direct evidence that the victim was aware of the media disclosures. For example, in *McKelvey v. Boeing North American, Inc.* the court took judicial notice of 117 newspaper, radio, and television reports concerning contamination at defendant's facility to show that anyone living in the Los Angeles area

---

development of a more serious medical problem than that which previously existed, identification of both the injury and its cause may be more difficult for a patient than if affirmative conduct by a doctor inflicts a new injury. Where a claim of medical malpractice is based on the failure to diagnose or treat a pre-existing condition, the injury is not the mere undetected existence of the medical problem at the time the physician failed to diagnose or treat the patient or the mere continuance of that same undiagnosed problem in substantially the same state. Rather, the injury is the *development* of the problem into a more serious condition which poses greater danger to the patient or which requires more extensive treatment. In this type of case, it is only when the patient becomes aware or through the exercise of reasonable diligence should have become aware of the development of a pre-existing problem into a more serious condition that his cause of action can be said to have accrued. . . .

Id. at 276–77 (emphasis in original); *see* New v. Armour Pharm. Co., 67 F.3d 716, 719–20 (9th Cir. 1995) (applying California law) (stating that statute of limitation does not run until plaintiff has knowledge of cause of harm such that plaintiff believes she is entitled to recourse); *cf.* Tarnowsky v. Socci, 856 A.2d 408, 415–16 (Conn. 2004) (holding that two year discovery period provided by statute did not commence until plaintiff knows or reasonably should know the identity of the tortfeasor); Yustick v. Eli Lilly & Co., 573 F. Supp. 1558, 1562 (E.D. Mich. 1983) (defendant must be identified as responsible for product which injured plaintiff before cause of action accrues).

[65] Olsen v. Bell Tel. Labs., Inc., 445 N.E.2d 609, 611 (Mass. 1983) (rejecting plaintiff's argument that cause of action did not accrue until he knew or should have known that his injuries became permanent because to adopt such a rule would negate fixed periods of limitation); *cf.* Stephens v. Dixon, 536 N.W.2d 755, 757 (Mich. 1995) (discovery rule not applicable to ordinary negligence when plaintiff merely misjudges severity of his injury).

[66] New v. Armour Pharmaceutical Co., 67 F.3d 716, 719 (9th Cir. 1995) (applying California law).

[67] *Browning, supra*, 613 N.E.2d at 1005 (holding that television program discussing problems that plaintiff's physician, the defendant, experienced with other patients and which problems were similar to plaintiff's complaints, constituted an alerting event for plaintiff, which commenced running of statute on plaintiff's claim).

would have known about pollution problems (for which plaintiffs were suing) at defendant's facility.[68]

The question of media attention is really part of a larger issue—inquiry notice. When does the plaintiff have sufficient information such that a prudent, reasonable person would inquire further?[69]

How insistent courts will be in addressing the issue of inquiry notice will vary because the issue is essentially one of "reasonableness" and reasonable minds will differ. For example, in *O'Brien v. Eli Lilly & Co.* it was held that the plaintiff (a DES baby) should have known that her physical complaints were DES related, even though her mother denied taking DES, because (1) plaintiff had cancer and (2) plaintiff had read a magazine article describing a possible link between DES and cancer, which she should have pursued.[70] A dissent criticized the majority's attribution of awareness to a young woman who had undergone a traumatic event, ovarian cancer requiring a hysterectomy.[71] A more relaxed approach was exhibited in *New v. Armour Pharmaceutical Co.*[72] when the court held that the plaintiff's claim that he contracted AIDS from contaminated blood was not time-barred even though he knew he was HIV positive and diligent inquiry would have disclosed cases in which hemophiliacs, such as plaintiff, were alleging that there was a cause/effect relationship between AIDS and contaminated blood plasma. The court held that plaintiff was not charged with the knowledge that being HIV positive leads to AIDS because court opinions, a magazine article, and an AIDS Update failed to find a conclusive link between being HIV positive and contracting AIDS.[73] *O'Brien* charges the plaintiff with knowledge of facts that would evidence defendant's liability when due diligence would have disclosed those facts; *New* tempers that approach by focusing on information that negates a connection between plaintiff's claims and another's wrongdoing, thus allowing a court to deem plaintiff's ignorance to be reasonable.

Because the discovery rule is predicated on both actual and constructive awareness, a number of courts have had to address whether the plaintiff's "repressed memory" of the events surrounding the injury operates to delay accrual? The issue has arisen in sexual molestation cases, usually involving

---

[68] 86 Cal. Rptr. 2d 645, 652–53 (Cal. App. 1999) (collecting decisions finding media publicity sufficient to trigger the statute of limitation under the "discovery" rule); see Winters v. Diamond Shamrock Chemical Co., 149 F.3d 387, 404 (5th Cir. 1998), *cert. denied*, 526 U.S. 1034 (1999) (same).

[69] Texas Soil Recycling, Inc. v. Intercargo Ins. Co., 273 F.3d 644, 649 (5th Cir. 2001) (applying Texas law) (noting that for purposes of the discovery rule the question is not actual knowledge but whether the plaintiff had knowledge of facts that would cause a reasonable person to diligently make inquiry to determine her legal rights).

[70] 668 F.2d 704, 707–09 (3d Cir. 1981).

[71] *Id.* at 713.

[72] 67 F.3d 716 (9th Cir. 1995).

[73] *Id.* at 721; *In re* Swine Flu Prods. Liab. Litig., 764 F.2d 637, 640–42 (9th Cir. 1985) (holding that additional fact finding required before attributing general community awareness to plaintiff).

minors. The general approach of courts has been to reject the "repressed memory" theory and leave the matter to the legislature.[74]

It is generally recognized that the discovery rule does not extend to the time the plaintiff realizes that a *viable* legal theory exists that she may assert to hold a defendant liable for her injuries.[75] On the other hand, the mere fact that the plaintiff has sustained an injury may not reasonably appraise her of the fact that she has a cause of action. Notwithstanding the various tests that proliferate in this area of the law, statute of limitation doctrine rests in many instances on fine distinctions and debatable policies.[76] It should come as no surprise that claims involving missed statutes of limitation have been the largest category in terms of claim frequency in the legal malpractice field.[77] Nonetheless, in an effort to summarize, with all the risks a summary entails, a concise statement of the discovery rule is found in *San Francisco Unified School District v. W.R. Grace & Co.*:

> The common law rule that a cause of action accrued on the date of injury has been modified by the discovery rule. Under the discovery rule, a cause of action does not accrue until the plaintiff either discovers the injury and its negligent cause or could have discovered the injury and cause through the exercise of reasonable diligence. The statute of limitations begins to run when the plaintiff suspects or should suspect that his or her injury was caused by wrongdoing—when the plaintiff has notice of information or circumstances that would put a reasonable person on inquiry. The plaintiff need not be aware of the specific facts necessary to establish the claim—these facts can be determined during pretrial discovery. Once a plaintiff suspects wrongdoing and therefore has an incentive to sue, he or she must decide whether to file suit or sit on his or her rights. When a suspicion exists, the plaintiff must go find the facts; he or she cannot wait for the facts to find him or her.[78]

[61.2.3] Continuing Injury or Violation

A defendant may engage in a course of sustained, protracted wrongdoing, such as conducting operations that constitute a nuisance or engaging in a pattern and practice of discriminatory hiring and retention policies. If

---

[74] *Doe v. Maskell*, *supra*, 679 A.2d at 1092; Lemmerman v. Fealk, 534 N.W.2d 695, 702 (Mich 1995). The decisions are collected in *S.V. v. R.V.*, 933 S.W.2d 1, 19–20 (Tex. 1996).

[75] Moll v. Abbott Labs., 506 N.W.2d 816, 828 (Mich. 1993); Peschel v. Jones, 760 P.2d 51, 56 (Mont. 1988).

[76] A good part of the variation in the decisions reflects the fact that the discovery rule is often tied to a statute that may cause a court to restrict its application. TRW Inc. v. Andrews, 534 U.S. 19 (2001) (construing discovery rule in Fair Credit Reporting Act to run from date of any harm to consumer's credit rating, not from date consumer learned of harm). In effect, under *TRW Inc.*, the consumer must monitor his credit. *See* Davis v. Monahan, 832 So. 2d 708 (Fla. 2002) (refusing to extend discovery rule to cause of action similar to those listed in the statute authorizing the discovery rule).

[77] Ronald E. Mallen & Jeffrey M. Smith, Legal Malpractice § 1.7, at 34 (5th ed. 2000).

[78] 44 Cal. Rptr. 2d 305, 309 (Cal. App. 1995) (citations omitted).

accrual rules were rigorously applied, the defendant might end up with a de facto license or prescriptive right to engage in wrongful conduct, in effect an acquired right to do wrong. To prevent this, jurisdictions recognize what is commonly known as the continuing injury or violation rule.[79]

This rule acts as a gloss on the basic rule that a claim accrues when facts that would support a cause of action are or should be apparent to the plaintiff. The continuing violation rule applies when the wrongful conduct is ongoing rather than a single event. It is important to distinguish between continuing injurious conduct, which triggers this rule, and continuing injury from a completed act or event, which does not. For example, if a defendant operates a nuisance, the wrongful conduct continues and is ongoing; thus, the continuing violation rule applies. The result is that each operative act constitutes a separate and distinct cause of action with its own statute of limitation.[80] It is commonly said that continuing nuisance claims are not subject to a limitation defense[81] but the statements must be viewed cautiously. Limitation doctrine may not affect the claim for injunctive relief, but it will affect a claim for damages.[82] Nuisance and trespass actions have developed a distinct remedial dichotomy, which turns on whether the nuisance or trespass is deemed permanent or temporary. This remedial dichotomy is heavily influenced by statute of limitation considerations, although the influence is indirect rather than direct. The point is discussed in greater detail in Section 93.1 ([Trespass] Temporary or Permanent) and Section 94.1 [Nuisance](Temporary or Permanent).

Under the continuing violation rule, a new claim accrues each day a violation occurs.[83] The necessary corollary to this rule is that while each new violation constitutes a separate cause of action, once the statutory period has run the plaintiff is without remedy as to that cause of action,[84] unless the rule is changed by the statute.[85]

Continuing injury from a completed course of conduct does not fall within this continuing violation rule. Once the defendant ceases operation of the nuisance the fact that injury continues, through expanded migration of buried pollutants to ground water or adjoining property, does not give rise

---

[79] The terms "continuing injury" and "continuing violation" are often used interchangeably; however "continuing violation" has a more precise usage in this context.

[80] Nelson v. C&C Plywood Corp., 465 P.2d 314, 325 (Mont. 1970) (holding that a new cause of action arose each time defendant dumped glue waste).

[81] Haas v. Sunset Ramblers Motorcycle Club, Inc., 726 N.E.2d 612, 614 (Ohio App. 1999).

[82] Simi Inv. Co. v. Harris County, Tex., 236 F.3d 240, 250 n.14 (5th Cir. 2000) (applying Texas law), cert. denied, 534 U.S. 1022 (2001).

[83] Hanover Shoe, Inc. v. United Shoe Machinery Corp., 392 U.S. 481, 502 n.15. (1968).

[84] Id. at 502 (plaintiff entitled to damages "for the entire period permitted by the applicable statute of limitations") (footnote omitted); Hanson v. Shell Oil Co., 541 F.2d 1352, 1361 (9th Cir.1976), cert. denied, 429 U.S. 1074, (1977) (limiting damages to the statutory period).

[85] State Dep't of Envtl. Protection v. Fleet Credit Corp., 691 So. 2d 512, 514 (Fla. App. 1997) (under federal and state environmental legislation, it is "ongoing contamination, not the initial disposal of wastes, that constitutes a continuing, but abatable, nuisance").

to new causes of action. It is the ongoing conduct and continuing harm that gives meaning to the continuing violation rule. As noted by one court:

> In deciding the date from which the cause of action accrued, we must determine whether the injury alleged by Telecasters was caused by a single or a continuing violation of the Act. Distinguishing between the two, the Supreme Court has held that a single violation necessarily occurs "within some specific and limited time span," whereas continuing violations "inflict continuing and accumulating harm." For this reason, exclusion from participation in an industry constitutes a continuing conspiracy, unless the exclusion is final in its impact. Thus, each refusal to deal gives rise to a claim under the antitrust laws.[86]

Decision applying the continuing violation gloss on the accrual rule may be difficult to organize and reconcile. Let's start with a simple example when the continuing violation rule does not apply. If a woman is rendered sterile by a physician's malpractice, the injury is certainly continuing, but that injury flows from a single, completed act and thus would not be an appropriate candidate for the continuing violation rule.[87] In *Pitts v. City of Kankakee* the court held that the continuing presence of a sign that identified the plaintiff's property as "SLUM PROPERTY" was not a continuing violation. The defendant allegedly placed the sign in retaliation against plaintiff's critical comments. The court held that the operate act was the defendant-city's retaliation; the placement of the sign was merely the manifestation of the retailiatory act. The act of retaliation were complete; hence, the continuing violation rule did not apply.[88]

In contrast with the above decisions is *Guardians Association of New York City Police Dept. Inc. v. Civil Service Comm'n of City of New York*, in which the operative act was the use of a discriminatory hiring examination and a resulting priority list. Even though the examination had been administered and the priority list established at an earlier date, each use of the list to make an employment decision was deemed to constitute a new violation and resulting cause of action for applicants who had lost an employment opportunity because of the discriminatory examination and

---

[86] Charlotte Telecasters, Inc. v. Jefferson-Pilot Corp., 546 F.2d 570, 572 (4th Cir. 1976) (citations omitted).

[87] Cyrus v. Nero, 546 N.E.2d 328, 331 (Ind. App. 1989) (distinguishing case from one in which injury was aggravated due to continuing failure to diagnose properly); Francis v. Hansing, 449 N.W.2d 479, 482 (Minn. App. 1989) (failure of physician to remove IUD did not constitute a continuing tort). There are a few cases to the contrary, Nieman v. NLO, Inc., 108 F.3d 1546, 1559 (6th Cir. 1997) (stating that "under Ohio law, a claim for continuing trespass may be supported by proof of continuing damages and need not be based on allegations of continuing conduct")), but they are better explained as cases when the court granted an injunction to redress the continuing injurious effects of past misconduct rather than examples of the continuing injury rule as a gloss on accrual doctrine.

[88] 267 F.3d 592, 595–96 (7th Cir. 2001) (analogizing to single publication rule for defamation actions), *cert. denied*, 536 U.S. 922 (2002).

resulting list.[89] Here the actual implementation of the wrongful policy created a new claim upon each implementation.[90]

In some contexts, the line between completed violation and continuing violation may be apparent. For example, an employee who is terminated from his employment and suffers continuing adverse consequences from that decision has sustained a completed violation.[91] On the other hand, a slight tweaking of the facts can produce uncertainty. For example, an employee who sustains on the job discrimination or harassment may or may not be able to assert a continuing violation claim. The application of the continuing violation rule to employment discrimination and harassment claims is a complex and evolving area of law that is beyond the scope of this work.[92]

[61.3]   Tolling

Tolling suspends the running of a statute of limitation. Tolling doctrine comes from two sources: (1) statutes and (2) equity. Most jurisdictions toll the running of statutes of limitation for certain, defined situations affecting the plaintiff, such as a legal disability (minority, insanity, or imprisonment), or absence from the state. The statutory rules can be quite tricky. For example, in California, the statute of limitation is tolled if the plaintiff is imprisoned when the action accrues,[93] but not if he is imprisoned after the action accrued.[94] Tolling may also be foreclosed if a court finds that the doctrine is inconsistent with the remedial program the legislature established and the limitation period the statute contains.[95]

---

[89] 633 F.3d 232, 250–51 (2d Cir. 1980).

[90] Bazemore v. Friday, 478 U.S. 385, 395–96 315 (1986) (holding that "[e]ach week's paycheck that delivers less to a black than to a similarly situated white is a wrong actionable under Title VII, regardless of the fact that this pattern was begun prior to the effective date of Title VII").

[91] Delaware State College v. Ricks, 449 U.S. 250, 258 (1980).

[92] Some recent decisions include: National Railroad Passenger Corp. v. Morgan, 536 U.S. 101 (2002) (distinguishing between discrimination and harassment claims insofar a continuing violation rule is concerned); Hildebrandt v. Illinois Dept. of Nat. Res., 347 F.3d 1014 (7th Cir. 2003) (reconciling *National Railroad* and *Bazemore*).

[93] Cal. Code Civ. P. § 352. *See* California Sav. & Loan Ass'n v. Culver, 59 P. 292, 294 (Cal. 1899) (holding that where plaintiff was insane when action accrued, recovered his sanity, and then relapsed into insanity, the relapse did not toll the applicable statute of limitations).

[94] Cal. Code Civ. P. § 357 (requiring that disability must exist at the time the cause of action accrues).

[95] Brice v. Secretary of Health & Human Services, 240 F.3d 1367 (Fed. Cir.) (holding that tolling is not allowed to abate statute of limitation period contained in National Childhood Vacine Act), *cert. denied sub nom.* Brice v. Thompson, 534 U.S. 1040 (2001); Lantzy v. Centrex Homes, 73 P.3d 517 (Cal. 2003) (rejecting tolling to extend absolute 10 year period within which to bring construction defect claims). California has a liberal tolling doctrine based on the principle of avoiding technical defaults when a party has not sustained any prejudice (*id.* at 523); the court did not foreclose tolling based on other grounds, such as equitable estoppel or fraudulent concealment, both of which are addressed in this section.

Non-statutory tolling principles are equitable in origin. The two most common bases for equitable (non-statutory) tolling are: (1) estoppel and (2) concealment.

Probably the most frequently invoked equitable tolling doctrine is estoppel. A representative case is *Muraoka v. Budget Rent-A-Car*.[96] In that case the court held that Budget was estopped from raising the statute of limitation defense when it (1) was the protagonist for the delay in settlement negotiations; (2) it intentionally misled plaintiff by promising that it would compensate him for his loss without the need to commence litigation; and (3) plaintiff relied on those representations and did not commence his action until after the statute of limitation had run.[97] The issue of estoppel is discussed in greater detail elsewhere,[98] but its frequent application to bar the running of the statute of limitation should not be overlooked.

Concealment (or fraudulent concealment) is another common equitable ground for tolling. Concealment to toll the running of the statute usually requires "affirmative acts" calculated (1) to mislead and hinder a plaintiff from obtaining information by reasonable inquiry, (2) to hinder or prevent the inquiry itself, or (3) to elude an inquiry altogether. The elements necessary to establish concealment to toll an applicable statute of limitation are similar to an action for fraud and, like the action for fraud, jurisdictions vary somewhat in the detail required to state the prima facie case. The essential elements are, however, common. They include: (1) wrongful concealment by the defendant; (2) failure by plaintiff to discover the true facts evidencing the action within the applicable statutory period of limitation; and (3) due diligence by the plaintiff until discovery of the action.[99]

The doctrine of fraudulent concealment "only serves to toll the statute of limitations as to those defendants who actively participate in the concealment . . . . A plaintiff cannot point to the deceptive practices of one defendant, and demand equitable tolling as to all."[100]

Many courts require that the acts constituting concealment be affirmatively directed at deflecting litigation.[101] In other words, the defendant's

---

[96] 206 Cal. Rptr. 476 (Cal. App. 1984).

[97] *Id.* at 480–81.

[98] Section 64 (Estoppel, Waiver, and Election).

[99] Landry v. Air Line Pilots Ass'n Int'l, AFL-CIO, 901 F.2d 404, 412–13 (5th Cir. 1990); Smith v. Boyett, 908 P.2d 508, 512 (Colo. 1995) (setting forth a five-part test: (1) the concealment of a material existing fact that in equity and good conscience should be disclosed; (2) knowledge on the part of the party against whom the claim is asserted that such a fact is being concealed; (3) ignorance of that fact on the part of the one from whom the fact is concealed; (4) the intention that the concealment be acted upon; and (5) action on the concealment resulting in damages).

[100] In the Matter of the Mediators, Inc., 190 B.R. 515, 525 (S.D.N.Y. 1995) (citations omitted); *aff'd on other grounds*, 105 F.3d 822 (2d Cir. 1997).

[101] Shropshear v. Corporation Counsel, 275 F.3d 593, 595 (7th Cir. 2001); Pocahontas Supreme Coal Co. Inc. v. Bethlehem Steel Corp., 828 F.2d 211, 218 (4th Cir. 1987).

action must be directed towards concealing from the plaintiff the fact that she has a cause of action as opposed to the facts that go directly to the existence of the cause of action. In these jurisdictions it is not enough that the action be "self concealing," although some jurisdictions accept the "self concealing" test.[102] The "self concealing" test is used in antitrust cases[103] and it is unclear to what extent a court would apply the test, with modification, to another factual context, such as product liability.

In professional malpractice actions, the issue is complicated by the affirmative disclosure obligations the professional may have to the client. If a physician, in response to a patient's inquiry, says the patient is "okay," does this amount to concealment if the patient is not okay, but the physician does not actually know that fact because the physician's malpractice prevented her from knowing the patient's true condition? Many court's resolve this problem by adopting a "culpability" standard to prevent transforming all "constructive" concealment cases (should have known) into "active" concealment (did know) cases, which would effectively nullify the statute of limitation.[104] Under this approach the professional must know she committed malpractice and either intentionally misrepresent the true facts to plaintiff or fail to disclose the true facts such as to impede the plaintiff's discovery of the malpractice.[105] There is only a fine line here between the discovery rule of due diligence[106] and the concept of concealment, even though concealment, as noted above, requires "culpability," while discovery does not. The distinction becomes even more difficult when the defendant owes affirmative disclosure obligations to the plaintiff because silence on the defendant's part may be labelled constructive fraud.[107]

There is a common gloss put on concealment that tolls the limitation period if the physician (or lawyer or other professional with a duty to disclose) treats or continues the professional relationship. If the rule were otherwise, the professional could defeat the claim by continuing the relationship and remaining silent until the limitation period expired. Continuing the relationship would also hinder the consumer from obtaining independent professional advice that would alert him to the claim.[108] There

---

[102] Hobson v. Wilson, 737 F.2d 1, 32–35 (D.C. Cir. 1984).

[103] Supermarket of Marlington, Inc. v. Meadow Gold Dairies, Inc., 71 F.3d 119, 122–23 (4th Cir. 1995).

[104] Hughes v. Glaese, 659 N.E.2d 516, 520–21 (Ind. 1995).

[105] *Smith v. Boyett, supra,* 908 P.2d at 513 nn.9–10 (collecting cases).

[106] McDonald v. United States, 843 F.2d 247, 248 (6th Cir. 1988) ("when a physician misinforms the patient that complications are not unusual occurrences and will improve, the statute of limitations is not activated" . . . . The reason for this rule is that a contrary "rule requiring patients to scrutinize their doctor's diagnosis or prognosis would impose an unfair burden on the patient . . . a patient's 'blameless ignorance' should not be held against him") (citations omitted).

[107] Lasley v. Helms, 880 P.2d 1135, 1138 (Ariz. 1994).

[108] Lockley v. Law Office of Cantrell, Green, Pekich, Cruz & McCort, 110 Cal. Rptr. 2d 877 (Cal. App. 2001).

are, however, a number of jurisdictions that reject tolling based on a continuing professional relationship.[109] Even jurisdictions that follow the doctrine require that the ongoing relationship be relevant to the complained of harm.[110]

Fraudulent concealment presupposes that the plaintiff is actually ignorant of the true facts. As with a basic fraud action, there is an element of reliance here. Consequently, if despite a defendant's continuing efforts to conceal the wrong, a plaintiff discovers or becomes aware of the wrongdoing and injury from independent sources, the limitation period commences.[111] Blameless ignorance is distinct from blissful ignorance. The defendant's culpability (fraudulent concealment) does not permit the plaintiff to hide behind the protection of the rule and close her eyes to what is visible or knowable.

Tolling can also arise when extraordinary, unforeseen events render timely commencement of a lawsuit within the applicable statute of limitation impossible. An example of this is *Lewis v. Superior Court.*[112] In *Lewis* the court held that although under the facts of that case tolling was not expressly statutorily required, statutes "must admit to implicit exceptions where compliance is impossible and manifest injustice would otherwise result." Plaintiff, a sole practitioner, was engaged in settlement efforts. He marked on his calendar, March 16, 1984, for filing a complaint if settlement was not reached. The applicable statute of limitation ran on March 17, 1984. On March 12, 1984, counsel was severely injured in an automobile accident, requiring his hospitalization. He did not recover consciousness until March 22, 1984, and suffered both short-and long-term amnesia. On April 16, 1984, he returned to work. On April 27, 1984, he discovered his failure to file timely, and filed the action that same day.

The court, after reviewing California case law recognizing bases for tolling besides those explicitly set forth by statute, noted that in certain circumstances, such as those presented in the case before the court, unusual catastrophes rendering timely filing impossible justified tolling the applicable period of limitation.[113] The court also observed that natural calamities, such as catastrophic fires or earthquakes, would justify tolling,[114] or extraordinary circumstances beyond the plaintiff's control.[115] Many courts

---

[109] Hunter, Maclean, Exley & Dunn v. Frame, 507 S.E.2d 411 (Ga. 1998) (rejecting continuing representation tolling rule).

[110] Gold v. Weissman, 8 Cal. Rptr. 3d 480 (Cal. App. 2004) (stating that continuing representation must relate to the claim the client wishes to assert against the lawyer).

[111] McCoy v. United States, 264 F.3d 792, 795 (8th Cir. 2001), *cert. denied*, 535 U.S. 1053 (2002); Sanchez v. South Hoover Hosp., 553 P.2d 1129, 1134 (Cal. 1976).

[112] 220 Cal. Rptr. 594 (Cal. App. 1985).

[113] *Id.* at 600.

[114] *Id. But cf.* Bennett v. Suncloud, 65 Cal. Rptr. 2d 80, 84 (Cal. App. 1997) (holding that under statute mere closing due to earthquake of proper branch court in which to file action did not toll statute of limitation unless main downtown courthouse in which action could also be filed was closed).

[115] Stoll v. Runyon, 165 F.3d 1238, 1242 (9th Cir. 1999).

have permitted equitable tolling when the plaintiff's physical or mental incapacity prevented him from commencing the lawsuit within the applicable limitation period.[116] There is, however, no "right" to invoke equitable tolling and in some cases tolling may be directly barred.[117]

[61.4] Merger of Law and Equity

As a general rule, the distinction between law and equity remains well respected with regard to the defenses of laches and statute of limitation; laches, as an equitable defense, is limited to equitable remedies.[118] The reason for this differentiation has been the perception that while both defenses are concerned with similar policies and goals, the focus of each is different. "[L]aches is premised on prejudice not only delay. Statutes of limitation are premised on delay, not prejudice. . . . [A] party may be unduly prejudiced by delay even though a statute of limitations does not bar a claim."[119]

Notwithstanding the above sentiments, laches has been applied to actions at law, although the applications have been rather erratic. Laches has been applied when concerns over extensive liability and a compelling desire for speedy adjudication of claims have been deemed of first order.[120] Laches has been applied to legal claims that are quasi equitable in the sense that the legal substance of the claim is based on equitable considerations.[121] Judge Posner has argued that laches, like other equitable defenses,[122] should be applied to actions at law,[123] and there are some cases to that effect.[124] Judge Posner's position has been criticized, however, on the ground that he overstates the scope of the cases he cites, ignoring the equitable nature of the legal claims to which courts have permitted the laches defense to be asserted.[125] The problem here as elsewhere is that both sides are correct. Many of the decisions applying laches to legal claims involve claims sometimes characterized as having an equitable side. For example, *Moore*

---

[116] Barrett v. Principi, 363 F.3d 1316 (Fed. Cir. 2004) (discussing appropriateness of invoking tolling based on mental illness and collecting decisions).

[117] Lampf, Pleva, Lipkind, Prupis & Petigrow v. Gilbertson, 501 U.S. 350, 363 (1991) (finding that equitable tolling was inconsistent with new structure of statute of limitation adopted by Court for 10b-5 claims).

[118] Cornetta v. United States, 851 F.2d 1372, 1376 (Fed. Cir. 1988) (stating that "[b]ecause laches is an equitable defense, it has traditionally been unavailable in actions at law brought within the applicable statute of limitations").

[119] Jackson v. Axton, 25 F.3d 884, 887 n.2. (9th Cir. 1994).

[120] Henry v. United States, 153 F. Supp. 285, 289–90 (Ct. Cl. 1957).

[121] F.D.I.C. v. Fuller, 994 F.2d 223, 224 (5th Cir. 1993).

[122] Byron v. Clay, 867 F.2d 1049, 1052 (7th Cir. 1989) (involving unclean hands).

[123] Martin v. Consultants & Administrators, Inc., 966 F.2d 1078, 1100–02 (7th Cir. 1992) (concurring opinion); Maksym v. Loesch, 937 F.2d 1237, 1248 (7th Cir. 1991).

[124] McDaniel v. Messerschmidt, 382 P.2d 304, 307 (Kan. 1963).

[125] Ashley v. Boyle's Famous Corned Beef Co., 66 F.3d 164, 168–69 (8th Cir. 1995); *cf.* Henry v. United States, 153 F. Supp. 285 (Ct. Cl. 1957) (rejecting argument that because dual systems have merged laches should be applied to bar legal remedy).

v. Phillips,[126] cited by Judge Posner in *Maksym v. Loesch,*[127] was an action for waste, a claim often referred to as being equitable in nature. Courts have also applied laches to claims by persons, such as mortgagees or receivers, who are traditionally within the jurisdiction of courts of equity. A number of decisions, however, simply state that laches may be applied to an action at law; these cases do not specifically acknowledge the gloss that the claim is equitable in nature.[128]

§ 62   UNCLEAN HANDS AND "IN PARI DELICTO"

The common theme that unites these defenses is a focus on the plaintiff's wrongful conduct. Several other defenses, such as fraud, illegality, and estoppel also fall within this category but are separately treated. Both unclean hands and "in pari delicto" assume a level of knowing, intentional misconduct, which, in part, distinguishes them from other fault-based defenses that have evolved into strict liability defenses. For example, a defense of fraud may be based in many jurisdictions on an innocent misrepresentation.[1] Estoppel may be based on an innocent misrepresentation.[2] Illegality may be asserted as a defense by a party that oppressed the innocent plaintiff.[3]

[62.1]   Unclean Hands

The general principle behind the defense of unclean hands is that a court should neither provide aid in the commission of a wrong nor relieve a party of the consequences of his participation in a wrong.[4] This principle is distinct from the concept that "he who seeks equity must do equity." The latter concept assumes that different equitable rights have arisen from the same subject matter or transaction, some in favor of plaintiff and some in favor of the defendant so that the plaintiff is required to recognize and provide for defendant's rights and his relief is granted only upon a showing that defendant's rights are protected.[5]

The general contours of the doctrine of unclean hands were set forth in *Precision Institute Manufacturing Co. v. Automotive Maintenance Machinery Co.:*

---

[126] 627 P.2d 831 (Kan. App. 1981).

[127] *Supra,* 937 F.2d 1237.

[128] Plaza Condo. Ass'n, Inc. v. Wellington Corp., 920 S.W.2d 51 (Ky. 1996) (involving action by association against developer to pay pro rata share of common expenses). The court found that defendant failed to show it had been prejudiced by plaintiff's delay. *Id.* at 54. The dissent argued the action was equitable in nature. *Id.* at 55.

[1] Section 65.1 (Fraud).

[2] Section 64 (Estoppel, Waiver, and Election).

[3] Section 65.2 (Illegality).

[4] DeGarmo v. Goldman, 123 P.2d 1, 6 (Cal. 1942).

[5] *Id.* at 6. The distinction is sometimes forgotten. Mudd v. Nosker Lumber, Inc., 662 A.2d 660, 664 (Pa. Sup. Ct. 1995) (stating that "[o]ne guilty of wrongdoing should be denied access to the court . . . ; "he who seeks equity must do equity") (citations omitted).

The guiding doctrine in this case is the equitable maxim that 'he who comes into equity must come with clean hands.' This maxim is far more than a mere banality. It is a self-imposed ordinance that closes the doors of a court of equity to one tainted with inequitableness or bad faith relative to the matter in which he seeks relief, however improper may have been the behavior of the defendant. That doctrine is rooted in the historical concept of [the] court of equity as a vehicle for affirmatively enforcing the requirements of conscience and good faith. This presupposes a refusal on its part to be 'the abetter of iniquity.'[6]

The unclean hands defense is not provided for the benefit of the defendant, but for the protection of the court. The integrity of the judicial process is said to be endangered when used to assist persons whose very presence before a court is the result of some fraud or inequity.[7] The consequences of this approach can be unfortunate when the wrongful conduct affects third parties. For example, assume both plaintiff and defendant are engaging in false advertising regarding their competing products.[8] If the court refuses to enjoin the advertising, because of the unclean hands defense, the consumer is left unprotected. The rationale behind this approach is that permitting equitable relief would allow one of the similarly situated parties to gain a competitive advantage to continue to advertise falsely while its competitor was enjoined.[9]

The defense of unclean hands is also said to have a deterrence quality. Wrongful conduct is thought to be more likely suppressed by leaving the parties without a remedy against each other rather than by enforcing "rights" at the insistence of one of the parties to the wrongful conduct.[10] This approach derives from the traditional view that the defense of unclean hands applies to facts involving only two parties, plaintiff and defendant, and one transaction involving both parties.[11] Not all cases today resemble

---

[6] 324 U.S. 806, 814 (1945) (citations omitted).

[7] Adams v. Manown, 615 A.2d 611, 616–17 (Md. 1992).

[8] Haagen-Dazs, Inc. v. Frusen Gladje, Ltd., 493 F. Supp. 73, 76 (S.D.N.Y. 1980) (holding that when both parties packaged their ice cream product to create misleading impression that each was of Scandinavian rather than domestic origin, injunctive relief would be denied on ground of unclean hands). *But see* Hot Wax, Inc. v. Turtle Wax, Inc., 191 F.3d 813, 825–26 (7th Cir. 1999) (stating that plaintiff's allegedly similar conduct to that ascribed to defendant—the false allegation that the product contains "wax" or exhibits "wax-like properties"—would not support defense of unclean hands; the evidence supported the district court's finding that plaintiff did not engage in "willful, egregious, or unconscionable conduct or bad faith," which was necessary to raise the defense in a Lanham Trademark action).

[9] Shatel Corp. v. Mao Ta Lumber & Yacht Corp., 697 F.2d 1352, 1355 (11th Cir. 1983) (stating that a court should not protect the exclusive right to use a name or mark that is misleading to the public); A.N. Chamberlain Medicine Co. v. H.A. Chamberlain Medicine Co., 86 N.E. 1025, 1026–27 (Ind. App. 1909) (stating that "[t]he exclusive privilege of deceiving or perpetrating a fraud upon the public is hardly a fit subject to be entertained in a court of equity, and certainly not one that such a court can be required to aid or sanction").

[10] Roman v. Mali, 42 Md. 513, 533–34 (1875).

[11] Smoketree-Lake Murray, Ltd. v. Mills Concrete Constr. Co., Inc., 286 Cal. Rptr. 435, 445 (Cal. App. 1991).

the strict duality that underlies the traditional view. Even in those traditional cases, we may question whether judicial views regarding the deterrence function of the defense of unclean hands are borne out in practice. Parties would have to be aware of the defense and its effect on their potential dispute for deterrence to apply. That is a large assumption.[12]

Courts require that the wrongful conduct, which dirties the plaintiff hands, be "connected" with the controversy before the court. The defense does not close equity's door to morally repugnant persons in general, but to those whose misconduct taints in some way the controversy before the court:

> Thus while 'equity does not demand that its suitors shall have led blameless lives,' as to other matters, it does require that they shall have acted fairly and without fraud or deceit as to the controversy in issue.[13]

How "connected" the taint must be, however, continues to divide the courts.

Many courts state that the "wrongdoing" must *directly* relate to the matter in controversy and affect the relationship between the parties.[14] There must be a direct nexus between the misconduct and the right that is the basis of the suit.[15] Misconduct directed at a third party will not support the defense of unclean hands. For example, assume plaintiff fraudulently conveys property to defendant to avoid paying his creditors, intending that defendant will reconvey the property to plaintiff after the dispute with the creditors has passed. If defendant refuses to reconvey the property to plaintiff and plaintiff sues in equity to compel reconveyance, does plaintiff's effort to defraud his creditors by understating his assets give him unclean hands in the reconveyance action? Courts have split whether the misconduct is sufficiently "connected" to support the defense.[16]

---

[12] Bistricer v. Bistricer, 659 F. Supp. 215, 217 (E.D.N.Y. 1987) (questioning efficacy of deterrence assumption).

[13] Precision Institute Manufacturing Co., supra, 324 U.S. at 814 (citations omitted); *see* Wilson v. S.L. Rey, Inc., 21 Cal. Rptr. 2d 552, 557 (Cal. App. 1993).

[14] Chauvin Int'l, Ltd. v. Goldwitz, 927 F. Supp. 40, 48 (D. Conn. 1996); DeRosa v. Transamerica Title Ins. Co., 262 Cal. Rptr. 370, 373 (Cal. App. 1989).

[15] Shondel v. McDermott, 775 F.2d 859, 869 (7th Cir. 1985):

> To apply unclean hands here thus would violate the principle that "ordinarily, the clean hands doctrine only applies when there is a direct nexus between the bad conduct and the activities sought to be enjoined." The linguistically fastidious may shudder at "nexus," that hideously overworked legal cliche, but there can be no quarrel with the principle.

(citation omitted); Warner Bros., Inc. v. Gay Toys, Inc., 724 F.2d 327, 334 (2d Cir. 1983).

[16] *Compare* Allstead v. Laumeister, 116. P. 296, 297 (Cal. App. 1911) (stating that the general rule is that equitable relief in the form of a resulting trust will not be granted in favor of one who has conveyed his property to another to accomplish a fraud against his creditors), *with* Beelman v. Beelman, 460 N.E.2d 55, 57 (Ill. App. 1984) (granting equitable lien in favor of decedent's estate against brother of decedent who had deeded property to brother to avoid IRS tax lien). This issue frequently arises in divorce litigation. Langdon v. Langdon, 525 N.Y.S.2d 649 (App. Dept. 1988) (involving husband who conveyed the residence to his wife

Similarly, assume plaintiff and defendant are business partners who keep inaccurate records for tax reporting purposes. The "records" substantially understate the profits of the business and its value, usually for tax reporting purposes. If the partners have a falling out and one partner seeks the equitable remedy of an accounting for profits, do the inaccurate records determine the value of the partners' interest in the business? If the partner seeks an accounting, does she have unclean hands to request the remedy that is not dependent on the inaccurate records? Again courts have split, but here we see a greater unwillingness to invoke the "unclean hands" defense.[17] Perhaps fraud against the government is implicitly seen as less serious or more foregiving than fraud against private parties?[18]

The defense of unclean hands may be avoided when the conduct, which dirties the plaintiff's hands, pertains to a different transaction than that before the court. The modern trend appears to be to insist upon a tight fit between the defense and the controversy. As noted by Judge Posner in *Shondel v. McDermott*:

> Unless courts insist on a tight connection between the object of the injunction and the misconduct of the plaintiff, suits for injunction will bog down in all sorts of collateral inquires. In this age of legalism, when relatively few plaintiffs are wholly free from any trace of arguable misconduct at least tangentially related to the objective of their suit, the right to injunctive relief, especially to preliminary injunctive relief, would have little value if the defendant could divert the proceeding into the byways of collateral misconduct.[19]

How "direct" the connection must be is difficult to state. California courts have developed a three prong test to refine the "directness" inquiry: (1) analogous case law, (2) the nature of the misconduct, and (3), the relationship of the misconduct to the claimed injuries.[20] The first factor "analogous case law" requires research as to how the defense has fared in analogous cases. How broadly (or narrowly) one defines what is analogous—a term

---

to avoid creditors' claims; trial court refused to award share of residence to husband as marital property in divorce proceedings); Farino v. Farino, 450 N.Y.S.2d 593, 594 (App. Dept. 1982) (involving husband who conveyed property to his brother to defraud his estranged wife and reduce award of alimony; brother refused husband's request for retransfer; court held that brother could raise defense of unclean hands in husband's suit for reconveyance).

[17] *Beelman, supra*, 460 N.E.2d at 57 (refusing to apply doctrine of unclean hands to parties effort to defeat federal tax lien by conveying property to another).

[18] *Id.* (referring to attempt to defraud the government as a "tactic"); *In re* Torrez, 827 F.2d 1299, 1301 (9th Cir. 1987) (involving Chapter 11 debtors who sought quiet title and turnover of farm property conveyed to them by their parents to allow parents to evade federal restrictions on acreage allotments, which qualified acreage for federally subsidized irrigation water. In permitting parents to obtain resulting trust in their favor the court noted that despite the parent's effort to evade the acreage limits, their conduct did not amount to "serious moral turpitude").

[19] 775 F.2d 859, 869 (7th Cir. 1985).

[20] Kendall-Jackson Winery, Ltd. v. Superior Court, 90 Cal. Rptr. 2d 743, 749 (Cal. App. 1999).

sufficiently vague to support several meanings—obviously impacts the case law one would argue is dispositive or helpful to disposing of the claim.[21] The second factor "nature of the misconduct" asks the court to assess the wrongfulness of the conduct. Does the misconduct violate important public policies? Is the misconduct malum per se or malum prohibitum? Conduct that is morally objectionable (malum per se) is more deserving of condemnation in equity through application of the defense than conduct that is legally, but not morally, wrong (malum prohibitum). The third factor "relationship of the misconduct to the injuries" addresses the degree to which the plaintiff is responsible (or benefitted from) the misconduct and the injuries. A party who is primarily responsible for his own losses has little room to complain that another should provide him with redress. The closer and more direct the plaintiff's misconduct is to his own injuries, the less willing a court should be provide him with an equitable remedy.[22]

The defense of unclean hands is most consistently successful when it appears that the plaintiff is seeking to use the litigation to profit from or avoid the consequences of his own wrongdoing. This was the situation in the "Highwayman's Case," a supposed suit between thieves seeking in effect declaratory relief as to how to divide the loot. The "case" was dismissed for "impertinence," the lawyer was fined, and both parties were executed.[23] While one is unlikely to find such extreme applications of the defense today, modern day highwaymen still make an occasional courtroom appearance, and achieve the same result, without the death penalty. For example in *Zappone v. Zappone* the parties had developed a practice of conveying and reconveying a piece of property to keep it from their respective spouses. As the matter was before the court, plaintiff was seeking a constructive trust. The court described the situation thusly:

> The question before the court is whether a constructive trust should be imposed. There is an equitable question, but there is no easy equitable answer. This is because both parties have behaved in a singularly inequitable fashion. Richard, who has the property in question, doesn't deserve to keep it. Ronald, who wants it, doesn't deserve to get it. Since they were jointly engaged in a fraudulent enterprise, the court declines to give affirmative assistance to either one.[24]

---

[21] *Cf.* Murillo v. Rite Stuff Foods, Inc., 77 Cal. Rptr. 2d 12, 21–22 (Cal. App. 1998) (holding that plaintiff's falsification of lawful immigration status to obtain employment was not sufficiently connected to her injuries from defendant's sexual harassment to warrant application of unclean hands defense). On the other hand, the *Murillo* court also noted that the defense of unclean hands would bar the former employee's wrongful discharge and breach of contract claims! *Id.* at 19.

[22] Bain v. Doctor's Co., 272 Cal. Rptr. 250, 258–59 (Cal. App. 1990) (barring legal malpractice action based on allegation that client's losses resulted from client following lawyer's advice to commit perjury at client's deposition).

[23] The "case" is discussed in *United States v. Kravitz*, 281 F.2d 581, 590 n.3 (3d Cir. 1960).

[24] 1993 Conn. Super. LEXIS 597 at *7–8 (Conn. Super. Ct., March 3, 1993).

Courts have barred plaintiffs from suing lawyers and liability insurance companies for damages arising out of the plaintiff's false testimony in a prior action that was allegedly encouraged or abetted by the lawyer[25] or insurer.[26] Similarly a plaintiff's unclean hands will often bar her from suing a lawyer or another on the ground that in reliance upon the defendant's advice, the plaintiff engaged in conduct that she knew or should have known was fraudulent and for which she later suffered a loss.[27] This application can raise difficult issues of imputation when the active wrongdoers are agents or employees and the defendant seeks to attribute the latter's wrongdoing to the plaintiff. This issue is discussed in Section 62.2 ("In Pari Delicto").

A former employee was held barred by unclean hands from asserting claims against his former employer based on the employer's alleged refusal to honor a promise that the employee could perform illegal acts without fear of being terminated from his employment.[28] On the other hand, if the employee is terminated for refusing to comply with a demand to perform an illegal act, courts are less willing to allow the unclean hands defense even though the employee may have participated and benefitted from the wrongful conduct in the past.[29] It is unclear whether these decisions disallowing the defense (1) are based on the court's perception that detection and deterrence of illegal conduct outweighs the policies that underlie the unclean hands defense,[30] (2) reflect a view that the employee by refusing to continue to engage in illegal conduct has purged herself of the wrongful conduct,[31] or (3) treat the employee's termination as distinct from the "connected" wrongful conduct.[32]

The unclean hands defense may be subject to public policy restrictions. In *Pieczynski v. Duffy* the court held that a former municipal employee could be barred from seeking reinstatement even though she was terminated from her employment for political reasons.[33] The court characterized the plaintiff as a "ghost" employee, which means being on the payroll without working. To permit reinstatement to such a "position" would be to perpetrate the continuation of fraud in the guise of vindicating constitutional guarantees.[34] In *McKennon v. Nashville Banner Pub. Co.* the plaintiff sued for

---

[25] Makela v. Roach, 492 N.E.2d 191, 195 (Ill. App. 1986) (unclean hands); *cf.* Pantely v. Garris, Garris & Garris, 447 N.W.2d 864, 868 (Mich. App. 1989) (in pari delicto).

[26] *Bain, supra*, 272 Cal. Rptr. at 258–59.

[27] Carmel v. Clapp & Eisenberg, P.C., 960 F.2d 698, 703–04 (7th Cir. 1992); Saks v. Sawtelle, Goode, Davidson & Troilo, 880 S.W.2d 466, 469 (Tex. Civ. App. 1994).

[28] Kiely v. Raytheon Co., 105 F.3d 734, 736–37 (1st Cir. 1997).

[29] Jacobs v. Universal Dev. Corp., 62 Cal. Rptr. 2d 446, 450–51 (Cal. App. 1997).

[30] Department of Public Welfare v. Superior Court, 496 P.2d 453, 456 (Cal. 1972).

[31] Stewart v. Jackson, 635 N.E.2d 186, 189–90 (Ind. App. 1994) (discussed at note 36, *infra*).

[32] Text and notes 19–22, *supra*.

[33] 875 F.2d 1331, 1332 (7th Cir. 1989 (noting that such a termination may violate principles expressed in *Elrod v. Burns*, 427 U.S. 347 (1976)).

[34] 875 F.2d at 1333 (noting that "[t]o that extent—but to that extent only—there is a defense of 'unclean hands' . . ."); Byron v. Clay, 867 F.2d 1049, 1051 (7th Cir. 1989) (same).

age discrimination. After plaintiff was terminated the employer discovered that plaintiff has engaged in misconduct that if known earlier would have justified plaintiff's termination. The Court refused to allow the defendant-employer to raise the defense of "after-acquired grounds" reasoning that it was in the nature of the unclean hands defense and the defense was inconsistent with the broad equitable remedies Congress authorized to interdict age discrimination in the workplace. [35]

The fact that a plaintiff's hands have been dirtied does not mean that they cannot be washed. For example, while a court may apply unclean hands to prevent a person from achieving through litigation an exclusive right or license to engage in wrongful conduct, if the plaintiff ceases engaging in wrongful conduct, the defense may be negated. [36] The fact that the plaintiff may have facilitated the defendant's misconduct is not a defense to unclean hands if the defendant was already predisposed to engage in the misconduct. [37]

[62.2] "In Pari Delicto"

The phrase "in pari delicto" is part of a larger phrase "in pari delicto potior est conditio defendentis," which means that "in cases of equal fault, the position of the defendant is stronger." [38] In pari delicto means "in equal fault" and is applied to those situations when the plaintiff's culpability regarding the matter at issue is equal to or greater than the defendant's culpability. Like the defense of unclean hands, the defense of in pari delicto is not designed to protect the defendant but to protect the integrity of the court. [39]

In order to establish the defense of in pari delicto the plaintiff's culpability must be equal to or greater than the defendant's. Mere delict or wrong on the plaintiff's part is insufficient. In pari delicto is not equivalent to the old contributory fault doctrine; moreover, it usually presupposes a greater amount or kind of wrongdoing than unclean hands:

---

[35] 513 U.S. 352, 360 (1995).

[36] Stewart v. Jackson, 635 N.E.2d 186, 189–90 (Ind. App. 1994) (holding that homeowner who violated restrictive covenants by using residence for business (day care center) could sue neighbor for violating covenant by neighbor's operation of day care center because homeowner had ceased and discontinued business prior to bringing suit); Estate of Blanco, 150 Cal. Rptr. 645, 649 (Cal. App. 1978) (holding that party may purge himself of taint and preclude application of defense of unclean hands; grantor whose transfer was tainted with fraud may purge fraud by disposing of affected creditor's claim by settlement or payment).

[37] Levi Strauss & Co. v. Shilon, 121 F.3d 1309, 1313 (9th Cir. 1997) (rejecting claim that assistance of plaintiff's investigator's in arranging "sting operation" against defendant constituted misconduct warranting assertion of defense of unclean hands).

[38] Evans v. Cameron, 360 N.W.2d 25, 28 (Wis. 1985).

[39] Feld & Sons, Inc. v. Pechner, Dorfman, Wolfee, Rounick & Cabot, 458 A.2d 545, 548 n.2 (Pa. Super. Ct. 1983) (noting that one purpose of the defense is to preserve the dignity of the court); Tri-Q, Inc. v. Sta-Hi Corp., 404 P.2d 486, 497 (Cal. 1965) (stating that purpose of defense is to protect the court from unwittingly lending its assistance to encouragement or consummation of conduct violative of public policy).

The doctrine of in pari delicto is the legal counterpart to the equitable doctrine of unclean hands. The doctrines are not, however, the same. The doctrine of unclean hands considers whether the party seeking relief has engaged in inequitable conduct that has harmed the party against whom he seeks relief. In pari delicto, in contrast, focuses on the relative culpability of the parties. The culpability element of the in pari delicto doctrine requires that the plaintiff has been guilty of illegal or fraudulent conduct. Just as importantly, the doctrine applies only where the plaintiff was equally or more culpable than the defendant or acted with the same or greater knowledge as to the illegality or wrongfulness of the transaction.[40]

Secondly, and of increasing importance today, application of the defense must not violate the public interest or public policy. This requirement is of ancient vintage.[41] Particularly in the context of statutory rights and remedies, courts have carefully navigated between common law concepts of fault and the desire not to frustrate legislative designs intended to validate larger public interests.[42] As noted in *Perma Life Mufflers, Inc. v. International Parts Corp.*: "[a] more fastidious regard for the relative moral worth of the parties would only result in seriously undermining the usefulness of the private action as a bulwark of antitrust enforcement."[43]

How these competing interests of plaintiff's culpability and the public interest should be balanced has proven to be highly complex and divisive; some jurisdictions avoid the issue altogether.[44] When the balancing test is applied, it is often devilishly difficult to determine how far the public interest reaches in disregarding a plaintiff's culpability. Statements in one case suggesting a broad prosecution,[45] may be met with limited acceptance in a later case.[46]

Some courts have responded to this development by distinguishing between the common law form of in pari delicto, which simply contemplates at least equal fault, and a policy-based form of in pari delicto that envisions a particularized kind of fault,[47] correlated to the remedial goals and

---

[40] General Car & Truck Leasing Sys., Inc. v. Lane & Waterman, 557 N.W.2d 274, 279 (Iowa 1996) (stating that client was equally culpable with law firm in filing false marks with the Patent and Trademark Office precluding action for legal malpractice) (citations omitted).

[41] 1 STORY, TREATISE ON EQUITY JURISPRUDENCE §§ 300, 423 (14th ed. 1918).

[42] Kiefer-Stewart Co. v. Joseph Seagram & Sons, 340 U.S. 211, 214 (1951) (refusing to dismiss antitrust claims on the ground that the plaintiff had, along with the defendant, violated the Sherman Act).

[43] 392 U.S. 134, 139 (1968).

[44] *Field & Sons, Inc., supra*, 458 A.2d at 550.

[45] *Perma Life Mufflers, Inc., supra*, 392 U.S. at 138 (suggesting that in pari delicto defense was not to be recognized in federal antitrust actions).

[46] Javelin Corp. v. Uniroyal, Inc., 546 F.2d 276, 278–79 (9th Cir. 1976) (recognizing rule announced in *Perma Life* only when "but for" actions of plaintiff, the wrongful conduct would not have occurred).

[47] General Leaseways, Inc. v. National Truck Leasing Ass'n, 830 F.2d 716, 720–21 (7th Cir. 1987).

purposes of the statute. In *Pinter v. Dahl*[48] and *Bateman Eichler, Hill Richards, Inc. v. Berner*[49] the Court limited the defense of in pari delicto to cases when (1) as a direct result of his own actions, the plaintiff bears at least substantially equal responsibility for the violation he seeks to redress, and (2) preclusion of suit would not significantly interfere with the effective enforcement of the securities laws and the protection of the investing public.[50] This standard is sufficiently comprehensive to accommodate other statutory schemes using private enforcement as a supplement to administrative regulation.

Like the defense of unclean hands, the defense of in pari delicto enjoys its greatest success when the claim and its effects are bilateral, *i.e.,* do not involve third parties or the public interest at large. Legal malpractice suits claiming losses incurred because the plaintiff-client engaged in fraudulent or wrongful activity encouraged or abetted by the defendant-lawyer is a frequent setting for the defense.[51] Conduct by the plaintiff that is immoral or unconscionable also increases judicial receptivity of the defense.[52] On the other hand, when the plaintiff is forced or coerced to engage in wrongful conduct, the case for the defense is reduced.[53]

In pari delicto, as well as the related defense of unclean hands, raises difficult problems of application when the active wrongdoer is an agent and the defendant seeks to attribute the wrongdoing to the plaintiff (principal). This issue arises most frequently in cases of agent (director or officer) misconduct that has inflicted loss on the principal (corporation) that the principal wishes to transfer in whole or part to a third party (law firm or accounting firm). Oftentimes the claim is asserted by a receiver, bankruptcy trustee, or creditor, which raises the additional argument whether there should be double imputation—first to the corporation, then to the receiver, trustee, or creditor?

---

[48] 486 U.S. 622, 634 (1988) (involving an action under § 12(b) of the Securities Act of 1933).

[49] 472 U.S. 299, 310–11 (1985) (involving a Rule 10(b)(5) action under the Securities Exchange Act of 1934).

[50] *Pinter, supra*, 486 U.S. at 638, 648–50 (holding that the policy behind the Securities Act limited the in pari delicto defense to situations where plaintiff functioned as a promoter rather than an investor since the purpose of the Act was to deter illegal activities and compensate victims of illegal activities; merely being a substantial factor in causing the sale of unregistered securities was insufficient to detract from the achievement of these objectives).

[51] *General Car & Truck Leasing Sys., Inc., supra*, 557 N.W.2d at 282–83; *Evans, supra*, 360 N.W.2d at 29; see Trustees of the AFTRA Health Fund v. Biondi, 303 F.3d 765, 783 (7th Cir. 2002) (holding that client could not recover indemnification from his own lawyers under theory of legal malpractice for fraud client perpetrated on another). The court relied on the fact that the client's claim was morally flawed and in any event the operative cause of the client's loss was his fraud, not his lawyer's malpractice. Section 52 (Indemnity).

[52] Jacobs v. Universal Dev. Corp., 62 Cal. Rptr. 2d 446, 451–52 (Cal. App. 1997) (holding that the defense is not appropriate where conduct is not based on an illegal or immoral act); In re Dow, 132 B.R. 853, 860 (S.D. Ohio 1991); City of New York v. Corwen, 565 N.Y.S.2d 457, 460 (App. Dept. 1990).

[53] Goldlawr, Inc. v. Shubert, 268 F. Supp. 965, 970, (E.D. Pa. 1967).

As a general rule, actions of corporate agents are imputed to the corporation, unless the agent's interest is completely adverse to the corporation, which usually involves situations when the agent's actions are designed and taken for the purpose of defrauding the corporation.[54] If the agent's wrongdoing falls outside this exception, the agent acts for the principal and the defense is good against the principal. If the principal seeks to transfer the loss to others, e.g., its lawyers or accountants, they may invoke the defense against the principal, assuming, of course, that the other elements of the defense are established. If, on the other hand, the exception applies, the defense is not good against the principal.

An exception to the adverse interest exception is the "sole actor" exception. If the agent is essentially defrauding himself by looting his own corporation, the rationale for the "adverse interest" exception dissipates.[55] In these cases, the defense is available against the principal.

The full development of these issues is beyond the scope of this work; however, some commentary is cited in the accompanying footnote.[56]

[62.3] Merger of Law and Equity

The defenses of unclean hands and in pari delicto had separate origins. Unclean hands was an equitable defense and was historically confined to actions in equity.[57] In pari delicto, on the other hand, was first recognized by Lord Mansfield in *Smith v. Bromley*,[58] although the equitable considerations that underlie in pari delicto[59] have caused a few courts to view it as having an equitable origin.[60]

Since the procedural merger of law and equity, several jurisdictions have recognized the equitable defense of unclean hands in actions at law. The earliest cases involved damages actions in matters that had an equitable connection, such as patent and trademark cases.[61] The principle has

---

[54] Long Island Sav. Bank v. United States, 54 Fed. Cl. 607, 618 (Fed. Cl. 2002).

[55] Official Committee of Unsecured Creditors v. R.F. Lafferty & Co., 267 F.3d 340, 359 (3d Cir. 2001).

[56] Irve J. Goldman, *Whose Cause of Action Is It Anyway?*, 23-Mar. Am. Bankr. Inst. J. 1 (2004); Practicing Law Institute, *Accountant's Liability After Enron: Bankruptcy* 1309 PLI/ Corp. 549 Part V (2002).

[57] Keystone Driller Co. v. General Excavator Co., 290 U.S. 240, 244 (1933); Meeks v. Meeks, 54 A.2d 334, 337 (1947).

[58] 2 Doug. 686, 99 Eng. Rep. 441 n. (N.P. 1760). Lord Mansfield also recognized that the defense was for the protection of the court, not for the benefit of the parties. Holman v. Johnson, 1 Cowp. 342, 343, 98 Eng. Rep. 1120, 1121 (K.B. 1775).

[59] Grodecki, *"In Pari Delicto Potior Est Conditio Defendentis"*, 71 L. Q. Rev. 254 (1955); John Wade, *Restitution of Benefits Acquired Through Illegal Transactions*, 95 U. Pa. L. Rev. 261 (1947).

[60] *Pinter, supra*, 486 U.S. at 632 (identifying in pari delicto as an equitable defense).

[61] Republic Molding Corp. v. B.W. Photo Utilities, 319 F.2d 347, 350 (9th Cir. 1963) (involving damages for patent and trademark infringement); Al-Ibrahim v. Edde, 897 F. Supp. 620, 625 (D.D.C. 1995) (applying defense to action for fraud because fraud is an equitable remedy).

become more accepted,[62] although the recognition of the defense of unclean hands to actions at law has not been complete.[63] The defense is most readily applied to actions at law when a plaintiff seeks both legal and equitable remedies for the same wrong.[64] The cases do not all identify this, however, as a precondition to application of the defense to actions at law.[65] The cases are few, but the movement is toward recognizing unclean hands as an available defense to legal claims.

The motivations for this movement are severalfold. First, there is the simple logicality of the fact of merger,[66] although many courts adhere to the rule that the merger is for procedural purposes only and does not extend to substantive doctrine; these courts still adhere to the traditional law-equity divide.[67]

Second, there is the belief that the defense of unclean hands embodies general principles of fairness and justice equally applicable, and therefore available, to actions at law as well as equity.[68]

Lastly, there is a strong overlap between unclean hands and in pari delicto both in terms of subject matter and approach. Both defenses emphasize the link between the plaintiff's culpability and the wrongdoing that is before the court. Both doctrines, through an emphasis on substantial justice and public policy, are increasingly being applied when the court believes that the benefits of applying the defense outweigh the costs.[69]

---

[62] Buchanan Home & Auto Supply Co. v. Firestone Tire & Rubber Co., 544 F. Supp. 242, 245 (D.S.C. 1981).

[63] Food Lion, Inc. v. Capital Cites/ABC, Inc., 951 F. Supp. 1233, 1234 (M.D.N.C. 1996) (applying North Carolina law) (stating that the "defense of unclean hands . . . is inapplicable . . . where plaintiff is not seeking an equitable remedy . . ."); Gratreak v. North Pac. Lumber Co., 609 P.2d 375, 378 (Or. App. 1980).

[64] Fibreboard Paper Products Corp. v. East Bay Union of Machinists Local 1304, 39 Cal. Rptr. 64, 96–97 (Cal. App. 1964) (involving claims for legal and equitable relief for losses caused by workplace violence by picket line employers); *Jacobs, supra*, 62 Cal. Rptr. 2d at 449 (noting that in California defense of unclean hands may "apply to legal as well as equitable claims and to both tort and contract remedies") (citations omitted).

[65] Unilogic, Inc. v. Burroughs Corp., 12 Cal. Rptr. 2d 741, 744 (Cal. App. 1993) (citing *Fibreboard* for the proposition that defense can be applied to claim seeking only tort conversion damages).

[66] Byron v. Clay, 867 F.2d 1049 (7th Cir. 1989) (Posner J.). Judge Posner has made the same argument in other contexts. Section 61.4 (Merger of Law & Equity) (involving equitable defense of laches).

[67] *Gratreak, supra*, 609 P.2d at 378 (questioning whether "procedural" merger should extend to "substantive" rules).

[68] *Buchanan Home & Auto Supply Co., supra*, 544 F. Supp. at 245; *see* Zechariah Chafee, *Coming Into Equity With Clean Hands*, 47 Mich. L. Rev. 1065, 1091–92 (1949):

> First, the clean hands maxim is not peculiar to equity, but is simply a picturesque phrase applied by equity judges to a general principle running through damage actions as well as suits for specific relief. This principle is that the plaintiff's fault is often an important element in the judicial settlement of disputes, as well as the defendant's fault.

[69] Lawler v. Gilliam, 569 F.2d 1283, 1292 (4th Cir. 1978) (in applying defense of unclean hands "[t]he question must be one of policy: which decision will have the better consequences

§ 63 DURESS AND UNCONSCIONABILITY

[63.1] Duress

The defense of economic duress permits a party to avoid (rescind) an obligation based on an act that was compelled because of the wrongful threat of another, which precluded the party's exercise of free will.[1]

Jurisdictions vary in their formulation of the elements of duress; nevertheless the basic structure is that the victim must show (1) that he was subject to a wrongful or unlawful act or threat and (2) that the act or threat deprived him of his unfettered will. In *Urban Plumbing & Heating Co. v. United States* the court stated:

> An examination of the cases, however, makes it clear that three elements are common to all situations where duress has been found to exist. These are: (1) that one side involuntarily accepted the terms of another; (2) that circumstances permitted no other alternatives; and (3) that said circumstances were the result of coercive acts of the opposite party . . . . The assertion of duress must be proven to have been the result of the defendant's conduct and not by the plaintiff's necessities.[2]

In *Troutman v. Facetglas, Inc.* the court stated a five-part test:

> (1) the coerced party must show he has been the victim of a wrongful or unlawful act or threat; (2) [the] act or threat must . . . [deprive] the victim of his unfettered will; (3) as a direct result, the [victim] must be compelled to make a disproportionate exchange . . . or to give up something for nothing; (4) the payment or exchange must be made solely for the [purpose] of protecting the [victim's] business or property interests; and (5) the [victim] must have no adequate legal remedy.[3]

In *Herndon v. First National Bank* the court articulated a three-part test which emphasized the wrongfulness of the conduct constituting the acts of duress:

> (1) a threat to do something which [the threatening party] has no legal right to do; (2) some illegal extraction, or some fraud or deception; and (3) the restraint is imminent and such as to destroy free agency without present means of protection [from the restraint].[4]

---

in promoting the objective of the securities laws by increasing the protection to be afforded the investing public . . . . Common law technicalities are to be avoided"); *Bain, supra,* 272 Cal. Rptr. at 257 (stating that "[t]he crux of [prior decisions] is not the use of in pari delicto as a litmus test. Rather . . . the 'true rule in such cases' is that under the circumstances there should be an application of that rule of equity . . .").

[1] 805 Third Avenue Co. v. M.W. Realty Assoc., 448 N.E.2d 445, 447 (N.Y. 1983); Chapter 15 (Rescission).

[2] 408 F.2d 382 (Ct. Cl. 1969) (citations omitted).

[3] 316 S.E.2d 424 427 (S.C. App. 1984) (brackets added).

[4] 802 S.W.2d 396, 399–400 (Tex. Civ. App. 1991) (brackets added).

A common theme that underlies these various formulations is that the defendant's threats must leave the plaintiff no reasonable alternative.[5] Whether a plaintiff had a reasonable alternative "is determined by examining whether a reasonably prudent person would follow the alternative course, or whether a reasonably prudent person might submit."[6] The pressure or coercion brought to bear upon the plaintiff need not be illegal, but may include an act that is wrongful in a moral sense.[7]

Duress requires more compulsion than the constraints encountered in daily life.[8] The fact that a person's difficult financial situation caused her to make concessions and agree to terms she would have preferred not to does not amount to duress.[9] Hard bargaining and financial pressure do not, without more, constitute duress.[10] The acts constituting duress cannot come from third parties, but must come from the party seeking to exploit the victim's vulnerability.[11]

The wrongful or unlawful act(s) that give rise to the claim of duress need not be committed in the very transaction the victim seeks to avoid. It is sufficient that the wrongful and unlawful act(s) relate and contribute to the victim's coercion, such that he is unable to resist the perpetrator's pressure. For example, in *Rich & Whillock, Inc. v. Ashton Development Inc.* a general contractor's misfeasance had caused the subcontractor to incur additional charges. When the subcontractor demanded reimbursement for

---

[5] Restatement (Second) of Contracts §§ 175 (1981) (stating that a contract is avoidable on grounds of duress if a party's assent is induced by an improper threat that leaves no reasonable alternative); 176 (defining improper threats).

[6] CrossTalk Productions, Inc. v. Jacobson, 76 Cal. Rptr. 2d 615, 623 (Cal. App. 1998).

[7] Rich & Willock; Inc. v. Ashton Dev., Inc., 204 Cal. Rptr. 86, 89 (Cal. App. 1984); Kaplan v. Kaplan, 182 N.E.2d 706, 709 (Ill. 1962).

[8] Reavis v. Slominski, 551 N.W.2d 528, 542 (Neb. 1996) (stating that "[t]he cases to date in which duress has been found to render the consent ineffective have involved those forms of duress that are quite drastic in their nature and that clearly and immediately amount to an overpowering of the will").

[9] Liebelt v. Liebelt, 801 P.2d 52, 55 (Idaho App. 1990) (holding that the fact that a party felt compelled to sign a prenuptial agreement because the other party insisted on it as a condition to marriage did not constitute duress, the threat of a refusal to marry is not wrongful in the eyes of the law); Machinery Hauling, Inc. v. Steel of West Virginia, 384 S.E.2d 139, 144 (W. Va. 1989).

[10] Willcutts v. Galeburg Clinic Ass'n, 560 N.E.2d 1, 5 (Ill. App. 1990); see Regent Partners, Inc. v. Parr Dev. Co., Inc., 960 F. Supp. 607, 612 (E.D.N.Y. 1997) (stating that "[a] defense of duress cannot be sustained by a contracting party who has simply been bested in contract negotiations by the 'hard bargaining' of another contracting party, even when the hard bargainer knowingly takes advantage of his counterpart's difficult financial circumstances") (citations omitted); Strickland Tower Maintenance, Inc. v. AT&T Communications, Inc., 128 F.3d 1422 (10th Cir. 1997) (same).

[11] Oskey Gasoline & Oil Co., Inc. v. Continental Oil Co., 534 F.2d 1281, 1286 (8th Cir. 1976) (stating that duress must emanate from coercive acts of opposing party); Blodgett v. Blodgett, 551 N.E.2d 1249, 1251–52 (Ohio 1990) (stating that "[t]o avoid a contract on the basis of duress, a party must prove coercion by the other party to the contract. It is not enough to show that one assented merely because of difficult circumstances that are not the fault of the other party"); Schmalz v. Hardy Salt Co. 739 S.W.2d 765, 768 (Mo. App. 1987).

the additional costs, the general contractor, knowing of the subsubcontractor's difficult financial situation, which had been exacerbated by the general's misfeasance, offered "$50,000 or nothing." The subsubcontractor accepted, but later sought relief on the ground of duress. The court agreed, finding that (1) the contractor knew there was no legitimate dispute over the amount due, but nevertheless (2) used the subsubcontractor's vulnerability the contractor's own actions had created (3) to exploit the situation to its benefit.[12]

At common law, duress was limited to transactions resulting from the victim's false imprisonment or from threats of physical violence or criminal prosecution.[13] Cases of this type still occur today, but the more common and modern form of duress is captured by the concept "economic" duress or coercion[14] or its close companion "business compulsion."[15] As noted in *Centric Corporation v. Morrison-Knudsen Company*:

> The rationale underlying the principle of economic duress is the imposition of certain minimal standards of business ethics in the market place. Hard bargaining, efficient breaches, and reasonable settlements of good faith disputes are acceptable, even desirable, in our economic system. However, the minimum standards are not limited to precepts of rationality and self-interest—they include equitable notions of fairness and propriety which preclude the wrongful exploitation of business exigencies to obtain disproportionate exchanges of value which, in turn, undermine the freedom to contract and the proper functioning of the system. The doctrine of economic duress comes into play only when conventional alternatives and remedies are unavailable to correct abberational abuse of these norms. It is available solely to prevent injustice, not to create injustice.[16]

It is generally recognized that it is not duress to threaten to do what one has a legal right to do.[17] Threatening to do what one does *not* have a right to do, or exploiting past wrongful conduct, may constitute duress. However,

---

[12] 204 Cal. Rptr. at 88–91. *See generally* Wendy Evans Lehmann, Annot., *Refusal To Pay Debt as Economic Duress or Business Compulsion Avoiding Compromise or Release,* 9 A.L.R. 4th 942 (1981).

[13] *See generally* 17 C.J.S. *Contracts* §§ 168–179; 25 Am. Jur. 2d *Duress and Undue Influence* §§ 22–29.

[14] Lawless v. Central Prod. Credit Ass'n, 592 N.E.2d 1210, 1217 (Ill. App. 1992).

[15] Barker v. Walter Hogan Enters., Inc., 596 P.2d 1359, 1360 (Wash. App. 1979) (stating that business compulsion is a species of duress "involving involuntary action in which one is compelled to act in such a manner that either he suffers a serious business loss or he is compelled to make a monetary payment to his detriment") (citation omitted).

[16] 731 P.2d 411, 413–15 (Okla. 1986) (footnote omitted).

[17] Griffith v. Geffen & Jacobsen, P.C., 693 S.W.2d 724, 728 (Tex. Civ. App. 1985) (stating that a threat to bring suit does not constitute duress if the defendant has a legal right to do so); Various Markets, Inc. v. Chase Manhattan Bank, N.A., 908 F. Supp. 459, 468 (E.D. Mich. 1995) (same).

exploiting another's financial predicament, not caused by one's own wrong-ful acts, is not duress.[18]

One issue that has caused difficulty here is whether the threat to prosecute criminally constitutes duress when the threat is used as a bargaining chip to secure an economic benefit. One line of decisions focuses on the element of choice. As long as the person's ability to make a voluntary choice remains, the use of the threat does not constitute duress:

> "[T]he assessment [of] whether real alternatives were offered is gauged by an objective standard rather than by the employee's purely subjective evaluation; that the employee may perceive his only option to be resignation . . . is irrelevant. Moreover, the mere fact that the choice is between comparably unpleasant alternatives . . . does not of itself establish that a resignation was induced by duress or coercion, hence was involuntary. Specifically, resignations can be voluntary even where the only alternative to resignation is facing possible termination for cause or criminal charges. Resigna-tions obtained in cases where an employee is faced with such unpleasant alternatives are nevertheless voluntary because the fact remains that plaintiff had a choice. [Plaintiff] could stand pat and fight. The one exception to this rule is where the employer actually lacked good cause to believe that grounds for the termination and the criminal charges existed.[19]

A competing line of decisions suggests that it is improper to use a threat of criminal prosecution to obtain a collateral advantage.[20] A third line of decisions presents a more nuanced approach. Under this approach, the critical issue is the victim's state of mind. A threat is coercive when it acts

---

[18] Goode v. Burke Town Plaza, 436 S.E.2d 450, 452–53 (Va. 1993) (stating that "[b]ecause the application of economic pressure by threatening to enforce a legal right is not a wrongful act, it cannot constitute duress") (citations omitted); Disctronics Ltd. v. Disc Mfg., Inc., 686 So. 2d 1154, 1163 (Ala. 1996) (threatening to force defaulting debtor into bankruptcy not duress); cf. Stefandel v. Sielaff, 575 N.Y.S.2d 304, 305 (App. Dept. 1991) (informing probation-ary employee that termination would jeopardize future employment did not vitiate on grounds of duress employee's election to resign rather than face termination); see note 11, supra.

[19] Hargray v. City of Hallandale, 57 F.3d 1560, 1568 (11th Cir. 1995) (citations omitted; brackets in original) (employment termination case). The court noted that whether an employee's resignation was obtained through coercion or duress will be influenced by the following:

> (1) whether the employee was given some alternative to resignation; (2) whether the employee understood the nature of the choice he was given; (3) whether the employee was given a reasonable time in which to choose; (4) whether the employee was permitted to select the effective date of the resignation; and (5) whether the employee had the advice of counsel.

Id. (citation omitted).

[20] Philliphine Export and Foreign Loan Guarantee Corp. v. Chuidian, 267 Cal. Rptr. 457, 466 (Cal. App. 1990) (stating that "[a]nother impermissible threat is a threat of criminal prosecution, which in contract as well as criminal law constitutes a plainly wrongful act and will avoid a bargain"); Germantown Mfg. Co. v. Rawlinson, 491 A.2d 138, 144 (Pa. Super. Ct. 1985) (stating that "[i]t is an affront to our judicial sensibilities that one person's ability to seek another's prosecution can be bartered and sold the same as commodities in the marketplace").

upon a person's fear such that his ability to exercise free choice is compro-mised.[21] The typical situation involves a spouse who is induced to co-sign a note or pledge to avoid the threatened prosecution of the other spouse for some alleged wrong.[22] Cognizant of the fact that transaction remorse may influence a party's recollection of the facts, courts usually insist that there be clear and convincing evidence that the threat actually induced the victim to engage in the transaction.[23]

The general rule is that duress is available as a defense, not as an inde-pendent cause of action.[24] Occasionally courts speaks of the tort of duress, but the context of the discussion is that the court is emphasizing the wrongfulness of the conduct; the court is not adopting duress as an affirmative cause of action.[25] Some of the confusion can be explained by the fact that duress is a grounds for rescission and restitution of money or benefits obtained from the victim by the perpetrator,[26] and the use of duress in this context may be seen by the court as an affirmative, offensive assertion of the doctrine.[27]

[63.2] Unconscionability

Unconscionability is the most idealistic of the equitable defenses. What could be more consistent with a jurisprudence based on the principle of individualized justice than a defense based on the concept that bargains that violate basic norms of morality and fairness as between individuals should not be enforced. As is the case, however, with "justice," so does "unconscionability" suffer from a lack of common agreement as to what the term means. A fair bargain for one, is often an unconscionable bargain for another.

The open-endedness of "unconscionability" has given most courts pause before accepting it without qualification. No jurisdiction at present permits an affirmative recovery based on unconscionable conduct: there is no "tort" of unconscionability. Unconscionability is a passive remedy; it allows a party to escape a bargain, but, by itself, does not create a bargain.

---

[21] Peavy v. Bank South, N.A., 474 S.E.2d 690 (Ga. App. 1996) (stating that the "mere threats of criminal prosecution, where neither warrant has been issued nor proceedings commenced, do not constitute duress . . . . The threatened prosecution must be for an act either criminal or which the party threatened thought was criminal. A mere empty threat does not amount to duress"); Smith v. Sneed, 638 So. 2d 1252, 1261 (Miss. 1994).

[22] Osage Corp., v. Simon, 613 N.E.2d 770, 774 (Ill. App. 1993).

[23] Warner v. Warner, 394 S.E.2d 74, 78 (W. Va. 1990) (conclusory allegations insufficient).

[24] NN Investors Life Ins. Co. v. Professional Group, Inc., 468 So. 2d 532, 533 (Fla. App. 1985) (*per curiam*) (rejecting tort of economic duress); *cf.* Boschette v. Bach, 925 F. Supp. 100, 101–02 (D.P.R. 1996) (holding that absent statutory authorization, no civil cause of action exists for extortion); Restatement (Second) of Torts § 871 (1965). There is a thoughtful discussion of the issue in *Machinery Hauling, Inc., supra,* 384 S.E.2d 139.

[25] *Lawless, supra,* 592 N.E.2d at 1217.

[26] Hurtt v. Stirone, 206 A.2d 624, 625 (Pa. 1965).

[27] *CrossTalk Productions, supra,* 76 Cal. Rptr. 2d at 623 (using duress to set aside modification of contract).

Unconscionability may, however, permit a party to redefine the bargain by removing unfavorable provisions and then enforcing the revised bargain against the defendant. Whether the defendant would have entered into the revised bargain is rarely considered. Perhaps enforcement of the "new" bargain is a penalty for including and seeking to enforce "unconscionable" terms? In this sense, unconscionability may be said to have an offensive rather than just a passive use.

Many courts limit unconscionability to equitable remedies, as a consequence the matter is resolved by the judge rather than the jury.[28] While the Uniform Commercial Code broadly expands the defense of unconscionable to contracts for the sale of goods regardless of the remedy sought, the UCC instructs that the determination is to be made "by the court."[29] Some jurisdictions have by statute broadly expanded the availability of the unconscionability defense. Here too the practice is to restrict consideration of the defense "to the court."[30]

Unconscionability may be seen as the absence of meaningful choice[31] and in this sense is related to other defenses such as duress or undue influence. Unlike those defenses, however, which focus on external pressure on the will or capacity of a person, unconscionability focuses directly on the bargain itself and seeks to determine if it is morally fair, *i.e.*, is the bargain so one-sided and the circumstances under which the bargain was reached so tilted against the person as to make it inequitable to enforce that particular bargain.[32]

The standard view is that the defense of unconscionability has both procedural and substantive components, each of which must be satisfied to establish unconscionability.[33] That dual requirement may be misleading,

---

[28] Section 20.2 (Right of Jury Trial); *see* Restatement (Second) Contracts § 208, cmt. f (1981); County of Asphalt, Inc. v. Lewis Welding and Engineering Corp., 444 F.2d 372, 379 (2d Cir.), *cert. denied*, 404 U.S. 939 (1971).

[29] U.C.C. § 2-302(1).

[30] Cal. Civ. Code § 1670.5.

[31] Ingle v. Circuit City Stores, Inc., 328 F.3d 1165, 1170 (9th Cir. 2003) (applying California law), *cert. denied*, 540 U.S. 1160 (2004); Earl of Chesterfield v. Janssen, 28 E.R. 82, 100 (K.B. 1750) (stating that an unconscionable agreement is one that "no man in his senses and not under delusion could make on the one hand, and no honest and fair man would accept on the other; which are unequitable and unconscientious bargains; and of such even the Common Law has taken notice").

[32] Campbell Soup Co. v. Wentz, 172 F.2d 80 (3d Cir. 1948):

> We are not suggesting that the contract is illegal. Nor are we suggesting any excuse for the grower in this case who has deliberately broken an agreement entered into with Campbell. We do think, however, that a party who has offered and succeeded in getting an agreement as tough as this one is, should not come to a chancellor and ask court help in the enforcement of its terms. That equity does not enforce unconscionable bargains is too well established to require elaborate citation.

Id. at 84 (footnote omitted).

[33] Samura v. Kaiser Foundation Health Plan, Inc., 22 Cal. Rptr.2d 20, 27 (Cal. App. 1993), *cert. denied*, 511 U.S. 1084 (1994); E.H. Ashley & Co. v. Willow Assocs., 907 F.2d 1274, 1278 (1st Cir. 1990) (applying Rhode Island law). The distinction appears to have been pioneered by Professor Leff. Arthur Allen Leff, *Unconscionability and The Code—The Emperior's New Clause*, 115 U. Pa. Rev. 485, 487, 509 (1967).

however, because courts will often balance the factors in the sense that a strong showing of one factor will compensate for a weaker showing as to the other.[34] In any event, it is a relative rare case when a showing of unconscionability as to one factor is not met with some indicia of unconscionability as to the other. Procedural and substantive are not mutually exclusive categories. Oppression or surprise (the typical showing to establish procedural unconscionability) will likely involve harsh or one-sided terms (the typical showing to establish substantive unconscionability) and vice versa.

[63.2.1] Procedural

Procedural unconscionability focuses on the way in which the bargain came about. Was the bargain a product of duress, deceit, sharp practices, etc. A bargain struck under such circumstances is seen as oppressive and unfairly subjecting the person to "surprise," which is to say the bargain includes terms that he did not contemplate and to which he did not give his considered assent. Perhaps the concept of surprise can be best summarized by the adage "what the bold print promises, the fine print cannot take away." Of course enforcement of such a view is hardly policy neutral and leaves much to the discretion of the court.

Influential factors in this area are whether the parties were of equal bargaining strength and whether the contract terms were offered on a "take it or leave it" basis, factors that underpin the so-called adhesion contract."[35] A finding that the parties were of unequal bargaining strength will assist, but not satisfy, the procedural unconscionability test. As noted by the California Supreme Court:

> To describe a contract as adhesive in character is not to indicate its legal effect. It is, rather, "the beginning and not the end of the analysis insofar as enforceability of its terms is concerned." Thus, a contract of adhesion is fully enforceable according to its terms unless certain other factors are present which, under established legal rules legislative or judicial operate to render it otherwise.[36]

Inequality in bargaining position will satisfy the procedural test when inequality deprives a party of meaningful choice,[37] which brings unconscionability close to duress.[38]

---

[34] *Samura, supra. But see* Vockner v. Erickson, 712 P.2d 379 (Alaska 1986) (affirming trial court's finding that transaction was unconscionable based on substantive unfairness alone).

[35] *Ingle, supra,* 328 F.3d at 1171; Lucier v. Williams, 841 A.2d 907, 911 (N.J. Super. Ct. A.D. 2004); *see* Todd D. Rakoff, *Contracts of Adhesion: An Essay in Reconstruction,* 96 Harv. L. Rev. 1173 (1983).

[36] Graham v. Scissor-Tail, Inc., 623 P.2d 165, 172 (Cal. 1981) (citations omitted).

[37] Davis v. M.L.G. Corp., 712 P.2d 985, 991 (Colo. 1986); A&M Produce Co. v. FMC Corp., 186 Cal. Rptr. 114, 121–22 (Cal. App. 1982).

[38] Section 63.1 (Duress).

[63.2.2] Substantive

Substantive unconscionability focuses on the bargain itself. Is it an unfair, one-sided, oppressive bargain? Commentators have challenged whether these considerations should be used to alter bargains struck by parties,[39] but the concepts appear to resonant well with courts, at least most courts most of the time.

What assortment of facts and interests will induce a court to find substantive unconscionability cannot be reduced to a rule. Unconscionability decisions necessarily interact with the relationships and the legal issues before the court. Unconscionability in the context of arbitration agreements tends to emphasize different concerns and different issues from insurance disputes. For example, with arbitration, substantive unconscionability findings have emphasized the non-neutrality of the arbitrator[40] or the absence of equivalency of remedy and redress provided to each party.[41] It must be emphasized that these points are contentious and provoke significant judicial disagreement as to the proper scope of each point.[42]

§ 64 ESTOPPEL, WAIVER, AND ELECTION

Estoppel and waiver are frequently treated as if they overlap, but they are definitionally distinct. Estoppel is designed to prevent the actor from profiting by exploiting action or inaction he has induced another to take; waiver, on the other hand, focuses on the conduct of the actor himself in disavowing a right.[1] Estoppel and waiver also share similarities with the concept of election. Election possesses both the detrimental reliance element of estoppel and the voluntary element of waiver; yet, in election neither concept is fully developed. Election exists as a freestanding doctrine in its own right and it is sometimes suggested as an explanation of, or alternative for, difficult applications of estoppel or waiver.[2] Estoppel,

[39] Russell Korobkin, *Bounded Rationality, Standard Form Contracts, and Unconscionability*, 70 U. Chi. L. Rev. 1203, 1203–06 (2003) (collecting conflicting commentary).

[40] *Graham, supra*, 623 P.2d at 175–76.

[41] Ting v. AT&T, 319 F.3d 1126, 1149 (9th Cir.) (applying California law), *cert. denied*, 124 S. Ct. 53 (2003).

[42] Carter v. Countrywide Credit Indus., Inc., 362 F.3d 294, 301 (5th Cir. 2004) (applying (Texas law) (rejecting contention that disparity in bargaining power supported procedural unconscionability conclusion); Iberia Credit Bureau, Inc. v. Cingular Wireless LLC, 379 F.3d 159 (5th Cir. 2004) (finding that arbitration provision that required only one party to the bargain to arbitrate was unconscionable, but the fact that the provision also limited remedies that were only valuable to one party to bargain did not render the provision unconscionable).

[1] Nassau Trust Co. v. Montrose Concrete Prods. Corp., 436 N.E.2d 1265, 1269–70 (N.Y. 1982).

[2] ROBERT E. KEETON & ALAN I. WIDISS, INSURANCE LAW § 6.1(b)(4), pp. 618–20 (Stud. ed. 1988) (arguing that application of estoppel and waiver doctrine in insurer-insured disputes to deprive insurer of defense to insured's claim is frequently misapplied; courts are imposing "involuntary choice" on the insurer and that legal consequence is better captured by the label "election").

waiver, and election are treated as remedy defenses, but the better term might be remedial defenses. Estoppel, waiver, and election do not directly affect the underlying right; rather, they invariably involve conduct or action that is distinct from that which created the right, but which in fairness and justice preclude recovery under, or enforcement of, the right.

[64.1] Equitable Estoppel

Equitable estoppel, or estoppel in pais, is the remedial defense form of estoppel. There are other forms of estoppel. These include judicial estoppel and collateral estoppel. Equitable estoppel requires proof of two elements. First, there must be misleading conduct in the form of words or actions by the party to be estopped. Second, the misleading conduct must induce the other party to act or refrain from acting in a way that is prejudicial to his legal interests.[3] Implicit within this formulation, although sometimes stated as separate parts of the test, are the requirements that the party claiming estoppel must have relied on the misleading conduct, and been without knowledge as to the true facts.[4] These latter elements are explicit in the requirement that the misleading conduct induce prejudice. If the party to be estopped neither relies nor is mislead because he knows the true facts, he is not induced by misleading conduct to his prejudice. The specific definition of estoppel, while important, must be kept in perspective, for it is the circumstances that control application of the doctrine.[5]

Because the usual tests for estoppel require misleading conduct, it is generally held that mere silence cannot raise an estoppel.[6] This principle is, however, not applied when from all the facts and circumstances it appears that silence did in fact induce prejudicial reliance and this was known to the party to be estopped, but nothing was done. This is known as "misleading silence." For example, when a patent owner objects to another party's actions as constituting a possible infringement and then remains silent in the face of continuing activity by the second party before seeking relief, courts have deemed the patent owner's silence to be misleading.[7] Silence may also support an estoppel when one has a duty to speak.[8]

---

[3] Rosenfield v. Metals Selling Corp., 643 A.2d 1253, 1265 (Conn. 1994); Berschauer/Phillips Constr. Co. v. Seattle Sch. Distr. No. 1, 881 P.2d 986, 994–95 (Wash. 1994).

[4] Airco Alloys Div., Airco Inc. v. Niagara Mohawk Power Corp., 430 N.Y.S.2d 179, 187 (App. Dept. 1980).

[5] Miskimen v. Kansas City Star Co., 684 S.W.2d 394, 401 (Mo. App. 1984).

[6] Hottel Corp. v. Seaman Corp., 833 F.2d 1570, 1573 (Fed. Cir. 1987); Waldrip v. Olympia Oyster Co., 244 P.2d 273, 277 (Wash. 1952).

[7] Meyers v. Asics Corp., 974 F.2d 1304, 1308–09 (Fed. Cir. 1992) (discussing cases but finding rule not applicable based on the record); see Peter Tiersma, The Language of Silence, 48 Rutgers L. Rev. 1 (1995) (discussing when "silence" may create reasonable expectation of assent or reliance).

[8] Anchor Packing Co. v. Grimshaw, 692 A.2d 5, 29 n.10 (Md. Ct. Sp. App. 1997) (stating that to establish estoppel by silence there must be both a duty and an opportunity to speak); Middleton v. Imperial Ins. Co., 666 P.2d 1, 5 (Cal. 1983) (involving a statutory duty to speak).

A "duty" may be imposed in order to achieve what the court believes to be a remedially just result.[9] Superior knowledge may create a duty to speak when the possessor of superior knowledge knows the other is ignorant of the true facts and that the other's ignorance will cause him to do what he would not do except for the possessor's silence.[10] Most commonly, however, a duty to speak arises out of a fiduciary or confidential relationship.[11]

Estoppel shares similarities with other defenses. For example in cases when the plaintiff has delayed commencing his lawsuit, resulting in prejudice to defendant, defendant may raise both laches and estoppel as defenses. Laches addresses specifically whether a plaintiff's delay in enforcing its rights for an unreasonable period of time has resulted in defendant's prejudice.[12] Estoppel may also apply when, in addition to the showing necessary for laches, there is added the fact that defendant was misled by plaintiff. Thus, it is sometimes said that laches is distinct from estoppel because laches involves injury due to inaction while estoppel involves injury due to misleading conduct.[13] Yet, as noted above, the plaintiff may be estopped by misleading "silence," and in that context little separates the two defenses.[14]

Equitable estoppel also shares similarities with "promissory estoppel." Promissory estoppel, however, creates a cause of action, while equitable estoppel raises a defense or bar to another's desired course of conduct. Where promissory estoppel is a sword, equitable estoppel is a shield, a shield that may be affirmatively asserted by a plaintiff to negate a defense.[15] The distinction, between equitable and promissory estoppel though fine, has important consequences, particularly when a party seeks to use estoppel doctrine to expand contractual obligations,[16] absent grounds, such

---

[9] Hartway v. State Board of Control, 137 Cal. Rptr. 199 (Cal. App. 1976) (stating that defendant's failure to provide claim forms or advise victims of time limits on suits for victim indemnification barred statute of limitation defense; indemnification was consistent with objective of legislation providing aid to victims of crime).

[10] Perlman v. First Nat'l Bank of Chicago, 305 N.E.2d 236, 245 (Ill. App. 1973); cf. Terrell Hills Baptist Church v. Pawel, 286 S.W.2d 204, 208 (Tex. Civ. App. 1956) (stating that estoppel by silence is available when there is some element of turpitude or negligence connected with the silence that operates to mislead the other party).

[11] Casa El Sol-Acapulco, S.A. v. Fontenot, 919 S.W.2d 709, 718 (Tex. Civ. App. 1996); Continental Potash, Inc. v. Freeport-McMoran, Inc., 858 P.2d 66, 77 (N. Mex. 1993); In re Windsor Plumbing Supply Co., Inc., 170 B.R. 503, 525–26 (E.D.N.Y. 1994) (collecting cases).

[12] Section 61.1 (Laches).

[13] Alber v. Standard Heating and Air Conditioning, Inc., 476 N.E.2d 507, 510 (Ind. App. 1985).

[14] Briarwood Apartments v. Lieblong, 671 S.W.2d 207, 209 (Ark. App. 1984) (stating that "[l]aches is a species of estoppel and rests upon the principle that if one maintains silence when in conscience he ought to speak, equity will bar him from speaking when in conscience he ought to remain silent").

[15] Jablon v. United States, 657 F.2d 1064, 1068 (9th Cir. 1981); Chemical Bank v. Washington Pub. Power Supply Sys., 691 P.2d 524, 540 (Wash. 1984).

[16] Watson v. Nortex Wholesale Nursery, Inc., 830 S.W.2d 747, 751 (Tex. Civ. App. 1992) (holding that equitable estoppel would not support plaintiff's claim against Nortex that Nortex's misrepresentation of the identity of plaintiff's employer (North Haven) precluded him from asserting a claim he may have against North Haven).

as fraudulent misrepresentation, supporting an independent action.[17] Conduct short of that necessary to constitute a cause of action entitling a party to damages may be sufficient to invoke an estoppel to restore the parties to the same relative position they would have occupied had the misleading action not occurred. "[T]he doctrine of equitable estoppel is founded on concepts of equity and fair dealing. It provides that a person may not deny the existence of a state of facts if he intentionally led another to believe a particular circumstance to be true and to rely upon such belief to his detriment."[18]

Unlike some defenses, such as laches and unclean hands, estoppel is universally recognized as a defense in both legal and equitable actions.[19]

Because estoppel is based on equitable considerations, it may be found inapplicable when its assertion as a defense, although warranted on the facts, would interfere with a higher equity or the public interest. For example, the defense of estoppel is frequently barred on the ground that recognition of the defense would not be in the best interests of a child who is innocent of the misconduct but who would be directly affected if the defense were permitted. Thus, the putative father may not resist paternity and support obligations by alleging an estoppel based on misrepresentation by the mother.[20] Similarly, a husband in a divorce proceeding has been deemed estopped from challenging the paternity of the children born during the marriage.[21] A person who has held himself out as the parent of a child may be estopped to deny his parentage insofar as child support is concerned.[22] This results even though it is difficult to find real detrimental reliance by the child; rather, the result is justified as a policy driven conclusion based on the child's needs and the putative parent's affirmative conduct.

Estoppel defenses have also been rejected or received with extreme caution when their recognition would threaten to upset a statutory balancing of interests.[23]

---

[17] Shaffer v. Hines, 573 S.W.2d 420, 422 (Mo. App. 1978) (stating that equitable estoppel "cannot be used to create a cause of action, if the cause of action did not otherwise exist"); Section 120 (Nature of Fraud) (particularly Section 120.2 (Promissory Fraud)).

[18] Strong v. County of Santa Cruz, 543 P.2d 264, 266 (Cal. 1975).

[19] Black v. TIC Inv. Corp., 900 F.2d 112, 115 (7th Cir. 1990); Brooks v. Cooksey, 427 S.W.2d 498, 503 (Mo. 1968).

[20] Murphy v. Myers, 560 N.W.2d 752, 755 (Minn. App. 1997) (rejecting defense that mother was estopped to claim defendant was father because mother falsely represented she was sterile); Section 4 (Public Policy); Section 125 ([Fraud] Personal Relationships).

[21] Fung v. Fung, 655 N.Y.S.2d 657, 659 (App. Dept. 1997).

[22] Marriage of Pedregon, 132 Cal. Rptr. 2d 861, 863–64 (Cal. App. 2003); Lynn v. Powell, 809 A.2d 927, 929–30 (Pa. Super. Ct. 2002).

[23] Wolin v. Smith Barney, Inc., 83 F.3d 847, 855 (7th Cir. 1996) (leaving open whether defense of estoppel is available in actions under ERISA for breach of fiduciary duty given that the statute provides a limitation period and further provides that fraudulent concealment tolls the limitation period); Doe v. Blue Cross & Blue Shield United of Wisc., 112 F.3d 869, 875 (7th Cir. 1997) (following *Wolin* and noting cases holding that ERISA forbids the conferral of benefits other than pursuant to a written plan).

[64.2] Waiver

Waiver is consistently defined as "the intentional relinquishment of a known right."[24] This means that in order to waive a right, the person doing so must be aware of the right and have the intent to give it up.[25] An implicit corollary to this principle is that the relinquishment must be free of coercion, duress, or overreaching.[26] If waiver doctrine were so restricted, it would pose vastly fewer problems in application. The fact is, however, that the waiver definition is less than helpful, and may be positively misleading, as to the actual scope of the doctrine in practice.

The fundamental problem is that courts have held that waiver may occur as a result of conduct that is inconsistent with the intent to hold and assert the right. In essence, a waiver may be implied.[27] The effect of recognizing an implied waiver is that a waiver becomes less dependent on establishing a person's actual intent to waive and more dependent upon a trier-of-fact's inference that conduct inconsistent with the believed intent to hold and assert a right means that the person has disclaimed the right.[28] This latter inference may, in fact, be directly contrary to the person's actual intent.

Adding to confusion over the precise scope of waiver doctrine is the principle that a waiver may be the result of inadvertent conduct by the person subject to the waiver.[29] The application of this concept tends to be very subjective; some courts embrace the concept,[30] other appear to reject it.[31]

Only a fine line separates equitable estoppel from implied waiver. Once a waiver can be inferred from a party's conduct, the reaction of the other party becomes significant. That reaction can often parallel or approximate the "reliance" element of estoppel.[32] Indeed, the confusion has been

---

[24] City of New York v. State of New York, 357 N.E.2d 988, 995 (N.Y. 1976); Novella v. Hartford Accident & Indemn. Co., 316 A.2d 394, 400 (Conn. 1972).

[25] *Novella, supra*, 316 A.2d at 400.

[26] Gonzalez v. Kokot, 314 F.3d 311 (7th Cir. 2002) (addressing enforceability of release of civil rights claim in exchange for dismissal of criminal charges; the court noted that for the release to be effective as a relinquishment of the claim the release had to be voluntary, free of prosecutorial misconduct, and not adverse to larger public interests regarding law enforcement), *cert. denied*, 539 U.S. 915 (2003).

[27] *In re* Sweet, 954 F.2d 610, 613 (10th Cir. 1992).

[28] Heller Int'l Corp. v. Sharp, 974 F.2d 850, 862 (7th Cir. 1992).

[29] Sielski v. Commercial Ins. Co. of Newark, 605 N.Y.S.2d 599, 600 (App. Dept. 1993).

[30] Griffiths v. CIGNA Corp., 857 F. Supp. 399, 406 (E.D. Pa. 1994) (applying Pennsylvania law) (holding that inadvertent admission that administrative remedies had been exhausted acted as waiver of right to raise defense of failure to exhaust remedies); *In re* Boldman, 147 B.R. 448, 451 (C.D. Ill. 1992) (finding an inadvertent waiver of the defense of sovereign immunity).

[31] *In re* United Marine Shipbuilding, Inc., 198 B.R. 970, 978 (W.D. Wash. 1996) (holding that the inadvertent release of funds did not act to waive right to set off). The court did note, however, that conduct inconsistent with the exercise of a right could be deemed a waiver. The conduct would have to have some element of knowing deliberateness. *Id.*

[32] Best Place Inc. v. Penn Am. Ins. Co., 920 P.2d 334, 353 (Haw. 1996) (noting that in context of insurance law, "the terms 'waive' and 'estoppel' have often been used without careful distinction, and thereby abused and confused").

captured by the tendency to treat implied waiver and estoppel as interchangeable.[33]

One significant distinction between waiver and estoppel is reversibility. A waiver, once executed, is frequently said to be irreversible.[34] An estoppel, on the other hand, may be reversible, if the status quo ante can be reestablished without prejudice to the party claiming the estoppel. These issues frequently arise in commercial transactions when the debtor has made and the creditor has accepted a late payment notwithstanding a clause in the contract requiring timely payment. If the acceptance is deemed a "waiver" of the timely payment clause, the clause is lost. Courts resist such an approach[35] relying instead on principles of estoppel and holding that acceptance of the late payment may estop the creditor from declaring the debt in default due to late payment and may estop the creditor from insisting on timely payment pursuant to the contract until notice of the intent to insist in the future on timely payment is communicated to the debtor.[36] The estoppel is irrevocable as to the accepted payment, but revocable upon proper notice as to future payments.

[64.3] Election

Election is a judicial doctrine that holds a party to a choice. The choice may be express and intended, in which case the doctrine resembles "waiver." The choice may be implied and unintended, in which case the doctrine resembles estoppel.

The most common manifestation of the doctrine of election is associated with the remedy of rescission. Discussion of the concept of "Election of Remedies" can be found there.[37] Here, we explore the concept of election as a bridge between waiver and estoppel and, perhaps, a better explanation of some of the more difficult applications of those doctrines, such as waiver without intent to relinquish and estoppel without detrimental reliance. Waiver doctrine provides a good example of the problem.

In a number of cases it appears that the concept of "waiver" is being used to address and prevent opportunistic behavior. For example, courts have,

---

[33] ACG, Inc. v. Southeast Elevator, Inc., 912 S.W.2d 163, 170 (Tenn. App. 1995) (stating that "[t]he elements of implied waiver are identical to the elements of equitable estoppel"); Hanover Ins. Co. v. Fireman's Fund Ins. Co., 586 A.2d 567, 573 (Conn. 1991) (stating that implied waiver and equitable estoppel by conduct are as so similar as to be "nearly indistinguishable").

[34] Nassau Trust Co. v. Montrose Concrete Prods. Corp., 436 N.E.2d 1265, 1269–70 (N.Y. 1982).

[35] Kessel v. Western Sav. Credit Union, 463 N.W.2d 629, 631 (N.D. 1990); United Missouri Bank South v. Cole, 597 S.W.2d 209, 212 (Mo. App. 1980).

[36] A.P. Development Corp. v. Band, 550 A.2d 1220, 1230–31 (N.J. 1988) (holding that landlord's habitual acceptance of late rent did not waive landlord's right to insist on timely payment, but acceptance of late rent without complaint made it necessary for landlord to give notice to tenant that strict construction of lease obligations would henceforth be insisted upon).

[37] Section 133 (Election of Remedies).

under a waiver theory, barred insurance companies from claiming additional reasons for denying coverage, beyond those initially asserted, after the insurer discovered that its initial objections were weak and unpersuasive.[38] These "opportunistic behavior" cases, however, can be generalized into rules that extend beyond the conduct they were initially designed to prevent.[39] An "opportunistic behavior" rule has no real attachment to waiver; it is based on policy considerations independent, and often contrary to, any insurer's actual intent.[40] Keeton and Widiss argued that use of estoppel and waiver doctrine was often a makeweight to reach a result the court believed was fair and just under the circumstances of the case.[41] They contended that the decision could be better explained as situations involving "involuntary choice."[42] The term "election" better captured this judicial decisional process than the concepts of "waiver" or "estoppel."[43] Keeton and Widiss did not see "election" as necessarily constraining judicial behavior or better predicting outcomes; rather, "election" was a better label and prevented continued misuse of "waiver" and "estoppel doctrines."[44]

The underlying theme of "election" is consistency. Having made a choice, whether voluntary or judicially imposed, a person must adhere to that choice and its consequences. Many decisions reflect a confusing melange of waiver, estoppel, and election, which makes it difficult to identify the true basis of the decision.[45] Decisions that apply estoppel without a showing of detrimental reliance or waiver without a showing of intentional relinquishment[46] are better explained as cases involving "election" rather than as applications of "estoppel" or "waiver." Nonetheless, one should not expect greater predictability using "election" than would be the case were one to use "waiver" or "estoppel." As noted by the Texas Supreme Court:

> The doctrine of election, although widely criticized, survives in wide-ranging branches of the law that stretch from the widow's election in probate law to the choice in contract law between a suit for damages and one for rescission. Election, an affirmative defense, has been held to bar remedies, rights, and inconsistent positions arising out of the same state of facts. The situations in which an

---

[38] Howard v. State Farm Mut. Auto Ins. Co., 496 N.W.2d 862, 870 (Neb. 1993).

[39] Village of Endicott, New York v. Ins. Co. of N. Am., 908 F. Supp. 115, 124 (N.D.N.Y. 1995) (stating that "the act by an insurer of disclaiming on certain grounds, but not others is deemed conclusive evidence of the insurer's intent to waive the unasserted grounds") (citation omitted).

[40] Bank Brussells Lambert v. Credit Lyonnais (Suisse) S.A., 160 F.R.D. 437, 442 (S.D.N.Y. 1995) (observing that "implied waivers are frequently found where the party can hardly be said to have intended to abandon the [right]" [brackets added]. The right involved was the attorney-client privilege.

[41] KEETON & WIDISS, INSURANCE LAW, *supra*, § 6.1(b)(4).

[42] *Id.* at 619.

[43] *Id.* at 619–20.

[44] *Id.*

[45] Potesta v. U.S. Fidelity & Guar. Co., 504 S.E.2d 135, 142–51 (W. Va. 1998) (noting and discussing confusion in this area).

[46] *Id.* at 145 n.13 (collecting decisions).

election might arise are so variable that an all-inclusive definition has been elusive, and discussions of the doctrine often borrow terms that may also appropriately relate to other affirmative defenses. For that reason, election is often confused with or likened to judicial estoppel, equitable estoppel, ratification, waiver or satisfaction. Those doctrines sometimes do not reach a situation that equity and good conscience need to reach through the doctrine of election.[47]

§ 65   FRAUD AND ILLEGALITY

[65.1]   Fraud

Fraud is usually discussed as a cause of action, but it has been long recognized as also a defense. There is little functional difference between an action to rescind a bargain based on the defendant's fraud[1] and the assertion of the defense of fraud to an action based on the bargain. In each instance, the party is contending that the bargain is unenforceable because it is infected with fraud.

The topic of fraud and misrepresentation is discussed at Chapter 14 of these materials. The central points to be understood here are first that when fraud is used to rescind, avoid, or obtain a declaration that a bargain is unenforceable due to fraud, it is not necessary that intent to deceive be established; innocent misrepresentations may suffice to avoid the bargain.[2]

The second point is that fraud is now a defense recognized both at law and in equity.

[65.2]   Illegality

It has long been recognized that no legal aid or assistance will be provided to parties to an illegal transaction.[3] For example, in *Wilson v. Adkins* the plaintiff sued for damages for breach of a promise to pay a sum of money in exchange for a bone marrow transplant. Relying on statutory law declaring such transactions illegal, the court denied recovery.[4]

The defense of illegality is based on the notion that one should not profit from her own wrongdoing. The problem here is to identify the type of illegal transactions that fall within this rule. When is it fair, just, and equitable that the plaintiff's claims be barred on account of plaintiff's wrongful

---

[47] Bocanegra v. Aetna Life Ins. Co., 605 S.W.2d 848, 850 (Tex. 1980).

[1] Section 136 (Grounds for Rescission).

[2] 27 Richard A. Lord, Williston on Contracts § 69.49 (4th ed. 2002). Intent to deceive (scienter) is usually required if a party seeks damages due to the fraud. Section 120.1 (Common Law Fraud).

[3] *In re* The Florida, 101 U.S. 37, 43 (1879) (stating that "[n]o court will lend its aid to a party who founds his claims for redress upon an illegal act"); 17 Am. Jur. 2d *Contracts* § 304 (1991).

[4] 941 S.W.2d 440, 441–42 (Ark. App. 1997) (relying on 42 U.S.C. § 274(e)).

conduct rather than defendant's lack of wrongdoing? As one court noted: "A rogue does not appeal to our conscience. Yet, even a rogue may have a cause of action. . . ."[5] The distinction between the unappealing rogue and the rogue with a cause of action has been difficult to find, criticized as arbitrary, and inconsistently applied.[6]

The critical question is often the connection between the wrongdoing and the cause of action.[7] A gambler who sues for personal injuries she sustained when she slipped and fell at a place where illegal gambling was being carried out will be viewed differently from a gambler who seeks recovery of the money lost while engaging in the activity[8] or the proprietor of the gambling establishment who seeks to recover money lent to enable gambling on credit.[9] To the extent gambling may no longer be viewed as an illegal transaction due to evolving civil standards of legal conduct, the ability to invoke the defense of illegality may be affected.[10] The fact that the plaintiff has committed a theft will preclude a legal claim by plaintiff to divide the loot with his accomplices when the illegal joint venture ceases,[11] but plaintiff's theft will not bar an action against law enforcement officers for excessive force in effecting plaintiff's arrest for his criminal activities.[12]

The defense of illegality extends not just to actions to recover damages, but often precludes any recovery even one for unjust enrichment.[13] This

---

[5] Manning v. Bishop of Marquette, 76 N.W.2d 75, 76 (Mich. 1956).

[6] Barker v. Kallash, 468 N.E.2d 39, 47 (N.Y. 1984) (dissenting opinion).

[7] *Manning, supra,* 76 N.W.2d at 76.

[8] *Id.* 77–78; National Sur. Co. v. Stockyards Nat'l Bank, 272 P. 470 (Colo. 1928) (stating that "every negotiable instrument given for a gambling consideration is void, even when held in due course . . . .").

[9] Carnival Leisure Indus., Ltd., v. Aubin, 938 F.2d 624, 626 (5th Cir. 1991) (refusing to enforce debt consisting of loans for gambling); Metropolitan Creditors Serv. of Sacramento v. Sadri, 19 Cal. Rptr. 2d 646, 651 (Cal. App. 1993) (refusing to enforce credit transactions facilitating legal gambling). *But see* Caribe Hilton Hotel v. Toland, 307 A.2d 85 (N.J. 1973). *See generally* Annot., *Law of Forum Against Wagering Transactions as Precluding Enforcement of Claim Based on Gambling Transactions Valid Under Applicable Foreign Law,* 71 A.L.R.3d 178 (1976).

[10] *See generally* Claudia G. Catalano, Annot., *Enforceability of Contract To Share Winnings From Legal Lottery Ticket,* 90 A.L.R. 4th 784 (1991).

[11] Byron v. Clay, 867 F.2d 1049, 1051 (7th Cir. 1989) (stating that "[i]n arguing that he, not Clay fils, should have the opportunity to defraud the people of Indiana, Byron is like the highwayman who sued his partner in crime for an accounting of the profits—and was hanged for his efforts"); *Manning, supra,* 76 N.W.2d at 77 (discussing infamous "Highwayman's Case") (discussed at Section 62.1 (Unclean Hands)).

[12] Graham v. Connor, 490 U.S. 386, 396 (1989) (recognizing a civil action for excessive force in effecting arrest, based on objective standards); Heflin v. Town of Warrenton, 944 F. Supp. 472, 474–75 (E.D. Va. 1996) (stating that an illegal act defense is inapplicable to excessive force suit, otherwise, the cause of action would be vitiated); *cf.* Smith v. City of Hemet, 394 F.3d 689 (9th Cir. 2005) (holding that plaintiff's conviction for resisting arrest did not preclude a Section 1983 action seeking damages for excessive force by arresting officers).

[13] Chandris S.A. v. Yanakakis, 668 So. 2d 180, 185 (Fla. 1995) (holding that lawyer's contingent fee agreement that did not comply with state's professional code was void and would not

refusal to permit actions to prevent unjust enrichment has been increasingly criticized of late. The competing policies were noted by Professor Birks:

> The objection to an otherwise good action in unjust enrichment is not illegality but stultification: to recognize an entitlement to restitution would make nonsense of the refusal to enforce the contract. It is true that the restitutionary action nearly always does prima facie have this stultifying tendency, for it will often operate as a safety net reducing the risks of illegal dealing or as a lever indirectly enforcing the illegal contract. However, this stultifying tendency can be neutralized by restricting the class of plaintiffs able to bring the restitutionary action and can be overridden if the effect of denying the restitutionary action would be to perpetrate a greater evil, as for instance by inflicting a wholly disproportionate penalty for the illegality.[14]

Professor Birk's approach has been largely adopted by the proposed Restatement (Third) of Restitution & Unjust Enrichment, which would generally permit restitution notwithstanding the illegality of the bargain or transaction unless restitution would "defeat or frustrate the policy of the underlying prohibition,"[15] or reward the "inequitable conduct" of the party seeking restitution.[16]

Like the defense of in pari delicto, the extent to which illegality will bar any remedy is heavily influenced by public policy concerns.[17] For example, in *Hydrotech Systems, Ltd. v. Oasis Waterpark* an unlicensed subcontractor was fraudulently induced to provide services and materials for the benefit of the general contractor. The general contractor disclaimed any liability on the ground that the subcontractor, as an unlicensed person, was statutorily barred from recovery. The court agreed, holding that the statutory bar not only precluded an action on the contract and an action for unjust enrichment, but also precluded an action for fraudulent inducement.[18] A similar harsh rule is applied in the context of bribes. There the

---

support a "quantum meruit" recovery); Al-Ibraham v. Edde, 897 F. Supp. 620, 624 (D.D.C. 1995) (denying restitution to a party who falsely represented to the IRS that gambling winnings were his and paid taxes that other individual should have paid).

[14] Peter Birks, *Recovering Value Transferred Under an Illegal Contract*, 1 Theoretical Inquiries L. 155, 155 (2000).

[15] Restatement (Third) of Restitution & Unjust Enrichment § 32(2) (Tentative Draft No. 3, 2004).

[16] *Id.* at § 32(3).

[17] *Cf.* Premier Elec. Constr. Co. v. Miller-Davis Co., 422 F.2d 1132, 1138 (7th Cir. 1970) (noting that "many factors are, therefore, relevant in determining whether participation by plaintiff in an illegal agreement constitutes a defense to his treble damage action").

[18] 803 P.2d 370, 372 (Cal. 1991); *cf.* Kashani v. Tsann Kuen China Enterprises Co., Ltd. 13 Cal. Rptr.3d 174 (Cal. App. 2004) (refusing to permit damages action for breach of contract to proceed when contract involved trade with Iran, which was prohibited by federal law); Spivak v. Sachs, 211 N.E.2d 329, 331 (N.Y. 1965) (holding that plaintiff was barred from recovering for services rendered pursuant to an illegal contract to practice law). Some

rule has developed that "in the absence of a statute, one who bribes another cannot recover the money or property transferred as part of the bribe."[19] It matters not whether the bribe was successful or unsuccessful.[20] On the other hand, the case law has generally permitted an employer to recover from its employee bribes taken in violation of the law.[21] Although the theories of recovery vary, the underlying principle appears to be the policy of deterring wrongdoing by depriving the wrongdoer of the benefit his conduct has engendered, when doing so will not reward an equally culpable party.[22]

§ 66   CHANGE IN POSITION AND HARDSHIP

The defenses of change in position and hardship are primarily used to negate a requirement to make restitution. The basic idea is that if the defense is available, the defendant has not been unjustly enriched.

[66.1]   Change in Position

The defense of change in position recognizes that when a defendant has innocently relied on the enrichment, the subsequent events should be considered to determine the extent of the defendant's actual enrichment, if any. For example, assume defendant is mistakenly credited with the sum of $10,000 and defendant then invests the money losing $5,000. Should that subsequent event, the loss of $5,000, be considered in determining the extent to which defendant was unjustly enriched by the mistaken payment?

The debate in this area has been over whether a causation requirement should be affixed to the change in position defense. In other words, must the defendant show that the enrichment *caused* the change in position, *i.e.*, but for the mistaken payment defendant would not have invested the monies and sustained the $5,000 loss.[1] Tying the change in position defense to a cause requirement may seem intuitively sound, but it can lead to the anomalous result that a defendant who squanders the monies mistakenly paid to him has a defense; whereas, a defendant who acquires necessities does not. The reason for the distinction is the intuition that the defendant

---

jurisdictions ameliorate this harsh result when a party was fraudulently induced to enter in an illegal contract or was the victim of fraud that was connected to the illegal bargain or transaction. Trees v. Kersey, 56 P.3d 765, 771–73 (Idaho 2002).

[19] State v. Gunzelman, 434 P.2d 543, 545 (Kan. 1967); Restatement (Third) of Restitution & Unjust Enrichment, *supra*, § 32, Illus. 11.

[20] State v. Adams, 471 N.E.2d 508, 509 (Ohio App. 1984); State v. Pierro, 470 A.2d 240, 242 (Conn. 1984).

[21] Western Elec. Co. v. Brenner, 360 N.E.2d 1091, 1094 (N.Y. 1977).

[22] *Cf.* Swig Weiler and Arnow Mgmt. Co. Inc. v. Stahl, 817 F. Supp. 400, 403 (S.D.N.Y. 1993) (stating that defendant could be liable under aiding and abetting violation of duty of loyalty by employee).

[1] *See generally* M.L. Cross, Annot., *What Constitutes Change of Position by Payee so as To Preclude Recovery of Payment Made Under Mistake*, 40 A.L.R.2d 997 (1955); Restatement of Restitution §§ 69, 142 (1937).

who squanders does so because of the mistaken payment; whereas, necessities, by their very nature, would have been acquired in any event, even absent the mistake.[2]

The second key element to the change in position defense is that the recipient of the mistaken payment be innocent, *i.e.*, without fault. The defense is usually denied if the recipient caused or materially contributed to the mistake. Innocence can be a somewhat exacting standard:

> [I]n determining whether the individual was at fault, SSA is to consider . . . whether he (1) received the overpayment as a result of (a) an incorrect statement he made that he knew or should have known was wrong, or (b) a failure to furnish information he knew or could have been expected to know was incorrect.[3]

If the defendant unreasonably refuses a demand to return the money or property, the defendant will not be able to assert the change in position defense as to events subsequent to the refusal.[4]

When the mistaken payment comes from a public entity, e.g., overpayment of social security or welfare assistance, the public agency usually has addressed the issue through administrative regulations and usually in terms that favor the recipient of the mistaken payment.[5]

[66.2] Hardship

Hardship, or perhaps more accurately "undue" hardship, is recognized as a defense to restitution, but the characteristics of the defense are somewhat unclear. The Restatement of Restitution does not separately describe a defense of hardship, but recognizes it obliquely in other contexts, such as whether restitution must be made after a judgment has been set aside.[6] The concept of "hardship" has not been particularly well received by courts. One court suggested that to sustain the defense, the defendant would have to show that restitution would result in her complete impoverishment, such that she would require public assistance.[7] The most frequent uses today of the hardship defense are in bankruptcy, where the hardship

---

[2] Paine Webber Inc. v. Levy, 680 A.2d 798, 799 (N.J. Super. Ct. L. 1995) ("Prejudice to payee does not occur when the payee has used the money to cover living expenses or to pay preexisting debt").

[3] Valente v. Sec'y Health & Human Services, 733 F.2d 1037, 1043 (2d Cir. 1984) (discussing "without fault" requirement in social security overpayment recoupment regulations); Restatement of Restitution § 142 cmt. c (1937).

[4] Goodbody & Co., Inc. v. Parente, 358 A.2d 32, 35 (R.I. 1976).

[5] 20 C.F.R. § 404.509 (2004) (Federal Old-Age, Survivors and Disability Insurance: Overpayments, Underpayments, Waiver of Adjustment or Recovery of Overpayments, and Liability of a Certifying Officer).

[6] Restatement of Restitution § 74 cmt. c (1937) (restitution of money paid in compliance with an order that is subsequently set aside must be made "unless restitution would be inequitable" and using "hardship" as example).

[7] Heron v. Heron, 703 N.E.2d 712, 716 n.4 (Mass. 1998).

defense has some limited application,[8] and criminal restitution, where an exception for "undue" hardship is often statutorily affixed to the penal restitution requirement.[9]

§ 67   ASSERTION OF DEFENSES AGAINST THE GOVERNMENT

Litigation with the government is different from litigation with private individuals. As a sovereign, the government possesses rights not held by private litigants. One of the privileges of sovereignty is the right to bring claims free of defenses, such as laches, estoppel, and unclean hands. Although the early rationale for this right lay in the government claim as sovereign per se, modern justifications tend to emphasize democratic principles. It is often asserted that recognition of remedy defenses would, in effect, permit governmental employees to act in a manner unauthorized by law.[1]

It should be emphasized that the reluctance to allow remedy defenses to government claims is usually applied to government enforcement actions. It appears to be at least tacitly accepted that when the government seeks legal redress for loss or injury, it is subject to remedy defenses.[2]

---

[8] 11 U.S.C. § 523(a)(8) (recognizing that "undue hardship" may permit partial discharge of student loans, but not defining what constitutes "undue hardship"). This statutory omission has generated the so-called *Brunner* test, which most courts follow:

> "[U]ndue hardship" require[s] a three-part showing: (1) that the debtor cannot maintain, based on current income and expenses, a "minimal" standard of living for herself and her dependents if forced to repay the loans; (2) that additional circumstances exist indicating that this state of affairs is likely to persist for a significant portion of the repayment period of the student loans; and (3) that the debtor has made good faith efforts to repay the loans.

Brunner v. New York State Higher Educ. Services Corp., 831 F.2d 395, 396 (2d Cir. 1987) (brackets added). *But cf.* In re Long, 322 F.3d 549, 553–54 (8th Cir. 2003) (rejecting *Brunner* in favor of a "totality of the circumstances" test). *See* Craig Peyton Gaumer, *Chaos in the Courts*, 23-May Am. Bankr. Inst. J. 8 (2004) (discussing bankruptcy "undue hardship" defense and noting disparate applications of *Brunner* test).

[9] *E.g.*, Ohio Rev. Code § 2929.22 (discussed in *State v. Young*, 684 N.E.2d 372, 373 (Ohio App. 1996)).

[1] Guaranty Trust Co. of New York v. United States, 304 U.S. 126, 132 (1938) (finding that "the great public policy of preserving the public's rights, revenues, and property from injury and loss [cannot be allowed to be compromised] by the negligence of public officers") (brackets added); *see* Heckler v. Community Health Servs. of Crawford County, Inc., 467 U.S. 51, 60 (1984):

> When the Government is unable to enforce the law because the conduct of its agents has given rise to an estoppel, the interest of the citizenry as a whole in obedience to the rule of law is undermined.

[2] Pan Am. Petroleum & Transp. Co. v. United States, 273 U.S. 456, 506 (1927) (holding that the government is subject to general principles of equity when invoking the equitable jurisdiction of the court); United States v. Vineland Chem. Co., Inc., 692 F. Supp. 415, 423 (D.N.J. 1988) (distinguishing between use of equitable defense to defeat claim for equitable relief and use of equitable defense to defeat enforcement action by government); *cf.* Miller v. Tony and Susan Alamo Found., 134 F.3d 910, 916 (8th Cir. 1998) (noting that when government intervenes to claim an interest in property, waiver of sovereign immunity does not extend beyond the property in controversy).

[67.1] Laches

The general rule is that the government's claims are not subject to the equitable defense of laches.[3] The rule is not, however, consistently applied, particularly when the government sues on behalf of specific individuals. Some federal courts have recognized a laches defense to claims brought by the Equal Employment Opportunity Commission when it brings claims and asserts rights of specific individuals rather than the public as a whole.[4] The distinction has been criticized and an alternative rationale has been offered that recognition of the laches defense is warranted due to the absence of a specific statute of limitation applicable to the EEOC cases.[5] In one case, the court strongly suggested it would rely on this reason for not extending the laches defense to a governmental claim that was subject to a statute of limitation defense.[6] The court did, nonetheless, note contrary authority for applying laches in cases governed by a statute of limitation[7] and decided the issue by finding that the laches defense was not well taken, even if it could be applied.[8]

Some courts have applied laches to government contract claims.[9] The defense seems to fare slightly better when the government comes to the claim as an assignee.[10] This issue is regularly litigated in claims arising out of defaulted student loans[11] and defaulted SBA loans.[12]

Laches has been recognized as a legitimate defense in a few contexts that clearly envision the government asserting a public interest, such as litigation involving public rights under the Voting Rights Act.[13] The preferable

---

[3] United States v. Summerlin, 310 U.S. 414, 416 (1940) (stating that "the United States . . . is not subject to the defense of laches in enforcing its rights"); Van Milligan v. Board of Fire & Police Comm'rs. of Village of Glenview, 630 N.E.2d 830, 833 (Ill. App. 1994); O'Reilly v. Town of Glocester, 621 A.2d 697, 703 (R.I. 1993). *But cf.* Scheble v. Missiouri Clean Water Comm'n, 734 S.W.2d 541, 560 (Mo. App. 1987) (questioning immunity of government entities from laches defense).

[4] Martin v. Consultants & Adm'rs, Inc., 966 F.2d 1078, 1090 (7th Cir. 1992) (collecting cases).

[5] *Id.*

[6] *Id.* 1090–91 (involving Employee Retirement Income Security Act (ERISA) claim, 29 U.S.C. §§ 1001–1461).

[7] *Id.* at 1091 (collecting cases).

[8] *Id.*

[9] *Compare* S.E.R. Jobs for Progress, Inc. v. United States, 759 F.2d 1, 3 (Fed. Cir. 1985) (recognizing laches defense), *with* United States v. Menatos, 925 F.2d 333, 335 (9th Cir. 1991) (rejecting recognition of laches defense), *and* United States v. St. John's General Hosp., 875 F.2d 1064, 1071 (3d Cir. 1989) (laches defense not recognized in government contract claim).

[10] United States v. Republic Ins. Co., 775 F.2d 156, 159 (6th Cir. 1985) (holding that government must take as part of its equitable assignment all defenses available against its predecessor subrogor). *But see* United States v. Robbins, 819 F. Supp. 672, 677–78 (E.D. Mich. 1993). In *United States v. California*, 507 U.S. 746, 756–57 (1993), the Court recognized that laches may apply when the claim is acquired by the government through subrogation.

[11] United States v. Menatos, 925 F.2d 333, 335 (9th Cir. 1991).

[12] United States v. La France, 728 F. Supp. 1116, 1122 (D. Del. 1990).

[13] United States v. State of Louisiana, 952 F. Supp. 1151, 1176–77 (W.D. La. 1997) (collecting cases and noting split in authorities as to whether laches defense is available in Section 5 case or available against the government).

approach in matters involving statutory remedies is to identify whether the defense of laches is consistent with the legislative program of rights and remedies.[14] If the defense is available under the statute, there is little reason to apply it only to private litigants, absent legislative instruction that a distinction between private and public plaintiffs is intended. If the defense is inconsistent with the statute, it is immaterial whether a private or public plaintiff in enforcing the statute.

When the plaintiff is acting as a private attorney general, asserting the larger public interests, the defense of laches has been rejected by many courts as inappropriate.[15]

[67.2]   Equitable Estoppel

The general rule is that the defense of equitable estoppel cannot be asserted against the government.[16] The general rule seems to permit more exceptions than with laches, perhaps due to estoppel's association with misconduct, whereas laches is associated simply with inaction. This approach is reflected in Supreme Court decisions. While the Court has emphasized that it has never expressly upheld the use by a lower court of the defense of estoppel,[17] the Court has carefully avoided absolutely foreclosing use of the defense against the government.[18] In cases when the

[14] *Id.* at 1177; Lancos v. Commomwealth Dep't of Transp., 689 A.2d 342, 347 (Pa. Comm. Ct. 1997).

[15] United States Interest Research Group v. Atlantic Salmon of Maine, 215 F. Supp. 2d 239 (D. Me. 2002):

> [L]aches is a disfavored defense in environmental cases because the plaintiff is not the only party to suffer harm by the alleged environmental damages. See *Portland Audubon Soc'y v. Lujan*, 884 F.2d 12331, 1241 (9th Cir. 1989) ("We have repeatedly cautioned against application of the equitable doctrine of laches to public interest environmental litigation. Laches must be invoked sparingly in environmental cases . . . . This approach has found unanimous support in the other circuits." (citing *Preservation Coalition, Inc. v. Pierce*, 667 F.2d 851, 854 (9th Cir. 1982)). ASM relies on the First Circuit decision in *Concerned Citizens on I-190 v. Sec'y of Transp.*, 641 F.2d 1 (1st Cir. 1981), to support its defense. However, this decision was not made in the context of a citizen suit under the Clean Water Act. Although, many courts find laches inappropriate in citizen suits under the Clean Water Act (*Student Pub. Interest Research Group, Inc. v. P.D. Oil & Chem. Storage, Inc.*, 627 F. Supp. 1074, 1085 (D.N.J.1986)) (stating that in citizen suits plaintiffs stand as private attorneys general, therefore laches should not apply to bar the suit), some courts allow the defense when the plaintiff has engaged in some affirmative misconduct. See, e.g., *Nat'l Wildlife Fed'n v. Consumers Power Co.*, 657 F. Supp. 989 1011 (D. Mich. 1987) reversed on other grounds, 862 F.2d 580 (6th Cir. 1988) (finding that because "plaintiff is in essence acting as a private attorney general in this matter, it probably is not subject to the doctrine of laches, at least absent a showing of come affirmative misconduct").

Id. at 258–59 (citations in original; brackets added).

[16] Office of Personnel Mgmt. v. Richmond, 496 U.S. 414, 419 (1990).

[17] *Id.* at 422.

[18] Heckler v. County Health Servs., 467 U.S. 51, 60 (1984) (noting that in some other case, affirmative misconduct by the government may be invoked through an estoppel defense); Office

Court has permitted a defendant to show as a defense that he was affirmatively misled by the government to his prejudice,[19] the term equitable estoppel was not used, a point emphasized in later cases.[20]

The Court has expressly held that the estoppel defense cannot be used to extract an appropriation of public money.[21] In this sense, however, the defense of estoppel becomes the equivalent of the action of promissory estoppel, which is traditionally held to be subject to the government's defense of sovereign immunity.[22] The commentators have been largely critical of the Court's approach in this area.[23]

When equitable estoppel against the government is recognized, it is subject to heavy proof obligations. The requirement most commonly imposed is that of "affirmative misconduct," which is intentional, wrongful behavior by the government through its employees.[24] A less demanding test has also been identified, however, focusing more on government error than positive misconduct.[25] Whichever test is used, it is clear that positive governmental action is required; the estoppel cannot be based on "mere inaction, delay or sloth on the part of the government."[26]

---

of Personnel Mgmt., supra 496 U.S. at 423 (stating that the Court has repeatedly "[left] for another day whether an estoppel claim could ever succeed against the Government") (brackets added). The day has not yet arrived.

[19] United States v. Pennsylvania Indus. Chem. Corp., 411 U.S. 655, 657 (1973) (involving application by administrative agency of its own regulations, which had been relied upon by the defendant); Moser v. United States, 341 U.S. 41, 46 (1951) (involving administrative interpretation of naturalization requirement relied upon by alien).

[20] Heckler, supra, 467 U.S. at 68 (Rehnquist, J., concurring).

[21] Office of Personnel Mgmt., supra, 496 U.S. at 414, 416, 434 (1990); Falso v. Office of Personnel Mgmt., 116 F.3d 459, 460 (Fed. Cir. 1997) (holding that under Office of Personnel Mgmt. the federal government cannot be estopped from denying benefits that are not permitted by law even when the claimant relies on the erroneous advice of a governmental official or agency). In Falso the plaintiff had been repeatedly assured by the federal agency that employed her that her part-time service would be credited as full-time service for purposes of calculating her retirement annuity. The plaintiff decided to retire on the basis of those representations. Plaintiff was not awarded benefits consistent with the representations. Because the representations were erroneous, her protest was denied.

[22] Jablon v. United States, 657 F.2d 1064, 1069–70 (9th Cir. 1981). But cf. id. at 1070 n.9 (collecting decisions suggesting possibility that promissory estoppel could be asserted against the government).

[23] See Alan I. Saltman, The Government's Liability For Actions of its Agents That are not Specifically Authorized: The Continuing Influence of Merrill and Richmond, 32 Pub. Contract L. J. 775 (2003). The author is not aware of any papers that have explored the "no estoppel against the government" from an agency costs perspective that might support at least a limited version of the prohibition.

[24] United States v. Ruby Co., 588 F.2d 697, 703–04 (9th Cir. 1978), cert. denied, 442 U.S. 917 (1979); cf. Ins. v. Hibi, 414 U.S. 5, 8 (1973) (per curiam) (noting that availability of "affirmative misconduct" as basis for estoppel against the government has been "left open").

[25] Akbarin v. Immigration and Naturalization Serv., 669 F.2d 839, 843 (1st Cir. 1982).

[26] INS v. Miranda, 459 U.S. 14, 19 (1982) (per curiam) (noting that even if "affirmative misconduct permitted an estoppel, "proof only that the Government failed to process "an application falls far short of establishing [affirmative misconduct]" (brackets added); Griffin, LTG Constr. Co. v. Reich, 956 F. Supp. 98, 108 (D.R.I. 1997) (requiring "at a minimum a compelling demonstration of conscious and aggravated misconduct").

The defense of equitable estoppel appears to fare slightly better when asserted against state governments rather than the federal government. For example, Connecticut courts have held that while estoppel against the government is limited and may be invoked only with caution, it may be asserted when (1) the action in question has been induced by an agent having authority in such matters and (2) when circumstances would make it highly inequitable or oppressive not to estop the government.[27] Although the test contains some constraining language, it effectively subjects the defense only to the court's equitable discretion. Other states have reached this conclusion directly.[28]

[67.3] Unclean Hands

The general rule is that the defense of unclean hands is not available against the government.[29] While private individuals "must turn square corners when dealing with the government,"[30] the converse is not always required. Corner-cutting by the government is often tolerated when the government represents the public as a whole and asserts public rights.[31] A few courts do, however see the issue differently:

---

[27] Kimberly-Clark Corp. v. Dubno, 527 A.2d 679, 684 (Conn. 1987). Unlike the federal courts, state courts are more likely to reject the sovereign immunity defense when raised against a claim of promissory estoppel. Minneapolis Teachers Retirement Fund Ass'n v. State, 490 N.W.2d 124, 128 (Minn. App. 1992) (applying promissory estoppel in context of funding pension plan); Pilot Oil Corp. v. Ohio Dep't of Transp., 656 N.E.2d 1379, 1382 (Ohio App. 1995) (holding that promissory estoppel doctrine may be applied when subject matter of promise is not illegal or ultra vires, but doctrine may not be applied when position taken is contrary to express statutory law); Utah State Univ. of Ag. & Applied Science v. Sutro & Co., 646 P.2d 715, 718 (Utah 1982) (stating that whether to permit defense is based on public policy considerations including whether subject matter is malum per se or merely ultra vires).

[28] City of Long Beach v. Mansell, 476 P.2d 423, 445 (Cal. 1970) (stating that "[i]t is settled that '[t]he doctrine of equitable estoppel may be applied against the government where justice and right require it' ") (citations omitted); see State ex rel Stenberg v. Moore, 571 N.W.2d 317, 322 (Neb. 1997) (holding that equitable estoppel would be applied against the state when "right and justice so demanded and in the interest of preventing a manifest injustice"). In Stenberg, the court applied principles of equitable estoppel to prevent the state from removing certain employees from the state retirement benefits program. The employees had been erroneously admitted into the plan over a period of 17 years until the error was discovered. The court found that the mere return of the employees premiums would, under the circumstances, not be fair. Id. at 322–23. Compare this result with that taken in Falso, supra, 116 F.3d 459, a federal case.

[29] United States v. Scott, 958 F. Supp. 761, 779 (D. Conn. 1997) (stating that "defense of unclean hands . . . against the government [is] strictly limited") (brackets added).

[30] Rock Island A.& L.R. Co. v. United States, 254 U.S. 141, 143 (1920) (stating that "men must turn square corners when they deal with the [g]overnment"). The phrase was again used in Federal Crop Ins. Corp. v. Merrill, 332 U.S. 380, 385 (1947), to bar a farmer from recovering federal crop insurance after the farmer was mistakenly told by a federal official that his crop was insured.

[31] United States v. Sutton, 795 F.2d 1040, 1062 (Temp. Emer. Ct. App. 1986); United States v. Martell, 844 F. Supp. 454, 459 (N.D. Ind. 1994); Kelley v. Thomas Solvent Co., 714 F. Supp. 1439, 1451 (W.D. Mich. 1989).

Moreover, we have insisted that in the exercise of statutory responsibilities, government must "turn square corners" rather than
exploit litigational or bargaining advantages that might otherwise
be available to private citizens. "[The government's] primary obligation is to comport itself with compunction and integrity, and in
doing so government may have to forego the freedom of action that
private citizens may employ in dealing with one another." We have
insisted that government adhere to strict standards in its contractual dealings. Therefore, DOT's failure to act with greater clarity
regarding the statute of limitations, its successful encouragement
of an administrative proceeding that redounded to its advantage
in terms of added investigation, complete discovery, fuller preparation in defense of the contractor's claim, as well as delay in payment,
and its subsequent attempt to seek a litigational advantage based
on Pangborne's inadvertence or false impression constituted conduct that seems inconsistent with the notion that government must
act fairly and "with compunction and integrity."[32]

The defense of unclean hands usually fails when asserted against the
government because its recognition would often frustrate the legislative
program or thwart the public interest.[33] The equitable defense is simply
conformed to the public interest and applied when it would further that
interest and rejected when it would not.[34] On the other hand, when the
government bargains for contractual benefits and rights, it is not uncommon for courts to consider the defense of unclean hands against the
government, without express discussion of the defense's limited applicability.[35]

---

[32] W.V. Pangborne & Co., Inc. v. New Jersey Dep't of Transp., 562 A.2d 222, 231 (N.J. 1989)
(citations omitted).

[33] United States v. Second Nat'l Bank of N. Miami, 502 F.2d 535, 548 (5th Cir. 1974).

[34] *Cf.* Mardan Corp. v. CGC Music Ltd., 600 F. Supp. 1049, 1058 (D. Ariz. 1984) (stating
that the "application of the clean hands doctrine . . . will not defeat the intent or purpose
of the Act . . . [d]efendants remain liable to the state or federal government . . . ."), *aff'd on
other grounds,* 804 F.2d 1454 (9th Cir. 1986). *Mardan Corp* involved the assertion of the
defense of unclean hands to an environmental clean up action under CERLA. Other courts
have found the defense inconsistent with the Act even when asserted against a private party.
Smith Land & Improvement Corp. v. Celotex Corp., 851 F.2d 86, 90 (3d Cir. 1988), *cert. denied,*
488 U.S. 1029 (1989).

[35] United States v. San Pedro, 781 F. Supp. 761, 775 (S.D. Fla. 1991) (government's unclean
hands barred rescission of plea bargain; assuming defendant breached agreement, government
induced and caused breach); Travelers Indem. Co. v. United States, 16 Cl. Ct. 142, 156 (1988)
(unclean hands could be asserted against government's laches defense to contract claim).

Chapter 8

REMEDIES FOR BODILY INJURIES

SYNOPSIS

§ 70 BODILY INJURY REMEDIES

The modern method for remedying bodily injury is the award of monetary damages to reflect what has been lost as a result of the injury. This usually includes: (1) lost income in the form of earnings or earnings potential; (2) money spent or liability incurred for medical treatment; and, (3) pain and suffering accompanying the injury. When injury has occurred to a close family member, many jurisdictions permit the other family member(s), particularly a spouse, to recover loss of consortium (companionship) damages.

Bodily injury claims have not been an area where injunctive relief is used. Bodily injury claims rarely present a threat of future harm based on a defendant's continuing conduct, so, there is nothing for the injunction to prevent. Nor for that matter can an injunction remediate the existing injury. Recently, jurisdictions have been receptive to issuing "personal security orders," which are usually invoked to protect family members from intra-family abuse,[1] but have also been applied to protect individuals, particularly public figures, from harassment and threats of harm by others.[2] Aside from the above and outside of established torts, such as nuisance[3] or contracted-for health care services,[4] efforts to obtain injunctive relief against perceived threats to bodily safety have been unsuccessful, primarily due to concerns over ripeness and justiciability.[5] The likelihood that the plaintiff will be subjected to physical assault is seen as too speculative to warrant the intervention of equitable relief.[6]

Restitution-oriented remedies have had no impact for private plaintiffs in this area. In the typical bodily injury claim the defendant does not derive a benefit from his misconduct. Even the occasional use of a restitutionary measure of damages is considered by the courts to be improper in this context.[7] Restitution is increasingly being used in connection with criminal

---

[1] *E.g.*, California Domestic Violence Prevention Act, Cal. Fam. Code § 6200 *et seq.* (providing that an order may be issued with or without notice to restrain a person for the purpose of preventing a reoccurrence of domestic violence); Oregon Family Abuse Protection Act, Or. Rev. Stat. §§ 107.700–107.732 (same).

[2] Mathew J. Gilligan, *Stalking the Stalker: Developing New Laws to Thwart Those Who Terrorize Others,* 27 Ga. L. Rev. 285 (1992). In *Champagne v. Gintick,* 871 F. Supp. 1527 (D. Conn. 1994) the court considered and rejected constitutional challenges to Connecticut's "Stalking" statute. These personal security orders can raise significant and difficult questions regarding rights of privacy and the public's "right" to know. Gallela v. Onassis, 353 F. Supp. 186 (S.D.N.Y. 1972), *modified and affirmed,* 487 F.2d 986 (2d Cir. 1973) (upholding injunction limiting access of photographer to Jackie Onassis, the former wife of President Kennedy, and her two children, but reducing the scope of the injunction due to First Amendment concerns).

[3] Heather K. v. City of Mallard, 887 F. Supp. 1249 (N.D. Iowa 1995) (enjoining nuisance that threatened health of nearby resident).

[4] Henderson v. Bodine Aluminum, Inc., 70 F.3d 958, 961 (8th Cir. 1995) (involving access to potentially life-saving medical treatment for terminally-ill plaintiff).

[5] Section 30 (Ripeness, Mootness, and Standing).

[6] *Cf.* City of Los Angeles v. Lyons, 461 U.S. 95, 105–06 (1983) (holding that to state justiciable controversy warranting equitable relief barring police from using a chokehold restraint, the plaintiff would have to demonstrate that it was the policy to apply a life endangering chokehold in violation of police department regulations in every encounter with citizens).

[7] Donahoo v. Turner Constr. Co., 833 F. Supp. 621, (E.D. Mich. 1993) (involving jury award

law actions, but the term "restitution" is here a misnomer. Typically, a convicted defendant is ordered, as part of the sentence, to pay a sum of money to the victim(s) of the crime. Although the term "restitution" is often used, the monetary sum is more in the nature of reparations or damages than disgorgement of a benefit or gain obtained by the defendant from the criminal activity. While criminal restitution can have a disgorgement aspect,[8] restitution is often applied in cases when the defendant has realized no gain or benefit from the crime but has inflicted a loss on the victim.[9] The situation is, however, different for defendants. When a defendant pays more than his fair share of a bodily injury damages award, that defendant may receive transfer payments from the other defendants to prevent their unjust enrichment.[10] Restitution-based theories have been used in some mass tort litigation, but the appropriateness of the theory in that context has been questioned.[11]

§ 71 LOST INCOME

A distinction is often drawn between earnings and earning capacity. The distinction is between what the plaintiff would have actually earned but for the injury, usually identified as "lost earnings or wages," and what the plaintiff could have or was capable of earning at the time of the injury, usually identified as impairment of earning capacity. There is also a temporal or permanency distinction between the two concepts. As noted by one court:

> We have defined the impairment of earning capacity as the perma-
> nent diminution of the ability to earn money. Consequently, an

---

of pain and suffering that was keyed to amount defendant saved by not posting flagman whose presence would arguably have prevented plaintiff's injury). The court held that defendant's benefit (costs avoided) was in no way related to plaintiff's pain and suffering. *Id.* at 623 (upholding award nonetheless on the ground there was sufficient other evidence to support the amount awarded).

[8] People v. Milne, 690 P.2d 829, 836 (Colo. 1984) (observing that criminal restitution takes the profit out of criminal activity).

[9] Mandatory Victims Restitution Act, 18 U.S.C. § 3663A(3)(b) (providing that restitution order shall require the defendant to compensate the victim for her financial losses, medical expenses, lost earnings etc); 18 U.S.C. § 2248(b)(1) (providing that court shall mandate restitution to cover victim's "losses"). In *People v. Keichler*, 29 Cal. Rptr. 3d 120 (Cal. App. 2005), the court ordered that criminal restitution include expenses incurred by the victim in participating in traditional Hmong (Laotian) healing ceremony that had cultural, rather than Western medical science, roots.

[10] Section 52 (Indemnity); Section 53 (Subrogation).

[11] Hanoch Dagan & James J. White, *Governments, Citizens, and Injurious Injuries*, 75 N.Y.U. L. Rev. 354 (2000) (discussing the use of restitution-oriented remedies in mass-tort litigation); Doug Rendleman, *Common Law Restitution in the Mississippi Tobacco Settlement: Did the Smoke Get in Their Eyes?*, 33 Ga. L. Rev. 847, 904–05 (1999) (discussing settlement of tobacco litigation between states and major tobacco companies and appropriateness of states' restitution claims); *see* Richard C. Ausness, *Public Tort Litigation: Public Benefit or Public Nuisance*, 77 Temple L. Rev. 825 (2004) (surveying the decisions and approaches used in mass tort, product liability litigation).

award of "lost earnings" does not satisfy an injured party's entitlement to compensation for lost earning capacity.[1]

The distinction is also important for pleading purposes. A jurisdiction may identify lost earnings and lost earning capacity as special or general damages. If identified as special damages, the loss must be specifically pleaded to be recoverable.

[71.1] Loss Earnings

A defendant who tortiously injures a plaintiff is liable for the wages the plaintiff was earning at the time of the injury but did not earn because of his injuries.

The recovery for lost earnings includes wages, bonuses, fringe benefits, pension contributions, etc., that the plaintiff more likely than not would have earned had she not been injured. If the injury partially incapacitated the plaintiff and she was able to work part time, her recovery is the difference between what she would have earned and what she did earn notwithstanding her injuries.

When the injury has resolved by the time of trial, it is common to characterize the claim as one for lost earnings as the injury is complete and there are no residual affects. When that is not the case because there are future losses,[2] the general tendency is to treat the claim as one involving impairment of earning capacity.

[71.2] Loss of Earning Capacity

The defendant is liable for earnings the plaintiff, by reason of her training and education, could have realized but for the injury, but was not, at the time of the injury, actually earning. While actual earnings are evidence of earning capabilities,[3] damages for lost earning capacity may be recovered even when the plaintiff had no actual earnings:

> Loss of earning power is an element of general damages which can be inferred from the nature of the injury, without proof of actual earnings or income either before or after injury, and damages in

---

[1] Grimes v. Haslett, 641 P.2d 813, 818 (Alaska 1982) (citation and footnote omitted); *see* Hilliard v. A.H. Robins Co., 196 Cal. Rptr. 117, 143 (Cal App. 1983) (stating that "[i]mpairment of the capacity or power to work is an injury separate from the actual loss of earnings); Athridge v. Iglesias, 950 F. Supp. 1187, 1193 (D.D.C. 1996); DeWall v. Prentice, 224 N.W.2d 428, 435 (Iowa 1974).

[2] Future losses are losses resulting from the injury that will be sustained by the plaintiff after the date of trial. Section 9.2 (Future Damages). These future losses could include (1) income that would have been earned after the date of trial; (2) medical expenses that will be actually incurred after the date of trial; and (3) pain and suffering that will be sustained after the date of trial.

[3] Crown Plumbing, Inc. v. Petrozak, 751 S.W.2d 936, 938–39 (Tex. Civ. App. 1988).

this respect are awarded for the loss of ability thereafter to earn money.[4]

In *Storrs v. Los Angeles Traction Co.* the California Supreme Court upheld a verdict, which included an award for past and future impairment of earning capacity, for a 75-year-old man who introduced no evidence of how much money he was earning, if any, at the time of injury, or at any time in the past. The court held that it was not necessary that there be evidence that he actually received wages or was capable of earning a specific sum in any particular employment. The court stated that it was for the jury to consider what plaintiff was *capable* of earning, not what he was actually earning.[5] Applying this approach, courts have upheld recovery of damages for lost earning capacity by unemployed persons,[6] retired persons,[7] domestic partners,[8] and minors,[9] and others with no earning history. Impairment awards have been particularly significant when young prodigies have been injured and, as a resulted, prevented from using their athletic[10] or artistic[11] talents to earn a livelihood.

While actual earnings are not required, a verdict for "earning impairment" in the usual case cannot rest on pure speculation; the plaintiff should introduce some evidence of earning capability and/or capacity.[12] Factors that may bear on the plaintiff's earning capacity before and after injury include age, health, education, training, experience, and opportunities for employment and promotion (including alternatives available in the post-injury condition). Also to be considered is the plaintiff's willingness to work as demonstrated by good faith efforts, due diligence, and meaningful

---

[4] Connolly v. Pre-Mixed Concrete Co., 319 P.2d 343, 346 (Cal. 1957) (involving amateur tennis star Maureen Connolly).

[5] 66 P. 72, 73 (Cal. 1901).

[6] Germ v. City & County of San Francisco, 222 P.2d 122, 135 (Cal. App. 1950) (involving a 50-year old unemployed inebriate, living on charity, who recovered $12,000 for loss of chance of work).

[7] *Storrs, supra,* 134 Cal. 91, 66 P. 72 (1901); *cf.* McLaughlin v. Chicago, M. St. P. & Pac. Ry., 143 N.W.2d 32, 39–40 (Wis. 1966) (finding that plaintiff priest could recover for impaired earning capacity based on employment as a teacher even though he had taken a vow of poverty and was not drawing a salary at the time he was injured).

[8] McCormack v. City & County of San Francisco, 14 Cal. Rptr. 79, 82–83 (Cal. App. 1961) (involving a 71-year old widow who presented no evidence of an occupation).

[9] Niles v. City of San Rafael, 116 Cal. Rptr. 733, 739 (Cal App. 1974) (involving a $4 million dollars verdict for an 11-year old rendered a quadriplegic; present discounted value of anticipated future wages allowed).

[10] *Connolly, supra,* 319 P.2d at 346.

[11] Maddox v. American Airlines, Inc., 115 F. Supp.2d 993 (E.D. Ark. 2000) (awarding $11.02 million for personal injuries to aspiring opera singer whose injuries occurred while she was in college and before she had embarked on an operatic career), *aff'd in part, rev'd in part,* 298 F.3d 694 (8th Cir. 2002), *cert. denied,* 537 U.S. 1192 (2003). Defendant did not contest the award as excessive on appeal.

[12] Corbett v. Seamons, 904 P.2d 229, 232 (Utah App. 1995) (stating that lost earning capacity must be proved with "reasonable certainty" but not "mathematical certainty"); *cf.* La Fever v. Kemlite Co., 706 N.E.2d 441, 455 (Ill. 1998) (stating that "[e]xpert testimony is not necessary to establish loss of future earnings ability").

attempts to find employment. Finally, the plaintiff must have skills that are valued in the marketplace. None of these factors is, however, conclusive and much is left to the discretion of the trier-of-fact.

When the plaintiff's earnings history is limited or non-existent, the court must engage in educated speculation regarding what the plaintiff would have accomplished as a wage earner over his or her lifetime. This situation presents itself most frequently in cases involving injured children, students, and homemakers. In general, "[t]he admissibility of evidence regarding future earning capacity is within the wide discretion of . . . trial judge[s]"[13] and this has led to a great diversity of decisions in this area. Most decisions evidence a willingness to exercise discretion liberally in favor of the plaintiff, finding that income and earnings opportunities would have been bountiful.[14] Occasionally, a court takes a more tightfisted approach.[15]

When the plaintiff has an earnings history, courts tend to indulge in less speculation than when the plaintiff, because of plaintiff's infancy or status as a student or homemaker, does not. In this context, courts have stated that the calculation of earning impairment may be influenced by the

---

[13] Oliveri v. Delta S.S. Lines, Inc., 849 F.2d 742, 745 (2d Cir. 1988) (brackets added).

[14] Athridge v. Iglesias, 950 F. Supp. 1187, 1193 (D.D.C. 1996) (finding that fact that 15 year old plaintiff's siblings were enrolled in professional degree programs substantiated plaintiff's claim that had he not been injured he would have gone to law school and become a lawyer; court found that based on the evidence plaintiff would have attained at least a college degree and there was a significant probability he would have obtained a professional degree); Pipgras v. Hart, 832 S.W.2d 360, 366 (Tex. Civ. App. 1992) (finding that in case of "a child who is too young to have earned money, the jury must determine lost earning capacity altogether from their common knowledge and sense of justice"); Alvis v. Henderson Obstetrics, S.C., 592 N.E.2d 678, 684 (Ill. App. 1992) (finding that when the jury found that the infant plaintiff had sustained permanent, disabling injury, the jury could infer future loss of earnings from the nature of the injury); Cranston v. Oxford Resources Corp., 571 N.Y.S.2d 733, 734 (App. Dept. 1991) (finding that a lost earnings award based on a career in law enforcement was not speculative even though the plaintiff was not in law enforcement; the plaintiff had passed all but one test for admission to the police academy); Ward v. La. & Ark. Ry., 451 So. 2d 597, 608 (La. App. 1984) (holding that an injured high school student was entitled to recover for loss of earning capacity even though she had not as yet entered the work force); Feldman v. Allegheny Airlines, Inc., 524 F.2d 384, 388 (2d Cir. 1975) (stating that future earnings award of college-educated 25 year old woman, who was unemployed when she was killed in plane crash, could be based on the fact that she had been capable of working full-time for forty years until she was 65, and planned to attend law school and would have continued to work part-time for an estimated eight years while raising children).

[15] Murphy v. United States, 833 F. Supp. 1199, 1208–09 (E.D. Va. 1993) (holding that plaintiff, a homemaker, who had worked as a secretary prior to marriage, failed to provide a reliable basis for the calculation of her earning impairment claim). The court rejected as arbitrary the dates plaintiff's expert used in his assumptions. *Id.* at 1208 (noting the expert's failure to use tables available to compute the normal work life expectancy of individuals such as plaintiff); *cf.* Boucher v. U.S. Suzuki Motor Corp., 73 F.3d 18, 21–22 (2d Cir. 1996) (stating that the opinion of the expert witness regarding lost income should be excluded as speculative "if it is based on unrealistic assumptions regarding the plaintiff's future employment prospects") (citations omitted). The court went on to find that was the case when the expert ignored the plaintiff's history of seasonal and intermittent employment and based the opinion on the assumption the plaintiff would have been employed on a permanent, full-time basis, year in and year out, had he not sustained the disabling injury. *Id.* at 22.

possibility of economic downturns,[16] the plaintiff's anticipated retirement date,[17] and the plaintiff's attitude toward work.[18] Even here, however, a plaintiff will be given substantial leeway. As noted in *Jones v. Wal-Mart Stores, Inc.*:

> There is no general rule regarding proof required for loss of earning capacity, other than that "each case is judged on its particular facts and the damages need be proved only to the degree to which they are ascertainable . . . ."

> The fact that the injured party earns as much as or more than he formerly did, especially in an employment relationship he had held for years (as in this case), does not bar him from recovering for loss of earning capacity . . . .

> Under Texas law a lessened earning capacity will be presumed when "one, formerly in good health and strength, is reduced to the state of a life-long cripple."[19]

A plaintiff's future earnings claim, whether based on lost earnings or impairment of earning capacity, will be based on his pre-injury work-life expectancy.[20] If plaintiff suffers from a pre-existing condition that will substantially affect his mortality, his earning capacity will be likewise affected.[21] Post-injury, but pretrial, events can also affect the calculation of

---

[16] Masinter v. Tenneco Oil Co., 929 F.2d 191, 194–95 (5th Cir. 1991) (finding that trial court did not abuse its discretion in reducing plaintiff's award by 25% to reflect likelihood plaintiff would have been laid-off in post-accident workforce's reduction in force).

[17] O'Shea v. Riverway Towing Co., 677 F.2d 1194, 1198 (7th Cir. 1982) (accepting 57 year old plaintiff's claim that she would have worked until age 70); Rosenbaum v. Lefrak Corp., 438 N.Y.S.2d 794, 799 (App. Dept. 1981) (rejecting 62 year old plaintiff's contention that he would have worked until 72); *cf. Masinter, supra,* 929 F.2d at 193–94 (holding that district judge did not abuse his discretion in rejecting expert's opinion that plaintiff would have worked to age 70).

[18] McGowan v. McGowan, 518 N.Y.S.2d 346, 351 (Sup. Ct. 1987), *aff'd and modified on other grounds,* 535 N.Y.S.2d 990 (App. Dept. 1988).

[19] 870 F.2d 982, 989–90 (5th Cir. 1989) (citations omitted); *see* Dombroski v. City of Atlantic City, 706 A.2d 242, 247 (N.J. Sup. Ct. A.D. 1998) (holding that "the mere fact that plaintiff [who sustained permanent and debilitating injuries] had his old job back with an increased salary did not foreclose diminished earning capacity damages") (brackets added). The court noted that the plaintiff could lose his present job and this factor could be considered by the expert in calculating the diminishment of earning capacity due to the earning plaintiff could have obtained before his injury and those earnings he would receive from the alternative employment to which he was relegated due to his injuries. 706 A.2d at 247–48.

[20] *In re* Joint E. and S. Dist. Asbestos Litig., 726 F. Supp. 426, 429–30 (E.D.N.Y. 1989) (following the majority rule that computes lost earnings based on the plaintiff's pre-injury life expectancy). The court collected authorities supporting the use of a pre-injury life expectancy and noted that only one jurisdiction (Iowa) has recently affirmed a contrary view. Beeman v. Manville Corp. Asbestos Disease Comp. Fund, 496 N.W.2d 247, 256 (Iowa 1993) (reaffirming view that plaintiff's future damages are based on his post-injury life expectancy).

[21] Jones v. Miles Labs., Inc., 700 F. Supp. 1127, 1133 (N.D. Ga. 1988) (finding that hemophiliac's claim against defendant for infecting him with AIDS (Acquired Immune Deficiency Syndrome) due to defendant's blood clotting product was limited to hemophiliac's pre-existing life expectancy, which court stated was short), *aff'd,* 887 F.2d 1576 (11th Cir. 1989).

lost earning. Thus, if plaintiff dies pretrial from an event unrelated to the defendant's misconduct, the lost earnings/impairment of earning capacity claim will end as of the date of plaintiff's death.[22]

The plaintiff's lifetime earnings may be calculated based on mortality and work-life expectancy tables prepared by the United States Department of Labor.[23] These materials can be used by the expert to form an opinion as to plaintiff's lost earnings or earning impairment. There is some authority that this opinion can be rendered by the plaintiff,[24] but this is an ill-advised approach for a plaintiff in most instances since his credibility on this matter will likely be poor.[25]

Some losses may fall between the cracks and not constitute loss of earnings or earnings impairment. For example, in *Snow v. Villacci* the question was the proper treatment of a lost earning opportunity. Plaintiff's injury caused him to be unable to begin or complete a training or educational program that would qualify the plaintiff for a higher rate of pay. The court saw the loss of earning opportunity as *sui generis*,[26] but that characterization would not prevent recovery as long as the plaintiff could show by reasonable evidentiary proof that had he not been injured he would have completed the program and seized the earning opportunity.[27]

---

[22] Zimny v. Lovric, 801 P.2d 259, 261–63 (Wash. App. 1990) (noting that a person's earnings become fixed as of the date of death and damages for impaired earning capacity cannot be recovered past the date of death). The court concluded:

> [W]e hold that where an injured person dies from causes unrelated to the injury litigated, the personal representative cannot recover damages for diminished earning capacity beyond the date of death. The cause of action survives, but damages become fixed and recovery may be had only for the period between the date of the accident and the date of the death from unrelated causes.

Id. at 263; Section 75.1 (Survival Actions).

[23] *Boucher v. U.S. Suzuki Motor Corp.*, *supra*, 73 F.3d at 23; *cf.* Jones v. Eppler, 266 P.2d 451, 456 (Okla. 1953):

> While, as suggested by defendants, this Court has never passed upon the question of admissibility of annuity tables in personal injury cases and the decision on this point will be one of first impression, yet the weight of authority is that standard life and annuity tables, no matter where found, if properly established and authenticated, are admissible in evidence in personal injury cases of permanent partial (or total) destruction of the earning capacity of the person negligently injured
>
> . . . .

[24] *La Fever v. Kemlite Co.*, *supra*, 706 N.E.2d at 454–55.

[25] Razzaque v. Krakow Taxi, Inc., 656 N.Y.S.2d 208, 209 (App. Dept. 1997) (noting that the lost earnings claim was speculative because the plaintiff's testimony was vague and unsubstantiated by any tax forms or W-2 forms).

[26] 754 A.2d 360, 364 (Me. 2000).

[27] *Id.* at 364–65. *See generally* William H. Danne, Jr., Annot., *Admissibility and Sufficiency, in Personal Injury or Wrongful Death Action, of Evidence as to Earnings or Earning Capacity From Position or Field For Which Person Has Not Fulfilled Education, Training, or Like Eligibility Requirement*, 2002 A.L.R. 5th 25 (not released for publication in ALR).

[71.3]   Self-Employed Plaintiffs

When the plaintiff is self-employed, determining the compensation she would have realized but for her injuries is more difficult than is the case for individuals who are employed by others and paid a salary. An employee's worth to the employer is fully evidenced by the compensation including fringe benefits, provided for the services rendered. The owner's compensation does not, however, simply reflect the value of her services. Self-employed persons must distinguish the value of their services to the business from that portion of their compensation that reflects the return on invested capital or the services of others when determining "earnings impairment," if any.[28] This does not mean that evidence of entity profits or income is never relevant to the determination of the self-employed person's loss of earnings or "earnings impairment claim." The critical focus is on whether the "earnings" were primarily the result of the plaintiff's services, not the labor of employees or a return on capital investment.

The preferred method of measuring lost earning capacity in the self-employed context is the cost of hiring a replacement to perform the task the plaintiff was responsible for before the injury.[29] Alternatively, the plaintiff may introduce evidence of lost profits as demonstrating her lost earning capacity when the capital invested in the business was relatively small and the profits resulted primarily from the personal skills and efforts of the plaintiff-owner, rather than from investment of capital or the skill of others.[30]

---

[28] Featherly v. Continental Ins. Co., 243 N.W.2d 806, 811–12 (Wis. 1976) (finding that evidence of lost profits alone was insufficient to establish plaintiff's lost earning capacity). *See generally* H.D. Warren, Annot., *Loss of Profits of a Business in Which Plaintiff is Interested as a Factor in Determining Damages in Action for Personal Injuries*, 12 A.L.R.2d 288 (1950).

[29] *Corbett v. Seamons, supra*, 904 P.2d at 233. *See generally* E. LeFevre, Annot., *Cost of Hiring Substitute or Assistant During Incapacity of Injured Party as Item of Damages in Action for Personal Injury*, 37 A.L.R.2d 364, 373–77 (1954). In *Claxton v. Lee*, 494 S.E.2d 80, 81–82 (Ga. App. 1997), the court suggested that the injured owner could evidence his lost earnings either by the cost of a substitute or by the additional wages paid to his employees while they compensated for his absence.

[30] *Corbett v. Seamons, supra*, 904 P.2d at 233–34 (collecting cases); *cf.* Croley v. Republican Nat'l Committee, 759 A.2d 682 (D.C. 2000) (reinstating $600,000 lost future earnings award for plaintiff who was a self-employed consultant). The court stated:

> In determining the loss of earnings or earning capacity of a self-employed individual or partner, consideration may be given to several factors, including loss of profits from the business, the cost of substitute labor, the value of the plaintiff's services, and plaintiff's draw against profits. Since Mr. Croley put his earnings into his computer company and was the sole employee of the company, under the circumstances, the best measure of his lost future earnings would be the value of his services. This value could be ascertained in two ways: (1) the amount of business he was able to obtain for his company, that is, the $532,000.00 covering a four year period, and (2) the testimony of an economic expert concerning what a person of his educational background, sex, and age would have earned had he not been injured. . . .

Id. at 692 (citation omitted).

[71.4] Children

A catastrophically injured child may recover "projected" future earnings even though the child has no earnings whatsoever and no track record on which to base an earnings projection.[31] This rule is a product of necessity; a contrary rule would preclude children, who suffered permanent, disabling injuries as a result of tortious conduct, from ever recovering for a loss of future earnings. In these cases, permitting awards based in large part on speculation is seen as the lesser evil.

The injured child's future earnings projection is normally based on United States Department of Labor lifetime earnings studies.[32] The critical issue in these cases is the assumptions the expert witness will make, and the court will accept, in calculating projected earnings over the child's lifetime. For example, in one case an infant ingested a caustic substance and sustained severe disabling injuries. In calculating future lost income the trial court accepted that the infant would have graduated from college and calculated her projected earnings from this baseline. The infant's family history gave no indication that she would attend, much less graduate, from college, but the trial court was prepared to base the earnings claim on the infant's lost opportunity, even though it was highly speculative. The appellate court disagreed.[33]

Somewhat less liberal, but still not ungenerous, assumptions were accepted by the court in *Hasson v. Ford Motor Co.*[34] In *Hasson* the injured plaintiff was a 19 year old college student who claimed $2,350,000 for lost future earnings based on what the California Supreme Court referred to

---

[31] Murray v. Sanford, 487 S.E.2d 135, 136 (Ga. App. 1997) (stating that while the general rule is that some evidence of earning capacity before and after the injury must be introduced, the rule is not applied to children who are too young to have a work or earnings history: "[i]n such cases, the amount of damages rests in the sound discretion of the jury"); *but cf.* Storrs, *supra*, 66 P. 72 (rejecting requirement of "before and after" proofs to claim by adult). Jordan v. Bero, 210 S.E.2d 618, 636–37 (W. Va. 1974) (holding that the infant plaintiff could recover lost earning capacity).

[32] *Niles v. City of San Rafael, supra*, 116 Cal. Rptr. at 739 (involving an 11 year old who was disabled by paralysis as a result of the accident). The court relied on a study of national average lifetime income compiled by the Department of Labor to calculate the lost income award. *See* text and notes 23–24, *supra*.

[33] Drayton v. Jiffee Chem. Corp., 395 F. Supp. 1081 (N.D. Ohio 1975), *as amended*, 413 F. Supp. 834 (N.D. Ohio 1976), *rev'd*, 591 F.2d 352, 364 (6th Cir. 1978) (finding that the trial judge's lost earnings award was deficient "in receiving and seriously considering projections which well outrun any reasonable prediction"). *But cf.* Andrews v. Reynolds Mem'l Hosp., 499 S.E.2d 846, 852 (W. Va. 1997) (affirming $1.75 million for lost earning of infant who died shortly after his premature birth). The court noted that the award was "within the range of estimated future earnings based on various life scenarios . . . established by the expert testimony of an economist at trial and . . . the economic and medical evidence . . . indicates that the infant . . . would statistically have had an average life expectancy and an average work-life expectancy, but for the alleged medial malpractice." *Id.* at 854. *See generally* D.E. Ytreberg, Annot., *Sufficiency of Evidence, in Personal Injury Actions, to Prove Impairment of Earning Capacity and to Warrant Instructions to Jury Thereon*, 18 A.L.R.3d 88 (1968).

[34] 650 P.2d 1171 (Cal. 1982), *cert. denied*, 459 U.S. 1190 (1983).

as the "speculative assumption" that the plaintiff would achieve his ambition of becoming a medical doctor. Although a college professor testified the plaintiff was capable of completing the necessary education requirements, the plaintiff had finished only one year of college and received a grade average of less than "B." Plaintiff's high school grades and Scholastic Achievement Test scores were unspectacular. The Supreme Court upheld the trial court's remittitur of $1,650,000 of the jury award of compensatory damages, which lowered the ultimate compensatory damages award to $5,850,000.[35]

Projecting a child's future potential earnings raises difficult social issues that rarely are addressed in the decided cases. For example, to what extent, if at all, should the trier-of-fact hear and consider evidence that the child's earnings capacity is affected by the child's race or ethnicity? By the earnings or educational level of the child's parent's or sibling? By the educational opportunities presented by the child's real life situation or hypothesized statistical life projection?

Courts have generally side stepped resolving the propriety of the use of a party's race in determining the amount of damages that should be awarded for lost earnings. For example, in *Childs v. United States* the court permitted the United States to present evidence and argue that the lost earnings award should be calculated based on the earnings of black males and black females, which are less than the earnings of white males and white females or earnings calculated using race neutral statistical tables.[36] The district judge noted that the use of race-based models was inconsistent with the position urged by the Department of Labor, that race and gender neutral models be used,[37] but the court did not reject or condemn the use of race and gender based models, merely their realiability.[38]

The Supreme Court has barred the use of race and gender based tables in calculating certain employee benefits.[39] The Courts decisions were, however, confined to employment relationships governed by Title VII of the Civil Rights Act of 1964, which expressly prohibits *employment* discrimination.[40]

---

[35] 650 P.2d at 1190; *Athridge v. Iglesias, supra,* note 14.

[36] 923 F. Supp. 1570, 1575–77 (S.D. Ga. 1996) (reciting testimony of expert witnesses concerning earnings potential of decedent black female 6 year old); *id.* at 1577–78 (same as concerning decedent unborn black male fetus).

[37] *Id.* at 1580 n.23 *citing Worklife Estimates, Effect of Race and Education,* Bulletin 2254, U.S. Dept. of Labor, Bureau of Labor Statistics (U.S. Printing Office, February, 1986).

[38] *Cf.* James v. Midkiff, 888 P.2d 5, 6 (Okla. App. 1994) (rejecting as irrelevant evidence concerning plaintiff's race, which permitted access to free medical care at Native American health clinic, on issue of duty to mitigate damages).

[39] Los Angeles Dept. Water & Power v. Manhart, 435 U.S. 702 (1978) (involving employer-sponsored employee benefit program in which annuity payments and benefits were disproportionate between males and females due to the use of gender based life expectancy tables); Arizona Governing Committee v. Norris, 463 U.S. 1073 (1983) (involving employer-sponsored employee retirement plan that required equal contributions from males and females but provided disproportionate benefits to males due to the use of gender based life expectancy tables).

[40] 42 U.S.C. § 2000e-2(a)(1).

Some jurisdictions require by statute that present value calculations be done by race-neutral life expectancy tables.[41]

[71.5] Homemaker

The unemployed homemaker is entitled to recover for loss of earning capacity.[42] The critical issue here is whether to use "opportunity" cost or "replacement" cost as the proper measure of damages for earning impairment of a homemaker. Evidence of either is usually admissible.[43] Replacement cost measures the value of the homemaker's service. Opportunity cost measures the value of any job or profession that the plaintiff may have given up to become a homemaker and to which the homemaker could have returned (presumably) in the future but for the injury. Each measure will lead to different awards because the income realized through outside employment will often be a significantly different amount from the amount of money needed to purchase substitutes to perform the homemaker's tasks. In some cases, the loss may include both replacement cost and opportunity cost measures, as, for example, when the homemaker could both work and perform parental duties.

[71.6] Aliens Subject to Deportation

A number of cases have addressed whether an alien's ability to recover for impairment of earning capacity should be affected by the possibility the alien will be deported to his country of origin. The issue is raised most often in the case of aliens whose presence in the United States is without documented legal status. The illegal presence of the plaintiff in the United States is not a bar to recovery of bodily injury damages.[44] Should the alien's impaired earnings recovery (future lost earnings) be based on earnings the alien could have obtained in the United States or should they be based on wages paid in the alien's country of origin? Some courts have stated that the possibility that the alien would be deported is a relevant factor in determining his lost earning capacity award.[45] The reason for this approach is that if the alien were deported his future earnings would have been based on work in the country of origin, not the United States; therefore, his

---

[41] Ariz. Rev. Stat. § 12-589B.

[42] Richmond v. Zimbrick Logging, Inc., 863 P.2d 520, 522 (Or. App. 1994); Arnett v. Thompson, 433 S.W.2d 109, 115 (Ky. 1968); Gotsch v. Market Street Ry., 265 P. 268, 271 (Cal. App. 1928).

[43] *Richmond v. Zimbrick Logging, Inc., supra,* 863 P.2d at 522; Schulz v. Chadwell, 558 S.W.2d 183, 188–89 (Ky. App. 1977); *see* Lambert v. Wrensch, 399 N.W.2d 369, 378 (Wis. 1987) (holding that wife could not recover for her loss of earning capacity when her husband's loss of consortium recovery had included the value of the wife's material services to the home during the time she was injured).

[44] Mischalski v. Ford Motor Co., 935 F. Supp. 203, 204–05 (E.D.N.Y. 1996); Janusis v. Long, 188 N.E. 228, 231 (Mass. 1933). *But cf.* text and notes 47–52, *infra* (discussing impact of Immigration Reform and Control Act of 1986).

[45] Collins v. New York City Health & Hosp. Corp., 607 N.Y.S.2d 387, 388 (App. Dept. 1994).

rightful position is based on earnings that would have been realized in the former country, not the latter.

Because of concern that the plaintiff's immigration status may prejudice his case, many courts limit the defendant's ability to raise the fact to cases when the defendant demonstrates a real possibility that the plaintiff may be deported. The test can be somewhat rigorous:

> [A] plaintiff's status as an illegal alien, in and of itself, cannot be used to rebut a claim for future lost earnings. The fact that a plaintiff is deportable does not mean that deportation will actually occur. Further, whatever probative value illegal alien status may have is far outweighed by its prejudicial impact. Therefore, in order to rebut such a claim defendants must be prepared to demonstrate something more than just the mere fact that the plaintiff resides in the United States illegally. Absent such a showing, a defendant will be precluded from presenting to the jury evidence which would indicate a plaintiff's immigration status.[46]

The Immigration Reform and Control Act of 1986 (IRCA) may make it more difficult for aliens without documented legal status to obtain lost earnings recoveries based on U.S. wage rates. IRCA prohibits employers from hiring aliens without documented legal status and requires that employers verify the identity and eligibility of each new-hire by examining appropriate documents before the new-hire begins work.[47] This statutory program received a significant boost in *Egbuna v. Time-Life Libraries, Inc.*[48] Egbuna quit his employment and then sought to be re-employed by his old employer. When he was refused, he sued under Title VII claiming the decision not to rehire him was in retaliation for assistance he had given a fellow employee on a sexual harassment claim. Without reaching the merits of the retaliation claim, the court held that Egbuna's undocumented status barred relief because IRCA made it illegal to hire or retain alien employees without documented legal status. The *Egbuna* court stated:

> Given Congress' unequivocal declaration that it is illegal to hire unauthorized aliens and its mandate that employers immediately

---

[46] Klapa v. O & Y Liberty Plaza Co., 645 N.Y.S.2d 281, 282 (Sup. Ct. 1996) (citations omitted); *see* Hernandez v. M/V Rajaan, 841 F.2d 582, 588, *as modified,* 848 F.2d 498, 499–500 (5th Cir. 1988) (finding no error to award future earnings and medical expenses based on U.S. rates to an alien illegally within the United States when it was established that the alien was probably entitled to remain in the United States), *cert. denied sub nom.* Hernandez v. Dianella Shipping Corp., 488 U.S. 1030 (1989) and 488 U.S. 981 (1989). *But cf.* Rodriguez v. Kline, 232 Cal. Rptr. 157, 158–59 (Cal. App. 1986) (suggesting that jury must, when awarding future earnings, take into account the possibility that the plaintiff, in the United States without lawful authority, may be deported).

[47] 8 U.S.C.A. § 1324a (West Supp. 1997).

[48] 153 F.3d 184 (4th Cir. 1998) (*en banc*); *cert. denied,* 525 U.S. 1142 (1999); *cf.* Hoffman Plastic Compounds, Inc. v. N.L.R.B., 535 U.S. 137 (2002) (holding that undocumented alien who is in the United States without proper authorization may not recover back pay award from the National Labor Relations Board, which otherwise could order such awards to a wrongfully terminated employee).

discharge unauthorized aliens upon discovering their undocumented status, we cannot reverse the district court's grant of summary judgment in favor of TLLI. To do so would sanction the formation of a statutorily declared illegal relationship, expose TLLI to civil and criminal penalties, and illogically create an entitlement simply because Egbuna applied for a job despite his illegal presence in this country and despite his having been statutorily disqualified from employment in the United States. In this instance, to rule Egbuna was entitled to the position he sought and to order TLLI to hire an undocumented alien would nullify IRCA, which declares it illegal to hire or to continue to employ unauthorized aliens.[49]

While *Ebunga* dealt squarely with an employee discharge/wrongful termination claim, the basic theme of the decision is that an alien without documented legal status cannot legally be employed as a matter of federal law. This theme can easily be extended to the personal injury context. If the employment contract and relationship are illegal, as *Ebunga* suggests because of IRCA, an award of lost earnings in U.S. dollars for bodily injury may be seen as inconsistent with IRCA.[50] If the alien cannot be legally employed in the United States, the future lost earnings award based on U.S. wage rates is not a measure of what was actually lost, unless the assumption is made that the alien's undocumented status would have remained concealed but for the accident and resulting injuries. On the other hand, given the goal of IRCA of deterring illegal immigration to the United States by foreclosing employment to aliens without proper legal status, there is a closer nexus between that goal and relief in a wrongful termination/retention action, as in *Ebunga,* then in the case of bodily injury claims. Immigrants no doubt come to the United States for jobs, but it is unlikely, to say the least, that they come to the United States to be involved in accidents, sustain bodily injury, and participate in the tort compensation system.

The application of IRCA outside of employment discrimination actions[51] have been mixed. The most common application has been in the area of workforce benefits, such as workers' compensation or disability,[52] but IRCA

---

[49] *Id.* at 188.

[50] Sections 62 (Unclean Hands and "In Pari Delicto"), 65.2 (Illegality) (discussing applications of defenses to claims by plaintiff who is illegally in the United States).

[51] And even within! *See* Rivera v. Nibco, Inc., 364 F.3d 1057, 1064 (9th Cir. 2004) (holding that discovery into a plaintiff's lawful or unlawful status in the United States may be denied by the district court).

[52] In *Dowling v. Slotnik*, 712 A.2d 396, 402–03 (Conn. 1998), *cert. denied*, 525 U.S. 1017 (1998), the court held that IRCA would not preempt the authority of a state to provide worker compensation benefits to an injured employee who was also an alien without documented legal status. *Compare* Correa v. Waymouth Farms, Inc., 664 N.W.2d 324 (Minn. 2003) (holding that alien illegally in the United States could recover workers' compensation despite alien's inability to satisfy diligent work search requirements due to alien's status), *with* Tarango v. State Indus. Ins. System, 25 P.3d 175 (Nev. 2001) *and* Del Taco v. Workers' Comp. Appeals Bd., 94 Cal. Rptr. 2d 825 (Cal. App. 2000) (both rejecting claims for vocational rehabilitation (job retraining) by alien worker illegally in the United States). *See generally* Marjorie A. Shields, Annot., *Application of Workers' Compensation Laws to Illegal Aliens*, 121 A.L.R. 5th 523 (2004).

has found application in the personal injury context.[53]

§ 72 MEDICAL EXPENSES

[72.1] Scope of Recovery

The recovery for medical expenses is limited to the reasonable value of the medical care and services provided. The amount actually paid or incurred is admissible evidence of the reasonable value of the services rendered. The proper amount to be awarded, however, is the reasonable value of services necessarily received, not the amount *billed*.[1] Nevertheless, when the plaintiff actually pays the bills, this is often deemed to be substantial evidence of the bills reasonableness.[2] Payment does not validate the providers' professional opinion regarding the reasonableness and necessity of the treatments provided. Payment does, however, serve to indicate that the plaintiff is not overtreating, which may be the case when the treatments are being provided free of cost to the plaintiff.[3] The amount actually received by the health care provider may or may not limit the plaintiff's recovery for medical expenses in personal injury actions, including bodily injury claims. This issue is addressed in Section 72.2 (Discounted Billing).

Medical expenses must be attributed to the injury and reasonably incurred. Courts generally are quite lenient in reviewing whether the plaintiff reasonably relied on a physician's representation that medical treatment was appropriate. However, there are limits. In *Monteleone v. Bahama Cruise Line, Inc.* the court held that plaintiffs future medical expenses were too speculative to award when her painful condition appeared to be permanent and without hope of medical amelioration. Under the assumption the medical treatment could provide no relief, the court was of the view that it would be unreasonable for her to receive compensation for treatment that would be of no medical value to her.[4]

---

[53] Balbuena v. IDR Realty, LLC., __ N.E.2d __ (N.Y. 2006) (holding that *Hoffman* preemption should not be read to apply to personal injury claim by alien injured while illegally in the United States). In *Rosa v. Partners in Progress, Inc.*, 868 A.2d 994 (N.H. 2005), the court held that in a claim of lost earnings capacity due to negligence evidence of the plaintiff's illegal status should not be admitted.

[1] Patterson v. Horton, 929 P.2d 1125, 1130 (Wash. App. 1997); Hanif v. Housing Auth. of Yolo County, 246 Cal. Rptr. 192, 194 (Cal. App. 1988).

[2] Lewis v. Alfa Laval Separation, Inc., 714 N.E.2d 426, 439 (Ohio App. 1998); Hughes v. Palermo, 911 S.W.2d 673, 675 (Mo. App. 1995).

[3] The admissibility of medical bills and their use to establish the reasonableness of the medical services provided can raise tricky evidentiary issues. In general, the bills alone cannot establish the reasonableness of the treatment. Shpigel v. White, 741 A.2d 1205, 1211 (Md. 1999). The bills may, however, be deemed sufficient to prove the costs of the treatment. *Patterson v. Horton, supra*, 929 P.2d at 1130–31.

[4] 664 F. Supp. 744, 746 (S.D.N.Y. 1987), *rev'd on other grounds*, 838 F.2d 63 (2d Cir. 1988); *see* Arthur v. Zearley, 992 S.W.2d 67, 77 (Ark. 1999) (giving of jury instruction regarding recovery of cost of future medical treatment was erroneous; plaintiff failed to introduce any evidence that future medical treatment was necessary and plaintiff testified that she was symptom and treatment free for the 3 years prior to trial).

Recoverable medical expenses include hospital expenses, physician fees (even if the physician is unlicensed),[5] nursing and attendant care, physical therapy, dental care, drugs, laboratory tests, wheelchairs, crutches, hospital beds for home use, prosthesis, glasses, transportation costs for medical treatment, etc.[6] The cost of tutoring and rehabilitation are also recoverable.[7] Most jurisdictions permit a recovery even when the services are rendered gratuitously by family providers, such as a spouse, children, or parents.[8] The recovery is based on the reasonable value of the services rendered. Although the plaintiff is not obligated to repay family providers, it is seen as unfair for the defendant to reap the benefits of the family members generosity.[9] The situation may be different when gratuitous services are rendered by non-family members. In this context, when there is no expense to the plaintiff, the plaintiff may not be allowed to claim as an item of his damages the reasonable value of the gratuitous services proved.[10]

A plaintiff's injury may give rise to future medical expenses, which is to say medical expenses that will be incurred after the date of trial. The plaintiff must establish her claim in a single proceeding and this includes future medical expense attributable to the injury.[11]

The presentation of a future medical expense claim bears the same burdens as a claim for future lost income. Both are economic losses; consequently both must be adjusted to present value.[12] The evidence must

---

[5] Gastine v. Ewing, 150 P.2d 266, 272 (Cal. App. 1944). This may, however, be limited to situations when the plaintiff has paid the medical fees because the physicians unlicensed status bars an action for the fees. Section 65.2 (Illegality).

[6] Meader by and through Long v. United States, 881 F.2d 1056, 1060–61 (11th Cir. 1989) (noting that the defendant is entitled to receive a credit for the salvage value of medical equipment furnished to the plaintiff when the equipment must be periodically replaced due to wear and tear, but that the defendant bears the burden of proof on the issue).

[7] Niles v. City of San Rafael, 116 Cal. Rptr. 733, 740 (Cal. App. 1974); cf. Lozada v. United States, 140 F.R.D. 404, 411 (D. Neb. 1991) (awarding future medical costs for profoundly damaged child as including respite for the child's parents), aff'd on other grounds, 974 F.2d 986 (8th Cir. 1992).

[8] Rodriguez v. McDonnell Douglas Corp., 151 Cal. Rptr. 399, 418 (Cal. App. 1978).

[9] Section 15.3 (Gratuitous Benefits) (discussing application of Collateral Source Rule to gratuitous benefits provided to the plaintiff).

[10] Peterson v. Lou Bachrodt Chevrolet Co., 392 N.E.2d 1, 5 (Ill. 1979) (holding that the plaintiff could not recover the value of free medical care provided by a charitable institution since the plaintiff had incurred no expense or liability for the medical services provided); cf. Helfend v. Southern Cal. R.T.D., 465 P.2d 61, 64 n.5 (Cal. 1970); see note 5, supra.

[11] Section 9.2 (Future Damages).

[12] Meader by and through Long v. United States supra, 881 F.2d at 1057–58; Section 9.3 (Discounting to Present Value). But cf. Sherbahn v. Kerkove, 987 P.2d 195, 201–02 (Alaska 1999) (holding that statute requiring that future medical expenses be discounted to present value did not apply because the plaintiff intended to spend the award immediately on medical treatment he could not otherwise afford, but would have undertaken and completed had he been financially able to do so). Although the treatments would occur in the future, it appears that the plaintiff in Sherbahn was going to pay for the treatments immediately and that amount was the basis of the award, although the point is not clear. Id. at 197, 201.

establish with reasonable probability that the plaintiff will require future medical treatment for her injuries; it is not sufficient to deal in conjecture.[13] On the other hand, the trier-of-fact is normally afforded some discretion in this area:

> To recover future medical expenses, a plaintiff has the burden of showing substantial evidence to establish with reasonable medical certainty future medical services are necessary. A jury can infer the reasonable cost of future medical expenses based upon record evidence of past medical expenses incurred by the plaintiff. Furthermore, a jury can infer the necessity of future nursing care based upon record evidence showing severe injuries sustained by a plaintiff and disabilities caused by those injuries.[14]

Plaintiff's evidence must show the reasonable estimated cost of the future medical treatment.[15] This evidence will normally require expert testimony.[16]

[72.2] Discounted Billing

In many cases, the provider of medical services has contractually agreed with a third party to accept, as payment in full, a smaller sum than that actually billed to the plaintiff. For example, a hospital may agree with Blue Cross/Blue Shield to accept payment for services at a capped rate (for example, $500/day for a room), while the plaintiff's bill shows the higher standard rate (for example, $750/day for a room). Should the medical expense award be based on the amount billed, which we may assume is a reasonable sum, or the amount the provider has agreed to accept from Blue Cross/Blue Shield? The decisional law in this area has exploded of late reflecting both the increased cost of medical care and the common use of health care provider agreements by which providers agree to reduced rates in exchange for listing as preferred providers by the insurer or funding entity. Legal issues involving these arrangements fall into several categories, each of which contains a split of authorities as to the proper resolution of the problem.

First, is the plaintiff-patient's recovery against the defendant tortfeasor for medical expenses determined by the reasonable value of services rendered (usually the amount billed at the standard, going rate) or the amount actually received by the provider pursuant to its contract with the

---

[13] Marchetti v. Ramirez, 688 A.2d 1325, 1328–29 (Conn. 1997) (stating that testimony by a medical expert that the plaintiff "might" need future treatment would be insufficient); Bankert by Bankert v. United States, 937 F. Supp. 1169, 1185 (D. Md. 1996) (stating that evidence that the plaintiff was "at risk" of developing problems that would require medical intervention was insufficient).

[14] Symington v. Mayo, 590 N.W.2d 450, 453 (N.D. 1999).

[15] Mendralla v. Weaver Corp., 703 A.2d 480, 485 (Pa. Super. Ct. 1997).

[16] Weber v. White, 681 N.W.2d 137, 142 (Wis. 2004); Lind v. Slowinski, 450 N.W.2d 353, 358 (Minn. App. 1990); *Mendralla v. Weaver Corp.*, *supra*, 703 A.2d at 485.

insurer? On this point some jurisdictions permit recovery based on "reasonable value,"[17] while other jurisdictions limit recovery to the amount actually paid and received.[18] Jurisdictions that adhere to recovery of "reasonable value" tend to emphasize the same concerns that underlie the Collateral Source Rule: any accommodation between the plaintiff, her insurer, and her health care provider is not for the benefit of the defendant tortfeasor.[19] Jurisdictions that restrict the plaintiff to the amount actually paid emphasize that the award should be based on the plaintiff's actual, rather than hypothetical, losses.[20]

Many of the decisions denying recovery of "reasonable value" have involved situations when the plaintiff's arrangement with the insurer provided that plaintiff would not be liable for any costs associated with the treatment, as is the case when plaintiff is covered by Medicaid,[21] but even here there is a split in the decisions.[22] Some courts, which generally refuse to permit the plaintiff to recover damages based on the written-off amount, reason that to recover based on the higher billed rate the plaintiff must incur some legal or moral obligation to pay the full amount claimed as medical expense damages.[23] Other courts emphasize that the plaintiff should not be allowed to recover the discounted amount of the medical expense bill unless she paid consideration for the medical benefits provided.[24] Thus, if the medical expense was paid pursuant to public assistance (e.g. Medicaid), plaintiff would be limited to the amount actual paid as her damages; otherwise, if she purchased the benefit directly or indirectly (employee benefits plan). Again, it must be emphasized, there is no consistent approach here.[25]

Second, the issue of recovery of the discounted portion of the bill also may arise when the claim is asserted by the health care provider to recover that amount from the tortfeasor (subrogation)[26] or from the patient (medical lien).[27] The critical issue here is whether the health care provider is bound to accept the amount it contractually agreed to "accept as full payment" or whether it may recover the "billed rate" (assuming that this rate is

---

[17] *See* Koffman v. Leichtfuss, 630 N.W.2d 201, 209 (Wis. 2001); Moorhead v. Crozer Chester Med. Ctr., 705 A.2d 452, 455 (Pa. Super. Ct. 1997).

[18] *Hanif, supra*, 246 Cal. Rptr. at 641–42; *see* Restatement (Second) of Torts § 911 cmt. h (1977).

[19] *Koffman, supra*, 630 N.W.2d at 209–10.

[20] *Hanif, supra*, 264 Cal. Rptr. at 641–42; Section 15.2 (Collateral Source or No Damage).

[21] McAmis v. Wallace, 980 F. Supp. 181, 184 (W.D. Va. 1997).

[22] Rose v. Via Christi Health System, Inc., 78 P.3d 798, 803–04 (Kan. 2003) (holding that defendant could not limit claim to amount paid by Medicare for medical treatment of plaintiff).

[23] *McAmis, supra*, 980 F. Supp. at 184.

[24] Bozeman v. State, 879 So.2d 692 (La. 2004).

[25] Haselden v. Davis, 579 S.E.2d 293, 296–97 (S.C. 2003) (holding that recovery of medical expenses is not limited to amount paid by Medicaid).

[26] Section 53 (Subrogation).

[27] Medical liens permit the health care provider to claim an interest in a recovery *by the plaintiff* against the tortfeasor. These medical liens may be statutory or consensual.

reasonable)? The issue normally arises in the context of medical liens that allow the health care provider (lienholder) to claim an interest in any recovery that the patient recovers against the tortfeasor.[28] The health care provider's lien rights permit it to recover the actual amount it agreed to accept. As noted previously, however, that amount is often deeply discounted from the "billed rate." The question thus arises whether the provider's lien rights permit it to recover all or a portion of the discount out of the patient's recovery. Rough justice suggests that the provider's ability to recover the discount from the patient's recovery should be limited to cases when the patient/plaintiff recovered the billed amount from the tortfeasor, but that approach does not appear to be driving the decisions; rather, the resolution of this problem parallels that presented under the law of subrogation,[29] except that the presence *here* of *statutory* rights (statutory liens) may enhance the lienholder's (providers) claim.[30]

Third, a significant complication in this field is the presence of federal law that may preempt state law regarding rights to, and priority of rights to, full compensation of medical expense.[31] A number of courts have held that federal law limits state created lien rights. The decisional law is rather uniform for Medicaid,[32] but somewhat mixed in the other prominent area (ERISA), which deals with employee-benefit plans.[33]

[72.3] Ownership of Claim

When the medical expenses are incurred on behalf of a child, the question may arise as to ownership of the damages claim. Because parents are responsible for providing life's necessities, including medical care, for their children, many courts hold that the medical expense claim belongs to the parents.[34] The parents may, however, waive or relinquish their claim in favor of the child.[35]

---

[28] *See* Parnell v. Adventist Health System/West, 109 P.3d 69, 74 (Cal. 2005) (holding that hospital's nonconsensual, statutory lien for actual value of services provided could not be asserted against patient's recovery when hospital had agreed to reduced compensation for services rendered).

[29] Section 53.3 ([Subrogation] Priorities).

[30] Carol A. Crocca, Annot., *Construction, Operation, and Effect of Statute Giving Hospital Lien Against Recovery From Tortfeasor Causing Injury*, 16 A.L.R. 5th 262 (1993); but see note 28, *supra*.

[31] 42 C.F.R. 447.20 (limiting the ability of providers to charge or recover amounts in excess of those authorized for Medicaid services).

[32] Lizer v. Eagle Air Med Corp., 308 F. Supp. 2d 1006, 1009–10 (D. Ariz. 2004) (holding the federal law prohibits Medicaid payee from seeking additional sum from *any entity or person*); Olszewski v. Scripps Health, 69 P.3d 927, 941–42 (Cal. 2003).

[33] *Compare* Liberty Northwest Ins. Corp. v. Kemp, 85 P.3d 871 (Or. App. 2004) (holding that state created rights were preempted by ERISA), *with* Trustees of AFTRA Health Fund v. Biondi, 303 F.3d 765 (7th Cir. 2002) (*contra*).

[34] Johns Hopkins Hosp. v. Pepper, 697 A.2d 1358, 1362–63 (Md. 1997); Lasselle v. Special Prods. Co., 677 P.2d 483, 486 (Idaho 1983).

[35] *Lasselle, supra*, 677 P.2d at 486 (noting that the waiver may be express or implied).

If the parents cannot assert the claim, the court will allow the child to do so rather than provide the defendant with a windfall.[36] This exception is generally limited, however, to the amount incurred on behalf of the child before the child becomes an adult and for which the parents are unable to pay.

[72.4] Medical Monitoring

Recovery of medical monitoring expenses is a recent development in American law.[37] When allowed, medical monitoring is seen as an element of consequential damages even though the plaintiff has not sustained a determinable, actual injury; rather, the plaintiff has been exposed to a hazardous substance that may cause future physical injury. Medical monitoring is designed to allow the plaintiff to receive timely notice if she develops the future injury so she can receive prompt medical treatment. Medical monitoring, however, is distinct from a claim for future injury and presupposes that the plaintiff is unable to establish to the requisite degree of proof that she will sustain future injury.[38]

Tests to determine whether a plaintiff may recover medical monitoring costs, without a showing of present injury or establishing the likelihood of future losses to the requisite degree of medical certainty, vary. Some jurisdictions have articulated fairly extensive prima facie tests.[39] Other jurisdictions permit recovery of medical monitoring on what appear to be only a "rational basis" test; there must be a clinical or medical basis for assuming a reasonable possibility that plaintiff's exposure may lead to the

---

[36] *John Hopkins Hosp.*, *supra*, 697 A.2d at 1363–66 (permitting the child to assert the claim when the parent's ability to do so was barred by the running of the statute of limitations; the limitations period was tolled, as to child, due to his minority).

[37] The claim became significant in the 1980s. Barnes v. American Tobacco Co., Inc., 984 F. Supp. 842, 864 (E.D. Pa. 1997) (discussing development of medical monitoring claims in Pennsylvania in the1980s), *aff'd*, 161 F.3d 127 (3d Cir. 1998), *cert. denied*, 526 U.S. 1114 (1999).

[38] Section 9.1 (Future Damage).

[39] Redland Soccer Club, Inc. v. Dep't of the Army, 696 A.2d 137 (Pa. 1997) (holding that to prevail on common law medical monitoring claim the plaintiff must satisfy a seven-element test). The elements are:

(1) exposure greater than normal background levels;

(2) to a proven hazardous substance;

(3) caused by the defendant's negligence;

(4) as a proximate result of the exposure, plaintiff has a significantly increased risk of contracting a serious latent disease;

(5) a monitoring procedure exists that makes the early detection of the disease possible;

(6) the prescribed monitoring regime is different from that normally recommended in the absence of the exposure; and

(7) the prescribed monitoring regime is reasonably necessary according to contemporary scientific principles.

Id. at 145–46; Hansen v. Mountain Fuel Supply Co., 858 P.2d 970, 979 (Utah 1993) (adopting an eight-part test that is substantially similar to the *Redland Soccer Club* 7-part test).

future losses, which medical monitoring will detect.[40] Probably, the majority of courts follow, in practice, a test that lies somewhere between the two above points. Under this approach, in order to recover medical monitoring expenses the plaintiff must establish:

1. Plaintiff was significantly exposed to a proven hazardous substance through the negligent actions of the defendant.

2. As a proximate result of exposure, plaintiff suffers a significantly increased risk of contracting a serious latent disease.

3. That increased risk makes periodic diagnostic medical examinations reasonably necessary.

4. Monitoring and testing procedures exist that make the early detection of the disease possible and beneficial.[41]

In fact, there is probably little difference between the various iterations of the test; the critical difference is in the application of the "significance" requirement[42] and whether the plaintiff demonstrates exposure only or actual contamination.[43] Whichever threshold test is used, however, it must be less than the future loss recovery test of reasonable certainty, otherwise medical monitoring will not have a distinct existence separate from the medical expenses that will usually be awarded for future losses resulting from injuries caused by the defendant.[44] Some jurisdictions require that in order for a plaintiff to recover medical monitoring costs, the plaintiff must establish the reasonable certainty of actual physical injury,[45] although in some of these cases the requisite injury is practically de minimis.[46]

---

[40] Abusio v. Consolidated Edison Co. of N.Y., 656 N.Y.S.2d 371, 372 (1997).

[41] *In re* R.R. Yard Litig., 916 F.2d 829, 852 (3d Cir. 1990), *cert. denied sub nom.* General Elec. Co. v. Knight, 499 U.S. 961 (1991); Ayers v. Town of Jackson, 525 A.2d 287, 312–13 (N.J. 1987).

[42] *See* text and notes 53–56, *infra.*

[43] *See* text and notes 47–49, *infra.*

[44] Patton v. General Signal Corp., 984 F. Supp. 666, 674 (W.D.N.Y. 1997) (stating that the burden of proof should be higher in an emotional distress "fear of contracting" case than on a medical monitoring case). The court noted:

> Exposure to a toxic substance might in some instances be enough to make medical monitoring advisable, but not enough to provide a rational basis for a fear that is severe enough to cause the plaintiff compensable emotional distress. Moreover, there could be cases in which the plaintiff cannot prove that a certain substance is present in his body, but could nevertheless present expert medical testimony that the plaintiff's exposure to that substance warrants future medical monitoring.

Id.

[45] Hinton v. Monsanto Co., 813 So.2d 827 (Ala. 2001); Hagerty v. L&L Marine Servs., Inc., 788 F.2d 315, 319 (5th Cir.), *modified,* 797 F.2d 256 (1986); Ball v. Joy Mfg. Co., 755 F. Supp. 1344, 1370–73 (S.D.W. Va. 1990), *aff'd,* 958 F.2d 36 (4th Cir. 1991), *cert. denied,* 502 U.S. 1033 (1992).

[46] Werlein v. United States, 746 F. Supp. 887, 901 (D. Minn. 1990) (finding that "chromosomal breakage" and "immunal system" damage constituted actual injury), *vacated on other grounds,* 793 F. Supp. 898 (D. Minn. 1992); Herber v. Johns-Manville Corp., 785 F.2d 79, 81–83 (3d Cir. 1986) (finding that "pleural thickening" in plaintiff's lungs after exposure to asbestos

Courts have debated whether a plaintiff must show that he has been contaminated by injurious substances before he may recover medical monitoring expenses. Courts generally require more than mere exposure, e.g., sustained or significant exposure; yet, courts appear to stop short of requiring actual contamination.[47]

The justification for not requiring proof of actual contamination lies in the general acceptance and application of the principle that a person who is the victim of another's misconduct may recover the costs of a medical examination to determine that he sustained no actual injuries.[48] Recovery turns on whether the medical examination was medically reasonable under all the circumstances. Medical monitoring presents a similar profile. If based on the scope, nature, and duration of the exposure, it would be medically reasonable to monitor the plaintiff, then the medical monitoring case is not, in principle, materially different from the garden-variety negligence case.[49] Medical monitoring asks whether that principle can be extended to warrant an award of the costs of monitoring individuals who have been *exposed* to an injurious agent, to determine if the exposure will at some point of time in the future result in injury in fact. The debate is over whether exposure, but not present injury in fact or a sufficient probability thereof,[50] warrants an award of damages that would facilitate early(ier) detection of injury if injury should occur, which it may not because there has been only exposure to injurious agents, not injurious exposure.

It has also been argued that medical monitoring is justified on the principle that a plaintiff should exercise reasonable efforts to avoid further injury.[51] The corollary here is that costs reasonably incurred to avoid or mitigate losses are recoverable to the extent they do not exceed the loss.[52] The problem with this argument is that it assumes the very fact it seeks to establish, which is that the plaintiff has sustained a loss, but some courts

---

constituted physical injury warranting medical monitoring). In both *Werlein* and *Herber* the identified "injuries" would generally not be recognized as actual injuries for purposes of compensation as bodily injury. Section 12 (Non-economic Damages), text and notes 24–31 (discussing "physical harm" requirement).

[47] *Patton, supra*, 984 F. Supp. at 674.

[48] Waltrip v. Bilbon Corp., 38 S.W.3d 873, 880 (Tex. Civ. App. 2001); Wainwright v. Fontenot, 774 So.2d 70, 77–78 (La. 2000); *Friends For All Children, Inc., supra*, 746 F.2d at 825.

[49] Redland Soccer Club, Inc. v. Dep't of the Army, 835 F. Supp. 803, 810 (M.D. Pa. 1993). The district court subsequently granted summary judgment for the defendant United States on the medical monitoring claim and the decision was affirmed on appeal. 55 F.3d 827, 848 (3d Cir. 1995) (finding that plaintiffs "failed to introduce evidence that their exposure required a different medical monitoring regimen than that which would normally be recommended for them absent exposure"), *cert. denied,* 516 U.S. 1071 (1996).

[50] Section 9.1 (Future Damage).

[51] *See generally* Amy Blumenburg, Note, *Medical Monitoring Funds: The Periodic Payment of Future Medical Surveillance Expenses in Toxic Exposure Litigation,* 43 Hast. L.J. 661, 678 (1992).

[52] Section 13.7 (Compensation for Mitigation Efforts).

have accepted the idea that mitigation to prevent or reduce foreseeable injury is compensable.[53]

While plaintiff need not establish actual contamination, a mere exposure is not sufficient. The decisions require that the plaintiff demonstrate that she sustained a significant exposure at a level or levels above normal background exposure levels. It is not enough for a plaintiff to show that her exposure came from the defendant's source if the exposure is no greater than normal background levels to which the general population is exposed.[54]

This "significance" standard is not necessarily an easy threshold to meet. For example, in *Abuan v. General Electric Co.* the court held that medical evidence that plaintiffs had been exposed to toxic substances and that the exposure had significantly increased their risk of future injuries, such as cancer and birth defects, was insufficient to rebut the defendants' motion for summary judgment on the medical monitoring claim.[55] The court held the proof was inadequate because it failed to state how significant or relative the increased risk was for plaintiffs over the general population.[56] On the other hand, the Third Circuit later deemed the *Abuan* standard as too rigorous and that it was not necessary that relative risk be quantified.[57]

§ 73   PAIN AND SUFFERING

[73.1]   Nature of the Loss

Pain and suffering are related concepts. Pain is commonly understood as referring to a physical sensation (usually caused by harmful stimuli); suffering is understood as referring to the mental and emotional response to an injury. "Pain and suffering" is a generic label used to identify a variety of non-economic harms, such as mental anguish, distress, agony, discomfort, loss of quality of life, disfigurement, etc., that may accompany bodily injury. Because one or more of these forms of pain and suffering is thought to be inherent in every instance of bodily injury, pain and suffering are usually characterized as general damages in the context of bodily injury claims.

The wisdom of compensating individuals for pain and suffering has been questioned. The critique focuses on the fact that the award does not really

---

[53] CUNA Mutual Life Ins. Co. v. Los Angeles County Metropolitan Transp. Authority, 133 Cal. Rptr. 2d 470 (Cal. App. 2003) (allowing recovery of costs incurred to protect building from damage due to subway construction).

[54] *In re* Paoli R.R. Yard PCB Litig., 113 F.3d 444, 459–60 (3d Cir. 1997).

[55] 3 F.3d 329, 334 (9th Cir. 1993) (applying Guam law), *cert. denied,* 510 U.S. 1116 (1994).

[56] *Id.* at 334–35. The court further noted that one of plaintiff's medical experts diminished his credibility by his view that any exposure to a toxic substance warranted medical monitoring of the exposed individuals. *Id.* at 335.

[57] *In re* Paoli R.R. Yard Litig., 35 F.3d 717, 788 (3d Cir. 1994), *cert. denied,* 513 U.S. 1190 (1995) (distinguishing *Abuan*).

restore the plaintiff to the position he would have occupied but for the bodily injury. Pain and suffering cannot be undone. The award cannot purchase a substitute, for there is no market for pain and suffering. As noted in *Consorti v. Armstrong World Industries*:

> Reasonable people of [Consorti's] age, in good mental and physical health, would have not traded one-quarter of [his] suffering for a hundred million dollars, much less twelve. While the law seeks by reasonable compensation to make a plaintiff whole, we must recognize that compensation for suffering can be accomplished only in a symbolic and arbitrary fashion. There are at least two serious shortcomings to the endeavor. First, money awards do not make one whole; they do not alleviate pain. Second, there is no rational scale that justifies the award of any particular amount, in compensation for a particular amount of pain.[1]

Academicians have also debated whether pain and suffering awards can be justified on the basis of substitution and deterrence. The substitution argument is that the award permits the plaintiff to purchase an amount of happiness that is equal to the amount of pain he suffered. The deterrence argument is that absent the awarding of pain and suffering damages defendants would engage in inefficient, risky behavior because they would not have to account for some of the harm (pain and suffering) their behavior inflicted on others.[2]

Pain and suffering is subjective: one person bears pain stoicly; another is extremely sensitive to the least painful stimuli. Unlike other forms of bodily injury, which can be corroborated by either visible inspection or medical technology, such as an x-ray, pain and suffering is not as easily subject to scientific or physical proof. However, while pain and suffering may be difficult to verify, that does not mean pain is not suffered. The difficulty remains, nonetheless, in documenting the experiencing of pain and suffering, for otherwise the trier-of-fact is left with little guidance to distinguish real claims of pain and suffering from those that are feigned, fanciful, or exaggerated.

The consistent policy in the United States has been to include pain and suffering as a component of bodily injury claims. The reasons are several-fold notwithstanding the critique that pain and suffering awards do not restore. One justification is that the tortfeasor who causes bodily injury and its resultant pain and suffering should be made to know that his breach

---

[1] 72 F.3d 1003, 1009 (2d Cir. 1995) (brackets added). *Judgment vacated on other grounds sub nom.* Consorti v. Owens-Corning Fiberglass Corp., 518 U.S. 1031 (1996); *see* 2 STEIN ON PERSONAL INJURY DAMAGES § 8.8, at 8–19 (3d ed. 1997).

[2] Joseph H. King, *Pain and Suffering, Noneconomic Damages, and the Goals of Tort Law*, 57 S.M.U. L. Rev. 163, 164 (2004) (arguing that "pain and suffering damages cannot be justified in any thoughtful way when one unprepossessedly considers such damages in the context of the goals of tort law"); David W. Leebron, *Final Moments: Damages For Pain and Suffering Prior to Death*, 64 N.Y.U. L. Rev. 256, 271–88 (1989) (rejecting compensatory goal as justifying pain and suffering award, but arguing that pain and suffering awards may be justified by tort goal of deterrence; *i.e.*, to encourage certain behaviors on the part of defendants).

of care has caused harm. The tortfeasor should receive a sanction sufficient to encourage the tortfeasor to conform his conduct to socially approved behavior. This is the deterrence argument noted earlier.

A second justification is that the injured party should be provided with sufficient funds to purchase at least an imperfect substitute, e.g., the purchase of happiness equal to the pain and suffering the plaintiff has endured as a result of the tortious conduct. While the injured party cannot transfer the experiencing of pain and suffering to another, he can use the pain and suffering award to purchase happiness in the future to offset the pain and suffering sustained. The two accounts can be roughly balanced. When the ability to purchase happiness is in equilibrium with the pain and suffering sustained, it may be said that the plaintiff has been "restored" to the position he would have achieved, absent the tortious conduct. While the restoration is approximate, it is the best the legal system can do and preferable to the alternative of no compensation, which may be perceived as a windfall to the defendant. This is the substitution argument mentioned earlier.

Lastly, there is the justification that pain and suffering awards are viewed by the general population as necessary and required aspects of the tort compensation system.[3] The failure to recognize such awards might generate popular dissatisfaction to the extent that the legal system would be viewed as nonresponsive to the needs and expectations of the average citizen.

[73.1.1] Ability to Appreciate

Should pain and suffering awards be limited to those who have the capacity to consciously and knowingly experience pain and suffering? For example, if the plaintiff is comatose, should the plaintiff's bodily injury award include pain and suffering? Several courts have held that comatose plaintiffs should not.[4] For these courts, an award for pain and suffering requires that the plaintiff be able to consciously experience the pain and suffering. There is a concern in some of these cases that the award will not be used by the plaintiff, but by others, such as the plaintiff's heirs, and thus be a windfall to them. This concern appears sporadically. Courts have awarded pain and suffering damages notwithstanding that the plaintiff will not be able to use the award for his own benefit.[5]

---

[3] Professor King, in his critique of the awarding of pain and suffering for personal injury, traces the development and rise of this form of damages to the development and rise of jury trial as the dominant method of dispute resolution, King, *Pain & Suffering, supra*, 57 S.M.U. Rev. at 169 & n.39, aided and abetted by more effective lawyering. *Id.* at 170.

[4] McDougald v. Garber, 536 N.E.2d 372, 374 (N.Y. 1989) (rejecting an award for pain and suffering to a comatose plaintiff on the ground that under the conditions the award served no compensatory purpose); Gregory v. Carey, 791 P.2d 1329, 1336 (Kan. 1990) (same); Stratis v. Eastern Airlines, Inc., 682 F.2d 406, 415 (2d Cir. 1982) (finding $1.2 million pain and suffering award for forty-two day stay at hospital (when the plaintiff was in a burn unit being treated for his injuries) to be excessive because the plaintiff became quadriplegic on the fourth day of his stay at the hospital and was unable to feel pain after that date).

[5] Rufino v. United States, 829 F.2d 354, 362 (2d Cir. 1987); Flannery v. United States, 297 S.E.2d 433, 438 (W. Va. 1981).

A significant number of courts have allowed the award of pain and suffering damages to comatose plaintiffs, albeit with some limitations and qualifications. Several justifications have been offered. First, a comatose victim suffers loss of enjoyment of life up to the date of her death. Some courts hold that this component of pain and suffering does not require conscious awareness.[6] Second, if the victim experienced pain and suffering before becoming comatose, a court may presume the situation continued.[7] Third, if the verdict does not distinguish between economic and non-economic damages, and the total award does not "shock the conscience" or otherwise evidence that in its totality the verdict is excessive, the court may uphold the whole verdict even though a component consists of the award of pain and suffering to a comatose plaintiff.[8]

Courts that permit plaintiffs to recover pain and suffering during a period in which they are comatose view the issue as one of legal entitlement, perhaps coupled with a skepticism over the limits of human knowledge and the direction decision making should be required to take when confronting such limits. For example, there are degrees of unconsciousness a comatose plaintiff may experience.[9] Courts requiring "awareness" as a condition for

---

[6] Holston v. Sisters of the Third Order of St. Francis, 618 N.E.2d 334, 337 (Ill. App. 1993), *aff'd on other grounds*, 650 N.E.2d 985, 996 (Ill. 1995); Eyoma v. Falco, 589 A.2d 653, 661–62 (N.J. Super. Ct. A.D. 1991). *But see McDougald, supra*, 536 N.E.2d at 374 (rejecting view that unconscious person may experience loss of enjoyment of life).

[7] *Holston, supra*:

> Defendant claims that most or all of the pain that Holston felt following her abdominal surgery was the expected discomfort following such surgery, and thus not compensable as being caused by defendant's negligence. After Holston lost consciousness, according to defendant, she could feel no further pain. Similarly, she was unable to appreciate her diminished brain functioning and disfigurement. Therefore, defendant argues, the jury's award of damages to Holston for her conscious pain and suffering and for disability and disfigurement was based on speculation.

> The appellate court in the case at bar stated that "the reasonable inference from the evidence of increasing pressure on the heart, rising pulse rate, and declining blood pressure was that decedent suffered more than she would have in a normal post-operative course. As award for decedent's suffering was appropriate. "We agree. The issue of Holston's physical pain and accompanying mental anguish was not limited to the period of time in which she may have lapsed into unconsciousness while she was receiving open heart surgery without an anesthetic. The evidence of her pain and suffering includes the time preceding the emergency surgery, when the pressure on her heart and respiratory system caused by the cardiac tamponade was building.

650 N.E.2d at 996 (citation omitted); Riser v. American Med. Intern'l, Inc., 620 So. 2d 372, 382 (La. App. 1993) (holding that $50,000 award for pain and suffering was not excessive for a victim who complained of pain for approximately 90 minutes before becoming comatose and dying 11 days later). The court noted that while comatose the victim stared at the ceiling, her tongue was ulcerated, her body jerked, and she made mumbling sounds. *Id.*

[8] Shaw v. United States, 741 F.2d 1202, 1208 (9th Cir. 1984) (applying Washington law).

[9] *See* Christian J. Borthwick, *The Permanent Vegetative State: Ethical Crux, Medical Fiction*, 12 Issues L. & Med. 167 (1996). This issue attained national attention in connection with efforts to end life support for Terry Schiavo. *In re* Schiavo, 780 So. 2d 176 (Fla. App. 2001); *see* Darren P. Mareiniss, M.D., *A Comparison of Cruzan and Schiavo: The Burden of Proof, Due Process, and Autonomy in the Persistently Vegetative Patient*, 26 J. Legal Med. 233 (2005).

recovery of pain and suffering do not require "appreciation" of the pain and suffering.[10] Courts have allowed pain and suffering claims on behalf of plaintiffs in a persistent, vegetative state based on evidence that the comatose person responded to stimuli.[11] In some cases the evidence of "awareness" has been rather slight and evocative.[12] In *Holston v. Sisters of Third Order of St. Francis* the Illinois Supreme Court upheld a pain and suffering award in favor of a comatose patient based on "the reasonable inference from the evidence of increased pressure on the heart, rising pulse rate, and declining blood pressure was that decedent suffered more than she would have in a normal post-operative course . . . ."[13] There are accounts of comatose patient's brains "lighting up" when shown photographs of familiar faces notwithstanding the lack of conscious brain activity.[14] Courts may well doubt their ability to know what the comatose plaintiff experiences and at what level a comatose person experiences sensitivity to external stimuli. Responses to this problem may simply reflect the court's confidence, misplaced or not, that triers-of-fact can know and distinguish between a person who is unable to experience pain and suffering from one who is simply unable to respond visibly to pain and to communicate his suffering to others.

Similarly situated with comatose plaintiffs are infants and those who are mentally or developmentally disabled. These individuals may be seen as unable to experience pain and suffering as does a normal adult or as unable to communicate their experiences as effectively as a normal adult. The characterization adopted will influence the willingness to award pain and suffering damages. The fairly consistent approach of courts, however, is to permit infants and the disabled to recover for pain and suffering.[15] The inability to verbalize a painful experience will not preclude a pain and suffering recovery; the necessary evidence may be provided by lay percipient witnesses and expert witnesses.[16]

---

[10] Ledogar v. Giordano, 505 N.Y.S.2d 899, 903 (App. Dept. 1986).

[11] Walsh v. Staten Island Obstetrics, 598 N.Y.S.2d 17, 19 (App. Dept. 1993) (finding that comatose 8 year old child who responded to stimuli had sufficient "awareness" to support $650,000 pain and suffering award).

[12] Cotilletta v. Tepedino, 573 N.Y.S.2d 396, 397 (Sup. Ct. 1991) (holding that lay testimony that victim-plaintiff was aware of her environment was sufficient to raise triable issue of fact notwithstanding expert medical opinion evidence that victim was in a deep comatose state from the time she was placed under anesthesia until her death).

[13] 650 N.E.2d at 996 (*quoting* underlying court of appeal opinion (citation omitted)); *see* note 7, *supra.*

[14] Frank Tallis, Hidden Minds: A History of the Unconscious (2002).

[15] Capelouto v. Kaiser Foundation Hosps., 500 P.2d 880, 884 (Cal. 1972) (holding that an infant could recover damages for pain and suffering on the same basis as an adult: "the inarticulate anguish of the infant serves as much a ground for recovery as the adult's most sophisticated description"); *see* Saguid v. Kingston Hosp., 623 N.Y.S.2d 341, 344 (App. Dept. 1995) (holding that a pain and suffering claim may be asserted by a new born infant); *cf.* Note, *The Science, Law, and Politics of Fetal Pain Legislation,* 115 Harv. L. Rev. 2010, 2010–15 (2002) (discussing debate whether a "fetus" can feel pain).

[16] *Capelouto, supra,* 500 P.2d at 885.

[73.1.2] Calculation of Award

The subjectivity surrounding pain and suffering awards leads courts to adopt a largely passive role and commit substantial discretion to the jury to reach an appropriate award under the circumstances. As noted by one court:

> [T]here is no definite and satisfactory rule to measure compensation for pain and suffering; the amount of damages must depend on the circumstances of each particular case. [C]ompensation for pain and suffering must be left to the sound discretion of the jury and the conclusion reached by it should not be disturbed unless the award is clearly excessive.[17]

Generally, the jury may infer the existence of pain and suffering from the nature of plaintiff's injuries, and this process may be abetted by lay testimony. Occasionally, however, a court will insist that plaintiff produce expert testimony, although this requirement is normally reserved for cases when the plaintiff's claim is unique.[18] The pain and suffering award must be individual to each plaintiff. Evidence of other awards to similarly situated individuals are not allowed, although such awards are used to "value" the case for settlement purposes and by the court to assess whether the award is excessive. Interestingly, other jurisdictions do permit juror consideration of comparative awards to reportedly good effect in reducing verdict variability.[19]

[73.1.3] Excessiveness

There has traditionally been no set standard for determining whether a pain and suffering award is excessive. The initial determination is committed to the trier-of-fact, and subsequent review is largely deferential. The length and intensity of the pain and suffering are of obvious significance. While there is no consensus as to when a verdict or award is excessive in the particular case, there does tend to develop, however, a general sense as to what the uppermost limit is for even the more horrific of injuries.[20] This "limit" is dynamic rather than static. The decided trend

---

[17] Advocat, Inc. v. Sauer, 111 S.W.3d 346, 354 (Ark. 2003) (citation omitted), *cert. denied*, 540 U.S. 1012 (2003); *see* Albrecht v. Metro Area Ambulance, 623 N.W.2d 367, 371 (N.D. 2001).

[18] *Compare* Roling v. Daily, 596 N.W.2d 72 (Iowa 1999) (holding that expert testimony was required to establish emotional damages resulting from vehicle collision in which plaintiff sustained moderate bodily injuries but his wife died and the distress claim was tied to the suffering and distress plaintiff experience as a result of his wife's death), *with* Larsen v. Pacesetter Sys., Inc., 837 P.2d 1273, 1295 (Haw. 1992) (stating that pain and suffering would be objectively obvious when plaintiff suffered "loss of limbs, sensory organs, or has been crippled or seriously disfigured," but if plaintiff's claims were subjective and not obvious, expert testimony may be required). Section 12.2.3 ([Non-economic Damages] Quality of the Evidence).

[19] Charles D. Cole, Jr., *Charging The Jury on Damages in Personal-Injury Cases: How New York Can Benefit From The English Practice*, 31 Syracuse J. Int'l L. & Com. 1, 14–18 (2004) (discussing English practice of permitting jurors to consider evidence of comparable awards for guidance).

[20] Trevino v. United States, 804 F.2d 1512, 1515 (9th Cir. 1986) (finding that $1 million

over the past several decades has been an upward ratcheting of the amount courts will treat as the uppermost limit of a pain and suffering award. For example, more recently than the decisions cited in footnote 20, which are from the mid-1980s, courts have awarded amounts significantly in excess of $1 million for pain and suffering.[21] These decisions are from the 1990s. More recently still, decisions from the late 1990s to the present have seen an additional increase.[22] Perhaps because pain and suffering, unlike emotional distress, is tied to actual physical injury, high pain and suffering awards appear to better withstand judicial scrutiny for excessiveness than pure distress awards.

A number of courts have addressed the extent to which the parties may attempt to objectify the pain and suffering award through the use of per diem arguments and the like. These are discussed in Section 12.2.2 ([Non-economic Damages] Discretion of the Decision Maker).

The general view is that awards for future pain and suffering do not have to be discounted to present value. While the award technically fits the criterion for discounting because the award is made before the harm is actually incurred, the view is that the pain and suffering award is not sufficiently concrete to warrant discounting. The belief seems to be that the trier-of-fact probably values future pain less than current or past pain; thus, a discounting of sorts has already taken place. This conclusion

---

was the maximum that could be awarded for pain and suffering to child born severely disabled with cerebral palsy that involved all four extremities, seizure disorders, and brain damage), *cert. denied,* 484 U.S. 816 (1987); Sosa v. M/V Lago Izabal, 736 F.2d 1028, 1035 (5th Cir. 1984) (finding that $1 million was uppermost that could be awarded for pain and suffering to plaintiff who was burned over 80% of his body).

[21] *In re* Joint E. and S. Dist. Asbestos Litig., 9 F. Supp. 2d 307, 317–19 (S.D.N.Y. 1998) (holding that $5 million award for plaintiff who endured 32 months of suffering caused by pleural mesothelioma resulting from exposure to asbestos was not excessive); Pantaleo v. Our Lady of the Resurrection Med. Ctr., 696 N.E.2d 717, 725–26 (Ill. App. 1998) (affirming as not excessive $1.6 million pain and suffering award in survival action based on 26 hours of suffering due to toxic shock syndrome prior to decedent's death); Bermeo v. Atakent, 671 N.Y.S.2d 727, 731 (App. Dept. 1998) (awarding $4.75 million for the past and future pain and suffering of a patient suffering hypoxic brain damage resulting from inadequate oxygen supply to the brain and acidosis during the plaintiff's premature birth); *In re* Asbestos Litig., 986 F. Supp. 761, 769–70 (S.D.N.Y. 1997) (finding that $2.6 million pain and suffering award was not excessive); Albert v. Paper Calmenson & Co., 515 N.W.2d 59, 66 (Minn. App.), *modified on other grounds,* 524 N.W.2d 460 (Minn. 1994) (holding that $2 million pain and suffering award for past and future injury was not excessive); *cf.* Ruiz Troche v. Pepsi Cola of Puerto Rico Bottling Co., 177 F.R.D. 82, 91 (D.P.R. 1997) (finding that $6 million award for pain and suffering of parents who lost their three minor children in a motor vehicle collision was not excessive).

[22] *Advocat, Inc., supra,* 111 S.W.3d 346 (reducing $15 million pain and suffering award to $5 million); Epping v. Commonwealth Edison Co., 734 N.E.2d 916 (Ill. App. 2000) (affirming $9 million pain and suffering award); Smith v. Ingersoll-Rand Co., 214 F.3d 1235 (10th Cir. 2000) (affirming $7 million pain and suffering award); Virginia Elec. And Power Co. v. Dungee, 520 S.E.2d 164 (Va. 1999) (affirming $20 million pain and suffering award); Olin Corp. v. Smith, 990 S.W.2d 789 (Tex. Civ. App. 1999) (affirming $5.58 million pain and suffering award); *cf.* Fertile v. St. Michael's Med. Ctr., 779 A.2d 1078 (N.J. 2001) (holding that $15 million pain and suffering was excessive, but that trial court remittitur to $5 million was not excessive); Section 8.2 (Excessiveness).

regarding the jury's approach to measuring pain and suffering is, of course, equal parts intuition and speculation; nevertheless, the subjective nature of the process by which the decision maker reaches its pain and suffering figure renders the award ill-suited for further adjustments by discounting to present value.[23] When pain and suffering awards are subject to a damages cap, one court has held that the cap should be applied prior to discounting.[24]

Under the Federal Tort Claims Act, the recovery of pain and suffering damages is determined by its availability under state law.[25]

[73.2] Loss of Enjoyment of Life

Loss of enjoyment of life refers to the plaintiff's inability, as a result of her injuries, to engage in life's pleasures, such as participating in sporting activities, walking, hiking, etc. As used here, the term should be distinguished from what is commonly referred to as "hedonic" damages,[26] although the distinction is not always adhered to by courts.[27] Loss of enjoyment of life refers to the loss of the capacity to enjoy and share in the amenities or pleasures of life as a result of the injuries sustained. A plaintiff paralyzed as a result of defendant's negligence will sustain not only pain and suffering as a result of his injuries, but his impaired mobility will prevent him, or at least make more difficult, his ability to engage in the everyday, normal personal and social activities of life.[28] Losses associated with sensory deprivation, such as injuries resulting in loss of touch, smell or hearing, also fall into this category.[29] A plaintiff will often attempt to communicate this loss to the trier of fact through the use of "A Day in the

---

[23] Friedman v. C&S Car Serv., 527 A.2d 871, 873–74 (N.J. 1987). The primary dissenter has been the Second Circuit. Oliveri v. Delta Steamship Lines, Inc., 849 F.2d 742, 751 (2d Cir. 1988) (stating that the court might reject discounting were it writing on a clear slate but the precedent that it discount was binding). The court did note that the discounting need not be as formal or as detailed as with respect to future lost earnings. Section 9.3 (Discounting to Present Value).

[24] Youngblood v. Sec'y of Dept. of Health, 32 F.3d 552 (Fed. Cir. 1994) (relying on language of the statute).

[25] Molzof v. United States, 502 U.S. 301 (1992).

[26] Section 73.4 (Hedonic Damages).

[27] Lewis v. Alfa Laval Separation Co., 714 N.E.2d 426, 433–38 (Ohio App. 1998) (permitting expert witness to base opinion on value of plaintiff's loss of enjoyment of life claim based on "willingness to pay"—an approach commonly used in "hedonic damages" calculations).

[28] See David Baldus, John McQueen & George Woodworth, *Improving Judicial Oversight of Jury Damages Assessments: A Proposal for the Comparative Additur/Remittur Review of Awards For Nonpecuniary Harms and Punitive Damages*, 80 Iowa L. Rev. 1109, 1236–37 (1995) (defining "loss of enjoyment of life" as including lifestyle limitations due to the injury preventing the plaintiff from participating in personal entertainment or recreational activities and impairing the plaintiff's ability to make and have friends, engage in sexual activity. etc.).

[29] Musick v. United States, 781 F. Supp. 445, 452 (W.D. Va. 1991) (involving loss of hearing and smell); Huff v. Tracy, 129 Cal. Rptr. 551, 553 (Cal. App. 1976) (involving injury to and impairment of sense of taste); Daugherty v. Erie R.R. Co., 169 A.2d 549, 552–53 (Pa. 1961) (involving injury to and impairment of senses of taste and smell).

Life" film which seeks to show how plaintiff's injuries have affected his daily, normal routines.[30]

Jurisdictions have adopted several positions regarding the recovery of loss of enjoyment of life damages. Some jurisdictions purport to reject this recovery altogether, but it is unclear how strongly this view is really held. The great majority of jurisdictions have responded favorably to allowing recovery for loss of enjoyment of life, although the enthusiasm of the embrace varies. Some of these jurisdictions suggest loss of enjoyment recoveries are limited to permanent, disabling injuries. Most jurisdictions, however, impose no such constraint. The major disagreement is whether the award of loss of enjoyment damages should be treated as part of the pain and suffering award or as an independent and separate recovery.

The slight majority position is to classify loss of enjoyment of life as a component of the pain and suffering award.[31] According to one survey approximately 19 jurisdictions include loss of enjoyment as a component of pain and suffering, approximately 16 allow it to be awarded separately, and approximately 11 allow for its consideration without taking a position whether it is included or separate from the pain and suffering award.[32] Separating loss of enjoyment of life from pain and suffering may lead to larger aggregate awards.[33]

An award for loss of enjoyment of life may depend on the plaintiffs' capacity to perceive and appreciate the curtailment of their active life. On this point, the jurisdictions are divided.[34]

When loss of enjoyment of life damages are permitted, the plaintiff's loss is measured by his actual impairment, not a hypothetical "good life" or a sanitized life. While the plaintiff may present the positive aspects of his

---

[30] Schiavo v. Owens-Corning Fiberglas Corp., 660 A.2d 515, 518 (N.J. Super. Ct. A.D. 1995) (permitting use of properly authenticated "Day in the Life" film when admission would aid the jury in understanding the nature and scope of plaintiff's injuries); Jones v. City of Los Angeles, 24 Cal. Rptr.2d 528, 530–33 (Cal App. 1993) (permitting use of "Day in the Life" film as long as film was relevant, not unduly prejudicial, nor cumulative of other evidence); Wagner v. York Hosp., 608 A.2d 496, 499–501 (Pa. Super. Ct. 1992) (permitting use of film that accurately portrayed plaintiff's daily experiences as a result of his injuries).

[31] *McDougald, supra*, 536 N.E.2d at 375–76 (collecting decisions holding that loss of enjoyment of life is a component of pain and suffering by treating the loss as a form of anguish over the inability to participate in life's pleasures); *see* Golden Eagle Archery, Inc. v. Jackson, 116 S.W.3d 757, 767 (Tex. 2003) (collecting decisions and describing single award as majority approach). *See generally* Annotation, *Loss of Enjoyment of Life As a Distinct Element or Factor in Awarding Damages for Bodily Injury*, 34 A.L.R.4th 293 § 3-4 (1981).

[32] *See* Michael Brookshire & Stan Smith, *Economic/Hedonic Damages: The Practice Book for Plaintiff and Defense Attorneys* 239 (1990).

[33] *See* Susan Poser, Brian H. Bornstein & E. Kiernan McGorty, *Measuring Damages for Lost Enjoyment of Life: The View From the Bench and the Jury Box*, 27 Law & Hum. Behv. 53 (2003) (reporting that larger verdicts were awarded by mock jurors who were specifically instructed on the topic of loss of enjoyment of life and who made separate awards for loss of enjoyment and pain and suffering).

[34] Ocasio v. Amtrak, 690 A.2d 682, 691 & n6 (N.J. Super. A.D. 1997) (noting split and collecting decisions); Section 73.1.1 ([Pain and Suffering]) Ability to Appreciate).

pre-injury lifestyle, the defendant may balance the portrayal by demonstrating, subject to undue prejudice considerations, the negative aspects of plaintiff's pre-injury lifestyle in order to show that, as a whole, there has been no loss of enjoyment.[35]

[73.3] Disfigurement

To disfigure means to make less complete, perfect, or beautiful in appearance or character. An injury may leave the plaintiff disfigured in this sense, for example, through an amputation of a limb, scar, or burn. It has been noted that this definition is but a beginning, not an end.[36] Courts have split whether the award for disfigurement is part of or separate from the general award for pain and suffering.[37] There is occasionally an inference or suggestion in the cases that the plaintiff must subjectively and negatively react to his disfigurement.[38] When expressly addressed, however, that suggestion or inference is rejected,[39] although the plaintiff's reaction to his disfigurement may influence the award.[40]

[73.4] Hedonic Damages

A number of commentators have discussed whether a plaintiff should be allowed to recover for the loss of life qua life.[41] This specific form of "loss

---

[35] *Ocasio, supra* (involving plaintiff's prior drug addition). The court noted:

> In sum, we conclude that a jury assigned the responsibility of determining the value of a loss of enjoyment of life should have had the opportunity to consider evidence that the Ocasio's mental and physical functions, customary activities and capacity to enjoy the pleasures of life were already restricted by a long-term addiction to drugs. Therefore, the trial court committed reversible error by allowing plaintiffs to paint a positive portrait of Ocasio's life while precluding defendants from presenting any evidence of its unpleasant and self-destructive aspects.

690 A.2d at 692; *see* Liimata v. Vest, 45 P.3d 310, 313–14 (Alaska 2002) (following *Ocasio*).

[36] Jones v. Wal-Mart Stores, Inc., 870 F.2d 982, 991 (5th Cir. 1989).

[37] *Compare* Preston v. Dupont, 35 P.3d 433, 441–42 (Colo. 2001) (noting that Colorado's general damages statute expressly provides that nothing in that statute shall be construed to limit the recovery for "disfigurement" and that provision controls pain and suffering damages cap in separate state medical malpractice legislation), *with* Smith v. Juneau, 692 So. 2d 1365, 1385 (La. App. 1997) (holding that "disfigurement and scarring has [sic] as an integral part of their substance the mental pain and anguish that accompany such disfigurement and scarring" and therefore separate awards would represent a duplicative recovery).

[38] Judd v. Rowley's Cherry Hill Orchards, Inc., 611 P.2d 1216, 1221 (Utah 1980) (stating that the pain and suffering award includes "humiliation and embarrassment resulting from the permanent scars and disability").

[39] *Jones, supra*, 870 F.2d at 991–92.

[40] *See* Neil Vidmar & Jeffrey Rice, *Assessments of NonEconomic Damage Awards in Medical Negligence: A Comparison of Jurors with Legal Professionals,* 78 Iowa L. Rev. 883, 894 (1993) (noting the positive correlation between the juror's total award and the pain and suffering award when jurors believed the scar truly embarrassed the plaintiff).

[41] *See* Andrew McClurg, *It's a Wonderful Life: The Case for Hedonic Damages in Wrongful Death Cases,* 66 Notre Dame L. Rev. 57 (1990).

of enjoyment of life" is usually referred to a "hedonic" damages[42] and is often tied to Adam Smith's view of human capital as a measure of one's life worth.[43]

American courts have in general rejected claims that loss of life, as opposed to impairment of the ability to enjoy life *while alive,* is compensable by damages.[44]

The one American court to explicitly accept this form of the hedonic damages concept is *Sherrod v. Berry,*[45] a decision that ultimately was reversed on other grounds by an *en banc* decision of the Seventh Circuit;[46] consequently, the trial court's position on hedonic damages was not addressed. The near unanimous position of other courts has been to reject the concept of hedonic damages.[47]

Much of the confusion in this area reflects the dual use of the term "hedonic damages" in related, yet distinct, contexts. When "hedonic damages" measures the value of life itself, it is rarely recognized. It is this usage of "hedonic damages" that is considered in this Section. "Hedonic damages" is also used to refer to the element of loss of enjoyment of life, a subset of pain and suffering, that is discussed in Section 73.2 (Loss of Enjoyment of Life). In that latter context, the recovery of "hedonic damages," as reflecting loss of life's enjoyment and pleasures, rather than life itself, is more generally accepted.

The reluctance to award damages for the value of life itself has been shaped by several factors. First, hedonic damages are seen as largely speculative and conjectural. Life's intrinsic value, it is said, makes it incommensurable.[48] Of course, life is priceless from an emotional or philosophical viewpoint; from an economic viewpoint, life's value is measurable. The primary methodology used is market risk surveys.[49] Market risk

---

[42] Loth v. Truck-A-Way Corp., 70 Cal. Rptr. 2d 571, 573, n.1 (Cal. App. 1998) (noting that the term "[h]edonic damages derives its name from the Greek word 'hedonikos' meaning pleasure or pleasurable. As interpreted by the courts around the United States, hedonic damages means either a loss of enjoyment of life or loss of life's pleasures") (citations omitted).

[43] *See* Ted R. Miller, *Willingness to Pay Comes of Age: Will the System Survive?*, 83 Nw. U. L. Rev. 876, 876–77 (1989).

[44] Willinger v. Mercy Catholic Med. Ctr., 393 A.2d 1188 (Pa. 1978):

> Unlike one who is permanently injured, one who dies as a result of injuries is not condemned to watch life's amenities pass by. Unless we are to equate loss of life's pleasures with loss of life itself, we must view it as something that is compensable only for a living plaintiff who has suffered from that loss.

Id. at 1191; Kemp v. Pfizer, Inc., 947 F. Supp. 1139, 1146 n.10 (E.D. Mich. 1996) (stating that "twenty-one cases in sixteen states, as well as three cases arising under federal law, have held that hedonic damages are not available in wrongful death actions" and collecting decisions).

[45] 629 F. Supp. 159 (N.D. Ill. 1985).

[46] 856 F.2d 802 (7th Cir. 1988) (en banc).

[47] *See* Reuben Slesinger, *The Demise of Hedonic Damages, in Tort Litigation,* 6 J. Legal Econ. 17 20–22 (1996) (collecting decisions).

[48] *See McClurg, supra,* 66 Notre Dame L. Rev. at 58 (noting that "life is priceless").

[49] *See* W. Kip Viscusi, *The Value of Risks to Life and Health,* 31 J. Econ. Lit. 1912 (1993) (surveying market risk studies and stating that estimates fall within range of $3–$7 million).

surveys are based on inferences as to how individuals adjust their wage demands to reflect the risk of death or serious bodily injury. For example, if an added assignment would increase risk by 1/100,000 and the average worker would demand an additional $50 as hazardous duty pay, then the inference drawn is that workers value their lives at $5 million ($50 divided by 1/100,000). This approach relies on assumptions of rationality, cognition, and freedom of choice that may be unjustified in fact.[50]

Second, notwithstanding the "market risk" approach, hedonic damages are perceived as non-economic and thus run counter to the legal system's general preference for limiting damages to events having definite economic consequences.[51] The exception for pain and suffering awards is not extended.

Third, although a few courts have permitted the recovery of hedonic damages in wrongful death cases, those decisions appear to be strongly influenced by the language of the jurisdiction's wrongful death statute rather than an appreciation and acceptance of the concept of hedonic damages.[52]

A somewhat broader attack on the concept of hedonic damages has been the refusal of some courts to permit testimony on the issue.[53] The attack is broader because it has been applied to the traditional loss of enjoyment of life cases when the plaintiff has survived his injuries.[54]

A related concept to damages for loss of life itself is damages for a shortening of life expectancy. Should a plaintiff recover damages if his life expectancy is shortened from 50 years, (plaintiff aged 25 would expect to live to age 75), to 20 years, (plaintiff age 25 can now expect to live to age 45), as a result of defendant's wrongdoing? Is the lost 30 years of life expectancy recoverable as damages? The general rule in the United States has been to reject such claims for much the same reasons courts reject

---

[50] *See* Joanne Linnerooth, *The Value of Human Life: A Review of the Models*, 17 Economic Injury 52 (1979). A more recent critique emphasizes the uncertainty of the economic projections that underlie the "willingness to pay" thesis. Victor E. Schwartz & Cary Silverman, *Hedonic Damages: The Rapidly Bubbling Cauldron*, 69 Brook L. Rev. 1037 (2004) (examining "hedonic damages" as a separate item of recovery and as part of the general pain and suffering loss of enjoyment of life category).

[51] *See* Brookshire & Smith, *Economic/Hedonic Damages, supra*, at 161 (noting that "[i]ntangible damages from profound injury have been difficult to quantify").

[52] Katsetos v. Nolan, 368 A.2d 172, 183 (Conn. 1976) (following provision in statute allowing for recovery of "just damages"); *see* Marcotte v. Timberlane/Hampstead Sch. Dist., 733 A.2d 394, 399 (N.H. 1999); Romero v. Byers, 872 P.2d 840, 845–47 (N.M. 1994); Montalve v. Lopez, 884 P.2d 345, 364 (Haw. 1994); *cf.* Durham v. Marberry, 156 S.W.3d 242 (Ark. 2004) (construing Arkansas survival statute to permit hedonic damages).

[53] Saia v. Sears Roebuck & Co., 47 F. Supp. 2d 141 (D. Mass. 1999) (finding that proposed expert testimony was not reliable); Ayers v. Robinson, 887 F. Supp. 1049, 1058–61 (N.D. Ill. 1995); *see* Joseph Kuiper, *The Courts, Daubert, and Willingness to Pay: The Doubtful Future of Hedonic Damages Testimony Under the Federal Rules of Evidence*, 1996 Univ. Ill. L. Rev. 1197.

[54] *Loth, supra*, 70 Cal. Rptr. 2d at 576–77.

"hedonic damages" for the loss of life itself, difficulty of measure and uncertainty over how to measure.[55]

This limitation on recoveries for shortened life expectancy applies to non-economic damages; economic damages for shortened life expectancy are customary.[56]

§ 74   LOSS OF CONSORTIUM

Historically, the action for loss of consortium protected the husband's property interest in his wife. As one court noted: "at common law the husband and wife were considered as one, and he was the one."[1] This male-centered view initially led many modern courts to reject all loss of consortium claims on the basis of gender discrimination.[2] That trend was soon corrected, however, and the modern trend is to permit both spouses to recover for loss of consortium.[3] A number of courts also permit children or parents or both to recover for loss of consortium resulting from injuries to the other, although the number is less than those that permit loss of consortium claims by spouses.[4]

When loss of consortium is recognized, it is based on the disruption of the protected relationship caused by the tortious conduct of a third party. While spousal and parental immunity has been abolished in most American jurisdictions, that development does not permit a loss of consortium claim when the disruption is caused by one of the parties to the protected relationship. The law protects the relationship from the acts of third parties, not from the acts of the parties themselves that disrupt their own relationship. This principle also extends to cases when the losses are caused by the spouse's, child's, or parent's comparative fault.[5]

---

[55] Morrison v. Stallworth, 326 S.E.2d 387, 393 (N.C. App. 1985); *cf.* Monias v. Endal, 623 A.2d 656, 660 (Md. 1993) (rejecting loss of services claim in loss of consortium claim for services that would not be provided due to victim's shortened life expectancy).

[56] Overly v. Ingalls Shipbuilding Inc., 87 Cal. Rptr. 2d 626, 631 (Cal. App. 1999); Section 71 (Lost Income).

[1] Acuff v. Schmit, 78 N.W.2d 480, 484 (Iowa 1956); see DuPont v. United States, 980 F. Supp. 192, 194 (S.D.W. Va. 1997) (discussing the historical development of loss of consortium claim); Hopson v. St. Mary's Hosp., 408 A.2d 260, 261–63 (Conn. 1979) (same).

[2] West v. City of San Diego, 353 P.2d 929, 934 (Cal. 1960) (declining to recognize husband's right to recover loss of consortium due to injuries to his wife because common law rule "was based upon the wife's subservient position in the marriage relationship whereas, under present day law, spouses are generally regarded as equals").

[3] Rodriguez v. Bethlehem Steel Corp., 525 P.2d 669, 673, 674 (Cal. 1974) (noting "dramatic reversal in the weight of authority on" the question whether the wife may recover for her loss of consortium due to her husband's injuries) (collecting decisions); see American Export Lines, Inc. v. Alvez, 446 U.S. 274, 284 n.11 (1980) (collecting decisions and noting that as of the date of the decision "[f]orty-one states and the District of Columbia allow recovery by a wife or couple" for loss of consortium).

[4] Section 74.3 (Parental and Filial Consortium).

[5] General Motors Corp. v. Doupnik, 1 F.3d 862, 866 (9th Cir. 1993) (noting that "a spouse does not have a legally cognizable duty of care to the other spouse regarding consortium").

The loss of spousal consortium claim today contains several elements. First, the claim recognizes the delicate and emotional elements of the relationship. These include love, solace, companionship, sexual relationships and procreation between spouses, and affection. The fact that these elements are non-economic has not deterred courts from recognizing that the trier-of-fact may award damages that substitute, as best as one can, for the intangible loss. Second, the loss of consortium claim permits the spouse to recover for the loss of services provided by the other spouse. These include assistance in maintaining the family home and caring for the children. In some jurisdictions, the two components are separately awarded as loss of consortium and loss of services damages.[6]

The fact that a spouse has been injured does not create a presumption that the other spouse has suffered a loss of consortium.[7] The other spouse must produce credible evidence that the injured spouse's condition had disrupted the marital relationship in either an emotional or economic context. The injury must also have occurred while the parties were married; a person cannot marry a cause of action.[8]

A jurisdiction's rules should be carefully reviewed when only the injured party brings suit to determine the extent to which a settlement or adjudication involving that party bars a subsequent loss of consortium claim by the injured party's spouse.[9]

[74.1] Loss of Services

The loss of consortium claim is commonly seen as compensation for non-economic losses, e.g., damage to companionship, love, etc.; however, the claim permits recovery of economic losses, here, loss of services. The recovery focuses on the economic value of the services the injured party

---

The court rejected the wife's efforts to recover for loss of consortium when her husband was found to 80% at fault for causing his quadriplegic condition, noting that "he is not a tortfeasor with respect to his wife's loss of consortium despite his own negligence in contributing to his quadriplegic condition." *Id.*; *see* Runcorn v. Shearer Lumber Prods., Inc., 690 P.2d 324, 329 (Idaho 1984) (reducing a spouse's loss of consortium award proportionally by the other spouse's comparative fault).

[6] Isern v. Watson, 942 S.W.2d 186, 197 (Tex. Civ. App. 1997).

[7] Seaman v. Wallace, 561 N.E.2d 1324, 1338–39 (Ill. App. 1990).

[8] Zwicker v. Altamont Emergency Room Physicians Medical Group, 118 Cal. Rptr.2d 912, 915 (Cal. App. 2002) (holding that wife who married her husband after he was injured could not maintain loss of consortium claim); Harris v. Sherman, 708 A.2d 1348, 1350 (Vt. 1998) (holding that the plaintiff who married her husband two months after the automobile accident that injured her husband could not maintain a loss of consortium action).

[9] *Buckley, supra*, 681 N.E.2d at 1290 (holding that a spouse who knowingly failed to prosecute loss of consortium claim was barred from doing so after the other spouse settled her bodily injury claim and released the defendant); *Hopson, supra*, 408 A.2d at 494 (holding that "because a consortium action is derivative of the injured spouse's cause of action, the consortium claim would be barred when the suit brought by the injured spouse has been terminated by settlement or by an adverse judgment on the merits"). *See generally* Michael Sullivan, Annot., *When Must Loss-of-Consortium Claim Be Joined With Underlying Personal Injury Claim*, 60 A.L.R.4th 1174 (1988).

provided to the holder of the consortium claim and which have not been provided because of the acts of the tortfeasor.

This loss of services recovery has ancient roots. It evolved out of the master's right to sue a tortfeasor who injured the master's servant and prevented the servant from providing services to the master. The recovery was recognized at common law,[10] but in the master-servant context it has atrophied of late.[11] Within the marital relationships and to a lesser extent within the family relationship,[12] however, the recovery of the economic value of the loss of services caused by the tortfeasor is alive and well.

The recovery of loss of services usually envisions the type of services the victim provides that would otherwise be purchased on the market, for example, housekeeping, transportation, instruction, etc.

The loss of services component of the loss of consortium claim can raise tricky issues of duplicatory recoveries because to some extent those same items may be included in the injured party's claim. For example, a husband may claim as part of his loss of consortium claim that he was unable to work because he had to care for his injured wife; the wife may claim, as her own damages, the reasonable value of the husband's services provided to her.[13] To award both would amount to a double recovery. The problem is resolved either by mandatory joinder of the loss of consortium claim to the injured party's claim or by requiring more specific delineation of the award to guard against double recovery.[14]

[74.2] Loss of Relationship

This aspect of the loss of consortium claim permits recovery for the non-economic attributes of the relationship that has been damaged by the

---

[10] PETER B. KUTNER & OSBORNE M. REYNOLDS, JR., ADVANCED TORTS 11–12 (2d ed. 1997).

[11] *Id.* at 230–34. The leading case here is *United States v. Standard Oil of California*, 332 U.S. 301 (1947), in which the Court refused to infer a right of action on the part of the United States to recover for economic losses (costs of hospitalization and pay) caused by defendant's negligence that injured a soldier). *See generally* Joel E. Smith, Annot., *Employer's Right of Action For Loss of Services or The Like Against Third Person For Tortiously Killing or Injurying Employee*, 4 A.L.R. 4th 504 (1981).

[12] Section 74.3 (Parental and Filial Consortium).

[13] *See generally* David Knotts, Annot., *Valuing Damages in Personal Injury Actions Awarded For Gratuitously Rendered Nursing and Medical Care*, 49 A.L.R.5th 685 (1997) (noting that many courts permit recovery against tortfeasors of reasonable value of nursing and medical services gratuitously provided the plaintiff by family members, relatives, or close friends). As for the husband's claim for economic losses resulting from his time off work, see Section 74.2 (Loss of Relationship).

[14] *Rodriguez, supra*, 525 P.2d at 683–85 (stating that the problem of a potential double recovery is easily abated by existing procedural safeguards); *cf.* Buckley v. National Freight, Inc., 681 N.E.2d 1287, 1290 (N.Y. 1997) (stating that whenever possible the loss of consortium claim should be asserted in the same action as the claim for bodily injury). *Buckley* collects decisions on this point noting a four-way split: some jurisdictions have a compulsory joinder rule; other jurisdictions encourage but do not mandate joinder; some jurisdictions permit the defendant to compel joinder; and a few jurisdictions suggest that joinder is only permissive. *Id.* at 1289–90.

tortfeasor. Loss of relationship damages usually include: (1) loss of sexual relationships between spouses; (2) loss of companionship, society, and guidance; (3) love and affection; and (4) solace and moral support.[15] The recovery largely parallels that of emotional distress.[16]

The loss of consortium claim is based on damage to a relationship and rights a party has in that relationship; consequently, economic loss sustained by the rightholder will not be recoverable under a loss of consortium claim. Economic claims in this area usually involve the spouse's loss of earnings caused by the need to care for the injured spouse. For example, in *Axen v. American Home Products Corp.* the court rejected a wife's economic loss claim that arose out of her decision to take early retirement to care for her injured husband.[17] As noted by the court:

> A careful review of case law in other jurisdictions reveals that the majority of courts have concluded that the only economic damages available to an uninjured spouse as part of a claim for loss of consortium are those damages incurred in replacing the material services and support previously provided by the injured spouse. A few jurisdictions have also included the reasonable cost of care provided to the injured spouse by the uninjured spouse, but the majority have followed the rule that those costs are more properly included in the injured spouse's claim. We need not decide whether Sandra Axen could recover the cost of providing care to her husband, however, because she sought only her lost income. On that claim, we adhere to the traditional rule and hold that lost income is not a proper subject of a damage award for loss of consortium.[18]

An example of the exception noted by the *Axen* court is *Biddle v. Griffin*.[19] In *Biddle* the husband had given up his job to care for his injured wife. The court permitted a recovery of the reasonable value of the services rendered to the wife in caring for her, subject to a cap of the husband's economic loss. This is consistent with the general rule that allows a party to recover from a tortfeasor the reasonable value of services gratuitously provided the injured victim.[20]

---

[15] Carlson v. Okerstrom, 675 N.W.2d 89, 111 (Neb. 2004); Black's Law Dictionary 304 (7th ed. 1999); *see* Lacy v. G.D. Searle & Co., 484 A.2d 527 (Del. Super. Ct. 1984):

> Generally, damages for loss of consortium damages encompass loss of society, companionship, affection, and sexual relations. However, damages are not limited to these claims and, in fact, involve many facets of the marital relationship. These include: aid, assistance, comfort, society, services, companionship, affection, fellowship, sexual relations, solace, conjugal life, all the assistance that accompanies the marriage relationship, love, physical and emotional support, contentment, satisfaction, and hopes and expectations relating to the marital existence.

Id. at 532 (citations omitted).

[16] Section 12.2 (Measuring Non-Economic Loss).

[17] 974 P.2d 224, 236–37 (Or. App. 1999), *cert. denied*, 528 U.S. 1136 (2000).

[18] *Id.* (footnote and citation omitted).

[19] 277 A.2d 691 (Del. Super. Ct. 1970).

[20] Section 15.3 (Gratuitous Benefits).

Loss of consortium may also involve increased obligations, such as increased care for the injured spouse and increased responsibility for the children.[21] Care must taken, however, not to confuse the non-economic aspects of these obligations, which are recoverable, from the economic aspects, which are either not recoverable[22] or are recoverable as part of the loss of services claim because the spouse is providing services that otherwise would have been provided by the injured spouse.[23]

[74.3] Parental and Filial Consortium

Most jurisdictions refuse to recognize loss of consortium claims for loss of parental consortium (claim by child[ren] for loss of relationship with parent(s)) or loss of filial consortium (claim by parent(s) for loss of relationship with child[ren]).[24]

With respect to loss of parental services (parental consortium claim), the award is generally limited to the period of the child's minority, which corresponds to the period the parent has a duty to support. In cases of handicapped or disabled children, the period for which loss of services may be recovered may be extended because the parental duty of support may extend into the period the disabled child is an adult.[25] The loss of parental consortium claim may also be limited by the requirement that the parent's injury be severely disabling.[26] The claim is further restricted to the relationship between parent and child; the loss of a stepparent or guardian will not suffice.[27]

---

[21] Kotta v. PPG Industries, Inc., 388 N.W.2d 160, 169 (Wis. 1986).

[22] *Axen, supra,* 974 P.2d 224.

[23] Section 74.1 (Loss of Services).

[24] Belcher v. Goin, 400 S.E.2d 830, 834 & n.5 (W. Va. 1990) (collecting decisions, observing that most states reject loss of parental consortium claims, but approving such recoveries in West Virginia).

[25] *Belcher, supra,* 400 S.E.2d at 841–42 (limiting loss of parental consortium claims to minor children or handicapped children of any age). *But see* Berger v. Weber, 303 N.W.2d 424, 427 (Mich. 1981) (rejecting limitation of loss of parental consortium to minor children of injured parent).

[26] Villareal v. State Dep't of Transp., 774 P.2d 213 (Ariz. 1989):

> Not all injuries to parents will result in a child's claim for loss of consortium. We limit our holding to allow loss of consortium claims only when the parent suffers serious, permanent, disabling injury rendering the parent unable to provide love, care, companionship, and guidance to the child. The parent's mental or physical impairment must be so overwhelming and severe that the parent-child relationship is destroyed or nearly destroyed. Hay, 145 Vt. at 537, 496 A.2d at 941 (parent rendered permanently comatose); Theama, 117 Wis. 2d at 514, 344 N.W.2d at 515 (father's permanent mental and physical injuries essentially deprived minor children of any further parent-child exchange).

Id. at 219 (citations in original).

[27] Ford Motor Co. v. Miles, 967 S.W.2d 377, 384 (Tex. 1998) (refusing to permit loss of consortium claim for injury to stepparent who assumed parental duties and relationship toward child).

A few jurisdictions recognize a cause of action for loss of filial consortium.[28] The action has been extended in some cases to injuries involving adult children.[29] The rationale for limiting claims to injuries to minor child is that at common law the father could sue tortfeasors for the loss of the minor child's services as a paid worker who could financially contribute to the maintenance of the household.[30] Repositioning the cause of action as protecting the parent-child relationship permits extending the action to the parents of injured adult children.[31] As in the loss of parental consortium cases, loss of filial consortium may be limited to claims involving severe or disabling injuries to the child.[32]

The vast disparity between acceptance of spousal consortium claims and the non-acceptance of parental and filial consortium claims cannot be grounded on foreseeability because a parent's or child's loss due to an injury to the other is no less foreseeable, nor less real and meaningful, than a spouse's loss when the other spouse is injured. Rather, the distinction is based on liability-limiting policies, namely, that a line must be drawn someplace and here seems to be a good spot.[33]

When a child or parent dies, many jurisdictions permit recovery of loss of companionship under the jurisdiction's wrongful death statute.[34]

---

[28] Mendillo v. Bd. of Educ. of Town of East Haddam, 717 A.2d 1177, 1182 n.10 (Conn. 1998) (collecting decisions). *See generally* Todd Symth, Annot., *Parent's Right to Recover For Loss of Consortium in Connection With Injury to Child,* 54 A.L.R.4th 112 (1988).

[29] Masaki v. General Motors Corp., 780 P.2d 566, 577–78 (Haw. 1989) (permitting action to be maintained for injury to adult child, but noting that majority of jurisdictions that recognize action for loss of filial consortium limit claims to injuries to minor children).

[30] Hall v. Hollander, 4 B. & C. 660, 107 Eng. Rep. 1206 (K.B. 1825); Section 74.1 (Loss of Services).

[31] *Masaki, supra,* 780 P.2d at 577:

> At common law, the child, like the wife, was relegated to the role of a servant and considered an economic asset to the family. In the modern family, however, children have become less of an economic asset and more of a financial burden to their parents. Today children are valued for their society and companionship. Thus, services have become only one element of the consortium action while the intangible elements of love, comfort, companionship, and society have emerged as the predominant focus of consortium actions.

(citations omitted).

[32]

> We find ourselves in agreement with those jurisdictions which have recognized that severe injury may have just a deleterious impact on filial consortium as death. These jurisdictions recognize that, in the case of a severely injured child, the quality of the parent-child relationship, as well as the parent's expectations of a normal family life, can be seriously impaired.

Id. (citations and footnote omitted).

[33] Sizemore v. Smock, 422 N.W.2d 666, 670 (Mich. 1988) (recognizing "that any attempt to draw a meaningful distinction on the basis of the sentimental aspects of the consortium claim . . . would be specious and unavoidably futile"). The court went on to state that the court must look beyond "logical analogies" and decide the matter on the basis of "public policy considerations and the social consequences of imposing yet another level of liability." *Id.*

[34] Section 75.2 (Wrongful Death Actions).

[74.4] Domestic Partners

At common law and in its modern revival, loss of spousal consortium claims could only be asserted by lawfully married spouses.[35] At least one court, however, has questioned this approach. In *Lozoya v. Sanchez* the New Mexico Supreme Court, the last court in the United States to recognize spousal loss of consortium claims[36] became the first state Supreme Court to recognize a loss of consortium claim by unmarried cohabitants.[37] Whether *Lozoya* will prove persuasive is unclear. One federal court refused to follow *Lozoya* as a predictor of how the State Supreme Court would resolve the issue of consortium claims by unmarried cohabitants.[38]

The general common law precludes loss of consortium claims by same-sex couples who are generally barred by state law from legally marrying. State "Domestic Partner" statutes may, however, change this result by extending the right to bring loss of consortium claims to registered partners.[39]

§ 75 REMEDIES WHEN THE PLAINTIFF DIES

At common law the death of either party abated many actions. Whether an action abated depended on the nature of the interest injured. If the interest to be protected was primarily a property interest, then the action survived the death of the plaintiff. If, on the other hand, the interest was primarily personal, it did not survive the plaintiff's death. Contract claims survived the plaintiff's death.[1] The rule was expressed in the latin maxim "action personalis moritur cum persona," which means a personal action dies with the person.[2] For purposes of personal injury actions, the death

---

[35] Schroeder v. Boeing Commercial Airplane Co., 712 F. Supp. 39 (D.N.J. 1989) (collecting decisions and concluding that the basic principle is well established that the absence of a legal marital relationship at the time of the loss precludes a loss of consortium claim).

[36] Romero v. Byers, 872 P.2d 840, 843 n.1 (N. Mex. 1994).

[37] 66 P.3d 948 (N. Mex. 2003):

> More convinced by the policies and rationale that favor recognizing the claim by unmarried cohabitants in certain circumstances, we conclude that the jury should have been allowed to consider Ms. Lozoya's claim.

[38] Robinson v. Hartzell Propeller, Inc., 276 F. Supp. 2d 412, 414 (E.D. Pa. 2003) (applying Pennsylvania law).

[39] *See* Vt. Stat. Ann. §§ 1204 (conferring on parties to a "civil union" all the same benefits, protections, and responsibilities under law that "are granted to spouses in a marriage"), 1204(e)(2) (including right to bring loss of consortium claim); Cal. Fam. Code § 297.5 (extending to same-sex registered domestic partners same rights, privileges, and protections as are afforded to spouses).

[1] Hambly v. Trott 98 Eng. Rep. 1136, 1138–39 (K.B. 1776) (distinguishing between contract actions and tort actions and distinguishing between torts by which property was acquired and those by which it was not); 3 WILLIAM BLACKSTONE, COMMENTARIES ON THE LAWS OF ENGLAND *302 (distinguishing between tort actions and contract actions); *see* Creighton v. Pope County, 54 N.E.2d 543, 547 (Ill. 1944) (distinguishing between property interests and personal interests).

[2] Percy Winfield, *Death As Affecting Liability in Tort,* 29 Colum. L. Rev. 239 (1929).

of the plaintiff resulted in the abatement and expiration of his cause of action for damages for bodily injury.[3] It made no difference whether or not the injury inflicted by the tortfeasor caused the plaintiff's death.[4]

The common law rule held sway until well into the twentieth century. England did not change its rule until 1934.[5] American States generally followed the English lead.[6] Compare this to the much earlier acceptance of wrongful death legislation to provide for the decedent's survivors.[7] The common law rule has now been changed in all American jurisdictions. The change has been accomplished by statutes that (1) provide for survival of the decedent's cause(s) of action (survival statutes) and (2) permit the assertion of claims for losses associated with the death of another (Wrongful Death Statutes). Survival statutes permit the decedent's estate to recover the decedent's pre-death damages. Wrongful Death statutes permit the decedent's survivors or his estate to recover for the losses sustained as a result of the decedent's death. The essential caveat to both situations, however, is that recovery is limited to the extent permitted by the statute.

[75.1] Survival Actions

Survival statutes change the common law rule by permitting the decedent's estate to maintain an action that had accrued during the decedent's lifetime. Survival statutes do not create causes of action; they merely maintain causes of action existing as of the date of the decedent's death.[8] The survival statute permits the decedent's representative to assert the decedent's pre-death claims,[9] subject to the limitation that damages must be confined to the pre-death period. The fact that the plaintiff while alive could have sued for his future losses related to his present injury does not permit the decedent's representative to do likewise. For example, the lost earnings award is measured by the decedent's earnings from the date of injury to the date of death, not to the date calculated by reference to the

---

[3] Ciarrocchi v. James Kane Co., 116 F. Supp. 848, 850 (D.D.C. 1953) (stating that "a personal right of action died with the person").

[4] Fidelity & Cas. Co. of N.Y. v. St. Paul Gas & Light Co., 188 N.W. 265, 265 (Minn. 1922).

[5] *See* Law Reform (Miscellaneous Provisions) Act of 1934, 24 & 25 Geo. 5, ch. 41, § 1(1).

[6] *E.g.*, California: Stats. 1949, Ch. 1380, § 2, p. 2400, codified at Civil Code § 956. The California provision is now at C.C.P. § 377.34. Survival actions are discussed at Section 75.1 (Survivial Actions).

[7] Lord Campbell's Act, 9 & 10 Vict., ch. 93 (1846). Wrongful death recoveries are discussed at Section 75.2 (Wrongful Death Actions).

[8] National Bank of Bloomington v. Norfolk & Western Ry. Co., 383 N.E.2d 919, 923 (Ill. 1978).

[9] Claims brought by persons other than personal representatives may be rejected. St. Paul Mercury Ins. Co. v. Circuit Court of Craighead County, 73 S.W.3d 584, 588 (Ark. 2002) (holding that *only* personal administrator of decedent's estate had standing to bring decedent's pre-death claim).

decedent's work-life expectancy.[10] Similarly, pain and suffering is limited to that experienced by the decedent prior to death.[11]

Initially, judicial interpretation of survival statutes tended to be restrictive, reflecting the dominance of the rule that statutes in derogation of the common law were strictly construed. The modern trend has been to apply survival statutes liberally.[12]

Survival statutes can provide a complex thicket as to which causes of action survive and which do not. Most significant is whether the statute is written expansively, *i.e.,* once the cause of action has accrued, the decedent's death does not cause the action to terminate, subject to stated exceptions, or whether the statute is written narrowly, *i.e.,* all causes of action expire with the death of the decedent except as expressly stated. It is common for survival statutes to preserve bodily injury claims, but not other personal injury claims, such as defamation or invasion of privacy. Since the statutory list is rarely exhaustive of potential causes of action, whether an unnamed cause of action survives is often a question of proper characterization. For example, in *Bryant v. Kroger Co.* the court characterized the decedent's loss of consortium claim as a type of personal property interest. As so characterized, the loss of consortium claim could be maintained post-death under Illinois's Survival statute.[13] The approach of characterization by analogy has been followed in other decisions involving such diverse causes of action as a decedent's claims for (1) professional malpractice,[14] (2) tortious interference,[15] and (3) economic support arising out of the wrongful death of another.[16]

Some survival statutes refer to "injuries to a person" or "personal injuries to a person." These statutes can present difficulties since the definitional phrases are subject to disparate interpretation. In *Allred v. Solaray, Inc.*

---

[10] Williamson v. Plant Insulation Co., 28 Cal. Rptr. 2d 751, 756 (Cal. App. 1994); *see* Miles v. Apex Marine Corp., 498 U.S. 19, 34–35, (1990) (holding that under general maritime law a survival action cannot include a recovery for decedent's lost future earnings because it would be duplicative of the award for loss of support in a wrongful death action); Jones v. Flood, 702 A.2d 440, 442 (Md. Sp. Ct. App. 1997), *aff'd,* 716 A.2d 285 (Md. 1998). The *Williamson* court did reserve the question whether the "loss of future earning capacity" was a loss that occurred during the decedent's lifetime, 28 Cal. Rptr. 2d at 756 n.5, but the distinction should be rejected. Section 9 (Future Losses).

[11] Wahlstrom v. Kawasaki Heavy Indus., Ltd., 4 F.3d 1084, 1093 (2d Cir. 1993), *cert. denied,* 510 U.S. 1114 (1994); Skoda v. West Penn Power Co., 191 A.2d 822, 829 (Pa. 1963). *See generally* 22 Am. Jur. 2d, *Damages* § 248.

[12] *E.g.,* McDaniel v. Bullard, 216 N.E.2d 140, 143 (Ill. 1966) (holding that the Illinois Survival statute "ought no longer be given . . . a narrow, technical construction").

[13] 570 N.E.2d 1209, 1213 (Ill. App. 1991).

[14] Nathan v. Touro Infirmary, 512 So. 2d 352, 354 (La. 1987). *But see* Hachmann v. Mayo Clinic, 150 F. Supp. 468, 469–70 (D. Minn. 1957) (holding that medical malpractice action did not survive plaintiff's death).

[15] Williams v. Palmer, 532 N.E.2d 1061, 1063–64 (Ill. App. 1988) (holding that tortious interference claim did survive the plaintiff's death).

[16] Katz v. Filandro, 739 P.2d 822, 827 (Ariz. 1987) (holding that loss of support claim did survive the death of a wrongful death beneficiary).

the decedent had prior to his death commenced litigation alleging workplace discrimination and the infliction of emotional distress. The applicable survival statute permitted survival of claims for "personal injuries to the person." The court noted that personal injury was not necessarily limited to bodily injuries; however, a claim of discrimination was deemed not to involve a claim of injury to the person, but an injury to rights or reputation; hence, it did not survive the plaintiff's death.[17]

When the plaintiff dies is also critical. In *Sullivan v. Delta Air Lines, Inc.*[18] the plaintiff sued for wrongful discharge and sought, among other remedies, recovery for emotional distress. Under California's Survival Statute, emotional distress damages do not survive the death of the plaintiff.[19] Plaintiff received a judgment for, among other things, emotional distress, but plaintiff died while defendant's appeal was pending. Defendant contended that since the proceedings were not final, plaintiff's death necessarily abated his emotional distress award. The court, relying on the common law rule, held that once the judgment was entered, plaintiff's subsequent death would not abate the award for emotional distress.[20]

The general rule is that an action for bodily injury does not survive when the injuries inflicted by the tortfeasor result in the victim's instantaneous death. In this situation, there are no pre-death damages.[21] There is, however, some contrary authority. In *Smith v. Whitaker* the New Jersey Supreme Court allowed the decedent's personal representation to assert a punitive damages claim even though the decedent had died instantaneously.[22] In *Koirala v. Thai Airways, Int'l Ltd.* the court held that "where

---

[17] 971 F. Supp. 1394, 1398 (D. Utah 1997) (applying Utah Survival statute). In *Reed v. Real Detective Pub. Co., Inc.*, 162 P.2d 133 (Ariz 1945) (involving a similarly worded survival statute), the court held that a defamation action involved injury to reputation, not to the person, and did not survive the death of the decedent. On the other hand, an action for invasion of privacy did involve personal injury because the wrong caused mental suffering to the plaintiff; consequently, the defamation claim was lost, but the privacy claim survived. *Id.* at 136–137. In *Camino v. New York News, Inc.*, 475 A.2d 528, 533 (N.J. 1984), the court held that a defamation action survived the death of the libelant based on New Jersey's survival statute, which allowed for survival of claims involving "trespass . . . to the person." *See generally* 1 C.J.S., *Abatement & Revival* § 141 (collecting decisions).

[18] 935 P.2d 781 (Cal. 1997).

[19] Such a limitation has been called "archaic" and the worst rule. Kuehn v. Childrens Hosp., Los Angeles, 119 F.3d 1296, 1302 (7th Cir. 1997) (Posner, J.). California is not alone in excluding pain and suffering awards from survivability. *See* Ariz. Rev. Stat. § 14-3110. The majority of states, however, disagree with this position and allow recovery of provable pre-death pain and suffering in a survival action.

[20] *Sullivan, supra,* 935 P.2d at 305 (concluding that amendment of the survival statute "did not abolish the common law rule that death after judgment does not abate any aspect of personal tort actions, including the right to recover damages for pain and suffering").

[21] Starkenburg v. State of Mont., 934 P.2d 1018, 1030–31 (Mont. 1997); Chapple v. Gangar, 851 F. Supp. 1481, 1486–87 (E.D. Wash. 1994) (stating that plaintiff must survive injuries resulting in his death for at least an appreciable measure of time for representatives to maintain a survival action for pre-death pain and suffering); Pease v. Beech Aircraft, 113 Cal. Rptr. 416, 422–23 (Cal. App. 1974).

[22] 734 A.2d 243 (N.J. 1999).

no wrongful death beneficiaries exist, the decedent's estate can receive an award of lost future earnings through a survival action even when in a case of virtual instantaneous death." The court reasoned that such a result better becomes the humane and liberal character of law, prevents the anomaly of a defendant being better off if his victim dies rather than simply being injured, and does not present a double recovery problem given the absence of a viable wrongful death action.[23]

If survival is required, how long the decedent must survive his injuries before he dies is unclear. As noted in *Ghotra v. Bandila Shipping, Inc.*:

> It is well-established that "pain and suffering substantially contemporaneous with death or mere incidents to it, as also the short periods of insensibility which sometimes intervene between fatal injuries and death, afford no basis for a separate estimation or award of damages" for predeath pain and suffering. Moreover, the Ninth Circuit has held that before a decedent's beneficiary may recover for the decedent's predeath pain and suffering, the beneficiary must show "that the decedent was conscious for at least some period of time after he suffered the injuries which resulted in his death." In *Ross Island Sand & Gravel*, this court stated that it would "not adopt a 'stop watch' approach to the question of whether a decedent remained conscious for a legally substantial period of time after he sustained the injuries," but that it would determine whether the decedent remained conscious for an "appreciable length of time" on a case by case basis.[24]

The case law in this area has been widely divergent. In *St Louis, Iron Mountain & S. Ry. Co. v. Craft* the Court stated that 30 minutes of consciousness after the decedent had been mortally injured in a railroad accident was "close to the borderline";[25] however, the decision is probably dated. More recently, courts have upheld substantial pre-death fright and distress awards when the period of consciousness was much less. For example, in *Bickel v. Korean Air Lines Co., Ltd.* the court upheld verdicts of $400,000, $1,350,000, and $1,000,000 for pre-death pain and suffering for three passengers who endured a 12 minute descent when their airplane was shot down after it intruded in the airspace of the former U.S.S.R.[26]

---

[23] 126 F.3d 1205, 1212 (9th Cir. 1997). *Koirala* may, however, have been implicitly overruled by *Dooley v. Korean Air Lines Co., Ltd.*, 524 U.S. 116 (1998) (holding that Death On the High Seas Act, 46 U.S.C. § 761 *et seq.* provides exclusive remedy for survivors and preempts survival claims under general Maritime law).

[24] 113 F.3d 1050, 1061 (9th Cir. 1997) (citations omitted) (concluding that the sole opinion evidence that the decedent was conscious for 10 seconds following his accident was insufficient to raise a triable issue of fact that the decedent was conscious and eligible to recover for his pre-death pain and suffering given the other evidence that he never regained consciousness after sustaining massive injuries from his accident), *cert. denied,* 522 U.S. 1107 (1988); Section 12.2.4 (Fear of Death).

[25] 237 U.S. 648, 655 (1915).

[26] 96 F.3d 151, 156 (6th Cir. 1996), *cert. denied,* 519 U.S. 1093 (1997).

In *Oldham v. Korean Air Lines Co., Ltd.* the court upheld awards of $100,000 to each of three passengers for their pre-death pain and suffering while in the same airplane as the *Bickel* plaintiffs![27] This well illustrates the subjectivity, and corresponding disparity, in awards of this nature. In *Wellborn v. Sears, Roebuck & Co.* the court affirmed a verdict of $1 million for pain and suffering for a boy who was trapped under a garage door for 3–5 minutes, according to the plaintiff's expert, before the boy died.[28] On the other hand, in *Randall v. Chevron, U.S.A.* the court reduced the pre-death pain and suffering award of a decedent, who suffered for approximately 25 minutes before he died, from $1 million to $500,000. The court distinguished *Wellborn* on the grounds that the decedent in *Wellborn* could have been trapped under the garage door for as long as several hours and the decedent was a child whereas in *Randall* the decedent was an adult.[29] In *Wall v. Progressive Barge Line, Inc.* the court upheld a $50,000 award for pre-death pain and suffering based on expert opinion testimony that the decedent was likely conscious for approximately 2 minutes before he drowned.[30]

[75.2] Wrongful Death Actions

The wrongful death action is to be distinguished from an action that survives the death of a person. As discussed in Section 75.1 (Survival Actions), when a person does not die instantaneously as a result of tortfeasor's wrong, that person's estate may possess a cause of action against the tortfeasor for damages sustained between the dates of injury and death. A wrongful death action, on the other hand, is a statutory action that matures on the death of the decedent and permits the holder(s) of the cause of action to recovery for the independent injury and loss resulting from the death of the decedent. Simply put, a survival action is the decedent's action, asserted by his estate for pre-death losses resulting from decedent's injuries; a wrongful death action is the statutory action for compensation for losses resulting from the death of the decedent.

There are two types of wrongful death statutes: loss to estate statutes and loss to survivors statutes. The differences are illustrated by the loss of support award. In the loss to estate approach, the decedent's work-life expectancy is determined. This figure is then multiplied by the decedent's projected earnings to estimate his lost earning capacity. The result is usually reduced to its present value by selecting the appropriate discount rate.[31] The focus is on what the decedent would have earned but for his death. In the loss to survivors approach, evidence is produced on the regular contributions made by the victim, while alive, to his or her survivors, such as parents, spouse, or children, and an estimate of this lifetime contribution

---

[27] 127 F.3d 43, 56–57 (D.C. Cir. 1997), *cert. denied,* 523 U.S. 1005 (1998).

[28] 970 F.2d 1420, 1428 (5th Cir. 1992).

[29] 13 F.3d 888, 901 (5th Cir. 1994), *modified on other grounds,* 22 F.3d 568 (5th Cir. 1994).

[30] 703 So. 2d 681, 690–92 (La. App. 1997).

[31] Section 9.3 (Discounting to Present Value).

is made, again normally subject to present value discounting. The focus is on what the survivors would have received but for the decedent's death. Under both approaches the decedent's lifetime earnings are reduced by the amount of money the decedent would have spent on himself during his lifetime, although this reduction is inherent in loss to survivors jurisdictions, but usually requires a statutory gloss in loss to estate jurisdictions. Both the loss to estate and loss to survivors approaches allow for the additional recovery of loss of society of the decedent and other economic losses as specified in the particular statutory plan.

Wrongful death actions date from 1846 with the passage of Lord Campbell's Act in England. [32] This statute changed the common law and provided that the survivors of a decedent would have a cause of action against persons responsible for the decedent's death. Lord Campbell's Act met with approval on this side of the Atlantic Ocean and most states enacted wrongful death statutes by the end of the nineteenth century. [33]

The consistent approach when interpreting wrongful death statutes has been to limit recoveries to pecuniary losses suffered by the survivors or the estate. [34] This approach has been adhered to even in the face of the rather strong argument that no pecuniary limitation was intended by the drafters of some of the original wrongful death statutes. [35] The limitation appears to be a product of the nineteenth and early twentieth century tendency to read narrowly statutes that altered or changed the common law, coupled with the weighty and consistent precedents that have developed on this point. The "pecuniary loss" requirement was an early construction of Lord Campbell's Act. [36] There is a modern willingness to permit hedonic damages and non-pecuniary recoveries, namely grief and sorrow experienced by the

---

[32] Lord Campbell's Act, 9&10 Vict., ch. 93 (1846); see Christopher Sprague, *Damages For Personal Injury and Loss of Life—The English Approach,* 72 Tul. L. Rev. 975 (1997).

[33] Farley v. Sartin, 466 S.E.2d 522, 525–26 (W. Va. 1995) (discussing development of wrongful death action in England and United States). Federal law also recognizes wrongful death actions under four theories. First, a federal statute that provides for personal injury recoveries, such as the Federal Employers Liability Act (FELA), 45 U.S.C.A. § 51 *et seq.,* also includes claims arising out of the death of a person covered by the Act. Second, federal law may create a specific wrongful death statute applicable to an area subject to federal law, such as the high seas. Death on the High Seas Act (DOSHA), 46 App. U.S.C.A. §§ 761–68. Third, the Supreme Court has recognized a common law basis for wrongful death actions under the general maritime law (Moragne v. Marine Lines, 398 U.S. 375 (1970), although this general action is subject to preemption to the extent a specific federal statute applies. Zicherman v. Korean Airlines Co., Ltd., 516 U.S. 217, 229 (1996) (noting that when specific federal statute applies (DOSHA) "neither state law, nor general maritime law can provide a basis for recovery . . ."). Lastly, federal law may mirror state law and provide a remedy consistent with state law when the injury is caused by a federal actor. Federal Tort Claims Act (discussed in Molzof v. United States, 502 U.S. 301 (1992)).

[34] *Zicherman, supra,* 516 U.S. at 224; Krouse v. Graham, 562 P.2d 1022, 1025 (Cal. 1977).

[35] *Krouse, supra,* 562 P.2d at 1025 (noting the removal of the term "pecuniary damages" from California's wrongful death statute and substitution of allowance of such damages as are "just" did not affect a change in the statute; recoveries were still limited to pecuniary losses).

[36] Blake v. Midland R. Co., 118 Eng. Rep. Reprint 35, 42 (Q.B. 1852).

survivors over the death of the decedent, but the willingness is presently confined to a few states that have modified their wrongful death statutes to permit such awards.[37] The general rule remains that wrongful death recoveries are limited to pecuniary losses, although in some jurisdictions the pecuniary loss requirement has been liberally and generously applied to include loss of society and companionship.[38]

In a wrongful death action the following items may be recoverable depending on the specific wrongful death statute in the jurisdiction:[39]

Loss of Support. This item consists of the contributions by the decedent that would have been made available during the life of the decedent to the wrongful death plaintiffs. This calculation usually reflects a deduction for the amount of money the decedent would have spent on his own needs and wants since those monies would not have been available for the plaintiffs.[40]

The fact that the decedent was not providing support may or may not be determinative as long as the plaintiff is legally entitled to support. For example, if a husband deserts his wife and fails to contribute to his wife's and children's support, the wife and the children may nonetheless maintain a wrongful death action for his death and claim loss of support,[41] but the fact that the decedent or survivor was an absentee family member may affect the calculation and allocation of the wrongful death award.[42] Ultimately, however, allocation of a wrongful death award among the legitimate wrongful death claimants may be controlled by statute.[43]

---

[37] Marcotte v. Timberlane/Hampstead School Dist., 733 A.2d 394, 399 (N.H. 1999) (construing New Hampshire's wrongful death statute to permit award for hedonic (loss of life damages). Hedonic damages are discussed at Section 73.4 (Hedonic Damages). Some wrongful death statutes permit recovery of grief and mental anguish. *See* Va. Code Ann. § 8.01-52.

[38] *See* text and notes 54–68, *infra.* This limitation does not, however, foreclose an independent action distinct from the wrongful death action. Jones v. Sanger, 512 S.E.2d 590 (W. Va. 1998) (permitting common law action for negligent infliction of emotional distress on the part of family member who witnessed death of loved one; award was not duplicative of nor barred by state wrongful death statute). Emotion distress recoveries are discussed at Section 12 (Noneconomic Damages).

[39] For a comprehensive collection of materials on the jurisdictional differences on the issue of wrongful death actions and damages, see STUART SPEISER, RECOVERY FOR WRONGFUL DEATH (3d ed. 1992).

[40] Wehner v. Weinstein, 444 S.E.2d 27, 36–38 (W. Va. 1994) (noting that the majority of American jurisdictions deduct the decedent's personal living expenses from her projected future earnings to determine the amount of support available to the plaintiff(s). The *Wehner* court concluded, nonetheless, that under the West Virginia statute the decedent's estimated living expenses need not be deducted in calculating the amount of income reasonably lost to the decedent as a result of her death caused by the defendant. *Id.* at 38.

[41] Sindelar v. Leguia, 750 A.2d 967, 97 (R.I. 2000); Saunders v. Consolidated Rail Corp., 632 F. Supp. 551, 553 (E.D. Pa. 1986); Powers v. Sutherland Auto Stage Co., 213 P. 494, 495 (Cal. 1923).

[42] Richardson v. Barber, 527 S.E.2d 8, 10–11 (Ga. App. 1989) (affirming allocation of wrongful death award based on relative closeness of each surviving parent to deceased child); *cf.* McTaggart v. Lindsey, 509 N.W.2d 881, 884 (Mich. App. 1994) (holding that no reasonable basis existed for loss of society claim when decedent had no meaningful family relationship with his surviving daughter).

[43] *See* 1 STEIN ON PERSONAL INJURY DAMAGES TREATISE § 3:52 (3d ed. 1992)

Evidence of the decedent's disposition toward work, inclination to support, provide services, personal habits of decedent (intemperance, gambling), disposition toward plaintiffs, e.g., was relationship harmonious or disharmonious, are all relevant, within bounds, in calculating the wrongful death award.[44] The fact that the wrongful death claimant is independently wealthy or destitute does not affect her claim for loss of support,[45] unless her right to bring a wrongful death claim is based on a required showing of dependency.[46]

Loss of support awards may also include governmental benefits the decedent would have received but for his death, such as social security benefits.[47]

Although most loss of support claims involve the death of a parent or spouse, courts have awarded loss of support in cases involving decedent children. In *Saavedra v. Korean Air Lines Company, Ltd.* the court upheld a $200,000 loss of support award in favor of the surviving parents of their child who died in the crash of a Korean Airliner shot down by military aircraft of the former U.S.S.R. The court noted that the surviving parents must have a reasonable expectation of future financial support. The court found that testimony by a cultural anthropologist regarding Japanese cultural patterns of children supporting their aged parents, coupled with the parent's testimony of expected support, was sufficient evidence to uphold the award.[48] The fact that a claim is allowed is not, however, a guarantee that it will be successful. For example, in *Bahl v. Talford*[49] the court rejected arguments that the surviving parents of decedent 11 and 16

---

[44] Drews v. Gobel Freight Lines, Inc., 557 N.E.2d 303, 308–09 (Ill. App. 1990), *aff'd*, 578 N.E.2d 970, 977 (Ill. 1991).

[45] Bagley v. Blue Flame Propane Co., Inc., 418 P.2d 333, 335 (Okla. 1966) (stating that "[t]he pecuniary loss one has suffered for a wrongful death is not mitigated by his or her wealth, means of support, financial independence or upon any other benefits received as a result of a death"); *see* Meyer v. Clark Oil Co., 686 S.W.2d 836, 839 (Mo. App. 1984) (Normile J., dissenting) (noting the general rule "that assets inherited from a deceased person do not diminish the damages suffered by his heirs from his wrongful death") (citations omitted).

[46] A wrongful death claimant's wealth may negate "dependency" and dependency may be required to claim the status of legitimate wrongful death claimant. *See* SPEISER, RECOVERY FOR WRONGFUL DEATH, *supra* at § 3.67.

[47] Wyatt v. United States, 470 F. Supp. 116, 117 (W.D. Mo. 1979), *aff'd*, 610 F.2d 545 (8th Cir. 1980). *See generally* Annotation, *Pension, Retirement Income, Social Security Payments, and the Like of Deceased as Affecting Recovery in Wrongful Death Actions*, 81 A.L.R.2d 949 (1962).

[48] 93 F.3d 547, 554–55 (9th Cir.) (applying DOSHA), *cert. denied*, 516 U.S. 217 (1996). The majority of American jurisdictions permit the parents of an adult child to maintain a wrongful death action for the death of the child. Mitchell v. Buchheit, 559 S.W.2d 528, 533–35 (Mo. 1977) (collecting cases and observing that at the time of the decision 26 states permitted actions for loss of contributions and benefits after majority age was reached; 6 states limited recovery to loss of services during the child's minority on the basis that the parent's right to services ceases on that date and any benefits after that date were speculative). This should be contrasted with the general unwillingness of most states to permit loss of filial consortium claims when the child is injured but not killed. Section 74.3 (Parental and Filial Consortium).

[49] 530 S.E.2d 347 (N.C. App. 2000).

years-old children could recover for loss of support. The court noted the absence of evidence that the children *intended* to provide for their parents. As noted by the court:

> [P]laintiffs were allowed to testify freely, yet presented no evidence Rene and Riana "had ever expressed an intent to provide any of [their] income to [their] parents." Indeed, during the directed verdict motion hearing, plaintiffs' counsel conceded his clients had brought forward "no absolute direct evidence" on the issue of what plaintiffs "could have expected to receive."[50]

It is not surprising that "direct evidence" would be lacking; few children are called upon, as children, to contemplate providing for their parents.

Loss of Services. This item consists of personal service, advice and training the decedent would have provided. These services include giving children piano lessons, directing the children's education, general home-making services, the value of the parent's moral, physical and intellectual training, instruction and nurture. These awards can be substantial. For example in *Morris v. Krauszer's Food Stores, Inc.* the court upheld a jury award of $1.5 million for loss of services of a mother of nine children. The children ranged in age from 7 to 18. The court noted:

> In a wrongful death case, reasonable compensation for the dependent survivors includes an amount to replace that which the decedent would have provided. However, compensation for intangible services such as guidance, advice and counsel "must be confined to what the marketplace would pay a stranger with similar qualifications for performing such services." The ages of the decedent's nine children at the time of her death ranged from seven to eighteen years. Plaintiff's expert calculated the loss of her services to her children at $677,500 which he based on the cost of paying someone to cook, clean, shop and launder. He valued the loss of guidance, instruction and training to her children at $45 an hour. He concluded that Morris would have been expected to provide these services until the youngest child was emancipated, which would have been another thirteen years. The jury's award of $1.5 million for loss of services was substantially more than the plaintiff's expert's calculation. However, the jury was entitled on this record to find that the expert was conservative in calculating the loss of such intangible services as guidance, training and counseling for so many children.[51]

If a parental claim for the wrongful death of a minor child included a request for recovery of loss of services, the general approach was to allow the tortfeasor to claim an offset for the child-rearing expenses avoided as a result of the child's death.[52] The offset would normally negate any loss

---

[50] *Id.* at 352 (citation omitted).

[51] 693 A.2d 510, 516 (N.J. Super. Ct. A.D. 1997).

[52] Bullard v. Barnes, 468 N.E.2d 1228, 1234 (Ill. 1984).

of services award unless the child had extraordinary earning capacity, such as an actor. The recent trend to use loss of society as the measure of the parent's loss has reduced the importance of the offset. The reason lies in the offsetting benefit rule discussed in Section 14 (Offsetting Benefits). When the expenses saved are a benefit that involve the same interest as the loss of services—economic advantage—an offset is permissible as the same interests are involved. Loss of society, while technically a pecuniary loss for inclusion in the wrongful death award, is usually deemed to involve sufficiently different interests to escape the offsetting benefits rule.[53] This issue has not, however, been resolved with certainty and the possibility that the loss of society award could be offset by "expenses saved" remains a possibility as long as loss of society is deemed pecuniary in nature.

Loss of Society. This item is related to, though distinct from, loss of services. It is analogous to loss of consortium and allows recovery for the loss of the decedent's love, companionship, comfort, affection, society, solace or moral support, any loss of enjoyment of sexual relations, or any loss of assistance in the operation or maintenance of the home.[54] Unlike the common law loss of consortium doctrine, loss of society is not limited to surviving spouses, but is available to surviving parents and children of the decedent. However, it is not usually extended outside this group.[55]

Because of its non-pecuniary nature, not all jurisdictions recognize an award for loss of society.[56] When the claim is allowed, awards can be substantial;[57] however, substantial awards are a possibility, not a certainty. In *Nelson v. County of Los Angeles* the court deemed excessive a $ 2 million loss of society award. The plaintiffs were the parents of an adult decedent with whom they had little contact and who had spent much of

---

[53] Selders v. Armentrout, 207 N.W.2d 686, 689 (Neb. 1973). *See generally* John Wagner, Jr., Annot., *Recovery of Damages For Loss of Consortium Resulting From Death of Child— Modern Status,* 77 A.L.R. 4th 411 (1991).

[54] McClain v. Owens-Corning Fiberglass Corp., 139 F.3d 1124, 1126 (7th Cir. 1998) (applying Illinois law).

[55] Mitchell v. United States, 141 F.3d 8, 19–20 (1st Cir. 1998); Section 74.3 (Parental and Filial Consortium).

[56] *Krouse v. Graham, supra,* 562 P.2d at 1025–27 (permitting recovery of loss of society while acknowledging the likely non-pecuniary quality of the award); 1 Speiser, Recovery for Wrongful Death, *supra,* at § 3.49 (stating that courts have denied loss of society recoveries for two reasons: first, the loss is not capable of measurement by any pecuniary standard and (2) the measure of the loss would include elements of passion and sympathy for the survivors).

[57] Lindsey v. Navistar Internat'l Transp. Corp., 150 F.3d 1307, 1319 (11th Cir. 1998) (affirming $5 million award for loss of society of young mother to surviving husband and two minor children); Currens v. Hampton, 939 P.2d 1138, 1143 (Okla. 1997) (upholding verdicts of $750,000 for each parent of 11 year old child for loss of society and destruction of parent-child relationship); Klinke v. Mitsubishi Motors Corp., 556 N.W.2d 528, 536–37 (Mich. App. 1996) (upholding verdict of $5 million for loss of decedent's services, gifts, society, and companionship based on "numerous witnesses who testified about their loss of society and companionship of the decedent," the 22 year old daughter of the surviving parents); Simmons v. University of Chicago Hosps. & Clinics, 617 N.E.2d 278, 288 (Ill. App. 1993) (upholding verdict for $1.6 million for loss of society of decedent infant who died minutes after birth), *aff'd,* 642 N.E.2d 107 (Ill. 1994).

his adult life in prison.[58] The court concluded that the award was necessarily based on impermissible factors of grief and distress, rather than permissible factors of society and companionship.[59]

The loss of society award is usually not reduced to present value.[60] The argument in favor of discounting to present value is that wrongful death awards are pecuniary in nature and courts have upheld loss of society awards on the basis that they are pecuniary.[61] Nonetheless, most jurisdictions look to loss of consortium law to determine whether the loss of society award should be discounted.[62] The result is that loss of society claims are treated as pecuniary for purposes of their allowance under wrongful death statutes, but as non-pecuniary for purposes of the application of discounting principles.[63]

Jurisdictions have split whether the remarriage of the surviving spouse is relevant to the loss of society claim. The traditional rule was that evidence of remarriage or the possibility of remarriage was irrelevant.[64] The rationale for this approach was threefold. First, damages should be determined as of the date the cause of action accrued, which was the date of death. Second, comparing the "value" of two marital relationships was viewed as speculative and inappropriate. Third, the benefits of a remarriage were deemed to be collateral to the matter before the court and the fortuity of the survivor's remarriage should not confer a windfall on the defendant.[65] While evidence of remarriage would not be considered in mitigation of damages, the court would not permit the remarried spouse to use her prior name.[66] Besides discriminating against women who customarily take the surname of their husband, the decision allowed the jury to speculate that either the plaintiff has remarried or resumed the use of her maiden name—neither factor being conducive to showing a loss of society.

The modern trend appears to permit evidence of the plaintiff's remarriage on the ground that the award should be for the actual loss, not a hypothetical loss.[67] Moreover, because the "value" of the first relationship must be

---

[58] 6 Cal. Rptr. 3d 650, 659 (Cal. App. 2003).

[59] *Id. See generally* Emile F. Short, Annot., *Parent's desertion, abandonment, or failure to support minor child as affecting right or measure of recovery for wrongful death of child*, 53 A.L.R. 3d 566, § 12 (1973).

[60] Drews v. Gobel Freight Lines, 578 N.E.2d 970 (Ill. 1991).

[61] *Krouse v. Graham, supra*, 562 P.2d at 1025–27.

[62] *Drews, supra*, 578 N.E.2d at 975–76.

[63] Section 9.3 (Discounting to Present Value) (noting general rule not to subject future non-economic losses to present subject value discounting).

[64] *See generally* Annotation, *Admissibility of Evidence of, or Propriety of Comment as to, Plaintiff Spouse's Remarriage, or Possibility Thereof, in Action for Damages For Death of Other Spouse*, 88 A.L.R.3d 926 §§ 2, 3[a] (1978) (collecting cases).

[65] Wood v. Detroit Edison Co., 294 N.W.2d 571, 573 (Mich. 1980).

[66] *Id.*

[67] Pasquale v. Speed Prods. Eng'g, 624 N.E.2d 1277, 1284 (Ill. App. 1993), *modification on other grounds,* 654 N.E.2d 1365 (Ill. 1995); Schaible v. Myers, 311 N.W.2d 297, 299–300 (Mich. 1981) (*per curiam*) (holding that it was proper to permit expert witness to consider plaintiff's remarriage in calculating her pecuniary loss from the death of her husband).

determined by the trier-of-fact, it is difficult to sustain the objection that comparing two relationships is speculative. If the comparison is speculative, it is inherent in what is being valued and measured—the marital relationship. Evidence that the plaintiff may remarry is not, however, generally admissible.[68] This is correct because a marital relationship in fact is different from the possibility of a relationship or a non-marital relationship. Comparing the two would be comparing apples to oranges.

Funeral and Burial Expenses. The reasonable value of funeral and burial expenses that have been paid or incurred as well as the cost of the funeral services are generally recoverable.[69] The claim for funeral or burial expenses, while often an item of estate administration, is not part of the decedent's survival claim unless the survival statute so provides. This results since the decedent did not have a claim while alive for funeral or burial expenses and the usual survival action only preserves those claims the decedent possessed.[70]

Loss of Inheritance. It appears that a majority of American jurisdictions permit recovery for loss of inheritance.[71] The measure of the loss may be different in loss to estate and loss to survivors jurisdictions.[72] The basis for the award is the amount of money the decedent would have accumulated, but for his death, and made available to his heirs or beneficiaries. The argument that such awards are speculative has been generally rejected,[73] but the plaintiff still must introduce proof that he had more than a mere expectancy of inheriting from the decedent. As noted in *C&H Nationwide, Inc. v. Thompson*:

> [I]f loss of inheritance damages are to be awarded, there must be evidence that plaintiffs would probably have been the beneficiaries of decedent's estate, and evidence from which the amount of that

---

[68] McClain v. Owens-Corning Fiberglass Corp., 139 F.3d 1124, 1129 (7th Cir. 1998) (stating that under Illinois authorities, which permit evidence of the plaintiff's remarriage, "whether or not McClain is cohabiting with someone is irrelevant to the question of the loss she suffered as a result of her husband's death").

[69] Keys v. Duke Univ., 435 S.E.2d 820, 822 (N.C. App. 1993); Francis v. Sauve, 34 Cal. Rptr. 754, 766–67 (Cal App. 1963).

[70] Harrison v. Burlington N. R.R., 750 F. Supp. 316, 321 (N.D. Ill. 1990); Nye v. Com., Dep't of Transp., 480 A.2d 318, 322 (Pa. Super. Ct. 1984).

[71] Yowell v. Piper Aircraft Corp., 703 S.W.2d 630, 633 (Tex. 1986). *See generally* James Tucker, Annot., *Wrongful Death Damages For Loss of Expectancy of Inheritance From Decedent*, 42 A.L.R.5th 465 (1996).

[72] Kulawik v. ERA Jet Alaska, 820 P.2d 627 (Alaska 1991):

> A beneficiary's ability to recover "prospective inheritance" presents a question of first impression in this state. Prospective inheritance represents that portion of the decedent's "probable accumulations" which a survivor could reasonably expect to inherit. Prospective inheritance is an item of damage available only under a "loss-to-the-survivor" theory of wrongful death damages, whereas probable accumulations is the measure under a "loss-to-the-estate" theory.

Id. at 631 (footnote and citation omitted).

[73] *Kulawick, supra*, 820 P.2d at 633; *Yowell, supra*, 703 S.W.2d at 633.

estate can reasonably be calculated. The necessity of some calculation is indicated by the fact that loss of inheritance damages are
economic in nature, and by the requirement in *Yowell* that only the
present value of the amount of an estate be awarded. Present value
is not simply a judgment call by the jury but a mathematical
calculation. Thus, loss of inheritance damages must be determined
as other economic damages are, rather than as damages for mental
anguish.[74]

An example of a situation where loss of inheritance is reasonably likely
is when the decedent had drafted testamentary documents that provided
a benefice to the plaintiff, but the decedent was unable to execute and
implement the testamentary devise before his death. One court extended
this to allow for a loss of inheritance claim when the decedent's death
resulted in an increase in federal estate taxes, which reduced the plaintiff's
inheritance.[75] On the other hand, when the survivors are elderly and the
decedent is young, a court may be unimpressed with the claim that the
survivors reasonably expected to claim an inheritance from the younger
decedent.[76]

The loss of inheritance claim may be subject to offset. In *Schaefer v.
American Family Mut. Ins. Co.* the court held that a plaintiff's recovery on
a life insurance policy covering the decedent should offset the plaintiff's loss
of inheritance claim.[77] Similarly, if the plaintiff's recovery is for the loss
of inter vivos gifts, that award should be deducted from the loss of
inheritance award unless there is evidence that the decedent would have
used funds other than those earned and saved in making the gifts.[78] When
loss of inheritance is allowed as an item of recovery, the proof standards
are high.[79] Loss of support awards usually decrease the amount of inheritance a plaintiff could have expected since money provided to others for
support would not have been saved for testamentary disposition. To award
both loss of support and loss of inheritance based on the same dollars would
amount to an impermissible double recovery.

---

[74] 903 S.W.2d 315, 323–24 (Tex. 1994).

[75] Pratt v. George Spalty Sons, Inc., 516 N.Y.S.2d 433, 435 (Sup. Ct. 1987); Section 17.5
(Enhanced Taxation as Additional Damages).

[76] Larson v. Cabrini Med. Ctr., 669 N.Y.S.2d 172, 177 (Sup. Ct. 1998) (noting that 69 and
70 year old parents of 35 year old decedent had no reasonable expectation of outliving their
son, whose life expectancy, according to standard mortality tables, was 40.1 years).

[77] 514 N.W.2d 16, 20–21 (Wis. App. 1994).

[78] *Oldham v. Korean Air Lines Co., Ltd., supra,* 127 F.3d at 54; *cf.* Luecke v. Mercantile
Bank of Jonesboro, 720 F.2d 15, 18 (8th Cir. 1983) (holding that the plaintiff's claim of loss
of annual gifts from the decedent would not be recognized when the gifts came from the
decedent's estate which plaintiff inherited. The annual gifts would have only diminished the
estate had the gifts continued. The evidence showed the decedent was retired and living off
her investment income). There are some broad statements to the contrary, but not in the
context of a specific claim for offset to avoid a double recovery. *See Meyer v. Clark Oil Co.,
supra,* note 45.

[79] Stathos v. Lemich, 28 Cal. Rptr. 462 (Cal. App. 1963).

Grief and Sorrow. Most jurisdictions do not allow a recovery by the survivors for their grief and sorrow resulting from the death of the decedent.[80] The rule has been changed in a few jurisdictions.[81] The reason for this limitation is the pecuniary orientation of wrongful death actions.[82] Nonetheless, some aspects of a recovery for grief and sorrow are no doubt included in most loss of society awards. While loss of society claims must be reduced to a pecuniary value, there is a substantial non-pecuniary element to the claim. The more the decedent was loved, and the greater the loss over her death, the more likely the trier of fact will measure loss of society generously. The relationship between loss of society and grief and sorrow has been noted even as courts have struggled to distinguish the two concepts. As noted by the Court in *Sea-Land Services, Inc. v. Gaudet*:

> Loss of society must not be confused with mental anguish or grief, which is not compensable under the maritime wrongful-death remedy. The former entails the loss of positive benefits, while the latter represents an emotional response to the wrongful-death. The difference between the two is well expressed as follows: When we speak of recovery for the beneficiaries mental anguish, we are primarily concerned, not with the benefits they have lost, but with the issue of compensating them for their harrowing experience resulting from the death of a loved one. This requires a somewhat negative approach. The fundamental question in this area of damages is what deleterious effect has the death, as such, had upon the claimants? In other areas of damage, we focus on more positive aspects of the injury such as what would the decedent, had he lived, have contributed in terms of support, assistance, training, comfort, consortium, etc.[83]

The distinction allows jurisdictions to include loss of society as a component of pecuniary-oriented wrongful death statutes, but when evaluated against concerns over certainty, the impact of sympathy, etc., the distinction between positive and negative consequences of a death are nebulous. If the jurisdiction permits an action for negligent infliction of emotional distress,[84] it is also necessary to distinguish grief and anguish over the loss of the decedent from distress caused by witnessing the death or arriving at the scene of the death of the decedent.[85]

Punitive Damages. Jurisdictions have split on whether punitive damages are recoverable in a wrongful death action. The issue turns on whether the

---

[80] *Krouse v. Graham, supra,* 562 P.2d at 1026; Kogul v. Sonheim, 372 P.2d 731, 732 (Colo. 1962); 1 SPEISER, RECOVERY FOR WRONGFUL DEATH, *supra,* at § 3.53.

[81] *E.g.,* S.C. Code § 15-51-10 *et seq.* (discussed in Garner v. Houck, 435 S.E.2d 847, 850 (S.C. 1993)); Nev. Rev. Stat. § 41.085.

[82] Person v. Behnke, 611 N.E.2d 1350, 1354 (Ill. App. 1993); *Krouse v. Graham, supra,* 562 P.2d at 1026.

[83] 414 U.S. 573, 587 n.17 (1974).

[84] Section 12.3 (Infliction of Emotional Distress).

[85] Stump v. Ashland, Inc., 499 S.E.2d 41, 51–52 (W. Va. 1997).

punitive damages award is deemed penal or compensatory[86] or authorized by the jurisdiction's wrongful death statute.[87] This is an issue that has tended to be captured by legislative amendment.[88]

A few jurisdictions still adhere to the rule that only punitive damages are available in wrongful death actions.[89]

The fact that a jurisdiction's wrongful death statute does not permit punitive damages does not control the availability of punitive damages under the state's survival statute.[90]

§ 76 CONCEPTION-RELATED CLAIMS

Within this section are a number of related, though, distinct claims. They include: wrongful birth, wrongful life, wrongful conception, and wrongful pregnancy. The terms are not always used consistently in the decisional law and commentary. Here, as elsewhere, it is important to look behind the label to the interest or right at issue and, from that perspective, evaluate the remedy available.

[76.1] Wrongful Birth/Wrongful Life

As used in these materials, and in most decisions, wrongful birth refers to an action brought by the parents of a birth-disabled child alleging that due to the defendant's misconduct the parents were denied the opportunity to make an informed decision whether to conceive the child or continue the

---

[86] Rubeck v. Huffman, 374 N.E.2d 411, 413 (Ohio 1978) (stating that "[s]ince punitive damages are 'assessed over and above that amount adequate to compensate an injured party' . . . they are, by definition, not available in a wrongful death action") (citation and footnote omitted); cf. In re Paris Air Crash, 622 F2d 1315, 1319 (9th Cir.) (stating that the state has a legitimate basis for excluding an award of punitive damages in wrongful death cases due to the danger of "excessive liability" and "the temptation for a jury to award punitive damages even when concrete elements of . . . intentional wrongdoing are absent"), cert. denied sub nom. Kalinsky v. General Dynamics Corp., 449 U.S. 976 (1980).

[87] Gionfriddo v. Avis Rent A Car Sys., Inc., 472 A.2d 306, 312 (Conn. 1984) (permitting the recovery of punitive damages under a wrongful death statute that allows "just damages"). The court concluded that under the Connecticut statute the proper focus was on the remedies the decedent would have if she survived her injuries. Id. at 311–12; McGowan v. Estate of Wright, 524 So. 2d 308, 309 (Miss. 1988) (holding that state's "just compensation" language permitted the awarding of punitive damages, in appropriate cases for wrongful death); Wills v. DeKalb Area Retirement Ctr., 530 N.E.2d 1066, 1071 (Ill. App. 1988) (stating that the Illinois wrongful death statute does not allow for the recovery of punitive damages).

[88] Gionfriddo, supra, 472 A.2d at 312 n.12 (noting jurisdictions where the legislature amended wrongful death statutes to bar punitive damages awards after the statute was judicially construed to permit such awards); Roach v. Jimmy D. Enters., Ltd., 912 P.2d 852, 855 (Okla. 1996) (noting the evolution in state wrongful death statute to allow for the award of punitive damages).

[89] Ala. Code § 6-5-410 (1975) (discussed in Cherokee Elec. Coop. v. Cochran, 706 So. 2d 1188, 1193 (Ala. 1997)).

[90] Pease v. Beech Aircraft Corp., 113 Cal. Rptr. 416, 423–24 (Cal. App. 1974); cf. Ballweg v. City of Springfield, 499 N.E.2d 1373, 1377 (Ill. 1986) (stating that punitive damages are not recoverable under the Illinois survival statute).

pregnancy after conception. The typical example of this type of case is the negligent performance of, or failure to conduct, testing for Tay Sachs, Sickle Cell Anemia, or other inheritable disease. As a consequence, a child is born with the disabling disease. A wrongful life action is similar to a wrongful birth action except that the claim is brought by the child for his or her impaired life as a result of being born with disabilities.[1]

Courts have regularly questioned whether to recognize these claims. The fundamental issue is whether life, however impaired, is preferable to the alternative the cause of action suggests, which is no life. This results since the assumption underlying of wrongful life and wrongful birth cases is that the wrong caused the life or birth! Courts have generally resisted treating life itself as a harm for which remedies should be provided to redress the poor quality of life.[2] Courts generally reject wrongful life claims on the ground that such a claim requires the court to value life impaired versus no life at all—a daunting moral and philosophical decision:

> [T]he implications of any such proposition are staggering. Would claims be honored, assuming the breach of an identifiable duty, for less than a perfect birth? And by what standard or by whom would perfection be defined?[3]

Courts have also rejected wrongful life claims due to the difficulty of valuing the immeasurable:

> Because children with genetic disorders . . . are impaired from the moment of conception, it is impossible for them to have a fundamental right to be born as whole individuals. Hence, the only alternative to their suffering, and the standard against which their compensation must be determined, is nonexistence.[4]

As noted by the New York Court of Appeals:

> Whether it is better never to have been born at all than to have been born with even gross deficiencies is a mystery more properly to be left to the philosophers and the theologians. Surely the law can assert no competence to resolve the issue, particularly in view of the very nearly uniform high value which the law and mankind has placed on human life, rather than its absence . . . .
>
> Simply put, a cause of action brought on behalf of an infant seeking recovery for wrongful life demands a calculation of damages dependent upon a comparison between the Hobson's choice of life in an

---

[1] Willis v. Wu, 607 S.E.2d 63 (S.C. 2004).

[2] Cowe v. Forum Group, Inc., 575 N.E.2d 630, 633 (Ind. 1991). *See generally* Gregory Sarno, Annot., *Recoverability of Compensatory Damages For Mental Anguish or Emotional Distress For Tortiously Causing Another's Birth*, 74 A.L.R. 4th 798 (1990).

[3] Becker v. Schwartz, 386 N.E.2d 807, 812 (N.Y. 1978).

[4] Siemieniec v. Lutheran General Hosp., 512 N.E.2d 691, 698 (Ill. 1987).

impaired state and nonexistence. This comparison the law is not equipped to make.[5]

On the other hand, denying a recovery may be seen as a moral and philosophical position. While life cannot be commodified, and while life itself may be priceless, the costs of disability are not.[6] Many courts have been sympathetic to the extraordinary economic costs incurred by parents in raising a disabled child.[7] The recovery has, however, been generally restricted to the economic costs associated with the pregnancy and with caring and raising the disabled child.[8] The recovery may be limited to the period of the child's minority because this period defines the parental duty of support and the parents have asserted the wrongful birth claim.[9] When, however, the parents will have support obligations after the child becomes an adult, which is often the case with disabled children, the extraordinary support award may run for the child's expected life.[10]

Courts have split on whether non-economic losses in the form of emotional distress may be awarded.[11] When distress damages have been awarded, it has often been to the parents, not the child, under a negligent infliction theory against the medical professional responsible for the wrongful birth.[12] Non-economic awards have also been subject to offset by some courts to the extent the parents receive benefits as parents from

---

[5] *Becker, supra*, 386 N.E.2d at 812; *see* Paretta v. Medical Officers For Human Reproduction, 760 N.Y.S.2d 639 645–46 (Sup. Ct. 2003) (holding that *Becker* reasoning would be extended to claim by child who alleged negligent in-vitro fertilization caused her birth-related disability: children would are "conceived with the help of modern technology" should not have more rights "than children conceived without medical assistance").

[6] The judicial reluctance to recognize wrongful life and wrongful birth actions based on the perception that a disabled life is preferable to no life has been criticized by commentators. *See* Deana A. Pollard, *Wrongful Analysis in Wrongful Life Jurisprudence*, 55 Ala. L. Rev. 327 (2004); F. Allan Hanson, *Suits For Wrongful Life, Counterfactual and the Nonexistence Problem*, 5 S. Cal. Interdiscip. L.J. 1 (1996).

[7] *Willis v. Wu, supra*, 607 S.E.2d 63 (collecting decisions accepting and rejecting wrongful life claims and noting that jurisdictions that allow the action limit recovery to extraordinary expenses needed to care for the disabled child, which brings the wrongful life claim in line with the wrongful birth claims, which has more adherents).

[8] *Willis v. Wu, supra*, 607 S.E.2d 63; Phillips v. United States, 575 F. Supp. 1309, 1314 (D.S.C. 1993); Schroeder v. Perkel, 432 A.2d 834, 841 (N.J. 1981). *But cf.* McAllister v. Ha, 496 S.E.2d 577, 583–84 (N.C. 1998) (allowing recovery of pregnancy-related expenses but denying recovery of extraordinary medical expenses incurred in raising the disabled child on the ground that "such extraordinary costs are simply part of child-rearing expenses for parents rearing an impaired child").

[9] Bader v. Johnson, 675 N.E.2d 1119, 1125 (Ind. App. 1997) (collecting decisions), *rev'd*, 732 N.E.2d 1212 (Ind. 2000).

[10] Arche v. United States Dep't of the Army, 798 P.2d 477, 482–83 (Kan. 1990) (collecting decisions).

[11] *Compare* Harbeson v. Parke-Davis, Inc., 656 P.2d 483, 492–93 (Wash. 1983) (permitting recovery), *with* Howard v. Lecher, 366 N.E.2d 64, 66 (N.Y. 1977) (rejecting emotional distress awards).

[12] Bader v. Johnson, 732 N.E.2d 1212, 1220–22 (Ind. 2000); Canesi ex rel. Canesi v. Wilson, 730 A.2d 805, 811 (N.J. 1999).

having a child.[13] The "offset" does not include any duty to mitigate by terminating the pregnancy.[14]

It is important to distinguish wrongful life/wrongful birth claims from injury in utero claims. If a defendant harms a fetus, causing the child to be born disabled or impaired, the child is entitled to a full recovery.[15] This would include future lost earnings based on a normal work-life expectancy.[16] This said, the dividing line between prenatal injury claims and wrongful birth claims is not always clear. For example, in *Saunders v. United States* a physician negligently advised Mrs. Saunders regarding her physical ability to have children and erroneously reassured her that she could have additional children. Mrs. Saunders became pregnant again and delivered a child who was disabled as a result of her physical ability to bear children.[17] The court found that the physician's negligence was the proximate cause of the child's birth impairment. Had Mrs. Saunders been properly advised she would either have had corrective surgery or elected not to have any more children. The majority characterized the action as one involving pre-natal injury:

> We consider this case to be analytically distinct from . . . other wrongful life cases . . . . [T]he critical difference in this case is that no incurable genetic defect was involved. In the California cases, although the doctors could have prevented the pregnancy, they could not have prevented the defect. In this case, had the doctor not been negligent, he could have prevented the injury. For this reason, we find this case to be more closely aligned with ordinary pre-natal injury cases, where the doctor's negligence more directly causes the injury.[18]

The dissenting judge thought that the matter was better characterized as a wrongful birth case and that the trial judge did not err in so concluding:

> Counsel urged the court to decide the case without resolving the question of whether, had Mrs. Saunders been fully informed, she would have had an operation and another child. The court decided

---

[13] *Compare* Eisbrenner v. Stanley, 308 N.W.2d 209, 213–14 (Mich. App. 1981) (permitting offset), *with Schroeder, supra,* 432 A.2d at 842 (rejecting offset). *Cf. Phillips, supra,* 575 F. Supp. at 1319 (discounting the parent's emotional distress award by 50% to reflect the benefit of having a child).

[14] Jones v. Malinowski, 473 A.2d 429, 437–38 (Md. 1984).

[15] Graham v. Keuchel, 847 P.2d 342, 364–65 (Okla. 1993); Womack v. Buchhorn, 187 N.W.2d 218, 222 (Mich. 1971). *See generally* Roland Chase, Annot., *Liability For Prenatal Injuries,* 40 A.L.R.3d 1222 (1972).

[16] 1st of Am. Bank v. United States, 752 F. Supp. 764, 780 (E.D. Mich. 1990); Ensor v. Wilson, 519 So. 2d 1244, 1273 (Ala. 1987).

[17] 64 F.3d 482 (9th Cir. 1995). Mrs. Saunders had a "septate uterus," an anomaly that reduces the space in which the fetus can grow and may predispose the mother to give birth prematurely. This occurred with respect to the child in question, Michael, Mrs. Saunders' third child, who was born premature. He suffered a hemorrhage on his second day of life leaving him profoundly disabled. *Id.* at 484.

[18] *Id.* at 485.

that she either would have had the operation or would not have had Michael. Again, it left the issue in equipoise. Thus, I cannot agree that as a matter of law this is simply a prenatal case. It is hybrid and could go either or neither way depending on the evidence. When it went neither way, the person who bore the burden of persuasion properly lost on that issue.[19]

The characterization was critical. As a wrongful birth matter, damages may be limited to extraordinary care and medical expenses during minority.[20] As a prenatal injury case, Michael Saunders, the plaintiff, was entitled to a full recovery for his bodily injuries.[21]

[76.2] Wrongful Conception/Wrongful Pregnancy

Wrongful conception or wrongful pregnancy involve claims by parents for the wrongful failure to provide effective birth control, which, as a consequence, has led to a pregnancy and the birth of an unplanned for child. Unlike the wrongful birth/wrongful life actions, the wrongful conception action usually involves a healthy, unimpaired child.

The costs of raising a healthy child in the United States today are substantial.[22] The decision to preclude a pregnancy is strong evidence that the parents elected not to bear those costs. Nevertheless, the general trend is to limit damages to those directly associated with the pregnancy itself, such as medical expenses, lost earnings while pregnant, loss of consortium, etc.,[23] and reject claims for child rearing costs, future lost earnings due to caring for the child, and emotional distress unless the child is born disabled.[24] The rationale for this limited recovery is judicial discomfort at treating parenthood as an injury. While the early view barring any recovery[25] has moderated,[26] the limited recoveries permitted evidence

---

[19] *Id.* at 487 (dissenting opinion).

[20] *See* note 8, *supra.*

[21] *See* note 16, *supra*; Sections 71.2 (Loss of Earnings Capacity), 73 (Pain and Suffering).

[22] One national magazine reported in 1998 that the average cost of raising a child in the United States, including the cost of college education and earnings foregone due to the demands of child rearing, was $2.78 million for the top third income bracket, $1.45 million for the middle third income bracket, and $0.761 million for the bottom third income bracket. *The Cost of Children*, U.S. News, March 30, 1998, at 50. Actual out-of-pocket expenses have been calculated as somewhat less. *The "Millennium Baby" Will Not Come Cheap*, L.A. Times, April 23, 1999, at C4 (discussing U.S. Dept. of Agriculture report that typical middle-income family will spend $156,690 over the next 17 years to raise a child born in 1999).

[23] Chaffee v. Seslar, 786 N.E.2d 705 (Ind. 2003) (permitting recovery of pregnancy related expenses, but rejecting recovery of ordinary costs of raising and educating a normal, healthy child); Emerson v. Magendantz, 689 A.2d 409, 411–12 (R.I. 1997) (collecting decisions).

[24] Bader v. Johnson, 732 N.E.2d 1212 (Ind. 2000); Section 76.1 (Wrongful Birth Wrongful Life).

[25] Christensen v. Thornby, 255 N.W. 620, 622 (Minn. 1934).

[26] *See generally* Russell G. Donaldson, Annot., *Recoverability of Cost of Raising Normal, Healthy Child Born as a Result of Physician's Negligence or Breach of Contract or Warranty*, 89 A.L.R. 4th 632 (1989); Gregory Sarno, Annot., *Tort Liability For Wrongfully Causing One to be Born*, 83 A.L.R. 3d 15 § 3(a) (1978) (collecting decisions permitting some damages recovery for birth of normal, healthy child).

continuing judicial unease with the claim. This unease can also be seen in the vigorous application of the offsetting benefits rule.[27] For example, in *Burke v. Rivo* the court recognized a right to recover the economic cost of raising a child borne after the defendant negligently performed a sterilization procedure on the mother.[28] The right of recovery was, however, burdened with an offset reflecting the benefits the parents would receive by having a child.[29]

---

[27] Section 14.1 (Tort Claims).

[28] 551 N.E.2d 1, 2–3 (Mass. 1990).

[29] *Id.* at 4–6. *See generally Donaldson*, Annot., *supra*, 89 A.L.R. 4th 632.

Chapter 9

REMEDIES FOR INJURY TO PERSONAL PROPERTY

§ 80 PHYSICAL DAMAGE

[80.1] Complete Destruction

The usual measure of damages for complete destruction of personal property is the fair market value of the property at the time it was destroyed.[1] Market value is determined based on the approaches discussed in § 7.0 (Value). When there is insufficient evidence to establish market value, other evidence, such as replacement cost, depreciation, expert opinion, and the amount of insurance, may be considered to determine the value of the property.[2] An example of these principles can be found in *The*

---

[1] Harris v. Peters, 653 N.E.2d 1274, 1275 (Ill. App. 1995); Amfac, Inc. v. Waikiki Beachcomber, Inv. Co., 839 P.2d 10, 32 (Haw. 1992); Griffin v. Bucknam, 184 P.2d 179, 183 (Cal. App. 1947).

[2] King Fisher Marine Serv., Inc. v. N.P. Sunbonnet, 724 F.2d 1181, 1185, *reh'g denied with opinion*, 729 F.2d 315 (5th Cir. 1984).

President Madison.[3] In that case, the court valued a boat specially designed for the local Skagit River by looking to the replacement cost of the boat. In so doing, the court refused to consider the market price at which the boat would sell on the Columbia River, because such buyers had different needs, and "could not give the owner, who needs these special features in his trade, the value of what he had lost."[4] In *King Fisher Marine Service, Inc.* the court found that because a barge lost at sea fulfilled the owner's unique legitimate needs as a drydock, the decision to award the owner the cost of replacement, rather than the price the owner paid for the barge only two days before the accident, was not clearly erroneous.[5]

The value of property may be determined by the owner's opinion of value, but this allowance goes to competency not weight. If the owner does not factually substantiate his opinion, it may be deemed to have no probative value.[6] Moreover, the trier of fact is not obligated to accept the owner's opinion, even if substantiated, as long as there is contrary evidence or the owner's credibility remains at issue,[7] which, given the owner's interest in the subject matter of the testimony, will invariably be the case.

The traditional rule in complete destruction cases was that the owner was not entitled to loss of use damages.[8] The rationale was that the owner should replace the destroyed property immediately. This approach was, in effect, a variant of mitigation principles. Because destroyed property should be immediately replaced, no loss of use damages would ordinarily be incurred. What sounded right in theory did not work out in practice. It is not always possible to replace immediately destroyed personal property. Substitutes may not be readily available or it may take some time to determine whether repair is possible or superior to replacement.[9] Whether property has been "destroyed" is not always self evident. The critical factor is often the cost of repair relative to the value of the property.[10] In such

---

[3] 91 F.2d 835 (9th Cir. 1937).

[4] *Id.* at 844.

[5] 724 F.2d at 1182.

[6] Sykes v. Sin, 493 S.E.2d 571, 574 (Ga. 1997). This allowance has not been altered by recent amendments to Fed. R. Evid. 701 addressing testimony by lay witnesses that it *not* be based on "scientific, technical, or other speculatized knowledge within the scope of [the expert witness rule]." Tampa Bay Shipbuilding & Repair Co. v. Cedar Shipping Co., 320 F.3d 1213, 1221–23 (11th Cir. 2003).

[7] Simmons v. Cuyahoga County Bd. of Revision, 689 N.E.2d 22, 24 (Ohio 1998).

[8] United Truck Rental Equip. Leasing, Inc. v. Kleenco Corp., 929 P.2d 99, 109 (Haw. App. 1996) (discussing traditional view).

[9] Fehlhaber v. Indian Trails, Inc. 286 F. Supp. 499, 506 (D. Del. 1968) (finding that common sense and justice dictate that the owners of horses injured in an accident were entitled to recover as damages expenses incurred while treating and resting the horses after the accident to determine whether they had any future value as race horses).

[10] Gaines Towing and Transportation, Inc. v. Atlanta Tanker Corp., 191 F.3d 633 (5th Cir. 1999):

> A vessel is considered a constructive total loss when the damage is repairable but the cost of repairs exceeds the fair market value of the vessel immediately before

cases, it may take time and investigation before the determination is made whether the property is repairable or destroyed. These considerations have induced many jurisdictions to reject the traditional rule and permit reasonable loss of use damages in cases of complete destruction of personal property.[11] The tendency is to treat the rejection of the old rule as categorical rather than just to recognize exceptions as warranted; hence, the modern approach is to permit loss of use damages when property has been destroyed regardless of whether it took time to determine the scope of injury, whether repairs were feasible, etc.

The damages award for complete destruction of personal property should reflect any salvage value the destroyed property possesses.[12] This reemphasizes that destruction is not simply a physical determination of the property's current condition but an economic decision that weighs the cost of repair against the pre-injury value of the property and the post-repair value of the property.

As a general rule, the owner may not recover emotional distress damages in connection with the destruction of or damage to personal property. The point is discussed in Section 82 (Pets).

[80.2] Partial Destruction

The measure of damage for injury to personal property is the difference between the value of the property immediately before and immediately after the injury, called diminution in value.[13] An alternative measure of diminution in value is the reasonable cost of repair.[14] In many jurisdictions the plaintiff is limited to the lesser of the two measures;[15] however, this "lesser of" test reflects less the recognition of cost of repair as a measure of property damage than it reflects an allocation of the burden of persuasion based on a presumption that, in many cases of partial loss, the cost of repair reflects the actual diminution in value.[16] The general measure of damages is

---

the casualty. In such a case repair is not economically practicable, and the market value of the vessel is the ceiling of recovery.
Id. at 635 (citations omitted).

[11] Reynolds v. Bank of Am., 345 P.2d 926, 927 (Cal. 1959); *see United Truck Rental, supra,* 929 P.2d at 109 (citing cases and commentators approving allowance of loss of use damages in complete loss cases). *But see* Mondragon v. Austin, 954 S.W.2d 191, 193 (Tex. Civ. App. 1997) (adhering to the rule of no loss of use damages in complete destruction case). The no loss of use damages rule in cases of complete destruction is also applied in Admiralty. *Gaines Towing and Transportation, Inc., supra,* 191 F.3d at 635.

[12] Coursey v. Broadhurst, 888 F.2d 338, 343 (5th Cir. 1989).

[13] Section 7.2 (Diminution in Value).

[14] Smith v. Hill, 47 Cal. Rptr. 49, 58 (Cal. App. 1965); Section 7.3 (Cost of Repair vs. Diminution in Value).

[15] Safeco Ins. Co. of Am. v. J&D Painting, 21 Cal. Rptr. 2d 903, 905 (Cal. App. 1993); Three and One Co. v. Geilfuss, 504 N.W.2d 393, 397 (Wis. App. 1993); Hogland v. Klein, 298 P.2d 1099, 1102 (Wash. 1956); Hauenstein v. St. Paul Mercury Indem. Co., 65 N.W.2d 122, 125, n.4 (Minn. 1954).

[16] Howard v. Wood Bros. Homes, Inc., 835 P.2d 556, 559 (Colo. App. 1992) (stating that

diminution in value; cost of repair is simply a "rule of thumb" means of determining the extent of diminution. This presumption is particularly strong when the repairs are made.[17] It is not necessary that the plaintiff establish both cost of repair and diminution in value. Plaintiff may select his remedy and the burden of persuasion lies with the defendant to show that plaintitff chose the greater of diminution in value or cost of repair rather than the lesser.[18]

In some cases, courts have allowed for recovery of the "cost of repair" as long as it does not exceed the pre-tort value of the property.[19] For example, assume plaintiff owns a used, 1995 transportation vehicle. The vehicle has a current fair market value of $10,000. Defendant negligently inflicts damage to the vehicle. The damage does not affect the economic utility of the vehicle nor does it affect the vehicle's market value. The "cosmetic" damage would not influence the price a buyer would pay for the vehicle. It would, however, cost the owner $1,000 to repair the cosmetic damage. That expenditure would not, however, add any economic value to the vehicle. Under the alternative cost of repair test, the owner could recover the cost of repair ($1,000) from the defendant as repair costs do not exceed the pre-injury value ($10,000). Under the majority "diminution in value" test the owner would recover no damages because the diminution in value ($0) is less than the cost of repair ($1,000).

The two tests reflect different views of economically sound actions. Under the alternative cost of repair test, which is the minority view, the pre-tort value fixes the economic value of the property for the owner. The owner engages in no economic waste as long as she does no more then replace in value what she had pre-tort. The majority "lesser of" test is that economic value cannot rest on an abstract view of property rights but must address the real productive capacities of property. Under this view, the true test of "economic detriment" caused by injury to property is the before and after differential because property "damage" must reflect a loss of economic utility.

When cost of repairs does not fully compensate a plaintiff for diminution in value, the plaintiff may recover any remaining diminution in value that remains, after repairs have been made.[20] In *Merchant Shippers Assn. v.*

---

evidence of cost of repair is probative of diminution in value), *modified on other grounds*, 862 P.2d 925 (Colo. 1993). *But cf.* McDaniel v. Linder, 990 S.W.2d 593, 596 (Ark. App. 1999) (deeming before and after appraisals to be best evidence of amount of property damage and relegating cost of repair to situations when market value proof is unobtainable).

[17] Pfingsten v. Westenhaver, 244 P.2d 395, 401–02 (Cal. 1952).

[18] Geddes & Smith, Inc. v. St. Paul Mercury Indem. Co., 407 P.2d 868, 870 (Cal. 1965).

[19] Hewlett v. Barge Bertie, 418 F.2d 654 (4th Cir. 1969), *cert. denied*, 397 U.S. 1021 (1970) (discussed in Section 7.3 (Cost of Repair vs. Diminution in Value)). In *Hewlett* a barge which was in a dilapidated but usable state was cosmetically injured by defendant. Plaintiff sought cost of repair damages, *i.e.*, the amount of money it would require to fix the minor dents in the barge. As a practical matter the injury did not lessen the economic value of the barge or interfere with the use to which it was being put, and was capable of being put, at the time of the collision.

[20] Parkway Co. v. Woodruff, 901 S.W.2d 434, 441 (Tex. 1995):

Kellogg Express & Draying Co. new precision machinery was damaged. The evidence showed that though repairs would put it in working order, it would be considered "secondhand" and would be difficult to sell in a limited market. It was held proper to award not only the cost of repair, but the difference between its value before the injury and after the repairs were made.[21] If, however, the owner of the property represents to others that it is "as good as new" after the repairs have been made, the owner may be estopped to claim additional damages.[22]

In partial destruction cases, the plaintiff and defendant must give due consideration to the proper evidentiary burdens that must be met. The plaintiff has the burden of showing the amount of loss using either cost of repair or diminution in value. If plaintiff selects cost of repair, evidentiary issues may turn on whether the repairs are made or not. When repair has not been made, invoices, bills, and receipts are generally inadmissible to establish liability for the repairs or that the estimated cost of repair is reasonable. If repairs are made, properly authenticated invoices, bills, and receipts may be admitted for the limited purpose of corroborating that the liability for repair was incurred and that the amounts charged were reasonable. The exception does not, however, extend to establishing that repairs were, in fact, made.[23] Some jurisdictions have modified their rules of evidence to permit the admission of repair estimates.[24]

The fact that the repairs are performed internally by the injured party with its own employees does not nullify or diminish that party's ability to recover those costs, including allocated overhead.[25]

The fact that the owner subsequently sells the damaged property for more than its post-injury value does not necessarily diminish the plaintiff's

---

Damages for diminution in value and damages for cost of repairs are not always duplicative. Diminution in value does not duplicate the cost of repairs if the diminution is calculated based on a comparison of the original value of the property and the value after repairs are made.

(citation omitted).

[21] 170 P.2d 923, 926 (Cal. 1946); *see* Smith v. Midland Risk Ins. Co., 699 So. 2d 1192, 1196 (La. App. 1997) (holding that post-repair diminution in value of vehicle due to fact of collision and repair was recoverable); Rosenfield v. Choberka, 529 N.Y.S.2d 455, 456 (Sup. Ct. 1988) (damages included loss in trade-in value even though automobile has been fully repaired).

[22] Kirkhof Elec. Co. v. Wolverine Express, Inc., 269 F.2d 147, 148 (6th Cir. 1959) (stating that because plaintiff admitted that transformers were as good as new after repair of damage incurred during transportation by defendant, a common carrier, plaintiff could not recover, in addition to repair costs, depreciation measured by deductions from original price that it had been compelled to make in order to procure customer acceptance of the repaired transformers); *cf.* Sullivan v. Pulkrabek, 611 N.W2d 162, 164 (N.D. 2000) (holding that owner who recovered full cost of repair from defendant's insurer could not claim diminution in value losses from defendant as measure of owner's property damage).

[23] Pacific Gas & Elec. Co. v. G.W. Thomas Drayage and Rigging Co., 442 P.2d 641, 648 (Cal. 1968).

[24] *E.g.*, NY CPLR 4533-a (repair estimates not in excess of $1000); Cal. R. Ct. 1613(b)(1) (Court-Annexed Arbitrations).

[25] Freeport Sulphur Co. v. The S/S Hermosa, 526 F.2d 300, 303 (5th Cir. 1976).

recovery against the defendant. The defendant may not expropriate an above market sale as his breach did not enable the plaintiff to obtain the above-market price.[26] On the other hand, the defendant is free to argue that the post-tort sale is at the property's pre-tort value and, thus, defendant did not inflict any economic harm on plaintiff.

[80.3] Loss of Use

The owner may also recover loss of use damages while the personal property is being repaired.[27] The normal measure of loss of use is the fair rental value of the property. This will either be: (1) the amount plaintiff could have realized by renting out the property in its pre-tort condition; or, (2) the reasonable cost of renting a substitute. Loss of use damages may be available, even where there is no actual "out-of-pocket" loss, because interference with the "right to use" is what is being compensated.[28]

In commercial cases, "actual pecuniary loss" may be required in order to recover loss of use damages.[29] The owner may be required to demonstrate an actual financial loss due to the unavailability of the property.[30] In many of these cases, analysis is complicated by the fact that sometimes the courts in commercial cases treat the issue as one of loss of profits rather than loss of use. As the former are consequential damages that must be shown to have been sustained, characterization can be key.[31] The reasoning in these cases is that when use has only a monetary value for the owner, compensation for loss of use should reflect the economic reality of the owner's position. A court should not award both "rental value" and "lost profits" as loss of use damages,[32] absent proof of actual special damages.

Recovery for loss of use is usually extended to lessees;[33] however, some courts require that the lessee have exclusive use or control over the

---

[26] Sullivan v. Young Bros. & Co., Inc., 893 F. Supp. 1148, 1161 (D. Me. 1995), *modified on other grounds*, 91 F.3d 242 (2d Cir. 1996); Section 14.1 ([Offsetting Benefits] Tort Claims).

[27] Valencia v. Shell Oil Co., 147 P.2d 558, 560 (Cal. 1944).

[28] Kuwait Airways Corp. v. Ogden Allied Aviation Servs., 726 F. Supp. 1389, 1396 (E.D.N.Y. 1989) (aircraft owner could recover loss of use damages even though it had not been required to obtain a substitute because it had replacement craft available).

[29] Mountain View Coach Lines, Inc. v. Hartnett, 415 N.Y.S.2d 918 (Sup. Ct. 1978) (involving an action for loss of use of bus resulting from accident). The owner was not allowed to recover rental value representing loss of use where no replacement vehicle was hired and plaintiff had extra buses repaired. *See* Brooklyn E. Dist. Terminal v. United States, 287 U.S. 170 (1932).

[30] CTI Int'l Inc. v. Lloyds Underwriters, 735 F.2d 679, 683-84 (2d Cir. 1984) (holding that defendant negated presumption that owner of property suffered loss of use damages by introducing evidence that plaintiff suffered no financial loss).

[31] *See generally* C. Marvel, Annot., *Recovery For Loss of Use of Motor Vehicle Damages or Destroyed*, 18 A.L.R.3d 497 (1968).

[32] Louisville & Nashville R.R. v. Bond Transfer & Storage Co., 190 So. 2d 696, 697 (Ala. 1966); *see* text and notes 39-42, *infra*.

[33] Koninklijke Luchtvaart Maatschaapij, N.V. (KLM Royal Dutch Airlines) v. United Techs. Corp., 610 F.2d 1052, 1057 (2d Cir. 1979).

property. [34]

Normally, the period for which loss of use damages are allowed is that reasonably required for making the repairs. [35] A longer time is sometimes permitted, as, for example, when there was delay in the arrival of new parts, [36] or when the plaintiff was financially unable to make repairs. [37] This analysis overlaps with mitigation of damages issues. [38]

Special damages may also be awarded as part of loss of use damages. In one case, a vehicle was damaged requiring repair. The owner was allowed to recover, as additional damages to loss of use, the wages paid the chauffeur while the vehicle was being repaired. [39] Although the argument could be made that this represents a windfall for the owner because he would pay the employee anyway, this treatment of the argument ignores that the owner has lost the benefit of the employee's services because of the damage to the vehicle.

In *Johnson v. Central Aviation Corp.* [40] the owner's airplane was damaged by a student pilot. In addition to seeking loss of use damages, plaintiffs alleged that, prior to the collision, they had agreed to sell the plane, which cost them $20,000, for $27,500, and that they were damaged in the sum of $7,500 as lost profits on the unconsummated sale. The court held that it was error to strike out this allegation. According to the court:

> There is nothing *necessarily* inconsistent with a claim for damages for loss of use of the plane and a claim for loss of profits upon sale, since both elements of damage might, in a proper case, if the proof warranted, be allowable. Thus, the time for delivery of the plane under the sale might be far enough in the future to enable the owner to use the plane for his own purposes for a period of time before being obligated to deliver it to the buyer in accordance with his selling agreement. [41]

This "loss of profits" is distinct from "loss of profits" used to measure "loss of use." "Lost profits" from the lost sale in *Johnson v. Central Aviation Corp.* are additional to loss of use damages, at least up to the point in time the airplane would have been sold. In this setting, however, the owner will have to make reasonable efforts to secure a substitute when doing so would enable the owner to avoid the loss. Thus, in the previous example involving

---

[34] Herzig v. Larson-Sawchak, 464 N.W.2d 754, 755-56 (Minn. App. 1991) (looking at lease agreement to determine if lessees had right to exclusive control and thus were analogous to owners).

[35] Menefee v. Raisch Improvement Co., 248 P. 1031, 1032 (Cal. App. 1926); *see* Florida Drum Co. v. Thompson, 668 So. 2d 192, 193 (Fla. 1996); Cress v. Scott, 868 P.2d 648, 651 (N. Mex. 1994).

[36] Lyle v. Seller, 233 P. 345, 346 (Cal. App. 1924).

[37] *Valencia v. Shell Oil Co., supra,* 147 P.2d at 561.

[38] Section 13 (Duty to Mitigate Damages).

[39] *Lyle, supra,* 233 P. at 346.

[40] 229 P.2d 114 (Cal. App. 1951).

[41] *Id.* at 117 (emphasis in original).

the chauffeur, the owner's unreasonable failure to secure a substitute vehicle for the chauffeur to operate may result in a failure to mitigate special damages in the form of the chauffeur's wages.[42]

§ 81 VALUE TO OWNER

In a limited number of cases property is said to have no market value; however, the statement is a misnomer. The property has a market value; however, for reasons of policy or for reasons of the moment, courts do not believe that in the circumstances the damages award should be based on market value. In this context, limiting the owner to "market value" may either lack economic substance or be socially unacceptable.[1]

Situations when courts have deemed market value not expressive of recoverable value include heirlooms and awards,[2] clothing,[3] furniture,[4] family records and photographs,[5] and personal jewelry.[6] These items are generally characterized as "personal effects" and recovery is based on the items general character and the fact that they are possessed for "the comfort and well being of the owner," not for their economic utility.[7]

In this context, some courts have permitted owners to recover based on a non-market measure—value to the owner.[8] Many jurisdictions while adopting this measure exclude sentimental value and direct that the jury be so instructed.[9] It is difficult to discern, nonetheless, how the trier of fact can separate "value to owner" from "sentimental value" in a manner that allows "value to owner" to have any meaning.[10]

The basis for allowing a non-market measure of damage reflects the view that certain items are imbued with strong human feelings that are not reflected in market clearing prices. In this sense, the property is outside

---

[42] Buchanan v. Leonard, 127 F. Supp. 120, 123 (D. Colo. 1954).

[1] This section builds on concepts earlier addressed in Section 7 (Value).

[2] Campins v. Capels, 461 N.E.2d 712, 720 (Ind. App. 1984).

[3] Id. at 719-720; Crisp v. Security Nat'l Ins. Co., 369 S.W.2d 326, 328 (Tex. 1963).

[4] Campins, supra, 461 N.E.2d at 719-20.

[5] Bond v. A.H. Belo Corp., 602 S.W.2d 105, 109 (Tex. Civ. App. 1980) (permitting recovery under "special value" measure for lost photographs and newspaper clippings collected by an adopted child who was searching for her biological parents and siblings).

[6] Williams v. Dodson, 976 S.W.2d 861, 865 (Tex. Civ. App. 1998).

[7] Williams, supra, 976 S.W.2d at 865 (holding that owner's desire to sell jewelry did not deprive owner of right to claim "value to owner" measure rather than market value: "the bracelet in question should be categorized based upon how it was generally held") (emphasis in original).

[8] Landers v. Municipality of Anchorage, 915 P.2d 614, 618 (Alaska 1996), citing Restatement (Second) of Torts § 911, cmt. e (1977) (involving loss of family photographs and videotapes).

[9] Taylor v. Jones County, 422 S.E.2d 890, 892-93 (Ga. App. 1992).

[10] Bond, supra, 602 S.W.2d at 106 (permitting recovery of sentimental value in calculating damages); Campins, supra, 461 N.E.2d at 721 (defining "sentimental value" as that normally generated by an item of personal property rather than a "mawkishly emotional" or "unreasonable attachment" to the property).

of any relevant market and must be measured, if it is to be measured at all, by a non-market measure.

The decisional law is not consistent in this area and this inconsistency is manifested in two ways. First, many jurisdictions do not permit the "value to owner" measure in any case. Here, the search is for an objective, albeit non-market, measure. In these contexts, damages to heirlooms, family records and photographs, and the like, will usually be determined by use of one of the following formulas:

- Original cost less depreciation due to age, condition or damage resulting from use or decay.[11]

- Replacement cost less depreciation.[12]

- Cost of repair or reproduction.[13]

- Market value.[14]

Second, inconsistency is found in those jurisdictions that permit recovery based on "value to owner" as to the types of personal property that qualify for a non-market measure of value. For example, most jurisdictions refuse to treat "pets" as within the value to owner rule and limit the owner's recovery for the death of family pets to the pet's market value.[15]

If an item has "value" to the "owner," it only makes sense to allow the owner to testify on the subject. Courts are, nonetheless, split on the issue.[16] When the owner is allowed to testify, he should state the reasons for his opinion as to "value." It should be noted that this "value to owner" opinion is different from the opinion on "market value," which the owner is generally permitted to give.[17]

---

[11] Some courts require evidence of depreciation, Vaughan v. Spurgeon, 308 A.2d 236, 238 (D.C. App. 1973) (involving damage to furniture and personal effects), while other courts assume a reasonable depreciation factor. Keeton v. Sloan's Moving & Storage Co., 282 S.W.2d 194, 199 (Mo. App. 1955) (involving damage to household furniture and personal effects).

[12] Restatement (Second) of Torts § 911(e) (1979).

[13] Airight Sales, Inc. v. Graves Truck Lines, Inc., 486 P.2d 835, 838 (Kan. 1971). This measure was suggested but not applied in *Williams v. Board of Educ. Clinton Community Unit School Dist. No. 15 of DeWitt County*, 367 N.E.2d 549, 553 (Ill. App. 1977). This measure is also commonly used when public property, such as bridges, roads, etc., is damaged or destroyed. Section 90.6 (Damage to Public Property).

[14] *Cf.* Hoffman v. Eastman Kodak Co., 278 P. 891, 891 (Cal. App. 1929) (involving loss of film taken on a trip to the Grand Canyon). The decision is limited because it relied primarily on principles of contract loss causation developed in *Hadley v. Baxendale*. Section 10.2.2 ([Loss Causation] Policy Considerations). In *Hoffman* the court found that the plaintiff had not informed the defendant of any special value of the film; hence, defendant's liability was limited to the actual cost of replacement film (retail market value). Because loss foreseeability is greater in commercial cases, a different rule has emerged there. Rhodes v. Ritz Camera Ctrs., 151 A.2d 262, 263 (D. C. App. 1959); Sarkesian v. Cedric Chase Photographic Labs., 87 N.E.2d 745, 746 (Mass. 1949); *see* text and notes 22–24, *infra*.

[15] Section 82 (Pets).

[16] *Campins, supra,* 461 N.E.2d 712; *Williams, supra,* 367 N.E.2d at 553-54.

[17] Section 80 (Physical Damage) (text and notes 6–7).

As in the case involving emotional distress damages,[18] courts are likely to review "value to owner" awards with a concern for excessiveness. In some cases, the courts have stated that a wide disparity between the non-market recovery and the damaged property's actual economic loss in value is near conclusive proof of excessiveness.[19] In those cases, however, the property (a family residence) had substantial economic value in its own right and it is unclear whether the court would extend the decision to cases involving property with minimal or no market value.[20]

In some commercial loss cases, the courts are willing to allow a non-market measure as long as the measure reasonably reflects an intuitive and commonsensical measure of the loss. Representative of these cases are those involving losses of film taken by commercial photographers. In valuing commercial photographs courts have examined factors such as: (1) uniqueness of the subject matter; (2) prestige of the photographer; (3) established use prices; (4) technical quality.[21] and losses of paintings or drawings by commercial artists.[22] The work often has no readily accessible market value; consequently, courts permit measure by such formulas as replacement cost, value to plaintiff, or other "rational" means.[23] A non-market measure has been used in cases where personal files were damaged that were used by the owner in his trade or profession.[24]

---

[18] Section 12.2.1 (Excessiveness).

[19] *Cf.* Hassle v. City of Poway, 24 Cal. Rptr. 2d 554, 559 (Cal. App. 1993) (refusing to allow cost of repair damages for a family residence that exceeded by a factor of three and one-half the actual injury (diminution in value). The court further stated that cost of repair would not be used whenever that measure "so vastly exceeds the harm done that it would as a matter of law be unreasonable to award. . . ." 24 Cal. Rptr. at 559.

[20] Carye Boca Raton Hotel and Club Ltd. Partnership, 676 So. 2d 1020, 1021-22 (Fla. App. 1996) (stating that when property that has value to owner has substantial economic value on its own right, the owner bears a heavy burden to persuade the court to use a non-market measure of damages); *cf.* Giacommo v. Tri-State Ins. Co., 595 N.W.2d 531 (Minn. App. 1999) (holding that "sweat equity" and uniqueness of antique motor vehicle did not permit an award over declared value of vehicle by owner when market value was "fully ascertainable").

[21] Miller v. Newsweek, 675 F. Supp. 872, 876 (D. Del. 1987) (citations omitted); *cf.* Gasperini v. Center For the Humanities, Inc., 66 F.3d 427, 428-29 (2d Cir. 1995) (finding that industry standard was a relevant consideration in determining the value of commercial transparencies; the industry standard was $1500 each. The court found, however, that it was improper to simply multiply the industry standard times the number of lost transparencies to arrive at a valuation; such a process created an excessive verdict because it excludes other relevant factors, such as the transparencies' uniqueness and the earnings of the plaintiff-photographer), *vacated on other grounds*, 518 U.S. 415 (1996) (holding that excessiveness issue is governed by state law in diversity action with appellate review limited to determining whether trial court abused its discretion in deciding motions for new trial), *on remand*, 972 F. Supp. 765 (S.D.N.Y. 1997) (reducing the verdict ($450,000) to $375,000), *vacated on other grounds*, 149 F.3d 137 (2d Cir. 1998).

[22] Rajkovich v. Alfred Mossner Co., 557 N.E.2d 496, 499 (Ill. App. 1990).

[23] *Id.* at 499. *See generally* W.E. Shipley, Annot., *Measure of Damages For Conversion or Loss of, or Damage to, Personal Property Having No Market Value*, 12 A.L.R.2d 902 (1950).

[24] *Williams v. Board of Educ. Clinton Community Unit School Dist. No. 15, supra,* 367 N.E.2d 549 (involving lecture notes, professional papers, and work product of football coach). The court stated that when, as here, there was no market for the property, "value is to be

The fact that property has "sentimental" value for which the law provides no compensation may support the claim that the remedy at law is inadequate and equitable relief is necessary to protect the property from harm.[25]

§ 82 PETS

The common law and the still dominant rule in the United States classifies pets as personal property;[1] consequently, if the pet is injured or killed, the loss is treated as damage to personal property. This limits the pet's owner to recovery of economic loss as calculated in Section 80 (Physical Damage).

The traditional approach is represented by *Nichols v. Sukaro Kennels* in which the court held that the proper measure of damages for injury to a pet was based on market value and rejected the "value to owner" test.[2] The *Nichols* court distinguished a prior decision finding that trees had intrinsic value warranting a non-market recovery.[3] The court concluded that unlike the ornamental and shade trees involved in the prior decision, the pet in *Nichols* had no intrinsic value other than his value as a family pet.[4] Damages for sentimental value, mental suffering, burial expenses, etc., are not recoverable under the market value approach.[5] Under the market value approach, pedigree and breeding do matter, as well as the pet's accomplishments, such as medals in shows. All of these may enhance the pet's economic value.[6] Courts have permitted non-market recoveries in cases

---

determined by some rational way and from such elements as are obtainable." 367 N.E. 2d at 553 (citation omitted). If the lost property could be replaced then replacement cost would be a suitable measure. *Id.* The court rejected, however, as speculative a valuation based on the coach's own personal opinion and that of "experts" whose opinions were not directly based on an accurate understanding of the contents of the coach's files that were lost. *Id.*

[25] *Cf.* Bumgarner v. Bloodworth, 738 F.2d 966, 968 (8th Cir. 1984) (finding that the state remedy was inadequate, and therefore permitted federal action, when the state remedy provided only damages, not the return of property with sentimental value).

[1] *See* Fackler v. Genetzky, 595 N.W.2d 884, 891-92 (Neb. 1999) (collecting cases). There is some authority that this is the modern common law rule and that originally some pets, particularly dogs, were deemed valueless! Citizens Rapid-Transit Co. v. Dew, 45 S.W. 790, 791 (Tenn. 1898):

> It is true, that at common law a dog was not considered as property, the reason given being that they were base in their nature, and kept merely for whims and pleasure. But this rule of law has not found favor in later days.

[2] 555 N.W.2d 689 (Iowa 1996); Section 81 (Value to Owner).

[3] Treating "trees" as an exception to the traditional test is a common mistake made by courts. Section 91.3 (Damage to Trees and Shrubs).

[4] *Nichols, supra,* 555 N.W.2d at 692; Krasnecky v. Meffen, 777 N.E.2d 1286, 1288-89 (Mass. App. 2002) (rejecting claim for distress damages to owners of sheep that were killed by defendant's dogs); *cf.* Stechler v. Homyk, 713 N.E.2d 44, 46-47 (Ohio App. 1998) (stating general rule that owner of personal property cannot recover distress damages on witnessing destruction or damage to that property).

[5] Zeid v. Pearce, 953 S.W.2d 368, 369 (Tex. Civ. App. 1997) (holding that owner could not recover distress damages for veterinary malpractice). *See generally* J. Connelly, Annot., *Measure and Elements of Damages For Killing or Injuring Dog,* 1 A.L.R.3d 997 (1965).

[6] Bueckner v. Hamel, 886 S.W.2d 368 (Tex. Civ. App. 1994) (allowing recovery of lost

involving injury to or loss of guide dogs. The problem, however, is that while guide dogs are of inestimable value to the blind, they are provided free; thus, it may be argued that the owner suffers no direct economic injury from the loss of the animal. Nonetheless, courts have affirmed jury verdicts awarding damages for loss of guide dogs.[7] Guide dogs require extensive training and the fact that they are provided free to the blind does not diminish the guide dogs economic value. The fact that the guide dog is provided free could be treated as subject to the collateral source rule and excluded from consideration in fixing the owner's loss.[8]

If the pet has unique economic value, e.g., "Morris the Cat" or "Lassie," and generates real economic loss to the owner as a result of injury to or loss of the pet, those losses should be recoverable.[9]

To state that the tradition rule does not comport with the views of many, if not most, pet owners would be a gross understatement. The relationship between pets and their owners, or companions or guardians as many prefer to be called, is but part of a larger reevaluation of the relationship between humans and animals.[10] Pets receive support after their owners divorce;[11] trusts for support after their owners die;[12] health insurance;[13] and legislative protection, some enacted, most still proposed.[14]

---

pecuniary value of two dogs based on evidence that owner had planned to breed dogs and that each dog could be expected to breed once a year and produce 6-8 puppies, whose market value ranged form $125-$400 for one dog (Dalmatian) and $125-$700 for the other dog (Australian Shepard)).

[7] Caskey v. Bradley, 773 S.W.2d 735 (Tex. Civ. App. 1989):

Bradley testified that the dog was a gift from Guide Dogs for the Blind. He further testified that the dog was his to use until the dog died or had to be destroyed. We are aware of no title requirement under Texas law for ownership of dogs. Bradley stated he had the dog for ten months prior to the accident. We believe this provides some evidence that Bradley owned the dog and thus was entitled to recover for it. Therefore, we modify the judgment to include an additional $1,250 for Bradley (one-half of the $2,500 value of the dog as determined by the jury).

Id. at 740. The reduction was based on the jury's finding that Bradley was 50% negligent.

[8] Section 15 (Collateral Source Rule).

[9] *Cf.* Pullman v. Land-O'Lakes, Inc., 262 F.3d 759, 765-66 (8th Cir. 2001) (affirming recovery of lost profits resulting from death and injury to dairy cows due to feed consultant's negligence).

[10] *See* Richard A. Epstein, *Animals as Objects, or Subjects, of Rights*, John M. Olin Law & Economics Working Paper No. 171 (2d Series), available at www.law.uchicago.edu/Lawecon/WkngPprs_151-175/171.rae.animals.pdf; Lynn A. Epstein, *Resolving Confusion in Pet Owner Tort Cases: Recognizing Pets' Anthropomorphic Qualities Under a Property Classification*, 26 So. Ill. L. Rev. 31 (2001); Steven M. Wise, *Recovery of Common Law Damages For Emotional Distress, Loss of Society and Loss of Companionship For the Wrongful Death of a Companion Animal*, 4 Animal L. 33 (1998).

[11] Doug Beasley, *Dog Support*, Edmonton Sun, June 18, 2004 (reporting monthly support award of $200 to ex-wife who obtained custody of couple's St. Bernard with, apparently, gourmet tastes); *cf.* Juelfs v. Gough, 41 P.3d 593 (Alaska 2002) (awarding custody of pet to divorcing husband because pet did not get along with divorcing wife's other pets).

[12] There is a website that addresses estate planning for pets maintained by Gerry W. Beyer at www.professorbeyer.com/Articles/Animals.htm.

[13] *Here and Now*, L.A. Times, July 12, 1999, at E2.

[14] *See* Elaine T. Byszewski, *Valuing Companion Animals in Wrongful Death Cases: A Survey*

This reexamination is beginning to have an effect on the consistent application of the common law rule. Several jurisdictions have recognized a "loss of companionship" remedy or allowed recovery based on the "special status" of the pet as somewhere between that of a person and property. The leading case here is *Campbell v. Animal Quarantine Station, Div. Of Animal Indus. Dep't of Agric., State of Hawaii, Board of Agric.*, which awarded distress damages arising out of the destruction of the family pet by the defendant notwithstanding the fact that the plaintiff did not witness the pet's destruction.[15] In *Brousseau v. Rosenthal* a widow, whose sole remaining companion, an eight year old dog, was killed at a boarding kennel, was allowed to recover "loss of companionship" damages for her dog's wrongful death notwithstanding that New York does not have a wrongful death statute for dogs.[16] In *La Porte v. Associated Independents* plaintiff recovered emotional distress and punitive damages when their 2 year old dachshund was killed by a deliberately thrown garbage can.[17] Many of these decisions, however, may have limited precedential value. For example, *Corso v. Crawford Dog and Cat Hospital, Inc.* involved a claim against a pet mortuary that agreed to provide a funeral for the plaintiff's pet dog, but when plaintiff's opened the coffin at the "funeral" she found a "cat in the casket."[18] Many of the decisions involved situations where the context suggested heightened awareness on the part of the defendant (veterinarian or pet hospital) that the plaintiff was emotionally attached to the pet. Some of the decisions involve exceptions to the general rule precluding non-economic damages for breach of contract when distress is a specifically foreseeable consequence of breach.[19] Some of the claims involve allegations of deliberate or reckless conduct that may elevate the claim to intentional tort for which distress damages are recoverable.[20]

Some courts have rejected market value as the proper measure of economic loss when pets are injured or killed in favor of the "value to owner" test.[21] For example, in *Hyland v. Borras* the plaintiff sued for veterinarian malpractice. The court stated that the replacement value of the pet was $500, but affirmed an award of $2500.[22] The court held:

---

of Current Court and Legislative Action and a Suggestion For Valuing Pecuniary Loss of Companionship, 9 Animal L. 215, 225-30 (2003).

[15] 632 P.2d 1066 (Haw. 1981).

[16] 443 N.Y.S.2d 285 (Sup. Ct. 1980).

[17] 163 So. 2d 267 (Fla. 1964); *see* Debra Squires-Lee, Student Note, *In Defense of Floyd: Appropriately Valuing Companion Animals in Tort,* 70 N.Y.U. L. Rev. 1059 (1995); Peter Barton & Frances Hill, *How Much Will You Receive in Damages From the Negligent or Intentional Killing of Your Pet Dog or Cat?*, 34 N.Y. L. Sch. L. Rev. 411 (1989).

[18] 415 N.Y.2d 182 (N.Y. City Civ. Ct. 1975).

[19] Section 142 (Distress Damages).

[20] Brown v. Muhlenberg Township, 269 F.3d 205, 218-19 (3d Cir. 2001) (stating that Pennsylvania would recognized cause of action for intentional infliction of emotional distress for deliberate killing of a pet); Kennedy v. Byas, 867 So.2d 1195 (Fla. App. 2004) (rejecting emotional distress claim for veterinarian malpractice and distinguishing *La Porte, supra*, as involving malicious, deliberate killing of pet).

[21] Section 81 (Value to Owner).

[22] 719 A.2d 662 (N.J. Super. Ct. A. D. 1998).

Most animals kept for companionship have no calculable market value beyond the subjective value of the animal to its owner, and that value arises purely as the result of their relationship and the length and strength of the owner's attachment to the animal. In that sense then, a household pet is not like other fungible or disposable property, intended solely to be used and replaced after it has outlived its usefulness. Plaintiff raised the dog from the time it was a puppy. Both parties stipulated that plaintiff loved her dog and devoted time, energy, and money to train and feed it, in order to bring it to the level of maturity it had attained at the time of the attack. It is purely a matter of "good sense" that defendants be required to "make good the injury done" as the result of their negligence by reimbursing plaintiff for the necessary and reasonable expenses she incurred to restore the dog to its condition before the attack.[23]

§ 83   DAMAGES FOR LOSS OR INTERFERENCE WITH POSSESSION

Loss or interference with possession of personal property may raise a number of discrete claims, such as conversion, replevin, trespass to chattels, and unjust enrichment. Each action carries with it certain remedial advantages and disadvantages that must be evaluated in the context of the specific facts of the claim.

[83.1]   Conversion

Conversion is a sale-oriented remedy. When a defendant wrongfully interferes with plaintiff's right of possession to, dominion of, or control over personal property, the law allows the plaintiff to treat the interference as a sale of the property to the defendant.[1] Conversion does not require the specific intent to convert the property of another. Any unauthorized and unlawful exercise of dominion and control over the personal property of another, which is inconsistent with the owner's rights, constitutes conversion.[2] The converter can act in "good faith;" it is only necessary that she "intend to do an act amounting to conversion."[3] On the other hand, the defendant's status as a "good faith" converter may militate the amount of damages awarded to the plaintiff.

The usual rule is that conversion is not available when the claim is that money was converted.[4] The reason for this rule is that money is fungible

---

[23] *Id.* at 664 (citations omitted).

[1] WILLIAM PROSSER & W. PAGE KEETON, THE LAW OF TORTS § 15 (5th ed. 1984).

[2] *In re* Moody, 899 F.2d 383, 385 (5th Cir. 1990) (applying Texas law).

[3] *Id.*; Fink v. Pohlman, 582 A.2d 539, 542 (Md. Ct. Spec. App. 1990) (holding that conversion cannot arise out of mere breach of contract; conversion requires the commission of a positive tortious act).

[4] 9310 Third Ave. Assocs., Inc. v. Schaffer Food Serv. Co., 620 N.Y.S.2d 255, 256 (App. Dept.

and quickly loses its separate identify when commingled. What cannot be separately identified cannot be bartered or sold—at least insofar as the common law is concerned. Money can, however, form the subject matter of a conversion action if it is sufficiently identified.[5] The money need not be specific notes or squirreled away in a bag to be "identified."[6] An earmarked account or fund may be converted, as may a check.[7] Conversion will lay when a third party has a paramount title or claim to specific money and the agent, who holds the monies, disburses the monies in derogation of the known claim.[8] In other words, if the plaintiff can "identify" the very money she lost, the law will allow her to maintain an action for conversion, but not otherwise.

In terms of compensatory damages, it will usually matter little whether the defendant's misappropriation of money is addressed through conversion or another form of relief, such as unjust enrichment (common count for money had and received). Conversion, however, permits the recovery of punitive damages when the requisite degree of misconduct can be shown.[9] Punitive damages may not be available for other means of redress.[10]

The fact that the property is intangible does not mean that conversion is unavailable. Courts have permitted conversion actions for stolen "securities"[11] and misappropriated "trade secrets."[12] This extension of conversion

---

1994) (rejecting claim for conversion of money "because monies alleged to have been converted . . . are not sufficiently identifiable . . . . The allegedly converted money is incapable of being 'described or identified in the same manner as a specific chattel' ") (citations omitted); Haas v. Town & Country Mortgage Co., 886 S.W.2d 225, 227 (Mo. App. 1994) (stating that conversion is limited to specific chattels; thus, a claim for money may not be asserted through conversion).

[5] Estate of T.K. Jackson v. Phillips Petroleum Co., 676 F. Supp. 1142, 1146 (S.D. Ala. 1987); see Ferguson v. Coronado Oil Co., 884 P.2d 971, 978 (Wyo. 1994) (finding that conversion of money would lie when there was an obligation to deliver the money in a specific manner; in such cases, money is identifiable although the specific bills and coins are not); Biermann v. Gus Shaffar Ford, Inc., 805 S.W.2d 314, 318 (Mo. 1991) (recognizing general rule but finding exception for funds placed in defendant's custody for a specific purpose, here a deposit on the purchase of a specific vehicle).

[6] Horbach v. Kaczmarek, 288 F.3d 969 (7th Cir. 2002):

An asserted right to money normally will not support a claim for conversion. Only if the money at issue can be described as "specific chattel"—in other words "a specific fund or specific money in coin or bills"—will conversion lie.

Id. at 978 (citations omitted).

[7] Decatur Auto Center v. Wachovia Bank, N.A. 583 S.E.2d 6, 8 (Ga. 2003) (check); Belford Trucking Co. v. Zagar, 243 So. 2d 646, 648 (Fla. App. 1970) (earmarked account).

[8] McCafferty v. Gilbank, 57 Cal. Rptr. 695, 700 (Cal. App. 1967) (finding conversion claim stated against lawyer who disbursed settlement funds to client in derogation of third party lien).

[9] Biermann, supra, 805 S.W.2d at 321-22 (upholding award of punitive damages for dealership's conversion of deposit on vehicle).

[10] Section 202.6 ([Punitive Damages] Equity).

[11] See generally Annotation, Nature of Property or Rights Other Than Tangible Chattels Which May be Subject of Conversion, 44 A.L.R.2d 927, 929 (1955) (noting that limitation of conversion to tangible property "has been discarded by most courts. . . .").

[12] FMC Corp. v. Capital Cities/ABC, Inc., 915 F.2d 300, 305 (7th Cir. 1990) (noting modern trend in "protecting against the misuse of confidential business information through conversion actions") (collecting decisions).

into intangible property has been particularly controversial with respect to the Internet.[13] On the other hand, the fact that property is tangible does not mean that conversion will always lie for the wrongful and unauthorized exercise of dominion and control over that property. This has been particularly true with regard to conversion claims involving the human body, its organs, or its genetic material.[14]

The usual measure of damages for conversion is the fair market value of the property at the time of the taking.[15] This should be contrasted with replevin damages which, when available, are usually determined by the value of the property as of the date of trial.[16]

When the property has a natural fluctuating value, such as market securities, many jurisdictions allow the plaintiff the "highest market price reached within a reasonable time after discovery of the conversion." This is the "New York" rule.[17] Some courts use the highest market price reached within a reasonable time from the date of the conversion.[18] Some courts, even in the context of property having a fluctuating value, do not use a valuation date other than the date of conversion;[19] while some use the highest market value between the date of conversion and the date of trial.[20]

---

[13] Kremen v. Cohen, 337 F.3d 1024, 1030 (9th Cir. 2003) (*en banc*) (holding that conversion would lie for the wrongful exercise of dominion and control over an internet domain name).

[14] Culpepper v. Pearl St. Bldg., Inc., 877 P.2d 877, 883 (Colo. 1994) (holding that no conversion claim could be stated when defendants mistakenly cremated plaintiff's son's body); Moore v. Regents of the Univ. of Cal., 793 P.2d 479, 488-89 (Cal. 1990), (holding that plaintiff could not state a cause of action for conversion of his body parts (spleen) based on the removal of the diseased spleen by surgeons); *cert. denied*, 499 U.S. 936 (1991). *But see* Hecht v. Superior Court, 20 Cal. Rptr.2d 275, 280-81 (Cal. App. 1993) (holding that decedent had property interest in his sperm that was frozen for later use and which he could devise to another); *cf.* Newman v. Sathyavagls-Waran, 287 F.3d 786 (9th Cir.) (holding that next of kin had a sufficient property interest in relative's corpse to warrant due process protection), *cert. denied*, 537 U.S. 1029 (2002). The underlying issue in *Newman* was the use of human cadavers for cornea harvesting.

[15] 50-Off Stores, Inc. v. Banque Paribas (Suisse), S.A., 180 F.3d 247, 254 (5th Cir. 1999) (applying Texas law), *cert. denied sub nom.* Lot$Off Corp. v. Chase Manhattan Bank, N.A., 528 U.S. 1078 (2000); Paves v. Corson, 765 A.2d 1128, 1135 (Pa. Super. Ct. 2000), *rev'd on other grounds*, 801 A.2d 546 (Pa. 2002); Welch v. Kosasky, 509 N.E.2d 919, 921 (Mass. App. 1987).

[16] *Welch, supra,* 509 N.E.2d at 922. Only a few jurisdictions recognize replevin damages as a generally available remedy. Section 83.2 (Replevin).

[17] Transcontinental Oil Corp. v. Trenton Prods. Co., 560 F.2d 94, 111 (2d Cir. 1977).

[18] Reed v. White, Weld & Co., 571 S.W.2d 395, 397 (Tex. Civ. App. 1978).

[19] George v. Coolridge Bank & Trust Co., 277 N.E.2d 278, 283 (Mass. 1971).

[20] Miller v. Kendall, 804 S.W.2d 933, 942 (Tex. Civ. App. 1991):

> In ordinary conversion cases, the measure of damages is the value of the converted property at the time of the conversion, but where the conversion is attended with fraud, willful wrong, or gross negligence, and the property converted is of changing or fluctuating value, the measure of damages is the highest market value between the conversion and the filing of the suit.

(citations omitted); Kaplan v. Cavicchia, 257 A.2d 739, 742 (N.J. Super. Ct. A.D. 1969) (finding conversion based on acts of gross negligence allowed plaintiff to use highest value between date of taking and date of judgment). Section 7.6.2 ([Value as a Function of Time] Fluctuating Value).

Many of the approaches are fact specific and the harshest approaches, which give the plaintiff the greatest amount of time within which to calculate the value of the property taken, are reserved for cases of deliberate conversion.[21] Because many of these claims involving property with fluctuating value also involve fiduciaries, the separate obligations of fiduciaries to manage property should be considered.[22] When a fiduciary breaches his duty of care by failing to properly manage securities and also breaches his duty of loyalty by converting securities, a plaintiff may have two different points in time at which she can measure damages for the loss.

When the converted property has "special value" to the owner, as in the case of family pictures, heirlooms, and the like, the owner may be permitted a recovery that reasonably reflects their non-market value.[23]

Because conversion operates as a forced judicial sale based on the defendant's wrongful exercise of dominion and control over the plaintiff's property, it is unclear whether the plaintiff must mitigate damages by accepting the return of the property from the converter. The usual assumption is that plaintiff retains unfettered discretion whether to accept the converted property because courts speak in terms of an "election."[24] If, however, the plaintiff elects to receive back the converted property, the measure of damages remains the value at the time of taking but the defendant is credited with the fair market value of the converted property at the time of the return less any claim by the plaintiff for loss of use during the period of deprivation.[25]

There is older authority that a plaintiff could not sue a good faith possessor of converted property for conversion until the plaintiff had made a demand on the defendant-possessor for the return of the property.[26] The modern application of this principle is, however, one of laches and appears to be limited to specific replevin.[27]

Recently, a number of courts have permitted distress damages awards for conversion of property.[28] One case, *Fredeen v. Stride*, involved a family pet and somewhat unusual facts.[29] Plaintiff's dog required surgery but

---

[21] *Kaplan, supra*, 257 A.2d at 742 (1969); *see* text and notes 40–42, *infra*; Section 8.7 (Harsh or Mild Measures).

[22] Marcus v. Otis, 168 F.2d 649, 654 (2d Cir. 1948); Section 113 (Breach of Fiduciary Duty).

[23] Ladeas v. Carter, 845 S.W.2d 45, 53 (Mo. App. 1992); Section 81 (Value to Owner).

[24] *Welch, supra*, 509 N.E.2d at 921.

[25] *Id.* (collecting cases). The conversion remedy here parallels replevin damages. Section 83.2 (Replevin).

[26] Autocephalous Greek-Orthodox Church of Cyprus v. Goldberg & Feldman Fine Arts, Inc., 917 F.2d 278, 294 n.2 (7th Cir. 1990) (Cudahy, J. concurring) (noting that a purpose of this rule was to permit the defendant to return the property to the rightful owner without recourse to litigation).

[27] *Id.* (discussing New York law).

[28] Gonzales v. Personal Storage, Inc., 65 Cal. Rptr. 2d 473, 481 (Cal. App. 1997) (permitting recovery of distress damages when defendant converts property that defendant knows or should know has special value to the owner).

[29] 525 P.2d 166 (Or. 1974) (permitting plaintiff whose pet had been converted by the defendant to recover emotional distress damages of $4,000).

plaintiff could not afford the procedure so she left the dog with the veterinarian with instructions that the dog was to be destroyed. The veterinarian's employees became fond of the dog and nursed it back to health. Plaintiff was not informed of these events. The veterinarian then gave the dog to a third party. Some time later plaintiff saw her dog with its new owner. Plaintiff called the veterinarian and he told her to contact the new owner about recovering her pet. She sued the veterinarian instead and recovered damages instead of her dog. This proves the adage "no good deed goes unpunished." Notwithstanding these decisions, the general rule remains that invasion of personal property interests does not warrant the recovery of non-economic damages, such as emotional distress.[30]

Most jurisdictions treat prejudgment interest as a component of the conversion damages award[31] and thus not subject to the normal rule that prejudgment interest in tort cases is discretionary.[32] One case where the "prejudgment interest" issue raised more attention than usual was *Iglesias v. United States*.[33] Iglesias successfully prevailed on a conversion claim against a bank. The property that was the subject of the conversion claim was subject to special tax treatment because the plaintiff was not a U.S. resident and the income from the property did not derive from sources within the United States. (The property was mutual fund shares in a foreign bank). The defendant bank (Citibank) wrongfully sold the shares to satisfy debts owed the bank by plaintiff. Plaintiff was awarded judgment against Citibank for the value of the shares as of the time of their taking plus interest. The bank paid the judgment; then the IRS entered the picture. The IRS contended that the interest awarded was taxable; plaintiff contended that the interest represented the tax free earning he would have realized on the investment. The court found in favor of the IRS. The court noted the sale orientation of the remedy and therefore concluded that the interest awarded was not a substitute for the loss of use of enjoyment of the property. The award of interest was to indemnify the plaintiff for the property converted and was not a substitute "either in amount or character for the yield the converted property would have produced."[34] As a result of his victory on the conversion theory, plaintiff saw his award reduced by $47,928.71, the amount of tax he owed on the interest he received.

A plaintiff's reasonable costs expended in efforts to recover his converted property may be awarded as additional damages.[35] An interesting application of this principle is *Gladstone v. Hillel* in which the court permitted recovery for time spent by plaintiff attempting to recover his converted

---

[30] Section 82 (Pets).

[31] Independence Flying Serv., Inc. v. Ailshire, 409 S.W.2d 628, 632[7] (Mo. 1966).

[32] Section 16.1 (Ascertainability: Liquidated v. Unliquidated Claims).

[33] 848 F.2d 362 (2d Cir. 1988).

[34] *Id.* at 365.

[35] Kraut v. Morgan & Bros. Manhattan Storage Co., 343 N.E.2d 744, 748 (N.Y. 1976) (permitting recovery of the amount paid as "ransom" to obtain the return of converted property); Section 13.7 (Compensation for Mitigation Efforts).

property.[36] The debate centered over whether litigation-related expenses could be included in this measure or whether they constituted a form of surrogate attorneys fees, which would not be recoverable in the general case.[37] The court found a middle ground:

> Under modern conditions, the legislative purpose of Civil Code section 3336 would be defeated by rigorously excluding all items having some connection with litigation. The statute should at least extend to efforts that had a purpose independent of the litigation, such as preparation of lists of missing property, inspection of inventories, meetings with appellants, contacts with law enforcement authorities, and inquiries regarding appropriate courses of action. The record of these items is sufficient to sustain the relatively modest award of $10,000 at issue here.[38]

This item of additional damages is in the nature of mitigation costs and usually capped by the fair market value of the property converted on the theory that it is not reasonable to spend more to avoid a loss than the loss itself. This item of recovery does not include attorneys fees expended in civil litigation to obtain the converted property.[39]

Whether the conversion is deemed willful or innocent can have a significant impact on the amount of compensatory damages awarded. The selection of the date to be used to fix the value of converted property will be influenced by whether the conversion was willful or innocent.[40] The decision whether a converter's liability is based on the value of the property when he exercised dominion and control over it, or whether he is also liable for any value he imparted to the property will also be influenced by the converter's culpability. For example, assume the defendant acquires timber wrongfully removed from plaintiff's land. At the time of acquisition the timber has a value of $100 per thousand board feet. Defendant mills the timber into wood and stores it on his property. In its improved state the timber (or wood) has a value of $200 per thousand board feet. If plaintiff sues defendant for conversion, is defendant's liability measured at $100 or $200 per thousand board feet? The general rule is that an innocent converter pays damages based on value at time of acquisition, while the willful converter pays damages based on his added value.[41] This is an area,

---

[36] 250 Cal. Rptr. 372 (Cal. App. 1988).

[37] Section 210 (Attorney's Fees—The "American Rule").

[38] *Gladstone, supra*, 250 Cal. Rptr. at 381; *see* Leonard E. Gross, *Time and Tide Wait For No Man: Should Lost Personal Time be Compensable?*, 33 Rutgers L. Rev. 683 (2002) (criticizing traditional common law rule that lost personal time resulting from defendant's wrongdoing is not compensable unless that lost is tied to a compensable loss, such as bodily injury).

[39] Harwood State Bank v. Charon, 466 N.W.2d 601, 605 (N.D. 1991); Section 211.4 ([Exception to the "American Rule"] Third Party Tort).

[40] *See* text and notes 15–21, *supra*.

[41] Young v. Faulkner, 492 S.E.2d 331, 332 & n.1 (Ga. App. 1997); Reynolds v. Pardee & Curtin Lumber Co., 310 S.E.2d 870, 876 (W. Va. 1983); Dethloff v. Zeigler Coal Co., 412 N.E.2d 526, 535 (Ill. 1980), *cert. denied*, 451 U.S. 910 (1981). *But see* Nelson v. All Am. Life & Fin. Corp., 889 F.2d 141, 148 (8th Cir. 1989) (stating that Iowa law does not distinguish between willful and innocent converters when awarding compensation).

however, where there are many individual exceptions due to statutory provisions.[42] Note that the difference in damages may create important tactical choices between use of specific remedies (replevin) versus substitutional remedies (conversion damages). If the owner can identify his property, he can recover possession (replevin) of the property, which has appreciated in value.[43] Replevin thus becomes the preferred remedy if a court would use a soft measure of damages that did not reflect the added value defendant gave to the property. On the other hand, the court might condition replevin on plaintiff compensating defendant for her work in enhancing the value of the property.[44] In that case, the remedies are brought back into equilibrium.

Identification of the converter as willful or innocent is thus often of critical importance.[45] Unfortunately, the law on the topic is difficult to define with particularity. Several factors appear, however, with some regularity in the decisions. They include: (1) was there reasonable doubt as to ownership and right to possession; (2) did the converter rely on advice of counsel after having made full complete disclosure to counsel of the facts; (3) was the converter acting in good faith and with honest intentions? When these factors are present, the Court will be more inclined to treat the conversion as innocent and not include "added value" into the damages calculation.

[83.2]   Replevin

At common law replevin was a specific remedy providing for the return of personal property that had been wrongfully taken.[46] Many jurisdictions

---

[42] Harris v. Nelson, 25 S.W.3d 917, 921-22 (Tex. Civ. App. 2000) (construing term "market value" in state treble damage statute applicable to the wrongful harvesting of trees belonging to another as including value added to converted property by the defendant). The *Harris* court emphasized several points set forth in the Legislative Analysis Report that accompanied the statute:

> The analysis informs us that theft was a primary concern of the legislature. As background, the analysis noted that (a) timber is the number one agricultural commodity in the eastern part of Texas; (b) high timber prices make the forests in East Texas a "prime target for timber thieves;" and (c) the Texas Forest Service estimates "timberland owners have lost millions of dollars worth of trees to thieves." The stated purpose of the bill's pertinent section was to "address the unauthorized harvesting of timber" and provide "punishment for violations."

Id. (citations omitted).

[43] Section 57 (Replevin).

[44] Section 86 (Good Faith Improvers of Personal Property).

[45] Grays Harbor County v. Bay City Lumber Co., 289 P.2d 975, 981 (Wash. 1955) (finding that the initial conversion was innocent; thus, plaintiff was limited to value as of the time of the initial taking). *Compare* Mineral Resources, Inc. v. Mahnomen Constr. Co., 184 N.W.2d 780 (Minn. 1971) (holding that innocent subsequent converter liable only for stumpage value even though original conversion was willful), *with* Masonite Corp. v. Williamson, 404 So. 2d 565 (Miss. 1981) (holding that when original conversion was willful; subsequent innocent converter was liable for "delivered" value of converted property received by him).

[46] Section 57 (Replevin).

continue to limit replevin to specific relief and derivative damages. A number of jurisdictions permit, however, the plaintiff to elect between specific and substitutional relief. If the plaintiff chooses the latter, her measure of recovery is the value of the property at the time of trial.[47]

Because replevin operates under the theory that the plaintiff was at all times the rightful possessor of the property, specific relief does not make the plaintiff completely whole. Plaintiff is entitled to his loss of use damages for the period of the detention.[48] The measure of loss varies. If the property has commercial utility, reasonable rental value may be allowed. The court may award interest on the value of the property during the period of detention as a surrogate measure of loss of use.[49]

When fair rental value is used as the measure of detention damages, the question of excessiveness is frequently raised because periods of detention can be long and the rental damages can seem disproportionate to the actual value of the property detained. The decisional law in this area is inconsistent. Loss of use damages that are approximately three times the value of the property wrongfully detained have been found to be excessive in some cases and proper in others. For example, in *Fran-Well Heater Co. v. Robinson*, which involved the wrongful withholding of oilfield equipment, the trial court calculated detention damages of approximately $5,000 (based on fair rental value over the twenty month detention period) against the equipment's actual market value of approximately $1,700. The appellate court thought the difference was disproportionate and excessive.[50] On the other hand, in *Harris v. Dixon Cadillac Co.*, which involved the wrongful detention of an automobile, the plaintiff sought loss of use damages even though she did not lease a substitute. The court affirmed an award of $7,500 for loss of use (approximately $5/day) even though the market value of the detained vehicle was only $2,500).[51]

The courts' concern with disproportionality may be questioned as it fails to acknowledge that payments over time may easily in the aggregate exceed what could be purchased for a lump sum price.[52] If the rental amounts are an accurate estimate of reasonable rental value, then the total owed does

---

[47] Guerin v. Krist, 202 P.2d 10, 17 (Cal. 1949); *cf.* Campbell v. Bausch, 395 S.E.2d 267, 269 (Ga. App. 1990) (permitting plaintiff to recover highest value of property between date of taking and date of trial when property is unlawfully detained up date of trial; if property is returned, plaintiff cannot claim post-return valuation date).

[48] Restatement (Second) of Torts § 931 (1977). *See generally* 66 Am. Jur. 2d *Replevin* 120.

[49] Allemang v. Kearney Farm Ctr., Inc., 554 N.W.2d 785, 788 (Neb. 1996) (stating that the ordinary measure of loss of use in replevin is interest on the value of the property during the period of wrongful taking or detention); Heg, Inc. v. Bay Bank & Trust Co., 591 So. 2d 1011, 1013 (Fla. App. 1991) (same). The plaintiff is allowed to claim loss of use damages under alternative formula when an award of interest does not adequately compensate her for the loss of use.

[50] 5 Cal Rptr. 900, 905 (Cal. App. 1960).

[51] 183 Cal. Rptr. 299, 302-03 (Cal. App. 1982).

[52] Morfeld v. Bernstrauch, 343 N.W.2d 880, 885 (Neb. 1984) (stating that "[t]he value of the use of a car may exceed the actual value of the car").

not become inaccurate, unreasonable, and excessive simply because it is large. The rental amounts may fail to reflect the lower rate normally charged for long term leases over short term leases, but this critiques the accuracy of the amount calculated as the fair rental measure, not the fact that loss of use damages exceed value lost. Courts are likely to raise intuitive concerns of excessiveness whenever the loss of use award exceeds the value of the property detained. Some courts require that plaintiff show that she was capable of using the property during the period of deprivation.[53] One court limited loss of use damages to the period the defendant actually used the property.[54]

Plaintiff may recover depreciation damage the property sustained during the period of detention.[55]

The plaintiff may be allowed consequential damages arising out of the detention of the property and consequent loss of use to the plaintiff.[56] There is a tendency in some of the cases to equate these loss of use damages with "special damages." As used here "special damages" means those damages that flow from but are additional to loss of use. For example, the farmer who cannot plant his crop because his tractor was wrongfully detained or taken by the defendant may suffer lost profits as a result.[57] Thus, in addition to the value of the loss of use of the tractor, a court may award consequential damages reflecting the value of the crops that were not planted or harvested. In some cases, the term "special damages" refers to the value of the use of the specific property wrongfully taken or withheld.[58]

---

[53] Korb v. Schroedel, 286 N.W.2d 589, 592 (Wis. 1980).

[54] White v. Gladden, 641 S.W.2d 738, 740-41 (Ark. App. 1982).

[55] *Morfeld, supra*, 343 N.W.2d at 884:

> Value of the use of the property is a just and recognized element of such damages, and the right to it should not be made nugatory by limiting its recovery to the event of a return. [I]f loss, deterioration or depreciation occur while the property is withheld, then the amount of such loss, damage or depreciation, to be conditioned, however, upon return of the property, the alternative judgment for the value being fixed as of the date of the taking. Moreover, the damages for detention must be such as grow out of the detention and are connected with or incident to the contest over possession.

(citation omitted); Slaughter v. Philadelphia Nat'l Bank, 290 F. Supp. 234, 237 (E.D. Pa. 1968) (stating that "[t]he general rule in an action for replevin, where the plaintiff has finally secured possession of the property, is that plaintiff may recover damages for the illegal detention of the stock. These damages are measured by the depreciation in the fair value of the property wrongfully held from the date of the demand to the date of the return"), *rev'd on other grounds*, 417 F.2d 21 (3d Cir. 1969); Hoff v. Lester, 200 P.2d 515, 519 (Wash. 1948) (same).

[56] *Cf.* Nora v. Safeco Ins. Co., 577 P.2d 347, 351 (Idaho 1978):

> We are aware that it would not be proper to allow lost business profit damages in every case involving conversion. The damages would only be proper when the person whose property has been converted shows that the conversion has resulted in lost business profits and shows with reasonable certainty the amount of these lost profits. The award of lost business profits in this particular case was proper.

[57] *Nora, supra*, 577 P.2d at 350-51 (using the above example as a case where consequential damages could be awarded if proven with sufficient certainty).

[58] Gemini Equip. Co. v. Pennsy Supply, Inc., 595 A.2d 1211, 1213-14 (Pa. Super. Ct. 1991) (using term "special damages" for claim of interest on value of detained property).

[83.3]   Trespass to Chattels

Trespass to chattels involves a less serious intrusion into the plaintiff's ownership and possessory interests in personal property than conversion. The distinction is hard to capture by a rule. In *Pearson v. Dodd* a newsman was given copies of documents that belonged to Senator Dodd. Senator Dodd sued for damages under various theories. The court rejected the conversion action since the newsman had not exercised dominion and control over Senator Dodd's property.[59] The reason for this position is that the possession of copies of papers (as opposed to the original documents) is not a sufficient interference with the owner's property to warrant redress through conversion.[60] Courts have been generally unwilling to extend the tort to ideas and thoughts[61] unless they had achieved a protected status, such as "trade secrets."[62]

The hallmark of the action for trespass to chattels is the requirement of actual damage as part of the prima facie case.[63] Nominal damages awards are not recognized. The higher burden imposed here than in cases of trespass to land reflects the greater protection afforded real property interests from intermedling over that afforded to personal property.[64] The *Pearson* decision is instructive on this point. The failure of the plaintiffs to show that they sustained actual damage as a result of the copying of the documents and dissemination of their contents resulted in the determination that they could not state a claim for trespass to chattels.[65]

A plaintiff asserting a claim for trespass to chattels maintains a continuing claim of ownership or right of possession, which, unlike conversion, entitles the plaintiff to claim damage to the chattel, such as physical injury and loss of use.[66]

---

[59] 410 F.2d 701 (D.C. Cir.), *cert. denied*, 395 U.S. 947 (1969).

[60] FMC Corp. v. Capital Cities/ABC, Inc., 915 F.2d 300, 303 (7th Cir. 1990), *citing* Harper & Row Publishers, Inc. v. Nation Enters., 723 F.2d 195, 201 (2d Cir. 1983), *rev'd on other grounds*, 471 U.S. 539 (1985).

[61] Intel Corp. v. Hamidi, 71 P.3d 296 (Cal. 20003) (rejecting theory of trespass to chattels as applicable to mass email communications that did not cause actual damage to plaintiff's computers and occupied only a small amount of the plaintiff's computer storage capacity).

[62] Burten v. Milton Bradley Co., 763 F.2d 461, 463 (1st Cir. 1985) (recognizing action for misappropriation of trade secrets); *cf.* Annis v. Tomberlin & Shelnutt Associates, Inc., 392 S.E.2d 717, 723 (Ga. App. 1990) (affirming award of damages for conversion of confidential information). *See generally* Uniform Trade Secrets Act (1995).

[63] CompuServe Inc. v. Cyber Promotions, Inc., 962 F. Supp. 1015, 1023 (S.D. Ohio 1997) (holding that defendant's use of plaintiff's proprietary computer equipment to send unsolicited e-mail constituted actionable trespass to chattels), *citing* Restatement (Second) of Torts § 218(d) (1977). *But see Intel Corp., supra*, 71 P.3d 296.

[64] Nominal damages are available when the trespass involves real property. Sections 93 (Trespass), 2.8 (Nominal Damages).

[65] *Pearson, supra*, 410 F.2d at 708.

[66] Restatement (Second) of Torts § 222A, cmt. c (1965) (recognizing that plaintiff may recover depreciation and loss of use damages when trespass results in those losses).

At common law the plaintiff suing for trespass to chattels had to accept the tender back of the property.[67] Formally, this differentiated trespass to chattels from the forced-sale concept of conversion.

§ 84 RETURN OF POSSESSION

[84.1] Replevin

The general nature of replevin is discussed at Section 57.1 (Nature of the Action).

[84.1.1] Superior Title or Equity in Another

When the owner seeks the return of her property through replevin, her claim to the property may be negated by a superior equity in the defendant in possession. If the defendant is a bona fide purchaser for value and without notice of plaintiff's rights in the property, replevin may be denied.[1] In some cases, such as with negotiable instruments, mere possession (*by a holder in due course*) may be sufficient to cut off a right of replevin.

One significant exception to the bona fide purchaser for value (BFP) rule (but not necessarily the holder in due course rule for negotiable instruments)[2] is the general rule that a thief cannot convey title, even to a BFP.[3] Consequently, a plaintiff may follow his property, as long and as far as necessary, in order to recover it through replevin, subject to the rule that he must be able to identify his property[4] and no subsequent possessor has a superior claim to the property.

---

[67] Prosser & Keeton, The Law of Torts 170-73 (5th ed. 1984).

[1] Paschal v. Hamilton, 363 So. 2d 1360, 1361 (Miss. 1978) (holding that bona fide purchaser for value took free of claim of original owner when transfer was from person who had voidable, but not void, title). A thief has only a void title that gives him nothing to convey.

[2] Brown v. Rosetti, 319 N.Y.S.2d 1001 (App. Dept. 1971) (*per curiam*) (holding that title to stolen bearer bonds could not be obtained unless bonds were acquired in the "usual course of business"). In *Brown*, the plaintiff, a commercial factor, acquired the bonds as security for an unpaid personal loan. The plaintiff did not deal in securities of that type. The court held that on the facts the plaintiff did not acquire the bonds in the usual course of business and therefore acquired no greater title than his debtor-customer.

[3] Suburban Motors, Inc. v. State Farm Mut. Auto Ins. Co., 268 Cal. Rptr. 16, 19 (Cal. App. 1990) (noting that a purchaser can only take those rights the seller possesses in the property; since a thief has neither title nor the power to convey title, even a BFP does not acquire title from a thief); *cf.* Creggin Group, Ltd. v. Crown Diversified Indus. Corp., 682 N.E.2d 692, 696-97 (Ohio App. 1996) (noting that when the owner has been "fraudulently induced" to convey property, the defrauder obtains "voidable title" and may convey good title to a bona fide purchaser for value); *Paschal, supra*, 363 So.2d 1360.

[4] Section 57.2 (Identification of Property (Accession and Confusion)).

[84.1.2]   Statutes of Limitation

The right to replevin property may be lost by operation of the statute of limitation or laches.[5] The statute begins to run on replevin at the time the defendant takes possession of the property or at the time the plaintiff demands the return of his property and is refused. The jurisdictions differ as to which rule to apply.[6] The differences are minimized by the fact that the first rule is subject to numerous limitations that, as a practical matter, substantially restrict its use. Nevertheless, the effect of the running of an applicable statute of limitation and its timely assertion by the defendant is to prevent the original owner from reclaiming her specific property, even if the property was stolen. While a thief cannot pass good title,[7] the passage of time can, as a practical matter.

Because the application of the statute of limitation deprives the true owner of his right to reclaim his property, the statute's application may work an injustice, particularly when property (such as works of art) have been stolen and kept out of public view for many years. One approach to this problem is to use the "demand and refusal" rule as the applicable rule for accrual of the statute of limitation.[8] This approach may be supplemented by principles of laches to determine if the claim is time barred.[9] The most prevalent approach, however, appears to be to apply the "discovery rule" and toll the statute of limitation until the true owner knows or should know the identity of the possessor of the stolen property.[10] The

---

[5] *In re* 1973 John Deere 4030 Tractor (Weaver v. Casey), 816 P.2d 1126, 1129 (Okla. 1991) (noting that 2 year statute applied to replevin action and gave defendant an affirmative defense to the remedy); Section 61 (Laches and Statutes of Limitation).

[6] *See* Stephen Foutty, Recent Development, Autocephalous Greek-Orthodox Church of Cypress v. Goldberg & Feldman Fine Arts, Inc.: *Entrenchment of the Due Diligence Requirement in Replevin Actions for Stolen Art*, 43 Vand. L. Rev. 1839, 1841–44 (1990) (collecting decisions).

[7] Natural Retailers Mut. Ins. Co. v. Gambino, 64 A.2d 927, 928 (N.J. Super. L. 1948):

> It is an elementary principle of law that no one can be deprived of his property except by his own voluntary act or by operation of law. The thief who steals a chattel acquires no title by such wrongful taking. The subsequent possession by the thief is a continuing wrong; and if during its continuance the wrongdoer enhances the value of the chattel by labor upon it or adds or substitutes new appliances or parts, the chattel in its enhanced value or changed condition with its substituted or added parts still belongs to the owner of the original chattel, and the original owner may retake it. And if the wrongdoer sells the chattel to an innocent purchaser, the latter obtains no title from the trespasser because the wrongdoer had none to give. The owner may still retake it in its improved or changed state.

(citations omitted).

[8] Kunstsammlungen Zu Weimar v. Elicofon, 678 F.2d 1150, 1161 (2d Cir. 1982) (stating that under New York law "an innocent purchaser of stolen goods becomes a wrongdoer only after refusing the owner's demand for [the goods'] return; until [d]emand is made and refused] the purchaser is considered to be in lawful possession") (citations omitted; brackets added).

[9] Republic of Turkey v. Metropolitan Museum of Art, 762 F. Supp. 44, 45 (S.D.N.Y. 1990); Solomon R. Guggenheim Foundation v. Lubell, 569 N.E.2d 426, 427 (N.Y. 1991).

[10] O'Keeffe v. Snyder, 416 A.2d 862, 869-70 (N.J. 1980) (involving painting lost in 1946 and found in 1976).

practical effect of using the discovery rule is to impose a due diligence obligation on the true owner. As noted in *O'Keeffe v Snyder*:

> The discovery rule shifts the emphasis from the conduct of the possessor to the conduct of the owner. The focus of the inquiry will no longer be whether the possessor has met the tests of adverse possession, but whether the owner has acted with due diligence in pursuing his or her personal property.[11]

In some cases, the demand and discovery rules are combined, thus extending significantly the period within which the rightful owner may act to reclaim the property.[12]

An interesting example of the application of the discovery rule occurred in *Erisoty v. Rizik*.[13] Defendants' parents owned the painting "Winter," an eighteenth century masterpiece by Corrado Giaquinto. The painting was stolen, along with several other paintings, in 1960. The loss was reported to law enforcement agencies and insurers. As part of the theft investigation, a number of organizations were contacted, including the Savoy Art Gallery, the Art Dealers Association of America, and the Hammer Gallery. The efforts to retrieve the stolen paintings were unsuccessful. In 1988, the painting was discovered in the trash having been separated into 5 pieces. The painting was partially restored and ultimately found its way to an auction house and was purchased by Erisoty in 1989. The sale had been publicly advertised and catalogues describing the painting were distributed. After acquiring the painting, Erisoty expended considerable time and effort further restoring the painting.

In 1992, defendant contacted an international organization devoted to preventing the circulation of stolen art. The organization was founded in 1976. Defendant had first learned of the organization in 1992. Through the efforts of the organization, the auction sale of the painting was discovered. The F.B.I. was involved and contacted Erisoty who turned the painting over to the agency. These events occurred in 1993. Litigation soon followed to determine the ownership interests in the painting. The court found that the applicable statute of limitation did not commence to run until defendants discovered the location of the painting and the identity of its possessor in 1993. Defendants' prior actions demonstrated reasonable diligence; consequently, defendants' claim of title was timely.

---

[11] *Id.* at 872 (noting that as long as the owner exercises due diligence but cannot locate the property or the identity of the possessor, the statute does not run).

[12] DeWeerth v. Baldinger, 836 F.2d 103, 106 (2d Cir. 1987), *cert. denied*, 486 U.S. 1056 (1988); *cf.* Johnson v. Gilliland, 896 S.W.2d 856, 859 (Ark. 1995) (involving action for conversion).

[13] 1995 U.S. Dist. LEXIS 2096 (E.D. Pa., February 23, 1995). This is a much truncated version of the tale.

[84.1.3] Pre-Trial or Judgment Remedy

At common law, replevin required that the plaintiff seize the property (chattel); indeed, seizure was necessary to vest the court with jurisdiction.[14] This pre-judgment seizure requirement led to several modern developments. First, there is the question whether a plaintiff may obtain a final judgment of replevin without first seizing the property at the commencement of the action. This was the common law approach for the final judgment was merely ancillary to the initial seizure. While many jurisdictions have by statute modified the common law rule to permit replevin without seizure,[15] the common law rule still has some adherents.[16]

The second development involved the application of constitutional due process guarantees to the seizure process. The common law rule, which was carried over in like form in its statutory counterpart—claim and delivery, was as follows:

> The plaintiff would apply for a writ of replevin from the court by supplying an affidavit alleging the right to immediate possession of the goods currently in the wrongful possession of a third party. If the affidavit satisfied the common law formalities, the court would issue the writ directing the sheriff to seize the chattel and to deliver the same to the plaintiff. Before the sheriff could serve the writ and seize the property, however, he had to obtain a bond from the plaintiff for twice the value of the goods sought to be replevied. Upon receiving possession, the plaintiff would bring the action in replevin seeking a judicial determination of his right to possession and any damages incurred by the defendant's wrongful retention of the chattel. Hence, replevin was a unique common law action that entitled a plaintiff to a prejudgment seizure of the chattel, leaving the merits of the plaintiff's claim of right to be tried later.[17]

Because the seizure could be accomplished ex parte and without a hearing, the procedure raised due process concerns, which the Supreme Court addressed in *Fuentes v. Shevin*. The Court held that common law replevin, which permitted debtor's property to be taken without prior opportunity to be heard, violated procedural due process guaranteed by the Fourteenth Amendment.[18]

In the aftermath of *Fuentes*, the states revised their pre-judgment seizure rules to bring them into compliance with the notice and hearing

---

[14] Doughty v. Sullivan, 661 A.2d 1112, 1118 (Me. 1995) (discussing common law restrictions on replevin).

[15] Cal. Civ. P. Code § 512.10-.120 (describing "Writ of Possession").

[16] *Doughty, supra,* 661 A.2d at 1119-20 (discussing modern versions of replevin and availability of remedy without seizure of property at the commencement of the action).

[17] *Id.* at 1118-19 (footnotes omitted).

[18] 407 U.S. 67 (1972).

requirements mandated by the Court. In an appropriate case, however, the notice and hearing requirement may be deferred until after the seizure.[19]

[84.2] Equitable Replevin

Replevin, when used to obtain the return of personal property, provides specific relief like an injunction. For that reason, equitable relief is not frequently invoked in this context because the remedy at law (replevin) is adequate, which is to say that it is as plain, complete, and efficient as equitable injunctive relief.[20] There are, however, a number of instances when the remedy of "equitable replevin" is available. The chief differences between the two forms of replevin are: (1) the availability of contempt to enforce equitable replevin decrees, and (2) the availability of a jury for legal replevin actions, although this second point is of little importance when the plaintiff seeks interim relief either through a pre-judgment attachment (legal replevin) or temporary injunction (equitable replevin).

Perhaps the most common use of equitable replevin is in connection with other equitable remedies. For example, a plaintiff may wish to rescind a transaction on the ground that her consent was procured by fraud, duress, or deceit. The rescission action often sounds in equity.[21] A common supplement to rescission of a transaction is the mutual return of consideration given. This can be facilitated by equitable replevin. For example, a plaintiff may be induced to sell common stock in a closed corporation through the fraud of company insiders. As part of the undoing of the transaction, plaintiff wishes the stock he sold returned to him. This can be accomplished by equitable replevin.[22]

Equitable replevin is also used in cases when the defendant has possession of sensitive or irreplaceable materials or goods. For example, the defendant may have possession of confidential business information belonging to his former employer,[23] or heirlooms or other unique artifacts, "which are prized for their associations rather than for their intrinsic value."[24] In both of these situations, recovery of the property has been accomplished in equity as well as at law.

---

[19] Sea Rail Truckloads, Inc. v. Pullman, Inc., 182 Cal. Rptr. 560, 562-63 (Cal. App. 1982) (holding that seizure of property may occur without notice when there is an imminent danger that the property will be destroyed); Section 31.6 (Notice and Hearing Requirements).

[20] Section 21 (Adequacy of the Remedy at Law/Irreparable Injury).

[21] Section 131.2 ([Forms of Rescission] Equity).

[22] Crist v. United Underwriters, Ltd., 343 F.2d 902, 903 (10th Cir. 1965) (involving defrauded seller who regained stock after undoing the transaction); Royal Air Properties, Inc. v. Smith, 312 F.2d 210, 213 (9th Cir. 1962) (same); Samia v. Central Oil Co. of Worcester, 158 N.E.2d 469, 478 (Mass. 1959) (ordering surrender and redistribution of wrongfully issued stock in closely held corporation).

[23] In re IBP Confidential Business Documents Litig., 754 F.2d 787, 789 (8th Cir. 1985) (involving business documents characterized by the court as containing "sensitive, confidential information about IBP's internal operations and business strategies").

[24] Charles Simkin & Sons, Inc. v. Massiah, 289 F.2d 26, 29 (3d Cir. 1961) (citation omitted).

Equitable replevin is sometimes available when the objective is to gain possession of specific property but not to test rights that the property represents. The common example here are stock certificates. A plaintiff has been allowed to use equitable replevin to obtain physical custody of the stock certificate without contesting the underlying ownership interest in the corporation which the certificate represents.[25] The certificate may have value as a pledge or collateral separate from its value as establishing an ownership interest in the corporation.

Equitable replevin may be necessary when the property to be recovered has been affixed or attached to other property. In such cases the sheriff may refuse to execute the writ; therefore, to effect redress the defendant may be ordered to deliver the property to the plaintiff.[26]

Equitable replevin, in the form of temporary injunctive relief, may be available.[27] In this context there is little functional difference between temporary injunctive relief (TRO or preliminary injunction) and the modern, constitutionally valid forms of pre-judgment seizure or attachment of property.[28]

§ 85   UNJUST ENRICHMENT AND RESTITUTION

The wrongful interference with the owner's exclusive right to possession and control of personal property may be addressed through unjust enrichment. The basic theory is that the defendant's wrongful conduct has conferred a benefit, which in fairness and justice he should convey to the true owner of the property. The usual vehicle for disgorging the benefit is the action for quasi contract.[1] While conversion treats the wrongful conduct as a "fictional sale," unjust enrichment treats the wrongful conduct as a "fictional contract." The "fictional contract" is the vehicle by which the defendant is held to have promised the plaintiff to deliver up the wrongful gains the defendant's wrongful conduct generated.[2]

---

[25] Somerville Nat'l Bank v. Hornblower, 199 N.E. 918, 920 (Mass. 1936) (permitting equitable replevin but not replevin to recover stock certificate). *Compare* Brennan v. W.A. Wills, Ltd., 263 F.2d 1, 2-3 (10th Cir.), *cert. denied*, 360 U.S. 902 (1959) (rejecting, under Colorado law, use of replevin to recover stock certificates in the name of another), *with* Baron v. Peoples Nat'l Bank of Secaucus, 84 A.2d 492, 493 (N.J. Co. Ct. 1951) (stating that replevin or equitable replevin may be used to recover stock certificates).

[26] Farnsworth v. Whiting, 72 A. 314 (Me. 1908).

[27] Pillsbury, Madison & Sutro v. Schectman, 64 Cal. Rptr. 2d 698 (Cal. App. 1997) (affirming grant of preliminary injunction requiring attorney representing law firm's employees to return confidential documents that were removed from law firm without the firm's consent or pursuant to lawful discovery).

[28] One potentially significant difference lies in the Federal Rules of Civil Procedure. Provisional relief, such as attachments, are governed by Rule 64, which references state law. Equitable remedies, such as temporary injunctions, are governed by Rule 65, which is self-contained and does not reference state law.

[1] Section 44 (Quasi Contract and Unjust Enrichment).

[2] Ablah v. Eyman, 365 P.2d 181, 191-92 (Kan. 1961).

The benefit of invoking unjust enrichment in this context lies in the calculus of the costs and benefits of a damages oriented remedy versus a gains oriented remedy. This is exemplified by *Olwell v. Nye & Nissen Co.*[3] In *Olwell* the defendant used machinery, stored by plaintiff on defendant's premises, without plaintiff's consent. A damages measure would focus on what plaintiff lost, here one can calculate conversion, or replevin, or trespass to chattels damages. A restitution measure would focus on defendant's benefit; what did the defendant gain or save by not contracting with the plaintiff for the benefit. Some measures of that benefit would overlap the damages measure. For example, we could say that defendant benefits by not paying a fair rental value for the machinery. This fair rental measure would duplicate loss of use damages.[4] On the other hand, benefit may be defined more capaciously, which is what happened in *Olwell*. The court characterized the benefit as the expenses saved by defendant in not having to employ an individual to do the tasks performed by the machine.[5] These avoided labor costs apparently exceeded the costs associated with using the machine.[6] This expense avoided measure, sometimes referred to as a "negative unjust enrichment," has been recognized in other decisions as a proper basis for restitution.[7]

The obvious reason for a plaintiff to seek recovery in restitution rather than damages is the prospect of a larger recovery. That presents, however, a dilemma for some courts. The usual measure of a plaintiff's recovery for tortious misconduct is compensatory and designed to place the plaintiff in the position she would have been in but for the misconduct by the defendant. A recovery in excess of the plaintiff's loss—the reason for selecting restitution over damages—is inconsistent with this goal and suggests a punitive measure. On the other hand, there is the belief that a tortfeasor should not be allowed to retain the profits realized by his wrongdoing as this might encourage the commission of tortious conduct. The issue was addressed in *Olwell*, but the court concluded that restitution was compatible with a compensation theory.[8] Some courts avoid the issue by assuming that damages to plaintiff and benefit to defendant are equal.[9] The awarding of restitution rather than damaged has received a little more consideration in connection with tortious interference cases, but no consensus has been achieved.[10] The competing considerations are not, however, reconcilable.

---

[3] 173 P.2d 652 (Wash. 1946).

[4] Sections 80.3 ([Physical Damage] Loss of Use), 83.2 ([Damages] Replevin), 83.3 ([Damages] Trespass to Chattels).

[5] *Olwell, supra,* 173 P.2d at 654.

[6] The defendant assigned as error the failure to award rental value rather than labor expenses avoided. *Id.* at 653. One assumes defendant would not argue for a greater measure over a lesser. One also assumes that if use of the machine was not cost effective, the defendant would not have wrongfully applied it to its business.

[7] Branch v. Mobil Oil Corp., 778 F. Supp. 35, 36 (W.D. Okla. 1991); *Ablah, supra,* 365 P.2d at 192 (referring to concept as the "resulting benefit" rule).

[8] *Id.* at 654.

[9] Zippertubing Co. v. Teleflex, Inc., 757 F.2d 1401, 1411 (3d Cir. 1985).

[10] *Compare* Developers Three v. Nationwide Ins. Co., 582 N.E.2d 1130, 1135 (Ohio App.

An election must be made based on the court's perception as to which approach better advances the values underlying the civil liability system.[11]

§ 86   GOOD FAITH IMPROVERS OF PERSONAL PROPERTY

The rights of a good faith improver to personal property are determined under the doctrine of accession and confusion, which is discussed in Section 57.2 (Identification of Property (Accession and Confusion)). The Good Faith Improver has primary application in the personal property context in the area of security interests (collateral). Do improvements made or affixed to property by the debtor in possession pass to the creditor who has a lien on the whole if the creditor forecloses and acquire the collateral? The answer to this question often turns on the ease with which the improvements may be separated from the property.[1]

1990) (finding "[o]n balance . . . the arguments against recovery of a defendant's profits more persuasive. . ."), *with* National Merchandising Corp. v. Leyden, 348 N.E.2d 771, 776 (Mass. 1976) (holding that a defendant should not "be heard to say that the unjust enrichment remedy is unfairly 'punitive' because the plaintiff may recover more than his exact loss, when use of a tort measure might allow the defendant to retain some part of his ill gotten gains. Here, as in other contexts, a plaintiff in proper cases may be permitted alternative routes of recovery").

[11] Section 41 (Restitution for Wrongdoing).

[1] Bucci v. IRS, 653 F. Supp. 479, 483 (D.R.I. 1987) (collecting decisions finding that creditor's liens did not attach to easily removable improvements to motor vehicle, such as mobile phone, new tires, radio, etc.); *In re* Lyford (General Motors Acceptance Corp.), 22 B.R. 222, 224–25 (D. Maine 1982) (finding that the creditor's lien attached to a factory-installed hydraulic boom and grapple attached to a truck chassis to pick up logs and load them onto truck). The fact that certain of the components were merely bolted, not welded to the chassis was not controlling given that separation would require two workers a full day or more to accomplish the task. *Cf.* Bancorp Leasing and Fin. Corp. v. Stadeli Pump & Constr., Inc., 739 P.2d 548, 553 (Or. 1987) (finding that the doctrine of accession did not apply to an engine placed in a vehicle; the court noted that while a vehicle without an engine was incomplete, the vehicle was capable of receiving a new engine with relative ease).

Chapter 10

REMEDIES FOR INJURY TO REAL PROPERTY

§ 90   PHYSICAL DAMAGE

The usual measure of damages for injury to real property, including structures and buildings,[1] is diminution in value, which is the difference

---

[1] Section 90.3 (Damage to Buildings).

between the market value of the property prior to the injury and its market value immediately thereafter.[2] Alternatively, the owner may seek cost of repair, restoration, or remediation as the measure of damages,[3] although some jurisdictions limit these measures to unique or special value property. As is the case with personal property, often the owner may use cost of repair as the measure of diminution in value. When the cost of repair is greater than the diminution in market value, some courts limit the recovery to the diminution in market value.[4] Other courts, however, permit recovery of reasonable remediation, restoration, or repair costs even though they exceed diminution in value.[5] This occurs when the court perceives that the diminution in value measure does not adequately reflect the actual detriment sustained[6] or under the impetus of legislation that emphasizes restoration of land to its pre-injury state as the preferred remedial goal.[7]

Real property damage claims should distinguish between injury to the realty itself, such as natural resource damage, and damage to improvements on the property, such as structures. The value of real property reflects the sum of both the value of the realty and the improvements. Damage to improvements may not dramatically affect the value of the property. In fact, the property may be worth more after the structure has been destroyed, as, for example, if the realty was going to be redeveloped. These cases can raise difficult valuation problems.[8]

[90.1]   Temporary or Permanent Injury

A gloss that is often applied in cases of damage to real property is that between permanent injury, on the one hand, versus non-permanent or

---

[2] Jordan v. Stallings, 911 S.W.2d 653, 663 (Mo. App. 1995); Kitzman v. Newman, 41 Cal. Rptr. 182, 188 (Cal. App. 1964); Restatement (Second) of Torts §§ 911, 929(i)(a) (1979); Section 7 (Value); Section 80 (Physical Damage).

[3] Green v. General Petroleum Corp., 270 P. 952, 955–56 (Cal. 1928).

[4] Lobozzo v. Adam Eidemiller, Inc., 263 A.2d 432, 437 (Pa. 1970).

[5] Orndorff v. Christiana Community Builders, 266 Cal. Rptr. 193, 195 (Cal. App. 1990) (involving damage to family residence); Revels v. Knighton, 805 S.W.2d 649, 650 (Ark. 1991) (involving damage to shade trees); Section 91.3 (Damage to Trees and Shrubs).

[6] Weld Cty. Bd. of Cty. Commrs., v. Slovek, 723 P.2d 1309, 1315–16 (Colo. 1986) (stating that no hard and fast rule can be identified which will determine with precision when it is appropriate to allow plaintiff to recover the greater of cost of restoration over diminution in value damages); Restatement (Second) of Torts § 929(1)(a) (1979) (stating that "in an appropriate case" the owner may elect between diminution in value or cost of restoration). What constitutes "an appropriate case" is not defined, but the comment identifies several factors, such as whether the real property constitutes a personal residence, whether the owner has personal reasons for restoring the property to its pre-injury condition, and whether the injury is repairable and at what cost. Id. at cmt. b.

[7] Section 91.1 (Environmental Injury).

[8] See ROBERT H. JERRY, UNDERSTANDING INSURANCE LAW § 46[b] (3d ed. 2001) (collecting decisions in which the insured structure, which is subject to be demolished or condemned, is damaged or destroyed by fire). As Professor Jerry notes, courts have reached conflicting conclusions as to whether the valuation should include the fact of imminent demolition or condemnation.

temporary injury, on the other. If the injury to real property is deemed to be permanent, the diminution in value measure is applied. If the injury to real property is deemed to be non-permanent, the cost of repair or remediation measure is used. The difference between permanent and non-permanent injury is, however, hard to define.[9] In theory, non-permanent injuries are those that are intermittent and occasional and which are repairable or abatable. Cost of repair is the preferred remedy because the injury is remediable and the cause of the injury can be terminated. Permanent injuries, on the other hand, are, in theory, fixed and immutable. The property will always be burdened with the injury. Since the injury is irremediable, the proper measure of damages is diminution in value.[10] As noted in *Kraft v. Langford*:

> The character of an injury as either permanent or temporary is determined by its continuum. Permanent injuries are those which are constant and continuous, not intermittent or recurrent. Temporary injuries are those which are not continuous but are "sporadic and contingent upon some irregular force such as rain." Another characteristic of a temporary injury is the ability of a court of equity to enjoin the injury causing activity. An injury which can be terminated cannot be a permanent injury. The concepts of temporary and permanent injuries are mutually exclusive and damages for both may not be recovered in the same action.[11]

The problem with the permanent versus non-permanent distinction is its implicit assumption that an injury can be deemed remediable or not without regard to the value of the thing to be repaired. Courts often speak as if the distinction and classifications are self-evident. The critical feature of the permanent versus non-permanent distinction is the realization that the distinctions are labels to be affixed at the end part of the analysis, not guidelines that can be used to resolve cases. Property becomes irremediable because it is deemed not worth the cost necessary to effect the repairs. In making this determination, the perspective is that of the reasonably prudent person.[12] Notwithstanding what should be an economic analysis,

---

[9] Miller v. Cudahy, 858 F.2d 1449, 1453 (10th Cir. 1988), *cert. denied,* 492 U.S. 926 (1985) (finding that the distinction between permanent and temporary damages "is at best problematical"). The court further noted that while no hard and fast rule can be adopted as to when damages are permanent or temporary, "the distinction remains a viable concept." *Id.* at 1453, *quoting* Olson v. State Highway Comm'n of Kansas, 679 P.2d 167, 172 (Kan. 1984). The court did not explain why the distinction remained viable in light of the problems and limitations noted. Sun Oil Co. v. Nunnery, 170 So. 2d 24, 31–32 (Miss. 1964) (stating that when damage to land is temporary and subject to remediation, cost of restoration is the proper measure of damages).

[10] McAlister v. Atlantic Richfield Co., 662 P.2d 1203, 1212 (Kan. 1983).

[11] 565 S.W.2d 223, 227 (Tex. 1978) (citations omitted).

[12] *Cf.* 15 R. ANDERSON, COUCH'S CYCLOPEDIA OF INSURANCE LAW § 54:62 (2d ed. 1966) (noting that one measure of "total loss" for insurance coverage purposes is the "restoration to use" test, *i.e.,* whether a reasonably prudent person would use the undamaged portion remaining after the loss as a basis for restoring the structure to its pre-loss condition). The issue here is whether a reasonably prudent person would repair the damaged property to its pre-injury condition or whether the injury would be declared total and the remains sold for their salvage value.

courts often attempt to project the patina of objective standards based on the nature of the injury. For example, in *Dougan v. Rossville Drainage District* the court identified three factors as guiding the classification of injury as temporary or permanent: (1) the nature of the causative structure; (2) the nature of the damages; and, (3) the ability to determine or estimate damages.[13] The difficulty with the test is its generality. The test tells a court what to look for, but doesn't provide any guidance as to how a court should interpret or evaluate what it finds. That process is more intuitive and contextual, and, hence, discretionary.

The use of permanent and non-permanent terminology is unfortunate because it suggests that the focus is on the nature of the injury, when the emphasis is more on the willingness of the court to permit the owner to expend more for cost of repair or remediation than the loss the owner actually sustained in terms of the economic value of the property (diminution in value). An alternative approach is to distinguish between permanent and non-permanent injuries based on the relationship between the cost of repair and the pre-injury value of the property.[14] This permits the owner to repair or remediate actual injury as long as the cost of doing so does not exceed the property's pre-injury value. While this approach is a distinct minority view in the personal property context,[15] it has a wider following in the real property field.[16]

The preference in real property cases for a measure that permits a recovery greater than the amount necessary to restore the owner to his prior economic position is more accepted than justified. Cultural and historical views of real property as a measure of the owner's wealth, status, and security may encourage courts to allow the owner to restore to herself that which she had before the injury, even if doing so is to some extent economically inefficient. Real property may be perceived as a scarce, unique resource that should be protected by non-market remedies. In addition, real property damages remedies are frequently influenced by legislation that has augmented the damages remedy available. Courts may treat this as a signal that real property damages remedies should be capaciously applied. On the other hand, the ideal of compensating wrongs in the cheapest, most cost-effective manner still retains some force here. Even when the permanent versus non-permanent distinction is drawn, and the injury is deemed

---

[13] 15 P.3d 338, 344 (Kan. 2000) (discussing temporary-permanent distinction in context of applying appropriate statute of limitation). The reference to "causative structure" is to whether the structure is permanent or removable as a practical matter.

[14] General Outdoor Adv. Co. v. LaSalle Realty Corp., 218 N.E.2d 141, 151 (Ind. App. 1966); Allied Hotels v. Barden, 389 P.2d 968, 973 (Okla. 1964).

[15] Section 80.2 ([Physical Damage] Partial Destruction).

[16] Restatement (Second) of Torts, § 929(1)(a) (1979) (permitting owner to recover damages based on diminution in value, or "at his election, in an appropriate case, the cost of restoration that has been or may be reasonably incurred").

non-permanent, a court may still apply, beneath the language of the test, a "lesser of" rule.[17]

When the court is willing to consider restoration costs that exceed diminution in value, the relevant factors mentioned by the Restatement, such as "an appropriate case" and "reasonably incurred," still leave much to individual discretion. For an injured party to recover restoration costs in excess of diminution in value, that party must show sufficient reasons supporting restoration and may be required to show that repairs actually will be made. The restoration costs must be reasonable in light of the special considerations presented and may not be disproportionate to diminution in value. A purely subjective preference for the land in its pre-tort condition will usually not qualify as a sufficient reason warranting restoration costs in excess of diminution in value.[18]

[90.2] Economic and Non-Economic Losses

Injury to real property may be valued by its consequences. For example, the presence of injury may be reflected in a reduction of the sales price when the damaged property is sold to a third person. In *Northridge Co. v. W.R. Grace & Co.* the buyer and seller negotiated a discount of the purchase price of a mall complex to reflect the costs of asbestos removal that the buyer would incur after the sale was consummated. The court held that the purchase price discount ($10 million) reflected the cost of contamination caused by the asbestos (diminution in value) and thus was properly charged to the defendant.[19]

The issue of annoyance, discomfort, and distress damages for injury to real property is one that is particularly vexing. Close attention must be paid to the form of action and the type of interest that has been injured. When the injury consists solely of physical injury to real property, there is language in some cases that annoyance, discomfort, and distress over those

---

[17] *E.g.,* Prashant Enters., Inc. v. State, 650 N.Y.S.2d 473, 476 (App. Dept. 1996) (involving damage to motel property resulting from overflow of a creek):

> Fundamentally, the proper measure of damages for permanent injury to real property is the diminution in the market value of the property by reason of that injury or, put another way, the difference between the value of the land before the injury and the value after the injury. In many cases, however, the cost of repairing the injury will be the proper measure of damages, so long as the cost of restoring the land to its former condition is less than the diminution in the market value of the whole property by reason of the injury. In such a case, the claimant is entitled to the cost of repair at the time the damages occurred.

(citations omitted).

[18] Lexington Ins. Co. v. Baltimore Gas & Elec. Co., 979 F. Supp. 360, 362–63 (D. Md. 1997) (noting that under Maryland law excess of diminution in value recovery may not be disproportionate to value of property). The court noted, however, that whether restoration costs were disproportionate was for the trier-of-fact to determine, *id.* at 364, and even if the costs were disproportionate they would be allowed if the owner had valid personal reasons for restoring the property to its original condition. *Id.*; Weld Cty. Bd. of Cty. Commrs v. Slovek, 723 P.2d 1309, 1317 (Colo. 1986).

[19] 556 N.W.2d 345, 350–51 (Wis. App. 1996).

losses are not separately comprehensible, outside of loss of use damages.[20] In *McBride v. Dice* the owners sought distress damages against a pest control company that negligently inspected the wrong residence for termite infestation. After the owners concluded their purchase, they discovered the residence they purchased, not the one defendant inspected, was infested with termites. They sought in addition to their economic damages $10,000 for inconvenience and discomfort. The court held that the owner's were limited to their economic losses only and that it was reversible error to allow damages for non-economic harm.[21]

The reasons for this rule are severalfold. First, there is the perception that witnessing or experiencing the destruction of property "is not nearly as devastating as witnessing or being involved in the loss of a close relative. . . ."[22] Such losses are not seen as *per se* inconsequential, but are simply deemed part of "life experience[s] that all [unfortunately] may expect to endure."[23]

Second, many courts believe that exposing defendants to distress damages in property damage cases (1) extends liability in a manner that unreasonably burdens the defendants; (2) raises concern over possible fraudulent claims; and (3) "removes any logical stopping point to a tortfeasor's liability."[24]

The above noted concerns largely replicate those that have been made and rejected in the personal injury context. They retain some vitality here, but how much is uncertain. For example, in *City of Tyler v. Likes* the court rejected recovery of distress damages arising out of the flooding of plaintiff's residence due to the defendant's negligence.[25] The court noted that while distress damages have been authorized in virtually all personal injury actions, the recovery of distress damages outside this area has been largely "ad hoc" resulting in case law that is in "an almost unparalleled state of confusion."[26] The court noted the special valuation rules applicable to property for which no market exists, noting that in such cases the owner's "feelings" for the property support a non-market measure.[27] The court concluded:

> The owner's feelings thus help determine the value of the destroyed item to the owner for purposes of property, not mental anguish, damages. Because a plaintiff whose property has been harmed can

---

[20] Blagrove v. JB Mechanical, Inc., 934 P.2d 1273, 1276 (Wyo. 1997) (noting that "[e]motional distress is not usually recoverable as an element of property damages unless an improper motive is involved").

[21] 930 P.2d 631, 633 (Kan. App. 1997).

[22] Kleinke v. Farmers Coop. Supply & Shipping, 549 N.W.2d 714, 716–17 (Wis. 1996); *Blagrove, supra*, 934 P.2d at 1276.

[23] *Kleinke, supra*, 549 N.W.2d at 717 (citation omitted).

[24] *Id.*

[25] 962 S.W.2d 489 (Tex. 1997).

[26] *Id.* at 495–96.

[27] *Id.* at 497.

ordinarily recover fully for that loss through economic damages, our reluctance to leave a legally injured plaintiff with no remedy at all, which has rightfully influenced courts to look favorably on awarding mental anguish damages, does not come into play in cases where the primary injury is to property.[28]

In effect, the court treated the distress claim as collapsed in the valuation claim under the "Value to Owner" test.[29]

An additional reason given by courts for not recognizing noneconomic damages is that the relationship between the parties is governed by contract and contract law should determine what remedies are available.[30]

Many courts, however, permit recovery of annoyance, discomfort, and occasionally distress damages for injury to real property,[31] particularly when the theories of nuisance or trespass are invoked.[32] These damages, when recognized, are usually tied to loss of use and the economic deprivation that accompanies loss of use. As noted in *Jarrett v. E.L. Harper & Son Inc.*, when plaintiffs sought annoyance and inconvenience damages resulting from destruction of their waterwell by defendant:

> Plaintiffs also seek to recover for loss of use of their property and allege annoyance, inconvenience and "general unpleasantness" as elements to be considered in proving loss of use. Ordinarily, loss of use is measured by lost profits or lost rental value. When that standard is difficult to apply because the property in question is not used commercially, it may be necessary to formulate a measure of damages that is more uniquely adapted to the plaintiffs' injury. Thus, we find that annoyance and inconvenience are properly considered as elements in the measure of damages that plaintiffs are entitled to recover, provided that these considerations are measured by an objective standard of ordinary persons acting reasonably under the given conditions.[33]

Non-economic damages are more readily granted when they are framed as annoyance or discomfort losses rather than distress losses, although the line between annoyance and distress is hard to define. Recovery of

---

[28] *Id.*

[29] Section 81 (Value to Owner).

[30] Section 142 (Distress Damages); *cf.* Orkin Extermination Co. Inc. v. DelGuidice, 790 So. 2d 1158 (Fla. App. 2001) (holding that homeowner could not recover "stigma" damages due to unsuccessful treatment by company of home for termites because contract did not provide for "stigma" damages); Section 186 (Negating Remedies by Contract).

[31] Horrisberger v. Mohlmaster, 657 N.E.2d 534, 538 (Ohio App. 1995); *Weld Cty. Bd. of Cty. Commrs., supra,* 723 P.2d at 1317–18.

[32] Birchler v. Castello Land Co., Inc., 942 P.2d 968, 972–73 (Wash. 1997) (recognizing recovery of distress damages for intentional trespass resulting in destruction of vegetation); Herzog v. Grosso, 259 P.2d 429, 433–34 (Cal. 1953) (permitting recovery of distress damages when trespass (blasting) caused distress (fear for safety) as a natural consequence of the defendant's conduct); Section 94.2.3 ([Nuisance] Annoyance and Discomfort Damages).

[33] 235 S.E.2d 362, 365 (W. Va. 1977).

non-economic losses is enhanced when the defendant's acts constitute a nuisance and injure the plaintiff in her use and enjoyment of her property. The willingness to award non-economic damages in nuisance cases, but not as willingly when the issue is direct damage injury to real property, is hard to square. It perhaps knows no better explanation than that offered by Maitland that the old "forms of action are buried but they still rule us from their graves."[34] A more liberal approach is suggested by *McGregor v. Barton Sand & Gravel, Inc.*[35] In *McGregor* the court noted precedent that suggested that distress damages were limited to nuisance claims but rejecting the limitation. The court held that the purpose of the suggestive caveat in the precedent was "only to dispel any understanding that the case decided anything beyond the immediate issue presented and to suggest that the general subject of emotional distress damages might eventually receive more extensive attention." In *McGregor* the court gave the issue more extensive attention and resolved:

> We conclude that the [precedent], allowing emotional distress damages for interference with the use and enjoyment of land, is as applicable in intentional trespass actions as in negligence or nuisance actions. No reason occurs to us why the same kind of injury resulting from the same kind of act should not be compensable solely because the actor's conduct is deliberate rather than negligent.[36]

The general rule is that the award of compensatory damages belongs to the person who owns the property at the time the injury or loss is sustained.[37]

[90.3] Damage to Buildings

The general rule regarding injury when the building is destroyed is diminution in value.[38] When the building is damaged, the usual measure is cost of repair or restoration,[39] subject to the principle that recovery may not exceed diminution in value. Whether the building has been destroyed or damaged is determined by reference to the relationship between the cost of repair and the pre-injury value of the building.[40] Limiting recoveries to diminution in value has been relaxed when residential buildings, such as

---

[34] F. Maitland, The Forms of Action at Common Law 2 (A. Clayton & W. Whittaker, eds. 1936), *quoted in* United States v. Benmar Transp. & Leasing Corp., 444 U.S. 4, 6 (1979).

[35] 660 P.2d 175 (Or. 1983).

[36] *Id.* at 181 (footnote omitted; bracket added). The "precedent" the court referred to was *Edwards v. Talent Irrig. Dist.*, 570 P.2d 1169 (Or. 1977).

[37] Florida Citrus Nursery, Inc. v. Department of Agric. & Cons. Affairs, 570 So. 2d 1355, 1356 (Fla. App. 1990) (stating rule and noting that the award only passes to the successor in interest or title through proper provision in a deed or by an assignment).

[38] Rittenhouse v. Tabor Grain Co., 561 N.E.2d 264, 272 (Ill. App. 1990).

[39] Linforth v. S.F. Gas. & Elec. Co., 103 P. 320, 322 (Cal. 1909).

[40] Section 90.1 (Temporary or Permanent Injury).

family homes, are involved.[41] The fact that the plaintiff makes the repairs itself, or with its own employees does not diminish the recovery[42] because the focus is on the reasonable costs of repair, not the identity of the repairer.

Repair of a building may require allocation of repair costs when the repairs add to the building's useful life. In *United States v. Ebinger* defendant (Ebinger) negligently set fire to a water cooling tower on top of a building. The tower was an integral part of the air conditioning system. Ebinger contended that the United States was limited to the pre-tort fair market value of the tower. The court (per Judge Friendly) disagreed:

> Although Ebinger does not question that it was cheaper to procure a new tower than to repair the old one, he claims that the value of the tower before the fire constituted the limit of the Government's recovery. The cases on which he relies . . . are based on the rationale that the plaintiff could have held its loss to the value of the property before the damage by abandoning rather than repairing it. The reasoning has no application when the damaged unit is an essential part of a larger whole. Despite the fact that the water tower was located above the building rather than within its four walls, it was a necessary and integral part of the building's air conditioning system. Under such circumstances it has been generally held that the defendant is not entitled to a credit merely because the plaintiff has acquired a new unit, presumably with a longer life expectancy than the old, if that was the cheapest course available. This can be justified by the consideration that the plaintiff should not be required to finance in part the premature replacement of equipment when there is no assurance that this will add to the realizable value of the property to which its appertains. . . . [W]e are not sure we would apply the established rule when this would be clearly inequitable, *e.g.* in a case where the damaged part was scheduled for early replacement, long before the expiration of the useful life of the whole. Here, however, the judge found that the old tower had 'a useful life expectancy of 20-25 years or perhaps longer' and while he estimated a somewhat longer useful life for the building, any increment in value by avoiding the possible need to replace the water tower a quarter of a century hence would be small and speculative. On the other hand, the trial court should have allowed credit for the maintenance expenses the new tower will save.[43]

Ebinger emphasizes that courts must be careful not to look at items of property in isolation when considering whether the costs of repair exceed pre-tort value. If an item is an integral part of a larger whole, it may be appropriate to examine whether costs of repair exceed the market value of the "larger whole," rather than the market value of the "item."

---

[41] Orndorff v. Christiana Community Builders, 266 Cal. Rptr. 193 (Cal. App. 1990).

[42] O'Tool v. Hathaway, 461 N.W.2d 161, 165 (Iowa 1990).

[43] 386 F.2d 557, 560-61 (2d Cir. 1967) (citations omitted); Section 7.5 (Betterment).

When the building or structure that has been damaged is unique, such as a church, courts have recognized that market value as measured by comparable sales may not provide adequate compensation because the market for the unique property is thin. In such cases, replacement cost less depreciation has been used.[44] To qualify for this measure, the property must meet several criteria to be considered legally unique: (1) the improvement must be unique and specially built for the specific purpose for which it is designed; (2) the improvement must have been designed for a special use and must be so specially used; (3) there must be no market for the type of property and no sales of property for such use; and (4) the improvement must be an appropriate improvement at the time of the injury and its use must be economically feasible and reasonably expected to be replaced.[45]

[90.4] Removal of or Damage to Fixtures

The measure of damages in cases of wrongful removal or destruction of fixtures is the market value of the fixture, separate and apart from the value of the real property or, in the alternative, the cost of restoring or replacing the fixture when that can be done at a reasonable cost not disproportionate to the injuries suffered and that cost is less than the diminution of value of the whole property.[46]

Where the fixtures are merely damaged, but not destroyed, then the proper measure of damages is the cost of their repair and reinstallation, so long as this does not exceed their actual value.[47]

[90.5] Condemnation Through Eminent Domain

The constitution requires that the government provide "just compensation" when taking private property for public benefit. The components of "just compensation" are not, however, prescribed by the constitution and jurisdictions vary in their approaches to this issue. This issue of valuing property for purposes of condemnation awards has developed into a specialized area of law, whose rules and governing principles are beyond the scope of this work. Some of the critical questions that arise in this area are: (1) valuation when there is a partial taking and the issue arising whether the taking has damaged the remaining property not damaged, *i.e.*, "severance" damage" (2) whether condemned property should be valued based on current use, planned-for use, or highest and best possible use; and (3)

---

[44] Matter of County of Suffolk, 392 N.E.2d 1236, 1237 (N.Y. 1979).

[45] *Id.* (involving specially built greenhouses and an adjoining residence, which the court found satisfied the test as specialty property).

[46] Givens v. Markall, 124 P.2d 839, 842 (Cal. App. 1942).

[47] Menzies v. Geophysical Serv., Inc., 254 P.2d 51, 53 (Cal. App. 1953); 3 MILLER & STARR, CURRENT LAW OF CALIFORNIA REAL ESTATE § 1752 *et seq.* (rev. ed. 1977) (discussing remedies for removal or destruction of fixtures from real property).

whether the owner should recover for "goodwill" when his business property is condemned and he is forced to relocate.[48]

[90.6]   Damage to Public Property

Difficult valuation issues can arise when the property damaged is publicly owned rather than privately owned. If the defendant damages or destroys a public bridge or highway wall, what is the proper measure of damages given the absence of a market for such property. The general approach here is to use cost of repair or replacement. As noted by one court in a case when an overweight truck damaged a public bridge:

> Where concepts of value in a commercial sense cannot be applied because a particular structure in the public domain simply doesn't have any such value, speculative or otherwise, the measure of damages must be the reasonable cost of replacement by a similar structure consistent with current standards of design.[49]

Alternatively, some jurisdictions adopt in effect a "broad evidence" test that allows the trier-of-fact to consider a number of factors to arrive at the "actual" or "real" value of property for which there is no market value. As noted by one court when defendant mistakenly caused a bridge to be torn down:

> Damages for the destruction of a public structure like a bridge cannot be determined by a reference to market value. That is because a destroyed bridge has no market value in the sense that a willing buyer or willing seller, even hypothetically, can be imagined. As one court put it, any attempt to apply a market value approach to property in the public domain like bridges "would be wholly speculative, the very pitfall to be avoided in proof of damages." Value to the owner is the ultimate standard of value to the plaintiff in a particular case. Market value is only a method of arriving at that value. The reason market value is the usual standard is because with most property one can make a loss good by going into the open market and buying an equivalent substitute. When that cannot be done, the courts usually resort to the actual or real value approach to establish value to the owner. Relevant evidence to prove actual or real value includes original cost, the age

---

[48] *E.g.*, State v. Whataburger, Inc., 60 S.W.3d 256 (Tex. Civ. App. 2001) (allowing loss profits recovery by owner of restaurant when government condemned building (restaurant) requiring restaurant to be razed and rebuilt notwithstanding government paid for rebuilding); *see* Lynda J. Oswald, *Goodwill and Going Concern Value: Emerging Factors in the Just Compensation Equation*, 32 B.C.L. Rev. 283 (1991). *See generally* Sandra L.K. Davidson, Annot., *Goodwill as Element of Damages For Condemnation of Property on Which Private Business is Conducted*, 81 A.L.R.3d 198 (1977) (discussing divergent views regarding recovery of goodwill in condemnation proceedings).

[49] Shippen Township v. Portage Township, 575 A.2d 157, 158 (Pa. Comm. Ct. 1990) (citation omitted).

of the property, its use and utility, its condition, and the cost of restoration or replacement.[50]

The recovery may also include the cost of temporary structures while the main structure is being repaired or replaced; however, this issue has been hotly debated and is often controlled by statute.[51]

The principles discussed here are not limited to bridges, but apply to other forms of public property, such as utility poles.[52] Some jurisdictions permit recovery based on full cost of replacement, while other jurisdictions do not.[53]

§ 91   NATURAL RESOURCE DAMAGE

[91.1]   Environmental Injury

Environmental damage has received significant attention over the last several decades; it has, however, a long history.[1] When real property has been contaminated and sustained environmental (natural resource) damage the preferred measure of redress is cost of restoration.[2] This is contrary to a general preference for diminution in value in property damage contexts and results from strong statutory incentives to remediate and restore land to an uncontaminated condition that have risen to the forefront in the United States since the 1970s. Although many of the decisions involve damage to public lands and liability theories that invoke trusteeship concepts insofar as public land is concerned, the same preference for cost of restoration has been evidenced when the government seeks the clean up, or reimbursement for the clean up, of contaminated private land.

---

[50] Vlotho v. Hardin County, 509 N.W.2d 350, 357 (Iowa 1993). *See generally* Christopher Vaeth, Annot., *Measure and Elements of Damages For Injury to Bridge*, 31 A.L.R. 5th 171 (1995).

[51] *See generally* Vaeth, Annot., *supra*, 31 A.L.R. 5th at §§ 9–10 (collecting decisions).

[52] Puget Sound Power & Light Co. v. Strong, 816 P.2d 716 (Wash. 1991).

[53] Portland General Elec. Co. v. Taber, 934 P.2d 538 (Or. App. 1987) (adopting "undepreciated" cost method, which is original cost less any depreciation actually taken). *Taber* collects and discusses decisions that have adopted the replacement cost or depreciation approaches. *Id.* at 540–42.

[1] Valerie Fogleman, *English Law—Damage to the Environment*, 72 Tulane L. Rev. 571, 573 (1997) (noting that "[c]riminal and civil liabilities for environmental damage in England and Wales have a long history").

[2] Ohio v. United States Dep't of the Interior, 880 F.2d 432, 444, 448 (D.C. Cir. 1989) (striking down regulations providing for diminution of damages measure as inconsistent with statutory requirements (CERCLA, 42 U.S.C. §§ 9601–9675) that the primary remedy be cost of restoration); Puerto Rico v. The SS Zoe Colocotroni, 628 F.2d 652, 675–76 (1st Cir. 1980), *cert. denied,* 450 U.S. 912 (1981) (holding that oil spill that damaged public lands should be remedied based on reasonable restoration costs, not diminution in damages); *see* Robert Copple, *The New Economic Efficiency in Natural Resource Damage Assessments*, 66 U. Colo. L. Rev. 675, 676–79 (1995) (arguing that common law approach to valuing physical injury component to natural resource damage is reasonable cost of restoration).

The scope of injury that can accompany environmental damage is quite broad; therefore, the "damages," remedy is quite extensive.[3] For example, the Comprehensive Environmental Response, Compensation and Liability Act (CERCLA) defines natural resource damage as injury to:

> land, fish, wildlife, biota, air, water, groundwater, drinking water supplies and other such resources belonging to, managed by, held in trust by, appertaining to, or otherwise controlled by the United States . . . any State or local government, any foreign government, any Indian tribe . . . .[4]

Besides cost of restoration, the defendant may also be required to compensate the plaintiff for loss of use.[5]

The Department of the Interior has developed a number of approaches for measuring the cost of restoration[6] and the quantification of compensable value, which is the amount of money necessary to compensate the public for the loss in services provided by the injured resource as a result of environmental damage.[7] Although these approaches pertain to "public lands"[8] as defined in the relevant statutes, the principles may be extended to private land, particularly when the plaintiff can demonstrate a real, as opposed to a merely generalized, interest in restoring the land to its pre-injury condition, as for example by a showing that plaintiff lives on or has the right to use the damaged land, used the land before it was damaged, and intends to resume use after the land is restored.[9]

[91.2] Stigma Damages

Even after remediation of the contamination, the owner may claim that the property's market value has been adversely affected by the fact that the property once was contaminated. This is the so-called "Brownlands" or

---

[3] Although phrased as "damages" the concept of a "restoration cost recovery" is actually equitable in nature and represents the monetary cost of compliance with an order to remediate the continuing environmental damage caused by the defendant. State v. Diamond Lakes Oil Co., 66 S.W.3d 613 (Ark. 2002) (holding that restoration cost was proper measure of damages for oil contamination of land resulting from adjacent gasoline service station because plaintiff was ordered to clean up the contamination by state environmental agency); see Heidi Wendel, Note, *Restoration as the Economically Efficient Remedy for Damage to Publicly Owned Natural Resources,* 91 Colum. L. Rev. 430, 447-48 (1991).

[4] 42 U.S.C. § 9601(16) (CERCLA); see 33 U.S.C. § 2701(20) (Oil Pollution Act).

[5] 42 U.S.C. § 9607(a)(4)(c); see Frank Cross, *Natural Resource Damage Valuation,* 42 Vand. L. Rev. 269, 281 (1989).

[6] 43 C.F.R. § 11.83 (1997).

[7] *Id.* at (b)(3) (cost-estimating methodologies), c(3)(2) (valuation methodologies). The valuation methodologies are not exclusive.

[8] Public land includes private land subject to government regulation, management, or control. *Ohio, supra,* 880 F.2d at 461.

[9] Roman Catholic Church v. Louisiana Gas Serv. Co., 618 So. 2d 874, 879–80 (La. 1993) (holding that plaintiff can recover restoration damages greater than diminution in value when there is "a reason personal to the owner for restoring the original condition or there is a reason to believe that plaintiff will, in fact, make the repairs" to the land).

"Brownfields" problem and the injury is frequently referred to as "stigma damage." Many courts have permitted recovery of this item of loss.[10] An interesting application of this principle occurred in *Terra-Products, Inc. v. Kraft General Foods, Inc.*[11] Terra-Products (Terra) sustained environmental damage to its property. Kraft General Foods (Kraft) remediated the damage at its expense; however, Terra contended that even after remediation the property's market value was less than its pre-contamination market value and sought that difference from Kraft. Kraft, which had already incurred remediation costs that greatly exceeded the pre-contamination value of the property, objected contending that Terra had received full compensation through restoration damages, which essentially treated the injury as temporary, and that Terra could not now shift gears and claim the injury was permanent and seek diminution in value damages.[12] The court rejected Kraft's argument and, in the context of environmental injury, the distinction between permanent and temporary injury to land.[13] The court affirmed use of both cost of restoration and diminution in value when necessary to restore the owner to her rightful position. This occurs when the owner can demonstrate that repairs to real property fail to restore the land to its former value:

> More specifically, in the context of environmental contamination of land a party should be entitled to recover as damages any proven reduction in the fair market value of real property remaining after remediation, *i.e.,* the remaining loss damages.[14]

Some courts reject the recovery of stigma damages in any case.[15] Some courts limit the recovery of stigma damages to situations when the owner

---

[10] Bradley v. Armstrong Rubber Co., 130 F.3d 168, 176 (5th Cir. 1997) (holding that Mississippi would recognize recovery of stigma damages, but finding that owner failed to produce convincing evidence that stigma affected the property's market value); *In re* Paoli R.R. Yard PCB Litig., 113 F.3d 444, 463 (3d Cir. 1997) (permitting parties to recover stigma damages when "stigma associated with their land will remain in place after any physical damage to their land has been repaired regardless of whether the repair is actually completed") (citation omitted).

[11] 653 N.E.2d 89 (Ind. App. 1995).

[12] *Id.* at 92; Section 90.1 ([Physical Damage] Temporary or Permanent Damage).

[13] 653 N.E.2d at 93; *cf.* Rudd v. Electrolux Corp., 982 F. Supp. 355 (M.D.N.C. 1997) (holding that recovery of stigma damages would not be allowed in cases of temporary injury to land (cost of repair is measure) but would be allowed in cases of permanent injury to land (diminution in value is measure)).

[14] 653 N.E.2d at 93 (citations omitted); Nashua Corp. v. Norton Co., 1997 U.S. Dist. LEXIS 5173 (N.D.N.Y., April 15, 1997) (permitting owner to recover stigma damages when it can do so by non-speculative evidence of such damage as a result of defendant's actions).

[15] *E.g.,* Santa Fe Partnership v. Arco Prods. Co., 54 Cal. Rptr. 2d 214, 220–21 (Cal. App. 1996). The court's opinion is, however, ambiguous. It may be read as only barring stigma damages in cases of a continuing, *i.e.,* abatable, nuisance. *Id.* In this context, however, the defendant is liable for the cost of remediation; therefore, even this limited reading would preclude the piggybacking of cost of restoration and stigma damages until remediation is completed. *See* Bartleson v. United States, 96 F.3d 1270, 1275 (9th Cir. 1996); *see also* Scribner v. Summers, 138 F.3d 471, 473 (2d Cir. 1998) (reading precedents narrowly and suggesting that presumption should be that remediation removes stigma). The development of the stigma

can show that the stigma caused special damages. As applied, however, that approach has proven to be imprecise. For example, in *Hammon v. City of Warner Robins* the court identified several items of loss as not constituting special damages for purposes of recovering stigma damages, but did not identify what types of loss items would qualify as special damages.[16]

It is generally required that stigma damage arise out of the actual environmental or natural resource injury to the owner's land.[17] When the actual physical injury is to the property of another, the plaintiff is generally barred from recovering stigma damages based on proximity to the contaminated area.[18] The rationale for this limitation has been the fear of open-ended liability, but this rationale is more a conclusion than a justification. Courts have recognized that loss of market value, resulting from even irrational public fears, may be compensable in some contexts.[19] Courts have failed to explain why "fears" are taken into account in some cases for calculating damages, but not other cases. The issue of stigma damages remains, to a large extent, a work in progress.

[91.3] Damage to Trees and Shrubs

When the injury is to fruit or ornamental trees or shrubbery, courts often permit a measure of recovery other than diminution in value of the land on which the trees are planted. Claims involving damage to, or destruction of, trees and shrubbery are sometimes treated as involving above market recoveries. On the one hand, the measure of loss remains that of restoring the plaintiff to her rightful position. This is not accomplished by replacing a fully grown shade tree with a sapling. The owner is entitled to recover

---

damages remedy is critiqued in E. Jean Johnson, *Environmental Stigma Damages: Speculative Damages in Environmental Tort Cases,* 15 J. Envir. L. 185, 186 (1996–97) (taking position "that stigma damages should not be recognized . . . because stigma damages are based solely on public perceptions—perceptions that can charge at any moment . . . . [W]here courts are inclined to award stigma damages, despite their speculative nature, . . . actual harm from the stigma [should be required]") (brackets added).

[16] 482 S.E.2d 422, 428 (Ga. App. 1997) (holding that inability to obtain loans, inability to refinance, and costs of litigation resulting from stigma would not qualify as special damages).

[17] Chance v. BP Chems., Inc., 670 N.E.2d 985, 993 (Ohio 1996) (rejecting claim of actual injury, necessary to sustain trespass action, when owner complained of use of deep wells to dispose of contaminates but could not demonstrate any actual migration of contaminants into the subsurface estate; mere fear of injury was insufficient).

[18] *Santa Fe Partnership, supra,* 54 Cal. Rptr. 2d at 224 (collecting decisions applying what court characterized as the uniform rule).

[19] Willsey v. Kansas City Power, 631 P.2d 268, 279 (Kan App. 1981); Reed v. King, 193 Cal. Rptr. 130, 133–34 (Cal. App. 1983); San Diego Gas & Elec. Co. v. Daley, 253 Cal. Rtpr. 144, 151 (Cal. App. 1988). *Compare* San Diego Gas & Elec. Co. v. Superior Court, 920 P.2d 669, 699 (Cal. 1996) (limiting *San Diego Gas & Elec. Co. v. Daley, supra,* to eminent domain cases and not applying decision to inverse condemnation cases; the court declined to approve or disapprove *Daley*), *with Nashua Corp., supra* (following decision of New York Court of Appeals permitting stigma damages in eminent domain case as applicable to environmental contamination case noting that "[t]here is no sound analytical basis for defining diminution property value in the context of nuisance different from the way it is defined in the taking context").

the reasonable value of replacing destroyed trees or shrubbery with identical or substantially similar trees or shrubbery.[20] On the other hand, the economic value of the land may not reflect the value of mature trees. In this sense, permitting the owner to recover restoration costs may be seen as allowing an above market recovery. The same debate occurs in the personal property context. In the real property context the dominant view is to permit restoration costs, whereas in the personal property context the tendency is to allow only the "lesser of" cost of restoration (repair) or diminution in value.[21] The difference lies in the common law's tradition of protecting real property rights more zealously than personal property rights.[22]

Damage to fruit trees may be measured by the tree's productive value[23] including lost profits,[24] or, in the case of both fruit trees and ornamental trees, the costs of restoration.[25] The costs of restoration may not, however, be disproportionate to the market value of the property. For example, in *Heninger v. Dunn*[26] the defendant bulldozed a road through the plaintiff's forested land, destroying or damaging 225 mature trees in the process. The market value of the land was $179,000; the cost of replacing the destroyed or damaged trees with mature trees was $241,000. While the court agreed with the principle that a plaintiff could recover restoration costs that exceeded the fair market value of the property,[27] the court held that given the disproportionality in amounts it would be unreasonable to do so in the case at hand.[28] The court noted that in such cases an alternative non-market measure, such as value to owner based on the aesthetic value of the property, could be used, again subject to the requirement that the recovery not unreasonably exceed the property's market value.[29]

Many jurisdictions continue, however, to measure recoveries for destruction to ornamental trees, and, to a lesser extent, to fruit trees by the traditional diminution in value test. Under this approach, the owner's recovery is based on the difference in market value of his property with and without

---

[20] Hassoldt v. Patrick Media Group, Inc., 100 Cal. Rptr. 2d 662, 672–73 (Cal. App. 2000).

[21] Section 80.2 (Partial Destruction).

[22] Section 91.1 (Environmental Injury).

[23] Sparks v. Douglas County, 695 P.2d 588, 591 (Wash. App. 1985).

[24] Pearce v. G.R. Kirk Co., 602 P.2d 357, 360 (Wash. 1979) (involving damaged Christmas trees). *See generally* Kristine Karnezis, Annot., *Measure of Damages For Destruction of or Injury to Fruit, Nut, or Other Productive Trees,* 90 A.L.R. 3d 800 § 2[a] (1980) (noting that the primary goal has been flexibility in approach to ensure adequate compensation).

[25] *See generally* Kristine Karnezis, Annot., *Measure of Damages for Injury to or Destruction of Shade or Ornamental Tree or Shrub,* 95 A.L.R. 3d 508 § 4[a] (1980).

[26] 162 Cal. Rptr. 104 (Cal. App. 1980).

[27] *Id.,* at 106-07.

[28] *Id.* at 109; G & A Contractors, Inc. v. Alaska Greenhouses, Inc., 517 P.2d 1379, 1385–87 (Alaska 1974); Samson Constr. Co. v. Brusowankin, 147 A.2d 430, 435 (Md. 1958).

[29] *Heninger, supra,* 162 Cal. Rptr. at 108-09.

the trees.[30] These jurisdiction adopt the economic utility viewpoint that is dominate in the personal property context.[31]

§ 92 EJECTMENT

Ejectment provides specific relief in the actual return of possession of real property and is discussed at Section 58 (Ejectment). These materials discuss the accompanying remedy of "mesne profits."[1]

In addition to specific relief, (recovery of the real property), a party bringing an action for ejectment may recover damages—called "mesne profits." Mesne profits means intermediate profits and refers to those profits that accrue between two periods in time, which in cases of ejectment means the period of time beginning with the accrual of the action for ejectment and the recovery of the property.[2] Mesne profits may be measured in a variety of ways: (1) reasonable rental value; (2) actual value to defendant; and (3) actual worth of the property to the plaintiff. The preferred measure is reasonable rental value.[3] If the defendant improved the property while he was in possession, mesne profits may be based on the improved condition of the property.[4] The defendant is, however, usually afforded an offset against the claim of mesne profits for the reasonable value of the improvements he has made to the property.[5] For example, assume defendant occupied the property for one year before his removal and during that year made improvements which: (1) cost $5,000, (2) raised the fair market value of the property $5,000, and (3) created a fair rental value of $1,000 per month for the property in its improved condition. Plaintiff's claim for mesne profits would be based on the fair rental value of the property in its improved condition, which is 12 times $1,000, or $12,000, less the value of the improvement, which here is $5,000. Thus, plaintiff would recover $7,000 as mesne profits.

---

[30] *See generally* Karnezis, Annot., *supra*, 90 A.L.R. 3d at § 2[a] (collecting cases), 95 A.L.R. 3d at § 2[a] (collecting cases).

[31] Section 80.2 (Partial Destruction).

[1] The term is pronounced "mean" as the s is silent.

[2] BLACK'S LAW DICTIONARY 1246 (Bryan A. Garner, ed. 8th ed. 2004).

[3] Fugate v. Rice, 815 S.W.2d 466, 471 (Mo. App. 1991); Dumas v. Ropp, 558 P.2d 632, 633 (Idaho 1977).

[4] Cracchiolo v. State, 706 P.2d 1219, 1227 (Ariz. App. 1985) (collecting decisions); Deakyne v. Lewes Anglers, Inc., 204 F. Supp. 415, 425 (D. Del. 1962). *But see* Mickle v. Kirk, 558 N.E.2d 1119, 1124 (Ind. App. 1990) (holding that good faith improver who purchased property at public auction, but who received defective title, should pay rental damages based on property's value at time improver acquired possession rather than based on value after improvements were made); Beaver v. Davis, 550 P.2d 428, 432 (Or. 1976) (limiting plaintiff's recovery of mesne profits to rental value of property without improvements made by defendant; ruling was controlled by state statute).

[5] Restatement of Restitution § 42 (1) (1937); *see* Prince v. Crow, 589 So. 2d 161, 163 (Ala. 1991) (noting that to recover offset, improver must act in good faith and without actual knowledge of plaintiff's superior title); Section 96 (Good Faith Improvers of Real Property).

Although ejectment is an action at law, many jurisdictions permit equitable defenses to be interposed.[6] On the other hand, ejectment's roots as a real property remedy may be invoked to negate otherwise applicable legal defenses, such as the duty to mitigate. As noted in *Smith v. Seamster*:

> The purpose of an action for ejectment is to test the right to possession of real property. To require the plaintiff to mitigate its damages by attempting to rent, let alone sell, the property over which it is trying to gain actual possession to incongruous with this purpose.[7]

Occasionally, courts use the term "equitable ejectment."[8] The concept refers to situations when an equity court had jurisdiction over the matter and ejectment was an appropriate remedy. Thus, "equitable ejectment" is simply the use of ejectment by an equity court. Whether the distinction survives the merger of law and equity is debatable.

§ 93   TRESPASS

Trespass involves any possessory intrusion onto the property of another.[1] Trespass may be used in cases when ejectment is available in theory but not in practice—as, for example, when the trespass is by an encroaching structure or when the defendant threatens a breach of the peace if the plaintiff or a judicial officer attempts to remove the encroaching structure, thus preventing peaceful removal. Trespass remedies are usually of two types: (1) substitutional (damages), and (2) specific (injunctive). Traditionally, the remedy of restitution was not used, but there is recent decisional law to the contrary.

---

[6] Jansen v. Clayton, 816 S.W.2d 49, 51–52 (Tenn. App. 1991) (involving equitable defense of laches); Bastian v. Brink, 45 N.W.2d 712, 714 (Minn. 1951) (stating that equitable defenses could be invoked); Smith v. Lanier, 34 S.E.2d 91, 96 (Ga. 1945) (involving defense of equitable title).

[7] 36 S.W.3d 18, 21 (Mo. App. 2000) (citation omitted).

[8] Owens v. Owens, 143 A.2d 123, 125 (Del. Ch. 1958) (charaterizing action in which wife sought to evict husband from family residence as "sound[ing] in equitable ejectment"), *rev'd in part on other grounds,* 149 A.2d 320 (Del. Ch. 1959); *cf.* Kelley v. United States, 19 Ct. Cl. 155, 160–61 (1989) (holding that court was without jurisdiction to consider plaintiff's claim, which court characterized as "sound[ing] in equity, that United States be ejected from land and offices it was leasing from plaintiff due to non-payment of rent").

[1] Trespass may also be characterized as the right to exclude others from one's property. When so characterized, many interesting problems may arise as courts attempt to balance the right to exclude with other values the intruders may claim to advance. *Compare* First Unitarian Church of Salt Lake City v. Salt Lake City Corp., 308 F.3d 1114 (10th Cir. 2002) (holding that private owner of land could not bar "expressive activity" on land when activity occurred on easement retained by city when it sold the land; the easement perserved the public forum character of the land, which the private owner was required to respect), *with* Albertson's Inc. v. Young, 131 Cal. Rptr. 2d 721 (Cal. App. 2003) (holding that supermarket in shopping center was not functional equivalent of traditional public forum; petitioners had no right to remain on premises to gather signatures for ballot proposition over objections of owner).

[93.1] Temporary or Permanent

The distinction between temporary and permanent injury, discussed at Section 90.1 (Temporary or Permanent Injury), is applicable to trespass damages claims. If the trespass is deemed permanent, the owner is limited to diminution in value damages and denied injunctive relief. Courts often describe "permanent" trespasses in terms of the ease and cost of removing or ceasing the trespass.[2] The characterization actually reflects different considerations, (here the desirability of injunctive relief), than suggested by the literal terms "temporary" and "permanent."[3] The characterization of the trespass as permanent or temporary can have significant collateral consequences.[4]

[93.2] Damages

A trespasser is liable in damages for all injuries proximately flowing from his trespass.[5] In this regard, it is important to identify the types of harm the trespass has engendered. The trespass may involve simply a temporary physical intrusion onto the land, as, for example, using the land as a pathway, in which case the measure of damages is reasonable rental value,[6] or nominal damages absent actual injury.[7] The intrusion may be more invasive, such as the physical encroachment on the land by a structure. In this context, the usual measure of damages is either diminution in value or reasonable rental value, often depending on whether the trespass is deemed permanent or non-permanent.[8] A trespass may consist of the

---

[2] L'Enfant Plaza East, Inc. v. John McShain, Inc., 359 A.2d 5, 6 (D.C. 1976) (noting ease by which underground structural encroachment was removed warranted characterization of trespass as temporary; consequently, an injunction could issue to secure that end).

[3] Section 90.1 ([Physical Damage] Temporary or Permanent Injury).

[4] *Id.* If the trespass is characterized as "permanent," the statute of limitation commences running at the beginning of the trespass; if the trespass is temporary, the limitation period runs with each trespass. Section 61.2.3 (Continuing Injury or Violation).

[5] United States v. Marin Rock and Asphalt Co., 296 F. Supp. 1213, 1219 (C.D. Cal. 1969); Bourdieu v. Seaboard Oil Co., 119 P.2d 973, 978 (Cal. App. 1941).

[6] Courts may temper the award based on the extent and nature of defendant's unauthorized use of plaintiff's property. If the trespass does not measurably interfere with plaintiff's use and enjoyment of the property, the court may limit the recovery to the diminution in rental value caused by the trespass. On the other hand, if the defendant has made profitable use of plaintiff's property, reasonable rental value is usually awarded. *See generally* 22 Am. Jur. 2d *Damages* § 263 (Temporary or Repairable Injuries Resulting From Trespass).

[7] The landowner will recover at least nominal damages for the actionable invasion of the right to exclusive possession. Section 2.8 (Nominal Damages). When the intrusion is physical, courts generally permit the trespass action to proceed without proof of "actual injury" to the owner, but the decisions are in conflict whether the same rule applies to intangible intrusions, *e.g.*, airborne, particulate emissions or electronics magnetic radiation. *See* Public Service Co. of Colorado v. Van Wyk, 27 P.3d 377 (Colo. 2001) (collecting decisions addressing whether plaintiff must allege and prove "actual injury" to land when suing on a trespass theory for electronic magnetic radiation damage).

[8] Jones v. Morrison, 458 S.W.2d 434, 439 (Tenn. App. 1970) (applying diminution in value measure after request for injunction to remove encroachment was denied; the court noted that

removal of natural resources, such as timber, coal, or oil and gas minerals. In this context the measure of damages turns on whether the trespass is deemed innocent or willful. If the trespass is innocent, a mild measure of compensatory damages is used; if the trespass is deemed willful, a harsh measure is used. The trespass may result in physical damage to the surface or subsurface estate. In this case the usual measure of damages is either diminution in value or cost of repair.[9] If a trespass causes mental distress to the owner, the defendant may be liable in damages for the plaintiff's mental distress and for any resulting illness or physical harm. The recovery of distress damages in this context is usually limited to extraordinary situations for the ordinary incursion onto the property of another is unlikely to cause distress damages that the law will recognize.[10] Some courts state that distress damages are available as a matter of right in trespass actions, but on the facts find that plaintiff has not made out a valid claim.[11]

Notwithstanding that damages for trespass are "essentially compensatory," there is a strong punitive element in trespass that is manifested in the distinction between willful and innocent trespassers noted in the prior paragraph. The distinction turns on defendant's intent. For example, in *Jim Thompson Coal Co. v. Dentzell* a coal company was found liable for willful trespass when it had failed to keep track of its mining operation maps— maps designed to ensure against trespasses, coupled with the fact that the company had notice of its trespass because its underground blasting operations produced discernible above ground manifestations.[12] On the other

---

in applying this formula the defendant, a willful trespasser, could not expect that a court would apply the willing buyer—willing seller model rather than one that was more protective of the plaintiff and his remaining property).

[9] Section 90 (Physical Damage).

[10] Hamman v. Southwestern Gas Pipeline, Inc., 821 F.2d 299, 306 (5th Cir. 1987) (holding that gas pipeline laid across plaintiff's land in violation of Natural Gas Pipeline Safety Act (49 U.S.C. § 1671 *et seq.*) constituted intentional trespass warranting distress damages under Texas law); *vacated in part on other grounds,* 832 F.2d 55; Kornoff v. Kingsburg Cotton Oil Co., 288 P.2d 507, 511 (Cal. 1955) (holding that once a cause of action for trespass or nuisance is established, an occupant of land may recover damages for annoyance and injury even if he or she has suffered no physical injury); *cf.* Belluomo v. KAKE TV & Radio, 596 P.2d 832, 842 (Cal. 1979) (allowing recovery of compensatory damages for injuries resulting from a publication of information acquired by trespass).

[11] *Compare* Gavcus v. Potts, 808 F.2d 596, 598 (7th Cir. 1986) (finding that plaintiff's claim for distress damages was lost because plaintiff failed to produce expert witness as to that claim), *with* Thompson v. Simonds, 155 P.2d 870, 875 (Cal. App. 1945) (holding that a plaintiff can recover damages for "pain, anxiety, inconvenience, [and] annoyance" resulting from the interference that defendant's trespass caused to plaintiff's free use of his land).

[12] 287 S.W. 548, 549 (Ky. 1926); *see Hamman, supra,* 821 F.2d at 305-06 (holding that the defendant who entered onto the property with notice of the plaintiff's lis pendens was a willful trespasser even though the defendant acted with the subjective good faith belief that plaintiff's claim was invalid; the defendant was bound by a settlement that recognized the plaintiff as the owner of the property and made the defendant's entry unauthorized); McGrath v. Hills, 662 A.2d 215, 219 (Me. 1995) (stating that the defendant's failure to take additional steps to ascertain the appropriate boundary lines and his continued action in removing gravel despite the dispute supported the lower court's finding that defendant acted willfully and with utter disregard and indifference to the plaintiff's rights).

hand, in *Rudy v. Ellis* the coal company was held to be an innocent trespasser where it acted under a lease later declared invalid.[13] The distinction between "willful" and "good faith" trespass are often complex though they are expressed as a simple pair of competing characterizations.[14]

With respect to damages for trespass involving the removal of minerals, the measure of damages for willful trespass is that the rightful owner is entitled to the full value of the mineral after its extraction without a reduction for the trespasser's production expenses.[15] This measure is clearly punitive.[16] Nonetheless, most jurisdictions do not prohibit an additional award of punitive damages.[17] Under this view, there is a difference between punitive damages and a punitive measure of compensatory or actual damages.[18] This view holds that different interests are being protected. The damages measure is protecting the plaintiff's interest in his property; the punitive damages measure is protecting the plaintiff (and the public) from malevolent conduct by others designed to injure. There is a dissenting view that takes the position that punitive damages and a punitive measure of damages are so close that to award both would be fundamentally unfair,[19] as would the blind use of one measure (punitive measure) when the use of the other (punitive damages) would not be warranted.[20]

When the trespass is labeled "innocent," two approaches have been recognized. The first approach measures damages based on the value of the mineral after extraction less the costs incurred by the trespasser in producing the mineral.[21] The second approach applies a royalty rate, *i.e.,*

---

[13] 236 S.W.2d 466, 469 (Ky. 1951).

[14] *See* Kelly Mark Easton, *The Measure of Damages For Mineral Trespass—A Kentucky Perspective*, 4 J. Min. L. & Pol'y 137, 139 (1988).

[15] Deltic Timber Corp. v. Great Lakes Chemical Corp., 2 F. Supp. 2d 1192, 1200 (W.D. Ark. 1998) (applying "harsh" measure and awarding plaintiff the value of the minerals after extraction and without an offset for the costs of production by the defendant); Section 8.7 (Harsh or Mild Measure).

[16] *Deltic Timber Corp., supra,* 2 F. Supp. 2d at 1200); Athens & Pomeroy Coal & Land Co. v. Tracy, 153 N.E. 240, 244 (Ohio App. 1925).

[17] *See generally* 58 C.J.S. *Mines & Minerals* § 117(g)(3)(b).

[18] Schafer v. Schnabel, 494 P.2d 802, 805–06 (Alaska 1972) (affirming finding that trespass was not so willful as to permit a punitive measure of damages).

[19] Martinez v. De Los Rios, 331 P.2d 724, 727 (Cal. App. 1958).

[20] Grays Harbor County v. Bay City Lumber Co., 289 P.2d 975, 978 (Wash. 1955) (comparing the punitive measure of damages with the award of punitive damages and noting their interchangeability):

> But whether the larger damages be frankly called vindictive damages, or are allowed on the last-mentioned ground without any express name, their nature is the same. It is obvious that the increased measure is allowed, not as compensation to the person wronged, but as punishment to the wrongdoer. It is not a mere question of terms, but of the inherent quality of the thing. The increased measure is punitive in its very nature, in that it exceeds the true measure of compensation. It is plain that the person whose trees are cut suffers exactly the same injury where the trespass is involuntary as where it is willful. In each case he suffers the loss of his trees.

[21] Georgia Marble Co. v. Therrell, 519 S.E.2d 900, 901-03 (Ga. 1999); Alaska Placer Co. v.

the exploitation value of the mineral before it is disturbed.[22] Courts may allow the plaintiff to elect between the two approaches; however, courts may limit the "profits" test to situations where the rightful owner is in a position to exploit the mineral resources.[23] The difference is this. A mineral rights' owner willing and able to develop minerals (or any resource for that matter) may be allowed to recover profits from a trespasser who wrongfully exacts the resource, whereas the mineral rights' owner without the ability to develop the resource may find his recovery limited to the property's mineral exploitation value, *i.e.*, the royalty. The theory is that when the trespasser has deprived the owner of a use of the property, which the owner was capable of exploiting, that deprivation identifies the owner's harm.[24]

If an innocent trespasser is to be allowed his reasonable costs of production, what are they? Courts tend to approach this on a case by case basis or use ambiguous phrases, such as whether the "cost" or "expense" was "reasonably calculated to be beneficial and productive." Normally, courts will be more tolerant of direct expenses incurred in production than of general overhead expenses.[25]

When the trespass involves the physical occupancy of another's land the usual measure of damages is fair rental value.[26] In cases where the use or occupancy is determined to be permanent, *i.e.*, not remedial by injunction,[27] the plaintiff's usual measure of damages is the fair market value of the portion of the premises used or occupied.[28] This calculation can be difficult for the occupied property may have unique value that is not

---

Lee, 553 P.2d 54, 57 (Alaska 1976). *See generally* Annot., *Right of Trespasser to Credit for Expenditures in Producing, as Against His Liability for Value of Oil or Minerals,* 21 A.L.R.2d 380, 384–85 (1952). If a "costs of extraction" test is used with respect to minerals in place there must be proper evidence of the cost of severance (production) in order that "profits" may be calculated. Maxvill-Glasco Drilling Co., Inc. v. Royal Oil & Gas Corp., 800 S.W.2d 384, 386–87 (Tex. Civ. App. 1990).

[22] *Deltic Timber Corp., supra,* 2 F. Supp. 2d at 1199; *Alaska Placer Co.,* 553 P.2d at 57–58; Sandy River Channel Coal Co. v. White House Coal Co., 101 S.W.2d 319, 320 (Ky. 1907).

[23] *Georgia Marble Co., supra,* 519 S.E.2d at 902–3; Hughett v. Caldwell County, 230 S.W.2d 92, 97 (Ky. 1950).

[24] *Georgia Marble Co., supra,* 519 S.E.2d at 902-03; National Lead Co. v. Magnet Cove Barium Corp., 231 F. Supp. 208, 218 (W.D. Ark. 1964). There is case law that a trespasser may be liable for destroying the speculative value of property, *e.g.*, by demonstrating that the land does not contain exploitable natural resources. *See* Humble Oil & Refining Co. v. Kishi, 261 S.W. 228, 232-33 (Tex. Civ. App. 1925), *aff'd on rehearing,* 291 S.W. 538 (Tex. 1927); 3 H. WILLIAMS, OIL & GAS LAW § 697.4 (1985).

[25] *Cf.* Clark-Montana Realty Co. v. Butte & Superior Copper Co., 233 F. 547, 577 (D. Mont. 1916), *aff'd,* 248 F. 609 (9th Cir. 1918), *aff'd,* 249 U.S. 12 (1919) (involving an accounting between adjoining mineral owners).

[26] United States v. Imperial Irrig. Dist., 799 F. Supp. 1052, 1066 (S.D. Cal. 1992) (noting that the proper measure of damages for trespass is the "fair rental value of the property, assuming that the property is being put to its highest and best use") (citation omitted); Montgomery Ward & Co. v. Andrews, 736 P.2d 40, 45 (Colo. App. 1987).

[27] Section 93.1 ([Trespass] Temporary or Permanent).

[28] Ravan v. Greenville County, 434 S.E.2d 296, 307 (S.C. App. 1993); Garey Constr. Co., Inc. v. Thompson, 697 S.W.2d 865, 867 (Tex. Civ. App. 1985).

reflected in the general diminution of value test.[29] The question becomes whether the portion of the property occupied should be given a higher value because of its location, which gives it special value to the occupier, or whether the property occupied should be deemed essentially equal in value, on a pro rata basis, to the property not occupied by the encroachment?[30] The decisional law here is not consistent; moreover, if the unique value of the property is recognized, courts fail to identify the criteria that should be used to measure that unique value the occupier has expropriated.

When the trespass inflicts injury that does not affect the property's market value, the owner may recovery intrinsic or non-market value in some jurisdictions[31] and nominal damages in most.[32]

[93.3] Injunction

Because trespass involves an invasion of the owner's use and enjoyment of real property, it is customary to find that the irreparable injury requirement has been met. In this sense, the normal remedy for the protection of a property right (particularly to remove an encroachment) is an injunction.[33] The legal remedy of ejectment will not be adequate in most

---

[29] Kratze v. Independent Order of Oddfellows, Garden City Lodge #11, 500 N.W.2d 115, 123 (Mich. 1993) (stating that "[b]ecause the trespass is permanent, the correct measure of damages is the diminution in value of the property itself as represented by the value of the property without the encroachment, minus the value of the property with the encroachment or, alternatively, the value of the strip of land on which the building sits"). On the facts, however, the court found that plaintiff suffered minimal damages since he agreed to pay his predecessor in title the same amount after plaintiff learned of the encroachment as he had been willing to pay before he learned of the encroachment. *Id.*

[30] Jones v. Morrison, 458 S.W.2d 434, 439 (Tenn. App. 1970) (holding that while diminution in value test should be used in case of willful trespass, "[t]he courts can hardly be expected to sanction such action by holding that, after one has unlawfully appropriated the property of another and erected a building thereon . . . the only remuneration the owner can claim or expect is the market value of the property taken as measured by the formula laid down in eminent domain cases involving a willing seller and a willing buyer").

[31] *Garey Constr. Co., Inc., supra*, 697 S.W.2d at 867; Section 81 (Value to Owner).

[32] Lake Mille Lacs Inv., Inc. v. Payne, 401 N.W.2d 387, 391 (Minn. App. 1987) (stating that once plaintiff demonstrated the existence of a trespass, plaintiff was entitled to nominal damages even in the absence of actual damages); Fairfield Commons Condominium Ass'n v. Stasa, 506 N.E.2d 237, 247 (Ohio App. 1985), *cert. denied sub nom.* Moriarty v. Fairfield Commons Condominium Ass'n, 479 U.S. 1055 (1987). *But see* Bradley v. American Smelting and Ref. Co., 709 P.2d 782, 791 (Wash. 1985) (eliminating the recovery of nominal damages in trespass actions because it encourages unnecessary litigation to vindicate insignificant, technical injury). *Bradley* involved the intrusion onto plaintiff's land of microscopic dust particles and the plaintiff sought to maintain the action in trespass rather than nuisance. The court's rejection of nominal damages and its requiring actual injury must be evaluated in that light. Section 98.2 ([Trespass] Damages) (text and notes 5-6).

[33] The seminal paper on the protection of property rights is Guido Calabresi & A. Douglas Melamed, *Property Rules, Liability Rules, and Inalienability: One View of the Cathedral*, 85 Harv. L. Rev. 1089, 1115-24 (1972). The paper has generated substantial commentary. *See* Louis Kaplow & Steven Shavell, *Property Rules v. Liability Rules: An Economic Analysis*, 109 Harv. L. Rev. 713, 757-73 (1996).

encroachment cases because the enforcing officer will not risk liability nor incur the cost of physically removing the encroaching structure from the plaintiff's land.[34] The unwillingness of sheriffs and marshals to enforce ejectment orders in these situations is frequently assumed.[35] Whether an injunction will issue requires, however, a careful balancing of the costs and benefits that would flow from the issuance of the injunction.[36] This is particularly true when the trespass consists of an encroachment onto the property of another.

An encroachment is a physical occupation that effectively transfers the use and benefit of the property occupied from the owner to the encroacher. Encroachments often look permanent,[37] but this does not mean that they are not removable. For example, in *Williams v. South & South Rentals*[38] a landowner constructed a two-story brick apartment building on his land. Nine years later he learned his building encroached one foot on the adjoining neighbor's property. He approached his neighbor to discuss an acceptable solution. The neighbor offered to sell the one-third acre property for $45,000, which was declined. The neighbor then sued for an injunction to remove the encroachment, which was granted.[39] It is often stated that a mandatory injunction is the proper remedy for a landowner "who seeks to compel the removal of an encroachment"[40] and injunctions will issue even though the encroachment is minor and compliance is costly.[41]

---

[34] Dundalk Holding Co. v. Easter, 137 A.2d 667 (Md.), *cert. denied,* 358 U.S. 901 (1958) (involving request for injunctive relief after earlier order of ejectment of encroaching building was unenforceable).

[35] *See* Doug Rendleman, *Irreparability Irreparably Damaged*, 90 Mich. L. Rev. 1642, 1657 (1992) (Book Review) (noting that "ejectment is also unsatisfactory because the sheriff cannot or will not remove the [encroachment]") (brackets added).

[36] Restatement (Second) of Torts § 941 (1979); Section 31.2.3 (Balancing of Hardships or Equities).

[37] City of Shawnee, Kan. v. AT&T Corp., 910 F. Supp. 1546, 1561 (D. Kan. 1995) (discussing differences between permanent and temporary (continuous) trespasses by encroaching structures):

> Courts have not agreed on the correct approach. In cases of actual encroachment, such as a building on the plaintiff's land, courts generally treat the trespass as permanent because of the lasting nature of the structure and because the defendant is not privileged to commit a second trespass to remove the offending item. The clearest case of a permanent trespass occurs when the trespassing structure is maintained as a necessary part of the operation of a public utility.

(citations omitted); Section 93.1 ([Trespass] Temporary or Permanent).

[38] 346 S.E.2d 665 (N.C. App. 1986).

[39] *Id.* at 668–69.

[40] Hanson v. Estell, 997 P.2d 426, 430 (Wash. App. 1999).

[41] Raph v. Vogeler, 695 A.2d 1066, 1069–70 (Conn. App. 1997) (affirming injunction ordering defendant to remove encroaching structure); Goulding v. Cook, 661 N.E.2d 1322, 1323–24 (Mass. 1996) (noting that court is not disposed to permit defendant to acquire property by paying damages for wrongful occupation); Urban Site Venture II Ltd. Partnership v. Levering Assocs. Ltd., Partnership, 665 A.2d 1062, 1065 (Md. 1995) (stating that preferred remedy for trespass caused by encroachment is injunction requiring encroachment's removal from plaintiff's land). *See generally* Annot., *Mandatory Injunction to Compel Removal of Encroachments By Adjoining Landowners*, 28 A.L.R.2d 679 (1953).

Whether a court will order a defendant to remove a trespassing encroachment often depends on a court's willingness to balance a property owner's right to exclusive use and enjoyment of the property against the cost of recognition of that right. Some jurisdictions refuse to balance, preferring the property owner's position because in these courts' view a balancing approach would sanction a form of "private eminent domain."[42]

Many jurisdictions, however, permit the equities of the situation to determine whether an injunction will issue. For these courts, the critical issues are twofold. First, will the cost of compliance with an order to remove an encroachment be disproportionate to the benefit the owner will realize by its removal? The analysis is based on monetary considerations: the monetary cost of removal versus the monetary value of the property occupied by the encroachment. Second, was the encroachment the product of a willful or innocent trespass? If the former, the injunction will usually issue; if the latter, the court may limit the owner to damages. Even with these considerations, the deck is stacked heavily against the trespasser. As noted previously, the preferred remedy for removal of an encroachment is an injunction[43] and the trespasser bears the burden in demonstrating that it acted innocently or in good faith.[44] In balancing the hardships (costs versus benefits of compliance), the courts require that for an injunction to be denied the costs be disproportionate to the benefits.[45] Courts also usually state that they will not balance at all if the encroachment was willful.[46] Factors weighting against the issuance of an injunction include: (1) the intrusion is minimal;[47] (2) the encroachment does not interfere with the value or use of the remaining property;[48] (3) the encroachment was the result of innocent mistake.[49] A good summary of the factors counseling against the

---

[42] *Goulding, supra*, 661 N.E.2d at 1324. The court did note that it was not adopting an absolutist position but would recognize extraordinary exceptions. *Id.* at 1324, *citing* Restatement (Second) of Torts § 941, cmt. c (1965) (discussing example of high rise which does not intrude over property line until the 10th story, the work was done in good faith by reputable engineers, and the total encroachment is only 4 inches).

[43] *Urban Site Venture II Ltd. Partnership, supra*, 665 A.2d at 1065.

[44] *Id.* at 1064; Christensen v. Tucker, 250 P.2d 660, 665 (Cal. App. 1952) (stating that while the judge has some discretion to deny an injunction to remove an encroachment, the presumption is that the defendant-encroacher is a wrongdoer and that doubtful cases should be decided in plaintiff's favor unless the defendant-encroacher establishes his innocence and perhaps even his freedom from negligence).

[45] *Kratze, supra*, 500 N.W.2d at 120.

[46] *Id.* at 121; Normandy B. Condominium Ass'n, Inc. v. Normandy C Ass'n, Inc., 541 So. 2d 1263, 1263 (Fla. App. 1989); Papanikolas Bros. Enter. v. Sugarhouse Shopping Ctr. Assocs., 535 P.2d 1256, 1259 (Utah 1975). *But cf.* Jones v. Morrison, 430 S.W.2d 668, 676-77 (Tenn. App. 1968) (holding that injunction against willful encroacher would not issue because injunction was a harsh and extreme remedy under the circumstances and the property owner had not promptly sought the aid of equity when the encroachment began).

[47] *Goulding, supra*, 661 N.E.2d at 1325 (noting that "courts will not enjoin truly minimal encroachments"); Newmark v. Vogelgesang, 915 S.W.2d 337, 339 (Mo. App. 1996) (same).

[48] *Urban Site Venture II Ltd. Partnership, supra*, 665 A.2d at 1067, *citing Dundalk Holding Co., supra; Newmark*, 915 S.W.2d at 339.

[49] *Urban Site Venture II Ltd. Partnership, supra*, 665 A.2d at 1066, *citing* Easter v. Dundalk Holding Co., 86 A.2d 404 (Md. 1952); *Newmark, supra*, 915 S.W.2d at 339.

granting of an injunction to remove an encroachment, and, thus, limiting the owner to damages, is found in *Hanson v. Estell*:

> Generally a mandatory injunction is the proper remedy for an adjoining landowner who seeks to compel the removal of an encroachment. Because this extraordinary injunctive relief is equitable in nature, the court may refuse to enjoin on equitable principles. In particular, the courts may withhold a mandatory injunction as oppressive when (1) the encroacher did not simply take a calculated risk, or negligently or willfully locate the encroaching structure; (2) the damage to the landowner is slight and the benefit of removal is equally small; (3) there is no real limitation to the property's future use; (4) it is impractical to move the encroaching structure; and (5) there is an enormous disparity in the resulting hardships. Contrary to the Estells' argument, the eminent domain provision, does not divest a court of equity of the power to refuse a mandatory injunction when the balancing equities listed above are clearly and convincingly proven.[50]

[93.4] Restitution

At common law, a trespasser was liable in damages, including nominal damages,[51] but it was understood that the trespasser was not required to account to the owner for any profits the trespasser realized as a result of the trespass.[52] The common law rule is recognized today.[53]

In some cases, however, the trespass results in *de minimis* injury to the owner, but produces significant benefits to the trespasser. For example, in *Raven Red Ash Coal Co. v. Ball*[54] the defendant coal company held an easement to transport coal across Ball's property. The easement applied to large mines on adjacent tracts of land. The company exceeded the easement by using it wrongfully to transport coal from several, smaller tracts. The additional usage could hardly be said to have damaged plaintiff's land to any extent greater than the land was already being subjected to by the easement. What, after all, is one or two more coal-carrying trucks to an estate already burdened by an easement that is subject to the carriage of a much larger number of coal-carrying trucks. The court recognized the common law rule, but refused to follow it, finding that the wrongful use

---

[50] *Supra*, 997 P.2d at 430–31 (citations omitted).

[51] Snow v. City of Columbia, 409 S.E.2d 797, 802 (S.C. App. 1991); Section 93.2 ([Trespass] Damages).

[52] Restatement of Restitution § 129 (1937) (stating that trespasser is not under a duty to disgorge benefits arising from wrongful use of plaintiff's land).

[53] *Cf.* Boudreaux v. Jefferson Island Storage & Hub, LLC, 255 F.3d 271 (5th Cir. 2001):

> The Boudreaux plaintiffs simply cannot assert a claim for unjust enrichment in the face of a claimed trespass, even if recovery for trespass is precluded . . . .

Id. at 275 (citations omitted) (applying Louisiana law).

[54] 39 S.E.2d 231 (Va. 1946).

of plaintiff's land demanded an appropriate remedy—here, disgorgement of the benefit the company derived from its unauthorized use of the easement.[55]

Similarly, in *Edwards v. Lee's Administrator*[56] the defendant had exploited for profit a cave which underlie both his and the plaintiff's land. The only entrance to the cave was on defendant's land, but defendant had constructed walkways and exhibits that encouraged the patrons to enter onto plaintiff's land, at least plaintiff's subterranean estate, as the patrons wandered about the cave. It was difficult to see how plaintiff had been damaged by the underground trespassing. While plaintiff could enjoin future trespasses, that remedy would not address past usage. The court held that under the circumstances the defendant should account to the plaintiff for the profits realized by exploitation of the cave.[57]

It is advisable when seeking a restitutional recovery of the benefits the trespasser derived by his unlawful entry, that plaintiff use the common count of money had and received. Framing the claim in trespass may induce a court to limit the plaintiff to damages.[58] The limitation unduly emphasizes form over substance, and violates the view in most jurisdictions that the remedy should follow the proof, not the pleadings;[59] nevertheless, there is no purpose served by inviting a court to commit error.

§ 94 NUISANCE

Nuisance liability is older than the concept of negligence and stems as much from early English common law concepts of property as from tort.[1] The "tort theory," however, has its adherents.[2] Age has not, however,

---

[55] *Id.* at 239 (finding that measure of benefit was prevailing rate of payment for purchase of the right of way).

[56] 96 S.W.2d 1028 (Ky. App. 1936).

[57] *Id.* at 1032-33; *see* Beck v. Northern Natural Gas Co., 170 F.3d 1018 (10th Cir. 1999) (holding that defendant was unjustly enriched when natural gas stored by defendant in one underground formation migrated (trespassed) into an adjoining formation under plaintiffs' land). As noted by the court:

The benefit that [defendant] received from the [plaintiffs] was the use of the [underground] formation without payment of rent . . . .

Id. at 1024 (brackets added).

[58] *Beck, supra,* 170 F.3d at 1024 (characterizing remedy as sounding in damages for benefit obtain by defendant in trespassing on plaintiffs' land and rejecting recovery of defendant's profits from the trespass); Payne v. Consol. Coal Co., 607 F. Supp. 378, 382 (D. Va. 1985) (recognizing Virginia precedent (*Raven Red Ash Coal Co., supra*) permitting plaintiff to recover, under restitution theory, benefits obtained by trespass, but noting that since plaintiffs chose to bring an action for trespass, they may receive only trespass damages).

[59] Fed. R. Civ. P. 54(c) (stating that except for a default judgment, "every final judgment shall grant the relief to which the party in whose favor it is rendered is entitled, even if the party has not demanded such relief in the party's pleadings").

[1] Tint v. Sanborn, 259 Cal. Rptr. 902, 907, 908 nn 1–2 (Cal. App. 1989).

[2] Fletcher v. City of Independence, 708 S.W.2d 158, 166 (Mo. App. 1986) (stating that "[a]n action for private nuisance rests on tort liability"); *see* Adkins v. Thomas Solvent Co., 487 N.W.2d 715, 720-23 (Mich. 1992) (describing common law origins of nuisance action).

brought enlightenment. Prosser once remarked that "[t]here is perhaps no more impenetrable jungle in the entire law than that which surrounds the word 'nuisance.'"[3] The remedies that accompany this action have proven to be equally difficult to cabin by legal rule.

Nuisance encompasses all manner of invasions of the plaintiff's private use and enjoyment of his land, including invasions that are (1) intentional and unreasonable, (2) negligent or reckless, or (3) actionable as an abnormally dangerous condition or activity.[4] The interference must be "substantial,"[5] but the activity does not have to be "unusual" to amount to a private nuisance.[6] The broad requirements of nuisance law are designed to regulate competing, simultaneous uses of nearby properties by unrelated owners, as, for example, the height or construction of a fence that separates adjoining owners.[7] Even natural objects may constitute a nuisance.[8] Because the requirements listed above impose different responsibility thresholds on a landowner, determining whether a particular use is a nuisance is often a difficult prediction.

The history of nuisance did have a significant impact on the remedies devised to address the tort. By the late medieval period, private nuisances could be addressed through the form of action "trespass on the case." This action, maintainable at law, provided only damages. To abate or enjoin a nuisance required the assistance of equity. The development of nuisance in two separate court systems contributed to the confusion Prosser described.

[94.1] Temporary or Permanent

Nuisances are often referred to as temporary (aka continuing) or permanent. Fixing one of the labels to a nuisance can have significant remedial repercussions. A nuisance is said to be classified as temporary or permanent based on the type and nature of harm inflicted on the plaintiff's property.[9] Whether an action is deemed temporary, on the one hand, or permanent, on the other hand, is, however, more an ending place than a beginning. The difference in classification is most apparent in the remedies available.

---

[3] WILLIAM PROSSER, HANDBOOK OF THE LAW OF TORTS, 571 (4th ed. 1971) (noting further that nuisance "has meant all things to all men").

[4] E.g., Barnes v. City of Thompson Falls, 979 P.2d 1275, 1278 (Mont. 1999); Copart Indus., Inc. v. Consol. Edison Co., 362 N.E.2d 968, 971 (N.Y. 1977); see Restatement (Second) of Torts § 822 (1979).

[5] E.g., Sharp v. 251st Street Landfill, Inc., 925 P.2d 546, 552 (Okla. 1996); Duff v. Morgantown Energy Assocs., 421 S.E.2d 253, 256-57 (W. Va. 1992).

[6] Tichnor v. Vore, 953 S.W.2d 171, 177-78 (Mo. App. 1997) (housing of 16 constantly barking dogs constituted an unreasonable use of property given the characteristics of the property and the neighborhood).

[7] See generally Deborah Tussey, Annot., Fence as Nuisance, 80 A.L.R. 3d 962 (1977).

[8] Wilson v. Handley, 119 Cal. Rptr. 2d 263 (Cal. App. 2002) (row of trees erected as "spite fence"), applying Cal. Civ. Code § 841.4.

[9] Bartleson v. United States, 96 F.3d 1270, 1275 (9th Cir. 1996) (applying California law).

A nuisance that is abatable, *i.e.,* will be enjoined by the court, is said to be temporary. A nuisance that will not be abated, but will be redressed only through an award of damages, is said to be permanent. Unfortunately, whether the label precedes the determination of the proper remedy, or vice versa, is about as difficult to ascertain as the proverbial firstness of the chicken or the egg.[10] What is reasonably practical under the circumstances is a case-specific test from which generalizations are hazardous. Since abatability determines the character of the nuisance, this approach leaves much discretion in the hands of the court to fashion case-specific remedies.

In attempting to give meaning to the temporary-permanent dichotomy, courts have used a variety of alternate phrasings. This has included frequency of the activity,[11] whether the activity has stabilized,[12] or whether the activity has acquired solidity of structure, analogous to an encroachment onto the plaintiff's land.[13] In many cases, the facts are capable of characterization and labeling as either a temporary or a permanent nuisance. What drives informed analysis is the calculation of the relative costs and benefits of abatement of the nuisance by an injunction as opposed to an award of damages. The assessment of the preferred remedy will then determine the label. If injunctive relief is found to be appropriate under the facts and circumstances of the case, the nuisance will be labeled temporary; if an injunction is not appropriate, because, for example, the benefits of the nuisance producing activities outweigh the costs imposed on the plaintiff(s) landowner(s), the nuisance will be deemed permanent and plaintiff(s) limited to damages.

Even if the nuisance is deemed temporary, the plaintiff may elect to recover damages instead of injunctive relief. A defendant may argue that plaintiff is limited to a single award because the nuisance is permanent.[14] A defendant would elect this tactic when the prospect of multiple awards based on the characterization of nuisance as temporary[15] exceeds in value the likely award based on the nuisance being deemed permanent. Although the analysis of whether the nuisance is temporary or permanent is usually conducted with reference to the costs and benefits of injunctive relief, the same approach can be used in evaluating the propriety of temporary nuisance damages versus permanent nuisance damages.

[10] *Cf.* Mangini v. Aerojet-General Corp., 912 P.2d 1220, 1227–28 (Cal. 1996) (discussing the concept of "abatability" and noting that the standard does not require all that is technically feasible but only that the nuisance can be abated by means that are reasonably practical under the circumstances).

[11] *Bartleson, supra,* 96 F.3d at 1275 (stating that "[a] nuisance is . . . generally considered continuing if it is an ongoing or repeated disturbance . . . that may vary over time") (citations and internal quotation marks omitted).

[12] Graveley Ranch v. Scherping, 782 P.2d 371, 374 (Mont. 1989) (stating that "a permanent nuisance is one where the situation has 'stabilized'").

[13] Sections 90.1 ([Physical Damage] Temporary or Permanent Injury), 93.1 ([Trespass] Temporary or Permanent).

[14] Section 94.2.2 (Permanent Nuisance Damages).

[15] Section 94.2.1 (Temporary Nuisance Damages).

[94.2] Damages

Measuring damages for a nuisance is complicated by the various ways in which a jurisdiction may characterize a nuisance. The characterization often influences how the court approaches the issue of damages and the application of the rules are often jurisdiction-specific. In *Weinhold v. Wolff* the "nuisance" was a hog farm that emitted odors. The court noted that several factors supported the characterization of the nuisance as permanent: (1) no technological control of the problem was feasible other than shutting down the activities causing the nuisance and the defendant intended to continue his operation unless enjoined; (2) enjoining the operation of the hog farm was not an equitable and practical solution.[16] As noted by the court in *Weinhold*: "The terms 'permanent' and 'temporary' are somewhat nebulous in that they have practical meaning only in relation to particular fact situations and can change in characterization from one set of facts to another."[17]

[94.2.1] Temporary Nuisance Damages

For a temporary nuisance, a plaintiff may seek to abate by injunction or, at its election and in addition, seek damages. When the plaintiff claims damages, the award will cover losses within the period of limitation prior to commencing the action and the date of trial.[18] Within that chronological limitation, the plaintiff may measure the loss by the diminution in value, diminished rental value, or reasonable cost of restoration.[19] In some cases, the plaintiff may elect his preferred remedy;[20] in other cases, the jurisdiction may adopt one of the above measures as the sole or preferred measure.[21] The plaintiff may also recover loss of use damages[22] and damages

---

[16] 555 N.W.2d 454, 463 (Iowa 1996); Miller v. Cudahy Co., 858 F.2d 1449, 1453–54 (10th Cir. 1988) (noting the "confused state of the law concerning the distinction between permanent and temporary nuisances," indicating that the "distinction" "remains a viable concept"(!), and concluding that "each case must be considered in its own factual setting") (citations omitted), *cert. denied*, 492 U.S. 926 (1989).

[17] 555 N.W. 2d at 463 (citation omitted).

[18] Briggs & Stratton Corp. v. Concrete Sales & Services, 29 F. Supp. 2d 1372 (M.D. Ga. 1998):

> In Georgia, a plaintiff asserting a claim for continuing nuisance can recover for any damages to his property that occurred within the four years before the action was filed.

Id. at 1377 (citations omitted). The period from the commencement of the action to the date of trial is covered by allegations in the complaint or by a supplemental pleading. Fed. R. Civ. P. 15(d).

[19] Porter v. Saddlebrook Resorts, Inc., 596 So. 2d 472, 474 (Fla. App. 1992).

[20] City of Phoenix v. Johnson, 75 P.2d 30, 37 (Ariz. 1938).

[21] Reeser v. Weaver Bros., Inc., 605 N.E.2d 1271, 1276 (Ohio App. 1992) (permitting plaintiff to use cost of remediation unless greater than diminution in value).

[22] Andersen v. Village of Little Chute, 549 N.W.2d 737, 742–43 (Wis. App. 1996); Henderson v. Spring Run Allotment, 651 N.E.2d 489, 494–95 (Ohio App. 1994); Moylan v. Dykes, 226 Cal. Rptr. 673, 680 (Cal. App. 1986); Section 80.3 (Loss of Use).

for discomfort and annoyance resulting from the nuisance.[23] Some jurisdictions permit consequential damages that proximately flow from loss of use.[24]

When a plaintiff seeks damages for a temporary nuisance, the court may not award future damages, i.e., damages for injury that will occur after the date of trial.[25] The availability of nominal damages has been recognized in a few cases.[26]

[94.2.2] Permanent Nuisance Damages

When the nuisance is characterized as permanent, the plaintiff must recover all damages (past, present, and future) that will result from the activity. The usual measure is diminution in value of the property due to the nuisance.[27] The plaintiff may recover consequential damages, such as a lost opportunity to sell the property, provided the plaintiff establishes these damages by reasonable, non-speculative evidence.[28] This lost sale is necessarily an above market sale since diminution in value will award to the plaintiff the difference between what his property is now worth and what it would be worth without the nuisance. Proving that the property could have been sold for more than its worth will be a daunting task.

When the nuisance causes environmental contamination, cost of remediation or restoration has tended to displace diminution in value as the preferred measure.[29] When the nuisance involves environmental injury, the cost of remediation may also be preferred.[30] Likewise in this context, the plaintiff may recover stigma damages based on the remaining diminution in value that will result even if reasonable remediation or restoration efforts are made.[31] Stigma damages should not be awarded when

---

[23] *Weinhold, supra,* 555 N.W.2d at 465–66; Washington Suburban Sanitary Comm'n v. CAE-Link, Corp., 622 A.2d 745, 760–61 (Md.), *cert. denied,* 510 U.S. 907 (1993); Fletcher v. City of Independence, 708 S.W.2d 158, 178 (Mo. App. 1986); *cf.* Sturges v. Charles L. Harney, Inc., 331 P.2d 1072, 1082 (Cal. App. 1958) (permitting mental distress damages); Section 94.2.3 ([Nuisance] Annoyance and Discomfort Damages).

[24] *Porter, supra,* 596 So. 2d at 474; State of Georgia v. City of East Ridge, Tennessee, 949 F. Supp. 1571, 1583 (N.D. Ga. 1996); Phillips v. Davis Timber Co., Inc., 468 So. 2d 72, 78 (Miss. 1985). *But cf. Weinhold, supra,* 555 N.W.2d at 466 (suggesting by implication that special damages are only available when the nuisance is labeled permanent).

[25] Santa Fe Partnership v. Arco Prods. Co., 54 Cal. Rptr. 2d 214, 220 (Cal. App. 1996); *see* Rudd v. Electrolux Corp., 982 F. Supp. 355, 372 (M.D.N.C. 1997) (noting position of some commentators that plaintiff could recover costs incurred to prevent future injury or abate the nuisance of its harmful effects), *citing* W. Page Keeton, et al., Prosser & Keeton on the Law of Torts § 89 at 640 (5th ed. 1984).

[26] Charles McCormick, Damages 89-90 (1935).

[27] *Miller, supra,* 858 F.2d at 1456 (applying Kansas law).

[28] Ravan v. Greenville County, 434 S.E.2d 296, 307 (S.C. App. 1993); *Reeser,* 605 N.E.2d at 1274. *Rudd, supra,* 982 F. Supp. at 372; *Weinhold, supra,* 555 N.W.2d at 465.

[29] Section 91 (Natural Resource Damage).

[30] Pepper v. J.J. Wellcome Constr. Co., 871 P.2d 601 (Wash. App. 1994) (rejecting "lesser of" rule and permitting plaintiff to recover cost of restoration as long as it does not exceed pre-nuisance value).

[31] Section 91.2 (Stigma Damages).

diminution in value rather than cost of remediation is used since stigma should be included in the measurement of diminution of value to which the property has been subjected by the nuisance.

[94.2.3] Annoyance and Discomfort Damages

Because nuisance involves a substantial and unreasonable interference with the plaintiff's use and enjoyment of his property, annoyance and discomfort damages are usually available in both temporary and permanent injunction cases.[32] Mere annoyance at the off-property activities of another will not create a nuisance, but an actual nuisance permits the award of damages for the annoyance and discomfort it causes.[33] A number of courts have limited annoyance and discomfort damages to actual occupiers of the property affected by the nuisance[34] and have limited the recovery of annoyance and discomfort damages to those well grounded in fact.[35] When annoyance and discomfort damages are allowed, it is recognized that they are non-economic in character and thus largely committed to the discretion of the trier-of-fact.[36]

[94.3] Injunction

When injunctive relief to abate a nuisance is considered, the most critical factor will usually be that of balancing the hardship. Unlike the situation with trespass, the willful-innocent distinction is less frequently applied to bar balancing of the hardship when considering whether to enjoin a nuisance. This probably reflects the realization that nuisance claims require the balancing of competing uses of neighboring property, whereas trespass represents a more direct expropriation of another's right to exclusive use and enjoyment of her property. Consequently, whether the nuisance will be enjoined reflects the considered balancing of several factors, including: (1) the nature and scope of the damage to plaintiff, (2)

---

[32] Thomsen v. Greve, 550 N.W.2d 49, 57 (Neb. App. 1996).

[33] Baker v. Westinghouse Elec. Corp., 70 F.3d 951, 955 (7th Cir. 1995) (applying Indiana law.

[34] *Reeser, supra*, 605 N.E.2d at 1279. *See generally* Tracy Bateman, Annot., *Nuisance as Entitling Owner or Occupant of Real Estate To Recover Damages for Personal Inconvenience, Discomfort, Annoyance, Anguish, or Sickness, Distinct From or in Addition to, Damages for Depreciation on Value of Property or its Use*, 25 A.L.R. 5th 568 (1995) (stating that general rule is to permit owner or occupier of real property to recover in nuisance action annoyance, distress, or discomfort damages, but noting exceptions, particularly for non-occupiers, claims against governmental entities, and for certain types of annoyance, distress, or discomfort claims, such as fear of enhanced risk of disease or sleeplessness).

[35] Boughton v. Cotter Corp., 65 F.3d 823, 832 (10th Cir. 1995) (holding that unfounded fear of contracting cancer was not compensable as element of annoyance and discomfort damages resulting from a nuisance) (applying Colorado law).

[36] Arvida/JMB Partners v. Hadaway, 489 S.E.2d 125, 129 (Ga. App. 1997) (stating that "[t]he measure of damages for 'discomfort, loss of peace of mind, unhappiness, and annoyance' of the plaintiff caused by maintenance of a nuisance is for the enlightened conscience of the jury") (citations omitted).

whether the nuisance can be fixed by methods other than ceasing the activity,[37] and (3) the costs of enjoining the activity on the defendant and third persons.[38]

There is language in some decisions that a court will only enjoin an actual nuisance, not an anticipatory nuisance.[39] The modern trend, however, is to evaluate the request in terms of ripeness and mootness.[40] If the threatened activity would constitute an abatable nuisance, and its occurrence is sufficiently likely to warrant injunctive relief, then the injunction should issue even against an anticipatory nuisance. The tendency, however, is to require a higher threshold of "likeliness" than in the usual case for injunctive relief. As noted in *Falkner v. Brookfield*:

> From the cited authorities and others it appears that equity will not enjoin an injury which is merely anticipated nor interfere where an apprehended nuisance is doubtful, contingent, conjectural or problematical. A bare possibility of nuisance or a mere fear or apprehension that injury will result is not enough. On the other hand, an injunction may issue to prevent a threatened or anticipated nuisance which will necessarily result from the contemplated act, where the nuisance is a practically certain or strongly probable result or a natural or inevitable consequence.[41]

If the court finds that the nuisance is abatable and that the plaintiff is entitled to injunctive relief, the plaintiff may also recover damages for past

---

[37] Cline v. Franklin Pork, Inc., 361 N.W.2d 566 (Neb. 1985):

> A court of equity will not usually enjoin the operation of a lawful business without regard to how serious may be the grievance caused thereby. In the first instance, at least, it will require the cause of the grievance to be corrected and will enjoin the conduct of the enterprise perpetually after it has been proven that no application of endeavor, science, or skill can effect a remedy where the owners cannot be induced to conduct it properly.

Id. at 571 (citation omitted).

[38] *See Weinhold, supra,* 555 N.W.2d at 467; O'Cain v. O'Cain, 473 S.E.2d 460, 465–66 (S.C. App. 1996); Parr v. Neal, 542 N.E.2d 1257, 1260 (Ill. App. 1989); York v. Stallings, 341 P.2d 529, 534–35 (Or. 1959).

[39] Duff v. Morgantown Energy Assocs., 421 S.E.2d 253, 258, n.9 (W. Va. 1992) (stating that equity will not interfere with activities not constituting a nuisance *per se* unless plaintiff proves the activity will amount to a nuisance "beyond all ground of questioning"). The court identified a nuisance *per se* as "an act, occupation, or structure which is a nuisance at all times and under any circumstances, regardless or location or surroundings"). *Id.* at 258 n.8 (citations omitted); McQuail v. Shell Oil Co., 183 A.2d 581, 584 (Del. Ch. 1962) (noting rule that court would not enjoin an anticipatory nuisance unless the activity would constitute a nuisance *per se*).

[40] Sections 30.1 (Ripeness), 30.2 (Mootness).

[41] 117 N.W.2d 125, 128 (Mich. 1962); *see* State *ex rel* Village of Los Ranchos de Albuquerque v. City of Albuquerque, 889 P.2d 185, 200 (N.Mex. 1994) (stating that anticipatory nuisance must be proven so as to make "any argument that it is not a nuisance highly improbable"); Roach v. Combined Utility Comm'n of City of Easley, 351 S.E.2d 168, 169 (S.C. App. 1986) (stating that evidence must show the "nuisance is inevitable from the proposed use of the premises or will necessarily result"). *But cf.* Sharp v. 251st Street Landfill, Inc., 925 P.2d 546, 549, 552 (Okla. 1996) (applying "reasonable probability" standard).

injury to the land caused during the time the nuisance was unabated,[42] subject to the rule that the plaintiff may only go as far back as the statute of limitation will allow.[43]

[94.4] Public vs. Private

At common law, the concept of public nuisance referred to "an act or omission 'which obstructs or causes inconvenience or damage to the public in the exercise of rights common to all her majesty's subjects.'"[44] In its modern formulation, public nuisance has two branches:

- acts which interfere with the use and enjoyment of the public use of property; and

- acts which are injurious to public health, safety, morals or welfare.[45]

When the nuisance is deemed a public nuisance, the ability of a non-governmental plaintiff to sue for redress is limited. The plaintiff is usually required to demonstrate that the public nuisance inflicts a "private and peculiar injury upon him, which is different from that inflicted on the general public."[46]

The verbal formulations of public nuisance are varied, but they all conform to and confirm the basic concept that a public nuisance "affects equally the rights of an entire neighborhood or community, although the extent of the injury may be unequal."[47] As noted in *Sharon Steel Corp. v. City of Fairmont*:

> A public nuisance is an act or condition that unlawfully operates to hurt or inconvenience an indefinite number of persons. The distinction between a public nuisance and a private nuisance is that the former affects the general public, and the latter injures one person or a limited number of persons only. Ordinarily, a suit to abate a public nuisance cannot be maintained by an individual in

---

[42] Stalely v. Sagel, 841 P.2d 379, 382 (Colo. App. 1992) (stating that "if the nuisance is abated by injunctive decree and there is no permanent damage to the property resulting from the nuisance while it existed, the proper measure of damages for any prior adverse affects upon the land's value is the loss of the property's rental value for the period during which the nuisance continued") (citations omitted); *cf.* Harris v. Town of Lincoln, 668 A.2d 321, 328 (R.I. 1995) (stating that "a plaintiff in a nuisance action is not required to elect between injunctive relief and monetary damages") (citation omitted).

[43] Section 94.2.1 (Temporary Nuisance Damages).

[44] KEETON, PROSSER & KEETON ON THE LAW OF TORTS, *supra* § 90, at 643 (citation omitted).

[45] The second branch is addressed in Section 27 (Injunction of Criminal Activity).

[46] Burns Jackson Miller Summit & Spitzer v. Lindner, 451 N.E.2d 459, 468 (N.Y. 1983).

[47] Miotke v. City of Spokane, 678 P.2d 803, 816 (Wash. 1984), *citing and quoting* R.C.W. 7.48.130.

his private capacity, as it is the duty of the proper public officials to vindicate the rights of the public.[48]

To constitute a public nuisance it is not necessary that all members of the public suffer actual injury: "[i]t is sufficient if it injures those of the public who may actually come in contact with it."[49] Plaintiff(s) may bring an action for public nuisance if they can show they are "specially affected" by the nuisance, in other words, that plaintiff(s) suffered a "special injury" which differentiates them from the larger public that has been injured by the nuisance.[50]

Special injury may be shown by *proximity*, which subjects the plaintiffs to substantially greater harm than visited on the public as a whole,[51] or the fact that plaintiff's land suffers a *disproportionate* burden of the injury from the public as a whole.[52] A showing that the public nuisance has *specially depreciated* plaintiff's property value has been held to demonstrate special injury.[53]

The fact that the plaintiff(s) self-identify a claimed injury as unique or special is not controlling as to whether they, as non-governmental entities, have standing to sue for a public nuisance. For example, in *Burns Jackson Miller Summit & Spitzer v. Lindner* two law firms sought damages on behalf of professional business entities against defendants for an illegal public strike by public transit workers. The court recognized that an additional expense in the performance of a specific contract caused by a public nuisance would satisfy the special injury requirement.[54] The court held, however, that "additional out-of-pocket expense" and "lost profit" were not

---

[48] 334 S.E.2d 616, 620 (W. Va. 1985) (citation and internal quotation marks omitted), *appeal dismissed*, 474 U.S. 1098 (1986); Atlanta Processing Co. v. Brown, 179 S.E.2d 752, 758 (Ga. 1971) (stating that "[a] public nuisance exists if the act complained of affects rights which are common to all within a particular area"); Restatement (Second) of Torts § 821B (1979) (stating that "[a] public nuisance is an unreasonable interference with a right common to the general public").

[49] *Atlanta Processing Co.*, *supra*, 179 S.E.2d at 758.

[50] Couture v. Board of Educ., 505 A.2d 432, 436 (Conn. App. 1986) (stating that "[t]o be considered public, the nuisance must affect an interest in common to the general public, rather than peculiar to one individual, or several"). *See generally* William Johnson, Annot., *What Constitutes Special Injury That Entitles Private Party to Maintain Action Based on Public Nuisance—Modern Cases*, 71 A.L.R. 4th 13 (1990).

[51] *Miotke*, *supra*, 678 P.2d at 816-17 (noting that waterfront owners would be affected to substantially greater extent than general public by sewage bypass pipe which permitted discharge of untreated sewage into waterway); Three Bills, Inc. v. City of Parma, 676 N.E.2d 1273, 1276 (Ohio App. 1996) (stating that "adjacent property owners have a special interest, inasmuch as they are beneficiaries of restrictive covenants, which enables them to maintain an action to enjoin misuse of public lands").

[52] Levene v. City of Salem, 229 P.2d 255, 262-63 (Or. 1951) (finding defendant liable under the theory of public nuisance for diverting a stream onto the plaintiff's land, among others, and flooding plaintiff's building).

[53] Concerned Area Residents for the Env't v. Southview Farm, 834 F. Supp. 1410, 1421 (W.D.N.Y. 1993) (applying New York law).

[54] 451 N.E.2d 459, 468 (N.Y. 1983).

sufficiently differentiated from that experienced by the greater community to be treated as "special injury."[55]

Similarly, in *Exxon Valdez Alaska Native Class v. Exxon Corp.* plaintiffs sought damages under a theory of public nuisance for losses sustained as a result of a massive oil spill.[56] Their "special injury" consisted of claims of cultural damage, particularly, the effect of the oil spill on the plaintiff's "subsistence way of life," which was dependent "upon the preservation of uncontaminated natural resources, marine life and wildlife." The court found that the claim was not sufficiently unique to the plaintiffs to enable them to maintain a public nuisance action:

> Admittedly, the oil spill affected the communal life of Alaska Natives, but whatever injury they suffered (other than the harvest loss), though potentially different in degree than that suffered by other Alaskans, was not different in kind. We agree with the district court that the right to lead subsistence lifestyle is not limited to Alaska Natives. While the oil spill may have affected Alaska Natives more severely than other members of the public, "the right to obtain and share wild food, enjoy uncontaminated nature, and cultivate traditional, cultural, spiritual, and psychological benefits in pristine natural surroundings" is shared by all Alaskans.[57]

The fact that many plaintiffs can claim "special injury" does not necessarily defeat their effort to maintain that, as to them, the public nuisance is a private nuisance:

> Defendants maintain that because plaintiffs purport to represent a group so numerous as a nationwide class of corn farmers, their damages cannot be considered special or unique. But the special damages requirement does not limit the absolute number of parties affected so much as it restricts the types of harm that are compensable. Class actions and special damages are not mutually exclusive.[58]

---

[55] *Id.* at 468–69. *But cf.* Farmer v. D'Agostino Supermarkets, Inc., 544 N.Y.S.2d 943, 947 (Sup. Ct. 1989) (requiring defendant to accept returns for refunds tendered by homeless persons and rejecting defendant's claim that injury to homeless persons, when defendant refused to accept returns, was generic rather than unique because economic harm was no different from that sustained by anyone refused a refund for a return).

[56] 104 F.3d 1196 (9th Cir. 1997).

[57] *Id.* at 1198 (*citing* Restatement (Second) of Torts § 821(C)(1), cmt. b (1979)); Comet Pelta, Inc. v. Pate Stevedore Co. of Pascagoula, Inc., 521 So. 2d 857, 861 (Miss. 1988) (stating that to show "special injury" the plaintiff's injury must be different in kind from that sustained by the general public but degree of harm cannot be totally disregarded because "someone experiencing a greater degree of harm will often be able to show particular harm").

[58] *In re* Starlink Corn Products Liability Litigation, 212 F. Supp. 2d 828, 848 (N.D. Ill. 2002). "Starlink" corn is a genetically modified foodstuff that was approved for livestock feed, but not human consumption. When traces of the product were found in foods eaten by humans there was a widespread substitution of domestic corn with non U.S. corn because of fears that the U.S. corn supply was contaminated. U.S. farmers sued the manufacturer of "Starlink" alleging, among other theories, the creation of a public nuisance that specially injured farmers. The claim withstood summary judgment for the reasons above noted. The court relied on Restatement (Second) of Torts § 821C (1979).

If the plaintiff(s) satisfy the special injury requirement, their remedies are as if they were suing for damages or to enjoin a private nuisance.

[94.5] Restitution

Traditionally, restitution has not been sought in nuisance. The focus of nuisance has been on the harm to the plaintiff's interest in the use and enjoyment of his property rather than the gains derived by the defendant in committing the nuisance. To the extent gains have been considered, it has been in connection with the determination whether defendant's operations constituted a nuisance or whether the defendant's operations should be enjoined as a nuisance.[59]

There have been a number of recent efforts, particularly in the area of mass tort, product liability, to allow a gains based recovery for nuisance, *i.e.*, to strip the defendant of the profits the defendant made as a result of his nuisance-producing activities. The effort has been generally criticized by commentators as a misuse of restitution[60] and this sentiment has been echoed by the courts.[61]

The criticisms have, however, been technical, rather than doctrinal. The objection has been that plaintiffs misstated or mischaracterized the basis of their gains-based claim (or relied on a statute that did not permit a gains-based recovery) rather than rejection of the theory altogether as inappropriate.

The use of restitution here is attractive for plaintiffs, particularly as the tradition means of obtaining a defendant's profits in mass tort claims—punitive damages—remains under sustained assault.[62] Restitution standards remain fairly pliable and absent forceful rejection of the remedy in the mass tort, product liability context by courts or legislatures—which has not yet occurred—one should expect to see continued efforts to use restitution to redress nuisance claims when the defendant has derived profits from its nuisance producing activities.[63]

§ 95 WASTE

Waste refers to anything that causes lasting damage to, or permanent loss of, a fee interest in real property or which destroys or lessens the value

---

[59] Section 94.3 ([Nuisance] Injunction).

[60] Doug Rendleman, *Common Law Restitution in the Mississippi Tobacco Settlement: Did the Smoke Get in Their Eyes?*, 33 Ga. L. Rev. 847 (1999); *see* Anthony J. Sebok, *Two Concepts of Injustice in Restitution For Slavery*, 84 B.U. L. Rev. 1405, 1423 (2004) (listing reasons why restitution (reparation) for slavery should not be recognized).

[61] United States v. Philip Morris USA, Inc., 396 F.3d 1190 (D.C. Cir. 2005) (rejecting restitution of tobacco company profits under RICO (Racketeer Influenced and Corrupt Organizations) action brought by the federal government).

[62] Chapter 23 (Punitive damages) (particularly Section 205 (Due Process Limitations on the Amount of the Award).

[63] Section 41 (Restitution for Wrongdoing).

of the fee interest.[1] The reason for the remedy is the need to protect the holders of future or succeeding estates against detriment and injury caused by improper conduct by the person in actual possession of the property.[2] Waste is usually classified as voluntary or permissive. Voluntary waste, which is also known as affirmative or commissive waste, is the deliberate, willful, or voluntary commission of acts constituting waste.[3] Permissive waste arises from neglect or omission, in other words the failure "under the circumstances, to exercise the ordinary care of a prudent man for the preservation and protection of the estate."[4] The common law also recognized a third form of waste known as ameliorative, which occurred when the possessor of the fee altered the premises so as to change the premises very character.[5] This form of waste, when recognized, permits recoveries even though the conduct increases the value of the property because the conduct is deemed to be inconsistent with the intent of the grantor.[6]

At common law, there were restrictions on who could maintain an action for waste. It was argued that waste could not be claimed against lessees for life or years because the owner of the reversion could have protected himself by provisions in the lease; rather, waste was available only against those who took their interest by operation of law, such as a tenant in dower or curtesy, or against tenants at will.[7] In many jurisdictions, the action for waste is now controlled by statute and the action for waste has been substantially expanded;[8] however, the action's common law heritage retains importance, particularly in two areas. First, may an action for damages be commenced before the expiration of the estate of the person committing waste? Second, when a statute provides treble damages for waste, does the statute apply to all forms of waste or only voluntary waste?

---

[1] 2 BLACKSTONE'S COMMENTARIES *281 (defining Waste as "a spoil or destruction in houses, gardens, trees, or other corporeal hereditaments, to the dishersion of him that hath the remainder or reversion"); see Keesecker v. Bird, 490 S.E.2d 754, 769 (W. Va. 1997).

[2] Hamilton v. Mercantile Bank of Ceder Rapids, 621 N.W.2d 401 (Iowa 2001):

> A claim for waste is an action at law brought by a remainderman against a tenant in lawful possession of land—usually a life tenant or tenant for a term of years—who is allegedly using the land in such a way as to diminish its value.

Id. at 409 (citations omitted).

[3] *Keesecker, supra,* 490 S.E.2d 754; Regan v. Moyle Petroleum Co., 344 N.W.2d 695, 697 (S.D. 1984); Moore v. Phillips, 627 P.2d 831, 834 (Kan. App. 1981).

[4] *Keesecker, supra,* 490 S.E.2d at 770; Lustig v. U.M.C. Indus., Inc., 637 S.W.2d 55, 59 (Mo. App. 1982).

[5] Restatement (Second) of the Law of Property § 12.2 (1977).

[6] 5 R. POWELL, REAL PROPERTY §§ 56-3 to -8, 56-17 to -19 (1989).

[7] Vollertsen v. Lamb, 732 P.2d 486, 491–93 (Or. 1987) (discussing action for waste at common law).

[8] *In re* Evergreen Ventures, 147 B.R. 751, 754 (D. Ariz. 1992) (noting that "[c]laims for waste have evolved far beyond the original English statutes and common law claims. No longer do courts require that a plaintiff in a waste action hold a future interest . . .") (citations and examples omitted), *modified on other grounds,* 174 B.R. 350 (Bankr. 9th Cir. 1994); Iowa Code § 658.1 (permitting action for waste against "tenant for life or years," among others); Cal. Civ. Code § 2929 (permitting mortgagee to sue mortgagor for waste when latter's acts impairs the value of the collateral that secures the loan).

Because waste involves a claim by one who does not have a right to immediate possession, concern may exist whether the claimant should be allowed to sue for damages before she has actually succeeded to the estate. For example, if the holder of a life estate outlives the contingent remainderman, the latter's interest expires. Permitting him to sue for damages while the holder of the life estate is alive might result in a windfall recovery for the contingent remanderman. The majority rule is that the contingency of the interest deprives that holder of a present claim for damages.[9] The holder of the contingent interest is limited to equitable relief to enjoin the commission of waste "to prevent the destruction of that which may become his."[10] When, however, the interest is not contingent but certain, or relatively certain, courts exhibit a greater willingness to allow an action for damages before the interest becomes possessory.[11] Because the essence of the action for waste is "to mediate between the competing interests of life tenants and remainderman,[12] some jurisdictions have developed a "bad faith" concept to identify when the life tenant abuses his right to use the property to the detriment of the holder of the remainder interest.[13]

It is not uncommon for statutes to permit treble damages for waste. Traditionally, treble damages have been limited to voluntary waste.[14] Similarly, when the statute authorizes a forfeiture of the estate for waste, a similar limitation to voluntary waste has been applied under the rationale that forfeitures are not favored and a statute authorizing a forfeiture should be strictly construed.[15]

The usual measure of damages for waste is the difference between the present value of the property and what it would have been worth had the property been maintained and repaired as it should have been.[16] The cost of repairing the damage has also been recognized as a proper measure of damages for waste, as long as the costs of repair do not exceed diminution in value.[17]

---

[9] *See generally* J.A. Bryant, Annot., *Right of Contingent Remainderman to Maintain Action for Damages for Waste*, 56 A.L.R.3d 677 §§ 2–3 (1974).

[10] Sermon v. Sullivan, 640 S.W.2d 486, 487–88 (Mo. App. 1982).

[11] Zauner v. Brewer, 596 A.2d 388, 395–96 (Conn. 1991) (permitting holder of indefeasibly vested reversion to sue life tenant for damages for permissive waste before expiration of life estate).

[12] RICHARD POSNER, ECONOMIC ANALYSIS OF LAW 83 (5th ed. 1998).

[13] Osuna v. Albertson, 184 Cal. Rptr. 338, 342–43 (Cal. App. 1982).

[14] *Regan, supra*, 344 N.W.2d at 697:

> In authorizing treble damages for waste, our statute does not distinguish between voluntary and permissive waste. Such open-ended statutes, however, are generally construed to contemplate voluntary waste only, applying where the acts complained of are willful, wanton or malicious

(citations omitted); *see* Fisher Properties, Inc. v. Arden-Mayfair, Inc., 726 P.2d 8, 23 (Wash. 1986) (declining to construe statute to provide treble damages for permissive waste).

[15] Larsen v. Sjogren, 226 P.2d 177, 182 (Wyo. 1951); Rzeszotarski v. Sanborn, 1996 Ohio App. LEXIS 2372 (Ohio App., June 7, 1996) (unpublished opinion).

[16] *Regan, supra*, 344 N.W.2d at 697.

[17] Jowdy v. Guerin, 457 P.2d 745, 749-50 (Ariz. App. 1969); Section 90 (Physical Damage).

When waste is committed on property used as collateral or security for a loan, the measure of damages is the amount by which the security or collateral is impaired, which is the extent to which, if at all, the value of the collateral or security is less than the indebtedness.[18] If the debt is still secured, even after the waste, by property that is of equal or greater worth than the debt, the interest of the creditor has not been impaired. This doctrine can be a trap for the unwary creditor who upon foreclosing on the collateral or security enters a "full credit bid" (a bid equal to the debt). Since the bid reflects the bidders opinion as to the fair market value of the property, the bidder is opining that the property, in its current condition, is equal in value to the debt; consequently, the creditor may not have been harmed by the commission of waste.[19]

Injunctive relief to enjoin the commission of waste is available,[20] but somewhat circumscribed. The irreparable injury requirement should not serve as an impediment here to obtaining equitable relief because the injury goes to land, which equity sees as unique.[21] Nonetheless, the availability of injunctive relief may be limited to cases involving equitable waste, which is unfortunately, a term of some imprecision. Some courts give it a narrow construction:

> Equitable waste is a nebulous term—a doctrine of obscure limitations. It is such as is cognizable only in a court of equity. It is said that it has reference to cases where, by the terms of the will, deed, settlement or lease, the tenant holds the land without impeachment of waste . . . .
>
> Thus, it is that equitable jurisdiction in this behalf seems to have been confined to wanton, malicious and unconscientious acts of the particular tenant injurious to the inheritance, in contravention of the presumed will of the creator of the limited estate.[22]

Other courts give the term a broader application, in effect, permitting equitable remedies when legal remedies would not be available:

> Some of the authorities indicate that even a contingent remainderman may enjoin what is known as equitable waste, and equitable waste has been defined as '[a] form of waste recognized by courts of chancery, usually defined as consisting in such acts as at law

---

[18] Cornelison v. Kornbluth, 542 P.2d 981, 992 (Cal. 1975).

[19] 333 West Thomas Medical Bldg. Enter. v. Soetantyo, 976 F. Supp. 1298, 1300–01 (D. Ariz.), aff'd, 111 F.3d 138 (9th Cir. 1997) (Table); cf. Nippon Credit Bank Ltd. v. 1333 North California Boulevard, 103 Cal. Rptr. 2d 421, 430 (Cal. App. 2001) (holding that lender could recovery under theory of waste for failure of debtor to pay real estate taxes debt though amount of taxes was added to debt lender acquired the property at the foreclosure sale and lender was still owed money "after application of the credit bid at the foreclosure").

[20] Sermon, supra, 640 S.W. 2d at 487–88; Wigal v. Hensley, 216 S.W.2d 792, 793–94 (Ark. 1949).

[21] Keesecker, supra, 490 S.E.2d at 769 n.16.

[22] Southern Real Estate and Fin. Co. v. City of St. Louis, 758 S.W.2d 75, 80 (Mo. App. 1988), quoting Camden Trust Co. v. Handle, 26 A.2d 865 (N.J. Eq. 1942).

would not be deemed to be waste under the circumstances of the case, but which, in the view of a court of equity, are so regarded from their manifest injury to the inheritance, although they are not inconsistent with the legal rights of the party committing them. Among the instances of equitable waste the following may be stated: where a mortgagor in possession fells timber on the estate and thereby renders the security insufficient; where a tenant for life, without impeachment of waste, pulls down houses, or does other waste wantonly and maliciously; and where tenants for life without impeachment of waste, or tenants in tail, after possibility of issue extinct, commit acts in destruction of the estate, or cut down trees planted for the ornament and shelter of the premises.'[23]

In some cases, the terms permissive waste and equitable waste appear to be interchangeable, although it is not clear if interchangeability is intended. For example, in *Rumiche Corp. v. Eisenreich*, the court defined permissive waste as the negligent failure to prevent waste and equitable waste as the failure to do what a prudent owner would do to avoid waste.[24] The court indicated that equity imposed only limited duties on the prudent, but failed to specify what those duties were. One notes an analogy between prudence and fiduciary duties, but one hesitates to extend or push the analogy too far.

The action for waste should be distinguished from the concept of economic waste. Economic waste, as a legal concept, generally refers to a remedy which is economically inefficient in the sense that the economic benefits derived from the remedy are outweighed by the costs imposed in providing the remedy.

§ 96 GOOD FAITH IMPROVERS OF REAL PROPERTY

At common law, as a general rule, the owner was under no obligation (outside of contract) to pay for improvement, enhancement, or value added to the property by an improver. As noted by Chancellor Kent: "Every occupant [of real property] makes improvement at his peril, even if he acts under a bona fide belief of ownership."[1]

The common law approach has been ameliorated to a significant extent by judicial easing of its harshness toward improvers, and in some cases by legislative modification of the common law. The result is that improvers of property stand in a much better position today to recover or receive credit for the value they impart to the true owner's property.

By the rigid rules of the common law, the improver of real property did so at his peril. If it turned out the improver was not the lawful owner, he was not entitled to compensation from the true owner although the

---

[23] Stephenson v. Kuntz, 49 S.E.2d 235, 248 (W. Va. 1948) (citation omitted).
[24] 352 N.E.2d 125, 128 (N.Y. 1976).
[1] 2 James Kent, Commentaries on American Law 334 (14th ed. 1896).

improvements may have been done in good faith and with the honest conviction that the land belonged to the improver.

Over time, incremental changes permitted the improver to receive credit for the value of their improvements as an offset against the true owner's claim for mesne profits that accompanied the action to eject the improver from the land.[2] Courts also began to condition the granting of ejectment on the willingness of the true owner to effect restitution for the value imparted to the real property by the improver. Although the action in ejectment was in law, rather than equity, the common law courts imported equitable doctrines and defenses to mitigate what increasingly was seen as the harshness of the common law's "no compensation" approach.[3] In essence, courts required the true owner to act equitably if he wished to be treated equitably with respect to the restoration of his estate to him. This is an adaptation of the equitable maxim that "he who seeks equity, must do equity."[4] Lastly, several jurisdictions have enacted so-called "Betterment" statutes which permit the improver to recover the value of his improvements directly against the true owner. As noted by Dickinson, the "Betterment" statutes vary widely:

> At present, forty-two jurisdictions have "betterment" or "occupying claimant" acts. Although the statutes of seven states simply reiterate the common law, most jurisdictions have expanded improvers' rights and afforded relief in situations not covered by common law, such as ejectment actions brought by owners to dispossess mistaken improvers. A few jurisdictions grant relief to improvers in any equitable action without regard to whether the suit is brought by the owner or the improver. Only two jurisdictions, however, allow improvers the right to initiate an independent legal action. Thus, on the whole, betterment acts restrict relief to a limited number of procedural situations.[5]

When an improver is permitted a recovery or offset for the value of the improvements made, two critical questions invariably arise. First, what state of mind must the improver have had when he made the improvements? Second, how is "value" measured?

The general requirement is that the improver must have acted in "good faith." This is essentially an equitable characteristic designed to distinguish

---

[2] Section 92 (Ejectment) (discussing recovery of mesne profits).

[3] Restatement of Restitution § 42 (1937). The application was easier when the true owner sought equitable relief, such as an action to quiet title or remove a cloud on title.

[4] James v. Bailey, 370 F. Supp. 469, 471 (D.V.I. 1974); cf. Kerr v. Miller, 977 P.2d 438 (Or. App. 1999) (holding that mortgagee in possession who improved property could recover under principle of unjust enrichment against mortgagor who exercised equity of redemption to recover property after foreclosure); see Section 168 (Installment Land Sale Contracts) (discussing equity of redemption).

[5] Kelvin Dickinson, *Mistaken Improvers of Real Estate*, 64 N.C.L. Rev. 37, 42–43 (1985) (footnote omitted). *See generally* Annotation, *Action to Recover Improvements Made on Land, Taxes or Interest Paid or Lien Discharged, by One Who Mistakenly Believed Himself the Owner*, 104 A.L.R. 577 (1936).

the improver from the volunteer or officious intermeddler. The usual formulation is that the improver must have acted under an honest, mistaken belief that he had a valid claim or title or right to improve the property. Inequitable conduct by the true owner is not required as a prerequisite to the improver's claim.[6]

Courts may distinguish between situations when betterment is used defensively rather than offensively to secure a positive recovery under a theory of unjust enrichment. The burden may be less in the former case (defensive use) than in the latter (offensive use).[7] Courts may require that the improver's entry onto the property be under a colorable claim of title for him to claim betterment either offensively or defensively.[8] In this context:

> The mere making of improvements does not of itself give rise to an equitable allowance . . . . In order to warrant compensation, the improver must have acted in good faith under color or claim of title so that the making of the improvements resulted from an innocent mistake. Thus, where the improver is a trespasser or otherwise occupies the property without claim of title, he cannot plead mistake as a ground for equitable relief.[9]

Other courts have rejected limiting betterment to improvers who operate under color of title. *Duncan v. Akers* involved a builder who mistakenly constructed house on an adjoining landowner's property due to mistakes by a surveyor in placing stakes. The court stated that its reliance on color of title in past decisions was not controlling. The court noted the unfairness of allowing the true owner to keep the improvement free of the bank loans that had been taken out to construct the house. It surveyed recent decisions and concluded "that the modern trend favors relief in equity to an innocent improver of another's real estate who acted under a mistake."[10]

What constitutes "good faith" or "innocent belief," in the absence of a colorable title requirement, is difficult to say. One consistent theme is that the improver will be denied a recovery or offset if he acts with knowledge or notice that he does not have title or that title is in dispute.[11] The fact

---

[6] Somerville v. Jacobs, 170 S.E.2d 805, 810 (W. Va. 1969).

[7] Wright v. Wright, 289 S.E.2d 347, 351 (N.C. 1982) (requiring that when betterment theory is used offensively the improver must show acquiescence of true owner in improver's good faith mistaken belief that improver owned the land, or the improver's actions were induced by person with close relationship to the true owner); Section 43 (Nature of Unjust Enrichment).

[8] Fouser v. Paige, 612 P.2d 137, 139 (Idaho 1980) (collecting decisions) (noting that improver who entered after receiving deed from person they thought had good title were operating under color of title).

[9] Vulovich v. Baich, 143 N.Y.S.2d 247, 250 (App. Dept. 1955) (citations omitted), *aff'd,* 135 N.E.2d 40 (N.Y. 1956).

[10] 262 N.E.2d 404, 405 (Ind. App. 1970); Section 44.3 (Connected Relationships).

[11] M.M. & G., Inc. v. Jackson, 612 A.2d 186, 192 (D.C. App. 1992) (collecting decisions holding that "good faith" means acting without actual or constructive knowledge of the claim of the true owner); *cf. Fouser, supra,* 612 P.2d at 140-41 (finding that actual notice of the title defect and true owner's interest defeated improver's claim for "good faith" status and reserving

that the improver acted negligently is not necessarily destructive of the claim of "good faith" improver; negligence is simply a factor to be taken into account in determining whether "good faith" exists.[12]

If an improver acts in "good faith," the measure of her restitutionary recovery or offset against the true owner must be calculated. The general rule is the benefit is determined by the difference in the value of the land with and without the improvements at the time of dispossession.[13] The cost of the improvements to the improver is not the basis for restitution,[14] although if the improvements are difficult to value, the case law does not prohibit the use of "cost of producing" the benefit as a surrogate measure of benefit. The improver is, however, generally limited to her costs as a cap on the measure of the true owner's unjust enrichment.[15] The extent to which the improvements are valuable to the improver is generally rejected as a measure of the benefit.[16]

The principles stated here may be modified when the improvements are valued as part of an accounting after rescission of a contract involving the sale of real property.[17]

---

question of "constructive notice" for another day); Blanar v. Blanar, 598 S.W.2d 381, 382 (Tex. Civ. App. 1980) (holding that in order to "qualify as a good faith improver under the equitable rule of 'betterments' [improver] must show not only that he believed he was the true owner of the land but also that he had a reasonable grounds for that belief") (citations and internal quotation marks omitted).

[12] Raab v. Casper, 124 Cal. Rptr. 590, 593 (Cal. App. 1975) (construing California's "Betterment" statute). *See generally* 42 C.J.S. *Improvements* § 7.

[13] Madrid v. Spears, 250 F.2d 51, 54 (10th Cir. 1957); *see* McKay v. Horseshoe Lake Hop Harvesters, Inc., 491 P.2d 1180, 1183 (Or. 1971).

[14] *McKay, supra,* 491 P.2d at 617.

[15] *Madrid, supra,* 250 F.2d at 54–55 (noting that " 'where the improver is permitted to recover for the improvements, he is entitled to the reasonable value of his labor and materials or to the amount which his improvements have added to the market value of the land, whichever is smaller' "), *quoting* Restatement of Restitution § 42 cmt. on Subs. (1).

[16] Mickle v. Kirk, 558 N.E.2d 1119, 1123 (Ind. App. 1990). *But cf. Kerr, supra,* 977 P.2d at 449:

> The general measure of restitution for improvements is the amount of the enhanced value of the property, or the actual and reasonable cost of the improvements, whichever is less. That measure applies, however, where the equities between the parties are equal—that is, where the owner is not guilty of inequitable conduct. Although no Oregon case previously has had occasion to consider the question, we hold that when a mortgagee in good faith has improved property in reliance on the mortgagor's inequitable conduct (here, explicit or implicit representations that he will not exercise his right to redeem, with a last minute change in that position), the better measure is the greater of the reasonable costs or increased market value. To prevent the owner's unjust enrichment, the owner not only should have to make the improver whole but also should disgorge the profits of the improver's efforts.

(citations and footnotes omitted).

[17] *Compare* Renner v. Kehl, 722 P.2d 262, 266-67 (Ariz. 1986) (holding that after rescission of land sale contract due to mutual mistake recovering seller must reimburse buyer for amount buyer's improvements enhanced value of real property), *with* W.H. Woolley & Co. v. Bear Creek Manors, 735 P.2d 910, 912 (Colo. App. 1986) (holding that improver was entitled to measure of value based on "reasonable value of services" provided even though improver materially

The rights of a good faith improver to personal property are determined under the doctrine of accession and confusion, which is discussed at Section 57.2 (Identification of Property).

---

breached agreement). It should be noted that in this latter case the measure was apparently less than that which would have been available under the market value enhancement approach. Section 134 ([Rescission] Restoration of Status Quo).

Chapter 11

REMEDIES FOR INJURY TO RELATIONSHIPS

SYNOPSIS

§ 100 ECONOMIC RELATIONSHIPS

The tort of interference with economic relationships is found in several forms: (1) inducing breach of contract; (2) inducing termination of a contract without breach, *e.g.*, an at-will relationship; (3) interference with contract performance; and (4) interference with prospective economic advantage (interference with an "expectancy" that does not constitute a present contractual right). Not all jurisdictions recognize all forms of the tort. The tort most often contains a scienter requirement. The defendant must intentionally and knowingly interfere in the plaintiff's economic relationship with another. Occasionally, a jurisdiction will recognize a claim for negligent interference with economic relationships, but that is a minority view.[1]

---

[1] The dominant rule is that scienter is required. Restatement (Second) of Torts § 767 (1979). A few courts have stated that negligence could support the tort if special factors or a special relationship existed between the parties. North Carolina Mut. Life Ins. Co. v. Plymouth Mut. Life Ins. Co., 266 F. Supp. 231, 235 (E.D. Pa. 1967) (plaintiff and defendant were parties to a reinsurance agreement; plaintiff complained that defendant's action with third parties caused plaintiff to incur greater costs; court found allegations stated claim for negligent interference). The negligent interference claim has been recognized in California. J'Aire Corp. v. Gregory, 598 P.2d 60, 63 (Cal. 1979). Many jurisdictions, however, apply the economic loss rule, when only negligence is alleged, to bar the claim. Garweth Corp. v. Boston Edison Co., 613 N.E.2d 92, 93–94 (Mass. 1993); Section 11 (Economic Loss Rule).

The tort of economic interference is an accumulation and expression of several longstanding common law doctrines.[2] The tort traces its modern origins to the English decision in *Lumley v. Gye*.[3] Johanna Wagner had contracted to perform exclusively at Lumley's "Her Majesty's Theatre" for three months. Gye induced Wagner to breach her contract and perform at his establishment "The Royal Italian Opera, Covent Garden." Lumley sued Gye for damages for inducing Wagner to breach. The court, drawing broadly from common law precedents involving "master-servant" relationships,[4] held Gye's actions were tortious even though they were unaccompanied by bodily injury or property damage.

From this humble beginning, the tort of interference with economic relationships has evolved into a broad ranging, albeit amorphous, doctrine. This results because of the inherent conflict between several basic policies subsumed within the tort. First, the tort must reconcile, on the one hand, enthusiasm for open competition within markets for goods and services with, on the other hand, the protection of the expectancies generated by contractual, or other, relationships. Second, the tort must calibrate the extent to which, if at all, impure motive on the part of the defendant will be sufficient to make interference actionable. As noted by one court:

> Every man has the legal right to advance himself before his fellows, and to build up his own business enterprises, and to use all lawful means to that end, although in the path of his impetuous movements he leaves strewn the victims of his greater industry, energy, skill, prowess, or foresight. But the law will not permit him to wear the garb of honor only to destroy.[5]

In this context, it is generally required that the predominant motive be the desire to destroy.[6] An alternative approach requires that the interference is accomplished by improper means, although the means need not be

---

[2] Top Serv. Body Shop, Inc. v. Allstate Ins. Co., 582 P.2d 1365 (Or. 1978):

> Tort claims for wrongful interference with the economic relationships of another have an ancient lineage. Their history has been traced from interference with members of another's household in Roman law or with his tenants in English law, with his workmen after the 1349 Ordinance of Labourers, with prospective workmen or customers, with existing contracts for personal services, and with contracts generally to contemporary forms not dependent on the existence of a contract.

Id. at 1368 (citations omitted).

[3] 2 El. & Bl. 216, 118 Eng. Rep. 749 (Q.B. 1853).

[4] The right of the master to claim damages against one who enticed the servant away from his employment was well recognized at common law under the action "per quod servitium amisit." Gareth H. Jones, *Per Quod Servitium Amisit*, 74 L. Q. Rev. 39 (1958).

[5] Farmers Coop. Elevator, Inc., Duncombe v. State Bank, 236 N.W.2d 674, 680 (Iowa 1975) (citation omitted); Leigh Furniture and Carpet Co. v. Isom, 657 P.2d 293, 307 (Utah 1982) (stating that "[t]he alternative of improper purpose (or motive, intent, or objective) will support a cause of action for intentional interference with prospective economic relations even where the defendant's means were proper").

[6] National Parcel Servs. v. J.B. Hunt Logistics, Inc., 150 F.3d 970, 971 (8th Cir. 1998) (applying Iowa law); *Leigh Furniture and Carpet Co., supra*, 657 P.2d at 307–08.

independently tortious.[7] Justification is context sensitive, but usually means that the interference was reasonable under all the circumstances.[8] Substantial confusion is generated in this area because whether the non-tortious means used were proper or improper, justified or not justified, is often influenced by an inquiry into the motive or intent of the defendant in acting as he did.[9] Means proper in one context may be improper in another context.[10] While courts have been resolving these issues on a case by case basis for over a hundred years, a general consensus on the proper elements of the torts has not yet crystalized. This confusion as to the proper reach of the tort is reflected in the cases. Most jurisdictions permit the action for tortious interference to be based either on improper motive or improper means.

The tort of interference with economic relationships is designed in basic form to protect the interests of A, in the continued enjoyment of A's economic relationship with B, against the degradation of that relationship by C. The paradigmatic case is *Lumley v. Gye*, which involved inducing breach of contract. A has a contract with B which C induces B to breach, thereby harming A. This form of interference is recognized as actionable in all jurisdictions. A related form of the tort is intentional interference with contractual relationships. Unlike the paradigmatic case, this form of the tort does not result in a breach but results in harm in decreased expectancies or higher costs of performance. For example, A employs B under a contract terminable at will. C induces B to leave A's employment to work for C. While B has not breached his contract, C has induced B to terminate the continuing contractual relationship with A. The expectancy in a contract terminable at will is legally sufficient to warrant protection against tortious interference in most jurisdictions.[11] Similarly, A may contract with B to perform a service, for example, wash the windows of B's building. C may interfere with that contract by making A's performance more expensive, as, for example, by causing soot and dirt from C's factory to be deposited on the windows on B's building.[12]

---

[7] *Leigh Furniture and Carpet Co., supra,* 657 P.2d at 305 (stating that test is whether the defendant acted "without justification"); *Top Serv. Body Shop, Inc., supra,* 582 P.2d at 1368–69.

[8] Potthoff v. Jefferson Lines, Inc., 363 N.W.2d 771, 776 (Minn. App. 1985).

[9] Hofmann Co. v. E.I. DuPont de Nemours and Co., 248 Cal. Rptr. 384, 391 (Cal. App. 1988).

[10] Guard-Life Corp. v. S. Parker Hardware Mfg. Corp., 406 N.E.2d 445, 448 (N.Y. 1980) (holding that litigation or the threat of litigation may support a claim of tortious interference when the litigant has no belief in the merit of the litigation or having some belief in the merits of the litigation institutes, or threatens to institute the litigation in bad faith intending only to harass the third parties and not bring the claim to a definitive and final adjudication).

[11] *See* Nordling v. Northern States Power Co., 478 N.W.2d 498, 505 (Minn. 1991). *See generally* James O. Person, Annot., *Liability For Interference With at Will Business Relationship,* 5 A.L.R. 4th 9 (1981).

[12] Northern Plumbing & Heating, Inc. v. Henderson Bros., 268 N.W.2d 296 (Mich. App. 1978):

> One is liable for commission of this tort who interferes with business relations of another, both existing and prospective, by inducing a third person not to enter into

As the formality of the legal relationship recedes, the extent to which the law will protect the relationship from interference recedes.[13] This is not to say the tort is not recognized in the absence of induced breach, for it is. The concession is that the court is more likely to treat the interferer's conduct as privileged or justified when breach is not induced. Likewise, when the tort is extended to protect prospective economic relationships, we see a greater willingness to favor competition rather than the stability of relationships by requiring that the plaintiff demonstrate to a greater extent that the defendant's conduct was not privileged or justified. As noted in *A-Abart Elec. Supply, Inc. v. Emerson Elec. Co.*:

> An individual with a prospective business relationship has a mere expectancy of future economic gain; a party to a contract has a certain and enforceable expectation of receiving the benefits of the contract. When a business relationship affords the parties no enforceable expectations, but only the hope of . . . benefits, the parties must allow for the rights of others. They therefore have no cause of action against a bona fide competitor unless the circumstances indicate unfair competition, that is, an unprivileged interference with prospective advantage.[14]

These substantive elements of the tort of interference with economic relationships are reflected in the remedies available. The most significant limitation is the special damages requirement, which requires that the plaintiff identify specifically some actual injury brought about by defendant's interference.[15] The "actual injury" requirement will not pose a difficulty in the paradigmatic or related cases because a specific contractual relationship exists and the harm to that relationship can be easily identified and quantified. For example, in *Lumley v. Gye* the injury to Lumley cause by Wagner's breach of her exclusive services contract is evident. If damages

---

or continue a business relation with another or by preventing a third person from continuing a business with another.
Id. at 299 (citation omitted); *see* Ad-Vantage Tel. Dir. Consult. v. GTE Directories, 849 F.2d 1336, 1349 (11th Cir. 1987) (stating that even if the plaintiff did owe the defendant money, the trier-of-fact could find a tortious interference claim based on the manner in which the defendant chose to collect its bills when those collection efforts interfered with the plaintiff's business relationships).

[13] Della Penna v. Toyota Motor Sales, U.S.A., 902 P.2d 740, 742 (Cal. 1995) (concluding that because intentionally interfering or inducing a breach of an existing contract is a wrong prima facie, no additional element of wrongdoing or wrongfulness need be proven to show the existence of a tort; when, however, the interference is with a prospective economic relationship, the conduct is not inherently wrongful and the plaintiff must show some wrongfulness independent of the defendant's interference, *e.g.*, that interference was not justified by competitive needs or interests).

[14] 956 F.2d 1399, 1404–05 (7th Cir. 1992) (applying Illinois law) (citations and quotation marks omitted).

[15] Lynch v. City of Boston, 180 F.3d 1, 19 (1st Cir. 1989) (loss of "honorary" position resulted in no pecuniary loss); Daniels v. Dean, 833 P.2d 1078, 1084 (Mont. 1992) (stating that necessary element of prima facie claim for tortious interference is "actual damages"); *cf.* Weinberg v. Mauch, 890 P.2d 277, 287 (Haw. 1995) (rejecting awarding of nominal damages in tortious interference cases; actual damage is required).

are difficult to calculate because the performances were never given, and thus, no baseline exists from which to calculate losses, that difficulty is simply inherent in any claim Lumley would bring, even one against Wagner for breach of contract.

When there is only a prospective economic relationship, the special damages requirement can prove to be the death knell of the action. The plaintiff must be able to identify and quantify the lost prospective economic relationship. This may be difficult when those prospective economic relationships are diffuse and diverse, as, for example, in cases of retail and wholesale patronage. If the defendant wrongfully refuses to supply plaintiff with a product the plaintiff resells to others, the plaintiff's ability to identify those "others" may influence whether the plaintiff will be able to state a claim for tortious interference. In *McGill v. Parker* owners and operators of carriage horses used in New York's Central Park brought an action against "animal rights activists" for interfering in the plaintiff's prospective economic relationships with "customers." The plaintiffs alleged that defendants discouraged patronage by claiming that plaintiffs mistreated their horses. The court held that the tortious interference claim failed because plaintiffs failed to identify specific customers and patronage lost as a result of defendants' conduct.[16]

Although courts have allowed alternative methods of proving "special injury" in trade disparagement cases,[17] those methods have not been specifically approved in tortious interference cases. In this context, the courts appear to be insistent on establishing the existence of the prospective advantage with direct and specific evidence of the person with whom the plaintiff expects to enjoy the prospective advance. This is consistent with the direct correlation between the strength of the plaintiff's expectancy and the willingness of the court to protect that expectancy.

Some courts have limited the tortious interference recovery to those damages that would be awarded in a breach of contract action.[18] This limitation flows from the initial recognition of the action as one for inducing breach of contract. The modern trend has been to view remedies for tortious interference as distinct from remedies for breach of contract.[19] Courts

---

[16] 582 N.Y.S.2d 91, 95 (App. Dept. 1992); *see* Anthony Distribs., Inc. v. Miller Brewing Co., 941 F. Supp. 1567, 1572 (M.D. Fla. 1996) (finding that plaintiff's tortious interference claim was defective because it failed to identify any customers lost as a result of defendant's actions) (applying Florida law).

[17] Brunswick Corp. v. Spinit Reel Co., 832 F.2d 513, 525 (10th Cir. 1987):

> Although damages may be awarded for a violation of section 43(a), the award is distinguishable from injunctive relief, because plaintiff bears a greater burden of proof of entitlement. Likelihood of confusion is insufficient; to recover damages plaintiff must prove it has been damaged by actual consumer confusion or deception resulting from the violation. Actual consumer confusion may be shown by direct evidence, a diversion of sales or direct testimony from the public, or by circumstantial evidence such as consumer surveys.

(citations omitted).

[18] Swaney v. Crawley, 157 N.W. 910, 911 (Minn. 1916).

[19] *Guard-Life Corp.*, *supra*, 406 N.E.2d at 453 n.6.

today, in general, recognize the availability of non-economic damages, such as distress damages or injury to reputation, for tortious inference claims.[20]

The fact that non-economic damages may be recoverable does not mean that they will be recovered. The allowance of a non-economic recovery was not the product of consensus.[21] While many courts authorize such recoveries in the abstract,[22] in the particular case the courts require a close nexus between the non-economic loss and the nature and type of relationship interfered with by the defendant. As noted in *Mooney v. Johnson Cattle Co., Inc.*:

> There are many kinds of contractual relations, however, just as there are many different settings for trespass or conversion. The claimed injury must be typical of the kind of contractual relationship involved in the case in order to come within the interests that the tort duty of noninterference is designed to protect, whatever other theory of recovery may also be available to the injured party. As already stated, these typical interests can differ when the disrupted relationship is employment, or a consumer purchase of a particular home or unique chattel, or a commercial transaction between entrepreneurs, or perhaps a wholly nonfinancial agreement. For instance, when the tort is applied in order to secure contractual arrangements and opportunities in the general economy, mental or emotional distress will not be a characteristic result of interference between corporate enterprises. The same may or may not be true of business dealings characteristically carried on by individuals.[23]

The basic remedy for tortious interference with economic relationships is the loss or diminution of the economic expectancy, usually the lost profits the plaintiff expected to enjoy as a result of his economic relationship with the third party. When tort remedies are permitted, as is the usual case, the plaintiff (A) in an inducing breach case may have a broader remedy against the interferor (C) than against the breaching party (B). A's recovery of her lost profits will be liberally allowed, as is the usual case when the action sounds in tort.[24] A may also recover consequential damages flowing from C's tortious conduct.[25]

---

[20] Mooney v. Johnson Cattle Co., Inc., 634 P.2d 1333, 1338 (Or. 1981), *citing* Restatement (Second) of Torts § 774A (1979).

[21] *Mooney, supra*, 634 P.2d at 1336 n.6 (discussing history leading to the adoption of Section 774A and noting the sparse decisional law on the issue at that time).

[22] Rite Aid Corp. v. Lake Shore Investors, 471 A.2d 735, 741 n.9 (Md. 1984) (collecting decisions approving recovery of non-economic damages as provided by Restatement (Second) of Torts § 774(A).

[23] 634 P.2d at 1338 (citations omitted).

[24] Hein Enters., Ltd. v. San Francisco Real Estate Investors, 720 P.2d 975, 981 (Colo. App. 1985). *But cf.* Sandare Chem. Co., Inc. v. Wako Int'l, Inc., 820 S.W.2d 21, 24 (Tex. Civ. App. 1991) (declining to permit plaintiff to use defendant's profits, which defendant realized after interfering in plaintiff's contractual expectancy, as a surrogate measure of plaintiff's loss).

[25] Kallok v. Medtronic, Inc., 573 N.W.2d 356 363–64 (Minn. 1998) (permitting recovery, as

The economic relationship will receive protection in equity against interference by the defendant.[26] Occasionally, references to the equitable doctrines that "equity will not enjoin a crime" and equity protects property rights, not personal rights" may be found in some of the cases. Neither doctrine should be applied to economic interference claims to restrict the availability of injunctive relief.[27] In the seminal *Lumley* matter, *Lumley* was able to obtain an injunction enjoining Wagner from performing for Gye at the Royal Italian Opera House.[28] The use of equitable remedies in this field is well grounded in practice and the history of the action.

In many cases, tortious interference is addressable, and enjoinable, as an unfair business practice. Moreover, when the interference is by a competitor who is required to be licensed, the general rule in the United States is to confer a broad power on holders of licenses to enjoin unauthorized competition without a required showing of direct injury.[29] In this regard, the equitable remedy of an injunction is broader than the legal remedy of damages to the extent that the identification of specific lost economic advantage (*e.g.*, lost sales, customers, or patronage) is not required.

Tortious interference with economic advantage will support an action for unjust enrichment and the disgorgement of the benefit the interferor obtained. In *Federal Sugar Refining Co. v. United States Sugar Equalization Board* the defendant Board induced the Kingdom of Norway to breach a contract to purchase sugar from the plaintiff and purchase sugar from the defendant Board instead. The profit the defendant Board made on the transaction was greater than the profit the plaintiff would have made had the Kingdom of Norway performed. The court permitted plaintiff to receive the defendant Board's profit as a restitutionary remedy.[30]

---

damages, of attorney's fees incurred by the plaintiff as a consequence of the defendant's tortious interference with a non-competition contract the plaintiff had with a third party); *Hein Enters., Ltd., supra*, 720 P.2d at 982 (permitting as consequential damages, loss of use of the purchase price caused by the defendant's interference in the performance of the contract for the sale of real estate).

[26] New England Patriots Football Club, Inc. v. University of Colo., 592 F.2d 1196, 1200 (1st Cir. 1979) (enjoining the defendant university from interfering with an employment contract between the plaintiff professional football team and its head coach, Charles Fairbanks). The university wished to hire Mr. Fairbanks as its head coach and had induced him to breach his contract with the plaintiff.

[27] In *Clark v. Crown Drug Co.*, 152 S.W.2d 145 (Mo. 1941) (involving unlawful competition in the sale of liquor), the court expressed some reluctance to enjoin the unlawful sale of liquor and invoked the equitable maxim to that effect. *Id.* at 146–47. The court, however, resolved the case on other grounds. In *Glover v. Malloska*, 213 N.W. 107, 108 (Mich. 1927), the court found that loss of customers, resulting from the defendant's tortious interference, would constitute a "property right" protectible in equity. Sections 25 ([Equitable Remedies] Nature of Rights Protected), 27 ([Equitable Remedies] Injunction of Criminal Activity).

[28] Lumley v. Wagner, 1 Deb. M. & G. 604, 42 Eng. Rep. 687 (Ch. 1852).

[29] *See generally* H.C. Lind, Annot., *Right to Enjoin Business Competitor From Unlicenced or Otherwise Illegal Acts or Practices*, 90 A.L.R.2d 7 (1963).

[30] 268 Fed. 575 (S.D.N.Y. 1920).

The ability to seek damages and restitution raises the issue of whether the plaintiff may recover both. The decisional law suggests that both damages and restitution should not be awarded.[31] There is some decisional law supporting awards of both the plaintiff's lost profits and the defendant's actual profits in the trademark area, but these have not been extended to tortious interference claims.

Tortious interference with economic advantage may support a claim for punitive damages.[32] The mere showing of intentional and knowing interference does not, however, satisfy the malice threshold for punitive damages.[33]

§ 101 SOCIAL AND PROFESSIONAL RELATIONSHIPS

For many individuals, membership in social groups, such as the Rotary, Masons, Elks Club, etc., are important facets of the life and lifestyle the person adopts for himself or herself. As social beings, our sense of self worth, and the perception of others of our worth, is measured, in some part, by those with whom we associate.[1] This desire is not only reflected in the

---

[31] Ramona Manor Convalescent Hosp. v. Care Enterps., 225 Cal. Rptr. 120, 130 (Cal. App. 1986) (stating that restitution should not be awarded when the plaintiff is made whole by a damages award).

[32] McLaurin v. Fischer, 768 F.2d 98, 105 (6th Cir. 1985) (applying Ohio law). See generally Sara Johnson, Annot., Punitive Damages For Interference With Contract or Business Relationship, 44 A.L.R.4th 1078 (1987).

[33] Sufrin v. Hosier, 128 F.3d 594 (7th Cir. 1997):

> A more difficult question is whether Illinois law allows the award of punitive damages in a case such as this. The mere fact that interference with contract is an intentional tort does not make an award of punitive damages permissible in Illinois; the defendant's misconduct must be worse than the minimum required to be guilty of the tort for an award of punitive damages to be proper . . . . But a rational jury could have found that Hosier's conduct was worse than the minimum required because it had a flavor of extortion, and extortion is not an element of the tort of intentional interference with contract.

Id. at 598 (citations omitted). Section 202 (Scope of Punitive Damages) (particularly Section 202.1 (Socially Deplorable Conduct)).

[1] Americans have had a longstanding commitment to social organizations. ALEXIS DE TOCQUE-VILLE, DEMOCRACY IN AMERICA, 513–17 (1966) (translated by George Lawrence; edited by J.P. Mayer). As noted by De Tocqueville:

> In the United States, political associations are only one small part of the immense number of different types of associations found there. Americans of all ages, all stations in life, and all types of disposition are forever forming associations. There are not only commercial and industrial associations in which all take part, but others of a thousand different types—religious, moral, serious, futile, very general and very limited, immensely large and very minute. Americans combine to give fetes, found seminaries, build churches, distribute books, and send missionaries to the antipodes. Hospitals, prisons, and schools take shape in that way. Finally, if they want to proclaim a truth or propagate some feelings by the encouragement of a great example, they form an association. In every case, at the head of any new undertaking, where in France you would find the government or in England some territorial magnate, in the United States you are sure to find an association.

Id. at 513.

individual's desire to associate, but also in the group's desire to control who may be included within the membership of the group, and who may not.[2] The ability to define a group is highly influenced by the power to exclude. The conflict in these cases is often between the group, which seeks to exercise its power to define who may be members of the group, and the individual who seeks to express his or her own sense of identity and self worth by inclusion within the group.

At common law, the rights of the group were generally preferred over those of the individual.[3] There is no generally recognized common law prohibition on discrimination insofar as groups are concerned.[4] The group could exclude individuals from membership for all manner of reasons, including race, sex, political affiliation, reputation, etc. Moreover, in making membership decisions, the group was not bound by any procedural due process requirements that attend to notions of a fair hearing or fair procedure. Arbitrary and capricious procedures were not actionable because, at common law, it was not perceived that such procedures adversely affected any "rights" held by the individual. However, the "group" could be required to adhere to its contractual obligations with its existing members. Thus, a legal distinction was recognized. The power to reject or exclude prospective members was absolute because prospective members had no "rights" to be admitted or any claim that their application be fairly considered. On the other hand, the power to eject or remove existing members was qualified to the extent the terms of membership specified how ejections or removals were to be conducted.[5] The contractual rights vested in existing members could not be unilaterally abridged by the group. Of course, the "rights" might be largely illusory to the extent the group retained in the organic contract or by-laws substantial, unfettered discretion over membership or delegated that discretion to a control group, such as the executive board or a presiding officer.

The recent trend has been to restrict the ability of groups to exclude individuals as prospective members or remove individuals who are existing members. This trend has been the product of several related, although independent, developments. First, at both the federal and state level, an

---

[2] Who actually exercises power within the group is outside the scope of this work.

[3] *Developments in the Law—Judicial Control of Actions of Private Associations*, 76 Harv. L. Rev. 986, 986–90 (1963).

[4] There was an exception for those involved in "public callings." *See* 3 WILLIAM BLACKSTONE, COMMENTARIES ON THE LAWS OF ENGLAND *164 (noting that a cause of action will lie against an innkeep or victualer who refuses to admit a traveler without cause).

[5] The nature of the rights as contractual or otherwise could vary. *Compare* Aspell v. American Contract Bridge League Memphis, Tenn., 595 P.2d 191, 193–94 (Ariz. App. 1979) (holding that "[t]he relationship between members of a voluntary association is contractual") and Garvey v. Seattle Tennis Club, 808 P.2d 1155, 1157 (Wash. App. 1991) (same), *with* Chisholm v. Hyattstown Volunteer Fire Dep't, 691 A.2d 776 (Md. Ct. Sp. App. 1997) (stating that "bylaws" of not-for-profit membership corporation did not form or constitute a contract between the members and the corporation; consequently, a member's proper remedy was not breach of contract but mandamus to require that the corporation follow its bylaws regarding the expulsion of a member).

immense body of statutory and regulatory law now controls the extent to which groups may control their internal membership by using criteria based on race, ethnicity, sex, or sexual orientation. In order to accommodate the competing First Amendment right of association, the application of these anti-discrimination statutes and regulations is based on the distinction between "public" and "private" groups. The anti-discrimination statutes and regulations apply to "public" groups but not "private" groups. The distinction between the "public" and the "private" is not, however, always agreed upon by courts.[6] Even among "public" groups, regulation by the state may be constrained when the group is organized for the achievement of "political" objectives,[7] or when the group's decision to exclude constitutes "expressive conduct" that is shielded from governmental control.[8]

The second means by which group self-control over membership has been restricted has been through the judicial development of enhanced review and scrutiny over membership decisions by groups that directly affect the economic interests of each member's professional occupation. Courts have imposed the requirement that good cause and fair procedures be employed when private groups have a larger agenda than simply facilitating purely social and fraternal associations. As noted by one court:

> While the courts should be loathe to intervene in purely private organizational matters, nonintervention is not justified where a quasi-public organization takes action and imposes penalties which carry the odor of public sanctions. It is clear that not all private associations are required to observe due process standards. However, such standards must be observed when a private association becomes quasi-public, assumes a public purpose of its own, incorporates and seeks the tax shelters and other protections of public law,

---

[6] *Compare* Warfield v. Penisula Golf & County Club, 896 P.2d 776 (Cal. 1995) (holding that a country club that permits the conduct of regular business between members and non-members is subject to California's state civil rights statutes as a place of public accommodation and may not exclude women from membership), *with* Curran v. Mount Diablo Council of the Boy Scouts of Am., 952 P.2d 218, 235 (Cal. 1998) (holding that the Boy Scouts are not an organization subject to California's state civil rights statutes because they are not a "business establishment"). The decisional law in this area is extremely complex since the public-private distinction is not always expressed in the statutory scheme. *See* Andrew M. Perlman, *Public Accommodation and the Dual Nature of the Freedom to Associate*, 8 Geo. Mason U. Civ. Rts. L.J. 111 (1997) (discussing constitutional limitations on the use of the "public accommodations" concept to override private decisions regarding membership in a group). *See generally* 15 Am. Jur. 2d *Civil Rights* §§ 35–36 (discussing public accommodations concept and ability of groups to control and direct their membership policies by themselves).

[7] Federal Election Comm'n v. Massachusetts Citizens for Life, 479 U.S. 238 (1986) (striking down campaign financing limitations on corporation organized and devoted to political activities); *see* Roberts v. United States Jaycees, 468 U.S. 609, 622 (1984) (noting that the Court has long protected the right of individuals to associate "in pursuit of . . . political, social, economic, educational, religious, and cultural ends"). The measure of protection afforded is outside the scope of these materials. *See* LAWRENCE TRIBE, AMERICAN CONSTITUTIONAL LAW § 15–17 (2d ed. 1988) (discussing issue).

[8] Boy Scouts of America v. Dale, 530 U.S. 640, 653–54 (2000).

or otherwise assumes a larger purpose or stature than pleasant, friendly and congenial social relationships.

[A] private organization, . . . if tinged with public stature or purpose, may not expel or discipline a member adversely affecting substantial property, contract or other economic rights, except as a result of fair proceedings which may be provided for in organization by-laws, carried forward in an atmosphere of good faith and fair play.[9]

Some courts express a reluctance to use the "due process" terminology believing that it should be reserved for government actors.[10] In some cases, this has induced courts to reject judicial review of private decision making based on "due process" concerns. In this context, all that is required is that the association follow its own stated procedures, such as they may be.[11]

Membership in a professional association is generally assumed to reflect some measure of competence, which may be relied on both by the general public and third parties who contract with professionals. This perception may cause some individuals to limit their relationships to professionals who are members of a specified group.[12] As a consequence, the association's control over its membership may be subjected to public control so that the interests of the public, and the professional to practice her profession, are protected.

The great majority of cases limit judicial intrusion into group membership decisions to professional groups and associations. The concept of "professional group and association" may, however, be broadly defined. For example, in *Ascherman v. Saint Francis Memorial Hospital* the court allowed an inquiry into the decision of a private hospital whether to allow a private physician to have staff privileges at the hospital. Because the private hospital provided a public function, it was held to have an obligation to private physicians to consider their applications for staff privileges fairly and objectively.[13] There is, however, contrary authority that limits the common law power of courts to intrude into membership decisions to cases raising legitimate claims of economic necessity,[14] although some courts will

---

[9] McCune v. Wilson, 237 So. 2d 169, 173 (Fla. 1970) (involving a chapter of the America Institute of Real Estate Appraisers).

[10] *See* Hartung v. Audubon Country Club, Inc., 785 S.W.2d 501, 503 n.1 (Ky. App. 1990).

[11] Indiana High Sch. Athletic Ass'n Inc. v. Reyes, 694 N.E.2d 249, 256 (Ind. 1997) (recognizing only limited exceptions to the Indiana rule that the association's bylaws and articles constitute the contract between the member and the group and are the exclusive means of defining that relationship).

[12] Pinsker v. Pacific Coast Soc'y of Orthodontists, 460 P.2d 495, 498 (Cal. 1969) (stating that while membership in defendant group was not essential to practice of orthodontics, membership would be economically advantageous because a member would receive more referrals from dentists, could charge higher fees, and take courses in professional education).

[13] 119 Cal. Rptr. 507, 509 (Cal. App. 1975) (stating that protection against arbitrary action extends to cases where decisions by a private hospital "impair the physicians right to fully practice his profession").

[14] Austin v. American Ass'n of Neurological Surgeons, 253 F.3d 967, 971–72 (7th Cir. 2001)

apply a more favorable standard for the individual who is expelled rather than simply excluded.[15]

Some courts have permitted judicial review of membership decisions by private groups even though the individual was unable to show that membership was of significant economic value. For example, in *Rutledge v. Gulian* the plaintiff complained that he had been wrongfully suspended from the Masons, a fraternal organization, for "un-Mason conduct." The court noted that:

> The rights accorded to members of an association traditionally have been assessed in terms of the property interests in the assets of the organization or in terms of contract rights. The modern trend, however, sees the member's valuable personal relationship to the organization as the true basis for judicial relief against wrongful expulsion.[16]

On the other hand, when merely "social" relationships are involved at least one court has suggested that this involves "one of the more remote objects of judicial scrutiny."[17]

When the associational interests affect economic or property rights, the distinction between admission cases, with their greater deference to the group, and expulsion cases, with their greater willingness to protect the individual, is given less weight.[18]

When an individual is found to have rights to participate as an ongoing member of the group, but her right of membership has been violated by group action, the traditional remedy is injunctive relief. The most common complaint in this area is that the group has either (1) failed to follow its own procedures or (2) the group's procedures are flawed, do not provide a fundamentally fair process for resolving the individual's membership claim,

---

(applying Illinois law) (rejecting claim that membership in professional association was economically important when plaintiff (1) continued to practice in area of specialty notwithstanding his expulsion and membership was not a precondition to the practice of the specialty; (2) plaintiff sought damages, not reinstatement; and, (3) plaintiff showed only a small economic impact resulting from the expulsion), *cert. denied*, 534 U.S. 1078 (2002); Salter v. New York State Psychological Assoc., 198 N.E.2d 250, 253 (N.Y. 1964) (requiring showing that admission into group is an "economic necessity" before permitting judicial scrutiny into "fairness" of the process). *See generally* Kathleen Dorr, Annot., *Exclusion of, or Discrimination Against, Physician or Surgeon by Hospital*, 28 A.L.R.5th 107 (1995).

[15] Treister v. American Academy of Orthopaedic Surgeons, 396 N.E.2d 1225, 1231, 1232 (Ill. App. 1979) (involving application for admission but indicating that a higher standard would be imposed in expulsion cases).

[16] 459 A.2d 680, 683 (N.J. 1983) (citation omitted); *see* Bay v. Anderson Hills, Inc., 483 N.E.2d 491, 493 (Ohio App. 1984) (*per curiam*) (holding that "member who an association seeks to expel is entitled to due process and natural justice which requires reasonable notice and hearing with the opportunity to defend the charges"). The fact that the expulsion was done pursuant to the literal terms of the associations' bylaws was insufficient when those bylaws failed to provide such process and procedure as due process and substantial justice require. *Id.* at 493.

[17] *Aspell, supra*, 595 P.2d at 195.

[18] *Ascherman, supra*, 119 Cal. Rptr. at 509. *But see Treister, supra*, 396 N.E.2d at 1332.

and should not be followed. In either case, injunctive relief can provide the individual with a full measure of relief: (1) the group can be ordered to comply with its internal rules, or (2) the group can be barred from applying a deficient set of rules.

Although there are relatively few cases that have actually awarded damages for wrongful interference with associational relationships, there appears to be a general acceptance of the principle that damages are available.[19] Moreover, the action is often deemed to sound in tort,[20] perhaps reflecting the idea that the group owes fiduciary-like duties to the individual.[21] These decisions all involve expulsions rather than refused admissions. To the extent the decisions appear to support a tort-based theory of recovery, damages should include non-economic recoveries, e.g., emotional distress, and may include punitive damages. If the action is deemed to sound in contract, a claim for recovery of non-economic damages may be available when the association is purely social, based on the theory that the object of the contract is to enhance non-economic interests. Those interests should be the measure of the loss in cases of breach.[22] This argument would not apply to professional associations, as the primary motive for the relationship is financial, not personal. Notwithstanding the above, the typical case in this area involves a claim seeking equitable relief ordering the plaintiff to be admitted to or reinstated in the association.[23]

In most cases when damages have been claimed, and in some cases in which injunctive relief has been sought, courts have imposed a requirement that the member exhaust all of the group's internal review and appeal procedures before seeking judicial relief.[24] Likewise, a member cannot rely

---

[19] *Austin, supra,* 253 F.3d at 971–72 (by implication); *Bay, supra,* 483 N.E.2d at 493.

[20] *Aspell, supra,* 595 P.2d at 195 (finding no cases that refuse to allow a tort action for wrongful expulsion from a social club, but finding only one case in which such an action was brought).

[21] *But see Austin, supra,* 253 F.3d at 968–69 (emphasizing contractual underpinnings of the relationships).

[22] *Cf.* Windeler v. Scheers Jewelers, 88 Cal. Rptr. 39, 44 (Cal App. 1970) (allowing distress damages for breach of bailment contract for jewelry of great sentimental value); Wynn v. Monterey Club, 168 Cal. Rptr. 878, 883–84 (Cal. App. 1980) (permitting distress damages for breach of a contract between a husband and two gambling establishments to exclude his wife from the establishments and not cash her checks); Section 142 (Distress Damages).

[23] *See Judicial Control of Actions of Private Associations, supra,* 76 Harv. L. Rev. at 1094 (noting that "[t]he difficult task of calculating the full value of the membership interest rarely arises, since a finding of wrongful expulsion normally results in a reinstatement order") (footnote omitted).

[24] Calabrese v. Policeman's Benevolent Ass'n, Local No. 76, 384 A.2d 579, 582–83 (N.J. Super. L. 1978) (holding that a court will entertain a challenge to a membership decision by a voluntary, private organization only after internal remedies have been exhausted); Westlake Community Hosp. v. Superior Court, 551 P.2d 410 (Cal. 1976) (same, but noting that the requirement may be excused when the group does not inform the member of the review and appeal procedures). *But cf.* Holder v. California Paralyzed Veterans Ass'n, 170 Cal. Rptr. 455, 460–61 (Cal. App. 1980) (construing *Westlake Community Hospital, supra,* as requiring member to bring successful mandamus action to require group to conform to its internal procedures before member may recover damages against the group for the wrongful failure to follow individual's membership decision). *See generally* 6 Am. Jur. 2d *Associations and Clubs* § 29.

on a claim that the group is biased against him as an excuse for not contesting the challenge to or rejection of his membership. If the member does not present a defense, the member may be deemed to have legally waived any claim that the process afforded him could not be fair.[25]

§ 102 PERSONAL RELATIONSHIPS

The common law provided rather extensive protection to personal relationships through a variety of actions that characterized the third party intruder as a wrongdoer, with accompanying remedies.[1] The actions were designed to protect personal, intimate relationships from third party interference. In the United States these actions have come to be known by their somewhat colorful names. Alienation of affections actions protected the spousal and parental claims of affection from destruction or diminishment by a third party. Criminal conversation protected the spouse's interest in the sexual fidelity of the other spouse.[2] The action for seduction protected the interest in the virginity of unmarried, female children. Originally, the action protected the father's interest in his daughter's virginity and freedom from pregnancy; however, beginning in the mid 1850s the action was modified, usually by statute, to allow the female to sue in her own right for her own injuries.[3] The action for breach of promise to marry protected the marriage partner's interest (usually the bride's) in the completion of what was seen as a critical and fundamental relationship for women, The breach of the promise to marry was perceived to inflict special injury upon women different in kind from that associated with breach of contract.

These actions developed out of a cultural and social milieu that is neither representative of, nor perhaps recognizable in, many parts of the United States today. Changes in cultural and social mores, coupled with the view that these personal torts were as often misused to extort settlements as to address legitimate grievances, led many states in the nineteenth and twentieth centuries to abolish, or at least modify, some or all of the personal torts. These statutes have come to be known as "Heart Balm" statutes, which are designed to preclude actions that pertain to a broken or sorrowful

---

[25] Garvey v. Seattle Tennis Club, 808 P.2d 1155, 1158 (Wash. App. 1991).

[1] Widley v. Springs, 840 F. Supp. 1259, 1261 (N.D. Ill. 1994) (stating that "[a]lthough a breach of promise [to marry] suit is an action on a contract, the damages that may be awarded more closely resemble tort damages") (citation omitted; brackets added), *modified on other grounds by* 47 F.3d 1475 (7th Cir. 1995).

[2] Criminal conversation was a strict liability tort. Liability attached even if the spouse was the aggressor and the tortfeasor was unaware of the spouse's martial status. Bearbower v. Merry, 266 N.W.2d 128, 131, 134 (Iowa 1978) (discussing knowledge issue); Norton v. MacFarlane, 818 P.2d 8, 16 (Utah 1991) (discussing aggressor issue). The *Norton* court stated that the primary reason for this tort lay in the "importance that feudal society placed on insuring that the right of inheritance . . . descended to legitimate children only." *Id.*

[3] *See* Jane Larson, *Women Understand So Little, They Call My Good Nature Deceit: A Feminist Rethinking of Seduction*, 93 Colum. L. Rev. 374, 382–83 (1993) (recounting the history of the action for seduction and noting its evolvement out of the father's ownership of the economic productivity of his minor children).

heart. The reason for the adoption of "Heart Balm" statutes is the belief that the law and the courts may not be an effective or desirable forum in which to attempt to redress these intimate, personal losses.[4]

When these actions are recognized, they are treated like torts and support tort-based remedies. Substantial awards are not uncommon when these personal torts are recognized,[5] with several recent verdicts in excess of $1 million.[6] Damages recoverable for personal torts overlap to some degree, but also vary; consequently, care must be taken to assess the law of the jurisdiction as to which personal torts, if any, are viable actions. It is also unclear to what extent the Supreme Court's decision in *Lawrence v. Texas*,[7] which recognizes a protected liberty interest in sexual intimacy between consenting adults, will compromise state efforts to deter sexually intimate conduct by civil awards rather than criminal sanction.

[102.1] Alienation of Affections

The action for alienation of affections allows the recovery of loss of marital consortium. The tort does not require that the tortfeasor destroy the marital relationship. As noted in *Norton v. MacFarlane*: "[a]ll that is necessary is that there be injury to consortium interests or diminution of affection."[8] Loss of consortium damages are thus the major component of the compensatory award.[9] Although there are few modern cases, the plaintiff should be allowed to recover distress damages.[10] However, care must be taken to ensure that distress damages are not duplicative of the loss of consortium

---

[4] Section 103 (Heart Balm Statutes).

[5] Veeder v. Kennedy, 589 N.W.2d 610 (S.D. 1999) (affirming award of $265,000 for alienation of affections); Vacek v. Ames, 377 N.W.2d 86, 89 (Neb. 1985) (affirming award of $100,000 for alienation of affections as not excessive). *See generally* Annot., *Excessiveness or Inadequacy of Damages For Alienation of Affections, Criminal Conversation, or Seduction*, 36 A.L.R.2d 548 (1954) (containing an extensive collection of awards).

[6] Oddo v. Presser, 592 S.E.2d 195 (N.C. 2004) (involving jury award of compensatory and punitive damages of $1.4 million for criminal conversation and alienation of affections by defendant of plaintiff's wife; although the court affirmed the granting of a new trial as to compensatory damages, the decision affected only a small part of the damages claimed); Hutelmyer v. Cox, 514 S.E.2d 554 (N.C. App. 1999) (affirming award of $1 million in favor of plaintiff wife against defendant who had an affair with the plaintiff's husband). There are several newspaper accounts of major awards in North Carolina for personal torts, but no reported appellate decisions of the awards. *E.g.*, Greensboro News & Record, November 10, 2001 (reporting $2 million verdict against defendant who had affair with plaintiff's husband).

[7] 539 U.S. 558 (2003) (holding that Texas statute that criminalized sodomy between consenting adults violated "liberty" interest protected by Fourteenth Amendment).

[8] 818 P.2d at 17 n.13.

[9] Section 74 (Loss of Consortium). If the relationship was weak before the intervention of the defendant, this will tend to depreciate the value of the claim. Jones v. Swanson, 341 F.3d 723 (8th Cir. 2003) (applying South Dakota law) (noting that "the evidence of Donna's pre-affair conduct and her dissatisfaciton with the marriage undermines Richard's claim for damages").

[10] *Hutelmyer, supra*, 514 S.E.2d at 561 (stating that in the area of personal relational torts "distress" damages are recoverable).

claim.[11] Punitive damages are available when the defendant's actions are motivated by actual malice.[12]

[102.2] Criminal Conversation

The tort of criminal conversation (or adultery) arises when one has sexual relations with the spouse of another. As with many family-based torts, criminal conversation arose out of the view that marital rights and relationships were property rights of the male; therefore, when a third party violated the male's right to exclusive sexual intercourse with his wife, a tortious invasion of property rights occurred.[13] Modernly, the tort has been broadened by dropping its male partiality and permitting either spouse to sue a third party who commits adultery with the plaintiff's spouse. The tort retains, however, its common law basis as a strict liability tort. As noted by one court:

> In truth, the tort is essentially a tort of strict liability. The tort is not designed to indemnify the aggrieved spouse for any loss to the marriage relationship. Indeed, a damage award may well be a complete windfall to the plaintiff. Moreover, there are no defenses, even if the offending spouse was the aggressor and wholly responsible for enticing the defendant into the act.[14]

More significantly, however, has been the abrogation of the tort in most jurisdictions. The primary reasons for this general abolishing of the tort of criminal conversation have been (1) the changed cultural view toward marital infidelity and (2) the perception that the tort of alienation of affections adequately protects the marital relationship from third party intrusions.

In jurisdictions where the tort of criminal conversation is still recognized, it may be redressed by damages. Because criminal conversation does not require actual loss of affection between the spouses, a recovery of damages may proceed from the commission of adultery itself. For example, in *Shaw v. Stringer* the court affirmed an award of punitive damages for criminal conversation even though a defense verdict of $0 was returned on the joined alienation of affections claim.[15]

---

[11] Strode v. Gleason, 510 P.2d 250, 253 (Wash. App. 1973) (recognizing recovery of distress damages against defendant who alienates affections of plaintiff's minor child against plaintiff).

[12] *Oddo, supra,* 592 S.E.2d 195 (affirming punitive damages awards of $500,000 for alienation of affection); Nelson v. Jacobsen, 669 P.2d 1207, 1219 (Utah 1983) (stating that "to recover punitive damages for the tort of alienation of affections the plaintiff must show 'circumstances of aggravation in addition to the malice implied by law from the conduct of defendant in causing the separation of [the spouses] which was necessary to sustain a recovery of compensatory damages'") (citations omitted); Section 202 (Scope of Punitive Damages).

[13] Neal v. Neal, 873 P.2d 871, 874 (Idaho 1994) (discussing history of the tort of criminal conversation).

[14] *Norton, supra,* 818 P.2d at 16.

[15] 400 S.E.2d 101, 103–04 (N.C. App. 1991). The jury awarded $125,000 in compensatory damages and $50,000 in punitive damaged on the criminal conversation claim.

The essential compensatory elements of the tort are nonpecuniary: (1) loss of consortium and (2) emotional distress.[16] When the adulterous relationship adversely affects the marital relationship, the aggrieved spouse may recover for loss of consortium in general. However, even if the marital relationship is not harmed, the aggrieved spouse may recover, at least in theory, for loss of sexual relations with the spouse and for emotional distress:

> The measure of damages in an action for criminal conversation is fair compensation to the plaintiff for the wrongful adultery with the spouse, "including such elements as pain, suffering, injury to his health, degradation and humiliation, to which, if properly pleaded, damages may be added as compensation for the loss or impairment of his right of consortium resulting from that adultery."[17]

As also noted in another decision:

> Damages . . . in an action for criminal conversation are compensatory, covering injury to the plaintiff's social position, disgrace in the community where he or she lives or was in business and dishonor to plaintiff and plaintiff's family. And, a single act of adultery is sufficient to entitle the husband of the woman to damages in an action against the adulterer for criminal conversation even though the husband sustains no further loss. Computations for the type of injury alleged here is always inexact and as Blackstone warned 'usually very large and exemplary.' This is so not only by virtue of the abstract nature of the injuries alleged but is further exacerbated by the emotion laden nature of the proceedings.[18]

In an appropriate case, the tort of criminal conversation will support an award of punitive damages,[19] for example, when the tortfeasor's conduct evidences the requisite actual malice in fact.[20]

Historically, the tort of criminal conversation would support equitable relief in the form of an injunction against the tortfeasor continuing to have a relationship with the adulterous spouse.[21] Nonetheless, there is a general

---

[16] Restatement (Second) of Torts § 685, cmts. d, g (1977); Rivers v. Rivers, 354 S.E.2d 784, 789 (S.C. 1987).

[17] Tarquinio v. Pelletier, 266 A.2d 410, 411 (Conn. Supp. 1970) (citation omitted); *Hutelmyer, supra*, 514 S.E.2d at 561 (same).

[18] Fadgen v. Lenkner, 365 A.2d 147, 150–51 (Pa. 1976) (citations omitted); Botwinick v. Annenberg, 198 N.Y.S. 151, 153 (App. Dept. 1923) (stating that "[t]he degradation which ensues, the distress and mental anguish which necessarily follow, are the real causes of recovery").

[19] *Fadgen, supra*, 365 A.2d at 150; McLean v. Mechanic, 447 S.E.2d 459, 462 (N.C. App. 1994).

[20] *Shaw, supra*, 400 S.E.2d at 103 (affirming award of punitive damages based on evidence that defendant persisted in visiting wife at the marital household and laughed when told by the wife that her husband (plaintiff) had learned of their affair); Section 202 (Scope of Punitive Damages).

[21] Witte v. Bauderer, 255 S.W. 1016 (Tex. Civ. App. 1923) (enjoining defendant from having anything further to do with plaintiff's wife). *See generally* 27A Am. Jur. 2d *Equity* § 62.

disinclination to invoke the court's equitable powers to enjoin willing parties from continuing a relationship. Courts may invoke ancient platitudes to achieve this result, as, for example, stating that equity will only protect property interests, not personal relationships.[22] The more salient justification was offered by the court in *Snedaker v. King*:

> The decree in this case is an extreme instance of government by injunction. It attempts to govern, control, and direct personal relations and domestic affairs. Among other restrictions placed upon the defendant by this decree is that of remaining away from any place where plaintiff's husband may be, and from interfering with plaintiff's efforts to communicate with her husband, and with her efforts to regain his love, esteem, support, and conjugal relation. It would be only a little more extreme if the husband had been made a party defendant, and a mandatory injunction decreed requiring him to discharge all the duties of companionship, affection, love, and all other obligations, legal and moral, assumed by him when he entered the conjugal relation.
>
> Such extension of the jurisdiction of equity to regulate and control domestic relations, in addition to the legal and statutory remedies already provided, in our opinion is not supported by authority, warranted by sound reason, or in the interest of good morals or public policy. The opening of such a wide field for injunctive process, enforceable only by contempt proceedings, the difficulty if not impossibility of such enforcement, and the very doubtful beneficial results to be obtained thereby, warrant the denial of such a decree in this case, and require a modification of the judgment in that respect.[23]

There is some relatively modern decisional law allowing injunctive relief in cases involving criminal conversation.[24] It is, however, difficult to envision such relief without the cooperation and assistance of the adulterous spouse. Such a requirement, in effect, transforms the lawsuit into one seeking protection against continued harassment of the adulterous spouse by the third party. It also raises serious questions whether the liberty interests of the parties subject to the injunction are being unconstitutionally infringed under *Lawrence v. Texas*.[25]

---

[22] Lyon v. Izen, 268 N.E.2d 436, 437 (Ill. App. 1971) (stating that spouse's interest in other spouse's love and affection is not a property right protectible in equity); Section 25 ([Equitable Remedies] Nature of Rights Protected).

[23] 145 N.E. 15, 16–17 (Ohio 1924). The contrary view is perhaps best evidenced by the dissenting judge in *Snedaker* who referred to the intruding third person as a "'*vampire*' who persists in her efforts to win the husband and father from the performance of his duties to his home and family." *Id.* at 17 (emphasis in original).

[24] Henley v. Rockett, 8 So. 2d 852, 855 (Ala. 1942) (affirming as not an abuse of discretion an injunction against the defendant's continued association with the plaintiff's spouse notwithstanding legislative abolition of the torts of criminal conversation and alienation of affections).

[25] Text and note 7, *supra*.

[102.3]   Seduction

The tort of seduction (fornication) involves having sexual relations with an unmarried female.[26] Technically, the tort consists of the act of inducing an unmarried woman to consent to unlawful sexual intercourse by enticement that overcomes her scruples.[27]

At common law, a seduced female could not recover damages in her own right; rather, the cause of action was held by her father alone. The reason for this rule was that the personal tort evolved out of the father's right to sue for his daughter's loss of services, usually because the daughter became pregnant, although pregnancy was not required to maintain the action.[28] This limitation has been abolished in many jurisdictions which now recognize the seduced female as the real party in interest. The seduced female's right of action was also compromised by her consent to sexual intercourse and by the defense of "in pari delicto."[29]

When the action for seduction is recognized today, it generally belongs to the seduced female, usually a minor; however, the parents of the seduced daughter *may* also obtain a recovery on their own behalf.[30] For this reason, decisions permitting only the father to recover damages[31] or obtain injunctive relief against the so-called "debaucher" of the daughter[32] can no longer be relied upon as good law.[33]

---

[26] Whether the female must be virginal prior to the seduction varies from jurisdiction to jurisdiction. Haeissig v. Decker, 166 N.W. 1085, 1085 (Minn. 1918) (stating that while "[s]eduction presupposes chastity . . . it would not do to hold that chastity once lost can never be regained").

[27] Breece v. Jett, 556 S.W.2d 696, 706 (Mo. App. 1977) (stating that the action for seduction is not limited to "impressionable young women," but may be maintained by mature women who acted prudently, exercised ordinary care, and "sacrificed [their] virtue through an influence which was calculated to lead astray an honest-minded woman").

[28] Magierowski v. Buckley, 121 A.2d 749, 754–55 (N.J. Super. Ct. A.D. 1956).

[29] *Id.* at 760; Section 62.2 ("In Pari Delicto"); *cf.* Martin v. Ziherl, 607 S.E.2d 367 (Va. 2005) (holding that claim for damages due to sexually transmitted disease was not barred by statute that criminalized fornication (sexual relations between unmarried persons)). Prior to the decision, Virginia courts had refused to recognize claims for the transmission of sexual disease because of the statute, which made the victim a criminal and thus barred the claim. At least Virginia is safe for lovers now!

[30] C.C. v. Roadrunner Trucking, Inc., 823 F. Supp. 913, 926 (D. Utah 1993) (citing Utah statute specifically permitting parental recovery for daughter's seduction); White v. Rhodes, 607 N.E.2d 75 (Ohio App. 1992) (stating that parents could recover at least nominal damages if tortious seduction of their daughter occurred); Boedges v. Dinges, 428 S.W.2d 930, 933 (Mo. App. 1968) (permitting parents to recover medical expenses in connection with pregnancy resulting from their daughter's seduction). *See generally* 70 Am. Jur. 2d *Seduction* § 78.

[31] *Haeissig, supra,* 166 N.W. at 1085 (affirming an award of $1500 to the father of a seduced daughter based on the father's mental anguish and "ruination" of his daughter's reputation, loss of his daughter's services, the costs of the daughter's confinement (the nature of which was not described), and the dishonor defendant's acts brought upon the father and the family).

[32] Stark v. Hamilton, 99 S.E. 861, 862 (Ga. 1919) (ordering that defendant no longer associate with plaintiff's minor daughter whom he had seduced and caused to leave her family residence).

[33] The fact that the tort can only be brought against men has led some courts to find that the tort violates equal protection guarantees. Edwards v. Moore, 699 So. 2d 220, 221 (Ala. App. 1997) (finding action for seduction to be constitutionally improper gender discrimination).

The seduced female may recover damages for injury to her reputation and emotional distress resulting from her seduction. She may recover economic losses, as consequential damages, such as loss of employment or position, resulting from her seduction.[34] Evidence of prior unchastity or prior bad character is admissible as to the amount of damages plaintiff sustained as a result of her seduction.[35] Substantial discretion is given to the trier-of-fact as to the measure of damages. As noted by one court:

> In seduction cases, because of the peculiar nature of the action and the various elements of damage both to the seduced female and to her parents, and, as expressed by some courts, a desire to avoid smoothing the way of seducers, appellate courts have generally shown great reluctance to interfere with the amount awarded by the jury. Largely on these grounds, verdicts have been sustained ranging up to $35,000.[36]

The tort of seduction will also support an award of punitive damages.[37]

[102.4]   Breach of Promise to Marry

Breach of promise to marry originated as a remedy for persons who had been induced to expend funds in reliance on another's promise of marriage, which was later rescinded or breached.[38] The modern evolution and tortification of the action reflects the increasing sentiment attached to the marital relationship, just as cultural and social mores have contributed to the rejection of the action in many jurisdictions.[39]

A promise to marry is essential to maintenance of the action. If no promise was made, an action for seduction may lie. Given the proclivities of human nature, breach of promise to marry and seduction were often combined.[40]

---

[34] Ryan v. Oswald, 278 N.W. 508, 512 (Neb. 1938).

[35] Kralick v. Shuttleworth, 289 P. 74, 80 (Idaho 1930).

[36] Graham v. Smith, 330 S.W.2d 573, 576 (Tenn. App. 1959). *See generally* W.E. Shipley, Annot., *Excessiveness or Inadequacy of Damages for Alienation of Affections, Criminal Conversation or Seduction,* 36 A.L.R.2d 548 (1954).

[37] Angie M. v. Superior Court, 44 Cal. Rptr. 2d 197, 204 (Cal. App. 1995); *Graham, supra,* 330 S.W.2d at 576; Owens v. Fanning, 205 S.W. 69, 72 (Mo. App. 1918); *cf.* Caccamisi v. Thurmond, 282 S.W.2d 633, 646 (Tenn. App. 1955) (stating that recovery of punitive damages is enhanced if seduction is accomplished under a promise of marriage).

[38] Jackson v. Brown, 904 P.2d 685, 686 (Utah 1995); *see* HOMER H. CLARK, JR., THE LAW OF DOMESTIC RELATIONS IN THE UNITED STATES 1–2 (2d ed. 1987).

[39] Gilbert v. Barkes, 987 S.W.2d 772, 776 (Ky. 1999) (abolishing action on ground, among others, that it is "an anachronism that has outlived its usefulness"); *Jackson, supra,* 904 P.2d at 686, *citing* CLARK, THE LAW OF DOMESTIC RELATIONS, *supra* at § 1; *see* Janet Larson, *Women Understand So Little, supra,* 93 Colum. L. Rev. at 472 n.85 (stating that the particular focus of reform legislation to abolish personal tort actions was directed at the action for breach of promise to marry).

[40] Luther v. Shaw, 147 N.W. 17, 18 (Wis. 1914) (affirming award to disappointed fiancee of punitive damages for breach of contract to marry and award to parents of fiancee of compensatory damages for the seduction of their daughter).

When the action for breach of promise to marry is recognized, the disappointed fiancee[41] can recover damages for mental anguish, harm to reputation, diminished marital prospects, and the loss of financial and social advantages that would have resulted from the marriage.[42] Punitive damages may also be awarded.[43] Given the prevalence of no-fault divorce, it is no doubt cheaper for a defendant to marry and then divorce then to never marry at all. As noted by one commentator:

> Under the current system of no-fault divorce, there will likely be no alimony and little or no marital property to divide if the marriage is very brief. If the man can marry on Monday and divorce on Tuesday with no real financial consequences, damages for a mere broken engagement would make no sense. During the heyday of breach of promise, however, divorce was only available with difficulty, typically for "fault."[44]

A number of jurisdictions recognize that a fraudulent promise to marry may be actionable notwithstanding the enactment of Heart Balm legislation.[45]

The legislative or judicial abolition of the action for breach of promise to marry does not preclude other actions, such as replevin[46] or unjust enrichment[47] to recover gifts or undo transactions made in contemplation

---

[41] Although the action is not limited to females, unlike, for example, the tort of seduction, I found no modern cases involving disappointed swains (suitors).

[42] Jacoby v. Stark, 68 N.E. 557, 558 (Ill. 1903); Morgan v. Muench, 156 N.W. 819, 823–24 (Iowa 1916). As noted in *Kuhlman v. Cargile*, 262 N.W.2d 454 (Neb. 1978):

> In awarding compensatory damages for breach of promise to marry, the trier of fact may consider the injury to the plaintiff's health, the effect of the breach on the plaintiff's feelings, mental suffering, wounded pride, humiliation, pain, and mortification. Loss of the pecuniary benefits of the promised marriage has also been held to be an element of damages, and evidence of the wealth of the defendant is admissible to show such loss. The wealth of the defendant, however, does not establish the measure of damages.

Id. at 459–60 (citations omitted). *See generally* J.P. Ludington, Annot., *Measure and Elements of Damages For Breach of Contract to Marry*, 73 A.L.R.2d 553 (1960).

[43] *Luther, supra,* 147 N.W. at 18; *Morgan, supra,* 156 N.W. at 823.

[44] Mary Coombs, *Agency and Partnership: A Study of Breach of Promise Plaintiffs*, 2 Yale J. L. & Feminism 1, 23 n.15 (1989).

[45] Tuck v. Tuck, 200 N.E.2d 554, 556 (N.Y. 1964). *But see In re* Marriage of Buckley, 184 Cal. Rptr. 290, 293–94 (Cal. App. 1982) (noting that California's Heart Balm statute (Cal. Civ. Code § 43.4) was specifically amended to include fraudulent promises to marry). Heart Balm legislation is discussed in Section 103 (Heart Balm Statutes).

[46] Vann v. Vehrs, 633 N.E.2d 102, 104 (Ill. App. 1994) (agreeing with what the court describes as the "majority view that a replevin suit for the return of an engagement ring and other gifts made on the condition of marriage is not an action for breach of a promise to marry").

[47] Dixon v. Smith, 695 N.E.2d 284, 288 (Ohio App. 1997) (stating that "the recovery of property transferred in reliance on a promise to marry is permitted upon the equitable theory of preventing unjust enrichment"). *But see* Bruno v. Guerra, 549 N.Y.S.2d 925, 926 (Sup. Ct. 1990) (refusing to allow an action by the father of the disappointed bride to recover from the defendant the cost of the canceled wedding reception because the defendant did not receive a benefit which represented any unjust enrichment). The result may be different if the court

of marriage when the condition (marriage) did not occur.[48]

Although there is a split in the authorities, the modern view appears to permit an action to recover "gifts" without regard to whether the plaintiff or the defendant decided not to go through with the wedding.[49] However, whether a "gift" was given in contemplation of marriage or otherwise may raise difficult issues of classification.[50]

§ 103 HEART BALM STATUTES

At the beginning of the twentieth century almost all American jurisdictions recognized one or more of the personal, sexual torts of alienation of affections, criminal conversation, seduction, or breach of promise to marry. However, beginning at the turn of that century a strong backlash developed against these torts, based largely on the perception that the actions were used more for extortion than redress.[1] The concern was described by one court:

> There is no doubt that in the history of romance a nation could be populated with the lovers and sweethearts (young and old) who have experienced genuine pain and agony because of the defection of their opposites who promised marriage and then absconded. Perhaps there should be a way to compensate these disillusioned souls, but it had been demonstrated that the action of breach of promise had been so misemployed, had given rise to such monumental deceptions, and had encouraged blackmail on such a scale, that the Legislature of Pennsylvania, acting in behalf of all the people, concluded that the evil of abuse exceeded to such an extent the occasional legitimate benefit conferred by a breach of promise suit that good government dictated its abolition.[2]

The result was the enactment in many jurisdictions of so-called "Heart Balm" or "Anti Heart Balm" statutes that abolished some or all of these torts. The term "Heart Balm" is a sardonic, derisive reference to a broken heart that lay at the root of the personal sexual torts of breach of promise

---

recognizes a "fictional" benefit. Earhart v. William Low Co., 600 P.2d 1344, 1349 (Cal. 1979) (stating that "performance at another's request may itself constitute a benefit"); Section 43 (Nature of Unjust Enrichment).

[48] See generally Elaine Tomko, Annot., Rights in Respect of Engagement and Courtship Presents When Marriage Does Not Ensue, 44 A.L.R. 5th 1 (1996).

[49] Lindh v. Surman, 742 A.2d 643, 645–46 (Pa. 1999); see In re Wilson, 210 B.R. 544, 546 (Bankr. N.D. Ohio 1997) (applying what court characterized as majority "no fault" rule regarding recovery of gifts given in contemplation of marriage when the marriage does not occur). See generally Tomko, Annot., supra, 44 A.L.R. 5th at §§ 20–25.

[50] Cooper v. Smith, 800 N.E.2d 372, 380–81 (Ohio App. 2003) (treating engagement ring as conditional gift in contemplation of marriage, but other gifts to fiancee and fiancee's mother are irrevocable unless expressly conditioned on marriage).

[1] See Nathan Feinsinger, Legislative Attack on "Heart Balm", 33 Mich. L. Rev. 979 (1935); Robert Kingsley, The "Anti-Heart Balm" Statute, 13 S. Cal. L. Rev. 37 (1939).

[2] Pavlicic v. Vogtsberger, 136 A.2d 127, 130 (Pa. 1957).

to marry, alienation of affections, seduction, and criminal conversation. The results of this backlash were quite successful. The majority of American jurisdictions have abolished all or some of the personal torts, most by statute, but a few by judicial action.

Although Heart Balm statutes are usually direct in their abolition of the common law actions, the actual impact on the ability of certain plaintiffs to maintain actions bordering, or even perhaps, overlapping, the abolished common law personal torts may be hard to gauge. For example, should a remedy be provided (1) when the personal, sexual tort is committed by one who stands as a fiduciary to the plaintiff; (2) when the defendant's conduct is outrageous and offensive such as to suggest maintaining the claim as one for the intentional infliction of emotional distress; or (3) when the defendant's misconduct is animated by fraud?

[103.1] Personal Tort Committed by Fiduciary

A potential or existing marital relationship may be disrupted or a sexual relationship may be initiated by one, such as a physician, pastor, or attorney, who stands in a fiduciary or quasi-fiduciary relationship to the party directly affected by the fiduciary's conduct. Courts have been generally willing to consider claims for breach of fiduciary duties in this context notwithstanding the enactment of Heart Balm statutes.[3] In this context, while the claim may parallel the sexual torts of alienation of affections, criminal conversation, or seduction, these courts characterize the "gist" of the action as involving breach of fiduciary duty.[4] As noted in *Erickson v. Christenson*:

> The tort of seduction provided recovery for damage to character and reputation, as well as for mental anguish and pecuniary losses. By contrast, plaintiff's claim alleges that Christenson misused his position as pastor and counselor to abuse her sexually, causing her not only emotional distress but also "loss of ability to trust other adults, to trust authority, and . . . in her ability to deal with religion and her faith in God." Accepting the allegations as true, the harm to plaintiff stemmed from Christenson's misuse of his position of trust, not from the seduction as such. Plaintiff has stated a claim.[5]

---

[3] Destefano v. Grabrian, 763 P.2d 275 (Colo. 1988) (involving a priest who allegedly engaged in sexual relations with the plaintiff's spouse during the time the priest was counseling the plaintiff and his spouse regarding their marriage); Cotton v. Kambly, 300 N.W.2d 627 (Mich. App. 1980) (involving psychiatrist who allegedly induced the plaintiff to engage in a sexual relationship with him as part of his prescribed therapy).

[4] *Destefano, supra*, 763 P.2d at 280–81; *Cotton, supra*, 300 N.W.2d at 628–29.

[5] 781 P.2d 383, 385 (Or. App. 1989) (citation omitted). *But see* Kling v. Landry, 686 N.E.2d 33, 40–41 (Ill. App. 1997) (distinguishing between the situation when an attorney exploits his position as an attorney to gain sexual favors from the client, which is actionable as a breach of fiduciary duty, from the situation when an attorney and a client engage in a consensual sexual relationship, which, by itself, is not actionable).

Not all jurisdictions recognize this exception to the Heart Balm statute.[6] When a cause of action, however, is recognized, the fiduciary duty, upon which the action is based, must be owed to the plaintiff.[7]

[103.2] Intentional Infliction of Emotional Distress

A recent development in the area of the personal, sexual torts has been the use of the action for Intentional Infliction of Emotional Distress [IIED] as a substitute for the abolished tort(s). The essential allegation is that the defendant's conduct, in alienating a spouse's affection, seducing a female, etc., was accomplished by sufficiently outrageous and offensive means as to constitute the independent tort of IIED. The jurisdictions have split as to whether a claim of IIED may be made to protect interests of the type subsumed under the personal, sexual torts.

It is difficult to ascertain whether the courts have adopted a case-by-case approach to the issue, rather than adopting a categorical rule.[8] In *Raftery v. Scott* the court asserted that the torts of IIED and alienation of affections were distinct causes of action and the presence of some "overtones of affection alienation does not bar recovery on the separate and distinct accompanying wrongdoing."[9] On the other hand, in *Koestler v. Pollard* the court held that the strong public policy behind the legislative abolition of the personal, sexual torts could not be bypassed by redressing the conduct as constituting outrageous and offensive acts perpetrated by the defendant on the plaintiff.[10] The critical issue for these latter courts is whether the plaintiff is simply relabelling an abolished tort (e.g., alienation of affections) as a modernly recognized tort (e.g., intentional infliction). A personal, sexual tort may cause emotional distress, but is the distress intended or

---

[6] Strock v. Pressnell, 527 N.E.2d 1235, 1242–43 (Ohio 1988) (noting that the enactment of the Heart Balm statute represented a policy decision by the legislature that amatory interests are not protected under the law and that the policy should not be eviscerated by the artful pleading of alternate theories of liability). *Strock* was factually similar to *Destefano, supra* note 3.

[7] Homer v. Long, 599 A.2d 1193, 1197 (Md. Ct. Sp. App. 1992) (refusing to permit the spouse of a patient to sue a physician for damages arising out of an alleged sexual relationship between the patient and the physician; the court held that no duty was owed by the physician to the plaintiff, who was the patient's spouse); Smith v. Pust, 23 Cal. Rptr. 2d 364, 370 (Cal. App. 1993) (involving therapist and reaching the same result as in *Homer, supra*).

[8] *Jackson, supra*, 904 P.2d at 688 (stating that plaintiff could take her claim to the jury that defendant's breach of his promise to marry was, under the circumstances, independently actionable as IIED); Van Meter v. Van Meter, 328 N.W.2d 497, 498 (Iowa 1983) (treating the issue as essentially for the jury).

[9] 756 F.2d 335, 339 (4th Cir. 1985) (applying Virginia law); Bartanus v. Lis, 480 A.2d 1178, 1182–83 (Pa. Super. Ct. 1984) (same); *cf.* Figueiredo-Torres v. Nickel, 584 A.2d 69, 76–77 (Md. 1991) (holding that patient could state IIED claim against physician who engaged in sexual relationship with patient notwithstanding abolition of tort actions for criminal conversation and alienation of affection).

[10] 471 N.W.2d 7, 10–11 (Wis. 1991); *see* McDermott v. Reynolds, 530 S.E.2d 902, 903–04 (Va. 2000); R.J. v. S.L.J., 810 S.W.2d 608, 609 (Mo. App. 1991); Pickering v. Pickering, 434 N.W.2d 758, 761 (S.D. 1989).

an incidental byproduct of the misconduct? An action may be maintained when the plaintiff can demonstrate that the defendant engaged in the conduct for the purpose of causing the plaintiff to suffer distress.[11] These cases will be difficult to prove.[12]

The abolition of spousal immunity, coupled with the recognition of "no fault" divorce, has generated a sizable body of decisions regarding the ability of one spouse to recover distress damages from the other spouse:

> [W]here a man and wife are involved in a marriage relationship, there could always exist a tort for intentional infliction of emotional distress where they had a argument. It could be over the family dog, who takes out the garbage, who forgot to pay the bills or who is spending too much money. In other words the law should not provide a basis for inter-familial warfare between husbands and wives where our courts would be flooded with litigation.[13]

Several jurisdictions have entertained claims of IIED between spouses; however, these jurisdictions, while recognizing the action in theory, have set the required outrageous and offensive behavior bar so high in this context as to preclude virtually all claims.[14] For example, in *Miller v. Ratner* plaintiff became seriously ill with breast cancer. Although the parties were not married, they had lived together in a "relationship" for 3 years. The plaintiff alleged that her boyfriend would awaken her while she was undergoing radiation treatments and verbally abuse her, telling her that she was a financial burden and would soon die. Her boyfriend's brother, apparently with her boyfriend's connivance, called the plaintiff, a "bitch," "whore," and a "one-breasted woman." The court held that the statements were not offensive enough to be actionable![15] Similarly, adulterous affairs by spouses with co-workers and family friends have been found to be insufficiently outrageous,[16] as have false representations of paternity.[17]

---

[11] Quinn v. Walsh, 732 N.E.2d 330, 338–39 (Mass. App. 2000).

[12] Padwa v. Hadley, 981 P.2d 1234 (N.Mex. App. 1999) (holding that intentional infliction of emotional distress could not be maintained against defendant (plaintiff's former friend(?)) who had serially and successfully seduced plaintiff's former wife, plaintiff's former fiancee, and plaintiff's current wife). *See generally* Marjorie A. Shields, Annot., *Action For Intentional Infliction of Emotional Distress Against Paramours*, 95 A.L.R.5th 445 (2002).

[13] *Pickering, supra,* 434 N.W.2d at 764 (Henderson, J.) (concurring and dissenting).

[14] McCulloh v. Drake, 24 P.3d 1162, 1169–70 (Wyo. 2001); Hakkila v. Hakkila, 812 P.2d 1320, 1326 (N.Mex. App. 1991) (collecting decisions). *See generally* George L. Blum, Annot., *Intentional Infliction of Emotional Distress in Marital Context*, 110 A.L.R.5th 371 (2003).

[15] 688 A.2d 976, 997 (Md. Ct. Sp. App. 1997).

[16] Ruprecht v. Ruprecht, 599 A.2d 604, 608 (N.J. Sup. Ct. 1991) (involving an 11 year affair by the wife with a coworker); Strauss v. Cilek, 418 N.W.2d 378, 379 (Iowa App. 1987) (involving a 5 year affair between the husband's friend and the husband's wife).

[17] Doe v. Doe, 747 A.2d 617, 625 (Md. 2000) and Richard P. v. Superior Court, 249 Cal. Rptr. 246, 249 (Cal. App. 1988) (both holding that husband had no claim against his wife for IIED based on her false representation to him that he was the biological father of their children); *cf. Koestler, supra,* 471 N.W.2d at 10–11 (rejecting husband's claims of fraud and intentional infliction of emotional distress against biological father of child the husband had been deceived into believing was his biological daughter); Section 103.3 ([Heart Balm Statutes] Fraud); Section 125 ([Fraud] Personal Relationships).

Some courts have permitted a spouse to claim IIED against the other spouse. In *Miller v. Miller* false representations regarding the paternity of the children were held to be actionable as IIED.[18] In *Whelan v. Whelan* the court permitted an IIED claim to go forward when the plaintiff alleged that her ex-husband had falsely told her during their marriage that he had tested positive for the HIV virus and that she should take their son to their former home in Canada because he did not want her to see him suffer and die.[19]

When the claim involves domestic violence, courts do not exhibit the same reluctance to become involved. Physical injury is seen as different in kind from pure economic loss or emotional distress; nonetheless, these claims are under reported and under represented.[20]

[103.3] Fraud

It is not uncommon that conduct that would amount to a personal, sexual tort also involves affirmative misrepresentations. False representations of love, devotion, fidelity, or honesty are frequently alleged to be part of the defendant's course of misconduct. For every sincere Swain there is, it appears, a lupine Lothario. The decisional law in this area generally refuses to allow fraud allegations to displace the policy behind Heart Balm statutes. In *Askew v. Askew* the husband complained that he would not have transferred property to his wife had his wife not falsely represented that she loved him and was sexually attracted to him. This type of fraud claim was deemed to be incompatible with the Heart Balm statute:

> We need not declaim generally on the topic of "sexual fraud," to be able to ascertain that the "sexual fraud" (as it were) in this case is not actionable . . . . Words of love, passion and sexual desire are simply unsuited to the cumbersome strictures of common law fraud and deceit. The idea that a judge, or jury of 12 solid citizens, can arbitrate whether an individual's romantic declarations at a certain time are true or false, or made with intent to deceive, seems almost ridiculously wooden. . . . "The judiciary should not attempt to

---

[18] 956 P.2d 887, 902 (Okla. 1998); *see* C.M. v. J.M., 726 A.2d 998 (N.J. Sup. Ch. 1999) (same). *But see* R.A.C v. P.J.S., 880 A.2d 1179, 1192 (N.J. Super. Ct. A.D. 2005) (disagreeing with *C.M. v. J.M.*).

[19] 588 A.2d 251, 252 (Conn. Sup. Ct. 1991).

[20] *See* Jennifer Wriggens, *Domestic Violence Torts*, 75 So. Cal. L. Rev. 121 (2001):

> People who commit domestic violence generally are, in theory, liable under intentional tort theories, in addition to whatever liability they may face under criminal law. But despite the frequency with which people are injured by "domestic violence torts," very few tort suits are brought to seek recovery from the harms domestic violence causes. This underenforcement is caused by several factors. First, standard liability insurance policies generally do not cover domestic violence torts. Second, many defendants have limited or no assets. Third, statutes of limitations are typically shorter for intentional torts than for negligence.

Id. at 124 (footnotes omitted).

regulate all aspects of the human condition. Relationships may take varied forms and beget complications and entanglements which defy reason." Love has been known to last a lifetime, but it has also been known to be notoriously evanescent. These are matters better left to advice columnists than to judges and juries. [C]ourts should not be in the business of probing a suitor's state of mind.[21]

In *Smith v. The National Railroad Passenger Corporation (Amtrak)* the court rejected a claim by the plaintiff that she had been induced to leave her employment and suffered resulting damages as a consequence of her male superior's false promise of marriage. The court held that the claim, while cast in terms of fraud and misrepresentation, was essentially one for breach of promise to marry which had been abolished in Pennsylvania. As noted by the court:

> While we do not condone the offensive conduct of defendant if in fact he acted as alleged, the court cannot provide plaintiff a remedy. Solace, comfort and restoration in matters of the heart and spirit must be sought and found elsewhere.[22]

In *Gubin v. Lodisev* the court refused to permit a fraud action by a wife against her husband on her claim that he only married her to gain entry into the United States.[23] In the movie "Green Card" a citizen and non-citizen marry to derail efforts by the Immigration & Naturalization Service to deport the non-citizen. Marriage, at least lawful, legitimate marriage, confers a lawful immigration status for the otherwise deportable non-citizen. In the movie, the "sham" marriage evolves into a loving relationship. Life may imitate art, but the law does not always provide a remedy when life does not provide a happy ending.

Some decisions have bucked this trend and have allowed fraud claims to be asserted when the misrepresentation arose out of the marital relationship.[24] Invariably, these claims also involve assertions that the conduct constitutes the intentional infliction of emotional distress[25] and it is

---

[21] 28 Cal. Rptr. 2d 284, 294 (Cal. App. 1994) (citations and footnotes omitted); *cf.* d'Elia v. d'Elia, 68 Cal. Rptr. 2d 324, 326–27 (Cal. App. 1997) (holding that state securities fraud laws did not apply to stock transfer that was part of marital settlement agreement because the husband's disclosure obligations arose out of family law not securities laws). The court indicated that result might be different if the transfer was not connected with the parties' divorce. *Id.*.

[22] 25 F. Supp. 2d 574, 575–76 (E.D. Pa. 1998).

[23] 494 N.W.2d 782, 784 (Mich. App. 1993) (noting that record demonstrated that the "defendant's actions were a blatant and crass attempt to fraudulently induce the plaintiff to marry him for no other reason than to obtain the means of lawful entry into the United States. This was the true reason for the breakdown in the marriage relationship"). The court held, nonetheless, that "[t]he fraud was so intimately involved with the marriage contract that it cannot be separated." *Id.*

[24] Koelle v. Zwiren, 672 N.E.2d 868, 875 (Ill. App. 1996) (permitting man to recover distress damages against woman who falsely represented that he was the father of her child).

[25] *Id.* (noting that the plaintiff sought compensation "for the losses he has suffered due to defendant's alleged fraud and for the pain and anxiety he has felt due to the alleged intentional infliction of emotional distress").

unclear whether the misrepresentation claim standing alone would permit the recovery of damages.[26]

§ 104   WRONGFUL ADOPTION

Recently some adoptive parents have sought damages or rescission based on the contention that they were induced to adopt based on material misrepresentations. Several jurisdictions have recognized the action when the adoption was induced by intentional misrepresentations or concealment of material facts, usually relating to the health or psychological stability of the child.[1] The courts have generally limited recoveries to economic losses,[2] although several courts have held that punitive damages may be recoverable.[3] The availability of rescission as a remedy in the wrongful adoption context has generally been conceded.[4] Courts, however, have also intimated that affirmance of the adoption is to be preferred over rescission.[5]

---

[26] Section 125 ([Fraud] Personal Relationships).

[1] Meracle v. Children's Serv. Soc'y of Wis., 437 N.W.2d 532, 537 (Wis. 1989) (holding that positive misrepresentations regarding child's health permitted damages action against agency); see D. Marianne Blair, *Getting the Whole Truth and Nothing But the Truth: The Limits of Liability For Wrongful Adoption*, 67 Notre Dame L. Rev. 851 (1992). *See generally* Harriet Dinegar Milks, Annot., *"Wrongful Adoption" Causes of Action Against Adoption Agencies Where Children Have or Develop Mental or Physical Problems That are Misrepresented or Not Disclosed to Adoptive Parents*, 74 A.L.R. 5th 1 (1999).

[2] *Meracle, supra*, 437 N.W.2d at 536; see Mohr v. Commonwealth, 653 N.E.2d 1104, 1106 n.4 (Mass. 1995) (affirming $200,000 damages award to adoptive parents, reduced from jury award of $3.8 million). The recovery was for the cost of treating the child's mental illness. *Id.* at 1109.

[3] Juman v. Louise Wise Servs., 663 N.Y.S.2d 483, 490 (Sup. Ct. 1997), *aff'd on other grounds*, 678 N.Y.S.2d 611 (App. Dep't 1998); Gibbs v. Ernst, 615 A.2d 851, 856 (Pa. Comm'n Ct. 1992), *aff'd in part, rev'd in part, on other grounds*, 647 A.2d 882 (Pa. 1994); Section 202.8 ([Punitive Damages] Public Entities and Not-For-Profit Organizations).

[4] Juman v. Louise Wise Servs., 608 N.Y.S.2d 612 (Sup. Ct. 1994) (stating that adoptive parents have the option of rescinding adoption or keeping child and seeking damages).

[5] *Juman*, 608 N.Y.S.2d at 615 (stating that in cases of rescission of adoption "everyone is hurt"); *cf.* Cesnik v. Edgewood Baptist Church, 88 F.3d 902, 909 (11th Cir. 1996) (stating that adoptive parents were not obligated to mitigate their damages by tendering child back to adoption agency and rescinding adoption), *cert. denied*, 519 U.S. 1110 (1997).

Chapter 12

REMEDIES FOR DEFAMATION

SYNOPSIS

§ 105 PRESUMED DAMAGES

The hallmark of defamation redress is the availability of presumed damages. Presumed damages are necessarily inferred from the commission of the tort of defamation and may be awarded without proof of any loss actually being sustained.[1] Moreover, the trier-of-fact has substantial discretion as to the amount of presumed damages that may be awarded, again without requiring any proof that would enable or assist in the calculation of the amount of damages. In some instances the amounts awarded are substantional;[2] however, the general award in this area is moderate.[3]

Defamation consists of the false and malicious publication of facts that tend to injure the reputation of another or hold him up to public ridicule, hatred, or contempt. At common law, when the publication of the defamatory material was by a writing it was referred to as "libel"; when the publication was oral, it was referred to as "slander." The distinctions are adhered to today but the application of the distinction to modern methods of electronic communication, such as e-mail, is not always clear.

The common law developed a number of classifications for addressing defamation claims. The two most critical, for remedial purposes, were *per se* and *per quod*. The distinction was essentially between words intrinsically

---

[1] Section 2.8 (Presumed Damages).

[2] Schmitz v. Aston, 3 P.3d 1184, 1190–99 (Ariz. App. 2000) (affirming $100,000 presumed damages award for defendant), *ordered not published*, 18 P.3d 1230 (Ariz. 2001).

[3] *Cf.* Nolley v. County of Erie, 802 F. Supp. 898 (W.D. N.Y. 1992) (awarding presumed damages of $3100 ($10 per day times 310 days) for plaintiff whose right of privacy was violated by disclosure of HIV status while plaintiff was incarcerated).

and inherently harmful, without the need of evidence to demonstrate injury to the plaintiff (*per se*), and words that depended on the facts and circumstances of the particular case, or the context in which the words were published or uttered, in order to demonstrate their defamatory import (*per quod*).[4] Material that was defamatory *per se* permitted the recovery of "presumed damages." In other words, damage or injury to the plaintiff's reputation, resulting from the defamatory words, was presumed and would support an award of damages. Material that was defamatory *per quod* required a showing that the words were defamatory and a showing of "special damages" flowing from the defamatory words before damages for reputational injury and other damages could be recovered. "Special damages" are actual pecuniary losses, such as loss of employment, that directly result from the defamatory statement.

The distinctions between material that was actionable *per se* or *per quod* has always reflected the larger culture. For example, at common law all libels (written defamatory words) were actionable *per se*, reflecting the permanency of written materials, the limited literacy of the population, and the likely audience of a libelous statement—the wealthier, better educated classes among whom the plaintiff might likely suffer from an injurious falsehood.[5] As literacy rates have climbed and as the modes of communication have evolved from print to mass media (e.g., radio, television, motion pictures), to electronic (e.g. the "internet"), the common law categories become difficult to maintain.

The availability of presumed damages in defamation actions has been under sustained attack because of concerns that the remedy is in conflict with larger First Amendment values. In *Gertz v. Robert Welch, Inc.*[6] the Court held that in a defamation action involving media defendants a court may not permit the recovery of presumed damages absent satisfaction of the *New York Times v. Sullivan*[7] scienter requirement, which is actual knowledge of the falsity of the communication or reckless disregard of the truth on the part of the defendant.[8] Several years later, in *Dun & Bradstreet, Inc. v. Greenmoss Builders, Inc.*,[9] the Court permitted recovery of presumed damages without requiring the satisfaction of the *New York Times v. Sullivan* standard when the defamatory words did not involve a matter of public concern. *Dun & Bradstreet, Inc.* was a plurality opinion and this generated some uncertainty as to the scope of the decision. By implication, presumed damages may be awarded in matters involving

---

[4] There are distinctions between slander *per se* and libel *per se* that are not addressed in these materials but which may be significant in evaluation of the substantive merits of the claim. Nazeri v. Missouri Valley College, 860 S.W.2d 303, 308 (Mo. 1993) (discussing the differences between slander *per se* and libel *per se*).

[5] Thorley v. Lord Kerry, 4 Taunt. 355, 128 Eng. Rep. 367, 370–71 (C.P. 1812) (holding that written words may be actionable when the same words, if spoken, would not be actionable).

[6] 418 U.S. 323, 349 (1974).

[7] 376 U.S. 254 (1964).

[8] *Id.* at 280.

[9] 472 U.S. 749, 763 (1985).

private, non-newsworthy matters and non-media defendants, and a number of courts so hold.[10] There is, however, a growing number of jurisdictions that have abolished presumed damages across-the-board.[11] In these jurisdictions, the plaintiff's compensatory damages recovery is limited to those damages that the plaintiff proves he actually sustained as a result of the defamatory material published by the defendant.

In some jurisdictions, the concept of defamation *per se* is separated from the concept of presumed damages. In these jurisdictions, defamatory material may be actionable *per se* even though the plaintiff does not introduce evidence of actual injury to reputation. In such cases, the plaintiff may recover for non-reputational injuries, such as emotional distress, according to proof, notwithstanding the absence of proof of reputational injury.[12]

§ 106 REPUTATIONAL INJURY

[106.1] General Principles

Injury to reputation, much like injury to emotional security, rejects exact measurement. Yet, the difficulties of proof do not negate the importance of the interest. One's reputation has been recognized throughout recorded history, from the Bible to Shakespeare, as well worth protecting.[1] Nonetheless, the attempt of modern defamation law to reconcile the conflicting goals of protecting reputations and protecting free speech has led to some controls on the quality of proofs that may be accepted as establishing reputational

---

[10] *See, e.g.*, Touma v. St. Mary's Bank, 712 A.2d 619, 622 (N.H. 1998); Nelson v. Lapeyrouse Grain Corp., 534 So. 2d 1085, 1092 n.3 (Ala. 1988). Both decisions treat the Court's decision in *Dun & Bradstreet, Inc.* as cutting back on the holding in *Gertz.*

[11] Khawar v. Globe Int'l, Inc., 965 P.2d 696 (Cal. 1998):

> Because in this defamation action Khawar is a private figure plaintiff, he was required to prove only negligence, and not actual malice, to recover damages for actual injury to his reputation. But Khawar was required to prove actual malice to recover punitive or presumed damages for defamation involving the Kennedy assassination.

Id. at 708, *cert. denied*, 526 U.S. 1114 (1999); United Ins. Co. of America v. Murphy, 961 S.W.2d 752, 756 (Ark. 1998) (holding that "the better and more consistent rule . . . is to require plaintiffs to prove reputational injury in all cases") (citations omitted); Zoeller v. American Family Mut. Ins. Co., 834 P.2d 391, 393 (Kan. App. 1992).

[12] Hearst Corp. v. Hughes, 466 A.2d 486, 495 (Md. 1983). *See generally* Earl Kellett, Annot., *Proof of Injury to Reputation as Prerequisite to Recovery of Damages in Defamation Action— Post* Gertz *Cases*, 36 A.L.R.4th 807 (1981).

[1] Proverbs 22:1 ("To be esteemed is better than silver or gold") or ("A good name is rather to be chosen than great riches"). The difference depends on the particular translation. In Shakespeare's great tragedy, "Othello," Iago says to Othello:

> Good name in man and woman, dear my lord, is the immediate jewel of their souls.
> Who steals my purse steals trash; 'Tis something, nothing; 'Twas mine, 'tis his, and has been slave to thousands; But he that filches from me my good name robs me of that which not enriches him, and makes me poor indeed.

Othello, Act 3, sc. 3.

injury. Many courts have expressed an unwillingness to permit proof of reputational injury to rest on the plaintiff's testimony alone.[2] Rather, "a plaintiff should offer some concrete proof that his reputation has been injured. One form of proof is that an existing relationship has been seriously disrupted, reflecting the idea that a reputation may be valued in terms of relationships with others . . . . Testimony of third parties as to a diminished reputation will also suffice to prove 'actual injury.' "[3] Concrete proof of reputational injury may be shown when the plaintiff suffers economic loss as a consequence of the defamation. In *Schlegel v. Ottumwa Courier* the court rejected an award of damages for reputational injury because the plaintiff failed to show that the defamation caused him any loss of business in his profession as a lawyer. The court agreed with the trial court's finding that "had [the lawyer's] reputation been damaged, it likely would have adversely affected his law practice."[4]

Injury to reputation is not, however, limited to proofs of economic consequences. It is sufficient if plaintiff establishes by competent proof that either people believed plaintiff to be guilty of the defamatory acts attributed to him or that people thought less of him as a result of the publication of the defamatory material.[5] The damages award may include both reputational injury[6] and the economic losses resulting from the defamatory statements. In *Sommers v. Gabor* the court upheld a compensatory damages award of $800,000 based on evidence that the plaintiff actress' fan club had received about 200 letters offering to "help" the plaintiff, which tended, according to the court, to show that the defamatory statements injured the plaintiff. The court also noted the testimony of plaintiff's publicist that the defamatory statement had harmed plaintiff's career.[7]

The jury is usually afforded substantial deference with respect to the calculation of economic damages once the defamatory content of the

---

[2] Sisler v. Gannett Co., Inc., 516 A.2d 1083, 1096 (N.J. 1986); *cf.* Richie v. Paramount Pictures Corp., 544 N.W.2d 21, 27 (Minn. 1996) (rejecting as inadequate testimony by the plaintiff that a previous good friend gave him the "cold shoulder" after the defamatory material was published).

[3] *Sisler, supra*, 516 A.2d at 1096.

[4] 585 N.W.2d 217, 224 (Iowa 1998).

[5] Little Rock Newspapers, Inc. v. Fitzhugh, 954 S.W.2d 914, 921 (Ark. 1997) (involving a lawyer falsely associated in a newspaper article with fraud arising out of the "Whitewater Affair"), *cert. denied*, 523 U.S. 1095 (1998), *cf.* Biondi v. Nassimos, 692 A.2d 103, 106 (N.J. Super Ct. A.D. 1997) (finding no reputational injury when the plaintiff presented no evidence that anyone refused to associate with him or that his business or personal relationships had been seriously disrupted). In *Biondi* it was alleged that the plaintiff had "mob connections." The court found insufficient, as proof of reputational injury, that individuals had called him "Godfather," "asked to kiss his ring," and asked him to "sit at the head of the table."

[6] Khawar v. Globe Intern., Inc., 965 P.2d 696, 699 (Cal. 1998) (affirming award of $100,000, among other damages, for injury to reputation), *cert. denied*, 526 U.S. 1114 (1999).

[7] 48 Cal. Rptr. 2d 235, 245 (Cal. App. 1995).

statement is confirmed in a manner consistent with constitutional safeguards. Economic damages awards can be substantial.[8]

[106.2] "Libel-Proof" Plaintiffs

A plaintiff's reputation may, by reason of her associations, position, or notoriety, be beyond the ability of the defendant to harm even by the utterance of demonstrably defamatory statements. While at common law such a plaintiff could claim "presumed damages," there is some support in the law today for the concept of the libel-proof plaintiff, *i.e.*, a plaintiff whose reputation is so bad that, as a matter of law, she cannot claim damages as a result of defamatory statements. Such "status" has been afforded to (1) career criminals,[9] (2) death-row inmates,[10] (3) disciplined professionals,[11] and (4) convicted assassins.[12] These categories are illustrative, not exclusive; criminal misconduct less than that of career criminal, capital felon, or convicted assassin may qualify one for the categorical status of "libel-proof."[13] A person's status as libel-proof is based on the facts and circumstances of the particular case. A court may conclude that a person is libel-proof only in connection with the particular matter.[14] A person who is libel-proof at one point in his life does not appear to be confined to that status forever. Redemption is available to some,[15] but apparently not to

---

[8] MMAR Group, Inc. v. Dow Jones & Co., Inc., 987 F. Supp. 535, 541–42 (S.D. Tex. 1997) (upholding a jury award of $22.7 million based on the destruction of the plaintiff's business caused by a defamatory newspaper article); Sprague v. Walter, 656 A.2d 890, 924–25 (Pa. Super. Ct. 1995) (affirming a compensatory damages award of $2.5 million). *See generally* Jay Zitter, *Excessiveness or Inadequacy of Compensatory Damages For Defamation*, 49 A.L.R.4th 1158 (1986). The verdict in *MMAR Group, Inc., supra*, was later reported to have been set aside because of misconduct (withholding of evidence) by the plaintiff. Wall Street Journal, April 9, 1999, at B6.

[9] Cardillo v. Doubleday & Co., Inc., 518 F.2d 638 (2d Cir. 1975); *see* Cerasani v. Sony Corp., 991 F. Supp. 343, 352,-53 (S.D.N.Y. 1998) (involving the person who was allegedly portrayed in the movie "Donnie Brasco").

[10] Coker v. Sundquist, 1998 Tenn. App. LEXIS 708 (Tenn. App., Oct. 23, 1998).

[11] Swate v. Schiffers, 975 S.W.2d 70, 74 (Tex. Civ. App. 1998) (involving a physician whose license to practice medicine had been taken away due to unprofessional conduct by the physician).

[12] Ray v. Time, Inc., 452 F. Supp. 618, 622 (W.D. Tenn. 1976), *aff'd*, 582 F.2d 1280 (6th Cir. 1978) (Table) (holding James Earl Ray, the convicted assassin of Dr. Martin Luther King, to be libel-proof).

[13] Cofield v. Advertiser Co., 486 So. 2d 434 (Ala. 1986) (involving a plaintiff who had numerous convictions for "theft").

[14] Jones v. Globe Int'l, Inc., 1995 U.S. Dist. LEXIS 22080 (D. Conn., Sept. 26, 1995) (involving a former employee of Marla Trump who publicly admitted a fascination with Ms. Trump's "shoes"); *cf.* Lamb v. Rizzo, 391 F.3d 1133, 1139 (10th Cir. 2004) (applying Kansas law) (stating that "libel-proof plaintiff" doctrine is most appropriately applied "as those cases, like Cardillo [*supra*], in which criminal convictions for behavior similar to that alleged in the challenged communication are urged as a bar to the claim") (brackets added).

[15] Da Silva v. Time, Inc., 908 F. Supp. 184 (S.D.N.Y. 1995):

Defendants' motion must be denied because a material issue of fact exists as to whether Da Silva's reputation could have and did suffer damage. Da Silva asserts

all.[16] Notwithstanding some judicial acceptance of the libel-proof plaintiff rule, its general acceptance in American law is, at present, unsettled.[17]

[106.3] Incremental Harm Rule

The incremental harm rule is sometimes confused with the libel-proof plaintiff rule. The incremental harm rule compares the harm to reputation resulting from non-actionable, "truthful," statements about the plaintiff with the harm to the plaintiff resulting solely from defamatory, "false," statements about the plaintiff.[18] The similarity is that the two rules identify a form of non-compensable defamation: the libel-proof plaintiff rule identifies a plaintiff whose reputation is so bad it can't be damaged further; the incremental harm rule asks whether the defamatory statements cause reputational injury meaningfully different from the reputational injury caused by non-actionable statements.

As with the libel-proof plaintiff doctrine, courts have struggled to apply the incremental harm rule. The issue arose in *Jewell v. NYP Holdings, Inc.* when news accounts erroneously identified the plaintiff as suspiciously involved in a bombing that occurred during the 1996 Summer Olympic Games in Atlanta, Georgia.[19] The court noted some concern over the doctrinal support for the incremental harm rule, but concluded that, as a diversity case, New York law controlled and New York would recognize the

---

by credible affidavit that, although she had been a prostitute in Recife, she had since developed a reputation there as a reformed prostitute by the time the photograph was taken and published. Moreover, Da Silva asserts she had developed a new reputation in her new community of Jaboatao des Guararapes as a wife and mother rather than as a prostitute. As such, a genuine issue of material fact exists as to whether her new reputation could have been and was tainted as a result of the published photograph.

Id. at 187.

[16] *Cf. Ray, supra,* 508 F. Supp. at 726 (holding that convicted assassin James Earl Ray was collaterally estopped from re-litigating finding that he was libel-proof).

[17] McBride v. New Braunfels Herald-Zeitung, 894, S.W.2d 6, 10 (Tex. Civ. App. 1994) (noting that "[t]he law presumes that one possesses good character and that even the limited good reputation of a person of a bad character could be worse"). The court further noted:

To justify applying the doctrine, the evidence of record must show not only that the plaintiff engaged in criminal or anti-social behavior in the past, but also that his activities were widely reported to the public.

Id. at 10 (citations omitted); *see* Liberty Lobby, Inc. v. Anderson, 746 F.2d 1563, (D.C. Cir. 1984) (Scalia, J.):

[T]he theory must be rejected because it rests upon the assumption that one's reputation is a monolith, which stands or falls in its entirety. The law, however, proceeds upon the optimistic premise that there is a little bit of good in all of us—or perhaps upon the pessimistic assumption that no matter how bad someone is, he can always be worse.

Id. at 1568, *vacated on other grounds,* 477 U.S. 242 (1986). *See generally* Eliot Katz, Annot., *Defamation: Who is "Libel-Proof,"* 50 A.L.R.4th 1257 (1987).

[18] Herbert v. Lando, 781 F.2d 298, 311 (2d Cir.), *cert. denied,* 476 U.S. 1182 (1986).

[19] 23 F. Supp. 2d 348, 349 (S.D.N.Y. 1998).

defense based on the considerable protection that New York courts have historically afforded defendants in defamation actions.[20] The court was also persuaded that the rule helps separate trivial claims from substantial claims, thus protecting speech by discouraging trivial claims of defamation.[21] The court also stated that the incremental harm rule is distinct from the "substantial truth" defense:

> The substantial truth defense is often confused with the incremental harm defense, but the two are distinct, and the distinctions should be clarified. Then-Judge Scalia recognized this distinction when . . . he noted the following: There may be validity to the proposition that at some point the erroneous attribution of incremental evidence of a character flaw of a particular type which is in any event amply established by the facts is not derogatory. If, for example, an individual is said to have been convicted of 35 burglaries, when the correct number is 34, it is not likely that the statement is actionable. That is so, however, not because the object of the remarks is "libel-proof," but because, since the essentially derogatory implication of the statement ("he is an habitual burglar") is correct, he has not been libeled. To summarize, the substantial truth defense dismisses a libel claim because a statement is not false and, therefore, an element of the cause of action has not been met. Although the defense is concerned with truth, it appears to have been confused with the incremental harm doctrine because of the manner in which truth is determined. As then Judge Scalia indicated, a court looks to the "implication" of the statement (in his example, that the putative plaintiff "is an habitual burglar") and compares that "implication" to the truth. The confusion flows from the implication analysis.[22]

---

[20] *Id.* at 389, 391. *But see* Masson v. New Yorker Magazine, Inc., 960 F.2d 896, 898–99 (9th Cir. 1992) (noting that the Supreme Court has rejected the claim that the "incremental harm" doctrine has a constitutional foundation and California courts have shown no enthusiasm for the doctrine).

[21] 23 F. Supp. 2d at 393.

[22] *Id.* at 393–94. *But see* Parry v. Mohawk Motors of Michigan, Inc., 236 F.3d 299 (6th Cir. 2000):

> Here, Plaintiff contends that Defendant Mohawk's characterization of Plaintiff as "immediately disqualified," once Mohawk became aware of the circumstances surrounding his drug test, amounted to defamation. Specially, plaintiff points to Mohawk pulling his card from the wall of dispatchable drivers. Although it was probably more accurate to characterize Plaintiff's status as a "refusal to test," this Court nevertheless concludes that the statement does not constitute a "false" statement because in defending against a defamation action, it is sufficient for the defendant to show that "the imputation is substantially true, or as it is often put, to justify the 'gist,' the 'sting,' or the substantial truth of the defamation." Here, the "gist" of the statement was that Plaintiff had not properly taken the drug test. Therefore, the statement does not constitute a "false" statement and cannot rise to the level of defamation.

Id. at 312–13 (citation omitted), *cert. denied*, 533 U.S. 951 (2001); Haynes v. Alfred A. Knopf, Inc., 8 F.3d 1222, 1228 (7th Cir. 1993) (Easterbrook, J.) (stating that the substantial truth defense is "based on a recognition that falsehoods which do no incremental damage to the plaintiff's reputation do not injure the only interest that the law of defamation protects").

The court concluded that much of the story regarding Mr. Jewell was non-actionable because it was substantially true. The court could not conclude, however, as a matter of law that the actionable defamatory statements did not incrementally add reputational injury to that Mr. Jewell already sustained as a result of the non-actionable statements.[23]

[106.4] Reputation Damages Without Defamation Claim

A reputational injury claim may be embedded in other actions, such as fraud or trespass. The issue occasionally arises whether the fraud or trespass action may support a claim for reputational damages recovery without satisfying the pleading and proof requirements of the tort of defamation. This occurred in the case of *Food Lion, Inc. v. Capital Cities/American Broadcasting Co.* In *Food Lion* agents of the defendant misrepresented their status to secure employment by plaintiff as part of an undercover investigation of the plaintiff. The court permitted the plaintiff to assert claims of fraud and trespass relating to the false employment applications, but rejected the plaintiff's efforts to recover consequential damages based on injury to reputation, which were recoverable under a theory of defamation. As noted by the court:

> [T]he fact that Food Lion's claims are not barred by the First Amendment does not mean that Food Lion may recover all of the damages that it has allegedly suffered. In the amended complaint, Food Lion alleges that it suffered damages as a result of ABC's wrongful or illegal acts as well as damages to its reputation from the publication of Prime Time Live. [T]his Court finds that Food Lion may recover damages caused by ABC's alleged wrongful and illegal acts. However, this Court also finds that . . . the First Amendment bars Food Lion from recovering publication damages for injury to its reputation as a result of the Prime Time Live broadcast.

> Food Lion seeks to recover for injuries alleged to have been caused by ABC's Prime Time Live broadcast. These alleged injuries are both reputational and non-reputational in nature. According to Food Lion, these alleged injuries were the result of ABC's unlawful gathering of information and subsequent publication. Food Lion does not allege that any of the alleged unlawfully obtained and published information was false. Instead, Food Lion contends that ABC's alleged wrongful actions in obtaining information about Food Lion are sufficient to allow Food Lion to recover both reputational and non-reputational damages regardless of whether the information published by ABC was true or false. [T]he Court disagrees with this contention.[24]

---

[23] 23 F. Supp. 2d at 395.

[24] 887 F. Supp. 811, 822 (M.D.N.C. 1995) (footnote omitted), *aff'd*, 194 F.3d 505, 522–23 (4th Cir. 1999) (holding that if a plaintiff seeks "publication damages," the plaintiff must satisfy the *New York Times v. Sullivan* "actual malice" requirement).

Reputational injury is occasionally compensated in breach of contract actions.[25] Reputational injury may be compensated under several specific torts, such as malicious prosecution.[26]

§ 107 NON-REPUTATIONAL DAMAGES

Courts have split as to whether emotional distress damages may be recovered in a defamation action absent proof of injury to reputation.[1] The split turns on the proper construction of a pair of Supreme Court decisions. As noted in *Schlegel v. Ottumwa Courier*:

> Although *Gertz* required a private figure plaintiff to prove "actual injury," the Court did not expressly mandate that the actual injury be to reputation. Thus, *Gertz* did not constitutionally mandate that damages be based on injury to reputation. In fact, two years later, the Supreme Court in *Time, Inc. v. Firestone* allowed recovery in a defamation action simply on a showing of emotional distress damages . . . . Simply put, the Federal Constitution does not bar recovery for a defamation action based solely on emotional distress damages.[2]

The court noted that several other courts continue to require, post *Gertz* and *Firestone*, reputational injury as a prerequisite to maintaining a defamation action.

Notwithstanding the uncertainty whether non-reputational injury may satisfy the "actual injury" standard when the "actual injury" requirement is constitutionally imposed,[3] the courts are in general agreement that if reputational injury is established, the plaintiff may recover non-reputational losses associated with the defamation as long as those losses result from the defamation. These non-reputational losses include: (1) emotional distress damages;[4] (2) economic losses, such as lost profits or destruction of one's business, credit, or profession,[5] and punitive damages.[6]

---

[25] Section 140 (General Principles Concerning Contract Remedies). The recovery may, however, raise loss causation issues. Section 10.2.2 ([Loss Causation] Policy Considerations) (at text and notes 19–21 (discussing *Redgrave v. Boston Symphony Orchestra, Inc.*)).

[26] Section 112 (Litigation Torts).

[1] Schlegel v. Ottumwa Courier, 585 N.W.2d 217, 224 (Iowa 1998); *cf.* Kassel v. Gannet Co., Inc., 875 F.2d 935, 947–49 (1st Cir. 1989) (applying New Hampshire law) (noting difficulty in resolving the issue because of the tension between the common law and constitutional rules regarding defamation).

[2] 585 N.W.2d at 223, *citing* Gertz v. Robert Welch, Inc., 418 U.S. 323 (1974), Time, Inc. v. Firestone, 424 U.S. 448 (1976).

[3] Section 105 (Presumed Damages).

[4] *See, e.g.*, Lickteig v. Alderson, Ondov, Leonard & Sween, 556 N.W.2d 557, 560 (Minn. 1996); Rozanski v. Fitch, 494 N.Y.S.2d 576, 577 (App. Dept. 1985).

[5] Scribner v. Waffle House, Inc., 14 F. Supp. 2d 873, 935 (N.D. Tex. 1998); Vinson v. Linn-Mar Community Sch. Dist., 360 N.W.2d 108, 120 (Iowa 1984); Claise v. Bernardi, 413 N.E.2d 609, 611 (Ind. App. 1980) (stating that damages for injury to one's credit is ordinarily recoverable in action for defamation).

[6] Khawar v. Globe Int'l, Inc., 965 P.2d 696 (Cal. 1998):

First Amendment considerations may constrain the availability of punitive damages for defamation.[7]

Recovery of compensatory, non-reputational damages may be constrained by the requirement that the plaintiff establish a causal link between the loss and the defamation. In *Benassi v. Georgia-Pacific* the court found that while the plaintiff had been defamed by being falsely called "drunk and misbehaving" in connection with her termination from her employment, the evidence failed to show that her inability to obtain a new job for approximately 5½ months, and the resulting distress, was caused by the defamation. The termination itself was not actionable. There was no evidence that prospective employers plaintiff contacted, but who did not hire her, had heard the defamatory statements. Furthermore, the one prospective employer who did hear the statements hired plaintiff anyway.[8] The case is different if the plaintiff is terminated from his employment due to the defendant's defamatory statement. In this context, failure to secure new employment goes to mitigation, not to the actuality of the loss.[9]

Another example of the difficulty a plaintiff may face in attempting to establish economic loss due to a defamatory statement is *Terillo v. New York Newsday*.[10] In *Terillo* the plaintiff demonstrated that a review of plaintiff's restaurant was an actionable defamatory statement; nonetheless, the defendant prevailed because the plaintiff was unable to establish that the restaurant suffered any loss of business as a result of the review. The plaintiff did allege that a particular patron no longer patronized the establishment, but the court found this proof to be inadequate.[11] The plaintiff could still recover "presumed damages."[12]

Having independently reviewed the record, we agree with the Court of Appeal that the evidence at trial strongly supports an inference that Globe purposefully avoided the truth and published the Globe article despite serious doubts regarding the truth of the accusation against Khawar. In short, we conclude that clear and convincing evidence supports the jury's finding that in republishing the Morrow book's false accusation against Khawar, Globe acted with actual malice—that is, with reckless disregard of whether the accusation was false or not.

965 P.2d at 712 (affirming the award of punitive damages).

[7] *Compare* Gertz, *supra* (holding that the First Amendment bars an award of punitive damages for false and defamatory statements unless the plaintiff shows "actual" malice), *with* Dun & Bradstreet, *supra* (holding that the First Amendment does not bar the awarding of punitive damages for false and defamatory statements absent a showing of "actual" malice when the statements do not involve matters of public concern).

[8] 662 P.2d 760, 766 (Or. App. 1983).

[9] Tosti v. Ayik, 508 N.E.2d 1368, 1370 (Mass.), *cert. denied sub nom.* UAW Local 422 v. Tosti, 484 U.S. 964 (1987).

[10] 519 N.Y.S.2d 914 (Civ. Ct. 1987).

[11] *Cf.* Aycock v. Padgett, 516 S.E.2d 907, 910 (N.C. App. 1999) (holding that plaintiff-candidate for elective office could not claim "loss of election" damages for defamation that he contended resulted in his defeat); *see* Southwestern Publishing Co. v. Horsey, 230 F.2d 319, 322 (9th Cir. 1956) (rejecting evidence of different results in two elections as proof that defamation caused plaintiff's defeat for elective office).

[12] Section 105 (Presumed Damages).

§ 108   ENJOINING A LIBEL

The availability of injunctive relief in this area is closely tied to the doctrine of prior restraints, which is discussed at Section 28 (Injunctions and Prior Restraints).

Even if a court does not apply the "prior restraints" doctrine to statements adjudicated to be actionable and defamatory, the plaintiff must demonstrate that injunctive relief is appropriate under the particular circumstances of the case. In this regard, the court still may follow the traditional rule that equity does not enjoin a libel.[1] The traditional rule continues to be applied in the United States despite the fact that England, the place of equity's origin and the source of the maxim, does not enforce the maxim with the rigor seen in American decisions.[2]

A party seeking a contempt citation for a violation of an order enjoining a libel bears a heavy burden of persuasion that the citation should issue.[3]

§ 109   DISPARAGEMENT

Defamation law exists primarily to protect the reputation of persons; disparagement law exists to protect the economic interests of a person when that person's trade or product is falsely maligned by the defendant.[1] The differences between defamation and disparagement (injurious falsehoods) were outlined in *Hurlbut v. Gulf Atlantic Life Ins. Co.*:

> More stringent requirements have always been imposed on the "plaintiff seeking to recover for injurious falsehood in three important respects—falsity of the statement, fault of the defendant and proof of damage." Regarding falsity, the common law presumed the defamatory statement to be false and truth was a defensive matter. The plaintiff in a business disparagement claim, however, must plead and prove the falsity of the statement as part of his cause of action. Regarding fault, the defendant in a defamation action was

---

[1] Hammer v. Trendl, 2002 U.S. Dist. LEXIS 25487 (E.D.N.Y., Oct. 10, 2002) (unpublished) (holding that damages were adequate remedy for alleged defamation rendering injunction unnecessary); Kisser v. Coalition For Religious Freedom, 1996 U.S. Dist. LEXIS 3906 (N.D. Ill., Mar. 29, 1996) (unpublished) (granting summary judgment for defendant on plaintiff's claim for an injunction against further publication of allegedly defamatory materials). The court cited the "rule" that equity will not enjoin a libel as the principle basis for the decision.

[2] Barres v. Holt, Rinehart and Winston, Inc., 378 A.2d 1148, 1150 (N.J. 1977) (Schreiber, J., dissenting):

> A more serious concern involves equity's refusal to enjoin publication of writings in advance because of infringement of freedom of the press. But this fear of censorship does not exist when a libel has been clearly established. Accordingly, the English courts have granted injunctions freely in that context. In England the use of even an interlocutory injunction has been sanctioned where the libel is clear.

(citations omitted); *see* Roscoe Pound, *Equitable Relief Against Defamation and Injuries to Personality*, 29 Harv. L. Rev. 640 (1916) (discussing English authorities).

[3] Lawrence-Leiter and Co. v. Paulson, 963 F. Supp. 1061, 1067 (D. Kan. 1997).

[1] McCarthy on Trademarks and Unfair Competition § 27:111 (4th ed. 2004).

held strictly liable for his false statement whereas the defendant in an action for business disparagement or injurious falsehood is subject to liability "only if he knew of the falsity or acted with reckless disregard concerning it, or if he acted with ill will or intended to interfere in the economic interest of the plaintiff in an unprivileged fashion." Finally, regarding damages, the common law required plaintiff in a defamation action to prove special damages in only a limited number of situations, whereas pecuniary loss to the plaintiff must always be proved to establish a cause of action for business disparagement.[2]

The critical issue here is the "special damages" requirement. The plaintiff must show "pecuniary loss directly attributable to the defendant's false statements."[3] Pecuniary loss is usually shown by evidence of loss of "specific sales," although many courts permit a plaintiff to establish the loss by evidence that sales after publication of the falsehoods were less than sales prior to the publication of the falsehoods regarding the product or trade.[4] Courts have generally rejected efforts to satisfy the pecuniary loss requirement by arguments that the business did not grow as fast as it would have had defendant not uttered the injurious falsehoods or that plaintiff had to devote resources to negate defendant's falsehoods.[5] The Restatement (Second) of Torts takes the position that the pecuniary loss requirement is satisfied when plaintiff incurs attorney's fees in prosecuting litigation to redress its good name,[6] but that view has not found favor with the courts.[7] The Restatement approach is inconsistent with the special damage requirement. If costs incurred in proving that defendant committed a tort could satisfy an essential element of the tort, essentiality is compromised. The tort must necessarily exist independent of plaintiff's efforts to prove the tort:

> Plaintiff cannot create a cause of action in disparagement through his own conduct where defendant has otherwise failed to provide him with one.[8]

---

[2] 749 S.W.2d 762, 766 (Tex. 1987) (citations omitted).

[3] Advanced Training Systems Inc. v. Caswell Equipment Co., Inc., 352 N.W.2d 1, 7 (Minn. 1984).

[4] Id. at 8.

[5] Id.

[6] Restatement (Second) of Torts § 623(b) (1976).

[7] See C.P. Interests Inc. v. California Pools, Inc., 238 F.3d 693, 695–96 (5th Cir. 2001) (predicting Texas law). supra, 352 N.W.2d at 8

[8] Advanced Training Systems, Inc., supra, 352 N.W.2d at 8. Attorney's fees might also be recoverable under a mitigation theory (Section 13.7 (Compensation for Mitigation Effort)), but this approach also assumes an actionable claim. Advanced Training Systems, Inc., id (rejecting claim that plaintiff's efforts to ameliorate defendant's false statements about plaintiff's product should be recoverable as mitigation damages). But see CUNA Mutual Life Ins. Co. v. Los Angeles County Metropolitan Transportation Auth., 133 Cal. Rptr. 2d 470 (Cal. App. 2003) (allowing recovery of mitigation expense to prevent harm that did not occur).

If the defendant's tortious misconduct *requires* the plaintiff to incur attorney's fees, those fees may be recoverable "as damages" flowing from the tortious conduct,[9] but that is different from treating the incurring of attorney's fees as satisfying an "actual injury" requirement that is part of the prima facie claim.

Disparagement claims will also support injunctive relief;[10] however, disparagement, like defamation, is subject to First Amendment constraints.[11] For example, in *Hajek v. Bill Mowbray Motors, Inc.* an automobile dealership obtained an injunction prohibiting a customer from driving a vehicle purchased from the dealership with the message painted on the vehicle that the dealership sold the customer a "lemon." The Texas Supreme Court overturned the injunction on state and federal constitutional grounds as an invalid prior restraint.[12]

---

[9] Section 211.4 ([Attorney's Fees] Third Part Tort).

[10] Carter v. Knapp Motor Co., Inc., 11 So. 2d 383, 385–86 (Ala. 1943); Menard v. Houle, 11 N.E.2d 436, 437 (Mass. 1937).

[11] Unelko Corp. v. Rooney, 912 F.2d 1049, 1058 (9th Cir. 1990) (involving disparagement claim brought against 60 Minutes correspondent Andy Rooney for critical comments regarding plaintiff's product, such as, "it didn't work").

[12] 647 S.W.2d 253, 255 (Tex. 1983); *see* J.Q. Office Equipment of Omaha, Inc. v. Sullivan, 432 N.W.2d 211, 213–14 (Neb. 1988) (same).

Chapter 13

REMEDIES FOR INJURY TO PERSONAL RIGHTS

SYNOPSIS

§ 110 PRIVACY

The right to privacy is of relatively recent vintage, tracing its genesis to an 1890 law review article by Louis Brandeis and Samuel Warren.[1] Yet, within 100 years the right has been widely adopted within the United States as common law[2] and as a statutory[3] and constitutionally protected interest.[4]

---

[1] *The Right to Privacy*, 4 Harv. L. Rev. 193 (1890). Privacy had pre-1890 antecedents. It was the central insight of the Brandeis-Warren article to collect and organize these antecedents into the right we now commonly call "privacy."

[2] Most jurisdictions recognize one or more of the four forms of action judicially created to protect privacy: (1) intrusion upon the plaintiff's physical solitude or reclusion; (2) promulgation of publicity concerning the plaintiff that violates ordinary decency; (3) placing the plaintiff in a false but not necessarily defamatory position in the public eye; or (4) appropriation of some element of the plaintiff's personality for a commercial use. Phillips v. Smalley Maintenance Servs., Inc., 435 So. 2d 705, 708 (Ala. 1983); Restatement (Second) of Torts §§ 652B (1977) (defining privacy action for intrusion), 652C (defining privacy action for misappropriation/publicity), 652D (defining privacy action for disclosure of private facts), 652E (defining privacy action for false light).

[3] Privacy Act, 5 U.S.C. § 552a (restricting the collection of data and records of individuals by the federal government); Federal Fair Credit Reporting Act, 15 U.S.C. § 1681 (restricting the use and dissemination of the credit history of individuals); Omnibus Crime Control and Safe Streets Act, 18 U.S.C. § 2511 (restricting use of eavesdropping or electronic methods of communication). The statutory remedy may be the exclusive remedy. Howell v. New York Post Co., 612 N.E.2d 699, 703–04 (N.Y. 1993) (noting that in New York actions for invasion of privacy are governed solely by sections of the civil rights laws prohibiting the use of a person's name, portrait, or picture for advertising or trade purposes without that person's consent).

[4] Roe v. Wade, 410 U.S. 113, 152 (1973) (holding that federal constitutional guarantees include a right of personal privacy); Hill v. National Collegiate Athletic Ass'n, 865 P.2d 633, 641–44 (Cal. 1994) (noting that California state constitution contains an express guarantee of the right of privacy, which the court held was applicable to non-governmental entities). The *Hill* court held, however, that the substance of the state constitutional right was no greater than that provided by the Fourth Amendment. *id.* at 650 n.9.

Notwithstanding the explosive growth of the right to privacy in the 100 years since the Brandeis-Warren article, the development of the privacy right remains muted and confused by conflicting goals and objectives. Recognizing one person's right to privacy is often seen as constraining another person's freedom to act[5] or need to know.[6] These conflicting goals, coupled with the fact that the right to privacy is valued subjectively and usually results in non-economic losses, has generated some uncertainty and imprecision in the creation of remedies to vindicate the privacy interest.

An example of this uncertainty is seen in the progress of an action brought against the United States by individuals claiming that their mail had been illegally intercepted and read by agents of the United States government before their mail was delivered.[7] The trial judge impaneled an advisory jury to assist in the valuation of the claims.[8] The trial judge commented on the recommendations of the advisory panel as follows:

> It was, nevertheless, instructive that this panel of average citizens—representing a broad range of economic, educational, social and political experience—uniformly found that the damages suffered by the plaintiffs in this case were substantial. Although the jurors were instructed that they could recommend nominal damages of one dollar if they found that the wrong done resulted only in slight harm, none chose this alternative. Three suggested that plaintiffs be awarded $10,000 each for their mental distress and for the encroachment upon their personal liberty; one suggested $2500; and the other eight jurors all agreed that $5000 was the compensation needed to make these plaintiffs whole.[9]

Nonetheless, the court deemed the advice unpersuasive[10] and awarded compensatory damages of $1,000 for mental anguish coupled with a

---

[5] Tyler v. Berodt, 877 F.2d 705 (8th Cir. 1989) (holding that a caller had no reasonable expectation of privacy when making a telephone call over a cordless telephone), *cert. denied*, 493 U.S. 1022 (1990). *Tyler* was decided under federal law, which has changed so that *Tyler* is no longer good law. *See* Electronic Communications Privacy Act, *infra*. Protection may be available under state law. State v. Faford, 910 P.2d 447, 452 (Wash. 1996) (holding that eavesdropping in on a cordless phone call violated state privacy law).

Privacy rights are often determined by reference to a growing body of statutory law. *See, e.g.*, 18 U.S.C. § 2510 (1), (12) (as amended 1994) (included cordless and cellular transmissions as protected communications under the Electronic Communications Privacy Act); Health Insurance Portability and Accountability Act of 1996, 42 U.S.C. § 210 (providing, effective April 2003, extensive privacy protection for medical records and information). There is an interesting paper exploring statutory approaches to privacy. James P. Nehf, *Incomparability and the Passive Virtues of Ad Hoc Privacy Policy*, 76 U. Colo. L. Rev. 1 (2005).

[6] Privacy Act, 5 U.S.C. § 552a (b)(1) (recognizing a "need to know" exception to protections guaranteed by the Act); *Howell*, *supra*, 612 N.E.2d at 705 (discussing the newsworthiness exception to New York's statutory privacy action).

[7] Birnbaum v. United States, 588 F.2d 319 (2d Cir. 1978), *modifying*, 436 F. Supp. 967 (E.D.N.Y. 1977).

[8] The action was brought under the Federal Torts Claims Act, 28 U.S.C. § 2402, under which no right to jury trial attaches.

[9] *Birnbaum*, *supra*, 436 F. Supp. at 988.

[10] This, of course, was within the court's prerogative, although the court did give the

mandatory letter of apology.[11] The Court of Appeal, in turn, directed that the court-ordered apology be stricken because the Federal Tort Claims Act only authorized monetary damages.[12] The Court of Appeal expressed reservation over the size of the compensatory damages award because, according to the court, had the plaintiffs not pursued the matter and confirmed the fact that their mail was being illegally opened by the CIA, they would not have sustained mental anguish in the first place.[13] Moreover, because the mail was going and coming from the former Soviet Union, the court held that the plaintiffs should have expected their mail would be opened somewhere along the route.[14] Nonetheless, the court reluctantly affirmed the award of $1,000 for compensatory damages as within the trial court's discretion:

> The District Court did find, however, that "the emotional distress these plaintiffs suffered was the sort that would be experienced by reasonable people under the almost unprecedented circumstances of these cases." Though we could view this finding as one merely of damage presumed from the circumstances, worth only the nominal sum of one dollar, we interpret the finding more generously as determining that these plaintiffs, whose demeanor the trial judge observed, actually suffered personal anguish. We give "due regard . . . to the opportunity of the trial court to judge of the credibility of the witnesses." Though the question of damages is close, we affirm the money judgments for $1,000 each, with the feeling that they represent the upper limit of allowable compensation in these cases.[15]

The differences exhibited between the advisory jury, trial judge, and appellate panel over the proper compensation for the wrong done to the *Birnbaum* plaintiffs well illustrates the difficulties inherent in attempting to identify the proper measure of damages in these cases. The issue may be further complicated by statutory constraints on the remedies available. For example, the Federal Privacy Act[16] permits the recovery of "actual damages" against the United States for violations of privacy by federal officials. Does "actual damages" include distress damages? Some courts

---

advisory panel less deference than appears to be the norm. Firemen's Ins. Co. v. Smith, 83 F. Supp. 668, 671 (W.D. Mo. 1949) (stating that recommendations of the advisory jury should be followed as long as they are supported by the evidence), *aff'd*, 180 F.2d 371 (8th Cir.), *cert. denied*, 339 U.S. 980 (1950). State practice is similar. Smith v. Williams, 575 S.W.2d 503, 506 (Tenn. App. 1978) (stating that recommendations of the advisory panel are entitled to "great weight"). *But see* Jacob's Banking Co. v. Campbell, 406 So. 2d 834, 848 (Ala. 1981) (stating that the recommendations of the advisory panel serve merely to enlighten the court and may be accepted or rejected at the court's discretion).

[11] *Birnbaum, supra,* 436 F. Supp. at 989.

[12] *Birnbaum, supra,* 588 F.2d at 335.

[13] *Id.* at 334. Apparently, for the Court of Appeal, "ignorance is bliss."

[14] *Id.*

[15] *Id.* at 334–35.

[16] 5 U.S.C. § 552a.

have held that it does not, reasoning that waivers of sovereign immunity should be narrowly construed.[17] Other courts, however, reason that distress damages should be allowed on the ground that remedial statutes should be broadly construed.[18] The point has enhanced significance today in light of the Court's decision in *Doe v. Chao*,[19] which required a plaintiff claiming a violation of the Federal Privacy Act demonstrate "actual injury" *before* the plaintiff can recover statutory damages.[20] A proof of actual damages is more likely to be satisfied if the plaintiff can claim distress injury resulting from the statutory violation than if the plaintiff must show economic loss.[21]

The availability of a damages award for invasion of privacy may be constrained by the same First Amendment concerns[22] that have dominated the law of defamation for the past 40 years since *New York Times v. Sullivan* was decided.[23] The difficulty here is that the extent to which an "actual malice" requirement, derived from *New York Times v. Sullivan*, applies to privacy torts is complicated by the various forms a privacy action can take. Some forms, e.g., "false light," are very close to defamation; others, e.g., intrusion, are not but may implicate "newsgathering" interests of the media and the public.[24]

The right to privacy may be protected by equitable relief. Perhaps the most notable case in this area involved Jacqueline Onassis, the former wife of President John F. Kennedy. Mrs. Onassis obtained an injunction against a press photographer, Mr. Gallela, limiting Mr. Gallela's access to Mrs. Onassis and her children. The difficulty in this area of fashioning injunctive relief is demonstrated by the Onassis-Gallela dispute. The courts had little difficulty finding that Mr. Gallela's activities constituted the hounding and harassment of Mrs. Onassis.[25] There was real difficulty, however, in

---

[17] Hudson v. Reno, 130 F.3d 1193, 1207 (6th Cir. 1997), *cert. denied*, 525 U.S. 822 (1998).

[18] Romero-Vargas v. Shalala, 907 F. Supp. 1128, 1134 (N.D. Ohio 1995).

[19] 540 U.S. 614 (2004).

[20] *Id.* at 620.

[21] The Court did not address whether "distress" would satisfy the "actual damages" requirement. The Court did allude to equating "actual damages" to "actual, quantifiable pecuniary loss," 540 U.S. at 615, but the point was raised in rejecting an argument proposed by plaintiff that an actual damages requirement should not be read into the statute, not that "actual damages" required pecuniary loss. *See generally* Brian Sheppard, Annot., *Award of Damages Under Privacy Act, 5 U.S.C. § 552A*, 189 A.L.R. Fed. 455 § 5 (2003) (collecting decisions holding that distress injury satisfies the "actual damages" requirement of the Privacy Act).

[22] Cox Broadcasting Corp. v. Cohn, 420 U.S. 469 (1975); Reader's Digest Ass'n v. Superior Court, 690 P.2d 610, 624 (Cal. 1984) (stating that "constitutional protection does not depend on the label given the stated cause of action; it bars not only actions for defamation, but also claims for invasion of privacy") (citation omitted), *cert. denied*, 478 U.S. 1009 (1986), *overruled on other grounds*, Gates v. Discovery Communications, Inc. 101 P.3d 552 (Cal. 2004); Section 105 (Presumed Damages).

[23] 376 U.S. 254 (1964).

[24] *See* 2 SMOLLA & NIMMER ON FREEDOM OF SPEECH § 24:5 (discussing application of First Amendment to privacy actions).

[25] Gallela v. Onassis, 487 F.2d 986, 994 (2d Cir. 1973), *modifying and affirming* 353 F. Supp. 196 (S.D.N.Y. 1972) .

drafting an order that respected Mrs. Onassis' and her children's right to privacy without unnecessarily infringing on Mr. Gallela's constitutional rights of speech, association, and travel. Ultimately, the appellate court substantially redrew (downwards) the geographic constraints imposed upon Mr. Gallela. The court reduced from 100 yards to 25 feet the distance Gallela was required to stay away from Mrs. Onassis.[26] The court generally upheld the constraints precluding Gallela from touching Mrs. Onassis, blocking her movement in public, or engaging in any act that might foreseeably or reasonably harm or frighten Mrs. Onassis.[27] Slightly more extensive constraints were placed on Mr. Gallela insofar as the children were concerned, but still less than imposed by the trial court. For example, the court reduced from 50 yards to 30 feet the distance Mr. Gallela was to keep away from the children and otherwise prohibited Mr. Gallela from entering the children's school or play area or engaging in conduct reasonably foreseen as placing the children's safety or well being in jeopardy or causing them to be frightened or alarmed.[28] It is unclear whether the change in tense from foreseeable (Onassis) to foreseen (children) was intended.

While injunctive relief is occasionally provided in this context,[29] the overarching First Amendment interests often hampers providing that remedy. The public interest in the subject to which a claim of privacy is asserted[30] makes equitable relief questionable because equitable relief is often deemed a "prior restraint."[31] This concept has been specifically applied to privacy claims. In *Berger v. Hanlon* the plaintiffs sought to enjoin the media from broadcasting the filming of a search conducted by law enforcement officials. The search was found to violate the plaintiffs' reasonable expectation of privacy; nonetheless, the injunction was refused as an invalid prior restraint.[32] The action proceeded, however, as a damages claim against the media defendants.[33]

---

[26] 487 F.2d at 993, 998.

[27] *Id.*

[28] *Id.* at 993, 999.

[29] Wolfson v. Lewis, 924 F. Supp. 1413, 1420, 1434–35 (E.D. Pa. 1996) (issuing a preliminary injunction barring the defendants, who worked for the television program "Inside Edition," from engaging in conduct that constituted harassment of the plaintiffs); Ali v. Playgirl, Inc., 447 F. Supp. 723 (S.D.N.Y. 1978) (enjoining an unauthorized publication of a nude portrait of the plaintiff).

[30] Time Inc. v. Hill, 385 U.S. 374, 387–88 (1967) (applying the *"New York Times v. Sullivan"* doctrine to false light invasion of privacy claims). *But cf. Briscoe v. Reader's Digest, supra* 483 P.2d at 43–44 (finding that an invasion of privacy claim for disclosing the plaintiff's prior criminal conviction was not barred by the *New York Times v. Sullivan* doctrine because the plaintiff was a private figure and the matter was not "newsworthy"); *see* text and notes 22–24, *supra.*

[31] Section 28 (Injunctions and Prior Restraints).

[32] 129 F.3d 505, 518 (9th Cir. 1997), *rev'd on other grounds,* 526 U.S. 808 (1999) (holding that damages claim could not be stated against government agents because they had "qualified immunity").

[33] Berger v. Hanlon, 188 F.3d 1155 (9th Cir. 1999) (on remand) (holding that private actors (media) were not entitled to qualified immunity afforded governmental actors).

A claim of invasion of privacy may support a claim for punitive damages.[34] As in the defamation context, the recovery of punitive damages may be substantially constrained when the privacy claim implicates constitutional values enshrined in the *New York Times v. Sullivan* doctrine.[35] A prevailing plaintiff may also recover attorney's fees in many cases involving a statutory privacy right.[36] Whether an award of fees to the prevailing party is mandatory or permissive depends on the language of the statute.[37] The statutory privacy action may contain its own statutory damages remedy. In that case, a court may refuse to permit both statutory and punitive damages to the extent it views the statutory damages remedy as essentially punitive.[38]

A court may also have discretion whether to award statutory damages for privacy violations, as, for example, when the violation was in good faith.[39]

There is no prohibition against use of the remedy of restitution upon finding that the defendant was unjustly enriched by the invasion of plaintiff's privacy,[40] although here, as elsewhere, the line between enrichment and damages is sometimes muddled.[41] As a practical matter, however, the restitution remedy has been limited to the misappropriation prong of the invasion of privacy tort.

---

[34] Bakker v. McKinnon, 152 F.3d 1007, 1013 (8th Cir. 1998). Punitive damages may also be authorized by statute. Minn. Stat. § 7.69(5) (authorizing an award of punitive damages for the violation of consumer privacy).

[35] Cantrell v. Forest City Publ'g, 419 U.S. 245, 251–52 (1974) (involving a false-light invasion of privacy claim).

[36] Chapter 24 (Attorney's Fees).

[37] *Compare* Reynolds v. Spears, 93 F.3d 428, 436 (8th Cir. 1996) (holding that court has discretion whether to award fees to prevailing party in federal wiretapping litigation (18 U.S.C. § 2511(1)(C)), *with* Abraham v. County of Greenville, S.C., 237 F.3d 386, 393 (4th Cir. 2001) (holding that the award of fees is mandatory).

[38] Clauson v. Superior Court, 79 Cal. Rptr. 2d 747, 749 (Cal. App. 1998) (permitting the plaintiff to claim punitive damages for both invasion of privacy (common law) and statutory damages for illegal wiretapping and eavesdropping (statutory), but noting that the plaintiff would be allowed only one recovery).

[39] *Compare Reynolds, supra*, 93 F.3d at 436 (holding court had discretion not to award statutory damage for violation of federal wiretapping statute when defendant had good faith belief in legality of conduct based on discussion with law enforcement officer that defendant could tap business phones used by employees), *with* Rodgers v. Wood, 910 F.2d 444, 448 (7th Cir. 1990) (contra).

[40] Section 40 (Restitution); *see* Wis. Stat. Ann. § 895.50 (stating that one whose privacy is unreasonably invaded is entitled to recovery damages or defendant's unjust enrichment).

[41] Cheatham v. Paisano Publications, Inc., 891 F. Supp. 381, 387 n.7 (W.D. Ky. 1995):

> Plaintiff also has asserted a claim for unjust enrichment. However, unjust enrichment in this circumstance merely forms a measure of damages in a right of publicity claim. It is not a separate cause of action. These damages stem from the theory that a defendant should not get for free that which has market value to the plaintiff and for which the defendant would normally have to pay. If Plaintiff is able to show she is entitled to damages, a part of any profits derived from T-shirt sales could be justified as unjust enrichment of Defendants' use of her image.

(citations omitted).

One of the ironies of the protection of privacy is that it probably finds its most frequent application in the protection of the individual's right to exploit himself, i.e., his right to publicity.[42] Because publicity entails profit, an aggrieved plaintiff may seek the defendant's profit through unjust enrichment.[43] The capturing of the defendant's profit as a remedy, however, is distinct from the requirement that the plaintiff demonstrate, in the misappropriation form of the privacy action, that the defendant appropriated to its own use or benefit the reputation, likeness, social standing, or other value of the plaintiff.[44]

The remedy of restitution could possibly be used in the developing "newsgathering tort" based on the profits from advertising revenue the defendant received.[45] So far there are no reported cases that such has been attempted. Perhaps this is due to the court's concerns over its ability to identify, segregate, and allocate the portion of profit attributable to the improper conduct from the total gross profit realized by the complete project.[46]

§ 111   CIVIL RIGHTS/CONSTITUTIONAL TORTS

Actions for civil rights violations/constitutional torts have grown exponentially over the past several decades. This growth has been driven by several factors. First, courts have generously interpreted federal and state constitutions as providing rights of action on behalf of aggrieved persons for redress of constitutional violations.[1] Second, the federal and state governments have enacted a plethora of statutes that operate to provide rights of action for all manner of civil rights violations.[2] By and large, both

---

[42] Crump v. Beckley Newspapers, Inc., 320 S.E.2d 70, 82–83 (W. Va. 1983) (discussing the "publicity" prong of right to privacy).

[43] Zacchini v. Scripps-Howard Broadcasting Co., 433 U.S. 562, 573 (1977) (noting that the publicity interest protected by the privacy action is closely akin to the goal of patent and copyright law that focuses on the right of the individual to reap the reward of his endeavors).

[44] Staruski v. Continental Telephone Co. of Vermont, 581 A.2d 266, 269 (Vt. 1990), *citing*, Restatement (Second) of Torts § 652C.

[45] *See* Nathan Siegel, *Publication Damages in Newsgathering Cases*, 19-Sum Communication Lawyer 11 (2001) (discussing decisions awarding economic and non-economic damages for newsgathering claims).

[46] Section 46 (Apportionment of Benefit). *But cf.* Hetter v. Eighth Judicial Dist. Court, County of Clark, 874 P.2d 762, 765 (Nev. 1994) (distinguishing between privacy and publicity prongs of invasion of privacy tort and noting that as to publicity prong, recovery is controlled by statutory remedies that preclude an action for restitution).

[1] Bivens v. Six Unknown Named Agents of Federal Bureau of Narcotics, 403 U.S. 388 (1971) (permitting private persons to sue federal officials and employees for violation of certain federal constitutional guarantees).

[2] *E.g.*, Voting Rights Act, 42 U.S.C. § 1973 *et seq.* (providing legal redress to banish racial discrimination that dilutes the right to vote); Federal Civil Rights Act, 42 U.S.C. § 1983 (permitting private persons to sue state officials and employees, and others acting under color of state law, for violation of federal constitutional and statutory guarantees); Section 3.3 (Statutory Remedies).

the constitutional and statutory actions provide for damages and injunctive relief.

The hallmark of constitutional tort litigation is the "actual damage" requirement. The Supreme Court has generally rejected the extension of the presumed damages rule to constitutional tort/civil rights litigation; rather, it has required that the plaintiff seeking redress in the form of damages for constitutional violations demonstrate that the violation resulted in the plaintiff's "actual injury."[3] The Court has not categorically ruled out presumed damages in all constitutional tort cases. It left open in *Stachura* the possibility that presumed damages could be awarded when the constitutional violation likely caused actual damage to the plaintiff, but the injury is "difficult to establish."[4] The one accepted exception to this actual damage requirement is in the context of denial of the right to vote. This exception dates from English practice, recognized in *Ashby v. White*,[5] in which the House of Lords reinstated an award of 200 pounds and held that the refusal of a voting official to permit a voter to exercise his franchise was actionable without proof of actual injury.

Some courts have read this exception narrowly. For example, in *Santana v. Registrar of Voters of Worcester*,[6] the court suggested that the federal right to vote decisions allowing presumed damages should be limited to their historical context of the discriminatory denial of the right to vote based on race. *Stachura*, however, broadly affirmed the federal voting rights precedents; it did not limit them.[7] Presumed damages awards for denial of the right to vote have not been insubstantial, but neither have they been overly generous.[8]

The post-*Stachura* decisional law has been split. Some courts have been hostile to the suggestion that presumed damages, outside the voting rights context, survive *Stachura*,[9] other courts see *Stachura* as leaving some room

---

[3] Memphis Community Sch. Dist. v. Stachura, 477 U.S. 299, 310 (1986); Section 105 (Presumed Damages).

[4] *Id.* at 311; *see* Jean Love, *Presumed General Compensatory Damages in Constitutional Tort Litigation: A Corrective Justice Perspective*, 49 Wash. & Lee L. Rev. 67 (1992) (arguing that *Stachura* left room for the award of presumed damages in some contexts of constitutional tort litigation).

[5] 1 Bro. Parl. Cas. 62, 1 Eng. Rep. 417 (H.L. 1704).

[6] 502 N.E.2d 132, 136 (Mass. 1986).

[7] *Stachura, supra*, 477 U.S. at 312, n.14.

[8] *Compare* Wayne v. Venable, 260 Fed. 64 (8th Cir. 1919) (affirming award of $2000 for denial of right to vote as not excessive), *with* Taylor v. Howe, 280 F.3d 1210 (8th Cir. 2002) (affirming awards of $500 to $2000 to various plaintiffs for denial of right to vote as not inadequate). According to The Inflation Calculator (*www.westegg.com / inflation /*), what would cost $2,000 in 1919 would cost $23,044.62 in 2003; conversely, what would cost $2,000 in 2003, would have cost $173.58 in 1919.

[9] Schneider v. Colegio de Abogados de Puerto Rico, 917 F.2d 620, 639 (1st Cir. 1990) (allowing only nominal damages award for the violation of First Amendment guarantees when the plaintiff offered no proof of actual injury), *cert. denied*, 502 U.S. 1029 (1992); Spence v. Board of Educ. of Christina Sch. Dist., 806 F.2d 1198, 1200 (3d Cir. 1986) (refusing to presume distress damages from violation of First Amendment constitutional right).

for presumed damages. [10] Perhaps presumed damages may be available as a "surrogate" for actual damages when there is evidence that the plaintiff suffered an actual injury resulting from the constitutional violation, but the difficulty lies in the ability to measure the scope and extent of the injury. [11] A similar approach has been taken with respect to nominal damages awards, [12] particularly when used to support an award of attorney's fees. [13]

The "actual damage" requirement means that the damages award must be designed to compensate the plaintiff for the harm resulting from the violation of the constitutional right. [14] The intrinsic value of the constitutional right may not be factored into the award. [15] This refusal to allow damages based on the intrinsic, inherent value of the constitutional right should not be taken as an expression of judicial reluctance to use damages awards to vindicate constitutional violations. As noted by the Court:

> [C]ompensatory damages may include not only out-of-pocket loss and other monetary harms, but also such injuries as "impairment of reputation . . . personal humiliation, and mental anguish and suffering." [16]

The calculation of compensatory damages in the constitutional/civil rights context is determined in accordance with the principles derived from the common law of torts. [17] Moreover, because compensatory damages in this area often involve non-economic harms, such as mental anguish and distress, substantial deference is given to the award made by the trier-of-fact. [18] The Court has rejected awarding damages based on the abstract value of the constitutional right, [19] but the question of "abstractness" has not been resolved. Lower courts have affirmed awards based on the

---

[10] Kerman v. City of New York, 374 F.3d 93, 129–30 (2d Cir. 2004) (affirming award of damages for loss of liberty attendant to illegal search and distinguishing *Stachura* as involving abstract rather than concrete injury); Hessel v. O'Hearn, 977 F.2d 299, 301–02 (7th Cir. 1992) (Posner, J.) (suggesting that *Stachura* may not bar presumed damages for 4th Amendment violations).

[11] Pembaur v. City of Cincinnati, 882 F.2d 1101, 1104 (6th Cir. 1989) (holding, post-*Stachura*, that "presumed damages may be appropriate" when they "approximate the harm that the plaintiff suffered and thereby compensate for harms that may be impossible to measure").

[12] Briggs v. Marshall, 93 F.3d 355, 360 (7th Cir. 1996) (noting different variants of nominal damages awards); Section 2.8 (Nominal Damages).

[13] Mercer v. Duke University, 401 F.3d 199, 204 (4th Cir. 2005); Section 213.2.2 (Actual Damages Award As Limit on Fees Award).

[14] *Stachura, supra*, 477 U.S. at 306–07.

[15] *Id.* at 308.

[16] *Id.* at 307, *quoting* Gertz v. Robert Welch, Inc., 418 U.S. 323, 350 (1974).

[17] *Stachura, supra*, 477 U.S. at 305.

[18] Section 12.2.2 ([Non-economic Damages] Discretion of the Decision Maker).

[19] *Stachura, supra*, 477 U.S. at 308–10 (concluding that it is improper to award compensatory damages based on the subjective appreciation of the abstract value of the constitutional right at issue).

generalized, but identifiable, consequences to the plaintiff of the constitutional violation. For example, in *City of Watseka v. Illinois Public Action Council* a political action committee had its First Amendment rights infringed by an anti-soliciting ordinance that limited door-to-door soliciting to the hours between 9:00 a.m. to 5:00 p.m. The court held that the committee could recover not only its lost revenue resulting from the restrictions on door-to-door soliciting, but that the committee could also recover the harm it suffered as a result of being prevented from exercising its First Amendment rights. These "harms" were identified as: (1) the inability to recruit new members; (2) the inability to disseminate its views; and (3) the inability to encourage others to support the committee's positions.[20] There seems to be little more to the identification of the "harm" than a fleshing out of the abstract value of the right in the context of its exercise. Nonetheless, such an approach may better register with the court as some form of "actual injury" required to sustain an award of compensatory damages.[21]

Compensatory awards for violations of a plaintiff's constitutional or civil rights must be linked to the interest protected. For example,[22] assume the plaintiff is required to submit to drug testing as a condition of continued employment with a municipal entity. Assume further that the plaintiff is in a non-safety sensitive position and that a court would find the required testing constitutionally deficient for that reason.[23] Assume finally that the plaintiff submits to the test, tests positive, and is discharged pursuant to a hearing during which the positive test result is used as evidence against him. May the plaintiff recover his lost wages if it is determined that the required drug testing was constitutionally deficient? The answer may well turn on why the drug testing program was constitutionally deficient. If the claim is that the required testing constituted an illegal search and seizure in violation of the Fourth Amendment, the answer may be that the lost wages claim is not redressable. Unlike the criminal justice system, where

---

[20] 796 F.2d 1547, 1558 (7th Cir. 1986), *aff'd memo opinion*, 479 U.S. 1048 (1987).

[21] *Kerman, supra*, 374 F.3d at 129–130 (treating individual loss of liberty while being subjected to illegal search as a concrete, actual injury, rather that an abstract injury seeking only vindication of the constitutional guarantee).

[22] The hypothetical is based on *Burka v. New York City Transit Authority*, 747 F. Supp. 214 (S.D.N.Y. 1990) (involving consolidated challenges to a mandatory urine testing policy for marijuana instituted by the Transit Authority for employees and applicants).

[23] *See* Chandler v. Miller, 520 U.S. 305, 313 (1997) (holding that the government must show "special need" to conduct suspicion-less drug testing of individuals); 19 Solid Waste Dep't Mechanics v. City of Albuquerque, 156 F.3d 1068 (10th Cir. 1998) (discussing the content of the "special need" test). The Court may have eroded much of the force of *Chandler* in *Board of Education of Independent School Dist. No. 92 v. Earls*, 536 U.S. 822 (2002), when it upheld a school's policy of suspicionless drug testing of high school athletes. The Court found that the interest in deterring and preventing drug use among schoolchildren satisfied the "special need" test. The Court relied on a pre-*Chandler* decision, Veronica School District No. 47J v. Acton, 515 U.S. 646 (1995), and it remains unclear whether the erosion of *Chandler* is limited to school-based testing or reflects a generally more lenient application across-the-board of the "special need" requirement. *See generally* John Bourdeau, Annot., *Supreme Court's Views on Mandatory Testing for Drugs or Alcohol*, 145 A.L.R. Fed. 335 (1998).

the "fruit of the poisonous tree" doctrine is liberally applied to bar the use of evidence obtained in violation of Fourth Amendment guarantees, many jurisdictions apply a more constrained approach in the civil context. While a person may sue for the damages directly associated with the illegal search and seizure, such as distress damages associated with the invasion of protected personal privacy, the remedy does not extend to bar subsequent use of the evidence;[24] therefore, the constitutional violation did not "cause" the loss of employment.

In order to recover lost wages resulting from the employment decision based on the positive drug tests, the plaintiff must show a constitutional deficiency separate from the taking of the tests. For example, in *Burka* the court held that the failure of the defendants to preserve the test results for independent testing by the plaintiff could constitute a Fourteenth Amendment procedural due process violation.[25] If the plaintiff was then terminated from his employment at a hearing based on the positive drug test result he was unable to challenge, the plaintiff could now claim his lost wages as damages. This results because the constitutional due process violation led directly to his loss of wages.

The approach taken in cases such as *Burka* is consistent with a "risk rule" approach urged by some commentators. Under this approach "compensation for violations of constitutional rights should encompass only constitutionally relevant injuries—that is, injuries within the risks that the constitutional prohibition seeks to avoid."[26]

Although, as noted in these materials, there are some exceptions, the general rule is that constitutional torts may be compensated only to the extent of actual injury and damages will not be presumed to flow from the constitutional violation. This principle has an enhanced application in the

---

[24] Boyd v. Constantine, 613 N.E.2d 511 (N.Y. 1993) (refusing to apply the exclusionary rule in administrative disciplinary proceedings to evidence obtained by the city police in violation of state police officers' constitutional rights). The court expressed the view that it was too remote that city police would foresee the subsequent disciplinary use of the illegally seized evidence at the time they conducted the search and seizure for an exclusionary rule to have any meaningful deterrence effect. Sheetz v. Mayor and City Council of Baltimore, 553 A.2d 1281, 1282 (Md. 1989) (stating that evidence obtained in violation of the Fourth Amendment is admissible in civil administrative discharge proceedings unless law enforcement officers acted in bad faith); *cf.* United States v. Janis, 428 U.S. 433, 447 (1976) (refusing to extend the exclusionary rule to federal civil proceedings when the evidence was obtained by state police without federal participation). This principle has been broadly extended by the Court. Pennsylvania Bd. of Probation and Parole v. Scott, 524 U.S. 357, 362 (1998) (noting that the Court has generally refused to extend the exclusionary rule outside the ambit of criminal trials).

[25] *Burka, supra,* 747 F. Supp. at 221.

[26] John Jeffries, Jr., *Damages For Constitutional Violations: The Relation of Risk to Injury in Constitutional Torts,* 75 Va. L. Rev. 1461, 1461 (1989). Professor Jeffries builds his argument on the thesis that civil liability for constitutional torts is fault based. This theme is critiqued in Sheldon Nahmod, *Constitutional Damages and Corrective Justice: A Different View,* 76 Va. L. Rev. 997 (1990).

procedural due process context.[27] The "actual injury" component for a due process violation does not necessarily include all losses that flow from the consequences of the constitutionally flawed process. If the results would have been the same even if the plaintiff had received fair process, then the consequences flowing from the flawed process, (plaintiff's termination or lost promotion), are not redressable through a damages award. When the due process violation does not affect the end result, plaintiff's remedies are limited to those resulting from the due process violation alone. This was demonstrated in the case of *Carey v. Piphus*.[28]

Piphus, a high school student, was summarily suspended from school based on the suspicion that he had been smoking marijuana. Piphus brought suit claiming that he had been deprived of procedural due process. There was no challenge to the lower court's ruling that the suspension violated Piphus' due process rights. Piphus contended, however, that the lower court had erred in refusing to award any damages. The Court partially agreed with Piphus. The Court noted that a party deprived of procedural due process guarantees could recover for actual injury associated with that deprivation, such as distress damages:

> "[W]e foresee no particular difficulty in producing evidence that mental and emotional distress actually was caused by the denial of procedural due process itself."[29]

However, if Piphus would have been suspended even had he received fair process, he could not recover for any damages flowing from his suspension, as opposed to the denial to him of procedural due process.[30]

Even if a plaintiff convinces a court that the result would have been different, she still must convince the court as to the magnitude of her losses. This may be difficult. For example, in *Marin v. Citizens Memorial Hospital* the court held that a physician who had been wrongfully denied staff privileges could not recover his resultant economic damages because they were too speculative.[31] The same result was reached in *Marks v. City Council of the City of Chesapeake, Virginia* when a "fortune teller" who was wrongfully denied a permit to practice his craft was limited to nominal damages—the court found that Marks' (the fortune teller) proof of lost business was unpersuasive.[32]

---

[27] Notwithstanding *Stachura*, *supra*, 477 U.S. 299, some lower courts treat the issue of awarding presumed damages for substantive due process violations as an open question. *E.g.*, Camfield v. City of Oklahoma City, 248 F.3d 1214, 1234 (10th Cir. 2001).

[28] 435 U.S. 247 (1978).

[29] *Id.* at 263

[30] *Id.* at 263; Rogers v. Kelly, 866 F.2d 997, 1000 (8th Cir. 1989) (finding that the plaintiff suffered no actual injury when he would have been terminated even if he had been afforded procedural due process).

[31] 700 F. Supp. 354, 361–62 (S.D. Tex. 1988).

[32] 723 F. Supp. 1155, 1164 (E.D. Va. 1988), *aff'd*, 883 F.2d 308 (4th Cir. 1989). Clearly, Marks was not surprised by the ruling!

The plaintiff can recover distress damages, subject to proof, flowing from the denial of due process.[33] Although there is decisional law stating that the plaintiff's testimony alone may support a distress damages award,[34] many courts state that there must be corroborating evidence, such as testimony by others or medical or psychological treatment.[35] Damages awards for distress occasioned by the violation of constitutional rights may be significant.[36] When the violation results in physical injury, or property damage, compensatory damages are recoverable as in other cases.[37] In cases when no actual injury is sustained, the plaintiff may recover nominal damages.[38]

While there is little caselaw, the accepted view is that mitigation of damages principles apply to civil rights/constitutional tort claims.[39] This is clearly true with respect to civil rights claims brought in the employment context under Title VII of the Civil Rights Act of 1964.[40]

As the prevailing party in Civil Rights/Constitutional Torts litigation, the plaintiff is entitled to attorney's fees almost as a matter of course.[41]

---

[33] *Carey, supra,* 435 U.S. at 264 n.20.

[34] Chalmers v. City of Los Angeles, 762 F.2d 753, 761 (9th Cir. 1985); *cf.* Bolden v. Southeastern Penn. Transp. Auth., 21 F.3d 29, 34 & n.3 (3d Cir. 1994) (holding that medical corroboration is not required to support an award of distress damages).

[35] Patterson v. P.H.P. Healthcare Corp., 90 F.3d 927, 938 (5th Cir. 1996) (collecting decisions requiring some corroboration of plaintiff's testimony regarding her distress damages), *cert. denied,* 519 U.S. 1091 (1997); Section 12.2 (Measuring Non-Economic Loss).

[36] DeNieva v. Reyes, 966 F.2d 480, 487 (9th Cir. 1992) (affirming distress damages award of $50,000 for the wrongful deprivation of a passport over an eleven day period); Walje v. City of Winchester, Ky., 827 F.2d 10, 12 (6th Cir. 1987) (affirming award of $5000 for distress to a firefighter who was suspended in violation of his First Amendment right of free speech).

[37] Ismael v. Cohen, 899 F.2d 183, 186–87 (2d Cir. 1990) (affirming award of $650,000 in compensatory damages to plaintiff injured as a result of excessive force by the police); Gutierrez-Rodriquez v. Cartegena, 882 F.2d 553, 577–78 (1st Cir. 1989) (affirming award of $4.5 million in compensatory damages to plaintiff left permanently paralyzed as a result of a police shooting); Chapters 8 (Remedies for Bodily Injury), 9 (Remedies for Injury to Personal Property).

[38] Gibeau v. Nellis, 18 F.3d 107, 110 (2d Cir. 1994); *Schneider, supra,* 917 F.2d at 639.

[39] Murphy v. City of Flagler Beach, 846 F.2d 1306, 1308–09 (11th Cir. 1988) (applying federal rule of mitigation to action brought under federal civil rights statute (42 U.S.C. § 1983)); Section 13 (Duty to Mitigate Damages).

[40] Carey v. Mt. Desert Island Hosp., 156 F.3d 31, 41 (1st Cir. 1998) (involving workplace discrimination claim brought under Title VII (42 U.S.C. § 2000e)); *cf.* Tyus v. Urban Search Management, 102 F.3d 256, 264 (7th Cir. 1996) (noting that under Federal Fair Housing Act (Title VI of Civil Rights Act of 1964 (42 U.S.C. § 3601)) mitigation of damages may be appropriate as to claims of lost housing, e.g., the plaintiff should attempt to find alternate housing; however, mitigation principles do not apply to intangible losses, such as injury resulting from the offensiveness of the discriminatory conduct) *cert. denied,* 520 U.S. 1251 (1997); Sections 13.2.2 ([Duty to Mitigate Damages] Employment Claims); 151 (Employee's Damages Remedies Against Employer), 152 (Reinstatement of Employee to Position).

[41] Newman v. Piggie Park Enter., 390 U.S. 400, 402–03 (1968) (stating that prevailing plaintiffs should receive attorney's fees award unless special circumstances render such an award unjust); Section 212 (Prevailing Party).

Prevailing defendants fare measurably less well insofar as the recovery of their attorney's fees is concerned.[42]

In an appropriate case demonstrating the requisite degree of actual malice,[43] a plaintiff may recover punitive damages against the individual defendants.[44] As a general rule, punitive damages are not recoverable against public defendants.[45] A municipality may indemnify a public official, such as a police officer, against a punitive damages award notwithstanding general proscriptions against indemnification for illegal acts.[46] The fact that the municipality has agreed to indemnify an individual against a punitive damages award does not itself expose the municipality to a punitive damages award, nor excuse the individual's liability for punitive damages.[47] The indemnity agreement may, however, expose the municipality to direct liability concerning the individual award.[48]

The ability to recover damages for civil rights/constitutional torts is subject to numerous constraints. The general immunity of municipal defendants from punitive damages awards has already been noted. The 11th Amendment generally immunizes the states from damages actions[49] and individual defendants may have absolute[50] or qualified immunity.[51] Whether the action is against the state, and thus subject to the 11th Amendment, or against an individual is not determined by the form of the action, but its substance:

---

[42] Christiansburg Garment Co. v. E.E.O.C., 434 U.S. 412, 421 (1978) (stating that the prevailing defendant in civil rights litigation should not recover a fees award unless the plaintiff's claim was frivolous or made in bad faith); Section 212 (Prevailing Party).

[43] Smith v. Wade, 461 U.S. 30, 56 (1983) (allowing punitive damages in civil rights claims under 42 U.S.C. § 1983 in cases of reckless indifference or callous disregard); Section 202.1 ([Punitive Damages] Socially Deplorable Conduct).

[44] See Michael Wells, *Punitive Damages For Constitutional Torts*, 56 La. L. Rev. 841 (1996).

[45] City of Newport v. Fact Concerts, Inc., 453 U.S. 247, 259, 271 (1981) (noting the general rule that punitive damages are not awarded against municipal defendants and extending the rule to statutory civil rights claims brought under 42 U.S.C. § 1983); Section 202.8 ([Punitive Damages] Public Entities and Not-For-Profit Organizations).

[46] Cornwell v. City of Riverside, 896 F.2d 398, 399 (9th Cir.), cert denied, 497 U.S. 1026 (1990) (applying federal law).

[47] Haile v. Village of Sag Harbor, 639 F. Supp. 718, 723 (E.D.N.Y. 1986).

[48] Bell v. City of Milwaukee, 746 F.2d 1205, 1271 (7th Cir. 1984) (noting that a municipality may waive immunity from liability for a punitive damages award); cf. Trevino v. Gates, 23 F.3d 1480, 1482–83 (9th Cir.) (holding that municipal officials who vote to authorize indemnification of police officers who are assessed punitive damages for civil rights violations may, by their vote, encourage violations of civil rights by immunizing the officers from the consequences of their conduct and by such votes expose themselves to punitive damages awards for encouraging civil rights violations), cert. denied, 513 U.S. 932 (1994).

[49] Erwin Chemerinsky, Federal Jurisdiction Ch. 7 (1989).

[50] Crooks v. Maynard, 913 F.2d 699, 700 (9th Cir. 1990) (holding that a state judge was absolutely immune from a civil rights claim based on the judge's actions in holding the plaintiff in contempt of court).

[51] Harlow v. Fitzgerald, 457 U.S. 800, 817–19 (1982) (holding that "government officials performing discretionary function generally are shielded from liability for civil damages insofar as their conduct does not violate clearly established statutory or constitutional rights of which a reasonable person would have known").

> The nature of a suit as one against the state is to be determined by the essential nature and effect of the proceeding . . . when the action is in essence one for the recovery of money from the state, the state is the real, substantial party in interest and is entitled to invoke its sovereign immunity from suit even though individual officials are nominal defendants".[52]

In this context, a damages action against a state actor in his official capacity is treated as an action against the state for 11th Amendment purposes.[53]

The federal government retains general immunity from damages actions unless its defense of sovereign immunity has been waived by statute.[54] Individual damages claims may be subject to absolute or qualified defenses distinct from *official* immunity. For example, in *Chappell v. Wallace* the Court held that enlisted black military personnel could not bring damages claims based on intentional racial discrimination against superior officers because such claims would interfere with "the unique disciplinary structure of the Military Establishment and Congress' activity in the field constitute 'special factors' which dictate" that a damages remedy pursuant to *Bivens* would be inappropriate.[55] The Court refuses to recognize a *Bivens* action by a federal military employee against his superior because the employment relationship was already subject to comprehensive regulation providing meaningful remedies.[56] Whether "special factors" counsel caution against allowing a *Bivens* action is decided on a case-by-case basis.[57] Similar results have been reached when claims are based on state constitutional guarantees.[58]

Equitable relief is commonly sought and frequently awarded in civil rights/constitutional tort litigation. Equitable relief requires direct judicial involvement in the execution of laws, at either the state or federal level, depending on whether state or federal actors are involved. For that reason, courts have interposed a number of justiciability constraints on the exercise

---

[52] Ford Motor Co. v. Department of Treasury of State of Indiana, 323 U.S. 459, 464 (1945).

[53] Kentucky v. Graham, 473 U.S. 159, 165–66 (1985) (distinguishing between "personal-capacity suits that seek to impose personal liability on a government official for actions he takes under color of state law" and "[o]fficial-capacity suits [which] represent only another way of pleading an action against an entity of which and officer is an agent") (brackets added).

[54] Loeffler v. Frank, 486 U.S. 549, 554 (1988) (holding that "[a]bsent a waiver of sovereign immunity, the Federal Government is immune from suit"). The waiver may be, but need not, be express. Morrison-Knudsen Co., Inc. v. CHG. Int'l, Inc., 811 F.2d 1209, 1223 (9th Cir. 1987) (stating that statutory language permitting agency to "sue or be sued" waives sovereign immunity of agency), *cert. denied*, 488 U.S. 935 (1987).

[55] 462 U.S. 296, 304 (1983); Section 3.3.2 ([Rights and Remedies] Implied Remedies) (discussing *Bivens* and its progeny)).

[56] Bush v. Lucas, 462 U.S. 367 (1983).

[57] Carlson v. Green, 446 U.S. 14, 16–19 (1980) (involving *Bivens* claims by prisoners); Schweiker v. Chilicky, 487 U.S. 412, 42–22 (1988) (involving *Bivens* claims by social security claimants for improper denial of benefits).

[58] Bonner v. City of Santa Ana, 53 Cal. Rptr. 2d 671, 676–77 (Cal. App. 1996) (refusing to recognize damages actions based on state due process guarantee to a homeless person whose belongings were summarily disposed of by the municipality; the court noted that redress was available through an action for conversion).

of equitable relief. As a practical matter, these justiciability constraints parallel those found in the law of remedies. Thus, concerns over ripeness and mootness have both a constitutional and remedial dimension, both of which are highly similar.[59] Judicial reluctance to exercise equitable jurisdiction is sometimes expressed in terms familiar to constitutional law scholars, such as political question,[60] standing,[61] and abstention.[62] At other times, terms are used that are more commonly found in the Remedies lexicon, such as concern over supervision of the equitable relief[63] or that equity will not interfere with personal rights.[64]

§ 112 LITIGATION TORTS

The common law developed two primary actions to redress misuse of legal process: (1) malicious prosecution and (2) abuse of process. One functional distinction between the torts is that abuse of process does not have a favorable termination" element, but malicious prosecution does. Abuse of process may be asserted as a counterclaim in the same action out of which the misuse of process arose. Malicious prosecution, on the other hand, requires that the underlying claim be favorably terminated before the malicious prosecution can be asserted; thus, precluding its assertion as a counterclaim to the maliciously prosecuted claim.[1] Several jurisdictions have combined the traditional torts of malicious prosecution and abuse of process into the unitary tort of wrongful use of legal proceedings.[2]

The tort of malicious prosecution is designed to compensate a person who is wrongfully hauled into court and forced to defend himself against a frivolous claim, i.e., one lacking probable cause, instituted with malice.[3] While the tort originated to redress the wrongful initiation or causing of criminal prosecutions, it has been extended in most jurisdictions to include the wrongful initiation or causing of civil actions.[4] Some jurisdictions

---

[59] CHEMERINSKY, FEDERAL JURISDICTION, *supra* at §§ 2.4 (Ripeness), 2.5 (Mootness); Section 30 (Ripeness, Mootness, and Standing).

[60] CHEMERINSKY, FEDERAL JURISDICTION, *supra* at § 2.6.

[61] *Id.* at § 2.3.

[62] *Id.* at Chapters 12 (discussing Abstention doctrine), 13 (discussing *Younger v. Harris* doctrine).

[63] Section 24 ([Equitable Remedies] Burden on the Court/Supervision).

[64] Section 25 ([Equitable Remedies] Nature of Rights Protected).

[1] Gordon v. Community First State Bank, 587 N.W.2d 343, 351 (Neb. 1998); Yaklevich v. Kemp, Schaeffer & Rowe Co., L.P.A., 626 N.E.2d 115, 119 & n.4 (Ohio 1994).

[2] Devaney v. Thriftway Mktg. Corp., 953 P.2d 277, 282–83 (N. Mex. 1997), *cert. denied*, 524 U.S. 915 (1998); Yost v. Torok, 344 S.E.2d 414 (Ga. 1986); *cf.* Simon v. Navon, 71 F.3d 9, 15 (1st Cir. 1995) (noting that "[t]he torts of abuse of process and malicious prosecution frequently are confused because of their close relationship") (citations omitted).

[3] Logan v. Caterpillar, Inc., 246 F.3d 912, 921–22 (9th Cir. 2001); Bertero v. National Gen. Corp., 529 P.2d 608, 613 (Cal. 1974); *see* Restatement (Second) of Torts § 653 (1977) (setting forth the elements of the cause of action for malicious prosecution.

[4] Lee v. Mitchell, 953 P.2d 414, 427 (Or. App. 1998) (noting that "[w]rongful initiation of a civil proceeding is the civil counterpart of a malicious prosecution action"); Sheldon Appel Co. v. Albert & Oliker, 765 P.2d 498, 501 (Cal. 1989).

reserve the term "malicious prosecution" for improper criminal prosecutions and use another term, e.g., "vexatious litigation," for improper civil prosecutions.

Abuse of process claims concern misuse of the tools the law affords litigants once they are in a lawsuit, regardless of whether there was probable cause to commence that lawsuit in the first place. Abuse of process claims typically involve improper or excessive attachments,[5] or improper use of discovery.[6] On the other hand, simply filing or maintaining a lawsuit for an improper purpose, such as obtaining a nuisance settlement or causing the defendant to incur litigation expenses, is generally not seen as an abuse of process.[7]

Damages recoverable for litigation torts are coextensive with the harm caused.[8] These include pecuniary damages caused by the tort, as for example, if the charge and prosecution cause the plaintiff to lose his job[9] or incur attorney's fees;[10] however, the decisions are less charitable when abuse of process is the litigation tort.[11] The amount of fees awarded is limited to the amount of attorney fees actually incurred because the award of fees is a measure of compensation, not an incentive to litigate.[12] However, it is not required that the fees have been paid to the attorneys as a condition

---

[5] White Lightning Co. v. Wolfson, 438 P.2d 345, 353–54 (Cal. 1968) (stating that claims for excessive attachments should be treated "as giving rise to a cause of action for abuse of process rather than for malicious prosecution"); *cf.* Suffield Development Associates Ltd. v. National Loan Investors, L.P., 802 A.2d 44, 49 (Conn. 2002):

> The plaintiff's amended complaint supports a claim for abuse of process because it alleged that the defendants had misrepresented the amount to which National was entitled as a matter of law under the stipulated judgment, inflated the amount owed, and thereby obtained an excessive execution all for the purpose of coercing the plaintiff into making payment to National. We conclude that such allegations may give rise to a claim for abuse of process because executions are properly obtained and used only in accordance with a valid judgment and in an appropriate amount.

[6] Younger v. Solomon, 113 Cal. Rptr. 113, 119 (Cal. App. 1974) (involving the use of interrogatories in a civil action to establish a charge of ambulance chasing made in State Bar disciplinary proceedings).

[7] Oren Royal Oaks Venture v. Greenberg, Bernhard, Weiss & Karma, Inc., 728 P.2d 1202, 1209 (Cal. 1986) (collecting decisions).

[8] There is an extensive annotation that collects numerous awards in malicious prosecution actions. Jay Zitter, Annot., *Excessiveness or Inadequacy of Compensatory Damages for Malicious Prosecution*, 50 A.L.R. 4th 843 (1987).

[9] Davis v. Local Union No. 11, 94 Cal. Rptr. 562, 568 (Cal. App. 1971).

[10] Kennedy v. Byrum, 20 Cal. Rptr. 98, 103 (Cal. App. 1962). *See generally* K. Potraker, Annot., *Attorney's Fees as Element of Damages in Action For False Imprisonment or Arrest, or For Malicious Prosecution*, 21 A.L.R.3d 1068 (1969).

[11] Spellens v. Spellens, 317 P.2d 613, 627 (Cal. 1957) (rejecting recovery of attorney's fees incurred in defending against improper legal process). *But cf.* Kizer v. Finch, 730 So.2d 1197 (Ala. 1998) (permitting recovery of attorney's fees due to the closeness between abuse of process and malicious prosecution actions). *Kizer* is problematic because it relies on authorities from Georgia, which has unified the litigation torts into a single tort, and from Florida where attorney's fees are governed by statute. Fla. Stat. Ann. § 57.105.

[12] Potraker, Annotation, *supra*, 21 A.L.R.3d at § 4; Section 213.2 (Limitations on Fees Awards).

to their recovery from the defendant; it is sufficient that the obligation to pay fees was incurred.[13]

Litigation torts permit the recovery of distress damages.[14] There is some decisional law that distress damages may be presumed to flow from the initiation or causing the malicious prosecution.[15] Malicious prosecution will also support a recovery for reputational injury.[16] Loss or injury to credit-worthiness caused by the wrongful act is also recoverable as an item of consequential damages; the malicious charge may adversely affect the willingness of lenders to extend credit to the plaintiff or may induce lenders to charge a higher rate.[17] While there are occasional statements that recoverable damages include physical injury traceable to the litigation tort, for example, the plaintiff is assaulted after being arrested as a result of the malicious charge,[18] the decisional law appears to treat the causal linkage as too remote when the issue is directly confronted.[19] However, loss of freedom resulting from the malicious prosecution is a compensable item of recovery.[20]

Jurisdictions have split as to whether a "special injury" rule should be incorporated into the prima facie case for malicious prosecution. The "special injury" rule requires "some physical interference with a party's person or property in the form of an arrest, attachment, injunction, or sequestration." As noted by one court:

> It is insufficient that a party has suffered the ordinary losses incident to defending a civil suit, such as inconvenience,

---

[13] Fust v. Francois, 913 S.W.2d 38, 47 (Mo. App. 1995).

[14] Thrift v. Hubbard, 974 S.W.2d 70, 81 (Tex. Civ. App. 1998); see Britton v. Maloney, 981 F. Supp. 25, 55 (D. Mass. 1997) (awarding distress damages when the malicious prosecution formed the basis of a civil rights claim under 42 U.S.C. § 1983).

[15] Fust, supra, 913 S.W.2d at 48.

[16] Thrift, supra, 974 S.W.2d at 80–81; Junior Food Stores, Inc. v. Rice, 671 So.2d 67, 76 (Miss. 1996), cert. denied, 429 U.S. 1091 (1997); Allard v. Church of Scientology, 129 Cal. Rptr. 797, 804 (Cal. App. 1976), cert. denied, 429 U.S. 1091 (1977); Young v. Jack Boring's Inc., 540 S.W.2d 887, 896 (Mo. App. 1976) (stating that in an action for malicious prosecution, damages are recoverable for every element of the injury including mental and physical suffering, injury to fame and reputation, and the general impairment of social standing).

[17] Sampson v. Hunt, 665 P.2d 743, 756 (Kan. 1983). See generally 54 C.J.S. Malicious Prosecution § 96.

[18] Babb v. Superior Court, 479 P.2d 379, 383 n.4 (Cal. 1971).

[19] Heban v. BFD, Inc., 621 F. Supp. 669, 670 (D. Ind. 1985) (stating that under Indiana law unless the defendant induced the mistreatment, the "plaintiff's treatment while in custody was not a proper element of damages"). See generally 52 Am. Jur. 2d, Malicious Prosecution § 99.

[20] Raysor v. Port Auth. of N.Y. and N.J., 768 F.2d 34, 39 (2d Cir. 1985) (stating that the fact of confinement alone entitled the plaintiff to at least nominal damages), cert. denied, 475 U.S. 1027 (1986); cf. Zok v. State, 903 P.2d 574, 577–78 (Alaska 1995) (discussing the issue in the context of the tort of false arrest).

embarrassment, discovery costs, and attorney's fees. The mere filing of a lawsuit cannot satisfy the special injury requirement.[21]

Although the "special injury" requirement has been questioned and critiqued as outmoded, many courts find that it serves as a necessary counterweight to discourage frivolous litigation, particularly given the general refusal in this country to award a prevailing defendant his attorney's fees incurred in the successful defense.[22]

Once the "special injury" element is met, the defendant is responsible for all losses caused by his wrong.[23]

The jurisdictions have split as to whether a loss of spousal consortium claim can be asserted in connection with a malicious prosecution action. The dispute is over whether loss of consortium should be allowed absent physical injury to the maliciously prosecuted spouse. Malicious prosecution claims do not generally result in bodily injury of the type normally supportive of a loss of consortium claim.[24]

The nature of litigation torts, particularly malicious prosecution, is that they naturally lead to claims for punitive damages. Malice is an element of the tort of malicious prosecution and while malice is not one of the elements of the tort of abuse of process, it may often be inferred from the required willful misuse of process. In either context, the proof of malice must meet the punitive damages standards.[25]

Some jurisdictions have adopted an enhancement statute that automatically increases the jury's award of malicious prosecution damages. These provisions tend, however to be somewhat limited.[26]

---

[21] Texas Beef Cattle Co. v. Green, 921 S.W.2d 203, 208–09 (Tex. 1996); (citation omitted); see Cult Awareness Network v. Church of Scientology Int'l, 685 N.E.2d 1347, 1350 (Ind. 1997) (applying the "special injury" rule and noting that the rule requires some injury or damage beyond that usually incurred in defending a lawsuit), cert. denied, 523 U.S. 1020 (1998).

[22] Engel v. CBS, Inc., 711 N.E.2d 626, 629–30 (N.Y. 1999); Section 210 (Attorney's Fees—The "American Rule").

[23] Texas Beef Cattle Co., supra, 921 S.W.2d at 209.

[24] Browning-Ferris Indus., Inc. v. Lieck, 881 S.W.2d 288, 294–95 (Tex. 1994) (concluding that physical bodily injury requirement should be imposed and rejecting contrary authority); see Barnes v. Outlaw, 964 P.2d 484, 486–87 (Ariz. 1998) (collecting decisions regarding requirement of physical injury to primarily injured spouse as necessary element of loss of consortium claim). The Barnes court decided not to impose such a requirement. 964 P.2d at 487.

[25] Bertero, supra, 529 P.2d at 624–25; Chapter 23 (Punitive Damages) (particularly Section 202 (Scope of Punitive Damages)).

[26] Camaj v. S.S. Kresge Co., 393 N.W.2d 875 (Mich. 1986) (discussing Michigan statute that permits trebling of damages award when defendant causes malicious prosecution action to be commenced in the name of another without that other person's consent). The court suggested that the reason for the statute was to redress "straw party" suits when the protagonist hid behind a judgment-proof initiator of the complaint. Id. at 877–78.

§ 113   BREACH OF FIDUCIARY DUTY

A fiduciary assumes duties to the beneficiary that go beyond mere fairness and honesty. A fiduciary must act on behalf of the beneficiary by giving the interests of the beneficiary priority over his (the fiduciary's) own interests.[1] Initially, the application of fiduciary obligations was limited to trustees subject to the jurisdiction of equity. Over time, fiduciary principles were extended to persons who, while not trustees in the strict, literal sense of the term, were seen as occupying a position that required they be held to some of the fiduciary's obligations. This is usually based on a finding of a "special relationship." The primary consequence of finding a special relationship is the importation of tort-based or tort-type remedies when one party breaches a commitment owed to the other party in the special relationship. Because the special relationship is not a true fiduciary relationship, the breaching party does not owe to the other party to the relationship the whole panoply of duties a true fiduciary owes to a beneficiary. Rather, the "relationship" is construed, as a matter of law, to impose on the breaching party obligations of good faith and fair dealing in the performance of its commitments arising out of the relationship. The closest analogy is that of quasi-contract. In that context, a contractual relationship is presumed in order to achieve a fair and just result between the parties.[2] In this context, the breaching party is a quasi-fiduciary, *i.e.*, one who is analogized to a real trustee for the purpose of obtaining a just result.

The special relationship situation has always been defined somewhat amorphously. It usually arises when the person in whom confidence is reposed (defendant) acquires control over the affairs of the plaintiff and the plaintiff, because of her situation, now finds herself vulnerable to the actions of the person in whom confidence is reposed.[3] How much "control" is sufficient to impose fiduciary-like obligations is difficult to gauge.[4] The

---

[1] Committee on Children's T.V. v. General Foods, Corp., 673 P.2d 660, 676 (Cal. 1983), *citing* Restatement (Second) of Trusts §§ 2, 170 (1959). The classic description is in Justice Cardozo's opinion in *Meinhard v. Salmon*:

> Many forms of conduct permissible in a workaday world for those acting at arm's length, are forbidden to those bound by fiduciary ties. A trustee is held to something stricter than the morals of the market place. Not honesty alone, but the punctilio of an honor the most sensitive, is then the standard of behavior. As to this there has developed a tradition that is unbending and inveterate. Uncompromising rigidity has been the attitude of courts of equity when petitioned to undermine the rule of undivided loyalty by the "disintegrating erosion" of particular exceptions.

164 N.E. 545, 546 (N.Y. 1928).

[2] Chapter 5 (General Principles Governing Restitution); Section 44 (Quasi Contract and Unjust Enrichment).

[3] Coca-Cola Bottling Co. of Elizabethtown, Inc. v. Coca-Cola Co., 696 F. Supp. 57, 75 (D. Del. 1988), *aff'd*, 988 F.2d 386, 400 (3d Cir.), *cert. denied*, 510 U.S. 908 (1993).

[4] *See* Wolf v. Superior Court, 130 Cal. Rptr. 2d 860, 864–65 (Cal. App. 2003) (holding that "the contractual right to contingent compensation in the control of another has never, by itself, been sufficient to create a fiduciary duty where one would not otherwise exist") (citations omitted).

general hallmark of a fiduciary-like relationship is the presence of a relationship of trust and confidence, in which one party exercises influence over the other party and thus renders the latter vulnerable to exploitation by the former.[5]

In some cases, this situation has occurred so frequently as to be reduced to a principle of law. Thus, partners owe fiduciary duties to one another;[6] officers and directors owe fiduciary duties to the corporation;[7] agents owe fiduciary duties to principals;[8] and attorneys owe fiduciary duties to clients.[9] In many other cases, however, whether fiduciary (or fiduciary-like) obligations exist depend on the facts and circumstances of the matter at hand. This has led to much uncertainty and confusion. As observed by one court:

> There are few legal concepts more frequently invoked but less conceptually certain than that of the fiduciary relationship. In specific circumstances and in specific relationships, courts have no difficulty in imposing fiduciary obligations, but at a more fundamental level, the principle on which that obligation is based is unclear. Indeed, the term "fiduciary" has been described as "one of the most ill-defined, if not altogether misleading terms in our law. . . ."[10]

A substantial body of decisional law has been generated on the issue of whether a confidential (or special)'relationship exists in a typical business or commercial relationship, such as to warrant recognition as a fiduciary relationship. Aside from the insured-insurer relationship, no consensus exists among American jurisdictions as to the type of relationships that qualify as "special" and therefore warrant tort-type damaged when the "relationship" is damages by the "quasi-fiduciary."[11] Some courts note a

---

[5] Richelle L. v. Roman Catholic Archbishop of San Francisco, 130 Cal. Rptr. 2d 601, 609 (Cal. App. 2003); Shervin v. Huntleigh Securities Corp., 85 S.W.3d 737, 740–41 (Mo. App. 2002).

[6] G.C.M., Inc. v. Kentucky Central Life Ins. Co., 947 P.2d 143, 149 (N. Mex. 1997).

[7] Anadarko Petroleum Corp. v. Panhandle E. Corp., 545 A.2d 1171, 1174 (Del. 1988).

[8] *Committee on Children's T.V.*, *supra*, 673 P.2d at 675 n.21 (noting that an agent owes fiduciary duties to the principal "even if the principal has greater bargaining strength").

[9] Dwyer v. Jung, 336 A.2d 498, 500 (N.J. Ch. Div. 1975) (noting that the relationship between an attorney and the client is "highly fiduciary on the part of counsel"), *aff'd*, 348 A.2d 208 (N.J. Super. Ct. A.D. 1975); CHARLES WOLFRAM, MODERN LEGAL ETHICS § 4.1 (1986).

[10] LAC Minerals Ltd. v. International Corona Resources, Ltd., 61 D.L.R. 4th 14, 26 (Can. 1989).

[11] *Compare* Careau & Co. v. Security-Pacific Bus. Credit, Inc., 272 Cal. Rptr. 387, 397–404 (Cal. App. 1990) (discussing the "special relationship" concept and concluding that it is infrequently applied outside the insurance setting), *with* Shea v. Esensten, 107 F.3d 625 (8th Cir.) (holding that an HMO has a fiduciary duty under ERISA to disclose to the HMO participants the incentive arrangements it has with its physicians regarding referrals to specialists), *cert. denied*, 522 U.S. 914 (1997). *But see* Neade v. Portes, 739 N.E.2d 496 (Ill. 2000) (declining to recognize an action for breach of fiduciary duties when a physician failed to disclose to his patient cost-cutting and profit incentives the physician had with his HMO; any *harm* sustained by the patient as a result of the arrangement between the physician and HMO was better addressed by a medical malpractice action than a breach of fiduciary duties action).

"technical" difference between a recognized fiduciary relationship, such as trustee and beneficiary or attorney and client, and a constructed fiduciary-like (or "confidential") relationship,[12] which is constructed factually on a case-by-case basis.[13] Nonetheless, when a fiduciary-like or confidential relationship is recognized, it is functionally and legally equal in remedy to the true fiduciary relationship.

Recognition of a fiduciary relationship subjects the fiduciary to higher duties of care toward the beneficiary than would be the case in an arms-length relationship. A fiduciary will have greater disclosure obligations and enhanced obligations to look after the interests of the beneficiary. To ensure the fiduciary's loyalty and devotion to the beneficiary's interests, transactions between the fiduciary and the beneficiary are presumed to be in violation of the fiduciary's duties to the beneficiary.[14] Although the presumption is rebuttable, the fiduciary has the burden of proof to demonstrate the fairness of the transaction.

A fiduciary's conduct is subject to significant legal sanction and liability if the fiduciary abuses her position of trust. The array of remedies is equal to the substantive doctrines that control the fiduciary's conduct. Most importantly, however, must be the recognition that fiduciary relationships do not require an express agreement or that the defendant specifically agree to serve as a fiduciary or assume fiduciary duties. As noted in *Paul v. North*:

> It has been recognized that a fiduciary relationship between parties does not depend upon some technical relation created by, or defined in, law. It exists in cases where there has been a special confidence reposed in one who, in equity and good conscience, is bound to act in good faith and with due regard for the interests of the one reposing the confidence.
>
> Fiduciary relationships recognized and enforceable in equity do not depend upon nomenclature; nor are they necessarily the product of any particular legal relationship. They may arise out of conduct of the parties evidencing an agreement to engage in a joint enterprise for the mutual benefit of the parties. But they necessarily spring from an attitude of trust and confidence and are based upon some form of agreement, either expressed or implied, from which

---

[12] *Richelle L.*, *supra*, 130 Cal. Rptr. 2d at 740.

[13] *Cf.* Atlantic Richfield Co. v. Farm Credit Bank of Wichita, 226 F.3d 1138 (10th Cir. 2000):

> However, that a fiduciary duty does not *necessarily* arise from a lessee-lessor relationship does not mean a fiduciary duty *never* arises from such a relationship. Colorado courts recognize that a variety of relationships can create fiduciary responsibilities under certain circumstances, even if those relationships are not fiduciary per se. These cases demonstrate that "the existence of a fiduciary or confidential relationship is generally a question of fact for the jury."

Id. at 1162.

[14] Watts v. Cumberland Hosp. Sys., Inc., 343 S.E.2d 879, 884 (N.C. 1986); Glass v. Burkett, 381 N.E.2d 821, 824 (Ill. App. 1978); Kanawha Valley Bank v. Friend, 253 S.E.2d 528, 530 (W. Va. 1979).

it can be said the minds have met in a manner to create mutual obligations.[15]

It should be noted that the sentiments expressed in *Paul v. North* are somewhat inconsistent with the conservative approach regarding creation and recognition of fiduciary and fiduciary-like relationships noted earlier. This duality in legal sentiment makes it difficult to predict outcomes here with a high degree of confidence. While courts are reluctant to adopt categorical approaches to recognizing fiduciary-like relationships, e.g., lender-debtor, courts are more willing to do so on an individual, case by case basis, e.g., this lender and this debtor in this particular financial transaction.[16]

Analysis of the remedies available for the breach of fiduciary duties is further complicated by some uncertainty as to whether the breach of fiduciary duties is independently actionable or whether the presence of a fiduciary relationship simply enhances the wrongfulness of the basic misconduct. The distinction is particularly significant for purposes of awarding equitable or legal remedies. Equity's traditional jurisdiction over fiduciaries has led to the providing of equitable remedies, such as disgorgement of profits, even though there was no actual injury sustained by the beneficiary as a result of the fiduciaries malfeasance.[17] When, however, legal remedies, such as damages, are sought, the focus tends to be on the underlying acts and whether those acts caused injury to the other party to the relationship. In this latter context, the defendant's fiduciary status simply enhances the available remedies. As noted by one court:

> While the expression "fiduciary relationship" is thus a defining element of the legal concept of a "trust," the same expression has been employed by analogy in other relationships that are not "trusts" in the strict or technical sense, *i.e.*, partnerships, agency, attorney-client, accountant-client, and others. This simply is a shorthand way of implying that the higher duties demanded of a fiduciary are applicable in that particular relationship—a relationship where "the law demands of one party an usually high standard of ethical or moral conduct with reference to another."[18]

---

[15] 380 P.2d 421, 426 (Kan. 1963) (citations omitted).

[16] *E.g.*, First Nat'l Bank of Cicero v. Sylvester, 554 N.E.2d 1063 (Ill. App. 1990) (recognizing duty of good faith and fair dealing on part of lender in lending money under letter of credit).

[17] Burrow v. Arce, 997 S.W.2d 229, 247 (Tex. 1999) (holding that client can seek forfeiture of fees earned by lawyer if lawyer is disloyal even though client suffers no injury); Rice v. Perl, 320 N.W.2d 407, 411 (Minn. 1982) (upholding the total disgorgement of attorney's fees because the attorney acted in bad faith by failing to disclose a relationship he had with the party settling the client's case even though the non-disclosure was unintentional *and* the client could not show that she had sustained any damage); *see* F.S.L.I.C. v. Molinaro, 889 F.2d 899, 903–04 (9th Cir. 1989) (holding that a bank director was liable for the profits he received when he engaged in an improper transaction with the bank he controlled and the transaction was improper because he was a fiduciary).

[18] Chien v. Chen, 759 S.W.2d 484, 495 (Tex. Civ. App. 1988) (citation omitted); *cf.* Restatement (Second) Torts § 874, cmt.b (1977):

When the breach of fiduciary duties subjects the fiduciary to a damages action for the resulting losses, the recovery may include economic[19] and non-economic losses, such as distress damages.[20] A few decisions have, however, refused to award "damages" for breach of fiduciary duty because of the equitable origins of the doctrine.[21]

The primary reason for asserting a breach of fiduciary duty claim, rather than a breach of contract or other common law tort claim, is usually to avail oneself of a more favorable remedy than is available when misconduct is committed by one who is not a fiduciary. For example, in California the measure of damages for common law fraud is the out-of-pocket rule. However, when the fraud is committed by a fiduciary, California permits use of the benefit-of-the bargain rule.[22]

The recovery of punitive damages for breach of fiduciary duties is usually permitted upon an appropriate showing of malice.[23] Care must be taken, however, to ensure that the appropriate level of malice exists to support the punitive damages award.[24] A breach of fiduciary duties may permit an award of punitive damages, but the breach alone does not compel such an award.[25]

Breach of fiduciary duty will support equitable relief in the form of an injunction.[26] The nature of most breaches, however, is that the relationship

---

The local rules of procedure, the type of relation between the parties and the intricacy of the transaction involved, determine whether the beneficiary is entitled to redress at law or in equity. The remedy of a beneficiary against a defaulting or negligent trustee is ordinary in equity; the remedy of a principal against an agent is ordinarily at law.

[19] Crowd Mgmt. Servs., Inc. v. Finley, 784 P.2d 104, 106 (Or. App. 1989) (affirming an award of damages for loss of business reputation and business opportunities, which the court equated to loss of goodwill, resulting from breach of fiduciary duty); *cf.* Augat, Inc. v. Aegis, Inc., 565 N.E.2d 415, 421 (Mass. 1991) (stating that an employee who breaches fiduciary duties owed to his employer is responsible for resulting losses to the employer).

[20] Chizmar v. Mackie, 896 P.2d 196, 203 (Alaska 1995) (noting and following the modern trend allowing the recovery of distress damages when a professional breaches a fiduciary duty owed to another).

[21] R.E.R. v. J.G., 552 N.W.2d 27, 30–31 (Minn. App. 1996) (rejecting a damages claim for breach of fiduciary duty against a minister who had an affair with the plaintiff's wife after the couple went to the minister for counseling because the damages sought (economic and non-economic losses) were legal in nature and an action for breach of fiduciary duty sounds in equity).

[22] Gray v. Don Miller & Assocs., Inc., 674 P.2d 253, 257 (Cal. 1984); Section 122.1 ("Out-of-Pocket" or "Benefit-of-the-Bargain" Measure).

[23] Material Supply Int'l, Inc. v. Sunmatch Indus. Co., Ltd., 146 F.3d 983, 993–94 (D.C. Cir. 1998); Cheek v. Humphreys, 800 S.W.2d 596, 599 (Tex. Civ. App. 1990) (stating that "[e]xemplary damages are proper where a fiduciary has engaged in self-dealing").

[24] Section 202 (Scope of Punitive Damages).

[25] Tomaselli v. Transamerica Ins. Co., 31 Cal. Rptr. 2d 433, 444 (Cal. App. 1994) (stating that "[a] breach of a fiduciary duty alone without malice, fraud or oppression does not permit an award of punitive damages") (citation omitted); Koester v. American Republic Invs., Inc., 11 F.3d 818, 823 (8th Cir. 1993) (applying Missouri law) (same). *But cf. Hawthorne, supra,* 917 S.W.2d at 936 (stating that "malice is not a required element of exemplary damages where there is an intentional breach of fiduciary duty").

[26] Preferred Meal Sys., Inc. v. Guse, 557 N.E.2d 506, 515–16 (Ill. App. 1990) (holding that

is severed and not continuing; therefore, there is no need for an injunction.[27] Equitable relief may, however, be necessary to require the fiduciary to turn over books and records or maintain confidences notwithstanding the termination of the relationship.[28]

Equity may also permit the use of constructive trust,[29] tracing,[30] and equitable accounting[31] and disgorgement orders,[32] as needed, to force a trustee to restore, return of turn over what he has wrongfully acquired.

---

an injunction would be a proper remedy when the defendants breached their fiduciary duties by forming a competing business); Leo Silfen, Inc. v. Cream, 278 N.E.2d 636, 639 (N.Y. 1972); cf. A.W. Chesterton Co., Inc. v. Chesterton, 128 F.3d 1, 8–9 (1st Cir. 1997) (holding that an injunction was a proper remedy to prevent a minority shareholder from breaching fiduciary duties owed to other shareholders of a Subchapter-S corporation). The breach involved the minority shareholder selling his shares so as to cause the corporation to lost its Subchapter-S status.

[27] Section 30.2 (Mootness).

[28] Maritrans GP, Inc. v. Pepper, Hamilton & Scheetz, 602 A.2d 1277, 1284–87 (Pa. 1980) (enjoining a law firm from undertaking the representation of new clients because of the substantial risk that the firm would breach its professional duty of confidentiality owed to a former client).

[29] Section 54 (Constructive Trust)

[30] Section 59 (Tracing Principles for Constructive Trusts, Equitable Liens, and Equitable Accounting).

[31] Section 55 (Equitable Accounting).

[32] Section 51 (Disgorgement Orders).

Chapter 14

FRAUD AND MISREPRESENTATION

§ 120   NATURE OF FRAUD

The cause of action for fraud remains one of the most comprehensive and confusing areas of the law. Fraud comes in many forms. It may be intentional, negligent, or innocent. It may induce a bargain or transaction or it may infect a course of conduct or relationship between two parties, a relationship that, in turn, may be between two adversaries, collaborators, or those in a confidential or fiduciary relationship. The fraud may be the basis of a damages claim by one who wishes to affirm the fraud-infected transaction, or a claim of fraud may underlay an effort to rescind the transaction and return the parties to the status quo ante—the position the parties would have been in had they not entered into the transaction. Fraud may be defined differently in specialized areas of the law, such as securities regulation or consumer-related business practices, from the definition applied to it in the common law context. For these reasons, care must be taken in defining fraud. Fraud is situation sensitive. The context in which the fraud claim is asserted and the remedial purpose of the action are highly significant in defining what fraud is and, conversely, whether, and what, fraud remedies are available in the particular case.

[120.1] Common Law Fraud

The common law fraud damages action required that the plaintiff plead and prove the following:

- **A false representation by the defendant of a past or present fact.** Fraud must relate to a past or existing fact. Expectations and predictions for the future are insufficient to amount to an actionable fraud.[1] In limited circumstances, however, opinions may be actionable as fraud.[2]

- **Defendant's knowledge of the falsity of the representation (scienter).** The mere fact that the representation is false does not raise a legal presumption that the speaker knew it was false.[3]

- **The representation was material to the transaction or bargain.** Materiality is usually understood to mean a representation that would induce a reasonably prudent person to rely on the representation. Because the materiality requirement might immunize a defendant who exploited an especially vulnerable person's receptivity to a false statement, many formulations of the above test substitute for "materiality" that the defendant intended to induce the plaintiff's reliance.[4] A defendant should not be allowed to knowingly exploit the weak, the meek, and the ignorant simply because they are influenced by what a reasonably prudent person would ignore.

- **Plaintiff did in fact rely on the representation.**

- **Plaintiff suffered actual damage from reliance on the misrepresentation.**

The common law test for fraud damages remains the most difficult pathway for a plaintiff. The strictness of the elements reflects, no doubt, unease with the use of a tort standard to police transactions and bargains that are the product of consensual agreements and thus ordinarily governed by the law of contract. Requiring a plaintiff to comply with a heightened burden helps to maintain the tort-contract distinction. Occasionally, the

---

[1] Trotter's Corp. v. Ringleader Restaurants, 929 S.W.2d 935, 940 (Mo. App. 1996).

[2] Trenholm v. Ratcliff, 646 S.W.2d 927, 930 (Tex. 1983) (noting that false opinion is actionable when the speaker purports to have special knowledge of facts that will occur or exist in the future); *cf.* Edmunds v. Valley Circle Estates, 20 Cal. Rptr. 2d 701, 706 (Cal. App. 1993) (same except that the party rendering the opinion must occupy the role of a fiduciary or other trusted person).

[3] Travelers Indemn. Co. v. Armstrong, 442 N.E.2d 349, 364 (Ind. 1982).

[4] Lubbe v. Barba, 540 P.2d 115, 117 (Nev. 1975).

misconduct basis of the tort action overwhelms the consensual basis of contract and a court may extend the damages remedy to negligent misrepresentations, and even innocent misrepresentations.[5] In cases of negligent and innocent misrepresentation, however, courts generally restrict the plaintiff to the out-of-pocket measure of damages.[6]

When fraud is the basis of rescission of the transaction or bargain, the claim of fraud may be based on intentional, negligent, or innocent misrepresentations.[7] This is sometimes distinguished as equitable fraud, as distinct from common law fraud when damages are sought.[8]

Negligent and innocent misrepresentations permitted relief in equity through rescission of the fraud-influenced bargain, but only intentional misrepresentations were actionable at common law. As noted above, the common law approach has been eased. Many jurisdictions now permit a damages action for negligent misrepresentation. The common law strictness is relaxed when fraud is committed by a fiduciary or one in a confidential relationship to the defrauded party. The common law restrictions may also be relaxed by consumer fraud legislation.[9]

These easings of the common law rule reflect the equitable origins of actions for rescission and claims involving fiduciaries. In fact, fraud as a cause of action originated in equity, but was adopted by the common law courts. As a civil damages action, fraud was severely limited by the common law courts, and was often labeled a disfavored action.[10] These comments are rarely, if ever, repeated today; yet, fraud remains an action that is significantly limited by courts.[11] This is largely due to the fraud action's allowance of tort-based remedies to consensual bargains.[12] The court imposed limits also reflect the realization that even an allegation of fraud can cause a defendant harm.[13]

---

[5] Section 120.3 (Negligent Misrepresentation).

[6] Section 122.1 ("Out-of-Pocket" vs. "Benefit-of-the-Bargain" Measure).

[7] Section 136 (Grounds for Rescission).

[8] Zirn v. VLI Corp., 681 A.2d 1050, 1060–61 (Del. 1996).

[9] Duran v. Leslie Oldsmobile, Inc., 594 N.E.2d 1355, 1360–61 (Ill. App. 1992) (noting that "[t]he majority of the elements of common law fraud have been eliminated by the Consumer Fraud Act, and it affords broader consumer protection than the common law action of fraud by prohibiting any deception or false promise").

[10] Bower v. Jones, 978 F.2d 1004, 1012 (7th Cir. 1992) (stating that "[p]romissory fraud is a disfavored cause of action in Illinois because fraud is easy to allege and difficult to prove or disprove").

[11] Section 121.3 (Economic Loss Rule); Section 125 ([Fraud] Personal Relationships).

[12] Breeden v. Richmond Community College, 171 F.R.D. 189, 199–200 (M.D.N.C. 1997) (noting that historically law has treated fraud as a "disfavored action" because it invokes attempts to "reopen settled transactions"); Kassab v. Michigan Basic Property Ins. Assoc., 491 N.W.2d 545, 568 (Mich. 1992) (dissenting opinion) (noting that fraud actions are disfavored and scrutinized by courts "because they often form the basis for 'strike suits' brought in the hope of forcing defendants to settle to avoid discovery expenses").

[13] Many jurisdictions require that allegations of fraud be pleaded in substantially more detail than other causes of action. Fed. R. Civ. P. 9(b).

[120.2]   Promissory Fraud

A party cannot convert a breach of contract claim into a fraud claim by alleging that the defendant falsely represented its intent to perform its contractual obligations. A party may, however, be able to assert, in limited circumstances, a fraud claim when she can show that the defendant *never* intended to perform its contractual obligations. This is a form of fraud in the inducement and is actionable as fraud in many jurisdictions.[14] The rationale for recognizing tort liability in this context was set forth in *Edgington v. Fitzmaurice*:

> The state of a man's mind is as much a fact as the state of his digestion. It is true that it is very difficult to prove what the state of a man's mind, at a particular time, is, but if it can be ascertained it is as much a fact as anything else. A misrepresentation as to the state of a man's mind is, therefore, a misrepresentation of a fact.[15]

The primary difficulty in promissory fraud cases is distinguishing among (1) promises as to what will be done in the future, (2) promises as to present facts and (3) promises as to present intent. Category (1) is actionable under breach of contract but usually not as fraud:

> "[S]tatements of intention made at the time of contracting are not fraudulent if, when made, such statements represent a person's true state of mind, even though later one changes one's mind.[16]

Category (2) is actionable as fraud; and category (3) is actionable as promissory fraud in jurisdictions that treat it as a form of category (2).[17]

Even if the court permits the plaintiff to base a fraud claim on proof that the defendant induced the plaintiff to enter into the contract without defendant having the then present intent to perform, the plaintiff must produce evidence that the defendant actually harbored that specific intent.[18] The mere fact of breach is not sufficient evidence that the defendant

---

[14] Formoso Plastics Corp., U.S.A. v. Presidio Eng'rs and Contrs., Inc., 960 S.W.2d 41, 48 (Tex. 1997) (holding that a "promise of future performance constitutes an actionable misrepresentation if the promise was made with no intention of performing at the time it was made"); Lazar v. Superior Court, 909 P.2d 981, 985 (Cal. 1996) (holding that an "action for promissory fraud may lie where a defendant fraudulently induces the plaintiff to enter into a contract"); Stewart v. Jackson & Nash, 976 F.2d 86, 88–89 (2d Cir. 1992) (holding that employee at will (lawyer) could assert a fraud claim against his employer (law firm) based on allegations that the employer fraudulently induced the employee to leave his prior employment and go to work for the employer).

[15] 29 Ch. Div. 459, 483 (Del. 1885).

[16] College Watercolor Group, Inc. v. William H. Newbauer, Inc., 360 A.2d 200, 206 (Pa. 1976) (citation omitted); Landes v. Sullivan, 651 N.Y.S.2d 731, 733 (App. Dept. 1997) (noting that "a representation of opinion or a prediction of something which is hoped or expected to occur in the future will not sustain an action for fraud").

[17] *Stewart, supra*, 976 F.2d at 88–89.

[18] O'Mary v. Mitsubishi Elecs. Am., Inc., 69 Cal. Rptr. 2d 389, 400 (Cal. App. 1997) (noting that terminated employee offered "no evidence to show that [employer] had no intent to perform [promise of lifetime employment] at the time it was made in the early 1980s) (brackets added);

harbored, at the time of contract formation, the fraudulent intent not to perform. As noted by one court:

> A fraudulent intent not to perform may not be inferred from the mere fact of the eventual failure to perform . . . . Other circumstances of a substantial character must be shown in addition to nonperformance to support the inference that the promissor never intended to perform.[19]

[120.3] Negligent Misrepresentation

Jurisdictions are divided as to whether to recognize a general duty to avoid negligent misrepresentations in the absence of the infliction of physical harm, i.e., when only economic loss results.[20] If a jurisdiction recognizes negligent misrepresentation as a basis for fraud damages, the defrauded party may proceed as if the misrepresentation were deliberate; however, the nature of the fraud claim as sounding in negligence, as opposed to intentional misrepresentation, may affect the amount of damages recoverable. As for economic damages the "out-of-pocket" measure finds general support in the decisional law in cases of negligent misrepresentation rather than the more generous "benefit-of-the-bargain" measure,[21] which is usually reserved for intentional misrepresentation. Moreover, comparative fault principles may reduce damages for negligent misrepresentation,[22] but if intentional misconduct is involved, an apportionment will not be made.[23] As to non-economic damages, a court may

---

cf. La Scola v. U.S. Sprint Comm., 946 F.2d 559, 567–68 (7th Cir. 1991) (holding that comments made to induce terminated employee to leave former employer and work for defendant were too indefinite and unverifiable to support claims of promissory fraud).

[19] The Communications Group, Inc. v. GTE Mobilnet of Oregon, 871 P.2d 502, 504 (Or. App. 1994) (citation omitted); Milwaukee Auction Galleries, Ltd. v. Chalk, 13 F.3d 1107, 1109 (7th Cir. 1994) (same); *Formoso Plastics Corp. U.S.A.*, *supra*, 960 S.W.2d at 48 (same); Restatement (Second) of Torts § 530, cmt. d (1977). A contrary decision, *Rosener v. Sears, Roebuck & Co.*, 168 Cal. Rptr. 237, 242 (Cal. App. 1980), *appeal dismissed,* 450 U.S. 1051 (1981), has not been followed. John Sebert, Jr., *Punitive and Nonpecuniary Damages in Actions Based Upon Contract: Toward Achieving the Objective of Full Compensation,* 33 U.C.L.A. L. Rev. 1565, 1607–13 (1986).

[20] Restatement (Second) of Torts § 311 (1965). Physical harm means bodily injury or property damage. Brogan v. Mitchell Intern., Inc., 692 N.E.2d 276, 278 (Ill. 1998).

[21] Burke v. Harman, 574 N.W.2d 156, 175–76 (Neb. App. 1998) (applying Restatement (Second) of Torts § 552B(1) (1977) and noting that the Restatement rejects, in this context, the benefit-of-the-bargain measure in favor of the out-of-pocket measure); Section 122.1 ("Out-of-Pocket" or "Benefit-the-Bargain" Measure).

[22] Esca Corp. v. Amerlinc Corp., 959 P.2d 651 (Wash. 1998).

[23] Welch v. Southland Corp., 952 P.2d 162, 163 (Wash. 1998) (noting that intentional acts are not included in statutory definition of fault in comparative fault statute). As between joint tortfeasors, courts are increasingly moving away from the traditional rule that prohibits comparing negligent and intentional misconduct. Hutcherson v. City of Phoenix, 961 P.2d 449 (Ariz. 1998). Whether this will encompass comparing levels of misconduct between a plaintiff-victim and defendant-intentional tortfeasor is unclear.

impose limitations that align the negligent misrepresentation action with the general action for negligence.[24]

In jurisdictions that treat negligent misrepresentations as actionable, to whom is the duty owed? When the gist of the claim is an actionable misrepresentation based on negligent conduct, courts have recognized several tests to determine if a duty was owed to the recipient of the misrepresentation. Some jurisdictions have adopted a privity or "near privity" requirement. In this context, a duty to avoid negligent misrepresentations is owed only to those in contractual privity or to those not in privity "who [rely] to [their] detriment on the [negligent misrepresentation and] only when [their] relationship with the [provider/supplier of the information is] so close as to approach that of privity."[25] At the other end of the continuum, a number of jurisdictions have adopted a pure tort foreseeability standard. In *Rosenblum v. Adler* the court held that a provider/supplier of information had a duty to all those whom that person (the auditor) should reasonably foresee as recipients from the company of the audit report for its proper business purposes, provided that the recipients rely on the audit report pursuant to those business purposes.[26] A third test strikes a middle ground. Drawing on the Restatement (Second) of Torts § 552, many courts have limited the scope of liability, to parties not in privity, to transactions or bargains: (1) the maker of the misrepresentation intends to influence, or (2) the maker of the misrepresentation knows that the party in privity, who receives the information, intends to use that information to influence another with regards to that bargain or transaction.[27]

---

[24] Branch v. Homefed Bank, 8 Cal. Rptr. 2d 182, 186 (Cal. App. 1992) (holding that in cases of negligent misrepresentation the fraud damages recovery should match that available in negligence actions generally. A plaintiff "incurring neither physical impact nor physical damage, and whose loss (other than emotional distress) is solely economic, is entitled neither to punitive damages nor to a recovery for emotional distress"); Pearson v. Simmonds Precision Prod., Inc., 624 A.2d 1134, 1137 (Vt. 1993) (same); *cf.* M.H. & J.L.H. v. Caritas Family Servs., 475 N.W.2d 94, 98 (Minn. App. 1991) (limiting, for public policy reasons, the cause of action for negligent misrepresentation in adoption cases to extraordinary expenses resulting from misrepresented facts, not the ordinary expenses of raising a child), *rev'd in part on other grounds,* 488 N.W.2d 282 (Minn. 1992). Those ordinary expenses would have been incurred whenever the adoptive parents retained custody of the child and, thus, affirmed the adoption contract.

[25] Ultramares Corp. v. Touche, 174 N.E. 441, 446 (N.Y. 1931) (Cardozo, J.) (brackets added). A party in "near privity" is one for whom the transaction is aimed and intended. White v. Guarente, 372 N.E.2d 315, 320 (N.Y. 1977) (holding that financial statement prepared by accountant for limited partnership pursuant to contract requiring partnership to provide accounting to limited partners was aimed and intended for limited partners; consequently, limited partner could sue accounting firm for negligent misrepresentation notwithstanding lack of privity).

[26] 461 A.2d 138, 153 (N.J. 1983). The holding was later repealed by the New Jersey legislature. N.J. Stat. Ann. § 2A-25 (West Supp. 1997). *See also* Citizens State Bank v. Timm, Schmidt & Co., 335 N.W.2d 361, 366 (Wis. 1983) (adopting tort foreseeability test).

[27] Bily v. Arthur Young & Co., 834 P.2d 745, 752, 758–59, 769 (Cal. 1992). This middle ground appears to be the majority view. Kohala Agric. v. Deloitte & Touche, 949 P.2d 141, 158–59 & n.33 (Haw. App. 1997). *See generally* Christine Guerci, Annot., *Liability of Independent Accountant to Investors or Shareholders,* 48 A.L.R.5th 389 (1997).

The duty to avoid making a negligent misrepresentation is different from the duty to avoid committing negligence, as is the issue of to whom is each duty owed. One may have a duty not to negligently misrepresent a fact to a person, but not owe a duty of care to that person. For example, a lawyer may owe a duty to a third person (non-client) not to misrepresent facts, as by an opinion letter, yet, not owe that third person a duty of care as to the preparation of the opinion letter.[28]

[120.4] Non-Disclosure as Fraud

Non-disclosure of material facts amounts to actionable fraud only when the non-disclosing party has a duty to disclose.[29] A duty to disclose will be found in four situations:

- a statute creates a duty to disclose.[30]

- a fiduciary or confidential relationship exists between the parties to the transaction or bargain.[31]

- **a disclosure has been made which is partially true and partially false.[32]**

- **one party has superior knowledge of the true facts and the other party to the bargain or transaction is unable to acquire that same information at a reasonable cost.[33]**

---

[28] *E.g.*, Goodman v. Kennedy, 556 P.2d 737 (Cal. 1976).

[29] Remington Rand Corp. v. Amsterdam-Rotterdam Bank, N.V., 68 F.3d 1478, 1483 (2d Cir. 1995).

[30] Cal. Civ. Code §§ 1102.6, 2079 (requiring sellers and brokers to disclose certain information in connection with sales of residential property).

[31] Hershey v. Donaldson, Lufkin & Jenrette Securities Corp., 317 F.3d 16, 20 (6th Cir. 2003) (applying Ohio law); *Remington Rand Corp, supra*, 68 F.3d at 1483–84.

[32] M.H. v. Caritas Family Services, 488 N.W.2d 282 (Minn. 1992):

We long ago recognized that even if one has no duty to disclose a particular fact, if one chooses to speak he must say enough to prevent the words from misleading the other party. We have also held that a duty to disclose facts may exist "when disclosure would be necessary to clarify information already disclosed, which would otherwise be misleading," particularly when a confidential or fiduciary relationship exists between the parties.

Id. at 288 (citations and footnote omitted) (involving adoption agency's failure to disclose the *entire* health history of the adoptee); Zimpel v. Trawick, 679 F. Supp. 1502, 1508–10 (W.D. Ark. 1988) (noting that a buyer normally does not have a duty to speak and disclose valuable information to the seller; however, once the buyer begins to speak, the buyer must speak the complete truth). In *Zimpel*, the defendant sought an oil and gas lease from an unsophisticated and nearly invalid owner of the mineral estate. Defendant correctly told the owner of the generally depressed conditions in the oil and gas industry, but failed to disclose that well drilling in the area indicated that the area held tremendous potential. The court treated the non-disclosure as actionable. A half truth may arise by conduct as well as speech. Donovan v. Aeolian Co., 200 N.E. 815, 816 (N.Y. 1936) (holding that the manner in which a product was displayed created a misleading impression that it was new, which the defendant had a duty to correct).

[33] Lewis v. Bank of America, 347 F.3d 587, 588 (5th Cir. 2003) (*per curiam*) (applying Texas

Non-disclosure liability is usually limited to cases when the non-disclosing party intends not to disclose. Jurisdictions, which recognize liability for negligent misrepresentations, may not recognize fraud liability for the negligent failure to disclose a material fact in the partial disclosure and superior knowledge contexts.[34]

Non-disclosure should also be distinguished from fraudulent concealment, although courts frequently use the terms non-disclosure and concealment interchangeably. Fraudulent concealment involves the active effort and conduct by a party to prevent another from discovering the true facts. While parties to an arms-length transaction or bargain usually do not have affirmative disclosure obligations and may exploit their adversary's information deficits to their profit, a party may not affirmatively impede, hinder, or subvert the adversary's detection of the true facts. For example, a seller does not have a duty to disclose obvious and patent defects in the product to be sold, but the seller cannot obscure the defects by applying a coat of paint or cover that hides and masks the defects from the buyer.[35] If seller does so, those acts would constitute fraudulent concealment and would be actionable if the concealed facts were material to the transaction.[36]

The right of a party to use her superior knowledge against the plaintiff may be compromised if the defendant acquired her knowledge improperly.[37]

---

law). It is usually required that the party with superior knowledge be aware of the fact that the other party is ignorant of the true state of affairs. *See* OnBank & Trust Co. v. F.D.I.C., 967 F. Supp. 81–88 (W.D.N.Y. 1997) (applying New York law). The duty effectively precludes one party from taking unconscionable advantage of another and may be likened to a pre-contractual implied covenant of good faith and fair dealing. *See* Banque Arabe et Internationale D'Investissement v. Maryland National Bank, 57 F.3d 146 (2d Cir. 1995) (applying New York law).

[34] Taggart v. Ford Motor Credit Co., 462 N.W.2d 493, 504 (S.D. 1990) (distinguishing between negligent misrepresentation, which is actionable, from negligent failure to disclose, which was not actionable). *But see* Wallerstein v. Hospital Corp. of Am., 573 So. 2d 9, 10 (Fla. App. 1990) (*per curiam*) (holding that adoptive parents could state a claim for negligent representation regarding the health of an adopted child based on a "should have known" standard).

[35] Van Deusen v. Snead, 441 S.E.2d 207, 209–10 (Va. 1994) (holding that action for fraud was stated when seller "put new mortar in cracks around the foundation" and "materials . . . in front of cracks in the basement" to prevent detection and diverting the buyer's attention).

[36] Restatement (Second) of Torts § 550 (1977) (treating fraudulent concealment as equivalent to the positive assertion that the concealed fact does not exist).

[37] Mallon Oil Co. v. Bowen/Edwards Associates, 965 P.2d 105 (Colo. 1998):

> Mallon argues that trespass creates a duty to disclose information, and that Boyce had a duty to disclose because he committed a geophysical trespass when he conducted the desorption tests. At common law, the general rule is that a person rightfully on property does not have a duty to disclose knowledge of the land to a seller of the land who does not have the same knowledge. However, this rule does not apply when the buyer acquires the information through improper means, such as trespass. Mallon asserts that a geophysical trespass occurred and that a duty exists in the case. However . . . no unlawful geophysical trespass occurred in this case. Thus, Boyce's desorption tests do not constitute "objective circumstances" that would create a duty on behalf of Boyce or BEA.

Id. at 111–12 (citations omitted).

§ 121 ELEMENTS OF FRAUD

[121.1] Materiality

To establish fraud, the plaintiff must show that the misrepresentation justifiably induced his reliance. To rely is not enough, the reliance must be reasonable. The law captures this requirement with the concept of materiality.

A statement is material if it would influence a reasonably prudent person. The "materiality" requirement is designed to insure that fraud claims are not predicated on insubstantial communications that while false are not seen as warranting legal intervention.

The materiality requirement is often difficult to pin down because there is a high degree of overlap between the particular elements of fraud and materiality can easily be subsumed within the analysis given the other factors. For example, whether a communication or statement as to product quality is material is often addressed as a question of fact or opinion[1] or as "puffery."[2]

Materiality is closely linked to reliance. Sometimes the materiality requirement is excused, as for example when a person *knowingly* preys on a vulnerable plaintiff by a false statement that would not influence a reasonably prudent person, but which does influence the vulnerable plaintiff and that is the fraudfeasor's intent.[3]

[121.2] Loss Causation

Liability for fraud damages is not unlimited; the loss must follow as the natural and proximate result of the defrauded party's reliance on the misrepresentation.[4] First, the plaintiff must show that defendant's misrepresentation caused him to act to his prejudice. In most cases, this causation element is satisfied by the reliance requirement, but occasionally reliance alone is insufficient, as, for example, when the plaintiff's action is a product of many factors, of which the misrepresentation is but one. In such cases, the plaintiff must demonstrate that the misrepresentation caused him to act as he did.[5] Causation also requires that when damages are sought, the

---

[1] American Italian Pasta Co. v. New World Pasta Co., 371 F.3d 387, 391 (8th Cir. 2004) (holding that phrase "America's Favorite Pasta, standing alone is not a statement of fact").

[2] San Leandro Emergency Med. Group Profit Sharing Plan v. Phillip Morris Companies, Inc., 75 F.3d 801, 811 (2d Cir. 1996) (stating that mere puffery cannot mislead a reasonable investor). Put another way, puffery would not influence a reasonably prudent investor as to whether the object of the puffery should be purchased or sold.

[3] Sections 120.1 (Common Law Fraud) (text and note 4), 121.4 (Reliance) (text and notes 27–30).

[4] Restatement (Second) of Torts § 548A (1977).

[5] Knepper v. Brown M.D., 50 P.3d 1209, 1221–22 (Or. App. 2002) (adopting "substantial factor" test to determine if defendant's false listing of physician as a "specialist" caused the plaintiff to be treated by the physician).

plaintiff must establish a linkage between the misrepresentation and the loss. This issue can be particularly difficult when the transaction or bargain's value is subject to external factors. If the plaintiff is fraudulently induced to purchase a business and the business subsequently fails, is the failure, and resulting loss, a consequence of the fraud or factors external to the fraud, such as plaintiff's business incompetence or general market conditions? In *Glass Design Imports, Inc. v. Import Specialties* defendant misrepresented the origin of products and exclusivity of a distributorship it offered to the plaintiff. As a consequence, defendant became liable for losses subsequently incurred by plaintiffs in the areas of loan losses, capital investment, legal expense and lost profits. The court concluded, however, that plaintiff's claimed losses of foregone salaries was not caused by the fraud: the plaintiffs "were not entitled to set salaries, rather, salaries are dependent upon profits and as investors they impliedly assumed the risk of the success or failure of their venture. There has been no 'but for' showing that the fraud caused the entire loss of salaries. . . ."[6]

The fact that fraud may have induced the transaction or bargain does not mean that all losses thereafter realized are deemed to have been "caused by" the fraud. This is simply a form of "Post Hoc, Ergo Propter Hoc" reasoning.[7] The loss must result from the fraud. As noted by one court:

> Defendant Madden cannot attempt to escape liability by alleging he wasn't on the scene at the time the second loan was made. One who engages in fraud, but is not involved in a subsequent overt act leading directly to additional damages, does not escape liability for those damages *if they flow from the initial fraudulent acts*.[8]

This point, while easy to state, is often difficult to apply. Let's start with an easy case. Assume a seller misrepresents the value of shares of stock and induces the buyer to pay more than the actual value of the stock based on its financial valuation. When that fact becomes known, and the market corrects based on the new information, the "loss" is due to the fraud. Conversely, if the stock's market value depreciates due to a general market decline or crash, that "down market" loss is not due to the fraud.[9] If a

---

[6] 867 F.2d 1139, 1143 (8th Cir. 1989). In *Sutter v. General Petroleum Corp.*, 170 P.2d 898, 903 (Cal. 1946), the court permitted recovery of loss of time and effort or loss of salary caused by fraudulent inducements to execute a lease. In *Sutter*, however, there were no other losses. Had the plaintiff not received compensation for the time he lost due to the fraud, the fraud would have gone unsanctioned.

[7] Literally, "after this, therefore, because of this." BRYAN GARNER, DICTIONARY OF MODERN LEGAL USAGE (2d ed. 1995). This form of argument or reasoning is recognized as based on a logical fallacy, a non-sequitur, for it confuses the concept of causation with that of correlation. However, some courts do permit inferences based on correlation alone, although these are usually in the context of statistical correlation, and even here the decisional law is diverse. At the very least, the correlation must be supported by a viable hypothesis that links the correlation to the effect shown. Carter v. Westinghouse Elec. Corp., 703 F. Supp. 393, 398–99 (W.D. Pa. 1988), *aff'd*, 877 F.2d 53 (3d Cir. 1989) (Table).

[8] National Consumer Coop. Bank v. Madden, 737 F. Supp. 1108, 1115 (D. Haw. 1990) (citations omitted) (emphasis added).

[9] Dura Pharmaceuticals, Inc. v. Broudo, 125 S. Ct. 1627 (2005) (holding that paying a higher

business fails because it is undercapitalized or lacks sufficient working capital due to cash management or accounts receivables problems, that loss may be attributable to the party who induced the buyer to purchase the business by misrepresenting the adequacy of the working capital or the quality of the assets or the business' income potential.[10] If on the other hand, the business fails due to a recession, loss causation is not satisfied.[11]

It is here that the differences between common law and equitable fraud are significant. Common law fraud required the intent to deceive and limited recoveries to losses resulting from the fraud. The action for fraud represented an affirmance of the fraud-infected transaction with damages the means by which the defrauded party was made whole. Equitable fraud, on the other hand, allowed the party to rescind the transaction. The focus in equity was on the inducement to enter into the transaction. When it was false, equity allowed the defrauded party to escape from the transaction.

When the intervening event is foreseeable, it does not cut-off the defendant's liability for fraudulent inducement. For example, in *Cicone v. URS Corp.* sellers were fraudulently induced to sell by oral misrepresentations made by buyer's counsel that the buyers would deem the sellers to be guaranteeing the information on the balance sheet only to the seller's best knowledge, when, in fact, the buyers intended to rely on the strict warranty contained in the contract. After the transaction was concluded, buyers made a claim based on a $200,000 understatement on the balance sheet, of which sellers were unaware. Sellers settled that claim and sued buyer's counsel for fraud. Counsel argued that the loss was caused by the settlement, not the misrepresentation. The court disagreed, holding that litigation and settlement was foreseeable and, thus, not a superceding event.[12]

[121.3] Economic Loss Rule

A number of courts have extended the "economic loss rule" to fraud actions.[13] The reason for this is the concern that tort-based remedies not preempt the consensual bargain (and contract remedies) to which the parties have agreed. Perhaps the safest formulation of a guiding principle

---

price due to fraud may be a necessary condition to a loss, but, standing alone, it is not a sufficient cause of a future loss; rather, the plaintiff must establish that the subsequent decline in price was the result of the fraud).

[10] Standard Chartered PLC v. Price Waterhouse, 945 P.2d 317, 344–45 (Ariz. App. 1997).

[11] Movitz v. First National Bank of Chicago, 148 F.3d 760, 763–64 (7th Cir. 1998) (discussed at Section 10.6 (Occurrence Causation vs. Loss Causation)).

[12] 227 Cal. Rptr. 887, 894–95 (Cal. App. 1986); *Madden, supra,* 737 F. Supp. 1108.

[13] McCutcheon v. Kidder, Peabody & Co., Inc., 938 F. Supp. 820, 824 (S.D. Fla. 1996) (holding that under Florida law, the economic loss rule barred recovery when plaintiff's fraud claim was interwoven with the contractual relationship between the parties). The claim centered on defendant's alleged failure to render truthful and accurate information and advice to plaintiff regarding his securities account at defendant's business. *Cf.* Medical Billing v. Medical Management Sciences, 212 F.3d 332, 338 (6th Cir. 2000) (applying Ohio law) (holding that fraud injury must be *unique* and *separate* from any injury resulting from breach of contract); Section 11 (Economic Loss Rule).

here is that the fraud claim must exist independent of the contract to be actionable. The misrepresentation, on which the fraud claim is based, must be outside or collateral to the contract.[14] How "independent" the fraud claim must be is a matter of some dispute. In *Robinson Helicopter Co. v. Dana Corp.* the California Supreme Court adopted a liberal interpretation of the requirement:

> [We have] held that a party's contractual obligation may create a legal duty and that a breach of that duty may support a tort action. We stated, [C]onduct amounting to a breach of contract becomes tortious only when it also violates a duty independent of the contract arising from principles of tort law. We went on to describe several instances where tort damages were permitted in contract cases. Tort damages have been permitted in contract cases where a breach of duty directly causes physical injury; for breach of the covenant of good faith and fair dealing in insurance contracts; for wrongful discharge in violation of fundamental public policy; OR WHERE THE CONTRACT WAS fraudulently induced. [I]n each of these cases, the duty that gives rise to tort liability is either completely independent of the contract or arises from conduct which is both intentional and intended to harm. . . . With respect to situations outside of those set forth above, we stated: Generally, outside the insurance context, a tortious breach of contract . . . may be found when (1) the breach is accompanied by a traditional common law tort, such as fraud or conversion; (2) the means used to breach the contract are tortious, involving deceit or undue coercion; or (3) one party intentionally breaches the contract intending or knowing that such a breach will cause severe, unmitigable, harm in the form of mental anguish, personal hardship, or substantial consequential damages. Focusing on intentional conduct gives substance to the proposition that a breach of contract is tortious only when some independent duty arising from tort law is violated. If every negligent breach of a contract gives rise to tort damages the limitation would be meaningless, as would the statutory distinction between tort and contract remedies.[15]

Other courts adopt a more restrictive interpretation, generally applying the economic loss rule to bargain related misrepresentation claims unless the misrepresentation *induced* the bargain.[16]

---

[14] AKA Distrib. Co. v. Whirlpool Corp., 137 F.3d 1083, 1086–87 (8th Cir. 1998) (collecting decisions).

[15] 102 P.3d 268, 273–74 (Cal. 2004) (citations and quotation marks omitted) (emphasis in original).

[16] Digicorp, Inc. v. Ameritech Corp., 662 N.W.2d 652 (Wis. 2003):

> Wisconsin recognizes a narrow fraud in the inducement exception . . . . We hold that, consistent with the *Huron Tool* decision, the economic loss doctrine acts as a bar where the fraud is interwoven with the contract, and not extraneous to it.

Id. at 657 (citations omitted).

The "economic loss rule" is not evenly applied to fraud claims, even in jurisdictions which recognize its application. Some jurisdictions apply the rule strictly, "bar[ing] all claims for fraud where the plaintiff has a remedy in contract for the breach."[17] Some jurisdictions limit the doctrines application to certain litigants, for example, permitting the fraud claim when it is brought against a defendant in the business of supplying information and the information was provided to the plaintiff to guide him in his business dealings with third parties.[18] There is also a debate whether the economic loss doctrine should be applied to disputes between commercial and non-commercial entities.[19]

Some jurisdictions reject the application of the "economic loss rule" to fraud claims.[20]

[121.4] RELIANCE

Reliance is a requirement when a party seeks fraud damages. A party cannot enter into a transaction with his eyes closed to available information and claim that he was deceived.[21] Whether an investigation is called for on the part of the recipient of the false information often depends on whether the true state of affairs is latent or patent.[22]

---

[17] Leisure Founders Inc. v. CUC Int'l, Inc., 833 F. Supp. 1562, 1572 (S.D. Fla. 1993) (applying Florida law).

[18] Gerdes v. John Hancock Mut. Life Ins. Co., 712 F. Supp. 692, 696 (N.D. Ill. 1989). Whether, under Illinois law, a defendant is in the business of supplying information is itself a difficult question for which additional tests have been created. *Id.* at 697–98; *see* Rankow v. First Chicago Corp., 870 F.2d 356, 364 (7th Cir. 1989).

[19] Werwinski v. Ford Motor Co., 286 F.3d 661, 672 (3d Cir. 2002) (applying Pennyslvania law) (rejecting argument that the economic loss doctrine is limited to disputes between commercial entities).

[20] Arthur D. Little Int'l, Inc. v. Dooyang Corp., 928 F. Supp. 1189, 1204 (D. Mass. 1996) (noting that "the Restatement (Second) of Torts § 552B(1) (1977) provides 'the correct rule' of damages for negligent misrepresentation cases" . . . and holding that "the economic loss rule does not apply in this context"). The context involved accounting services. The court further noted that if the economic loss rule were applied "tort law would not exert significant financial pressure to avoid negligence." *Id., quoting* Barber Lines A/S v. M/V Donau Maru, 764 F.2d 50, 56 (1st Cir. 1985).

[21] Lazard Freres & Co. v. Protective Life Ins. Co., 108 F.3d 1531 (2d Cir.) (holding that the deliberate bypassing of critical relevant information that would have corrected the misrepresentation undermined the claim of reliance), *cert. denied*, 522 U.S. 864 (1997); Lewis v. Cohen, 603 A.2d 352, 354–55 (Vt. 1991) (holding that the buyer's knowledge of the seller's outstanding debts and checkered financial history rendered unjustified the buyer's reliance on the seller's representations of business value); *cf.* Simmons v. Pilkenton, 497 S.E.2d 613, 616 (Ga. App. 1998) (holding that the buyer failed to exercise due diligence in relying on the seller's representation of lot size when the correct (albeit smaller) lot size was provided in the written contract documents); *but cf. Cicone, supra* text and note 12.

[22] *Compare* Fleisher v. Lettvin, 557 N.E.2d 383, 389 (Ill. App. 1990) (stating that the seller's advisement to the purchaser not to overload the electric system was sufficient to put the purchaser on notice of possible problems with the electrical system and required the purchaser to investigate further so that the purchaser could not recover for the alleged fraudulent concealment of water damage to the electrical system), *with* Payne v. O'Quinn, 565 So. 2d 1049, 1052 (La. App. 1990) (holding that termite damage to a house was a latent defect that the purchaser could not have discovered by a simple inspection; the purchaser was entitled to rely on the seller's report that the old termite damage had been treated).

The victim of fraud does not have a general duty to conduct an investigation to verify the accuracy of facts represented to him as true by the fraudfeasor. As noted by one court:

> A party may justifiably rely on a misrepresentation even when he could have ascertained its falsity by conducting an investigation. This rule applies whether the investigation would have been costly and required extensive effort or could have been made without "any considerable trouble or expense." This pragmatic rule of conduct is at the heart of millions of commercial transactions conducted daily in this nation which rely on the honesty and truthfulness of representation made by the parties.[23]

The fact that the falsity of the misrepresentation could have been discovered by a search of public records does not negate a claim of reliance, absent some alerting event that would cause a reasonable person to doubt the accuracy of the fact(s) represented.[24] If, however, the plaintiff conducts an investigation, the investigation may foreclose a claim of reliance,[25] as long as the defendant does not interfere.[26]

The general rule is that plaintiff's reliance on defendant's fraudulent conduct must be both actual and justifiable.[27] Care must be taken, however, not to read too much into the notion of "justifiable." A defendant will not be allowed to exploit a vulnerable party and escape liability by claiming a prudent party would not have been misled. Whether reliance is justified is determined "with reference to the specific intelligence and experience of the aggrieved party rather than a reasonable-man standard."[28] A defendant may not knowingly exploit the susceptibility and naivete of a vulnerable person and then seek to escape responsibility by blaming the victim for his loss. Even when the plaintiff is negligent, a feature of many successful frauds, the plaintiff's mistakes will not negate a finding of "justifiable" reliance. As noted by one court:

> Negligence in reliance upon a misrepresentation is not a defense where the misrepresentation was intentionally made to induce reliance upon it. Only [i]f the conduct of the plaintiff [in relying

---

[23] Sanford Inst. for Sav. v. Gallo, 156 F.3d 71 (1st Cir. 1998) (citation omitted); Holmes v. Couturier, 452 N.W.2d 135 (S.D. 1990) (holding that the buyer could rely on the seller's statements that sanitary and electrical systems were in working order and the buyer was not required to investigate and verify the information).

[24] Cao v. Nguyen, 607 N.W.2d 528, 533–34 (Neb. 2000); *Lazard Freres & Co., supra*, 108 F.3d at 1543.

[25] Czarnecki v. Roller, 726 F. Supp. 832, 842 (S.D. Fla. 1989) (holding that buyer could not have relied on any misrepresentation regarding the quality of the subject of the bargain (yacht) in light of buyer's own independent investigation).

[26] Homer v. Guzulaitis, 567 N.E.2d 153, 157 (Ind. App. 1991) (applying Minnesota law) (holding that plaintiffs did not waive their right to damages by conducting an appraisal when defendant's conduct thwarted the effectiveness of the appraisal).

[27] Haralson v. E.F. Hutton Group, Inc., 919 F.2d 1014, 1025–26 (5th Cir. 1990).

[28] Midland Nat'l Bank v. Perranowski, 299 N.W.2d 404, 412 (Minn. 1980)

upon a misrepresentation] in light of his own intelligence and information was manifestly unreasonable will he be denied recovery.[29]

A different approach may be applied, however, when the plaintiff is not seen as vulnerable.[30]

The fact that the plaintiff learns about the true facts during the executory period of the transaction or bargain does not mean that there can be no reliance.[31] Nevertheless, a court may find that facts discovered during the executory (or escrow) period preclude a finding of reliance, particularly when the deal contains opt-out provisions that permit a party to walk away if the investigation discloses new facts.[32] The critical issue is whether termination of the bargain or transaction on discovery of the fraud would be economically reasonable or unreasonable under the facts.[33] Severe enforcement of this termination rule could put the defrauded party in a catch-22 situation: complete the transaction but lose the fraud claim if there is a misrepresentation or hold up the transaction and risk being held in breach if there is no misrepresentation. Rescission remedies have similar termination requirements.[34]

A party who disclaims reliance on the defendant's representations may be held to his word even if fraud infects the bargain.[35] How broadly and

---

[29] Winn v. McCulloch Corp. 131 Cal. Rptr. 592, 601 (Cal. App. 1976) (citations and quotation marks omitted); *see* Lockard v. Carson, 287 N.W.2d 871, 878 (Iowa 1980) (same); *cf.* Field v. Mans, 516 U.S. 59, 73–74 (1995) (holding that fraud exception to bankruptcy discharge required *justifiable but not reasonable* reliance by defrauded creditor of bankrupt debtor).

[30] Nappe v. Anschelewitz, Barr, Ansell & Bonello, 460 A.2d 161, 165–66 (N.J. Super. Ct. A.D. 1983) (noting that plaintiff's reliance was not justified when the non-disclosed fact of so-called "sweetheart leases" was obvious or would have been disclosed by a limited investigation), *rev'd on other grounds,* 477 A.2d 1224 (N.J. 1984). The fact that plaintiff was represented by counsel in at least one of the underlying transactions was not treated as outcome determinative. 469 A.2d at 163; *see Homer, supra,* 567 N.E.2d at 157 (noting that plaintiffs, while college educated, were not "sophisticated business people").

[31] Jue v. Smiser, 28 Cal. Rptr. 2d 242, 244–46 (Cal. App. 1994) (noting that reliance is determined at inception of transaction or bargain and the misrepresenter should not be permitted to force the relying party either to consummate the deal and waive the claim for damages or sue for rescission).

[32] Atari Corp. v. Ernst & Whinney, 981 F.2d 1025, 1030–31 (9th Cir. 1992) (applying California law); Section 133.3 (Election).

[33] *In re* Usery, 123 F.3d 1089, 1097 (8th Cir. 1997) (stating that "a party to an executory contract who discovers fraud may not go forward and compound the damages, but instead must terminate the relationship and sue for damages at that point," but further stating that termination is subject to principle of economic reasonableness), *citing* Clements Auto Co. v. Servs. Bureau Corp., 444 F.2d 169, 184 (8th Cir. 1971).

[34] Sonnenberg v. Security Mgmt. Corp., 599 A.2d 820, 823 (Md. 1992) (noting the debate in the law regarding the duty of a defrauded party who discovers fraud during the executory phase of a bargain or transaction), *citing* Annotation, *Proceeding Under Executory Contract After Discovering Fraud as Waiver of Right to Recover Damages for the Fraud,* 13 A.L.R.2d 807 (1950); Section 132 (Demand for Rescission).

[35] Meehan v. United Consumers Club Franchising Corp., 312 F.3d 909, 912 (8th Cir. 2002) (stating that "it is simply unresonable to continue to rely on representations after stating in writing that you are not so relying"), *quoting* Hardee's of Maumelle, Ark., Ind. v. Hardee's Food Sys., Inc., 31 F.3d 573, 576 (7th Cir. 1994).

strictly these "no-reliance" disclaimers should be read remains, however, a matter of some debate.[36]

There may be no reliance when the plaintiff is under a preexisting duty to do what the plaintiff alleges he was induced to do by the misrepresentation.[37] This concept has been applied to claims brought by insurance companies against their policyholders for the costs in investigating fraudulent (exaggerated) claims presented by the policyholder. Some courts have held that such claims are barred because of the insurance company's contractual duty under the insurance policy to investigate all claims.[38] There is, however, some caselaw in the non-insurance area that states that investigative costs incurred as a result of fraud are recoverable as consequential damages.[39]

Reliance is usually required when the plaintiff seeks to rescind the bargain or transaction.[40] In limited circumstances, the reliance requirement may be relaxed, usually by statute.[41]

A link between reliance and causation has been noted by some courts. In this context, a court may look at the plaintiff's reliance and the plaintiff's conduct to determine whether, under the circumstances, and in light of the information available, the loss was the plaintiff's own responsibility.[42] The point was addressed at some length in *City Solutions, Inc. v. Clear Channel Communications, Inc.*:

---

[36] F.T.C. v. Minuteman Press, 53 F. Supp. 2d 248, 262–63 (E.D.N.Y. 1998) (rejecting argument that disclaimer precluded reliance; disclaimers only barred representations it expressly purported to disclaim); *cf.* AES Corp. v. Dow Chemical Co., 325 F.3d 174, 180–81 (3d Cir. 2003) (refusing to enforce "no-reliance" disclaimer in sale of securities because enforcement would violate 1934 Securities Exchange Act prohibition of ex-ante waivers of liability). *But cf.* Harsco Corp. v. Segui, 91 F.3d 337, 343 (2d Cir. 1996) (enforcing disclaimer in action under 34 Securities Exchange Act).

[37] Manufacturer's Hanover Trust v. Ward, 857 F.2d 1082, 1083 (6th Cir. 1988) (holding that a lender must "investigate creditworthiness and ferret out ordinary credit information" before the lender may claim reliance on a debtor's misrepresentation).

[38] Truck Ins. Exch. v. Kafka, 911 F. Supp. 313, 315–16 (N.D. Ill. 1995); Handel v. United States Fid. & Guar. Co., 237 Cal. Rptr. 667, 696 (Cal. App. 1987).

[39] Sutter v. General Petroleum Corp., 170 P.2d 898, 902–03 (Cal. 1946).

[40] *Simmons, supra,* 497 S.E.2d at 616 (stating that the buyer's failure to prove reliance in support of rescission operated to preclude the remedy); Allstate Fin. Corp. v. Utility Trailer of Ill., Inc., 936 F. Supp. 525, 528 (N.D. Ill. 1996) (involving rescission of a settlement agreement).

[41] Northwestern Mut. Life Ins. Co. v. Iannacchino, 950 F. Supp. 28, 31 (D. Mass. 1997) (stating that, under Massachusetts law, an insurance company need not prove reliance in order to rescind an insurance policy for misrepresentation).

[42] Runnemead Owners, Inc. v. Crest Mortgage Corp. 861 F.2d 1053, 1058–59 (7th Cir. 1988) (finding that the plaintiff, a sophisticated businessman, had not justifiably relied on oral representations by the defendant's chairman that the loan committee would approve plaintiff's loan when those oral representations were inconsistent with the written terms of the qualified loan commitment letter); *cf.* Buchanan v. Geneva Chervenic Realty, 685 N.E.2d 265, 268–69 (Ohio App. 1996) (holding that the fact that the buyer did not notice problems, which were discoverable through reasonable diligence, until after the buyer moved into the residence did not transform the "problems" into "latent defects" which the seller had the duty to disclose).

Under California law, [a] complete causal relationship between the fraud or deceit and the plaintiff's damages is required. An essential element in recovery for deceit is proof of the plaintiff's justifiable reliance on the defendant's fraudulent representations. Reliance exists when the misrepresentation or non-disclosure was an immediate cause of the plaintiff's conduct which altered his or her legal relations, and when without such misrepresentation or non-disclosure he or she would not, in all reasonable probability, have entered into the contract or other transaction. It is not . . . necessary that [a plaintiff's] reliance upon the truth of the fraudulent misrepresentation be the sole or even the predominant or decisive factor in influencing his conduct . . . . It is enough that the representation has played a substantial part, and so has been a substantial factor, in influencing his decision.[43]

§ 122 DAMAGES

[122.1] "Out-of-Pocket" or "Benefit-of-the-Bargain" Measure

Fraud general damages are measured by either the out-of-pocket or benefit-of-the-bargain measure. Under the out-of-pocket measure, the defrauded party recovers the difference between the value parted with (usually the consideration) and the value received.[1] Under the benefit-of-the-bargain measure, the defrauded party recovers the difference between what that party would have received had the representation(s) been true and the value of what was actually received.[2] The benefit-of-the-bargain measure, as applied by the courts, is not the same as the bargain expectancy. An example will help illustrate the point. Assume Dan represents to Pat that a product has a value of $20 and that Dan will sell the product to Pat for $18. Dan knows the representation is false and that the value of the product is $10. Pat believes Dan and purchases the product for $18. Pat's bargain expectancy was $2 (value represented ($20) less purchase price ($18)). Under the out-of-pocket measure, Pat's damages are $8 (value paid ($18) less value actually received ($10)). Under the benefit-of-the-bargain measure, Pat's damages are $10 (value represented ($20) less value actually received ($10)). The fraud benefit-of-the-bargain and contract benefit-of-the-bargain measures meet, however, when the contract claim is based on "breach of warranty."[3] That is not surprising given the substantial overlap between the two actions.[4]

---

[43] 365 F.3d 835, 840 (9th Cir. 2004) (citations and quotation marks omitted).

[1] Kenly v. Ukegawa, 19 Cal. Rptr. 2d 771, 773 (Cal. App. 1993).

[2] DCD Programs, Ltd. v. Leighton, 90 F.3d 1442, 1449 (9th Cir. 1996); Estate of Korf. v. A.O. Smith Harvestore Prods., 917 F.2d 480, 483 (10th Cir. 1990) (*per curiam*).

[3] Chattos Systems, Inc. v. National Cash Register, 670 F.2d 1304, 1306 (3d Cir. 1982).

[4] Gary L. Monserud, *Rescission and Damages For Buyer Due to Seller's Fraudulent*

The purpose of tort damages is to compensate the injured party for her loss; however, the "loss" is not self defining. Under the benefit-of-the-bargain measure, the "loss" is conceptualized as restoring the plaintiff to the position she would have occupied if the representations had been true.[5] Under the out-of-pocket measure, the "loss" is conceptualized more in the nature of making the person whole from a balance sheet point of view: the defrauded party gave $18 and received $10; therefore, $8 is needed to make the party whole in the sense of having $18. Under the out-of-pocket approach there is a strong sense here of indemnity as the true measure of the loss:

> The purpose of an action for deceit is to indemnify the party injured. All elements of profit are excluded. The true measure of damage is indemnity for the actual pecuniary loss sustained as the direct result of the wrong.[6]

There are good arguments that can be made in support of both measures. The proponents of benefit-of-the-bargain contend that unless the defrauded party is restored to the position she would have assumed if the representation were true, the defrauding party will have no disincentive to commit fraud. If the out-of-pocket measure is used and if the fraud is discovered, the parties are merely restored to the status-quo. To the proponents of the benefit-of-the-bargain rule, such a limited remedy saps tort of much of its deterrence value for the wrongdoer risks only the fruits of her fraud. The defendant can simply replay the fraud on a new, unsuspecting victim knowing that there is no financial penalty if the fraud is discovered. Proponents of the out-of-pocket rule, on the other hand, assert that this measure best accomplishes the redress of injury function of tort. The defrauded party is indemnified for the loss and her total wealth is equal to what she would have had but for the fraud. To proponents of the out-of-pocket measure, the benefit-of-the-bargain measure produces a windfall for the defrauded party by giving her more than she actually lost. Three arguments substantially parallel those made against, and in favor of, awarding contract expectancies.[7]

Reconciling the two viewpoints is impossible; indeed, while many jurisdictions express a preference for one measure over the other, a large number of jurisdictions accept both measures.[8] In jurisdictions that recognize both

---

Inducement of An Articles 2 Contract For Sale, 1998 Colum. Bus. L. Rev. 331, 438 (discussing Llwellyn's efforts to bring warranty and fraud actions into alignment in the Uniform Commercial Code); JAMES J. WHITE & ROBERT S. SUMMERS, HANDBOOK OF THE LAW UNDER THE UCC § 9–1, at 327 (2d ed. 1980) (noting similarities between fraud and breach of warranty actions).

[5] Ambassador Hotel Co., Ltd. v. Wei-Chuan Investment, 189 F.3d 1017, 1032 (9th Cir. 1999) (applying California law); Wilhoite v. Franklin, 570 So. 2d 1236, 1237 (Ala. App. 1990).

[6] Reno v. Bull, 124 N.E. 144, 146 (N.Y. 1919); *see Ambassador Hotel Co., Ltd., supra*, 189 F.3d at 1032.

[7] Section 6.1 (Expectancy Interest).

[8] Turnbull v. LaRose, 702 P.2d 1331, 1336 (Alaska 1985) (holding that "[a] plaintiff should

measures, which measure is used in a particular case is a product of finding the measure that best achieves the ends of justice, as defined by the court in the particular case.[9] For example, in *Gold v. Dubish* the plaintiff left his previous employment in reliance on the defendant's representations that the bargain would be completed.[10] The court held that the benefit-of-the-bargain measure should not be used because the fraud-infected bargain (purchase of the defendant's business) was not consummated; rather, out-of-pocket damages, based on lost earnings and expenses incurred in securing alternative employment, could be awarded under a reliance theory. Initially, election between "benefit-of-the-bargain" and "out-of-pocket" damages did not include consideration of the defendant's culpability; however, modern courts limit the "benefit-of-the bargain" measure to intentional misrepresentations.[12]

[122.2] Consequential Damages

Consequential, or special, damages are generally recoverable when they are foreseeable and directly traceable to and result from the fraud.[13]

Damages for fraud include the costs incurred in preparing for, performing, or passing up other business opportunities, as well as costs incurred in making reasonable efforts to mitigate damages.[14] Because damages are

---

have the opportunity to use either measure . . ."); *cf.* Johnson v. Naugle, 557 N.E.2d 1339, 1343 (Ind. App. 1990) (holding that the plaintiff may receive the benefit-of-the-bargain measure or the cost of repairing the property to make it conform to the representations, depending on whether the injury is permanent or temporary):

> If the injury is temporary in the sense that restoration can cure the harm, the reasonable cost of repair may serve the need and provide adequate and fair compensation. If the damage is permanent and beyond full repair, the variance in the value of the property before and after injury often affords the better guide to a just award. It all depends upon the character of the property and the nature and extent of injury.

Id., quoting Cushman v. Kirby, 536 A.2d 550, 554 (Vt. 1987). *See generally* J.F. Rydstrom, Annot., Comment Note, *"Out of Pocket" or "Benefit of Bargain" As Proper Rule of Damages For Fraudulent Representations Inducing Contract For the Transfer of Property*, 13 A.L.R.3d 875 (1968).

[9] Martin v. Brown, 566 So. 2d 890, 891–92 (Fla. App. 1990); Zeliff v. Sabatino, 104 A.2d 54, 56–57 (N.J. 1954).

[10] 549 N.E.2d 660, 667 (Ill. App. 1989); *cf.* Midwest Home Distrib., Inc. v. Domco Indus., Ltd., 585 N.W.2d 735, 742 (Iowa 1998) (holding that Iowa recognizes both measures and that plaintiff should recover under benefit-of-the-bargain measure when no out-of-pocket losses are sustained otherwise defendant will not be deterred from committing fraud).

[12] Section 120.1 ([fraud] Common Law Fraud).

[13] Arthur Anderson & Co. v. Perry Equip. Corp., 945 S.W.2d 812, 817 (Tex. 1997); Gyldenvand v. Schroeder, 280 N.W.2d 235, 239 (Wis. 1979); *cf.* Usery v. Usery, 123 F.3d 1089, 1096 (8th Cir. 1997) (stating that under Missouri law, a "defrauded party may recover special damages necessarily incurred solely by reason of the fraud") (citations omitted); Redstone v. Goldman Sachs & Co., 583 F. Supp. 74, 76 (D. Mass. 1984) (stating that under Massachusetts law the plaintiff may recover lost profits resulting from the fraud). Section 6.4 (General Damages v. Special or Consequential Damages).

[14] Ostano Commerzanstalt v. Telewide Sys., Inc., 880 F.2d 642, 648 (2d Cir. 1989); *cf. Midwest Home Distrib., Inc., supra*, 585 N.W.2d at 742 (awarded as part of "benefit-of-the-bargain" damages).

tort-based, the general rule is to use tort proximate cause concepts rather than contract foreseeability principles. Thus, in one recent case, a court awarded lost future earnings resulting from damage to a business owner's reputation arising out of bookings cancellations caused by the defendant's misrepresentations.[15] This should be compared with the rule that reputation damages are not generally awarded in breach of contract actions.[16]

[122.3] Pecuniary Loss Requirement

It is frequently stated that a fraud damages recovery is dependent on a showing of actual pecuniary loss.[17] Such statements must, however, be viewed cautiously. Some jurisdictions permit recovery of nominal damages for fraud; other jurisdictions, however, reject this view and bar nominal damages awards.[18] The more accurate view of the case law is that to state a claim for common law fraud usually requires a showing of damage caused by the fraud. Confusion arises because the terms "damage," "damages" and "injury" are used interchangeably. They are distinct. Injury is the invasion of a legal right; damage is the loss or hurt which results from injury; and, damages are the amount awarded to compensate for damage.[19]

The actual damage need not constitute general or direct damages, but may be redressed as consequential damages.[20] Thus, if the defendant misrepresents the performance ability of a product, but the product is worth what the plaintiff paid, in an out-of-pocket jurisdiction the plaintiff will have sustained no general or direct damages. If, however, as a result of the misrepresentation, the plaintiff was unable to bid for a contract with a third party, the lost profits from that third party contract would satisfy the actual damage or injury requirement.

Fraud damage may consist of the fact that the plaintiff was fraudulently induced to enter into a bargain in which he did not receive what he bargained for because of the fraud. The resulting damage may not be subject to specific measure. In any case, the defrauded party's damage should not be confused with his damages. When "damage" has been sustained as a

---

[15] Finley v. River N. Records, Inc., 148 F.3d 913, 918–20 (8th Cir. 1998).

[16] Section 10.2.2 ([Loss Causation] Policy Considerations), *discussing* Redgrave v. Boston Symphony Orchestra, Inc., 855 F.2d 888 (1st Cir. 1988), *cert. denied*, 488 U.S. 1043 (1989).

[17] Dornberger v. Metropolitan Life Ins. Co., 961 F. Supp. 506, 543 (S.D.N.Y. 1997) (applying New York law and stating that "[a]n action for damages requires the showing of some concrete pecuniary loss"); Nab v. Hills, 452 P.2d 981, 987 (Idaho 1969) (stating that "[w]e do not doubt that an action to recover monetary damage occasioned by fraud necessitates a showing of actual pecuniary damage, although what the measure of that damage may be, is open to question").

[18] *See* note 13, *supra*.

[19] Section 9.1 (Future Damage).

[20] Stout v. Tunney, 586 P.2d 1228, 1235 (Cal.1978); Section 122.2 ([Fraud] Consequential Damages).

result of fraud, a claim for at least nominal damages, or in the alternative rescission, should be recognized. [21]

[122.4] Distress Damages

The availability of emotional distress damages for fraud has been extensively debated. Again the problem is centered in fraud's contract-tort duality. In a contract action, distress damages are usually unavailable since contract damages are generally limited to economic losses. [22] Distress damages are more consistent with tort-based theories of recovery. [23] The distinction is reflected in the cases. Some courts bar distress damages. [24] Some courts permit distress damages in contexts where the plaintiff can show that she would have received distress damages in a breach of contract action. [25] Many courts, however, simply apply tort-causation tests in considering the availability of distress damages in tort. [26] As one commentator has noted:

> No judicial consensus exists on the propriety of awarding damages
> for emotional distress in fraud cases. Many jurisdictions limit
> damages for fraud to pecuniary injuries; this view has had the most
> influence on legal commentators and treatise writers. Nevertheless,
> a substantial group of jurisdictions has awarded emotional distress
> damages in fraud cases. Few of the decisions on either side of this
> issue have examined closely other jurisdictions' treatment of the

---

[21] *See generally* 37 Am. Jur. 2d *Fraud and Deceit* § 285 (noting split in jurisdictions whether rescission should be permitted absent a showing of pecuniary loss. In Earl v. Saks & Co., 226 P.2d 340, 346 (Cal. 1951), the court held that the pecuniary loss requirement would be satisfied for purposes of rescission "if the facts show that material *injury* will necessarily ensue from the fraud") (emphasis added). In Jakway v. Proudfit, 109 N.W.2d 388 (Neb. 1906), the court distinguished between a misrepresentation as to identity of property loss requirement was only applied when rescission was sought for the latter (quality) misrepresentation. The proposed Restatement (Third) of Restitution & Unjust Enrichment § 13 (T.D. No. 1, 2001), rejects the pecuniary loss requirement for rescission based on fraud. *Id.* at cmt. e.

[22] Section 142 (Distress Damages).

[23] Section 12 (Non-economic Damages).

[24] Brogan v. Mitchell Int'l, Inc., 692 N.E.2d 276, 278 (Ill. 1998) (holding that there is "no broad duty to avoid misrepresentations that cause only emotional harm"); Juman v. Louise Wise Servs., 663 N.Y.S.2d 483, 488–89 (Sup. Ct. 1997) (rejecting claim of distress damages in connection with fraud inducing plaintiffs to adopt child); Bates v. Allied Mut. Ins. Co., 467 N.W.2d 255, 260 (Iowa 1991) (stating that emotional distress damages are not available in a cause of action for fraud: "fraud is an economic tort which only protects pecuniary losses").

[25] *Kilduff, supra,* 593 A.2d at 485 (concluding that a defrauded party may recover distress damages when "the defendant should have realized that its conduct involved an unreasonable risk of causing emotional distress and that that distress, if it were caused, might result in illness or bodily harm") (citation omitted); Section 142 (Distress Damages).

[26] Phinney v. Perlmutter, 564 N.W.2d 532, 546 (Mich. App. 1997) (holding that in cases of common law fraud the defendant is liable for consequential damages, including distress damages, which are the natural consequence of the wrongful act, whether foreseeable or not, and which might reasonably have been anticipated); *cf.* Cook v. Children's Medical Group, Inc., 756 So. 2d 734, 740 (Miss. 1999) (recognizing recovery of distress damages for fraud); Sea-Land Service, Inc. v. O'Neal, 297 S.E.2d 647, 653 (Va. 1982) (same).

issue, and most of these decisions have not analyzed the policies favoring or opposing the award of emotional distress damages in fraud cases.[27]

[122.5] Attorney's Fees and Punitive Damages

In causes of action for common law fraud, the recovery of attorneys fees is governed by the "American Rule," which limits the recovery of attorneys fees by prevailing parties to cases when the recovery of fees is allowed by statute, contract, or other limited exceptions.[28]

Punitive damages may be recoverable in cases of common law fraud[29] and attorneys fees may be recoverable as a component of the punitive damages award.[30] Statutory causes of action for fraud often expressly allow for the recovery of attorney's fees by successful litigants.[31]

[122.6] Statutory Fraud Actions

The scope and extent of liability for misrepresentations may be substantially expanded by statute. For example, under the common law, a product endorser probably has no liability for innocent or perhaps even negligent misrepresentations regarding the product's quality or suitability.[32] The result may be different under consumer-oriented, anti-fraud statutes.[33]

[122.7] Fiduciary Actions

When the defrauded party sues the fiduciary for fraud,[34] the tendency is to allow benefit-of-the-bargain damages even if the jurisdiction usually

---

[27] Andrew Merritt, *Damages For Emotional Distress in Fraud Litigation: Dignitary Torts in a Commercial Society,* 42 Vand. L. Rev. 1, 2 (1989) (arguing that distress damages should be awarded as a matter of course in fraud actions). *See generally* Steven Gaynor, Annot., *Fraud Actions: Right to Recover For Mental or Emotional Distress,* 11 A.L.R.5th 88 (1993).

[28] Cantu v. Butron, 921 S.W.2d 344, 354 (Tex. Civ. App. 1996) (noting that in cases of common law fraud, the prevailing party does not recover its attorney's fees as actual damages); Chapter 24 (Attorney's Fees) (particularly Section 211 (Exceptions to the "American Rule")).

[29] Section 202.2 ([Punitive Damages] Fraud).

[30] *Cantu, supra,* 921 S.W.2d at 354–55.

[31] Oparaocha v. Sun Co., Inc., 3 F. Supp. 2d 4, 9 (D.D.C. 1998) (involving Federal Petroleum Marketing Practices Act and District of Columbia Retail Service Station Act); Schorsch v. Fireside Chrysler-Plymouth, Mazda, Inc., 677 N.E.2d 976, 978–79 (Ill. App. 1997) (involving Consumer Fraud Act); Cieri v. Leticia Query Realty, Inc., 905 P.2d 29, 45 (Haw. 1995) (involving Consumer Protection Act).

[32] Kramer v. Unitas, 831 F.2d 994, 998 (11th Cir. 1987) (applying Florida law).

[33] *In re* Diamond Mortgage Corp., 118 B.R. 588 (Bankr. N.D. Ill. 1989) (holding that the Illinois Consumer Fraud statute imposed a duty to investigate and verify on all product or service endorsers); Ramson v. Layne, 668 F. Supp. 1162, 1165–66 (N.D. Ill. 1987) (holding that the plaintiff-investor stated a claim under the Illinois Consumer Fraud and Deceptive Practices Act against the actor-endorser (Lloyd Bridges) who was involved in the promotion of a product).

[34] Section 113 (Breach of Fiduciary Duty).

applies the out-of-pocket measure.[35] Recovery may also be enhanced by the general rule that presumes that transactions between a fiduciary and the beneficiary constitute a breach of trust.[36] Although the presumption is rebuttable, the effect is to place the full burden on the fiduciary to demonstrate that the transaction or bargain was fair, just, and equitable for the beneficiary.

The existence of a fiduciary relationship may also expose the tortfeasor to fraud damages when, absent the fiduciary relationship, no remedy or cause of action would be recognized. For example, many jurisdictions have adopted "Heart Balm" statutes that reject common law actions for alienation of affection, seduction, etc.[37] If, however, the alienator or seducer is a fiduciary, the statutory immunity may not apply.[38]

§ 123 INJUNCTIVE RELIEF

Because many frauds involve one-time, executed transactions, injunctive relief is not frequently sought by private parties. The economic nature of the tort suggests that money damages are adequate.[1] In most instances, the likelihood that the victim will be defrauded again by the defendant is sufficiently remote to make the claim for injunctive relief moot.[2] When, however, the fraud has continuing injurious consequences, which an injunction may abate, resort to equity is freely recognized. Examples of these situations include an action to enjoin payment of a promissory note (letter of credit) that was acquired by fraud;[3] an action to prevent the foreclosure of property when the mortgage or deed of trust was procured by fraud;[4] or, an action to enjoin the defendant from accepting a bid,

---

[35] Section 122.1 ("Out-of-Pocket" vs. "Benefit-of-the-Bargain" Measure).

[36] Studniewski v. Kryzanowski, 584 N.E.2d 1297, 1300 (Ohio App. 1989); Deist v. Wachholz, 678 P.2d 188, 198 (Mont. 1984) (statutory presumption); cf. Merchant v. Foreman, 322 P.2d 740, 745 (Kan. 1958) (stating that transactions between fiduciaries and beneficiaries will be "viewed with suspicion" and "scrutinized").

[37] Section 103 (Heart Balm Statutes).

[38] Richard H. v. Larry D., 243 Cal. Rptr. 807, 810 (Cal. App. 1988) (stating that "[we] do not think the [heart balm] statute was intended to lower the standard of care which psychiatrists owe their patients, nor to permit them to avoid liability for breach of their professional and fiduciary responsibilities, or commit fraud."); Barbara A. v. John G., 193 Cal. Rptr. 422, 428 (Cal. App. 1983) (holding that the abolition of the action for seduction did not bar an action against an attorney for sexual intercourse with his client when the action was based on battery and misrepresentation); cf. Destefano v. Grabrian, 763 P.2d 275, 282–83 (Colo. 1988) (holding that the heart balm statute did not bar a couple's claim of breach of fiduciary duty against a clergyman who had sexual relationship with the wife while counseling the couple for marital problems); Section 103.1 (Personal Tort Committed by Fiduciary).

[1] Section 21 (Adequacy of the Remedy at Law/Irreparable Injury).

[2] Section 30.2 (Mootness).

[3] Jurisco, Inc. v. Bank South, N.A., 492 S.E.2d 765, 769 (Ga. App. 1997).

[4] Darnell v. Myers, 1996 Del. Ch. LEXIS 162 *5 (Del. Ch., Dec. 6, 1996) (unpublished) (stating that "[i]n general, a court of equity has the power to enjoin the foreclosure of a mortgage when the mortgagee is guilty of fraud . . .") (citation to unpublished memorandum opinion omitted).

allegedly procured by fraud, to the detriment of another bidder, the plaintiff.[5]

The most common use of injunctive relief to abate fraud is in civil suits by law enforcement officials to enjoin deceptive or fraudulent practices in the marketplace.[6]

§ 124 RESTITUTION

Fraudulent transactions between fiduciaries and beneficiaries and between those in a quasi-fiduciary, or confidential, relationship, have been frequently remedied by recourse to restitution. In this regard, courts have been particularly sensitive to ensure that no individual take advantage of his or her own wrongdoing, even if the wrongdoer has no contractual privity with the victim. Thus, agents, who for their own benefit, act deceptively toward third parties, ostensibly on behalf of their principals, may be required to disgorge to the third parties any benefits they obtained from the third party. This was the situation in *Ward v. Taggart*.[1]

The plaintiff, Ward, requested a real estate broker, Thomsen, to look for attractive investment property in Los Angeles. Another real estate broker, Taggart, told Thomsen that he (Taggart) had an exclusive listing for 72 acres of land owned by Sunset Oil. Ward directed Thomsen to submit an offer for the land through Taggart for $4,000 per acre. Taggart promised to convey the offer to Sunset Oil but later informed Thomsen that the company would not accept less than $5,000 per acre. Upon receiving this advice, Ward authorized Thomsen to make an offer on those terms. Thomsen communicated the offer to Taggart and Taggart ultimately informed Ward that Sunset accepted the offer. At the closing, however, title to the property appeared in the name of one of Taggert's associates. Taggart offered elaborate explanations for this development, and Ward purchased the property. Afterwards, Ward learned that Taggart had never held a listing on the property and had never presented his $4,000 offer to Sunset. The court noted: "Instead, he [Taggart] presented his own offer of $4,000 per acre, which Sunset accepted. [Taggart] falsely represented to [Ward] that the least Sunset would take for the property was $5,000 per acre, because [Taggart] intended to purchase the property from Sunset himself and resell it to plaintiffs at a profit of $1,000 per acre. All the reasons [Taggart] gave for the unusual handling of the sale were fabrications."[2] The court held that on these facts Ward could obtain restitution from Taggart of the profit Taggart derived from the deception. Disgorgement of profits was ordered even though (1) no privity of contract existed between Ward

---

[5] Hill Int'l, Inc. v. National R.R. Passenger Corp., 957 F. Supp. 548, 556 (D.N.J. 1996).

[6] United States v. Fang, 937 F. Supp. 1186 (D. Md. 1996) (involving health insurance reimbursement false claims); Securities and Exch. Comm'n v. Moran, 922 F. Supp. 867, 896 (S.D.N.Y. 1996) (involving securities fraud); People v. Federated Radio Corp., 154 N.E. 655 (N.Y. 1926) (involving state "Blue Sky" laws); Section 27 (Injunction of Criminal Activity).

[1] 336 P.2d 534 (Cal. 1959).

[2] *Id.* at 536.

and Taggart, (2) Ward was willing to pay the price Taggart represented, and (3) Ward received exactly what he bargained for. The fact remained, however, that Taggart obtained his profits by misrepresenting his status and authority and for that reason he could not retain his ill-gotten gains.

Restitutionary remedies may permit the defrauded party to capture any profit the defrauding fiduciary has acquired. Because the fiduciary can exploit inside information, it is not uncommon for these fraud claims to involve the plaintiff (seller) suing the defendant (fiduciary-buyer) seeking to recapture that which plaintiff sold defendant for an allegedly inadequate price. One significant example of this is *Janigan v. Taylor*.[3] The plaintiffs, former shareholders of Boston Electro Steel Casting, Inc. (BESCO), were induced to sell their shares to the defendant, the President and General Manager of BESCO. The sale price was $40,000. Several years later, defendant resold the stock for $700,000. The court found that the initial transaction was infected with fraud and ordered defendant to disgorge the profit ($660,000) he had made on the latter transaction. If plaintiffs had sued for damages, their recover would have been limited to the difference between what they received and what they parted with at the time of the sale to defendant. It is unlikely the actual value of the shares at that time was worth $700,000 for the court noted that defendant expended considerable effort in raising the value of the corporation after he acquired the shares, an effort for which he derived no credit against the recovery.[4]

There is nothing inherent in the fraud cause of action that necessarily precludes restitution; nonetheless, restitution is generally sought in claims involving fiduciary fraud rather than as a general fraud remedy. This probably is more a consequence of remedy selection by litigants than a conscious policy choice by courts. Litigants seek restitution against fiduciaries or those in fiduciary relationships because restitution is better than damages. For example, in *Hicks v. Clayton* plaintiffs sought to impose a constructive trust (a restitutionary action) on property they had been fraudulently induced to convey to the defendant.[5] Although the defendant was a lawyer, and thus a fiduciary of sorts to the plaintiffs who were his former clients, the fiduciary status played no role in the court's decision to grant the remedy of a constructive trust. Restitution was sought because a damages award would have been worthless given the defendant's insolvency. Restitutionary remedies have been recognized in other instances, such as *In re Telronics*, when no fiduciary relationship existed.[6]

Restitution is available when the fraud is committed by a fiduciary or one in a confidential relationship with the victim of the fraud.[7] Outside

---

[3] 344 F.2d 781 (1st Cir.), *cert. denied*, 382 U.S. 879 (1965).

[4] *Id.* at 786 (noting that it is "more appropriate to give the defrauded party the benefit even of windfalls than to let the defrauding party keep them").

[5] 136 Cal. Rptr. 512, 520–21 (Cal. App. 1977) (discussed at Section 54 (Constructive Trust)).

[6] 649 F.2d 1236, 1239 (7th Cir. 1981), *discussed in* Section 59.3.2 ([Tracing Principles for Constructive Trusts, Equitable Liens, and Equitable Accounting] Tracing and Equal Treatment).

[7] Section 113 (Breach of Fiduciary Duty).

that area, the availability of restitution is controversial, if at all, largely because of the absence of decisions on the point. If restitution is being used only to restore to the victim what she lost, the point is probably uncontroversial because here restitution provides no more redress than damages. *Hicks v. Clayton* and *In re Teltronics* fall into this category. When, however, restitution is being used to effect disgorgement, as in *Ward v. Taggart* and *Janigan*, the point becomes more controversial, as the disgorgement cases demonstrate,[8] because restitution now permits the plaintiff to recover more than she lost and perhaps even more than she hoped to gain. The issue is discussed in more detail in Section 41 (Restitution for Wrongdoing).

§ 125 PERSONAL RELATIONSHIPS

While fraudulent misrepresentations are not consistent with sound public policy, vindicating and remediating the victim's injuries may violate a higher and greater public policy.[1] In this context, the preference may be to leave the victim of the misrepresentation without a remedy.

Private, intimate relationships are an area where courts have generally refused to recognize fraud claims,[2] unless the wrongdoer is a fiduciary. In *Perry v. Atkinson* the court refused to allow a fraud claim based on the defendant's intentionally false promise to impregnate his girlfriend *later* in order to persuade his girlfriend to have an abortion *now*. The court held that tort liability will not flow from the decision whether to have or conceive a child.[3] As another court noted in this context:

> It does not lie within the power of any judicial system, however, to remedy all human wrongs. There are many wrongs which in themselves are flagrant. For instance, such wrongs as betrayal, brutal words, and heartless disregard of the feelings of others are beyond any effective legal remedy and any practical administration of law. To attempt to correct such wrongs or give relief from their effects "may do more social damage than if the law leaves them alone."[4]

---

[8] Section 51 (Disgorgement orders).

[1] Section 4 (Public Policy).

[2] *See* Jeffrey Kobar, Note, *Heartbalm Statutes and Deceit Actions,* 83 Mich. L. Rev. 1770 (1985) (noting disagreement among courts whether deceit actions for damages resulting from breach of a promise to marry (promissory fraud) are actionable).

[3] 240 Cal. Rptr. 402, 405 (Cal. App. 1987) (noting that such decisions "would encourage unwarranted governmental intrusion into matters affecting the individual's right to privacy") (citation omitted); *see* Conley v. Romeri, 806 N.E.2d 933 (Mass. App. 2004) (holding that woman whose biological clock was ticking could not sue man who falsely represented that he wanted a family when what he wanted (and had gotten) was a vasectomy).

[4] Stephen K. v. Roni L., 164 Cal. Rptr. 618, 619 (1980) (citation omitted); *see* McBride v. Boughton, 20 Cal. Rptr.3d 115, 123 (Cal. App. 2004) (rejecting claim for restitution of money spent on care of child by man who was fraudulently induced to believe that the child was his biological offspring because to do so would frustrate public policies—"the enforcement of parents' obligations to support their children, and the protection of children's interest in the stability of their family relationships") (citations omitted); Day v. Heller, 653 N.W.2d 475 (Neb. 2002) (rejecting damages claim by former husband against former wife that she misrepresented husband's status as biological father of her child).

These public policy considerations can lead to situations when misrepresentation by one party is actionable, but a similar misrepresentation by the other party is not. For example, assume a man fraudulently induces a woman to have sexual relations with him by a false representation that he is sterile. His fraud may vitiate her consent and result in his action being deemed a battery if she sustains physical injury as a result of the sexual relations.[5] On the other hand, assume a woman falsely represents that she is unable to conceive to induce a man to have sexual relations with her. As a result, the woman later gives birth to a child and sues the man for child support. The man interposes the defense of misrepresentation. In this setting, the court will reject the defense because it would hinder the public policy of providing for the child.[6] On the other hand, the man could probably sue for battery under the vitiated consent theory if he suffered actual injury as a result of having sexual intercourse with the woman, e.g., he contracted a sexually transmitted disease.

Fraud claims will fail not just in the personal relationship arena, but also when the state has a public policy that would be frustrated if the fraud claim were recognized. For example, when the fraud claim would allow evasion of the jurisdiction's heart balm statute,[7] licensure requirement,[8] or open court policy,[9] the claim may be rejected on public policy grounds.

---

[5] Barbara A. v. John G., 193 Cal. Rptr. 422, 426 (Cal. App. 1983) (involving a false representation of sterility by the man, an attorney, to his client; the client later became pregnant and suffered injuries from an ectopic pregnancy); cf. Lockhart v. Loosen, 943 P.2d 1074, 1080 (Okla. 1997) (stating that if a defendant knowing she has a sexually transmitted, communicable disease has a sexual relationship with a married man, that defendant owes a duty of disclosure to her sexual partner and her partner's wife if the defendant knows her partner is married).

[6] Pamela P. v. Frank S., 449 N.E.2d 713, 714 (N.Y. 1983) (holding that misrepresentation had no relevance to a father's duty to support his child).

[7] Doe v. Doe, 747 A.2d 617, 621 (Md. 2000) (holding that husband's claims for fraud and distress resulting from wife's adultery and lies were no different from common law criminal conversation, which had been abolished in Maryland); Section 103 (Heart Balm Statutes).

[8] Hydrotech Systems, Ltd. v. Oasis Waterpark, 803 P.2d 370, 375–76 (Cal. 1991) (rejecting fraud claim by unlicenced contractor against owner who allegedly knowingly hired the contractor with the intent to use the licensure requirement to avoid paying for the work performed); Section 65.2 (Illegality) (discussing Hydrotech and contrary decisions permitting fraud action to proceed).

[9] Hatch v. TIG Ins. Co., 301 F.3d 915 (8th Cir. 2002) (holding that exclusive remedy for discovery misrepresentations was sanctions in the underlying case in which the discovery was conducted); cf. Home Ins. Co. v. Zurich Ins. Co., 116 Cal. Rptr. 2d 583 (Cal. App. 2002) (holding that misrepresentation regarding policy limits that was relied on to settle litigation was absolutely privileged under state litigation immunity law (Cal. Civ. Code § 47(b)) and would not permit action for fraud damages).

Chapter 15

RESCISSION (DISAFFIRMANCE) OF BARGAIN

§ 130 NATURE OF RESCISSION

Recession permits a party to a bargain to disaffirm and undo the bargain. Rescission is fundamentally different from damages actions, which are predicated on the affirmance of the bargain. In seeking damages, the plaintiff elects to retain the bargain, even with its deficiencies, and sue the defendant for the bargain-related injuries, such as the plaintiff's lost expectancy. Rescission is based fundamentally on restoration. The bargain or transaction is undone and the parties are restored to their pre-bargain positions, as much as possible. Rescission is all about "giving up" and "getting back" and when it is fair and just to do so. An example may help illustrate the point.

Assume buyer acquires, through an initial public offering, 1000 shares of X Corp at \$100/share. Because of a fraudulent statement in X Corp's prospectus, the stock has been artificially inflated by \$10/share. In other words, the true value of the stock is $90/share. If buyer sues for fraud damages, buyer would receive $10,000 ($10 times 1000 shares). The $10,000 when added to buyer's 1000 shares at $90/share would equal $100,000 and make buyer whole. Fraud damages would be buyer's affirmance remedy and under these hypothetical facts would compensate buyer for his fraud-related losses. Under rescission, buyer would return the 1000 shares to X Corp and X Corp would return the $100,000 to buyer. Using damages (affirmance remedy) buyer would have assets worth $100,000, consisting of 1000 shares of X Corp stock ($90,000) plus $10,000 in cash damages; using rescission (disaffirmance remedy) buyer would have assets worth $100,000, consisting of $100,000 in cash. From a "balance sheet" perspective, both damages and rescission take buyer to the same place, given the factual assumptions used.[1]

If the hypothetical facts are changed, however, the equality between affirmance and disaffirmance remedies may disappear. Assume that 10 days after buyer's purchase, a conflict in Southwest Asia between India and Pakistan drives the entire market downward; the Dow drops 3000 points and X Corp's stock is worth only $60/share. Fraud damages would now provide buyer only $70,000 ($10,000 + $60,000 (1000 shares at $60/share)).[2] Rescission, however, gives buyer $100,000! Recall that X Corp. returns buyer's $100,000 purchase price; buyer returns to X Corp. the now depreciated stock buyer received. Rescission gives buyer $30,000 more than a fraud damages action would!

A remedy that permits such a significant shift in fortunes is subject to misuse and abuse. The plaintiff may attempt a "wait and see" game: affirm if X Corp's share price remains steady or rises with a bull market; disaffirm if the share price drops, as in the hypothetical or in a bear market. In addition, it may be difficult to detect the rescinding party's true motive for disaffirming. The rescinding party may be suffering from "buyer remorse" rather than objective injury related to the bargain or sale. For example, minor defects in a newly purchased product may be magnified by the buyer in the hope of escaping a bargain the buyer now regrets, not because of deficiencies with the product, but because the product no longer meets the buyer's "wants." Concerns that rescission may be misused or abused have led courts to develop a number of rules and principles that operate to constrain the availability of the remedy.

Rescission is available for both executory (ongoing) and executed (completed) bargains and transactions. However, the law's interest in the stability of consensual bargains may limit the availability of rescission when the bargain is fully completed. For example, many jurisdictions refuse

---

[1] The hypothetical ignores transaction costs, such as attorney's fees. The assumption is that transaction costs are equal for each remedy. That assumption may not hold in the real world. To the extent it does not, the buyer's decision whether to pursue affirmance or disaffirmance remedies may be affected.

[2] Buyer's fraud damages are limited to $10/share because the fraud caused that loss; the additional declined was not fraud related, but "conflict" related. Section 121.2 ([Fraud] Loss Causation).

to allow rescission of a deed for failure of consideration.[3] Similarly, a breach of warranty claim may not support rescission due to the doctrine of "merger by deed."[4] In both of these situations, stability of titles is offered as the justification for the restriction of disaffirmance remedies for completed transactions.[5]

In order to establish an equitable right to rescind a bargain, the rescinding party must establish that timely notice of rescission was provided to the other party,[6] return or offer to return the consideration the rescinding party received,[7] and restore any benefit derived from possession of the consideration when retention of that benefit would constitute unjust enrichment.[8] In addition, rescission is subject to the rule that the plaintiff not have lost his right to rescind by operation of the doctrine of election of remedies.[9] The scope of rescission remedies may be affected by the basis of the claim for rescission.[10]

§ 131   FORMS OF RESCISSION

Rescission is available in both law and equity, although the form and scope of the remedy differs in each system.

---

[3] Anchor v. O'Toole, 94 F.3d 1014, 1025 (6th Cir. 1996) (applying Ohio law); Fry v. Emmanuel Churches of Christ, Inc., 839 S.W.2d 406, 409–10 (Tenn. App. 1992).

[4] Knight v. Breckheimer, 489 A.2d 1066, 1068 (Conn. App. 1985) (stating that "acceptance of a deed in pursuance of articles of agreement for the conveyance of land is prima facie the completion of the contract and all stipulations contained therein . . . are merged in the deed although omitted therefrom"); Pryor v. Aviola, 301 A.2d 306, 308 (Del. Super. Ct. 1973) (recognizing the general rule that once the contract has been executed and the deed issued, "the rights of the parties are to be determined by the covenants of the deed and not by the agreement of sale"). The doctrine does not apply to the extent the parties intend the contract provision to survive the deed and not be incorporated into it. Town of Nags Head v. Tillet, 336 S.E.2d 394, 397 (N.C. 1985) (permitting rescission of a sales contract and cancellation of the deed for failure of consideration when deed specifically stated that conveyance was pursuant to the contract and subject to its terms). The doctrine of "merger by deed" may not apply in cases when rescission is sought on the basis of mistake or fraud. Link v. Breen, 649 N.E.2d 126, 128 (Ind. App. 1995); Reed v. Hassell, 340 A.2d 157, 160 (Del. Super. Ct. 1975); see Southpointe Dev. Inc. v. Cruikshank, 484 So. 2d 1361, 1362 (Fla. App. 1986) (not applying doctrine of merger in case involving mistake).

[5] State, by Pai v. Thom, 563 P.2d 982, 989 (Haw. 1977) (noting that "[t]o hold that a vendor of real property could, upon vendee's failure to pay the purchase price, repudiate his deed and recover the property, would render real estate titles dangerously uncertain with ensuing unfortunate consequences"). The vendor was limited to an action for the unpaid price, coupled with an implied lien that was good against the original vendee and an encumbrancer *with notice*, but rescission was not available. *Id.*

[6] Section 132.1 (Notice Requirement).

[7] Section 133.2 (Tender Requirement).

[8] Sections 134 (Restoration of the Status Quo), 135.2 (Disgorgement of Benefits Received).

[9] Section 133 (Election of Remedies).

[10] Sections 135.2 (Disgorgement of Benefits Received), 136 (Grounds for Rescission).

[131.1] Law

For rescission at law the essential requirement traditionally has been the return, or tender by the rescinding party, of the consideration to the defendant.[1] If the defendant did not reciprocate, the rescinding party could then sue the defendant in quasi contract because the defendant's retention of both (1) the initial consideration received in the bargain or transaction and (2) the returned (tendered) consideration constituted unjust enrichment for which restitution was warranted. For example, assume the bargain to be rescinded involved the sale of 1000 shares of X Corp stock for $100,000. Legal rescission required the plaintiff-buyer to tender the consideration (stock) to the defendant-seller and demand the return of the consideration the buyer initially provided ($100,000). When the seller refused, the buyer could sue in quasi contract (using the common count of "money had and received") on the theory that the defendant had "impliedly" promised to return to plaintiff his consideration ($100,000); therefore, restitution was appropriate to require the defendant to disgorge what the defendant unjustly retained. Legal rescission exposes the rescinding plaintiff to substantial risk since she has divested herself of what she received in the bargain without, at the same time, receiving back her initial consideration. A plaintiff seeking rescission at law can not protect herself by making a conditional tender—the condition being immediate reciprocity or tender into an escrow. The tender has to be unconditional.[2]

The rescinding plaintiff's claim is also subject to the vagaries of litigation and the risk that even if successful she might not be able to collect on her judgment. As a practical matter, rescission at law works best when the consideration received by the plaintiff is valueless—hence nothing is lost by tendering it back—or rescission in equity is not available.

There is some decisional law supporting the position that the tender rule for rescission at law could be suspended in the interests of justice.[3]

[131.2] Equity

Rescission in equity is more user-friendly, to borrow a current phrase. A tender is not required. The equity court will order relief on such grounds

---

[1] Maumelle Co. v. Eskola, 865 S.W.2d 272, 274 (Ark. 1993) (stating that "[t]o maintain an action at law, the tender must be done at or prior to the time of the commencement of the action") (citations omitted); Stefanac v. Cranbrook Educ. Community, 458 N.W.2d 56, 80 (Mich. 1990) (noting that tender of consideration was a prerequisite to rescission at law) (dissenting opinion).

[2] *Maumelle, supra*, 865 S.W.2d at 274; *see* text and note 4, *infra*.

[3] Remediation Servs., Inc. v. Georgia-Pacific Corp., 433 S.E.2d 631, 636 (Ga. App. 1993) (stating that tender requirement would not be imposed when rescinding party received nothing of value or was less than amounts owed to the rescinding party by the non-rescinding party); Crews v. Cisco Bros. Ford-Mercury, Inc., 411 S.E.2d 518, 520 (Ga. App. 1991) (holding that a tender back to the seller was not required when the rescinding party was liable to third party creditors who financed the sale, tender would not extinguish that obligation, and, tender would have given the seller both the buyer's money and the property sold).

as are fair, just, and proper. The reason for this difference lies in the differences between law and equity:

> The chancellor had the power to cancel or rescind a contract. A person could, therefore, bring an action seeking cancellation of a contract or release, as distinguished from an action claiming that the contract or release had been rescinded . . . .

> The chancellor could guard against unjust enrichment of the rescinding party by conditioning a decree of rescission on the rescinding party's return of consideration received . . . .

> An action at law, by contrast, proceeded on the theory that the rescinding party had, himself, rescinded the contract. Courts of law were thought to lack the power to render conditional judgments. Consequently, tender was considered a precondition to the institution of an action at law—a formality perfecting the rescinding party's rescission.[4]

There are occasional statements in the decisions that rescission in equity is subject to the irreparable injury requirement.[5] These statements are, however, rarely dispositive of the decision. The better view is that the availability of rescission in equity turns on the merits of the claim not on the absence of an adequate remedy at law. If rescission is warranted on the facts, equity will provide a remedy; if rescission is not warranted, equity will not provide a remedy. Thus, in *Coalville City v. Lundgren*, a decision purporting to apply the irreparable injury requirement to rescission in equity, the court refused rescission because the breach was non-material and it was impossible to return the parties to the status quo ante. Only in this context was a damages remedy, based on affirmance, adequate.[6] In most modern decisions, the irreparable injury requirement is either ignored,[7] stated as a requirement in the disjunctive,[8] or mentioned but not

---

[4] *Stefanac, supra*, 458 N.W.2d at 79–81 (dissenting opinion) (citations and footnotes omitted).

[5] Coalville City v. Lundgren, 930 P.2d 1206, 1210 (Utah App. 1997) (stating that "the equitable remedy of rescission is inappropriate when a legal remedy such as damages is adequate").

[6] *Id.* at 1210.

[7] Transamerica Ins. Fin. Corp. v. North Am. Trucking Ass'n, Inc., 937 F. Supp. 630, 635 (W.D. Ky. 1996) (noting availability of rescission in equity without discussing the irreparable injury requirement).

[8] Laniewicz v. Rutenberg Constr. Co., 580 So. 2d 203, 204 (Fla. 1991) (involving rescission of a land sale contract and stating that rescission "is an ancient equitable [remedy] devised by the courts where monetary damages are inadequate or when one party, having a right, elects that remedy") (brackets added); Joyce v. Davis, 539 F.2d 1262, 1265 (10th Cir. 1976) (stating that rescission is available "where there is substantial breach, irreparable injury, or where damages would be inadequate") (applying Colorado law); Overland v. LeRoy Foods, Inc., 113 N.Y.S.2d 124 (Sup. Ct. 1952):

> Cancellation of contract is a recognized field of equity jurisdiction. Generally speaking, however, in order to obtain relief in a court of equity, the case presented must embrace facts bringing it within some of the recognized heads of equity jurisdiction, such as fraud, accident, mistake, duress, undue influence, or the like;

really applied.[9]

Some jurisdictions, such as California, have adopted a statutory form of rescission that is a hybrid of both the law and equity forms.[10]

§ 132 DEMAND FOR RESCISSION

Rescission of a bargain requires that the rescinding party give timely notice of the intent to rescind. This requirement is sometimes confused with the tender and the election of remedies requirements. The concepts of notice, tender, and election are distinct; yet, the confusion is understandable for the concepts are often applied to similar facts and serve similar ends.

[132.1] Notice Requirement

Notice of the intent to rescind must be given within a reasonable time after the rescinding party learns, or should have learned, that it possessed a right to rescind; however, the mere passage of time does not make notice untimely.[1] The notice requirement is, thus, analogous to the doctrine of laches. Unlike laches, however, the promptness requirement is not a defense but an element of the plaintiff's case. In some jurisdictions, the failure to provide prompt notice of the intent to rescind will cause rescission to be lost.[2] In other jurisdictions, the link with laches is stronger, and a prejudice requirement is imposed.[3] In this latter context, prejudice may be shown, again as with laches, by a showing that evidence was lost, the costs of proof increased, the risks inherent in the transaction were unfairly shifted to the defendant by reason of the delay, or the ability to restore the parties to the status quo ante was impaired.[4]

When the notice-prejudice principle is applied, there is little to distinguish the notice requirement from the "election of remedies" concept. In many of the decisions, it is not completely clear whether a "prejudice"

---

or it must be shown that the complainant, if denied equitable relief, will sustain an injury for the redress of which a court of common law can afford no adequate remedy.

Id. at 126, *aff'd*, 114 N.Y.S.2d (App. Dept. 1952).

[9] *See* text and note 6, *supra* (discussing *Coalville City v. Lundgren*).

[10] Cal. Civ. Code § 1690 *et seq.*; *cf.* Dinsmore-Thomas v. F.D.I.C., 139 F.3d 904 (9th Cir. 1998) (unpublished opinion available at 1998 U.S. App. LEXIS 2777) (stating that a "court may modify statutory rescission procedures").

[1] Knudsen v. Jensen, 521 N.W.2d 415, 420 (S.D. 1994) (noting that the "element of time is not conclusive in and of itself").

[2] Allen v. West Point-Pepperell, Inc., 908 F. Supp. 1209, 1218 (S.D.N.Y. 1995) (applying New York law).

[3] *Knudsen, supra*, 521 N.W.2d at 420.

[4] *Id.* at 421 (noting that critical party had moved out-of-state during the period notice was delayed); Gannett Co. v. Register Publ'g Co., 428 F. Supp. 818, 827, 839–40 (D. Conn. 1977) (finding that rescinding party had changed the essential character of business during period notice was delayed).

requirement is being applied with respect to the notice or the election requirement.[5]

The rescinding party may have a justification for the delay that causes the delay to be characterized as reasonable.[6] For example, the efforts of the parties to negotiate a compromise may justify delay, as may the defendant's promise to rectify or repair the problem that has induced the other party to consider rescission as a remedy. The rescinding party is also allowed a reasonable period of time to investigate the facts to determine that a right to rescind exists. The requirement that notice be timely does not require the rescinding party to act rashly. On the other hand, the rescinding party may not rely on negotiations or assurances that the problem will be remedied to delay indefinitely the decision to demand rescission. As noted in *Gannett Co. v. Register Publishing Co.*:

> The better approach, appropriate to a remedy as drastic as rescission, takes into account all the facts and circumstances that bear on reasonableness, with due regard for the sensitive nature of settlement negotiations and the policy reasons for protecting them. Though discussions may continue over months or even years, the acts and omissions of the parties must retain their normal legal significance . . . . Time no more stands still during settlement negotiations culminating with a rescission demand than it does when the statute of limitations runs during settlement. The fact that the parties agree, as they apparently did at the commencement of negotiations in this case, that settlement talks will be "without prejudice" and understand that participation in the negotiations will not of itself lessen their substantive rights does not always relieve the would-be rescinder of his duty to take the steps the law requires to preserve his rescission remedy. Legally significant acts and omissions can operate of their own force to terminate the right to rescission. The pendency of settlement discussions is simply one circumstance, albeit an important one, in determining the reasonableness of what the rescinding party did or failed to do.[7]

Even courts that apply a pure "promptness" requirement may excuse "delay" when the delay cannot be seen as having harmed the defendant in any significant way relevant to the action for rescission.[8] Thus, the "promptness" requirement has been eased when the rescinding party does not possess property that could be returned or restored to the defendant.[9] In these cases, notice simply informs the defendant that disaffirmance of the bargain is desired.

---

[5] Section 133 (Elections of Remedies).

[6] *See generally* J.H. Tigges, Annot., *Circumstances Justifying Delay in Rescinding Land Contract After Learning of Ground of Rescission,* 1 A.L.R.3d 542 (1966).

[7] 428 F. Supp. 818, 835–36 (D. Conn. 1977).

[8] *Id.* at 836 (noting that absence of rescission demand might be excused when the value and the condition of the property remained constant).

[9] *Allen, supra,* 905 F. Supp. at 1219 (collecting New York decisions not applying "promptness" requirement for notice in rescission action).

[132.2] Tender Requirement

As noted previously, for common law actions, whether a tender is required usually turns on whether the rescission claim is brought in equity or at law.[10] When, however, the underlying claim is of statutory origin, the tender issue may be seen as part of the larger statutory scheme and thus controlled by it, rather than whether the form of the action sounds in equity or law.[11]

A statute may create a right to rescind without expressly adopting or incorporating a tender requirement. For example, the Federal Truth in Lending Act confers a right on debtors to rescind loans when the creditor fails to comply with its statutory duties. The pure exercise of the right to rescind would allow the debtor to retain the loan proceeds. In this context, courts have recognized an inherent equitable power to condition the debtor's right of rescission on the debtor's tender to the creditor of the principal of the loan.[12]

§ 133 ELECTION OF REMEDIES

The election of remedies concept can arise in a variety of contexts. Election may be applied to require a party to choose among cumulative statutory or common law rights. In this context, the doctrine operates as a preemption rule.[1] For example, a plaintiff may not be permitted to simultaneously pursue alternate remedies provided under the Federal Labor-Management Relations Act (5 U.S.C. §§ 7101–035) and the Equal Employment Opportunity Act (42 U.S.C. § 2000e et seq.).[2] Similarly, an

---

[10] Section 131 (Forms of Rescission).

[11] Oubre v. Entergy Operations, Inc., 522 U.S. 422, 427–28 (1998) (holding that under the Older Workers Benefit Protection Act (29 U.S.C.A. § 626(b)(1)) workers who released their former employers from employment-related liability in exchange for severance packages need not tender back their benefits before seeking rescission of the releases on the ground the releases are statutorily defective). Rescission of the releases was necessary before the former employees could sue for discriminatory termination and severance in violation of the Age Discrimination in Employment Act (29 U.S.C. § 621 et seq.).

[12] F.D.I.C. v. Hughes Dev. Co., Inc., 938 F.2d 889, 890 (8th Cir. 1991), cert. denied sub nom. Hughes Dev. Co., Inc. v. Great Plains Capital Corp., 502 U.S. 1099 (1992); Brown v. Nat'l Permanent Fed. Sav. & Loan Ass'n, 683 F.2d 444, 449 (D.C. Cir. 1982); see Elwin Griffith, Truth in Lending—The Right of Rescission, Disclosure of the Charge, and Itemization of the Amount Financed in Closed-End Transactions, 6 Geo. Mason L. Rev. 191 (1998):

> The first step in the rescission process requires the consumer to notify the creditor in writing that he is rescinding. When he does that, the security interest on the consumer's property is automatically void, regardless of whether it is perfected, and the consumer is not liable for any amount, including any finance charge. Although Regulation Z does not put any qualification on the voiding of the security interest, creditors have frequently argued for a kind of conditional rescission that makes the voiding of the lien contingent on the consumer's tender of creditor's funds.

Id. at 223 (footnotes omitted).

[1] Kansas State Bank v. Citizens Bank, 737 F.2d 1490, 1498 (8th Cir. 1984).

[2] Vinieratos v. United States Dep't of the Air Force, 939 F.2d 762 (9th Cir. 1991):

employee injured in a work-related accident may be required to elect between claiming worker's compensation benefits or suing the employer for damages on the ground that the injury is not covered by worker's compensation.[3] If the failed transaction involved real property, rescission may be subordinated to a foreclosure action. Foreclosure is an equitable remedy designed to protect the interests of all parties to the contract.[4] When the debtor has established equity in the property, the court may require the use of a remedy (e.g. judicial foreclosure) that affords the breaching party greater rights than would a simple rescission action.[5]

Second, election of remedies also operates to prevent duplicate remedies for a single injury. Here, the concept refers to the choice a plaintiff has (1) in affirming the bargain and seeking damages or specific performance as the remedy for the defendant's breach or wrong, or (2) disaffirming the bargain and retracting her consent through an action for rescission. A buyer will be denied a disaffirmance remedy (rescission) if the remedy is sought after the buyer has been awarded damages for breach of contract, which presumes affirmance of the contract.[6]

Third, election of remedies is sometimes invoked to prevent parties from seeking inconsistent theories of relief, although much of the force of this application has been sapped by the modern allowance of inconsistent pleadings.[7]

Fourth, election of remedies is closely related to judicial estoppel, both of which may be invoked to bar a party from taking inconsistent positions in related judicial proceedings.[8]

Under the terms of the Act a federal employee [with exclusive union representation] who alleges employment discrimination must elect to pursue his claim under either a statutory procedure [(*e.g.*, the EEO process)] or a union-assisted negotiated grievance procedure [unless the grievance procedure specifically excludes discrimination claims]; he cannot pursue both avenues, and his election is irrevocable.

Id. at 768 (brackets added).

[3] Medina v. Herrera, 927 S.W.2d 597, 598–99 (Tex. 1996) (holding that as a matter of law employee's claiming of worker's compensation benefits barred claim against the employer).

[4] Looney v. Farmers Home Admin., 794 F.2d 310, 312 (7th Cir. 1986) (applying Indiana law).

[5] S.B.D., Inc. v. Sai Mahen, Inc., 560 N.E.2d 86, 87 (Ind. App. 1990).

[6] Baker v. Wade, 949 S.W.2d 199 (Mo. App. 1997).

[7] *In re* Grain Land Coop., 978 F. Supp. 1267, 1278 (D. Minn. 1997) (noting that bar on inconsistent pleading "has been eviscerated by the permissive rules of pleading under Fed. R. Civ. P. 8(a) and 8(e)(2)"), *quoting Kansas State Bank, supra,* 737 F.2d at 1499; *see* Desjardins v. Van Buren Community Hosp., 37 F.3d 21, 23 (11th Cir. 1994) (stating that "[t]here are many situations, especially at the outset of litigation, where a party is free to assert a position from which it later withdraws—or even to assert, in the alternative, two inconsistent positions of its potential claims or defenses"); Fort Vancouver Plywood Co. v. United States, 860 F.2d 409, 415 (Fed. Cir. 1988).

[8] Gens v. Resolution Trust Co., 112 F.3d 569, 572 (1st Cir. 1997), *cert. denied,* 522 U.S. 931 (1997) (stating that "[t]he companion doctrines of judicial estoppel and election of remedies essentially preclude a party from asserting a legal or factual position 'inconsistent' with its position in a prior proceeding") (footnote and citation omitted); Section 133.2 (Judicial Estoppel).

The primary purpose of election of remedies is to prevent double recoveries for a single wrong.[9] Under this approach, a party should be permitted to delay electing between affirmance remedies and disaffirmance remedies until the entry of final judgment. Many decisions support this approach.[10] As noted by one court:

> The doctrine of election of remedies prevents a party from obtaining double redress for a single wrong. The doctrine "refers to situations where an individual pursues remedies that are legally or factually inconsistent." As a general rule, three elements must be present for a party to be bound to an election of remedies: (1) two or more remedies must have existed at the time of the election, (2) these remedies must be repugnant and inconsistent with each other, and (3) the party to be bound must have affirmatively chose, or elected, between the available remedies.[11]

On occasion a court will hold a plaintiff to a remedy election prior to the entry of final judgment,[12] although the emerging trend is to forebear when a plaintiff has satisfied the notice and tender requirements. Ultimately, however, a choice between inconsistent or duplicative remedies must be made. A party cannot receive a judgment for both affirmance damages and rescission. At that point all courts will require an election; however, the plaintiff usually can select the more favorable of the two options.[13]

Invocation of an election requires a showing that basic fairness demands an election. While an election of remedies is not per se either a waiver or an estoppel, (thus the technical requirements for finding a waiver or an estoppel need not be met), the facts must show a legitimate reason for forcing an election prior to the announcement of verdict or judgment. In this regard, the decisions disagree whether delay alone, or delay accompanied by prejudice, is sufficient to find or force an election prior to entry of judgment.[14]

---

[9] *Gens, supra*, 112 F.3d at 573, n.3 (collecting decisions).

[10] *Id.*; Christensen v. Eggen, 577 N.W.2d 221, 224 (Minn. 1998).

[11] Latman v. Burdette, 366 F.3d 774, 781–82 (9th Cir. 2004) (citations omitted); *cf.* York v. Association of Bar of City of New York, 286 F.3d 122, 127–28 (2d Cir. 2002) (holding that having elected to raise state-based claims of unlawful discrimination practices before a state administrative agency, the plaintiff has elected her remedy and may not litigate the same claims in federal court).

[12] *In re* Beglinger Trust, 561 N.W.2d 130, 131–32 (Mich. App. 1997); Butcher v. Cessna Aircraft Co., 850 F.2d 247, 248 (5th Cir. 1988) (applying Mississippi law), *cert. denied,* 489 U.S. 1067 (1989); Section 64 (Estoppel, Waiver, and Election).

[13] Far W. Fed. Bank v. Office of Thrift Supervision, 119 F.3d 1358, 1365 (9th Cir. 1997); Dopp v. HTP Corp., 947 F.2d 506, 515 (1st Cir. 1991), *aff'd in part, rev'd in part on other grounds sub nom.* Dopp v. Pritzker, 38 F.3d 1239 (1st Cir. 1994); Continental Sand & Gravel, Inc. v. K & K Sand & Gravel, Inc., 755 F.2d 87, 93 (7th Cir. 1985).

[14] *Compare In re* Beglinger Trust, *supra,* 561 N.W.2d at 132 (noting that "prejudice is not required under the general rule of election"), *with* Sharpe v. F.D.I.C., 126 F.3d 1147, 1153 (9th Cir. 1997) (noting that under California law, a defendant may not force the plaintiff to an election of remedies prior to judgment unless the "plaintiffs' actions cause substantial prejudice to the defendant"). The same split as to the role of "prejudice" applies to the notice requirement. Section 132 (Demand for Rescission).

The modern, and surely the superior, view is that the defendant ought to be required to demonstrate that the plaintiff has gained a benefit, imposed a detriment, or acted inconsistently to defendant's prejudice before an election of remedies will be found or forced prior to entry of judgment. If a plaintiff sues for breach of contract, a court may require an election when the plaintiff's indecision put the defendant unreasonably at risk as to whether she should continue to perform under the contract. Continued performance by the defendant would be proper if the plaintiff sought affirmance remedies, but wasteful if the plaintiff wishes to rescind.[15] Similarly, if the plaintiff, with knowledge of all the relevant facts, continues to reside on and improve real property without disclosing or demanding rescission, a court may find an election to affirm since the plaintiffs have not only openly acted in a manner that could be deemed a ratification of the bargain, but, by their conduct, have increased the costs that will be incurred in restoring the parties to the status quo.[16] Finally, the election must be between remedies, not rights.[17]

As noted previously, election of remedies bars duplicative recoveries for the same wrong. The bar does not apply when inconsistent claims arise from independent wrongs. A suit for trespass to try title, (which is predicated on the plaintiff's claim of title), is independent from a claim against a title insurance company for failure of title. The "trespass" involves a separate and independent wrong from the claim against the title insurance company on the title policy. Both claims may be prosecuted without a required election.[18]

---

[15] Medcom Holding Co. v. Baxter Travenol Lab, Inc., 984 F.2d 223, 229 (7th Cir. 1993) (discussing principle, but finding that election of remedies doctrine did not apply to case at hand).

[16] Grube v. Daun, 570 N.W.2d 851, 859–60 (Wis. 1997) (forcing an election on similar facts to those in the text).

[17] PVI, Inc. v. Ratiopharm GmBH, 253 F.2d 320, 327 (8th Cir. 2001) (stating that under Delaware law plaintiff was not required to elect between breach of contract action and contractual right of appraisal). As noted by the court:

> The appraisal process was not a remedy for Ratiopharm's breach of contract; it was merely a contractual method for determining the value of the Martec stock. The process was not intended to determine the validity of Ratiopharm's submission, and thus could not redress Ratiopharm's breach other than by awarding PVI the right to buy the stock at PVI's proposed price if that price was closer to the expert's valuation than Ratiopharm's inappropriately low submission.

Id.

[18] American Sav. & Loan Ass'n v. Musick, 531 S.W.2d 581, 588 (Tex. 1975); see Thornton, Summers, Biechlin, Dunham & Brown, Inc. v. Cook Paint & Varnish, 82 F.3d 114, 117–18 (5th Cir. 1996) (applying principles of Musick, supra, and finding that the duty owed by a retained insurance defense law firm to the plaintiff as a client was different from the duty owed by an insurance company to the plaintiff as a policyholder to provide defense counsel); Birchler v. Castello Land Co., Inc., 942 P.2d 968, 971 (Wash. 1997) (holding that claim for distress damages for destruction of property is not duplicative of statutory treble damages remedy for destruction or damage to same property).

Election of remedies is an affirmative defense that must be asserted or it will be deemed waived.[19]

[133.1]   Interim Relief

Some jurisdictions have held that seeking interim equitable or provisional relief, consistent with affirmance remedies, constitutes an election.[20] Although the distinction is not always articulated, the better view is that seeking interim relief to preserve the status quo, as opposed to obtaining a pre-trial advantage, should not be deemed an election.[21] Thus, an interim injunction to maintain the status quo while seeking to enforce arbitration rights should not be deemed an election of affirmance remedies simply because the arbitration is based on a contract provision.[22] On the other hand, seeking a pre-judgment attachment, and the leverage attachment provides, could be deemed an election when the interim remedy confers strategic advantage to the plaintiff at the expense, and to the detriment, of the defendant.[23]

[133.2]   Judicial Estoppel

Election of remedies is related to judicial estoppel.[24] Judicial estoppel bars a party from obtaining an advantage by taking one position before a court and then seeking a second advantage by later taking an inconsistent

---

[19] Medina v. Herrera, 927 S.W.2d 597, 600 (Tex. 1996); North Carolina Fed. Sav. & Loan Ass'n v. Ray, 382 S.E.2d 851, 855–56 (N.C. App. 1989); *Medcom Holding Co.*, *supra*, 984 F.2d at 228 n.2.

[20] State *ex rel.* Hilleary & Partners, Ltd. v. Kelly, 448 S.W.2d 926, 931–32 (Mo. App. 1969) (holding that a plaintiff who had obtained temporary injunctive relief based on the contract could not later claim that the contract was invalid).

[21] Jim-Bob, Inc. v. Mehling, 443 N.W.2d 451, 461 (Mich. App. 1989) (stating that "[b]asing a determination of plaintiff's election of remedies on the entry of a preliminary injunction forces plaintiff into the untenable position of seeking the injunction to preserve the status quo and thereby being relegated to seeking only specific performance or foregoing the injunction and risking being forced to seek damages in a situation in which the legal remedy may be inadequate").

[22] Preiss/Breismeister v. Westin Hotel Co.–Plaza Hotel Div., 437 N.E.2d 1154 (N.Y. 1982) (Memorandum Decision).

[23] *Cf.* Estrada v. Alvarez, 240 P.2d 278, 281 (Cal. 1952) (holding that obtaining the advantage of an attachment on a contract claim constituted an election barring the plaintiff from seeking tort-based damages for fraud involving the same general facts as constituted the contract claim). *But cf.* Modoc Mineral & Oil Co. v. Cal-Vada Drilling & Exploration Co., 46 Cal. Rptr. 508, 512 (Cal. App. 1965) (holding that securing an attachment did not constitute an election because California law specifically allowed the rescission action and the defendant had failed to plead election as an affirmative defense). In *Waffer Int'l Corp. v. Khorsandi*, 82 Cal. Rptr. 2d 241 (Cal. App. 1999), the court rejected the contention that seeking pre-judgment attachment warranted finding an election consistent with that interim remedy. The court emphasized the limitations placed on pre-judgment attachment, which carefully protect the defendant. *Id.* at 243, 246.

[24] *Gens, supra*, 112 at 572 (noting that "[t]he companion doctrines of judicial estoppel and election of remedies essentially preclude a party from asserting a legal or factual position 'inconsistent' with its position in a prior proceeding") (citations and footnote omitted).

and incompatible position. For example, a party who seeks disability benefits based on her inability to work a position may be barred from later claiming that she was the victim of discrimination, which denied her employment or a promotion to the position she now claims she was capable of performing.[25]

Judicial estoppel is designed to prevent litigants from playing "fast and loose with the courts,"[26] or from "speak[ing] out of both sides of her mouth with equal vigor and credibility before [the] court."[27] However, because inconsistent pleading is specifically permitted by the Federal Rules of Civil Procedure, the scope and application of judicial estoppel is difficult to define, much less predict. Some courts have suggested that they will not apply the doctrine.[28] Many courts require that the earlier inconsistent position was adopted by the court, *i.e.*, that the litigant successfully persuaded the court to accept her factual or legal position, before a judicial estoppel will be found.[29] The general approach is to permit the trial court to exercise its discretion whether to find an estoppel.[30]

An equitable reason should exist before a judicial estoppel will be found. Merely asserting inconsistent positions should be insufficient to trigger the doctrine, even if one of the positions is accepted by the court. The touchstone should be whether, as a result of successfully asserting a prior position,

---

[25] Rissetto v. Plumbers & Steamfitters Local 343, 94 F.3d 597, 600 (9th Cir. 1996) (involving a plaintiff who sought to assert an age discrimination claim after receiving worker's compensation benefits). There is a split of authorities as to whether this practice raises a judicial estoppel.

[26] Russell v. Rolfs, 893 F.2d 1033, 1037 (9th Cir. 1990), *cert. denied,* 501 U.S. 1260 (1991).

[27] Reigel v. Kaiser Found. Health Plan of N.C., 859 F. Supp. 963, 970 (E.D.N.C. 1994) (brackets added); *see* Barger v. City of Cartersville, Ga., 348 F.3d 1289, 1294–96 (11th Cir. 2003) (holding that debtor's failure to list employment discrimination claim as asset in bankruptcy raised a judicial estoppel barring subsequent assertion of the claim after the debtor secured a bankruptcy discharge). As noted by the court:

> [I]t is difficult to argue that Barger should not be judicially estopped from asserting the discrimination claims she failed to disclose in her bankruptcy petition. Barger appeared to gain an advantage when she failed to list her discrimination claims on her schedule of assets. Omitting the discrimination claims from the schedule of assets appeared to benefit her because, by omitting the claims, she could keep any proceeds for herself and not have them become part of the bankruptcy estate. Thus, Barger's knowledge of her discrimination claims and motive to conceal them are sufficient evidence from which to infer her intentional manipulation.

Id. at 1295 (footnote omitted). There was a dissent that argued that the debtor's failure to list the claim was inadvertent, rather than manipulative; therefore, an estoppel should not be raised. *Id.* at 1297 (Barkett, J., dissenting). Raising an estoppel due to failure to list "assets" in a bankruptcy is not uncommon. Hamilton v. State Farm Fire & Cas. Co., 270 F.3d 778 (9th Cir. 2001).

[28] *In re* BCD, Corp., 119 F.3d 852, 858 (10th Cir. 1997).

[29] *Rissetto, supra,* 94 F.3d at 600–01 (collecting decisions); Prilliman v. United Air Lines, Inc., 62 Cal. Rptr. 2d 142, 153–58 (Cal. App. 1997) (collecting decisions).

[30] *Russell, supra,* 893 F.2d 1033; *cf.* New Hampshire v. Maine, 532 U.S. 742, 750–51 (2001) (noting that the doctrine of judicial estoppel is "probably not reducible to any general formulation of principle").

inconsistent from that now taken, the party has unfairly prejudiced the other party or unfairly gained an advantage that a court could not adequately redress if the second position was allowed to be asserted. It should also be kept in mind that we are not addressing situations where the interests of finality, as raised by the doctrine of res judicata/collateral estoppel are implicated. Judicial estoppel, and election of remedies for that matter, involve matters still in litigation; thus, the penultimate question is whether the party should be deemed bound by a litigation position prior to final resolutions of the entire dispute. [31]

[133.3]   Election

A party's conduct may lock her into a position from which she cannot escape. As noted in *Gaugert v. Duve*:

> [C]ontrary to the trial court's understanding, the doctrine of election of rights is not available only if the breach is the result of fraud. In fact, prior Wisconsin decisions appear to have employed the doctrine of election of rights, although they have never expressly referred to it as such, in cases where there is a lack of consideration or a lack of mutuality and the party has a choice of either performing or not performing. If a party chooses to continue performance, these cases hold that the party gives up the right to later terminate the contract on grounds of either lack of consideration or lack of mutuality. [32]

The types of situations noted in the above-quoted materials illustrate a basic, commonsensical tenet. A party cannot be allowed to play "heads, I win; tails, you lose." When (1) the bargain-related deficiency is known, (2) the nonbreaching party can reasonably avoid the bargain, and (3) the deficiency does not encompass a future bargained-for performance, the nonbreaching party who proceeds with the transaction is hard pressed to contend later that the consideration received was inadequate. If there was a loss, it was not caused by the inadequacy of the consideration or lack of mutuality. The non-breaching party was aware of these "deficiencies" during the executory stage, but consciously chose to proceed and complete the bargain. [33]

---

[31] Judicial estoppel is related to the doctrine of "the law of the case." The law of the case doctrine holds that "when a court decides upon a rule of law, that decision should continue to govern the same issues in subsequent stages in the same case." Arizona v. California, 460 U.S. 605, 618 (1983); Pit River Home & Agric. Coop. Ass'n v. United States, 30 F.3d 1088, 1097 (9th Cir. 1994) (stating that the law of the case doctrine is designed "to maintain consistency and avoid reconsideration, during the course of a single, continuing lawsuit, of those decisions that are intended to put a matter to rest"). Both doctrines are discretionary and subject to displacement to secure the ends of justice. Christianson v. Colt Indus. Operating Corp., 486 U.S. 800, 815–16 (1988).

[32] 579 N.W.2d 746, 750 (Wis. App. 1998); Section 121.4 (Reliance).

[33] *See* RICHARD A. LORD, 13 WILLISTON ON CONTRACTS § 39.32 (Election) (4th ed. 2002); Section 64.3 (Election) (discussing the issue in the context of a remedy defense).

A related, albeit converse, concept is the statement that rescission will not lie when the breaching party has provided complete and full performance.[34] This statement is, however, overbroad, although occasionally applied. The better view is to examine the issue in terms of the feasibility of restoring the parties to the status quo ante rather than adopting a blanket rule.[35] A similar concern is expressed when the buyer claims breach, but continues to use the goods provided by the contract. In such cases, the seller may contend that the buyer's continued use of the goods constitutes an election of affirmance remedies.[36] The point is addressed in Section 134 (Restoration of the Status Quo).

§ 134 RESTORATION OF THE STATUS QUO

Restoring the parties to the "status quo ante" (the position each would have occupied had the bargain not been entered into) is the objective of rescission.[1] From this it follows that the inability of the court to restore the status quo may be a valid reason for denying rescission.[2] Restoration, however, need not be strict; when equity and fairness demand, substantial restoration is adequate.[3] The notice and tender requirement, and the election of remedies doctrine, are all tied in part to the restoration goal. The earlier rescission is unequivocally sought, the less likely it will be that restoration will be rendered difficult or impossible by the passage of time and events.

Whether the inability to restore the parties to the status quo will bar rescission is dependent on a number of factors. When the plaintiff has been instrumental in preventing the restoration of the status quo, courts will often deny rescission, sometimes by directly addressing the restoration requirement, sometimes indirectly by raising the election of remedies bar. For example, when a business is sold and the buyer makes substantial changes in the manner of operating the business, the changes may be characterized as conduct evidencing the intent to affirm the bargain or as change precluding the restoration of the status quo.[4] Characterization may turn

---

[34] *In re* Ivan Boesky Sec. Litig., 825 F. Supp. 623, 636–37 (S.D.N.Y. 1993), *aff'd*, 36 F.3d 255 (2d Cir. 1994) (holding that recovery by rescission of fees paid to party to study restructuring plan would not be permitted when services had already been provided by that party).

[35] Section 134 (Restoration of the Status Quo).

[36] *See* John R. Bates, *Continued Use of Goods After Rejection or Revocation of Acceptance: The UCC Rule Revealed, Reviewed, and Revised*, 25 Rutgers L.J. 1, 64 (1993) (criticizing treatment of the issue under the UCC and noting that courts are split over the proper approach to the problem).

[1] Schwartz v. Rose, 634 N.E.2d 105, 108–09 (Mass. 1994); Kracl v. Loseke, 461 N.W.2d 67, 75–76 (Neb. 1990); Potter v. Oster, 426 N.W.2d 148, 152 (Iowa 1988).

[2] Luciani v. Bestor, 436 N.E.2d 251, 255 (Ill. App. 1982).

[3] Vermilyea v. BDL Entrprises, Inc., 462 N.W.2d 885, 889 (N.D. 1990). *See generally* 13 Am. Jur. 2d *Cancellation of Instruments* § 33.

[4] Gannett Co. v. Register Publ'g Co., 428 F. Supp. 818, 827, 839–40 (D. Conn. 1977) (involving a change in operation of a newspaper from afternoon to morning); Caruso v. Moy, 81 N.W.2d 826, 831 (Neb. 1957) (involving a change in the motif and operation of a restaurant from Chinese-American to Italian-American).

on whether the rescinding party knew or should have known of the grounds to rescind when the changes were made. Knowledge, actual or constructive, should be required before the election of remedies doctrine is applied; an "election" presupposes some level of cognition and awareness.[5] Conversely, when the restoration goal cannot be achieved due to the defendant's misconduct, the requirement is often excused.[6] As noted by one court:

> The rule is in fact that neither the defrauding party nor the purchaser may retain an unfair advantage; there is no room for either party to "have its cake and eat it, too."[7]

The mere fact that restoration is difficult or even impossible does not mean that rescission is unavailable. A court may order rescission under whatever conditions justice and equity may require to protect the interests of both parties.[8] As noted by one court:

> Defendants also argue rescission of the contract was inappropriate because they presented evidence that some of the equipment which made up the sale was no longer in existence. However, return of the actual property is not necessary. Upon seeking rescission of a contract, a party must return the property received or the reasonable value thereof if return of the property is impossible. Thus, any property that Defendants proved missing can be valued and credited against the consideration actually paid by Harts.[9]

Restoration to the status quo ante is a general rule, not an absolute requirement. The guiding principle is to act equitably:

> The rule that he who desires to rescind a contract must restore whatever he has received under it is one of justice and equity . . . and must be reasonably construed and applied. The object of the rule is theoretically to place the parties in status quo; but the rule is equitable, not technical, and does not require more than that such restoration be made as is reasonably possible and such as the merits of the case demand.[10]

Restoration of the status quo will also require that benefits realized and detriments sustained by the parties as a result of the bargain be accounted for or redressed. If the rescission involves a sale of a residence, the buyers and sellers must account for the benefits each realized, such as the benefit the rescinding buyer realized as a result of any occupancy of the residence

---

[5] Section 133 (Election of Remedies).

[6] International Ins. Co. v. Sargent & Lundy, 609 N.E.2d 842, 853 (Ill. App. 1993).

[7] Crews v. Cisco Bros. Ford-Mercury, Inc., 411 S.E.2d 518, 520 (Ga. App. 1991) (citation omitted).

[8] J.C. Penney Co. v. Schulte Real Estate Co., 197 N.E. 458, 460 (Mass. 1935).

[9] Hart v. Steel Prods., Inc., 666 N.E.2d 1270, 1276 (Ind. App. 1996); Braman Dodge, Inc. v. Smith, 515 So. 2d 1053, 1054 (Fla. App. 1987) (permitting rescission, even though restoration to the status quo is impossible, when the equities between the parties may be balanced).

[10] International Software Solutions, Inc. v. Atlanta Pressure Treated Lumber Co., 390 S.E.2d 659, 661 (Ga. App. 1990).

before rescission is accomplished or the benefit the sellers realized because the buyers were in possession of the residence as owners, such as payment of property taxes, mortgages, maintenance of the property, etc.[11]

This accounting for benefits can raise difficult issues of valuation when the rescinding party improved the property that will now be returned to the original owner as a result of the rescission of the bargain. If the rescinding party redecorated the residence, how should the "improvements" be measured: (1) cost to the rescinding party, (2) market value before and after, or (3) value to the defendant? Courts have generally preferred the neutrality of the market value approach, although the culpability of the defendant may be a significant factor.[12]

A party seeking rescission is not required to maintain the property for the non-rescinding party. Of course, property not maintained may deteriorate, suffer damage, or be lost. These risks precede the determination whether rescission will be allowed, but their allocation is uncertain. If rescission is granted, the risk lies with the non-rescinding party because that party should have assumed control of the property, after notice was given, to protect her interest. If rescission is denied, the risk of loss is with the party who unsuccessfully sought to rescind the transaction.

Because there is a risk of error in gauging whether rescission will be granted, a rescinding party may elect to continue to hold the property, which is the subject of the bargain to be rescinded, rather than leave the property unattended. When this is done the rescinding party holds the property as a bailee. The rescinding party must be careful that his continued use of the property is not deemed so inconsistent with the claim of rescission that the remedy is lost. For example, in *Gasque v. Mooers Motor Car Co., Inc.* the court held that a buyer who continued to operate a motor vehicle and drove it 2600 miles after the notice of recission was given had acted so inconsistently with the claim for rescission as to lose it.[13] The court

---

[11] Cardiac Thoracic and Vascular Surgery, P.A. Profit Sharing Trust v. Bond, 840 S.W.2d 188, 193 (Ark. 1992) (noting that "[w]ithout question . . . a purchaser entitled to rescission has some obligation to the vendor for the purchaser's possession and/or use of the property. . ."). The court held that the purchaser's obligation to make restitution was limited to cases where the purchaser derived an actual benefit. When the purchaser only partially occupied the premises, restitution would be limited to that pro rata share. *Id., citing* Restatement of Restitution § 157 (1937) (and collecting cases); *cf.* Metcalfe v. Talarski, 567 A.2d 1148 (Conn. 1989) (holding that a buyer rescinding a real estate bargain was not required to account for the value of the use and occupancy of the premises because the buyer only had possession of the premises, but had not actually used the premises; on the other hand, the buyer was required to account for rents received).

[12] Renner v. Kehl, 722 P.2d 262, 267 (Ariz. 1986) (holding that the measure of the value of improvements would be the difference in market value with and without improvements rather than the cost to the rescinding party of making the improvements when rescission was based on mutual mistake rather than culpability of the defendant); *cf.* Grill v. Hunt, 7 Cal. Rptr. 2d 768, 772 (Cal. App. 1992) (stating that the normal rule requiring the non-rescinding party to carry the burden of proof as to any entitlement to restitution or offset should not be applied when rescission is not based on culpable misconduct); Section 8.7 (Harsh or Mild Measures); Section 136 (Grounds For Rescission).

[13] 313 S.E.2d 384, 389 (Va. 1984) (stating that "after giving notice of revocation, the buyer

distinguished decisions involving mobile homes on the ground that requiring the rescinding party to vacate the "home" would cause undue hardship and would not "be the best means of safeguarding the property for a seller who refuses to take it back." According to the court, use of the property should be distinguished from maintenance of the property insofar as the party's right to rescind is concerned.[14] On the other hand, for many buyers the use of goods, particularly a motor vehicle, may be as necessary as a residence, mobile or otherwise.[15] In such cases, rather than denying rescission a court may allow the seller a reasonable recovery (usually as a "set-off" against the purchase price that the seller returns) for the value of the buyer's use.[16]

If the rescinding party maintains property and rescission is granted, the rescinding party must account to the non-rescinding party for any profits

---

holds the goods as bailee for the seller. The buyer cannot continue to use them as his own and still have the benefit of rescission; his continued use becomes wrongful against the seller, unless induced by the seller's instructions or promises"). This is the general rule. *See generally* L.S. Tellier, Annot., *Use of Article by Buyer as Waiver of Right to Rescind for Fraud, Breach of Warranty, or Failure of Goods to Comply With Contract*, 41 A.L.R.2d 1173 (1955). The Uniform Commercial Code adopts this approach. O'Shea v. Hatch, 640 P.2d 515 (N. Mex. 1982):

> Where a buyer notifies a seller of revocation of acceptance of goods, and receives no instructions from the seller concerning the return or disposition of the property, the buyer is entitled to retain possession of such property. Continued possession and reasonable use of property after the buyer has notified seller of revocation of acceptance, under the U.C.C. does not as a matter of law constitute waiver of the right to revoke acceptance.

> The Uniform Commercial Code, specifies that a buyer, after having given seller notice of rejection of goods within a reasonable time, may not then exercise acts over the property amounting to dominion or ownership, and a buyer who does not have a security interest in such property is under a duty after rejection to hold the goods with reasonable care for a time sufficient to permit the seller to remove them. Continued use of such property, however, will not negate the claim of revocation of acceptance in every case particularly where defendants fail to contact plaintiffs to arrange for removal of such property, or to show how any delay may have prejudiced them, or to show that the delay could have been avoided.

Id. at 522 (citations omitted); *see* John R. Bates, *Continued Use of Goods After Rejection or Revocation of Acceptance: The UCC Rule Revealed, Reviewed, and Revised*, 25 Rutgers L.J. 1 (1993) (criticizing the UCC approach and advocating that a "reasonable use" rule be applied, which would preserve rescission remedies for the disappointed buyer).

[14] *Gasque, supra*, 313 S.E.2d at 389–90.

[15] *Cf.* Stridiron v. I.C., Inc., 578 F. Supp. 997, 1002 (D.V.I. 1984) (noting that when continued use was inevitable and reasonable under the circumstances, rescission would not be denied). The general rule may not apply when statutory rescission under a consumer protection statute (*e.g.*, "Lemon Law") is involved. *E.g.*, Page v. Chrysler Corp., 687 N.E.2d 9, 10–11 (Ohio App. 1996) (holding that state "Lemon Law" required refund in full without offset for reasonable use). State "Lemon Laws" vary tremendously and each should be reviewed carefully. *Cf.* Maitland v. Ford Motor Co., 816 N.E.2d 1061, 1066–67 (Ohio 2004) (holding that Attorney General's set off policy must be used when consumer's "Lemon Law" claim is arbitrated).

[16] *Ex Parte* Stem, 571 So. 2d 1112, 1114–15 (Ala. 1990) (stating that continued use is "wrongful" but not so wrong as to cause buyer to lose right to rescind; injury from wrongful use should be monetized); Johnson v. General Motors Corp., 668 P.2d 139, 1050–51 (Kan. 1983) (same).

realized during the period of actual maintenance.[17] The rescinding party maintains the property, however, at its risk and cannot recover for losses sustained from maintaining the property, except to the extent the maintenance benefits the non-rescinding party. On the other hand, the accounting of profits envisions that the rescinding party's efforts and industry in creating the profits will be recognized.[18]

§ 135   SCOPE OF REMEDY OF RESCISSION

Rescission is not limited to restoration. A number of courts have recognized that a rescinding party may recover damages, including punitive damages. Recovery by the rescinding party of the non-rescinding party's profits has also been allowed.

[135.1]   Rescission Damages

Restoration of the "status quo ante," even with an accounting to balance the equities, may not fully redress the harm sustained by the rescinding party that resulted from the conduct that justified rescission. While recovery of the bargain expectancy would be inconsistent with the nature of rescission, compensating the rescinding party for her out-of-pocket losses caused by the misconduct justifying rescission is not inconsistent with disaffirmance. As noted in *Groothand v. Schlueter*:

> [T]here is no bright line rule for returning parties to the status quo after a court grants a rescission. The result can differ depending on the circumstances . . . . [T]he result in both cases came down to an equitable balancing of benefits. We believe the same principle should apply to consequential damages when a court sits in equity. Rescission is an equitable remedy, and the decision by a court as to whether to award consequential damages unrelated to the contract should be driven by the equitable principles of fairness and

---

[17] *Cardiac Thoracic and Vascular Surgery, P.A. Profit Sharing Trust, supra*, 840 S.W.2d at 193 (noting that rescinding party must account only to the extent she derives actual benefit); Section 46 (Apportionment of Benefit).

[18] *Cf.* Lu v. Grewal, 30 Cal. Rptr. 3d 623, 629 (Cal. App. 2005) (holding that tenants who abandoned lease were not entitled to offset against unpaid rent the profits earned by the landlord who reentered and operated business on the leased premises). As noted by the court:

> Respondents are not entitled to the benefit of appellant's hard work and capital in making the property productive; nor should appellant be punished for bringing the abandoned property back to life. An owner of commercial real property is not required, by virtue of a tenant's breach, to run the business located there at the expense of using time and capital business elsewhere. A tenant has an interest neither in the value of the land, nor in the value of the landowner's business ventures. A tenant's right not to pay damages for rent that he proves could have been earned had the property been released at fair market value does not convert a landowner's ability—or inability—to successfully run a business into an offset against the tenant's breach.

Id. at 629.

justice. Courts in equity must remain free to consider all equitable considerations and to fashion flexible remedies to meet the needs of justice on a case by case basis.[1]

Some courts have stated that "damages" may not be recovered in a rescission action.[2] Such statements must be reviewed carefully. The rescinding party's out-of-pocket expenses, which can be identified as benefitting the non-rescinding party, may be included within the balancing of equities and accounts that is part of the restoration to the status quo ante accomplished by rescission and recovered as such.[3] In some cases, the concept of "out-of-pocket" expenses has been treated quite broadly by the courts to include "opportunities foreborn or lost" as a result of having entered into the now disaffirmed transaction.[4] In this context, there is a significant overlap between rescission damages and reliance damages.

[135.2] Disgorgement of Benefits Received

While restoration of the direct benefits received as a result of a rescinded bargain is well recognized, there has been little judicial discussion how far beyond that point, if at all, restitution should be taken. The principle that a rescinding party who operates or maintains a business that will be returned to the seller must account for profits earned but not losses sustained has been recognized; however, discussions of other indirect benefits have been rare.[5] For example, a party (A) may license another (B) to use a procedure, service, or information delivery system developed by A. Pursuant to the license, B is able to revise its own procedures, independent of the licensed product, and become vastly more profitable. If the licensing contract is rescinded, should A receive, as a restitutionary remedy, any or all of the benefits (increased profits) realized, and realizable in the future, by B and attributable to the license?

When the rescission action is based on culpable wrongdoing, the commentators are in general agreement that the principle of disgorgement should extend deeper.[6] This approach is also reflected in certain areas of the case

---

[1] 949 S.W.2d 923, 931 (Mo. App. 1997) (citation and internal quotes omitted; brackets added).

[2] Metcalfe v. Talarski, 567 A.2d 1148, 1154–55 (Conn. 1989) (holding that since theory of rescission is that contract never existed, a rescinding party may not claim reliance damages after exercising the rights to rescind).

[3] Id. at 1153–54 (holding that trial court did not abuse its discretion in awarding the rescinding party its cost in installing a heating system, the benefit of which would be realized by the seller after the real estate bargain was rescinded).

[4] Runyan v. Pacific Air Indus., Inc., 466 P.2d 682, 693 (Cal. 1970) (permitting recovery of salary rescinding party would have earned had he not entered into bargain with defendant).

[5] The point has received greater discussion in the academic literature. *Compare* E. Allan Farnsworth, *Your Loss or My Gain? The Dilemma of the Disgorgement Principle in Breach of Contract,* 94 Yale L.J. 1339, 1341 (1985) (suggesting that courts should be reluctant to order disgorgement in breach of contract/rescission actions since a breach is not a wrong), *with* John Dawson, *Restitution or Damages,* 20 Ohio St. L.J. 175 (1959) (arguing that complete disgorgement is the preferable remedy when the wrongdoer's gains exceed the victim's losses).

[6] Douglas Laycock, *The Scope and Significance of Restitution,* 67 Texas L. Rev. 1277, 1289 (1989); GEORGE PALMER, THE LAW OF RESTITUTION § 2.12, pp. 164–65 (1978).

law, such as securities fraud.[7] It has found few applications, however, outside the securities fraud area. This is most likely due to the harshness of the remedy, the realization that any downstream profits realized were not likely the result solely of the bargain,[8] and the fact that rescission may be based on non-culpable conduct, e.g., mistake.[9]

[135.3]　Punitive Damages

The jurisdictions have split as to whether punitive damages may be awarded in an action for rescission. Two objections have been raised. First, rescission may be based on conduct, such as mistake or failure of consideration, that will not support a punitive damages award. This hurdle is pervasive across the law, however, and not restricted to rescission actions.[10] The second hurdle is more problematic. Traditionally, punitive damages were not available in equity.[11] While the modern trend is to allow punitive damages in equity,[12] the nature of rescission may limit the availability of punitive damages.

An action for rescission is not founded *per se* on the notion of actual injury, but on the premise that equity should act to abrogate the bargain between the parties and restore them to the status quo ante because of defendant's inequitable conduct. Equity is not concerned with the rescinding party's actual injury (or pecuniary loss) so much as equity seeks to avoid injury by undoing the bargain to protect the innocent party. This is not to suggest that "injury" is immaterial, for it is not; however, the injury element is not viewed in the same light as it is in the damages context. As noted by one court:

> Defendants argue that plaintiff has failed to allege injury. The injury element of a fraud claim is interpreted differently depending on whether the remedy sought is damages or rescission. An action for damages requires the showing of some concrete pecuniary loss. By contrast, a substantial body of case law indicates that an action

---

[7] Affiliated Ute Citizens of Utah v. United States, 406 U.S. 128, 155 (1972); Jordan v. Duff & Phelps, Inc., 815 F.2d 429, 442 (7th Cir. 1987), *cert. denied*, 485 U.S. 901 (1988); Janigan v. Taylor, 344 F.2d 781, 786 (1st Cir.), *cert. denied*, 382 U.S. 879 (1965).

[8] Section 46 (Apportionment of Benefit); Section 51 (Disgorgement Orders).

[9] *Cf. Runyan, supra*, 466 P.2d 682 (holding that when rescission was based on equitable considerations (*e.g.*, the defendant's culpable misconduct) disgorgement of benefits would be permitted, but when recission was based on non-culpable misconduct, rescission remedy would be limited to return of consideration).

[10] Chapter 23 (Punitive Damages) (particularly Section 202 (Scope of Punitive Damages)).

[11] Pedah Co. v. Hunt, 509 P.2d 1197, 1199 (Or. 1973) (stating that great weight of authority denied recovery of punitive damages in equity since the objective of equity is to do justice between the parties). There is the further consideration that equity acts without a jury. Section 202.6 ([Punitive Damages] Equity). If legal and equitable claims are joined, the presence of the equitable claim should not prevent the award of punitive damages on the legal claims. Rexnord, Inc. v. Ferris, 657 P.2d 673, 675 (Or. 1983).

[12] *See generally* Jay Zitter, Annot, *Punitive Damages: Power of Equity Court to Award*, 58 A.L.R.4th 844 § 3 (1988).

to rescind a contract for fraudulent inducement does not require a showing of injury in the traditional sense which is required in an action for damages. Though a plaintiff seeking rescission on the ground of fraud need not show actual pecuniary loss, he must still show injury in some sense.[13]

This may raise problems since "actual injury" is a prerequisite for a punitive damages recovery.[14]

[135.4] Losing Contracts

If the plaintiff is able to rescind a losing contract, *i.e.*, a contract on which plaintiff would incur a loss in performing, the plaintiff obtains significant benefits. First, additional performance costs are avoided.[15] Second, plaintiff may be able to recoup her cost of performance from the defendant under a restitution theory.[16] Either of these options is more palatable when the defendant engaged in conduct that is tortious[17] or which materially contributed to plaintiff's losses, such as "change orders" that increased plaintiff's cost of performance beyond that initially specified in the contract.[18]

The extent to which, if at all, a plaintiff should recover more than his consideration, (or a pro rata share of the contract price when plaintiff provided services for a fee), remains of matter of significant academic debate and judicial disagreement. The issue is covered elsewhere in these materials in the sections cited in the footnotes of this subsection.

§ 136 GROUNDS FOR RESCISSION

Rescission is not available as a matter of right when a party's bargain related expectations have been adversely affected by the defendant's conduct. In order to maintain an action for rescission the plaintiff must invoke a proper basis for the claim. These include: (1) fraud, deceit, or

---

[13] Dornberger v. Metropolitan Life Ins. Co., 961 F. Supp. 506, 543 (S.D.N.Y. 1997) (citations omitted); *see* Dehring v. Northern Mich. Exploration Co., Inc., 304 N.W.2d 560, 566 (Mich. App. 1981) (stating that pecuniary loss is not a necessary element of a rescission action for fraud); Nab v. Hills, 452 P.2d 981, 987 (Idaho 1969) (stating that when fraud is used to support an action for damages, the plaintiff must show actual pecuniary harm; when fraud is used to support an action for rescission, proof of monetary damage is unnecessary—"[w]hat must be demonstrated is damage or injury as those words are used in their broader sense"); *cf.* Adickes v. Andreoli, 600 S.W.2d 939, 946 (Tex. Civ. App. 1980) (holding that rescission for fraud is available even if rescinding party has not suffered a pecuniary loss if such a loss will be suffered unless bargain is rescinded); Section 121.3 ([Fraud] Economic Loss Rule).

[14] Section 203 (Actual Injury Requirement).

[15] Section 162 (Contractor's Remedies); Section 163 (Losing Contracts and Restitution).

[16] Section 41 (Restitution for Wrongdoing).

[17] Section 41.1 ([Restitution for Wrongdoing] Tortious Conduct).

[18] Section 41.2 ([Restitution for Wrongdoing] Breach of Contract); Section 162.3 ([Contractor's Remedies] Change Orders).

misrepresentation; (2) failure of consideration or material breach of contract; (3) mistake; (4) duress or undue influence, particularly by a fiduciary; and (5) illegality.

Care must be taken, however, in applying substantive theories of liability to the rescission action. In some cases, the rescission claim may be based on conduct that is less culpable than that required for affirmance remedies. This is the case with fraud. In many jurisdictions, fraud damages requires a showing of fault, either the intent to deceive or negligence.[1] Rescission, on the other hand, will often be available for innocent misrepresentations.[2] In other cases, the rescission remedy will require a higher threshold. For example, it is often held that the breach must be "substantial" when a party seeks rescission as a remedy for breach of contract.[3]

In the case of mistake, duress, and illegality, the sole remedy provided is that of rescission. The plaintiff either takes the bargain as it is, "warts and all," or rescinds. Affirmance damages are not available for the redress of mistake, duress, or illegality.[4] These grounds usually go to the question whether a bargain was formed and it is perhaps perceived by the courts to be fundamentally inconsistent to seek damages when the gist of the action denies the requisite bargaining intent or state of mind.[5] Mistake usually must be mutual for rescission; occasionally, however, unilateral mistake will permit rescission, particularly when the defendant takes advantage of the plaintiff's mistake,[6] but sometimes even absent that element of exploitation.[7]

---

[1] Section 120 (Nature of Fraud).

[2] Herzog v. Capital Co., 164 P.2d 8, 9–10 (Cal. 1945) (noting that an integration clause in a contract may protect the innocent seller from innocent oral misrepresentations, but the integration clause will not prevent rescission when innocent misrepresentations are material and induce reliance); cf. Van Lare v. Vogt, Inc., 683 N.W.2d 46 (Wis. 2004) (holding that economic loss rule barred damages action based on innocent misrepresentation). Several of the justices sparred in concurring opinions whether an innocent misrepresentation would satisfy the "inducement" requirement.

[3] Harris v. Desisto, 932 S.W.2d 435, 444 (Mo. App. 1996) (stating that "[to] justify a rescission, the breach must relate to a vital provision going to the very substance or root of the agreement, and cannot relate simply to a subordinate or incidental matter") (citations and internal quotation marks omitted).

[4] The availability of illegality as a ground for rescission may be compromised by the unwillingness of the court to provide redress to either party to a bargain infected with illegality. Section 65.2 (Illegality).

[5] Dairyland Power Coop. v. United States, 16 F.3d 1197, 1202 (Fed. Cir. 1994) (stating that to rescind contract for mutual mistake, the plaintiff must establish that: (1) the parties to the contract were mistaken in their belief regarding a fact; (2) that mistaken belief constituted a basic assumption underlying the contract; (3) the mistake had a material effect on the bargain; and (4) the contract did not put the risk of the mistake on the party seeking rescission). As to the elements for duress, see Section 63.1 (Duress); as to the elements for illegality, see Section 65.2 (Illegality).

[6] Wellman Sav. Bank v. Adams, 454 N.W.2d 852, 855 (Iowa 1990) (holding that a bargain can be rescinded for unilateral mistake when the defendant acted inequitably with awareness of the other's mistake).

[7] Donovan v. RRL Corp., 27 P.3d 702, 706 (Cal. 2001) (permitting rescission of newspaper

Occasionally, courts speak of damages for mistake but the true remedy is not damages but restitution for unjust enrichment due to mistaken payments. When the negligence of the defendant leads the plaintiff to mistakenly under-collect money from another, damages may be recovered, but here the cause of loss is negligence not mistake.[8]

Rescission is available if a condition to a bargain, transaction, agreement, or promise is unfulfilled. This issue commonly arises in connection with broken engagements. Although most jurisdictions have abolished the common law action of breach of promise to marry,[9] restitution is still available under the theory of rescission. For example, in *Fierro v. Hoel* an engagement ring was given in contemplation of marriage. The condition never occurred. The court allowed rescission and return of the ring holding that the gift was impliedly conditional. The court rejected an inquiry into the reasons why the marriage did not occur holding that fault was irrelevant.[10]

---

offer that contained inaccurate price due to newspaper's error when dealer acted in good faith, defendant did not have actual or constructive knowledge of the mistake, and enforcement of the contract would be inequitable); Powder Horn Constructors, Inc. v. Florence, 754 P.2d 356 361–65 (Colo. 1989) (holding that contractor could rescind mistaken bid prior to acceptance by defendant when mistake was material, contractor exercised due care, and defendant was not prejudiced).

[8] Laclede Gas Co. v. Solon Gershman, Inc., 539 S.W.2d 574, 577 (Mo. App. 1976) (holding that defective meter did not estop utility from collecting underpayments from defendant-landlord, but that landlord could offset against added payments, monies it could have collected from tenants if meter had properly functioned). *But see* Wisconsin Power & Light Co. v. Berlin Tanning & Mfg. Co., 83 N.W.2d 147 (Wis. 1957) (rejecting damages counterclaim when utility mistakenly bills landlord).

[9] Section 102.4 (Breach of Promise to Marry); Section 103 (Heart Balm Statutes).

[10] 465 N.W.2d 669,672 (Iowa App. 1990); Section 102.4 (Breach of Promise to Marry).

Chapter 16

BREACH OF CONTRACT REMEDIES— AFFIRMANCE OF BARGAIN OR TRANSACTION

§ 140 GENERAL PRINCIPLES OF CONTRACT REMEDIES

The measure of contract remedies is significantly influenced by the identity of the non-breaching party. Whether the non-breaching party is the buyer or the seller, the employer or the employee, or the owner or the contractor will have a significant impact on the form and shape of the remedy provided. This occurs because the parties to a contract have different expectations and interests regarding the subject matter of the contract; consequently, breach affects them in different ways. The buyer seeks to obtain the specific subject matter of the contract, which may or may not be easily substituted for by like or equivalent goods. The seller, on the other hand, seeks to exchange the subject matter of the contract for something else, usually cash or cash equivalent. These different goals identify the parties' contract expectations and shape the consequences each will sustain if the promised performance of the other party to the contract is not met.

The available remedies for breach of contract are (1) examined in terms of damages, injunction (specific performance), and restitution, (2) in terms of the type of contract, such as employment contract or construction contract, and (3) from the perspective of the non-breaching party to that contract. It is particularly important, however, to correlate the discussion of contract remedies with the treatment of the specific remedy, such as damages,[1] specific performance,[2] and rescission.[3] This chapter provides a

---

[1] Chapter 2 (General Principles Concerning Compensatory Damages).

[2] Chapter 20 (Specific Performance).

[3] Chapter 15 (Rescission (Disaffirmance) of Bargain).

broad overview. Subsequent chapters examine remedies in the context of specific contract relationships, including: (1) employment,[4] contruction,[5] and sale of real property.[6] Remedies associated with relationships that have been subject to uniform codification, e.g., contracts for the sale of goods, or tend to exhibit wide jurisdictional variations, e.g., lease agreements, are not addressed. The omissions evidence that much of the law in this area is subject to reconceptualization within the area of concern in which the contract operates. Employment, construction, and sales of realty were selected to present general issues. Within each of these areas lie further refinements, exceptions, and areas of specialization that are beyond the coverage of this work.

A second significant consideration regarding contract remedies is the issue of fault. It is frequently noted that the tort concept of fault plays no role in the enforcement of contract claims.[7] Contract liability is said to be strict.[8] This concept of strict liability is often extended to the issue of remedies for breach of contract,[9] but caution must be exercised. While the rule of strict liability is generally accurate, exceptions are significant.[10] On the other hand, the exceptions, while significant, are not consistently applied, nor consistently applauded.

Most prominent in this latter context is the efficient breach doctrine. Adherents of this approach generally decry allowing enhanced remedies based on notions of fault-based breach because such enhanced remedies would deter efficient breaches.[11] The determination as to whether a jurisdiction recognizes fault as a basis for enhancing contract-based remedies cannot be stated to have general acceptance or general rejection.[12] This

---

[4] Chapter 17 (Breach of Employment Contract).

[5] Chapter 18 (Breach of Construction Contract).

[6] Chapter 19 (Breach of Contract to Sell Real Property).

[7] Martini v. Beaverton Ins. Agency, Inc., 838 P.2d 1061, 1066 (Or. 1992).

[8] Patton v. Mid-Continent Sys., Inc., 841 F.2d 742, 750 (7th Cir. 1988) (stating that "liability for breach of contract is, prima facie, strict liability. That is, if the promisor fails to perform as agreed, he has broken his contract even though the failure . . . was in no way blameworthy"); Restatement (Second) of Contracts § 309 (1981).

[9] 3 E. Allan Farnsworth, Farnsworth on Contracts § 12.8, at 190 (1990) (stating that "contract law is, in its essential design, a law of strict liability, and the accompanying system of remedies operates without regard to fault").

[10] See Romero v. Mervyn's, 784 P.2d 992, 999-1002 (N. Mex. 1989) (upholding punitive damages award for breach of contract based on agent-promisor's knowledge at the time the contract was made that his principal would not be able to perform).

[11] Richard Posner, Economic Analysis of Law 118-20, 128-29 (4th ed. 1992).

[12] Compare Timothy Sullivan, Punitive Damages in the Law of Contract: The Reality and the Illusion of Legal Change, 61 Minn. L. Rev. 207, 219 (1977) (stating that "[t]he functional purposes of contract damages . . . are obscured by a thick overlay of judicial decisions and scholarly commentary which uncritically recite that the object of damages in contract is solely to compensate for pecuniary loss"), with Eric Mills Holmes, The Four Phases of Promissory Estoppel, 20 Seattle U. L. Rev. 45 (1996):

> Tort may be abandoning its great flywheel of fault for strict liability, compensation systems, and no-fault; fault, in turn however, is being absorbed into contract.

concept of enhanced damages based on fault-based breaches is also picked up by the concept of "bad faith" breach of contract, particularly, the implied covenant of good faith and fair dealing. This motion of "bad faith" breach has made substantial advances in American law. It occupies large parts of insurance contract remedies and has made substantial inroads into employment contract litigation. The application of "bad faith" liability has been most successful when the contract is said to be relational and exposes one party to exploitation by the other.[13]

A third consideration involves the common law rule that barred a party in breach of his contract from seeking an affirmative recovery against the non-breaching party. A buyer in breach of his contract to purchase was often barred from seeking recovery of any of his down payment, even if the seller sustained no damages from the breach.[14] Theis common law rule is, however, in decline. The dominant position today is that a plaintiff in breach of his contractual obligations may recover based on principles of unjust enrichment.[15] In other words, the breaching plaintiff must make the non-breaching defendant whole by covering any losses the defendant sustained as a result of the plaintiff's breach. However, if the non-breaching defendant, after being made whole, still retains funds or property belonging to the breaching plaintiff, the plaintiff may require the defendant to disgorge the "net of loss" funds or property to the plaintiff to the extent necessary to prevent the defendant's unjust enrichment.

Finally, contract remedies usually do not include non-economic losses; however, this rule is subject to some significant exceptions that are discussed in Section 141 (Bad Faith Breach) and Section 142 (Distress Damages).

Contract, using fault notions, seems to be embracing equitable principles such as the exerciser concept of unconscionability and the additur of good faith. The result of this mix is three varieties of contract breach: (1) the amoral classical contract breach with Hadley-limited damages; (2) the bad-faith breach for which not only compensatory but all non-punitive damages proximately caused by the breach are recoverable; and (3) the fraudulent or oppressive [unconscionable] breach for which punitive damages are allowed.

Id. at 71, n.78.

[13] Section 141 (Bad Faith Breach).

[14] *See generally* 77 Am. Jur. 2d *Vendor and Purchaser* § 649 (stating traditional common law rule).

[15] Vines v. Orchard Hills, Inc., 435 A.2d 1022 (Conn. 1980):

The right of a contracting party, despite his default, to seek restitution for benefits conferred and allegedly unjustly retained has been much disputed in the legal literature and in the case law. Although earlier cases often refused to permit a party to bring an action that could be said to be based on his own breach; many of the more recent cases support restitution in order to prevent unjust enrichment and to avoid forfeiture.

Id. at 1025-26 (citations omitted).

§ 141 BAD FAITH BREACH

[141.1] Tort-Based Remedies

The concept that contractual duties must be performed in good faith is well established in the law.[1] What is a relatively recent extension, or deviation depending on one's point of view, is the idea that the bad faith breach of implied contractual obligations, (the implied covenant of good faith and fair dealing), may permit tort-based, rather than contract-based, remedies. The development of this bad faith doctrine has proceeded along two paths. The first path is the idea that bad faith breach of contract may consist of wrongfully denying that any contractual obligation exists in the first place.[2] Although this idea enjoyed some initial acceptance, it has failed to maintain much traction as a tort-based remedy.[3]

The second pathway has been more successful. Borrowing from principles established to measure and control the relationship between trustee and beneficiary, many jurisdictions, but in varying circumstances, allow tort-based remedies for the bad faith breach of contract when the breaching and non-breaching party stand in a confidential or special relationship to one another.[4] The most pronounced example of this is the application of the concept of bad faith breach to the insurer-insured relationship.[5] The traditional, common law rule for failure to pay money allows for limited remedies.[6] Absent the theory of bad faith, insurer breach of contract by the failure to pay policy proceeds would limit the insured to recovery of the

---

[1] *See* Steven Burton, *Breach of Contract and the Common Law Duty to Perform in Good Faith*, 94 Harv. L. Rev. 369, 369 (1980) (noting that "[a] majority of American jurisdictions, the Restatement (Second) of Contracts, and the Uniform Commercial Code (U.C.C.) now recognize the duty to perform a contract in good faith as a general principle of contract law") (footnotes omitted).

[2] Seaman's Direct Buying Serv., Inc. v. Standard Oil Co., 686 P.2d 1158, 1167 (Cal. 1984) (recognizing "that a party to a contract may incur tort remedies when, in addition to breaching the contract, it seeks to shield itself from liability by denying, in bad faith and without probable cause, that the contract exists").

[3] Freeman & Mills, Inc. v. Belcher Oil Co., 900 P.2d 669, 670 (Cal. 1995) (overruling *Seaman's Direct Buying Serv., Inc., supra*); State, Dept. of Natural Resources v. Transamerica Premier Ins. Co., 856 P.2d 766, 774, n.6 (Alaska 1993) (declining to adopt *Seaman's Direct Buying Serv., Inc., supra*, tort-based theory of damages for bad faith denial of contract).

[4] Section 113 (Breach of Fiduciary Duty).

[5] Careau & Co. v. Security-Pacific Bus. Credit, Inc., 272 Cal. Rptr. 387, 397-404 (Cal. App. 1990) (surveying California decisions and concluding that the allowance of tort-based remedies for breach of contract is generally limited to the insurer-insured context).

[6] Loudon v. Taxing Dist., 104 U.S. 771, 774 (1881) (holding that an aggrieved party in a contract action involving the failure to pay a sum of money is entitled only to the amount owed and any interest that has accrued during the delay period); 11 SAMUEL WILLISTON, A TREATISE ON THE LAW OF CONTRACTS § 1410, at 604-06 (Walter H. E. Jaeger ed., 3d ed. 1968) (citing several cases in which the only relief awarded in a suit for nonpayment of a debt was the debt itself plus interest from the time due). The common law rule is fading even as a limiting contract damages remedy. Section 141.2 ([Bad Faith Breach] Contract-Based Remedies).

proceeds plus prejudgment interest. Bad faith liability dramatically increases the insurer's liability for breach for failure to pay.

Bad faith, which exposes a breaching insurer to tort-based remedies, is recognized in many American jurisdictions.[7] Recognition of tort-based remedies for bad faith breach is influenced, however, by the context in which the insurer's misconduct occurs. Insurer breach for the failure to settle a third party's claim against the insured remains one situation in which the insurer's tort liability is consistently recognized. This situation involves an insurer that has contractually assumed the exclusive control of the insured's defense of the third party's claim; thus, placing the insured in a vulnerable position because the consequences of insurer breach are borne by the insured, who cannot protect herself. This situation most easily coheres with notions of confidentiality and "special relationship" to warrant tort-based recoveries based on fiduciary principles.[8]

Insurer breach that causes the delayed receipt of policy proceeds by the insured will subject the insurer to tort-based remedies in many jurisdictions, but not as many as in the failure to settle context.[9] Here the insurer-insured relationship is simply bilateral and without the aspect of control that makes the insured especially vulnerable to insurer breach, as in the failure to settle context. The failure to pay or delayed payment of policy benefits claim is essentially the form of most contractual disputes; yet, many courts have extended tort-based remedies to this situation. The rationales for the extension are that: (1) insurance contracts are contracts of adhesion; (2) the relationship between insurer and insured is unequal; (3) the primary purpose of insurance contracts is non-economic, *i.e.*, the preservation of the insured's peace of mind; and (4) the quasi-public status of insurers.[10]

The concept of tortious breach of the implied covenant of good faith and fair dealing has been extended by a few jurisdictions beyond the insurance context. The primary extensions have been in the area of employee-employer disputes[11] and lender-borrower disputes.[12] The extension has,

---

[7] STEPHEN ASHLEY, BAD FAITH ACTIONS LIABILITY AND DAMAGES at App. II (1984 and current supplement) (listing jurisdictions recognizing a bad faith action in this context).

[8] Section 113 (Breach of Fiduciary Duty); *see* Carma Developers (California), Inc. v. Marathon Dev. Cal., Inc., 826 P.2d 710, 726 (Cal. 1992) (noting that "[t]he covenant of good faith finds particular application in situations where one party is invested with discretionary power affecting the rights of another. Such power must be exercised in good faith") (citations omitted).

[9] Approximately 25 jurisdictions recognize tort-based remedies in this "delayed receipt" context. Nichols v. State Farm Mut. Auto. Ins. Co., 306 S.E.2d 616, 619 (S.C. 1983).

[10] James Fischer, *Why Are Insurance Contracts Subject to Special Rules of Interpretation?: Text v. Context*, 24 Ariz. St. L. J. 995 (1992); *see* Foley v. Interactive Data Corp., 765 P.2d 373, 389-401 (Cal. 1988). Foley also suggested that the inability to cover, *i.e.*, secure insurance coverage for known, existing losses, served to distinguish insurance contracts from other contracts. *Id.* at 396.

[11] ASHLEY, BAD FAITH ACTIONS, *supra* at § 11:7 (Bad Faith in Wrongful Discharge Cases) (surveying cases and noting that "[t]he courts have relied upon a variety of reasons for refusing to extend the cause of action for bad faith [to wrongful discharge]") (brackets added). Some

however, been cautious and most jurisdiction treat the concept of tortious bad faith as limited to the insurance area as traditionally defined.[13]

The components of a "bad faith breach" are difficult to define. Some jurisdictions use an objective standard: did the defendant act in a reasonably prudent manner. Other jurisdictions define bad faith more subjectively as referring to the defendant's state of mind when committing the breach. At the definitional level, the decisions are inconsistent and confusing.[14]

The recognition of tort-based remedies for bad faith breach of contractual obligation means that the plaintiff can recover extra-contractual damages. These include: (1) the amounts due under the contract;[15] (2) extra-contractual economic losses, e.g., consequential damages;[16] emotional

---

jurisdictions that accept the theory restrict it to what the court characterizes as "conduct [that] goes well beyond the bounds of ordinary breach." Smith v. Cladianos, 752 P.2d 233, 235 (Nev. 1988) (brackets added).

[12] *See generally* Lori J. Henkel, Annot., *Bank's Liability For Breach of Implied Contract of Good Faith and Fair Dealing*, 55 A.L.R.4th 1026 (1987) (noting limited acceptance of lender liability for tortious breach and collecting decisions).

[13] Cates Constr., Inc. v. Talbot Partners, 980 P.2d 407 (Cal. 1999) (rejecting extension of tortious breach of implied covenant of good faith and fair dealing to surety on construction performance bond).

[14] Taylor v. State Farm Mut. Auto. Ins. Co., 854 P.2d 1134, 1142 (Ariz. 1993) (stating that "cases demonstrate the uninterrupted recognition that bad faith has components of both tort and contract and underscore the lack of consensus in the area"); Bollinger v. Nuss, 449 P.2d 502 (Kan. 1969):

> The result is that under the negligence test the insurer must conduct itself with that degree of care which would be used by an ordinarily prudent person in the management of his own business, with no policy limits applicable to the claim. Likewise, under the good faith test, the insurer must in good faith view the situations as it would if there were no applicable policy limits . . . .
>
> . . . [I]t would appear that the two rules have tended to merge. In the final analysis, the question of liability depends upon the circumstances of the particular case and must be determined by taking into account the various factors present . . . .

Id. at 511-12 (involving "failure to settle"); *cf.* Garret v. Bank West, 459 N.W.2d 833, 845 (S.D. 1990) (stating that the commercial requirement of "[g]ood faith is an 'excluder.' It is a phrase without general meaning . . . of its own and serves to exclude a wide range of heterogeneous forms of bad faith. In a particular context the phrase takes on specific meaning, but usually this is only by way of contrast with the specific form of bad faith actually or hypothetically ruled out"), *quoting* Summers, *Good Faith in General Contract Law and the Sales Provision of the Uniform Commercial Code*, 54 Va. L. Rev. 195, 201 (1968).

[15] This is the basic contract remedy. *See* note 6, *supra*; Section 141.2 ([Bad Faith Breach] Contract-Based Remedies).

[16] Hart v. Prudential Property & Cas. Ins. Co., 848 F. Supp. 900, 902 (D. Nev. 1994) (noting that Nevada allows the recovery of all consequential damages when there has been a showing of bad faith by the insurer); Farmers Group, Inc. v. Trimble, 658 P.2d 1370, 1374 (Colo. App. 1982) (holding that a claim for impairment of credit damages may be actionable if the injury arose from the other party's negligence), *aff'd*, 691 P.2d 1138 (Colo. 1984); BARRY R. OSTRANGER & THOMAS R. NEWMAN, HANDBOOK ON INSURANCE COVERAGE DISPUTES § 12.10(a) (5th ed. 1992) (surveying jurisdictions that allow recovery for economic loss in insurance bad faith actions).

distress damages;[17] (3) punitive damages,[18] and (4) in some jurisdictions, attorney's fees.[19]

When the bad faith breach sounds in tort rather than contract another consequence may be a broader measure of consequential damages due to the different "foreseeability" tests used.[20] The broader "foreseeability" test may be applied even when a jurisdiction treats "bad faith breaches" as giving rise to contract-based remedies rather than tort-based remedies, but permits, notwithstanding the common law rule, a recovery of consequential damages.[21] In other words, a finding of bad faith may encourage a court to apply contract-based remedies broadly when, absent bad faith, the court would limit the non-breaching party's recovery to the payment of the sum of money owed, plus interest.

[141.2] Contract-Based Remedies

There have been relatively few decisions addressing contract remedies available for bad faith breach of implied obligations of contractual good faith and fair dealing. The critical issue is whether breach of an implied obligation should give rise to contract-based remedies less than, equal to, or greater than those available for the breach of an express term of the contract. In the insurance context, the traditional approach law has tended to equalize contract-based remedies for the two forms of breach.[22] More recently, however, courts have begun to expand contract-based remedies for breach of the implied obligation of good faith so that they more closely approximate tort-based remedies. This expansion has, however, been limited to economic losses.[23] Some jurisdictions have achieved nearly the

---

[17] Merlo v. Standard Life & Accident Ins. Co., 130 Cal. Rptr. 416, 423 (Cal. App. 1976); OSTRANGER & NEWMAN, INSURANCE COVERAGE DISPUTES, *supra* at § 12.10(d); ASHLEY, BAD FAITH ACTIONS, *supra* at § 8:04-:05; John Bauman, *Emotional Distress Damages and the Tort of Insurance Bad Faith*, 46 Drake L. Rev. 717 (1998).

[18] State Farm Mut. Auto. Ins. Co. v. Engelke, 824 S.W.2d 747, 754 (Tex. Civ. App. 1992); ASHLEY, BAD FAITH ACTIONS, *supra* at § 8:06.

[19] Brandt v. Superior Court, 693 P.2d 796, 800 (Cal. 1985) (holding that the insured in a bad faith action may recover attorney's fees expended in recovering the policy benefit due but not attorney's fees expended in securing consequential or extra-contractual damages). *But see* Bernhard v. Farmers Ins. Exch., 915 P.2d 1285, 1290-91 (Colo. 1996) (rejecting *Brandt*). Some jurisdictions do not recognize the *Brandt* limitation and permit the recovery of all attorney's fees incurred in prosecuting the bad faith action against the insurer. Polselli v. Nationwide Mut. Fire Ins. Co., 126 F.3d 524, 532 (3d Cir. 1997) (applying Pennsylvania law and collecting decisions on both sides of the issue).

[20] Billings v. Union Bankers Ins. Co., 918 P.2d 461, 466-67 (Utah 1996) (finding error in a jury instruction that allowed a broader measure of consequential damages in contract-based action for bad faith (breach of implied covenant of good faith) than for breach of express term of insurance contract). The court stated that the broader measure should be reserved for tort actions. *Id.* at 466; Sections 10.2.2 ([Loss Causation—Contracts] Policy Considerations); 10.3.2 ([Loss Causation—Torts] Policy Considerations).

[21] Section 141.2 ([Bad Faith Breach] Contract-Based Remedies).

[22] Billings v. Union Bankers Ins. Co., 918 P.2d 461, 466-67 (Utah 1996).

[23] Jonathan Neil & Assocs., Inc. v. Jones, 94 P.3d 1055 (Cal. 2004):

same results by rejecting the common law rules limiting recoveries in failure to pay cases and allowing the insured to recover consequential *economic* damages based on breach of contract.[24] A few courts permit recovery of non-economic losses or punitive damages when only a contract remedy is available.[25]

The concept of bad faith has also been applied to preliminary negotiations, but here the tendency has been to limit recoveries to reliance losses and reject the recovery of expectancy losses. As noted by one court:

> Many courts enforce promises to negotiate in good faith, although there is no clear majority rule. Most courts that do so limit relief to reliance damages: *i.e.*, expenses incurred in negotiating, drafting, or preparing to perform a contract scuttled by another's bad-faith negotiating conduct. Most deny expectation damages: *i.e.*, expected profits on the hoped-for contract.[26]

Even if future loss profits are abstractly available, the fact that the breach involved an agreement to be rather than an agreement in place may cause a court to treat the lost profits claim as "remote" and non-recoverable.[27]

When the context involves bad faith breach of express contractual obligations, courts have awarded lost expectancies and the decisions do not reflect the same concern that remedies be limited to the reliance interest as in the failure to negotiate fairly cases.[28] This distinction reflects a

---

The Joneses contend that the very act of billing a retroactive excess premium created such financial uncertainty as to compel them to close their business. Assuming someone in a similar position to the Joneses can prove that, notwithstanding their resort to available administrative remedies, the excessive premium charge compelled them to close their business, lost profits would be available even when the implied covenant of good faith and fair dealing sounds only in contract, so long as the lost profits were among "the natural and direct consequences of the breach."

Id. at 1069 (citation omitted).

[24] *See* Marquis v. Farm Family Mut. Ins. Co., 628 A.2d 644, 650-52 (Me. 1993) (stating principle); Olson v. Rugloski, 277 N.W.2d 385, 387-88 (Minn. 1979) (permitting the recovery of consequential economic damages when the insurer breached the insurance contract by unreasonably delaying payment, but requiring proof that the insurer committed an independent tort before permitting an award of punitive damages); Lawton v. Great Southwest Fire Ins. Co., 392 A.2d 576, 579-81 (N.H. 1978) (rejecting a bad faith action in tort for failure to pay because the insurer does not control the insured's fate as it does in third-party failure to settle cases, but allowing recovery for consequential economic damages).

[25] *See* Douglas G. Houser, Ronald J. Clark & Linda M. Bouldan, *Good Faith as a Matter of Law—An Update on the Insurance Company's "Right to be Wrong"*, 39 Tort Trial & Ins. Prac. L. J. 1045, 1057 (2004).

[26] Brady v. State, 965 P.2d 1, 11 (Alaska 1998) (footnotes omitted).

[27] Vestar Development II, LLC. v. General Dynamics Corporation, 249 F.3d 958, 961-62 (9th Cir. 2001) (applying California law).

[28] Sons of Thunder, Inc. v. Borden, Inc., 690 A.2d 575, 589 (1997) (permitting the recovery of one year of lost profits as expectancy damages based on the defendant's failure to act in good faith in exercising its right to terminate the contract); *cf.* Canusa Corp. v. A&R Lobosco, Inc., 986 F. Supp. 723, 731-32 (E.D.N.Y. 1997) (finding that bad faith breach of a requirements contract entitled the plaintiff to the recovery of lost profits as consequential damages).

differentiation between a vested expectation in an existing contract and the much more limited expectation that necessarily exists in the "hoped-for" contract being negotiated. Moreover, even as to contracts themselves, as Professor Speidel observes, "the appropriate remedies for bad faith breach vary with the circumstances."[29]

§ 142   DISTRESS DAMAGES

A consistent theme of contract remedies is that they emphasize economic loss. It is a mantra, often intoned by courts, that contract remedies do not redress non-economic injuries, such as distress[1] or reputational injury[2] damages. Courts invoke several reasons for the prohibition of non-economic recoveries in breach of contract actions. The courts have suggested that non-economic damages are speculative, unforeseeable, and likely to result in windfalls to the plaintiff.[3] The looseness of these arguments has not gone unnoticed. Exceptions to the traditional rule are recognized, particularly when the infliction of emotional distress is a likely result of the breach.[4] Thus, contracts touching upon or relating to matters that directly affect (1) the comfort, happiness, or personal welfare of the plaintiff or (2) the affection, self-esteem, or tender feelings of the plaintiff have the potential to give rise to a valid claim for non-economic damages on breach.[5]

A California decision illustrates the types of contracts that fall within or without the approach stated in the prior paragraph:

> The rule against emotional distress damages for breach of contract has been applied in California to bar such damages, for example, for breach of a choral singer's employment contract, in an action for rescission of a real estate gift on the ground of undue influence, and for a bank's breach of its contractual obligation to buy automobile insurance for a borrower. The exceptional contracts for whose breach distress damages have been allowed include the agreement of two gambling clubs with a husband to exclude his wife from the clubs and not to cash her checks, a mortician's contract to preserve

---

[29] Richard Speidel, *The "Duty" of Good Faith in Contract Performance and Enforcement*, 46 J. Legal Educ. 537, 542 (1996).

[1] Kewin v. Massachusetts Mut. Life Ins. Co., 295 N.W.2d 50, 55 (Mich. 1980); Restatement (Second) of Contracts § 353 cmt. a (1981).

[2] Volkswagen Interamericana, S.A. v. Rohlsen, 360 F.2d 437, 446 (1st Cir.) (involving the wrongful termination of an employee in breach of an employment contract), *cert. denied*, 385 U.S. 919 (1966). *But see* Redgrave v. Boston Symphony Orchestra, Inc., 855 F.2d 888, 894 (1st Cir. 1988) (allowing the recovery of what the court characterized as reputation injury in a breach of performance contract action if the non-breaching performer identified specific professional opportunities she lost as a result of the breach), *cert. denied*, 488 U.S. 1043 (1989). In *Redgrave* the plaintiff claimed that she was effectively "blacklisted" because of her political views.

[3] E. ALLAN FARNSWORTH, CONTRACTS § 12.17 (1992); Restatement (Second) Contracts § 353 (1981).

[4] FARNSWORTH, CONTRACTS, *supra* at § 12.17.

[5] Wynn v. Monterey Club, 168 Cal. Rptr. 878, 883 (Cal. App. 1980).

a dead body and to ship cremated remains, a cemetery's agreement to keep a burial service private and protect the grave site from vandalism, and a bailment for jewelry of great sentimental value where that value was made known to the bailee.[6]

Professor Sebert observed that many of these cases are reconcilable by recognizing a personal/commercial dichotomy, but suggested that the distinction was underexplanatory and, while a factor, could not account for the cases without further development.[7] The primary difficulties lay (1) in the imprecision over the dividing line between personal and commercial and (2) in that the personal/commercial distinction was essentially a vehicle for determining the foreseeability of distress damages.[8]

"Foreseeability" is a marvelously imprecise term; nevertheless, it is the best we currently can do to identify when distress dangers will be awarded for breach of contract. Although the decisions are few and the rationales vary, it is possible to identify some recurring themes in this area. First, courts consistently find that it is foreseeable that a breach of a contract to provide funeral or burial services will induce distress, which is compensable at law.[9] Courts have also awarded distress damages when the contract involved a confidential or special relationship, such as that between insurer and insured,[10] but have resisted extending the concept into other areas, such as employment and commercial relationships.[11] Contracts involving vanities (e.g., cosmetic surgery) may generate distress damages awards when performance is not up to contract expectations,[12] as may contracts involving matters of intimate, personal detail.[13] Distress damages have been awarded in matters involving (1) the breach of a "no-molestation" provision in a divorce agreement that prohibited the spouse from interfering in the other spouse's privacy and personal affairs;[14] (2) breach of an

---

[6] Kwan v. Mercedes-Benz of N. Am., Inc., 28 Cal. Rptr. 2d 371, 380 (Cal. App. 1994) (citations omitted) (refusing to award non-economic damages to the buyer of a defective automobile notwithstanding the personal nature of the acquisition). See generally Gregory G. Sarno, Annot., Recoverability of Compensatory Damages for Mental Anguish or Emotional Distress For Breach of Service Contract, 54 A.L.R.4th 901 (1987), at § 2(a) (extensive annotation that collects and categorizes decisions regarding the recoverablity of distress damages for breach of contract).

[7] John Sebert, Punitive and Non-pecuniary Damages in Actions Based Upon Contract: Toward Achieving the Objective of Full Compensation, 33 U.C.L.A. L. Rev. 1565, 1594 (1986).

[8] Id. at 1594–96.

[9] Ross v. Forest Lawn Memorial Park, 203 Cal. Rptr. 468 (Cal. App. 1984).

[10] Crisci v. Security Ins. Co., 426 P.2d 173 (Cal. 1967).

[11] Section 141.1 ([Bad Faith Breach] Tort-Based Remedies).

[12] Cf. Steward v. Rudner, 84 N.W.2d 816 (Mich. 1957) (allowing distress damages against physician who breached promise to deliver baby by caesarean section).

[13] Molien v. Kaiser Foundation Hosp., 616 P.2d 813 (Cal. 1980) (defendant misperformed test for venereal disease and erroneously informed plaintiff that he tested positive). In Molien the claim was stated as one for the negligent infliction of emotional distress, but the duty originated in a contract for health care between the parties.

[14] Reis v. Hoots, 509 S.E.2d 198, 205 (N.C. App. 1998) (upholding $30,000 verdict).

agreement to provide child-care services;[15] and, (3) breach of a contract not to allow the plaintiff's spouse entry to a gambling establishment.[16]

As a general rule, attorney's fees incurred in prosecuting or defending a breach of contract action are not recoverable as costs or damages unless the contract or a statute so provides.[17] There are a few cases that have permitted the recovery of attorney's fees in breach of contract actions based on general principles of equity,[18] but they are exceptional and have not been followed.

---

[15] Lane v. Kindercare, 588 N.W.2d 715, 717–18 (Mich. App. 1998).

[16] *Wynn, supra,* 168 Cal. Rptr. at 883-84; *see* Diana Digges, *Stakes Rise in "Compulsive Gambling" Suits,* Lawyer Weekly U.S.A. (November 21, 2001) (discussing recent settlements of claims that gambling establishments breached agreement to bar compulsive gamblers from their casinos).

[17] Sections 210 (Attorney's Fees—The "American Rule"), 211.2 (Contractual Authorization).

[18] Baja Energy, Inc. v. Ball, 669 S.W.2d 836, 838-39 (Tex. Civ. App. 1984); Department of Transp. v. Arapaho Constr. Co., 349 S.E.2d 196, 200 (Ga. App. 1986), *aff'd on other grounds,* 357 S.E.2d 593 (Ga. 1987).

Chapter 17

BREACH OF EMPLOYMENT CONTRACT

SYNOPSIS

§ 150 EMPLOYMENT CONTRACTS

The relationship between employer and employee is pervasively addressed by both the common law and by statute. The focus of these materials is, however, rather narrow in that it is limited to remedies for breach of the employment contract. The issue is addressed first from the perspective of the employee who is wrongfully discharged from his employment. Both contract and tort remedies are addressed because this is an area where tort-type remedies have made some inroads notwithstanding the contractual underpinnings of the relationship. The issue is then addressed from the perspective of the employer whose employee fails to conform to her contractual obligations. The analysis here is generally based on contract remedies; however, some employee breaches will generate tort-type remedies because of the employee's quasi-fiduciary relationship with the employer.

[150.1] Common Law Principles

In the absence of a collective bargaining arrangement, a fixed term contract of employment, or some form of guaranteed employment, such as civil service or tenure, the employment relationship is terminable at will by either party. The American rule that employment contracts for an indefinite term are terminable at will may be contrasted with the English Rule that such contracts were presumptively for a term of one year.[1] A

---

[1] The history of the American and English approaches is discussed in Lex K. Larson, 1 Unjust Dismissal § 2.02 (1991). Larson is critical of the historical support for the American

relationship that is terminable at will ordinarily creates lesser expectations than a relationship whose termination is subject to some constraints, such as good cause. The invocation and incorporation of fault-based theories of liability (tort) into this area has been seen most frequently in employment relationships that substantive contract law would deem terminable at will. Tort-based liability provides redress for the at-will employee's lost expectancy of continued employment, an expectancy contract law would not recognize.[2]

[150.2] Statutory Rights

The 20th Century experienced significant government involvement in the employer-employee relationship. While freedom of contract has been the dominant theme of the common law, the modern law of employment relations is largely a course in statutory law, with an emphasis on protecting employees. Today, the doctrine of employment at will is substantially encumbered by public policies that prohibit discrimination, harassment, and non-accommodation of employees. The content of this public law allows employees[3] many more opportunities to claim remedies for an employer breach of duty, a duty increasingly imposed not by private contract but by public law.

Whether an employer-employee relationship exists and whether it has been breached is a subject that is outside the scope of this work. The questions addressed here focus on remedies available when the relationship is improperly disturbed. The identification of remedy must, however, be understood as tentative absent a fuller investigation of the source and scope of the duty that has been breached.[4]

---

rule, characterizing it as "invented" by an early American Treatise writer Horace Wood. *Id.* at § 2.04; *see* Gunther Peck, Book Review, *Contracting Coercion? Rethinking the Origins of Free Labor in Great Britain and the United States*, 51 Buff. L. Rev. 201, 203 (2003) (discussing use of penal sanctions in 19th Century Britain against employees who breached their contractual term of employment).

[2] Section 141.1 ([Bad Faith Breach] Tort-Based Remedies).

[3] As a general rule, public protection extends to employees only. If the person is deemed an independent contractor (Shah v. Deaconess Hospital, 355 F.3d 496, 499 (6th Cir. 2004)), or an employer (Schmidt v. Ottawa Medical Center, P.C., 322 F.3d 461, 466 (7th Cir. 2003)), statutory protection may not exist. Classification is critical; unfortunately, in some significant areas, proper classification is more an art than science. *See* Clackamas Gastroenterology Assocs., P.C. v. Wells, 538 U.S. 440 (2003) (holding that whether physician-shareholders who owned entity were to be deemed employees or employer was determined by the issue of "control"). The issue there was significant because if the physician-shareholders were counted as employees, the entity met the 15 employee threshold that would trigger application of Title VII, 42 U.S.C. § 2000e(b). *See* Stephanie Greene & Christine Neylon O'Brien, *Who Counts?: The United States Supreme Court Cites "Control" as the Key to Distinguishing Employers From Employees Under Federal Employment Antidiscrimination Laws*, 3 Colum. Bus. L. Rev. 761 (2003).

[4] Section 3.1 (Relationship Between Rights and Remedies).

[150.3]   Restitution Remedies

An employee who is terminated from his employment generally does not have a claim for restitution. The relationship between employee and employer is defined by contract, express or implied-in-fact, and courts are not inclined to allow recovery outside of those permitted by the law of contract.[5] The limited exception here has been tort-based recoveries,[6] but this too has emphasized damages, not benefits received.

Even if restitution were available, this remedy is not attractive to employees. The remedy would be quantum meruit, but that remedy does not permit a recovery for services that would have been rendered, but were not because of the employee's discharge. The recovery is limited to the value of services already rendered, but for which no payment has been received.[7] The approach is different when the employee breaches and that issue is separately treated at Section 155 (Employer's Remedies for Employee's Breach of Duty).

Quantium meruit is most frequently invoked by attorneys who have been retained on a contingent fee basis and have been discharged prior to the contingency (settlement or judgment) being realized. The rule in American jurisdictions is that the attorney-client relationship is terminable by the client at anytime.[8] To maximize the client's freedom to be represented by counsel of her choice, the right to terminate is not burdened in most jurisdictions by the obligation to pay damages. The obligation to pay damages would tend to restrain clients from terminating the client-lawyer relationship.[9]

Quantum meruit is an equitably oriented remedy that permits a service provider to recover the reasonable value of the services provided notwithstanding the absence of a contractual right of recovery.[10] The measure of what constitutes the "reasonable value of services rendered" is elastic. Courts will evaluate a number of factors in determining the availability and amount of any quantum meruit recovery, including (1) whether the lawyer was terminated for good cause;[11] (2) whether the lawyer completed

---

[5] Section 41 (Restitution for Wrongdoing) (particularly Section 41.2 (Breach of Contract)).

[6] Section 141 (Bad Faith Breach).

[7] In *Chodos v. West Publishing Co.*, 292 F.3d 992 (9th Cir. 2002), the court did permit a disappointed author to recover in restitution (quantum meriut) when his publisher breached the agreement to publish the author's work. *Chodos* is not an employment contract case and the court's allowance of restitution was heavily influenced by the fact that the author's damages were speculative; nonetheless, *Chodos* may evidence a willingness to consider restitution when services are actually rendered in the employment context, but not paid for by the employer. Section 44 (Quasi Contract and Unjust Enrichment). Another use of the remedy of restitution through quantium meruit arises when a fund is created through the attorney's efforts. Section 211.3 ([Attorney's Fees] Common Fund).

[8] CHARLES WOLFRAM, MODERN LEGAL ETHICS § 9.5.2, at 545 (1986).

[9] WOLFRAM, MODERN LEGAL ETHICS, *supra*, § 9.5.2, at 545–46; *see* text and notes 14–15, *infra*.

[10] Section 44 (Quasi Contract and Unjust Enrichment).

[11] Arce v. Burrow, 958 S.W.2d 239, 249–50 (Tex. Civ. App. 1997) (holding that whether an attorney discharged for cause should recover all or only a portion of his fees must be determined on a case-by-case basis). The court noted:

essentially all the required services before she was fired;[12] and (3) whether the lawyer or the client terminated the relationship.[13]

The quantum meruit recovery represents a balancing of the client's right to terminate the attorney-client relationship and the recognition that exempting the client from any obligation to pay fees would both create incentives for the opportunistic firing of counsel and unjust enrichment of clients if they received the benefits of representation (settlements or judgments) without any obligation to pay for those benefits.[14] Quantum meruit resolves that problem by allowing the attorney to recover the reasonable value of the services rendered if the contingency is satisfied, *i.e.*, the matter settles or judgment is awarded and collected.[15] A minority view allows the discharged attorney, who is terminated without good cause, to recover the reasonable value of services without showing that the contingency (settlement or judgment) has been satisfied.[16]

When two or more attorneys have represented the client, the aggregate fees awarded, (quantum meruit and contract), to all the attorneys may exceed the amount the client originally agreed to pay the discharged attorney for the prosecution of the claim.[17] The jurisdictions have not resolved

---

[I]n determining the amount, if any, of the fee forfeiture, the entity assessing forfeiture should consider: (1) the nature of the wrong committed by the attorney or law firm; (2) the character of the attorney's or firm's conduct; (3) the degree of the attorney's or firm's culpability, that is, whether the attorney committed the breach intentionally, willfully, recklessly, maliciously, or with gross negligence; (4) the situation and sensibilities of all parties, including any threatened or actual harm to the client; (5) the extent to which the attorney's or firm's conduct offends a public sense of justice and propriety; and (6) the adequacy of other available remedies.

Id. at 250 (*relying on* Restatement (Third) of the Law Governing Lawyers § 49), *aff'd in part rev'd in part on other grounds sub nom.* Burrow v. Arce, 997 S.W.2d 229 (Tex. 1999); O'Rourke v. Cairns, 683 So. 2d 697, 704 (La. 1996) (holding that an attorney discharged for cause could still recover under quantum meruit, but that the recovery should be reduced to reflect the fact of any misfeasance).

[12] Taylor v. Shigaki, 930 P.2d 340, 343 (Wash. App. 1997) (holding that when an attorney is discharged without cause after substantially performing the duties owed to the client, the attorney may recover the full fee); Searcy, Denney, Scarola, Barnhart & Shipley, P.A. v. Scheller, 629 So. 2d 947, 954 (Fla. App. 1993) (holding that when a lawyer had successfully obtained a judgment for the client before being discharged for cause, the quantum meruit recovery should be equal to the contracted for fees less any damages sustained by the client as a result of discharging the attorney).

[13] Auguston v. Linea Aerea Nacional-Chile, S.A., 76 F.3d 658, 662 (5th Cir. 1996) (applying Texas law) (holding that a lawyer who withdraws from the representation without good cause loses all rights to compensation).

[14] *Taylor, supra,* 930 P.2d at 343.

[15] WOLFRAM, MODERN LEGAL ETHICS, *supra,* § 9.5.2, at 547.

[16] Skeens v. Miller, 628 A.2d 185, 188 (Md. 1993) (discussing majority and minority positions regarding when cause of action for quantum meruit accrues on behalf of the discharged lawyer employed under a contingent fee contract). *See generally* George Blum, Annot., *Limitation to Quantum Meruit Recovery, Where Attorney Employed Under Contingent Fee Contract is Discharged Without Cause,* 56 A.L.R.5th 1 (1998).

[17] Joseph Perillo, *The Law of Lawyers' Contracts is Different,* 67 Fordham L. Rev. 443, 458 (1998) (noting significant uncertainty whether "when a second lawyer is retained on a contingency basis, the award of fees to two lawyers may exceed the larger of the two contingency retainers").

whether this improperly abridges the client's freedom to discharge counsel without financial penalty. In *La Mantia v. Durst* the court limited the total fees recovery to the contract rate when the client was kept by a departing attorney and the fee was allocated between the predecessor firm and the departing attorney.[18] The principle has been generally applied to cases when the client discharges one attorney and retains another.[19] The specific issue of an excess of contract rate recovery was not at issue in the cited case, although the suggestion was that it would not be allowed, else it would penalize the client who elected to exercise her right to discharge counsel.[20]

§ 151   EMPLOYEE'S DAMAGES AGAINST EMPLOYER

In the case of employer breach, the employee recovers her lost expectancy, which is the compensation the employee would have earned over the contract term. The justification for this approach is that the remedy should approximate what the plaintiff would have received had the contract been fully performed.[1] Compensation includes all applicable fringe benefits,[2] such as bonuses, pension contributions, or vacation pay.[3] If the employee was furnished an automobile, the award may include the replacement value of the use of the automobile, including all accessory benefits, such as insurance or gasoline furnished by the employer.[4]

When the employment contract is for a fixed term, the amount of damages may be calculated with reference to that term. This would include additional periods of employment the employee had the option to claim, and would have claimed, but for the employer's breach.[5] The general rule in

---

[18] 561 A.2d 275, 277–79 (N.J. Super. Ct. A.D. 1989).

[19] *Kopelman and Assocs., supra,* 473 S.E.2d at 919–20 (discussing cases).

[20] *Id.* at 917, n.7, 918; *see* note 12, *supra.*

[1] Birk v. Board of Educ. Flora Comm. Unit Sch. Dist. No. 3, 457 N.E.2d 1065, 1069 (Ill. App. 1983), *aff'd on other grounds,* 472 N.E.2d 407 (Ill. 1984).

[2] Adams v. Frontier Airlines Fed. Credit Union, 691 P.2d 352, 354 (Colo. App. 1984); *see* 2 MARK A. ROTHSTEIN ET AL., EMPLOYMENT LAW § 9.24, at 583 (1994) ("[A] major element of damages in any discharge action is the compensation (wages, salary, commissions, or other payments, plus fringe benefits) the employee lost by reason of the discharge."); JOEL FRIEDMAN & GEORGE STRICKLER, JR., THE LAW OF EMPLOYMENT DISCRIMINATION 652–53 (3d ed. 1993) (same).

[3] Worrell v. Multipress, Inc., 543 N.E.2d 1277, 1283 (Ohio 1989). *See generally* 22 Am. Jur. 2d *Damages* § 115; 82 Am. Jur. 2d *Wrongful Discharge* § 236. An interesting application of this principle is *Sposato v. Electronics Data Sys. Corp.,* 188 F.3d 1146, 1148 (9th Cir. 1999) (applying California law) (holding that wrongfully terminated employee, who was killed while lawsuit was pending, could recover face value of life insurance policy the employee could obtain as a fringe benefit of employment), *cert. denied,* 528 U.S. 1189 (2000).

[4] Potter v. Village Bank of New Jersey, 543 A.2d 80 88 (N.J. Super. Ct. A.D. 1988); *Adams, supra,* 691 P.2d at 354. *But see* Voiter v. Church Point Wholesale Beverage Co., Inc., 760 So. 2d 451, 460 (La. App. 2000) (treating use of automobile as *lesser* fringe benefit, not integral to employment benefits package, and not recoverable item of damage when discharged employee no longer needed automobile to provide services for employer).

[5] Oldenkott v. American Elec., Inc., 92 Cal. Rptr. 127, 130–31, *cert. denied,* 402 U.S. 975 (1971); Dumes v. Harold Laz Advertising Co., 409 P.2d 307 (Ariz. App. 1965) (same).

the United States is that the employee is not limited to the amount of damages that accrue as of the time of trial, but may include future losses, (those that accrue after trial),[6] subject to the requirement that those future losses be discounted to present value.[7] Under the minority rule, the employee is limited to the amount of damages that accrue as of the earlier of the completion of the term of the employment contract or the date of trial.[8]

The contract term may be indefinite. The employee may be promised that she will not be discharged except for good cause, but no specific term of employment is set. An example of this open-ended employment would be civil service or academic tenure. In these cases, the term for which damages are awarded is committed to the discretion of the trier-of-fact.[9]

The period of time for which damages may be calculated when the employee is hired for an indefinite term may be quite long. In *Bruno v. Detroit Institute of Technology* the employee was a tenured professor. The court found that the professor was improperly terminated in violation of his tenure rights. The professor was entitled to future damages based on a view of the professor's tenure that gave him a vested interest in his position until he retired:

> Clearly, having attained tenured status, plaintiff is entitled to continuous employment by defendant until retirement. The proper measure of damages . . . to put the injured party in as good a position as he would have had if performance had been rendered as promised. The proper method of computing these future damages is: (1) On the basis of past experience, project the anticipated level of compensation for similarly situated associate professors at defendant institution for each of the years until the date at which plaintiff would have retired had he been allowed to continue his employment relationship at defendant institution; (2) On the basis of past experience, project the anticipated earnings of plaintiff premised upon good-faith attempts on plaintiff's part to secure employment in his chosen profession; (3) Subtract the anticipated earnings of plaintiff for each of the years from the anticipated salary he would have received at defendant institution in the corresponding year; (4) Reduce the difference for each year to its worth as of the date

---

[6] *See generally* C.P. Jhong, Annot., *Recovery of Damages by Employee Wrongfully Discharged Before Expiration of Time Period Fixed in Employment Contract as Embracing Entire Term of Contract or as Limited to Those Damages Sustained Up to Time of Trial*, 91 A.L.R.2d 682 (1963), § 2 (observing that the rule that limits recovery to damages sustained up to the time of trial is based on concerns that future losses are contingent and speculative; the rule that permits recovery of post-trial damages is based on the view that while concern over contingent and speculative damages is legitimate, the employee should be allowed to recover all damages that can be proved).

[7] Section 9.3 (Discounting to Present Value).

[8] Munoz v. Expedited Freight Sys., Inc., 775 F. Supp. 1181, 1186–87 (N.D. Ill. 1991) (applying Illinois law).

[9] O'Dell v. Basabe, 810 P.2d 1082, 1098–99 (Idaho 1991).

of the filing of the complaint; and (5) Take the sum of these properly mitigated and reduced figures.[10]

There are certain terms of art that are encountered in this area. They include the terms "front pay" and "back pay." "Front pay" refers to future earnings. Future earnings are post trial earnings the employee would have earned had she not been the subject of a wrongful termination or employment action. "Back pay" refers to past earnings. Past earnings are earnings that accrued prior to the trial but which plaintiff did not receive as a result of the employer's wrongful termination or employment action.

The trier-of-fact's discretion as to future lost earnings is not unbounded.[11] The exercise of discretion must rest on an adequate factual record to permit a reasonable trier-of-fact to conclude that the employee would have worked for the term upon which damages are calculated. Factors the trier-of-fact should consider include: the employee's age, work competence, and intention to continue working for the employer.[12] Some courts suggest that for the indefinite term cases, the trier-of-fact should use the "average duration of employment" for workers like the plaintiff.[13] The rationale of this

---

[10] 215 N.W.2d 745, 749 (Mich. App. 1974) (citations, footnote, and quotation marks omitted).

[11] Horney v. Westfield Gage Co., 211 F. Supp. 2d 291 (D. Mass. 2002), aff'd in part and rev'd in part on other grounds, 77 Fed. Appx. 24 (1st Cir. 2003) (2003 U.S. App. LEXIS 20776):

> Front pay awards [future lost earnings] are targeted at compensating the plaintiff from the conclusion of trial until she can obtain comparable employment elsewhere. However, the court is not supposed to catapult [the plainti[ff] into a better position than [she] would have enjoyed in the absence of discrimination. Since future damages are inherently speculative, the court must keep a close eye on the circumstances of the particular case.
>
> Although front pay is not subject to a federal statutory damage cap, the First Circuit has expressed serious concern about speculative and excessively lengthy front pay awards under federal law. An award of front pay that extends over many years to an estimated retirement date should be examined carefully . . . since the greater the period of time upon which a front pay award is calculated in a case involving an at-will employee the less likely it is that the loss of future earnings can be demonstrated with any degree of certainty or can reasonably be attributed to the illegal conduct of the employer. To be sure, the court in Cummings upheld a $665,000 award, which constituted fourteen years of front pay. But that age discrimination case was based solely on an open-ended state law and the court expressed grave doubts as to the sustainability of a front pay award of so great a duration under federal law. Moreover, in contrast to the facts here, the plaintiff in Cummings was a fifty-five year old manager with fifteen years of experience at the company and an annual salary at termination of over $88,000.
>
> The First circuit is not alone in its concern for avoiding excessive front pay awards. [T]he importance of the court's scrutiny of front pay awards is underscored by the facts that many jurisdictions do not allow juries to make front pay awards, leaving that task to the judge.

Id. at 322–23 (citations omitted; brackets added).

[12] Sealand Serv., Inc. v. O'Neal, 297 S.E.2d 647, 652 (Va. 1982).

[13] Panhandle E. Pipeline Co. v. Smith, 637 P.2d 1020, 1025 (Wyo. 1981); cf. Hayes v. Trulock, 755 P.2d 830 (Wash. App. 1988):

> The employees here argue that an appropriate award would have been 2 years' front

approach is that there is a substantial risk that indefinite term contracts would turn into lifetime employment contracts if the trier-of-fact is allowed to rely on the employee's stated intentions, post-breach, that he would have stayed with his employer until retirement, but for the wrongful termination. Such testimony is difficult to refute because it is based on the plaintiff's state of mind. Other courts, however, have resisted policy generalizations and leave the calculation of future losses to case by case determination:

> We reject defendant's argument [that the evidentiary burden can be satisfied only by presenting statistical or other comparable evidence]. [W]e impose no such evidentiary requirement. Either party might have chosen to present statistical or other comparable evidence of the average duration of employment in the relevant industry in an attempt to persuade the jury that plaintiff either would or would not have continued in defendant's employ until retirement or for some other period. [T]he weakness of a plaintiff's evidence may be explored by contrary evidence. However, the fact that such evidence may be probative of the front pay issue does not make it a necessary element of plaintiff's evidentiary showing.
>
> Plaintiff presented evidence that his job satisfaction was high, that defendant was satisfied with plaintiff's work before he experienced his job-related back problems, and that he had received positive performance evaluations and merit salary increases. We agree with the Court of Appeals that the jury reasonably could infer from that evidence that both parties wanted the arrangement to continue indefinitely. Plaintiff's vocational rehabilitation expert testified that persons in supervisory positions in plaintiff's field normally are hired from within the company, creating a reasonable inference that plaintiff probably would not have left defendant's employ to seek out a similar position elsewhere. The record also contains evidence respecting the other factors that enter into a calculation of front pay, including the amount that plaintiff would have earned in defendant's employ, offset by the amount that plaintiff is expected to earn in the future, reduced to present value. We conclude that plaintiff's evidence was sufficient to permit an inference that plaintiff's employment with defendant would have continued until the end of plaintiff's work life expectancy, which the jury found to be age 63 based on "work life expectancy" tables. We hold that the trial court did not err in denying defendant's motion to strike plaintiff's claim for front pay.[14]

pay. However, the record on appeal fails to show any evidence presented by them to support such an award. Although it is known that the employees who were hired to replace the plaintiffs continued in their employment following the sale of the business, it is unknown what the duration of their employment has been. In addition, the plaintiffs did not provide the trial court with any evidence showing the average duration of employment of convenience store employees. In the absence of any such evidence, this court cannot say that the trial court below abused its discretion. *Id.* at 834.

[14] Tadsen v. Praegitzer Indus., Inc., 928 P.2d 980, 985 (Or. 1996) (citations omitted; brackets added).

The concern over extended, long term liability for indefinite term contracts is ameliorated by the employee's duty to mitigate damages.[15]

A number of jurisdictions have recognized the tort of "bad faith" discharge. The boundaries of this tort are difficult to find. Courts usually state that "bad faith" breach requires more than a "mere" breach of the employment contract.[16] However, as in the insurance bad faith context, the difference between a mere breach and a bad faith breach resists reduction to a rule capable of even application and having predictive value.[17]

Another difficulty encountered here is that the concept of "bad faith" is expressed in ways that may or may not generate tort-based recoveries. When wrongful discharge is based on specific public policy grounds, for example, the discharge of an employee in retaliation for filing a work-injury claim,[18] tort-based remedies are common. The situation is murkier when the recovery is based on the breach of the implied covenant of good faith and fair dealing. Jurisdictions that permit a claim for breach of the implied covenant have split as to whether the remedy for the breach lies in contract or tort.[19]

When tort-based remedies are recognized, the recovery may include distress damages and punitive damages.[20] The claim for distress damages is stronger if the employee can demonstrate that the employer intended by the termination to inflict emotional distress on the employee rather than the distress being only incidental to a wrongful discharge. Many jurisdictions, however, refuse to impose additional proof burdens on the employee before allowing recovery of non-economic losses, particularly when the

---

[15] Section 13.2.2 ([Duty to Mitigate Damages] Employment Claims).

[16] K-Mart Corp. v. Ponsock, 732 P.2d 1364, 1369 (Nev. 1987) (holding that the improper motive of the employer in discharging an employee to avoid paying the employee retirement benefits constituted "bad faith"); Prout v. Sears-Roebuck & Co., 772 P.2d 288, 292 (Mont. 1989) (finding that if the employer discharges the employee for dishonesty, the employee must be given an opportunity to rebut the charge; the employer may not use a false charge to terminate an "at will" employee).

[17] Section 141 (Bad Faith Breach).

[18] Hansen v. Harrah's, 675 P.2d 394, 396–97 (Nev. 1984) (collecting decisions upholding tort action for wrongful discharge because failure to provide tort-based remedies would operate as condonation of employer's frustration of employee's right to access state-mandated remedial scheme for workplace injuries).

[19] Noye v. Hoffman-La Roche, Inc., 570 A.2d 12, 14–15 (N.J. Super. Ct. A.D. 1990) (collecting decisions and noting split among jurisdictions that: (1) recognize an implied covenant of good faith and fair dealing in the employment contracts and permit tort damages; (2) recognize an implied covenant but reject tort damages; and (3) refuse to recognize an implied covenant in the employment context).

[20] Travis v. Gary Community Mental Health Ctr., Inc., 921 F.2d 108, 111 (7th Cir. 1990) (affirming an award of distress and punitive damages for the retaliatory discharge of an employee who testified against his employer), cert. denied, 502 U.S. 812 (1991); Niblo v. Parr Mfg., Inc., 445 N.W.2d 351, 355–56 (Iowa 1989) (stating that distress damages may be recovered when an employee is discharged in retaliation for employee's threat to file work-injury claim). See generally Francis Dougherty, Annot., Damages Recoverable For Wrongful Discharge of At-Will Employee, 44 A.L.R.4th 1131 (1987).

wrongful termination claim involves discharges in violation of public policy.[21]

Employee wrongful termination actions often include statutory claims for discrimination, harassment, etc. The statutory provisions should be examined as they may supplement and/or confirm common law remedies for wrongful termination.[22]

§ 152 EMPLOYEE REINSTATEMENT TO POSITION

An employee who is wrongfully terminated may seek equitable relief in the form of reinstatement to her position, including all promotions and advancements the employee would have received but for the wrongful termination. This is a modern trend reflected in the availability of reinstatement as an arbitration remedy and the policy preferences found in statutes prohibiting work-place discrimination.[1]

Reinstatement is an alternative remedy to an award of lost future earnings (front pay). The difficulty in calculating future losses in wrongful discharge cases has led some courts to speak of reinstatement as a preferable remedy to a damages award of front pay.[2] The concern is over the uncertainty, and consequent need to speculate, as of the date of trial, both as to the likely path the employee's "career" would have taken had he not been discharged (insofar as front pay is concerned) and the path his career will take now that he has been discharged (insofar as mitigation of damages is concerned). Reinstatement moots these concerns.

Notwithstanding the attractiveness of reinstatement, the common law rejected the remedy:

---

[21] *Niblo, supra*, 445 N.W.2d at 355–56 (collecting decisions and holding that retaliatory discharged employee need not demonstrate that his distress was severe to recover his distress damages); *cf.* Zhang v. American Gem Seafood, Inc., 339 F.3d 1020, 1043 (9th Cir. 2003) (suggesting that discrimination claims might support higher punitive/compensatory damages ratios because of highly reprehensible nature of the employer's misconduct), *cert. denied*, 541 U.S. 902 (2004); Section 205.3 (Ratio Between Compensatory Award and Punitive Damages Award).

[22] Salinas v. O'Neill, 286 F.3d 827 (5th Cir. 2002) (affirming award of $300,000 for distress damages for claim of employment-related race discrimination and job retaliation under Title VII; evidence that employee suffered from sleeplessness, anxiety, stress, marital problems, and humiliation as a result of the employer's action provided substantial evidence for the award); *see* Michelle Curcuzza, *Evaluating Emotional Distress Damages Awards*, 65 Brooklyn L. Rev. 393, 403–11 (1999) (discussing damages available to prevailing plaintiff in discrimination cases).

[1] Martha West, *The Case Against Reinstatement in Wrongful Discharge*, 1988 Ill. L. Rev. 1, 2 (noting that "[r]einstatement, accompanied by back pay, however, has been the traditional remedy for employees illegally discharged under federal labor relations law or discharged without "just cause" under collective bargaining agreements"); Lea VanderVelde, *Making Good on VACA's Promise: Apportioning Back Pay to Achieve Remedial Goals*, 32 U.C.L.A. L. Rev. 302, 337–38 (1984).

[2] Julian v. City of Houston, Tex., 314 F.3d 721, 728 (5th Cir. 2002). The court also noted that in "failure to promote cases" the employee should be "instated" to the position she would have occupied but for the employer's wrongful conduct. *Id.*

Historically, the common law has not allowed employees discharged in breach of an employment contract to seek the equitable remedy of reinstatement. Instead, an employee working under an express contract for a definite term who is discharged in breach of that contract may sue for contract damages.[3]

The reason for the bar seems to lie in the equitable doctrine of mutuality: because the employer could not obtain injunctive relief requiring a breaching employee to return to work,[4] it was thought to be unfair to allow the employee to obtain injunctive relief (reinstatement) ordering the employer to take the employee back.[5] Moreover, the employee's loss was money (lost wages); therefore, damages (money) was seen as an adequate remedy.[6]

The common law bias against reinstatement has been rejected when the discharge violates statutory or constitutional guarantees, such as when employment decisions are based on race or gender. In some non-statutory cases, the common law rule has not been applied when the employee's discharge is said to violate public policy.[7]

When reinstatement is allowed as a remedy, the general rule is that the appropriate remedy, as between reinstatement or front pay, is committed to the discretion of the court. Reinstatement presupposes the ability to maintain a normal working relationship and if that is absent, reinstatement may not be appropriate. As noted in *Feldman v. Philadelphia Housing Authority*:

> PHA argues that the district court erred by permitting an award of front pay instead of ordering Feldman reinstated at PHA. The equitable remedy of reinstatement is available for discharges that violate 42 U.S.C. § 1983, and reinstatement is the preferred remedy to cover the loss of future earnings. However, reinstatement is not the exclusive remedy, because it is not always feasible, such as when there exists "irreparable animosity between the parties." When reinstatement is not appropriate, front pay is the alternate remedy.[8]

---

[3] West, *Wrongful Discharge, supra*, 1988 Ill. L. Rev. at 2; *see* SeaEscape Ltd., Inc. v. Maximum Mktg. Exposure, Inc., 568 So. 2d 952, 954 (Fla. App. 1990); Zannis v. Lake Shore Radiologists, Ltd., 392 N.E.2d 126, 128–29 (Ill. App. 1979); Sprunt v. Members of the Bd. of Trustees of the Univ. of Tenn., 443 S.W.2d 464, 466 (Tenn. 1969).

[4] Section 154 (Employer's Injunction Against Employee).

[5] Section 173 (Mutuality of Remedy).

[6] Section 21.2.2 ([Adequacy of the Remedy] Economic Harm).

[7] Munoz v. Expedited Freight Sys., Inc., 775 F. Supp. 1181, 1191–92 (N.D. Ill. 1991) (applying Illinois law).

[8] 43 F.3d 823, 831 (3d Cir. 1994) (citations omitted); *see* Rabkin v. Oregon Health Sciences University, 350 F.3d 967, 977 (9th Cir. 2003) (stating that it was not an abuse of discretion for the district court to deny plaintiff reinstatement "to a leadership position he held at the discretion of his superiors at OHSU [defendant]") (brackets added). The court further stated "that reinstatement may be inappropriate 'where discord and antagonism between the parties [make] it preferable to fashion relief from other available remedies.'" *Id.* (brackets in original).

The availability of reinstatement reflects more than judicial concern over the calculation of future losses. It also reflects awareness of the importance of employment to the discharged employee, particularly when the discharge arises out of a violation of the employee's civil rights or constitutional guarantees:

> When a person loses his job, it is at best disingenuous to say that money damages can suffice to make that person whole. The psychological benefits of work are intangible, yet they are real and cannot be ignored . . . . We also note that reinstatement is an effective deterrent in preventing employer retaliation against employees who exercise their constitutional rights. If an employer's best efforts to remove an employee for unconstitutional reasons are presumptively unlikely to succeed, there is, of course, less incentive to use employment decisions to chill the exercise of constitutional rights.[9]

If an employee is granted reinstatement, the rights of third parties must be considered. Should an innocent employee be "bumped," demoted, or discharged to make room for the reinstated employee? The decisional law has developed several approaches to this problem. Under one approach, the rights of the innocent co-employee may be deemed superior to those of the wrongfully discharged employee. Under this approach, reinstatement may be denied if the remedy would harm the employment of the innocent co-employee.[10] Under the second approach, the rights of the innocent co-employee may be subordinated to those of the wrongfully discharged employee. The wrongfully discharged employee will be reinstated and the "innocent" co-employee will be "bumped" from her position.[11] A third approach attempts to accommodate both the innocent co-employee and the wrongfully discharged employee. Under the third approach, the innocent co-employee is not "bumped," but the wrongfully discharged employee is paid as if he occupied the position to which he seeks reinstatement *and* he is reinstated or promoted to that position at the first opportunity.[12]

Notwithstanding the doctrinaire language in some decisions, the general approach appears to recognize that the issue of reinstatement, particularly when innocent third parties are concerned, is committed to the discretion of the court.[13] Factors that tend to be treated as influential include: (1)

---

[9] Allen v. Autauga County Bd. of Educ., 685 F.2d 1302, 1306 (11th Cir. 1982).

[10] Shortt v. County of Arlington, Va., 589 F.2d 779, 782 (4th Cir. 1978) (stating that federal law "neither requires nor authorizes 'bumping' of incumbent employees from jobs to which they have been promoted . . .").

[11] Hayes v. Shalala, 933 F. Supp. 21, 25 (D.C. Cir. 1996), *citing* Lander v. Lujan, 888 F.2d 153, 157 (D.C. Cir. 1989).

[12] Spagnuolo v. Whirlpool Corp., 717 F.2d 114, 121 (4th Cir. 1983). *But see* Doll v. Brown, 75 F.3d 1200, 1205 (7th Cir. 1996) (criticizing *Spagnuolo* as having "no basis in the statute or in equitable principles and [as] contrary to the Supreme Court's decision in *Franks* [v. Bowman Transp. Co., 424 U.S. 747, 774–79 (1976)]") (citations omitted; brackets added).

[13] *Doll, supra,* 75 F.3d at 1205 (noting that the "effect on innocent third parties is a factor to be taken into account in the formulation of an equitable remedy"; however, the court rejected a per se rule against "bumping" based on third party effects.

the frequency of openings to the position to which the plaintiff would be reinstated;[14] (2) whether the plaintiff will be employed during the waiting period for reinstatement;[15] (3) whether the plaintiff's reinstatement will create friction with other employees;[16] or, (4) whether the circumstances have so changed since the date of termination as to make reinstatement inequitable to the defendant-employer.[17]

The usefulness and practicality of the remedy of reinstatement has been questioned by several commentators. Professor West noted that reinstatement is a generally ineffective remedy if it takes place more than a few months after the employee's termination. Approximately 50% of the reinstated employees leave their employment within a year of being reinstated due to their perception of employer harassment.[18] Another study, involving reinstatement in the collective bargaining context, was even more pessimistic:

> First, only about 40% of the employees for whom reinstatement was ordered actually took their jobs back. The major reason given by employees for declining reinstatement was fear of employer retaliation, a factor that may well also have affected some of those who said that they had simply found better jobs. The employees' fears were apparently well founded; of employees who did go back, nearly 80% were gone within a year or two, and most blamed their departure on vindictive treatment by the employer.[19]

A wrongfully terminated employee cannot recover both front pay and reinstatement.[20] Opting for reinstatement, therefore, may prove to be economically disadvantageous to the employee, given the evidence that, in practice, reinstatement has marginal real value.

---

[14] Davis v. City of Waterloo, 551 N.W.2d 876, 885 (Iowa 1996) (factor favoring reinstatement).

[15] Granziel v. City of Plainfield, 652 A.2d 227, 231–32 (N.J. Super. Ct. A.D. 1995) (factor favoring reinstatement).

[16] Thomas v. National Football League Player's Ass'n, 131 F.3d 198, 207 (D.C. Cir. 1997) (factor against reinstatement).

[17] *Doll, supra,* 75 F.3d at 1205.

[18] West, *Reinstatement, supra,* 1988 Ill. L. Rev. at 29.

[19] Paul Weiler, *Promises to Keep: Securing Workers' Rights to Self-Organization Under the NLRA,* 96 Harv. L. Rev. 1769, 1792 (1983) (footnotes omitted).

[20] Smith v. World Inc. Co., 38 F.3d 1456 (8th Cir. 1994); Flynn v. Shoney's Inc., 850 S.W.2d 458, 461 (Tenn. App. 1992). Front pay and reinstatement may, however, both be awarded when the employee's reinstatement is delayed. *See* Selgas v. American Airlines, Inc., 104 F.3d 9 (1st Cir. 1997):

> Where reinstatement is not immediately available as a remedy, either due to the plaintiff's condition, or due to conditions at the employer that preclude the plaintiff's return (such as hostility of other employees, or the need for an innocent employee to be "bumped" in order to reinstate the plaintiff), front pay is available as an alternative to compensate the plaintiff from the conclusion of trial through the point at which the plaintiff can either return to the employer or obtain comparable employment elsewhere.

Id. at 12 (citations omitted).

Time is also a factor. As noted by Weiler:

> Time is the crucial variable in reinstatement cases. If the [National Labor Relations] Board can secure reinstatement quickly, the wrongfully discharged employee is likely to accept the offer. In time, however, the employee generally obtains another job, which he will be reluctant to leave for the bleak prospects at his old position. Thus, he becomes progressively less likely to assert his reinstatement rights. Only about 5% of reinstatement offers obtained after six months are in fact accepted.[21]

The effect of time on the effectiveness and efficiency of permanent injunctive relief may require reevaluation of the general unwillingness to provide temporary injunctive relief in the wrongful discharge cases.[22] In *Scott, on Behalf of N.L.R.B. v. Pacific Custom Materials Inc.*, the court placed particular emphasis on the effect of time on the efficacy of the remedy of reinstatement as a reason for favoring temporary injunctive relief restoring employees to their jobs pending trial.[23]

The employer may limit the employee's damages claim by offering to reinstate the employee to her position from which she was wrongfully discharged.[24] The reinstatement offer may not impose new conditions at variance with the original contract of employment;[25] however, the employer need not offer better terms, only equivalent terms.[26] The employer need not include in the offer of reinstatement the affirmative relief that the court may award at trial, such as lost seniority, as long as the offer is without prejudice to the lawful interests of either the employee or employer.[27] The employer must show that the offer of reinstatement is equivalent, which is consistent with the treatment of mitigation as an affirmation defense.[28] If the employee questions the sincerity of the offer of reinstatement or its bona fideness, the employee's challenge must rest on concrete evidence, not speculation.[29] On this issue, the emerging view is that the employee has the burden of proof.[30] The unreasonable refusal of an unconditional offer

---

[21] Weiler, *Promises to Keep, supra*, 96 Harv. L. Rev. at 1792–93 (footnote omitted; brackets added).

[22] Sampson v. Murray, 415 U.S. 61, 90 (1974) (holding that "temporary" loss of income associated with termination from employment would not be deemed "irreparable"); Section 31.2.2 ([Temporary Injunctive Relief] Irreparably Injury).

[23] 939 F. Supp. 1443, 1455–56 (N.D. Cal. 1996).

[24] Giandonato v. Sybron Corp., 804 F.2d 120, 124 (10th Cir. 1986).

[25] Pichignau v. City of Paris, 70 Cal. Rptr. 147, 149 (Cal. App. 1968). *See generally* William Danne, Jr., Annot., *Nature of Alternative Employment Which Employee Must Accept to Minimize Damages For Wrongful Discharge*, 44 A.L.R.3d 629 (1972).

[26] Fair v. Red Lion Inn, 943 P.2d 431, 440 (Colo. 1997).

[27] Rasheed v. Chrysler Corp., 517 N.W.2d 19, 25 (Mich. 1994).

[28] Section 13.2.2 ([Duty to Mitigate Damages] Employment Claims).

[29] *Fair, supra*, 943 P.2d at 440–42 (noting that the failure of the plaintiff-employee to substantiate her claims that she justifiably rejected her employer's offer of reinstatement meant that she acted unreasonably in rejecting the offer).

[30] *Rasheed, supra*, 517 N.W.2d at 31 (stating that this position is a "middle ground" approach).

of reinstatement forfeits the employee's claim to damages that accrue after that date.[31]

An emerging issue is whether the employer can contest the remedy of reinstatement based on misconduct by the employee. In *McKennon v. Nashville Banner Publishing Company* the Supreme Court held that employee misconduct, discovered post-termination by the employer, would not preclude a discrimination claim. The Court rejected the argument that because the discovered misconduct provided lawful grounds for termination, the discrimination claim was mooted.[32] The Court commented, however, on the role of employee misconduct on available remedies for employment discrimination. The Court stated:

> The proper boundaries of remedial relief in the general class of cases where, after termination, it is discovered that the employee has engaged in wrongdoing must be addressed by the judicial system in the ordinary course of further decisions, for the factual permutations and the equitable considerations they raise will vary from case to case. We do conclude that here, and as a general rule in cases of this type, neither reinstatement nor front pay is an appropriate remedy. It would be both inequitable and pointless to order the reinstatement of someone the employer would have terminated, and will terminate, in any event and upon lawful grounds.[33]

A dispute in the caselaw is also evidenced with respect to when the misconduct must occur. Some courts hold that it must be pre-termination; other courts allow for consideration of post-termination misconduct.[34]

§ 153   EMPLOYER'S DAMAGES AGAINST EMPLOYEE

The usual measure of damages to the employer for the employee's breach of an employment contract is the cost of obtaining a replacement employee.[1] The damages are limited to the remaining term of the employment contract. Unlike the case of employer breach of indefinite term employment agreements,[2] the employee retains the unfettered right to terminate an at will relationship, although there may be post-term limitations placed on the employee.[3]

---

[31] Denesha v. Farmers Ins. Exch., 161 F.3d 491, 502 (8th Cir. 1998); *Fair, supra,* 943 P.2d at 438 (collecting decisions).

[32] 513 U.S. 352, 360–61 (1995).

[33] *Id.*

[34] Sellers v. Mineta, 358 F.3d 1058 (8th Cir. 2004) (collecting decisions). The *Sellers* court concluded that post-termination misconduct by the employee could be considered when determining the appropriate remedy.

[1] *See generally* H.B. Chermside, Annot., *Employer's Damages For Breach of Employment Contract by Employee's Terminating Employment,* 61 A.L.R.2d 1008 (1958).

[2] Section 151 (Employee's Damages Against Employer).

[3] Section 154 (Employer's Injunction Against Employee) (discussing employer's ability to limit employment of former employee).

The recovery for replacing the employee, who breaches a contract of employment for a fixed term, consists of several factors. First, the employer may recover the difference between the contract rate for the defendant-employee and the market rate the plaintiff-employer will be required to pay to obtain a substitute for the remainder of the term.[4] The fact that the replacement employee may be more experienced, competent, or efficient than the breaching employee does not entitle the breaching employee to an offset. "Any additional value the [employer] may have received from the replacement's greater experience was imposed on it and thus cannot be characterized as a benefit."[5] On the other hand, the replacement must perform the duties of the breaching employee, even if he does so more efficiently. The breaching employee is not responsible for that portion of the replacement's compensation that reflects work not required of the breaching employee.[6]

Second, the employer may recover the cost of training the new employee to perform the breaching employee's duties.[7] It may be argued that recovery of training and hiring costs should not be allowed because they are duplicative of costs the employer would have incurred in any event on the termination of the contract. That the costs were accelerated by the breach should be seen as too insignificant to warrant recovery—"de minimis non curat lex" (the law does not deal with trifles). The courts have, however, consistently decided otherwise.

Third, the cost of advertising and interviewing the replacement employee may be recoverable, subject to the same observation as was made above with regard to costs of training the replacement employee.

Courts have exhibited some reluctance in awarding consequential damages for the employee's breach. The reluctance is based on the rule of *Hadley v. Baxendale*.[8] The concern is that the losses were not within the contemplation of the parties at the time of contract formation.[9]

The concern, but perhaps not the reluctance, may pale when the employes's services are unique. For example, if an actor or professional athlete breaches an employment contract, the likelihood of consequential damages is highly foreseeable. The actor's breach may delay production or perhaps even terminate the production resulting in losses to the employer-producer

---

[4] Handicapped Children's Educ. Bd. of Sheboygan Cty. v. Lukaszewski, 332 N.W.2d 774, 778 (Wis. 1983). ·

[5] *Id.* at 779.

[6] Roth v. Speck, 126 A.2d 153, 156 (D.C. App. 1956).

[7] Med + Plus Neck and Back Pain Center, S.C. v. Noffsinger, 720 N.E.2d 687, 691 (Ill. App. 2000); *cf.* Ryan v. Orris, 463 N.Y.S.2d 883, 885–86 (App. Dept. 1983) (enforcing a liquidated damages provision in an employment agreement against a departing physician employee because of the difficulty in measuring the costs invested in training the departing employee and in training his replacement).

[8] Section 10.2.2 ([Loss Causation—Contracts] Policy Considerations).

[9] *Med + Plus Neck and Back Pain Center, supra,* 726 N.E.2d at 692; Southern Ariz. Sch. for Boys, Inc. v. Chery, 580 P.2d 738, 741–42 (Ariz. App. 1978).

of the film. There are few reported decisions. In *Stadium Pictures, Inc. v. Walker* the court held that there was a triable issue of fact whether the parties to a motion picture employment contract contemplated the losses the employer would incur to third parties, who had agreed to produce and promote the picture, if the employee breached by refusing to perform.[10]

In *Lemat Corp. v. Barry* Rick Barry breached a contract to play professional basketball with the San Francisco Warriors so he could play for more money with a team in a rival league. The Warriors secured an injunction against Barry's playing for the rival league and sought damages for financial losses resulting from Barry's refusal to play, primarily diminished attendance receipts the Warrior's attributed to the loss of their star performer. The trial court refused to award damages because it had granted the employer's request for injunctive relief. The appellate court affirmed. The court observed that damages for lost attendance may have been appropriate if the equitable relief had not been sought or had been denied.[11] The observation is patently wrong; the granting of equitable relief was not inconsistent with the employer's claim that Barry's breach had caused it to suffer attendance losses.[12] The court further confused the issue by suggesting that the losses were "speculative and uncertain and practically impossible to ascertain."[13] Yet the lost attendance damages were easy to calculate using a "before and after" test. While the correlation of the loss in attendance to Barry's departure is not capable of ironclad determination, that is not the test.[14] Indeed, courts frequently note that the risk of error in this context should be borne by the defendant, not the plaintiff.[15]

The absence of reported decisions directly on point should not obscure, however, the strength of the argument in a particular case that the

---

[10] 229 N.Y.S. 313, 313–14 (App. Dept. 1928).

[11] 80 Cal. Rptr. 240, 246 (Cal. App. 1969).

[12] *See* Washel v. Bryant, 770 N.E.2d 902, 905–06 (Ind. App. 2002) (holding that the plaintiff was not required to elect between a liquidated damages award and injunctive relief against a employee who breached a non competition provision of an employment contract). The court noted:

> [R]egardless of what constitutes a "violation," the liquidated damages clause in this agreement does not preclude injunctive relief because money damages will not remedy the ongoing violation of the covenant.

Id. at 907. On the other hand, it might be argued that "damages" reflects the amount a party must pay for the privilege of breaching the contract. In the context of liquidated damages there is some risk the parties may miscalculate and set an amount that over-estimates (or underestimates) the costs of breach to the non-breaching party. Section 183 (Liquidated Damages as Exclusive or Non-exclusive Remedy).

[13] *Lemat Corp.*, *supra*, 80 Cal. Rptr. at 246.

[14] Section 8.1 (Certainty); Section 8.3 (Lost Profits).

[15] Bigelow v. RKO Radio Pictures, Inc., 327 U.S. 251, 264 (1946); *cf.* Turbines, Inc. v. Thompson, 684 N.E.2d 254, 257–58 (Ind. App. 1997) (noting that the proper measure of damages for breach of a non-compete contract is "net profits" lost). When the business is cyclical, which renders it difficult to calculate net losses, the court may permit the trier-of-fact to award the plaintiff a fractional amount of gross receipts as a surrogate for lost net profits. *Id.* (permitting recovery of 25% of gross receipts).

breaching employee is liable for consequential damages. For example, the actress Kim Basinger was sued by Main Line Pictures over her alleged breach of an oral agreement to appear in a film "Boxing Helena." A jury concluded that a valid contract existed and that Ms. Basinger's breach had caused Main Line to incur additional pre-production expenses and lost profits. In other words, the film would have been more successful if Ms. Basinger, rather than the replacement actress, had performed the role Ms. Basinger contracted to play. The jury, valued the losses at $8.9 million.[16] The award was subsequently set aside for error on an issue unrelated to the measure of damages.[17]

§ 154   EMPLOYER'S INJUNCTION AGAINST EMPLOYEE

Courts have been reluctant to order defendant-employees to perform their employment contracts.[1] The reasons for this reluctance are severalfold:

> Such an order would impose upon the court the prodigious if not impossible task of passing judgment on the quality of performance. It would also run contrary to the Thirteenth Amendment's prohibition against involuntary servitude. Courts wish to avoid the friction and social costs which result when the parties are reunited in a relationship that has already failed, especially where the services involve mutual confidence and the exercise of discretionary authority. Finally, it is impractical to require judicial oversight of a contract which calls for special knowledge, skill, or ability.[2]

Professor Laycock argues that the primary objection to specific performance of personal services contracts is that courts should not "make a human being work." The objection to coerced employment is based on a "substantive law commitment to free labor."[3] In this context, employment contracts are

---

[16] Donna Parker, *Boxing Scores Basinger KO*, Hollywood Reporter, March 25, 1993, at 1. A portion of the award ($1.5 million) was based on the theory of "bad faith" denial of a contract, a cause of action subsequently rejected by the California Supreme Court in *Freeman & Mills, Inc. v. Belcher Oil Co.*, 900 P.2d 669 (Cal. 1995); Section 141 (Bad Faith Breach).

[17] Main Line Pictures, Inc. v. Basinger (Cal. App. 1994) (unpublished) (1994 W.L. 814244) (reversing judgment because the special verdict forms used the ambiguous "and/or" in allowing the jury to find that either Ms. Basinger or her professional corporation had contracted with the plaintiff Main Line Pictures, Inc.).

[1] Restatement (Second) of Contracts § 367(1) (1981) (stating the general rule that "[a] promise to render personal service will not be specifically enforced"). The exception to the policy are generally centered in labor activity subject to collective bargaining and strikes affecting entire industries or a substantial part thereof that threaten "national security." 29 U.S.C.A. § 176.

[2] Woolley v. Embassy Suites, Inc., 278 Cal. Rptr. 719, 727 (Cal. App. 1991) (citations omitted). *See generally* 71 Am. Jur. 2d *Specific Performance* § 164. The concerns expressed here may be compared to the reverse situation when the employee seeks reinstatement to her employment. Section 152 (Employee Reinstatement to Position) (identifying reinstatement as preferred remedy and requiring specific proof of workplace hostility and animosity that would preclude satisfactory workplace relationship before denying reinstatement).

[3] Douglas Laycock, *The Death of the Irreparable Injury Rule*, 103 Harv. L. Rev. 687, 746 (1990) (noting that policy of free labor has "nothing to do with the adequacy of the legal remedy"; specific performance is denied because the remedy is too good).

broadly construed to include all contracts calling for the rendition of personal services.[4]

While courts have historically refused to specifically enforce personal services contracts, they have exhibited a willingness to order the defendant-employee not to work for another if that work would constitute a breach of contract. This form of equitable relief is often referred to as a "negative" injunction.[5] A negative injunction is not available simply because the employee breaches; equitable remedies are not available for all contract breaches. The employer must demonstrate a proper case for the exercise of equitable relief.[6]

Injunctive relief will be limited to situations when the services of the employee are unique and allowing the employee to work for another would impose substantial harm on the employer not readily capable of monetary assessment or collection.[7] The reason for this requirement is that restrictions on an individual's right to offer her services for gainful employment are disfavored. As noted by one court:

> An employer may not simply forbid his employee from subsequently operating a similar business. The employer must have an interest which he is trying to legitimately protect. There must be some reason why it would be unfair to allow the employee to compete with the former employer. The employee should only be enjoined if he has gained some advantage at the employer's expense which would not be available to the general public.[8]

---

[4] Hopkins v. Price Waterhouse, 920 F.2d 967, 980 (D.C. Cir. 1990) (noting that the common law refusal to enforce personal service contracts included partnership agreements, but holding that the matter was governed by the broader remedies provided by federal law barring workplace discrimination).

[5] Safety-Kleen Systems, Inc. v. Hennkens, 301 F.3d 931 (8th Cir. 2002) (affirming injunction barring former employer from working for competitor of employer in violation of non-competition agreement); Nassau Sports v. Peters, 352 F. Supp. 870, 875–76 (E.D.N.Y. 1972) (enjoining a professional athlete employed by a team in the established National Hockey League from playing for a team in a competing professional hockey league (the fledgling "World Hockey League")); cf. American Broadcasting Cos., Inc. v. Wolf, 420 N.E.2d 363, 367 (N.Y. 1981) (noting that "if the services to be rendered are of an unusual or unique nature, then the situation is more clearly one in which an adequate remedy at law does not exist") (citation omitted).

[6] Chapters 3 (General Principles Concerning Equitable Relief), 4 (Injunctions), 20 (Specific Performance).

[7] BDO Seidman v. Hirshberg, 712 N.E.2d 1220, 1223 (N.Y. 1999); see Nelson v. Agro Globe Eng'g. Inc., 578 N.W.2d 659, 663 (Iowa 1998) (stating that equity will grant an injunction "only if the services of the employee are unique and extraordinary and he or she cannot be readily replaced"); Nassau Sports, supra, 352 F. Supp. at 876 (stating that "[t]he primary requisite for enforcing either the contract or the option clause is that the player be an athlete of exceptional talent") (citations omitted).

[8] Norlund v. Faust, 675 N.E.2d 1142, 1154 (Ind. App. 1997) (citation omitted) (noting that the protection of trade secrets would constitute the type of interest the employer would have a legitimate interest in protecting).

Moreover, unless the services are unique, they are easily replaceable, which undermines the claim that the employer was irreparably injured by the employee's breach.[9]

In assessing the availability of a negative injunction courts have distinguished, to some extent, between (1) negative injunctions to prevent the employee from working for another during the term of the contract and (2) negative injunctions to prevent the employee from working for another in breach of a post-employment covenant not to compete. As a rule, courts are more receptive to requests for negative injunctions to prevent employees from working elsewhere during the term of the employment contract than when the employer seeks to prevent a former employee from breaching a post-term of employment covenant not to compete. Courts will imply a covenant not to compete during the term of the contract to prevent a unique or highly valued employee from working elsewhere.[10] In general, courts will not imply post-term of employment covenants not to compete.[11] Post-term of employment restrictions must be express or there must exist independent equitable reasons to bar the former employee from working at the particular job, such as the protection of trade secrets or confidential information.[12] In this context, courts emphasize the likelihood of disclosure.[13] Courts have divided whether the "likelihood of disclosure" issue should be influenced by the concept of "inevitable disclosure," which is to say that the former employee would disclose the protected information to the new employer regardless of promises made or intentions stated.[14]

---

[9] *Nelson, supra,* 578 N.W.2d at 663.

[10] *American Broadcasting Cos., Inc., supra,* 420 N.E.2d at 367 (noting that a negative injunction to prevent a current employee from working elsewhere will issue when "the circumstances justified implication of a negative covenant") (citations omitted).

[11] This refusal springs from two sources. First, is the common law's historic hostility to post-term of employment restrictions as improper restraints on labor and human capital. *See* Katherine Stone, *Knowledge at Work,* 34 Conn. L. Rev. 721, 739–41 (2002). Second, is the requirement that the restriction be reasonable as to term, scope, and duration. *See* text and notes 15–17, *infra.* The failure to provide an express restriction that meets these requirements will not be cured by a judicially created default rule; however, an express provision that is unreasonable may be modified by the court to cure the deficiency. *See* text and notes 18–25, *infra.*

[12] *American Broadcasting Cos., Inc., supra,* 420 N.E.2d at 367; *see* Pepsico, Inc. v. Redmond, 54 F.3d 1262, 1270–71 (7th Cir. 1995) (affirming an injunction barring a former employee, who had not executed a covenant not to compete, but who did possess trade secrets, from working for a competitor). The court compared the former employer to a coach and the former employee as a player who goes to play for a rival "playbook in hand" "before the big game." *Id.* at 1270.

[13] Air Prods. and Chems., Inc. v. Johnson, 442 A.2d 1114, 1119–20 (Pa. Super. Ct. 1982). *See generally* P. Guthrie, Annot., *Employee's Duty, in Absence of Express Contract, Not to Disclose or Use in New Employment Special Skills or Techniques Acquired in Earlier Employment,* 30 A.L.R.3d 631 (1970).

[14] *Compare Pepsi Co., Inc., supra* (accepting "inevitable disclosure" doctrine and upholding injunction barring employee from working with competitor to prevent disclosure), *with* Marietta Corp. v. Fairhurst, 754 N.Y.S. 2d 62, 65 (App. Dept. 2003) (refusing to adopt "inevitable disclosure" doctrine). Oftentimes, however, the courts professed adoption or rejection of the doctrine of "inevitable disclosure" may be colored by external facts. *See, e.g., Pepsi Co., Inc., supra,* 54 F.3d at 1270 (noting lack of candor on part of former employee and new employer as supporting invocation of "inevitable disclosure" doctrine).

To secure equitable enforcement of a covenant not to compete, the covenant must impose no more than a reasonable restriction on the employee's ability to secure work. The "reasonableness" restriction is usually analyzed in terms of (1) the scope of activities barred by the covenant, (2) the geographic space or extent of the covenant, and (3) the duration or length of time the covenant is applicable to the former employee.[15] Alternatively, the Restatement (Second) of Contracts formulates the test more abstractly as a rule of reason test. The restraint is unenforceable if it is (1) greater than necessary to protect the former employer's legitimate interests; or (2) the former employer's need is outweighed by the hardship the former employee will face if the restraint is enforced *and* enforcement will likely injure the public.[16]

Whether a covenant not to compete is a reasonable restraint in terms of scope of activities prohibited, geographic space covered by the covenant, and the covenant's duration is determined based on the facts of the individual case.[17]

If the non-competition provision is unreasonable as to scope, space, or duration, courts have split whether the provision may be construed so that it is reasonable or must be deemed invalid. Jurisdictions that permit reformulation of the terms of the non-compete provision to make them reasonable (or refuse to allow a challenge to the reasonableness of the provision unless, as applied, the provision would be unreasonable as to the defendant),[18] do so for two primary reasons. First, the ability to construe non-competition provisions to make them reasonable "permits public policy to be served in the most effective manner."[19] Second, permitting

---

[15] Wolff v. Wolff, 490 N.E.2d 532, 533 (N.Y. 1986); Reiman Assocs., Inc. v. R/A Adver., Inc., 306 N.W.2d 292, 295 (Wis. App. 1981). See generally C.T. Drechsler, Annot., *Enforceability of Restrictive Covenant, Ancillary to Employment Contract, as Affected by Territorial Extent of Restrictions*, 43 A.L.R.2d 94 (1955).

[16] Restatement (Second) of Contracts § 188 (1981).

[17] Webcraft Techs., Inc. v. McCaw, 674 F. Supp. 1039, 1045–46 (S.D.N.Y. 1987) (holding that when the plaintiff engaged in an unusual and specialized business, a worldwide covenant not to compete or solicit customers for a two year period was reasonable); see Stone, *Knowledge*, *supra*, 34 Conn. L. Rev. at 741–746 (discussing reasons for divergent judicial approaches toward employee restraints).

[18] For example, if a reasonable geographic space limitation would prohibit competition in the state of Texas, a defendant competing against the plaintiff in Texas could not challenge the broader, literal provision, *e.g.*, no competition within the entire United States. However, a defendant competing against the plaintiff in Arizona could challenge the provision.

[19] Hopper v. All Pet Animal Clinic, Inc., 861 P.2d 531 (Wyo. 1993):

> Both the employer and the employee invest in success by expressing a commitment to one another in the form of a reasonable covenant not to compete. For the employer, this commitment may mean providing the employee with access to trade secrets, customer contacts or special training. These assets of the business are entitled to protection. For the employee, who covenants as part of a bargained for exchange, the covenant provides notice of the limits both parties have accepted in their relationship. The employee benefits during his tenure with the employer by his or her greater importance to the organization as a result of the exposure to the trade secrets, customer contacts or special training.

Id. at 546.

modification is perceived as being equitably superior to an all or nothing approach.[20]

Jurisdictions that refuse to construe unreasonable non-compete provisions to make them reasonable and enforce them as modified contend it is not the business of courts to rewrite the contract entered into between the parties.[21] Some jurisdictions limit this approach to contracts that are indivisible. "[I]f the covenant is clearly separated into parts and some parts are reasonable and other are not, the contract may be held divisible and the reasonable restrictions may be enforced."[22]

Even jurisdictions that permit judicial reformation of the non-competition provision recognize that the power should be exercised with constraint so as not to encourage employers to draft onerous provisions knowing that the worst sanction they would face is a judicially redrafted reasonable restraint. As noted by the New York Court of Appeals:

> The issue of whether a court should cure the unreasonable aspect of an overbroad employee restrictive covenant through the means of partial enforcement or severance has been the subject of some debate among courts and commentators. A legitimate consideration against the exercise of this power is the fear that employers will use their superior bargaining position to impose unreasonable anti-competitive restrictions, uninhibited by the risk that a court will void the entire agreement, leaving the employee free of any restraint. The prevailing, modern view rejects a per se rule that invalidates entirely any overbroad employee agreement not to compete. Instead, when, as here, the unenforceable portion is not an essential part of the agreed exchange, a court should conduct a case specific analysis, focusing on the conduct of the employer in imposing the terms of the agreement. Under this approach, if the employer demonstrates an absence of overreaching, coercive use of dominant bargaining power, or other anti-competitive misconduct, but has in good faith sought to protect a legitimate business interest, consistent with reasonable standards of fair dealing, partial enforcement may be justified.[23]

If a defendant breaches a non-competition provision, the courts have split as to whether they possess the power to extend the term of the provision so as to deprive the defendant of the benefit of her breach. As noted in *Thermatool Corp. v Borzym*:

> [C]ourts have reasoned that the additional restraint time is necessary to give one party an opportunity to regain the customers that it lost when the other party breached the agreement. An additional

---

[20] *Id.* at 547 (collecting decisions).

[21] Federated Mut. Ins. Co. v. Bennett, 818 S.W.2d 596, 599 (Ark. App. 1991); Beit v. Beit, 63 A.2d 161, 165 (Conn. 1949).

[22] Smart Corp. v. Grider, 650 N.E.2d 80, 83 (Ind. App. 1995).

[23] *BDO Seidman, supra,* 712 N.E.2d at 1226 (citations omitted).

rationale for extending an agreement not to compete beyond its stated expiration date after a party had violated it is that a contrary result would reward the breach of contract. Some courts, however, have refused to prolong a non-competition agreement beyond its expiration date. The predominant rationale for rejection of this relief has been that the parties did not expressly provide for it in the original agreement.[24]

The court concluded that the better approach was to permit extension.[25]

Many jurisdictions have codified rules regarding the availability of negative injunctions in connection with personal services contracts or covenants not to compete. For example, California has adopted a broad public policy declaring that contracts that purport to restrict a person's ability to earn a livelihood are illegal.[26] Several statutory exceptions exist, including covenants not to compete in connection with a sale of business goodwill[27] and actions involving employees possessing unique or specialized talents who have signed guaranteed minimum payments contracts.[28]

§ 155   EMPLOYER'S REMEDIES FOR EMPLOYEE'S BREACH OF DUTY

An employee owes fiduciary duties of loyalty and obedience to the employer.[1] As Justice Frankfurter once noted, however, to state that a

---

[24] 575 N.W.2d 334, 337 (Mich. App. 1998) (citations omitted); Section 33.3 ([Permanent Injunction] Time Frame of Relief).

[25] *Thermatool Corp., supra,* 575 N.W.2d at 338; *see* Presto-X-Co. v. Ewing, 442 N.W.2d 85, 90 (Iowa 1989) (extending the restraint period, which would have shortly expired, to one year from the date of the opinion); *cf.* J.H. Goldberg Co., Inc. v. Stern, 385 N.Y.S.2d 427, 432 (App. Dept. 1976) (adding the period of time the defendant was in breach of a non-competition provision to the durational term of the provision to prevent the defendant from profiting from her breach).

[26] Cal. Bus. & Prof. Code § 16600.

[27] Cal. Bus. & Prof. Code § 16601. The transaction must be bona fide and not a sham designed to evade the basic public policy of the State. Bosley Med. Group v. Abramson, 207 Cal. Rptr. 477, 481–82 (Cal. App. 1984) (refusing a negative injunction in favor of a controlling person who required the defendant-employee, as a condition of employment, to execute a stock purchase agreement with a non-competition clause upon buy-out and which gave the controlling person sole authority to demand execution of the buy-out provisions on 5 days notice to the defendant).

[28] Cal. Civ. Code § 3423:

An injunction may not be granted:

. . . .

(e) To prevent the breach of a contract . . . other than a contract in writing for the rendition of personal services from one to another where the promised service is of a special, unique, unusual, extraordinary or intellectual character, which gives it peculiar value, the loss of which cannot be reasonably or adequately compensated in damages in an action at law, and where the compensation for the personal services is as follows . . . .

[1] *See* Phansalkar v Andersen Weinroth & Co., L.P., 344 F.3d 184, 200 (2d Cir. 2003); Central Sec. and Alarm Co., Inc. v. Mehler, 918 P.2d 1340, 1345–46 (N. Mex. App. 1996); Augat, Inc. v. Aegis, Inc., 565 N.E.2d 415, 419 (Mass. 1991).

person has a fiduciary duty only begins the analysis. It still must be ascertained to whom the duty is owed, what obligations are owing, in what respects have the obligations not been discharged, and what are the consequences of the breach of duty?[2]

Justice Frankfurter's observation has particular importance here. An employee may breach his duty of loyalty to his employer in different ways. The employee may (1) set up a competing business to that of his employer, (2) accept bribes or kickbacks, (3) expropriate to himself or others business opportunities belonging to the employer, (4) cause other employees to leave, (5) fail to discharge his responsibilities as an employee competently and diligently due to conflicts of interest, etc. In each of these cases, the employer may seek redress either by way of damages, or, due to the employee's fiduciary status, by way of restitution for unjust enrichment.

The damages recoverable for the employee's breach of duty are based on the actual loss sustained by the employer. This loss is usually measured by the decline in business and resulting profits that are caused by the defendant's breach. In *Williamson v. Palmer* the court upheld an award of $10,000 against the defendant who breached a covenant not to compete.[3] The plaintiffs' proof showed that during the period of the defendant's breach of the covenant not to compete, sales dropped by over $11,000, projected annual growth rates were not achieved, and 15 customers were lost.[4]

In many cases, however, determining actual losses will prove to be difficult. A court may be less willing than the *Williamson* court to attribute a downturn in sales to the breaching employee's competing business. In some cases, the effect on sales and profits may be difficult to establish, as in cases when the employee accepts a bribe or kickback to approve a contract with a third party. Courts do allow an alternative restitutionary measure of recovery based on the profits the defendant realized as a result of his breach of duty.[5] Because this is a restitutionary remedy, rather than a damages remedy, the focus is on the defendant's unjust enrichment. An accounting for profits may be required to identify the extent to which the "profit" is the product of the defendant's use of his skills and resources, the benefits of which he may be entitled to retain.[6]

---

[2] S.E.C. v. Chenery, 318 U.S. 80, 85–86 (1943). The question whether the status of employee and agent are equivalent or different for purposes of determining either's fiduciary duties to the principal/employer are beyond the scope of this work. Condon Auto Sales & Service, Inc. v. Crick, 604 N.W. 2d 587, 599-600 (Iowa, 1999) (discussing differences between agent and employee regarding duty of loyalty).

[3] 404 S.E.2d 131 (Ga. App. 1991). The covenant was given to the buyers of the business by the defendant seller. While the case does not involve an employee breach of a covenant not to compete, damages calculation do not turn in this context on the identity of the defendant.

[4] *Williamson, supra*, 404 S.E.2d at 133.

[5] Scobell, Inc. v. Schade, 688 A.2d 716, 719–20 (Pa. Super. Ct. 1997); Chernow v. Reyes, 570 A.2d 1282, 1285 (N.J. Super. Ct. A.D. 1990) (holding that a disloyal employee is liable for the profits earned in a competing business to which the employee referred business while the employee was employed by the plaintiff); Section 40 (Restitution).

[6] Section 46 (Apportionment of Benefit). *See generally* Michael Rosenhouse, Annot., *Proper Measure and Elements of Damages For Misappropriation of Trade Secrets*, 11 AL.R.4th 12 (1981), at § 28.

The use of a damages or restitutionary remedy may lead to different results. When, for example, the remedy of restitution is based on the assumption that the defendant diverted sales from the plaintiff to himself, this does not mean that the recoveries (damages or restitution) are the same because the sales are the same. The plaintiff's profit margins may differ from the defendant's profit margins. Even though the plaintiff's recovery is limited to the net profits lost,[7] if the plaintiff can prove that he would have earned the entire gross profit without any additional expense, the gross profit equals the plaintiff's net profits.[8] Moreover, the offsets the defendant may be allowed, (in an action based on its unjust enrichment), will not necessarily correlate with the defendant's actual cost of producing the profit.[9] Which remedy is superior thus depends on the individual facts.

A disloyal or disobedient employee may be required to disgorge all compensation received from the employer, *i.e.,* salary forfeiture.[10] This often draconian remedy is made available because the essence of a fiduciary obligation is that of devotion to another "founded on the highest and truest principles of morality."[11] The breach of this moral obligation may warrant that the deficient fiduciary not receive any money for his services, else his wrongdoing would be rewarded.[12] And it is a settled principle of equity, from which fiduciary duties arise, that no person should be allowed to profit from her own wrongdoing.[13]

On the other hand, the harshness of salary forfeiture has not been ignored by the courts. Several meliorating concepts may apply, such that either forfeiture is avoided or forfeiture of the employee's salary is partial rather than total. First, a court may require that the employer show that the period of employee disloyalty coincides with the period of time that salary

---

[7] Section 8.3 (Lost Profits).

[8] *Central Sec. and Alarm, supra,* 918 P.2d at 1347 (collecting authorities). The court further noted:

> When the plaintiff's overhead or expenses are fixed and no savings accrued to the plaintiff because of the defendant's breach, deducting a portion of these amounts to determine the plaintiff's award would not achieve the purpose of compensatory damages to place the plaintiff in as good a position as if there had been no breach. Therefore, the only expenses which should be deducted from lost gross profit are incremental expenses, i.e., only those additional expenses that Central would have incurred had it handled the additional Lionel business.

Id. (citations omitted).

[9] Section 46 (Apportionment of Benefit).

[10] *In re* Ivan F. Boesky Sec. Litig., 36 F.3d 255, 264–65 (2d Cir. 1994) (stating that "[a] principal is entitled to restitution of compensation paid if an agent breaches its duties of loyalty or obedience") (citations omitted); Jet Courier Serv., Inc. v. Mulei, 771 P.2d 486, 499–500 (Colo. 1989); *cf.* Restatement (Second) of Contracts §§ 393 cmt. f, 399 cmt. k, 456 (1981); Restatement (Second) of Agency § 469 cmt. a (1958).

[11] Little v. Phipps, 94 N.E. 260, 261 (Mass. 1911) (citation omitted).

[12] *Phansalkar, supra,* 344 F.3d at 199–200 (noting that sanction for faithless servant is loss of all compensation from the date the employee's disloyalty began).

[13] Estate of O'Keefe, 583 N.W.2d 138, 140 (S.D. 1998); Yost v. Rieve Enters., Inc., 461 So. 2d 178, 184 (Fla. App. 1984).

forfeiture is sought. While total forfeiture is allowed, the salary is treated as being earned in increments. The misconduct must overlay a salary increment to warrant forfeiture of salary for that period.

An example of this approach is *Simulation Systems Technologies, Inc. v. Oldham.* Oldham breached his employment contract by forming a competing business to his employer. The court noted that the employer could seek a forfeiture, but the employer had to identify the salary periods within which the breaches of duty occurred:

> [Oldham's] acts during his employment that were in violation of his legal duty were his sales and attempted sales of services competitive with plaintiff's. According to the cited sections of the Restatement (Second) of Agency, plaintiff was entitled to recover compensation paid to defendant Oldham for those specific two-week or half-month periods during which he committed his disloyal acts. But the trial court is correct that the record is totally devoid of evidence which pinpoints the pay period in which each disloyal act was committed and of evidence that shows the amount of compensation apportioned to that period. Accordingly, the trial record does not support the theory of recovery which plaintiff expouses.[14]

Another consideration relied upon by the courts is the nature of the employee's violation. Breaches that go to core values underlying the fiduciary principle, such as transactions involving a conflict of interest, are more likely to justify a total forfeiture than breaches, which, while wrongful, are not seen as central to the employee's fiduciary obligations and duties.[15] An example of this can be found in attorney fee forfeiture cases where the courts have largely limited total forfeiture to cases involving an attorney's conflict of interest and have treated other breaches, usually those surrounding fees, as warranting, at most, partial forfeiture.[16] Related to

---

[14] 634 A.2d 1034, 1037 (N.J. Super. Ct. A.D. 1993). The Restatement references are to the Restatement (Second) of Agency §§ 456, 469 (1958).

[15] *Phansalkar, supra*, 344 F.3d at 202–03 (noting pervasiveness of breach of duty by disloyal employee). On the other hand, in *Cameco, Inc. v. Gedicke*, 728 A.2d 783 (N.J. 1999), the court adopted a more forgiving approach):

> [T]he egregiousness of the employee's conduct may affect the employer's right to withhold or recoup the employee's compensation. If the employee directly competes with the employer, aids the employer's direct competitors or those with interest adverse to the employer's interests, participates in a plan to destroy the employer's business, or secretly deprives the employer of an economic opportunity, the employee may forfeit the right to compensation. In contrast, if the employee's breach is minor, involves only a minimal amount of time, or does not harm the employer, the employee may be entitled to all or substantially all of his or her compensation.

Id. at 791 (citations omitted; brackets added).

[16] *Compare* Asbestos Claims Facility v. Berry & Berry, 267 Cal. Rptr. 896, 907 (Cal. App. 1990) (reaffirming, albeit in *dicta*, that a lawyer with a disqualifying conflict of interest may not receive any fee), *with* Coons v. Kary, 69 Cal. Rptr. 712, 714 (Cal. App. 1968) (holding that while the attorney's contingent fees' agreement was unenforceable because the client was being represented in a marital dissolution action, (for which use of contingent fee arrangements is not permitted), the attorney could, nonetheless, recover on the basis of quantum meruit). *See* Restatement (Third) of the Law Governing Lawyers § 37 (2000).

this concept is the position and responsibilities of the employee. The more critical and central the employee to the success of the employer's business, the more likely the court will permit total rather than partial forfeiture. As noted by one court:

> All of the out-of-state cases on which plaintiff relies deal with employees or other agents whose positions were far more responsible, whose duties were far more critical to their employers' or principals' businesses, and whose misconduct was far more pervasive and reprehensible than Oldham's. We are content to wait until we are presented with a case comparable to those before deciding whether the forfeiture rule which plaintiff enunciates is consistent with *Joseph Toker, Inc.*, or, if not, should be adopted in its stead.[17]

Finally, the culpability of the fiduciary is often a factor. Total forfeiture is more likely to be reserved for deliberate and knowing breaches. When the employee breaches through negligence, inadvertence, or mistake, the case for a draconian sanction (forfeiture) is reduced,[18] but not always avoided.[19]

---

[17] *Simulation Sys. Techs., Inc.*, *supra*, 634 A.2d at 1039.

[18] *Cameco, Inc.*, *supra*, 728 A.2d at 791 (discussed at note 15, *supra*); Boston Children's Heart Found., Inc. v. Nadal-Ginard, 73 F.3d 429, 435–36 (1st Cir. 1996) (noting that the court may ameliorate the harshness of total forfeiture when the defendant establishes that her breach of duty was not egregious).

[19] *Boston Children's Heart Found., Inc.*, *supra*, 73 F.3d at 435 (stating that total forfeiture is the "baseline" position for employee breaches of fiduciary duties).

Chapter 18

BREACH OF CONSTRUCTION CONTRACT

§ 160 CONSTRUCTION CONTRACTS

The business of construction in the United States is a vast enterprise ranging from home repair and remodeling to massive public works projects. Gross revenues exceed half a trillion dollars. The magnitude of business and diversity among the participants has led to an immense body of law addressing the specialized needs of the construction industry. The scope of these materials is, however, limited to a general survey of the remedies available to owners and contractors when the construction contract is breached.[1]

Construction contract remedies, like contract remedies in general, are designed to place the nonbreaching party in the position she would have occupied had the breach not occurred. This position is different for the two principal parties to the construction contract—the owner and the builder-contractor—because each party has different expectations regarding the contract. To account for this differentiation, these materials are organized along the lines of (1) the owner's remedies when the contractor breaches and (2) the contractor's remedies when the owner breaches.

Construction contract disputes often turn on whether the contractor has "substantially performed" his contractual obligations. If the contractor has substantially performed, he can recover the contract price even though he

---

[1] A good overview of the substantive theories of liability applicable to construction contract litigation is provided by William Jones, *Economic Losses Caused by Construction Deficiencies: The Competing Regimes of Contract and Tort*, 59 U. Cin. L. Rev. 1051 (1991).

has breached, less the amount required by the owner to cure the gap between substantial performance and full performance. This substantial performance rule is an exception to the common law rule barring a plaintiff in breach of his contractual obligations from recovery of breach of contract damages.[2] The reason for the exception was that it was perceived as being "unreasonable to condition recovery upon strict performance when minor defects or omissions could be remedied by repair."[3] If, on the other hand, the contractor has not substantially performed, the owner's damages are measured by the increased cost to the owner of having the contracted-for-work performed by another.[4] Not much divergence from the contract requirements will be tolerated. As noted by one court:

> It is well established under Massachusetts law that a contractor "cannot recover on the contract itself without showing complete and strict performance of all its terms." Failing complete performance, a contractor "who in good faith substantially performs a contract may recover in quantum meruit." "It is equally well established that 'an intentional departure from the terms of the contract without justification or excuse in matters other than those so trifling as to be properly regarded as falling within the rule of de minimis will bar all recovery for materials supplied and work performed.' "[5]

As the above quote evidences, some courts treat the substantial performance doctrine as sounding in unjust enrichment rather than contract. Unjust enrichment may be allowed for the breaching contractor who fails to even substantially perform, but here the measure of recovery may be based on the increase in the affected property's value due to the contractor's partial performance[6] rather than quantum meruit.[7]

The substantial performance doctrine influences construction contract remedies in another way. When there is a discrepancy between the work promised and the work performed, what type of discrepancy allows the owner the remedy of replacement of the deficient work with conforming work? This was the issue in the often cited case of *Jacob & Youngs, Inc. v. Kent*.[8] The contractor agreed to build a house for Kent, using in the construction a certain quality of piping: "wrought-iron pipe" that "must be well galvanized, lap welded pipe of the grade known as 'standard pipe' of Reading manufacture."[9] Notwithstanding the contractual promise, the contractor used other piping in much of the construction. Kent demanded that the "nonconforming piping" be removed and replaced. The contractor

---

[2] Section 140 (General Principles Concerning Contract Remedies).

[3] National Chain Co. v. Campbell, 487 A.2d 132, 135 (R.I. 1985).

[4] *Id.*

[5] U.S. Steel v. M. DeMatteo Constr. Co., 315 F.3d 43, 48 (1st Cir. 2002) (citations omitted).

[6] BRUNER & O'CONNOR ON CONSTRUCTION LAW § 19:72 (2002).

[7] "Quantum meruit" permits recovery based on the reasonable value of the services rendered. Section 44 (Quasi Contract and Unjust Enrichment).

[8] 129 N.E. 889 (N.Y. 1921) (Cardozo, J.).

[9] *Id.* at 890.

refused, on the argument that the piping used was of "like quality and kind" to that specified in the contract. Kent refused to pay contending that the nonconforming piping should be removed and replaced. The cost of doing so would have been high, given that the piping had been embedded in the partially constructed house. The court was thus confronted with the choice of giving the owner a cost of repair or restoration remedy, which would give the owner what he had contracted for, or compensating the owner solely for the economic harm caused by the breach, *i.e.*, the difference in value between the house with the specified piping and the house with the replacement piping. This choice requires the court to identify what the parties intended and whether that intent should be fully protected by the courts.[10] This struggle between different conceptions of the "rightful position" is played out in other areas of the law.[11]

In many construction contracts the parties have gone to great lengths to control by contract provision the allocation of losses associated with either party's breach. These provisions, which include waivers of consequential damages, waiver of delay damages, liquidated damages provisions, usually control against judge-made common law remedies rules.[12] The discussion in the following materials assumes the absence of such contractual remedies provisions.

If the work to be performed under a construction contract requires that the contractor be licensed, the lack of a license bars the contractor from any recovery in damages or unjust enrichment.[13] The fact that the owner knew the contractor was unlicenced and intended to use this fact to refuse payment has been found by some courts to be immaterial.[14] The extent to which an unlicenced contractor will be denied a remedy is, however, highly dependent on the licensure provisions of the jurisdiction.[15]

---

[10] Section 161.2 ([Owner's Remedies] Defective or Deficient Performance).

[11] Personal property injury: Section 80.2 ([Physical Damage] Partial Destruction) (discussing whether courts should use a pure diminution in value rule to measure losses to personal injury caused by the physical injury or whether courts should permit reasonable cost of repair even though it may exceed diminution in value. Fraud: Section 122.1 ([Fraud] "Out-of-Pocket" or "Benefit-of-the-Bargain" Measure).

[12] Lynn Axelroth, *Mutual Waiver of Consequential Damages—The Owner's Perspective*, 18 Construction Lawyer 11 (Jan. 1998); Gary Snodgrass, *Waiver of Subrogation and Allocation of Risk in Construction Contracts*, 62 Def. Couns. J. 95 (1995); Scott Tyler, Student Note, *No (Easy) Way Out: "Liquidating" Stipulated Damages For Contracts Delay in Public Construction Contracts*, 44 Duke L.J. 357 (1994); Mark Fleder & Peter Smith, *Defending Against The Contractor's Delay Damages Claim*, 391 PLI/Real 387 (1993); Chapter 21 (Agreed Remedies).

[13] Cudahy v. Cohen, 661 N.Y.S.2d 171, 173 (Dist. Ct. 1997); Kreischer v. Armijo, 884 P.2d 827, 831 (N. Mex. App. 1994); Revis Sand & Stone, Inc. v. King, 270 S.E.2d 580, 582 (N.C. App. 1980); Section 65.2 (Illegality).

[14] Hydrotech Sys., Ltd. v. Oasis Waterpark, 803 P.2d 370, 372 (Cal. 1991) (holding that unlicenced contractor could not sue owner for fraud based on owner's deceitful intention at time of contract formation not to pay for services rendered because contractor was unlicenced); *Cudahy, supra*, 661 N.Y.S.2d 171.

[15] Dotson v. Gaidos, 736 S.W.2d 119, 120 (Tenn. App. 1987) (holding that Tennessee statute that barred mechanics lien remedy if lienholder exaggerated amount for which he claimed a lien did not bar unlicenced contractor from recovery on the debt); Section 65.2 (Illegality) (noting "fraud" exception to defense of illegality is recognized by some jurisdictions).

§ 161 OWNER'S REMEDIES FOR CONTRACTOR'S BREACH

The owner's remedies will vary somewhat depending on the nature of the contractor's breach.

[161.1] Incomplete Performance

When the contractor fails to complete the project, as for example by abandoning the project, the normal remedy is the additional cost to the owner to complete the project. For there to be an appreciable loss, the cost of completion must exceed the contract price. For example, assume the following:

- Original Contract Price: $100,000
- Amount Paid to Original Contractor: $ 40,000
- Amount Paid to Replacement Contractor: $ 70,000

In this context, the owner incurred an additional cost of $10,000 as a result of the contractor's breach. The $10,000 would be the amount of the owner's general damages for the contractor's breach. If, on the other hand, the replacement contractor required only $60,000 to complete the work, the owner has sustained no damages; the owner has paid no more for the work than she agreed to pay, which is $100,000. If the replacing contractor does the work for $30,000, the owner sustains a windfall. She pays only $70,000 for work she agreed to pay $100,000. Under these circumstances, the original contractor may seek recovery.[1]

Construction contracts are usually complex legal documents and construction projects often require the coordination of diverse but interrelated elements for long periods of time. The project itself is often dynamic, changing as the parties interact at the job site.[2]

When the contractor's breach prevents the owner from renting out the premises to be constructed or built by the contractor, the owner may recover lost rentals as part of its damages.[3] In this context, rental value simply reflects the loss of use of the premises caused by the contractor's breach and reflects the awarding of damages for loss of expectancy.[4] Similarly, when the contractor's breach prevents a profitable resale of the property, lost profits may be recovered;[5] however, the recovery must take into

---

[1] Section 163 (Losing Contracts and Restitution). The fact that the contractor is in breach may deny him a remedy that would permit him to recover more than the contract price. Section 160 (Construction Contracts) (text and notes 5–6).

[2] Change Orders are common and are often addressed in the construction contract itself. Section 162.3 (Change Orders).

[3] Gregory v. Weber, 626 P.2d 392, 395–96 (Or. App. 1981).

[4] Ambrose v. Biggs, 509 N.E.2d 614, 616–17 (Ill. App. 1987).

[5] Cf. Bull v. Pinkham Engineering Assocs., Inc., 752 A.2d 26, 33 (Vt. 2000) (affirming award

account subsequent profits earned when the property is ultimately sold,[6] unless the owner can qualify for "loss volume seller" status.[7]

Construction costs are often time-sensitive and tend to be heavily influenced by inflationary trends in the economy. Cost to complete damages may be heavily influenced by the date of measure, e.g., breach date or trial date. The usual contract remedies approach is that the cost to complete is determined as of the date of breach.[8] Any increase in actual costs has traditionally been seen as includable within an award of prejudgment interest.[9] A few courts have, however, permitted the plaintiff to measure cost of completion as of the date of trial, although these decisions appear to be limited to periods of intense inflationary pressures.[10] The identification of the point in time to measure cost to complete damages is different from the issue whether the time period to complete the construction was unreasonably long, which resulted in higher costs to complete.[11]

The courts have split as to whether the owner's cost of completion recovery is limited to the reasonable cost of completion or is allowable up to the actual cost of construction unless actual cost is economically wasteful. The modern trend appears to be to place "reasonable cost" as the upper boundary of the owner's cost of completion damages but to assign to the breaching contractor the burden of proof that the actual cost of completion is unreasonable.[12] In effect, actual cost of completion, consistent with the specifications of the construction contract, is presumptively reasonable, although the presumption is rebuttable.

A few jurisdictions have allowed the owner to obtain specific performance to require the contractor to complete the work consistent with the terms of the contract. These decisions almost all involve unique factual situations.[13] The court in *City Stores Co. v. Ammerman* did order specific

---

of lost profits against surveyor whose negligence deprived owner of access to portion of property he wished to develop). The court also upheld and award of attorneys fees as damages for the owner's costs in legal proceeding needed to correct defendant's errors. *Id.* at 36; Section 211.4 ([Attorney's Fees] Third Party Tort).

[6] Section 14 (Offsetting Benefits).

[7] Section 8.5 (Lost Volume Seller).

[8] Section 7.6 (Value as a Function of Time).

[9] Section 16 (Prejudgment Interest).

[10] Anchorage Asphalt Paving Co. v. Lewis, 629 P.2d 65, 68–69 (Alaska 1981) (holding that trial court did not abuse its discretion in awarding cost of repair damages measured as of the date of trial when inflation amounted to 81% over the relevant period); Seaman Unified Sch. Dist. No. 345, Shawnee County v. Casson Constr. Co., 594 P.2d 241, 247 (Kan. App. 1979).

[11] *Cf.* New York State Thruway Auth. v. John Civetta Constr. Corp., 62 A.D.2d 530, 405 N.Y.S.2d 778, 780 (1978) (finding that 2 year length of time required to repair a bridge, after the defendant's tractor-trailer damaged it, was not unreasonable; therefore, the plaintiff was entitled to recover the full cost of repairs even though the cost of repair increased due to inflation within the 2 year period).

[12] Marshall v. Schultz, Inc., 438 So. 2d 533, 534 (Fla. App. 1983); Kirkpatrick v. Temme, 654 P.2d 1011, 1012–13 (Nev. 1982).

[13] Home Am., Inc. v. Atkinson, 392 So. 2d 268, 270 (Fla. App. 1980) (holding that specific

performance in a garden variety builder breach case. The court relied on the specificity in the relevant contract documents detailing the parties' obligations as reducing the court's concern over ongoing supervision.[14] The dominant tendency, however, is to reject specific performance because of concerns that granting the remedy will require prolonged and continuous oversight and supervision of the construction project by the court.[15] This approach has been followed even when the parties contractually agreed to the specific performance remedy.[16] Because the primary concern is with ongoing judicial supervision, specific performance of a construction contract against the contractor-builder stands the best, albeit still marginal, chance of success when the contract specifications are complete and detailed and the work required to be done is simple or, at least, routine.[17]

[161.2] Defective or Deficient Performance

The contractor may breach the construction contract by failing to perform to the standards of quality demanded by the contract. Breach may involve either workmanship or materials used. Although the basic remedy (cost to complete) is the same as in the failure to complete case,[18] the defective performance cases sometimes raise the issue whether the owner should be allowed "cost to complete damages" or whether the owner should be relegated to the "difference in value between the work as promised and the work as performed," in other words, an "economic loss" model. The issue is raised in cases when the cost to complete remedy is deemed to be economically inefficient. In some of the cases, the court may also be influenced by the perception that the owner is opportunistically seeking to exploit technical breaches to escape her contractual obligations to the

---

performance was available remedy for the builder's breach when the builder agreed to build a house and convey it to the purchaser). The court noted that the court could order the builder to "correct the construction deficiencies." *Id.*; *cf.* Grayson-Robinson Stores v. Iris Constr. Corp., 168 N.E.2d 377, 378–79 (N.Y. 1960) (enforcing arbitral award of specific performance); Chapter 20 (Specific Performance).

14 266 F. Supp. 766 (D.D.C. 1967), *aff'd*, 394 F.2d 950, 956 (D.C. Cir. 1968); Section 24 ([Equitable Remedies] Burden on the Court/Supervision); *see* Peter Linzer, *On the Amorality of Contract Remedies—Efficiency, Equity and the Second Restatement*, 81 Colum. L. Rev. 111, 139 n.101 (1981) (collecting decisions that have held or intimated that specific performance of a construction contract against the contractor-builder would be granted).

15 Franklin Point, Inc. v. Harris Trust and Sav. Bank, 660 N.E.2d 204, 206 (Ill App. 1995); Petry v. Tanglwood Lakes, Inc., 522 A.2d 1053, 1056–57 (Pa. 1987). *See generally* Wade Habeeb, Annot., *Specific Performance of Lease of, or Binding Option to Lease, Building or Part of Building to be Constructed*, 38 A.L.R.3d 1052 (1971).

16 Franklin Point, Inc., *supra*, 660 N.E.2d at 208; Section 185 (Specifying Injunction Relief by Contract).

17 *See generally* Habeeb, Annot., *supra*, 38 A.L.R.3d 1052; 71 Am. Jur. 2d *Specific Performance* § 150. Both authorities rely extensively, however, on *Grayson-Robinson Stores, Inc.*, *supra*, 168 N.E.2d 377, which involved an arbitral award of specific performance.

18 Freeman & Co. v. Bolt, 968 P.2d 247, 255 (Idaho App. 1998) (applying cost of completion rule when contractor substantially performed but work contained minor defects); Section 161.1 ([Owner's Remedies] Incomplete Performance).

contractor. This issue can be explored using the claims raised by "disappointed" buyers in the case of *Grossman Holdings, Ltd. v. Hourihan.*[19] The Hourihans contracted to purchase a home in a planned development. Both the model of the home and the office drawing of the home showed the house to have a southeastern exposure. The house as constructed, however, had a northeastern exposure. During the construction phase, the Hourihans brought the discrepancy to the contractor-builder's attention and objected to the change. The change was claimed to be important to the Hourihans because they wished to "obtain the optimal benefit of the prevailing winds which would minimize the need for air conditioning as well as for esthetic reasons."[20]

The "cost to complete" remedy would give the Hourihans what they claim they wanted and regarded as essential to the contractor-builder's performance. It would do so, however, at the cost of demolishing the work done and reorienting the house so that it faced in the desired direction. The "difference in value" approach would make the Hourihans economically whole by giving them the difference between the market value of the house as constructed and the house as promised, but at the cost of denying them the house they claimed to have purchased.

Resolution of this problem follows no set script. The problem parallels difficulties found in other areas of the law, such as whether to award non-economic damages in cases involving destruction or damage to personal property[21] or whether to award non-economic damages for breach of contract.[22] In these contexts, the court must determine whether the subjective affection the owner claims for the property or subject matter of the contract warrants recognition. The approaches, across the categories, are: (1) to prefer a strict economic approach;[23] (2) to limit exceptions to situations where, as a general rule, the subjective affection for the item in question has cultural relevance and is not perceived as opportunistic[24] or

---

[19] 414 So. 2d 1037 (Fla. 1982), *rev'g*, 396 So. 2d 753–54 (Fla. App. 1981).

[20] This fact was disclosed in the Court of Appeal decision. 396 So. 2d at 754.

[21] Section 81 (Value to Owner); Section 82 (Pets).

[22] Section 140 (General Priniciples Concerning Contract Remedies); Section 142 (Distress Damages).

[23] *Hourihan, supra,* 414 So. 2d at 1038–39 (rejecting cost to complete damages to reorient direction of house when reorientation would require demolition and substantial rebuilding). *See generally* John Ludington, *Modern Status of Rule as to Whether Cost of Correction or Difference in Value of Structures is Proper Measure of Damages For Breach of Construction Contract,* 41 A.L.R.4th 131 (1986).

[24] Section 81 (Value to Owner) (noting that the cases that allow a non-market basis of recovery to owner of property are generally limited to property to which the plaintiff has a personal and sentimental attachment, such as heirlooms, personal memorabilia, etc.); Section 142 (Distress Damages) (noting that the cases that allow distress damages for breach of contract are generally limited to claims involving a plaintiff who has a personal and intimate connection with the subject matter of the contract, such as contracts involving funeral arrangements for a loved one).

the claimed loss bears some proportionality to the actual market value loss of the item in question.[25]

The factor of disproportionality has played a significant role in determining whether an owner may recover cost to repair or restore damages or is limited to a difference in value recovery. A fundamental concern is the avoidance of "economic waste," which is the expenditure of money for repair or restoration that is disproportionate to the result to be achieved.[26] As noted by one court:

> "Economic waste" is a term of art which has not been defined in Indiana. Other jurisdictions have described economic waste as "the destruction of usable property," "substantial undoing" of the contractor's work, and a situation wherein "the cost of reconstruction exceeds the original cost of construction." "Economic waste exists only when the cost to repair measure for damages would result in unreasonable duplication of effort. Further, economic waste is not present and the difference in value measure cannot be used unless the building would be substantially destroyed by completely remedying the defects."[27]

For example, it would be economically wasteful to spend $100,000 to demolish and redirect the house in *Hourihan* if the difference in value between a house with a southeastern exposure, as opposed to a northeastern exposure, was only $10,000. More leeway may be afforded an owner who is forced to complete the contract after the contractor has ceased working before full performance is rendered. On the other hand, less leeway may be given to the owner who seeks to undo what has already been built and rebuild in strict compliance with the terms of the contract.[28]

In *Hourihan* the implementation of a cost of repair remedy would have entailed severe and extreme destruction of usable property for minimal economic gain. It is perhaps noteworthy that in *Hourihan* no mention was made of any significant price disparity among homes in the planned development with different exposures. One is left with the strong impression that providing the cost of repair measure would have generated significant demolition and rebuilding expenses, with no net economic gain between the before and after value of the structures.

In order for the contractor to avoid cost of repair damages that are disproportionate to "difference in value," a number of courts have required that the contractor must have substantially performed the contract and that

---

[25] Housley v. City of Poway, 24 Cal. Rptr. 2d 554, 559 (Cal. App. 1993) (refusing to allow cost of repair damages for a family residence that exceeded the difference in value measure by a factor of 3½).

[26] *See* Carol Chomsky, *Of Spoil Pits and Swimming Pools: Reconsidering the Measure of Damages for Construction Contracts*, 75 Minn. L. Rev. 1445, 1463 (1991).

[27] Willie's Constr. Co., Inc. v. Baker, 596 N.E.2d 958, 962 (Ind. App. 1992) (citations omitted); Restatement (Second) of Contracts § 348(2)(b) (1981).

[28] Pennington v. Rhodes, 929 S.W.2d 169, 173–74 (Ark. App. 1996), *citing* Restatement (Second) of Contracts § 348 cmt. c (1981).

the structure that is built "substantially conforms to the contract specifications and only a minor defect exists which does not substantially lower the value of the structure."[29] Notwithstanding frequent assertions that courts should not promote results that are economically wasteful, the general trend is to reserve the economic waste argument for the most extreme "expense to benefit" situations.[30]

When the objective of the construction contract is manifestly aesthetic or personal to the owner, courts, in general, do not limit the owner to "difference in value." As noted by one court:

> Plaintiffs contracted to build a custom home at significant expense which, in fact, exceeded the fair market value of the home as completed per the drawings.
>
> . . . It is clear from the record that the aesthetic appearance of the home, both inside and out, was of utmost importance to plaintiffs. Our review of the photographs of the home as constructed compared with the design drawings convinces us that plaintiffs did not get the benefit of their bargain and that requiring defendants to remedy the problem would not, under these particular circumstances, result in unreasonable economic waste. Accordingly, we find that the Supreme Court applied the appropriate measure of damages.[31]

Many jurisdictions have permitted an owner to recover stigma damages—consisting of the long-term negative perception of the property—when the defendant's trespass or nuisance activities has caused physical harm to the property, such as its contamination.[32] Whether this approach will be extended to contract remedies for defective construction is unclear. In *McAlonan v. U.S. Home Corp.*[33] and *Anderson v. Bauer*[34] the courts permitted owners to obtain both cost of repair damages and diminution in value when the repairs did not restore the property to its promised market value. However, while the courts have allowed post-remediation diminution in value recoveries, the decisions have not expressly referred to "stigma" damages. The basis for the post-remediation diminution in value was not explained in *McAlonan*. In *Anderson* the court simply referenced the fact that the public was now aware of "water problems" associated with the properties in question.[35] It is unclear whether the post-remediation diminution in

---

[29] City of Charlotte v. Skidmore, Owings and Merrill, 407 S.E.2d 571, 580 (N.C. App. 1991) (citation omitted).

[30] *Willie's Constr. Co., Inc., supra*, 596 N.E.2d at 962 (stating that "in only extreme cases should the court find that the cost to repair involves economic waste"); Chomsky, *Of Spoil Pits, supra*, 75 Minn. L. Rev. at 1463.

[31] Lyon v. Belosky Constr., Inc., 669 N.Y.S.2d 400, 401–02 (App. Dept. 1998) (citation omitted) (holding that cost of replacement was the proper measure of damages).

[32] Walker Drug Co., Inc. v. La Sal Oil Co., 972 P.2d 1238, 1246 (Utah 1998) (stating that awarding stigma damages for "contamination" represents the majority view); Section 91.2 (Stigma Damages).

[33] 724 P.2d 78, 79 (Colo. App. 1986).

[34] 681 P.2d 1316, 1324 (Wyo. 1984).

[35] 681 P.2d at 1324. *See generally* Charles Stott, Student Comment, *Stigma Damages: The*

value award was the product of adverse perception or publicity regarding the event or was the consequence of damage that remediation could not correct. The latter is actual damage that exists after repairs have been affected and is recoverable as actual injury as long as the total award does not exceed diminution in value. [36] When stigma damage reflects perception or restoration exceeds diminution in value, the case for avoidance of economic waste argues that damages should not be awarded. There is, however, substantial decisional law to the contrary. [37] These decisions more typically involve environmental torts; however, there are some construction breach decisions that raise this issue with divergent results. [38]

§ 162 CONTRACTOR'S REMEDIES FOR OWNER'S BREACH

The owner may breach the construction contract in several ways. For example, the owner may wrongfully terminate or abandon the project, wrongfully terminate or bar the contractor from the worksite, wrongfully interfere in the contractor's performance, or refuse to pay either on the original contract for work performed or for additional work approved by change orders.

[162.1] Anticipatory Breach by Owner

When the owner repudiates the contract before any work has been performed, the contractor's normal recovery is limited to its lost profit (expectancy interest), but in many cases limiting recovery to lost profits would

---

Case For Recovery in Condominium Construction Defect Litigation, 25 Cal. W. L. Rev. 367, 378–79 (1988–89) (noting that neither *McAlonan* nor *Anderson* developed fully the reasons for awarding post-remediation diminution in value recoveries).

[36] Murray v. McCoy, 949 S.W.2d 613, 615 (Ky. App. 1996); W.G. Slugg Seed & Fertilizer v. Paulsen Lumber, 214 N.W.2d 413 (Wis. 1974) (noting that if the repair process does not fully restore the property, a diminution in value award may be entered to close the gap):

> The proper rule for measuring recoverable difference between substantial and complete performance of a building contract is not necessarily the costs of tearing down the defective work and rebuilding it so as to conform to the contract. It is the reasonable cost of remedying defects, so far as that can be done practicably, and the diminution value of the building so completed because of defects not so remediable.

Id. at 416 (citation omitted).

[37] *See* James R. Cox *Reforming the Law Applicable to the Award of Restoration Damages as a Remedy For Environmental Torts*, 20 Pace Env'l L. Rev. 777 (2003) (arguing that restoration costs should be the dominant remedy when property is contaminated). How far courts will go in allowing recoveries that exceed diminution in value is a matter of debate. BRUNER & O'CONNOR ON CONSTRUCTION LAW §§ 19.30, 19.59 (2002) (collecting decisions).

[38] *Compare* Aas v. Superior Court, 12 P.3d 1125 (Cal. 2000) (rejecting cost of repair and diminution in value claims against contractor for negligent workmanship when alleged construction defects had not caused any property damage; owners were limited to contract remedies), *with* New Bellum Homes, Inc. v: Griffin, 784 So. 2d 139 (Miss. 2001) (affirming excess of diminution in damage award in breach of warranty case brought by owner against contractor).

be undercompensatory. Lost profit is the difference between the contract price and the contractor's cost of performing the contract. In other words:

Costs to construct + profit = contract price

The cost to construct includes labor costs, material costs, and overhead. Overhead is defined as "those costs which are expended for the benefit of the business as a whole and which usually accrue over time."[1] In other words, the portion of the overhead costs that would have been absorbed by the particular contract with the owner must now be spread out and absorbed by other work the contractor has available. These fixed, general costs of doing business must now be borne by fewer contracts. The owner's breach causes the contractor harm in addition to the loss of profit when the contractor was relying on the contract price to defray fixed expenses that must be paid regardless of the owner's breach.[2] To the extent the expenses can be avoided, e.g., supplies for the contract not purchased or contract for supplies cancelled, the contractor must act reasonably to mitigate damages.[3]

Calculating overhead costs with sufficient precision to warrant recovery can be a daunting task. Formulas have been developed to calculate overhead that should be allocated to the particular contract. The tests can be quite complicated.[4]

---

[1] Wickham Contracting Co. v. Fischer, 12 F.3d 1574, 1578 (Fed. Cir. 1994). Examples of overhead include: rent, administrative costs, insurance, etc. *See generally* S. Shapiro, Annot., *Comment Note: Overhead Expense As Recoverable Element of Damages*, 3 A.L.R.3d 689 (1966).

[2] Autotrol Corp. v. Continental Water Systems Corp., 918 F.2d 689 (7th Cir. 1990) (Posner, J.):

> The question of the proper treatment of overhead expenses arises more frequently in cases in which the plaintiff is seeking not the expenses themselves—they have not been incurred—but the price of a contract that has not yet been fully performed, and the defendant asks that the overhead expenses assigned by the plaintiff on the uncompleted portion of the contract be deducted, on the theory that they were saved by the breach and therefore that their inclusion would exaggerate the plaintiff's loss. The proper analysis of that case is symmetrical with the property analysis of our case. If the plaintiff can either cut his overhead expenses or recover them in a substitute contract, then he indeed has not lost them as a result of the breach and they should not be figured in his damages. But if he cannot do either of these things—if in other words these really are fixed costs—then the breach gives him no scope to economize and there should be no deduction.

Id. at 693–94 (citations omitted).

[3] Section 13 (Duty to Mitigate Damages).

[4] West v. All State Boiler, Inc., 146 F.3d 1368, 1372 (Fed. Cir. 1998) (approving use of the "Eichleay Formula," which allocates indirect overhead on a proportionate basis among all the contractor's contracts). The formula comes from *Appeal of Eichleay Corp.*, 60–2 B.C.A. (CCH) P2688, 1960 ASBCA LEXIS 1207 (Armed Serv. Bd. Contract App. 1960). In that case, the Board of Contract Appeals applied a formula suggested by the appellant contractor with some minor modifications. The basic approach is as follows:

> Appellant has based its claim on an allocation of the total recorded main office expense to the contract in the ratio of contract billings to total billings for the period of performance. The resulting determination of a contract allocation is divided into

The concept of overhead is further complicated by the fact that it is surrounded by many qualifying terms and the terms are not used consistently. Overhead may be referred to as general, direct, unabsorbed, extended, etc.[5] This lack of consistency makes it impossible to reconcile all of these usages, and the formulas that have been adopted in connection with the various usages.

The contractor must establish that absent the owner's breach the contract price would have covered the overhead expense; however, how rigorously the courts will enforce this requirement varies.[6] The contract price is not always self-evident in construction cases. For example, the parties may enter into a "cost plus" contract, in which the owner agrees to pay the contractor the actual cost of performance plus. The "plus" may be "profit," "overhead," or both. The contract itself should specify the components of the calculation, e.g., whether general overhead is included, and, if so, what elements of general overhead qualify for inclusion.[7] The "plus" may be a specified amount or a percentage of the actual costs incurred in performing the contract. Usually the "cost plus" arrangement is used when building costs are uncertain and the contractor is unwilling to bid the job because she cannot calculate her costs to perform within a reasonable margin of error; hence, there is a substantial risk she may underbid. The owner is usually protected against the upward billing pressures "cost plus" contracts impose by a guaranteed maximum price.

[162.2] Partial Performance By Contractor

When the contractor has begun performance before the owner breaches, the damages recovery must now explicitly consider the cost of labor and materials expended in performance as a component of the recovery. It may be helpful to visualize again the components of the contract price:

> a daily rate, which is multiplied by the number of days of delay to arrive at the amount of the claim. This method of computation relies primarily on the duration of the suspension as the criterion for allocating the contract expenses of the main office. The same formula has been used by the Court of Claims. In other cases the daily rate and total for the delay period have been determined after allocation of contract overhead according to monthly gross.

1960 ASBCA LEXIS at *11–12 (citations omitted).

[5] *Compare* Southwestern Eng'g Co. v. Cajun Elec. Power Coop, Inc., 915 F.2d 972, 978 (5th Cir. 1990) (distinguishing between extended and unabsorbed overhead), *with* Linda Shapiro & Margaret Worthington, *Use of The Eichleay Formula to Calculate Unabsorbed Overhead For Government-Caused Delay Under Manufacturing Contacts*, 25 Pub. Cont. L. J. 513, 536 n.46 (1996) (noting that terms are used interchangeably or synonymously).

[6] *Autotrol Corp., supra*, 918 F.2d at 695 (stating that because the contractor is being asked to establish a counterfactual "he should not be subjected to too demanding a burden of proof").

[7] Freeman & Co. v. Bolt, 968 P.2d 247, 251 (Idaho App. 1998) (stating that the term "cost" as used in a "cost plus contract" does not "with respect to the inclusion of overhead" have any fixed, settled legal meaning). The court surveyed decisions from other jurisdictions on the point. Peterson Painting & Home Improvement, Inc. v. Znidarsic, 599 N.E.2d 360, 362 (Ohio App. 1991) (stating that when owner agreed to pay contractor "cost plus 10%" to remodel a home, overhead expense was an item of cost, not of the 10%).

Costs to construct + Profit = Contract price

In the partial performance case, the cost to construct is broken down into two categories:

Costs already incurred + Costs to be incurred to complete construction = Costs to construct

When the work has been performed pursuant to the original contract, the contract price provides a baseline against which the cost of the labor and materials may be calculated. An example may help. To simplify matters I hve excluded consideration of overhead, the issue discussed in Section 162.1 (Anticipatory Breach by Owner). Assume the contractor and the owner enter into a construction contract. The contract price is $100,000 and the calculated profit is $10,000; thus, the contractor anticipates that she can perform the work for $90,000. After 50% of the work has been completed, the owner breaches. The contractor should recover $55,000. This consists of $45,000 for labor and materials (50% times $90,000) plus the $10,000 profit. The $45,000 represents the contractor's damages incurred in performing the contract. The $10,000 represents the contractor's expectancy based on the contract.[8] The schematic can be restated now as a damages formula.

Costs incurred + Profit = Damages
($45,000) + ($10,000) = ($55,000)

Progress payments are advance payments of the contract price based on the percentage of work done against the contract price. Usually the percentage of work done is greater than the percentage of the contract price, e.g., when 25% of the work is done, 20% of the contract price is paid. The difference is the "holdback" and is designed to assure that the contractor has an incentive to complete the work and that a fund exists to pay for corrective work. If progress payments have been made, the owner receives a credit against the award:

Costs incurred + Profit − Payments made = Damages

An alternative model, which achieves the same result, is to award the contractor the contract price, less the amount it would cost under the contract to complete the construction.[9] If the contractor had performed 50% of the work, she would recover $55,000, based on the contract price ($100,000), less remaining work (50% of $90,000, or $45,000). In other words:

---

[8] J.R. Loftus, Inc. v. White, 649 N.E.2d 1196, 1198 (N.Y. 1995) (noting that "the general measure of damages for the plaintiff contractor is expectancy damages").

[9] Blaine Econ. Dev. Auth. v. Royal Elec. Co., Inc., 520 N.W.2d 473, 477–78 (Minn. App. 1994).

Contract Price − Cost to complete = Damages

Under either approach, insofar as the measure of damages is concerned, the contractor's actual cost of performing the contract is disregarded. The damages calculation is based on the percentage of work done measured against the contract price for the work, not the actual cost of the work. If the contractor bid too low and would suffer a loss under the contract, (it required the actual expenditure of $60,000 to produce 50% of the work required under the contract, rather than the anticipated cost of $45,000), contract damages remedies do not permit the transfer of that risk to the owner simply because the owner breached. Under the contract damages approach, the underbidding contractor suffers a $5,000 loss after recovering $55,000 in damages because the contractor expended $60,000 to perform. The result may, however, be different if the contractor is allowed to invoke unjust enrichment and restitution theories against the owner.[10]

It is important to remember that these formulas do not consider the point made earlier that the contractor may have been relying on the contract price to defray a portion of his fixed expenses. If that is the case, the damages calculation needs to be adjusted to consider that factor. This point is addressed in Sections 162.1 (Anticipatory Repudiation by Owner), 162.4 (Delay in Completion or Disruption in Work).

[162.3]   Change Orders

When the contractor has performed additional work for which the owner is responsible, as, for example, pursuant to a change order, the contractor is entitled to recover the fair price of the additional work.[11] How to determine the "fair" price of the extra work is, however, often a factually difficult problem. A number of approaches have been used. One approach is the "actual cost" method under which the contractor proves the actual costs incurred in performing the extra work, as determined from the contractor's books and records.[12] A second approach is the "total cost" approach under which the contractor subtracts the bid or contract price of the entire undertaking from the actual final cost incurred in the completion of the project to determine the amount to be allocated to "extra work."[13] A third approach is referred to as the "measured mile." This approach compares the cost of work when the contractor was not disrupted or interfered with by the owner and the period of disruption and interference.[14] The fourth approach is the broad evidence or "jury-decides" approach under which the

---

[10] Section 163 (Losing Contracts and Restitution).

[11] Thomas Galligan, Jr., *Extra Work in Construction Cases: Restitution, Relationship, and Revision*, 63 Tulane L. Rev. 799 (1989).

[12] New Pueblo Constructors, Inc. v. State, 696 P.2d 185, 194 (Ariz. 1985).

[13] Huber, Hunt & Nichols, Inc. v. Moore, 136 Cal. Rptr. 603, 621–22 (Cal. App. 1977).

[14] *See* Steven C. Bennett, *Construction Contract Damages: The "Measured Mile" Methodology*, 16 Touro L. Rev. 77 (1999).

trier-of-fact is presented with all the evidence and opinions of witnesses, lay and expert, and allowed to determine the value of the extra work.[15]

The "total cost" approach (approach #2 above) is often said to be disfavored because of the lack of proof that the total increased costs were related to the specific breach.[16] Nonetheless, the approach is often used when certain qualifying conditions have been met. As noted by one commentator:

> Although many courts have questioned the [total cost] method's application, most courts now accept the total cost method if a four part test is met. The total cost method hinges on proof that (1) the nature of the particular losses make it impossible or highly impractical to determine them with a reasonable degree of accuracy; (2) the plaintiff's bid or estimate was realistic; (3) its actual costs are reasonable; and (4) it was not responsible for the expenses.[17]

The broad evidence approach may be likewise limited to cases when the contractor is unable to prove its claim by "direct and specific proof."[18]

Change orders or owner breach may require the contractor to work under more adverse conditions than would have otherwise been the case. This may result in a decline in productivity. Although the recovery of damages for productivity decline has been recognized in the decisions, the factual proof needed to substantiate the claim tends to be rigorous.[19]

---

[15] Dawco Contr., Inc. v. United States, 930 F.2d 872, 881 (Fed. Cir. 1991); *see* Power Constructors, Inc. v. Taylor & Hintze 960 P.2d 20, 41 (Alaska 1998) (discussing various methodologies).

[16] Fairbanks N. Star Borough v. Kandik Constr., Inc. & Assocs., 795 P.2d 793, 799 (Alaska 1990).

[17] Bernhard Aaen, *The Total Cost Method of Calculating Damages in Construction Cases*, 22 Pacific L. J. 1185, 1185 (1991) (footnote omitted; brackets added). The test is derived from *WRB Corp. v. United States*, 183 Ct. Cl. 409, 426 (1968), *quoted in* Frost Constr. Co. v. Lobo, Inc., 951 P.2d 390, 397 (Wyo. 1998).

[18] Joseph Pickard's Sons Co. v. United States, 532 F.2d 739, 742 (Ct. Cl. 1976).

[19] Thomas Shea, *Searching For the Standard of Productivity: Loss of Efficiency Damages in Construction Cases*, 15 Ohio N.U. L. Rev. 225 (1988):

> There are several approaches that can be used to prove damages in complex construction cases involving inefficiency or the loss of productivity where actual cost data is not available. Under each of these methods, a standard is developed and used to gauge the loss of productivity. These are referred to as the standards approaches:
>
> A) Productivity Comparison Method;
> B) Estimated Evaluation Method;
> C) Total Cost Method;
> D) Modified Total Cost Approach;
> E) Should Have Cost Approach;
> F) Jury Verdict Method.

Id. at 226 (footnote omitted). The various methodologies are discussed in the article.

[162.4]   Delay in Completion or Disruption in Work

The owner's interference or breach may delay the contractor's completion of the project. Delay may increase the contractor's actual costs, for example, by increased materials costs, scheduling difficulties, idled equipment and employees, and affect the contractor's ability to spread its overhead across all the contracts (business) the contractor could perform, but for the breach by the owner. As a general rule, the contractor may recover the additional costs actually incurred as a result of unexcused delay caused by the owner. These delay costs are usually "divided between direct added costs on the delayed project and indirect impacts upon other aspects of the contractor's business."[20] As to the indirect impacts, the contractor will confront the same difficulties of proof noted earlier insofar as overhead calculations are concerned.[21]

There is decisional law stating that the contractor may recover consequential damages arising out of unexcused delay.[22] That language, however, should be read within the context of the construction dispute for the recovery usually refers to the direct and indirect costs incurred by the contractor as a result of the breach. It is not, however, a double recovery for the contractor to recover both overhead and lost profit from other jobs not undertaken because of the owner' breach. The "lost profits" from the jobs not undertaken must be proven with the requisite legal certainty.[23]

The presence of a guaranteed maximum price may influence the allocation of the burden of proof on damages. For example, in *Sage Street Associates v. Northdale Constr. Co.* the terminated contractor sued the owner for damages. The contractor had been working under a "cost plus" contract with a guaranteed maximum price. The presence of the maximum price provision required, that in order for the contractor to earn a profit, the contractor had to be able to complete the work at or near, but not in excess of, the maximum price. The court held that the contractor was not required to prove the actual completion cost of the project; rather, the contractor only had to establish that a breach had occurred, thus, entitling the contractor to its profit, and what its total reimbursable costs, if any, were.[24] The

---

[20] Ian A.L. Strogatz, William J. Taylor & Gavin P. Craig, *Pricing the Delay: Whom Do I Sue and What Do I Get?* 17-Oct Construction Law. 4, 8 (1997).

[21] Kenneth Cushman & Joyce Hackenbrach, *Delays and Disruptions*, 357 PLI/Real 11 (1990) at 50 (noting that the critical issue in the delay case is tying the contractor's added costs to the delay caused by the owner's interference or breach); Section 162.1 (Anticipatory Breach by Owner) (discussing recovery of overhead costs as damages).

[22] M.A. Lombard & Son Co. v. Public Bldg. Comm'n of Chicago, 428 N.E.2d 889, 891–92 (Ill. App. 1981).

[23] *Fairbanks N. Star Borough, supra,* 795 P.2d at 798 (noting that while mathematical precision is not required, the contractor must prove damages "with reasonable certainty"); *Autotrol Corp., supra,* 918 F.2d at 695 (stating that when the contractor is required to establish what would have happened had the owner not breached, the court should not require "too demanding a proof").

[24] 863 S.W.2d 438, 442 (Tex. 1993) (distinguishing a "cost plus" contract from a "fixed price" contract. Under the latter (fixed), the contractor must establish that it would have earned a "profit" by proving its cost to complete the project. Under the former (cost-plus), the contractor's profit is either a contractually defined percentage of the costs or a flat fee added to the costs).

burden of proof lay with the owner to show that the cost to complete the project would have exceeded the guaranteed maximum; thus, ensuring that the contractor would not have realized a profit even in the absence of breach.

§ 163   LOSING CONTRACTS AND RESTITUTION

The ability of a contractor to recover in restitution when the owner breaches has generated significant disagreement among courts and commentators. The major points of the debate are discussed in Section 41 (Restitution for Wrongdoing), particularly Sections 41.2 (Breach of Contract) and 41.3 (Other Examples of Restitution in Contractual Settings). This section examines the issue in the specific context of a contractor versus owner dispute.

The critical issues in the contractor versus owner dispute are (1) whether the contractor should be able to ignore the price term set forth in the contract that established the contractor-owner relationship and (2) what circumstances warrant disregarding the price term. On the first issue, we should exclude those cases when the parties have redefined their relationship by contract modifications, e.g., "change orders."[1] When the court finds that the contractor's work was the result of the parties' bargain, the remedy remains on the contract even though the parties may not have specified a new price term. In this context, the courts will impose a default term (price) for the parties.[2]

A number of courts have permitted the contractor to recover under the theory of unjust enrichment when the owner breaches before the contractor renders full performance.[3] The theory is that the owner's breach permits the contractor to rescind the contract and recover the value of the benefit the contractor's performance conferred on the owner. The theory has been strongly criticized,[4] but it has been adopted, nonetheless, by many courts.[5]

---

[1] Section 162.3 (Change Orders).

[2] Section 162.3 (Change Orders) (discussing four methodologies courts use to determine price term for work done pursuant to change orders).

[3] Full performance is universally seen as limiting the contractor to an action for the contract price. Restatement (Second) of Contracts § 373(2), cmts. a, d (1979); 3 E. ALLAN FARNSWORTH, CONTRACTS § 12.20 (1990).

[4] Andrew Kull, *Disgorgement For Breach, the "Restitution Interest," and the Restatement of Contracts*, 79 Tex. L. Rev. 2021 (2001):

> A host of additional considerations, relating primarily to the stability of the contractual exchange, counsel against a rule that offers escape from an unfavorable bargain as a remedy for the defendant's (improbable) breach. Whether judged in the light of contract or restitution principles, the remedy is incongruous for these reasons, *inter alia*: (1) It treats a breaching defendant as if he had induced the plaintiff's consent to the underlying transaction by fraud. (2) It makes the contractual risk allocation contingent on substantial performance. (3) It is supracompensatory and therefore punitive. (4) It levies a form of disgorgement that might be appropriate for a profitable and opportunistic breach in circumstances where, by definition, the defendant's conduct cannot even be profitable. (5) It makes the defendant's breach

When unjust enrichment and restitution are allowed under the rationale that the owner's breach permits the contractor to rescind, the question turns to when rescission will be allowed. As a general rule, courts permit rescission when the defendant engages in a substantial breach of the contract.[6] The owner's fundamental contractual obligation is to pay for the contractor's performance. The owner may substantially breach by refusing to pay for work done by the contractor or barring the contract from the worksite. On the other hand, if the contract is a losing contract for the contractor, it is an advantageous contract for the owner; therefore, a breach by the owner in these cases would be unexpected.[7] This may explain the overlap between construction disputes involving "change orders" and the contractor seeking rescission and restitution. The presence of change orders, which alter the contractor's initial contract obligations, in some cases substantially so, may be implicitly treated as a material departure from the contract by the owner to support rescission by the contractor.[8] Many courts require that the contractor establish that the owner acted in such a way as to manifest the intent or purpose to abandon the contract.[9]

---

more desirable to the plaintiff than the defendant's performance. (6) It is inconsistent with the treatment of the defendant whose material breach consists in the failure to pay money. (7) It is inconsistent with the rule that reliance damages cannot exceed contractual expectation. (8) It is inconsistent with the law's treatment of the plaintiff in breach. (9) It purports to find unjust enrichment in an event (defendant's breach and plaintiff's consequent release from an onerous obligation) that is beneficial to the plaintiff and costly to the defendant. (10) It is inconsistent with the broad proposition that the measure of enrichment between parties to a valid contract is fixed by the contract.

Id. at 2041 n.49; Section 41.2 ([Restitution] Breach of Contract); Section 135.4 ([Rescission] Losing Contracts).

[5] Salo Landscape & Constr. Co., Inc. v. Liberty Elec. Co., 376 A.2d 1379 (R.I. 1977):

[A]n owner or prime contractor who fails to pay an installment due on a construction contract is guilty of a breach that goes to the essence of the contract and that entitles the injured party to bring an action based on a quantum meruit theory for the fair and reasonable value of the work done.

Id. at 1382 (citations omitted); Royal Manor Apartments v. Powell, 523 S.W.2d 909, 911 (Ark. 1975) (same).

[6] Section 136 (Grounds for Rescission).

[7] *See* Cray Research Inc. v. Department of the Navy, 556 F. Supp. 201 (D.D.C. 1982).

[8] The courts and commentators are divided as to whether the contractor's claim should sound in contract or unjust enrichment. *See* Kull, *Disgorgement*, *supra*, 79 Tex. L. Rev. 2021; Section 162.3 (Change Orders).

[9] Amelco Electric v. City of Thousand Oaks, 38 P.3d 1120 (Cal. 2002) (distinguishing between "abandonment theory" and "cardinal change" theory):

The United States Federal Court of Claims has historically recognized government breach of contract liability under the doctrine of cardinal change. Here, Amelco asserts the abandonment doctrine is coextensive with the cardinal change doctrine. In fact, the theories are fundamentally different. [O]nce the parties cease to follow the contract's change order process, and the final project is materially different from the project contracted for, the contract is deemed inapplicable or abandoned and is set aside. The plaintiff may then recover the reasonable costs for all of its work. There is little, if any, separation between the theory of liability and the measure of damages.

Jurisdictions are split whether the contract price limits the quantum meruit recovery.[10] If the owner' breach was willful, the chances increase that the quantum meruit recovery will not be limited by the contract price.[11] Unjust enrichment is the contractor's preferred remedy when she has entered into an unprofitable contract because the remedy allows the contractor to transfer her contract losses to the owner.

The typical claim for restitution by a contractor involves owner breach. Courts have, however, permitted a breaching contractor to seek restitution against an owner to prevent unjust enrichment.[12] Restitution recoveries by the breaching contractor was also supported by Corbin.[13] In this context, however, the contractor is limited to the contract price and he cannot shift the cost of a losing contract to the non-breaching owner.[14]

Under the cardinal change doctrine, the cardinal change "constitutes a material breach of the contract." The contractor may recover breach of contract damages for the additional work. There is no hint in any Federal Circuit or Court of Claims case to which we have been directed that the terms of the federal contract are held inapplicable or set aside for the period prior to the breach, or that the government's payments for other work not affected by the cardinal change are suddenly compensated on a quantum meruit basis.

Id. at 907 (citations omitted); *see* Aaron P. Silberman, *Abandonment and Cardinal Changes on State and Local Construction Projects*, 39 Procurement Lawyer 17 (Spring 2004).

[10] Section 41.2 ([Restitution] Breach of Contract).

[11] Ballard v. Krause, 248 So. 2d 233, 234–35 (Fla. App. 1971) (stating that "[t]he contract price generally is the upper limit where the contractor sues in quantum meruit, but in the event the owner's breach is willful, the contractor may recover his outlay even if it exceeds the contract price").

[12] Kreyer v. Driscoll, 159 N.W.2d 680, 683 (Wis. 1968) (permitting a breaching contractor to recover to avoid windfall to the owner). Quantum meruit has been allowed even though the contractor had not substantially performed, although under limiting circumstances. Peters v. Halligan, 152 N.W.2d 103, 109–10 (Neb. 1968) (permitting partially performing contractor to recover in quantum meruit when contract was divisible and contractor substantially performed as to one part (construction of basement), but breached as to other part (construction of trailer addition); Section 44.4 ([Restitution] Recovery by Party in Breach of Contract).

[13] 5 Arthur Corbin, Corbin on Contracts § 1125 (1964).

[14] *Kreyer, supra*, 159 N.W.2d at 683 (limiting the recovery of the breaching contractor to the excess of benefit over harm he has caused but in no event "exceeding a ratable proportion of the agreed compensation").

Chapter 19

BREACH OF CONTRACT TO SELL REAL PROPERTY

SYNOPSIS

§ 165 BREACH OF CONTRACT TO SELL REAL PROPERTY

Contracts to sell real property come in a variety of forms as extensive and creative as the human mind can conceive. No survey set of materials could realistically plumb the myriad ways real property transactions are structured for financing, taxation, and other reasons. In the following sections, the remedies of the disappointed buyer and the disappointed seller are sketched and discussed with the goal of identifying general approaches to each party's remedies for breach.

§ 166 BUYER'S REMEDIES

The buyer has three remedies when the seller breaches the contractual obligation to sell real property: (1) damages; (2) specific performance; and (3) restitution, usually by way of rescission but occasionally by way of disgorgement of profits realized by the seller from the breach.

[166.1] Damages

American jurisdictions have recognized two approaches in the assessment of the buyer's damages remedy for the seller's breach. One approach, the "English Rule," derives from *Flureau v. Thornhill*, and limits the buyer to recovery of his reliance interest, unless the seller acted in "bad faith."[1] The

---

[1] 2 W. Bl. 1078, 96 Eng. Rep. 635 (K.B. 1776).

817

reliance interest measure allows recovery of money paid by the buyer, such as a down payment, and the expenses incurred in preparation for performance, such as the cost associated with examining title. The "English Rule" does not permit recovery of the buyer's expectancy, unless the breach is in bad faith.

The reasons for the adoption of this limitation on remedy are not entirely clear. *Flureau* involved a claim of loss arising out of the buyer's costs of raising the capital to pay for the property that the seller was not able to convey due to a defect in title. As noted by one court:

> It is difficult to understand how that case, which simply involved highly speculative damages, could have been accorded the authoritative position it has enjoyed for the past 173 years.[2]

In *Yates v. James* the court suggested that in England the rule was "sustained upon the ground that the purchaser should investigate the title before he is justified in taking any other step."[3] This rationale was further explained in *Donovan v. Bachstadt*:

> The English principle developed because of the uncertainties of title due to the complexity of the rules governing title to land during the eighteenth and nineteenth centuries. At that time the only evidence of title was contained in deeds which were in a phrase attributed to Lord Westbury, "difficult to read, disgusting to touch, and impossible to understand." The reason for the English principle that creates an exception to the law governing damages for breaches of executory contracts for the sale of property is no longer valid, and the exception should be eliminated.[4]

Even jurisdictions that adopted the "English Rule" recognized that not all breaches were equal. Expectancy damages would be recoverable by the buyer when the seller's breach is due to circumstances within his control, such as his refusal to convey notwithstanding his possession of good title or his conveyance of the property to a third party notwithstanding his contract with the buyer.[5] These failures to convey good title were often treated by courts as within the "bad faith" exception.

Whether the seller's breach was in "bad faith" presented a difficult issue for the courts given the general notion that contract liability is strict and not based on fault.[6] No consensus ever developed as to when a seller's

---

[2] Raisor v. Jackson, 225 S.W.2d 657, 658 (Ky. App. 1949) (rejecting prior authorities and permitting the buyer to recover his expectancy without regard to whether the seller's breach was in good or bad faith). The decision surveys the English decisions following *Flureau v. Thornhill*.

[3] 26 P. 1073, 1074 (Cal. 1891).

[4] 453 A.2d 160, 164 (N.J. 1982) (citation omitted).

[5] Soloman v. Western Hills Dev. Co., 312 N.W.2d 428, 433 (Mich. App. 1981) (noting that cases invoking the "English Rule" are generally limited to cases when the seller was unable to convey good title).

[6] George Cohen, *The Fault Lines in Contract Damages*, 80 Va. L. Rev. 1225 (1994) (arguing

breach was in "bad faith," thus relieving the buyer of the limitations on his remedy. The *Flureau* court actually equated recovery of the expectancy with actions sounding in fraud. This restriction was not adopted by other courts. Cases involving the refusal of the seller's spouse to join in the conveyance illustrate the lack of consensus. The jurisdictions split as to whether the spouse's failure constituted "bad faith" on the part of the contracting spouse. As noted in *Raisor v. Jackson*:

> While the question presented is not novel, it is one of broad significance. Research indicates that numberless courts for many years have wrestled with the problem and have reached differing results. In our own jurisdiction we find conflicting decisions.[7]

If the buyer improves the property prior to the defect in title being discovered, the rule is to allow a recovery based on principles of unjust enrichment and this approach has been carried over to contract actions when the seller breaches by failing to provide good title.[8]

While the "English Rule" enjoyed wide acceptance in this country in the past, the modern trend and majority rule is to allow the disappointed buyer to recover his expectancy regardless of whether the seller's breach is deemed in good faith or bad faith. The buyer's expectancy is measured by the difference between the contract price and the fair market value of the property.[9] The usual reference date is the date the seller's performance is due under the contract,[10] but there are qualifications when the breach consists of anticipatory repudiation.

When the seller anticipatorily repudiates the contracts the courts have split as to the use of the breach date or the anticipated performance (settlement) date as the appropriate reference date. In *Jenkins v. Brice* the court opted for the date of breach:

> We find no law suggesting that in the case of an anticipatory breach the fair market value should be determined at the time the contract was to be performed (closing was to take place on December 1). The Brices introduced the November 1 sale price, and the court used this figure to calculate damages. The time of the breach was in July, when Jenkins told the Brices' agent he was not going forward with

---

that the awarding of the expectancy interest in breach of contract action is frequently influenced by the absence or presence of "bad faith" on the part of the defendant notwithstanding the basic premise that contract liability is strict); Section 8.7 (Harsh or Mild Measures); Section 140 (General Principles Concerning Contract Remedies).

[7] *Raisor, supra*, 225 S.W.2d at 657–58.

[8] Horton v. O'Rourke, 321 So. 2d 612, 613 (Fla. App. 1975). *Horton* calculated the amount of the benefit based on the cost of providing the benefit. *Id.* at 613. On this point, the decision was subsequently overruled. Levine v. Fieni McFarlane, Inc., 690 So. 2d 712, 713 (Fla. App. 1997) (stating that in Florida unjust enrichment is measured by the benefit to the owner not the cost to the improver).

[9] Ackerman v. McMillan, 477 S.E.2d 267, 268 (S.C. App. 1996); McCarty v. Lingham, 146 N.E. 64, 67 (Ohio 1924).

[10] Section 7.6 (Value as a Function of Time).

the purchase. There is no evidence that the November price is an accurate gauge of the fair market value in July.[11]

On the other hand, in *McKenna v. Woods* the court opted for the settlement date:

> In the case of anticipatory breach, however, the inquiry more appropriately focuses on the date of performance contemplated by the contract, rather than on the earlier date of anticipatory breach. To do otherwise would be inconsistent with the general principle governing contract remedies, namely, protecting the injured party's expectation interest by putting him in as good a position as he would have been in had the contract been performed. That principle involves measuring damages based on the value of the promised performance on the date that performance is to be rendered, and that measurement is no different for an anticipatory breach.[12]

In most cases, the values on the two dates are likely to be the same and the inconsistent rules appear more a trap for the unwary plaintiff who fails to introduce evidence of the market value of the property with reference to the critical date, as was the case in *Jenkins v. Brice*. In cases when the difference in dates matters, *e.g.*, the market is rising, the settlement date is the preferable rule for the reason noted in *McKenna v. Woods*:

> Furthermore, the defendant's proposal would encourage breaches. If the date of repudiation were used to measure damages, a seller of real estate would be induced to commit an anticipatory breach whenever he is contractually obligated to convey real property in a rising market, so that he, rather than the buyer, would reap the incremental appreciation accruing from the time of the repudiation to the time of promised performance. To prevent this scenario, the date of performance must govern.[13]

In addition to the buyer's expectancy, the buyer has also been allowed to recover his reliance damages, including money paid to the seller and expenses incurred in preparing to perform, such as the costs of examining title.[14] This appears on its face to amount to overcompensation as the buyer would have incurred the expenses had the seller performed and the recovery of the buyer's expectancy gives buyer the benefit she reasonably expected to receive from the bargain. A more accurate measure of the buyer's position when the buyer recovers her expectancy would be that no recovery should be allowed for expenses actually incurred. If the expenses were not incurred, the breaching seller should receive an offset to avoid buyer's unjust enrichment.[15]

---

[11] 499 S.E.2d 734, 737 (Ga. App. 1998).

[12] 574 A.2d 836, 840 (Conn. App. 1990) (citation omitted).

[13] *Id.* at 840.

[14] *Donovan, supra*, 453 A.2d at 166.

[15] Section 140 (General Principles Concerning Contract Remedies) (text and notes 14–15, discussing right of breaching party to bring action for unjust enrichment after non-breaching party has been whole by damages award).

The buyer may also recover consequential damages, such as lost profits from a failed resale of the property by the buyer to a third party that has been nullified by the seller's non-performance.[16] The buyer must show that the consequential damages were reasonably contemplated at the time of contract formation.[17] The recovery of the buyer's expectancy and lost resale profit may, however, constitute a double recovery whenever the resale profit would include any difference between the contract price with the seller and the property's fair market value. For example, if the contract price is $100, the fair market value is $150, and the resale price is $200, the lost profit from the resale is $100 (resale price ($200) less contract price ($100)). If the buyer also received his expectancy of $50 (market value ($150) less contract price ($100)), the buyer would receive $50 more than he would have received if the contract was fully performed by the seller. In other words, if seller performs, buyer receives the $100 resale profit; if seller breaches and the buyer receives both the resale profit and the expectancy, the buyer receives $150. The additional $50 is unwarranted enrichment and should not be awarded.

Liquidated damages and limited remedy clauses are frequently encountered in contracts to purchase and sell real property.[18] There is some authority that prohibits a party in "bad faith" breach from invoking a "liquidated damages" "limited liability" provision to restrict or reduce the ability of the non-breaching party to recover its actual losses.[19] It is, moreover, at least an open question in many jurisdictions whether an implied obligation of good faith can be used to nullify or modify agreed remedies provisions.[20]

[166.2] Specific Performance

The buyer is customarily allowed to claim specific performance of the contract on the legal fiction that each piece of real property is unique; therefore, the remedy at law is per se inadequate.[21] The buyer may seek damages and specific performance; however, care must be taken to avoid a double recovery. The buyer may not obtain both expectancy damages and specific performance as that would allow him to capture the "benefit" twice: once as damages and again as the difference between the consideration he

---

[16] *Donovan, supra*, 453 A.2d at 166.

[17] Section 10.2 ([Loss Causation] Contacts).

[18] Chapter 21 (Agreed Remedies).

[19] BGW Dev. Corp. v. Mount Kisco Lodge No. 1552 of the Benevolent and Protective Order of Elks of the U.S. of Am., Inc., 669 N.Y.S.2d 56, 60 (App. Dept. 1998) (stating that "[a] vendor of real property who breaches the contract of sale in bad faith cannot limit the damages recoverable by the injured purchaser by relying on a contractual limitation . . .") (citations omitted); Wolofsky v. Waldron, 526 So. 2d 945, 946 (Fla. App. 1988) (same).

[20] *Cf.* Super Valu Stores, Inc. v. D-Mart Food Stores, Inc., 431 N.W.2d 721, 726 (Wis. App. 1988) (holding that a party cannot use the implied duty of good faith to claim a breach of contract when the breach consists of acts specifically authorized by the contract).

[21] Section 170 ([Specific Performance] Introduction).

paid and the value he received pursuant to the remedy of specific performance. The buyer may, however, recover specific performance and damages for losses not connected with the value of the property or the costs of completing the contract had seller not breached. For example, it is not a double recovery for buyer to receive specific performance *and* damages for lost profits or rents caused by the seller's breach of the purchase agreement.[22]

The remedy of specific performance is discussed in Chapter 20 (Specific Performance).

[166.3]   Restitution

The seller who breaches her contract with the buyer by selling the property to a third party may have to account to the buyer for those resale profits. For example, seller agrees to sell Blackacre to buyer for $100. Blackacre has a market value of $105. Thereafter, seller breaches the contract and sells Blackacre to a third party for $110. The buyer's lost expectancy is $5 ($105 (market value) less $100 (contract price)). A few courts have permitted the buyer to recover the profit the seller made as a result of the breach, which is $10 ($110 (resale price) less ($100 (contract price)).[23] If this remedy is sought, it should be in lieu of the buyer recovering the lost expectancy; otherwise the buyer would recover the lost expectancy twice— once as general damages ($5) and again in the difference between the resale price ($110) and the contract price ($100), or $10. The total ($15) is greater than the amount buyer would have received had seller performed or had buyer made the resale.

The recovery of the breaching seller's profit is vastly underutilized. This is probably due to the fixation on damages; the recovery of the seller's profit is unlikely to be seen as part of the buyer's damages. The measure of damages for the breach of a contract to sell property is the sum that will put the buyer in the position the buyer would have been in had the seller performed. Unless the profitable resale was available to the buyer, and reasonably contemplated by the buyer and seller at the time of contract formation, the resale profit is not an item the buyer can recover as damages.

Recovery of the resale profit is properly characterized in most cases as a restitutionary remedy to prevent unjust enrichment. Yet, even in this context, whether disgorgement of the profit should be required is a difficult question involving the evaluation and assessment of the seller's wrongdoing[24] and the determination whether the seller should receive a financial credit for his efforts in effecting the sale to the third party.[25] Nonetheless,

---

[22] Section 177 ([Specific Performance] Damages).

[23] Middelthon v. Crowder, 563 So. 2d 94, 95 (Fla. App. 1990); *see* Lawrence Berkovich, *To Pay or Convey?: A Theory of Remedies for Breach to Real Estate Contracts*, 95 Ann. Surv. Am. L. 319 (1995) (discussing the relationship of lost profits recovery and the theory of efficient breach).

[24] Section 51 (Disgorgement Orders).

[25] Section 46 (Apportionment of Benefit).

disgorgement of profit from wrongful interference in a party's contract expectancies has wide support in the decision law.[26] No legal rule flatly prohibits recovery of the seller's profit from breach, although the lack of precedent may deter some courts from allowing a recovery on this theory.[27]

§ 167 SELLER'S REMEDIES

[167.1] Damages

The seller's general measure of damages for the buyer's breach of the contract to purchase real property is the difference between the contract price and the fair market value of the property.[1] The seller's expectancy is based on an above market sale price. The difference between the contract price and the lower market value of the property then becomes the lost expectancy for the seller. In seller breach cases the situation is just the reverse. The buyer acquired the property for less than its market value; therefore, the difference between the contract price and the higher market value of the property measures the buyer's lost expectancy. In either case, for there to be a lost expectancy, there must be a contract price—market price differential. If the sale is at the market, there is no lost expectancy, measurable in money, if there is a breach. In the prior section dealing with seller breach, the usual case involved a rising market that created an incentive for sellers to breach and capture a higher resale price. In cases of buyer breach, the typical case involves a falling market. In a falling market the buyer hopes to purchase an equivalent for less and this creates an incentive to breach the higher cost contract. Alternatively, the falling market may make it more difficult for the buyer to secure necessary financings, e.g., lower appraisal value requires greater down payment to qualify for acceptable loan interest rates, which prevents buyer from completing the transaction.

The reference date for determining market value is the day the buyer's performance was due.[2] When the seller resells the property within a reasonable time, that resale price is evidence of the market value of the property as of the date of the buyer's breach.[3] What constitutes a reasonable time will vary with the circumstances of the case. In *Roesch v. Bray* the parties entered into a contract to sell a home for $65,000. The buyers

---

[26] Section 100 (Economic Relationships). Admittedly, the decisions in Section 100 involve third party interference, not interference by a party to the contract. Nonetheless, while the distinction supports not extending tort liability to the contracting party for interference, the distinction does not preclude restitution from the breaching contracting party of a direct benefit achieved by breach.

[27] Section 41.2 ([Restitution] Breach of Contract).

[1] Abrams v. Motter, 83 Cal. Rptr. 855, 863–64 (Cal. App. 1970).

[2] Gilomen v. Southwest Mo. Truck Ctr., Inc., 737 S.W.2d 499, 501 (Mo. App. 1987) (stating that the proper measure of damages for the buyer's breach is "the difference between the contract price and the value of the realty on the day the contract should have been completed).

[3] Kemp v. Gannett, 365 N.E.2d 1112, 1113 (Ill. App. 1977).

breached and the sellers resold the home a year later for $63,500. The trial court refused to allow the seller to use the resale as evidence of market value as of the date of the breach because the 1 year separation was too great. The court of appeal reversed:

> At the time of appellees' breach in the instant case, the housing market was moving rather slowly since interest rates were very high. Therefore, it would not be unreasonable to assume that the resale price tendered in August 1983 was the best indicator of the market value of the home in 1982. Furthermore, we cannot conclude that the resale of the home one year after appellees' breach was unreasonable due to the market condition. It is also apparent that the resale price obtained by appellants, $63,500, was, in fact, very close to the purchase price offered by appellees. That is, the eventual sale price in 1983 is a measure of the value of the property in August 1982, and this value is most favorable to appellees. Based on the evidence before us, we conclude that the resale price is as ". . . favorable a bid as the value of the property will admit to."[4]

A few jurisdictions have adopted by analogy the approach of the Uniform Commercial Code, which permits the seller of goods to recover damages based on the difference between the contract price and the resale price.[5] In jurisdictions that adopt the U.C.C. approach, the resale price is not simply evidence of the value of the property as of the date of the buyer's breach; the resale price is a component of the measure of the seller's actual damages.[6]

If the resale price is greater than the contract price, the buyer's breach has not caused the seller a lost expectancy. Thus, a buyer who breaches in a rising market, because, for example, the price turns out to be beyond the buyer's means, will often escape a damages action. The breach allows the seller to resell the property at a higher price and the increase realized offsets all the losses caused by the breach.[7] An exception is sometimes

---

[4] 545 N.E.2d 1301, 1303 (Ohio App. 1988) (citation omitted); see Crown Life Ins. Co. v. American Nat'l Bank & Trust Co. of Chicago, 830 F. Supp. 1097, 1100 (N.D. Ill. 1993) (applying Illinois law) (stating that "[t]he price paid at a fair forfeiture sale is presumptively considered to be market value"), aff'd, 35 F.3d 296 (7th Cir. 1994); Section 166.1 (Buyer's Remedies] Damages) (text and notes 11–13, discussing use of breach date or settlement date when seller anticipatorily repudiates the contract).

[5] U.C.C. § 2–706 (permitting the seller, when the resale is made in good faith and in a commercially reasonable manner, to recover from the buyer the difference between the contract price and the resale price as damages). This measure has been adopted by the Uniform Land Transactions Act, but there are few decisions applying the damages provision of the Act. See Gerald Korngold, Seller's Damages From a Defaulting Buyer of Realty: The Influence of the Uniform Land Transactions Act on the Courts, 20 Nova L. Rev. 1069 (1996).

[6] Kuhn v. Spatial Design, Inc., 585 A.2d 967, 970–71 (N.J. Super. Ct. A.D. 1991) (allowing the seller to recover damages based on the difference between the contract price and the resale price when the relevant transaction occurred in a declining real estate market); Grossman v. Lowell, 703 F. Supp. 282, 284 (S.D.N.Y. 1989) (same but without the declining market caveat).

[7] Section 14.2 ([Offsetting Benefits] Contract Claims).

recognized here for "lost volume" sellers. A "lost volume seller" is one who, as a practical matter, is deemed to be able to supply every potential purchaser with conforming goods. If the plaintiff can claim the status of "lost volume seller" she can claim both the profit she would have realized on the failed sale and the profit she realized on the second sale. Courts and commentators have developed various approaches to determine whether a seller qualifies as a "lost volume seller."[8] It is unlikely that a seller of real property will fall into the "lost volume seller" category. The possible exception would be a large scale developer with hundreds, if not thousands, of units for sale.

The seller is entitled to recover prejudgment interest on the amount recoverable as general damages (lost expectancy), which here is the difference between the contract price and the value of the property.[9] This interest award is provided because damages are ascertainable and certain.[10] An interest award, based on the contract purchase price, should not be allowed when the seller elects to keep the property and recover damages. As noted in *Abrams v. Motter*:

> When a seller, [faced with] the buyer's refusal to purchase, ultimately seeks damages only, he relieves the buyer of his obligation, and the law substitutes for the seller's rights under the contract (1) the property free of the buyer's right to purchase, and (2) the loss of bargain damages.[11]

The seller is usually allowed to recover as consequential damages the additional costs and expenses incurred as a result of his putting the property back on the market. These costs and expenses include maintenance of the property, payment of taxes, mortgages, etc.[12] The additional expenses must, however, be related to the effort to resell the property. If the seller decides to reside in the property or lease, rather than resell, the property, recovery of maintenance and other post-breach expenses will not be allowed.[13]

---

[8] Section 8.5 (Lost Volume Seller).

[9] 21 West, Inc. v. Meadowgreen Trails, Inc., 913 S.W.2d 858, 881 (Mo. App. 1995); *Abrams, supra*, 83 Cal. Rptr. at 864.

[10] Section 16.1 ([Prejudgment Interest] Ascertainability: Liquidated vs. Unliquidated Claims).

[11] *Abrams, supra*, 83 Cal. Rptr. at 864 (brackets added); *see* Cook v. Brown, 428 So. 2d 59 61 (Ala. App. 1982) (following *Abrams*). The result is different if the seller seeks specific performance. In this situation the seller was entitled to the contract price on the date of performance and is entitled to interest on that sum to compensate for delayed receipt.

[12] Karakehian v. Boyer, 900 P.2d 1273, 1281 (Colo. App. 1994) (allowing recovery of mortgage interest paid by seller while attempting to resell the property); Allen v. Enomoto, 39 Cal. Rtpr. 815, 819 (Cal. App. 1964) (allowing recovery of expenses incurred for fire insurance, mortgage interest, and property taxes while attempting to resell).

[13] *Abrams, supra*, 83 Cal. Rptr. at 870–71:

> However, the vendor in Allen did not occupy the subject property after the vendee's breach . . . . In the instant case Abrams continued to live in the Angelo residence for a dual purpose: (1) To enjoy its use; and (2) to keep it in presentable condition

When the additional expenses are caused by buyer's breach, the seller must also establish that they were within the reasonable contemplation of the parties at the time of contract formation before those expenses are recoverable as consequential damages.[14] In *Turner v. Benson* the court permitted the seller to recover as damages the additional costs and expenses of maintaining two residences after the buyer breached.[15] The court found that the buyers were aware of the seller's intention to purchase another house as a result of a conversation between two of the parties during the negotiation before the contract was entered into by the parties. It was sufficient that the buyers were informed of the seller's intentions; the sellers did not state that they had purchased a home.[16]

In order to secure payment of the purchase price the seller retains a lien in the real property that is the subject of the contract. The lien may be express, but is always implied in the absence of express treatment in the contract.[17] The lien is usually seen in installment land sale contracts when the seller retains title, but the buyer receives possession during the executory period of the bargain.[18] When the parties contemplate a fully executed transaction after a short escrow period, it is a misnomer to speak of a vendor's lien for the seller simply retains her interest in the land until it is conveyed at the completion of the bargain on the close of escrow.[19]

[167.2] Specific Performance

The buyer's breach of a contract to purchase real property has traditionally entitled the seller to obtain specific performance.[20] The seller's remedy of specific performance tends, however, to be more restricted than is the case with the buyer's action for specific performance. Courts more frequently find that a damages action will adequately protect the seller's interest

---

for prospective purchasers and to protect its valuable exterior and interior appointments. This was Abrams' choice. After the breach he sought a damage remedy, regained his equitable interest in the subject property and could utilize it in any way he saw fit. He cannot charge the expenses of normal occupation to the breaching vendee. If, however, at the trial of this matter, Abrams can isolate certain expenses that were unnecessary to such use but were reasonably related to the process of effecting a resale, these may be charged to Motter.

(footnote omitted).

[14] Section 10.2 ([Loss Causation] Contracts).

[15] 672 S.W.2d 752 (Tenn. App. 1984).

[16] *Id.* at 755–56. *But see* Buschman v. Clark, 583 So. 2d 799, 800 (Fla. App. 1991) (applying the "reasonable contemplation" test rigorously and denying post-breach expenses based on the failure to demonstrate that they were within the reasonable contemplation of the parties at the time of contract formation).

[17] Krajeir v. Egidi, 712 N.E.2d 917, 925 (Ill. App. 1999). *See generally* 77 Am. Jur. 2d *Vendor and Purchaser* § 589.

[18] Section 168 (Installment Land Sale Contracts).

[19] Butler v. Wilkinson, 740 P.2d 1244, 1256 n.6 (Utah 1987).

[20] BD Inns v. Pooley, 266 Cal. Rptr. 815, 818 (Cal. App. 1990); *see* 2 E. ALLAN FARNSWORTH, FARNSWORTH ON CONTRACTS § 12.6 (1990).

because the object of the contract—from the seller's vantage point—is the receipt of money for property.[21] This, of course, would not be the case if the buyer and seller were exchanging properties, e.g., Blackacre for Whiteacre.

[167.3] Restitution

A seller may take possession of the property due to the buyer's breach, but, thereafter, the buyer may cure the breach and claim the property. If the seller improves the property while in possession, the seller may seek to recover the cost or the reasonable value of the improvements. The common law rule was that the seller could not claim reimbursement for improvements; however, the modern trend is to allow recovery if the seller can claim the status of "good faith improver,"[22] which should be the case here when the seller reclaims after the buyer breaches.[23]

§ 168 INSTALLMENT LAND SALE CONTRACTS

Installment land sale contracts (contracts for deeds) are seller financed real property transactions. The installment land sale contract is an ubiquitous device. As noted by a leading commentator in the field:

> For most of this century, the contract for deed has been the most pervasively used substitute for the mortgage or deed of trust. First, some terminology is important. Depending on the jurisdiction, this financing device is also called an "installment land contract," an "installment sale contract," a "bond for deed" or a "long-term land contract." A contract for deed is not an "earnest money contract" or a "binder." The latter device is simply an executory contract for the sale of land and does not serve a mortgage function; rather, it governs the rights and obligations of the parties during the short period between the time of its signing and the closing of the transaction. At the closing, a deed is delivered to the purchaser who usually executes and delivers a purchase money mortgage to an institutional lender or, in some situations, to the vendor. Indeed, it is usually at this stage that a contract for deed is executed to serve as a substitute for a mortgage to the vendor. While a precise definition of the contract for deed is elusive, it is perhaps appropriately described as "a contract for the purchase and sale of real estate under which the purchaser acquires the immediate right to possession . . . and the vendor defers delivery to a deed until a later time to secure all or part of the purchase price."[1]

---

[21] Section 170 ([Specific Performance] Introduction).

[22] Kerr v. Miller, 977 P.2d 438, 444–45 (Or. App. 1999).

[23] Section 96 (Good Faith Improvers of Real Property).

[1] Grant Nelson, *The Contract For Deed as a Mortgage: The Case For the Restatement Approach*, 1998 B.Y.U. L. Rev. 1111, 1112 (footnote omitted).

The installment land sale contract combines both a mortgage and a contract to sell property in a single instrument. Its primary benefit to the parties to the transaction is that it permits an alternative to conventional financing and may permit transactions that otherwise would fail for lack of conventional financing of the purchase price.[2] As traditionally understood, under the installment land sale contract the buyer pays the balance of the purchase price over time in installments. At the conclusion of the term, the seller issues the deed to the property. The seller's property secures the debt owed by the buyer. If the buyer defaults at any time, the seller may foreclose on the security and keep both the property and the prior payments. In effect, the defaulting buyer forfeits all his interest in the property and his payments.

The forfeiture provision made the installment land sale contract attractive to sellers. While the buyer's breach provided several remedies, such as specific performance, damages (including the unpaid balance), and rescission, the seller's ability to recover the property and keep the payments received was the preferred remedy in many situations.[3]

While the forfeiture provision was harsh, it has, up until relatively recent times, consistently been enforced.[4] The modern trend, however, has been to substantially reduce the effectiveness of land sale contracts to the seller. In many jurisdictions, either by legislation or by the exercise of equity, the ability of the seller to declare a forfeiture upon the buyer's default has been sharply curtailed.[5] The legislative response has been to condition the seller's ability to take a forfeiture by providing the buyer with a statutory cure period.[6] The judicial approach has been to treat the installment land sale contract as an equitable mortgage that the buyer has on the seller's land.[7] The seller's ability to foreclose and forfeit the buyer's interest in the property is, thus, subject and subordinate to the buyer's equitable rights in the property.

The buyer's equitable rights in the property may entitle the buyer to reinstate the contract by tendering the delinquent installment, and an

---

[2] *Id.* at 1112–13.

[3] Grant Nelson & Dale Whitman, *The Installment Land Contract—A National Viewpoint*, 1977 B.Y.U. L. Rev. 541, 542 (1977).

[4] Nelson, *Contract For Deed as a Mortgage*, *supra*, 1998 B.Y.U. at 1113–14 (noting that "forfeiture provision was routinely enforced"). Professor Nelson's article contains an excellent review of the justifications for and criticisms of the forfeiture rule).

[5] *Id.* at 1120–22 (noting legislative and judicial efforts to restrict seller's forfeiture remedy).

[6] Gregory Henriksen, Student Comment, *Perfecting Oregon's Land Sale Contract: Beyond Notice & Cure*, 76 Or. L. Rev. 945, 951–52 (1997) (discussing the various approaches of the jurisdictions that have enacted legislation on mandatory "cure" periods).

[7] Hicks v. Dunn, 622 So. 2d 914, 915 n.1 (Ala. 1993) (stating that "[a] bond for title is an executory contract for the sale of land which creates an equitable mortgage on the land") (citation omitted); Brooks v. Hackney, 404 S.E.2d 854, 858 n.1 (N.C. 1991) (noting that "the law normally grants buyers of real property who use the installment land contract method the right to an equitable mortgage . . ."); Wagner v. Wyoming Prod. Credit Ass'n, 773 P.2d 927, 931 (Wyo. 1989) (same).

amount sufficient to compensate the seller for losses caused by the buyer's default, thereby curing the default. The remedy is not available, however, as a matter of right. The buyer must show that it is equitably just that she be allowed to cure her default. Factors the courts have considered in determining the strength of the buyer's equitable right include: (1) whether the buyer has taken possession; (2) whether the buyer's breach was willful; and (3) the proportion of the total obligation the buyer had paid to the seller.[8] The extent to which the seller contributed to the default is also frequently cited as a factor.[9]

Treatment of the relationship as creating an equitable mortgage is designed not just to protect against forfeiture but also to protect the interests of the seller. As noted in *McFadden v. Walker*:

> It bears emphasis, of course, that we are here dealing with an equitable remedy that is carefully hedged around with protections to the person against whom it is invoked. The contract must be just and reasonable, and the consideration adequate, the vendor must be assured that he too will receive the benefit of his bargain, and the defenses of laches and unclean hands are available to preclude a defaulting vendee from seeking an unfair advantage over an innocent vendor.[10]

When the buyer is unable to demonstrate that the seller's interests will be adequately protected if the buyer is allowed to cure and resume performance, the buyer's equitable interest may permit her to recover, to prevent unjust enrichment, the difference between her payments and the seller's damages.[11] The seller's damages included not only the expectancy loss, but also the use value of the property. If the buyer used or occupied the property, this restitutionary recovery might be negligible because the defaulting buyer would have to account for the reasonable rental value of the property during her use or occupancy.

In *Petersen v. Hartell* the court adopted an approach that gave the defaulting buyer a near absolute right to defeat forfeiture of the buyer's interest by tendering full and immediate performance. If the defaulting buyer paid the balance of the contract price, the seller's expectancy would be completely satisfied. Moreover, full and complete performance avoided concerns that were associated with reinstatement. In reinstatement, the seller must continue to deal with the previously defaulting buyer. When the full contract price is tendered, however, the seller-buyer relationship is terminated by the completion of the contract. As noted by the court:

---

[8] McFadden v. Walker, 488 P.2d 1353, 1357 (Cal. 1971).

[9] Bartley v. Karas, 197 Cal. Rptr. 749, 755 (Cal. App. 1983). *See generally* Charles Marvel, Annot., *Sufficiency of Tender of Payment to Effect Defaulting Vendee's Redemption of Rights in Land Purchased*, 37 A.L.R.4th 286 (1981); L.S. Tellier, Annot., *Redemption Rights of Vendee Defaulting Under Executory Land Sale Contract After Foreclosure Sale or Foreclosure Decree Enforcing Vendor's Lien or Rights*, 51 A.L.R.2d 672 (1957).

[10] *McFadden, supra*, 488 P.2d at 1356–57 (citations omitted).

[11] *See generally* James Pearson, Annot., *Modern Status of Defaulting Vendee's Right to Recover Contractual Payments Withheld by Vendor as Forfeited*, 4 A.L.R.4th 993 (1981).

[W]e conclude that where the seller of land retains title only as security for amounts payable under an installment sale contract, a vendee who wilfully defaults in one or more payments after having paid a substantial part of the purchase price nonetheless retains an absolute right to redeem the property by paying the entire balance of the price and any other amounts due. If the seller seeks to quiet title on account of the default, the right of redemption may be exercised before judgment or within a reasonable time thereafter set by the court. If the contract on its face "does not require conveyance of title within one year from the date of formation of the contract" the right [of redemption] may be exercised as soon as the seller gives notice of election to terminate the contract on account of the default. Since it appears from the record that plaintiffs have such a right of redemption and have exercised it by timely tender of the entire balance due, the judgment must be reversed.[12]

Not all jurisdictions expressly embrace *Petersen*. Professor Nelson suggests that the defaulting buyer's right to pay the balance is widely recognized.[13] An earlier annotation that predates Professor Nelson's work, suggests a less than unqualified right to pay the unpaid balance;[14] however, as noted previously, when the seller's expectancy is fully satisfied, it is difficult to justify allowing the seller to rely on the default to accomplish a complete forfeiture of the buyer's interest. The modern trend here reflects Professor Nelson's view.

The vendor's right to declare a forfeiture of an installment land sales contract may be subject to tax liens filed against the vendee's interest in the property.[15]

---

[12] 707 P.2d 232, 234 (Cal. 1985) (citations omitted; brackets added).

[13] Nelson, *Contract for Deed as a Mortgage, supra*, 1998 B.Y.U. L. Rev. at 1122 (stating that "[n]umerous courts have held that a purchaser in default has the right to defeat forfeiture by tendering the contract balance") (footnote omitted).

[14] *See generally* Allen Korpela, *Specific Performance of Land Contract Notwithstanding Failure of Vendee to Make Required Payments on Time*, 55 A.L.R.3d 10 (1974).

[15] Orme v. United States, 269 F.3d 991, 994–95 (9th Cir. 2001) (holding that forfeiture of installment land sales contracts are subject to federal requirements of timely notice to the IRS (26 U.S.C. § 7425(b)); otherwise the lien is not discharged by the sale).

Chapter 20

SPECIFIC PERFORMANCE

SYNOPSIS

§ 170 INTRODUCTION

Specific performance is a form of permanent equitable injunctive relief that orders the nonperforming party to the contract to perform. Specific performance gives the plaintiff exactly what she bargained for—the other contracting party's performance. By the same token, specific performance denies the non-performing party the power to substitute a damages recovery for performance. This deprivation has generated substantial debate among commentators as to whether specific performance impairs efficiency.[1]

To obtain specific performance, the plaintiff must demonstrate the entitlement to equitable relief. The critical element tends to be the requirement that the remedy at law be inadequate.[2] The usual test in bargain situations is whether damages would allow the non-breaching party to acquire the very thing, or its equivalent, promised under the bargain. The more unique the thing promised, the more difficult it would be for the non-breaching party to obtain an equivalent through the award of money damages.[3] Land is often treated as the prototypical measure of uniqueness under the legal fiction that each piece of real property is unique; therefore,

---

[1] Thomas Ulen, *The Efficiency of Specific Performance: Toward a Unified Theory of Contract Remedies*, 83 Mich. L. Rev. 341 (1984).

[2] Allegheny Energy Inc. v. DQE, Inc., 171 F.3d 153, 159 (3d Cir. 1999) (applying Pennsylvania law); Triple-A Baseball Club v. Northeastern Baseball, 832 F.2d 214, 223–24 (1st Cir. 1987) (applying Maine law) (finding that a contract to purchase a minor league baseball team was specifically enforceable because the subject matter of the contract was unique and not easily replaceable with a substitute); Section 21 (Adequacy of the Remedy at Law/Irreparable Injury).

[3] *Allegheny Energy Inc.*, *supra*, 171 F.3d at 160, n.9.

specific performance of a contract to acquire real property is specifically enforceable as a matter of course.[4] The legal fiction is beginning to erode, but it remains a powerful presumption in favor of specific performance of contracts to acquire real property.

A few courts have denied specific performance to buyers of real property who intend to resell the property on the ground that in such cases a damages award representing the lost expectancy is adequate.[5] This exception to the customary award of specific performance to the non-breaching buyer has been criticized as focusing too much on collateral issues to the bargain the parties struck.[6] The ability of the non-breaching party to recover a resale expectancy is also questionable given the presence of the Rule of *Hadley v. Baxendale*, for it will not always, or perhaps even often, be the case that a profitable resale is within the reasonable contemplation of the parties at the time of contract formation.[7] How often does it happen that the seller contracts with the buyer at a price less than the seller reasonably anticipates he could obtain from another party? Moreover, the non-breaching buyer's inability to perform on his contract with the third party because of the seller's breach may subject the buyer to damages on that third party contract. Specific performance avoids that problem by enabling the buyer to perform his related obligations on the contract with the third party.[8]

The seller's remedy of specific performance is frequently justified by reference to the doctrine of mutuality of remedies, i.e., because the buyer can obtain specific performance when the seller breaches, equity ought to permit the seller to obtain specific performance when the buyer breaches.[9] The implied, and sometimes express, understanding is that, absent the doctrine, the seller of property would not be entitled to specific performance because the seller seeks money and money is fungible.[10] A damages award should adequately compensate the disappointed seller for any losses occasioned by the buyer's refusal to perform, such as lost profits on the sale and the added costs of reselling the property.[11] However, in some cases,

---

[4] Restatement of Contracts § 360, cmt. 1 (1932). The "uniqueness" concept is critiqued in Nancy Perkins Spyke, *What's Land Got to Do With it?: Rhetoric and Indeterminacy in Land's Favored Legal Status*, 52 Buff. L. Rev. 387 (2004).

[5] Miller v. LeSea Broad., Inc., 87 F.3d 224, 230 (7th Cir. 1996) (applying Wisconsin law) (stating that "[i]n a case in which, although the contract is for the sale of an entire business, the buyer's negotiations to resell the property enable his loss from the breach to be exactly monetized, the case for specific performance collapses") (citations omitted).

[6] Justus v. Clelland, 651 P.2d 1206, 1207–08 (Ariz. App. 1982).

[7] Section 10.2 ([Loss Causation] Contracts).

[8] Ace Equip. Co., Inc. v. Aqua Chem., 73 Pa. D.&C. 2d 300, 20 U.C.C. Rep. Serv. 392 (Comm. Pleas Ct. 1975) (noting that a person's liability to another on a related contract if specific performance is not awarded is a reason for granting specific performance in the first instance).

[9] Section 173 (Mutuality of Remedy).

[10] Centrex Homes Corp. v. Boag, 320 A.2d 194, 196–97 (N.J. Super. Ct. Ch. Div 1974) (rejecting "mutuality of remedy" as ground for granting seller specific performance of contract for sale of real property to buyer).

[11] Section 167.1 ([Seller's Remedies] Damages).

the seller's legal remedies may be inadequate. The property may be difficult to sell or the defendant-purchaser better suited than the plaintiff to resell the property. Under such circumstances, it may not be an abuse of discretion for the court to find the remedy at law is inadequate and award specific performance for the seller, without recourse to the doctrine of mutuality.[12]

Specific performance is not limited to contracts for the sale of real property. It is generally available when the remedy at law for breach of contract is inadequate. Contracts for the sale of goods may be specifically enforced when the goods are unique.[13] Specific performance has been made available to enforce novel agreements, such as agreements to engage in nonbinding ADR (Alternative Dispute Resolution)[14] to enforce a collective bargaining agreement,[15] an agreement to merge two companies,[16] and perhaps even agreements to negotiate in good faith.[17]

Because specific performance is an equitable remedy, it may be lost when the plaintiff has engaged in inequitable behavior related to the bargain the plaintiff seeks to specifically enforce.[18]

§ 171 CERTAINTY

To be specifically enforceable the contract should be complete and the terms clear, definite, and unequivocal.[1] It is sometimes suggested that the

---

[12] *Allegheny Energy Inc., supra,* 171 F.3d at 160 n.9 (noting that property need not be inherently unique, but may "become unique by virtue of its context") (citation omitted).

[13] Bander v. Grossman, 611 N.Y.S.2d 985 (Sup. Ct. 1994) (recognizing availability of specific performance of contract to sell rare automobile). Specific performance was not awarded, however, in *Bander* because the dealer sold the vehicle to a third party before relief could be ordered. *See generally* Andrea Nadel, Annot., *Specific Performance of Sale of Goods Under UCC § 2-716,* 26 A.L.R.4th 294 (1981). Section 2-716 provides that specific performance may be granted when the goods are unique "or in other proper circumstances." This latter gloss has been underused but has potentially broad scope. Copylease Corp. of Am. v. Memorex Corp., 408 F. Supp. 758, 759 (S.D.N.Y. 1976) (applying California law) (suggesting that buyer under requirements contract may have remedy of specific performance when competing goods were inferior in quality).

[14] AMF, Inc. v. Brunswick Corp., 621 F. Supp. 456, 462–63 (S.D.N.Y. 1985) (requiring specific enforcement of agreement to obtain a non-binding advisory opinion before commencing litigation when there is a reasonable expectation the dispute will be settled by the procedure).

[15] Sheet Metal Workers' Intern. Ass'n v. Herre Bros. Inc., 201 F.3d 231, 249–50 (3d Cir. 1999).

[16] *Allegheny Energy Inc., supra,* 171 F.3d 153.

[17] *Cf.* Gilling v. Eastern Airlines, Inc., 680 F. Supp. 169, 170 (D.N.J. 1988) (sanctioning a party for failing to participate in non-binding dispute resolution procedures in good faith). The program was court ordered and this factor may limit the persuasive value of the decision. *See generally* Richard English, Annot., *Alternative Dispute Resolution: Sanctions For Failure to Participate in Good Faith in, or Comply With Agreement Made in, Mediation,* 43 A.L.R.5th 545 §§ 2[b], 6, 32[b] (1996).

[18] Phillips v. Homfray, 6 L.R. Ch. App. 770 (1871) (denying specific performance of a contract for sale to a purchaser of land who had trespassed to test for subsurface coal); Chapter 7 (Remedy Defenses) (particularly Sections 62.1 (Unclean Hands), 63.2 (Unconscionability), 65 (Fraud and Illegality)); Section 174 ([Specific Performance] Fairness).

[1] Coale v. Hilles, 976 S.W.2d 61, 65 (Mo. App. 1998); Boese v. Knight, 802 P.2d 675, 677 (Or. App. 1990). *See generally* 81A C.J.S. *Specific Performance* § 29.

contract must be clearer and more certain to obtain specific performance than damages.[2] How diligent and consistent the courts are in applying this admonition is difficult to state. The decisions are conflicting as to whether even so basic a requirement as price must be expressly delineated in order to secure specific performance of the agreement.[3] If the contractual language is uncertain or the issue unprovided for, recourse may be had to parol evidence.[4]

Even though the contract is silent, an essential term may be determined by reference and specific performance granted. For example, in *Tonkery v. Martina* the court found that a contract, which gave the plaintiff the option to purchase property "at a price 'equal to that offered by any bona fide third party purchaser' " or at a "price to be determined by an appraisal method," was specifically enforceable.[5]

The certainty requirement may be addressed as an element of the prima facie case or as an affirmative defense. If specific performance requires that the contract be more certain than necessary to support a damages action at law, the concept of an equitable defense of uncertainty is plausible. If, however, the certainty standard is the same in both contexts, it would appear to be part of the plaintiff's prima facie case.

Uncertainty sufficient to bar the remedy of specific performance should only be applied when the uncertainty or incompleteness prevents the court from knowing what to enforce. By this approach, no distinction should exist between remedies available at law or in equity for the breach of a contract based on the principle that the contract is uncertain.[6]

A contract that vests substantial discretion in the breaching defendant as to the manner of its performance is a less attractive candidate for specific

---

[2] *See* Cinman v. Reliance Fed. S. & L. Ass'n, 508 N.E.2d 239, 244 (Ill. App. 1987); Yackey v. Pacifica Dev. Co., 160 Cal. Rptr. 430, 434 (Cal. App. 1979). *But see* Hennefer v. Butcher, 227 Cal. Rptr. 318, 322 n.4 (Cal. App. 1986) (criticizing "more certainty" principle and stating that in general the cases applying the principle involved contracts that were too uncertain to support an action at law for damages).

[3] *Compare* Idol v. Little,, 396 S.E.2d 632, 633–34 (N.C. App. 1990) (granting specific performance of an option renewal provision in a lease that was silent as to rent; the court stated that the amount of rent was impliedly the same as that due under the original lease), *with* Cann v. Metropolitan Atlanta Rapid Transit Dist., 396 S.E.2d 515, 517 (Ga. App. 1990) (stating that the failure to specify the amount of rent due if the option renewal provision in the lease was exercised precluded specific performance). *See generally* W.E. Shipley, Annot., *Validity and Enforceability of Contract Which Expressly Leaves Open For Future Agreement or Negotiation the Terms of Payment For Property*, 68 A.L.R.2d 1221 (1959).

[4] *Coale, supra,* 976 S.W.2d at 66.

[5] 562 N.Y.S.2d 895, 895 (App. Dept. 1990), *aff'd,* 577 N.E.2d 1042 (N.Y. 1991). *See generally* J.R. Harvey, Annot., *Requisite Definiteness of Price to be Paid in Event of Exercise of Option For Purchase of Property*, 2 A.L.R.3d 701 (1966) at § 2 (noting that the absence of the specific price does not preclude specific performance when the contract provides a formula or reference for determining the option price).

[6] Okun v. Morton, 250 Cal. Rptr. 220, 227 (Cal. App. 1988) (stating that modern trend disfavors holding contracts unenforceable due to uncertainty). *See generally* 17A Am. Jur. 2d *Contracts* § 193 (stating that the determination is favored that the contract is sufficiently certain to be enforceable).

performance than a contract that contains defined objectives against which the defendant's performance may be measured.[7]

§ 172 ABILITY TO PERFORM

Specific performance will not be ordered when the defendant is unable to comply with the order. A party may lawfully contract to sell property she does not own; however, her failure to obtain legal title precludes, as a practical matter, specific performance.[1] In such a case, the disappointed buyer is limited to an action for damages. The reason for this rule is that because inability to comply is a defense to contempt, the order to perform would be, at the outset, an unenforceable order.[2]

Specific performance may be lost by post-breach events that deprive the breaching party of the power to perform, such as bankruptcy. In such cases, however, the court may allow the plaintiff to measure damages on a date other than the usual breach-date rule, for example, the date specific performance became unavailable.[3] Other dates may, however, be deemed by the court to be appropriate. In *Bander v. Grossman* the buyer sought monetary specific performance based on the value of the goods (rare Astin-Martin automobile). The buyer claimed the value of the goods as of the date they were resold by the seller to a third party ($185,000) rather than the contract price ($40,000). Buyer argued that the resale date was the correct valuation date because as of that date seller's performance became impossible.[4] The court declined to adopt the resale date suggested by the buyer, which was when specific performance would normally be decreed;[5] rather, the court adopted the date of trial as the valuation date.[6] The court was concerned with the significant fluctuations in value experienced by the automobile during the course of the litigation.[7] The court did not so much reject the buyer's offered date as find that, under the circumstances, a trial date valuation was more equitable due to the substantial price fluctuations the vehicle had experienced between the contract date and the trial.

---

[7] Woolley v. Embassy Suites, Inc., 278 Cal. Rptr. 719, 727 (Cal. App. 1991) (refusing to order specific performance of management contract because it would cause court to be intrusively involved in day-to-day operation of business that required high degree of mutual confidence between plaintiffs and defendants); Section 24 (Burden on Court/Supervision).

[1] Walgren v. Dolan, 276 Cal. Rptr. 554, 556 (Cal. App. 1990) (stating the principle but granting specific performance when the beneficiary of the trust, holding the equitable interest, could compel the trustee, holding the legal title, to convey the property subject to the contract of sale).

[2] Sections 192.2 (Ability to Comply), 194.3 (Ability vs. Willingness to Comply).

[3] *Cf.* Beard v. S/E Joint Venture, 587 A.2d 239, 244 (Md. 1991) (holding that when the debtor secures the rejection of an obligation after filing for bankruptcy, the date of breach for the purpose of determining damages is the day immediately before the filing of the bankruptcy petition).

[4] 611 N.Y.S.2d 985 (Sup. Ct. 1995).

[5] U.C.C. § 2–716. This valuation date allows the buyer to capture any resale profit obtained by the seller as a result of the breach. Section 166.3 ([Buyer's Remedies] Restitution).

[6] 611 N.Y.S.2d at 989.

[7] *Id.*

The fact that the defendant voluntarily disables herself from being able to specifically perform, such as by selling the subject matter of the contract to a bona fide purchaser for value, does not improve the plaintiff's claim for specific performance, just the opposite.[8] The obligation lies with the plaintiff seeking specific performance to protect the claim by filing a lis pendens or securing temporary injunctive or provisional relief preventing the defendant from engaging in actions that compromise the defendant's ability to perform its contractual obligations. The inability to perform issue must be contrasted with the issue of specific performance with an abatement of the consideration when the breaching party is capable of partial performance.[9]

An order for specific performance of contractual obligations does not exist in a vacuum. The ordered performance may be just part of the defendant's total obligations in the area. Care must be taken that the order does not unnecessarily or impermissibly subject the defendant to conflicting obligations. For example, in *Davis v. Sun Refining & Marketing Co.* the defendant failed to remove material from underground storage tanks as it had agreed to do when it sold the property. The plaintiff sought specific performance of the obligation, which the court agreed was proper. The defendant's conduct had, however, created a site contamination problem subject to the jurisdiction of the fire marshal.[10] The court found that the order should be reconciled with the fire marshal's authority. This was accomplished by keeping in place the basic order to perform, (which was to remove the material that the defendant had contractually obligated itself to remove), but to delete from the order specific criteria, such as timelines for compliance, that might infringe on the fire marshal's authority:

> [I]t is at least plausible that Sun's completion of the task in accordance with the requirements set forth by the fire marshal could take more than one year. Therefore, it appears to us that the trial court's requirement that the cleanup be completed within one year potentially conflicts with the regulations adopted by the fire marshal.[11]

§ 173 MUTUALITY OF REMEDY

It was traditionally the rule that in order to secure specific performance the plaintiff had to show that there was mutuality of remedy. Mutuality of remedy meant that either party could obtain specific performance of the contract. Mutuality of remedy is different from mutuality of obligation, which renders a contract illusory because the other party has not obligated itself to perform.[1] The origins of the mutuality of remedies requirement

---

[8] Canton v. Monaco Partnership, 753 P.2d 158, 160 (Ariz. App. 1987).

[9] Section 176 (Abatement).

[10] 671 N.E.2d 1049, 1054–55 (Ohio App. 1996) (noting Ohio provisions vesting in the Fire Marshal the authority to regulate corrective action in this area).

[11] *Id.* at 1055.

[1] Federal Sign v. Texas S. Univ., 951 S.W.2d 401, 408–09 (Tex. 1997).

are obscure but may have evolved out of the equitable notion that equity and symmetry are complimentary concepts.[2]

Mutuality of remedy has been given both a negative and a positive application. The negative version of mutuality of remedy restricts a court from ordering specific performance unless both parties to the contract can obtain specific performance of the other's obligation. For example, some courts refuse to permit a franchisee to secure specific performance of the franchise agreement because, were the tables turned, the franchisor could not obtain specific performance against the franchisee.[3] This results even though, in all other respects, the franchisee has a valid claim for specific performance.

The positive version of mutuality of remedy permits one party to obtain specific performance if the other party could have obtained specific performance against the first party. For example, courts routinely permit a buyer of real property to obtain specific performance based on the notion that real property is unique.[4] Under the positive view of mutuality of remedy, the buyer's right to claim specific performance entitled the seller to a like remedy, even though the seller's actual interest was limited to the cash consideration to be paid by the buyer. As noted by one court:

> While the inadequacy of the damage remedy suffices to explain the origin of the vendee's right to obtain specific performance in equity, it does not provide a rationale for the availability of the remedy at the instance of the vendor of real estate. Except upon a showing of unusual circumstances or a change in the vendor's position, such as where the vendee has entered into possession, the vendor's damages are usually measurable, his remedy at law is adequate and there is no jurisdictional basis for equitable relief. The early English precedents suggest that the availability of the remedy in a suit by a vendor was an outgrowth of the equitable concept of mutuality,

---

[2] Cannefax v. Clement, 786 P.2d 1377, 1390 n.37 (Utah App. 1990) (Bullock, dissenting) (noting the irony that equity, which evolved as a response to the strict formalism of the common law came to "have a penchant for wholly abstract logical symmetry"), aff'd, 818 P.2d 546 (Utah 1991); JOHN POMEROY'S EQUITY JURISPRUDENCE § 2191, p. 4922 n.35 (4th ed. 1919) (noting the obscurity of the doctrine's origins).

[3] Burger Chef Sys., Inc. v. Burger Chef of Fla., Inc., 317 So. 2d 795, 796–97 (Fla. App. 1975) (reversing a grant of specific performance to a franchisee against the franchisor because the personal nature of the services rendered by the franchisee would preclude the specific performance remedy for the franchisor against the franchisee).

[4] Walgreen Co. v. Sara Creek Property Co., 966 F.2d 273, 278 (7th Cir. 1992); see Coale v. Hilles, 976 S.W.2d 61, 68 (Mo. App. 1998) (stating that "a tract of land is regarded as unique, entitling purchaser to specific performance . . . irrespective of special facts showing inadequacy of purchaser's legal remedy") (citation omitted); Pruitt v. Graziano, 521 A.2d 1313, 1314 (N.J. Super Ct. A.D. 1987) (involving a condominium unit and reaching the same result as Coale for the same reason); Sections 166.2 ([Buyer's Remedies] Specific Performance), 167.2 ([Seller's Remedies] Specific Performance).

i.e., that equity would not specifically enforce an agreement unless the remedy was available to both parties.[5]

It should be observed that whether specific performance was denied due to negative mutuality or granted due to positive mutuality turned on how the court chose to look at the situation. There was no rule of preference for choosing between the two approaches. One is reminded of the lament of Kipling's jaguar whose mother had told him that if he should find a tortoise he should scoop the tortoise out of its shell and if he found a hedgehog (of the porcupine family) he should hold it underwater until the hedgehog uncoiled, but had failed to tell her son how to distinguish a tortoise from a hedgehog.[6] Consider, for example, a seller who contracts for liquidated damages in her contract to sell real property. Does the presence of the liquidated damages clause bar the seller from claiming irreparable injury necessary to support a claim for specific performance? If so, should the seller's actions now preclude the buyer's claim for specific performance under the doctrine of mutuality? Courts have not always permitted sellers to preclude buyers of their remedy of specific performance by such feats of legal legerdemain,[7] but this illustrates the dangers that an unconstrained love for symmetry can engender.

The modern trend has been to reject mutuality of remedies as a condition to obtaining specific performance.[8] The reason for the original rule is now seen as an imperfect effort to assure that if specific performance was ordered, it would operate justly and fairly on both parties.[9] More particularly, the rule assured that if the defendant were ordered to specifically perform, the defendant would be assured of the plaintiff's reciprocal performance. As noted by Cardozo:

---

[5] Centex Homes Corp. v. Boag, 320 A.2d 194, 196–97 (N.J. Super. Ct. Ch. Div. 1974) (citations and footnote omitted); Baruch v. W.B. Haggerty, Inc., 188 So. 797, 799 (Fla. 1939). Had the courts not adopted this gloss on the mutuality rule, the negative version of the rule would have applied and denied the buyer specific performance of the contract.

[6] RUDYARD KIPLING, THE BEGINNING OF THE ARMADILLOS, IN JUST SO STORIES FOR LITTLE CHILDREN 101–02 (1902).

[7] Jay Vee Realty Corp. v. Jaymar Acres, Inc., 436 So. 2d 1053, 1055 (Fla. App. 1983) (noting that "a seller of land may contractually limit his remedy to liquidated damages and forego the remedy of specific performance without destroying mutuality of remedy"); *cf.* Section 166.1 ([Buyer's Remedies] Damages) (text and note 22, discussing refusal of some courts to permit party who breaches in "bad faith" from invoking favorable "agreed remedy" provision).

[8] Restatement (Second) of Contracts § 363 cmt. c (1981); 5A ARTHUR CORBIN, CORBIN ON CONTRACTS § 1180 (1964).

[9] This was Pomeroy's justification for the mutuality of remedies rule. POMEROY'S EQUITY JURISPRUDENCE, *supra* at § 2191:

> Equity will not compel specific performance by a defendant, if after performance the common-law remedy of damages would be his sole security for the performance of the plaintiff's side of the contract. The court will not grant specific performance to plaintiff and at the same time leave defendant to the legal remedy of damages for possible future breaches on plaintiff's part. This rule, it is believed, covers the circumstances in equity where, according to the weight of authority, the court refuses its aid for lack of mutuality.

Id. at 4923–24 (footnotes and quotation marks omitted).

If there ever was a rule that mutuality of remedy existing, not merely at the time of the decree, but at the time of the formation of the contract, is a condition of equitable relief, it has been so qualified by exceptions that, viewed as a precept of general validity, it has ceased to be a rule to-day. What equity exacts to-day as a condition of relief is the assurance that the decree, if rendered, will operate without injustice or oppression either to plaintiff or to defendant. Mutuality of remedy is important in so far only as its presence is essential to the attainment of that end. The formula had its origin in an attempt to fit the equitable remedy to the needs of equal justice. We may not suffer it to petrify at the cost of its animating principle.[10]

Rather than use the mutuality of remedies rule to address the concern of reciprocal performance, courts consider the issue directly. If there is inadequate security that the party seeking specific performance will perform, the court may withhold ordering specific performance until that security is provided.[11] If the plaintiff has already performed, then the concern is nonexistent and the court will order defendant to specifically perform if the other requirements for the remedy are met. For example, in *Henderson v. Fisher* the court found that plaintiffs, who had performed personal services pursuant to a contract with the defendant's decedent, were entitled to specific performance of the decedent's promise to convey property to them in exchange for their performance.[12] The court noted that even though the decedent could not have secured specific performance of the plaintiffs' personal services, the fact of plaintiffs' actual and completed performance relieved the court of any concern that it could not be assured of the plaintiffs' reciprocal performance.[13]

§ 174 FAIRNESS

One of the enduring hallmarks of equity is the notion of fairness. Equity will not grant specific performance unless the agreement itself is fair.[1] Fairness, or its absence, can manifest itself in many ways. It is usually equated with notions of good faith and the doctrine of unconscionability. In this regard, fairness has a procedural component. Was the agreement reached by means and methods that were fair and just, e.g., did the plaintiff achieve the bargain she wishes to specifically enforce in good faith or did

---

[10] Epstein v. Gluckin, 135 N.E. 861, 862 (N.Y. 1922) (Cardozo, J.) (citations omitted) (refusing to apply the mutuality of remedies requirement to an assignor seeking specific performance).

[11] Stamatiades v. Merit Music Serv., Inc., 124 A.2d 829, 834 (Md. 1956).

[12] 46 Cal. Rptr. 173 (Cal. App. 1965). The defendant was the Administratrix of the decedent's estate.

[13] *Id.* at 179 (noting that "contracts which lack mutuality at their inception may be specifically enforced after the want of mutuality is removed by the performance by one party of his obligation under the contract") (citations omitted).

[1] Estate of Looney, 975 S.W.2d 508, 519–20 (Mo. App. 1998).

she exploit the defendant's vulnerable position?[2] Fairness also has a substantive component. Is the agreement fair and just as to its terms or is it one-sided in the plaintiff's favor? How far the concept of fairness (or good faith or unconscionability) should be taken has received diverse judicial applications.[3] Courts have, however, consistently recognized one particular application of the fairness doctrine to specific performance actions. The consideration paid by the plaintiff must bear a reasonable relationship to the value realized by the plaintiff from the defendant's reciprocal performance.

Assume that plaintiff-buyer agrees to purchase property from defendant-seller. Plaintiff promises to pay, and defendant agrees to accept, $100 for the property. The property has, in fact, a fair market value of $500, a difference of 1:5. Some courts treat this difference as precluding specific enforcement because, notwithstanding the contract, it is unfair to order a defendant to perform when he will receive only, as consideration, 20% of what his performance is objectively worth based on the property's fair market value.[4]

How extreme a difference is necessary to generate a finding of inadequacy cannot be reduced to a mathematical formula. First, this is an area committed to the trial judge's discretion and discretion necessarily envisions variation in result.[5] Second, mere inadequacy will not in many jurisdictions suffice to render specific performance unfair unless inadequacy is coupled with additional inequitable conduct. In other words, merely entering into a bad bargain or unwise transaction does not automatically render specific performance of that bargain unfair. For example, in *Kuntz v. Kuntz* the court ordered specific performance of an agreement to convey an uncle's farmland and other farm assets to the uncle's nephew notwithstanding that the price was below market.[6] The court, nonetheless, enforced the bargain finding that it was the bargain the parties intended and was not the product of undue influence. Third, when inadequacy of consideration alone is deemed sufficient to preclude specific performance, courts often require that the inadequacy be extreme or that it shock the

---

[2] Lundgren v. Gray, 671 N.E.2d 967, 970–71 (Mass. App. 1996) (affirming the trial court's rejection of a request for specific performance by an ex-husband against his ex-wife based on the trial court's findings that the ex-husband had created a situation of Byzantine complexity to take advantage of his ex-wife); Double AA Corp. v. Newland & Co., 905 P.2d 138, 141–42 (Mont. 1995) (declining to award specific performance even though the consideration was fair because the seller was pressured to act, was the victim of erroneous information and bad advice, and, generally, was unsophisticated in business matters).

[3] Section 63.2 (Unconscionability).

[4] Miller v. Coffeen, 280 S.W.2d 100, 103 (Mo. 1955) (denying specific enforcement of the contract for the sale of a residence having a fair market value of $11,000 to $12,000 for a consideration of $2,400).

[5] Linderkamp v. Hoffman, 562 N.W.2d 734, 735 (N.D. 1997); Chatterton v. Luger, 158 P.2d 809, 816 (Idaho 1945); Section 23 (Equitable Discretion).

[6] 595 N.W.2d 292, 297 (N.D. 1999).

conscience of the court.[7] Again, like the proverbial Chancellor's Foot, different courts are "shocked" at different thresholds.[8]

The concern over equivalency between consideration given by the plaintiff and value received from the defendant is tempered by several factors. First, equivalency is determined as of the date of the agreement. As noted in *Robert Lawrence Associates, Inc. v. Delvechhio*:

> [E]quity, in deciding whether to grant specific performance in enforcing a contract, will consider the fairness of an agreement in accordance with the circumstances as they existed at the time of the execution of the contract even though the property contracted to be sold becomes considerably more valuable at the time performance is due. Specific performance of a contract will not be refused because there has been an increase in the value of the property contracted for between the date of the contract and the time when execution is demanded where (1) the parties anticipated such an increase . . . and . . . (2) the contract at the time it was made was a reasonable and fair one.[9]

Second, some flexibility will be allowed when the consideration provided is not easily and objectively determinable. In *Henderson v. Fisher* the plaintiffs agreed to care for an 86 year old person for his lifetime in exchange for the transfer of property to plaintiffs upon the person's death. The person died shortly after the plaintiffs commenced performance. Plaintiffs sought specific performance of the agreement against the decedent's estate. In addressing the claim that the consideration provided was inadequate, given the short period of actual performance, the court rejected the idea that a rigid comparison based on "actual value conferred" should be the test:

> [T]he proper test to apply in determining adequacy of consideration in a contract involving the transfer of property is not whether the promisor received the highest price obtainable for his property, but whether the price he received is fair and reasonable under the circumstances. Moreover, in addition to the value of the property to be conveyed, the court may consider such factors as the relationship of the parties, their friendship, love, affection, and regard for each other, and the object to be obtained by the contract.[10]

---

[7] *Id.*:

> The evidence shows George Kuntz intended to sell his farm assets for less than full market value and give a "good deal" to his nephews, so they could "make it." In light of his evident purpose, there is no evidence the parties' agreement was not, as to George Kuntz, "just and reasonable," as required for specific performance.

(citations omitted). *See generally* Annotation, *Right to Specific Performance as Dependent Upon Fairness of Contract or Adequacy of Consideration Therefor*, 65 A.L.R. 7, 86 (1930).

[8] Annot., *Right to Specific Performance, supra* at 91; 71 Am. Jur. 2d *Specific Performance* § 78.

[9] 420 A.2d 1142, 1151 (Conn. 1979) (citations omitted).

[10] 46 Cal. Rptr. 173, 178 (Cal. App. 1965) (citations omitted).

The court stated that at the time the contract was entered into the decedent was in good health, had a life expectancy of some duration beyond that actually experienced, and had a warm and longstanding relationship with the plaintiffs; therefore, there was adequate consideration to support the specific performance action.[11]

§ 175 FLEXIBILITY

Specific performance will not be ordered when the performance sought would be impossible, tortious, or criminal.[1] The court may, however, not deem itself as being strictly bound by the terms of the contract. Equitable relief may be provided so as to meet the needs of justice as dictated by the circumstances of the case.[2] When property, subject to a contract of sale, is condemned by a public agency, thus precluding performance by the seller, the court may order that the condemnation proceeds be paid to the buyer.[3] Similarly, a court may grant partial specific performance even though partial specific performance is not provided for by the contract. For example, the seller may agree to convey a tract of land, but it turns out that the tract is subject to a valid claim as to a portion of the tract by a third person. In such cases, the court may order the conveyance of the unimpaired portion of the tract with an abatement of the purchase price.[4]

§ 176 ABATEMENT

The defendant's inability to comply fully with its contractual obligations does not necessarily negate specific performance. The court may adjust the consideration to reflect the diminished value the plaintiff will receive if the defendant is able to only partially perform his contractual undertaking. For example, assume defendant contracts to sell to plaintiff a 100 acre tract of land but breaches and sells 5 acres of the tract to a third party "bona fide purchaser for value." Should the plaintiff be denied specific performance entirely because the defendant cannot perform completely? Similarly, if defendant agrees to sell the same 100 acre tract, but prior to the close of escrow the parties discover that the tract actually contains only 88 acres, should this mistake deprive either party of the remedy of specific performance? A response to these types of problems is to allow specific performance, but with an abatement of the purchase price (consideration) to reflect the defendant's limited ability to perform.

---

[11] *Id.*

[1] Rogers v. Davis, 34 Cal. Rptr. 2d 716, 720 (Cal. App. 1994); Section 172 (Ability to Perform).

[2] *Rogers, supra,* 34 Cal. Rptr. 2d at 720, *citing,* Restatement of Contracts § 359, cmts. c, d; Section 23 (Equitable Discretion).

[3] *Rogers, supra,* 34 Cal. Rptr. 2d at 721 (noting that "as the equitable owners of the property at the time of the foreclosure sale, plaintiffs would be entitled, in equity, to the sale proceeds under the doctrine of equitable conversion") (citations and footnote omitted).

[4] Wilcox v. Wyandotte World-Wide, Inc., 493 P.2d 251, 256 (Kan. 1972); Section 176 (Abatement).

A party who cannot completely perform his contractual commitments may be required to perform to the extent he can.[1] In this context, the disappointed non-breaching party may affirm the contract and seek specific performance of what the breaching party is able to do; alternatively, the non-breaching party may sue for damages or rescission. As noted in *Botticello v. Stefanavicz*:

> The rule we have applied under similar circumstances is that "the vendee, if he so elects, is not only entitled to have the contract specifically performed to the extent of the vendor's ability to comply therewith by requiring him to give the best title he can or convey what he has, but he may compel the vendor to convey his defective title or deficient estate, and at the same time have a just abatement out of the purchase price for the deficiency of title, quantity, or quality of the estate to compensate for the vendor's failure to perform the contract in full . . . .[2]

The right to claim specific performance with an abatement is not, however, unlimited. The discrepancy between what was promised and what can be provided may be so great as to cause the court to believe that it would be enforcing either (1) a totally different contract from that actually entered into by the parties or (2) a contract the breaching party would not have entered into had the true facts been known at the time of contract formation.[3] For example, assume the plaintiff agrees to buy a tract of unimproved real property that both plaintiff-buyer and defendant-seller believe to be 10 acres in size. The purchase price is $100,000 and the property is encumbered by a mortgage of $90,000. It turns out that the property contains only 8 acres and the plaintiff seeks specific performance with an abatement of the purchase price to $80,000 to reflect the quantity discrepancy. If the court ordered specific performance in this context, the defendant would be required to pay the $10,000 difference to clear the encumbrance to convey good title to the plaintiff. Transforming the contract from a sale $10,000 over existing encumbrances to one $10,000 below existing encumbrances could be deemed the substitution of an agreement the defendant would not have entered into for the agreement the defendant did accept. Such a radical transformation of the bargain may be perceived by the court

---

[1] Firebaugh v. Hanback, 443 S.E.2d 134, 137 (Va. 1994); D-K Investment Corp. v. Sutter, 96 Cal. Rptr. 830, 836 (Cal. App. 1971).

[2] 411 A.2d 16, 22 (Conn. 1979) (citations omitted).

[3] *Id.*:

> [T]he court may confine the vendee's relief to damages, where under the circumstances the granting of specific performance would be inequitable, particularly where the rights of third parties are concerned." Since no third parties are here involved, the form of relief to be accorded must take into account the plaintiff's preference as well as the court's own discretion, "depending upon the equities of the case and based on reason and sound judgment."

as unfair within the context of the court's discretion to provide an equitable remedy.[4]

How the abatement should be calculated is a matter committed to the court's discretion.[5] A critical factor is the nature of the discrepancy, for example, has the plaintiff lost something of significant importance, such as roadway access or mineral or water rights, as a result of the defendant's inability to perform completel? In the hypothetical sale of a 100 acre tract mentioned earlier, the ability to convey only 88 acres due to mistake over the actual size of the tract may not significantly reduce the value of the tract beyond the pro rata reduction in acreage. On the other hand, in the alternative scenario, the loss of 5 acres may significantly affect the value of the tract because of the location of the 5 acres within the tract.[6]

The reason for the discrepancy may be significant. Was the discrepancy innocent or the product of deliberate wrongdoing on the part of the defendant?[7] While the use of "fault" as a factor for determining remedy has been criticized in bargain setting,[8] the moral basis of equity jurisdiction provides a justification for the use of the concept when determining the terms and conditions for specific performance.[9]

The intent and objectives of the parties in entering into the agreement is a consideration. An example of this is the so-called "per-acre"/ "in gross" approach. This approach asks whether the objective of the parties in entering into a sale of real property was to acquire a specific number of acres, i.e., a definitive quantity of land, or whether the parties' objective was to transfer a tract of land? When the parties intend a sale of a definite quantity of acreage, courts apply the "per acre" rule. Under this approach, any discrepancy in the size of the actual conveyance, unless it is so great as to warrant the denial of specific performance, will be adjusted by a pro rata reduction in the purchase price. As noted in *Dixon v. Morse*:

> The rule is well settled that: 'Where a sale of land is by the acre
> or specific quantity, as where it is at so much an acre or foot, and

---

[4] Dlug v. Woolbridge, 538 P.2d 883, 885–86 (Colo. 1975) (limiting the plaintiff-buyer to the remedies of rescission or specific performance at contract price notwithstanding a substantial discrepancy in acreage the defendant-seller could convey because the consideration the seller would receive if the abatement was allowed would give the seller less than the actual value of the land the seller could convey). *But see* Simpson v. Johnson, 597 P.2d 600, 605 (Idaho 1979) (permitting recovery of damages notwithstanding a substantial discrepancy between the acreage promised and the amount of acreage actually conveyed).

[5] Chesapeake Builders, Inc. v. Lee, 492 S.E.2d 141, 145 (Va. 1997).

[6] Smith v. Hornkohl, 90 N.W.2d 347, 353 (Neb. 1958) (stating that specific performance with an abatement would be refused when it would produce inequity or would make a new contract between the parties); *cf.* Reigart v. Fisher, 131 A. 568, 571 (Md. 1925) (holding that specific performance will not be compelled when the discrepancy between what was promised and the actual performance is substantial).

[7] *Chesapeake Builders, Inc., supra*, 492 S.E.2d 146 (noting the absence of bad faith on the part of the defendant in failing to perform completely).

[8] Section 140 (General Principles Concerning Contract Remedies).

[9] Chapter 3 (General Principles Concerning Equitable Relief).

it is evident that the quantity, or number of acres, specified is of the essence of the contract, the purchaser is entitled to an abatement of the purchase price for a deficiency in the quantity represented to be sold. . . . And whether the vendor knowingly misrepresented the number of acres is immaterial.[10]

Thus, if 100 acres are promised, but only 88 acres are delivered, the plaintiff would pay 88% of the agreed purchase price.

When the parties intend a sale in gross, the courts are reluctant to permit any abatement when the discrepancy is small and the plaintiff has received essentially what he contracted for—the tract.[11] When, however, the discrepancy is significant, an abatement will be allowed by some jurisdictions;[12] however, in this context, the countervailing consideration of unfairness in requiring the defendant to perform a substantially different contract must be considered.[13]

Whether a sale is "per acre" or "in gross" depends primarily upon the intention of the parties.[14] This intention is derived from a number of factors including: (1) the negotiations of the parties; (2) the method by which the purchase price is stated;[15] (3) the manner of describing the property;[16] and, (4) the language of the contract.[17]

§ 177 DAMAGES

The issue of damages will arise in specific performance actions in two ways. First, if the court denies specific performance (the equitable remedy),

---

[10] 463 P.2d 284, 285 (Idaho 1969) (citations and quotation marks omitted). The court's reference to "immateriality" is with respect to the remedy of specific performance with an abatement, not to the availability of a fraud damages action. Chapter 14 (Remedies for Fraud and Misrepresentation).

[11] Barnosky v. Petteys, 373 N.Y.S.2d 674, 676 (App. Dept. 1975) (rejecting abatement for 29 acre discrepancy). *See generally* C.T. Drechsler, Annot., *Relief by Way of Rescission or Adjustment of Purchase Price For Mutual Mistake as to Quantity of Land, Where the Sale is in Gross*, 1 A.L.R.2d 9 (1948).

[12] Flygare v. Brundage, 302 P.2d 759, 764 (Wyo. 1956) (permitting abatement notwithstanding finding that sale was "in gross" when seller innocently misrepresented that property conveyed contained 13 acres when, in fact, it only contained 7.93 acres).

[13] *See* text and notes 3–4, *supra*. *See generally* Annotation, *Measure and Elements of Damages Recoverable From Vendor Where There Has Been Mistake as to Amount of Land Conveyed*, 94 A.L.R.3d 1091 (1980) (collecting decisions).

[14] Ewing v. Bissell, 777 P.2d 1320, 1323 (Nev. 1989).

[15] For example, was the price stated as a lump sum or as a price per acre? *Dixon, supra,* 463 P.2d at 287. When the lump sum price is a multiple of the number of acres conveyed, the sale may be deemed as being "per acre." *Id.*

[16] *Id.* at 286:

It has been held that where the land conveyed is described by metes and bounds or government survey, and the deed or contract also contains a specification of the number of acres, the legal description controls over the stated acreage, the acreage becoming merely descriptive.

(citations omitted).

[17] *Ewing, supra,* 777 P.2d at 1323.

does the court have the power to award damages for breach of contract (the legal remedy)? Second, if the court grants specific performance, may the court also award compensation to redress the consequences of the defendant's non-performance of its contractual obligations? A variant of this second alternative is when the defendant is ordered to specifically perform but refuses to comply. In such situations, damages may be all the plaintiff can obtain, particularly if the court is unwilling to use coercive contempt remedies to secure compliance with the order to specifically perform.

The first situation raises an issue of equity power that is addressed in Section 20 (The Historical Relationship Between Law and Equity). There it is noted that the modern approach is to permit the court to award damages as long as equitable jurisdiction was invoked in good faith by the plaintiff.[1]

The second situation involves awarding of compensation incidental to the granting of specific performance and is well recognized in equity. The issue is not of power but of discretion or measurement. When there is a delay in the completion of the parties' obligations under the contract because of the need to secure an order of specific performance, the objective of the court should be to place the parties in the position they would have been had performance been accomplished as contemplated under the contract. For example, when the seller fails to timely convey or transfer property to the buyer, the buyer has lost the benefit of possession and ownership during the period of delayed performance and the seller has lost the use and enjoyment of the purchase price. Although courts occasionally describe the award as one of damages, it may be more accurate in some contexts to describe the remedy as involving an accounting.[2] The non-performing seller may have maintained the subject matter of the contract during the period of delay and were the seller's contributions ignored, the buyer would be unjustly enriched. The form of recovery largely parallels that provided when the court grants rescission.[3] The general principles applicable were cogently stated in *D-K Investment Corp. v. Sutter*:

> Under this rule a purchaser should be treated as the owner of the property from the date of performance fixed by the contract; is entitled to the rents and profits from the property thereafter; but is required to pay the purchase price as of that date which would entail the loss of the use of the purchase funds during the period performance is delayed. On the other hand, a seller is entitled to use of the purchase funds from the date of completion fixed by the contract, which would amount to interest on the purchase price from that date for the period performance was delayed; but is not entitled to the rents and profits received during that period; and is chargeable with the rents and profits received less taxes and other authorized expenses. Where, as in the case at bench, the seller is

---

[1] Section 20.2 (Right of Jury Trial).

[2] Bissonnette v. Hanton City Realty Corp., 529 A.2d 139, 143 (R.I. 1987).

[3] Section 134 (Restoration of Status Quo).

in default, he is entitled to interest on the purchase funds only to the extent it is an offset against rents and profits from the property during the period of delayed performance. Also, where, as in the case at bench, the buyer has retained use of the purchase funds from the date of completion fixed by the contract, he is not entitled to the rents and profits during that period except as the amount of the latter exceeds the amount of the interest on the purchase funds withheld. In any event, as noted, the rents and profits with which the seller is chargeable are the net rents and profits.[4]

In this context, it can be confusing to use the term "damages" because the objective of the court is to place the parties in the position they would have been in had the contract been performed and adjust the relationship to prevent unjust enrichment rather than compensate the plaintiff for a harm caused by the defendant's wrongdoing.[5]

In other contexts, however, the award is one for damages. For example, if the defendant promises clear title but a structure on the premises encroaches onto adjoining property, the cost of acquiring title to the encroached land is recoverable as an award of compensatory damages.[6]

The interplay between abatement and damages can have interesting remedial implications. Assume the parties contracted to sell 20 acres but the defendant cannot convey 5 of the acres having sold them to a BFP. The purchase price is $100,000. Plaintiff acquires the 5 acres from the BFP for $40,000. Under the abatement approach, plaintiff would pay defendant $75,000 (15/20 × $100,000) for the interest defendant could convey. After acquiring the missing 5 acres, plaintiff's total cost of acquisition for the property would be $115,000 ($75,000 + $45,000), or $15,000 over the contract price. Using a damages approach, plaintiff's acquisition costs for the missing 5 acres would be set off against the purchase price; thus, plaintiff would pay $100,000 for the 20 acres ($60,000 to defendant ($100,000 − $40,000) and $40,000 to the third party).[7] Alternatively, the cost of

---

[4] 96 Cal. Rptr. 830, 837; (Cal. App. 1971); *see* Smith v. McKee, 859 P.2d 1061, 1064 (N. Mex. 1993) (rejecting the seller's claim for interest on the purchase price in connection with the buyer's successful specific performance action because an award of interest would reward the seller's wrongdoing). Not awarding interest results in the buyers' enrichment to the extent they retain the use of funds that would have been transferred to the seller but for the seller's breach. Section 44.4 ([Unjust Enrichment] Recovery by Party in Breach of Contract).

[5] BD Inns v. Pooley, 266 Cal. Rptr. 815, 820 (Cal. App. 1990).

[6] Campbell v. Karb, 740 P.2d 750, 752–53 (Or. 1987) (stating that the cost of acquiring outstanding title is the measure of damages for the breach of the seller's covenant against encumbrances).

[7] Gonzales v. Garcia, 552 P.2d 468, 470 (N. Mex. 1976):

Based upon plaintiffs' purchasers' complaint two remedies with attendant measures of damages are available to them. First, since purchasers utilized the theory of breach of the covenant of seisin of the executed contract, and since purchasers eventually acquired title to the deficient land from the actual titleholder, the measure of damages in this case generally is the purchase price for the outstanding title, provided it was reasonable in amount and did not exceed the consideration paid by the purchaser to the vendor-in-deficiency, plus reasonable expenses to obtain the

acquiring the missing 5 acres could be placed on the defendant.[8]

Damages is the proper classification when the defendant's breach has caused the plaintiff to lose a prospective benefit, such as a resale, or to incur a cost, such as remediating a deficiency the seller represented not to exist.[9] The fact that the plaintiff commences the action in equity does not reduce, however, her evidentiary obligations regarding proof of damages.[10]

---

title to the deficient acreage. If, as here, the third party who has actual title conveyed that title to the purchaser before that purchaser brought the action for breach of the covenant of seisin against the vendor-in-deficiency, the measure of damages has been held to be the amount expended to acquire that title.

(citations and footnote omitted).

[8] *Cf.* Friede v. Pool, 14 N.W.2d 454, 459 (Minn. 1944) (rejecting the seller's action for specific performance with abatement to reflect the inability of the seller to perform completely because the "omitted" acreage had strategic locational significance). In *Friede* the seller was unable to convey clear title because of a claim of adverse possession to a small disputed strip of property. The seller sought an abatement of the price based on the percentage relationship between the 1.8 acres to the total conveyance (160 acres). The court held that this would unfairly shift to the buyer the risk that he could clear the adverse claim for the amount of the abatement. The court held that the risk belonged to the seller and denied specific performance with abatement unless the seller could convey clear title to the entire 160 acres.

[9] Stoll v. Grimm, 681 N.E.2d 749, 758 (Ind. App. 1997) (finding that the trial court properly abated the purchase price by the amount it cost the buyers to bring the property into conformity with the sellers representations). *But see* Arnold v. Leahy Home Bldg. Co., Inc., 420 N.E.2d 699, 705–06 (Ill. App. 1981) (rejecting abatement of the purchase price for the cost of repairing defective construction and stating that the court would not recognize under Illinois law the recovery of special damages incidental to the award of equitable relief (specific performance)).

[10] Pirchio v. Noecker, 82 N.E.2d 838, 840 (Ind. 1948) (limiting recovery of damages incidental to an award of specific performance to those within the Rule of *Hadley v. Baxendale*, i.e., within the reasonable contemplation of the defendant at the time of contract formation). *But cf.* Reis v. Sparks, 547 F.2d 236, 239 (4th Cir. 1976) (stating that the Rule of *Hadley v. Baxendale* is limited to actions for damages at law and does not apply to actions in equity). To the extent the recovery is based on principles of restitution rather than damages, as appeared to be the case in *Reis*, the position is defensible. Care should be exercised, however, before extending the statement generally. The general tendency appears to moot the issue by finding that the item was within the parties' reasonable contemplation. Bevan v. J.H. Constr. Co., Inc., 669 P.2d 442, 444 (Utah 1983); Section 166.1 ([Buyer's Remedies] Damages).

Chapter 21

AGREED REMEDIES

§ 180 INTRODUCTION

The topic of "Agreed Remedies" is very broad in American law. The initial tendency is to view the topic as involving only "liquidated damages," but that is unduly restrictive. "Agreed Remedies" includes all consensual efforts to control court determined remedies. Arbitration provisions,[1] waiver of jury trial,[2] forum selection clauses,[3] etc., are forms of "Agreed Remedies,"

---

[1] *E.g.*, Circuit City Stores, Inc. v. Adams, 532 U.S. 105 (2001) (holding that Federal Arbitration Act applied to employment contracts, except those of transportation workers); *see* Charles L. Knapp, *Taking Contract Private: The Quiet Revolution in Contract Law*, 71 Fordham L. Rev. 761 (2002) (discussing growth of arbitration and change in judicial attitude towards predispute, contractual arbitration from hostility to, at times, enthusiastic embrace).

[2] *See generally* Jay M. Zitter, Annot., *Contractual Jury Trial Waivers in State Court Cases*, 42 A.L.R.5th 53 (1996); Debra T. Landis, Annot., *Contractual Jury Trial Waivers in Federal Civil Cases*, 92 A.L.R. Fed. 688 (1989). Both annotations note the general tendency to uphold the waiver, absent evidence that to do so would be inequitable, *e.g.*, the waiver is unconscionable, was procured by duress, etc. *But cf.* Grafton Partners L.P. v. Superior Court, 116 P.3d 479 (Cal. 2005) (holding that predispute waiver of jury trial was invalid because statute authorizing waiver, Cal. Civ. Code § 631, did not include predispute waiver).

[3] *In re* Automated Collection Technologies, Inc., 156 S.W.3d 557 (Tex. 2004) (enforcing forum

although they address the scope of available remedies indirectly rather than directly. The focus here, however, is on provisions that attempt to effect directly the remedy available for breach of contract. The emphasis is on remedies; the materials do not address contractual efforts to control a legal standard of care, as, for example, through the use of an exculpatory, indemnity, or hold harmless agreement.[4]

§ 181 LIQUIDATED DAMAGES

[181.1] Damages or Penalty

A true liquidated damages provision is distinguishable from a penalty clause. Courts haves consistently refused to enforce penalties designed to coerce performance of a contractual obligation.[1] This reflects the law's general willingness to tolerate breaches of contract as long as the non-breaching party is made whole. Admittedly, the tolerance is not complete. In some cases, the court will order specific performance of the contract rather than allow a party to breach and pay damages.[2] A few jurisdictions permit punitive damages for malicious breach of contract.[3] Penalty clauses, on the other hand, require a party to incur greater costs not to breach than the costs that breach imposes on the other party to the contract.[4] Penalty

---

selection clause requiring litigation to be conducted in Pennsylvania; the complaint was brought by a Pennsylvania corporation against a Texas corporation; the Texas corporation didn't want to litigate in Texas; the Texas Supreme Court agreed). *See generally* Francis M. Dougherty, Annot., *Validity of Contractual Provisions Limiting Place or Court in Which Action May be Brought*, 31 A.L.R.4th 404 (1984) (stating that courts are increasingly willing to enforce forum selection clauses—a change from the past).

[4] The provisions are usually upheld unless they propose to exempt a party from his intentional, deliberate misconduct or the provision violates the public interest. What constitutes the state's "public interest" may be difficult to determine. *Compare* Tunkl v. Regents of the Univ. of Cal., 383 P.2d 441, 445–46 (Cal. 1963) (setting forth six factor test to determine whether activity subject to exculpatory clause qualified as within the public interest), *with* Wolf v. Ford, 644 A.3d 522, 526–27 (Md. Sp. Ct. App. 1994) (rejecting *Tunkl* factors approach and adopting test based on the totality of the circumstances in a particular case evaluated against the backdrop of current societal expectations). In Westlye v. Look Sports, Inc., 22 Cal. Rptr. 2d 781, 795–800 (Cal. App. 1993), the plaintiff sought damages which he claimed resulted from improperly adjusted ski bindings. The court held that an exculpatory clause in the rental agreement applied to the negligence claims; however, as to the strict liability claims, state public policy existed to protect consumers from defective products. Consequently, the exculpatory clause was unenforceable as to the strict liability claims. In *Wolf v. Ford, supra*, the court upheld and exculpatory clause that exonerated a broker and his firm for investor losses, absent a showing that the losses were caused by the broker's (or firm) gross negligence or intentional misconduct).

[1] Hoag v. McGinnis, 22 Wend. Rep. 163, 166 (N.Y. 1839) (stating that to permit parties, in their unbridled discretion, to use penalties as damages "would lead to the most terrible oppression in pecuniary dealings").

[2] Chapter 20 (Specific Performance) (particularly Section 170 ([Specific Performance] Introduction).

[3] Section 202.5 ([Punitive Damages] Breach of Contract).

[4] Scavenger Sale Investors, L.P. v. Bryant, 288 F.3d 309, 311 (7th Cir. 2002) (Easterbrook,

clauses impose these greater costs regardless of the value of the perfor-mance, the ability of a damages award to make the injured party whole, or the reason for the breach. From this viewpoint, penalty clauses may be seen as encouraging conduct that is economically wasteful and abetting conduct that the law either wishes to discourage or discourage conduct the law wishes to encourage.[5] A liquidated damages provision, on the other hand, is simply an agreed method of computing damages if a party breaches and fails to provide the promised performance. In effect, it is a pre-breach stipulation between the parties to accept the agreed sum in lieu of court determined damages. Alternatively, it may be seen as an optional form of performance: a party may exchange the promised performance with the stipulated sum.

At common law, the test for distinguishing between an enforceable liquidated damages provision and an unenforceable penalty clause was threefold: (1) did the parties intend the provision to be a penalty or an alternative measure of damages on breach (the "intent" element); (2) was it difficult at the time of contract formation to determine the amount of damages that would reasonably and probably flow from a breach (the "uncertainty" requirement); and, (3) did the damages specified bear a reasonable relationship to the damages anticipated (the "ballparking" requirement). Some decisions today still assert the threefold test,[6] but many jurisdictions articulate a two-part test, using the "uncertainty" and "ball-parking" components and dropping an express reference to the "intent" element.[7] Some courts characterize the issue of the parties' intent as irrelevant.[8] The latter approach is consistent with the objective theory of contract. If the liquidated damages provision satisfies the "uncertainty" and "ballparking" requirements, the fact that one or both of the parties harbored a subjective intent that the provision punish a breach, or deter a breach by its penal aspects, is irrelevant.[9] If the parties understood the provision

---

J.) ("In contract law a 'penalty' is a payment that exceeds a reasonable estimate of the loss from the breach"), *citing* E. ALLAN FARNSWORTH, FARNSWORTH ON CONTRACTS § 12.18 (2d ed. 1998).

[5] *Compare* Diosdado v. Diosdado, 118 Cal. Rptr. 2d 494 (Cal. App. 2002) (holding that an agreement that imposed liquidated damages, including an amount to compensate for emotional distress, for a spouse's infidelity during the marriage, constituted a penalty on a errant spouse for breaching the promise of sexual fidelity and was contrary to the public policy underlying no-fault divorce), *with* Konzelman v. Konzelman, 729 A.2d 7 (N.J. Super. Ct. A.D. 1999) (holding that provision in divorce property settlement agreement terminating spousal support if ex-spouse cohabited with another was enforceable and not violative of state public policy as an infringement of the court's equity power over matrimonial matters).

[6] Habif, Arogeti & Wynne, P.C. v. Baggett, 498 S.E.2d 346, 356 (Ga. App. 1998); Walker v. Graham, 706 P.2d 278, 281 (Wyo. 1985).

[7] Space Master Int'l, Inc., v. City of Worcester, 940 F.2d 16, 17–18 (1st Cir. 1991); Truck Rent-A-Center, Inc. v. Puritan Farms 2nd, Inc., 361 N.E.2d 1015, 1018 (N.Y. 1977); Restate-ment (Second) of Contracts § 356(1), cmt. b (1979).

[8] *In re* Graham Square, Inc., 126 F.3d 823, 829 (6th Cir. 1997).

[9] Samson Sales, Inc. v. Honeywell, Inc., 465 N.E.2d 392, 392 (Ohio 1984) (syllabus).

to act as a penalty to secure performance, it is unlikely that the "uncertainty" and "ballparking" requirement would be met.[10]

At common law, the presumption was that a stipulated damages provision was a penalty rather than an alternative, agreed to method for calculating compensatory damages.[11] Today, it is fair to say that, to the extent a presumption exists, it is just the reverse. The general rule is that liquidated damages provisions are valid and enforceable;[12] consequently, the burden rests on the party challenging the provision to demonstrate that the provision is unenforceable as a penalty.[13]

An exception to this modern approach lies with consumer contracts where vestiges of the old approach remain.[14]

The essential feature of any argument that a liquidated damages provision is enforceable is reasonableness. Reasonableness is often measured in terms of proportionality between the agreed remedy and the harm avoided.

---

[10] Circle B. Enterps., Inc. v. Steinke, 584 N.W.2d 97, 101 (N.D. 1998) (noting that characterization of the provision by the parties as a penalty was not conclusive); Weber, Lipshie & Co. v. Christian, 60 Cal. Rptr. 2d 677, 682 (Cal. App. 1997) (noting that the parties' subjective intent that a provision be intended as a penalty was not controlling; the validity of the provision as an agreed remedy is determined by the language of the agreement and the circumstances surrounding its execution).

[11] Aristides N. Hatzis, *Having the Cake and Eating it Too: Efficient Penalty Clauses in Common and Civil Contract Law*, 22 Int'l Rev. Law & Econ. 381 (2002):

> Common law was not always reluctant to enforce penalty clauses and forfeitures stipulated by the contracting parties. Until at least the late 17th century and the development of a rule by the Court of Chancery which enjoined them as unconscionable, penal bonds were readily enforced by Common law courts. Penal bonds were sealed instruments designed to secure performance by embodying a promise to pay a stipulated sum of money (usually twice the value of the contract itself) in case of breach, regardless of the actual damages caused by the breach. Another common practice from the law of mortgages was the forfeiture of the property by the mortgagee if the borrower failed to pay off the loan and interest on the due date, even though it could have been worth much more than the amount due. This Equity rule was adopted by courts of law and led to the enacting of statutes in both England and the United States forbidding the enforcement of penalty clauses.

Id. at 384 (citation and footnotes omitted); *see* XCO Intern. Inc. v. Pacific Scientific Co., 369 F.3d 998, 1001–03 (7th Cir. 2004) (Posner, J.) (discussing treatment of liquidated damages provisions by common law).

[12] Kahuna Group, Inc. v. Scarano Boat Bldg., Inc., 984 F. Supp. 109, 117 (N.D.N.Y. 1997) (stating that "a court should not interfere with the agreement of the parties, absent some persuasive justification").

[13] *Id. But cf.* Rattigan v. Commodore Int'l, Ltd.; 739 F. Supp. 167, 169–70 (S.D.N.Y. 1990) (stating that in doubtful cases the judicial tendency is to characterize an agreed remedy provision as a penalty rather than a liquidated damages clause, but further noting that the burden of establishing that the provision is a penalty rests on the breaching party); Lake River Corp. v. Carborundum Co., 769 F.2d 1284, 1289 (7th Cir. 1985) (stating that Illinois courts resolve doubtful agreed remedies provisions as penalties rather than as liquidated damages).

[14] *See* Cal. Civ. Code § 1671(c) (excepting certain consumer contracts from the general rule, § 1671(b), that the burden is on the breaching party to establish that the consensual remedy is invalid).

For example, in *Ridgley v. Topa Thrift & Loan Ass'n* the court addressed a provision that required payment of 6 months interest if a loan was paid prior to maturity, but waived the fee if the loan was in force for 6 months before payment of the loan principal *unless the borrower had made a late interest payment or otherwise defaulted.* [15] The court held that the highlighted portion of the provision constituted a penalty because it was disproportional to any damages the lender was likely to realize as a result of a late payment or default. The fact that the lender could have insisted on a prepayment penalty clause but agreed to the less restrictive limitation, at the request of the borrower, was deemed irrelevant. [16] On the other hand, an early termination clause requiring a lessor to pay the depreciated value of the leased goods, i.e., the difference between the realized and residual value of the leased automobile, was enforced in *Baez v. Banc One Leasing Corp.* [17] If the lease was fully performed, the lessor would have recaptured all of the depreciation in the lease payments; however, depreciation is usually greater at the beginning of the lease than at the end. Because leased payments are level, this creates an imbalance if the lessee terminates the lease early, which was the case in *Baez*. The liquidated damages provision protected the lessor by allowing it to recapture all of the depreciation up to the time the lessee relinquished possession of the vehicle.

One critical fact in *Ridgley*, as contrasted with *Baez*, was that in form and substance the *Ridgley* prepayment penalty was "imposed as a penalty for the [debtor's] default in being tardy with one or more monthly interest payments and not to compensate [the lender] for its lost future interest payments or extra administrative expenses attendant to re-lending this money." [18] In *Baez* there was no breach; the lender conditioned the debtor's ability to exercise the early termination clause by requiring that accrued, but unpaid, depreciation be paid. [19] Also illustrative of this point is *Lake Ridge Academy v. Carney* in which the defendant-parents entered into a contract requiring them to pay the full year's tuition under the school reservation agreement, which also gave parents the option to cancel the contract before a specific date without incurring liability. The parents failed to give notice to the school by that certain date that their child would not be attending the school. The court enforced the full tuition provision finding that the timing of the notice was tied to the likelihood the seat would go "empty" for the school year and the school would lose revenue it might have been able to cover had timely notice been provided by the parents. [20]

---

[15] 953 P.2d 484, 488–89 (Cal. 1998).

[16] *Id.* at 486.

[17] 348 F.3d 972, 974 (11th Cir. 2003) (applying federal and Georgia law), *aff'g* Torres v. Banc One Leasing Corp., 226 F. Supp. 2d 1345 (N.D. Ga. 2002).

[18] *Ridgley v. Topa Thrift & Loan, supra*, 953 P.2d at 484; Raffel v. Medallion Kitchens of Minn., Inc., 139 F.3d 1142, 1146 (7th Cir. 1998) (finding that a provision that caused seven months of abated rent to become due and payable if the tenant failed to make timely rent payments was disproportionate to any harm caused by the breach and was therefore a penalty).

[19] Section 181.2 (Penalty or Condition).

[20] 613 N.E.2d 183, 187–88 (Ohio 1993).

The concern that the amount of agreed damages may be disproportionate to the potential loss is largely based on the fear that performance secured by a disproportionate sanction will encourage conduct that is socially and economically unproductive. As noted in *Truck Rent-A-Center*:

> A promisor would be compelled, out of fear of economic devastation, to continue performance and his promisee, in the event of default, would reap a windfall well above actual harm sustained.[21]

The concerns voiced in *Truck Rent-A-Center* have been critiqued, most notably perhaps in Judge Posner's opinion in *Lake River Corp. v. Carborundum Co.* when he argued that over-deterrence is a matter best left to the parties themselves because they are in the best position to weigh the gains and losses from breach.[22] Nonetheless, Judge Posner concluded that traditional analysis should prevail:

> On this view the refusal to enforce penalty clauses is (at best) paternalistic—and it seems odd that courts should display parental solicitude for large corporations. But however this may be, we must be on guard to avoid importing our own ideas of sound public policy into an area where our proper judicial role is more than usually deferential. The responsibility for making innovations in the common law of Illinois rests with the courts of Illinois, and not with the federal courts in Illinois. And like every other state, Illinois, untroubled by academic skepticism of the wisdom of refusing to enforce penalty clauses against sophisticated promisors, continues steadfastly to insist on the distinction between penalties and liquidated damages.[23]

Courts usually reject an absolute "sophisticated party" exception to liquidated damages analysis.[24] On the other hand, the fact that *both* parties to the agreement are sophisticated, are represented by counsel, and there is evidence that the liquidated damages provision was specially negotiated has been noted by several courts in upholding very severe liquidated damages provisions.[25]

---

[21] 361 N.E.2d at 1018.

[22] 769 F.2d 1284, at 1288–89 (7th Cir. 1985).

[23] *Id.* at 1289 (citation omitted).

[24] *Id.*; *see In re* Trans World Airlines, Inc., 145 F.3d 124, 135 (3d Cir. 1998).

[25] Uzan v. 845 WN Unlimited Partnership, 778 N.Y.S.2d 171, 173 (App. Dept. 2004) (upholding contract provision that allowed owner (Donald Trump) to retain 25% deposit ($8 million) on contract to purchase four units in a luxury apartment building (for $32 million) after the buyers backed out of the deal); Metlife Capital Fin. Corp. v. Washington Ave. Assoc. L.P., 732 A.2d 493, 496 (N.J. 1999) (stating that liquidated damages provision negotiated by "sophisticated" parties was entitled to presumption of reasonableness); Gordonsville Energy, L.P. v. Virginia Electric and Power Co., 512 S.E. 811, 818 (Va. 1999) (stating that liquidated damages provision negotiated by sophisticated parties represented by counsel was a valid waiver of their right to object to liquidated damages provision as a penalty clause).

[181.2] Penalty or Condition

A liquidated damages clause may be difficult to distinguish from a failure of consideration or condition. Proper characterization is not always easy. In *Prince William Professional Baseball Club v. Boulton* the contract provided for a $650,000 payment conditioned on Boulton's adherence to a post-employment non-competition agreement. Boulton breached and his former employer refused to pay the $650,000. Boulton contended that the provision was a penalty masquerading as a liquidated damages clause because the sanction for breach ($650,000) was disproportionate to any damages actually sustained. The court disagreed. It held that the provision was an important aspect of the contract for the employer and that its breach excused the employer's duty to pay the $650,000.[26] The issue arises with some frequency in the context of post-employment non-competition clauses; however, most courts address and resolve the question as one involving "reasonable" post-employment restraints rather than an enforceable liquidated damages provision.[27] This situation may be contrasted with the approach in *Ridgley v. Topa Thrift and Loan* when the loss of benefits due to a late payment (breach) was deemed a penalty rather than a reasonable restriction on the availability of the benefit as in *Baez v. Banc One Leasing Corp.* Both decisions are discussed in Section 181.1 (Damages or Penalty).

The characterization of an acceleration clause as a penalty was before the court in *Justine Realty Co. v. American National Can Co.*[28] An acceleration clause sets the amount of damages due at the time of default on an installment obligation. The court held that while an acceleration clause that simply made all future installments immediately due and payable upon a material breach or default would be a penalty, that situation was not before the court. An acceleration clause that includes a rebate of the interest inherent in the installments, i.e., simply requires immediate payment of the principal sum plus accrued interest, would not be penalty.[29]

Part of the difficulty in distinguishing liquidated damages provisions from other contract forms, such as conditions, may be in the way we identify and define the problem. For example, consider two ways to promote timely performance of a remodeling contract. Owner promises contractor $100 if the work is done on time, but a $10 offset if it is not. Alternatively, owner promises contractor $90 with a $10 bonus if the work is done on time. The difference is one of form, not substance, but it is much more likely that the first description will be deemed a penalty than the second description of the bargain.[30] There is also a framing heuristic between gains (bonuses)

---

[26] 882 F. Supp. 1446, 1453 (D. Del 1995). The opinion was subsequently withdrawn apparently because the parties settled the dispute. 910 F. Supp. 143 (D. Del. 1995).

[27] Tatom v. Ameritech Corp., 305 F.3d 737, 744–45 (7th Cir. 2002) (applying Illinois law). Section 154 (Employer's Injunction Against Employee), text and notes 15-17.

[28] 976 F.2d 385 (8th Cir. 1992) (applying Illinois law). •

[29] *Id.* at 389.

[30] *See generally* Annotation, *Contractual Provision for Per Diem Payments For Delay in Performance as One for Liquidated Damages or Penalty*, 12 A.L.R. 4th 891 (1982).

versus losses (penalties) that tends to bias decisionmaking in favor of the former (gains) over the latter (penalties or losses). [31]

Whether a provision is a valid liquidated damages provision or a penalty is a question of law for the court, not the trier-of-fact. [32]

An agreed damages amount that fails to reflect any calibration with the foreseeable types and kinds of breaches is at greater risk of being characterized as a penalty. For example, a provision providing that the maker of a check would pay double if the check bounced is usually seen as a penalty. The amount of the check bears only an indirect connection with the damages a payee might realize if the check is returned for non-sufficient funds or other irregularity. [33]

A liquidated damages clause may be enforceable in some situations even though the amount of damages is ascertainable to some degree; thus, the "uncertainty" requirement is unsatisfied. For example, a construction contract may provide for liquidated damages equal to fines that would be imposed by a public entity if the project is not completed on time. If a subcontractor's breach causes the contractor to incur the fines, the clause is enforceable even though the amount of the fines is predetermined by statute or regulation. [34] In these contexts it might be more accurate to characterize the provision as an indemnity or hold harmless provision, but the use of liquidated damages terminology is common.

When a liquidated damages provision is declared to be unenforceable as a penalty, the general view is to permit the non-breaching party to recover her actual damages. [35]

Liquidated damages provisions must be expressly contracted for by the parties; courts will not infer such arrangements from the parties' relationship. [36]

---

[31] Jeffrey J. Rachlinski, *The "New" Law and Psychology: A Reply to Critics, Skeptics, and Cautious Supporters*, 85 Cornell L. Rev. 739, 754 (2000) (discussing liquidated penalties and bonuses and the judicial reaction to them).

[32] Daniel Int'l Corp. v. Fischbach & Moore, Inc., 916 F.2d 1061, 1050 (5th Cir. 1990); Vernitron Corp. v. CF 48 Assocs., 478 N.Y.S.2d 933, 934 (App. Dept. 1984).

[33] Lawyer's Title Ins. Corp. v. Dearborn Title Corp., 939 F. Supp. 611, 616–17 (N.D. Ill. 1996) (noting that the maker "would have to wait an extremely long time to replace a bounced check before [the payee] would be entitled to interest of 100%. The court further noted that when "the [damages] estimate greatly exceeds a reasonable upper estimate of what the damages are likely to be, it is a penalty") (citation omitted), *vacated on other grounds*, 118 F.3d 1148 (7th Cir. 1997).

[34] Taos Constr. Co. v. Penzel Constr. Co., 750 S.W.2d 522, 526–27 (Mo. App. 1988). The court noted that "it is proper for a prime contractor to 'pass on' to a subcontractor liquidated damages caused by a subcontractor." *Id.* at 527.

[35] *See* Kingston Contractors v. WMATA, 930 F. Supp. 651, 656 (D.D.C. 1996); Hackett v. JRL Dev., Inc., 566 So. 2d 601, 603 (Fla. App. 1990); Shapiro v. Grinspoon, 541 N.E.2d 359, 366 (Mass. App. 1989).

[36] *See* Lafarge Corp. v. Wolff, Inc., 977 S.W.2d 181, 188 (Tex. Civ. App. 1998).

A party enjoying the benefit of a valid, enforceable liquidated damages clause is usually held to be under no duty to mitigate.[37] On the other hand, the absence of a duty to mitigate may encourage courts to read liquidated damages provisions severely to find them unreasonable.[38] If that occurs, the obligation to mitigate damages, as a limitation on the recovery of actual damages, will come into play.[39]

[181.3] Timing of Decision

Jurisdiction differ whether the reasonableness analysis is based only on what was known at the time of contract formation or includes what is known at the time of breach. The basic "uncertainty" and "ballparking" requirements focus on what the parties knew at the time of contract formation.[40] Under this view, if the liquidated damages provision was reasonable when entered into, it would not become unreasonable by the mere passage of time or the effect of time on the nature of the consequences of breach, e.g., damages turn out, in fact, to be easily determinable at the time of breach. This may be characterized as the "single look" rule.[41] On the other hand, a number of jurisdictions employ a "double look" test. These latter jurisdictions reject a pure "time of contract formation" perspective and subject the liquidated damages provision to a further and additional requirement that the liquidated damages amount not be disproportionate to the amount of damage actually sustained.[42] This requirement is distinct from, but often confused with, the issue whether the non-breaching party must sustain an actual loss to invoke the liquidated damages provision.[43]

---

[37] *Lake Ridge Academy*, *supra*, 613 N.E.2d at 190 (reasoning that if a party's damages are uncertain in amount and difficult to prove the same infirmity must affect the party's ability to mitigate); Koenings v. Joseph Schlitz Brewing Co., 377 N.W.2d 593, 601 (Wis. 1985). *But see* Browning-Ferris Indus. of Neb., Inc. v. Eating Establishment-90th & Fort, Inc., 575 N.W.2d 885, 890 (Neb. App. 1998) (stating that "a contracting party [cannot] negate a general duty to mitigate damages by merely inserting a liquidated damages provision in a contract").

[38] AFLAC, Inc. v. Williams, 444 S.E.2d 314, 317 (Ga. 1994) (noting that required payment, as liquidated damages, which failed to take into account non-breaching party's duty to mitigate, evidenced that provision was a penalty rather than a legitimate effort to estimate damages arising from a breach). If this approach is adopted, then the non-breaching party should not be required to mitigate post-breach, as suggested in the *Browning-Ferris Indus. of Neb.* decision cited in note 37 as that would amount to double counting of the mitigation requirement, which was already factored into the liquidated damages sum.

[39] Section 13 (Duty to Mitigate Damages).

[40] Section 181.1 (Damages or Penalty) (text and notes 6–10, discussing "uncertainty" and "ballparking" concepts).

[41] JKC Holding Co., LLC. v. Washington Sport Ventures, 264 F.3d 459, 468 (4th 2001); (applying New York law); United States v. Ponnapula, 246 F.3d F.3d 576, 584 (6th Cir. 2001); (applying Tennessee law); *cf.* Honey Dew Associates, Inc. v. M & K Food Corp., 241 F.3d 23, 28 n.3 (1st Cir. 2001) (applying Massachusetts law).

[42] Wallace Real Estate Inv., Inc. v. Groves, 881 P.2d 1010, 1017 (Wash. 1994); *see* Kelly v. Marx, 694 N.E.2d 869, 872–74 (Mass. App.) (containing an Appendix collecting "single look" and "double look" jurisdictions), *rev'd*, 705 N.E.2d 1114 (Mass. 1999) (adopting "single look" approach).

[43] Section 182 (Liquidated Damages: Compensable Damage Requirement) (discussing the two concepts).

§ 182 LIQUIDATED DAMAGES: COMPENSABLE DAMAGE REQUIREMENT

Jurisdictions have divided on whether the breach must inflict a loss on the non-breaching party in order to permit enforcement of a liquidated damages provision. One view denies recovery of liquidated damages when there is no compensable damages.[1] The other view holds that the situation existing at the time of contract formation controls. If the liquidated damages provision was valid then; it does not become invalid because the parties' reasonable assumptions are not borne out in fact.[2] This latter view is supported by the argument that requiring compensable damage at the time of breach ignores the reality that legally awardable damages may be undercompensatory in fact and not reflect the uncompensated transaction costs that the non-breaching party may sustain.[3]

There is oftentimes some confusion between the question whether actual injury is required and the question as to the appropriate point(s) in time when the issues of "uncertainty" and "ballparking," (which constitute the reasonableness requirement), should be made.[4] A jurisdiction that requires actual injury may or may not require that the determination of uncertainty and reasonableness be made at the time of contract formation rather than, or in addition to, at the time of breach. For example, the Restatement (Second) of Contracts takes the view that liquidated damages are available if the specified amount is reasonable and difficult to determine at the time of contract formation (the time the loss is anticipated) or at the time of breach (the time of actual loss).[5] The Uniform Commercial Code expresses a similar view.[6] The judicial preference appears to favor the time of contract formation approach.[7]

A jurisdiction that does not require actual loss at time of breach as a condition to enforcement of a liquidated damages clause may, nonetheless, consider the amount of damage sustained to determine if the liquidated damages provision is excessive.[8] Such a jurisdiction is a "double look" jurisdiction as discussed in Section 181.3 (Timing of Decision).

---

[1] Colonial at Lynnfield, Inc. v. Sloan, 870 F.2d 761, 765 (1st Cir. 1989) (refusing to enforce liquidated damages provision when no loss was sustained as a result of the breach); see 301 Dahlgren Ltd. Partnership v. Bd. of Supervisors of King George County, 396 S.E.2d 651, 653 (Va. 1990).

[2] Kelly v. Marx, 705 N.E.2d 1114, 1117 (Mass. 1999); Mechanical Air Eng'g Co. v. Totem Constr. Co., 801 P.2d 426, 428 (Ariz. App. 1989); see 24 RICHARD A. LORD, WILLISTON ON CONTRACTS §§ 65:15, 65:17 (4th ed. 2002) (stating that time of contract formation rule is majority rule).

[3] Wallace Real Estate Inv., Inc. v. Groves, 881, 881 P.2d 1010, 1016–17 (Wash. 1994).

[4] Section 181.1 (Damages or Penalty) (defining terms).

[5] Restatement (Second) of Contracts § 356(1) (1981).

[6] U.C.C. § 2-718(1).

[7] See Gregory Scott Crespi, *Measuring "Actual Harm" For the Purpose of Determining the Enforceability of Liquidated Damages Clauses*, 41 Houston L. Rev. 1579, 1580–87 (2005).

[8] *Wallace Real Estate Inv. Inc., supra,* 881 P.2d at 1017.

§ 183   LIQUIDATED DAMAGES AS EXCLUSIVE OR NON-EXCLUSIVE REMEDY

A liquidated damages clause may by its terms provide that it is the exclusive remedy for breach or that it is non-exclusive and supplemental, i.e., the non-breaching party may forego the benefits of the clause and seek to recover its actual damages. When an election is permitted, the decision will rest pragmatically, for the non-breaching party, on which damages measure will be greater.

The liquidated damages clause is often silent as to whether it is exclusive or non-exclusive.[1] Jurisdictions have split as to the effect of silence on the right of the non-breaching party to elect to claim actual damages or recover under the liquidated damages provision. One view holds that the valid stipulation of damages in a contract is a pre-breach arrangement that is binding on the non-breaching party post-breach.[2] A second approach treats the liquidated damages provision as subservient to other interests the law deems paramount when there is a breach. For example, in *Bafile v. Borough of Muncy* the court permitted the non-breaching seller to claim the liquidated damages amount, which the seller held as a down payment, as an offset against the actual damages incurred as a result of the buyer's breach of a contract for the purchase of real property. The court stated that limiting the seller to the amount specified in the contract as liquidated damages would operate as a disincentive for the seller to mitigate his damages.[3] In this context, the liquidated damages provision acts more as security for the judgment than as a consensual allocation of the costs of breach. If actual damages are less than the liquidated damages amount, under this approach the defaulting buyer should receive the difference, otherwise the seller would be unjustly enriched. A third approach permits recovery of both actual damages and liquidated damages when the two are not duplicatory.[4]

The problem with the approaches is that the exclusivity issue cannot be resolved in isolation. Treating the liquidated damages remedy as non-exclusive raises difficult issues going to the very justification of liquidated damages as an alternative method of performance or agreement as to damages.[5] Sometimes the interconnectivity of the analysis is acknowledged; most often it is ignored.

The matter of exclusivity is also addressed in the Uniform Commercial Code, but with no greater clarification. Section 2-719 of the Code provides that the parties to a contract for the sale of goods have relative freedom to specify whether contract remedies are exclusive or supplemental, subject

---

[1] McDonagh v. Moss, 565 N.E.2d 159, 160–61 (Ill. App. 1990).

[2] Domestic Linen Supply & Laundry Co. v. Kenwood Dealer Group, Inc., 672 N.E.2d 184, 190 (Ohio App. 1996).

[3] 588 A.2d 462, 463–64 (Pa. 1991).

[4] Construction Contracting & Mgmt., Inc. v. McConnell, 815 P.2d 1161, 1167–68 (N. Mex. 1991) (characterizing liquidated damages as "delay" damages and recognizing that award of liquidated sum and non-delay actual damages would be proper).

[5] Section 181.1 (Damages or Penalty).

to certain exceptions, including Section 2-718, which sets forth the UCC's position on liquidated damages. Thus, the question arises whether the parties must *expressly* state in the contract that the liquidated damages provision is the exclusive remedy for it to be so? In *Northern Illinois Gas Co. v. Energy Cooperative, Inc.* the court took the position that Section 2-719 did not control because that section dealt with a "limitation on a remedy," such as an exclusion of consequential damages, whereas a liquidated damages provision was "an agreed upon formula for calculating the amount of money damages owed."[6] Professor Laycock questions whether the distinction drawn in *Northern Illinois* is sound: "A clause that eliminates 96 percent that is overcompensatory, of the damages is a pretty effective limitation of remedies, isn't it?[7] Professor Laycock's insight is one way of seeing the case. It treats liquidated damages provisions that are undercompensatory as limitations of remedies, but a liquidated damages provision that is overcompensatory, relative to actual loss, would not, by definition be a "limitation" on a remedy; it would be an "expansion" on a remedy. As such, the undercompensatory provision would be subject to Section 2-719, but the overcompensatory provision would not be. Whether the UCC envisions this distinction cannot be determined from the text or history of the provision.

The traditional approach, which rests largely on custom and practice, treats all liquidated damages provisions as distinct from limitations on a remedy. Liquidated damages attempt to provide by contract an amount that is "plain on its face";[8] whereas a limitation on a remedy is more abstract and categorical, such as the waiver of consequential damages. Of course, this approach does not fully address the reference to Section 2-718 in Section 2-719. If liquidated damages are truly different in kind from limitations on a remedy, the "subject to" language in Section 2-719 is difficult to understand. On the other hand, the "subject to" language of Section 2-719 can be seen as preserving otherwise available remedies in the event the liquidated damages provision is deemed unenforceable. This approach preserves the distinction between liquidated damages and limitations on a remedy while preventing the "subject to" language from being wholly ignored. It is also consistent with the approach outlined in the Official Comment to Section 2-719, although the specific issue discussed here is not addressed in the comment. At present, the matter remains a puzzle, with courts finding the liquidated damages clause that is silent on the subjects to be either exclusive or non-exclusive on a case-by-case basis, with no consensus yet achieved.

---

[6] 461 N.E.2d 1049, (Ill. App. 1984). On the waiver of consequential damages, see Section 186 (Negating Remedies by Contract).

[7] Douglas Laycock, Modern American Remedies 90 (3d ed. 2002). *Northern Illinois* is discussed in Section 184 (Liquidated Damages as Overcompensatory or Undercompensatory) at text and notes 7–8.

[8] Oxford English Dictionary 1012 (2d ed. 1991) (stating that the older, 18th century, usage of the meaning of term "liquidate" is "[t]o make clear or plain (something obscure or confused); to render unambiguous; to settle "differences, disputes").

In some cases, the express reservation of the right to sue for actual damages, when coupled with a liquidated damages clause in the same agreement, has been held to evidence that the liquidated damages clause was intended as a penalty rather than as a substitute for performance.[9] Under this approach expressly providing that the liquidated damages provision is supplemental raises the chances it will be deemed a penalty. The rationale is that at the time of breach, the non-breaching party would seek to recover on the liquidated damages clause whenever it provided a greater recovery than an actual damages recovery. The rationale may be seen as incomplete because it fails to distinguish between damage and damages. A plaintiff will rationally elect the liquidated damages clause when it provides a greater, and perhaps less expensive, recovery than the expected recovery of damages for actual injury. Recoverable compensatory damages may not equal actual damage for reasons applicable to the law of remedies, as, for example, because of legal constraint, such as the rule of *Hadley v. Baxendale*,[10] or the inability of the non-breaching party to carry its factual burden of proof as to consequential damages.[11] Moreover, transaction costs in the form of litigation expenses are likely greater for actual loss proofs than for liquidated damages proofs. The presence of a reservation of the right to seek actual damages is not compelling evidence that a companion liquidated damages clause is a penalty. On the other hand, under the "substitute performance" or "stipulated damages" approach, treating the liquidated damages provision as "supplemental" undermines the justification for enforcing the provision in the first place.[12] If the breaching party has the "right" to exercise an option and substitute the liquidated damages recovery for its performance, allowing the non-breaching party to claim actual damages is inconsistent with that "right."

Exclusivity versus non-exclusivity questions can also arise with the issue of injunctive relief. A number of courts have permitted both liquidated damages and injunctive relief. The underlying rationale is that the court sees the liquidated damages clause as "security" for performance rather than as an alternative form of performance. For example, in *Kohrs v. Barth* the seller sought specific performance of a real estate contract; the buyer contended that the liquidated damages clause was the exclusive remedy for breach; thus, specific performance was barred. The court rejected, on the facts, the exclusivity argument:

> In the instant case, the contract is not alternative in its nature (specific performance of the contract could not be enforced because, by the contract as construed by the court, either party had the option to pay a penalty instead of complying with the other terms of the contract). It does not give to the buyer the option to do the act or to pay a certain sum but, instead, calls for a certain act to

[9] Lefemine v. Baron, 573 So. 2d 326, 328–30 (Fla. 1991).

[10] Sections 10.2.2 ([Loss Causation—Contract] Policy Considerations).

[11] Section 8 (Measuring Compensatory Damages).

[12] Section 181.1 (Damages or Penalty).

be done with a sum annexed as damages to secure performance of the act. Hence, the provision for liquidated damages does not prevent specific performance.[13]

Similarly, an employer may seek specific performance of a contractual noncomplete provision in addition to, or in lieu of, liquidated damages.[14] As noted in *Washel v. Bryant*:

> The parties' agreement contemplates an injunctive remedy when it states, in pertinent part: "Should this [noncompetition] provision be enforced against [Bryant] in any proceeding, the parties to this Agreement agree that no bond shall be posted by [Washel] in order to obtain an injunction order." The liquidated damages clause then provides: "The parties agree that because damages for any violation of Provisions 6 and 7 of this Agreement may be difficult to prove, the parties stipulate that any violation of Provision 6 or 7 shall subject the breaching party to liquidated damages of $5,000 for each violation."
>
> The trial court's findings take an either-or approach with respect to legal and equitable relief. That is, the findings suggest that the court must choose between the two remedies as if they were mutually exclusive. The court concluded in its finding twenty-one that "to grant a permanent injunction would deprive both Washel and Bryant of the benefit of their negotiated bargain" for the liquidated damages clause, a legal remedy. We cannot agree. Rather, to disallow injunctive relief would deprive Washel of the benefit of Bryant's covenant not to compete. Nowhere does the agreement state or imply that liquidated damages shall be the exclusive remedy.[15]

The argument that providing for injunctive relief is not inconsistent with also providing for liquidated damages is aided by the fact that injunctive relief may not fully restore the plaintiff to its rightful position. An injunction that prevents future injury may not redress already committed acts that have caused present injury. The plaintiff may recover in damages for that present injury.[16] Given that, use of a liquidated damages clause to

---

[13] 570 N.E.2d 1273, 1276 (Ill. App. 1991) (citations omitted); Duckwall v. Rees, 86 N.E.2d 460, 462 (Ind. App. 1949).

[14] *In re* Udell, 18 F.3d 403, 408 (7th Cir. 1994); Sections 153 (Employer's Damages Remedies Against Employee), 154 (Employer's Injunction Against Employee). In this situation, however, there is a greater chance that the cost of breach to the breaching party will be treated as a loss due to failure of a condition rather than a penalty for breach. Section 181.2 (Penalty or Condition).

[15] 770 N.E.2d 902, 905–06 (Ind. App. 2002) (citations to record omitted). *Washel* appears to rely on the "intent" theory that has generally been abandoned. Section 181.1 ([Specific Performance] Damages or Penalty). In *Lemat Corp. v. Barry*, 80 Cal. Rptr. 240 (Cal. App. 1969), the court refused to award damages and injunctive relief to an employer against its employee who had breached a contract in order to play for a rival professional team. Section 153 (Employer's Damages Against Employee) (text and notes 10–14, discussing *Lemat Corp. v. Barry*).

[16] Section 177 (Damages).

stipulate those damages would not amount to double or inconsistent recovery against the defendant.

§ 184   LIQUIDATED DAMAGES AS OVERCOMPENSATORY OR UNDERCOMPENSATORY

Whether a liquidated damages clause overcompensates or undercompensates an actual injury sustained on breach of a contract should not directly determine the validity of the liquidated damages provision. Overcompensation or undercompensation does, however, affect the types of arguments that may be directed towards enforcement or non-enforcement of the liquidated damages provision.

When the liquidated damages clause overcompensates, relative to actual injury, the claim will be made by the breaching party that the clause provides excessive compensation in the nature of a penalty rather than as substituted performance. For example, in *Truck-Rent-A-Center v. Puritan Farms 2nd, Inc.* a milk delivery truck lease required the lessee (Puritan), on breach of its commitments, to pay one-half of all rentals that would have been due had the agreement run its full course. This amount of liquidated damages was $92,341.79. The amount of actual injury sustained as a result of the breach of the lease by Puritan was, however, only $48,134.17.[1] Notwithstanding this imbalance, the court enforced the clause on the ground that it provided a reasonable estimate, at the time of contract formation, of the damage that the lessor would sustain if the lessee breached.[2] Because the liquidated damages clause is often seen here as providing greater compensation than necessary to make the plaintiff whole,[3] this is the most common setting for the argument that the clause acts as a penalty to coerce performance.[4]

When the liquidated damages clause undercompensates, relative to actual injury, the non-breaching party will seek to recover its actual losses and the defendant-breaching party will contend that the plaintiff is limited to the exclusive remedy of the liquidated damages clause.[5] In *H.S. Perlin Co. v. Morse Signal Devices* the court upheld a damages clause in a burglary

---

[1] 361 N.E.2d 1015, 1019 (N.Y. 1977). This resulted because Puritan could have exercised an option permitting it to terminate the lease by paying the $48,134.17; hence, the lessor's actual injury could not rise higher than the "buy-out" amount. *Id.* at 1016.

[2] *Id.*, at 1017.

[3] Section 181 (Liquidated Damages).

[4] Telenois, Inc. v. Village of Schaumburg, 628 N.E.2d 581 (Ill. App. 1993) (holding that a $100,000 deposit required of a cable company to ensure that it performed fully its contractual obligations to install cable within the municipality was an unreasonably large liquidated damages clause that acted as a penalty). Defendant admitted that it required the deposit to ensure that the plaintiff's past history of poor performance would not be repeated. *Id.* at 585 (holding that clause fixing damages merely as "security" for performance is a penalty under Illinois law).

[5] Section 183 (Liquidated Damages as Exclusive or Non-exclusive Remedy).

alarm lease that limited the lessee's recovery to $250 in case of breach even though actual losses were allegedly $958,000.[6] Perhaps the classic case in this area, at least in terms of the differential between liquidated and actual damages, is *Northern Illinois Gas Company v. Energy Cooperative, Inc.*[7] Northern agreed to buy 56 million barrels of naphtha from Energy over a 10 year period. Northern used the naphtha to produce natural gas. When the United States ended price controls on natural gas (after the contract was entered into), Northern found it was much cheaper to buy gas than produce it from naphtha. Northern breached. Energy claimed actual damages of approximately $330 million. Northern invoked the liquidated damages clause which would limit Energy's damages to approximately $13 million. The jury awarded actual damages of $305.5 million. The court held the clause was valid and the exclusive remedy on Northern's breach and rejected Energy's argument that the clause was optional because it was not labeled as the exclusive remedy in the contract.[8] As a result, Energy's judgment was reduced to $13 million, a reduction of approximately $290 million!

§ 185 SPECIFYING INJUNCTIVE RELIEF BY CONTRACT

Traditionally, courts have resisted efforts by the parties to control the exercise of equitable jurisdiction. The primary concern has been that the court should reserve the right to preserve its jurisdiction and authority and to limit the exercise of its power, particularly injunctive relief, to those situations that the court believes are consistent with the public interest. As noted by one court:

> We do not wish to express the view that an agreement for the issuance of an injunction, if and when a stipulated state of facts arises in the future, is binding on the court to that extent. Such an agreement would serve to oust the inherent jurisdiction of the court to determine whether an injunction is appropriate when applied for and to require its issuance even though to do so would be contrary to the opinion of the court.[1]

---

[6] 258 Cal. Rptr. 1 (Cal. App. 1989). As suggested in *H.S. Perlin,* and discussed in Section 186 (Negating Remedies by Contract), undercompensatory damages clauses are frequently drafted as limited remedies rather than as liquidated damages clauses. Mahoney v. Tingley, 529 P.2d 1068 (Wash. 1975) (holding that when stipulated sum limits the injured party's loss there is no penalty, though the result may be undercompensatory). The result was the clause was enforced even though lower courts had held that damages were reasonably capable of ascertainment. Here again we see some uncertainty as to differences between "liquidated damages" and "limitation of remedy" provisions. Section 183 (Liquidated Damages As Exclusive or Non-Exclusive Remedy), text and notes 6-8.

[7] 461 N.E.2d 1049 (Ill. App. 1984).

[8] *Id.* at 1056. *See generally* Debora Threedy, *Liquidated and Limited Damages and the Revision of Article 2: An Opportunity to Rethink the U.C.C.'s Treatment of Agreed Remedies,* 27 Idaho L. Rev. 427 (1990-91) (discussing the U.C.C.'s treatment of agreed remedies that are overcompensatory or undercompensatory relative to actual damages).

[1] Stokes v. Moore, 77 So. 2d 331, 335 (Ala. 1955); *see* Ed Bertholet & Assocs., Inc. v. Stefanko, 690 N.E.2d 361, 363–64 (Ind. App. 1998); Section 24 (Burden on Court/Supervision).

A few courts have recognized that the parties may contractually provide for injunctive relief for breach of contract,[2] but there is also contrary authority.[3] It is customary for parties to stipulate to the granting or extension of injunctive relief once litigation has commenced. There would appear to be no a priori reason why the stipulation for injunctive relief could not be made ex ante rather than ex post, as long as the court was otherwise satisfied that the contractual terms were enforceable, e.g., not the product of duress, unfairness, etc. The court could also refuse to enter a stipulated order that exceeded the court's jurisdiction or presented special problems of supervision, but these concerns would be present in any case seeking injunctive relief and should not affect the core issue of the parties' ability to stipulate to the prima facie case.

Some recent cases exhibit a greater willingness to allow equitable remedies, particularly specific performance, to be the subject of the pre-dispute consensual allocation. As noted in *Marco & Co., L.L.C. v. Deacon-ess/Billings Clinic Health System*:

> The language of this provision of the vendor agreement is clear and unambiguous. In their most ordinary and popular sense, the words of this provision provide the non-breaching party with an election of remedies. If the non-breaching party elects an equitable remedy, it would include a temporary restraining order or injunction, and specific performance. Marco's and Deaconess's predecessors in interest mutually agreed to these terms when they entered into this contract. We conclude that there exists no public policy, misinterpretation, or bad faith that would prevent the enforcement of the clear terms of this contract.[4]

An interesting application of this principle occurred in *Leet v. Totah*.[5] The court upheld a limited remedy clause[6] that confined the non-breaching party to either the return of his down payment or specific performance. The court noted that specific performance was an appropriate agreed remedy given the complexity of the transaction; moreover, the transaction's numerous contingencies made the calculation of damages for breach difficult.[7] The court did not address nor suggest difficulty in ordering specific performance insofar as the transaction's complexity and contingencies were concerned.

How far the courts will take this development is unclear. The issue arises most frequency when a specific contract remedy for equitable relief is

---

[2] Hockenberg Equip. Co. v. Hockenberg's Equip. & Supply Co. of Des Moines, Inc., 510 N.W.2d 153, 158 (Iowa 1993).

[3] Sonny's Pizza, Inc. v. Braley, 612 So. 2d 844, 846 (La App. 1992) (holding parties may not stipulate to injunctive relief because it would unfairly allow them to use summary rather than ordinary proceedings, thus expediting their own case at the expense of other litigants and would circumvent statutory language codifying the prima facie case for injunctive relief).

[4] 954 P.2d 1116, 1119 (Mont. 1998).

[5] 620 A.2d 1372 (Md. 1993) (involving purchase of real property).

[6] Section 186 (Negating Remedies by Contract).

[7] *Leet, supra.*

combined with an arbitration clause. The question arises whether the parties may specify that an inherent judicial power may be exercised by a non-judicial actor. On this point, the jurisdictions are divided and much depends on whether the dispute involves public or private matters.[8]

§ 186 NEGATING REMEDIES BY CONTRACT

It is helpful to distinguish between a contractual agreement, such as a "hold harmless," indemnity, or exculpatory contract or provision, that seeks to limit or avoid a party's liability for tortious conduct,[1] and a contractual provision that limits the liability of the breaching party to the non-breaching party for breach of contract, including breach of warranty.[2] This section addresses the latter type of provision.

Contract limitation of remedies provisions seek to prevent a non-breaching party from recovering all that the law would permit on proof of a breach. The provision may be phrased in the negative, such as by barring recovery of consequential damages or lost profits, or the provision may be phrased in the positive but as words of limitation, such as by limiting recovery to the return of the consideration or a specified sum. In the latter case, there is little that separates a limitation on remedy from a liquidated damages provision. The difference remains, however, that a liquidated damages provision is, at root, an effort to predict a plaintiff's actual damages should the defendant breach. A limited remedy, on the other hand, usually reflects a successful effort by the defendant to specify a recovery that is far less than the plaintiff's actual, potential damages arising from breach.

---

[8] Broughton v. Cigna Health Plans of California, 988 P.2d 67, 75–76 (Cal. 1999). In *Broughton* the party opposing arbitral authority noted that the arbitrator lacks the power "to modify or vacate its [injunctive] decree . . . ." *Id.* at 75; *see* Section 36 (Modification of Injunctions). The party supporting arbitral authority noted that the arbitrator's injunction could be modified or vacated by a court through the initiation of a new arbitral proceeding that a court could review. *Id.* at 76. The court avoided resolving the issue:

> We need not decide the broad question framed by the Court of Appeal and by plaintiffs as to whether an arbitrator may ever issue a permanent injunction. We conclude on narrower grounds that the injunction plaintiffs seek in the present case is indeed beyond the arbitrator's power to grant. The CLRA plaintiff in this case is functioning as a private attorney general, enjoining future deceptive practices on behalf of the general public. We hold that under such circumstances arbitration is not a suitable forum, and the Legislature did not intend this type of injunctive relief to be arbitrated.

Id. CLRA refers to Consumer Legal Remedies Act, Cal. Civ. Code § 1750 *et seq.*

[1] These agreements received a mixed reception from the courts. Perhaps the most accurate general statement is that these agreements, while not favored, are not automatically void as against public policy. K-Lines, Inc. v. Roberts Motor Co., 541 P.2d 1378, 1383 (Or. 1975); Section 180 ([Agreed Remedies] Introduction) (text and note 4).

[2] The distinction blurs when the breach of contract is also deemed to constitute an independent tort. Estey v. MacKenzie Eng'g, Inc., 927 P.2d 86, 89 (Or. 1996) (refusing to apply a contractual limitation on liability for breach of contract to a negligence action predicated on the same conduct that constituted the breach absent more specific draftsmanship by the contracting parties).

Contract limitation of remedies has been most extensively developed in the Uniform Commercial Code. The use of contractual limitations of remedies is, however, pervasive and not limited to the sale of goods.

[186.1] Contracts for the Sale of Goods

The Uniform Commercial Code (U.C.C.) provides two ways in which a seller may limit its liability to the disappointed buyer. First, the seller may disclaim implied but not express warranties.[3] In some jurisdictions, however, the disclaimer may extend to express warranties.[4] Second, the seller may seek to limit or exclude certain remedies. The distinction is important. A disclaimer limits the opportunity for the buyer to claim a breach. A limitation of remedies limits what the buyer may claim and recover for a breach.[5] Often disclaimers and limitations are packaged together as part of the seller's effort to reduce its exposure should the goods sold to the buyer not meet the buyer's expectations or the seller's representations. Notwithstanding the combining of disclaimers and limitations as a package, the emphasis here remains on contract limitation of remedies.

A typical limitation of remedies provides that the buyer's sole recourse is to return the goods to the seller for repair or replacement. Should the seller be unable to repair or replace, the buyer may then recover his consideration. Consequential damages may also be expressly excluded.[6]

Whether a limitation of remedy is enforceable is addressed under the U.C.C. by determining whether it has failed of its essential purpose, *i.e.*, whether the buyer has lost the substantial value of the bargain.[7] When this occurs is not easy to define. If the seller completely breaches, such as by failing to deliver goods altogether, a court will likely find that a limited repair remedy, such as an exclusive remedy of repair or replacement of goods, is not applicable because the implied condition is that the goods be delivered.[8] If goods are delivered, however, and they prove to be unsatisfactory and incapable of being made satisfactory, whether the buyer has been deprived of the substantial value of the bargain depends on the facts and the degree to which the product delivered deviates from the product promised by the contract.[9]

---

[3] U.C.C. § 2-316.

[4] *E.g.*, Hydra-Mac, Inc. v. Onan Corp., 450 N.W.2d 913, 916 (Minn. 1990) (*citing* Minn. Stat. § 336. 2-316 (1988)).

[5] JAMES WHITE & ROBERT SUMMERS, UNIFORM COMMERCIAL CODE § 12-11, at 669 (4th ed. 1995).

[6] U.C.C. § 2-719.

[7] UCC, § 2-719 cmt.1.

[8] Hawaiian Tel. Co. v. Microform Data Sys., Inc., 829 F.2d 919, 924–25 (9th Cir. 1987).

[9] Boston Helicopter Charter, Inc. v. Agusta Aviation Corp., 767 F. Supp. 363, 373–74 (D. Mass. 1991) (collecting decisions); *see* Jonathan Eddy, *On the "Essential" Purpose of Limited Remedies: The Metaphysics of U.C.C. Section 2-719(2)*, 65 Cal. L. Rev. 28 (1977). *See generally* 67 Am. Jur. 2d. *Sales* § 1247.

A related issue is whether the failure of the limited "repair or replace" remedy, because the remedy provided fails of its essential purpose, causes other limitations, such as the exclusion of consequential damages, to fail. The jurisdictions have split on the issue.[10] However, even if the jurisdiction treats the limited remedy and the exclusion of consequential damages as independent provisions, the failure of the limited remedy is relevant to the validity of the exclusion of consequential damages.[11] In *Ritchie Enterprises v. Honeywell Bull, Inc.* the court found that the failure of the seller to repair the goods would not cause the limited remedy to fail of its essential purpose if there were back-up remedies. As noted by the court:

> Although an occasional decision holds that return of the purchase price is a remedy that fails of its essential purpose if the consequential damages far exceed that amount, these cases misread Section 2-719(2) and confuse the concepts of unconscionability with failure of essential purpose. The better reasoned decisions hold that refund of the purchase price prevents a limited remedy from failing of its essential purpose . . . .

> A backup remedy providing the aggrieved buyer with a replacement unit free from defects should blunt the argument that the repair—or—replace remedy has failed of its essential purpose. Or to put the matter another way, the backup remedy does not fail of its essential purpose even though the front-line remedy does . . . .

> Of course the backup remedy may also fail of its essential purpose. For example, the seller may refuse to refund the purchase price after failure of the front-line repair-or-replacement remedy. Or the seller might conceal facts regarding the breach of warranty until such time that rescission by the buyer could not be pursued as a backup remedy because it would cause severe financial strain.[12]

In *S.M. Wilson & Co.* the court found that the limited repair remedy did not fail of its essential purpose to the extent necessary to nullify the exclusion of consequential damages when the seller tried conscientiously, but unsuccessfully, to repair the goods. The court noted that the parties

---

[10] *Compare* Chatlos Sys. Inc. v. National Cash Register Corp., 635 F.2d 1081, 1086 (3d Cir. 1980) (holding that the failure of the limited repair remedy of its essential purpose did not require negation of the independent exclusion of consequential damages), *and* S.M. Wilson & Co. v. Smith Int'l, Inc., 587 F.2d 1363, 1375 (9th Cir. 1978) (concluding that although the limited repair remedy failed of its essential purpose, the failure was not so total and fundamental as to require the exclusion of consequential damages to be expunged), *with* RRX Indus., Inc. v. Lab-Con, Inc., 772 F.2d 543, 546–47 (9th Cir. 1985) (finding that the "total and fundamental" failure of the limited repair warranty caused the consequential damages exclusion to be expunged).

[11] Kearney & Trecker Corp. v. Master Engraving Co., Inc., 527 A.2d 429, 435–36 (N.J. 1987) (noting that whether the failure of the limited remedy affects the exclusion of consequential damages "depends upon the specific circumstances and the probable intention[s] of the parties") (citations omitted).

[12] 730 F. Supp. 1041, 1049 (D. Kan. 1990) (applying Massachusetts law), *quoting* CLARK, THE LAW OF PRODUCT WARRANTIES ¶ 8.04[2](d) at 8-60–8-61.

were of equal bargaining power, the goods (tunnel boring machine) was a complex piece of equipment, and the buyer knowingly accepted the risk of loss.[13]

If the exclusion of consequential damages survives the failure of the limited remedy, the exclusion may still be nullified if its enforcement would be unconscionable.[14] It is not unconscionable to exclude consequential damages when there is a reasonable business reason to do so, as, for example, when the potential exposure would be great, relative to the value of the contract, or the amount of consequential damages is difficult to quantitify.[15] The impact of allowing consequential damages on the seller's pricing structure is a valid consideration,[16] as is the relative sophistication of the parties to the contract.[17] As noted by one court, unconscionability is a product of several factors, including:

> The good faith of the parties; the nature of the injuries suffered by the plaintiff; whether the plaintiff is a substantial business concern; the parties' relative sophistication; whether there is an element of surprise in the inclusion of the challenged clause; and the conspicuousness of the clause.[18]

An exclusion of "consequential" damages is valid to the extent the non-breaching party has suffered "consequential" damages. The exclusion, by its terms, will not preclude the award of general damages and in some cases the line between the two is fine. For example, in *Chatlos Sys. Inc. v. National Cash Register* the court enforced an exclusion of consequential damages provision in a case when a computer software system failed to work as represented. On remand, the buyer obtain a substantial recovery for lost benefit of the bargain based on the difference between the value of the program as represented and the value of the program actually received.[19] Similarly, in *Inacom Corp. v. Sears, Roebuck and Co.* defendant Sears breached its contract with Inasom by discontinuing the supply of a product Inacom needed to perform a contract it had with a third party. The court permitted Inacom to recover the added performance costs Inacom incurred on its third party contract, notwithstanding a consequential damages exclusion, on the ground that the added costs were recoverable mitigation expenses.[20]

---

[13] 587 F.2d at 1375.

[14] U.C.C. § 2-719(3).

[15] Canal Elec. Co. v. Westinghouse Elec. Co., 973 F.2d 988, 997–98 (1st Cir. 1992) (applying Massachussetts law).

[16] *Kearney & Trecker Corp., supra*, 527 A.2d at 437.

[17] *Richie Enterps., supra*, 730 F. Supp. at 1050.

[18] Damin Aviation Corp. v. Sikorsky Aircraft, A Div. of United Techs. Corp., 705 F. Supp. 170, 177 (S.D.N.Y.), *aff'd*, 880 F.2d 1318 (2d Cir. 1989).

[19] 670 F.2d 1304, 1305 (3d Cir. 1982); Section 8.2 (Excessiveness) (discussing *Chatlos Sys. Inc.*'s allowance of a general damages recovery).

[20] 254 F.3d 683, 691 (8th Cir. 2001); Section 13.7 (Compensation For Mitigation Efforts).

[186.2] Other Contracts

Contractual provisions restricting and reducing the non-breaching party's remedies are found in a wide array of contractual arrangements. Because the U.C.C.'s Article 2 is not applicable to transactions not involving a sale of goods, the approach of courts when considering limited remedies clauses in a context other than a sale of goods has tended to rely on notions of unconscionability. For example, in *Moler v. Melzer* a home buyer sought damages against a building inspector hired by the home buyer to inspect the residence to be purchased. The inspector allegedly failed to detect several structural deficiencies and the home buyer sued for the cost of repairing those deficiencies. The inspector successfully invoked a contractual provision limiting the inspector's liability to the cost of the inspection.[21] The court found that because the limitation was not illegal, violative of public policy, or induced by fraud it was enforceable. Moreover, because the terms were clear and unambiguous, entered into between parties of roughly equal bargaining and economic power, and not a product of monopoly, it was not unconscionable to enforce the limitation. The court noted:

> Here, the clause limiting Apex's liability was not hidden; it appears as the last of six short provisions, each of which is accompanied by a box to be checked by the client after he or she has read the provision. And just before the signature line, the client must check a box indicating he or she has read the foregoing provisions: "The client agrees to permit the inspector to perform the inspection of the property according to the terms listed above without change as read and understood."[22]

There is some decisional law holding that the limited remedy must be supported by a separate consideration to be enforceable.[23] Those decisions appear to be aberrational and likely reflect a judicial effort to extricate consumers from bad bargains.[24] There is no reason why a particular provision of a contract needs to be supported by a consideration separate from that given for the contract as a whole.[25]

The issue of the enforceability of limited remedy clauses has arisen frequently in the context of fire alarm and burglary alarm contracts. The standard contract usually limits recovery for breach, e.g., when the alarm

---

[21] 942 P.2d 643 (Kan. 1997). The provision provided: "In the case that the client should become dissatisfied with the inspection, it's [sic] findings, or future occurrences, the client will hold the inspector . . . liable for the cost of the inspection only." *Id.* at 644.

[22] *Id.* at 645.

[23] Schaffer v. Property Evaluations, Inc., 854 S.W.2d 493, 495 (Mo. App. 1993) (expunging a limited remedy in a home inspection contract entered into by the home buyer and an inspector that limited recovery to the cost of the inspection).

[24] *Moler, supra,* 942 P.2d at 645 (stating that *Schaffer, supra* note 23, "is leading a parade of one").

[25] Sasco, Inc. v. Wells Fargo Alarm Servs., Inc., 969 F. Supp. 535, 539 (E.D. Mo. 1997) (noting that "one item of consideration may support more than one promise") (citation omitted).

fails to function as promised or warranted, to a small sum on the order of $50–$100. The losses resulting from the breach are often enormous relative to the limited remedy. While these clauses are often referred to in the contracts as liquidated damages clauses, they are in fact limited remedies clauses as no real effort is made to calculate the plaintiff's actual, potential losses if the defendant breaches.[26]

Courts have split on the enforceability of a limited remedy clause in a fire alarm or burglary alarm contract, although the dominant view is to uphold the provision. The minority approach refuses to enforce the provision. In *Samson Sales, Inc. v. Honeywell, Inc.* the court characterized the limited remedy as a liquidated damages clause and, as so characterized, refused to enforce the provision as a penalty.[27] It is difficult to characterize an undercompensatory award (plaintiff claimed actual damages of $68,303) as a penalty. Usually the term "penalty" is reserved for liquidated damages clauses that provide an excessive recovery relative to actual loss. Nonetheless, the court was clearly troubled by the disparity between the amount provided by the contract and the amount of loss reasonably to be contemplated by a breach:

> [T]he stated sum of $50 in the contract involved in this case is manifestly disproportionate to either the consideration paid by Samson or the possible damage that reasonably could be foreseen from the failure of Honeywell to notify the police of the burglary. [I]t is beyond comprehension that the parties intended that damages in the amount of $50 should follow the negligent breach of the contract.[28]

Notwithstanding *Samson Sales, Inc.,* the great majority of courts have consistently upheld limited remedy provisions in fire alarm and burglary alarm contracts against claims that they are unconscionable or violative of public policy.[29] The reason for this position was stated in *Guthrie v. American Protection Industries*:

> Most persons, especially operators of business establishments, carry insurance for loss due to various types of crime. Presumptively

---

[26] Schrier v. Beltway Alarm Co., 533 A.2d 1316, 1321 (Md. App. 1987) (noting that when the purpose of the provision is to limit the party's liability to a specified amount rather than provide a sum certain for breach, the provision is a limitation on liability not a liquidated damages clause); Section 183 (Liquidated Damages as Exclusive or Non-exclusive Remedy), (text and notes 5–8, discussing *Northern Illinois Gas Co.*)

[27] 465 N.E.2d 392 (Ohio 1984). The clause provided: "In the event of loss . . . [c]ompany's liability . . . shall be limited to the sum of [$50] as liquidated damages . . . and this liability shall be exclusive." *Id.* at 393.

[28] *Id.* at 394 (citation omitted); *see* Mattegat v. Klopfenstein, 717 A.2d 276, 280 (Conn. App. 1998) (same).

[29] *Schrier, supra,* 533 A.2d at 1319 (collecting cases upholding clauses and noting only one dissenting decision—*Samson Sales, Inc.*); *see* North River Ins. Co. v. Jones, 655 N.E.2d 987, 992–93 (Ill. App. 1995) (involving a fire alarm contract). *See generally* Martin J. McMahon Annot., *Liability of Person Furnishing, Installing, or Servicing Burglary or Fire Alarm System For Burglary or Fire Loss,* 37 A.L.R.4th 47 (1985).

insurance companies who issue such policies base their premiums on their assessment of the value of the property and the vulnerability of the premises. No reasonable person could expect that the provider of an alarm service would, for a fee unrelated to the value of the property, undertake to provide an identical type of coverage should the alarm fail to prevent a crime.[30]

The limited remedy must be a product of a bargaining process, although the parties need not address specifically the issue of the limited remedy in their negotiations. A limited remedy or limited liability provision printed on the back of a parking ticket given a patron who parks her car at a garage does not become part of the bargain or bailment.[31] A similar approach has been applied to more complicated contracts containing limitations on remedy for breach. For example, in *Wallis v. Princess Cruises, Inc.* the court refused to apply a $60,000 limitation of recovery provision printed on the reverse side of a cruise ship ticket to a claim brought under the federal Death on the High Seas Act for a passenger who had fallen overboard and drown.[32] The court applied a "reasonable notice" test[33] and found that the limitation was insufficiently specific to reasonably inform a passenger that the limitation would apply to a wrongful death claim against the cruise line.[34] There is admittedly a fine line here between the decisions in this area, where courts have scrutinized limitation of remedy provisions and often found them wanting, and the fire and burglary alarm cases, home inspection cases, and lost film cases (discussed *infra*), where courts have been much more receptive to the provisions.

Limited remedy provisions have had general success in connection with lost film or photographs. In *Fotomat Corp. of Florida v. Chanda* the court upheld a limited remedy provision in a contract under which a film processor agreed to transfer deteriorating movie film to videotape. The nature of the movie film, whether personal or business related, was not disclosed in the opinion, although the suggestion in the opinion is that the film was personal. The film was lost by Fotomat. The court held that the limited remedy provision was not unconscionable as there was no showing

---

[30] 206 Cal. Rptr. 834, 836 (Cal. App. 1984). One may question the assumption of the court that an alarm company and an insurer are providing "an identical type of coverage." The insurer's exposure under a standard form contract is much greater than the alarm company's single exposure for breach. Insurers cover many risks; the alarm company covers but one.

[31] American Auto Ins. Co. v. Dayton Parking Co., 79 N.E.2d 687, 688 (Ohio App. 1947). *See generally* Annotation, *Liability For Loss of Automobile Left at Parking Lot or Garage*, 13 A.L.R.4th 362 § 2 (1981) (stating that the majority of courts have held disclaimers of liability and limited remedy provisions printed on parking tickets or posted on premises to be ineffective).

[32] 306 F.3d 827 (9th Cir. 2002).

[33] *Id.* at 835:

[T]he proper test of reasonable notice is an analysis of the overall circumstances on a case-by-case basis, with an examination not only of the ticket itself, but also of any extrinsic factors indicating the passenger's ability to become meaningfully informed of the contractual terms at stake.

[34] *Id.* at 836–37.

that the provision was commercially unreasonable given the cost of the services and the supplies to be provided.[35] The court noted:

> The reasonableness of the clause is demonstrated by the huge loss claimed by Dr. Chanda, compared to the cost of the service. Without a doubt the film had peculiar value to the plaintiff. Some of it was irreplaceable and all of it was of great sentimental value, but that unknown "tiger" is the very reason for the inclusion of the limitation of liability provision in the transaction. There is no way the processor can conceive of the risk it takes in accepting film for processing absent an explicit agreement to accept such risk. When the customer is made aware of the provision for limitation of liability and nevertheless proceeds with the transaction he has assented to an agreement for which there is a commercial need, if the cost of the service is to be made reasonable.[36]

A similar result was reached in *Collins v. Click Camera & Video, Inc.*, which also involved lost movie film left with the defendant for transfer onto videotape. The court rejected contentions that the limited remedy provided in the contract between the parties[37] violated public policy and was unconscionable. As to the public policy contention, the court noted:

> In determining whether an exculpatory provision is void as against public policy, courts have considered, inter alia, whether the goods or services contracted for are necessary for a person's living needs; whether the supplier assumes a quasi-public function in providing the goods; whether the supplier has been granted a monopoly in providing a specific service; and whether the limitation provision is such that the customer is in a position to assent to its terms.[38]

The court found that none of the factors applied to the matter before the court. As to the unconscionability contention, the court found that the substantive unconscionability argument was unpersuasive as the limited remedy was commercially reasonable for the reasons set forth in the quote above from *Guthrie v. American Protection Industries.*[39] As to the procedural prong of the unconscionability test,[40] the court held that the critical factors were those that bore on the relative bargaining position of the contracting parties. These factors included: "age, education, intelligence, business acumen and experience, relative bargaining power, who drafted the contract, whether the terms were explained to the weaker party, whether

---

[35] 464 So. 2d 626 (Fla. App. 1985).

[36] *Id.* at 631.

[37] 681 N.E.2d 1294 (Ohio App. 1993). The movie film consisted of 28 reels of Super 8 movie film, much of which depicted images of the plaintiff's daughter during her early childhood. The cost of the service, which constituted the limited remedy, was $234.28. Plaintiff sought in excess of $25,000 in damages.

[38] *Id.* at 1298.

[39] *Supra*, text and note 30.

[40] Section 63.2 (Unconscionability).

alterations in the printed terms were possible, whether there were alternative sources of supply for the goods in question."[41] The court held that procedural unconscionability was not demonstrated:

> Collins is a Harvard graduate, with extensive business and contracting experience. He admits he saw the limitations clause, but failed to read its contents. Therefore, he did not attempt to negotiate for less onerous terms, and the record does not indicate whether he could have obtained such terms had he tried. Assuming arguendo, that he could not have bargained with Click Camera to alter the terms of its limitations clause, this inability alone is insufficient to establish procedural unconscionability. There were certainly other places where Collins could have taken his film and, despite the fact that limitations clauses are standard in the film processing industry, there is no evidence that no one was willing to negotiate with Collins as to these terms. Furthermore, because the object of the bailment did not relate to one of the necessaries of life, Collins was not required, as a practical matter, to have entered into the bailment contract with anyone. He could have kept his film if he found the limitation of liability to be unacceptable.[42]

A contrary result was reached in *Mieske v. Bartell Drug Co.*[43] when the court upheld a trial court's ruling that a limited remedy provision in a contract to splice 32 50-foot reels of developed movie film into 4 reels was not binding on the plaintiffs because of unconscionability. The limited remedy capped defendant's responsibility at the "cost of the film." The trial court's decision was made after considering evidence on the point, the content of which was not specified in the opinion. Moreover, the jury was given the discretion to find the limited remedy "conscionable" but declined.[44]

One of the more unusual liquidated damages/limited remedy cases is *Laudig v. Laudig*, which involved a post-nuptial agreement.[45] The wife agreed that if she engaged in sexual intercourse with anyone other than her husband within a period of 15 years, while the two were married and living together, the wife would waive her marital property rights in consideration for the payment of $10,000 and $1,000 a year for 15 years. The court held that the "agreement" barred the wife from any right to additional marital assets under the Pennsylvania divorce code. The agreement was enforceable in a divorce action even though it did not specifically address a divorce proceeding. Moreover, the court held that the agreement did not violate public policy because there was no reason why the parties

---

[41] *Collins, supra,* 621 N.E.2d at 1299; *cf.* Wallis, *supra,* 306 F.3d at 835–36 (using a "totality of the circumstances" approach to determine if party received reasonable notice of limitation on recovery provision of contract).

[42] *Id.* (citation omitted).

[43] 593 P.2d 1308 (Wash. 1979).

[44] *Id.* at 1314.

[45] 624 A.2d 651 (Pa. Super. Ct. 1993).

could not by contract affect a distribution of marital property different from that provided by Pennsylvania's equitable distribution rules. That said, the decision cannot be substantiated as a liquidated damages case. The payments were fixed if the wife breached her promise of fidelity. The purpose of the agreement was "to limit the assets the wife would receive in the event she resumed her adulterous conduct."[46] No effort was made to estimate or determine the likely damages that would flow from the breach of the promise of fidelity. The purpose of the contract was to encourage the wife's fidelity by the threat of a draconian sanction if she breached. In this case, in Pennsylvania, it worked; however, that is not always the case. Usually claims of the type made by the husband could not be successfully presented.[47]

Increased concerns over possible exposure to punitive damages awards have led to efforts to contractually negate the right to claim punitive damages. Inasmuch as the decision to award punitive damages rests on public policy considerations, efforts to restrict by contract public rights will receive strict scrutiny by courts.[48] That has been the case; however, there is some decisional law permitting waiver.[49]

[186.3] "AS IS" Clause

"As Is" clauses are rather inscrutable. The common, lay understanding that the buyer takes the property "warts and all," without recourse, is inaccurate. "As Is" usually has a more limited meaning; moreover, the clause may be preempted by duties of disclosure owed by the seller to the buyer.

The general effect of an "As Is" clause is to exclude all implied warranties and to constitute a "representation" by the seller that the property may or may not be defective, but that if the buyer nonetheless buys, he does so solely at his own risk.[50] When an "As Is" clause is contained in a sale of

---

[46] *Id.* at 654 (stating husband's testimony).

[47] Sections 102 (Personal Relationships), 103.0 (Heart Balm Statutes), 181 (Liquidated Damages) (text and note 5, discussing *Disdado v. Disdado*, 118 Cal. Rptr. 2d 494 (finding a similar type of agreement to violate California's no-fault divorce laws).

[48] *Ex Parte* Thicklin, 824 So. 2d 723 (Ala. 2002):

> Whether a provision in a contract immunizing a party from liability for punitive damages is substantively unconscionable as violating public policy in that it "attempt[s] to alter in an impermissible manner fundamental duties otherwise imposed by the law" appears to be a question of first impression in Alabama. However, the absence of precedential authority does not prevent the Court from recognizing unconscionability as a defense to the enforcement of such a provision in an arbitration agreement so long as any such newly announced rule condemning a provision immunizing a party from liability for punitive damages applies to all contracts, regardless of the contemplated method of dispute resolution.

Id. at 731 (footnote omitted).

[49] *Cf.* Investment Partners L.P. v. Glamour Shots Licensing, Inc., 298 F.3d 314, 318 n.1 (5th Cir. 2002) (stating that "[p]rovisions in arbitration agreements that prohibit punitive damages are generally enforceable").

[50] Arthur Leff, *The Leff Dictionary of Law: A Fragment*, 94 Yale L. J. 1855, 2067 (1985) (defining "As Is").

goods, the provisions of the UCC respecting disclaimers of implied warranties must be addressed.[51]

The presence of an "As Is" clause does not permit the seller to affirmatively and intentionally misrepresent the condition and quality of the property to be sold and then seek to avoid those statements by an "As Is" provision in the agreement. As noted by one court:

> Most states do not permit an "as is" clause to shield a seller who has fraudulently misrepresented the condition of property or who has intentionally concealed known defects. The rationale of these authorities is obvious. A person who makes affirmative false representations to consummate a sale should not be able to shield himself from liability by hiding behind the "as is" contractual language in a sales contract.[52]

Consensus breaks down, however, when the misrepresentation is not intentional, but negligent or innocent. When the seller affirmatively, but negligently, misrepresents, an "As Is" clause may be insufficient to shift the risk of loss to the buyer.[53] The decisions are more favorable to the seller when the basis of the claim is negligent non-disclosure of a material fact. In this context, the presence of an "As Is" clause, coupled with the right to inspect, is often seen as sufficient to shift the risk of loss to the buyer for all non-disclosed defects,[54] but not from proactive duties to disclose, such as those created by operation of statute.[55]

The presence of an "As Is" clause will not relieve a party of a duty imposed by law to disclose certain facts. This point is illustrated by *Katz v. Department of Real Estate*.[56] Katz, a real estate broker, acquired real property subject to orders issued by the local Department of Building & Safety to rectify certain problems. Katz then sold the property as a "fixer upper" without disclosing the existence of the orders, but without affirmatively misrepresenting the status or condition of the property on this point.

Katz's license as a broker was suspended as a consequence of his conduct in this matter. He contended that his conduct did not support the license suspension. The court disagreed:

---

[51] Janet Richards, *"As Is" Provisions—What Do They Really Mean?*, 41 Ala. L. Rev. 435 (1990).

[52] Mackintosh v. Jack Matthews & Co., 855 P.2d 549, 551–52 (Nev. 1993) (citations omitted); *see* DRR, L.L.C. v. Sears, Roebuck & Co., 949 F. Supp. 1132, 1137 (D. Del. 1996); Richey v. Patrick, 904 P.2d 798, 803 (Wyo. 1995); Shapiro v. Hu, 233 Cal. Rptr. 470, 476 (Cal. App. 1986).

[53] Restatement (Second) of Torts § 552 (1977). *Compare* Stonecipher v. Kornhaus, 623 So. 2d 955, 964 (Miss. 1993) (holding that "As Is" clause precluded negligent misrepresentation claim), *with* Wagner v. Cutler, 757 P.2d 779 (Mont. 1988) (holding that an "As Is" clause did not preclude a claim of negligent misrepresentation). *See generally* Frank Wozniak, Annot., *Construction and Effect of Provision in Contract For Sale of Realty by Which Purchaser Agrees to Take Property "As Is" or in its Existing Condition*, 8 A.L.R.5th 312 § 4 (1993).

[54] *Richey, supra*, 904 P.2d at 803–04; Nussbaum v. Weeks 263 Cal. Rptr. 360 (Cal. App. 1989) (holding that the buyer had no duty to disclose information he acquired as a public official to the seller even though the knowledge acquired enabled the buyer to obtain a good deal).

[55] Section 120.4 ([Fraud] Duty to Disclose); *see* text and notes 56–57, *infra*.

[56] 158 Cal. Rptr. 766 (Cal. App. 1979).

Katz concedes his lack of candor, but contends that it is legally immaterial because Young and McGregor were under a duty to make an independent investigation of the state of the property. This duty, he insists, was compelled by two factors: (1) the parties' understanding that the property was being sold "as is"; and (2) his express disclaimer of warranties relating to municipal regulations. We disagree. An "as is" provision, "generally speaking, . . . means that the buyer takes the property in the condition visible to or observable by him." "It . . . does not in itself protect . . . or absolve (a seller) from liability for . . . passive concealment." Accordingly, there exists no reason why McGregor should have taken the provision to mean that he relied on Katz's silence at his own peril. Further, . . . a principal under a positive duty to make a disclosure "cannot escape liability for his failure to do so by relying on a provision in the agreement of sale that there are no other representations except those therein expressed . . . ."[57]

----

[57] *Id.* at 769 (citations omitted); *see* Loughrin v. Superior Court of San Diego County, 19 Cal. Rptr. 2d 161, 164 (Cal. App 1993) (holding that an "As Is" clause will not protect against the failure to make statutorily required disclosures).

Chapter 22
CONTEMPT

§ 190 NATURE OF CONTEMPT

Contempt is a manifestation of the power of a court to protect itself and its orders. Contempt generally arises in one of two settings. First, a party (the contemnor) may act disrespectfully toward a judicial body or engage in acts that constitute the obstruction of justice. Second, the contemnor may disobey a judicial order. The emphasis in these materials is on the second setting. The line between the two settings is not, however, always clear or well-marked. Disobedience of an order may be deemed "disrespectful." False testimony may be treated as a crime or as the equivalent of a refusal to testify.[1] For this, and many other reasons, the law of contempt has been deemed "a mess."[2]

Courts often refer to their inherent power of contempt.[3] The idea that courts possess inherent power to punish for contempt goes back to the very beginning of the Republic.[4] At times courts identify the contempt power as rooted in the common law;[5] at other times, they suggest that the contempt power is reserved to the judiciary as part of the constitutional doctrine of separation of powers.[6]

Notwithstanding the argument of inherent power, courts recognize that the contempt power is limited by statute,[7] though perhaps it was not always so. For example, one commentator reported an instance of severe and non-reviewable punishment for contempt:

> [In] 1631, a man threw a brickbat at the Chief Justice after being convicted of a felony. Though he missed the judge, his right hand was cut off and fixed to the gibbet [gallows] and he was immediately hanged in the presence of the court.[8]

---

[1] United States v. Arredondo, 349 F.3d 310, 319–20 (6th Cir. 2003) (noting, however, that the "falsity" must be apparent and not require reference to extrinsic evidence). *See generally* J.A. Bock, Annot., *Perjury or False Swearing as Contempt*, 89 A.L.R.2d 1258 (1963), at § 2 (stating that many decisions uphold the broad principle that perjury may be punished by contempt, but that many decisions require something more than false testimony such as that the perjury constitute an actual obstruction of justice).

[2] Earl Dudley, *Getting Beyond the Civil/Criminal Distinction: A New Approach to the Regulation of Indirect Contempts,* 79 Va. L. Rev. 1025, 1025 (1993) (noting that "[t]he literature on contempt of court is unanimous on one point: the law is a mess") (footnote omitted).

[3] Young v. United States *ex rel* Vuitton et Fils S.A., 481 U.S. 787, 795 (1987).

[4] United States v. Hudson, 11 U.S. 32, 34 (1812); Anderson v. Dunn, 19 U.S. 204, 217 (1821).

[5] *See In re* Williams, 306 F. Supp. 617, 619 (D.D.C. 1969).

[6] Gompers v. Buck's Stove and Range Co., 221 U.S. 418, 450 (1911). The separation of powers argument has been criticized. *See Ex parte* Grossman, 267 U.S. 87, 119–20 (1925); Felix Frankfurter & James Landis, *Power of Congress Over Procedure in Criminal Contempts in "Inferior" Federal Courts—A Study in Separation of Powers,* 37 Harv. L. Rev. 1010, 1012–23 (1924).

[7] *Arredondo, supra,* 349 F.3d at 316; United States v. Powers, 629 F.2d 619, 624 (9th Cir. 1980); CHARLES WRIGHT, FEDERAL PRACTICE & PROCEDURE: CRIMINAL 2D § 701, at 808 (1982):

> [T]he subject of contempt is a favorite matter of legislative action. Ever since 1831 Congress has been speaking to the matter, curtailing the contempt power in some instances and making it applicable to new areas in others. In the Advisory Committee Note to Rule 42 when it was originally adopted, 34 statutes were cited relating to contempt. No doubt many more have been enacted since.

[8] RONALD L. GOLDFARB, THE CONTEMPT POWER 13–14 (1963) (*citing* Anon. (1631) Dy. 1886; brackets added). The validity of the story is shrouded in the mists of history.

Constitutional strictures increasingly have affected the use of the contempt power in significant ways.[9] As a practical matter, the argument over the existence of an inherent power to punish for contempt has importance today insofar as a statute or rule purports to limit the contempt power. In this regard, courts have required that the limitation on the contempt power be explicit, not implied.[10]

Contempt is often seen as a natural remedy when a judicial order is violated. The essential feature of the order is the command to do or not do something.[11] A judicial decision that does not command, as, for example, a court imposed money judgment, is not usually enforceable by contempt.[12] However, the fact that the order requires the payment of money does not preclude the use of contempt to enforce the order in appropriate cases, as, for example, when the order of payment is imposed as a sanction[13] or as an equitable remedy, such as an order to pay support or restitution.[14]

§ 191   TYPES OF CONTEMPT

Contempt is perhaps best described as sui generis, neither civil nor criminal in nature, even though both of those labels are used to describe certain categories of contempt."[1] Nevertheless, the "best description" is not the one most often used. Characterization of contempt as civil or criminal is longstanding and basic to an understanding of the law of contempt.

A contempt finding is criminal if its primary effect is to punish; it is civil if its primary effect is remedial. Whether contempt is criminal or civil should be determined by examing the substance of the proceeding and the character of the relief that will be provided. The "effect" test should be distinguished from a "purpose" test, which was rejected as marking the line between civil and criminal contempt by the Supreme Court in *Hicks ex rel. Feiock v. Feiock.*[2] The Court was concerned that a "purpose" test would be

---

[9] Codispoti v. Pennsylvania, 418 U.S. 506 (1974) (stating that the right to jury trial attaches whenever the aggregate sentence for contempt, imposed in a single proceeding, exceeds six months); Mayberry v. Pennsylvania, 400 U.S. 455 (1971) (stating that in certain circumstances, due process requires that a vilified judge recuse himself from presiding over contempt proceedings involving the vilification).

[10] United States v. Fidanian, 465 F.2d 755, 757 (5th Cir.), *cert. denied,* 409 U.S. 1044 (1972); *Williams, supra,* 306 F. Supp. at 619.

[11] Section 34 (Specificity of Injunctive Relief).

[12] Combs v. Ryan's Coal Co., Inc., 785 F.2d 970, 980 (11th Cir.) (noting that appropriate remedy for failure to pay money judgment is a writ of execution, not a contempt citation), *cert. denied sub nom.* Simmons v. Combs, 479 U.S. 853 (1986).

[13] Loftus v. Southeastern Pa. Transp. Auth., 8 F. Supp. 2d 464, 468 (E.D. Pa. 1998) (involving a monetary sanction against an attorney for litigation-related misconduct); *cf.* Boarman v. Boarman, 556 S.E.2d 800 (W. Va. 2001) (holding that spouse could assign attorney's fees award to her attorney; however, spouse could not assign personal right to have award enforced by contempt); Section 193.1 (Order).

[14] Section 191.2 (Civil Contempt).

[1] Mitchell v. Stevenson, 677 N.E.2d 551, 559 (Ind. App. 1997) (citations omitted); Warner v. Second Judicial Dist. Court, State of Nev., County of Washoe, 906 P.2d 707, 7–9 (Nev. 1995).

[2] 485 U.S. 624, 631–32 (1988) (rejecting efforts to characterize contempt as civil or criminal

too subjective and impossible for reviewing courts to implement evenly when examining the correctness of the underlying proceedings. The Court did state, however, that the purpose of the sanction was a relevant, albeit not controlling, factor that could be considered in the characterization of contempt as civil or criminal. The distinction drawn in *Feiock* between effect and purpose is fine and is not always observed by courts.[3]

The classification of contempt as either criminal or civil will determine whether: (1) the conduct in question is subject to the contempt power at all; (2) the procedures to be used in adjudicating the conduct, as, for example, the burden of proof;[4] and (3) the sanctions to be imposed. The analysis can get circuitous, with contempt classified by the way it is treated and the way it is treated determined by its classification. Depending on how the court found out about the conduct in question, the adjudication procedures (summary or non-summary) being used, and the sanctions involved, identical conduct may be characterized as criminal or civil contempt. For example, the obstruction of court proceedings resulting from the refusal of a witness to give testimony as ordered is punishable as criminal contempt; however, the court, having ordered the witness to testify, may punish the same refusal to do so as civil contempt.

[191.1]   Criminal Contempt

Criminal contempt is punitive in nature. It is applied to conduct that is directed against the dignity and authority of the court.[5] Those affronts may occur in either criminal or civil proceedings. Criminal contempt is itself a crime and, thus, falls under many of the same rules and requirements applicable to criminal proceedings in general.[6] Substantive crimes may also evolve out of the same conduct as that which constitutes criminal contempt. In some circumstances, the contemnor may be punished for the substantive offense and for contempt without violating double jeopardy.[7]

---

primarily by looking at the underlying purpose of the sanction and adopting an approach that examined the substance of the proceedings and the character of the relief the proceedings will afford or have afforded).

[3] *E.g.*, Garrison v. Cassens Transport Co., 334 F.3d 528, 543 (6th Cir. 2003) (stating distinction between criminal and civil contempt as based on whether the "purpose" of the contempt is to punish or remedy).

[4] The burden of proof cannot be shifted to the defendant if the proceedings are criminal in nature, Mullaney v. Wilbur, 421 U.S. 684, 701 (1975); however, the burden of proof may be shifted to the defendant in civil matters. United States v. Rylander, 460 U.S. 752, 757 (1983).

[5] Yates v. United States, 355 U.S. 66, 72 (1957); Falstaff Brewing Corp. v. Miller Brewing Co., 702 F.2d 770, 778 (9th Cir. 1983).

[6] Bloom v. Illinois, 391 U.S. 194, 201 (1968).

[7] *Compare* Ellis v. State of Indiana, 634 N.E.2d 771, 774 (Ind. App. 1994) (holding that "the principles of double jeopardy do not preclude the subsequent prosecution of a person for engaging in conduct which constitutes an unlawful act simply because a trial court has invoked the power of direct contempt to protect itself against gross violations of decorum"), *with* Griffin v. United States, 598 A.2d 1174, 1177 (D.C. 1991) (holding that "[t]he record makes clear that it was the same conduct which formed the basis of the contempt conviction that formed the basis for the subsequent conviction for obstructing justice. This violates the Double Jeopardy

[191.2]   Civil Contempt

Civil contempt is identified by its remedial effect. [8] Civil contempt can be used to compel obedience to a court order for the benefit of the complainant or compensate the complainant for injuries resulting from noncompliance with the underlying order. Thus, either a coercive order or a compensatory order may remedy civil contempt. [9]

§ 192   CLASSIFICATION OF CONTEMPT AS CRIMINAL OR CIVIL

The same conduct may justify a court's resorting to coercive (civil contempt) as well as punitive (criminal contempt) measures. [1] "Punishment" of conduct as both a civil and a criminal contempt does not violate the double jeopardy clause. [2] Jointly trying the civil and criminal contempt charges is not a ground for reversal unless shown to result in substantial prejudice, [3] although one circuit has commented on the "difficulties of trying civil and criminal contempt cases together" and intimated that bifurcation would be preferable. [4] When it is unclear whether the contempt proceeding and judgment are criminal or civil, and when the judgment contains an admixture of criminal and civil elements, the criminal aspects of the order usually fix its character. [5] While appellate courts lament the failure of trial

---

Clause). The court in *Griffin* relied, however, on the "same conduct" test of *Grady v. Corbin*, 495 U.S. 508 (1990), that was later disapproved in *United States v. Dixon*, 509 U.S. 688, 704 (1993).

[8] Shillitani v. United States, 384 U.S. 364, 368–70 (1966); Gompers v. Buck's Stove & Range Co., 221 U.S. 418, 441 (1911).

[9] Perfect Fit Indus. v. Acme Quilting Co., 673 F.2d 53, 56–57 (2d Cir.), *cert. denied*, 459 U.S. 832 (1982) (noting that sanctions imposed on contemnor may properly serve to coerce future compliance or to remedy past noncompliance); United States v. Asay, 614 F.2d 655, 659 (9th Cir. 1980).

[1] United States v. United Mine Workers of America, 330 U.S. 258, 299 (1947); Mitchell v. Stevenson, 677 N.E.2d 551, 560 (Ind. App. 1997) (noting that disobedience of a court order can constitute either civil or criminal contempt).

[2] United States v. Marquardo, 149 F.3d 36, 39 (1st Cir. 1998); United States v. Hughey, 571 F.2d 111, 114–16 (2d Cir. 1978).

[3] *United States v. United Mine Workers, supra*, 330 U.S. at 299–300.

[4] United States v. Rylander, 714 F.2d 996, 998 (9th Cir.), *cert. denied*, 460 U.S. 752 (1983). In *Rylander* the court relied on several procedural differences it identified as existing between civil and criminal contempt, such as (1) the right to counsel, (2) the right not to take the witness stand, and (3) the proof beyond a reasonable doubt standard. Many courts recognize a right to counsel in civil contempt proceedings when imprisonment is sought as a coercing remedy. Ridgway v. Baker, 720 F.2d 1409, 1413–14 (5th Cir. 1983) (rejecting government's argument that possibility of imprisonment is irrelevant because contemnor had the keys of his prison in his own pocket); United States v. McAnlis, 721 F.2d 334, 337 (11th Cir. 1983), *cert. denied*, 467 U.S. 1227 (1984) (stating that "the right to counsel exists if the litigant loses his physical liberty if he loses the litigation . . . . We do not dispute McAnlis' right to counsel at the contempt proceeding because imprisonment is a possibility").

[5] Penfield Co. v. SEC, 330 U.S. 585, 591 (1947); Falstaff Brewing Corp., *supra* 702 F.2d at 778.

judges to indicate clearly the nature of the contempt order as criminal or civil,[6] when trial judges do so characterize the nature of the contempt proceedings, that characterization may be given little weight by appellate courts.[7]

To fix the character of the order as criminal or civil there must be something more than the always present incidental effect of every contempt order—the vindication of judicial authority and the benefits derived from sanctions as deterrents against future repetition of disobedient acts. The incidental presence of either effect does not fix the criminal or civil character of the contempt. Sections 192.1 through 192.4 describe the factors that help to fix the character of contempt for disobedience of a court order as criminal or civil. They evidence the modern tendency to favor objective measures over a subjective purpose or intent test.[8]

[192.1] Nature of Sanction

In cases of criminal contempt, the court imposes on the defendant-contemnor a fixed term of imprisonment or an unconditional fine payable to the court.[9] A fine that compensates the complainant for injury caused by the contemnor's disobedience of a court order usually identifies the proceedings as involving civil contempt. Similarly, incarceration of the contemnor for an indefinite term, but only for so long as the contemnor disobeys the court order, is a feature of civil contempt. A fixed, unconditional term of imprisonment or sanction marks the proceedings as involving criminal contempt.

A difficult issue arises when the court imposes by order a coercive fine. If the order vindicates the court's authority, the order is for criminal contempt.[10] If, however, the order is entered after due consideration of the character and magnitude of the harm threatened by continued contumacy (e.g., refusal to obey), the fine imposed is reasonably related to that threatened harm, and the order is conditional, *i.e.,* the contemnor may purge the contempt and obtain prospective relief from the contempt judgment, then the contempt order is civil in nature.[11]

---

[6] United States v. North, 621 F.2d 1255, 1265 (3d Cir.) (*en banc*), *cert. denied sub nom.* Eyler v. United States, 449 U.S. 866 (1980)).

[7] TWM Mfg. Co. v. Dura Corp., 722 F.2d 1261, 1270 n.8 (6th Cir. 1983) (trial judge's characterization not determinative); United States v. Powers, 629 F.2d 619, 626 (9th Cir. 1980) (but one fact to consider); Southern Ry. v. Lanham, 403 F.2d 119, 124 (5th Cir. 1968) (judge's characterization not conclusive).

[8] Gregory v. Depte, 896 F.2d 31, 39 (3d Cir. 1990), *citing Hicks ex rel. Feiock, supra,* 485 U.S. 624.

[9] *Falstaff Brewing Corp., supra,* 702 F.2d at 779.

[10] United States v. UMWA, *supra,* 330 U.S. at 303–04; *In re* Grand Jury Proceedings, 658 F.2d 211, 217 (3d Cir. 1981); Commodity Future Trading Comm'n v. Premex, Inc., 655 F.2d 779, 785 (7th Cir. 1981); United States v. Asay, 614 F.2d 655, 659 (9th Cir. 1980).

[11] *Shillitani, supra,* 384 U.S. at 370; Perfect Fix Indus. v. Acme Quilting Co., 673 F.2d 53, 57 (2d Cir.), *cert. denied,* 459 U.S. 832 (1983); United States v. Spectro Foods Corp., 544 F.2d 1175, 1182 (3d Cir. 1976). *But cf.* International Union, United Mine Workers of America v. Bagwell, 512 U.S. 821 (1994) (discussed in Section 194.4 (Coercive Fine)).

The district court has great latitude in setting the amount of a coercive fine. As noted by one court:

> When the purpose is compensatory, the order should be fashioned so as to reimburse the injured party for his actual damages. When, however, the purpose is coercive, the district court has broad discretion to design a remedy that will bring about compliance. Several factors should be considered in the exercise of this discretion, including the "character and magnitude of the harm threatened by continued contumacy, . . . the probable effectiveness of any suggested sanction in bringing about (compliance)," and the "amount of (the contemnor's) financial resources and the consequent seriousness of the burden of (him)." Ultimately, however, the overriding consideration is whether the coercive fine was reasonably set in relation to the facts and was not arbitrary.[12]

The fact that the sanction is payable to the plaintiff as compensation for his damages is a factor that usually leads the court to characterize the contempt as civil.[13] On the other hand, if the fine is unconditionally payable to the court, this is seen as a factor warranting treatment of the contempt as criminal.[14] When a coercive fine is payable to the court, other factors, primarily the conditional nature of the sanction, may persuade courts to treat the sanction as civil rather than criminal.[15] The fact that payment of the fine is made to the court may, however, cause an appellate court to see the issue differently as involving criminal rather than civil contempt.[16]

Efforts to direct the payment of fines to complainants rather than the court have been generally unsuccessful. In *Law v. National Collegiate Athletic Assn.* the trial court imposed a 25% surcharge on the attorneys fees awarded the complainant. The attorneys fees were incurred as a result of discovery abuses by the defendant. The court held that the surcharge (but not the underlying fees) was a fine because there was no evidence it was compensatory.[17] The surcharge was unconditional and could not be purged. It was not argued that the sanction was to induce compliance as coercive civil contempt. Because the surcharge was a fine, the court held that it could only be valid as a sanction for criminal contempt, but since the protections afforded for criminal contempt were not provided, the surcharge was reversed.

---

[12] *Perfect Fit Indus., supra,* 673 F.2d at 57 (citations omitted); IBM Corp. v. United States, 493 F.2d 112 (2d Cir. 1973), *cert. denied,* 416 U.S. 955 (1974).

[13] Roe v. Operation Rescue, 919 F.2d 857, 868 (3d Cir. 1990).

[14] *Hicks ex rel. Friock, supra,* 485 U.S. at 632.

[15] *Id.* (noting that the fact that the fine is paid to the court does not require that contempt be deemed criminal when the contemnor can avoid paying the fine simply by performing the affirmative act required by the order).

[16] *Falstaff Brewing Corp., supra,* 702 F.2d at 779; Section 194.6 (Recipient of Collected Fine).

[17] 134 F.3d 1438, 1443 (10th Cir. 1998). Section 194.4 (Coercive Fine).

[192.2] Ability to Comply

Inability to comply constitutes a complete defense to coercive civil contempt, but not necessarily to criminal contempt in cases when the inability to comply is self-induced.[18] Consequently, whether or not the contemnor can comply with the order will help identify the underlying proceeding as either criminal or civil contempt. As noted by one court:

> No matter how reprehensible the conduct is it does not "warrant issuance of an order which creates a duty impossible of performance, so that punishment can follow." If the record establishes that there in fact is a present inability to comply with a production order, the "civil [contempt] inquiry is at an end" insofar as the court may coerce compliance because obedience to the order is no longer within the contemnor's power.[19]

[192.3] Initiation By Court or Party

An action for civil contempt may be initiated only by an aggrieved party or by an individual with an interest in the right to be protected.[20] This distinguishes civil contempt proceedings from criminal contempt proceedings, which may be initiated (1) by the government on its own initiative or on the relation of one who has an interest in the enforcement of the order or (2) by the court on its own initiative.[21] When there has been no party, or interested person, initiating the contempt proceedings, the proceedings must be for criminal contempt. The converse, however, is not necessarily true. Party, or interested person, initiation does not bind the court, which may, on its own, transform a request for civil contempt into criminal contempt proceedings.

[192.4] Consequence of Incorrect Characterization

A frequent ground on which a judgment of contempt is set aside is that the wrong procedure was used. If the matter is really a criminal contempt, it is reversible error to treat it as a civil contempt for purpose of procedural

---

[18] *In re* Marc Rich & Co., A.G., 736 F.2d 864, 866 (2d Cir. 1984):

> Civil contempt is a coercive sanction, and thus a person held in civil contempt must be able to comply with the court order at issue. Individuals unable to comply, because of their own bad faith actions or otherwise, may be subject to criminal sanctions, but may not be held in civil contempt. The burden of proving "plainly and unmistakably" that compliance is impossible rests with the contemnor.

(citations omitted); SEC v. Ormont Drug & Chem. Co., 739 F.2d 654 (D.C. Cir. 1984) (same).

[19] *Falstaff Brewing Corp., supra,* 702 F.2d at 781 (citation omitted).

[20] MacNell v. United States, 236 F.2d 149 (1st Cir.), *cert. denied,* 352 U.S. 912 (1956). *But cf.* United States v. McAnlis, 721 F.2d 334, 337 (11th Cir. 1983) (noting that the fact that judge initiated civil contempt not reversible error in absence of contemnor showing prejudice), *cert. denied,* 467 U.S. 1227 (1984).

[21] *Civil and Criminal Contempts in the Federal Courts,* 17 F.R.D. 167, 172 (1955).

due process.[22] The issue can be trickier than just the format of the proceedings. For example, in *Hicks ex rel. Feiock v. Feiock* the Court addressed the application of a statutory presumption that a party subject to an order to provide support would be deemed continuously able to comply until it was determined otherwise. The Court held that the presumption could not be applied in cases of criminal contempt because it would undercut the state's burden of proving the contemnor's guilt beyond a reasonable doubt; however, the presumption could be applied to civil contempt.[23]

Proper characterization can be complicated by the mixing of one or more of the above factors, some of which point to the proceedings being labelled "criminal"; others which point to the proceedings being labelled "civil." For example, a contempt order may blend fixed sanctions with a purge clause. A court may impose a determinant sentence of imprisonment or fine, but then provide that the sentence or fine may be purged if the contemnor either brings herself into compliance with the court order or engages in no future violations of the court order. Although the two situations are often treated as similar, they are different. A sanction designed to bring a contemnor into compliance is a true conditional order. If the contemnor immediately complies, no fine will accrue and if compliance takes some time, fines will accrue only during that time period. The second situation assumes that the defendant is in compliance, but holds over the defendant's head the Damoclean sword of a fixed, determined sanction if the order is violated. The purge clause is prospective only and only in the sense of avoidance. If the order is violated, the contemnor cannot purge herself of the imposed sanction because by violating the order she has caused the sanction to be activated.

While there are similarities between the two forms of conditional contempt, the differences are greater. Both forms are designed to ensure compliance and deter violations of court-adjudicated rights. The second, determinable form of coercive contempt does so, however, by creating a fixed, determinable sanction for non-compliance. The sanction is non-purgible except in the same way that any penal sentence or fine is non-purgible, which is to avoid engaging in prohibited behavior.

The Supreme Court suggested in *International Union, United Mine Workers of America v. Bagwell* that predetermined fines in coercive contempt contexts would be treated as criminal contempts.[24] The *Bagwell* decision is discussed in Section 194.4 (Coercive Fine).

---

[22] In federal courts, civil contempt is governed by the Federal Rule of Civil Procedure. *See* Rogers v. Webster, 776 F.2d 607, 610 (6th Cir. 1985). Criminal contempt is governed by the Federal Rules of Criminal Procedure. Fed. R. Crim. Proc. 42.

[23] 485 U.S. at 637–38.

[24] 512 U.S. 821, 836 (1994) (stating that "the fact that the trial announced the fines before the contumacy, rather than after the fact, does not in itself justify respondents' conclusion that the fines are civil or meaningfully distinguish these penalties from the ordinary criminal law").

§ 193 ELEMENTS OF CIVIL CONTEMPT

The general elements necessary to sustain a finding of civil contempt for disobedience of an order are as follows:

- There must be an order;
- The contemnor must have prior knowledge of the order;
- The terms of the order must be clear and definite;
- There must be proof of non-compliance,
- The proof of non-compliance must be by clear and convincing evidence.

Criminal contempt includes all of the above and also requires that the contempt be willful and the proof of the elements meet the "beyond a reasonable doubt" standard.[1]

[193.1] Order

The basic requirement for contempt based on disobedience of an order is that there be an order, the hallmark of which is language of an "operative command capable of enforcement" rather than an abstract statement of rights, duties, or obligations.[2] In *Ashcraft v. Conoco, Inc.* a reporter published material that had been placed under seal by the court. A special prosecutor sought contempt. The court denied the requested sanction on the ground that no order had been entered that the reporter had violated.[3] The court had placed a confidentiality admonition on the documents. The Special Prosecutor apparently argued to the court that the admonition alone was sufficient to support contempt and did not rely on the underlying orders.[4] The court found that, as such, the essential element of contempt, an enforceable order, was lacking.[5]

[193.2] Prior Knowledge

A person cannot be held in contempt of an order of which he is unaware.[6] While knowledge is required, the degree of knowledge required is based on context and reasonableness. As noted in *Perfect Fit Industries*:

[I]gnorance of the term of a decree would ordinarily preclude a finding of contempt. Nevertheless, a party to an action is not

---

[1] Chapman v. Pacific Tel. & Tel. Co., 613 F.2d 193, 195 (9th Cir. 1979).

[2] International Longshoremen's Ass'n, Local 1291 v. Philadelphia Marine Trade Ass'n, 389 U.S. 64, 73 (1967) (stating that decree, though purporting to be an order, could not support contempt when the decree lacked language of operative command). Section 34 (Specificity of Injunctive Relief).

[3] 218 F.3d 288 (4th Cir. 2000).

[4] *Id.* at 296–97.

[5] *Id.* at 297–98 (reversing judgment of contempt entered by district court).

[6] Perfect Fit Indus. v. Acme Quilting Co., 646 F.2d 800, 808 (2d Cir. 1981), *aff'd after remand,* 673 F.2d 53 (2d Cir), *cert. denied,* 459 U.S. 832 (1982).

permitted to maintain a studied ignorance of the terms of a decree in order to postpone compliance and preclude a finding of contempt. The party and his counsel have a duty to monitor the progress of the litigation and to ascertain the terms of any order entered against the party. Unexcused failure to do so may justify a finding of contempt when the party knows that some order has been entered against him.[7]

[193.3]   Order Must be Clear and Definite

The order the defendant is alleged to have violated must be definite, clear, and leave no reasonable doubt or uncertainty in the mind of the defendant regarding his duties and obligations under the order.[8] Put another way, "[t]he basic inquiry is 'whether the parties subject to the injunctive order understand their obligations under the order.'"[9]

[193.4]   Non-Compliance

The general and federal rule is that the plaintiff need only show the defendant contemnor's non-compliance with the order. Inability to comply constitutes a defense to civil contempt for which the contemnor has the burden of proof.[10] A few decisions express a more restrained approach. Some jurisdictions suggest that the order the contemnor is charged with violating must contain a finding of ability to comply, though the finding may be implied. For example, if a parent is charged with violating a support order, the proceedings leading to the support order likely addressed the defendant's ability to pay the amount of support ordered by the court; therefore, the proceeding will support the implicit finding of ability to comply.[11] On the other hand, if the order simply requires the payment of

---

[7] *Id.*; Section 35 (Person Bound by Injunction).

[8] McMullan v. McMullan, 710 So. 2d 1045, 1046 (Fla. App. 1998); ACLI Gov't Sec., Inc. v. Rhoades, 989 F. Supp. 462, 465 n.4 (S.D.N.Y. 1997), *aff'd,* 159 F.3d 1345 (2d Cir. 1998) (Table); Glover v. Johnson, 934 F.2d 703, 707 (6th Cir. 1991).

[9] Landmark Legal Foundation v. E.P.A., 272 F. Supp. 2d 70, 75 (D.D.C. 2003) (citation omitted); Section 34 (Specificity of Injunctive Relief).

[10] United States v. Rylander, 460 U.S. 752, 757 (1983); NLRB v. Trans Ocean Export Packing, Inc., 473 F.2d 612 (9th Cir. 1973):

> [I]nability to comply with a judicial decree constitutes a defense to a charge of civil contempt, the federal rule is that one petitioning for an adjudication of civil contempt does not have the burden of showing that the respondent has the capacity to comply. The contrary burden is upon the respondent. To satisfy this burden the respondent must show "categorically and in detail" why he is unable to comply.

Id. at 616 (citations omitted); Moss v. Superior Court, 950 P.2d 59, 61 (Cal. 1998) (holding that inability to comply (pay child support) is an affirmative defense that must be established by the alleged contemnor by the preponderance of the evidence); *see* State *ex rel.* Udall v. Wimberly, 884 P.2d 518, 523 (N. Mex. App. 1994); Balaam v. Balaam, 187 N.W.2d 867, 872 (Wis. 1971).

[11] *See* Sodones v. Sodones, 314 N.E.2d 906, 913 (Mass. 1974) (involving an order to pay alimony); *In re* S.L.T., 180 So. 2d 374, 379 (Fla. App. 1965) (involving an order to pay child support).

money, the ability to pay may not be implied.[12] Some courts require that the plaintiff must establish, at the contempt hearing, the contemnor's ability to comply.[13]

Obedience to a court order must be complete. Subject to an exception noted *infra*, partial or even substantial compliance may not avoid a finding of contempt.[14] There is no pure "good faith" exception to compliance, at least as to civil contempt.[15] The rule may be otherwise in criminal contempt.[16] Substantial or partial compliance only becomes a defense to contempt when it is all the contemnor can reasonably and in good faith do under the circumstances. Although some courts occasionally assert that "substantial compliance" is a defense,[17] the more complete and accepted statement is that substantial compliance is sufficient when that is all that can be expected under the circumstances. As noted in *General Signal Corp. v. Donallco, Inc.*:

> [S]ubstantial compliance with a court order is a defense to an action for civil contempt . . . . If a violating party has taken all reasonable steps to comply with the court order, technical or inadvertent violations of the order will not support a finding of civil contempt.[18]

---

[12] Mitchell v. Flynn, 478 A.2d 1133, 1135 (Me. 1984) (finding that order to pay taxes and mortgage interest contained no implication of ability to pay); Roy v. Levanthal, 360 N.E.2d 688, 689 (Mass. App. 1977) (stating that "[a] simple order or judgment for the payment of money does not . . . carry any implication of ability to pay").

[13] *Mitchell, supra*, 478 A.2d at 1135 (stating that while the burden of production may shift to the contemnor, the burden of persuasion on the issue of ability to comply is on the plaintiff).

[14] Vacco v. Consalvo, 670 N.Y.S.2d 703, 708 (Sup. Ct. 1998); *see* Petties v. District of Columbia, 897 F. Supp. 626, 629 (D.D.C. 1995) (stating that "[c]ivil contempt is a remedial device intended to achieve full compliance with a court's order").

[15] Peterson v. Highland Music, Inc., 140 F.3d 1313, 1323 (9th Cir. 1998) (rejecting defendants' excuses as to why their repeated refusals to comply were not their fault), *cert. denied sub nom.* Gusto Records, Inc. v. Peterson, 525 U.S. 983 (1998); Food Lion, Inc. v. United Food and Commercial Workers Int'l Union, AFL-CIO-CLC, 103 F.3d 1007, 1017–18 (D.C. Cir. 1997) (noting that "good faith alone is insufficient to excuse contempt"); Doe v. General Hosp., 434 F.2d 427, 431 (D.C. Cir. 1970) (holding that physician's good faith misunderstanding as to scope of preliminary injunction did not constitute a defense to a civil contempt order for violating that injunction).

[16] United States v. Armstrong, 781 F.2d 700 (9th Cir. 1986):

> Appellants misinterpret the nature of the "good faith" defense to a charge of criminal contempt. [A] defendant's good faith belief that he is complying with the order of the court may prevent a finding of willfulness . . . .

Id. at 706 (footnote and citations omitted); United States v. Greyhound Corp., 508 F.2d 529, 531–32 (7th Cir. 1974) (stating that a willful violation is a volitional act that the contemnor knew was wrongful). The *Greyhound Corp.* court defined "willfulness" as excluding situations when the contemnor acted in the "good faith pursuit of a plausible though mistaken alternative" to full compliance. *Id.* at 532; *cf.* United States v. Lynch, 952 F. Supp. 167 (S.D.N.Y 1997) (holding as finder of fact that protestors charged with criminal contempt for their conduct at abortion clinic did not willfully violate court order because they "acted out of a sense of conscience and sincere religious convictions").

[17] Wolfard Glassblowing Co. v. Vanbragt, 118 F.3d 1320, 1321 (9th Cir. 1997) (stating that in order "to succeed in its motion for civil contempt, [plaintiff] had to show . . . that Zodiac violated the consent judgment beyond substantial compliance").

[18] 787 F.2d 1376, 1379 (9th Cir. 1986).

The same is true with partial compliance.[19] Perhaps the most accurate statement of the principles stated here is that normally a court order demands full and complete compliance; however, less than full and complete compliance should not subject a party to contempt when that party has performed in good faith to the best of his ability.[20] The court always retains discretion to reduce or remit a contempt sanction based on the nature of the party's efforts to comply.[21]

[193.5] Clear and Convincing Evidence

The federal and majority state rule is that the plaintiff must establish the elements of civil contempt by clear and convincing evidence.[22] A number of state jurisdictions, however, apply the preponderance standard.[23] In jurisdictions that apply the clear and convincing evidence standard, a defense to a charge of civil contempt, such as inability to comply, can usually be satisfied by meeting the preponderance standard.[24]

§ 194 COERCIVE CIVIL CONTEMPT

The line between coercive civil contempt and criminal contempt is illusive. Coercive civil contempt is designed to secure compliance with a court order. The court may impose sanctions, such as imprisonment or fines, to induce the contemnor to comply with the order. A court may not, however, impose sanctions under the guise of inducing compliance that are disproportionate to the advantages gained by compliance.[1] The general principle is

---

[19] Department of Health and Rehabilitative Servs. v. Beckwith, 624 So. 2d 395, 397 (Fla. App. 1993).

[20] Harris v. City of Philadelphia, 47 F.3d 1311, 1324 (3d Cir. 1995) (noting that "[t]here is general support for the proposition that a defendant may not be held in contempt as long as it took all reasonable steps to comply") (citation omitted); Durfee v. Ocean State Steel, Inc., 636 A.2d 698, 704 (R.I. 1994) (noting that "[s]ubstantial compliance must 'depend on the circumstances of each case, including the nature of the interest at stake and the degree to which non-compliance affects that interest' ") (citation omitted); Glover, supra, 934 F.2d at 708.

[21] Maher v. Maher, 393 N.W.2d 190, 195 (Minn. App. 1986) (holding that contemnor could purge himself of contempt and secure remission of remaining sentence if he agreed to repayment schedule of past due and unpaid support obligations).

[22] Wolfard Glassblowing Co., supra, 118 F.3d at 1322; Food Lion, Inc., supra, 103 F.3d at 1016; Durfee, supra, 636 A.2d at 704; In re Ayer, 695 N.E.2d 1180, 1183 (Ohio App. 1997); Middleton v. Middleton, 620 A.2d 1363, 1370 (Md. 1993); Von Hake v. Thomas, 759 P.2d 1162, 1172 (Utah 1988).

[23] State of Tenn. v. Winningham, 958 S.W.2d 740, 742 (Tenn. 1997); Marian Shop, Inc. v. Baird, 670 A.2d 671, 672 (Pa. Super. Ct. 1996); In re Harvey, 464 S.E.2d 34, 36 (Ga. App. 1995).

[24] Moss, supra, 950 P.2d at 77 (holding that affirmative defense of inability to comply can be proven by preponderance of the evidence); Matter of Elder, 763 P.2d 219, 222 (Alaska 1988); Haynes v. Kaiser, 1996 Ohio App. LEXIS 4603 (Ohio App., Oct. 18, 1996) (unreported).

[1] United States v. United Mine Workers of America, 330 U.S. 258, 304 (1947) (noting that the appropriate level of coercive sanction is determined by "the character and magnitude of the harm threatened by continued contumacy, and the probable effectiveness of any suggested sanction in bringing about the result desired").

that "only [t]he least possible power adequate to the end proposed should be used in contempt cases."[2] This principle does not prescribe a preference for civil contempt over criminal contempt;[3] rather, it expresses the concern that the civil contempt remedy itself be measured and tailored to the mischief at hand. This is simply a variation on the theme that a coercive sanction, or any sanction for that matter, should not be disproportionate to the harm or injury that compliance will avoid or remedy.[4]

A sanction that is designed as a remedy to secure compliance may be difficult to differentiate from a sanction designed to punish. The distinction may also be complicated by the fact that in the case of fines or other monetary sanctions, such as the payment of attorneys fees or the costs of supervision through a monitor or receiver, the exaction of the sanction will occur after compliance has been secured or the effort to secure compliance has been abandoned as futile. Payment of the sanction will appear to be designed to punish for past contumacy if the court uses the viewpoint of the time of payment, rather than the time the sanction was threatened.

The essential element of coercive civil contempt is its conditional nature. Coercive civil contempt is designed to achieve compliance. Once compliance is achieved, or is no longer feasible, the need for coercive civil contempt disappears. The conditional nature of coercive civil contempt is referred to as the ability to "purge" oneself of contempt.[5] This "purge" factor is critical and its absence will usually defeat an effort to characterize the sanction as civil rather than criminal.[6]

[194.1] Procedure for Obtaining Coercive Sanction

A court order commands a party to do or desist from doing something; however, court orders rarely specify the sanctions that will be imposed to secure compliance or punish for their violation. If a party violates a court order, it is usually necessary to have the party first adjudicated as being in contempt of court. After being held in contempt, the court will then impose the conditional sanction, "comply or else." As noted in *Thomas v. Woollen*:

> It is not to be anticipated that the lawful orders of the court will be violated but rather that they will be obeyed. If they are violated, however, the remedy is by way of attachment or a rule to show cause. In either event, the matter and alleged offender is again

---

[2] Spallone v. United States, 493 U.S. 265, 276 (1990) (citation and internal quotation marks omitted); Young v. United States *ex. rel.* Vuitton & Fils, S.A., 481 U.S. 787, 801 (1987) (same).

[3] United States v. Roach, 108 F.3d 1477, 1483 (D.C. Cir.), *cert. denied*, 522 U.S. 983 (1997), *modified on other grounds on reconsideration*, 136 F.3d 794 (D.C. Cir. 1998).

[4] *Cf.* Section 181.1 ([Liquidated Damages] Damages or Penalty) (noting that liquidated damages provision that provides compensation disproportionately greater than harm expected, or incurred, from breach is likely to be deemed a penalty clause and not enforced).

[5] *Bagwell, supra*, 512 U.S. at 829.

[6] Jones v. State, 718 A.2d 222, 230–31 (Md. 1998).

brought to the attention of the court for appropriate action. There must be some prima facie showing that the order has been violated. There may be intervening circumstances that rendered compliance impossible or circumstances surrounding the violation may have rendered it relatively innocent. These are factors that should be taken into account in determining whether or not there has been a contempt and, if so, what the penalty should be. They cannot be determined in advance. To anticipate the breach, assess the penalty and provide for the execution, it appears to us, amounts to the abandonment by the trial court of its responsibility in this area and should not be sanctioned.[7]

An example may help illuminate the procedure. Assume the defendant was ordered to remove an encroaching structure, but failed to do so. The plaintiff may now have the defendant cited for contempt of court, for disobedience of the court's order to remove the encroaching structure.[8] If the defendant is found to have violated the order, he will be held in contempt of court. The court can, if criminal process were provided, sanction the disobedience as a criminal contempt. Alternatively, or additionally,[9] the court can now impose a conditional sanction designed to coerce compliance, such as a daily fine requiring the defendant to pay $1,000 per day until the encroaching structure is removed. If after 10 days, the defendant removes the encroachment, the conditional sanction will abate. The defendant has, however, accrued $10,000 in sanctions ($1,000 × 10 days). At a third hearing the court will determine whether to collect the sanction. It is here that the overlap between coercive contempt and criminal contempt is most visible. The sanction has ceased having a coercive function because compliance has been achieved.[10] From the viewpoint at this last stage, requiring payment of the $10,000 appears to be penal. If, however, the $10,000 is viewed as a penalty or punishment it can only be exacted if criminal due process was afforded at the prior stage when the defendant was held in contempt. Moreover, if, at the last stage of the process, the $10,000 sanction is deemed penal rather than remedial, that characterization will undermine the coercive nature of the conditional sanction. The defendant, subject to the conditional sanctions, will know, at the second stage of the process, that she can argue at the third stage that the aggregate sanction must be reduced to achieve a just punishment function. This knowledge, or reasonable belief, that the sanction may be discounted in the future may undermine the coercive effect of the order on the contemnor in the present.

---

[7] 266 N.E.2d 20, 23 (Ind. 1971) (citations omitted).

[8] This is often done by a request for an Order to Show Cause (OSC) why the defendant should not be held in contempt. *In re* Grand Jury Proceedings, 142 F.3d 1416, 1424 (11th Cir. 1998) (discussing procedure for enforcing injunctions in federal courts).

[9] Double Jeopardy principles do not apply to coercive confinement pursuant to civil contempt. *Ex Parte* Hudson, 917 S.W.2d 24, 26 (Tex. 1996); Section 191.1 (Criminal Contempt).

[10] Ochoa v. United States, 819 F.2d 366, 369 (2d Cir. 1987) (noting that coercive sanctions end as soon as the contemnor "ceases his contumacious behavior").

The process may be illustrated by the following timeline:

   *   *   *   *

Stage 1	Stage 2	Compliance	Stage 3
Order to remove encroachment issued.	Contempt finding made based on defendant's failure to comply with earlier order. Conditional sanction imposed.		Sanction collected for period of noncompliance.

It should be noted that the problem arises because of the delay encountered between imposing and collecting a monetary fine. When imposition and exaction are simultaneous, as is the case when the defendant is conditionally imprisoned, the sanction is seen as coercive, as long as it is perceived as capable of producing compliance.[11] Once the defendant complies, he is released from prison. The collection of the sanction (imprisonment) is not deferred, as is the case with monetary sanctions.

Courts have not developed a consistent approach to this issue of collecting coercive monetary sanctions. In some cases, the court evaluates the sanction based on its impact at the time it is exacted; at other times the focus is on the time the sanction was threatened.[12]

[194.2]   Coercive Imprisonment

A contemnor may be imprisoned in order to secure compliance with a court order. In theory, the length of imprisonment is indefinite; the contemnor is often said to hold the keys to his own cell. This means that once the contemnor brings himself into compliance, he will be freed.[13] Under this rationale a party who is imprisoned for failing to comply with an order to pay is not incarcerated because he is a debtor, but because he is a contemnor.[14] From this viewpoint, the contemnor imprisons himself by his refusal to comply, but only for so long as he refuses to comply. The justification is perhaps too good by a half. While a contemnor may bring himself into compliance, the fact remains that his imprisonment is the product of a court order. This open-ended deprivation of liberty is not taken lightly and courts have struggled to balance the competing goals that are raised, in this context, between securing compliance for its own sake (and the values that compliance will bring into existence) and the recognition

---

[11] Section 194.2 (Coercive Imprisonment).

[12] Section 194.4 (Coercive Fine).

[13] Gregory v. Depte., 896 F.2d 31, 37 (3d Cir. 1990).

[14] *E.g.*, Watson v. Givens, 758 A.2d 510, 515 (Del. Fam. Ct. 1999); *cf.* Marshall v. Mathei, 744 A.2d 209, 217 (N.J. Super. Ct. A.D. 2000) (recognizing writ of *capias ad satis faciendum*, which permits arrest of judgment-debtors who have means to satisfy outstanding judgments, but refuse to do so, as analogous to contempt proceedings and an exception to prohibition on imprisonment for debt).

that deprivation of liberty is a significant sanction. The length of imprisonment may become disproportionate to the values compliance would secure; moreover, the sanction may, in fact, have no real coercive value since the contemnor may prefer imprisonment to compliance.

While a conditional sanction of imprisonment may have a formal "purge" element, *i.e.,* compliance will secure the contemnor's immediate release from imprisonment, the "purge" element may be illusory. A recalcitrant witness imprisoned for refusing to provide testimony may base the refusal to comply on any number of grounds, some of which may be deemed principled or otherwise. A father may refuse to disclose the location of a child he is accused of physically abusing. [15] A wife may refuse to disclose to her husband the location of their child on the ground that the husband has abused the child. The refusal may persist even though the court finds the charge of abuse to be without a sound factual basis. [16] A news reporter may refuse to disclose a source due to the reporter's belief that his information should be protected from disclosure because it came from a confidential source. [17] A witness may refuse to provide testimony to a Grand

[15] *In re* King, 756 P.2d 1303 (Wash. 1988) (holding that father's imprisonment for over 11 months for refusing to disclose child's whereabouts had not lost its coercive potential).

[16] Morgan v. Foretich, 564 A.2d 1, 11 (D.C. 1989) (holding that since there was no realistic possibility of substantial likelihood that wife would disclose location of child, order had lost its coercive effect and wife should be released from prison after spending 25 months incarcerated). A rehearing was granted and the opinion was vacated. 564 A.2d at 20–21. The reason for the vacation was that Congress enacted the District of Columbia Civil Contempt Imprisonment Limitations Act of 1989, Pub. L. No. 101-97, 103 Stat. 633 (1989). The law was directed toward the contemnor and designed to secure her release from confinement. Randal White, Student Comment, *Civil Contempt and Congressional Interference in the Case of Morgan v. Foretich,* 95 Dick. L. Rev. 353 (1991). In *Anyanwu v. Anyanwu,* 771 A.2d 672 (N.J. Super. Ct. A.D. 2001), a father was incarcerated for refusing to facilitate the repatriation of his children to this county from Nigeria. The Appellate Division reversed a release order issued by the lower court. The Appellate Division found that the father had not demonstrated that the order of imprisonment had lost its coercive effect. The father, a professor at a New Jersey State University, had been imprisoned since August 14, 1997, a period of 3 1/2 years. It was reported that the father was released in early 2002. (www.indypressny.org/article.php.3?Article ID = 83) (visited April 26, 2005).

[17] Farr v. Superior Court, 99 Cal. Rptr. 342 (Cal. App. 1971), *cert. denied,* 409 U.S. 1011 (1972) (involving a purported confession by one of the defendants in the Manson murder trial). Farr had received the information from a person subject to a "gag" order. When Farr refused to disclose to the judge who the source was, Farr was imprisoned for contempt. The court rejected Farr's claims that his right to protect his confidential sources was protected by the First Amendment. *Id.* at 349. Notwithstanding the decision, Farr persisted in his refusal to disclose. He was again imprisoned. On further review the trial court determined that further imprisonment would have no coercive effect. The court proceeded to try Farr for criminal contempt, but the first effort ended in an acquittal and a second effort was deemed barred by the double jeopardy clause. *In re* Farr, 134 Cal. Rptr. 595, 598 (Cal. App. 1976) (discussing the procedural history of the effort to hold Farr in contempt of court for refusing to disclose his source(s)). A recent report in the Columbia Journalism Review reports the case of Vanessa Leggett who spent 168 days in prison rather than surrender her notes pursuant to a grand jury subpoena and court order. (www.cjr.org) (visited March 26, 2002). A more recent case involves New York Times reporter Judith Miller who has refused to comply with a court order to testify regarding the disclosure of Valerie Plame's status as a C.I.A. employee. Adam Liptak, *Reporter Jailed After Refusing to Name Source,* New York Times (July 7, 2005), available at

Jury because she believes that the prosecutor is abusing his office to make a case for impeachment against the President.[18] A witness may refuse to testify based on claims of fear of danger to personal safety[19] or religious belief.[20] A person may refuse to obey a court order for naked self-interest.[21] This last ground appears to account for an increasing number of recent cases involving defendants who have moved their assets offshore as part of "asset protection programs" and seek to avoid repatriation of the assets pursuant to court order.[22] In some cases, refusal appears to be based on pure spite.[23] In all of these cases, a court must decide whether the conditional order has lost its coercive effect, all the while knowing that a favorable ruling may encourage other future contemnors in their recalcitrance.

The analysis here is different from that employed in the usual ability to comply case. In the typical ability to comply case the issue is whether in fact the defendant has the proverbial "keys" to his cell in his pocket.[24] Here

---

www.nytimes.com/2005/07/07/politics/07leak.html (visited July 9, 2005) (registration required); *cf. In re* Grand Jury Subpoena, Judith Miller, 397 F.3d 964 (D.C. Cir.) (rejecting claim that there is a federally recognized journalist's evidentiary privilege regarding sources), *cert. denied sub nom.* Miller v. United States, 125 S. Ct. 2977 (2005).

[18] *In re* Grand Jury Subpoena, 97 F.3d 1090 (8th Cir. 1996) (upholding subpoena issued to Susan McDougal seeking her testimony in connection with special independent counsel's investigation of "Whitewater" activities involving President Clinton). Ms. McDougal spent 18 months in prison for refusing to provide testimony and cooperate with independent counsel's investigation. Ms. McDougal was subsequently charged by independent counsel with obstruction of justice and criminal contempt for her refusal to testify. Ms. McDougal was acquitted of the charge of obstruction of justice and the jury deadlocked on charge of criminal contempt. Washington Post, April 13, 1999, at A01.

[19] Catena v. Seidl, 343 A.2d 744 (N.J. 1975) (involving a contemnor who refused to provide testimony claiming that doing so would subject him to physical retribution by those against whom he provided testimony).

[20] Simkin v. United States, 715 F.2d 34, 36 (2d Cir. 1983) (involving witness who refused to testify on the ground that informants were viewed with disdain under Jewish law and liturgy). The court held that while fear of reprisal was not a valid reason for refusing to comply with an order to testify, the trial court should consider all the facts that went into the witness's recalcitrance to determine if the order had lost its coercive effect. *Id.* at 38–39; *see* Tara Adams Ragone, Student Comment, *In Contempt of Contempt? Religious Motivation as a Reason to Mitigate Contempt Sanctions*, 1999 Ann-Survey of Amer. Law 295.

[21] United States v. McNulty, 446 F. Supp. 90, 92 (N.D. Cal. 1978) (refusing to grant release to contemnor who refused to repatriate Irish Sweepstakes winnings to the United States to satisfy federal tax liens). The contemnor was subsequently released when the judge concluded that continued incarceration would not result in compliance. KENNETH YORK, JOHN BAUMAN & DOUG RENDLEMAN, REMEDIES, CASES AND MATERIALS 159 (5th ed. 1991).

[22] *E.g., In re* Lawrence, 279 F.3d 1294 (11th Cir. 2002) (affirming order of coercive imprisonment for debtor who refused to repatriate assets in offshore trust); Sections 31.5 (Freeze Orders), 194.3 (Ability vs. Willingness to Comply).

[23] *E.g.,* H. Beatty Chadwick v. Janecka, 312 F.3d 597 (3d Cir. 2002) (discussing Mr. Chadwick's unsuccessful efforts to prove that an order that he place $2.5 million in an escrow account, reflecting money belonging to his ex-wife, had lost its effectiveness). Mr. Chadwick is reported to have spent 10 years in prison for his continuing contempt. BOSTON.COM NEWS, March 22, 2006, *Millionaire Held for Contempt For 10 Years,* available at *www.boston.com / news / nation / article / 2006 / 03 / 22 / millionaire_held_for_contempt_for_10_years /*

[24] Pompey v. Cochran, 685 So. 2d 1007, 1015 (Fla. Ct. App. 1997).

the issue is not whether the contemnor has the keys, for he does; rather, the issue is whether the contemnor has the willingness to insert the "key" and unlock the cell door. The situation should also be distinguished from the risk to the contemnor of compliance, which is properly a function of whether the order should be entered in the first place.[25]

Coercive imprisonment can be quite lengthy,[26] although most incarcerations are short. Most individuals probably find that non-compliance is easy to claim but the consequences of non-compliance are difficult to experience. In cases involving recalcitrant witnesses, once the testimony is no longer needed, the reason for coercive contempt ends. Thus, if the trial has concluded, compliance with a trial subpoena is no longer needed. Similarly, once a Grand Jury term has expired, compliance with that Grand Jury's subpoena is no longer needed. In some cases involving recalcitrant witnesses, the court has expressed a rough rule of thumb that an incarcerated contemnor should be allowed an evidentiary hearing to demonstrate the unlikelihood that continued imprisonment will induce compliance within the usual term of a Grand Jury.[27]

The availability of a hearing is different from determining the point that the order has lost its coercive effect. On this latter point "no hard and fast rule or fixed period of time has been set."[28] The issue is resolved on a case by case basis and with some disagreement as to the factors a court ought to consider in determining whether an order is likely to be complied with if the contemnor remains confined. In *Sanders v. Shepard* the court upheld the continued imprisonment of the contemnor who had already spent seven years in jail for abducting and refusing to tell authorities the location of his daughter. Unlike *Morgan,* the contemnor in *Sanders* had kidnapped his daughter from the mother and had spent 3 years in prison for child-abduction. His coercive imprisonment term began after the abduction sentence concluded.[29] As one court noted, the type of findings rendered in this context are sui generis and unlikely to generate predictive rules:

> The determination to be made by the District Judge is far removed from traditional factfinding. What is called for is obviously not a retrospective determination of a historical fact, nor even a prospective determination of a future fact, such as the amount of medical expenses a tort victim will incur. The determination is not even akin

---

[25] In the Matter of Grand Jury Proceedings Impanelled May 1988, 894 F.2d 881 (7th Cir. 1990) (holding that before ordering witness under a grant of immunity to testify when the witness expressed concerns over his physical safety and fear of retaliation, the court should ensure that if the witness' fear is reasonable, the government has taken reasonable steps to protect the witness and his family before ordering him to testify).

[26] *E.g., Chadwick, supra* note 23 (8 years in prison); *Catena, supra* note 19 (5 years in prison); *Anyanwu, supra* note 16 (3 1/2 years in prison).

[27] Acceturo v. Zelinski (State Grand Jury Investigation), 576 A.2d 900, 904 (N.J. Super. Ct. A.D. 1990)..

[28] *Id.* at 903.

[29] 630 N.E.2d 1010, 1015 (Ill. App.) (noting that contemnor had provided no evidence that he could not or would not comply with court's order), *aff'd,* 645 N.E.2d 900 (Ill. 1994).

to fact-finding as to a future hypothetical matter, such as the profits a plaintiff would have made but for a defendant's actionable wrong-doing. Instead, the district judge is obliged to look into the future and gauge, not what will happen, but the prospect that something will happen.[30]

[194.3] Ability Versus Willingness to Comply

The inability to comply with an order is a complete defense to civil contempt. A court may order a person to do what he has the power to do and may back up that order with the sanction of coercive contempt; however, the court may not order the defendant to do what he cannot do and then punish him for failing to do it. The necessary limitation on coercive contempt is that there must be the ability to comply. It would be a monstrous injustice to imprison a person until she complies with the order she is incapable of complying. We would treat as a moral and legal abomination an order of coercive confinement based on a person's failure to comply with an order that required her to run a 1-minute mile, high jump 15', or fly by flapping her arms. The examples are extreme, but the point they make is not. Ability to comply is basic to coercive contempt. This principle has early antecedents.[31]

Inability does not mean undesirability. A party may be required to do that which he can do even though it would require significant lifestyle changes. In *Moss v. Superior Court of Riverside County* the court held that a parent who claimed inability to comply with support orders and willfully refused to find work could be sanctioned through coercive contempt. The court noted:

> We conclude therefore, that neither the constitutional prohibition of involuntary servitude nor the bar to imprisonment for debt precludes imposition of a contempt or criminal sanction on a parent who, having the ability to do so, willfully fails to pay court-ordered child support, or when necessary to make payment possible willfully fails or refuses to seek and accept available employment for which the parent is suited by virtue of education, experience, and physical ability.[32]

---

[30] *In re* Parrish, 782 F.2d 325, 327 (2d Cir. 1986). *But cf.* Matter of Crededio, 759 F.2d 589, 592 (7th Cir. 1985) (requiring that the trial judge, in evaluating the continuing effectiveness of penal incarceration to induce compliance, must make a "conscientious assessment of the relevant factors" and an "individualized determination that [the contemnor's] incarceration has not lost its coercive effect") (brackets added). *Crededio* can be read as casting the burden of proof on the plaintiff to demonstrate the efficacy of continued imprisonment.

[31] Cash v. Quenichett, 52 Tenn. 737, 741 (1871).

[32] 950 P.2d at 76. While there are some older decisions to the contrary, *see Ex Parte Hamberg*, 217 P. 264 (Id. 1923), the modern trend is consistent with *Moss. But cf.* Street v. Street, 480 S.E.2d 118, 122 (Va. App. 1997) (holding that parent who voluntarily reduced his income and thereby rendered himself unable to pay support ordered by court was not subject to coercive contempt absent evidence that reduction was contumacious). The issue of coercive contempt may be superceded when a jurisdiction "criminalizes" the failure to pay support. *E.g.*,

Inability also does not man unwilling. The "obstinant" contemnors who prefer imprisonment over compliance are "willingness to comply" cases, not "ability to comply" cases.[33] A persistent and unyielding recalcitrance evidences the futility of the remedy, not that the contemnor lacks the ability to comply if he wanted to comply.[34]

The burden of demonstrating "inability" is usually placed on the defendant.[35] A person cannot assume that a change in circumstances will automatically excuse his required compliance with a court order. The proper approach is to seek modification of the order based on changed circumstances.[36]

[194.4] Coercive Fine

A court may seek to insure compliance with its order by threatening a monetary fine that will be exacted if the order is not obeyed. As noted earlier, in the case of coercive fines there is invariably a delay between the point in time the fine is "threatened" and the point in time the fine is "exacted," with the defendant's violation of the order in between.[37] The combination of a "purge" factor and fixed fines to induce prospective compliance has raised a complicated issue of proper characterization of contempt as criminal or civil. That was the issue addressed by the Court in the *Bagwell* case.[38]

Bagwell involved a strike that turned violent. The mine owners ("company") obtained a comprehensive injunction addressing many of the

---

United States v. Craig, 181 F.3d 1124, 1127 (9th Cir. 1999) (holding that a court in ordering restitution of past due child support, upon violation of Federal Child Support and Recovery Act, 18 U.S.C. § 228, is not required to inquire into financial capability of determination to pay restitution award; if defendant is unable to pay, he should seek modification of support order). The Child Support Act makes it unlawful for a person to willfully fail to pay a past-due support obligation with respect to a child who resides in another state.

[33] Section 194.2 (Coercive Imprisonment).

[34] *Compare* King v. Dept. of Social & Health Service, 756 P.2d 1303 (Wash. 1988) (ordering release of wife who was incarcerated for not complying with order to disclose location of her child; the court found that the wife did not know where the child was located and, therefore, the wife could not comply with the order), *with* Anyanwu, *supra*, 771 A.2d at 680 (noting that "defendant is not held in the Norris County Correctional Facility for failure to perform the feat of producing his living child in a New Jersey courthouse. Since 1997, he has been required only to make good efforts to comply with orders toward effectuating that result"). *Cf.* United States v. Williams, 121 F.3d 615, 620–21 (11th Cir. 1997) (holding that there was sufficient evidence that defendant "willfully" failed to pay child support when he took lower paying job to evade support obligations).

[35] Staffon v. Staffon, 587 S.E.2d 630 (Ga. 2003) (holding that support obligation is not excused or diminished for incarceration due to voluntary criminal conduct); In re Marriage of Thurmond, 962 P.2d 1064 (Kan. 1998) (noting that cases evidence three approaches to the problem whether incarceration for commission of a crime warrants a reduction in support obligations: (1) the no-justification approach; (2) the complete-justification approach; and, (3) the one-factor approach).

[36] Section 36 (Modification of Injunctions).

[37] Section 194.1 (Procedure for Obtaining Coercive Sanction).

[38] International Union, United Mine Workers of America v. Bagwell, *supra*, 512 U.S. 821.

violent acts that were occurring during the strike and containing a schedule of escalating fines if there were future violations of the injunction. The injunction was, however, violated on numerous occasions. Due to escalating fines in the injunction, the fines ultimately aggregated over 60 million dollars. The parties then settled the dispute and ended the strike. The opinion is silent, but it is customary in these settings for the company to waive any claim it has to fines or damages arising out of the strike. The trial court vacated the fines payable to the company, but did not vacate the fines payable to the affected counties and the state. The non-vacated fines were upheld by the Virginia Supreme Court, but the Supreme Court reversed.

There are several factors that make *Bagwell* a difficult case. The trial court levied a conditional fine that the union could avoid by complying with the injunction. In this sense, the violation of the injunction looked like a case of coercive civil contempt. On the other hand, the injunction itself was quite detailed in terms of the type of conduct it prohibited and the level of fine that would be imposed. Once the injunction was violated, the sanction was uniform and fixed for the violation. Lastly, the fine was paid to the government. In this sense, the violation of the injunction looked like a case of criminal contempt. The problem the Court confronted was that the very nature of coercive contempt using conditional fines is that once the injunction is violated, the punishment becomes fixed.[39] If that alone was sufficient to cause the contempt to be deemed criminal, coercive contempt using conditional fines would be largely abolished. Coercive contempt could be limited to orders that imposed mandatory ("Thou shall") as opposed to prohibitory ("Thou shall not") obligations.[40]

The precise holding of *Bagwell* is somewhat unclear. The Court reversed the fine because the contempt was deemed "criminal" and the union had not been provided process appropriate to a criminal proceeding. The Court identified a number of factors relative to the characterization of the contempt proceedings as "criminal," but did not identify any rank order of importance or preference regarding the factors. The openness of the Court's opinion permits several possible readings of *Bagwell*: a broad holding and a narrow holding.

Broad holding:	All fixed, determinate fines are criminal sanctions notwithstanding the ability to avoid the sanction by complying with the order or to purge the sanction by bringing oneself into compliance with the order.

---

[39] Section 194 (Coercive Civil Contempt).

[40] Chandler v. James, 180 F.3d 1254, 1268 (11th Cir. 1999) (Tjoflat, J. concurring), *judgment vacated on other grounds sub nom.* Chandler v. Siegelman, 530 U.S. 1256 (2000). Judge Tjoflat's narrow view of the contempt power is critiqued by Doug Rendleman, *Irreparability Resurrected?: Does a Recalibrated Irreparable Injury Rule Threaten the Warren Court's Establishment Clause Jurisprudence*, 59 Wash. & Lee. L. Rev. 1348, 1388 (2002). Judge Tjoflat's distinction was raised by the union in *Bagwell*. The Court discussed the point in *Bagwell* and did not reject it out of hand. 512 U.S. at 835.

Narrow   The decision is limited to cases involving ongoing
holding: disputes and complex transactions that the court
              attempts to regulate and control by an injunction
              that prescribes a detailed code of conduct.

Adoption of the "Broad holding" would not nullify coercive contempt using conditional fines. It would, however, require that the contemnor be afforded criminal due process when the defendant was found to be in contempt. Adoption of the "Narrow holding" would permit coercive fines to be exacted in proceeding at which civil due process was afforded the contemnor as long as the case was not factually comparable to *Bagwell*. How close to *Bagwell* the proceedings and injunction could come before stepping over to the criminal due process side is unresolved.[41]

In *Evan v. Williams* the court gave *Bagwell* a liberal reading. The court downplayed the fact, as had the Court in *Bagwell*, that the court announced the fines prospectively so that the defendant could avoid the fine by complying with the order.[42] Rather, the court emphasized that the fines were fixed and determinate and that "once imposed, there was no opportunity to eliminate it through future compliance" even though it could have been avoided by initial compliance.[43] The court also refused to limit *Bagwell* to cases involving extraordinary fines.[44]

These points would suggest a large, preemptory role for *Bagwell*. On the other hand, the court ultimately grounded its decision in what it ascertained as the salient aspect of *Bagwell*—the injunction that acts as a "detailed code of conduct."[45] When an injunction effectively transmutes into a legislative-type control over a party's conduct, the case for treating the order different from a statute is diminished. It is, ultimately, the nature of the order that controls.[46]

---

[41] *Compare* People v. Operation Rescue Nat'l, 80 F.3d 64 68 n.7 (2d Cir.), *cert. denied sub nom.* Broderick v. United States, 519 U.S. 825 (1996) (holding that "under *Bagwell* a noncompensatory fine is civil, and thus may ordinarily be imposed in the absence of a criminal trial '. . . if the contemnor is afforded an opportunity to purge' "), *with* N.O.W. v. Operation Rescue, 37 F.3d 646, 661 (D.C. Cir. 1994) (requiring that all noncompensatory fines be imposed in proceedings in which contemnors are afforded protections available in criminal contempt proceedings). In *Crowe v. Smith*, 151 F.3d 217, 226–28 (5th Cir. 1998), *cert. denied sub nom. In re* Wright, 526 U.S. 1158 (1999), the court held that all substantial fines paid to the court must be exacted through processes that afford the defendant criminal due process. The court suggested that a $5,000 fine would trigger the requirement. *See* Mackler Productions v. Cohen, 146 F.3d 126, 129 (2d Cir. 1998) (same involving $10,000 fine).

[42] 206 F.2d 1292, 1295–96 (D.C. Cir. 2000).

[43] *Id.* at 1296.

[44] *Id.* (holding that a fine of $5 million was "serious" for purposes of *Bagwell*).

[45] *Id. citing Bagwell*, 512 U.S. at 836.

[46] *See* 3A Charles Alan Wright, Nancy J. King & Susan R. Klein, Federal Practice & Procedure Criminal 3d § 704 (3d ed. 2004).

[194.5] Excessiveness

The contempt sanction, whether a daily fine (coercive civil contempt) or fixed penalty (criminal contempt), must be calibrated to the seriousness of the misconduct, the damage that has resulted, and the good that preventing further misconduct will generate. Excessive fines and penalties raise questions of proportionality and reasonableness that traditionally have been considered components of fundamental fairness. On the other hand, a fine or penalty must be large enough to catch the contemnor's attention.

Large fines and penalties are not uncommon in cases where parties have disobeyed court orders.[47] The general approach of courts has been to review claims of excessiveness on a case-by-case basis. The courts have suggested that, with respect to coercive fines, the fine should be set at the least amount necessary to secure compliance. However, many of the cases involve injunctions/orders issued by federal courts requiring state officials to bring their conduct in conformity with federal law. It is unclear if the "least amount" principle is a general guideline or one limited to cases involving contempt sanctions imposed on state officials by federal courts and, thus, influenced by principles of federalism as well as concerns over remedies.

The size of the fine is a factor the Court has identified as marking the boundary between civil and criminal contempt.[48] The size of the fine may also trigger a right to jury trial; however, the Court has not identified when a contempt fine triggers a right to jury trial in the context of criminal contempt. In *Muniz v. Hoffman* the Court held that a $10,000 fine against a union did not give rise to a right to jury trial.[49] The Court emphasized that the union had 13,000 members, which substantially diluted the impact of the fine. The types of fines that, to date, have been found sufficiently "serious" to warrant treatment of the contempt as criminal rather than civil[50] would appear to satisfy the "seriousness" trigger for jury trial.[51]

[194.6] Recipient of Collected Fines

When a coercive sanction results in the collection of fines imposed for the period of non-compliance, the rule is that the fines are payable to the court, not the parties.[52] Occasionally, courts state that a coercive sanction will be paid to a party, but as the court noted in *New York State National*

---

[47] New York State Nat'l Org. for Women v. Terry, 886 F.2d 1339, 1351 (2d Cir. 1989) (involving daily fine of $25,000 for each future violation of court order), *cert. denied*, 495 U.S. 947 (1990); Margaret Meriwether Cordray, *Contempt Sanctions and the Excessive Fines Clause*, 76 N.C.L. Rev. 407, 417 & n.44 (1998) (collecting decisions).

[48] *Bagwell, supra*, 512 U.S. at 836; *see Evans, supra* 206 F.3d at 1296. Both decisions are discussed in Section 194.4 (Coercive Fines).

[49] 422 U.S. 454, 477 (1975).

[50] *Bagwell, supra*, 512 U.S. 821 ($52 million); *Evans, supra*, 206 F.3d 1292 ($5 million).

[51] *See* Mindy Boyce, *Right to Jury Trial*, 89 Geo. L.J. 1515, 1517 n. 1559 (2001) (collecting decisions on when fine or sanction triggers Sixth Amendment right to jury trial).

[52] *Hicks ex rel. Feiock, supra*, 485 U.S. at 632.

Org. for Women v. Terry, those decisions "are either distinguishable or indicate merely that a complainant's evidentiary burden is not great in the contempt context."[53] The reference to "evidentiary burden" refers to compensatory contempt and suggests that the "fine" was actually designed and intended to compensate the plaintiff for losses resulting from the contemnor's disobedience of the court order.[54] The fact that the "fine" is paid to the court is also a factor that courts rely on when characterizing the contempt as criminal rather than civil.[55]

§ 195   COMPENSATORY CONTEMPT

The remedy of contempt may be used in many jurisdictions to compensate a party for losses caused by the contumacious conduct.[1] Some jurisdictions do not, however, recognize compensatory damages as a remedy for contempt.[2]

When compensatory contempt is available, the "willfulness" of the contempt may be a significant factor. While willfulness is not an element of civil contempt,[3] the contemnor's state of mind in engaging in the contumacious conduct is a factor the court may take into account in determining the appropriate level and amount of compensation to be awarded.[4]

It is often stated that compensatory contempt is limited to "actual damages," but the statement must be limited to situations when damages are sought.[5] Many courts have permitted "disgorgement of profits" as a

---

[53] 886 F.2d 1339 1353–54 (2d Cir. 1989), *cert. denied,* 495 U.S. 947 (1990). The court held that the "district court abused its discretion when it allocated this coercive sanction to plaintiff N.O.W." *Id.* at 1353; *In re* Dinnan, 625 F.2d 1146, 1149 (5th Cir. 1980), *per curiam* (stating that "[a] coercive, non punitive fine payable to the clerk of the court is an appropriate tool in civil contempt cases"); Winner Corp. v. H.A. Caesar & Co., 511 F.2d 1010, 1015 (6th Cir. 1975) (dicta) (holding that a coercive fine should be paid to the court not the complainant).

[54] Connolly v. J.T. Ventures, 851 F.2d 930, 932 (7th Cir. 1988) (noting that when "compensation is intended, a fine may be imposed payable to the complainant") (citation omitted).

[55] *Mackler Productions, Inc., supra,* 225 F.3d at 142; Section 192 (Classification of Contempt as Criminal or Civil).

[1] McComb v. Jacksonville Paper Co., 336 U.S. 187, 191 (1949).

[2] H.J. Heinz Co. v. Superior Court of Alameda Cty., 266 P.2d 5, 12 (Cal. 1954) (holding that since an order of contempt is designed to vindicate the dignity and authority of the court, not the private rights of individuals, compensatory contempt would not be allowed); Keuper v. Beechen, Dill & Sperling Bldr., 704 N.E.2d 915 (Ill. App. 1998). *See generally* Annotation, *Right of Injured Party to Award of Compensatory Damages or Fines in Contempt Proceedings,* 85 A.L.R.3d 895 (1978).

[3] Manhattan Indus., Inc. v. Sweater Bee By Banff, Inc., 885 F.2d 1, 5 (2d Cir. 1989), *cert. denied sub nom.* Banff, Ltd. v. Salant Corp., 494 U.S. 1029 (1990); Section 193 (Elements of Civil Contempt).

[4] Canterbury Belts, Ltd. v. Lane Walker Rudkin, Ltd., 869 F.2d 34, 39 (2d Cir. 1989); Section 8.7 (Harsh or Mild Measures).

[5] City of New York v. Local 28, Sheet Metal Workers, Int'l Assn, 170 F.3d 279, 284 (2d Cir. 1999); Gemco Latino Am. v. Seiko Time Corp., 61 F.3d 94, 100 (1st Cir. 1995).

remedy for compensatory contempt.[6] Some courts have permitted remedies for contempt in the nature of specific performance.[7]

Compensatory damages can include:

- Out-of-pocket expenses;[8]
- Statutory damages;[9]
- Lost profits;[10]
- Lost wages;[11]
- Lost revenue.[12]

A few decisions have addressed whether officers of a corporation can be personally liable for compensatory contempt when assisting the corporation in violating the order. In *Parker v. United States*[13] the court found the corporate officer personally liable when, on the facts, he had intended by his actions to cause a loss and had engaged in the conduct over a long period of time to render the corporation incapable of complying with the order. The court rejected efforts to fasten personal liability based merely on the defendant's status as corporate officer. Status liability was, however, upheld in *Connolly v. J.T. Ventures*.[14] The *Connolly* court affirmed a finding of personal liability holding that as officers, the defendants were bound by the order and could be punished to the same extent as the corporate defendant.[15]

The fact that a fine is incremental, *e.g.*, daily, does not mean that it cannot be compensatory. A fine may have both coercive *and* compensatory attributes; as long as the compensatory aspect "corresponds to some degree with the amount of damages," it is proper and enforceable.[16]

In *F.T.C. v. Kuykendall*[17] the court considered the interplay between the Supreme Court's decision in *Bagwell*, which constrained the ability of courts

---

[6] Colonial Williamsburg Found. v. Kittinger Co., 792 F. Supp. 1397, 1407 (E.D. Va. 1992) (collecting decisions recognizing remedy of "disgorgement of profits"), *aff'd*, 38 F.3d 133 (4th Cir. 1994); *cf. Manhattan Indus., Inc., supra*, 885 F.2d at 6 (permitting measuring of monetary sanction through use of unjust enrichment theory).

[7] Hart v. McChristian, 36 S.W.3d 357, 364 (Ark. 2000) (upholding compensatory contempt order that defendant file application with the FCC to transfer broadcast license to plaintiff).

[8] Time Warner Cable of New York City v. U.S. Cable T.V., Inc., 920 F. Supp. 321, 329 (E.D.N.Y. 1996) (awarding plaintiff actual costs incurred in seizing and preventing distribution of "black boxes" used to intercept plaintiffs signal notwithstanding that plaintiff suffered no actual statutory damages caused by the illegal importation of the boxes).

[9] *Id.* at 331 (awarding statutory damages of $10,000 per unit for sale of cable signal descrambler facilitated by contemnor violation of consent decree).

[10] Connolly v. J.T. Ventures, 851 F.2d 930, 933–34 (7th Cir. 1988).

[11] *City of New York, supra*, 170 F.3d at 284.

[12] American Airlines, Inc. v. Allied Pilots Association, 228 F.3d 574, 585 (5th Cir. 2000).

[13] 126 F.2d 370, 379 (1st Cir. 1942).

[14] 851 F.2d 930.

[15] *Id.* at 935; Section 35 (Person Bound by Equitable Relief).

[16] Paramedics Electromedicina Commercial, Ltda v. GE Medical Systems Information Technologies, Inc., 369 F.3d 645, 658 (2d Cir. 2004) (citation omitted).

[17] 371 F.3d 745 (10th Cir. 2004) (*en banc*).

to use civil coercive contempt to secure compliance with detailed, complex orders,[18] and civil compensatory contempt. The court held that in cases of civil *compensatory* contempt the reasoning of *Bagwell* was not applicable. While the similarities between coercive and criminal contempt warranted that in close cases the defendant be afforded criminal due process, that approach did not apply to compensatory contempt even though the order was complex and the fine was large ($39 million).[19]

The court further noted that the fines did not lose their compensatory character because they included some non-compensatory relief or because the plaintiff F.T.C. was asserting claims on behalf of third party consumers.[20]

To recover in compensatory contempt a party must establish a violation of the order by clear and convincing evidence.[21] Once contempt has been established, however, the general understanding is that the amount of damages need only be proven by a preponderance of the evidence.[22]

§ 196 ATTORNEY'S FEES

Many jurisdictions permit the recovery of attorney's fees for prosecuting a civil contempt action.

Some decisions require that the contemnor willfully violate the order before attorney's fees are recoverable.[1] Although stated at times as a requirement, the "willfulness" element may be more appropriately characterized as a justification for awarding fees.[2] Other decisions suggest a more flexible standard committing the matter to the discretion of the court.[3]

---

[18] *Bagwell*, 512 U.S. 821 (discussed in Section 194.4 (Coercive Fine)).

[19] *Kuykendall*, 371 F.3d at 752 & n.3 (noting language in *Bagwell* when the Court emphasized that the challenged fines were not compensatory).

[20] *Id.* at 753.

[21] *Id.* at 756–57:

> [T]he FTC has the burden of proving by clear and convincing evidence, (1) that a valid order existed, (2) that the defendant[s] had knowledge of the order, and (3) that the defendant[s] disobeyed the order

(citations and quotation marks omitted); *American Airlines, Inc., supra*, 228 F.3d at 578 (same).

[22] McGregor v. Chierico, 206 F.3d 1378, 1387 (11th Cir. 2000 (collecting decisions).

[1] Manhattan Indus., Inc. v. Sweater Bee By Banff, Inc., 885 F.2d 1, 8 (2d Cir. 1989), (stating that "courts in this Circuit generally 'award the reasonable costs of prosecuting the contempt, including attorney's fees,' only where violation of a court order is found to be wilful") (citations omitted), *cert. denied sub nom.* Banff, Ltd. v. Salant Corp., 494 U.S. 1029 (1990).

[2] Hester Indus., Inc. v. Tyson Foods, Inc., 985 F. Supp. 236, 250 (N.D.N.Y. 1997), *vacated on other grounds,* 160 F.3d 911 (2d Cir. 1998); *cf.* Police Commissioner of Boston v. Gows, 705 N.E.2d 1126, 1129 (Mass. 1999) (stating that award of fees is inconsistent with the "American Rule" that generally denies a fees award to the prevailing party; therefore, a fees award should be reserved for "rare and egregious cases"); Section 210 (Attorney's Fees—The "American Rule").

[3] Food Lion, Inc. v. United Food and Commercial Workers Int'l Union, AFL-CIO, 103 F.3d 1007, 1017 n.14 (D.C. Cir. 1997) (collecting decisions and noting conflict but not deciding issue since fees had not yet been awarded; thus, issue was not ripe for adjudication); Colonial Williamsburg Found. v. Kittinger Co., 38 F.3d 133, 137 (4th Cir. 1994).

Some jurisdictions reject the award of attorney's fees to the prevailing party, applying the "American Rule," that absent a contract or statute, each party bears its own litigation costs, including attorney's fees. [4]

An award of attorney's fees has also been justified as within the ambit of compensatory contempt. [5] The decision itself is somewhat ambiguous as to the reason for awarding attorney's fees; however, if fees are awarded as damages, the award should comport with general rules for allowing the recovery of attorney's fees as damages. [6]

§ 197   DEFENSES TO CONTEMPT

A person charged with contempt based on disobedience of a court order may assert the defense that the order was issued without, or in excess of, the court's subject matter jurisdiction. Such an order is void and of no legal effect. [1]

An alleged contemnor may also defend on the ground that he did not in fact violate the order. For example, in *United States v. Cutler* the court applied the collateral bar rule to prohibit the contemnor from contesting the constitutional validity of a "gag order" he had violated in connection with a criminal prosecution he was defending. [2] The court did, however, permit the contemnor to question whether he had in fact violated the terms of the "gag" order which prohibited the contemnor "from discussing the merits of the [case] with the media only if his comments were reasonably likely to 'interfere with a fair trial or otherwise prejudice the due administration of justice' ". [3] Moreover, because First Amendment rights were involved, the court applied a more rigorous scrutiny to the factual finding of contempt, although the court ultimately upheld the finding of contempt and the sanction imposed. [4] In this regard, the defendant may be aided by the tendency to read orders narrowly and resolve ambiguities in favor of the contemnor. [5]

---

[4] *See generally* A.S. Klein, Annot., *Allowance of Attorneys' Fees in Civil Contempt Proceedings,* 43 A.L.R.3d 793 (1972); Section 211 (Exceptions to the "American Rule").

[5] Reed v. Hamilton, 39 S.W.3d 115, 119 (Tenn. App. 2000).

[6] Section 211.4 ([Attorney's Fees] Third Party Tort).

[1] People v. Gonzales, 910 P.2d 1366, 1374 (Cal. 1996).

[2] 58 F.3d 825, 832–33 (2d Cir. 1995); Section 198 (Collateral Bar Rule).

[3] *Id.* at 833.

[4] *Id.* at 834 (noting that to sustain a charge of criminal contempt "the government ha[s] to prove beyond a reasonable doubt that: (1) the court entered a reasonably specific order; (2) defendant knew of that order; (3) defendant violated that order; and (4) his violation was willful") (citations omitted).

[5] Sections 34 (Specificity of Injunctive Relief), 193.3 (Order Must be Clear and Definite).

§ 198 COLLATERAL BAR RULE

[198.1] Scope and Nature of Collateral Bar Rule

The "collateral bar rule" prohibits many legal challenges to the validity of the order by one who is charged with violating the order. The rule is ordinarily limited to criminal contempts. A person charged with civil contempt is usually permitted to defend on the ground that the order she is charged with violating is invalid or erroneous.[1] However, it is not always clear whether a contempt citation will generate a civil or criminal contempt sanction. The limitation, therefore, may not be beneficial for cautious individuals who will be adverse to the risk that if they violate the order they will be held in criminal contempt. Moreover, a few decisions do not respect the distinction between civil and criminal contempt and apply the collateral bar rule to civil contempt.[2]

The collateral bar rule requires that a party comply with the order if the party wishes to challenge the validity of the order. The force of the rule was made evident in the cases of *Walker v. City of Birmingham*[3] and *Shuttlesworth v. City of Birmingham*,[4] both of which arose out of civil rights protests in the 1960s against racial discrimination in the South.

Numerous individuals and civil rights groups wished to engage in protest demonstrations on Good Friday and Easter Sunday in Birmingham, Alabama. City officials obtained an ex parte TRO on the Wednesday before Good Friday. The TRO was based on a Birmingham city ordinance that vested substantial discretion in local officials as to when a parade (public demonstration) permit should be granted "in the public welfare." The TRO application made conclusory allegations that the protests would endanger public safety.[5] There was no material difference in language between the

---

[1] *In re* Establishment Inspection of Hern Iron Works, 881 F.2d 722, 726 n.11 (9th Cir. 1989).

[2] Southern Ill. Med. Bus. Assocs. v. Camillo, 567 N.E.2d 74, 83 (Ill. App. 1991). Reasons for applying the collateral bar rule to civil contempt were noted in *Garry v. Garry*, 467 N.Y.S.2d 175 (Sup. Ct. 1983):

> The reason for this is obvious: the orderly administration of justice requires that parties not be permitted to make private, unreviewable decisions as to whether a judgment should be obeyed. Admittedly, there is authority to the contrary, suggesting that a party charged with civil contempt, but not criminal contempt, may collaterally attack the order or judgment violated. But, as the latter treatise points out, collateral attack, where permitted, has been often justified "when some overriding policy would be impaired by a failure to permit such a challenge," *e.g.,* "when the judgment or order being challenged attempts to restrain or inhibit constitutionally protected conduct." Also, there has been some expression of judicial concern that a party who obtained an erroneous judgment should not be permitted to receive a windfall in fines imposed for the contempt.

Id. at 180 (citations omitted).

[3] 388 U.S. 307 (1967).

[4] 394 U.S. 147 (1969).

[5] *Walker, supra,* 388 U.S. at 309.

ordinance and the TRO, which was granted. The next day, Thursday, notice of the TRO was served on various individuals involved in the protests and a press conference was held later in the day, at which time several individuals disclosed their intent to protest notwithstanding the TRO. Similar sentiments were voiced at a meeting that Thursday night. Protest demonstrations were held on Good Friday and Easter Sunday notwithstanding the TRO and without any effort to seek a stay, modification, or vacating of the order. The protests were generally peaceful.[6]

On Monday, the officials who had procured the TRO began proceedings to have certain individuals, who had received notice of the TRO, held in contempt of court for violating the TRO [the *Walker* defendants]. Other individuals were charged with violating the city ordinance on which the TRO was based [the *Shuttlesworth* defendants]. Both groups of defendants alleged that the city's efforts to bar the protests violated First Amendment guarantees. In *Shuttlesworth* a unanimous Supreme Court agreed that the ordinance was clearly violative of First Amendment guarantees. In *Walker* the defendants fared less well for the Court, by a 5 to 4 majority, upheld the lower state court's refusal to allow the defendants' claim that the TRO was constitutionally defective. The reason for this refusal was the collateral bar rule. Because the *Walker* defendants had violated the TRO, they could not challenge its constitutional validity. The *Shuttlesworth* defendants, who had violated the similarly worded ordinance, could challenge the ordinance's constitutionality, and did so successfully.

The justification for the collateral source bar is said to be the judiciary's need to preserve its authority and dignity, coupled with the fact that the legal system itself provides mechanisms for the further review of a judicial order either by the court that issued the order or by a reviewing court of appeal.[7] A number of jurisdictions have found this argument unpersuasive when it involves a constitutionally defective order. As noted by the Texas Supreme Court in *Ex Parte Tucci*:

> Underlying our state law is the principle that speech delayed often translates into speech denied. The Texas approach represents the converse of the federal collateral bar rule, which was relied upon in Walker v. City of Birmingham, to bar the release of Dr. Martin Luther King, Jr. and others from the Birmingham jail for disregarding unconstitutional restrictions upon their civil rights marches. Citizens must not "be muffled pending outcome of . . . proceedings" to dissolve an injunction, since [t]he ability to exercise protected protest at a time when such exercise would be effective must be as

---

[6] These two cases are part of a larger tapestry that illustrates the Civil Rights movement in the South in the 1960s. Among those arrested on Good Friday was Dr. Martin Luther King, Jr. During his incarceration he wrote his memorable "Letter From a Birmingham Jail," a letter that helped catapult Dr. King to the leadership position of the Civil Rights movement until his assassination in 1968.

[7] *Walker*, 388 U.S. at 314, *citing and quoting,* Howat v. Kansas, 258 U.S. 181 (1922), and *citing* United States v. United Mine Workers of America, 330 U.S. 258 (1947).

protected as the beliefs themselves . . . . It is a flagrant denial of constitutional guarantees to balance away this principle in the name of "respect for judicial process." To preach "respect" in this context is to deny the right to speak at all. Nor is Texas alone in recognizing the unduly restrictive nature of a collateral bar rule.[8]

Under the approach adopted in *Tucci,* even if the court that issued the order possessed subject matter jurisdiction over the matter and personal jurisdiction over the parties, an order that exceeds the court's power, "whether that power be defined by constitutional provision, express statutory declaration, or rules developed by the courts," renders the order void.[9]

[198.2] Exceptions to Collateral Bar Rule

Courts that follow the collateral bar rule have identified several exceptions to its application. The exceptions, however, appear to be more available in theory than in practice. The exceptions require satisfaction of substantial legal hurdles by the contemnor who seeks to avoid the collateral bar rule.

The first exception is that the collateral bar rule will not be applied when the order, which was disobeyed, was "transparently invalid or had only a frivolous pretense to validity."[10] This is a limited exception. A strong presumption is given to validity.[11] Moreover, this exception is further limited by the requirement that the contemnor make "good faith efforts to seek emergency relief" before violating the order and must show "compelling circumstances justifying his decision to ignore the order."[12]

A second exception has been recognized when there is no effective procedure available to obtain judicial review of the order before it is violated.[13] This exception was applied in *United States v. Ryan.* The Court held that *Walker* does not apply in the context of a subpoena duces tecum because one to whom a subpoena is directed may not appeal from a motion

---

[8] 859 S.W.2d 1, 2 (Tex. 1993) (citing decisions from California, Washington, and Arizona).

[9] Del Papa v. Steffen, 915 P.2d 245, 249 (Nev. 1996) (*quoting In re* Berry, 436 P.2d 273, 280 (Cal. 1968)), *cert. denied sub nom. In re* Whitehead, 519 U.S. 1107 (1997).

[10] *Walker, supra,* 388 U.S. at 315 (suggesting exception); Matter of Providence Journal Co., 820 F.2d 1342 (1st Cir. 1986), *modified on other grounds,* 820 F.2d 1354 (1st Cir. 1987), *cert. dismissed,* 485 U.S. 693 (1989).

[11] *Matter of Providence Journal Co., supra,* 820 F.2d at 1347–48.

[12] *Cutler, supra,* 58 F.3d at 833. The exception was, however, recognized in *State v. Alston,* 887 P.2d 681 (Kan. 1994) (holding that "gag" order was transparently invalid when the trial court failed to make the requisite *Nebraska Press* findings). The *Alston* court also noted that information for which the contempt was issued was a matter of public record and the order was issued without a full and fair hearing. The *Nebraska Press* findings are that a judge may not issue a "gag" order barring or limiting news coverage of a public trial unless the judge evaluates and examines (1) the nature and extent of the pretrial news coverage; (2) whether other measures would be likely to mitigate the effects of unrestrained pretrial publicity; and (3) the effectiveness of a "gag" order in actually preventing disclosures. *Id.* at 686, *citing* Nebraska Press Ass'n v. Stuart, 427 U.S. 539, 562 (1976).

[13] *Walker, supra,* 388 U.S. at 315 n.6 (suggesting exception).

to quash but must either comply or refuse to do so and contest the validity of the subpoena).[14] As noted in *Ryan*:

> We think that respondent's assertion misapprehends the thrust of our cases. Of course, if he complies with the subpoena he will not thereafter be able to undo the substantial effort he has exerted in order [to] comply. But compliance is not the only course open to respondent. If, as he claims, the subpoena is unduly burdensome or otherwise unlawful, he may refuse to comply and litigate those questions in the event that contempt or similar proceedings are brought against him. Should his contentions be rejected at that time by the trial court, they will then be ripe for appellate review. But we have consistently held that the necessity for expedition in the administration of the criminal law justifies putting one who seeks to resist the production of desired information to a choice between compliance with a trial court's order to produce prior to any review of that order, and resistance to that order with the concomitant possibility of an adjudication of contempt if his claims are rejected on appeal.[15]

Since the contemnor is required to disobey the subpoena to secure appellate review of its validity, fundamental fairness requires that disobedience not cause him to lose challenges to the subpoena's validity. Notwithstanding the acceptance of the exception, it may be given cursory application.[16]

A third exception involves claims that compliance would cause irreparable injury.[17] Application of the irreparable injury exception appears, however, to be limited to situations where no immediate appellate review is available. There appears to be little real difference in practice between the second and third exceptions. As noted by the Court in *Maness*:

> When a court during trial orders a witness to reveal information, however, a different situation may be presented. Compliance could cause irreparable injury because appellate courts cannot always 'unring the bell' once the information has been released. Subsequent

---

[14] 402 U.S. 530 532–83 n.9 (1971), *citing* Cobbledick v. United States, 309 U.S. 323 1940).

[15] *Id.* at 532–33 (citations and footnotes omitted).

[16] *E.g.*, Mullally v. City of Los Angeles, 49 Fed. Appx. 190 (9th Cir. 2002) (invoking collateral bar rule to deny a challenge to the validity of a protective order). Mullally was convicted of criminal contempt for violating the order, which prevented disclosure of information regarding criminal conduct by members of the Los Angeles Police Department. The court relied entirely on the "transparently invalid" argument and did not discuss the non-appealability exception even though protective orders, which are not appealable because they are simply pretrial discovery or judicial housekeeping orders, fall within the exception. *See generally* Sean P. McBride, Student Comment, *The Collateral Bar Rule and Rule 26 Protective Orders: Overprotection of Judicial Discretion*, 35 Ariz. St. L.J. 1029 (2003).

[17] Maness v. Meyers, 419 U.S. 449, 460–63 (1975) (stating that the contemnor could challenge the order to testify notwithstanding the fact that he violated the order because the basis of his claim was the privilege against self-incrimination and the contemnor would suffer irreparable injury if he was required to speak to preserve a challenge to the order's validity).

appellate vindication does not necessarily have its ordinary consequences of totally repairing the error. In those situations we have indicated the person to whom such an order is directed has an alternative:

[W]e have consistently held that the necessity for expedition in the administration of the criminal law justifies putting one who seeks to resist the production of desired information to a choice between compliance with a trial court's order to produce prior to any review of that order, and resistance to that order with the concomitant possibility of an adjudication of contempt if his claims are rejected on appeal.[18]

There is also, for lack of a better term, an *ad hoc* category of exceptions. This category encompasses cases when the collateral bar rule is simply ignored. For example, in *Johnson v. Virginia* there was a standing order maintaining racially segregated seating in state courtrooms. The contemnor (Johnson), who was African-American, violated the order by refusing to move from the section reserved for Whites. Johnson did not seek review of the order before violating it. The Court permitted Johnson to challenge the validity of order in his criminal contempt case, which he did successfully.[19] The *Johnson* decision may be limited. It may be an example of a transparently invalid order. Even though that may not have been the case in 1963, it is certainly the case today. Why the *Walker* defendants were treated differently is a mystery.

[198.3]   "Jurisdiction to Determine Jurisdiction" Rule

It is universally recognized that a court that lacks subject matter jurisdiction cannot issue a valid order; consequently, such an order may be challenged by a contemnor without regard to the collateral bar rule.[20] A significant exception to this rule, however, is the counterrule that a court has jurisdiction to determine whether it has jurisdiction! Even if the court does not have subject matter jurisdiction over the matter, it has subject matter jurisdiction to consider whether it has jurisdiction over the matter; therefore, orders issued to permit the court to consider the matter are valid and not void. Such orders are, therefore, subject to the collateral bar rule.

The "jurisdiction to consider jurisdiction" exception could literally swallow the rule. Some formulations and applications of the "jurisdiction to consider jurisdiction" exception appear to adopt such an approach. A more restrained view appears, however, to dominate. Under the restrained approach, the order must relate to the effort by the court to determine if

---

[18] *Id.* at 460, *citing, inter alia, Cobbledick* and *Ryan*.

[19] 373 U.S. 61 (1963).

[20] United States v. United Mine Workers of America, 330 U.S. 258, 293 (1947); Mead Sch. Dist. 354 v. Mead Educ. Ass'n, 534 P.2d 561, 564–65 (Wash. 1975) (discussing tests and approaches used to determine if court that imposed contempt had jurisdiction to issue the order that was disobeyed).

it has jurisdiction. For example, *United States v. Thompson*[21] involved the issuance of a subpoena to a witness outside the United States and the subsequent noncompliance by the witness. The court stated:

> The Government further argues, relying on United States v. United Mine Workers, and United States v. Bryan, that even assuming the district court was without power or jurisdiction to order a grand jury subpoena under § 1783, Thompson could not ignore with impunity such an order which was valid on its face. In the United Mine Workers case it was held that except in circumstances of plain usurpation, a United States District Court has the authority to determine its own jurisdiction in a matter before it, and to maintain the status quo, as by issuance of a temporary restraining order, pending the determination of that issue. The Supreme Court concluded, therefore, that even should the district court be ultimately found, in such a case, to lack jurisdiction over the parties or the subject matter, it had power to punish violations of its prior restraining order as contempt. Here, however, the court was not seeking to preserve existing conditions pending a jurisdictional determination. Similarly inapposite is United States v. Bryan, which dealt with the failure of a witness under subpoena to raise objections to the competence of the body before which he appeared to testify. That decision did not touch the question of the validity of the subpoena which was issued or the power or jurisdiction of the body issuing it. We hold, therefore, that a mandate is void which is beyond the power and jurisdiction of the issuing court and that the court may not punish for its violation. Thus, the power and jurisdiction of the court to issue a subpoena may be raised for the first time in a proceeding to punish for contempt.[22]

An order maintaining the status quo while the court determines if it has jurisdiction would be valid, but this concession would not extend to an order that afforded a party substantial relief.

§ 199 ATTEMPTED CONTEMPTS

[199.1] Anticipatory Contempt

The general rule is that a coercive sanction requires that the contemnor be in violation of the order at the time of the contempt proceeding. An example of this rule is *United States v. Johnson*.[1] In *Johnson* a defendant, Timothy Neal, was involved in a bank robbery. He initially agreed to provide testimony against other defendants, but reneged, apparently out of concern for his physical safety. Neal was then tried and convicted of bank

---

[21] 319 F.2d 665 (2d Cir. 1963).

[22] *Id.* at 667–68 (citations omitted).

[1] 736 F.2d 358 (6th Cir. 1984).

robbery. The government then sought his testimony. At a hearing on the government's motion to compel testimony, Neal refused, but his refusal was indefinite. As noted by the court: Neal was found in contempt based on "his statement that he will in the future refuse to testify at a trial that has not yet begun."[2] The court held that such a statement could not be the basis for a coercive sanction:

> [I]mposing coercive imprisonment upon the statement that testimony will not be given in the future is certainly a greater exercise of power than imposing a similar sanction upon an actual demand for, and refusal of, testimony . . . . The inquiry by the court as to whether the witness will testify at a future date is itself an exercise of power not normally used in contempt proceedings.[3]

Another way of looking at the problem is to imagine that Neal promised at the hearing that he would testify, but thereafter Neal changed his mind. Contempt would not lie for his breach of promise because a promise is not an order.[4] Stating a present intent not to testify in the future is no different from stating a present intent to testify in the future. In either case, the witness remains free to change his mind between the date of the promise and the date his testimony is required. Given that freedom, contempt is not an appropriate sanction.

[199.2] Evasion of Anticipated Order

Contempt sanctions may be sought to address efforts undertaken by a party before an order is issued to frustrate the implementation of the order that is ultimately entered. This issue has proved to be nettlesome. There is substantial authority that holds that it is not contumacious to engage in conduct before a court order is entered (and which is encompassed by the prospective order) that results in the party being unable to comply with the court order when it is subsequently entered. For example, in *Ex Parte Guetersloh* a property owner, with knowledge that the court would soon enter an order prohibiting certain uses of his property, engaged in those uses.[5] The trial court held him in criminal contempt, the court of appeals affirmed, but the Texas Supreme Court reversed. The court found that the defendant's pre-order actions could not be deemed contumacious:

> An alleged contemnor cannot be held in constructive contempt of court for actions taken before the court reduces its order to writing. The property owners' association argues that the thrust of the court of appeals' contempt finding is that Guetersloh continued building on the property without approval after the trial court issued the

---

[2] *Id.* at 360.

[3] *Id.* at 363; *see* United States v. West, 21 F.3d 607, 608–09 (5th Cir. 1994) (holding that an attorney could not be held in criminal contempt for stating that he would not pay a fine that had been imposed, but which was not yet due).

[4] State v. Matos, 640 A.2d 1176, 1182 (N.J. Super. Ct. A.D. 1994).

[5] 935 S.W.2d 110 (Tex. 1996) (*per curiam*).

injunction. However, the order clearly states that Guetersloh is being punished in part for an act that occurred before the injunction. We cannot segregate the permissible from the impermissible reason for holding Guetersloh in contempt, and therefore the 180-day sentence cannot stand.[6]

If a party acts with awareness of the pendency of an order, he acts at his peril for the court may require him to remediate his conduct and restore the status quo,[7] but the usual view is that his conduct is not contumacious.

In some cases, however, the courts exhibit an intolerance for deliberate, pre-order conduct that frustrates the court's ability to provide equitable relief. For example, in *Griffin v. County School Board of Prince Edward County, Virginia*[8] the defendant had closed the public schools to evade desegregation mandates and made tuition grants to white parents so that their children could attend segregated private schools. The district court enjoined the payment of tuition grants until the public schools were reopened. Subsequently, the court ordered the public schools reopened. The Supreme Court ultimately affirmed the order and the matter was remanded to the district court for further proceedings.

The district court considered several motions regarding unpaid tuition grants. Ultimately, the district court entered a permanent injunction barring reimbursement or payment of tuition grants for the 1963-64 school year, but the court declined to enjoin future grants. Because the public school had "reopened," the prior order enjoining tuition payments was no longer operative. An appeal was taken regarding the refusal to enjoin future grants.

Because the Court of Appeal was not in session, the Chief Judge, through the Clerk of the Court, requested a stipulation that no tuition grants would be made pending the appeal. The Board refused to so stipulate. Communications between the Clerk and the State Attorney General suggested a satisfactory stipulation that the grants would not be paid before the normal time for processing and paying grants, which would be after the schools opened in September, 1964. The status of this "stipulation" was not clear and, in any event, the Board was not a party to it. The appellate opinion is silent as to whether the State Attorney could bind the Board, but the point was not relied on in the opinion.

---

[6] *Id.* at 111 (citation omitted).

[7] Schnepper v. American Info. Techs., Inc., 483 N.E.2d 987 (Ill. App. 1985):

> [A]fter the suit for injunction has been filed and the court has acquired jurisdiction of the person, if the defendant does any act which the complainant seeks to enjoin, he acts at his peril and is subject to the power of the court to compel a restoration of the status quo ante or to grant such other relief as may be proper under the particular circumstances of the case.

Id. at 988–89 (citations omitted); *cf.* Porter v. Lee, 328 U.S. 246, 251 (1946) (stating that "[i]t has been long established that where a defendant with notice in an injunction proceeding completes the acts sought to be enjoined the court may by mandatory injunction restore the status quo").

[8] 363 F.2d 206 (4th Cir.), *cert. denied*, 385 U.S. 960 (1966).

During this time period (August 4-5, 1964) the Board met and ordered that the tuition grants be entered and that one-half of the tuition grants for the 1964-65 school year be made before September 1, 1964. White parents were notified of the Board's action and the checks were distributed and largely negotiated by 9:00 a.m., August 5, 1964. The effort resulted in the disbursement of $180,000 as tuition grants to white parents so as to enable them to enroll their children in private schools. The effect of the disbursements would be less money for, and fewer white children in, the public schools.

The Court of Appeal treated the Board's action as contumacious even though no order had been entered. The court relied on the point that the Board's actions had "impaired the appeal."[9] The authorities on this point are somewhat sparse and it is not inaccurate to note that there was nothing directly on point that supported the court's position that a contempt had occurred. For example, the court relied on *Merrimack River Savings Bank v. City of Clay Center*,[10] in which an injunction was issued barring the destruction by the municipality of public utility poles and wires. The action was dismissed on jurisdictional grounds; however, during the appellate process the injunction was kept in place. Ultimately, the Supreme Court upheld the dismissal; however, during the period the appellant could petition for a rehearing and before the injunction expired or was vacated, the municipality destroyed the poles and wires. For this, the municipality was held in contempt. *Merrimack River Savings Bank* can be expansively construed for the court did suggest in dicta that the presence of the injunction was not controlling:

> "[I]rrespective of any such injunction actually issued the willful removal beyond the reach of the court of the subject-matter of the litigation . . . [on] appeal . . . is, in and of itself, a contempt of the appellate jurisdiction of this court."[11]

On the other hand, a narrower construction consistent with both the facts of *Merrimack River Savings Bank* and the general case law is also available. In *Reliance Ins. Co. v. Mast Constr. Co.*, the court noted:

> Generally speaking, a person who violates an injunction or temporary restraining order during its pendency is subject to a compensatory civil contempt judgment, even if the injunction or restraining order later terminates due to passage of time or mootness.[12]

What was clear in *Griffin*, however, was the continued obstinacy of the Board and others in resisting desegregation. In such cases, one should not be surprised when the precedents are expansively construed to achieve what the court believes is a "just" result, particularly when the court

---

[9] *Id.* at 211.

[10] 219 U.S. 527, 535–36 (1911).

[11] *Id.* at 535–36.

[12] 84 F.3d 370, 376 (10th Cir. 1996) (citations omitted).

perceives the acts to be deliberate efforts to frustrate any relief the court may order.[13]

An interesting application of the "evasion" issue occurred in *Doe, 1-13 ex rel. Doe Sr., 1-13 v. Bush.*[14] The district court failed to certify a class, but that did not prevent the district court from finding the defendants in contempt for failing to provide class-wide redress.[15] The court found that there existed an "implied" class based on the parties' conduct and expectations regarding the litigation and its outcome.[16] The court also noted *its* expectations, based on prior appeals, that the remedy would be system-wide rather than just limited to the plaintiffs before the court.[17]

The question of the "scope" of injunctive relief is discussed elsewhere in these materials, but it is not unusual that an injunction will benefit others than those who are party's before the court.[18] *Doe, 1-13 ex. rel. Doe Sr.* permits that, in such cases, the party(ies)' may use contempt to secure the benefits of the injunction for others. It would seem that the non-parties should also be able to use contempt if they are deemed proper third party beneficiaries of the order, but that issue remains open, as does the acceptance of the *Doe, 1-13 ex rel. Doe Sr.* approach.

---

[13] City of Cleveland v. City of Fairview Park, 582 N.E.2d 1053, 1055 (Ohio App. 1989) (applying *Griffin* when conduct "was intended to destroy jurisdiction by rendering the action moot and so preclude the impact of any adverse decree that might have resulted from the remand"); Griffin v. State Bd. of Educ., 296 F. Supp. 1178, 1182 (E.D. Va. 1969) (distinguishing and refusing to apply *Griffin* rationale when "the disbursements were made in utmost good faith, wholly without defiance of judicial decree and devoid of any semblance of maneuver to escape one"). Interestingly, the author of *Griffin v. State Bd. of Educ.* was also the author of *Griffin v. County Sch. Bd. of Prince Edward County, Va.*, discussed *supra*, text and notes 8–9.

[14] 261 F.3d 1037 (11th Cir. 2001), *cert. denied sub nom.* Kearney v. Does 1-13, 534 U.S. 1104 (2002).

[15] The district court did certify a class in *Doe*, but it was after the defendants had been found in contempt and the case was on appeal. The plaintiffs in *Doe* were developmentally disabled individuals who had been placed on waiting lists for entry into intermediate care facilities. They brought a § 1983 suit on behalf of themselves and those similarly situated alleging that the long waiting lists violated the Medicaid Act and the Social Security Act. 261 F.3d at 1041–42. Plaintiffs filed a motion for certification, but there was no ruling. In 1996, the district court granted summary judgment for the plaintiffs. The judgment was for the plaintiffs only; the motion for certification was impliedly denied. *Id.* at 1043. The Eleventh Circuit affirmed. *Id.* Two months later, the plaintiffs sought to enforce the summary judgment by filing a motion for contempt, alleging that there were 600 individuals on waiting lists in violation of the previous court order. The district court found the defendants in contempt; the defendants appealed claiming that they were not obligated to comply with the order on a class-wide basis, because the suit was never certified as a class action. *Id.* at 1048. Then in 2000, approximately 3 months after defendants appealed the contempt citations, the district court certified the class. *Id.* at 1041. Defendants also appealed that order and both appeals were consolidated.

[16] *Id.* at 1049–51.

[17] *Id.* at 1051.

[18] Section 33.1 ([Permanent Injunctions] Scope of Relief).

Chapter 23

PUNITIVE DAMAGES

SYNOPSIS

§ 200 INTRODUCTION

Punitive or exemplary damages can trace a lineage from the Code of Hammurabi and the Old Testament. Exodus 22:1 reads: "If a man shall steal an ox or a sheep and kill it, he shall restore five oxen for an ox, and four sheep for a sheep." Unlike the "eye for an eye" concept, which is compensatory (in an egalitarian sense) in tone, this passage from Exodus is clearly retributive. It is an eye for an eye, plus some teeth as added compensation![1]

The early common law recognized that compensation for civil wrongs often included the payment of a civil penalty to the crown as well as compensatory damages to the plaintiff.[2] This merger of compensatory and punitive was reflected in the substantial deference given jury awards. The idea of damages as generally limited to compensation did not crystallize until the end of the eighteenth century.[3] Punitive damages as a distinct remedy begins at this time.[4] Punitive damages received early recognition in American courts after the War of Independence with England.[5] Today, almost all American jurisdictions permit the award of punitive damages in civil actions.[6]

Notwithstanding this level of general acceptance, no remedial issue has received more public, judicial, and scholarly analysis and criticism than punitive damages. The constitutionality of the remedy has been addressed by the Supreme Court several times in the last two decades. In the most significant of the cases in which the Court considered the constitutionality of punitive damages awards, the Court held in *BMW of North America, Inc. v. Gore* that under certain conditions an award could violate the due process guarantee of the 14th Amendment.[7] The *BMW* decision, in turn, has spawned a swarm of decisions in this area and encouraged a cottage industry in the study of the subject. Punitive damages have been analyzed, studied, critiqued, and defended.[8] It is probably the only remedy to have

---

[1] Transportation Ins. Co. v. Moriel, 879 S.W.2d 10, 36–37 (Tex. 1994) (Doggett, J., concurring) (describing the history of punitive damages in Western law).

[2] Gail Heriot, *An Essay on the Civil-Criminal Distinction With Special Reference to Punitive Damages*, 7 J. Contemp. Legal Issues 43, 43–44 (1996) (discussing early common law forms of action of tort and appeal of felony and noting their civil-criminal hybrid nature); *see* Norman T. Braslow, *The Recognition and Enforcement of Common Law Punitive Damages in a Civil Law System: Some Reflections on the Japanese Experience*, 16 Ariz. J. Int'l & Comp. L. 312, 313–44 (1999) (discussing availability of "punitive" damages in some ancient legal systems and at common law).

[3] SEDGWICK ON DAMAGES § 349 (8th ed. 1891).

[4] Wilkes v. Wood, 98 Eng. Rep. 489, 498–99 (K.B. 1763) (upholding jury award in excess of actual damages); Huckle v. Money, 95 Eng. Rep. 768, 769 (K.B. 1763) (same).

[5] Coryell v. Colbaugh 1 N.J.L. 77 (1791) (discussed in SEDGWICK ON DAMAGES, *supra* at § 351).

[6] Richard A. Seltzer, *Punitive Damages in Mass Tort Litigation: Addressing The Problems of Fairness, Efficiency and Control*, 52 Fordham L. Rev. 37, 44 (1983) (stating that all but four states recognize punitive damages awards).

[7] 517 U.S. 559 (1996); Section 205.1 (*BMW* and *Campbell*).

[8] A. Mitchell Polinsky & Stephen Shavell, *Punitive Damages: An Economic Analysis*, 111

received a critique in a magazine devoted to scientific inquiry.[9] The critics and defenders of punitive damages have debated whether the remedy poses a danger to law (and society) as we know it, or is so inconsequential as to be essentially harmless.[10] As with most things in life, the truth probably lies somewhere in between.[11]

§ 201 PURPOSE OF PUNITIVE DAMAGES

[201.1] Punish

Punitive damages are designed to punish, and justified on that ground. As noted in *Molzof v. United States*:

> Although the precise nature and use of punitive damages may have evolved over time, and the size and frequency of such awards may have increased, this Court's decisions make clear that the concept of "punitive damages" has a long pedigree in the law. "It is a well-established principle of the common law, that in actions of trespass and all actions on the case for torts, a jury may inflict what are called exemplary, punitive, or vindictive damages upon a defendant, having in view the enormity of his offense rather than the measure of compensation to the plaintiff."[1]

The punitive function brings the civil law system close to the criminal law system; nonetheless, courts have resisted the temptation to apply criminal process to punitive damages claims.[2]

Harv. L. Rev. 869, 954 (1998) (reaching the primary conclusion that punitive damages "should be imposed when deterrence otherwise would be inadequate because of the possibility that injurers would escape liability"); Paul Mogin, *Why Judges, Not Juries, Should Set Punitive Damages*, 65 U. Chi. L. Rev. 179 (1998) (arguing that the Seventh Amendment does not require that punitive damages awards be determined by the jury and that, as a matter of policy, authority to award and set the amount of punitive damages should be sited in the judge not the jury); David Crump, *Evidence, Economics, and Ethics: What Information Should Jurors be Given to Determine the Amount of a Punitive Damage Award*, 57 Md. L. Rev. 174 (1998) (arguing that awarding punitive damage should encourage the deterrence goal of law and that tying awards to the blameworthiness of the defendant is counterproductive); Stephen Daniels & Joanne Martin, *Myth and Reality in Punitive Damages*, 75 Minn. L. Rev. 1 (1990) (analyzing the social agendas of the defenders and critics of punitive damages awards).

[9] Richard Mahoney & Stephen Littlejohn, *Innovation on Trial: Punitive Damages Versus New Products*, 246 Science 1395 (Dec. 1989) (arguing that the fear of punitive damages, coupled with a legal regime predicated on uncertainty, discourages new product innovation and introduction into the market).

[10] *Compare*, National Law Journal, July 29, 1991 (discussing studies that state that punitive damages are awarded infrequently and when awarded are frequently reversed or reduced), *with Punitive Jury Still Out*, Business Insurance, May 27, 1996, at 1 (suggesting that punitive damages awards remain a significant concern for American business).

[11] *See Symposium: Reforming Punitive Damages*, 38 Harv. J. Legis. 469 (2001). The Symposium contains an excellent summary of the positions, and conflicts of opinion and data, regarding punitive damages. Robert A. Klinck, *The Punitive Damages Debate, id.* at 469–476.

[1] 502 U.S. 301, 306 (1992) (citations omitted).

[2] *E.g.*, Browning-Ferris Indus. of Vt. Inc. v. Kelco Disposal, Inc., 492 U.S. 257, 262–76 (1989) (rejecting effort to apply 8th Amendment "excessive fines" clause to punitive damages claim).

Current challenges to punitive damages have not focused so much on the punishment function as on the ability of lay jurors to appropriately inflict punishment in a civil context. The idea that civil law may punish in some circumstances seems to be generally accepted;[3] it is the execution of the idea that draws criticism.[4]

For a punitive damages award to punish, the award should touch the defendant so that he is aware of the sanction and its purpose. Although that principle is well enshrined in criminal law,[5] it is less well received on the civil law side.[6] While punishment is closely tied to punitive damages, the idea of punishment is not unique to punitive damages. The idea that punishment is an appropriate component of the remedy is seen at a number of points in the civil law,[7] but punishment here remains the exception rather than the rule.

Finally, punishment as a justification can be situation specific or general: should the defendant be punished because he committed a bad act or because he is a bad person. If the latter, can either party introduce evidence of "other" good or bad acts? The general rule is to deny "other acts" evidence.[8] On the other hand, a court has suggested that other act evidence would be admissible under the theory of mitigation.[9]

[201.2] Deter

Punitive damages are also designed to deter wrongful conduct by the defendant or others.[10] Ironically, the deterrence rationale has been the

---

[3] *See* David G. Owen, *The Moral Foundations of Punitive Damages*, 40 Ala. L. Rev. 705 (1989); Stein on Personal Injury Damages §§ 4:3, 7:92 (3d ed. 1997).

[4] *See* Cass Sunstein, Daniel Kahneman & David Schkade, *Assessing Punitive Damages*, 107 Yale L. Rev. 2071 (1998).

[5] *E.g.,* Ford v. Wainwright, 477 U.S. 399, 409 (1986) (holding that 8th Amendment prohibits execution of prisoner who is presently insane because, among other reasons, the disability prevents the prisoner from appreciating the reason for his punishment); *cf.* Atkins v. Virginia, 536 U.S. 304 (2002) (holding that 8th Amendment prohibits execution of prisoners who are mentally retarded).

[6] G.J.D. v. Johnson, 713 A.2d 1127, 1129 (Pa. 1998) (noting split in decisions regarding the survivability of a punitive damages claim against a defendant who dies). *See generally* Jay M. Zitter, Annot., *Claim For Punitive Damages in Tort Action as Surviving Death of Tortfeasor or Person Wronged*, 30 A.L.R.4th 707 (1984); Section 75.1 (Survival Actions).

[7] Andrew Kull, *Restitution's Outlaws*, 78 Chi-Kent L. Rev. 17 (2003) (arguing that in a number of contexts restitution includes a punitive function and component); Sections 8.7 (Harsh or Mild Measure), 41 (Restitution for Wrongdoing), 46.2 (Defendant's Culpability), 51 (Disgorgement Orders).

[8] Wohlwend v. Edwards, 796 N.E.2d 781 (Ind. App. 2003) (rejecting effort to introduce subsequent arrests of defendant for DUI in case seeking punitive damages).

[9] Norwest Bank, New Mexico, N.A. v. Chrysler Corp., 981 P.2d 1215, 1225 (N. Mex. App. 1999) (holding that defendant could introduce evidence that it promoted use of seat belts, even though failure to use seat belts was not admissible with respect to compensatory damages claim); *see* Crump, *Evidence, Economics, and Ethics, supra*, 57 Md. L. Rev. at 226 (discussing "other evidence" problem). The "other evidence" issue has also become part of the due process test applied to punitive damages awards. Section 205.1 (*BMW* and *Campbell*).

[10] Stein on Personal Injury Damages, *supra* at § 4:4.

focus of many critics of punitive damages awards who contend that punitive damages are inefficient and provide inaccurate incentives.[11] Some commentators contend that the very threat of punitive damages may discourage individuals from engaging in prudent risk calculations because jurors may disagree with the assessment and use that risk-benefit calculation to award punitive damages.[12] Notwithstanding academic criticism of the deterrence rationale, the intuitive appeal of deterrence remains and courts continue to recite it as a justification for awarding punitive damages.[13]

The deterrence rationale supports the awarding of punitive damages when the defendant's misconduct is difficult to detect. In such circumstances, not all victims may seek redress; therefore, compensatory damages alone may not deter because paying only some of the victims even their full damages may not deter the defendant when overall violations are profitable.[14]

[201.3] Compensate

Some jurisdictions overtly tie punitive damages to a compensatory goal. As noted by the Michigan Supreme Court:

> In Michigan, exemplary damages are recoverable as compensation to the plaintiff, not as punishment of the defendant. Our review of the precedent indicates that those cases which permit recovery of exemplary damages as an element of damages involve tortious conduct on the part of the defendant. An award of exemplary damages is considered proper if it compensates a plaintiff for the "humiliation, sense of outrage, and indignity" resulting from injuries "maliciously, wilfully and wantonly" inflicted by the defendant. The theory of these cases is that the reprehensibility of the defendant's conduct both intensifies the injury and justifies the award of exemplary damages as compensation for the harm done to the plaintiff's feelings.[15]

[11] W. Kip Viscusi, *Punitive Damages: How Jurors Fail to Promote Efficiency*, 39 Harv. J. Legis. 139 (2002).

[12] Steven Garber, *Punitive Damages and Deterrence of Efficiency—Promoting Analysis: A Problem Without a Solution*, 52 Stan. L. Rev. 1809 (2000).

[13] *E.g.*, State Farm Mut. Auto. Ins. Co. v. Campbell, 538 U.S. 408, 415 (2003) (stating that "punitive damages . . . are aimed at deterrence and retribution") (citations omitted). *See generally* 22 Am. Jur. 2d *Damages* § 542.

[14] Perez v. Z. Frank Oldsmobile, Inc., 223 F.3d 617, 621–22 (7th Cir. 2000), *cert. denied*, 531 U.S. 1153 (2001); *see* Robert D. Cooter, *Punitive Damages For Deterrence: When and How Much?*, 40 Ala. L. Rev. 1143, 1149-6 (1989). In *Grimshaw v. Ford Motor Co.*, 174 Cal. Rptr. 348, 383 (Cal. App. 1981), the court expressly noted that the danger that compensatory damages might not deter otherwise profitable violations was particularly acute in commercial relationships.

[15] Kewin v. Massachusetts Mut. Life Ins. Co., 295 N.W.2d 50, 55 (Mich. 1980) (citations omitted); *cf.* Walker v. Dickerman, 993 F. Supp. 101, 106 (D. Conn. 1997) (identifying purpose behind Connecticut's punitive damages law as being compensatory and limiting award to attorney fees incurred by the plaintiff).

Judge Posner built on this compensation rationale by suggesting in a recent case that punitive damages should be available when a compensatory damages award would not adequately redress the harm inflicted on the plaintiff by the defendant:

> One function of punitive damages awards is to relieve the pressures on an overloaded system of criminal justice by providing a civil alternative to criminal prosecution of minor crimes. An example is deliberately spitting in a person's face, a criminal assault but because minor readily deterrable by the levying of what amounts to a civil fine through a suit for damages for the tort of battery. Compensatory damages would not do the trick in such a case, and this for three reasons: because they are difficult to determine in the case of acts that inflict largely dignitary harms; because in the spitting case they would be too slight to give the victim an incentive to sue, and he might decide instead to respond with violence—and an age-old purpose of the law of torts is to provide a substitute for violent retaliation against wrongful injury—and because to limit the plaintiff to compensatory damages would enable the defendant to commit the offensive act with impunity provided that he was willing to pay, and again there would be a danger that his act would incite a breach of the peace by his victim.[16]

Judge Posner further argued that when compensatory damages adequately compensate the plaintiff, the case for punitive damages is reduced.[17] Judge Posner used as an example the Exxon Valdez oil spill in Alaska. Compensatory damages claims exceeded $1 billion. Judge Posner suggested that the size of the compensatory damages award is significant:

> When punitive damages are sought for billion-dollar oil spills and other huge economic injuries, the considerations that we have just canvassed fade. As the Court emphasized in *Campbell*, the fact the plaintiffs in that case had been awarded very substantial compensory damages—$1 million for a dispute over insurance coverage—greatly reduced the need for giving them a huge award of punitive damages ($145 million) as well in order to provide an effective remedy.[18]

There is an intuitive appeal to the "size is important" argument, but we can't really evaluate size in isolation. A large compensatory award may or may not fully redress the plaintiff's injuries because of limits on compensatory damages awards.[19]

The "size matters" argument may also be questioned under the deterrence rationale. A large award may not deter because violations may still be

---

[16] Mathias v. Accor Economy Lodging, Inc., 347 F.3d 672, 676–77 (7th Cir. 2003)

[17] *Id.*

[18] *Id.*

[19] Chapter 2 (General Principles Concerning Compensatory Damages) (particularly Sections 8 (Measuring Compensatory Damages), 10 (Loss Causation), 11 (Economic Loss Rule) and 12 (Non-economic Damages).

profitable or covered by insurance. It is not surprising that many punitive damages awards seek to strip defendants of the profits gained by the misconduct.[20]

§ 202   SCOPE OF PUNITIVE DAMAGES

Not all acts of misconduct permit an award of punitive damages. Punitive damages are reserved for conduct that is outside the pale. Unfortunately, there is no agreement as to where the pale begins or ends; rather, jurisdictions tend to use general categories, (e.g., fraud, wanton and willful), tempered with a case-by-case approach. In general, punitive damages are reserved for outrageous conduct.[1] How outrageous conduct should be redressed has not, however, been reducible to a precise rule.[2] This section examines some of the general considerations jurisdictions use to determine if punitive damages are appropriate.

[202.1]   Socially Deplorable Conduct

Punitive damages are generally limited to cases when the defendant has engaged in socially deplorable conduct, such as fraud, or has acted wrongfully with an improper motive or intent, such as the desire to harass, vex, or annoy. This improper motive or intent is usually referred to as malice. This form of malice (often referred to as "actual malice") should be further distinguished from legal malice. Actual malice is a positive state of mind, evidenced by the positive desire and intention to injure another, actuated by hatred or ill-will towards that person. Legal malice is malice that the law presumes, infers from, or imputes to certain acts.[3]

Actual malice can be evidenced in many ways. Factors that will tend to show its presence include: (1) the defendant's awareness of the likelihood or certainty of harm from its misconduct; (2) the profitability of the defendant's misconduct; (3) the duration of the misconduct; and, (4) defendant's response when being informed of misconduct committed by its agents and employees.[4] It is not enough that the defendant engaged in wrongful

---

[20] *BMW of North Amererica v. Gore, supra,* 417 U.S. 559, 564 (1996) (noting that lower court calculated amount of punitive damage by referring to money earned by selling repaired, slightly damaged vehicles as new without disclosure of prior damages); *cf. In re* Exxon Valdez, 270 F.3d 1215, 1238–39 (9th Cir. 2001) (noting that "the jury may well have decided that for such egregious conduct the company responsible ought to have a year without profit). In the famous Pinto exploding gas tank case, Grimshaw v. Ford Motor Co., 179 Cal. Rptr. 348 (Cal. App. 1981), the jury award equaled the amount of money Ford saved by not providing a safer gas tank for its "Pinto" model automobile. In each of the above cases, the punitive damages award was reduced or vacated for other reasons.

[1] *E.g.,* Sharp v. Case Corp., 595 N.W.2d 380 (Wis. 1999).

[2] Cass R. Sunstein, *Outrage,* 2002 Utah L. Rev. 717, 718 ("The simplest lessons are that punitive damages are rooted in outrage; that levels of outrage command a degree of agreement among diverse Americans, at least in some domains; but that people have a great deal of difficulty in 'mapping' their outrage onto a bounded scale").

[3] Holmes v. Wegman Oil Co., 492 N.W.2d 107, 112–13 (S.D. 1992).

[4] Ramirez v. IBP, Inc., 950 F. Supp. 1074, 1078–80 (D. Kan. 1996) (applying Kansas law), *aff'd,* 145 F.3d 1346 (10th Cir. 1998) (table).

conduct; rather the defendant must act, or fail to act, with the intentional or reckless disregard for the "rights" of others.[5] Mere inaction or inattentiveness to duty that results in harm to another is generally insufficient to permit an award of punitive damages.[6] A defendant's subjective good faith belief that his conduct is legal may defeat a claim for punitive damages.[7]

In some instances, jurisdictions have relaxed the malice threshold for awarding punitive damages to recklessness or even gross negligence.[8] More recently, however, the trend, consistent with tort reform legislation, has been to raise the threshold, as by requiring that the jury find that the defendant's conduct was despicable or that the punitive damages facts be established by a heightened evidentiary standard.

[202.2] Fraud

Courts have consistently recognized that fraud based on the deliberate intent to deceive can support an award of punitive damages.[9] When fraud is based on a lesser standard, such as negligence, punitive damages are generally barred.[10]

Some jurisdictions may limit the contexts in which fraud will support an award of punitive damages.[11]

---

[5] It is generally not required that the defendant's misconduct be specifically directed at the plaintiff as long as it is directed to a group or class of which the plaintiff is a member. Strenke v. Hogner, 694 N.W.2d 296, 306–07 (Wis. 2005).

[6] Brueckner v. Norwich University, 730 A.2d 1086, 1095–96 (Vt. 1999) (rejecting claim that university was liable for punitive damages for fraternity hazing death of student).

[7] Gile v. United Airlines, Inc., 213 F.3d 365 (7th Cir. 2000):

> Punitive damages depend not on the egregiousness of the defendant's misconduct, or its callousness in denying reasonable accommodation, but instead run from a culpable state of mind regarding whether that denial of accommodation violates federal law.

Id. at 375 (citations omitted).

[8] Williams v. Wilson, 972 S.W.2d 260, 263–64 (Ky. 1998) (permitting recovery of punitive damages for gross negligence); Palais Royal, Inc. v. Gunnels, 976 S.W.2d 837, 851 (Tex. App. 1998) (same).

[9] Walston v. Monumental Life Ins. Co., 923 P.2d 456, 466–67 (Idaho 11996) (stating that punitive damages may be awarded when the defendant has committed fraud or has engaged in deceptive business practices for a profit that pose a danger to the public); *cf.* Palm Beach Atl. College v. First United Fund, 928 F.2d 1538, 1546 (11th Cir. 1991) (noting that "[w]hether a fraudulent act is sufficiently outrageous so as to justify an award of punitive damages is a question for the jury") (citations omitted). *See generally* M. David LeBrun, Annot., *Recovery of Punitive Damages in Action by Purchasers of Real Property Charging Fraud or Misrepresentation,* 19 A.L.R.4th 801 (1981).

[10] Reid v. Moskovitz, 255 Cal. Rptr. 910, 912 (Cal. App. 1989) (stating that punitive damages cannot be awarded in cases of negligent misrepresentation).

[11] Walker v. Sheldon, 179 N.E.2d 497, 499 (N.Y. 1961) (permitting punitive damages in cases "where the fraud, aimed at the public generally, is gross and involves high moral culpability").

[202.3] Intentional Infliction of Harm

Courts have found that deliberate conduct that exposes others to the risk of physical injury may support a punitive damages award. For example, in *Granite Construction Co. v. Rhyne* the court upheld an award of punitive damages against a contractor who had entered into a contract with the State of Nevada to protect highway users by providing protective fencing to keep livestock off the highway. The contractor knowingly failed to do so and as a result a motorist was injured when livestock entered onto the highway and collided with his vehicle. The court held that this conduct demonstrated the requisite conscious and deliberate disregard of the safety of others to support an award of punitive damages. [12] The court further observed that the contractor's deliberate decision to bypass the fencing requirement to complete the construction contract on time to avoid "burdensome financial penalties" added further support for the award. [13]

[202.3.1] Bodily Injury

The deliberate infliction of bodily injury upon another is well recognized as grounds for an award of punitive damages. [14] Again the requisite "malice" may often be demonstrated by conscious indifference or reckless disregard of the rights of another. [15]

[202.3.2] Property Damage

Although it is frequently asserted that punitive damages are available in cases of property damage or destruction, the assertion may suggest more than it can deliver. In most cases, the basis for the punitive damages claim is not the malicious injury to the property, but the malicious intrusion into the plaintiff's emotional security. Destruction of the property is often a means to an end—intentional infliction of emotional distress—not an end unto itself. [16]

Punitive damages for injury to property has been recognized when the misconduct violated the plaintiff's rights to the property. The most common example is conversion, [17] but this approach essentially parallels the

---

[12] 817 P. 2d 711, 713 (Nev. 1991).

[13] *Id.*

[14] *E.g.*, Rufo v. Simpson, 103 Cal. Rptr.2d 492 (Cal. App. 2001) (upholding $25 million punitive damages award for the slaying of two individuals by the defendant).

[15] *E.g.*, Smith v. Wade, 461 U.S. 30 (1983) (involving civil rights action under 42 U.S.C. § 1983); *Strenke, supra*, 694 N.W.2d 296 (involving motor vehicle collision, which resulted in bodily injury being sustained by the plaintiff; the defendant had a blood alcohol content of 0.269% and pled "no contest" to a charge of DUI).

[16] *E.g.*, Richardson v. Fairbanks North Star Borough, 705 P.2d 454, 456 (Alaska 1985) (discussing relationship between intentional infliction claim and punitive damages in context of killing of pet by city officials, but upholding lower court's determination that intentional infliction claim was not supported by the evidence nor could a punitive damages claim be asserted against a municipality without express statutory authorization).

[17] *E.g.*, Management Computer Serv., Inc. v Hawkins, Ash, Baptie & Co., 557 N.W.2d 67, 82–83 (Wis. 1996) (finding defendant's misconduct supported an award of punitive damages for acts amounting to conversion of plaintiff's property).

protection of economic interests discussed in Section 202.3.3 (Economic Loss). A number of courts have suggested that malpractice resulting in property damage may support a punitive damages claim if the other requirements, *e.g.*, malice, are met,[18] but again the focus is on a different legal interest than the owner's interest in the property.

[202.3.3] Economic Loss

Punitive damages may be awarded in claims involving economic torts, such as inducing breach of contract, insurance bad faith, etc.,[19] when the tort is committed with the requisite "actual malice."

[202.3.4] Other Invasion of Right

Punitive damage may be available when the defendant maliciously violates the "rights" of another. The most common basis for such claims involve violations of constitutional or statutory rights.[20] The statutory standard must be reviewed to determine if the requirements for imposing punitive damages differ from the common law test.[21] The statute or constitutional text must be examined to determine whether it allows punitive damages in the first place.[22] The malicious violation of rights established by the common law may also provide a basis for punitive damages. Intentional infliction of emotional distress is one example noted earlier,[23] but the example is illustrative not exclusive. The malicious disregard of the rights of another may support an award of punitive damages, when the "right" is that of privacy,[24] reputation,[25] or relationship.[26]

---

[18] *E.g.*, Levine v. Knowles, 197 So. 2d 329 (Fla. App. 1967) (veterinary malpractice); Section 82 (Pets).

[19] *See generally* Sara Johnson, Annot., *Punitive Damages For Interference With Contract or Business Relationship*, 44 A.L.R.4th 1078 (1987); Section 202.5 (Breach of Contract).

[20] Erwin v. County of Manitowoc, 872 F.2d 1292, 1299 (7th Cir. 1989) (recognizing punitive damages for civil rights violations (42 U.S.C. § 1983)).

[21] Smith v. Wade, 461 U.S. 30, 51 (1983) (rejecting heightened proof requirements for punitive damages for a violation of the Civil Rights statute, 42 U.S.C. § 1983; reckless disregard standard was sufficient to sustain a punitive damages award); *cf.* Kolstad v. American Dental Ass'n, 529 U.S. 526, 535 (1999) rejecting requirement of proof of "egregious" conduct before punitive damages could be awarded in employment discrimination case).

[22] Getty Petroleum Corp. v. Bartco Petroleum Corp., 858 F.2d 103, 113 (2d Cir. 1988) (holding that Lanham Act, 15 U.S.C. § 1060, does not authorize an award of punitive damages for the willful infringement of a registered trademark), *cert. denied*, 490 U.S. 1006 (1989).

[23] *E.g.*, Prince v. Bear River Mut. Ins. Co., 56 P.3d 524 (Utah 2002) (noting emotional distress must be based on facts that would support award of punitive damages).

[24] *E.g.*, Rohrbaugh v. Wal-Mart Stores, 572 S.E.2d 881 (W. Va. 2002) (involing improper employer mandated substance abuse testing).

[25] *E.g.*, Gertz v. Robert Welch, Inc., 418 U.S. 323, 349 (1974) (permitting punitive damages against publisher if plaintiff can satisfy *New York Times Co. v. Sullivan* (376 U.S. 254 (1964)) standard); *see* Fahnestock & Co. v. Waltman, 935 F.2d 512, 516 (2d Cir. 1991) (affirming award of $100,000 in punitive damages for defamation), *cert. denied*, 502 U.S. 1120 (1992); Park v. First Union Brokerage Services, Inc., 926 F. Supp. 1085, 1087 (M.D. Fla. 1996) (upholding an arbitration panel award of $500,000 in punitive damages for injury to reputation); Constant

Courts general permit punitive damages whenever the defendant commits a tort under circumstances that demonstrate a wanton or willful disregard of the rights of another.[27]

[202.4] Aiding and Abetting

Punitive damages may be assessed against an aider and abettor of misconduct that qualifies for punitive damages; however, the jurisdiction may require that the aider and abettor be legally capable of committing the misconduct for which punitive damages are awarded.[28] For example, a non-fiduciary who aids and abets a fiduciary's breach of duty may not be capable of committing the breach of duty herself because the aider is not a fiduciary. Under these circumstances, no punitive damages should be awarded against the non-fiduciary based on her status as an aider and abettor.[29]

[202.5] Breach of Contract

It is generally recognized that punitive damages are not available for a breach of contract.[30] The basis for this rule is the principle that contract damages adequately compensate the non-breaching party for the breach-related losses and restore her to her rightful position. Imposing punitive damages would run counter to this principle and would also impose a penal sanction for breach, which the law has historically rejected.[31] When,

---

v. Spartanburg Steel Products, Inc., 447 S.E.2d 194 (S.C.) (affirming jury verdict of $100,000 in punitive damages in defamation action), *cert. denied*, 513 U.S. 1017 (1994).

[26] *E.g.*, Wolf v. Wolf, 690 N.W.2d 887, 893–94 (Iowa 2005) (affirming award of $25,000 in punitive damages for ex-wife's tortious interference with her ex-husband's custodial rights).

[27] Kelsay v. Motorola, Inc., 384 N.E.2d 353, 359 (Ill. 1978) (wrongful discharge claim: punitive damages allowed to deter employer from dismissing employees who file workers compensation claims).

[28] JAMES GHIARDI & JOHN KIRCHER, PUNITIVE DAMAGES: LAW & PRACTICE § 9.09 (1985).

[29] *Cf.* Applied Equip. Corp. v. Litton Saudi Arabia, Ltd. 869 P.2d 454 (Cal. 1994) (holding that a party to a contract cannot be liable for aiding and abetting the tort of inducing breach of contract because a party to a contract owes no tort duty to refrain from interference with that party's contractual performance); Section 202.9 (Vicarious Liability).

[30] Trammell v. Vaughan, 59 S.W. 79 (Mo. 1900). *But see* Paiz v. State Farm Fire & Cas. Co., 880 P.2d 300, 307 (N. Mex. 1994) (stating that in a breach of contract case, punitive damages are available "on a showing of bad faith, or at least a showing that the breaching party acted with reckless disregard for the interests of the non-breaching party"). *Cf.* Given v. Field, 484 S.E.2d 647, 652 (W. Va. 1997) (upholding award of $5.5 million punitive damages award in breach of contract action for failure to pay royalties to inventor). The court noted that the manufacturer never paid the inventor any royalties and attempted to conceal the invention's success and its contractual duty to pay. Section 141 ([Breach of Contract] Bad Faith Breach).

[31] Section 181 (Liquidated Damages).

however, the defendant's breach also constitutes an independent tort, such as fraud[32] or larceny,[33] punitive damages may be awarded.

Many jurisdictions permit an award of punitive damages when the obligation arises out of contract, but the breach involves a duty imposed by law. The two most common examples of this development are: (1) breach of the implied covenant of good faith and fair dealing by an insurer;[34] and, (2) breach of confidence.[35]

[202.6] Equity

Jurisdictions have split as to whether a court of equity may award punitive damages,[36] although the modern trend appears to allow their recovery in equity.[37] Equity courts often awarded legal relief incidental to equitable relief. When punitive damages have been awarded in equity, the authorities are not always clear as to the basis for awarding punitive damages. Does it rest on the court's equity power or in its power to award legal relief incidental to equitable relief?

Some courts hold that when one is proceeding solely in equity, punitive damages are not available.[38] The rejection of punitive damages flows from the history and tradition of equity. The Chancellor did not award punitive

---

[32] Scott v. Jenkins, 668 A.2d 958, 959–60 (Md. Ct. Sp. App. 1995) (stating that "actual malice" required for award of punitive damages may be shown by "fraud").

[33] Pinnacle Envtl. Sys., Inc. v. R.W. Granger & Sons, Inc., 665 N.Y.S.2d 473, 475 (App. Dept. 1997) (permitting punitive damages claim based on diversion of funds subject to state construction lien law: "the unauthorized disbursement of trust assets, without satisfying the claims of contractors or subcontractors, constitutes larceny . . . and 'thus, would clearly satisfy the high threshold of moral culpability necessary to support a punitive damages award' ") (citations omitted).

[34] There are many forms of "insurer bad faith." *See* STEPHEN ASHLEY, BAD FAITH ACTIONS (1984); ROBERT H. JERRY II, UNDERSTANDING INSURANCE LAW §§ 99[c] (3d ed. 2002) (discussing availability of punitive damages for failure of insurer to pay policy proceeds to insured), 110[h][4] (discussing availability of tort damages, including punitive damages, for insurer's breach of duty to defend insured), 112[f] (discussing remedies, including punitive damages, for insurer's failure to settle third party claim against insured).

[35] *E.g.*, Berkla v. Corel Corp., 302 F.3d 909, 918 (9th Cir. 2002) (discussing conflicting California authorities as to availability of punitive damages for breach of confidence arising out of contractual relationship). Section 113 (Breach of fiduciary Duty).

[36] *See generally* Jay Zitter, Annot., *Punitive Damages: Power of Equity Court to Award*, 58 A.L.R.4th 844 (1988).

[37] *E.g.*, Medasys Acquisition Corp. v. SDMS, P.C., 55 P.3d 763, 76–78 (Ariz. 2002) (holding that "an election of an equitable remedy need not preclude an award of punitive damages" and collecting authorities supporting that position).

[38] Santos v. Bogh, 298 So. 2d 460, 461 (Fla. App. 1974); Dekle v. Vann, 223 So. 2d 30, 31 (Ala. 1969); *cf.* Tuxedo Beach Club Corp. v. City Fed. Sav. Bank, 749 F. Supp. 635, 649–50 (D.N.J. 1990) (rejecting attempt to impose punitive damages against entity in receivership because effect of award would be passed through to innocent creditors of the entity). The punitive damages were sought for wrongful conduct before the receiver was appointed. *But cf.* Lussier v. Mau-Van Development, Inc., 667 P.2d 804, 825 (Haw. App. 1983) (rejecting traditional view and allowing award of punitive damages in equitable shareholder derivative action).

damages and the purpose of equity was not to punish but to ensure fairness between the parties.[39] On the other hand, when a statute authorizes an award of punitive damages for certain types of conduct, the statute may trump the equitable characterization of the claim.[40] When the claim involves malfeasance by a trustee, some courts have rejected efforts to impose punitive damages, relying instead on the court's power to surcharge the trustee by reducing the trustee's commissions.[41]

[202.7]　Arbitration

Jurisdictions have split as to whether punitive damages may be awarded in arbitration.[42] In general, federal courts have been more receptive to allowing arbitrators to award punitive damages than state courts.[43] The primary arguments against allowing punitive damages awards in arbitration are (1) the private rather than public nature of the dispute resolution and (2) the absence of an objective standard by which to measure the award.[44] This second concern is overstated insofar as it is based on a perception that compensatory damages are more objective than punitive damages; moreover, recent decisions have reduced the discretion afforded the trier-of-fact in determining punitive damages. Perhaps a more persuasive argument is that the lack of meaningful review of the arbitrator's award would vest nearly complete and unfettered discretion as to the amount of punitive damages in the arbitrator, particularly in light of recent decisions applying due process limitations to punitive damages awards.[45]

[202.8]　Public Entities and Not-For-Profit Organizations

The overwhelming majority of American jurisdictions reject the award of punitive damages against public entities.[46] The same result is often

---

[39] Zitter, *supra*, *Punitive Damages*, at § 2 (noting reasoning that equity "should not become a forum for inflicting vengeance, penalties, or damages of a vindictive or punitive nature").

[40] *Cf.* Ward v. Taggart 336 P.2d 534, 538 (Cal. 1959) (holding that claim for unjust enrichment did not preclude claim for punitive damages as claim was within statute (Cal. Civ. Code § 3294) authorizing punitive damages for misconduct committed by defendant).

[41] Kann v. Kann, 690 A.2d 509, 520 (Md. 1997).

[42] *Compare* Garrity v. Lyle Stuart, Inc., 353 N.E.2d 793, 794 (N.Y. 1976) (holding that allowing arbitrator to award punitive damages violated public policy), *with Ex Parte* Costa & Head Atrium, Ltd., 486 So. 2d 1272 (Ala. 1986) (rejecting contention that submission of fraud and punitive damages claim to arbitration violated public policy). *See generally* Timothy Travers, Annot., *Arbitrator's Power to Award Punitive Damages*, 83 A.L.R.3d 1037 (1978).

[43] *E.g.*, Mastrobuono v. Shearson Lehman Hutton, Inc., 514 U.S. 52, 60–61 (1995) (upholding arbitral award of punitive damages); Raytheon Co. v. Automated Bus Systems, Inc., 882 F.2d 6, 11–12 (1st Cir. 1989) (joining other federal circuits in allowing arbitrators to award punitive damages and rejecting decisions by several states that have denied arbitrators the power to award punitive damages).

[44] *Garrity*, *supra*, 353 N.E.2d at 795–96.

[45] Section 205 (Due Process Limitations on Amount of Award).

[46] Alaska Housing Fin. Corp. v. Salvucci, 950 P.2d 1116, 1122–23 (Alaska 1997) (noting

achieved when a jurisdiction provides the public entity with an immunity for any willful or wanton misconduct by its agents.[47]

The immunity extended to a public entity from a punitive damages award does not necessarily extend to public officials.[48] The genesis of the immunity doctrinally lies in the defense of sovereign immunity. In order to assert a claim for punitive damages against a public entity, most jurisdictions require an explicit waiver of the defense.[49]

With regard to not-for-profit organizations, including religious organizations, the decisional law is more favorable for the award of punitive damages. For example, in *Mrozka v. Archdiocese of St. Paul and Minneapolis* the court refused to extend the public entity exception to a religious organization. The court noted that there is "no common law rule exempting religious or non-profit organizations from punitive damages awards."[50] The

---

that an award of punitive damages would only punish "innocent taxpayers"). The court also noted that the active wrongdoer (public official) would not be deterred by a punitive damages award against the public entity and that the "responsiveness of our democratic institutions make punitive damages awards against governments unnecessary." *Id.* at 1124. *But cf.* Bain v. City of Springfield, 678 N.E.2d 155, 159 (Mass. 1997) (holding that Massachusetts' anti-discrimination statute, defining employer to include municipalities and generally authorizing punitive damages, allows the award of punitive damages against public entities).

[47] *In re* Chicago Flood Litig., 680 N.E.2d 265, 273 (Ill. 1997).

[48] Ramirez v. United States, 998 F. Supp. 425, 438 (D.N.J. 1998) (noting that while under New Jersey's Tort Claims Act public entities are not subject to punitive damages awards, "a public official may be held liable" when actual malice is established on the official's part in committing the tortious act); *Alaska Housing, supra*, 950 P.2d at 1124:

> [T]here is available a more effective means of deterrence. By allowing juries and courts to assess punitive damages in appropriate circumstances against the offending official, based on his personal financial resources, the statute directly advances the public's interest in preventing repeated constitutional deprivations. In our view, this provides sufficient protection against the prospect that a public official may commit recurrent constitutional violations by reason of his office. The Court previously has found, with respect to such violations, that a damage remedy recoverable against individuals is more effective as a deterrent than the threat of damages against a government employer.

citing and quoting, City of Newport v. Fact Concerts, 453 U.S. 247, 266–67 (1981).

[49] *E.g.*, Krohn v. New York Police Dept., 811 N.E.2d 8, 11–12 (N.Y. 2004) (holding that statutory provision authorizing punitive damages for violations of municipality's Human Rights Law did not operate to permit punitive damages claim against municipality for violation of that law absent express reference to the municipality in the law); *cf.* Barnes v. Gorman, 536 U.S. 181, 186–87 (2002) (holding that public entities that accept federal funds, and thus become subject to federal legal obligations, do not also become subject to punitive damages awards authorized by that same federal law). *Barnes v. Gorman* involved a claim for compensatory and punitive damages by a disabled plaintiff who sought relief under Title VI of the 1964 Civil Rights Act and the Americans With Disabilities Act (ADA). The Court also held, however, that punitive damages were not available under Title VI or, because the ADA is modeled on the 1964 Civil Rights Act, the ADA. *Id.* at 188–190.

[50] 482 N.W.2d 806 810 (Minn. App. 1992). The court collected authorities supporting the awarding of punitive damages against religious and not-for-profit organizations. *Id.* at 810–11.

court also rejected First Amendment challenges to the awarding of punitive damages against religious entities.[51]

[202.9] Vicarious Liability

There is, at present, no constitutional prohibition against liability for punitive damages being based on legal attribution.[52] Jurisdictions disagree over whether to allow and how to limit vicarious liability for punitive damages.[53]

Under what circumstances should punitive damages lie against a defendant who did not directly commit the wrongful act? This is always the problem with a legal entity. Should the misconduct of the insurance adjuster be attributed to the insurer? Should the misconduct of the lawyer be attributed to the law firm. Should the misconduct of the employee be attributed to the employer? When civil liability for actual harm is concerned, the law attributes responsibility broadly and generally, as the doctrines of respondeat superior and agency well evidence.[54] When it comes to punitive damages, however, the modern trend is to be much more restrictive. The central idea here is that punishment should be reserved for those who have moral guilt based on actual responsibility for the wrongdoing. Passive action, even passive tolerance or awareness, may be insufficient unless the passivity can be seen as encouragement, abetting ratification, or endorsement.[55]

A showing that agents of another (principal) have the requisite state of mind to support an award of punitive damages against them does not mean

---

[51] *Id.* at 811–12 (rejecting federal and state constitutional challenges to the awarding of punitive damages); Section 105 (Presumed Damages) (discussing application of the First Amendment to punitive damages claims for defamation).

[52] Pacific Mut. Life Ins. Co. v. Haslip, 499 U.S. 1, 14–15 (1990) (rejecting argument that attribution to principal (insurer) of liability for punitive damages for acts of agents (insurance adjustor) based on principles of respondeat superior violated 14th Amendment due process).

[53] 2 J. GHIARDI & J. KIRCHER, PUNITIVE DAMAGES: LAW AND PRACTICE § 24.01 (1998) (discussing disagreement). *See generally* 22 Am. Jur. 2d, *Damages* § 788.

[54] *E.g.*, McLachlan v. Bell, 261 F.3d 908 (9th Cir. 2001):

Even "willful and malicious torts of an employee" can be within the scope of his employment, and that may be so even where the employee's torts violate the employer's express rules and confer no benefit on the employer. Thus, for example, torts have been found to be within the scope of employment where an employed truck driver beat a motorist with a wrench, a traveling salesman beat a motorist with whom he had a near-accident, and a contractor's employee threw a hammer at a subcontractor.

Id. at 911 (footnotes omitted) (applying California law). Not all jurisdiction view the principle of vicarious liability so broadly. Andrews v. United States, 732 F.2d 366, 370 (4th Cir. 1984) (applying South Carolina law) (requiring that to invoke vicarious liability agent's actions that give rise to liability must have been primarily motivated by desire to serve the principal); *see* text and notes 56–57, *infra* (discussing Restatement approach).

[55] *E.g.*, Tolle v. Interstate Systems Truck Lines, Inc., 356 N.E.2d 625, 627–28 (Ill. App. 1976) (rejecting allowance of claim for punitive damages based on principle of respondeat superior when agent was not managerial level employee and principal did not ratify agent's conduct).

that the award can be automatically extended to the principal (*e.g.*, legal entity). Liability must be properly imputed to the principal for the acts of the agent. The general rule is reflected in the Restatement (Second) of Agency, which among other things, authorizes punitive damages "against a . . . Principal because of an [agent's] act . . . if . . . the agent was employed in a managerial capacity and was acting in the scope of employment."[56] The Restatement goes on to state that even intentional, specifically forbidden torts are within the scope of employment if the conduct is "the kind [the employee] is employed to perform," "occurs substantially within the authorized time and space limits," and "is actuated, at least in part, by a purpose to serve the principal."[57]

The actions of directors and senior officers of a legal entity, at least those actions within the scope of the director or senior officers' employment, can usually be directly attributable to the principal/legal entity. The more difficult issue involves "managers" or "management agents" or those who occupy a "managerial role." Who are these people? The California Supreme Court addressed the question in *White v. Ultramar.*[58] The court held that in amending Civil Code Section 3294, the Legislature intended to limit punitive damage liability to those employees who exercise substantial independent authority and judgment over decisions that ultimately determine the entity's policy, *i.e.*, "managing agent."

The *White* court emphasized that the determination of whether employees act in a managerial capacity does not necessarily hinge on their level in the corporate hierarchy. The critical inquiry is the degree of discretion the employee possesses in making decisions that will ultimately determine corporate policy. The *White* court disagreed with the proposition that the agent's power to hire or fire employees was, by itself, sufficient to attribute the agent's mental state to the principal/legal entity. The scope of an employee's discretion and authority, such as to bind the principal to the agent's acts for purposes of a punitive damages award, is a question of fact to be decided on a case-by-case basis.

The entity's decision to designate a particular employee or office as the person or place responsible for acting on certain matters *e.g.*, harassment complaints, may be sufficient to impute notice and knowledge to the entity when notice is given to the designated person or office.[59] A punitive damages claim based on the failure to take corrective action may now be assertable against the principal/legal entity.

---

[56] Restatement (Second) of Agency § 217C (c) (1958); Briner v. Hyslop, 337 N.W.2d 858 (Iowa 1983) (collecting decisions approving and rejecting award of punitive damages against principal based solely on fact claim arose based on act(s) of agent within course and scope of employment). *See generally* 22 Am. Jur. 2d *Damages* § 592.

[57] Restatement (Second) of Agency §§ 29(1), 230, cmt. b (1958).

[58] 981 P.3d 563 (Cal. 1999). *White* is illustrative of the problem; not all courts can be expected to resolve the issues the same way.

[59] Swinton v. Potomac Corp., 270 F.3d 794 (9th Cir. 2001), *cert. denied*, 535 U.S. 1018 (2002); Deters v. Equifac Credit Information Services, 202 F.3d 1262 (10th Cir. 2000).

Even if the agent qualifies as a "managing agent," the principal/legal entity may still be able to refute the attribution of punitive damages liability if the principal/legal entity engaged in good faith efforts to prevent the type of conduct that is being attributed to it by the managing agent. In *Kolstad v. American Dental Assn.*, a workplace sex discrimination case, the Court held that broad attribution of liability for punitive damages under the law of Agency would not apply when the manager's decisions, which formed the basis of the discrimination claim, are contrary to the principal's good faith efforts to comply with Title VII:

> Applying the Restatement of Agency's "scope of employment" rule in the Title VII punitive damages context, moreover, would reduce the incentive for employers to implement anti-discrimination programs. In fact, such a rule would likely exacerbate concerns among employers that § 1981's "malice" and "reckless indifference" standard penalizes those employers who educated themselves and their employees on Title VII's prohibition.

> In light of the perverse incentives that the Restatement's "scope of employment" rule create, we are compelled to modify these principles to avoid undermining the objectives underlying Title VII. [60]

The *Kolstad* majority did not, however, explain why the attribution of liability for punitive damages would discourage "good faith" compliance programs; it merely cited an amicus brief.

[202.10] Multiple Punitive Damages Awards

There is no prohibition against multiple punitive damages awards based on the same course of conduct being given to different plaintiffs. [61] The court may, however, consider the aggregate amount of punitive damages to determine whether, in their entirety, the point has been reached when the award has become excessive. [62] A prerequisite, however, to consideration of excessiveness is that the trier of fact be first presented with the evidence of the prior punitive damages awards. [63] The prejudicial aspects of this evidence on the defendant's contention that punitive damages are not warranted may be ameliorated by bifurcation of the liability and amount phases of the punitive damages portion of the trial. [64]

The defendant will be required to show that it has paid the prior punitive damages award in order to claim that additional awards would be excessive. [65]

---

[60] 527 U.S. 526, 545–46 (1999); *cf. Deters, supra*, 202 F.3d at 1271(holding that *Kolstad* did not apply to case of "direct liability," *i.e.*, misconduct was by managing agent).

[61] Scheufler v. General Host Corp., 126 F.3d 1261, 1271–72 (10th Cir. 1997).

[62] Owens-Corning Fiberglas Corp. v. Malone, 972 S.W.2d 35, 40–41 (Tex. 1998); Stevens v. Owens-Corning Fiberglas Corp., 57 Cal. Rptr. 2d 525, 535 (Cal. App. 1996).

[63] *Stevens, supra*, 57 Cal. Rptr. 2d at 535–36 (collecting decisions).

[64] *Id.* at 536.

[65] *Id.* at 537 (refusing to take judicial notice of other punitive damages awards entered

Professor Denemark has proposed an interesting solution to this problem. He suggests that courts approach the problem as they do claims of contribution: allow the jury to decide, then apply a credit to the jury's award for past punitive damages claims paid by the defendant involving the same misconduct.[66]

§ 203 ACTUAL INJURY REQUIREMENT

It is oftentimes stated that "actual damages" or an award of compensatory damages is a prerequisite to an award of punitive damages. This is also referred to as the "actionable injury" requirement. A number of jurisdictions assert adherence to this prerequisite[1] and it has been identified as the majority or dominant view.[2] The rationale for this view is that it is not appropriate to punish a defendant unless the defendant has inflicted actionable injury on the plaintiff; allowing punitive damages in the absence of actionable injury is perceived to provide a "windfall" to the plaintiff.[3] Other jurisdictions simply require that the plaintiff show actual damage or injury rather than actionable injury.[4] Actionable injury may be shown in a number of ways, for example, by an award of compensatory damages,[5] restitution,[6] offset,[7] presumed damages,[8] or nominal damages,[9] but not

---

against the defendant because the court "would not have enough information to gauge the actual impact of the awards in those cases because we have no evidence that [defendant] has paid the awards"); *Owens-Corning Fiberglas Corp.*, supra, 972 S.W.2d at 41 (holding that evidence of unpaid punitive damages awards is not admissible because unpaid awards neither punish nor deter). The court rejected the Restatement (Second) of Tort's (§ 908 cmt. e) suggestion that unpaid awards should be considered. *Id.* at 41–42.

[66] Howard A. Denemark, *Seeking Greater Fairness When Awarding Multiple Punitive Damages For a Single Act by a Defendant*, 63 Ohio St. L. J. 931 (2002).

[1] Chaiken v. Eldon Emmor & Co., Inc., 597 N.E.2d 337, 349 (Ind. App. 1992):

   [T]he purpose for the predicate award of compensatory damages, to foreclose recovery absent some harm, is fulfilled by proof of the injury and damage. The general rule is based upon two grounds: (1) a court will not punish conduct, no matter how reprehensible, which in fact causes no legal injury; and (2) no separate cause of action for punitive damages exists, punitive damages are derivative of actual damages.

(footnote omitted).

[2] *See generally* Richard Tinney, Annot., *Sufficiency of Showing of Actual Damages to Support Awards of Punitive Damages—Modern Cases*, 40 A.L.R.4th 11, 18–19 (1986).

[3] People Helpers Found., Inc. v. Richmond, 12 F.3d 1321, 1327 (4th Cir. 1993).

[4] City of Shawnee, Kansas v. AT&T Corp., 910 F. Supp. 1546, 1562 (D. Kan. 1995); *see* Restatement (Second) of Torts § 908 cmt. c (adopting no injury requirement). Note the distinction between "actual damages" and "actual damage." Section 9.1 (Future Damage); Section 9.2 (Future Damages).

[5] *People Helpers Found., Inc.*, supra, 12 F.3d at 1327.

[6] Ward v. Taggart, 336 P.2d 534, 538 (Cal. 1959).

[7] Esparza v. Specht, 127 Cal. Rptr. 493, 496–98 (Cal App. 1976); *Chaiken*, *supra*, 597 N.E.2d at 349.

[8] Grossman v. Goemans, 631 F. Supp. 972, 973 (D.D.C. 1986); Leyendecker & Assocs., Inc. v. Wechter, 683 S.W.2d 369, 372–75 (Tex. 1984); Clark v. McClurg, 9 P.2d 505, 506 (Cal. App. 1932).

all courts accept all of the above as satisfying an actionable injury requirement.

The issue whether a front or back pay award will support a punitive damages award under the federal Civil Rights Act has generated diverse positions. The problem arises because while the Act, as amended in 1991, permits the award of compensatory damages, the Act and judicial decisions exclude front and back pay awards from the definition of "compensatory" damages.[10] If a plaintiff receives only a front or back pay award, may the plaintiff also recover punitive damages?

One position holds that punitive damages can only be considered when the plaintiff has received an award of compensatory damages.[11] This view is closest to the so-called majority, "actionable injury" view.[12] A second position holds that front or back pay is sufficiently similar to compensatory damages to permit an award of punitive damages; the exclusion of back pay from inclusion within statutory compensable damages was to prevent double compensation, not prevent punitive damages.[13] This view is aligned with the actionable injury requirement: a loss of wages is an actionable injury, functionally equivalent to compensatory damages. It also reflects that the plaintiff sustained actual injury, for which she has been compensated.[14] The fact that federal courts have traditionally treated back pay awards as a form of equitable relief is not dispositive.[15] A third position holds that a plaintiff may recover punitive damages even in the absence of an award of monetary damages either in the form of compensatory damages or lost wages.[16] The rationale for this approach is that it is

---

[9] Jacque v. Steenberg Homes, Inc., 563 N.W.2d 154 (Wis. 1997) (permitting recovery of punitive damages when only nominal damages awarded for intentional trespass to land); Pulla v. Amoco Oil Co., 882 F. Supp. 836, 875 n.33 (S.D. Iowa 1994) (collecting decisions holding that award of nominal damages will support an award of punitive damages), *modified*, 72 F.2d 648 (8th Cir. 1995). There is some disagreement as to the type of nominal damages that will support an award of punitive damages. Some jurisdictions state that only nominal damages awarded due to measurement difficulties will support an award of punitive damages; when nominal damages are awarded simply because the plaintiff was a prevailing party, punitive damages may not lie. Shell Oil Co. v. Parker, 291 A.2d 64, 71–72 (Md. 1972); Section 2.8 (Nominal Damages).

[10] Civil Rights Act of 1991, 105 Stat. 1071, 1072–74, codified at 42 U.S.C. § 1981a.

[11] Allison v. Citgo Petroleum Corp., 151 F.3d 402, 417–18 (5th Cir. 1998).

[12] Text and notes 1–2, *supra*.

[13] Corti v. Storage Technology Corp., 304 F.3d 336, 341–42 (4th Cir. 2002).

[14] *E.g.*, Salitros v. Chrysler Corp., 306 F.3d 562, 575 (8th Cir. 2002) (stating that when the plaintiff has suffered an actual economic loss in the form of lost wages the general rule, that punitive damages cannot be awarded where the plaintiff fails to recover compensatory damages, should not be applied).

[15] Albermarle Paper Co. v. Moody, 422 U.S. 405, 417–18, 442–48 (1975) (Rhenquist, J. concurring); Mitchell v. Robert DeMario Jewelry, Inc., 361 U.S. 288, 291–93 (1960); *cf.* Mertens v. Hewitt Assoc., 508 U.S. 248, 256 (1993) (treating restitutionary relief as equitable in nature); Russell v. Northrup Grumann Corp., 921 F. Supp. 143, 151–53 (E.D.N.Y. 1996) (stating that courts generally treat back pay awards as restitutionary in nature and thus a form of equitable relief).

[16] Cush Crawford v. Adchem Corp., 271 F.3d 352, 357–59 (2d Cir. 2001).

"unseemly" that the defendant escape accountability for his malicious misconduct simply because the plaintiff has fortuitously managed to escape injury.[17] This approach goes even beyond the actual injury approach as it rejects the injury requirement altogether; rather, the focus of inquiry is the defendant's misconduct and state of mind.

Under the "actual injury" approach the key factor should be the fact of damage, not damages. For example, in *Topanga Corp. v. Gentile* the plaintiff brought an action for rescission due to fraud. In considering the plaintiff's claim for punitive damages, the court stated: "[T]he fact that plaintiffs were not given a grant of monetary damages of a certain amount is not determinative [of the issue of punitive damages]. Plaintiff was indeed damaged by defendant's fraud for defendants had, as the result of the fraud, received stock in an amount not commensurate with the value of their contribution to the corporation."[18]

§ 204 WEALTH OF THE DEFENDANT

Jurisdictions have split on whether evidence of the defendant's wealth is necessary for determining a just measure of punitive damages.[1] Judge Posner argued in *Kemezy v. Peters* that evidence of the defendant's wealth was unnecessary because wealth and the purposes he identified as underlying the punitive damages award were not commensurate. Judge Posner stated in the opinion for the court:

> What is striking about the purposes that are served by the awarding of punitive damages is that none of them depends critically on proof

---

[17] *Id.* at 359. *See generally* Jeffrey Scot Fowler, Annot., *Punitive Damages in Actions For Violations of Title VII of the Civil Rights Act of 1964 (42 U.S.C. § 1981a; 42 U.S.C.A. §§ 2000e et seq.)*, 150 A.L.R. Fed. 601 (1998).

[18] 58 Cal. Rptr. 713, 719 (Cal. App. 1967) (brackets added); *see* Medasys Acquisition Corp. v. SDMS, P.C., 55 P.3d 763, 767–68 (Ariz. 2002) (same). *But see* Estate of Jones v. Kvamme, 449 N.W.2d 428 (Minn. 1989):

> It is likely that the jury awarded punitive damages because it felt its original award of out-of-pocket damages of $125,000 would insufficiently compensate the estate for the stock while at the same time allowing Kvamme to retain the fruits of his misrepresentation, namely, the considerable dramatic appreciation of the stock. Here, the rescission of the transaction and the imposition of a constructive trust, rather than the compensation for out-of-pocket damages, has the effect of adequately restoring the estate to the status quo ante.

Id. at 432.

[1] *Compare* Bennis v. Gable, 823 F.2d 723, 734 n.14 (3d Cir. 1987) (stating that while the defendant's wealth "may be relevant to the imposition of punitive damages, it can hardly be said that the defendant's financial status was an element of plaintiff's cause of action to be proved before punitive damages could be awarded") (citations omitted), *and* Woods-Drake v. Lundy, 667 F.2d 1198, 1204 n.9 (5th Cir. 1982) (same), *and* Zarcone v. Perry, 572 F.2d 52, 56 (2d Cir. 1978) (same), *with* Adams v. Murakami, 813 P.2d 1348 (Cal. 1991):

> A reviewing court cannot make a fully informed determination of whether an award of punitive damages is excessive unless the record contains evidence of the defendant's financial condition.

Id. at 1351 (citations omitted). *Adams* is discussed at text and notes 5–10, *infra.*

that the defendant's income or wealth exceeds some specified level. The more wealth the defendant has, the smaller is the relative bite that an award of punitive damages not actually geared to that wealth will take out of his pocketbook, while if he has very little wealth the award of punitive damages may exceed his ability to pay and perhaps drive him into bankruptcy. To a very rich person, the pain of having to pay a heavy award of damages may be a mere pinprick and so not deter him (or people like him) from continuing to engage in the same type of wrongdoing. What in economics is called the principle of diminishing marginal utility teaches, what is anyway obvious, that losing $1 is likely to cause less unhappiness (disutility) to a rich person than to a poor one. But rich people are not famous for being indifferent to money, and if they are forced to pay not merely the cost of the harm to the victims of their torts but also some multiple of that cost they are likely to think twice before engaging in such expensive behavior again. Juries, rightly or wrongly, think differently, so plaintiffs who are seeking punitive damages often present evidence of the defendant's wealth. The question is whether they must present such evidence—whether it is somehow unjust to allow a jury to award punitive damages without knowing that the defendant really is a wealthy person. The answer, obviously is no. A plaintiff is not required to seek punitive damages in the first place, so he should not be denied an award of punitive damages merely because he does not present evidence that if believed would persuade the jury to award him even more than he is asking.[2]

Judge Posner would permit the defendant to introduce evidence of his wealth, unless the defendant would be indemnified against the punitive damages award.[3] Judge Posner argued that a contrary rule would be inefficient because the costs of misconduct would be shifted from the wrongdoer to the indemnitor.[4]

The California Supreme Court adopted the contrary position in *Adams v. Murakami*. The court held that evidence of the defendant's wealth is necessary to enable the court to determine "whether the amount of damages exceeds the level necessary to properly punish and deter."[5] According to the court:

> The question cannot be answered in the abstract. The reviewing court must consider the amount of the award in light of the relevant facts. The nature of the inquiry is a comparative one. Deciding in

---

[2] 79 F.3d 33, 35–36 (7th Cir. 1996) (citation and parenthetical omitted).

[3] *Id.* at 37:

> The defendant should not be allowed to plead poverty if his employer or an insurance company is going to pick up the tab.

(citations omitted).

[4] *Id., rejecting* Michael v. Cole, 595 P.2d 995, 997 (Ariz. 1979).

[5] *Adams*, 813 P.2d at 1350.

the abstract whether an award is "excessive" is like deciding whether it is "bigger," without asking "Bigger than what?"[6]

The court went on to hold that the burden of producing evidence of defendant's wealth should be placed on the plaintiff.[7] The court offered several justifications. First, punitive damages are extra-compensatory and thus in the nature of a "windfall" or "boon" to the plaintiff; therefore "[i]t is not too much to ask of a plaintiff seeking such a windfall to require that he or she introduce evidence that will allow [a determination] whether the amount is appropriate. . . ."[8] Second, forcing the defendant to introduce evidence of his wealth requires that he "[bid] against himself" and could be construed as a tacit admission of liability.[9]

One may question whether the California Supreme Court resolved the fairness issue correctly. The court's concern that the defendant may be required to "bid against itself" or engage in conduct that could be construed as a "tacit admission" of liability is endemic. Every time a defendant introduces a damages proof, it runs the same risk identified by the court; yet, courts often criticize defendants for not introducing a damages proof.[10]

Is it fair to require the plaintiff to invade the personal financial data of the defendant and present that information in court as a component of the prima facie case for punitive damages?[11] Evidence of the defendant's wealth is more easily accessible to the defendant rather than the plaintiff; consequently, the burden of production would normally be the defendant's. Resolving the conflicting interests of personal wealth retention and privacy would appear to be better assigned to the party who bears the risk (defendant), not the party who would reap the benefit. If evidence of a defendant's wealth is relevant to assessing whether a particular punitive damages award will punish in the particular case, the burden of producing evidence on that point should lie with the party who will be most directly affected by the outcome—the defendant.

When evidence of defendant's wealth is to be considered, how do you measure wealth? The general rule is to consider the defendant's "net worth."[12] As noted by one district court:

---

[6] *Id.* at 1350–51.

[7] *Id.* at 1357. The defendant may, however, engage in conduct that discharges plaintiff's burden. Davidov v. Issod, 92 Cal. Rptr. 2d 897, 905 (Cal. App. 2000) (holding that defendant, by disobeying a valid court order that he produce any records that would reflect his financial condition, "waived any right to complain of the lack of such evidence").

[8] 813 P.2d at 1357–58 (brackets added). If "equity abhors forfeitures," it appears that "law abhors windfalls."

[9] *Id.* at 1358 (brackets added).

[10] *E.g.*, Texaco v. Pennzoil Co., 729 S.W.2d 768, 861 (Tex. Civ. App. 1987) (noting that Texaco "presented no expert testimony to refute the claims [regarding damages] but relied on its cross-examination of Penzoil's experts to attempt to show that the damages model used by the jury was flawed") (brackets added), *cert. dismissed*, 485 U.S. 994 (1988).

[11] *Id.* at 1364–65 (Mosk, J., dissenting).

[12] Downey Savings & Loan Assn v. Ohio Cas. Ins. Co., 189 Cal. App. 3d 1072, 234 Cal. Rptr. 835, 851 (1987) (stating that "[a] defendant's net worth is generally considered the best measure of his wealth for the purpose of assessing exemplary damages"), *cert. denied*, 486 U.S. 1036 (1988).

Under Kansas punitive damage standards, however, the amount of profit received as a result of intentional wrongdoing is not the ceiling of punitive damage liability. To the contrary, if evidence of a defendant's financial status is introduced, the deterrent effect of punitive damages is served only by references to the net wealth of the wrongdoer. Otherwise, a manufacturer could continue to "gamble" with low revenue, "high risk" products, secure in the knowledge that any future punitive liability could always be mitigated by a compartmentalization of profits.[13]

More recently, however, some courts had evidenced a tendency to relax the "net worth" requirement. For example, O.J. Simpson was assessed over $25 million in punitive damages for the slaying of his ex-wife and a young man. The verdict was in excess of his current worth, net or otherwise. The court disagreed, however, that it was excessive:

> Although net worth is the most common measure of the defendant's financial condition, it is not the only measure for determining whether punitive damages are excessive in relation to the condition. [N]et worth is subject to easy manipulation, and blind adherence to that or any single standard could lead to awards that fail to deter and punish, or deter and punish too much.

> Furthermore, the court that compiled a list of cases in an attempt to discover a formula for determining whether a given percentage of net worth is excessive ultimately concluded there is no formula, and that each case must be decided on its own fact . . . .

> The evidence here, viewed in the light most favorable to the judgment, shows that Simpson is a wealthy man, with prospects to gain more wealth in the future. The enormity of his misconduct shows that a large amount of punitive damages is necessary to punish him and deter him. There is no formula based on net worth for determining what amount is too much. The fundamental underlying principle is that punitive damages must not be so large they destroy the defendant. Evidence unique to this case shows this award will not destroy Simpson economically. He has pension funds worth $4.1 million that are exempt from execution to pay this award. Despite the award of punitive damages. Simpson can continue to enjoy a comfortable living.[14]

The O.J. Simpson case was identified by the court as "unusual," but the approach adopted has been carried over to more routine cases. For example, in *Zaxis Wireless Communications v. Motor Sound Corp.* the claim was simply one of fraud; the defendant fraudulently induced the plaintiff to

---

[13] Mason v. Texaco, Inc., 741 F. Supp. 1472, 1504 (D. Kan. 1990) (citation omitted), *aff'd*, 948 F.2d 1546 (10th Cir. 1991), *cert. denied*, 504 U.S. 910 (1992).

[14] Rufo v. Simpson, 103 Cal. Rptr. 2d 492, 528–29 (Cal. App. 2001) (citations and footnotes omitted). In that case, plaintiff's expert testified that Simpson's net worth was $15.7 million, which apparently included Simpson's future earnings capacity. *Id.* at 527–28.

retain the defendant as its subagent. The jury awarded $300,000 in punitive damages; defendant contended that it had a negative net worth of $6.3 million.[15] The court was unimpressed with defendant's claim of inability to pay:

> In this case the jury considered net worth and a variety of other factors included on the financial documents presented by Zaxis to conclude Motor Sound had the ability to pay a punitive damage award of $300,000. The evidence showed Motor Sound earned hundreds of millions of dollars in 1997 and 1998 but had a net loss. The financial documents in evidence revealed the net worth calculation included accumulated depreciation of approximately $4.9 million and a note to the sole shareholder of $6 million. Although this represents a loss for accounting purposes, it did not impact Motor Sound's ability to pay a damage award as would, for example, salary and wage expenses.[16]

What percentage of the defendant's wealth can be claimed by the punitive damages award is difficult to predict. The easiest cases are those when the award claims the increase in defendant's wealth caused by the misconduct—a disgorgement of profits measure.[17] When the award is not related to defendant's increase in wealth, courts have suggested that awards that

---

[15] 107 Cal. Rptr. 2d 308, 310 (Cal. App. 2001). The negative net worth was based on a $6 million debt owed to the defendant's sole owner and accumulated depreciated of $4.9 million. *Id.*

[16] *Id.* at 312–13.

[17] Cummings Med. Corp. v. Occupational Med. Corp. of Am., Inc., 13 Cal. Rptr. 2d 585 (Cal. App. 1992):

> The defendant's profits from misconduct are objectively based and uniquely appropriate as the basis for punitive damages. For example, an insurer who knowingly induces an individual to purchase a grossly inadequate policy for an unreasonable sum undoubtedly "profits" from the use of excess premiums it improperly gained. Removing the gain in such a case, in addition to requiring the insurer to compensate the plaintiff for its actual losses, makes it less likely the defendant will repeat the conduct. A gain-based measure of this sort sends a clear signal to defendants that such misconduct does not pay and, thus, serves the deterrent function of punitive damages. Of course, a gain-based measure of punitive damages may not always adequately serve the deterrent function. A defendant may, for example, escape effective deterrence if its conduct is rarely challenged in litigation. But even if taking away the defendant's ill-gotten gains may sometimes not be enough to deter similar conduct, it is never too much.

Id. at 590 (citations omitted). *But cf.* Kenly v. Ukegawa, 19 Cal. Rptr. 2d 771, 775–77 (Cal. App. 1993) (holding that award of "net profits" as punitive damages is subject to defendant's ability to pay: "An award based solely on the alleged 'profit' gained by the defendant, in the absence of evidence of net worth, raises the potential of its crippling or destroying the defendant, focusing as it does solely on the assets side of the balance sheet . . . ."). The court's concern in *Kenly* appears overcautious and unduly sensitive to the tortfeasor who, under the court's approach, may keep some of his ill-gotten gains if he can show repayment would be disruptive. Section 51 (Disgorgement orders).

claim more that several percent of the defendant's net wealth are suspect,[18] but as the O.J. Simpson case evidences, every principle has its exception.[19]

Difficulties can be encountered when the defendant's financial condition is consolidated with that of a non-party. In *Dangerfield v. Star Editorial, Inc.* the plaintiff, a well-known comedian, successfully sued the defendant for defamation. The trial court awarded nominal damages for emotional distress, presumed damages of $45,000, but $0 for punitive because plaintiff did not submit evidence of the financial net worth of the defendant "Star."

On appeal plaintiff argued that evidence of Star's corporate parent ("GP") was relevant to Star's financial condition. The court agreed with the trial court that the evidence was not relevant:

> Including GP's financial condition in the determination of punitive damages for Star is not appropriate. Dangerfield's introduction of GP's net worth, without isolating Star's balance, cannot sustain punitive damages without litigating alter ego. Furthermore, the district court dismissed GP from the action on the merits. Given that the evidence presented showed that Star operated at a net loss, Dangerfield failed to establish Star's ability to pay punitive damages. The district court did not err when it declined to award punitive damages against Star.[20]

§ 205 DUE PROCESS LIMITATIONS ON AMOUNT OF AWARD

Concerns over the subjectivity of punitive damages awards have generally been voiced in terms of excessiveness. Courts have always evaluated punitive damages awards on their own terms and with an eye to the retributive and deterrence functions of the award. Not surprisingly, there has been variation among the jurisdictions regarding the amount of deference to be afforded the trier-of-fact.[1] Traditionally, the test whether a punitive damages claim was excessive focused on the factors that served to justify and measure the award. The fit between the punishment and the

---

[18] Cash v. Beltmann N. Am. Co., 900 F.2d 109, 111 n.3 (7th Cir. 1990) (stating that typical ratio for a punitive damages award to be defendant's net wealth is 1% and reducing award of $137,409, which represented 8.29% of defendant's net worth, to $75,000, which was approximately 4.5% of defendant's net worth); *see* Velop, Inc. v. Kaplan, 693 A.2d 917 (N.J. Super. Ct. A.D. 1997) (finding that punitive damages awards that claimed 2.9% and 2.4% of defendant's net worth were reasonable); Michelson v. Hamada, 36 Cal. Rptr. 2d 343, 359 (Cal. App. 1994) (stating that punitive damages awards "generally are not allowed to exceed 10 percent of the net worth of the defendant") (citation omitted).

[19] Text and notes 14–15, *supra*.

[20] 97 F.3d 1458 (9th Cir. 1996) (Table), *citing* Tomaselli v. Transamerica Ins. Co., 31 Cal. Rptr. 2d 433, 441 (Cal. App. 1994), *cert. denied*, 520 U.S. 1196 (1997).

[1] Amfac, Inc. v. Waikiki Beachcomber Inv. Co., 839 P.2d 10, 36–37 (Haw. 1992) (noting that an award of punitive damages is committed to the discretion of the trier-of-fact); Section 208 (Discretion as to the Scope and Size of the Award).

misconduct was a natural focus. How depraved was the defendant's conduct?[2] Did the punitive damages award sting or did it mulct the defendant.[3]

Recently, the Supreme Court has added an additional, albeit somewhat overlapping, layer of review. The review is additional because it derives from 14th Amendment due process. It is overlapping because the components of the due process test mirror to a substantial, but not complete, extent the traditional factors used by courts to determine whether an award of punitive damages is excessive. The critical point, however, is that today a punitive damages award must satisfy two tests: first, the traditional factors must be examined to determine if punitive damages are warranted and, if so, what is an appropriate award. These factors are discussed in Sections 202.0 through 204.0 and basically require (1) the requisite degree of malice, fraud, or willful and wanton misconduct by the defendant;[4] (2) actual or actionable injury by the plaintiff;[5] and, (3) an appropriate relationship between the award and the defendant's wealth.[6] Second, the court must determine that the punitive damages awarded are not excessive in light of 14th Amendment due process requirements. This 14th Amendment test is the subject of this section.

[205.1] *BMW* and *Campbell*

The Supreme Court defined the due process limitations on punitive damages awards in two recent decisions: *BMW of North America v. Gore*[7] and *State Farm Mut. Auto. Ins. Co. v. Campbell.*[8]

In *BMW* the plaintiff's (Gore's) car was damaged while it was being transported to a dealership in Alabama. BMW repaired the car and it was sold to Gore without disclosure of the prior damage.[9] After the purchase, Gore learned that his vehicle had been "repaired" prior to the sale and he sued for fraud. A jury awarded him $4,000 in compensatory damages and $4 million in punitive damages, which the Alabama Supreme Court reduced to $2 million and affirmed. The Alabama Supreme Court justified the award, in part, on the basis that the BMW repair program was a company policy and involved vehicles distributed throughout the United States.

The Supreme Court reversed. The Court held that it violated due process of law for a state to award punitive damages based on a defendant's out-of-state conduct when the illegality or wrongfulness of the conduct in those other states had not been established.[10] In addition to this quasi territorial

---

[2] Section 202 (Scope of Punitive Damages).

[3] Section 204 (Wealth of the Defendant).

[4] Section 202 (Scope of Punitive Damages).

[5] Section 203 (Actual Injury Requirement).

[6] Section 204 (Wealth of the Defendant).

[7] 517 U.S. 559 (1996).

[8] 538 U.S. 408 (2003).

[9] 517 U.S. at 562–63.

[10] *Id.* at 572.

restriction, the Court established a three-factor test for determining excessiveness: (1) the degree of reprehensibility of the defendant's conduct;[11] (2) the ratio of punitive damages to compensatory damages;[12] and, (3) the difference between the punitive damages remedy and the civil penalties authorized or imposed in similar cases.[13] These factors are more fully discussed in Sections 205.2 through 205.4.

In *Campbell* the insurer (State Farm) declined to settle within the policy limits an automobile accident claim in which its insured (Campbell) was viewed by both State Farm's investigators and witnesses to have been the cause of one person's death and another's permanent disability. A Utah jury returned a judgment against Campbell for over three times the $50,000 policy limit. Although State Farm had initially told Campbell it would cover him if the verdict exceeded his policy limits, it subsequently refused to do so; one of State Farm's adjusters told Campbell he should sell his home to pay the judgment. Campbell settled the personal injury claim and turned his attention to State Farm. At some point in time, State Farm reconsidered and paid the excess judgment, but Campbell was not mollified. The Campbells sued State Farm for bad faith, fraud, and intentional infliction of emotional distress. A jury awarded the Campbells $2.6 million in compensatory damages and $145 million in punitive damages, which the trial court reduced to $1 million and $25 million, respectively, but which the Utah Supreme Court reinstated in full. The United States Supreme Court held that the punitive damage award of $145 million was excessive and violated the due process clause of the 14th Amendment. The Court was critical of what it perceived to be Utah's attempt to expose and punish the perceived deficiencies of State Farm's claim adjustment practices throughout the United States. The Court, in a refinement of the approach it had taken several years earlier in *BMW*, held that Utah did not have a legitimate interest in imposing punitive damages to punish a defendant for unlawful acts committed outside the State.[14] The Court also commented on the three factors earlier raised in *BMW* for evaluating whether the

---

[11] *Id.* at 575.

[12] *Id.* at 577–81.

[13] *Id.* at 583.

[14] 538 U.S. at 421:

> A State cannot punish a defendant for conduct that may have been lawful where it occurred. Nor, as a general rule, does a State have a legitimate concern in imposing punitive damages to punish a defendant for unlawful acts committed outside of the State's jurisdiction. Any proper adjudication of conduct that occurred outside Utah to other persons would require their inclusion, and, to those parties, the Utah courts, in the usual case, would need to apply the laws of their relevant jurisdiction.

(citations omitted). The Court did not foreclose the use of out-of-state conduct for other purposes, e.g., to demonstrate knowledge of the conduct on the part of defendant or authorization or ratification of the conduct. *See* Jim Gash, *Punitive Damages, Other Acts Evidence, and the Constitution*, 2004 Utah L. Rev. 1191 (proposing a framework for analyzing when "other act" evidence would be admissible in a punitive damages case under Fed. R. Evid. 404(b) or a state equivalent).

punitive damages award is excessive. These factors, including the *Campbell* gloss, are discussed in Sections 205.2 through 205.4.

[205.2] Reprehensibility of the Defendant's Conduct

The Court has identified this factor as "[p]erhaps the most important indicium of the reasonableness of a punitive damages award."[15] Punitive damages are usually awarded for conduct that ranges from that taken in conscious disregard of the rights of others[16] to that which is despicable.[17] While there is an intuitive relationship between the reprehensibility of the conduct and the size of the punitive damages award—all other things being equal, despicable conduct deserves a larger sanction than conscious disregard—the test lacks certainty or even a pretense of certainty. Reprehensibility is a value judgment that does not translate easily to an objective scale. Perhaps, reprehensibility, like obscenity, is better seen than described.[18]

The Court did note in *BMW* that the reprehensibility concept encompassed economic torts; however, in *Campbell* the Court signaled that conduct involving or raising a substantial risk of bodily injury will be deemed more serious and more deserving of sanction than pure economic torts.[19] How this signal will be read by lower courts is unclear.[20]

In evaluating the reprehensibility of the conduct, the trier-of-fact may consider other similar acts committed by the defendant within the

---

[15] *Campbell, supra*, 538 U.S. at 419, *quoting BMW v. Gore; But cf.* Union Pacific R.A. Co. v. Barber, 149 S.W.3d 325, 347 (Ark. 2004) (stating that "[t]he three *Gore* criteria are to be given equal weight)").

[16] "Conscious disregard" involves conduct by a defendant who, while aware of the probable harmful consequences of his actions, proceeds to act thereby willfully and deliberately failing to avoid those consequences. Mock v. Michigan Millers Mut. Ins. Co., 5 Cal. Rptr. 2d 594, 609 (Cal. App. 1992). The threshold is also captured by the "reckless indifference" standard. Smith v. Wade, 461 U.S. 30, 37, 51 (1983) (upholding jury instruction permitting award of punitive damages for civil rights violations under 42 U.S.C. § 1983 when the conduct of the defendant "is shown to be a reckless or callous disregard of, or indifference to, the rights or safety of others"). The Court rejected a requirement that the defendant's conduct be animated by an actual intent of ill will, spite, or intent to injury. *Id.* at 48–49. A few jurisdictions permit punitive damages claims to be based on "gross negligence," which represents a less reprehensible level of conduct than "reckless disregard." Section 202.1 (Socially Deplorable Conduct).

[17] "Despicable" involves conduct by a defendant that is so vile, base, contemptible, miserable, loathsome, and wretched that it would be looked down upon and despised by all ordinary, decent people. *Mock, supra*, 5 Cal. Rptr. 2d at 609.

[18] Rush v. Scott Specialty Gases, Inc., 930 F. Supp. 194, 201 (E.D. Pa. 1996) (noting that "the difference between very bad behavior and completely amoral conduct may be easy to see, [but] it is not so easy to draw lines between conduct falling between the two extremes") (brackets added), *rev'd on other grounds*, 113 F.3d 476 (3d Cir. 1997).

[19] *Campbell, supra*, 538 U.S. at 409, 419 (noting that the Campbell's injuries did not involve personal injuries or threats to health and safety).

[20] *Compare* Continental Trend Resources, Inc. v. OXY USA, Inc., 101 F.3d 634, 643 (10th Cir. 1996) (reducing punitive damages award of $30 million for tort of intentional interference with prospective economic advantage to $6 million), *cert. denied*, 520 U.S. 1241 (1997), *with* Neibel v. TransWorld Assur. Co., 108 F.3d 1123, 1126, 1132 (9th Cir. 1997) (describing fraud directed at vulnerable targets ("Joe Lunch Bucket") as clearly reprehensible).

jurisdiction. Conduct that is repeated or recidivist may be punished more severely than conduct that is isolated or limited. The critical issue here is how similar must the other conduct be to permit consideration in the punitive damages action. In the aftermath of *BMW* and *Campbell* the trend has been to require a high degree of similarity: the other conduct must be of the type that was directed at the plaintiff and formed the basis of the punitive damages claim.[21] This point is further developed in Section 205.5 (Other Factors).

[205.3] Ratio Between Compensatory Award and Punitive Damages Award

Traditionally courts have examined the ratio between punitive damages and compensatory damages to determine if the punitive damages award is excessive. Many courts have also looked at the ratio between punitive damages and the defendant's wealth for the same purpose,[22] but the Court rejected this latter ratio as part of the due process test.[23] The Court has not, however, been altogether clear what role, if any, the defendant's wealth could play in determining whether a punitive damages award is excessive.[24] The resolution of the dilemma appears to be that while a defendant's wealth is not part of the *BMW-Campbell* test, wealth is a part of the basic excessiveness test.[25] This approach may, however, impose limits on the scope of review of punitive damages awards.[26] In neither context, moreover, have the courts identified an optimal ratio. As noted in one decision:

---

[21] *E.g.*, Williams v. ConAgra Poultry Co., 378 F.3d 790, 797–98 (8th Cir. 2004) (holding that other acts evidencing racial workplace prejudice were not admissible because they were not directed towards plaintiff, but actions directed towards plaintiff were admissible even if he was not aware of them at the time the acts occurred).

[22] Devlin v. Kearny Mesa AMC/Jeep/Renault, Inc., 202 Cal. Rptr. 204, 211 (Cal. App. 1984) and Wollersheim v. Church of Scientology of Cal., 6 Cal. Rptr. 2d 532, 547 (Cal. App. 1992) (depublished on hearing being granted by California Supreme Court), both contain appendices collecting decisions and discussing the ratios between punitive damages and actual damages and punitive damages and defendant's wealth. Unfortunately, the opinions are now both dated.

[23] *Campbell*, *supra*, 538 U. S. at 427: "The wealth of a defendant cannot justify an otherwise unconstitutional punitive damages award." (citation omitted). The Court did, however, cite this factor approvingly in Pacific Mut. Life Ins. Co. v. Haslip, 499 U.S. 1, 21 (1991).

[24] *E.g.*, Eden Elec., Ltd. v. Amana Co., L.P., 258 F. Supp.2d 958 (N.D. Iowa 2003):

> Contrary to various media accounts of the opinion, it may still be proper for the jury to consider the financial condition of a defendant. The Supreme Court actually held that the "wealth of a defendant cannot justify an otherwise unconstitutional punitive damages award." Thus, the fact that a defendant is a wealthy corporation does not mean that a court is free to disregard the *Gore* analysis of determining whether an award is violative of the Fourteenth Amendment. [I]f punitive damages are to continue to serve the broader functions of deterrence and retribution, the defendant's wealth must be a consideration in calculating any award.

Id. at 972 (citations omitted).

[25] *Id.* at 974 (stating that the defendant's wealth is *a* factor the court may consider, but may not override the *BMW-Campbell* criteria).

[26] Section 206 (Standard of Review of Award).

We have examined a number of appellate decisions in an effort to determine whether we could discern from the cases a single formula for calculating punitive damages. For those with a mathematical bent, the attached appendix reflects part of our research. Frankly, we are unable to find that formula. Instead of making a mathematical breakthrough we discovered what everyone probably already knows: the formula does not exist.

* * * *

[T]he calculation of punitive damages does not involve strict adherence to a rigid formula. It involves, instead, "a fluid process of adding or subtracting depending on the nature of the acts and the effect on the parties and the worth of the defendants. Juries within this framework have a wide discretion in determining what is proper . . . ."[27]

The Court's decision in *BMW* promised a reappraisal of this flexibility. While the Court expressly rejected the invitation to "draw a mathematical bright line" ratio,[28] it raised an intimation that ratios more than 10-1 between punitive damages and actual damages would be suspect.[29]

That "intimation" in *BMW* received renewed emphasis in *Campbell* when the Court noted that a single digit ratio between punitive and compensatory damages is the norm.[30] The Court also stated that when compensatory damages are substantial even lesser ratios can test the limits of due process.[31]

---

[27] *Devlin, supra,* 202 Cal. Rptr. at 208–09, 210.

[28] 517 U.S. at 583. This is the consistent approach of courts that have addressed the issue outside the 14th Amendment context. Northrup v. Miles Homes, Inc. of Iowa, 204 N.W.2d 850, 861 (Iowa 1973) (rejecting requirement that there be a set mathematical ratio between actual and punitive damages). Most jurisdictions expressly require, however, that the ratio be reasonable, although some degree of disproportionality is inherent in a "reasonableness" approach.

[29] 517 U.S. at 582.

[30] 538 U.S. at 425:

[T]he principles it has now established demonstrate, however, that, in practice, few awards exceeding a single-digit ratio between punitive and compensatory damages, to a significant degree, will satisfy due process.

[31] *Id.*:

[B]ecause there are no rigid benchmarks that a punitive damages award may not surpass, ratios greater than those we have previously upheld may comport with due process where "a particularly egregious act has resulted in only a small amount of economic damages." *Ibid* (posting that a higher ratio might be necessary where "the injury is hard to detect or the monetary value of noneconomic harm might have been difficult to determine"). The converse is also true, however. When compensatory damages are substantial, then a lesser ratio, perhaps only equal to compensatory damages, can reach the outermost limit of the due process guarantee. The precise award in any case, of course, must be based upon the facts and circumstances of the defendant's conduct and the harm to the plaintiff.

(citation omitted).

What impact these "suggestions" will have in practice is hard to say. A number of courts have labored to devine whether a correct ratio has been achieved. Some courts have embraced the ratios.[32] Other courts suggest that the ratios should be kept at a distance. In a decision that has generated significant attention, Judge Posner downplayed the notion that the Court has established a default ratio; rather, the ratios are merely an aid to analysis, not a substitute.[33] Judge Posner's view appears to be more consistent with the *BMW-Campbell* test than the alternative default approach. As the Court stated in *BMW*:

> [L]ow awards of compensatory damages may properly support a higher ratio than high compensatory awards, if, for example, a particularly egregious act has resulted in only a small amount of economic damages. A higher ratio may also be justified in cases in which the injury is hard to detect or the monetary value of noneconomic harm might have been difficult to determine.[34]

Absent these supporting factors, some courts have had little difficulty finding high ratios to be excessive.[35] A ratio of approximately 13:1 was found excessive absent additional facts, such as reprehensibility, warranting a larger award.[36] Even a single digit award may raise questions of

---

[32] *E.g.*, Diamond Woodworks, Inc. v. Argonaut Ins. Co., 135 Cal. Rptr. 2d 736 (Cal. App. 2003):

> *Campbell, BMW* and *Haslip* all suggest that in the usual case, *i.e.*, a case in which the compensatory damages are neither exceptionally high nor low, and in which the defendant's conduct is neither exceptionally extreme nor trivial, the outer constitutional limit on the amount of punitive damages is approximately four times the amount of compensatory damages.

Id. at 762; Daka Inc. v. McCrae, 839 A.2d 682, 697–98 (D.C. 2003) (identifying 4:1 as the default ratio).

[33] Mathias v. Accor Economy Lodging, Inc., 347 F.3d 672 (7th Cir. 2003):

> The Supreme Court did not, however, lay down a 4-to-1 or single-digit-ratio rule—it said merely that "there is a presumption against an award that has a 145-to-1 ratio," and it would be unreasonable to do so. We must consider why punitive damages are awarded and why the Court has decided that due process requires that such awards be limited. The second question is easier to answer than the first. The term "punitive damages" implies punishment, and a standard principle of penal theory is that "the punishment should fit the crime" in the sense of being proportional to the wrongfulness of the defendant's action, though the principle is modified when the probability of detection is very low (a familiar example is the heavy fines for littering) or the crime is potentially lucrative (as in the case of trafficking in illegal drugs). Hence, with these qualifications, which in fact will figure in our analysis of this case, punitive damages should be proportional to the wrongfulness of the defendant's actions.

Id. at 676 (citation omitted).

[34] 517 U.S. at 582.

[35] Pulla v. Amoco Oil Co., 72 F.3d 648, 659 (8th Cir. 1995) (250,000:1). *But cf.* text and notes 38–43, *infra*.

[36] Schimizzi v. Illinois Farmers Ins. Co., 928 F. Supp. 760, 786 (N.D. Ind. 1996) (reducing a punitive damages award of $600,000 against actual damages of $45,000 (13:1 ratio) to $135,000 (3:1 ratio); *cf.* Ace v. Aetna Life Ins. Co., 139 F.3d 1241, 1248–49 (9th Cir. 1998) (finding that 13:1 ratio was far beyond that previously approved by Alaskan courts), *cert. denied*, 525 U.S. 930 (1998).

excessiveness![37]

When supporting factors are present, ratios substantially in excess of 10:1 have been upheld. For example, in *Wilson v. IBP, Inc.* the court upheld a punitive damages award of $2 million against $4,000 actual damages (500:1) based largely on the wealth of the defendant.[38] In *Watson v. Johnson Mobile Homes* a 175:1 ratio was reduced to 37.5:1 ($4,000 compensatory, $150,000 punitive) on facts that evidenced defendant preyed on unsophisticated victims.[39] In *Hampton v. Dilliard Dept. Stores, Inc.* the court upheld a 20:1 ratio ($56,000 compensatory, $1.1 million punitive) on facts that evidenced deliberated racial discrimination in stopping, searching, and restraining a minority customer suspected of shoplifting.[40] In *Mathias v. Accor Economy Lodging, Inc.* the court affirmed a 37.2:1 ratio ($5,000 compensatory, $186,000 punitive) when the facts evidenced that defendant deliberately and knowing rented rooms that were infested with bedbugs.[41]

A high ratio may be tolerated in cases in which nominal damages are awarded.[42] If strict adherence to a reasonable ratio is required, punitive damages would effectively be barred in nominal damages cases; yet, it is these cases in which sizable punitive damages awards may be most important.[43]

It is unclear to what extent, if at all, the trier-of-fact may consider the "potential" for harm that defendant's conduct presented when calculating

---

[37] *E.g.*, Rhone-Poulenc Agro, S.A. v. Dekalb Genetics Corp., 538 U.S. 974 (2003), *vacating and remanding* 272 F.3d 1335 (Fed. Cir. 2001) in light of *Campbell*. *Rhone-Poulenc Agro* involved a 3:1 ratio in a patent infringement, fraud, trade secret misappropriation claim in which plaintiff was awarded $15 million in compensatory damages. On remand the court upheld the award. 345 F.3d 1366 (Fed. Cir. 2003), *cert. denied sub nom.* Dekalb Genetics Corp. v. Bayer Crop Science, S.A., 540 U.S. 1183 (2004).

[38] 558 N.W.2d 132, 148 (Iowa 1996) (involving suit for defamation arising out of workplace injury of the plaintiff), *cert. denied*, 522 U.S. 810 (1997).

[39] 284 F.3d 568 (5th Cir. 2002).

[40] 247 F.3d 1091 (10th Cir. 2001), *cert. denied*, 534 U.S. 1131 (2002).

[41] 347 F.3d 672 (7th Cir. 2003).

[42] Williams v. Kaufman County, 352 F.3d 994, 1016 (5th Cir. 2003) (stating that "any punitive damages-to-compensatory damages *ratio analysis* cannot be applied effectively in cases when only *nominal* damages have been awarded") (emphasis in original); Lee v. Edwards, 101 F.3d 805, 811 (2d Cir. 1996) (stating that the Court's statement in *BMW v. Gore* that 500:1 ratio was "breathtaking . . . does not necessarily control the fair ratios in a [federal civil rights] case").

[43] Edwards v. Jewish Hosp. of St. Louis, 855 F.2d 1345, 1352 (8th Cir. 1988) (noting that "[t]o apply the proportionality rule to a nominal damages award would invalidate most punitive damages awards because only very low punitive damages awards could be said to bear a reasonable relationship to the amount of a nominal damages award"); *cf. Lee, supra*, 101 F.3d at 811 (noting that the Court's decision in *BMW v. Gore,* reinforces the view that greater disproportionality must be tolerated in nominal damages cases: "violations of civil rights may very well be 'particularly egregious' acts that result in only 'a small amount of economic damages' or injuries whose monetary value is 'difficult to determine.' Because the compensatory award here was nominal, any appreciable exemplary award would produce a ratio that would appear excessive by this measure") (citation omitted).

an appropriate punitive damages award.[44] The *Campbell* Court did suggest that "potential harm" was a valid consideration.[45]

The focus on the size of the ratios has tended to obscure a related issue—the content of the ratio. When comparing the punitive damages award to the compensatory damages award, what damages are counted as compensatory damages? Does the compensatory damages component of the ratio include all compensatory damages awarded or only those compensatory damages that are connected to the specific misconduct that led to the punitive damages award? Suppose, for example, that a professor is the victim of sexual harassment and is also terminated from her employment in breach of her tenure rights. She sues the University and receives an award of $100,000 for distress damages associated with the harassment claim, $1 million for her lost earnings on her breach of contract claim and $5 million in punitive damages for the sexual harassment. Is the ratio 50:1 ($100,000 compensatory, $5 million punitive) or 4.5:1 ($1.1 million compensatory, $5 million punitive)?[46]

In *Textron Financial Corp. v. National Union Fire Ins. Co.* the defendant insurer was sued in tort and contract for wrongful denial of coverage. The court affirmed a jury finding that defendant was properly subject to punitive damages for the misconduct of its managing agent; however, the court disagreed with the jury's assessment of the amount of damages.[47] The court agreed with the defendant that in assessing whether the proportionality ratio between compensatory and punitive damages was correct the court should only count the damages awarded for the acts (fraud, bad faith) that supported the punitive damages claim, not the damages awarded for breach of contract, which here was the amount due under the policy. The court reasoned that the awards were separate and had been treated as such by the parties:

> Here, the parties held separate trials on the breach of contract count and the tort claims and the jury returned separate awards on them. In addition, the jury's finding that defendant acted with oppression, fraud, or malice applied solely to the latter two counts. Thus, our

---

[44] *Pulla, supra,* v. Amoco Oil Co., 882 F. Supp. at 887 (upholding punitive damages award that bore a 250,000:1 ratio to actual damages because "the award bore a reasonable relationship to the potential harm [defendant's] conduct could have caused") (brackets added), *modified,* 72 F.3d 648 (8th Cir. 1995) (holding that 250,000:1 ratio was excessive due to "limited offensiveness of Amoco's actions and the unlikelihood of any serious potential harm from its conduct").

[45] 538 U.S. at 418 (stating that "the disparity between the actual or potential harm suffered by the plaintiff and the punitive damages award" is the relevant consideration).

[46] Front and back pay awards may or may not be considered part of compensatory damages for punitive damages purposes. Section 203 (Actual Injury Requirement) (text and notes 10–17).

[47] 13 Cal. Rptr. 3d 586, 603–04 (Cal. App. 2004).

consideration of the disparity between plaintiff's actual harm and the punitive damage award must be limited to its tort relief.[48]

On the other hand, in *Bains LLC v. Arco Products Co.* the court included breach of contract damages in the proportionality analysis even though the breach of contract did not support the punitive damages claim.[49] The court put particular emphasis on the connectiveness between the contract and punitive damages claims:

> On the facts of this case, in determining the correct amount of punitive damages, the jury could properly consider not only the one dollar in nominal damages awarded for discrimination under § 1981, but also the $50,000 in compensatory damages awarded for breach of contract. The conduct was intertwined and the jury could conclude that, even if Tim Reichert would have terminated Flying B based on the safety reports that Al Lawrence gave him, those safety reports would never have come to Reichert had Lawrence not decided to back up his racist leadman or to exercise his authority to lock Flying B out of the terminal. Thus we take $50,000 as the harm suffered.[50]

---

[48] *Id.* at 604. The court further noted:

As a corollary to its attack on the constitutionality of the punitive damage award, defendant argues consideration of the proportionality of the punitive damages to compensatory damages must focus on the amount awarded for breach of the implied covenant of good faith and fair dealing and for fraud ($89,744), excluding the sum plaintiff recovered on the contract claim ($75,670.40). This argument has merit.

Id. The court relied on a cursory statement in *Diamond Woodworks, Inc., supra*, 135 Cal. Rptr. 2d at 761 n.35, that only compensatory damages awarded on the same causes of action that supported the punitive damages award should be considered in the proportionality analysis.

[49] 405 F.3d 764 (9th Cir. 2005). In *Bains LLC* plaintiffs, d/b/a, "Flying B," alleged and proved discrimination directed at them due to their nationality by employees of the defendant. The court found, however, that the termination of the contract with defendant was distinct from the discrimination claim:

Flying B was terminated by a manager who did not know that the company's principals and most of its drivers were Sikhs, so the jury could have found that the breach of contract damages compensated for the harm from the contract's termination. But the jury could have concluded from the evidence that, had Reichert not terminated Flying B for safety violations, Davis and Lawrence would have found a way to terminate Flying B anyway. The jury could have found that routine or debatable safety violations were flagged for Reichert because of Davis' racial animus, whereas the same violations committed by a non-Sikh company would be ignored. Possibly the jury found that under the contract Flying B was entitled to thirty-days notice, that ARCO's immediate termination of the contract without notice cost Flying B around $50,000 in damages, and that putting the same $50,000 under both the § 1981 and the breach of contract causes of action would be double counting. The jury might therefore have put the damages under the breach of contract claim, but signified its agreement with Flying B on the § 1981 claim with its affirmative verdict on that claim.

Id. at 772. The reference in the quote to § 1981 is to 42 U.S.C.A. § 1981, which prohibits discrimination in the making and enforcing of contracts.

[50] *Id.* at 776.

Although the ratio analysis is usually made with respect to the compensatory damages award and the punitive damages award, the *Campbell* Court suggested that courts could use a broader "actual injury" test.[51] The question whether courts should use damages or damage as the basis for computing a proper punitive damages award is addressed in Section 203 (Actual Injury Requirement).

[205.4] Comparable Misconduct Penalties

This factor directs courts to compare the punitive damages award with "the civil or criminal penalties that could be imposed for comparable misconduct."[52] When using this factor the first issue is whether the comparison should be to the entire comparable penalty or just the civil fine provisions. While the maximum authorized civil fines are often small when compared to civil punitive damages awards for comparable conduct, the deprivation of liberty sanctions through imprisonment or probation may make the punitive damages award "pale in comparison."[53] In the aftermath of *BMW*, the decisional law applied this factor inconsistently. In one decision, the court found that the possibility of 5 years imprisonment was insufficient to prevent a reduction of the punitive damages award.[54] In another case, a $1.5 million punitive damages award was sustained in part because the comparative criminal sanction provided for imprisonment for up to 20 years.[55] The difference between 5 and 20 year sentences is surely significant, but how this correlates to a meaningful comparison with a punitive damages award on anything but an intuitive basis is unclear.

The Court's decision in *Campbell* appears to endorse those courts that adopted the restrictive interpretation.[56] The Court deleted any reference to criminal penalties in its recitation of the criterion and downplayed the role of such penalties in the discussion immediately following the quoted language:

> The existence of a criminal penalty does have bearing on the seriousness with which a State views the wrongful action. When used to determine the dollar amount of the award, however, the criminal penalty has less utility. Great care must be taken to avoid use of the civil process to assess criminal penalties that can be imposed only after the heightened protections of a criminal trial

---

[51] *See* text and note 45, *supra*.

[52] *BMW, supra*, 517 U.S. at 583.

[53] Food Lion Inc. v. Capital Cities/ABC Inc., 984 F. Supp. 923, 936 (N.C. 1997).

[54] Lister v. Nationsbank of Del., N.A., 494 S.E.2d 449, 459 (S.C. App. 1997).

[55] Talent Tree Personnel Serv. Inc. v. Fleenor, 703 So. 2d 917, 927 (Ala. 1997). *But cf.* Mathie v. Fries, 121 F.3d 808, 816–17 (2d Cir. 1997) (involving $500,000 punitive damages award against public official (prison director of security) who sexually assaulted an inmate). The court noted that the criminal sanction was a maximum penalty of 25 years, but found the award excessive when compared to other similar misconduct awards. The court reduced the award to $200,000. *Id.*

[56] 538 U.S. at 428.

have been observed, including, of course, its higher standards of proof. Punitive damages are not a substitute for the criminal process, and the remote possibility of a criminal sanction does not automatically sustain a punitive damages award.[57]

The Court in *Campbell* emphasized the civil "fine" that was available to punish the misconduct engaged in by the defendant insurer and strongly hinted that fines were the appropriate point for comparison.[58] The civil fine is a closer approximation of the punitive damages award than the term of imprisonment. The desire to downplay the emotive and speculative harm associated be imprisonment may be driving the Court's refinement of this criterion.

Courts have also drawn comparisons with other punitive damages awards,[59] however, the variables between punitive damages awards and the dangers of selection bias are so great that the value of this approach must be questioned. There may be some cases, however, where a tighter fit may exist.[60]

The complexity inherent in comparing the defendant's misconduct with "comparable" criminal and civil sanctions suggests that this element of the constitutional test for excessiveness should not be included when instructing the jury. The better practice is to use the factor as a post-verdict consideration.[61]

---

[57] *Id.*

[58] *Id.; see* Colleen P. Murphy, *Comparison to Criminal Sanctions in the Constitutional Review of Punitive Damages*, 41 San Diego L. Rev. 1443 (2004). It is unclear whether the Court meant to limit reference to "civil" as opposed to "criminal" fines. States have considerable leeway to characterize a sanction as civil or criminal, so the distinction cannot be in the name or form of the sanction.

[59] *Lee, supra*, 101 F.3d at 812–13; Guzman v. Tower Dev. Inc., 133 F.3d 927 (9th Cir. 1997) (Table); Cherokee Elec. Coop. v. Cochran, 706 So. 2d 1188, 1194–05 (Ala. 1997).

[60] Geuss v. Pfizer, Inc., 971 F. Supp. 164, 178 (E.D. Pa. 1996) (noting that under the Americans with Disability Act "damages for compensatory and punitive damages are capped at different amounts depending on the size of the employer," *citing* 41 U.S.C. § 1981 a (b)(3)). The court noted that the total award was within the damages cap; nonetheless, the court found the punitive damages award of $150,000 to be excessive and issued a remittur of $132,500. *Id.; cf.* Lust v. Sealy, Inc., 383 F.3d 580, 590 (7th Cir. 2004) (noting that Congress's limit on damages that may be awarded for violations of the Civil Rights Act requires greater judicial scrutiny of punitive damages awards in this area to protect against excessive awards).

[61] Geressy v. Digital Equip. Corp., 950 F. Supp. 519, 521 (E.D.N.Y. 1997):

> The charge should therefore, arguably, include all three Gore factors (reprehensibility; disparity between harm and the punitive damage award; and civil and criminal remedies available for similar actions). Nevertheless, there are too many complicating and prejudicial factors in asking a lay jury to consider the third element, potential legal penalties in other civil and criminal actions. Reference to possible criminal (and even administrative penalties such as those of the Occupational Safety and Health Act (OSHA) of which the jury was aware) and to other civil awards, were therefore omitted from the Gore portion of the charge.

[205.5] Other Factors

The three factors discussed in Sections 205.2 through 205.4 address the constitutional test enunciated by the Court in *BMW v. Gore.* The factors are, however, neither unique nor exclusive.[62] In *Campbell* the Court noted several additional factors a court could consider in determining whether the punitive damages award violated 14th Amendment due process. The Court did not expressly expand the *BMW* three part test; rather, the Court placed the factors within the first criterion of the test—degree of reprehensibility. In evaluating the punitive damages award, the Court stated that a court must consider whether (1) the harm was physical rather than economic; (2) the tortious conduct evinced an indifference to or a reckless disregard of the health or safety of others; (3) whether the conduct involved repeated actions or was an isolated incident; and (4) whether the harm resulted from intentional malice, trickery or deceit, or merely accident.[63]

As noted previously, reprehensibility, ratios, and comparability have long played a role in evaluating punitive damages awards for excessiveness. Many jurisdictions have embellished on these factors. Courts may look at the defendant's ability to pay the punitive damages award.[64] Courts may also consider the deterrence value of the award, which may be negligible if the defendant is deceased or no longer in business.[65] Whether the defendant has engaged in remedial or mitigative efforts is relevant,[66] as is the converse, which is to say has the defendant attempted to conceal the harm or stonewall investigations into its wrongdoing.[67] Other factors that have been identified by courts as relevant to the inquiry as to appropriateness of the size of the punitive damages award include: (1) potential harm to others;[68] (2) the profitability of defendant's misconduct and the desire to separate the defendant from his ill-gotten gains;[69] (3) costs of

---

[62] Bowden v. Caldor, Inc., 710 A.2d 267, 278 (Md. 1998) (noting that common law legal principles developed by the court to evaluate whether a punitive damages award is excessive "may be the same as requirements imposed by other courts as a matter of constitutional law, we have no reason at this time to consider minimum constitutional requirements in the area").

[63] *Campbell, supra,* 538 U.S. at 419.

[64] *Bowden, supra,* 710 A.2d at 278 (stating that "[a] second very important principle . . . is that the award of punitive damages 'should not be disproportionate to . . . the defendant's ability to pay' "); *Lee, supra,* 101 F.3d at 813 (stating that "one purpose of punitive damages is deterrence and that deterrence is directly related to what people can afford to pay"); *cf.* City of Newport v. Fact Concerts, Inc., 453 U.S. 247, 270 (1981) ("[E]vidence of a tortfeasor's wealth is traditionally admissible as a measure of the amount of punitive damages that should be awarded").

[65] *Bowen, supra,* 710 A.2d at 279.

[66] *Id.* (collecting decisions).

[67] *Mattias, supra,* 347 F.3d at 675.

[68] TXO Production Corp. v. Alliance Resources Corp., 509 U.S. 443, 460 (1993) (stating that a large punitive damages award may be justified to punish and deter conduct that poses a substantial threat of injury or harm to others); Green Oil Co. v. Hornsby, 539 So. 2d 218, 223–24 (Ala. 1989); *cf. Bains LLP, supra,* 405 F.3d at 776 ("Potential harm to others is best considered when victims are not in a position to vindicate the wrongs against themselves, not where, as here, they are in such a position").

[69] *Green Oil Co., supra,* 539 So. 2d at 223–24; *see* Owens-Corning Fiberglas Corp. v. Malone, 972 S.W.2d 35, 40–41 (Tex. 1998) (involving the defendant's profitability).

litigation;[70] (4) the duration of the misconduct,[71] and (5) the effect of the misconduct on the plaintiff and others.[72]

There are many variations of the factors a jurisdiction may select as its test for determining whether a punitive damages award is excessive. In the end, the reasonableness of a punitive damages award is determined on a case-by-case basis.[73] Moreover, because the basic focus is on the "reasonableness" of the award, one must expect and accept substantial diversity (and disagreement) as to what constitutes a reasonable award under the circumstances.

§ 206 STANDARD OF REVIEW OF AWARD

In *Cooper Industries, Inc. v. Leatherman Tool Group, Inc.* the Supreme Court held that punitive damages awards, unlike compensatory damages awards, should be subject to a de novo standard of review.[1] The Court reasoned that unlike compensatory damages, the assessment of punitive damages does not present a question of historical or predictive fact tried by the jury; therefore, appellate review of a punitive damages award does not implicate Seventh Amendment concerns.[2] In addition, differences in the institutional competence of trial and appellate judges does not warrant differential appellate review. Non deferential review only applies, however, to the constitutional factual aspects of an appeal from a judgment containing an award for punitive damages. Unlike the measure of compensatory loss, an award of punitive damages has a constitutional dimension and an expression of moral condemnation. With respect to the non-constitutional aspects of the punitive damages award, e.g., whether punitive damages should be awarded and, if so, how much, deferential review of the award is often stated to be the norm.[3]

The Court noted in *Cooper Industries, Inc.* that in some circumstances a closer fit between punitive and compensatory damages might warrant

---

[70] *Mathias, supra,* 347 F.3d at 677; *Green Oil Co., supra,* 539 So. 2d at 223–24.

[71] Minn. Stat. § 549.20, subd. 3(3).

[72] Utah Foam Prods. Co. v. Upjohn Co., 930 F. Supp. 513, 525 (D. Utah 1996), *aff'd,* 154 F.3d 1212 (10th Cir. 1998); *see* text and notes 10, 13–14, *supra* (discussing Court's limitation on state's use of defendant's out-of-state activities to calculate punitive damages award).

[73] Management Computer Servs., Inc. v. Hawkins, Ash, Baptie & Co., 557 N.W.2d 67, 82 (Wis. 1996).

[1] 532 U.S. 424, 436 (2001).

[2] *Id.* at 437.

[3] Amfac, Inc. v. Waikiki Beachcomber Inv. Co., 839 P.2d 10, 36–37 (Haw. 1992). *See generally* Jane Massey Draper, Annot., *Excessiveness or Inadequacy of Punitive Damages Award in Personal Injury or Death Cases,* 12 A.L.R. 5th 195 (1993), at § 3:

> [C]ourts have adopted the view that the amount of punitive or exemplary damages awarded in an action involving personal injury or death is left to the sound discretion of the trier of fact and absent a showing of passion or prejudice such award will not be set aside on the grounds of excessiveness or inadequacy.

Section 208 (Discretion as to Scope and Size of the Award).

treatment of the issue as one encompassed by the Seventh Amendment.[4] The court suggested those circumstances might involve a case when a statute stipulated that punitive damages must be an amount "necessary to obtain economically optimal deterrence" or were to be awarded as a prescribed multiple of awarded compensatory damages.[5]

The de novo review permitted by *Cooper Industries, Inc.* applies to the 14th Amendment due process test established in *BMW* and refined in *Campbell.*[6]

Because *Cooper Industries, Inc.* dealt with a punitive damages claim brought in federal court, it was not resolved whether the decision is binding on the states or simply a supervisory decision by the Court over inferior *federal* courts. At present, all the courts that have considered the issue have treated *Cooper Industries, Inc.* as a constitutional decision binding on the states, rather than a supervisory decision binding only on the federal courts.[7] In *Simon v. San Paolo U.S. Holding Co., Inc.* the Court vacated and remanded a state court punitive damages award for reconsideration in light of *Cooper Industries, Inc.*[8] This suggests that the *Cooper Industries, Inc.* rule is one of constitutional due process even though the decision itself largely navigated Seventh Amendment jurisprudence—a jurisprudence that is not binding on the States.[9]

If the court finds that the punitive damages award is unconstitutionally excessive, it may remand or issue a remittitur,[10] although there is disagreement whether "remittitur" is the correct term:

> A constitutionally reduced verdict, therefore, is really not a remittitur at all. A remitittur is a substitution of the court's judgment for that of the jury regarding the appropriate award of damages. The court orders a remittitur when it believes the jury's award is *unreasonable* on the facts. A constitutional reduction, on the other hand, is a determination that the law does not permit the award. Unlike a remittitur, which is discretionary with the court and which we review for an abuse of discretion, a court has a mandatory duty

---

[4] *Cooper Industries, Inc., supra*, 532 U.S. at 440 n.13.

[5] *Id.*

[6] *Id.* at 436 (holding that a court "should apply a de novo standard of review when passing on a district court's determination of the constitutionality of punitive damages awards").

[7] Roth v. Farner-Bocken Co., 667 N.W.2d 651, 665 n4 (S.D. 2003); Central Bering Sea Fisherman's Assn. v. Anderson, 54 P.3d 271 (Alaska 2002); Sand Hill Energy v. Ford Motor Co., 83 S.W.3d 483 (Ky. 2002), *cert. granted and judgment vacated sub nom.* Ford Motor Co v. Estate of Smith, 538 U.S. 1028 (2003) (vacating and remanding for consideration in light of *Campbell*); Aken v. Plains Elec. Generation and Transmission Coop., Inc., 49 P.3d 662 (N.M. 2002); St. John v. Coisman, 799 So. 2d 1110 (Fla. App. 2001); *see* Lisa M. White, Student Comment, *A Wrong Turn on the Road to Tort Reform: The Supreme Courts Adoption of De Novo Review in* Cooper Industries v. Leatherman Tool Group, Inc., 68 Brook. L. Rev. 885 (2003).

[8] 532 U.S. 1050 (2001).

[9] Minneapolis & St. L. R. Co. v. Bombolis, 241 U.S. 211, 216 (1916).

[10] *E.g.*, Leatherman Tool Group, Inc. v. Cooper Industries, Inc., 285 F.3d 1146, 1151 (9th Cir. 2002).

to correct an unconstitutionally excessive verdict so that it conforms to the requirements of the due process clause.[11]

§ 207 MULTIPLE DAMAGES AWARDS

[207.1] Augmented Damages

Many statutory remedies provide for the doubling or trebling of compensatory damages awards. The general purpose behind augmented damages provisions is deterrence. It is often argued that the best deterrent fixes the amount to be levied against the malefactor as the product of the harm caused divided by the possibility of detection and punishment.[1] Augmenting the compensatory damages award is seen as one way of correcting for under-detection of misconduct. Augmented damages are also justified as valid efforts to fix actual damages[2] and as retribution for the wrong committed by the defendant.[3]

The problem of characterization is complicated because a court may characterize augmented damages as being remedial in one context, but punitive in another context.[4] The characterization is situation sensitive rather than based on a principled understanding of the role of augmented

---

[11] Johnson v. Combuston Eng'g, Inc., 170 F.3d 1320, 1331 (11th Cir.) (citations and footnote omitted) (emphasis in original), *cert. denied sub nom.* Combustion Eng'g, Inc. v. McGill, 528 U.S. 931 (1999); *see* Ross v. Kansas City Power & Light Co., 293 F.3d 1041, 1049–50 (8th Cir. 2001) (same).

[1] For example, if the harm caused is $100 and the likelihood of detection and punishment is 50%; the proper sanction is $200 ($100 ÷ ½).

[2] Mitsubishi Motors Corp. v. Stoler Chrysler-Plymouth, Inc., 473 U.S. 614 (1985):

> Notwithstanding its important incidental policing function, the treble-damages cause of action conferred on private parties by § 4 of the Clayton Act . . . seeks primarily to enable an injured competitor to gain compensation for that injury. "Section 4 is in essence a remedial provision . . . . Of course, treble damages also play an important role in penalizing wrongdoers and deterring wrongdoing . . . . It nevertheless is true that the treble-damages provision, which makes awards available only to injured parties, and measures the awards by a multiple of the injury actually proved, is designed primarily as a remedy."

Id. at 635–36 (*quoting* Brunswick Corp. v. Pueblo Bowl-O-Mat, 429 U.S. 477, 485–86 (1977); *see* Robert H. Lande, *Are Antitrust "Treble Damages" Really Single Damages?*, 54 Ohio St. L. J. 115, 118 (1993) (arguing that "antitrust damages awards are approximately equal to, or less than, the actual damages caused by antitrust violations" due to the substantial injuries that are not captured by standard compensatory damages measurement).

[3] *E.g.*, Concrete Spaces, Inc. v. Sendere, 2 S.W.3d 901, 907 (Tenn. 1999) (stating that "multiple damages are punitive in nature"); Section 207.2 (Augmented Damages and Punitive Damages).

[4] *Compare Mitsubishi Motors Corp., supra,* 473 U.S. at 635–36 (treble damages are essentially remedial), *with* Vermont Agency of Natural Resources v. United States *ex rel.* Stevens, 529 U.S. 765, 785–86 (2000) (characterizing treble damages provision of False Claims Act as punitive) and Texas Indus., Inc. v. Radcliff Materials, Inc., 451 U.S. 630, 639 (1981) (suggesting that antitrust treble damages are punitive).

damages. Unless the legislature has spoken clearly,[5] augmented damages can be characterized as having primarily a deterrence, remedial, or penal function, much like "New Shimmer" of Saturday Night Live fame that was both a floor wax and a dessert topping!

[207.2] Augmented Damages and Punitive Damages

The relationship between augmented damages and punitive damages is unclear, at best. One distinction is that punitive damages are discretionary, whereas augment damages tend to be automatic once the statutory standards for their awarding have been met. As noted by one court:

> The plaintiff has no right to exemplary damages, which are in the sole discretion of the trier of fact. On the other hand, the treble damages award authorized in [the statute] is mandatory once the plaintiff has met his burden of showing [a violation]. Nowhere in [the statute] are treble damages referred to as "exemplary." In addition, all exemplary damages awarded under [the statute] are limited to an amount equal to the amount of actual damages unless the defendant has continued the wrongful behavior during the pendency of the case or has acted in a willful and wanton manner during the pendency of the case that has further aggravated the plaintiff's damages. The treble damages provision of [the statute] clearly falls outside the scope of that provision since, once the conduct is proved, the treble damages award is automatic.[6]

Beyond this point, the distinctions grow murky. Some jurisdictions treat punitive and augmented damages as flip sides of the same coin.[7] The augmented portion of the award is deemed punitive; therefore an award of augmented damages and punitive damages is deemed duplicative.[8] Other courts, while recognizing the overlap between augmented and punitive damages, have found that dual awards are permissible under the statutory remedial scheme creating the augmented remedies. For example, in *Neibel v. TransWorld Assurance Company* the court addressed the permissibility of augmented damages awards under RICO (Racketeer Influenced Corrupt

---

[5] *E.g.*, Itin v. Ungar, 17 P.3d 129, 132 (Colo. 2000) (holding that recovery of treble damages under state's Civil Theft statute required plaintiff to prove that defendant committed criminal act).

[6] Farmers Group, Inc. v. Williams, 805 P.2d 419, 427 (Colo. 1991) (citations omitted; brackets added).

[7] Multi-Channel v. Charlottesville Cable, 108 F.3d 522, 528 (4th Cir. 1997) (applying Virgina law); Palm Beach Atl. College v. First United Fund, 928 F.2d 1538, 1545 (11th Cir. 1991) (applying Florida law).

[8] Fineman v. Armstrong World Indus., 980 F.2d 171, 218 (3d Cir. 1992) (precluding dual award of trebled damages under federal antitrust remedies and punitive damages under state law when both remedies arose out of same conduct), *cert. denied*, 507 U.S. 921 (1993); Lexton-Ancira Real Estate Fund, 1972 v. Heller, 826 P.2d 819, 822–23 (Colo. 1992) (barring dual award of trebled damages under state Deceptive Practices Act and punitive damages for common law fraud when both claims arose from same facts).

Organizations Act) and punitive damages under state law for the same conduct. The court noted:

> [W]e cannot ignore the text of RICO itself, which states: "Nothing in this title shall supersede any provision of Federal, State, or other law imposing criminal penalties or affording civil remedies in addition to those provided for in this title." The Supreme Court has interpreted this section to mean that "under RICO, the States, remain free to exercise their police powers to the fullest constitutional extent in defining and prosecuting crimes within their respective jurisdictions." The wording of the statute convinces us that the same reasoning should apply to civil as well as criminal cases. Since Congress has spoken clearly on this issue, we are bound by its wishes. We hold that a plaintiff may receive both treble damages under RICO and state law punitive damages for the same course of conduct.[9]

Some jurisdictions treat augmented damages as entirely compensatory.[10] This viewpoint avoids the conclusion that an award of augmented and punitive damages are necessarily duplicatory. As noted by one court:

> In addition, although it is unclear what damages are being compensated by the multiple damages provision, that fact alone does not necessarily make the provision punitive and thus duplicative of punitive damages. Legislative history indicates that one objective the legislature sought to achieve through enactment of subdivision 2 was the enticement of the private bar into bringing claims based on violations of the [Minnesota Human Rights Act]. We conclude, therefore, that multiple compensatory damages are not duplicative of punitive damages where at least one objective of multiple compensatory damages is nonpunitive. Thus, the trial court's award of both punitive damages and double actual damages does not constitute an unfair double recovery for punitive damages.[11]

If the jurisdiction treats the augmented damages award as punitive two approaches have been recognized. One approach allows the plaintiff to submit both claims to the trier-of-fact and claim the greater.[12] The other approach treats the augmented damages claim as penal and bars submission of a punitive damages claim to the trier-of-fact when both claims are based on the same conduct.[13] The plaintiff may elect to not assert the augmented

---

[9] 108 F.3d 1123, 1130–31 (9th Cir. 1997) (citations omitted).

[10] Phelps v. Commonwealth Land Title Ins., 537 N.W.2d 271, 275 (Minn. 1995).

[11] Id. at 277 (citations omitted; brackets added). See generally Lisa K. Gregory, Annot., Plaintiff's Rights to Punitive or Multiple Damages When Cause of Action Renders Both Available, 2 A.L.R.5th 449 (1992).

[12] Concrete Spaces, Inc., supra, 2 S.W.3d at 907–09 (permitting election after jury has rendered verdicts so that plaintiff can compare recoveries under punitive damages and augmented damages); Eastern Star. Inc. v. Union Bldg. Materials, 712 P.2d 1148, 1160 (Haw. App. 1985).

[13] Johnson v. Tyler, 277 N.W.2d 617, 618–19 (Iowa 1979).

damages claim in order to present the punitive damages claim, but that election will cost the plaintiff all other remedies available under the augmented damages claim, such as attorneys' fees.[14]

Because the augmented award is based on a multiple (doubling or trebling) of the compensatory damages award, the issue may arise as to the proper crediting of settlements and offsets against the augmented award. The basic issue is whether the credit should be taken before or after the compensatory award is augmented. The difference can be significant. For example, assume a plaintiff brings a statutory deceptive practices action against an automobile dealer arising out of the purchase of a used vehicle. Assume the compensatory recovery involves rescission of the transaction, *e.g.*, return of the vehicle, plus damages of $5,000. Assume further that the use value of the vehicle to the plaintiff before the vehicle is returned is $2,000, which the defendant-dealer is entitled to take as a credit.[15] If the credit is taken before trebling, plaintiff will recover damages of $9,000 ($5,000 minus $2,000) × 3). If, on the other hand, trebling occurs before the credit is applied, plaintiff will recover $13,000 (($5,000 x 3) minus $2,000). The difference, $4,000, reflects the before versus after calculation.

As a general rule, courts have trebled awards and then applied the credit when settlements by other parties are offset against the plaintiff's recovery.[16] The rationale for this approach was set forth in *Hydrolevel Corp. v. American Society of Mechanical Eng'rs, Inc.*:

> First, the antitrust laws provide that the plaintiff should receive three times the proven actual damages. If settlement proceeds are deducted before trebling, the plaintiff total award is less than what the law allows. Since antitrust defendants are joint tortfeasors, each is liable to complete the total deserved damages irrespective of fault. Second, . . . one purpose of the trebling provision is to encourage private plaintiffs to bring suit. Any ultimate recovery totaling less than three times proven damages would weaken the statutory incentive through judicial construction. Third, deduction of settlement proceeds before trebling would discourage settlement by making litigation relatively more profitable for plaintiffs; every dollar received in settlement would cause a three dollar reduction in the judgment at trial.[17]

---

[14] Kelco Disposal, Inc. v. Browning-Ferris, 845 F.2d 404, 411 (2d Cir. 1988) (stating that when a party elects a remedy and foregoes another, that party foregoes the entire remedy, including the provision that attorneys fees be awarded to the prevailing party), *aff'd on other grounds sub nom.* Browning-Ferris Indust. of Vermont v. Kelco Disposal, Inc., 492 U.S. 257 (1989).

[15] Section 134 (Restoration of Status Quo).

[16] This is the federal rule. Flinkote Co. v. Lysfford, 246 F.2d 368, 397–98 (9th Cir.), *cert. denied*, 355 U.S. 835 (1957) (involving antitrust litigation); Liquid Air Corp. v. Rogers, 834 F.2d 1297, 1310 (7th Cir. 1987) (involving civil racketeering claims), *cert. denied*, 492 U.S. 917 (1989).

[17] 635 F.2d 118, (2d Cir. 1980), *aff'd on other grounds*, 456 U.S. 556 (1982).

Although the court was addressing antitrust trebling provisions, the reasoning has been applied to other augmented damages claims.[18]

The jurisdictions have split as to whether the credit should be taken before or after augmentation when the credit involves an offset. The claims frequently arise under state unfair practices consumer protection laws and the split reflects judicial attention to specific language in the jurisdiction's consumer protection statute.[19]

§ 208 DISCRETION AS TO THE SCOPE AND THE SIZE OF AWARD

Punitive damages are awarded not as a matter of right but to punish and deter. While punitive damages express the trier-of-fact's indignation at the defendant's misconduct, the indignation must be not only rightful but restrained.[1] When punitive damages awards are the product of passion or prejudice, they will be set aside.[2] Within these broad guidelines much is committed to the discretion of the trier-of-fact[3] and that discretion may find expression in punitive damages awards that are specifically tailored to the particular case. For example, in *Schwenk v. Kavanaugh* two prosecutors were found to have improperly obtained the defendant's confidential psychiatric records in violation of the defendant's constitutional rights. The court noted the strong public interest in the protection of medical records, and of psychiatric records in particular. Nonetheless, the court awarded only $1 in nominal damages and $1 in punitive damages against each prosecutor. The court held that economic deterrence would not be advanced by a larger award because the prosecutors would be indemnified by their employers![4] Moreover, the matter had received widespread attention in the press, which the court believed provided sufficient deterrence:

---

[18] *In re* National Mortgage Equity Pool Certificates Sec. Litig., 636 F. Supp. 1138, 1151 (C.D. Cal. 1986) (quoting *Hydrolevel Corp.* and applying rationale to civil racketeering claim); *cf.* Stewart Title Guar. Co. v. Sterling, 822 S.W.2d 1, 9 (Tex. 1991) (applying the same reasoning to a claim under the Texas Insurance Code).

[19] *Compare* Taylor v. Volvo North Am. Corp., 451 S.E.2d 618, 628–30 (N.C. 1994) (applying offset, for use of vehicle, before augmentation), *with* Davis v. Wholesale Motors, Inc., 949 P.2d 1026, 1042–43 (Haw. App. 1997) (applying offset, for use of vehicle, after augmentation).

[1] Coster v. Crookham, 468 N.W.2d 802, 810–11 (Iowa 1991).

[2] Scala v. Moore McCormack Lines, Inc., 985 F.2d 680, 684 (2d Cir. 1993) ("While a jury has broad discretion in measuring damages, it may not abandon analysis for sympathy for a suffering plaintiff and treat an injury as though it were a winning lottery ticket.") (citations and internal quotes omitted).

[3] Amfac, Inc. v. Waikiki Beachcomber Inv. Co., 839 P.2d 10, 36–37 (Haw. 1992). *See generally* Jane Massey Draper, Annot., *Excessiveness or Inadequacy of Punitive Damages Award in Personal Injury or Death Cases*, 12 A.L.R.5th 195 § 3 (1999) (noting that general view is to commit decision as to whether to award punitive damages and, if so, the amount to the discretion of the trier-of-fact).

[4] 4 F. Supp. 2d 116, 118 (N.D.N.Y. 1998). It is unclear whether a policy of reimbursement is admissible. Freeman v. City of Santa Ana, 68 F.3d 1180, 1190 (9th Cir. 1995) (holding that trial judge did not abuse her discretion in excluding evidence of public entity's policy of indemnifying officers against any punitive damages awards on grounds that prejudicial effect outweighed evidence's probative value).

Appearing in an article discussing conduct which warrants punitive damages, with a wide circulation among the bench and bar, must be considered punitive to the attorneys whose conduct is the subject of the article. Further, the threat of appearing in another such article provides sufficient deterrence to these defendants. The deterrent effect of the New York Law Journal article is as powerful, if not more so, as any monetary award would be. Moreover, the deterrent effect of this type of article extends not only to the defendants in this case, but literally across the country to all of the readership of the New York Law Journal.[5]

A number of courts have upheld allowing the trier-of-fact to consider the litigation expenses the plaintiff has incurred in seeking redress against the defendant. For example, in *St. Luke Evangelical Lutheran Church, Inc. v. Smith* the court upheld the practice, notwithstanding the prevailing rule that each side to the litigation bear its own non-taxable costs, including attorneys fees.[6] The court noted that the modern trend was to permit the trier-of-fact to consider such evidence and in its discretion include those expenses in the punitive damages award.[7]

§ 209 TORT REFORM—PUNITIVE DAMAGES

Tort reform legislation has had a significant impact on punitive damages. In 1995 the American Tort Reform Association reported that 31 states have enacted punitive damages reforms since 1986.[1] The impact has been in several areas. Many states now require that plaintiffs establish their punitive damages claim by clear and convincing evidence rather than the traditional preponderance of the evidence standard. A second reform elevates the standard for establishing punitive damages by setting a minimum threshold of wantonness or despicability before punitive damages may be awarded. Third, the procedural rules for pleading and proving punitive damages have been modified, often requiring more detailed pleading of punitive damages and bifurcating the trial so that punitive damages are tried separately from compensatory damages. Some jurisdictions are now going further and holding a separate hearing to determine the extent to which, if at all, the punitive damages award is covered by insurance.[2] This stage is designed to measure the actual impact of the punitive damages award on the defendant to determine if it will truly punish and deter.[3] Some

---

[5] *Schwenk, supra,* 4 F. Supp. 2d at 118.

[6] 568 A.2d 35 (Md. 1990); Section 210 (Attorney's Fees—The "American Rule").

[7] *St. Luke Evangelical Lutheran Church, supra,* 568 A.2d at 41, *citing* Restatement (Second) of Torts § 914 (1979).

[1] Tort Reform Record, December 31, 1995.

[2] ROBERT JERRY III, UNDERSTANDING INSURANCE LAW, § 65(e) (3d ed. 2002) (discussing split in jurisdictions as to whether insurance coverage may be extended to punitive damages awards).

[3] Jurisdictions have split on the issue of pre-trial discovery of defendant's wealth when bifurcation is ordered. *Compare* Tillery v. Lynn, 607 F. Supp. 399, 402 (S.D.N.Y. 1985)

jurisdictions cap punitive damages awards, usually in the $250,000–$350,000 range, and some jurisdictions require that punitive damages awards be shared with the state on a percentage basis.[4]

(permitting pretrial discovery of defendant's wealth prior to determination of liability for punitive damages), *with* Davis v. Ross, 107 F.R.D. 326, 327 (S.D.N.Y. 1985) (delaying discovery of defendant's wealth until determination is made by jury that plaintiff is entitled to punitive damages).

[4] Jurisdictions have split on the constitutionality of the "sharing with the state" reform. *Compare* Kirk v. Denver Pub'g Co., 818 P.2d 262, 270 (Colo. 1991) (holding provision violative of state constitution prohibitions on the taking of private property without compensation), *with* Mack Trucks, Inc. v. Conkle, 436 S.E.2d 635, 638–39 (Ga. 1993) (holding that state's claim to 75% of punitive damages awards did not violate equal protection clauses of state and federal constitutions). The Georgia statute considered in *Conkle* only applied to products liability claims. In *Gordon v. State of Florida*, 585 So. 2d 1033, 1035 (Fla. App. 1991), *cert. denied*, 507 U.S. 1005 (1993), the court squarely rejected a taking challenge to the Florida statute claiming up to 60% of punitive damages. *See generally* Sonja Larsen, Annot., *Validity, Construction, and Application of Statutes Requiring That Percentage of Punitive Damages Awards Be Paid Directly to State or Court-Administered Fund*, 16 A.L.R.5th 129 (1994). Some commentators see this "reform" as not only illusory, but as potentially leading to larger punitive damages awards. Victor E. Schwartz, Mark A. Behrens & Cary Silverman, *I'll Take That: Legal and Public Policy Problems Raised By Statutes That Require Punitive Damages Awards to be Shared With the State*, 68 Mo. L. Rev. 525 (2003). Perhaps it is somewhat probative of the point that when California adopted a "share with the state" statute, the Governor included projected revenues from the statute as a significant component of his program to cure California's budget deficit. James J. Farrell & Jeremy G. Suiter, *Assessing the Impact of the New Law on Punitive Damages*, 28-APR L.A. Law. 14 (2005) (discussing Cal. Civ. Code § 3294.5).

Chapter 24

ATTORNEY'S FEES

§ 210   ATTORNEY'S FEES—THE "AMERICAN RULE"

The common law rule in the United States is that each party in a civil action pays her own attorney's fees. This rule is known as the "American Rule"[1] and has been long established in the United States.[2] The rule that each party bears the cost of its attorney expenses should be distinguished from public welfare or public subsidy programs that provide legal assistance to certain categories of individuals, such as indigents. Although the "American Rule" has been extensively debated and critiqued, it remains the dominant rule in civil litigation in the United States today.[3] The competing rule is the so-called "loser pays," or "English Rule," which permits limited shifting of the cost of representation incurred by the prevailing party to

---

[1] John Leubsdorf, *Toward a History of the American Rule on Attorney Fee Recovery*, 47 Law & Contemp. Probs. 9 (1984).

[2] Arcambel v. Wiseman, 3 U.S. 306 (1796); Day v. Woodworth, 54 U.S. 363 (1851).

[3] Alyeska Pipeline Serv. Co. v. Wilderness Soc'y, 421 U.S. 240, 247–62 (1975).

the losing party.[4] Alaska has adopted a general rule of "loser pays,"[5] but it is apparently the only state to have done so.[6]

The "American Rule" is identified with the goal of favoring access to courts. As noted by the Court:

> In support of the American Rule, it has been argued that since litigation is at best uncertain one should not be penalized for merely defending or prosecuting a lawsuit, and that the poor might be unjustly discouraged from instituting actions to vindicate their rights if the penalty for losing included the fees of their opponents' counsel.[7]

Law, and its production by such means as verdicts, judgments, and opinions, is seen as a public good in the sense that the statement and clarification of law benefits not just the parties to the dispute, but the public as a whole. Encouraging disputants to bring their contest before a tribunal for resolution rather than engaging in self help, discourages breaches of the peace and the social disruption resulting from not redressing wrongdoing. Both of these goals are enhanced if the cost of access to tribunals is kept low. Not saddling the plaintiff with the successful defendant's attorney's fees reduces the cost of entry and thus encourages plaintiffs to litigate. Of course, this is not an unmitigated good, or even perceived as a "good" by all concerned. However, the values identified with the "American Rule" have continued to outpace the reasoning underlying the "English Rule" that the costs of litigation should be borne by the party that erroneously inflicted them.[8]

The "American Rule" is not, however, monolithic; it includes a number of exceptions, several of which are quite capacious. The main exceptions include: (1) statutory authorization; (2) contractual authorization; (3) common fund; (4) third party tort; and, (5) bad faith; each of which is discussed in Section 211 (Exceptions to the "American Rule").

§ 211 EXCEPTIONS TO THE "AMERICAN RULE"

[211.1] Statutory Authorization

The "American Rule" has seen its most significant and extensive erosion by federal and state legislation that expressly authorizes the award of

---

[4] John Vargo, *The American Rule on Attorney Fee Allocation: The Injured Person's Access to Justice*, 42 Am. U. L. Rev. 1567, 1570–74 (1993) (discussing English and American colonial experience with the allocation of the expense of litigation between parties to the lawsuit).

[5] McDonough v. Lee, 420 P.2d 459, 460–61 nn. 5–6 (Alaska 1966) (noting that the Alaska "loser" pays rule developed out of territorial legislation ratified by the state legislature shortly after statehood was achieved).

[6] Monzingo v. Alaska Air. Group, Inc., 112 P.3d 655, 665 (Alaska 2005).

[7] Fleischmann Distilling Corp. v. Maier Brewing Co., 386 U.S. 714, 718 (1967).

[8] *Symposium on Fee Shifting*, 71 Chi.-Kent L. Rev. 415–697 (1995).

attorney's fees to the prevailing party in civil litigation. Statutory authorization of a fees award may partake of a number of formats and forms in the service of several different purposes or goals.

In terms of "format," statutes allow a recovery of attorney's fees in one of three ways. First, the statute may refer to the recovery of costs and a reasonable attorney's fee. In this format the recovery of attorney's fees is separate and independent of the recovery of costs[1] and the recovery of attorney's fees is specifically authorized. Second, the statute may refer to the recovery of costs, including attorney's fees. In this format, attorney's fees are recoverable as part of the recovery of costs. However, when attorney's fees are appendaged to costs, limitations and constraints on the recovery of costs may limit the recovery of fees.[2] Third, the statute may authorize the recovery of costs and expenses, including attorney's fees. It is not clear under this format whether attorney's fees are independently and separately authorized, as in the first format, or as an appendage to costs, as in the second format.[3]

In terms of "purpose," statutes authorize that the cost of representation incurred by the prevailing party be borne by the non-prevailing party for several distinct reasons. One purpose is to encourage litigation of a specific type by decreasing the cost of accessing the civil justice system and by encouraging attorneys to accept representation by the prospect of the recovery of a statutory fee. A second purpose is to punish the non-prevailing party for having engaged in the inappropriate and socially unproductive conduct condemned or discouraged by the statute with the fees shifting provision. A third purpose is to compensate the prevailing party for the transactions costs incurred in seeking redress. Unless litigation transaction costs are reimbursed, a prevailing party may not be made whole as a result of the non-prevailing party's legal wrong. For example, if D inflicts $100 of harm on P and it costs P $30 to recover damages of $100, P's net recovery is $70. From this perspective P has not been made whole by an award of compensatory damages.

Fees award statutes come in a variety forms. Some statutes only allow one party to recover fees; other statutes permit either party to the dispute

---

[1] "Costs" refers to specific items of litigation expense that are reimbursed to the prevailing party as a result of statutory grant, including court rules. Not all litigation costs are recoverable—attorney's fees, under the "American Rule" are a good example, as are time away from work, distraction, distress, etc., caused by litigation. Recoverable costs usually include such items as filing fees, costs of service of process, and fees for witnesses, but not including expert witnesses, unless court appointed. See 28 U.S.C. § 1920(1)–(5).

[2] For example, costs are usually not awarded in the absence of a judgment. Moreover, even if a judgment is entered, the court retains substantial discretion over the awarding ("taxing") of the costs of litigation. See, e.g., Wilkerson v. Johnson, 699 F.2d 325, 330 (6th Cir. 1983); Poe v. John Deere Co., 695 F.2d 1103, 1108 (8th Cir. 1982); EEOC v. Pierce Packing Co., 669 F.2d 605, 609 (9th Cir. 1982); SCA Servs. v. Lucky Stores, 599 F.2d 178, 180 (7th Cir. 1979); Section 212 (Prevailing Party).

[3] The three formats, and examples from federal statutes, are discussed in Justice Brennan's dissenting opinion in Marek v. Chesny, 473 U.S. 1, 43–44 (1985).

to recover fees.[4] Some statutes require only that the party prevail; other statutes require that the claim or defense be exceptional in some sense, for example, the plaintiff's position must be unusually strong or weak[5] or the benefits of the litigation must transcend the plaintiff's personal interest in the dispute.[6]

[211.2]   Contractual Authorization

It is generally recognized that parties to a contract may agree to the recovery of attorney's fees incurred by the non-breaching party as an item of compensable damages. The policy of freedom of contract warrants enforcement of the provision. It is not uncommon, however, for contractual provisions regarding attorney's fees to be drafted so as to favor only one of the contracting parties. For example, a lease may permit the prevailing landlord to recover her attorney's fees against the tenant, but not expressly permit the prevailing tenant to recover his attorney's fees against the landlord in contractual disputes over the lease. One-sided attorney's fees provisions have been enforced by the courts.[7] A number of jurisdictions have, however, enacted statutes mandating that whenever a contractual provision makes recovery of attorney's fees available only for one party, the provision will be applied for the benefit of all parties.[8] The purpose of these statutes is to prevent oppressive and opportunistic use of one-sided attorney's fees provisions. These factors may induce a court to either deny enforcement of a one-sided attorney's fee's provision or allow for mutuality, even in the absence of a statute, when the equities of the matter so demand.

---

[4] For example, under the Civil Rights Attorney Fees statute, 42 U.S.C. § 1988, a prevailing plaintiff is entitled to a fees award without more, but a prevailing defendant recovers fees only if the plaintiff's claims are "groundless, without foundation, frivolous, or unreasonable." McCarthy v. Mayo, 827 F.2d 1310, 1318 (9th Cir. 1987). Under the Fair Labor Standards Act, 29 U.S.C. § 216 (b), only the prevailing plaintiff may recover fees.

[5] United States v. Manchester Farming Partnership, 315 F.3d 1176 (9th Cir. 2003) (addressing question whether successful defendant in criminal case brought by United States could recover fees under Hyde Amendment, which permits recovery if criminal prosecution was "vexatious" under the Act); United States v. Tamko Roofing Products v. Ideal Roofing, 282 F.3d 23, 29–34 (1st Cir. 2002) (discussing Lanham Act requirement that fees can be awarded to prevailing party "in exceptional cases").

[6] E.g., Hammon v. Agran, 120 Cal. Rptr. 2d 646 (Cal. App. 2002) (discussing requirement that to recover fees under California's private attorney general statute the public benefits of the litigation must "transcend" the prevailing parties personal interests in the matter). In *Hammon* a candidate for public office secured a ruling that portions of a voter pamphlet filed by a rival candidate were misleading. The court allowed an award of fees finding that important public interests in the proper interpretation of the state Election Code were vindicated.

[7] Estate of Szorek, 551 N.E.2d 697, 700–01 (Ill. App. 1990) (enforcing one-sided attorney's fees provision contained on Bank signature card). The court noted that the party to be burdened by the provision had the opportunity to read the provision and obtain any assistance she needed. *Id.*

[8] E.g., Cal. Civ. Code § 1717, *discussed in* Santisas v. Goodin, 951 P.2d 399, 406 (Cal. 1998); Fla. Stat. § 57.105(2), *discussed in* County Waste, Inc. v. Public Storage Mgmt., Inc., 582 So. 2d 87 (Fla. App. 1991); Rev. Code Wash. § 7.84.330, *discussed in* Hemenway v. Miller, 807 P.2d 863, 873 (Wash. 1991).

For example, in *Ecco-Phoenix Electric Corp. v. Howard J. White, Inc.* the contract contained a one-sided attorney's fees clause that required the subcontractor to bear any attorney's fees incurred by the contractor "should litigation be necessary to enforce any term or provision of this agreement." The court held that a one-sided clause might encourage vexatious or frivolous litigation and thus would be contrary to public policy.[9] The court, however, did not base its decision directly on a finding that a one-sided clause violated public policy. The court held that the provision was "ambiguous." Employing the rule of contra proferentum (construction against the drafter), the court limited the clause to litigation made necessary by the subcontractor.[10]

The contractual attorney's fees provision will be construed according to its terms,[11] but the provision is often written quite broadly, for example, providing for the recovery of fees for actions seeking to enforce any right under or on the contract. When this general language is combined with a mutuality statute, the scope of recoverable fees may be very broad. If a party is successful in canceling or rescinding the contract, attorney's fees may be awarded on the theory that had the other party prevailed, she would have been entitled to attorney's fees "under the contract."[12] An attorney's fees clause will not, however, be implied from an agreement.[13]

One of the more difficult areas here is when a contractual authorization of attorney's fees meets a statutory provision that directly or indirectly addresses fees awards. In *Wong v. Thrifty Corp.* the court held that an Offer of Compromise under California law that was accepted by the plaintiff controlled a contractual attorney's fees provision that had more limited language and would not, on its terms, have permitted a recovery.[14]

---

[9] 461 P.2d 33, 36 (Cal. 1969).

[10] *Id.* at 39.

[11] *E.g.*, Moallem v. Coldwell Banker Commercial Group, Inc., 31 Cal. Rptr. 2d 253, 255 (Cal. App. 1994) (refusing to allow attorney's fees to successful party who sued broker for negligence notwithstanding attorney's fees provision in the contract). The court noted that the provision favored only the broker, the action sounded in negligence not contract, and the provision limited recovery to any "legal action relating to the contract." *Id.* at 255. The court distinguished cases reaching a contrary result by noting that the provisions in those cases were broader. *Id.* (noting that "[i]n all of those cases . . . the contract provisions . . . provided for attorney['s] fees to whichever party prevailed . . .").

[12] Katz v. Van Der Noord, 546 So. 2d 1047, 1049 (Fla. 1989); *see* Mackintosh v. California Fed. S. & L. Ass'n, 935 P.2d 1154, 1162 (Nev. 1997) (agreeing with *Katz*); Hastings v. Matlock, 217 Cal. Rptr. 856, 866 (Cal. App. 1985) (stating that an action for rescission is an "action on the contract" for purposes of California's contracted-for attorney's fees mutuality statute (Cal. Civ. Code § 1717)); *cf.* Thompson v. Miller, 4 Cal. Rptr. 3d 905 (Cal. App. 2003) (defendant who relied on *contract language to defeat claim* asserted by plaintiff could not invoke contract provision authorizing an award of fees to "[t]he prevailing party in any dispute under the Agreement" because *plaintiff's claim* was not within the language of the contract).

[13] Prudential-Bache Secs., Inc. v. Depew, 814 F. Supp. 1081, 1082 (M.D. Fla. 1993) (refusing to imply contractual authorization for an award of attorney's fees to prevailing party out of broad remedies clause in AAA standard arbitration agreement).

[14] 118 Cal. Rptr. 2d 276, 278 (Cal. App. 2002) (holding that the statutory definition of prevailing party replaced the narrower definition of the contract); Carver v. Chevron USA, 118

[211.3] Common Fund

The "common fund" exception to the "American Rule" is based on the principle that when a party has employed counsel and thereby created a fund, which will benefit third parties, the third parties should be required to assume a fair share of the attorney's fees incurred in the fund's creation. This principle is "based on the equitable notion that those who have benefitted from litigation should share its costs."[15] Shareholders who pursue a successful derivative action may recover their attorney's fees if they can show that they have conferred a substantial "benefit" to the corporation by their efforts.[16] Similarly, class representatives who pursue litigation that benefits the entire class may shift responsibility for the payment of attorney's fees to the "fund" created by the recovery.[17] The use of the terms "benefit" and "fund" illustrate a common problem in this area. When a monetary "fund" is created, awarding fees out of the "fund" is usually not questioned, although the measure of the fees may be.[18] On the other hand, when no "fund" is created, but a "benefit" is said to have been realized as a result of the litigation, should third parties be responsible for the costs of "benefit" creation?[19]

In *First Interstate Bancorp Consol. Shareholder Litigation*, the court accepted that a "benefit" need not be a tangible monetary benefit in the sense of a discrete fund.[20] However, if a benefit can be created in such circumstances, how should that benefit be valued or monetized for purposes of a fees award? In *First Interstate* the litigation arose out of a hostile takeover that was ultimately successful. Plaintiffs argued that a "fund" existed and could be measured by the difference between the initial proposal and the aggregate value of the consideration ultimately paid, here $3.5 billion or, alternatively $1.4 billion under a different formula. The court rejected each approach because it did not find that the litigation was directly an effective cause in the price increase the acquirer (Wells Fargo) paid.

Cal. Rptr. 2d 569 (Cal. App. 2002) (holding that statute (Cartwright Act) preempted contract provision governing recovery of attorney's fees). In *Carver* gasoline franchisees sued and lost on their claim that Chevron breached its leases, committed fraud, and violated the Cartwright Act. Chevron claimed $5 million as defense costs under its lease provision providing for recovery of attorney's fees by a prevailing party. The court held, however, that the Cartwright Act's limitation on fee recoveries to prevailing "plaintiffs" controlled; the fact that the claims involved a breach of lease was held to be legally insignificant.

[15] Skelton v. General Motors Corp., 860 F.2d 250, 252 (7th Cir. 1988), *cert. denied*, 493 U.S. 810 (1989) (citation omitted); *see* John Dawson, *Lawyers and Involuntary Clients: Attorney Fees From Funds*, 87 Harv. L. Rev. 1597, 1603–04 (1974).

[16] *In re* First Interstate Bancorp Consol. Shareholder Litigation 756 A.2d 353, 359 (Del. 1999).

[17] Boeing Co. v. Van Gemert, 444 U.S. 472, 481 (1980).

[18] Section 213.1 (Calculation of Fees Award); *see* text and notes 26–33, *infra*.

[19] Sections 42 (Restitution for Unjust Rnrichment), 43 (Nature of Unjust Enrichment).

[20] 756 A.2d 353.

The court did find a "benefit," however, in plaintiffs' litigation that deterred First Interstate's board from agreeing to a friendly merger and presented the opportunity of Wells Fargo's higher priced "hostile" merger:

> By their action, the plaintiffs were not seeking damages, or monetary relief. Primarily, their complaint sought injunctive relief constraining the operation of certain aspects of the First Interstate/ FBS merger agreement and compelling the defendant directors to act in accordance with their fiduciary duties in responding to the hostile takeover effort mounted by Wells Fargo. Ultimately, the directors acted to abandon the First Interstate/FBS merger agreement and to enter into a superior merger agreement with Wells Fargo. Assuming, for the purposes of this argument, some causal relationship between the litigation and these actions, the litigation may be seen to have benefitted the First Interstate stockholders, as a whole, in some unquantifiable, but nonetheless real, sense. The barriers to the superior offer were overcome and the First Interstate rights plan used in a way to achieve the optimal outcome. Plaintiffs argue that, under the authority of *Richman*, such a benefit may support an award of fees *from the corporate treasury*.[21]

The "common fund" as opposed to "common benefit" approach would have created other problems. The defendant was First Interstate and the consideration had long been distributed, so the "fund" itself no longer existed. Could First Interstate, as opposed to the shareholders, be seen to have derived monetary benefit, (the fund), from the plaintiffs efforts. The court intimated that it could not, but was not required to decide the issue because it found no causal link between the litigation and any "fund."[22] The calculation of the value of the benefit and the amount of fees that would be paid by the recipient of the benefit, here the successor corporation, was not addressed by the court.[23] The extension of the "common fund" concept to "common benefits" has been criticized as unwarranted and unwise.[24]

The common fund recovery is an application of principles of unjust enrichment and restitution. Unlike other exceptions to the "American Rule," when attorney's fees are paid by the defendant in addition to actual damages, in common fund cases the fees are extracted from the recovery;

---

[21] *Id.* at 358 (emphasis added).

[22] *Id.* at 357–59.

[23] An interesting example of this problem was demonstrated in *O'Neil v. Church's Fried Chicken, Inc.*, 910 F.2d 263, 265 (5th Cir. 1990) (applying Texas law). The court held that as a result of the derivative action the corporation received an increased price per share in the tender offer. That benefit, however, was actually realized by the prior shareholders. Nonetheless, the benefit was received by the corporation, which remained liable for the attorney's fees under the common fund approach. As a practical matter, the court's approach resulted in the buyer paying for counsel whose efforts required them to pay a higher price for the corporation! *Id.* at 267 (stating in justification that benefit to prior shareholders was diffused equally and that the buyer acquires liabilities as well as assets).

[24] Lloyd C. Anderson, *Equitable Power to Award Attorney's Fees: The Seductive Appeal of "Benefit"*, 48 S.D. L. Rev. 217 (2003).

thus, the fund pays the fees, not the opposing party. This viewpoint, while technical in the sense that all monies, including monies for the fund, come from the defendant, is significant as a cap on attorney's fees recoveries. The defendant's payment to the fund caps its liability; that is not the case when the defendant pays attorney's fees in other contexts.[25] As noted, previously, however, this result may not fully apply in common "benefit" as opposed to common "fund" cases when the defendant is deemed the "beneficiary" of plaintiff's efforts.

Two methodologies have developed to determine attorney's fees in common fund cases: the lodestar and percentage methods. Under the lodestar approach, the court calculates the "lodestar" figure by multiplying the hours reasonably expended by counsel times a reasonable hourly rate.[26] Under the percentage method, the court allocates a portion of the fund to pay for attorney's fees. The normal portion runs in the 20–30% range.[27] However, when valuation of the fund is difficult due to non-cash contributions by the settling defendants, courts tend to decrease the portion allocated to attorney's fees.[28] The non-cash contributions frequently consist of discount coupons exchangeable for future goods or services from the settling defendants.

The percentage share approach has gained numerous adherents,[29] although many courts state that whether the lodestar or percentage approach is used depends on the facts of the case.[30] Several jurisdictions have expressly rejected the percentage approach on the ground that it is biased in favor of contingent risk factors, applicable to contingent fee cases,

---

[25] It is, however, not uncommon in "common fund" cases for the defendant to agree to pay, in addition to the "fund" amount, the attorney's fees awarded by the court. This approach is practically a necessity whenever the settlement does not include the payment of cash.

[26] Hensley v. Eckerhart, 461 U.S. 424, 433 (1993). The lodestar may be adjusted by various factors used to calculate attorneys fees in statutory fees cases, although how much variance is permissible remains a contested issue. Section 213.1 (Calculation of Fees Awards).

[27] Swedish Hosp. Corp. v. Shalala, 1 F.3d 1261, 1272 (D.C. Cir. 1993) (approving 20% figure and noting that majority of awards are between 20% and 30%); Paul, Johnson, Alston & Hunt v. Graulty, 886 F.2d 268, 272 (9th Cir. 1989) (suggesting a 25% figure as a benchmark).

[28] Hanlon v. Chrysler Corp., 150 F.3d 1011, 1029–30 (9th Cir. 1998) (affirming fees award totaling 4.5% of the fund ($5.2 million) when action settled, no class member received cash, but class counsel and defendant valued settlement at $115 million).

[29] In re Guyana Dev. Corp., 201 B.R. 462, 479 n.10 (Bankr. S.D. Tex. 1996) (stating that "current trend among the courts of appeal favors the use of the percentage method to calculate an award of attorneys' fees in common fund cases") (citations omitted); Goodrich v. E.F. Hutton Group, Inc., 681 A.2d 1039, 1047 (Del. 1996) (same).

[30] Life Assur. Society of the United States, 307 F.3d 997 (9th Cir. 2002) ("Reasonableness is the goal, and mechanical or formulaic applications of either method, where it yields an unreasonable result, can be an abuse of discretion . . . . Courts may compare the two methods of calculating attorney's fees in determining whether fees are reasonable.") Id. (citations omitted); In re Washington Pub. Power Supply Sys. Sec. Litig., 19 F.3d 1291, 1296 (9th Cir. 1994) (stating that "in common fund cases, no presumption in favor of either the percentage or lodestar method encumbers the district court's discretion to choose one or the other"); Rawlings v. Prudential-Bache Properties, Inc., 9 F.3d 513, 516 (6th Cir. 1993) (same).

that are not applicable to common fund cases. For these jurisdictions, the lodestar approach more equitably sets the allowable attorney's fees.[31]

Because attorney's fees are paid under the common fund rationale to avoid unjust enrichment, payment of the fees should be proportional to the actual recovery of monies or property that constituted the fund.[32] When property is received, attorney's fees should be based on the actual, going value of the property, not a hypothetical value, unless that hypothetical value has been approved by all interested parties, and even here, the court is not bound by the valuation.[33]

In order to recover under the common fund theory, the fund must be created by the attorney's efforts and otherwise demonstrate that absent payment the fund beneficiaries would be unjustly enriched.[34] Some

---

[31] Kuhnlein v. Department of Revenue, 662 So. 2d 309, 313–14 (Fla. 1995). *See generally* Caroline Krivacka, Annot., *Method of Calculating Attorneys' Fees Awarded in Common Fund or Common Benefit Cases—State Cases,* 56 A.L.R.5th 107 (1998).

[32] *See* Democratic Central Committee of the Dist. of Colum. v. Washington Metro. Area Rapid Transit Commn, 38 F.3d 603, 606 (D.C. Cir. 1994); *cf.* Wolff v. Ampacet Corp., 284 Ill. App. 3d 824, 673 N.E.2d 745, 748 (1996) (stating that "if no fund has been placed under the control of the court, then the court lacks authority to award fees") (citations omitted).

[33] *Hanlon, supra,* 150 F.3d at 1029–30; *In re* Synthroid Marketing Litig., 325 F.3d 974, 979 (7th Cir. 2003) (stating that district court erred in rejecting 22% of recovery as a benchmark for awarding fees resulting from class action $88 million settlement). The district court relied on the fact that bids for the right to be appointed class attorney in some security cases fall below 22%. *Id.* at 977, 979. The court of appeal found this unpersuasive. The appellate court found no evidence of any lack of competition for legal services that would suggest market rates are inaccurate measures of the value of legal services provided. *Id.* The court further noted that the "bid" procedure was an inappropriate reference here:

> There is, moreover, considerable question just what is being auctioned in bidding to represent a class. Normally an auction specifies the precise product to be sold (a particular painting, a share of stock in a named corporation, or 5,000 cubic yards of concrete having defined attributes). For legal services, however, it is hard if not impossible to hold the quality dimension constant. Contingent-fee arrangements are used when it is difficult to monitor counsel closely; otherwise some different arrangement, such as hourly rates, is superior.
>
> Lawyers will earn a competitive return even at the lower level of compensation, but the class may be worse off. Large and sophisticated purchasers of legal services, such as Exxon/Mobile and General Motors, do not acquire legal services at auction; even clients able to monitor lawyers closely may be worried about the effect of the auction process on quality. So it is not possible to say, without other evidence of a kind missing in this record, that the outcome of auctions for the right to represent other classes in other litigation shows that the 22% contingent fee agreed to in arm's-length transactions between well informed parties in this case is "too high."

Id. (the 22% "agreed to in arm's-length transactions" was the amount the health insurer class privately negotiated with counsel they retained to represent their interests in the litigation; the focus at this part of the case was on the fees awards for counsel for the consumer class, which had not negotiated a fee arrangement).

[34] Village of Clarendon Hills v. Mulder, 663 N.E.2d 435 (Ill. App. 1996):

> An attorney may collect attorney fees under the common fund doctrine only if: (1) the fund from which fees are sought was created as a result of legal services performed by the attorney; (2) the claimant of the fund did not participate in its creation; and (3) the claimant benefitted or will benefit from its creation.

jurisdictions construe the common fund rule narrowly simply because it is an exception to the "American Rule."[35]

[211.4] Third Party Tort

When a person commits a wrongful act that she can reasonable foresee will require the plaintiff to prosecute or defend a lawsuit, the expenses incurred in connection with that lawsuit, including reasonable attorney's fees, are recoverable damages. This exception to the "American Rule" is actually much narrower than the above definition might suggest.[36] The key word is not "foresee" but "require." The litigation must be compelled or caused by the wrongful act. The fact that litigation is necessary to vindicate rights infringed by the wrongful act is not sufficient. For example, the exception would not apply to the typical personal injury action. Even though litigation to redress personal injury grievances is commonplace, and even if the defendant is unrealistic and intransigent about resolving the grievance and therefore forces recourse to litigation, the legal wrong does not cause litigation, it causes personal injury.

The line between attorney's fees as recoverable damages due to the tort of another and attorney's fees as simply a non-recoverable expense under the "American Rule" is not bright and crisply defined. The distinction between litigation that is compelled or required, on the one hand, and litigation that is necessitated or needed to vindicate a legal right, on the other hand, is a distinction that is difficult to make consistently.

Attorney's fees may be recovered when the legal wrong causes litigation and the plaintiff is required to incur attorney's fees in that litigation. Attorney's fees incurred in proceedings before a taxing authority to obtain refunds of tax penalties assessed as a result of the defendant's negligence have been deemed to lie within this exception.[37] Attorney's fees incurred by a lienholder in a quiet title action against a purchaser necessitated by defendant's acts of conversion have been held to be within the exception.[38]

Id. at 440; *cf. Swedish Hosp. Corp*, 1 F.3d at 1272 (limiting recovery of attorney's fees out of fund in part because of perception that counsel "piggybacked" on the work of others). *But cf.* Kline v. Eyrich, 69 S.W.3d 197 (Tenn. 2002) (holding that passive beneficiaries (children) of wrongful death action brought by surviving spouse were required to pay portion of their award to attorney for surviving spouse under common fund doctrine; children had no privilege to hire separate counsel to protect their interests).

[35] *Village of Clarendon, supra*, 663 N.E.2d at 440 (noting limitation and refusal of Illinois courts to extend doctrine to situation when attorney assisted hospitor-creditor in securing payment of its lien for services provided the patient-debtor). The attorney represented the patient-debtor and secured a recovery from the tortfeasor; the recovery was used in part to satisfy the lien. Some jurisdictions allow a recovery under the common fund theory in this setting. Section 53.5 (Duties to Fund Creators).

[36] Missouri Property & Cas. Ins. Guar. Ass'n v. Pott Indus., 971 S.W.2d 302, 306 (Mo. 1998) (stating that the third party tort exception is limited to "cases involving 'very unusual circumstances' or where the natural and proximate result of a breach of duty is to involve the wronged party in collateral litigation") (citation omitted).

[37] Sorenson v. Fio Rito, 413 N.E.2d 47, 52 (Ill. App. 1980).

[38] Collins v. First Fin. Servs., Inc., 815 P.2d 411, 415 (Ariz. 1991).

Reasonable attorney's fees may be recoverable when a third party tortiously interferes with the plaintiff's contract rights with another and, as a direct consequence of that interference, the plaintiff is drawn into litigation with the other party to the contract to determine their rights, duties, and obligations under the contract.[39] The common theme in all of these examples is that the defendant's wrongdoing required the plaintiff to incur attorney's fees in an action involving a third party.

This third party tort exception to the "American Rule" distinguishes between attorney's fees incurred as a result of the defendant's wrongdoing and attorney's fees incurred to establish the wrongfulness of the defendant's doings. The tortious interference example may help illustrate the distinction. Reasonable attorney's fees incurred in determining the rights, duties, and obligations of the contracting parties might be recoverable; however, attorney's fees incurred to establish that the defendant tortiously interfered would not be recoverable. Assume a real estate Broker interfered with a real estate purchase agreement between Seller and Buyer, Buyer refused to perform, and Seller sued Buyer for specific performance. Did Broker's misconduct *require* Seller to incur litigation expenses? The "Third Party Tort" exception to the "American Rule" allows for the recovery of attorney's fees when the Third Party's (Broker's) negligence necessarily causes litigation. When, however, litigation is not caused by the negligence but by another's (Buyer's) actions or intransigence, attorney's fees are not recoverable under this exception. If the distinction appears evanescent, it is. The argument against recovery of attorney's fees goes like this. In the hypothetical, Broker's delict did not cause or require litigation. Buyer refused to perform and no facts indicate that this refusal was directly due to Broker's doings. Broker's negligence did not require or cause Seller to incur litigation expenses against Buyer. Many courts would find this hypothetical case to be outside the Third Party Tort exception to the "American Rule."[40] Possibly to the contrary is *Tetherow v. Wolfe*. In *Tetherow* the plaintiff vendor sued the defendant real estate broker for the broker's failure to properly prepare a real estate sale contract. The court approved as an item of damages the attorney fees the vendor had expended defending a suit brought by the purchaser of the real estate to recover the down payment.[41] In both *Tetherow* and the hypothetical case, the Broker's

---

[39] DP Solutions, Inc. v. Rollins, Inc., 353 F.3d 421, 430–31 (5th Cir. 2003) (applying Texas law involving covenant not to compete); Lee v. Aiu, 936 P.2d 655, 669–70 (Haw. 1997).

[40] *Cf.* Hitachi Credit America Corp. v. Signet Bank, 166 F.3d 614, 631 (4th Cir. 1999) (applying Virginia law) (stating that to recover attorney's fees when a defendant's breach of contract has forced the plaintiff to maintain or defend a suit with a third person, "[t]he employment of counsel must be a direct and necessary consequence of the breach . . . . If the damages that result from defendant's breach are consequential rather than direct, they are not compensable").

[41] 392 N.W.2d 374, 379 (Neb. 1986). The court cited the Restatement (Second) of Torts § 914(2) (1979), which states, "One who through the tort of another has been required to act in the protection of his interests by bringing or defending an action against a third person is entitled to recover reasonable compensation for loss of time, attorney fees and other expenditures thereby suffered or incurred in the earlier action."

negligence has prevented Seller from completing and consummating the sale with Buyer. Seller's unsuccessful effort at specific performance does not appear to be materially different from Buyer's successful action to recover the down payment. Both actions are resolved favorably to Buyer due to Broker's negligence. *Tetherow* seems to suggest that if a party's negligence or breach confuses another persons legal rights or status vis à vis another person, litigation required to clarify that confusion over rights and status falls within the "Third Party Tort" exception. Under the *Tetherow* rationale, Seller would be entitled to recover his attorney's fees incurred in the specific performance action if Broker's interference confused Seller's rights vis à vis Buyer.

Some courts have suggested that when the defendant's wrongdoing requires the plaintiff to seek the remedy of rescission or cancellation, attorney's fees incurred in that action are recoverable. These cases appear, at least for the present, to be aberrations rather than mainstream. Moreover, in these cases there are additional themes that may better support the award of attorney's fees than the third party tort exception.[42]

It is not necessary that the compelled litigation be successful; it is only necessary that it be compelled. Thus, in the quiet title action discussed above,[43] a senior lienholder brought a quiet title action after the junior lienholder wrongfully sold the collateral to a third party. The sale (conversion) necessitated the quiet title action. The action was unsuccessful because the court found the third party to be a bona fide purchaser for value; nonetheless, the senior lienholder was permitted to recover its reasonable attorney's fees incurred in the quiet title action because the quiet title action was caused by the junior lienholder's wrongdoing.

[211.5] Bad Faith

The "bad faith" exception to the "American Rule" has been largely limited to claims against insurance companies for the failure to provide benefits promised by the insurance contract. As stated in one case:

> When an insurer's tortious conduct reasonably compels the insured to retain an attorney to obtain the benefits due under a policy, it follows that the insurer should be liable in a tort action for that expense. The attorney's fees are an economic loss—damages— proximately caused by the tort. These fees must be distinguished from recovery of attorney's fees qua attorney's fees, such as those attributable to the bringing of the bad faith action itself. What we consider here is attorney's fees that are recoverable as damages

---

[42] Shapiro v. Sutherland, 76 Cal. Rptr. 2d 101, 111–12 (Cal. App. 1998) (suggesting recovery of attorney's fees would be allowed when rescission was caused by defendant's fraud or misrepresentation); Murphy v. Murphy, 694 A.2d 932, 935 (Me. 1997) (recognizing right to recover attorney's fees in action against defendant for breach of fiduciary duty); Section 211.5 ([Attorney's Fees] Bad Faith).

[43] *Collins, supra,* 815 P.2d at 415 (discussed at text and note 38, *supra*).

resulting from a tort in the same way that medical fees would be part of the damages in a personal injury action.

When a pedestrian is struck by a car, he goes to a physician for treatment of his injuries, and the motorist, if liable in tort, must pay the pedestrian's medical fees. Similarly, in the present case, an insurance company's refusal to pay benefits has required the insured to seek the services of an attorney to obtain those benefits, and the insurer, because its conduct was tortious, should pay the insured's legal fees.[44]

Even in this limited context the "bad faith" exception has received mixed acceptance.[45] It is difficult to identify a principled limitation of the bad faith exception that confines it to cases of insurer breach. On its face, the exception would largely swallow the "American Rule."[46] The restriction of the exception to cases of insurer breach appears to be more practical than principled, absent a more thorough rethinking of the validity and efficiency of the "American Rule."

The "bad faith" exception should be distinguished from cases awarding the insured the costs incurred, including reasonable attorney's fees, when the insurer breaches its contractual obligation to provide a defense. In this setting, the award of reasonable attorney's fees is standard because the award reflects the expectancy interest of the insured in the contract.[47]

[211.6]   Inherent Power

Courts have inherent power to create proper sanctions to redress litigation misconduct.[48] This authority is, however, also a limitation, at least

---

[44] Brandt v. Superior Court, 693 P.2d 796, 798–99 (Cal. 1985) (citations and internal quotation marks omitted); Section 141 (Bad Faith Breach).

[45] *Compare* DeChant v. Monarch Life Ins. Co., 547 N.W.2d 592, 595–96 (Wis. 1996) (collecting cases and holding that insured may, in the absence of a statute, recover attorney's fees incurred to obtain the benefits of an insurance contract tortiously denied (*i.e.,* denied in "bad faith") by the insurer), *with* Bernhard v. Farmers Ins. Exch., 915 P.2d 1285, 1290 (Colo. 1996) (rejecting approach that would permit the insured to recover reasonable attorney's fees whenever the insurer tortiously withheld any benefit).

[46] *See Bernhard, supra:*

> Bernhard's claim for attorney fees incurred in bringing a bad faith breach of insurance contract action does not fit into any exception to the American Rule recognized in Colorado. Furthermore, we decline to carve out an additional exception since we find no principled way to create such an exception while still upholding the general principles of the American rule. We therefore conclude that an insured must bear the cost of attorney fees incurred in bringing a bad faith breach of insurance contract action. We affirm the court of appeals and remand the case for further proceedings consistent with this opinion.

915 P.2d at 1291.

[47] *Id.* at 1290–91 (limiting recovery of attorney's fees to situations where the insured was denied a defense by the insurance company and thus was deprived of a specific contract benefit); Olympic S.S. Steamship Co. Inc. v. Centennial Ins. Co., 811 P.2d 673, 681 (Wash. 1991) (same).

[48] Chambers v. NASCO, Inc., 501 U.S. 32 (1991) (sanctioning "bad faith" litigation misconduct).

for federal courts—the award must be tied to the litigation misconduct, not the underlying conduct that constitutes the claim.[49] Some states have adopted a broader standard that effectively melds the "bad faith" and "inherent power" standards.[50]

§ 212 PREVAILING PARTY

Attorney's fees are awarded to "prevailing" parties. Prevailing parties are those who are successful, although "success" is sometimes loosely and expansively defined. Prevailing parties may be either plaintiffs or defendants; care must, however, be taken. The use of the term "prevailing party" for attorney's fees purposes may differ from the general context.[1] Moreover, in many contexts, the prevailing defendant will be denied attorney's fees because of the belief that an award would discourage responsible plaintiffs from seeking access to courts.[2] Of course, the cost of this approach is the inevitable presence of some irresponsible plaintiffs.

The tendency is to read the term "prevailing party" broadly in the context of awarding attorney's fees, although the broadness varies depending on whether the fee award is based on statute or contract or other. The broadest constructions of the term occur in the statutory authorization cases because of the underlying policy that lawsuits are to be encouraged, not discouraged. Thus, the Supreme Court has stated that in civil rights litigation a plaintiff "prevails" by succeeding on "any significant issue in litigation which

---

[49] Towerridge, Inc. v. T.A.O., Inc., 111 F.3d 758, 766–67 & n.5 (10th Cir. 1997) (citing other circuits as having reached the same conclusion).

[50] In re Trust, 823 A.2d 1 (N.J. 2003) (holding that bad faith by trustee in inducing settlor suffering from dementia to modify will and trusts to detriment of beneficiaries warranted award of attorney's fees); cf. Morganroth & Morganroth v. DeLorean, 213 F.3d 1301, 1317–18 (10th Cir. 2000) (noting that under diversity jurisdiction, question may be controlled by state law, which may permit recovery of attorney's fees for non-litigation related bad faith).

[1] Compare Cal. Civ. P. Code, § 1032(a) (4) (defining "prevailing" party as including "the party with a net monetary recovery, a defendant in whose favor a dismissal is entered, a defendant where neither plaintiff nor defendant obtains any relief, and a defendant as against those plaintiffs who do not recover any relief against that defendant"), with Cal. Civ. Code § 1717(b)(2) (stating that for purposes of determining who is the prevailing party, in cases involving contractual provisions authorizing the recovery of attorney's fees, "where an action has been voluntarily dismissed or dismissed pursuant to a settlement of the case, there shall be no prevailing party for purposes of this section"). See generally Thomas Goger, Annot., Dismissal of Plaintiff's Action as Entitling Defendant to Recover Attorneys' Fees or Costs as "Prevailing Party"or "Successful Party," 66 A.L.R.3d 1087 § 2 (1975) (noting split in the decisions as to understanding of the term "prevailing party").

[2] Christiansburg Garment Co. v. EEOC, 434 U.S. 412, 422 (1978) (stating that a "plaintiff [in a Title VII action] should not be assessed his opponent's attorney's fees unless a court finds that his claim was frivolous, unreasonable or groundless, or that the plaintiff continued to litigate after it clearly became so"); Velasquez v. City of Abilene, 725 F.2d 1017, 1023 (5th Cir. 1984) (stating that awarding attorney's fees to prevailing defendants as a matter of course would have a "chilling effect on suits to redress constitutional violations that would be disastrous").

achieves some of the benefit the parties sought in bringing suit."[3] A plaintiff must, however, achieve some success as a result of the lawsuit.

For example, in *Gingras v. Lloyd* the plaintiffs sought to prevent the State of Connecticut from closing a hospital that administered to the special rehabilitative needs of persons afflicted with tuberculosis and other chronic disabilities. Through plaintiffs' efforts, a committee of special masters was appointed by the court to review the proposed shutdown. The committee agreed with the State, the hospital was closed, and all relief requested by the plaintiffs except for attorney's fees, was denied by the trial court. On the request for fees, the trial court stated that while the master's report confirmed the soundness of the State's plan and position, the report helped the court reach a decision and helped the state bureaucracy move more efficiently and awarded fees for that reason.[4] The Court of Appeal held that these reasons were insufficient to permit a fees award. As to the assistance to the court rationale, the court held that the appointment of masters "is neither success on an issue in the litigation nor the type of productive prodding that might bring the plaintiffs within the ambit of [42 U.S.C.] § 1988."[5] As to the making the "bureaucracy more efficient" rationale, the court found that no facts demonstrated that the "suit itself resulted in any cognizable benefit."[6] In this posture, the court held that no basis for a fees award existed.

If the litigation serves as a "catalyst" toward achieving the object of the litigation, may the plaintiff be deemed a prevailing party for purposes of a fee award? In *Buckhannon Board & Care Home, Inc. v. West Virginia Dept. Health & Human Resources* the plaintiff received all the relief it requested; however, it received that relief from the legislature rather than the courts.[7] Under the traditional test plaintiff was not a "prevailing party" and would not be entitled to claim attorney's fees.[8] Prior to *Buckhannon*

---

[3] Texas State Teacher's Ass'n v. Garland Indep. Sch. Dist., 489 U.S. 782, 791–92 (1989) (construing 42 U.S.C. § 1988). This approach has been applied to other statutory attorney's fees provisions. Union of Concerned Scientists v. U.S. Nuclear Regulatory Comm'n, 840 F.2d 957, 959 (D.C. Cir. 1988) (involving 28 U.S.C. § 2412(D), Equal Access to Justice Act. *See generally* Francis Dougherty, Annot., *Who is "Prevailing Party" so as to be Entitled to Award of Attorneys' Fees by Court Under Equal Access to Justice Act (28 U.S.C.A. § 2412(D))*, 105 A.L.R. Fed. 110 (1991).

[4] 740 F.2d 210, 211 (2d Cir. 1984) (relying on the trial judge's statement).

[5] *Id.* at 213. *Compare* San Francisco NAACP v. San Francisco Unified School District, 284 F.3d 1163, 1166 (9th Cir. 2002) (holding that court has discretion to award attorney's fees to prevailing party for work undertaken to monitor and enforce compliance with consent decree whether in same, or separate, collateral action and regardless of whether the party is successful in the post-decree work), *with* Alliance to End Repression v. City of Chicago, 356 F.3d 767, 770–71 (7th Cir. 2004) (holding that attorney's fees should not be awarded to party whose post-decree work related to the consent decree was unsuccessful and resulted in no further action being undertaken by the court).

[6] *Gingras, supra*, 740 F.2d at 213.

[7] 532 U.S. 598 (2001).

[8] Hanrehan v. Hampton, 446 U.S. 754 (1980) (holding that a prevailing party is one who has been awarded some relief by the court and this requires that the "party has prevailed on the merits of at least some of his claims").

Board many of the circuits had adopted the "catalyst" test, which permitted recovery of fees when the litigation served as a "catalyst" toward achieving the object the litigation. In *Buckhannon Board* the Court rejected the "catalyst" test when the statute used the term "prevailing party." The Court repudiated the "catalyst" test because it found that the test "allows an award where there is no judicially sanctioned change in the legal relationship of the parties." According to the Court:

> A defendant's voluntary change in conduct, although perhaps accomplishing what the plaintiff sought to achieve by the lawsuit, lacks the necessary judicial imprimatur on the change. Our precedents thus counsel against holding that the term "prevailing party" authorizes an award of attorney's fees without a corresponding alteration in the legal relationship of the parties. [9]

The Court rejected the argument that the legislative history of Civil Rights Attorney's Fees Award Act [10] supported a reading of "prevailing party" that included the catalyst theory. The Court stated that it "doubt[ed] that the legislative history could overcome what we think is the rather clear meaning of the term 'prevailing party.'" [11] The Court also rejected arguments that the catalyst theory is necessary to prevent defendants from unilaterally mooting an action before judgment in an effort to avoid an award of attorney's fees and that rejection of the theory will deter plaintiffs with meritorious but expensive cases from bringing suit. [12]

Although *Buckhannon Board* rested on specific fee shifting statutes, its holding has been applied to other fee shifting statutes that use the operative term "prevailing party." [13] On the other hand, the limits of *Buckhannon Board* should be understood. First, the decision applies to federal fee-shifting statutes that use the operative term "prevailing party." Many federal fee-shifting statutes use the phrase, but many do not. These other

---

[9] 532 U.S. at 605.

[10] 42 U.S.C. § 1988. The plaintiffs requested attorney's fees under the Fair Housing Amendment Act of 1988, 42 U.S.C. § 3601 *et seq.*, and the Americans With Disabilities Act of 1990, 42 U.S.C. § 12101 *et. seq.* All three statutes use the term "prevailing parties," but the legislative record was more developed on this point in the Civil Rights Attorney's Fees Awards Act.

[11] 522 U.S. at 607 (brackets added).

[12] *Id.* at 608 ("We are skeptical of these assertions, which are entirely speculative and unsupported by any empirical evidence.")

[13] *E.g.*, Bennett v. Yoshina, 259 F.3d 1097 (9th Cir. 2001) (applying *Buckhannon Board* to 42 U.S.C. § 1988, Civil Rights Attorney's Fees Awards Act); Perez-Arellano v. Smith, 279 F.3d 791, 794–95 (9th Cir. 2002) (applying *Buckhannon Board* to Equal Access to Justice Act, 28 U.S.C. § 2412(d)(1), which allows an award of fees to litigants who prevail in action against the federal government); *see* Union of Needletrades, Industrial and Textile Employees v. United States Immigrant and Naturalization Service, 336 F.3d 200, 205–06 (2d Cir. 2003) (applying *Buckhannon Board* to FOIA (Freedom of Information Act) claim, 5 U.S.C. § 552(a)(4)(E); J.C. v. Regional School Dist. 10 Bd. of Education, 278 F.3d 119 (2d Cir. 2002) (stating that while *Buckhannon Board* dealt with the Fair Housing Amendment Act and Americans with Disabilities Act, it has much wider application because Congress used the operative term "prevailing parties" in many fees-shifting statutes).

statutes authorize courts to award attorney's fees "in the interests of justice" or "whenever appropriate." Awards under these statutes are not necessarily constrained by *Buckhannon Board*.[14] *Buckhannon Board* has had the greatest impact in civil rights litigation because the applicable statutes tend to use the phrase "prevailing parties." *Buckhannon Board* has not had as significant an impact in other areas, such as environmental law, because the applicable statutes in that field tend to use broader language regarding the awarding of fees.[15]

Second, *Buckhannon Board* is not a rule of constitutional dimension; states may construe their own attorney's fees awards statute to include the "catalyst" theory.[16]

Third, *Buckhannon Board* primarily applies when the plaintiff seeks injunctive or declaratory relief and the case effectively is mooted by the defendant's actions (or a third party's), which negates the need for injunctive or declaratory relief. A plaintiff may avoid or reduce *Buckhannon Board's* impact if she can assert a claim for monetary relief. Alternatively, or in addition to monetary relief, the plaintiff may ask the court to retain jurisdiction to monitor defendant's compliance with its promised changes in conduct that effectively mooted the claim by giving the plaintiff what she requested.

Fourth, a payment of money through settlement may be sufficient to confer "prevailing party status on the plaintiff." The majority in *Buckhannon Board* noted that settlements enforced through consent decrees would confer prevailing party status because they represent a "court-ordered chang[e] [in] the legal relationship between [the plaintiff] and the defendant.[17] The Court, however, disavowed its previous endorsement of the extension of the rule to "private" settlement in *Farrar v. Hobby* (noting the absence of judicial approval and oversight and that the *dicta* in Farrar extending the rule may have ignored limiting language in *Maher v. Gagne*.[18] Notwithstanding this sentiment many lower courts continue to treat private settlements with the retention of jurisdiction to enforce the settlement as sufficient to confer "prevailing party" status on the plaintiff.[19] There is Ninth Circuit precedent that can be read as even dispensing with the "retention of jurisdiction" requirement.[20] Some courts have suggested

---

[14] Sierra Club v. EPA, 322 F.3d 718 (D.C. Cir. 2003) (awarding fees, after private settlement, under Clean Water Act, which authorizes the award of attorney's fees "whenever appropriate"), *cert. denied*, 540 U.S. 1104 (2004).

[15] *Id.* at 725 (collecting decisions).

[16] Graham v. Daimler Chrysler Corp., 101 P.3d 140, 148 (Cal. 2004).

[17] 532 U.S. at 604.

[18] *Id.* at 604 n.7, *citing* Farrar v. Hobby, 506 U.S. 103 (1992), Maher v. Gagne, 448 U.S. 122 (1980).

[19] Truesdell v. Philadelphia Housing Authority, 290 F.3d 159 (3d Cir. 2002).

[20] Richard S. v. Dept. of Developmental Services, 317 F.3d 1080 (9th Cir. 2003); Barrios v. Calif. Interscholastic Fed'n, 277 F.3d 1128, 1134 n.5 (9th Cir.) (stating that *Buckhannon Board* only rejected catalyst theory and did not preclude an award of attorney's fees to a plaintiff who prevailed in a private settlement), *cert. denied*, 537 U.S. 820 (2002).

that the settlement must be confirmed in a consent decree, a mere "retention of jurisdiction" to enforce the settlement may be insufficient, but the "suggestion" seems to have been rejected elsewhere in the same decision in which it is made.[21]

Fifth, a court may balkanize the proceedings, deem the plaintiff the prevailing party as to a portion of the proceeding, and award fees as to that portion.[22] This approach has been used to allow for recovery of attorney's fees by a plaintiff who obtained temporary injunctive relief even though the plaintiff subsequently lost on the merits on his substantive claims.[23] Several courts have, however, rejected the position that success at an interim phase of the litigation is sufficient to confer prevailing party status.[24]

If the catalyst test is adopted, the plaintiff must show that (1) the lawsuit was a material, significant factor in causing the defendant to change its conduct in the direction desired by the litigation; and, (2) the claims asserted by the plaintiff were at least colorable.[25] For example, assume the plaintiff challenges a defendant county's method of calculating general relief as being inconsistent with current law. After the lawsuit is filed, the county changes it practices so that they now conform to law as contended

---

[21] T.D. v. La Grange School District No. 102, 349 F.3d 469 (7th Cir. 2003) (implying that mere retention of jurisdiction to enforce private settlement would not satisfy *Buckhannon Board*). According to the court the settlement agreement may confer prevailing party status when it is "sufficiently analogous" to a consent decree, as when it contained mandatory language, bore the signature of the district court judge, was entitled an "order," and provided for "judicial enforcement." *Id.* at 478–79; Smyth v. Rivero, 282 F.3d 268, 281 (4th Cir. 2002) (stating that settlement agreement that was embodied in a court order and contained the obligation to comply, backed-up by the court's authority would satisfy *Buckhannon Board*). While neither decision expressly refuted the claim that retention of jurisdiction to enforce the award was insufficient; both decisions contained language indicating a retention might be sufficient. *T.D., supra*, 349 F.3d at 476; *Smyth, supra*, 282 F.3d at 280–81; *see* Robertson v. Giulani, 346 F.3d 75 (2d Cir. 2003) (reversing lower court decision that held that unlike consent decree, a court does not exercise "judicial approval and oversight" when it retains jurisdiction to enforce a settlement after dismissing a suit pursuant to the settlement). The Court of Appeal held that settlement with retention of jurisdiction was sufficient to confer "prevailing party" status under *Buckhannon Board. Id.* at 80–81.

[22] *T.D., supra*, 349 F.3d at 479 (permitting plaintiff who prevailed at administrative hearing to recover attorney's fees for that phase even though plaintiff could not recover fees for the trial phase because the post-hearing settlement was insufficient to confer prevailing party status on plaintiff).

[23] Watson v. County of Riverside, 300 F.3d 1092 (9th Cir. 2002), *cert. denied*, 538 U.S. 923 (2003). The injunction barred use of a report at plaintiff's termination hearing that plaintiff was compelled to write. Notwithstanding his success in obtaining the injunction, he was terminated.

[24] John T. *ex rel.* Paul T. v. Delaware County Intermediate Unit, 318 F.3d 545 (3d Cir. 2003) (holding that disabled student plaintiff who secured a preliminary injunction *and* a contempt order against the defendant was not a prevailing party; the preliminary injunction merely maintained the status quo and the contempt order provided relief for violation of the order, not relief under the Individual With Disabilities Education Act); *Smyth v. Rivero*, 282 F.3d 268 (4th Cir. 2002) (same).

[25] Nadeau v. Helgemoe, 581 F.2d 275, 280–81 (1st Cir. 1978).

by the plaintiff. As a result of the changes, plaintiff's lawsuit is mooted. If the court found that plaintiff's lawsuit was a significant factor in the county's decision, the court could award the plaintiff its attorney's fees as the "prevailing party" under the catalyst theory.[26]

The court is not obligated to find a "cause and effect" relationship between the lawsuit and the policy change. For example, in *Stanley v. California State Lottery Comm'n* the court held that the catalyst theory was not available when the lawsuit prods the defendant to change its practices, but the plaintiff loses on the merits of the claim.[27] Stanley complained that the Lottery Commission sold instant scratch game tickets promising prizes that had already been redeemed by previous winners. The claims were rejected on the merits, but the Lottery Commission ceased the practice nonetheless. Stanley sought and was awarded attorney's fees by the trial court. The Court of Appeal reversed holding that the "term 'successful party' cannot be stretched that far."

To be identified as a "prevailing party" does not require that the plaintiff secure a large recovery. Nominal damages awards are sufficient.[28] Courts may, however, scrutinize nominal damages recoveries to ensure that the award of fees does not go to a party who effectively "lost" the case. In *Farrar*, the Court's majority questioned whether a plaintiff who sought $17 million in damages, but who received $1 in nominal damages, achieved anything other than a moral victory that might negate the claim for attorney's fees in its entirety.[29] The Court did not resolve the issue, but lower courts, post-*Farrar*, have done so. For example, in *Romberg v. Nichols* the plaintiffs claimed that law enforcement officials had violated their constitutional rights by conducting a warrantless search of their home.[30] Plaintiffs sought $2 million in damages; they were awarded $1 nominal damages. During closing argument, their counsel had specifically asked for $1 in damages. The court found that this last minute pitch to the jury to provide a base for an award of attorney's fees, for what was in effect a losing effort, would not support an award of fees.[31]

It would be a mistake, however, to read *Romberg* and *Farrar* too broadly on this point. It is the change in strategy from damages to attorney's fees

---

[26] Hartman v. Winnebago County, 561 N.W.2d 768, 774–75 (Wis. App. 1997) (affirming trial court's award of attorney's fees on similar facts as in the hypothetical), *rev'd on other grounds*, 574 N.W.2d 222 (Wis. 1998).

[27] 4 Cal. Rptr. 3d 861 (Cal. App. 2003) (unpublished).

[28] *Farrar supra*, 506 U.S. at 112 (holding that "a plaintiff who wins nominal damages is a prevailing party under [42 U.S.C.] § 1988"). When attorney's fees are available, either by statute or by contract, an award of nominal damages is usually sufficient to qualify the plaintiff as a "prevailing party." Ventura v. Ford Motor Co., 433 A.2d 801, 812 (N.J. Super. Ct. A.D. 1981) (involving Magnuson-Moss Warranty Act, 15 U.S.C. §§ 2301–2312); Section 2.8 (Nominal Damages).

[29] 506 U.S. at 114–15.

[30] 48 F.3d 453 (9th Cir. 1994), *cert. denied*, 516 U.S. 943 (1995).

[31] *Id.* at 455 (citation omitted); *see* Pino v. Locascio, 101 F.3d 235, 238 (2d Cir. 1996) (rejecting fees award when plaintiff sought $21 million and received $1).

that appears to drive the courts' antipathy to a fees award. When the plaintiff receives a vindication of his constitutional rights, the decision will have significant effects on others, but the plaintiff's actual damages are meager, a fees award may be substantial, notwithstanding that only nominal damages were awarded.[32] In other cases, nominal damages may support a low fee rather than no fee at all.[33] In some cases, nominal damages may support a large fee, as when the case creates a new rule of official conduct on public or private duty that benefits the general public as a whole.[34]

A few cases have permitted the plaintiff to be designated a "prevailing party" even though no affirmative relief was obtained. For example, in *Gudenkauf v. Stauffer Communications, Inc.* the plaintiff sued for wrongful termination claiming violation of several federal statutes. The jury found that the termination was motivated in part by plaintiff's pregnancy, but that she would have been terminated from her employment in any event.

---

[32] *E.g.*, Lucas v. Guyton, 901 F. Supp. 1047 (D.S.C. 1995) (involving a death row inmate who was beaten by correctional officers during the course of a prison altercation):

> It is this court's opinion that the jury's award of nominal damages in the amount of ten cents, which may appear on its face to be *de minimis* victory, was in realty a significant accomplishment under the very unique circumstances of this case. It is hard to imagine a more repugnant or unsympathetic client to put before a jury. See Wilcox v. City of Reno, 42 F.3d 550, 557 (9th Cir. 1994) (awarding attorney's fees under § 1988 and recognizing the unsympathetic nature of the plaintiff, who was a convicted felon, drunk at the time of the alleged excessive police force incident and who had just broken a beer bottle on a woman's face). Although the jury was not told the specific circumstances of the double murder that Cecil Lucas committed in 1983, the jury was aware that Plaintiff was on death row and could reasonably conclude that those on death row are usually there for a good reason. The evidence before the jury also demonstrated that Plaintiff had a history of self inflicted injury and had the unfortunate habit of fighting with correctional officers. The day of the incident, Plaintiff admitted to being drunk, swinging the first punch, possibly having spit at Officer Harvey, and violently resisting the officers' efforts to take him to the isolation cell. All of plaintiff's corroborating witnesses, whose testimony was read by deposition, were death row inmates—not the type of people that are usually seen to be overly credible. The mere fact that the jury was able to look past these highly prejudicial and negative factors and render a verdict for Plaintiff, was far from a de minimis or pyrrhic victory. Instead, Plaintiff's verdict was a vindication of an important constitutional right and merits compensation for his attorney. The overall success that Plaintiff obtained "goes well beyond" the ten cent verdict.

Id. at 1052. The *Wilcox* decision cited in *Lucas* involved a nominal damages award of $1 against law enforcement officials who punched the plaintiff twice in the face during the course of making an arrest. *Wilcox*, *supra*, 42 F.3d at 551–52.

[33] Dillenbeck v. Hayes, 830 F. Supp. 673, 675 (N.D.N.Y. 1993) (awarding a low fee rather than no fee to a plaintiff who received a nominal damages award but who established by his lawsuit that it is unconstitutional for the police to use K-9 police dogs to assist in controlling an inmate who refuses to get off the telephone).

[34] Muhammad v. Lockhart, 104 F.3d 1069, 1070 (8th Cir. 1997) (noting that plaintiff succeeded in establishing either that defendant violated due process in conducting prison discipline hearings or inflicted cruel and unusual punishment by outfitting inmates with ill-fitting shoes); Cabrera v. Jakabovitz, 24 F.3d 372, 393 (2d Cir.) (noting that plaintiff's litigation achieved new rule of liability for landlords regarding racial steering by real estate brokers employed by landlords), *cert. denied*, 513 U.S. 876 (1994).

Because of this latter finding, plaintiff was denied reinstatement, back pay, or damages.[35] Nonetheless, because plaintiff's termination had been motivated in part by her pregnancy, itself a violation of the Pregnancy Discrimination Act,[36] she was awarded attorney's fees.[37] The court found that *Farrar v. Hobby* was not applicable:

> It is therefore clear that Congress' stated purpose in enacting the statutes governing mixed motive cases supports an award of attorney's fees in those cases notwithstanding the lack of a damages award. A verdict for a plaintiff in a mixed motive Title VII case constitutes a victory on a significant legal issue that furthers a public goal, a goal that is advanced notwithstanding the fact that a plaintiff recovers no damages. As Justice O'Connor acknowledged in her concurrence in *Farrar*, "[w]hen construing a statute, this Court is bound by the choices Congress has made, not the choices we might wish it had made." Accordingly, we conclude that recovery of damages is not a proper factor (time and labor expended) upon which to assess the propriety of granting a fee award in a mixed motive case. Moreover, we agree with the district court that, as under section 2000e-5(k), a plaintiff who prevails under section 2000e-2(m) should ordinarily "be awarded attorney's fees in all but special circumstances."[38]

The *Grudenkauf* court did reduce the lodestar attorney's fees award by 50% to reflect the plaintiff's limited(!) success.[39] There are contrary decisions regarding whether Title VII actions, involving employment discrimination, are an exception to *Farrar*.[40] In any event, decisions such as *Grudenkauf* should be recognized as being extremely limited and tied quite securely to the particular facts and statutes involved.

§ 213 AWARD OF FEES

[213.1] Calculation of Fees Award

There is "no pat formula for computation of fee-shifting awards;"[1] rather, courts balance a number of factors to achieve a reasonable fee under the circumstances.[2] The dominant approach is the "lodestar" method, which was described in *Van Gerwin v. Guarantee Mut. Life Co.*:

---

[35] 158 F.3d 1074, 1076 (10th Cir. 1998).

[36] 42 U.S.C. § 2000e-5(k).

[37] 158 F.3d at 1082.

[38] *Id.* at 1081, *citing Farrar*, 506 U.S. 103.

[39] *Id.* at 1077.

[40] Sheppard v. Riverview Nursing Ctr., Inc., 88 F.3d 1332, 1335–38 (4th Cir.), *cert. denied*, 519 U.S. 993 (1996); Bristow v. Drake St., Inc., 41 F.3d 345, 352–53 (7th Cir. 1995).

[1] Krewson v. City of Quincy, 74 F.3d 15, 17 (1st Cir. 1996).

[2] Gates v. Rowland, 39 F.3d 1439, 1449 (9th Cir. 1994); Schofield v. Trustees of the Univ. of Penn., 919 F. Supp. 821, 826 (E.D. Pa. 1996).

The lodestar/multiplier approach has two parts. First, a court determines the "lodestar" amount by multiplying the number of hours reasonably expended on the litigation by a reasonable hourly rate. The party seeking an award of fees must submit evidence supporting the hours worked and the rates claimed. A district court should exclude from the lodestar amount hours that are not reasonably expended because they are "excessive, redundant, or otherwise unnecessary."[3]

In both calculating and challenging the lodestar, the parties will use a number of factors developed by courts and largely duplicative of factors used to assess the reasonableness of fees under Professional Rules of Conduct that govern the practice of law.[4] These factors were set forth in *Johnson v. Georgia Highway Express* and include:

(1) the time and labor required to litigate the suit; (2) the novelty and difficulty of the questions presented by the lawsuit; (3) the skill required properly to perform the legal service; (4) the preclusion of other employment opportunities for the attorney due to the attorney's acceptance of the case; (5) the customary fee for such services; (6) whether the fee is fixed or contingent; (7) time limitations imposed by the client or the circumstances; (8) the amount in controversy involved and the results obtained; (9) the experience, reputation, and ability of the attorney; (10) the "undesirability" of the case; (11) the nature and length of the attorney's professional relationship with the client; and (12) awards in similar cases.[5]

The *Johnson* factors were approved by the Supreme Court in *Hensley v. Eckerhart.*[6] The basic requirement remains, however, that the fees awarded must be reasonable and not excessive.[7]

The first *Johnson* factor multiplied by a reasonable rate, usually the market rate, is the lodestar itself. Much ink and paper has been used

---

[3] 214 F.2d 1041, 1045 (9th Cir. 2000) (citations and footnote omitted).

[4] *E.g.*, ABA Model Rules of Professional Conduct 1.5 (2002).

[5] 488 F.2d 714, 717–19 (5th Cir. 1974). A similar approach is evidenced in common fund cases. *In re* Cendant Corp. PRIDES Litig., 243 F.3d 722 (3d Cir.), *cert. denied sub nom.* Kirby McInerney & Squire, LLP v. Joanne A. Aboff Family Trust, 534 U.S. 889 (2001). These include (1) the presence or absence of substantial objections by members of the class to the settlement terms and/or fees requested by counsel; (2) the skill and efficiency of the attorneys involved; (3) the amount of time devoted to the case by counsel for the prevailing party; (4) the complexity and duration of the litigation; (5) the range of awards in similar cases; (6) the comparison of the percentage method with the lodestar method; and (7) disclosure by the district court of its reasoning and application of "fee awards jurisprudence." *Id.* at 735. The reference to "fee award jurisprudence" is deliberate. This is an intensely litigated area of the law. *See* Alan Hirsch & Diane Sheehey, *Awarding Attorney's Fees and Managing Fee Litigation* (Monograph) (2d ed. 2005). The monograph is available at the Federal Judicial Center and, as of August 6, 2005, can be downloaded for free.

[6] 461 U.S. 424, 429–30 (1983).

[7] *Cf.* Smart SMW of New York v. Zoning Comm'n, Town of Stratford, 9 F. Supp. 2d 143, 151 (D. Conn. 1998) (stating that "lawyers should not expect their clients to foot the bill so they can acquire the knowledge necessary to litigate these cases").

discussing whether the remaining factors are used to justify the lodestar (by defining the reasonableness of the time expended and the hourly rate claimed), or may be used to enhance the lodestar. While the Supreme Court has frowned on enhancement,[8] that grimace has not been consistently adopted by lower courts.[9] By the same token, the courts have often frowned on downward departures from the lodestar. The Ninth Circuit has held that adjustments of the lodestar are the exception, not the rule.[10] The reluctance to adjust the lodestar to reflect quality of work is based upon the view that the factor is "generally considered at the lodestar stage in determining what is a reasonable hourly rate."[11]

The prevailing party must "maintain billing time records in a manner that will enable a reviewing court to identify distinct claims."[12] The time records must be contemporaneous and specify the date, time expended, and the nature of the work done. The degree of specificity required varies from

[8] City of Burlington v. Dague, 505 U.S. 557, 562, 567 (1992) (rejecting enhancement for contingency that litigation would be unsuccessful on ground that enhancement "would likely duplicate in substantial part factors already subsumed in the lodestar").

[9] E.g., Gomez v. Gates, 804 F. Supp. 69, 75–76 (C.D. Cal. 1992) (awarding attorney's fees based on 1.75 multiplier of lodestar due to the "undesirability" of the case—a factor not considered in City of Burlington v. Dague, supra); cf. Florin v. Nationsbank of Ga., 34 F.3d 560, 564–65 (7th Cir. 1994) (limiting City of Burlington to statutory fee awards cases and not applying rationale to "common fund" cases).

[10] Fischel v. Equitable Life Assur. Society of the United States, 307 F.3d 997, 1007 (9th Cir. 2002); see Ferland v. Conrad Credit Corp., 244 F.3d 1145, 1149 (9th Cir. 2001) (per curiam) (holding that district court must provide reasoned justification for the fees award, particularly when a reduction in the lodestar is imposed). The Ferland court chastised the district court for internal inconsistencies in its treatment of the fees request. Id. The Ferland court also criticized what it characterized as the "meat-axe approach" to reduction of fees. Id. The Ferland decision also collects Ninth Circuit precedent as to when it will (or will not) permit across-the-board reductions in the lodestar. Cf. In re Synthroid Marketing Litig., 325 F.3d 974, 979 (7th Cir. 2003) (stating that if class counsel invested too many hours, dallied when preparing the settlement, or otherwise ran the meter, the loss falls on counsel themselves). In Synthroid Marketing, however, counsels' fees award was based on a percentage of the award rather than the lodestar.

In common fund cases the issue has been whether there should be a default percentage that should be assessed against the fund to compensate counsel. E.g., Goldberger v. Integrated Resources, 209 F.3d 43 (D.C. Cir. 2000) (holding that the district court has discretion to use either lodestar or percentage method in common fund cases). The court found no abuse of discretion in the district court's use of a lodestar and rejected out-of-hand the claim that 25% of the fund was a reasonable benchmark for fees awards. Id. at 51 (characterizing the request as a disguised bid for a fees multiplier of 6). The court also questioned the use of 25% as a benchmark in common fund cases. Compare Id. (questioning whether "common fund plaintiffs in an efficient legal market would agree to" a 25% rate), with Synthroid Marketing supra, 325 F.3d at 979 (finding that 22% percentage rate was efficient, market rate based on conduct of sophisticated parties in the negotiation of their contingent fees agreements).

[11] Van Gerwen, supra, 214 F.3d at 1046 (citing Blum v. Stenson, 465 U.S. 886, 899 (1984) and further noting that "[t]o factor quality of representation into the multiplier risks double counting"). Id. The appellate court imposed a very heavy burden on the district court to justify a downward departure from the lodestar. Id. (stating that the district court must make a "detailed finding based on specific evidence that the quality of service was inferior in light of the hourly rate selected in setting the lodestar amount").

[12] Hensley, supra, 461 U.S. at 437.

court to court, but, at the minimum, counsel must identify the "general subject matter of his time expenditures."[13]

Accurate maintenance of time records is also necessary because not all aspects of the lawsuit may qualify for an attorney's fees recovery. For example, the prevailing party may prevail on only a portion of the complaint and lose on other portions. In this context, the billings must enable the court to differentiate between fees expended on the successful aspects of the case from fees expended on unsuccessful aspects. Of course, attorney time can rarely be so neatly compartmentalized. When a complaint presents a common core of facts from which claims and legal theories are presented, it is necessary to distinguish between related and unrelated claims. One approach permits the prevailing party to recover all of her fees, even though some of the claims are unsuccessful, when the claims are related.[14] When, however, distinctly different claims are based on separate facts and theories, no fees should be awarded for work expended on the unsuccessful claims.[15]

Courts have developed some formulaic approaches when multiple claims are presented, but only some of the claims provide for attorney's fees. In *Schultz v. Hembree*[16] the court noted but rejected one option, which it characterized as the marginal fees approach:

> The court asks what fees would have been incurred had the shifting claims not been brought, and awards only those fees exceeding that amount. Under this method, the prevailing party only recovers fees for work devoted solely to shifting claims, not fees attributable in any way to ordinary claims. The converse approach focuses on the total fees related to the shifting claims. Under this method the court determines what fees are wholly unrelated to the shifting claims, and awards all the rest. The prevailing party recovers its fees for all work somehow related to the shifting claims, but nothing for work that does not relate to those claims at all.[17]

The court noted that the "marginal" approach was flawed because invariably work done on the attorney's fees claims will benefit the non-attorney's

---

[13] *Id.* at 437 n.12. The court may reduce the award due to the failure to keep contemporaneous records. *Id.* at 438 n.13 (approving 30% reduction to fees request).

[14] Nanetti v. University of Ill. at Chicago, 944 F. 2d 1416, 1419 (7th Cir. 1991) (permitting recovery of fees based on time spent for joint preparation even when only one claim resulted in a recovery); *cf.* Gulfstream III Assocs., Inv. v. Gulfstream Aerospace Corp., 995 F.2d 414, 420 (3d Cir. 1993) (finding that if (1) the fees incurred in other litigation were for work product actually used in current litigation, (2) the time spent in other litigation was "inextricably linked" to issues in present litigation, and (3) the plaintiff was not previously compensated, the court may include the work product in the fees award). See text and notes 20-24, *infra*.

[15] Dee v. Sweet, 460 S.E.2d 110, 113 (Ga. App. 1995), *citing* Lerman v. Joyce Int'l, Inc., 10 F.3d 106, 114 (3d Cir. 1993).

[16] 975 F.2d 572 (9th Cir. 1992).

[17] *Id.* at 576. The reference to "shifting claims" means those claims for which statutory attorney's fees may be awarded.

fees claims and vice-versa. The court adopted what it characterized as an intermediate position:

> We hold that the prevailing party may recover that amount in fees it would have incurred had the shifting claims been litigated by themselves. This amount may well differ from the amount actually expended in advancing (or defending against) the claim in the context of the multiple-claim litigation. It might be less, if the parties would have litigated the shifting claims less vigorously, or compromised them early in the litigation. Or it might be more, as the parties may have devoted more resources to the shifting claims had they not been distracted by others. In any event, this method avoids both overcompensating and under-compensating the prevailing party, because the fees award is pegged precisely to the claim under which it is authorized.[18]

Unfortunately, the claims that support attorney's fees cases were not litigated by themselves; consequently, the fees award must be based on a hypothetical case. As noted by the dissenting judge in *Schultz*: "[the majority's rule] will require a host of discretionary, subjective, and obtuse judgments . . . in reaching an allowed award."[19]

A related problem is whether compensation should include work done in related litigation that benefits the main case. In *Armstrong v. Davis* the party sought attorney's fees for an amicus brief filed in another case before the Supreme Court that raised issues that could prove dispositive in the main case. The court held:

> In *Hasbrouck*, an antitrust case, we approved the award of attorney's fees to the plaintiffs for their counsel's preparation of an amicus brief to the Supreme Court in a case involving different parties, because, we held, the award of fees should cover "every item of service which, at the time rendered, would have been undertaken by a reasonably prudent lawyer to advance or protect his client's interest" in the case at bar.[20]

The court rejected arguments that the rule was limited to antitrust claims, as in *Hasbrouck*. The court also rejected arguments that *Hasbrouck* was distinguishable because in *Hasbrouck* the lawyer had actually filed an amicus brief; in *Armstrong* the lawyer sought fees for representing another party in a separate proceeding for which he didn't receive fees because ultimately his client was not the prevailing party, losing on a motion for summary judgment after a successful appeal.[21] The *Armstrong* court held that the representation of another served the client's interests here.

On the other hand, in *Tsotaddle v. Absentee Shawnee Housing Authority*, the court drew a sharp distinction between work on the claims that allowed for a fees award and other work. As noted by the court:

---

[18] *Id.* at 577 (footnote omitted).

[19] *Id.* at 579.

[20] 318 F.3d 965, 971 (9th Cir. 2003) (citations omitted).

[21] *Id.* at 971–72; *Gulfstream III Assocs., Inv., supra* note 14 (same).

We find, however, that the Housing Authority's contention regarding apportionment of the attorney fees has more merit. Even if Mr. Murdock's successful defense of Ms. Tsotaddle's claims was crucial to his success on the cross-claims he asserted against the Housing Authority, the claims themselves are separate and distinct and involved totally different issues and evidence. The only basis for recovery of attorney fees by Mr. Murdock for defeating other claims would involve his successful defense of counterclaims by the Housing Authority that were asserted as a setoff to his claim. However, the Housing Authority did not assert any counterclaims against Mr. Murdock for purposes of setoff.[22]

The calculation and allocation of fees between claims for which fees are allowed and claims for which fees are not allowed remains fundamentally a matter committed largely to the trial court's discretion. As noted by one commentator:

> The process of disallowing hours that do not contribute materially to the favorable results obtained is no less intuitive or arbitrary than the process of regulating hours generally. To put the matter bluntly, judges' decisions to disallow hours are discretionary and highly impressionistic.[23]

The observation is reflected in practice when the allocation is generally committed to the trial judge's discretion and reviewed under the deferential abuse of discretion standard.[24]

The determination of the hourly rate component of the lodestar is based on the market rate for the "relevant legal community." As noted in *Barjon v. Dalton*:

> Generally, the relevant community is the forum in which the district court sits. However, rates outside the forum may be used "if local counsel was unavailable, either because they are unwilling or unable to perform because they lack the degree of experience, expertise, or specialization required to handle properly the case."[25]

In cases where a "specialist" was retained, outside rates may be used.[26] In some cases, the "relevant legal community" may be identified as a

---

[22] 20 P.3d 153, 162 (Okla. App. 2000).

[23] Charles Silver, *Unloading the Lodestar: Toward A New Fee Award Procedure,* 70 Tex. L. Rev. 865, 955 (1992) (footnoted omitted).

[24] Pinkham v. Camex, Inc., 84 F.3d 292, 294 (8th Cir. 1996).

[25] 132 F.3d 496, 500 (9th Cir. 1997) (citations omitted), *cert. denied,* 525 U.S. 827 (1998); *cf.* Hamilton Mut. Ins. Co. v. Perry,. 705 N.E.2d 731 (Ohio App. 1997) (holding that it was not an abuse of discretion to use the entire state rather than an 11 county area to calculate a reasonable hourly rate).

[26] Guckenberger v. Boston Univ., 8 F. Supp. 2d 91, 103 (D. Mass. 1998); *cf.* Davis County Solid Waste Management and Energy Recovery Special Service District v. EPA, 169 F.3d 755, 757–58 (D.C. Cir 1999) (holding that usual appropriate billing rate is market rate prevailing at the locale of the court deciding the case, but recognizing an exception when an out-of-state lawyer is retained because of that lawyer's special expertise or the unwillingness of the local

national market, particularly when practitioners freely provide similar if not identical legal services across state or jurisdictional geographic boundaries.[27]

In determining the actual rate the reference is the "prevailing market rate," which is the rate "prevailing in the community for similar services of lawyers with reasonably comparable skills, experience, and reputation.[28] The lawyer's usual and customary billing rate is relevant, but not controlling.[29] The antagonism between market rate and billing rate is possibly a reflection of the fact that these cases often involve situations when the lawyer has billed a below-market fee or no fee and the need (or desire) here is to identify a "reasonable" rate to replicate what a private for-profit lawyer would have billed,[30] but this lawyer did not.

bar to take the case). In *Davis County* the court recognized a *new* exception to the locale rule when (1) the locale rate is substantially higher than the home rate and (2) the work done at the locale is minimal. The court rejected both reasons offered by out-of-state counsel for using the forum market rates in all cases: (1) administrative ease; and (2) neutrality; nonetheless, the court stated a preference for the use of locale market rates unless a strong case could be made for using home rates. In *Mathur v. Board of Trustees of Southern Illinois Univ.*, 317 F.3d 738 (7th Cir. 2003), the court held that Chicago counsel who successfully litigated a civil rights claim in downstate Illinois should be paid at the Chicago (home) market rate rather then the lower downstate (locale) rate. Using the lower downstate rate would make it more difficult for downstate claimants to secure representation; however, and consistent with this rationale, the court stated that this higher out-of-locale rule would not apply if the claimant bypassed equally competent local counsel in favor of higher priced outside counsel. *Id.* at 743–44.

[27] Steiner v. Hercules, Inc., 835 F. Supp. 771, 787 (D. Del. 1993) (identifying the "relevant legal community" in securities fraud litigation as the "national legal community that practices securities litigation"); *In re* Unisys Corp. Retiree Med. Benefits ERISA Litig., 886 F. Supp. 445, 477–78 (E.D. Pa. 1995) (applying *Steiner* to ERISA class action); *cf. Barjon, supra*, 132 F.3d at 501 (suggesting that national legal market may exist for federal civil rights claims under 42 U.S.C.§ 1983, *citing* Casey v. City of Cabool, Mo., 12 F.3d 799 (8th Cir. 1993)), *cert. denied*, 513 U.S. 932 (1994); Finkelstein v. Bergna, 804 F. Supp. 1235, 1242–45 (N.D. Cal. 1992) (holding that hourly rate for successful civil rights litigation should be set with reference to comparably complex matters litigated in federal courts).

[28] *Blum, supra*, 465 U.S. at 895; Dillard v. City of Greenoboro, 213 F.3d 1347 (11th Cir. 2000) (holding that attorney for prevailing party in voting rights cases would be paid at his usual and customary rate of billing ($200/hr.) rather than the market rate ($290 to $350/hr.) he had been awarded in other voting rights cases). The court stated that "[p]rior awards are not direct evidence of market behavior; the court is not a legal souk." *Id.* at 1355. The court stated that prior awards possess "inferential evidentiary value" but that value is inferior to the evidence of the lawyer's actual billing rate. *Id.* The record did state that the only evidence offered as to billing rates in the locale for lawyers of counsel's caliber was $190–225/hr., which placed on upper limit of $225/hr. as to what the district court could award. *Id.*; United States *ex rel* Averback v. Pastor Medical Associates, P.C., 224 F. Supp. 2d 342 (D. Mass. 2002) (holding that physician-lawyer who represented prevailing party in False Claims Act health care fraud action could recover at rate of $175/hr., rather than $325 for experienced litigators). The lawyer was employed primarily as a physician and had the legal experience of a third year associate. The court allowed a small upward adjustment to reflect the lawyer's medical billing experience, which was helpful in handling a health care fraud action.

[29] Gay Officers Action League v. Puerto Rico, 247 F.3d 288, 296 (1st Cir. 2001).

[30] Section 213.2.3 (Retainer as Limit on Fees Award); *cf. Mathur, supra*, 317 F.3d at 743 (noting that attorney's usual billing rate is presumptively appropriate as a measure of market rate and other evidence should be used only when lawyer cannot provide his actual billing rate).

In calculating the "market rate" the comparison should be "apples to apples;"[31] however, some courts will depart from this approach.[32] Note that this can result in some disharmony with the approach discussed in the prior paragraph. A different result may accompany use of the lawyer's usual billing rate, the market rate for those who practice in the subject matter area before the court, or the blended market rate for all practitioners, e.g., commercial litigation lawyers.

[213.2] Limitations on Fees Awards

In addition to the various factors that are balanced to determine the reasonable attorney's fees to be awarded in a case, a number of factors further constrain either the availability or the amount of fees that may be claimed by a prevailing party. When the limitation is imposed by statute, it is, of course, uniformly applied, although differences in the understanding of the limitation, and, therefore, its application, can be expected to arise in practice.

[213.2.1] Substantially Justified

In fee awards against the United States based on the Equal Access to Justice Act (EAJA), a prevailing party may recover attorney's fees against the United States unless the United States shows that its litigation position

---

[31] *E.g.*, Cooper v. Casey, 97 F.3d 914 (7th Cir. 1996) (holding that proper comparison for purpose of determining prevailing market rates" in civil right claim was rate in lawyer civil rights community, not lawyer commercial community).

[32] Yahoo, Inc. v. Net Games, Inc., 329 F. Supp. 2d 1179 (N.D. Cal. 2004):

> [T]he average market rate in the local legal community as a whole is a better approximation of the hourly rate that would be charged by reasonably competent counsel than the actual billing rate charged by a single attorney. Like the hypothetical "reasonably competent attorney," attorneys billing at the average rate will not be unusually skilled or experience but those attorneys typically capable or rendering the required services. Further, an average market rate combines the rates charged by private, non-profit and government attorneys from a variety of practice areas.

Id. at 1185–86. The court then went on to reject the claim that the billing rates of high priced counsel should be used:

> Much of what plaintiff has submitted to support its fee application would lead the court to a result the Supreme Court rejected. The experience of plaintiff's counsel and the high fees charged by the elite segments of the bar, to which plaintiff's papers attest, simply do not bear on the amount of a "reasonable fee."
>
> Rather, these premia reflect what counsel's clients are willing to pay to secure the services of a particular lawyer and thus diminish the risk of loss or for a variety of subjective reasons. Conversely, a lawyer may agree to take on a matter and charge a below-average rate because of the importance of the case, its notoriety and a host of other intangible factors. These considerations are properly reflected in the agreement between the lawyer and the client, but not in the court's award of a fee. A "reasonable fee" award does not necessarily equate to what the client agrees to pay.

Id. at 1188. Compare this approach to the preference for the market rate expressed in these materials at text and notes 25–30.

was "substantially justified."[33] In most jurisdictions, the United States' position was "substantially justified" if the position was "reasonable," although some jurisdictions impose a more stringent standard.[34] The fact that a court determined that the United States' position in one context was "arbitrary and capricious," as, for example, under the Administrative Procedure Act, does not mean that the government's position is unreasonable insofar as a fees award is concerned. Terms that are "words of art," as is the term "arbitrary and capricious" in the context of Administrative Law, are not necessarily dispositive of the inquiry. The government's position may be found to be "arbitrary and capricious" and thus in violation of the law; yet, the government's position may still be deemed "substantially justified" so as to deny to the prevailing plaintiff a recovery of attorney's fees.[35]

[213.2.2] Actual Damages Award as Limit on Fees Award

Courts have divided on the issue of whether an attorney's fees award may exceed the damages award. One line of decisions holds that statutory attorney's fees need not bear a reasonable relationship to the amount of damages awarded. For example, in *Beaulieu v. Dorsey* the court affirmed an award of more than $18,000 in fees and expenses on a claim for which the plaintiff recovered $610.[36] The action was brought under the state's Unfair Trade Practices Act and the court noted that because the purpose of the Act is to encourage litigation that might otherwise be deterred by economic considerations, the amounts involved and results obtained by the plaintiff are not controlling.[37]

---

[33] 28 U.S.C.A. § 2412, (d)(1)(A)–(B).

[34] F.E.C. v. Rose, 806 F.2d 1081, 1087 (D.C. Cir. 1986) (noting that the government's position is justified if it acted "slightly more than reasonably"). *See generally* Kevin Brown, Annot., *What Constitutes Substantial Justification of Government's Position so as to Prohibit Awards of Attorneys' Fees Against Government Under Equal Access to Justice Act (28 U.S.C.A. § 2412(D)(1)(A))*, 69 A.L.R. Fed. 130 (1984), at § 2.

[35] *F.E.C. v. Rose, supra*, 806 F.2d at 1087–88. *But cf. id.* at 1081 (noting that contrary language in Committee Report, stating that a finding that the government's position is arbitrary and capricious will rarely support a finding that the government's position was substantially justified, was inconsistent with the statutory text); *see* Gregory C. Sisk, *The Essentials of the Equal Access to Justice Act: Court Awards of Attorney's Fees For Unreasonable Governmental Conduct (Part One)*, 55 La. L. Rev. 217 (1994), (*Part Two*) 56 La. L. Rev. 1 (1995).

[36] 562 A.2d 678 (Me. 1989).

[37] *Id.* at 679; *see* Tuf Racing Products, Inc. v. American Suzuki Motor Corp., 223 F.3d 585 (7th Cir. 2000):

> The fact that the attorneys' fees awarded exceed the damages award is not decisive either. Because the cost of litigating a claim has a fixed component, a reasonable attorney's fee in the sense of the minimum required to establish a valid claim can exceed the value of the claim. Yet one purpose of fee shifting is to enable such claims to be litigated, and the purpose would be thwarted by capping the attorneys' fees award at the level of the damages award. There is no evidence that the $391,000 that Tuf expended to establish its claim—an amount that was, incidentally, little

Another approach is evidenced in the dissenting and concurring opinions in *City of Riverside v. Rivera* in which the dissenting Justices indicated that the attorney's fees award must be made proportional to the award of actual damages unless the plaintiff's success also advances the public good.[38] Four Justices concluded in a plurality opinion that requiring "proportionality" would be inconsistent with the legislative intent behind the the Civil Rights Attorney's Fees Award statute to encourage private litigation to enforce constitutional and statutory rights.[39] Four other Justices dissented and argued that a proportionality requirement would help ensure that litigation was conducted in an efficient and cost effective manner relative to the objectives and goals of the litigation.[40] Justice Powell concurred in the judgment. While he appeared to agree with the plurality's position that proportionality was not required, he placed primary emphasis on the trial court's findings.[41] The gloss of the public good, which the dissenting Justices urged, has been expressly adopted in some jurisdictions under the "private attorney general" rationale.[42]

A different problem is presented when the plaintiff claims an amount as damages that would support a large fee, but recovers only a fraction of that amount at trial. In this context, the actual award may be treated as a relevant factor in calculating a reasonable fees award. In other words, the results achieved by the litigation are a relevant, though not necessarily controlling factor, in the awarding of reasonable attorney's fees.[43] While

---

more than a third as great as Suzuki's expenditure in defending against it—was more than was reasonably necessary for Tuf to prevail.

Id. at 592 (citation omitted). *See generally* Francis M. Dougherty, Annot., *Propriety of Amount of Attorney's Fees Awarded to Prevailing Parties Under Civil Rights Attorney's Fees Awards Act of 1976* (42 U.S.C.A. § 1988), 118 A.L.R. Fed. 1 (1994).

[38] 477 U.S. 561 (1986).

[39] *Id.* at 576–80.

[40] *Id.* at 595 (noting that it is unlikely "that Congress intended to turn attorneys loose to spend as many hours as possible to prepare and try a case that could reasonably be expected to result only in a relatively minor award of monetary damages").

[41] *Id.* at 583–84; *see* Quaratino v. Tiffany & Co., 129 F.3d 702, 708 (2d Cir. 1997) (rejecting arguments that *Farrar v. Hobby*, discussed at Section 212 (Prevailing Party) (text and notes 28–31), overruled the position of the plurality in *City of Riverside*).

[42] Section 211.1 ([Attorney's Fees] Statutory Authorization).

[43] Sheffer v. Experium Information Systems, 290 F. Supp. 2d 538 (E.D. Pa. 2003):

In the instant case, Plaintiff sought $300,000.00 in damages, comprised of a $50,000.00 claim for actual damages, arising out of purported credit denials and emotional distress, and $250,000.00 for statutory and punitive damages. Despite Plaintiff's request, the jury awarded the nominal amount of $1,000.00. Although this Court cannot be certain of the basis for the $1,000.00 award, the only testimony at trial specifically assigning a monetary value to any of Mr. Sheffer's purported damages consisted of testimony regarding a $1,000.00 retainer that Mr. Sheffer paid to Mr. Lyons' law firm. Thus, it appears that the award, rather than indicating the jury's valuation of Mr. Sheffer's compensatory damages, was in fact designed to reimburse Mr. Sheffer for his out-of-pocket expenses associated with this lawsuit. Furthermore, the $1,000.00 judgment Mr. Sheffer derived from this lawsuit is significantly less than the $30,000.00 amount Sears' offered in settlement.

Id. at 551; *see Tuf Racing Products, Inc.*:

the lodestar may be adjusted to reflect the results achieved, many courts adopt the " 'strong presumption' that the lodestar figure represents a reasonable fee."[44]

[213.2.3]   Retainer as Limit on Fees Award

If the attorney has entered into a retainer with the client, does the retainer control or may the court award fees based on the market rate? It is generally assumed that an attorney's ordinary billing rate reflects the market rate.[45] The extent to which the prevailing plaintiff and her attorney should be tied to the billed rate is, however, unclear. Some courts have recognized that the billed rate is not conclusive on the issue of reasonableness, but should be compared to the community rate for similar work by equally experienced counsel.[46] These cases, however, usually address the problem whether the billed rate should be awarded when it exceeds the community rate.[47]

Does the fees arrangement between the prevailing party and her attorney place a ceiling on what constitutes, and may be recovered as, "reasonable" fees? For example, assume Attorney usually bills at the hourly rate of $150, but agrees, out of compassion for Plaintiff, to accept a fixed fee of $5,000. Attorney expends 300 hours on the matter before it is resolved in a manner that entitles plaintiff to an award of attorney's fees. Should Plaintiff receive the lodestar, $45,000 ($150 × 300 hours), or the fixed amount, $5,000, as her reasonable fees recovery? There is decisional law on both sides of the issue.

Several cases in this circuit do suggest that a plaintiff's failure to obtain at least 10 percent of the damages it had sought will weigh heavily against any award of attorney's fees. Indeed, *Perlman v. Zell* states this in a way that makes it sound like a rule, although the cases it cites for the rule treat it, rather, merely as a factor to consider along with other factors weighing for or against an award of attorneys' fees. Since a defendant must take seriously a large demand and prepare its defense accordingly, it is right to penalize a plaintiff for putting the defendant to the bother of defending against a much larger claim than the plaintiff could prove. But here the plaintiff scaled back its claim before trial and obtained more than 10 percent of the scaled-back demand from the jury. That seems to us enough to take the case out of the "rule" for which Suzuki contends.

223 F.3d at 592 (citations omitted); *see also* Atkins v. Apfel, 154 F.3d 986, 987–88 (9th Cir. 1998). In *Atkins*, the court held that the district court's decision awarding attorney's fees for work done on an unsuccessful appeal would be remanded because the trial court failed to consider the results achieved on appeal in determining fees. *Id.* at 989–90.

[44] *Quaratino, supra*, 129 F.3d at 705.

[45] McDonald v. Armontrout, 860 F.2d 1456, 1459 (8th Cir. 1988). *McDonald* involved the prevailing party's effort to recover at the billed rate; it did not involve the specific issue whether the billed rate limited the recovery.

[46] Shakopee Mdewakanton Sioux Community v. City of Prior Lake, Minn., 771 F.2d 1153, 1160 (8th Cir. 1985), *cert. denied sub nom.* City of Prior Lake, Minnesota v. Shakopee Mdewakanton Sioux Community, 475 U.S. 1011 (1986).

[47] Buffington v. Baltimore County, Md., 913 F.2d 113, 130 (4th Cir. 1990), *cert. denied,* 499 U.S. 906 (1991); Section 213.1 (Calculation of Fees Awards) (text and notes 25–32, discussing "market" rate determination).

In *Blanchard v. Bergeron* the Supreme Court came down strongly in favor of calculating reasonable fees without being bound by the fees arrangement between the prevailing party and her counsel. As noted by the Court:

> Respondent cautions us that refusing to limit recovery to the amount of the contingency agreement will result in a "windfall" to attorneys who accept [42 U.S.C.] § 1983 actions. Yet the very nature of recovery under [42 U.S.C.] § 1988 is designed to prevent any such "windfall." Fee awards are to be reasonable, reasonable as to billing rates and reasonable as to the number of hours spent in advancing the successful claims. Accordingly, fee awards, properly calculated, by definition will represent the reasonable worth of the services rendered in vindication of a plaintiff's civil rights claim. It is central to the awarding of attorneys fees under [42 U.S.C.] § 1988 that the district court judge, in his or her good judgment, make the assessment of what is a reasonable fee under the circumstances of the case. The trial judge should not be limited by the contractual fee agreement between plaintiff and counsel.[48]

Blanchard was, however, decided under the federal civil rights fees statute, 42 U.S.C. § 1988(b), and that provision does not expressly require that the attorney's fees have been "incurred." When the statute uses the term "incurred," many courts have relied on that language as imposing a ceiling on the fees award to the amount of the prevailing party's actual liability to its attorney.[49]

Whether the fees arrangement should limit the prevailing party's fees recovery can raise interesting, but difficult, policy choices. First, should the fees arrangement apply to public interest litigation maintained by public interest organizations? These organizations traditionally provide free, or deeply discounted, representation to parties to advance the organization's public interest agenda through legal action. The organizations rely heavily on fees awards to fund litigation. In general, courts have recognized that fees arrangements in this context should not limit fees recoveries; discounting fees below market rates would deter attorney's from accepting and prosecuting cases the fees awards statutes are designed to incentivize.[50] To encourage representation in this situation courts permit a reasonable

---

[48] 489 U.S. 87, 96 (1989) (brackets added); Board of Trustees of the Hotel & Restaurant Employees Local 25 v. JPR, Inc., 136 F.3d 794, 801 (D.C. Cir. 1998) (applying decisional law interpreting civil rights fees statute, 42 U.S.C. § 1988, to ERISA claim and holding that prevailing party was not limited to contract rate but could recover fees based on "market" rate). The ERISA fees provision, 29 U.S.C. § 1132(g)(2), does not contain the term "incurred."

[49] *E.g.*, Marre v. United States, 38 F.3d 823, 828–29 (5th Cir. 1994) (collecting decisions); Finney v. Department of Corrections, 434 S.E.2d 45, 47 (Ga. 1993) (holding that the prevailing party under the state Fair Employment Practices Act claim was not entitled to attorney's fees when her attorney represented her at no cost and, thus, she incurred no liability for fees). While the court expressed some reluctance to rule as it did, and noted the countervailing policies warranting an award of fees to a successful litigant in this context, the court concluded that those arguments were better addressed to the legislature. *Id.*; Section 4 (Public Policy).

[50] Pitts v. Holt, 710 N.E.2d 155, 157 (Ill. App. 1999).

fee regardless of the deal struck between the lawyer and the client.[51] This exception has been acknowledged as being applicable even when the fees statute limits recovery or when it requires that the fees obligation be "incurred."[52]

Second, should fees be awarded when the prevailing party is represented by an attorney-employee? The question was answered in the affirmative in *PLCM Group, Inc. v. Drexter* in which the court held that an entity that elects to be represented by in-house counsel, rather than a private lawyer or law firm, may recover the same amount of fees as the entity would have paid outside counsel to represent it.[53]

If a prevailing party can recover fees based on its use of in-house counsel, should the recovery be based on "market rates" or the actual cost of employing counsel, *e.g.*, counsel's salary and allocated overhead prorated to reflect time expended on the matter? The court in *PLCM Group, Inc.* emphasized the general acceptance and the ease of administrating the lodestar approach as opposed to an "actual cost" approach.[54] It rejected the argument that the lodestar approach represented a "windfall" for the entity not on the merits, but based on the failure of the defendant to establish what the entity's actual costs of counsel were relative to the amount awarded as reasonable fees under the lodestar approach.[55] At the same time it strongly suggested that efforts to establish the actual cost of employing in-house counsel should be rebuffed:

> We do not want a [trial] court, in setting an attorney's fee, [to] become enmeshed in a meticulous analysis of every detailed facet of the professional representation. It . . . is not our intention that the inquiry into the adequacy of the fee assume massive proportions, perhaps dwarfing the case in chief. Indeed, such wholly ancillary litigation on the question of salaries and costs and the

---

[51] Student Pub. Interest Research Group, Inc. v. AT&T Bell Labs., 842 F.2d 1436, 1445 (3d Cir. 1988) (involving 42 U.S.C. § 1988(b)).

[52] *See generally* Gregory Sarno & Anne Payne, Annot., *Recoupment of Attorney Fees, Under Equal Access to Justice Act (EAJA) (28 U.S.C.A. § 2412), by Litigant Represented by Counsel to Whom no Fee is Paid by Litigant*, 121 A.L.R. Fed. 291 (1994) (noting that "incurred" rule has not generally been applied when litigant is represented by a public interest organization's counsel). In *Gisbrecht v. Barnhard*, 535 U.S. 789 (2000), the Court addressed a statute that permits lawyers who represent claimants on Social Security claims to use contingent fee agreements, but limits the fee percentage to 25%. The lower court had used a lodestar approach to setting the fees award and calculated a "reasonable" fee, based on hourly rates, that was less than the lawyer would recover under the contingent fee agreement with the client. The lower court awarded fees based on a $125/hr. rate; under the fee agreement, the lawyer would realize an effective hourly rate of $188 to $283 in the three cases before the Court. The Court held that because the statute authorized the 25% rate, the statute controlled the disposition of the fees award and displaced the lodestar approach. *Id.* at 793; *see* Dansereau v. Ulmer, 955 P.2d 916, 918 (Alaska 1998) (noting that public interest litigants can recover fees at the market rate rather than at the statutory rate).

[53] 997 P.2d 511 (Cal. 2000).

[54] *Id.* at 519–20.

[55] *Id.* at 520.

internal economics of a law office could lead to an increase rather than a diminution of the costs of fee awards . . . .

Requiring trial courts in all instances to determine reasonable attorney fees based on actual costs and overhead rather than an objective standard of reasonableness, i.e., the prevailing market value of comparable legal services, is neither appropriate nor practical; it would be an unwarranted burden and bad public policy.[56]

The lodestar approach has been extended to fees claims by governmental entities that use their in-house staff.[57] Some courts have, however, rejected use of the lodestar approach because of the "windfall" possibilities.[58]

In *Wisconsin v. Hotline Indus., Inc.* the court permitted a recovery, but capped the award to the proportional share of the salaries of the attorneys who handled the case and related overhead costs, not market rates. The reason for the limitation was that the award was based on improper removal and the statute (28 U.S.C. § 1447(c) permits recovery of "actual expenses, including attorneys fees incurred as a result of the removal." The court held that this language limited recovery to actual outlays.[59] The court noted, however, that the fee shifting statute was unique and that the lodestar would have been used if not for the specific statutory language.[60]

In the analogous situation involving the employment of non-attorney staff, such as law clerks and paralegals, courts have generally used the "market" (billing to client) rate rather than the "cost of employing" (salary) rate.[61]

---

[56] *Id.* (citations and quotation marks omitted).

[57] Balkind v. Telluride Mountain Title Co., 8 P.3d 581 (Colo. App. 2000); *see* Wisconsin v. Hotline Indus., Inc., 236 F.3d 363, 365–66 (7th Cir. 2000) (collecting decisions).

[58] Softsolutions, Inc. v. Brigham Young University, 1 P.3d 1015 (Utah 2000):

Courts that have considered what is a reasonable attorney fee award for services of in-house counsel have, in some cases, awarded fees using a cost-plus rate. Other courts have employed a market-rate formula. We are convinced that a cost-plus rate is the more reasonable measure of attorney fees to in-house counsel, and is consistent with the public policy that the basic purpose of attorney fees is to indemnify the prevailing party and not to punish the losing party by allowing the winner a windfall profit.

Id. at 1107 (footnote omitted).

[59] 236 F.3d 363, 366–67 (7th Cir. 2000).

[60] *Id.* ("Section 1447(c) is unusual among fee-shifting statutes"); *cf.* Bond v. Blum, 317 F.3d 385, 399–400 (4th Cir.) (recognizing that entity that is represented in litigation by in-house counsel may recover fees award as prevailing party based on market rates), *cert. denied*, 540 U.S. 820 (2003).

[61] Williams v. Bowen, 684 F. Supp. 1305, 1308 (E.D. Pa. 1988) (permitting under "Equal Access to Justice Act" the recovery of law clerk expense at the market rate rather than the cost of employment rate); *cf. In re* Job, 198 B.R. 763 (Bankr. 9th Cir. 1996) (suggesting that an attorney-party who used associate attorneys could recover at the associates' billing rate rather than their salary; however, the issue was not decided), *rev'd on other grounds,* 117 F.3d 1425 (9th Cir. 1997). *But cf.* Burka v. United States Dep't of Health & Human Resources, 142 F.3d 1286, 1291 (D.C. Cir. 1998) (holding that pro se attorney could not recover, as prevailing

Courts have, in general, refused to allow the wealth of the prevailing party to influence the amount of fees awarded.[62] There are some decisions that consider the parties' wealth to calculate the amount, but not the entitlement, to fees; however these decisions are limited to situations when the prevailing defendant seeks to recover attorney's fees against the non-prevailing plaintiff.[63]

A court may not decrease an attorney's fees request to reflect (mandate) a pro bono contribution by counsel. Such a decrease is flatly inconsistent with Supreme Court precedent,[64] unless the decrease reflects duplication or overstaffing resulting from the pro bono nature of the work.[65]

[213.3] Pro Se Attorney Litigants

Alaska appears to be the only American jurisdiction to allow an attorney-party appearing pro se (as her own attorney) to recover attorney's fees as the prevailing party.[66] Other jurisdictions have allowed fees recoveries by pro se attorneys, but usually in contexts other than those involving attorney's fees statutes or contract provisions.[67]

Although there is some case law permitting a pro se attorney to recover attorney's fees when she is the prevailing party, the dominant modern rule is to deny a fees recovery in this context. In many of the decisions, the courts have relied on the presence of the term "incur" in the fees statute or contract provision and observed that a party cannot incur a liability to oneself but only to another.[68] More broadly, however, allowing an attorney-party to

party, fees for the services of his lawyer colleagues who worked on his case). The court distinguished cases when the other lawyers were unaffiliated with the pro se attorney. In *Burka* the court noted: "Burka controlled the legal strategy and presentation, he was the only attorney to enter an appearance in the case, and his colleagues worked under his direction. These are material differences." *Id.*; Section 213.3 (Pro Se Attorney Litigants).

[62] Jones v. Wilkinson, 800 F.2d 989, 991 (10th Cir. 1986) (involving 42 U.S.C. § 1988):

[Section] 1988 has purposes other than encouraging lawyers to take on a case, such as "penalizing obstructive litigation by civil rights defendants and generally deterring civil rights violations." These other purposes of § 1988 compel us to say that the ability of a party to bring suit without a fee award is not a special circumstance rendering a fee award unjust.

(citation omitted), *aff'd,* 480 U.S. 926 (1987); Herrington v. County of Sonoma, 883 F.2d 739, 742–43 (9th Cir. 1989); Duncan v. Poythress, 777 F.2d 1508, 1511 (11th Cir. 1985) (*en banc*).

[63] Miller v. Los Angeles County Bd. of Educ., 827 F.2d 617, 621 (9th Cir. 1987).

[64] *Blum, supra,* 465 U.S. at 894–95 (stating that courts should avoid decreasing fees award "because the attorneys conducted the litigation more as an act of pro bono publico than as an effort at securing a large monetary return") (citations omitted).

[65] Alexander v. Boyd, 929 F. Supp. 925, 935, 943 (D.S.C. 1995), *aff'd,* Burnside v. Boyd, 89 F.3d 827 (4th Cir. 1996) (Table); Section 213.1 (Calculation of Fees Awards).

[66] Pratt & Whitney Canada, Inc. v. Sheehan, 852 P.2d 1173, 1181 (Alaska 1993).

[67] Harkleroad v. Stringer, 499 S.E.2d 379, 382 (Ga. App. 1998) (involving fees awarded as sanctions for abusive litigation); Ziobron v. Crawford, 667 N.E.2d 202, 207–08 (Ind. App. 1996) (involving fees awarded under "third party tort" exception to the "American Rule").

[68] Katz v. Trope, 902 P.2d 259, 263 (Cal. 1995).

recover fees based on the time she spent handling her case would discriminate against a non-attorney party who appeared on his own behalf.[69] Even when the fees statute does not use the term "incur," as, for example, the federal civil rights fees statute, 42 U.S.C. § 1988(b), the Court in *Kay v. Ehrler* held that an attorney-party may not recover fees as the prevailing party for the time she spent litigating her case.[70]

The courts are split whether the rule barring the recovery of fees by attorneys appearing pro se applies to attorneys who are related to parties. In *Matthew v. Dekalb County School System* the court stated that lawyer-parents who successfully represent their children in proceeding under the Individuals With Disabilities Education Act (IDEA) may recover attorney's fees.[71] The district court distinguished *Kay v. Ehler* because in that case the lawyer-parent sued under civil rights statutes and did not present the child as a real party in interest. The comments in *Matthew* proved to be dicta, however, because the child was not a prevailing party. In *Woodside v. School District of Philadelphia Bd. of Education* the court denied fees to a lawyer-parent who successfully represented his disabled child in IDEA proceedings.[72] The court stated that the better rule was the one that "encourages parents to seek independent, emotionally detached counsel for their children's IDEA actions.[73]

A lawyer who retains another member of his firm to represent him was allowed by one court to recover the reasonable value of the lawyer's services based on "market" rates.[74] One is left to speculate how "emotionally detached" or "objective" a colleague is when representing a fellow member of the firm.[75] It should be noted that the IDEA cases discussed in this section involved the representation of minors; a different result may be expected if the child is an adult and legally capable of making his own

---

[69] *Id.* at 267 (noting that "Legislature did not intend to allow doctors, architects, painters, or other non-attorneys to receive compensation for the valuable time they spend litigating a contract matter on their own behalf").

[70] 499 U.S. 432, 435 & n.5 (1991). Although the Court addressed the issue under 42 U.S.C. § 1988(b), it has been broadly applied to all federal fees statutes.

[71] 244 F. Supp. 2d 1331 (N.D. Ga. 2003). IDEA is codified at 20 U.S.C. § 1400 *et seq.*

[72] 248 F.3d 129 (3d Cir. 2001).

[73] *Id.* at 131. *Compare* McLaughlin v. Boston Sch. Comm., 976 F. Supp. 53, 64 (D. Mass. 1997) (awarding attorney's fees to father of student-plaintiff who represented daughter in civil rights action against defendant, but noting conflicting authority, which it declined to follow); *with* Erickson v. Bd. of Educ. of Baltimore County, 162 F.3d 289, 293 (4th Cir. 1998) (holding that a child is the real party in interest in action brought under IDEA; however, the child, as the prevailing plaintiff, could not recover attorney's fees based on legal representation provided by his attorney-parent). The *Erickson* court held that the case fell within the exception when "special circumstances can render such an award unjust" because of the "special and close relationship between a parent and his or her child." *Id.* at 293–94, *citing Kay v. Ehler*, *supra*, 499 U.S. 432.

[74] Gilbert v. Master Washer & Stamping Co., Inc., 104 Cal. Rptr. 2d 461, 468 (Cal. App. 2001) (holding that introduction of "objective third party as counsel" warranted award of fees).

[75] *Burka*, *supra*, 142 F.3d at 1292 (holding that "a pro se attorney-litigant is not entitled to an award of attorney's fees for work performed by other attorneys on the case where the other attorneys worked in the attorney-litigant's firm under the attorney-litigant's direction").

selection of counsel to represent his interests. On the other hand, if the adult child is disabled the court may not believe that the "clients" decision is independent of parental influence.

There is sparse case law (largely pre-*Kay v. Ehrler*) that has permitted a *non-attorney* prevailing party appearing pro se to recover attorney's fees.[76] This approach is outweighted by the great weight of authority denying an attorney's fees recovery to a non-attorney for time spent representing himself.[77]

A client who retains a non-admitted lawyer may lose the claim for reasonable attorney's fees even though the client is a prevailing plaintiff.[78]

§ 214   STANDING TO COLLECT FEES AWARD

The general rule is that the right to collect an attorney's fees award belongs to the party and can be waived by the party without incurring a breach of duty to the attorney.[1] In *Flannery v. Prentice*, however, the court adopted a different view. It held that a fees award under the California Fair Employment and Housing Act belonged to the attorney who earned the fee, not the prevailing plaintiff-client.[2] Nonetheless, *Flannery* represents a distinct minority view.

To be distinguished from the issue of ownership is the issue of rights to the fees award itself. Once a party collects an attorney's fees recovery, the attorney's rights, if any, to the fees arises. As noted in *Image Technical Service, Inc. v. Eastman Kodak Co.*:

> Our recent opinion in *Virani* articulates a similar dilemma in the context of evaluating a fee award under the False Claims Act. Like the antitrust law, the FCA provides that successful plaintiffs "shall" receive reasonable attorneys' fees from defendants. Such language [o]n its face seems to say that the plaintiff can recover the attorneys' fee for himself. What then of the attorney? Are not the fees for his services and should not he, if anyone receive them? It is usually assumed that the answer to the latter question is "Yes, of course,

[76] Celeste v. Sullivan, 734 F. Supp. 1009 (S.D. Fla. 1990), *rev'd,* 988 F.2d 1069 (11th Cir. 1992).

[77] Benavides v. Bureau of Prisons, 993 F.2d 257, 259–60 (D.C. Cir. 1993) (involving Freedom of Information Act claim and disallowing fees recovery by non-attorney prevailing party representing himself under rationale of *Kay v. Ehrler, supra*), *cert. denied,* 510 U.S. 996 (1993); Demarest v. Manspeaker, 948 F.2d 655, 655 (10th Cir. 1991), *cert. denied,* 503 U.S. 921 (1992); see generally Vincent Waldman, Note, *Pro Se Can You Sue?: Attorney Fees For Pro Se Litigants,* 34 Stan. L. Rev. 659 (1982).

[78] Z.A. v. San Bruno Park School District, 165 F.3d 1273 (9th Cir. 1999); Sections 65.2 (Illegality), 214 (Standing to Collect Fees Award) (text and notes 3–5, discussing whether lawyer with conflict of interest should receive fees award).

[1] Evans v. Jeff D., 475 U.S. 717, 730–31 (1986) (involving civil rights fees statute 42 U.S.C. § 1988).

[2] 28 P.3d 860 (Cal. 2001); *cf.* Bishop v. Burgard, 764 N.E.2d 24, 30–32 (Ill. 2002) (holding that attorney owns the claim for reimbursement for his services in creating a common fund).

how could it be otherwise." That assumption simply tends to be in the background of decision making about fees. Yet there are times when someone will ask that a usually unacknowledged part of the background be brought to the forefront and perused before it recedes again into relative obscurity. While "in general, statutes bestow fees upon parties, not upon attorneys . . . weighty authority demonstrates that the client himself is not entitled to keep the fees which are measured by and paid on account of the attorney's services." *Virani* concluded that under the FCA the client's right to a reasonable fee was actually a "power" to demand such a fee, and after the client exercised that power the attorney had a right to the fees.[3]

The distinction between "ownership" and "rights to" is based on the view that control over the claim to the fee should lie with the client, not the lawyer. Once the fees award exists, however, the lawyer's right to the fees is superior to the clients.[4] *Flannery* is also within this distinction in that the dispute in that case was not over the claim for fees, but how much of the fees award could be claimed by the attorney.[5]

The decisions are uniform that an attorney may not intervene in a matter to argue that the waiver of attorney's fees by the client is collusive.[6] There

---

[3] 136 F.3d 1354, 1358–59 (9th Cir. 1998) (citations omitted) (involving claim of fee forfeiture arising out of unconsented to conflict of interest). The issue involved ownership of statutory fees earned by "conflicted" counsel. The law firm represented the plaintiff against the defendant. Defendant successfully disqualified the law firm because the firm had represented a division of defendant in other matters. The plaintiff prevailed at trial and the court awarded attorney's fees, including $400,000 for the law firm's work prior to its disqualification representation. Should the $400,000 be paid to the party, to counsel, or not paid at all? The court held that the conflict negated the claim for attorney's fees! *Id.* at 1359 (denying fees award because conflict arose out of duty owed to law firm's former client, which was the party which would have to pay the fees award). The court suggested the result may be different if the conflict arose out of a breach of duty owed to the prevailing party. *Id.*

[4] *E.g.*, JTH Tax, Inc. v. H&R Block Eastern Tax Services, Inc., 28 Fed. Appx. 207, 2002 U.S. App. LEXIS 477 (4th Cir. 2002) (*per curiam* (unpublishd) (distinguishing *Images Technical Services, Inc.*, *supra*, on the ground that in *Images Technical Services, Inc.* the client was not seeking reimbursement of money it had paid as fees and thus "the court was appropriately concerned that a fee award would provide compensation to conflicted counsel . . . or bestow a sizable windfall on the plaintiff"). The *JTH Tax, Inc.* court held that those concerns were not present when the firm had been paid for its work by the prevailing plaintiff and the plaintiff was seeking reimbursement from the defendant under a fee-shifting statute).

[5] 28 P.3d at 812. The parties had a contingent fee arrangement. The client received an award of compensatory damages and attorney's fees. The attorney wanted the entire fees award; the client wanted both awards to be aggregated and the attorneys to be paid from the aggregated amount based on the contingent rate, which would leave a substantial portion of the fees award for plaintiff.

[6] Willard v. City of Los Angeles, 803 F.2d 526, 527–28 (9th Cir. 1986) (rejecting contention that settlement of a private civil rights action could not be conditioned on a fees waiver by the plaintiff and holding that the plaintiff's attorney could not intervene in the dispute to contest the waiver); *see* Panola Land Buying Assn. v. Clark, 844 F.2d 1506 (11th Cir. 1988) (rejecting an effort by an attorney for the prevailing party to challenge a fees waiver when fees could be awarded, absent the waiver, under Equal Access to Justice Act, 28 U.S.C. § 2812); Zeisler v. Neese, 24 F.3d 1000, 1001 (7th Cir. 1994) (same result involving federal Truth in Lending Act, 15 U.S.C. § 1640(a)(3)).

is dicta, however, in *Evans* that suggests that an attorney may take an assignment of the client's fees claim.[7] Whether a pre-waiver assignment by an attorney would be permissible under governing Rules of Professional Conduct has not been resolved, even though it has been noted:

> Although respondents contend that Johnson, as counsel for the class, was faced with an 'ethical dilemma' when petitioners offered him relief greater than that which he could reasonably have expected to obtain for his clients at trial (if only he would stipulate to a waiver of the statutory fee award), and although we recognize Johnson's conflicting interests between pursuing relief for the class and a fee for the Idaho Legal Aid Society, we do not believe that the "dilemma" was an "ethical" one in the sense that Johnson had to choose between conflicting duties under the prevailing norms of professional conduct. Plainly, Johnson had no ethical obligation to seek a statutory fee award. His ethical duty was to serve his clients loyally and competently.[8]

Many ethical dilemmas can be "made to disappear" once it is assumed that the attorney will not give in to the dark side of self interest. When counsel takes a pre-settlement assignment of the attorney's fees claim from her client, counsel will necessarily place herself in a potential conflict with the client over the settlement counsel must negotiate on the client's behalf.[9] Counsel may also have taken an improper interest in the subject matter of the litigation.[10] While ethics opinions and courts have focused on the propriety of defense counsel tendering a fee waiver,[11] little attention has been given to the propriety of plaintiff's counsel taking the pre-settlement assignment of fees from her client.[12]

---

[7] 475 U.S. at 731 (noting that Congress has not expressly precluded the assignment of fees claims).

[8] *Id.* at 727–28 (footnote omitted).

[9] *See* CENTER FOR PROFESSIONAL RESPONSIBILITY, ANNOTATED MODEL RULES OF PROFESSIONAL CONDUCT 19, 50 (4th ed. 1999) (collecting authorities finding that attorney constraints on client's absolute right to settle are violative of attorney's professional duty of loyalty to the client and unenforceable; and noting that the simultaneous negotiation of the client's claim and the lawyer's fees constitutes a conflict of interest).

[10] *Id.* at 135–36 (noting general prohibition against attorney obtaining proprietary interest in client's cause of action).

[11] Coleman v. Fiore Bros., Inc., 552 A.2d 141, 146–47 (N.J. 1989) (holding that in actions involving consumer fraud, public interest counsel must settle claim before negotiating fees and defense counsel may not insist on a waiver of fees as a condition for settlement); Edward Sherman, *From "Loser Pays" to Modified Offer of Judgment Rules: Reconciling Incentives to Settle With Access to Justice*, 76 Tex. L. Rev. 1863, 1896 (1998) (collecting ethics opinions on propriety of tenders by defense counsel of settlement conditioned on plaintiff's fees waiver and discussing effect of *Evans* on that position).

[12] In Pony v. City of Los Angeles, 433 F.3d 1138 (9th Cir. 2006) the court held that client's statutory right to fees was not assignable to counsel; an assignment in the retainer agreement was void under California law. The court relied on California's general prohibition on the assignment of personal injury claims (*id.* at 1143–44) and did not discuss *Flanner, supra*, 28 P.3d 860.

The jurisdictions have split as to whether the fees award can be paid directly to the attorney(s) or must be paid to the party for the party's endorsement or payment over to the attorney(s).[13] In most cases this will not pose a problem because the award would be deposited into the client trust account. When the client-attorney relationship has been severed or destroyed, direction of the award may be critical, or, at the very least, provide one side or the other with some leverage to resolve any dispute over fees. Payment to the client also raises the issue as to whether the fees award is subject to the claims of the client's creditors other than the attorney.

---

[13] The decisions are collected in *Heston v. Secretary of Health and Human Services*, 1997 U.S. Claims LEXIS 257 (Ct. Cl., October 3, 1997). The decision of the Special Master in *Heston* was that payment should be made directly to counsel given the breakdown in the client-lawyer relationship. The decision was, however, overturned by the trial judge. Heston v. Secretary of Health and Human Services, 41 Fed. Cl. 41, 48 (1998) (holding that fees must be awarded to the client).

TABLE OF CASES

[References are to page numbers. Primary cases appear in all capital letters.]

[References are to page numbers. Primary cases appear in all capital letters.]

[References are to page numbers. Primary cases appear in all capital letters.]

[References are to page numbers. Primary cases appear in all capital letters.]

[References are to page numbers. Primary cases appear in all capital letters.]

C

[References are to page numbers. Primary cases appear in all capital letters.]

[References are to page numbers. Primary cases appear in all capital letters.]

[References are to page numbers. Primary cases appear in all capital letters.]

[References are to page numbers. Primary cases appear in all capital letters.]

[References are to page numbers. Primary cases appear in all capital letters.]

[References are to page numbers. Primary cases appear in all capital letters.]

[References are to page numbers. Primary cases appear in all capital letters.]

E

[References are to page numbers. Primary cases appear in all capital letters.]

[References are to page numbers. Primary cases appear in all capital letters.]

[References are to page numbers. Primary cases appear in all capital letters.]

[References are to page numbers. Primary cases appear in all capital letters.]

G

[References are to page numbers. Primary cases appear in all capital letters.]

[References are to page numbers. Primary cases appear in all capital letters.]

H

[References are to page numbers. Primary cases appear in all capital letters.]

[References are to page numbers. Primary cases appear in all capital letters.]

[References are to page numbers. Primary cases appear in all capital letters.]

[References are to page numbers. Primary cases appear in all capital letters.]

K

[References are to page numbers. Primary cases appear in all capital letters.]

[References are to page numbers. Primary cases appear in all capital letters.]

[References are to page numbers. Primary cases appear in all capital letters.]

[References are to page numbers. Primary cases appear in all capital letters.]

[References are to page numbers. Primary cases appear in all capital letters.]

M

[References are to page numbers. Primary cases appear in all capital letters.]

[References are to page numbers. Primary cases appear in all capital letters.]

[References are to page numbers. Primary cases appear in all capital letters.]

[References are to page numbers. Primary cases appear in all capital letters.]

[References are to page numbers. Primary cases appear in all capital letters.]

[References are to page numbers. Primary cases appear in all capital letters.]

O

[References are to page numbers. Primary cases appear in all capital letters.]

[References are to page numbers. Primary cases appear in all capital letters.]

[References are to page numbers. Primary cases appear in all capital letters.]

[References are to page numbers. Primary cases appear in all capital letters.]

[References are to page numbers. Primary cases appear in all capital letters.]

[References are to page numbers. Primary cases appear in all capital letters.]

[References are to page numbers. Primary cases appear in all capital letters.]

[References are to page numbers. Primary cases appear in all capital letters.]

[References are to page numbers. Primary cases appear in all capital letters.]

[References are to page numbers. Primary cases appear in all capital letters.]

[References are to page numbers. Primary cases appear in all capital letters.]

[References are to page numbers. Primary cases appear in all capital letters.]

[References are to page numbers. Primary cases appear in all capital letters.]

X

Y

Z

[References are to page numbers. Primary cases appear in all capital letters.]

INDEX

[References are to page numbers.]

[References are to page numbers.]

[References are to page numbers.]

[References are to page numbers.]

[References are to page numbers.]

[References are to page numbers.]

[References are to page numbers.]

[References are to page numbers.]

[References are to page numbers.]

[References are to page numbers.]

[References are to page numbers.]

O

[References are to page numbers.]

[References are to page numbers.]

[References are to page numbers.]

[References are to page numbers.]

[References are to page numbers.]